11e

UNDERSTANDING MANAGEMENT

Richard L. Daft
Vanderbilt University

Dorothy Marcic
Columbia University

CENGAGE

Australia • Brazil • Mexico • Singapore • United Kingdom • United States

Understanding Management, **Eleventh Edition**
Richard L. Daft and Dorothy Marcic

Senior Vice President, Higher Education Product Management: Erin Joyner

Vice President, Product Management: Mike Schenk

Product Director: Bryan Gambrel

Senior Product Manager: Michael Giffen

Senior Content Manager: Julia Chase

Learning Designer: Courtney Wolstoncroft

Product Assistant: Nick Perez

Production Service: SPi-Global

Marketing Manager: Audrey Wyrick

Digital Delivery Lead: Drew Gaither

Manufacturing Planner: Ron Montgomery

Intellectual Property Analyst: Diane Garrity

Intellectual Property Project Manager: Nick Barrows

Senior Art Director: Bethany Bourgeois

Internal Designer: Ted & Trish Knapke/Ke Design/ Bethany Bourgeois

Cover Designer: Bethany Bourgeois

Cover Image credit: iStock-531318564

Front and Back Matter Images: iStock-531318564

For product information and technology assistance, contact us at **Cengage Customer & Sales Support, 1-800-354-9706** or **support.cengage.com.**

For permission to use material from this text or product, submit all requests online at **www.cengage.com/permissions.**

Library of Congress Control Number: 2018961051

ISBN-13: 978-0-357-03382-1

Cengage
20 Channel Center Street
Boston, MA 02210
USA

Cengage is a leading provider of customized learning solutions with office locations around the globe, including Singapore, the United Kingdom, Australia, Mexico, Brazil, and Japan. Locate your local office at: **www.cengage.com/global**

Cengage products are represented in Canada by Nelson Education, Ltd.

To learn more about Cengage platforms and services, register or access your online learning solution, or purchase materials for your course, visit **www.cengage.com.**

Printed at CLDPC, USA, 01-21

To my grandchildren: Nelson, Phoenix, Roman, and Samantha,
Who bring me perfume-colored taffy and rainbow-scented flowers
And fill my world with light-years of happiness.
—Dorothy Marcic

The World of Innovative Management

Today's managers and organizations are being buffeted by massive and far-reaching competitive, social, technological, and economic changes. Any manager who believed in the myth of stability was rocked out of complacency several years ago when, one after another, large financial institutions in the United States began to fail, automakers filed for bankruptcy, the housing market collapsed, European economies faced financial devastation, and a global economic recession took hold and wouldn't let go. Business schools, as well as managers and businesses, are still scrambling to cope with the aftermath, keep up with fast-changing events, and evaluate the impact that this volatile period of history will have on organizations in the future. This edition of *Understanding Management* addresses themes and issues that are directly relevant to the current, fast-shifting business environment.

We revised *Understanding Management*, 11th edition, with a goal of helping current and future managers find innovative solutions to the problems that plague today's organizations—whether they are everyday challenges or once-in-a-lifetime crises. The world in which most students will work as managers is undergoing a tremendous upheaval. Ethical turmoil, the need for crisis management skills, e-business and mobile commerce, economic instability, rapidly changing technologies, globalization, outsourcing, increasing government regulation, social media, global supply chains, cybercrime, and other challenges place demands on managers that go beyond the techniques and ideas traditionally taught in management courses. Managing today requires the full breadth of management skills and capabilities. This text provides comprehensive coverage of both traditional management skills and the new competencies needed in a turbulent environment characterized by economic turmoil, political confusion, and general uncertainty. *Understanding Management* focuses especially on small business and entrepreneurship. The theme of the 11th edition is the food business from farming through grocery, restaurants, and waste management. Since the typical undergraduate student is from a demographic very interested in food and its production, these new examples should be of great interest.

In the traditional world of work, management's job was to control and limit people, enforce rules and regulations, seek stability and efficiency, design a top-down hierarchy, and achieve bottom-line results. To spur innovation and achieve high performance, however, managers need different skills. Managers have to find ways to engage workers' hearts and minds as well as take advantage of their labor. The new workplace asks that managers focus on building trust, inspiring commitment, leading change, harnessing people's creativity and enthusiasm, finding shared visions and values, and sharing information and power. Teamwork, collaboration, participation, and learning are guiding principles that help managers and employees maneuver the difficult terrain of today's turbulent business environment. Rather than controlling their employees, managers focus on training them to adapt to new technologies and extraordinary environmental shifts and thus achieve high performance and total corporate effectiveness.

Our vision for this edition of *Understanding Management* is to present the newest management ideas for turbulent times in a way that is interesting and valuable to students while retaining the best of traditional management thinking. To achieve this vision, we have included the most recent management concepts and research and have shown the contemporary application of management ideas in organizations. At the end of many major chapter sections, we have added a "Remember This" feature that provides a quick review of the salient concepts and terms students should remember. Within each chapter, a feature called "Green Power" highlights how various organizations are responding to the growing demand for socially and environmentally responsible ways of doing business. Thoughtful or inspiring quotes within each chapter—some

from business leaders, others from novelists, philosophers, and everyday people—help students expand their thinking about management issues. The combination of established scholarship, new ideas, and real-life applications gives students a taste of the energy, challenge, and adventure inherent in the dynamic field of management. We have worked together with the Cengage staff to provide a textbook that is better than any other at capturing the excitement of organizational management.

We revised *Understanding Management* to provide a book of utmost quality that will create in students both respect for the changing field of management and confidence that they can understand and master it. The textual portion of this book has been enhanced through the engaging, easy-to-understand writing style and the many new in-text examples, boxed items, and short exercises that make the concepts come alive for students. The graphic component has been enhanced with several new and revised exhibits and updated photo essays that illustrate specific management concepts. The well-chosen photographs provide vivid illustrations and intimate glimpses of management scenes, events, and people. The photos are combined with brief essays that explain how a specific management concept looks and feels. Both the textual and graphic portions of the textbook help students grasp the often abstract and distant world of management.

Focus on Innovation: New to the 11th Edition

A primary focus for revising the 11th edition has been to relate management concepts and theories to events in today's turbulent environment by bringing in present-day issues that real-life managers face. Sections that are particularly relevant to fast-shifting current events are marked with a "Hot Topic" icon.

Learning Opportunities

The 11th edition includes several innovative pedagogical features to help students understand their own capabilities and learn what it is like to manage in an organization today. Each chapter in MindTap begins with an interactive self-assessment questionnaire that directly relates to the topic of the chapter and enables students to see how they respond to situations and challenges typically faced by real-life managers. These short questionnaires provide feedback to the students that compares them with their classmates and give students insight into how they would function in the real world of management. "Remember This" bullet-point summaries at the end of many major chapter sections give students a snapshot of the key points and concepts covered in that section. The end-of-chapter questions have been carefully revised to encourage critical thinking and application of chapter concepts, and "Apply Your Skills: Group Learning" exercises give students the opportunity to apply concepts while building teamwork skills. Ethical dilemma scenarios and our "You Make the Decision" branching activities in MindTap help students sharpen their diagnostic skills for management problem solving and thinking like a manager. Finally, the test bank has been expanded with hundreds of all-new questions.

Chapter Content

Within each chapter, many topics have been added or expanded to address the current issues that managers face. Chapter text has been tightened and sharpened to provide greater focus on the key topics that count most for management today. The essential elements concerning operations and information technology, subject matter that is frequently covered in other courses, have been combined into an appendix for students who want more information about these topics.

Chapter 1 includes a discussion of some of the high-impact events and changes that have made innovative management so critical to the success of organizations today and into the future. This introductory chapter broaches the concept of the bossless organization and discusses making the leap from being an individual contributor in the organization to becoming a new manager and getting work done primarily through the efforts of others. It touches upon the skills and competencies needed to manage organizations effectively, including issues such as managing one's time, maintaining appropriate control, and building trust and credibility.

Chapter 1 also provides solid coverage of the historical development of management and organizations. It begins with an overview of the historical struggle within the field of management to balance the machinery and the humanity of production. The chapter includes sections on managing the technology-driven workplace and managing the people-driven workplace and ends with a consideration of social business as one current answer to the historical struggle. The section on managing the technology-driven workplace includes information on big data analytics and supply chain management. Managing the people-driven workplace includes discussions of the bossless trend and using engagement to manage millennial employees.

Chapter 2 contains an updated view of current issues related to the environment and corporate culture, including a discussion of organizational ecosystems, the growing importance of the international environment, and trends in the sociocultural environment, including changing social views toward issues such as same-sex marriage and the legalization of marijuana. The chapter also describes how managers shape a high-performance culture as an innovative response to a shifting environment.

Chapter 3 takes an updated look at the shifting international landscape, including the growing clout of China and India and the proposed Trans-Pacific Partnership as well as what these changes mean for managers around the world. The chapter includes a new look at the shifting geography of the *Fortune* Global 500 companies, describes the importance of cultural intelligence (CQ) and a global mind-set, and considers communication challenges, incorporating a new discussion of the role of implicit communication. The chapter includes a section on social entrepreneurship, discusses the bottom-of-the-pyramid (BOP) concept, and considers how the global supply chain brings new ethical challenges for managers in companies based in the United States and other Western countries.

Chapter 4 makes the business case for incorporating ethical values in the organization and looks at the role that managers play in creating an ethical organization. The chapter includes an updated discussion of the state of ethical management today, the pressures that can contribute to unethical behavior in organizations, the difference between "giving" and "taking" corporate cultures, and criteria that managers can use to resolve ethical dilemmas. The chapter considers corporate social responsibility issues as well, including new discussions of conscious capitalism, greenwashing, and benefit corporations.

Chapter 5 provides a discussion of the overall planning and goal-setting process. The chapter describes the socially constructed nature of goals and how managers decide which goals to pursue. It also outlines the criteria for effective goals and talks about the value of key performance indicators. The chapter covers some of the benefits and limitations of planning and goal setting and includes a discussion of using management by means (MBM) to lessen the problem of too much pressure to attain goals. The final section describes innovative approaches to planning to help managers plan in a fast-changing environment.

Chapter 5 continues the focus on the basics of formulating and implementing strategy, including the elements of strategy and Michael E. Porter's competitive strategies. In addition, the chapter explains the Boston Consulting Group (BCG) matrix and diversification strategy.

Chapter 6 gives an overview of managerial decision making, including decision-making models, personal decision styles, and a revised and updated discussion of biases that can cloud managers' judgment and lead to bad decisions. The chapter includes a new section on quasirationality and a short discussion of the 5 Whys technique. The final section looks at innovative group decision making, including the concept of evidence-based decision making, avoiding groupthink and escalating commitment, and using after-action reviews.

Chapter 7 discusses basic principles of organizing and describes both traditional and contemporary organizational structures in detail. The chapter includes a discussion of the strengths and weaknesses associated with each structural approach and looks at new positions such as chief digital officer (CDO) and social media director. It also offers a discussion of how companies are changing their physical space to enhance relational coordination and horizontal collaboration.

Chapter 8 focuses on the critical role of managing change and innovation in today's business environment and includes a revised and expanded discussion of disruptive innovation and the ambidextrous approach. The chapter describes the bottom-up approach to innovation and the use of innovation contests and explains the horizontal linkage model for new product development. In addition, it describes how some companies are using an innovation by acquisition strategy and discusses open innovation and crowdsourcing. The final sections of the chapter examine the reasons why many people resist change and discuss techniques for implementing change effectively.

Chapter 9 reflects the shifting role of human resource management (HRM) in today's turbulent economic environment. The chapter includes new discussions of talent management, the techniques of blind hiring and fast track hiring, and the types of training and development most desired by young professionals. The chapter also discusses pre-hire testing, using big data to make hiring or compensation decisions, acqui-hiring (acquiring start-ups to get the human talent), and using social media and internships for recruiting. The section on training and development has been updated and includes a discussion of social learning.

Chapter 9 also has a revised section that reflects the most recent thinking on organizational diversity issues. This part includes an updated discussion of demographic changes occurring in the domestic and global workforce and how organizations are responding. It also includes a new section on the challenges that minorities face in organizations, including the problem of unconscious bias. The chapter contains an expanded discussion of challenges that women face, including a revised section on the glass ceiling and the "bamboo ceiling" and delves into the importance of mentoring and employee affinity groups for supporting diverse employees.

Chapter 10 continues its solid coverage of the basics of understanding individual behavior, including personality, attitudes, perception, and emotions. In addition, the chapter includes a section on the value and difficulty of self-awareness, techniques for enhancing self-awareness and recognizing blind spots, and an expanded discussion of the concept of emotional contagion. The chapter also describes self-management and gives a step-by-step guide to time management. The section on stress management has been enhanced by a discussion of challenge stress versus threat stress and revised sections describing ways that both individuals and organizations can combat the harmful effects of too much stress.

Chapter 11 examines contemporary approaches to leadership, including Level 5 leadership, authentic leadership, and servant leadership. The chapter also discusses charismatic and transformational leadership, task versus relationship leadership behaviors, gender differences in leadership, the importance of leaders discovering and honing their strengths, and the role of followers. The section on leadership power has been enhanced with a discussion of the differences between *hard* versus *soft* power.

Chapter 12 covers the foundations of motivation and incorporates sections on positive versus negative approaches to motivating employees and the use of intrinsic versus extrinsic rewards. The chapter also describes motivational methods such as the making progress principle, employee engagement, and building a thriving workforce.

Chapter 13 explores the basics of good communication and includes discussions of using social media for communication, the importance of radical candor, using redundant communication for important messages, and practicing powerful body positions to enhance nonverbal communication. The chapter also discusses the role of listening and asking questions. It includes a section on creating an open communication climate and an expanded and enriched discussion of communicating to influence and persuade.

Chapter 14 takes a fresh look at the contributions that teams make in organizations. It also acknowledges that work teams are sometimes ineffective and explores the reasons for this, including such problems as free riders and lack of trust. The chapter looks at the difference between putting together a team and building teamwork, covers the types of teams, and includes a look at using technology effectively in virtual teams. It also discusses how factors such as team diversity, member roles, norms, and team cohesiveness influence effectiveness. The section on team norms has been enriched by a discussion of the value of promoting norms of psychological safety and equal participation for effective teamwork. There is also a section on negotiation and managing conflict, including an explanation of task versus relationship conflict and a new look at different ways of expressing conflict.

Chapter 15 provides an overview of financial and quality control, including the feedback control model, Six Sigma, International Organization for Standards (ISO) certification, and use of the balanced scorecard. The chapter includes a discussion of zero-based budgeting, an explanation of quality partnering, and a step-by-step benchmarking process. The chapter also addresses the current issue of electronic monitoring.

You can find an appendix, "Managing Start-Ups and New Ventures" in the eBook.

In addition to the topics listed previously, this text integrates coverage of the Internet, social media, and new technology into the various topics covered in each and every chapter.

Organization

The chapter sequence in *Understanding Management* is organized around the management functions of planning, organizing, leading, and controlling. These four functions effectively encompass both management research and the characteristics of the manager's job.

Part 1 introduces the world of management, including the nature of management, issues related to today's chaotic environment, historical perspectives on management, and the technology-driven workplace.

Part 2 examines the environments of management and organizations. This section includes material on the business environment and corporate culture, the global environment, and ethics and social responsibility.

Part 3 presents two chapters on planning, including organizational goal setting and planning, strategy formulation and execution, and the decision-making process.

Part 4 focuses on organizing processes. These chapters describe dimensions of structural design, the design alternatives that managers can use to achieve strategic objectives, structural designs for promoting innovation and change, the design and use of the human resource function, and how the approach to managing diverse employees is significant to the organizing function.

Part 5 is devoted to leadership and control. The section begins with a chapter on understanding individual behavior, including self-awareness and self-understanding. This foundation paves the way for subsequent discussions of leadership, motivation of employees, communication, and team management.

Part 6 describes the controlling function of management, including basic principles of total quality management (TQM), the design of control systems, and the difference between hierarchical and decentralized control.

Innovative Features

The major goals of this solution are to offer better ways to convey management knowledge to the reader, while providing opportunities for students to "think and act like a manager". To this end, the book and MindTap® include several innovative features that draw students in and help them contemplate, absorb, and apply management concepts. Cengage has brought together a team of experts to create and coordinate color photographs, video cases, beautiful artwork, and learning activities for the best management textbook and digital learning solution on the market.

Text and Ebook Features

Chapter Outline and Objectives. Each chapter begins with a clear statement of its learning objectives and an outline of its contents. These devices provide an overview of what is to come and can be used by students to guide their study and test their understanding and retention of important points.

Self-Assessments. Available in the book/e-book and MindTap, self-assessments grab students' attention immediately by giving them a chance to participate in the chapter content actively. The students answer personal questions related to the topic and score the assessment based on their answers. These self-assessments provide insight into what to expect and how students might perform in the world of the new manager.

Take Action. At strategic places within the chapter, students are invited to "Take Action" to complete a self-assessment that relates to the concepts being discussed.

Green Power. A "Green Power" box in each chapter highlights how managers in a specific company are innovatively addressing issues of sustainability and environmental responsibility. Examples of companies spotlighted in these boxes include Whole Foods Market, Cargill Foods India, Burt's Bees, Enel, Coca-Cola, Acciona, Procter & Gamble, Nike, Bean and Body, Intel, and PepsiCo.

Concept Connection Photo Essays. A key feature of the book is the use of photographs accompanied by detailed photo essay captions that enhance learning. Each caption highlights and illustrates one or more specific concepts from the text to reinforce student understanding of the concepts; they also convey the vividness, immediacy, and concreteness of management events in today's business world.

Contemporary Examples. Every chapter of this book contains several examples of management incidents. They are placed at strategic points in the chapter and are designed to illustrate the application of concepts to specific companies, including bossless organizations and other innovative designs. These in-text examples—indicated by the title "Sunny Side Up"—include well-known U.S. and international organizations, including Tesla Motors, the Golden State Warriors, Google, The Container Store, and General Motors (GM), as well as lesser-known companies and not-for-profit organizations, including Yokohama Nursery Company, the Ackerman Institute for the Family, Buurtzorg, and Upper West Side Yoga and Wellness.

Recipe for Success. A "Recipe for Success" box in each chapter addresses a specific topic straight from the food business that is of special interest to students. The new examples include Second Harvest Food Bank, Starbucks, and Kraft Foods as well as start-up organic farms, Vegan donut bakers, a Paleo bakery, two food trucks, craft services for a TV series, and various other small, and often scrappy, food companies. The boxes heighten student interest in the subject matter and provide an auxiliary view of management issues not typically available in textbooks.

Video Cases. Each chapter in MindTap and in the MindTap eReader includes a video case that illustrates the concepts presented in the text. These 15 "On the Job" videos (one per chapter) enhance the classroom experience by giving students the chance to hear from real-world business leaders so they can see the direct application of the management theories they have learned. Companies discussed include Tough Mudder, Bissell Brothers Brewery, Black Diamond Equipment, Camp Bow Wow, Theo Chocolate, and many more innovative organizations. Each video case explores critical managerial issues, allowing students to synthesize material they've just viewed. The video cases sections culminate with several questions that can be used to launch classroom discussion or can be assigned as homework. Suggested answers are provided in the Instructor's Manual.

Exhibits. Several exhibits have been added or revised in this edition to enhance student understanding. Many aspects of management are research based, and some concepts tend to be abstract and theoretical. The many exhibits throughout this book enhance students' awareness and understanding of these concepts. These exhibits consolidate key points, indicate relationships among concepts, and visually illustrate concepts. They also make effective use of color to enhance their imagery and appeal.

Remember This. At the end of each major section of a chapter is a "Remember This" bullet-point summary of the key concepts, ideas, and terms discussed in that section. The "Remember This" feature gives students an easy way to review the salient points covered in the chapter.

Glossaries. Learning the management vocabulary is essential to understanding contemporary management. This process is facilitated in three ways. First, key concepts are boldfaced and completely defined where they first appear in the text. Second, brief definitions are set out at the end of each major section in the "Remember This" list for easy review and follow-up. Third, students can access flashcards and the glossary in the MindTap product.

Discussion Questions. Each chapter closes with discussion questions that will enable students to check their understanding of key issues, to think beyond basic concepts, and to determine areas that require further study.

Apply Your Skills Exercises. End-of-chapter exercises called "Apply Your Skills" provide self-tests and exercises for students and opportunities to experience management issues in a personal way. These exercises take the form of questionnaires, scenarios, and activities.

Small Group Breakout Exercises. "Apply Your Skills: Group Learning" exercises at the end of each chapter give students a chance to develop both team and analytical skills. Completing the small-group activities will help students learn to use the resources provided by others in the group, to pool information, and to develop a successful outcome together. The "Small Group Breakouts" provide experiential learning that leads to deeper understanding and application of chapter concepts.

Off-Site Learning. "Apply Your Skills: Action Learning" offers students a chance to apply concepts from the chapter either individually or in groups.

Case for Critical Analysis. Also appearing at the end of each chapter is a brief but substantive case that offers an opportunity for student analysis and class discussion. These cases are based on real management problems and dilemmas, but the identities of companies and managers have been disguised. These cases allow students to sharpen their diagnostic skills for management problem solving.

MindTap® Management Features

MindTap® for Daft/Marcic's *Understanding Management*, 11th edition, is the digital learning solution that helps instructors engage and transform today's students into critical thinkers. Through paths of dynamic assignments and applications that you can personalize, real-time course analytics, and an accessible reader, MindTap helps you turn cookie-cutter into cutting-edge, apathy into engagement, and memorizers into higher-level thinkers. The control to build and personalize your course is all yours, letting you focus on the most relevant material while also lowering costs for your students. Stay connected and informed in your course through real-time student tracking that provides the opportunity to adjust the course as needed based on analytics of interactivity in the course.

Online Self-Assessments. Each chapter starts with short interactive self-assessment questionnaires. Students see how they respond to situations and challenges typically faced by real-life managers and get feedback that compares them with their classmates and provides insight into how they would function in the real world.

Videos. Concept clips help students gain understanding from short, detailed animations that address core concepts with narrated audio. These videos are found in MindTap and the MindTap eReader. On the Job videos give students an inside look into various companies and organizations.

Chapter Assignment. Auto-graded questions powered by *Aplia*, offer detailed feedback and a rotating pool of questions of varying complexity to help students learn to think like managers.

Chapter Quiz. These quizzes test students' knowledge of chapter concepts.

You Make the Decision. These activities let students make real-world business decisions and experience the results of their decisions to help them think like managers.

Experiential Team Task Exercises. Team Tasks (group projects) are designed to develop collaboration, communication and critical thinking skills. Powered by *YouSeeU*, instructors are provided with options for grading and rubrics, and options for setting up and monitoring groups. Students leverage tools for scheduling meetings, collaborating, setting milestones, and uploading documents or videos.

Study Tools: Practice Tests. Students can select which chapters or sections to include in a practice test that mimick's the test experience.

Affordable and Flexible Options for Students

**CENGAGE
UNLIMITED**

Cengage Unlimited is the first-of-its-kind digital subscription designed specially to lower costs. Students get total access to everything that Cengage has to offer on demand—in one place. That's 20,000 eBooks, 2,300 digital learning products, and dozens of study tools across 70 disciplines and over 675 courses, currently available in select markets. Details can be found at www.cengage.com/Unlimited.

Students can also use Cengage.com to select from rent or buy options for the textbook, ebook and MindTap.

Of Special Interest to Instructors

Instructors will find a number of valuable resources available on our online instructor resource center accessed through Cengage.com. These include the following:

Instructor's Manual. Designed to provide support for instructors new to the course as well as innovative materials for experienced professors, the Instructor's Manual includes chapter outlines, annotated learning objectives, lecture notes, and sample lecture outlines. In addition, the Instructor's Manual includes answers and teaching notes to end-of-chapter materials.

Cengage Testing Powered by Cognero. Cognero is a flexible online system that allows you to author, edit, and manage test bank content from multiple Cengage solutions; create multiple test versions in an instant; and deliver tests from your LMS (Learning Management System), your classroom, or wherever you want. The test bank has been expanded with hundreds of new questions.

PowerPoint Lecture Presentation. The PowerPoint Lecture Presentation enables instructors to customize their own multimedia classroom presentation. The material is organized by chapter and can be modified or expanded for individual classroom use.

Acknowledgments

From Richard Daft: I want to extend special appreciation to my assistant, Linda Roberts, here at Vanderbilt. Linda provided excellent support and assistance on a variety of projects that gave me time to write. I also want to acknowledge an intellectual debt to my colleagues, Bruce Barry, Mark Cannon, David Owens, Ty Park, Ranga Ramanujam, Joe Ryan, Bart Victor, and Tim Vogus. Thanks also to Deans Eric Johnson and Richard Willis, who have supported my writing projects and maintained a positive scholarly atmosphere in the school.

I'd like to pay special tribute to my longtime editorial associate, Pat Lane. I can't imagine how I would ever complete my part of a comprehensive revision without her. Pat provided truly outstanding help throughout every step of writing this edition of *Understanding Management*. She skillfully drafted materials for a wide range of chapter topics, boxes, and cases; researched topics when new sources were lacking; and did an absolutely superb job with the copyedited manuscript and page proofs. Her commitment to this text enabled us to achieve our dream for its excellence.

I also want to acknowledge the love and support from my daughters—Danielle, Amy, Roxanne, Solange, and Elizabeth—who make my life special during our precious time together.

Thanks also to BJ, Kaitlyn, Kaci, Emily, Nelson, Samantha, Roman, and Phoenix for their warmth and smiles that brighten my life.

Richard L. Daft
Nashville, Tennessee

From Dorothy Marcic: As a human who operates in community, I have many wonderful people surrounding me who give me continuous support, and this includes my assistants, Allison Greer O'Bryant and Emileena Pedigo. Friends and colleagues who gave invaluable encouragement and assistance include Bill Franzblau, Bob and Debbie Rosenfeld, Valerie Rutstein, Linda Assaf, Haley Swindall, Jamibeth Margolis, Janice Maffei, Deb Victoroff, Wendi Momen, Kathleen McEnerny, Ron Browning, Silvy and Ron Gray, Janet Conrad, Kate DeStefano Weisman, Peter McIntosh, Franz Grebacher, Gail Phanuf, Peter Neamann, Victoria Marsick, Marie Volpe, Karen Streets-Anderson, Andi Seals, Adrienne Corn, Mark and Maxine Rossman, Adrienne Ewing-Roush, Hillary Chapman, Kenneth Ferrone, Aram Ferdowsi, Nikki Gundry, and Lishy Price. And Dick Daft, whose collaboration on this book is greatly satisfying. How can one do such a project without family love and support? My sister, Janet Mittelsteadt, is a true friend; my cousins, Shannon Stordock Hecht, Donna Stordock, Rick and Bill Stordock, Marilyn Nowak, Michael Shoemaker (the genealogist who has helped me find my own roots), and Katherine Runde (who is so precious), and Tony, Iskandar, and Eden Hai. There is no way to imagine my life without my three beautiful daughters—Roxanne, Solange, and Elizabeth, along with my amazing sons-in-law, Thomas Williams and Ryan Lash—who have taught me more than all my degrees combined, and then my lovely stepdaughters, Danielle and Amy. And finally, what I see now as the crowning aspect of life, my four grandchildren, Nelson, Phoenix, Roman, and Samantha. You light up my life.

Dorothy Marcic
New York, NY

We would also like to continue to acknowledge those reviewers who have contributed comments, suggestions, and feedback on this and all previous editions:

David C. Adams
Manhattanville College

David Alexander
Christian Brothers University

Erin M. Alexander
University of Houston–Clear Lake

David Arseneau
Eastern Illinois University

Reginald L. Audibert
California State University–Long Beach

Hal Babson
Columbus State Community College

Reuel Barksdale
Columbus State Community College

Gloria Bemben
Finger Lakes Community College

Pat Bernson
County College of Morris

Andy Bertsch
Minot State University

Art Bethke
Northeast Louisiana University

Frank Bosco
Marshall University

Burrell A. Brown
California University of Pennsylvania

Paula Buchanan
Jacksonville State University

Deb Buerkley
Southwest Minnesota State University

Thomas Butte
Humboldt State University

Peter Bycio
Xavier University, Ohio

Diane Caggiano
Fitchburg State College

Douglas E. Cathon
St. Augustine's College

Peggy Cerrito
Augsburg College

Camille Chapman
Greenville Technical College

Bruce Charnov
Hofstra University

Jim Ciminskie
Bay de Noc Community College

Gloria Cockerell
Collin College

Dan Connaughton
University of Florida

Bruce Conwers
Kaskaskia College

Jack Cox
Amberton University

Byron L. David
City College of New York

V. J. Daviero
Pasco Hernando Community College

H. Kristl Davison
University of Mississippi

Richard De Luca
William Paterson University

Robert DeDominic
Montana Tech

Mark DeHainaut
California University of Pennsylvania

Granison Eader
Manor College

Joe J. Eassa, Jr.
Palm Beach Atlantic University

John C. Edwards
East Carolina University

Mary Ann Edwards
College of Mount St. Joseph

Paul Ewell
Bridgewater College

Mary M. Fanning
College of Notre Dame of Maryland

Janice M. Feldbauer
Austin Community College

Merideth Ferguson
Baylor University

Daryl Fortin
Upper Iowa University

Karen Fritz
Bridgewater College

Michael P. Gagnon
New Hampshire Community Technical College

Richard H. Gayor
Antelope Valley College

Dan Geeding
Xavier University, Ohio

James Genseal
Joliet Junior College

Peter Gibson
Becker College

Alexandra Giesler
Augsburg College

Yezdi H. Godiwalla
*University of
Wisconsin–Whitewater*

Carol R. Graham
*Western Kentucky
University*

Gary Greene
Manatee Community College

James Halloran
Wesleyan College

Ken Harris
*Indiana University
Southeast*

Martin Hart
*Manchester Community
College*

Kathy Hastings
Greenville Technical College

Paul Hayes
*Coastal Carolina Community
College*

Dennis Heaton
*Maharishi University of
Management, Iowa*

Stephen R. Hiatt
Catawba College

Jeffrey D. Hines
Davenport College

Bob Hoerber
Westminster College

Betty Hoge
Bridgewater College

James N. Holly
*University of Wisconsin–
Green Bay*

Genelle Jacobson
Ridgewater College

Jody Jones
*Oklahoma Christian
University*

C. Joy Jones
Ohio Valley College

Kathleen Jones
University of North Dakota

Sheryl Kae
Lynchburg College

Jordan J. Kaplan
Long Island University

J. Michael Keenan
Western Michigan University

Jerry Kinard
Western Carolina University

Renee Nelms King
Eastern Illinois University

Gloria Komer
Stark State College

Paula C. Kougl
Western Oregon University

Cynthia Krom
Mount St. Mary College

Sal Kukalis
*California State University–
Long Beach*

Mukta Kulkarni
*University of Texas–San
Antonio*

Donna LaGanga
*Tunxis Community
College*

William B. Lamb
Millsaps College

Ruth D. Lapsley
*Lewis-Clark State
College*

Robert E. Ledman
Morehouse College

George Lehma
Bluffton College

Joyce LeMay
Bethel University

Cynthia Lengnick-Hall
*University of Texas–San
Antonio*

Gilda Lewis
University of Memphis

Janet C. Luke
*Georgia Baptist College of
Nursing*

Jenna Lundburg
Ithaca College

Walter J. MacMillan
Oral Roberts University

Iraj Mahdavi
National University

Myrna P. Mandell
*California State University,
Northridge*

Daniel B. Marin
Louisiana State University

Michael Market
Jacksonville State University

Joan McBee
Southern Oregon University

Wade McCutcheon
East Texas Baptist College

James C. McElroy
Iowa State University

Tom D. McFarland
Tusculum College

Dennis W. Meyers
*Texas State Technical
College*

Alan N. Miller
*University of Nevada–
Las Vegas*

Irene A. Miller
*Southern Illinois
University*

Tom Miller
Concordia University

W J Mitchell
Bladen Community College

Daniel Morrell
*Middle Tennessee State
University*

James L. Moseley
Wayne State University

Micah Mukabi
Essex County College

David W. Murphy
*Madisonville Community
College*

Nora Nurre
Upper Iowa University

Ross O'Brien
Dallas Baptist University

Tomas J. Ogazon
St. Thomas University

Allen Oghenejbo
Mills College

John Okpara
Bloomsburg University

Linda Overstreet
Hillsborough Community College

Michael Payne
Milwaukee School of Engineering

Ken Peterson
Metropolitan State University

Lori A. Peterson
Augsburg College

Clifton D. Petty
Drury College

James I. Phillips
Northeastern State University

Marliss Platz
Cankdeska Cikana Community College

Michael Provitera
Barry University

Linda Putchinski
University of Central Florida

Abe Qastin
Lakeland College

Kenneth Radig
Medaille College

Gerald D. Ramsey
Indiana University Southeast

Holly Caldwell Ratwani
Bridgewater College

Barbara Redmond
Briar Cliff College

Tommie Redwine
Clatsop Community College

William Reisel
St. John's University–New York

Barbara Ribbens
Illinois State University

Terry L. Riddle
Central Virginia Community College

Linda Ridley
Hostos Community College

Walter F. Rohrs
Wagner College

Meir Russ
University of Wisconsin–Green Bay

Marcy Satterwhite
Lake Land College

Don Schreiber
Baylor University

Kilmon Shin
Ferris State University

Daniel G. Spencer
University of Kansas

Gary Spokes
Pace University

M. Sprencz
David N. Meyers College

Shanths Srinivas
California State Polytechnic University, Pomona

Barbara Stasek
Pasco Hernando Community College

Jeffrey Stauffer
Ventura College

William A. Stower
Seton Hall University

Mary Studer
Southwestern Michigan College

James Swenson
Moorhead State University, Minnesota

Thomas Sy
California State University–Long Beach

Irwin Talbot
St. Peter's College

Andrew Timothy
Lourdes College

Frank G. Titlow
St. Petersburg Junior College

John Todd
University of Arkansas

Kevin A. Van Dewark
Humphreys College Linn Van Dyne Michigan State University

Philip Varca
University of Wyoming

Dennis L. Varin
Southern Oregon University

Gina Vega
Merrimack College

George S. Vozikis
University of Tulsa

Noemy Wachtel
Kean University

Peter Wachtel
Kean University

Bruce C. Walker
Northeast Louisiana University

Kevin Wayne
Rivier College

Mark Weber
University of Minnesota

Emilia S. Westney
Texas Tech University

Rhonda Wetzler
Illinois Central College

Irene Wilder
Jefferson Community College

Stan Williamson
Northeast Louisiana University

Alla L. Wilson
University of Wisconsin–Green Bay

Ignatius Yacomb
Loma Linda University

Imad Jim Zbib
Ramapo College of New Jersey

Vic Zimmerman
Pima Community College

About the Authors

Courtesy of the Author

Richard L. Daft, Ph.D., is the Brownlee O. Currey, Jr., Professor of Management and Principal Senior Lecturer in the Owen Graduate School of Management at Vanderbilt University. Professor Daft specializes in the study of organization theory and leadership. He is a fellow of the Academy of Management and has served on the editorial boards of the *Academy of Management Journal, Administrative Science Quarterly,* and *Journal of Management Education.* He was the associate editor-in-chief of *Organization Science* and served for three years as associate editor of *Administrative Science Quarterly.*

Professor Daft has authored or co-authored more than a dozen books, including *Building Management Skills: An Action-First Approach* (with Dorothy Marcic, South-Western, 2014), *The Executive and the Elephant: A Leader's Guide for Building Inner Excellence* (Jossey-Bass, 2010), *Organization Theory and Design* (South-Western, 2016), *The Leadership Experience* (South-Western, 2018), and *Fusion Leadership: Unlocking the Subtle Forces That Change People and Organizations* (Berrett-Koehler, 2000, with Robert Lengel). He has also written dozens of scholarly articles, papers, and chapters in other books. His work has been published in *Administrative Science Quarterly, Academy of Management Journal, Academy of Management Review, Strategic Management Journal, Journal of Management, Accounting Organizations and Society, Management Science, MIS Quarterly, California Management Review,* and *Organizational Behavior Teaching Review.* Professor Daft is listed among the world's most highly cited authors in the fields of economics and business. In addition, he is an active teacher and consultant.

Professor Daft has taught management, leadership, organizational change, organizational theory, and organizational behavior. He has served as associate dean, produced for-profit theatrical productions, and helped manage a start-up enterprise. He has been involved in management development and consulting for many companies and government organizations, including the American Banking Association, Bridgestone/Firestone, Bell Canada, the National Transportation Research Board, the National Academy of Science, the Tennessee Valley Authority (TVA), Pratt & Whitney, State Farm Insurance, Tenneco, the U.S. Air Force, the U.S. Army, J. C. Bradford & Co., Central Parking System, Entergy Sales and Service, Bristol-Myers Squibb, First American National Bank, United Methodist Church, Oak Ridge National Laboratory, and the Vanderbilt University Medical Group.

Francois Bonneau

Dorothy Marcic, Ed.D, M.P.H., M.F.A., is a professor at Columbia University and former faculty member at Vanderbilt University. Dr. Marcic is also a former Fulbright Scholar at the University of Economics in Prague and the Czech Management Center where she taught courses and did research on leadership, organizational behavior, and cross-cultural management. She has taught courses at the Monterrey Institute of International Studies and has taught courses or given presentations at the Helsinki School of Economics, Slovenia Management Center, College of Trade in Bulgaria, City University of Slovakia, Landegg Institute in Switzerland, the Swedish Management Association, Technion University in Israel, and the London School of Economics. Other international work includes projects at the Autonomous University in Guadalajara, Mexico, and a training program for the World Health Organization in Guatemala. She has served on the boards of the Organizational Teaching Society, the Health Administration Section of the American Public Health Association, and the *Journal of Applied Business Research.*

Dr. Marcic has authored 18 books, including *Organizational Behavior: Experiences and Cases* (South-Western Publishing, 6th edition, 2001), *Management International* (West Publishing, 1984), *Women and Men in Organizations* (George Washington University, 1984), and *Managing with the Wisdom of Love: Uncovering Virtue in People and Organizations* (Jossey-Bass, 1997), which was rated one of the top 10 business books of 1997 by *Management General,* as well as *Love Lift Me Higher* (George Ronald, 2011). Her most recent book is a true crime thriller about

the murder of her uncle and is called *With One Shot: Family Murder and a Search for Justice.* In addition, she has had dozens of articles printed in such publications as *Journal of Management Development, International Quarterly of Community Health Education, Psychological Reports,* and *Executive Development.* She has recently been exploring how to use the arts in the teaching of leadership and has a book, *RESPECT: Women and Popular Music,* which serves as the basis for the musical theater production *Respect: A Musical Journey of Women (*also titled *This One's for the Girls,* which has played in over 75 cities and also the Off-Broadway *SISTAS: The Musical,* in its eighth year Off-Broadway.

Professor Marcic has conducted thousands of seminars on various business topics and consulted for executives at AT&T Bell Labs, the governor and cabinet of North Dakota, the U.S. Air Force, Slovak Management Association, Eurotel, Hallmark Corp, Viacom, Czech Ministry of Finance, the Cattaraugus Center, USAA Insurance, State Farm Insurance, the Salt River–Pima Indian Tribe in Arizona, and Viacom.

Brief Contents

Contents

Chapter 3   Managing in a Global Environment   86

Chapter 4   Managing Ethics and Social Responsibility   118

Part 3 Planning 150

Chapter 5 Planning and Goal Setting 150

Chapter 6 Managerial Decision Making 190

Part 5 Leading 364

Chapter 10 Understanding Individual Behavior 364

Chapter 13 Managing Communication 478

Chapter 14 Leading Teams 512

Part 6   Controlling   548

Chapter 15 Managing Quality and Performance   548

PART 1

Chapter 1

The World of Innovative Management

iStock.com/oscarhdez

Chapter Outline

Learning Outcomes

After studying this chapter, you should be able to:

1.1 Describe five management competencies that are becoming crucial in today's fast-paced and rapidly changing world.

1.2 Define the four management functions and the type of management activity associated with each.

1.3 Explain the difference between efficiency and effectiveness and their importance for organizational performance.

1.4 Describe technical, human, and conceptual skills and their relevance for managers.

1.5 Describe management types and the horizontal and vertical differences among them.

1.6 Summarize the personal challenges involved in becoming a new manager.

1.7 Define 10 roles that managers perform in organizations.

1.8 Explain the unique characteristics of the manager's role in small businesses and nonprofit organizations.

1.9 Summarize the historical struggle between managing the "things of production" and the "humanity of production."

1.10 Describe the major components of the classical and humanistic management perspectives.

1.11 Discuss the management science approach and its current use in organizations.

1.12 Explain the major concepts of systems thinking and the contingency view.

1.13 Provide examples of contemporary management tools and explain why these trends change over time.

1.14 Describe the management changes brought about by a technology-focused workplace, including the role of big data analytics and supply chain management.

1.15 Explain how organizations are implementing the ideas of bossless workplaces and employee engagement to facilitate a people-focused workplace.

1.16 Explain how social business is bridging the historical struggle between managing the "things of production" and the "humanity of production."

Are You Ready To Be a Manager?

Before reading this chapter, please circle either "Mostly True" or "Mostly False" for each of the following five statements.

1 I am good at multitasking.

Mostly True ◀ ·················· ▶ Mostly False

[page 16]

2 I'd be a good manager because I enjoy telling people what to do.

Mostly True ◀ ·················· ▶ Mostly False

[Page 5]

3 I get easily distracted if I have frequent interruptions in my work.

Mostly True ◀ ·················· ▶ Mostly False

[page 17]

4 I like to be systematic when solving problems.

Mostly True ◀ ·················· ▶ Mostly False

[page 25]

5 I have a keen awareness of other people's needs.

Mostly True ◀ ·················· ▶ Mostly False

[Page 31]

Discover Your Management Approach

Welcome to the world of management. Are you ready for it? This questionnaire will help you see whether your priorities align with the demands placed on today's managers.

Instructions: Rate each of the following items based on your orientation toward personal achievement. Read each item and based on how you feel right now, check either Mostly True or Mostly False.

	Mostly True	Mostly False
1. I enjoy the feeling I get from mastering a new skill.	_____	_____
2. Working alone is typically better than working in a group.	_____	_____
3. I like the feeling I get from winning.	_____	_____

To complete and score the entire assessment, visit MindTap.

"In the late 1980s, it seemed inconceivable that Bon Jovi would last five years," wrote one music historian. Yet more than three decades after the rock group was founded, it is still one of the world's top-selling bands. In 2014, Jon Bon Jovi was ranked No. 4 on *Forbes*'s list of the year's highest-paid musicians, and the December 2015 announcement of the band's 14th album had classic rock fans eagerly anticipating another concert tour.[1] Bon Jovi has been so successful partly because its lead singer and namesake is a consummate manager. For example, as the group prepared for the launch of its most recent tour, Jon Bon Jovi was hidden away in the arena at the Mohegan Sun casino in Uncasville, Connecticut, for days, overseeing nearly 100 people organized into various teams such as lighting, sound, and video. It is an activity that he performs again and again when the band is touring, managing a tightly coordinated operation similar to setting up or readjusting a production line for a manufacturing business. Yet Bon Jovi is also performing other management activities throughout the year—planning and setting goals for the future, organizing tasks and assigning responsibilities, influencing and motivating band members and others, monitoring operations and finances, and networking inside and outside the organization (in perhaps the most prestigious example, he was appointed to President Barack Obama's White House Council for Community Solutions). *Efficiency* and *effectiveness* are key words in his vocabulary. "Jon is a businessman," said former comanager David Munns. "He knows how to have a great-quality show, but he also knows how to be efficient with money."[2]

Jon Bon Jovi was smart enough to hire good people who could handle both production activities and the day-to-day minutiae that go along with a global music business. However, it took several years to develop and hone his management skills. He assumed top management responsibilities for the band in 1992, about 10 years after founding it, because he had a vision that his professional managers weren't supporting. "Most of my peers wanted to be on the cover of *Circus* [a magazine devoted to rock music that was published from 1966 to 2006]," he said. "I wanted to be on the cover of *Time*."[3]

The nature of management is to motivate and coordinate others to cope with diverse and far-reaching challenges. One surprise for many people when they first step into a management role is that they are much less in control of things than they expected to be. Many new managers expect to have power, to be in control, and to be personally responsible for departmental outcomes. However, managers, who depend on subordinates more than the reverse, are evaluated on the work of other people rather than on their own achievements. Managers set up the systems and conditions that help other people perform well.

In the past, many managers exercised tight control over employees. But the field of management is undergoing a revolution that asks managers to do more with less, to engage employees' hearts and minds as well as their physical energy, to see change rather than stability as natural, and to inspire vision and cultural values that allow people to create a truly collaborative and productive workplace. This textbook introduces and explains the process of management and the changing ways of thinking about the world that are critical for managers.

Management matters, as substantiated by a McKinsey Global Institute study. In collaboration with the Centre for Economic Performance at the London School of Economics and partners from Stanford and Harvard Universities, McKinsey collected data over a dozen years from roughly 14,000 organizations in more than 30 countries. The data show that well-managed companies have higher productivity, higher market value, and greater growth, as well as a superior ability to survive difficult conditions.[4] By reviewing the actions of some successful and not-so-successful managers, you will learn the fundamentals of management. By the end of this chapter, you will recognize some of the skills that managers use to keep organizations on track, and you will begin to understand how managers can achieve astonishing results through people. By the end of this book, you will understand the fundamental management skills for planning, organizing, leading, and controlling a department or an entire organization.

1-1 Management Competencies for Today's World

Management is the attainment of organizational goals in an effective and efficient manner through planning, organizing, leading, and controlling organizational resources as Jon Bon Jovi does for his rock band and as chairman of the Jon Bon Jovi Soul Foundation, a nonprofit organization that supports community efforts to combat poverty and homelessness. You will learn more about these four basic management functions later in this chapter.

There are certain elements of management that are timeless, but environmental shifts also influence the practice of management. In recent years, rapid environmental changes have caused a fundamental transformation in what is required of effective managers. Technological advances such as social media and mobile apps, the move to a knowledge/information-based economy, the rise of virtual work, global market forces, the growing threat of cyber crime, and shifting employee and customer expectations have led to a decline in organizational hierarchies and more empowered workers, which calls for a new approach to management that may be quite different from managing in the past.[5] Exhibit 1.1 shows the shift from the traditional management approach to the new management competencies that are essential in today's environment.

Instead of being a *controller*, today's effective manager is an *enabler* who helps people do and be their best. Today's managers learn to "design the rules of the game without specifying the actions of the players."[6] Managers shape the cultures, systems, and conditions and then give people the freedom to move the organization in the direction it needs to go. Managers help people get what they need, remove obstacles, provide learning opportunities, and offer feedback, coaching, and career guidance. Instead of "management by keeping tabs," they employ an empowering leadership style. Much work is done in teams rather than by individuals, so team leadership skills are crucial. People in many organizations work at scattered locations, so managers can't monitor behavior continually. Some organizations are even experimenting with a bossless design that turns management authority and responsibility over to employees. Managing relationships based on authentic conversation and collaboration is essential for successful outcomes. Social media represent a growing tool for managers to enhance communication and collaboration in support of empowered or bossless work environments. In addition, managers sometimes coordinate the work of people who aren't under their direct control, such as those in partner organizations, and they sometimes even work with competitors. They have to find common ground among people who might have disparate views and agendas and align them to go in the same direction.

"I was once a command-and-control guy, but the environment's different today. I think now it's a question of making people feel they're making a contribution."

—JOSEPH J. PLUMERI, FORMER CHAIRMAN AND CEO OF WILLIS GROUP HOLDINGS

Exhibit 1.1 State-of-the-Art Management Competencies for Today's World

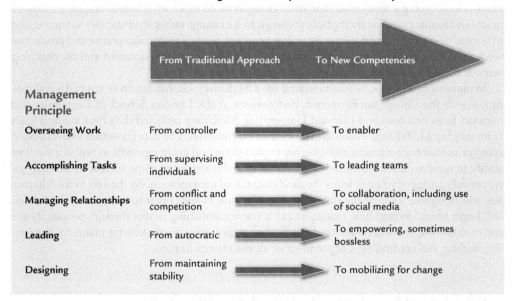

Management Principle	From Traditional Approach	To New Competencies
Overseeing Work	From controller	To enabler
Accomplishing Tasks	From supervising individuals	To leading teams
Managing Relationships	From conflict and competition	To collaboration, including use of social media
Leading	From autocratic	To empowering, sometimes bossless
Designing	From maintaining stability	To mobilizing for change

Also, as shown in Exhibit 1.1, today's best managers are "future facing." That is, they design the organization and culture to anticipate threats and opportunities from the environment, challenge the status quo, and promote creativity, learning, adaptation, and innovation. Industries, technologies, economies, governments, and societies are in constant flux, and managers are responsible for helping their organizations navigate through the unpredictable with flexibility and innovation.[7] Today's world is constantly changing, but "the more unpredictable the environment, the greater the opportunity—if [managers] have the . . . skills to capitalize on it."[8]

There are managers in all types of organizations who are learning to apply the new management skills and competencies, and you will learn about some of them throughout this textbook. Consider how coaches of the Oregon Ducks football team are applying new management ideas.

Sunny Side Up } **Oregon Ducks**

"It's awesome," the Oregon Ducks starting center told a reporter. "There's leadership everywhere you go. We call it horizontal leadership." Hroniss Grasu now plays for the Chicago Bears of the National Football League (NFL), but he spent four years as starting center for the University of Oregon Ducks.

The Ducks are known for doing things differently. Instead of a hierarchical organization with the head coach at the top, Ducks coaches, administrators, and players are considered equals and collaborators. When head coach Mark Helfrich was asked about the team's leadership, he quickly mentioned about 10 names of players who had stepped forward as vocal leaders. A freshman can call out a senior just as easily as a senior star can challenge a new player. The lowliest graduate assistant is treated with the same respect and esteem as a high-level staff member. "It's so different here," said player

Bralon Addison. "Everybody's just 'one' and I like that so much about this team."

Another way in which the Ducks are different is that coaches have done away with the traditional approach of yelling at players in favor of a softer, more caring method of correction and motivation. "When you put your arm around a guy and say, 'This is how it could be done better,' they understand you care about them and you just want what's best for the team," said Marcus Mariota, the Ducks Heisman Trophy–winning former quarterback. "Those guys already understand that they did wrong."

Former defensive coordinator Nick Aliotti says things weren't that way when he coached for the Ducks. "I would raise my voice at times," he admits. "But society has changed." By the end of his career with Oregon, Aliotti says he rarely raised his voice because players were no longer responding to that kind of communication.[9]

The approach the Oregon Ducks coaches use to interact with a new generation of football players is also being used more often in other types of organizations. Research has found that the "drill sergeant approach" doesn't go over well with the "Millennial" generation (those born in the 1980s and 1990s), so managers in all types of organizations are using a softer, more collaborative style of management.[10]

The shift to a new way of managing isn't easy for traditional managers who are accustomed to being "in charge," making all the decisions, and knowing where their subordinates are and what they're doing at every moment. Even more changes and challenges are on the horizon for organizations and managers. This is an exciting and challenging time to be entering the field of management. Throughout this book, you will learn much more about the new workplace, about the new and dynamic roles that managers are playing in the twenty-first century, and about how you can be an effective manager in a complex, ever-changing world.

Remember This

- Managers get things done by coordinating and motivating other people.
- Management is often a different experience from what people expect.
- **Management** is defined as the attainment of organizational goals in an effective and efficient manner through planning, organizing, leading, and controlling organizational resources.
- Turbulent environmental forces have caused a significant shift in the competencies required for effective managers.

- Traditional management competencies could include a command-and-control leadership style, a focus on individual tasks, and a standardization of procedures to maintain stability.
- New management competencies include being an enabler rather than a controller, using an empowering leadership style, encouraging collaboration, leading teams, and mobilizing for change and innovation.
- The Oregon Ducks football team illustrates some of the new management competencies.

1-2 The Basic Functions of Management

Every day, managers solve difficult problems, turn organizations around, and achieve astonishing performances. To be successful, every organization needs good managers. The famed management theorist Peter Drucker (1909–2005), often credited with creating the modern study of management, summed up the job of the manager by specifying five tasks, as outlined in Exhibit 1.2.[11] In essence, managers set goals, organize activities, motivate and communicate, measure performance, and develop people. These five manager activities apply not only to top executives such as Mark Zuckerberg at Facebook, Ginni Rometty at IBM, and Kenneth Chenault at American Express but also to the manager of a restaurant in your hometown, the leader of an airport security team, a supervisor at a Web hosting service, or the director of sales and marketing for a local business.

The activities outlined in Exhibit 1.2 fall into four fundamental management functions: planning (setting goals and deciding activities), organizing (organizing activities and people), leading (motivating, communicating with, and developing people), and controlling (establishing targets and measuring performance). Depending on their job situation, managers perform numerous and varied tasks, but they all can be categorized within these four primary functions.

Exhibit 1.2 illustrates the process of how managers use resources to attain organizational goals through the functions of planning, organizing, leading, and controlling. Chapters of this book are devoted to the multiple activities and skills associated with each function, as well as to the environment, global competitiveness, and ethics that influence how managers perform these functions. Ineffective control can damage an organization. A good example comes from the U.S. Secret Service, which has been embroiled in a public relations nightmare for several years, partly due to a breakdown of managerial control. For example, in March 2015, after a night out drinking,

"Good management is the art of making problems so interesting and their solutions so constructive that everyone wants to get to work and deal with them."

—PAUL HAWKEN, ENVIRONMENTALIST, ENTREPRENEUR, AND AUTHOR OF *NATURAL CAPITALISM*

Exhibit 1.2 What Do Managers Do?

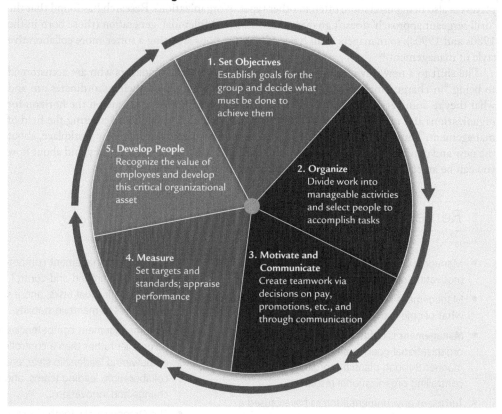

1. Set Objectives
Establish goals for the group and decide what must be done to achieve them

2. Organize
Divide work into manageable activities and select people to accomplish tasks

3. Motivate and Communicate
Create teamwork via decisions on pay, promotions, etc., and through communication

4. Measure
Set targets and standards; appraise performance

5. Develop People
Recognize the value of employees and develop this critical organizational asset

SOURCE: Based on "What Do Managers Do?" *The Wall Street Journal Online*, http://guides.wsj.com/management/developing-a-leadership-style/what-do-managers-do /(accessed August 11, 2010), article adapted from Alan Murray, *The Wall Street Journal Essential Guide to Management* (New York: Harper Business, 2010).

Don Bartletti/Getty Images

Concept Connection

John Stonecipher finds that as the president and CEO of Guidance Aviation, a high-altitude flight school in Prescott, Arizona, his job involves all four management functions. Once he's charted the course for the operation (**planning**) and put all the necessary policies, procedures, and structural mechanisms in place (**organizing**), he supports and encourages his 50+ employees (**leading**) and makes sure that nothing falls through the cracks (**controlling**). Thanks to his strengths in all of these areas, the U.S. Small Business Administration named Stonecipher a National Small Business Person of the Year.

two senior agents in a government car hit a security barrier at an active bomb investigation near the White House. Although officers on duty wanted to administer a sobriety test, a supervisor told the officers to let the offending agents go home. This event, combined with numerous other allegations of agent misconduct and "morally repugnant behavior," has put the Secret Service in a harsh spotlight. Two directors have resigned under pressure, and numerous agents and top executives have been fired or demoted. One response from managers has been to create stricter rules of conduct, rules that apply even when agents are off duty.[12]

Remember This

- Managers perform a wide variety of activities that fall within four primary management functions.
- Recent U.S. Secret Service agency scandals can be traced partly to a breakdown of management control.

1-3 Organizational Performance

The definition of management also encompasses the idea of attaining organizational goals in an efficient and effective manner. Management is so important because organizations are so important. In an industrialized society where complex technologies dominate, organizations bring together knowledge, people, and raw materials to perform tasks that no individual could do alone. Without organizations, how could technology be provided that enables us to share information around the world in an instant; electricity be produced from huge dams and nuclear power plants; and millions of songs, videos, and games be available for our entertainment at any time and place? Organizations pervade our society, and managers are responsible for seeing that resources are used wisely to attain organizational goals.

Our formal definition of an **organization** is a social entity that is goal directed and deliberately structured. *Social entity* means being made up of two or more people. *Goal directed* means designed to achieve some outcome, such as make a profit (Target Stores), win pay increases for members (United Food & Commercial Workers), meet spiritual needs (Lutheran Church), or provide social satisfaction (college sorority Alpha Delta Pi). *Deliberately structured* means that tasks are divided, and responsibility for their performance is assigned to organization members. This definition applies to all organizations, including both for-profit and nonprofit ones. Small, offbeat, and nonprofit organizations are more numerous than large, visible corporations—and just as important to society.

Based on our definition of management, the manager's responsibility is to coordinate resources in an effective and efficient manner to accomplish the organization's goals. Organizational **effectiveness** is the degree to which the organization achieves a *stated goal*, or succeeds in accomplishing what it tries to do. Organizational effectiveness means providing a product or service that customers value. Organizational **efficiency** refers to the amount of resources used to achieve an organizational goal. It is based on how much raw material, money, and people are necessary for producing a given volume of output. *Efficiency* can be defined as the amount of resources used to produce a product or service. Efficiency and effectiveness can both be high in the same organization.

Many managers are using mobile apps to increase efficiency, and in some cases, the apps can enhance effectiveness as well.[13] For example, Square is revolutionizing small business by enabling any smartphone to become a point-of-sale (POS) terminal that allows the user to accept credit card payments. Millions of small businesses and entrepreneurs in the United States and Canada who once had to turn customers away because they couldn't afford the fees charged by credit card

Green Power

A Local Market in a Box Can a huge corporation that is frequently targeted by environmental activists be a force for social good? Coca-Cola CEO Muhtar Kent believes so. The company has set specific goals to improve the well-being of the communities in which it operates, achieve water neutrality in its products and production, and empower women entrepreneurs. One tangible project is the Ekocenter, an off-the-grid, modular "community market in a box" that is run by a local female entrepreneur. At the Ekocenter, customers can charge their mobile devices, send a fax, access the Internet, pick up educational materials on hygiene and health issues, and buy basic products. Each Ekocenter has solar panels to provide consistent power and reduce the environmental footprint.

With plans for 150 Ekocenters in Africa, Asia, and Latin America, the purpose is to stimulate the local economies and provide some of the most remote and distressed communities in the world access to things many of us take for granted, such as safe drinking water, electric power, and Internet access. The local markets in a box will ultimately create 600 new jobs, mostly for local women entrepreneurs.

SOURCE: Based on Eric J. McNulty, "Teaching the World to Do More Than Sing," *Strategy + Business* (September 8, 2015), http://www.strategy-business.com/article/00358?gko=a9ace (accessed February 15, 2016).

Recipe for Success } **General Mills**

Sales at General Mills have been lagging, but thanks to extensive and thoughtful cost-cutting and smart strategic decisions, profits haven't suffered. General Mills managers pay attention to both efficiency and effectiveness.

To reduce overhead expenses, managers have cut hundreds of jobs at corporate headquarters, closed factories, and sold off the struggling Green Giant and Le Sueur brands. An annual efficiency program that concentrates on reducing waste and improving productivity has saved $2.4 billion over the past five years. But CEO Ken Powell knows cutting costs isn't enough. "To have a sustainable business model, you have to have growth," he says.

General Mills managers are pumping money into products that meet changing consumer tastes. Powell says Millennial consumers, a growing part of the company's customer base, have "different food values" and pay much more attention to what goes into their food. The company recently bought the natural and organic food maker Annie's, reduced sugar by 25 percent in its original Yoplait yogurt, and introduced several new products under the Nature Valley brand. General Mills has also cut salt from many of its products and banished artificial colors and flavors from all of its cereals. Gluten-free Chex is the company's fastest-growing cereal, so managers cut gluten from Cheerios and are rolling out more gluten-free products.

General Mills managers strive to find a balance between efficiency and effectiveness to stay competitive in the rapidly changing food industry. "I've been doing this a long time, and I've never seen it this fast," Powell said.[14]

companies can now use Square to process credit cards. Customers get their need to pay with a card met, and businesses get a sale that they might have missed.[15]

All managers have to pay attention to costs, but severe cost cutting to improve efficiency—whether it is by using cutting-edge technology or old-fashioned frugality—can sometimes hurt organizational effectiveness. The ultimate responsibility of managers is to achieve high **performance**, which is the attainment of organizational goals by using resources in an efficient *and* effective manner. Consider the example of General Mills, maker of Cheerios cereal and Betty Crocker dessert mixes.

Powell knows he and his managers must both run an efficient operation as well as adapt their company's products to give customers what they want. Compare the approach of General Mills managers to what happened at music company EMI. Weak sales led managers to focus on financial efficiency, which successfully trimmed waste and boosted operating income. However, the efficiencies damaged effectiveness by reducing the company's ability to recruit new artists, who are vital to record companies, and also led to internal turmoil that caused some longtime acts like the Rolling Stones to leave the label. Thus, the company's overall performance suffered. After struggling for several years, the century-old music company was split in two and sold for $4.1 billion to Universal Music Group and Sony Corporation.[16]

Remember This

- An **organization** is a social entity that is goal-directed and deliberately structured.
- Good management is important because organizations contribute so much to society.
- **Efficiency** pertains to the amount of resources—raw materials, money, and people—used to produce a desired volume of output.
- **Effectiveness** refers to the degree to which the organization achieves a stated goal.
- Some managers are using mobile apps to increase efficiency; one example is Square, which is used to process credit and debit card payments with a smartphone.
- **Performance** is defined as the organization's ability to attain its goals by using resources in an efficient and effective manner.
- Managers at General Mills are concerned both with keeping costs low (efficiency) and providing products that meet changing consumer tastes (effectiveness).

1-4 Management Skills

A manager's job requires a range of skills. Although some management theorists propose a long list of skills, the necessary skills for managing a department or an organization can be placed in three categories: conceptual, human, and technical.[17] As illustrated in Exhibit 1.3, the application of these skills changes dramatically when a person is promoted to management. Although the degree of each skill that is required at different levels of an organization may vary, all managers must possess some skill in each of these important areas to perform effectively.

Human skills are increasingly important for managers at all levels and in all types of organizations.[18] Even at a company such as Google, which depends on technical expertise, human skills are considered essential for managers. Google analyzed performance reviews and feedback surveys to find out what makes a good manager of technical people and found that technical expertise ranked dead last among a list of eight desired manager qualities, as shown in Exhibit 1.4. The exhibit lists eight effective behaviors of good managers. Notice that almost all of them relate to human skills, such as communication, coaching, and teamwork. People want managers who listen to them, build positive relationships, and show an interest in their lives and careers.[19] A recent study found that human skills were significantly more important than technical skills for predicting manager effectiveness.[20] Another survey compared the importance of managerial skills today with those from the late 1980s and found a decided increase in the role of skills for building relationships with others.[21]

JERRY LAMPEN/Getty Images

Concept Connection

Holding degrees in both physics and economics, entrepreneur Elon Musk certainly possesses his share of **technical skills**. He designed and created the first viable electric car—the Tesla roadster—as well as the Web-based payment service PayPal and a spacecraft that will enable private citizens to travel to outer space. But it is his stellar **conceptual skills** that allow him to lead the innovative companies that are making these products and services available to people worldwide.

Exhibit 1.3 Relationship of Technical, Human, and Conceptual Skills to Management

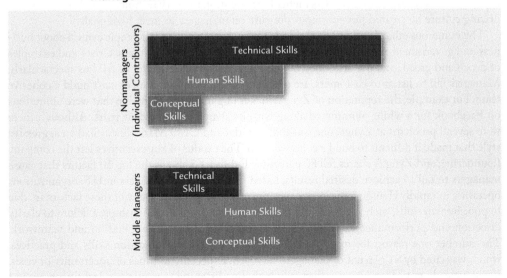

Exhibit 1.4 Google's Rules: Eight Good Behaviors for Managers

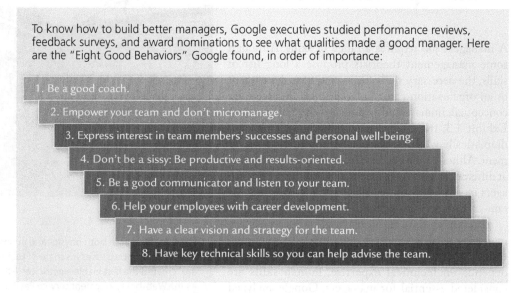

To know how to build better managers, Google executives studied performance reviews, feedback surveys, and award nominations to see what qualities made a good manager. Here are the "Eight Good Behaviors" Google found, in order of importance:

1. Be a good coach.
2. Empower your team and don't micromanage.
3. Express interest in team members' successes and personal well-being.
4. Don't be a sissy: Be productive and results-oriented.
5. Be a good communicator and listen to your team.
6. Help your employees with career development.
7. Have a clear vision and strategy for the team.
8. Have key technical skills so you can help advise the team.

SOURCE: "Google's Quest to Build a Better Boss," by Adam Bryant, published March 12, 2011, in *The New York Times*. Courtesy of Google, Inc.

1-4a When Skills Fail

Good management skills are not automatic. Particularly during turbulent times, managers really have to stay on their toes and apply all their skills and competencies in a way that benefits the organization and its stakeholders—employees, customers, investors, the community, and so forth. In recent years, numerous highly publicized examples have shown what happens when managers fail to apply their skills effectively to meet the demands of an uncertain, rapidly changing world.

Everyone has flaws and weaknesses, and these shortcomings become most apparent under conditions of rapid change, uncertainty, or crisis.[22] Think of the recent diesel emissions scandal at Volkswagen. In the early 2000s, CEO Martin Winterkorn announced a bold strategy to triple Volkswagen's sales in the United States in just a decade and become the world's largest automaker by 2018. The company reached the goal years earlier, surpassing Toyota in July 2015—but Winterkorn had just two months to savor the victory. He resigned and several other high-level managers were fired after Volkswagen was discovered to have used software in diesel vehicles designed to cheat U.S. emissions tests. Although Winterkorn says he had no knowledge of the trickery, others say the former CEO's meticulous attention to every technical detail and the hard-driving culture he created put enormous pressure on managers to meet high goals.[23]

The numerous ethical and financial scandals of recent years have left people cynical about business and government managers and even less willing to overlook mistakes. Crises and examples of deceit and greed grab the headlines, but many more companies falter or fail less spectacularly. Managers fail to listen to customers, are unable to motivate employees, or can't build a cohesive team. For example, the reputation of Zynga, maker of games like Farmville that were ubiquitous on Facebook for a while, plummeted along with its share price in recent years. Although there were several problems at Zynga, one was that founder and CEO Mark Pincus had an aggressive style that made it difficult to build a cohesive team. The exodus of key executives left the company floundering, and Zynga's shares fell 80 percent.[24] Exhibit 1.5 shows the top 10 factors that cause managers to fail to achieve desired results, based on a survey of managers in U.S. organizations operating in rapidly changing business environments.[25] Notice that many of these factors are due to poor human skills, such as the inability to develop good work relationships, a failure to clarify direction and performance expectations, or an inability to create cooperation and teamwork. The number one reason for manager failure is ineffective communication skills and practices, which was cited by 81 percent of managers surveyed. Especially in times of uncertainty or crisis, if managers do not communicate effectively, including listening to employees and customers and showing genuine care and concern, organizational performance and reputation suffer.

Exhibit 1.5 Top Causes of Manager Failure

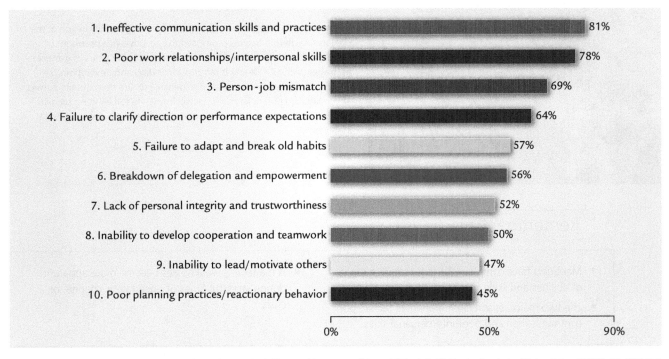

1. Ineffective communication skills and practices	81%
2. Poor work relationships/interpersonal skills	78%
3. Person-job mismatch	69%
4. Failure to clarify direction or performance expectations	64%
5. Failure to adapt and break old habits	57%
6. Breakdown of delegation and empowerment	56%
7. Lack of personal integrity and trustworthiness	52%
8. Inability to develop cooperation and teamwork	50%
9. Inability to lead/motivate others	47%
10. Poor planning practices/reactionary behavior	45%

SOURCE: Adapted from Clinton O. Longenecker, Mitchell J. Neubert, and Laurence S. Fink, "Causes and Consequences of Managerial Failure in Rapidly Changing Organizations," *Business Horizons* 50 (2007): 145–155, Table 1.

An important determinant of the manager's job is the hierarchical level. Exhibit 1.6 illustrates the three levels in the hierarchy. The manager's job differs as the level increases. First-level managers are more concerned with employee performance, middle managers with putting plans into place and top managers is strategy, as shown in Exhibit 1.6.

Exhibit 1.6 Management Levels in the Organizational Hierarchy

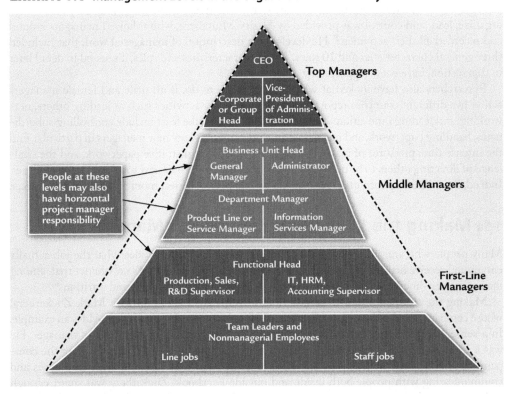

SOURCE: Adapted from Thomas V. Bonoma and Joseph C. Lawler, "Chutes and Ladders: Growing the General Manager," *Sloan Management Review* (Spring 1989): 27–37.

Dennis Ku/Shutterstock.com

Concept Connection

Perhaps one of the best-known leaders in baseball is Billy Beane of the Oakland A's. Before he was promoted to executive vice president of baseball operations in late 2015, Beane served for 17 years as **general manager** of the A's. Beane is famous for finding and developing talented young players who are less expensive to hire than the big names, which allowed him to keep his payroll low while still winning six division titles. Beane was the subject of the best-selling book and hit film *Moneyball*.

Remember This

- Managers have complex jobs that require a range of abilities and skills.
- The two major reasons that managers fail are poor communication and poor interpersonal skills.
- A manager's weaknesses become more apparent during stressful times of uncertainty, change, or crisis.

1-5 What Is a Manager's Job Really Like?

"Despite a proliferation of management gurus, management consultants, and management schools, it remains murky to many of us what managers actually do and why we need them in the first place," wrote Ray Fisman, a Columbia Business School professor.[26] Unless someone has actually performed managerial work, it is hard to understand exactly what managers do on an hour-by-hour, day-to-day basis. One answer to the question of what managers do to plan, organize, lead, and control was provided by Henry Mintzberg, who followed managers around and recorded all their activities.[27] He developed a description of managerial work that included three general characteristics and 10 roles. These characteristics and roles, discussed in detail later in this section, have been supported by other research.[28]

Researchers also have looked at what managers *like* to do. Both male and female managers across five different countries report that they most enjoy activities such as leading others, networking, and leading innovation. Activities that managers like least include controlling subordinates, handling paperwork, and managing time pressures.[29] Many new managers in particular find the intense time pressures of management, the load of administrative paperwork, and the challenge of directing others to be quite stressful as they adjust to their new roles and responsibilities. Indeed, the initial leap into management can be one of the scariest moments in a person's career.

1-5a Making the Leap: Becoming a New Manager

Many people who are promoted into a manager position have little idea what the job actually entails and receive little training about how to handle their new role. It's no wonder that, among managers, first-line supervisors tend to experience the most job burnout and attrition.[30]

Making the shift from individual contributor to manager is often tricky. Mark Zuckerberg, whose company, Facebook, went public a week before he turned 28 years old, provides an example. In a sense, the public has been able to watch as Zuckerberg has "grown up" as a manager. He was a strong individual performer in creating the social media platform and forming the company, but he fumbled with day-to-day management, such as interactions with employees and communicating with people both inside and outside Facebook. Zuckerberg was smart enough to hire seasoned managers, including former Google executive Sheryl Sandberg, and cultivate

Exhibit 1.7 Making the Leap from Individual Performer to Manager

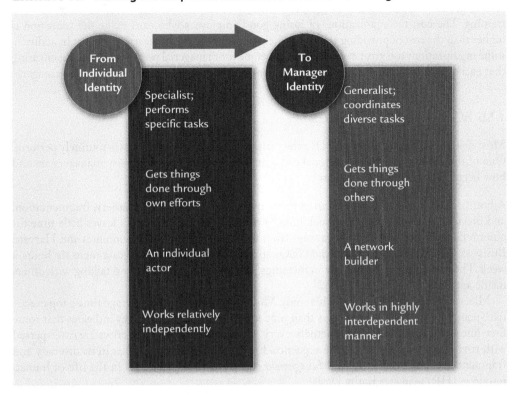

From Individual Identity

Specialist; performs specific tasks

Gets things done through own efforts

An individual actor

Works relatively independently

To Manager Identity

Generalist; coordinates diverse tasks

Gets things done through others

A network builder

Works in highly interdependent manner

SOURCE: Based on Linda A. Hill, Exhibit 1.1, "Transformation of Identity," *Becoming a Manager: Mastery of a New Identity*, 2d ed. (Boston, MA: Harvard Business School Press, 2003), p. 6.

advisors and mentors who have coached him in areas where he is weak. He also shadowed David Graham at the offices of The Post Company (the publisher of *The Washington Post* before it was purchased by Jeff Bezos) for four days to try to learn what it is like to manage a large organization. Now that Facebook is a public company, Zuckerberg is watched more closely than ever to see if he has what it takes to be a manager of a big public corporation.[31]

Harvard professor Linda Hill followed a group of 19 managers over the first year of their managerial careers and found that one key to success is to recognize that becoming a manager involves more than learning a new set of skills. Rather, becoming a manager means a profound transformation in the way people think of themselves, called *personal identity*, which includes letting go of deeply held attitudes and habits and learning new ways of thinking.[32] Exhibit 1.7 outlines the transformation from individual performer to manager. The individual performer is a specialist and a "doer." His or her mind is conditioned to think in terms of performing specific tasks and activities as expertly as possible. The manager, on the other hand, has to be a generalist and learn to coordinate a broad range of activities. While the individual performer strongly identifies with his or her specific tasks, the manager has to identify with the broader organization and industry.

In addition, the individual performer gets things done mostly through his or her own efforts and develops the habit of relying on self rather than others. The manager, though, gets things done through other people. Indeed, one of the most common mistakes that new managers make is wanting to do all the work themselves, rather than delegating to others and developing others' abilities.[33] Hill offers a reminder that, as a manager, you must "be an instrument to get things done in the organization by working with and through others, rather than being the one doing the work."[34]

Another problem for many new managers is that they expect to have greater freedom to do what they think is best for the organization. In reality, though, managers find themselves hemmed in by interdependencies. Being a successful manager means thinking in terms of building teams and networks and becoming a motivator and organizer within a highly interdependent system of people and work.[35] Although the distinctions may sound simple in the abstract, they are anything but. In essence, becoming a manager means becoming a new person and viewing oneself in a completely new way.

Visit MindTap for "Self-Assessment: Are You a Winner?" to see how your priorities align with the demands placed on a manager.

Many new managers have to make the transformation in a "trial by fire," learning on the job as they go, but organizations are beginning to be more responsive to the need for new manager training. The cost to organizations of losing good employees who can't make the transition is higher than the cost of providing training to help new managers cope, learn, and grow. In addition, some organizations use great care in selecting people for managerial positions, including ensuring that each candidate understands what management involves and really wants to be a manager.

1-5b Manager Activities

Most new managers are unprepared for the variety of activities that managers routinely perform. One of the most interesting findings about managerial activities is how busy managers are and how hectic the average workday can be.

Visit MindTap for "Self-Assessment: How Do You Manage Your Time?" to see how good you are at time management.

Adventures in Multitasking   Managerial activity is characterized by variety, fragmentation, and brevity.[36] The widespread and voluminous nature of a manager's tasks leaves little time for quiet reflection. A recent study by a team from the London School of Economics and Harvard Business School found that the time CEOs spend working alone averages a mere six hours a week. The rest of their time is spent in meetings, on the phone, traveling, and talking with others inside and outside the organization.[37]

Managers shift gears quickly. In his study, Mintzberg found that the average time a top executive spends on any one activity is less than nine minutes, and another survey indicates that some first-line supervisors average one activity every 48 seconds![38] Significant crises are interspersed with trivial events in no predictable sequence. Every manager's job is similar in its diversity and fragmentation to what *Workforce Management* described as a typical day in the life of human resources (HR) manager Kathy Davis:[39]

- 6:55 a.m.—Arrives at work early to begin investigating a complaint of sexual harassment at one of the factories, but as she's walking to her office, she bumps into someone carrying a picket sign that reads "Unfair Hiring! Who Needs HR?" Spends a few minutes talking with the young man, who is a temp that she had let go due to sloppy work.
- 7:10 a.m.—Finds the factory shift supervisor and a security staff member already waiting outside her door to discuss the sexual harassment complaint.
- 7:55 a.m.—Sue, a member of Kathy's team who has just arrived and is unaware of the meeting, interrupts to let Kathy know there is someone picketing in the hallway outside her office and the CEO wants to know what's going on.
- 8:00 a.m.—Alone at last, Kathy calls the CEO and explains the picketing situation, and then she begins her morning routine. Checking voice mail, she finds three messages that she must respond to immediately, and she passes four others to members of her team. She begins checking e-mail but is interrupted again by Sue, who reminds her that they have to review the recent HR audit so that the company can respond promptly and avoid penalties.
- 9:15 a.m.—As she is reviewing the audit, Kathy gets a call from manager Pete Channing, asking if she's sent the offer letter to a prospective hire. "Don't send it," Pete said, "I've changed my mind." Weeks of interviewing and background checks, and now Pete wants to start over!
- 11:20 a.m.—Kathy is getting to the end of her critical e-mail list when she hears a commotion outside her door and finds Linda and Sue arguing. "This report IT did for us is full of errors," Linda says, "but Sue says we should let it go." Kathy agrees to take a look at the IT department's report and discovers that there are only a few errors, but they have critical implications.

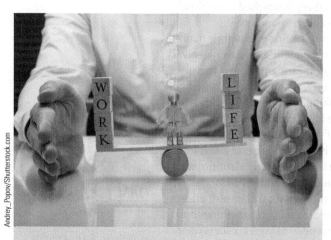

Andrey_Popov/Shutterstock.com

Concept Connection

New managers sometimes find themselves overwhelmed by the various activities, multiple responsibilities, long hours, and fast pace that come with management. A manager's **life on speed dial** requires good **time management skills**. Managers must also find ways to maintain a healthy balance between their work and personal lives.

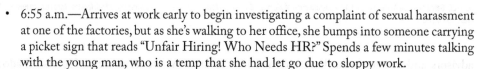

- 12:25 p.m.—As she's nearing the end of the IT report, Kathy's e-mail pings an "urgent" message from a supervisor informing her that one of his employees will be absent from work for a few weeks "while a felony morals charge is worked out." This is the first she's heard about it, so she picks up the phone to call the supervisor.
- 1:20 p.m.—Time for lunch—finally. She grabs a sandwich at a local supermarket and brings one back for the picketer, who thanks her and continues his march.
- 2:00 p.m.—Meets with CEO Henry Luker to review the audit and IT reports, discuss changes to the company's 401(k) plan, and talk about ideas for reducing turnover.
- 3:00 p.m.—Rushes back to her office to grab her keys so that she can drive to a meeting with the manufacturing facilities manager, who has asked Kathy to "shadow" him and share ideas about training and skills development.
- 3:15 p.m.—As she gets out of her car at the facility, Kathy runs into a man who had attended a supervision training course a few months earlier. He tells her that the class really helped him—there are fewer misunderstandings, and the staff seems to respect him more.
- 3:30 p.m.—Arrives right on time and spends the next couple of hours observing and asking questions, talking to employees to learn about the problems and obstacles they face.
- 5:40 p.m.—All is quiet back in the HR department, but there's a message from Sue that Kathy has an appointment first thing tomorrow morning with two women who had gotten into a fight in the elevator. Sighing, Kathy returns to her investigation of the sexual harassment complaint that she had begun at 7:00 that morning.

Life on Speed Dial   The manager performs a great deal of work at an unrelenting pace.[40] Managers' work is fast paced and requires great energy. Most top executives routinely work at least 12 hours a day and spend 50 percent or more of their time traveling.[41] Calendars are often booked months in advance, but unexpected disturbances erupt every day. Mintzberg found that the majority of executives' meetings and other contacts are ad hoc, and even scheduled meetings are typically surrounded by other events such as quick phone calls, scanning of e-mail, or spontaneous encounters. During time away from the office, executives catch up on work-related reading, paperwork, phone calls, and e-mail. Technology, such as e-mail, text messaging, smartphones, tablets, and laptops, has intensified the pace. Brett Yormark, the National Basketball Association (NBA)'s youngest CEO (he heads the Brooklyn Nets), typically responds to about 60 messages before he even shaves and dresses for the day, and employees are accustomed to getting messages that Yormark has zapped to them in the wee hours of the morning.[42]

The fast pace of a manager's job is illustrated by Michelle Davis, an analytics director at Fair Isaac Corporation (FICO). As a middle manager at this company, which is best known for calculating consumer credit scores, Davis oversees three direct reports and three other subordinates assigned to her teams. On a typical day, she arrives at work at 6:00 a.m. so she can pick up her children in the early afternoon, and she uses the first hour and a half of quiet time to catch up on messages and respond to urgent requests for data. At 7:30, she has her first meeting, often a conference call with the analytics board of directors. Then Davis leads an hour-long training session for a few dozen staffers on new analytics products, staying longer to answer questions and talk about how clients might use the data. At 10:30 a.m., she checks in with senior members of the product development and product management teams and sorts out various problems. Lunch is a quick stop at the company cafeteria and then on to present a few slides at the monthly lunch-and-learn session. Davis squeezes in an hour or so of hands-on work time before it's back to more meetings. Afternoon meetings often run long, meaning she has to scramble to pick up her three children. While the kids

Concept Connection

As the executive vice president of marketing at Microsoft, Tami Reller plays a number of significant interpersonal roles. She serves as the top **leader** for the company's bevy of marketers on functions like advertising, media usage, and distribution, and she is often Microsoft's **liaison** with the public, providing information about Windows and other products.

eat snacks and play in the backyard, Davis catches up on e-mail and phone calls. After dinner with her husband, she tries to stay away from work, but admits that she keeps an eye on her text messages until bedtime.[43]

Where Does a Manager Find the Time?   With so many responsibilities and so many competing demands on their time, how do managers cope? One manager who was already working 18-hour days five days a week got assigned another project. When the CEO was informed of the problem, he matter-of-factly remarked that by his calculations, she still had "30 more hours Monday through Friday, plus 48 more on the weekend." That is surely an extreme example, but most managers often feel the pressure of too much to do and not enough time to do it.[44] *The Wall Street Journal's* "Lessons in Leadership" video series asked CEOs of big companies how they managed their time, and it found that many of them carve out time just to think about how to manage their time.[45] Time is a manager's most valuable resource, and one characteristic that identifies successful managers is that they know how to use time effectively to accomplish the important things first and the less important things later.[46] **Time management** refers to using techniques that enable you to get more done in less time and with better results, be more relaxed, and have more time to enjoy your work and your life. New managers in particular often struggle with the increased workload, the endless paperwork, the incessant meetings, and the constant interruptions that come with a management job. Learning to manage their time effectively is one of the greatest challenges that new managers face. The "Sunny Side Up" box offers some tips for time management.

Sunny Side Up } Time Management Tips for New Managers

Becoming a manager is considered by most people to be a positive, forward-looking career move, and indeed, life as a manager offers appealing aspects. However, it also holds many challenges, not the least of which is the increased workload and the difficulty of finding the time to accomplish everything on one's expanded list of duties and responsibilities. The following classic time management techniques can help you eliminate major time-wasters in your daily routines.

- **Keep a To-Do List**. If you don't use any other system for keeping track of your responsibilities and commitments, at the very least you should maintain a to-do list that identifies all the things that you need to do during the day. Although the nature of management means that new responsibilities and shifting priorities occur frequently, it's a fact that people accomplish more with a list than without one.

- **Remember Your ABCs**. This is a highly effective system for prioritizing tasks or activities on your to-do list:

  - An "A" item is something highly important. It *must* be done, or you'll face serious consequences.
  - A "B" item is a *should do*, but consequences will be minor if you don't get it done.
  - "C" items are things that would be nice to get done, but there are no consequences at all if you don't accomplish them.
  - "D" items are tasks that you can delegate to someone else.

- **Schedule Your Workday**. Some experts propose that every minute spent in planning saves 10 minutes in execution. Take your to-do list a step further and plan how you will accomplish each task or project you need to handle. Planning to tackle the big tasks first is a good idea because most people are at peak performance early in the day. Save the e-mails and phone calls for less productive times.

- **Do One Thing at a Time**. Multitasking has become the motto of the early twenty-first century, but too much multitasking is a time-waster. Research has shown that multitasking *reduces* rather than enhances productivity. The authors of one study suggest that an inability to focus on one thing at a time could reduce efficiency by 20 to 40 percent. Even for those whose job requires numerous brief activities, the ability to concentrate fully on each one (sometimes called *spotlighting*) saves time. Give each task your full attention, and you'll get more done and get it done better, too.

SOURCES: Based on information in Pamela Dodd and Doug Sundheim, *The 25 Best Time Management Tools & Techniques* (Ann Arbor, MI: Peak Performance Press, Inc., 2005); Brian Tracy, *Eat That Frog: 21 Great Ways to Stop Procrastinating and Get More Done in Less Time* (San Francisco: Berrett-Koehler, 2002); Joshua S. Rubinstein, David E. Meyer, and Jeffrey E. Evans, "Executive Control of Cognitive Processes in Task Switching," *Journal of Experimental Psychology: Human Perception and Performance* 27, no. 4 (August 2001): 763–797; Sue Shellenbarger, "Multitasking Makes You Stupid: Studies Show Pitfalls of Doing Too Much at Once," *The Wall Street Journal* (February 27, 2003); and Ilya Pozin, "Quit Working Late: 8 Tips," *Inc.* (June 26, 2013), http://www.inc.com/ilya-pozin/8-ways-to-leave-work-at-work.html (accessed August 19, 2013).

1-5c Manager Roles

Mintzberg's observations and subsequent research indicate that diverse manager activities can be organized into 10 roles.[47] A **role** is a set of expectations for a manager's behavior. Exhibit 1.8 describes activities associated with each of the roles. These roles are divided into three conceptual categories: informational (managing by information), interpersonal (managing through people), and decisional (managing through action).

One of Mintzberg's roles is disseminator, which means scanning for information and knowing what to share and with whom. Equifax failed, as shown in this chapter's "Half-Baked Management" box.

Each role represents activities that managers undertake to ultimately accomplish the functions of planning, organizing, leading, and controlling. Although it is necessary to separate the components of the manager's job to understand the different roles and activities of a manager, it is important to remember that the real job of management isn't practiced as a set of independent parts; all the roles interact in the real world of management.

Exhibit 1.8 **Ten Manager Roles**

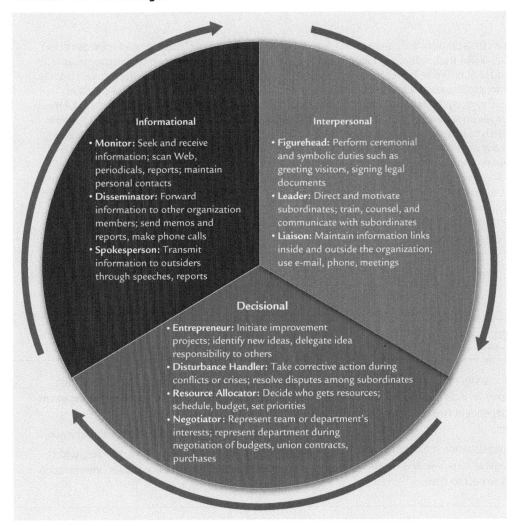

SOURCE: Adapted from Henry Mintzberg, The *Nature of Managerial Work* (New York: Harper & Row, 1973), pp. 92–93; and Henry Mintzberg, "Managerial Work: Analysis from Observation," *Management Science* 18 (1971), B97–B110.

Half-Baked Management ⟩ Equifax

Equifax is one of the three main credit bureaus in the United States. Anyone who has a credit rating is in the database of usually two or three of these Bureaus.

So when Equifax disclosed in September 2017 that the personal data of 143 million consumers' (roughly 44 percent of the U.S. population) had been hacked from its servers, people were shocked. Breached were social security numbers, birth dates, drivers' license numbers, credit card numbers, and addresses. Not only were individuals at risk, but alo theft of resources from retirement accounts was highly possible. If that weren't bad enough, it was reported that Equifax knew of the breach in May and had told no one, preventing the 143 million people from taking precautions against losing their assets. So much for credit bureaus making a positive contribution to the economy.

SOURCE: E.B. MARK and A. Hahn, Cybersecurity for Retirement Plans. *Employee Relations Law Journal, New York* 43, no. 4 (Spring 2018): 67–71.

Recipe for Success ⟩ Second Harvest Food Bank of Middle Tennessee

It's a good problem to have, but it's still a problem that needed to be solved. People like to donate during the holidays, and food donations to Second Harvest Food Bank of Middle Tennessee swell to nearly double what the nonprofit organization receives during the rest of the year. It was a huge logistical challenge for the operation, which depends largely on volunteers. Second Harvest, like other food banks, needs to deliver perishable items before they expire and save as many canned and dried foods as it can to distribute in the months when donations tend to decline.

Second Harvest managers didn't have the millions of dollars Amazon.com or Walmart stores have poured into specialized inventory management systems, but with the cost of technology declining, they were able to buy logistics software from Exact Macola. Exact Macola has donated upgrades to the software since that initial purchase and has begun donating its software to other food banks nationwide. The software records when food products are received and their "use-by" dates. Volunteers and employees rely on automated alerts to let them know when goods are expiring and where they are located in the warehouse. The ability to know in an instant what needs to be used immediately and what can be stored for later use helps Second Harvest get the most out of its limited space, says Dennis Easter, the agency's information systems director. Managers have also been able to use data on food distribution to decide on where to build two new facilities, which are projected to save $500,000 in transportation costs.[48]

Remember This

- Becoming a new manager requires a shift in thinking from being an individual performer to playing an interdependent role of coordinating and developing others.

- Because of the interdependent nature of management, new managers often have less freedom and control than they expect to have.

- The job of a manager is highly diverse and fast paced, so managers need good **time management** skills.

- A **role** is a set of expectations for one's behavior.

- Managers at every level perform 10 roles, which are grouped into informational roles, interpersonal roles, and decisional roles.

1-6 Managing in Small Businesses and Nonprofit Organizations

Small businesses are growing in importance. Hundreds of small businesses open every month, but the environment for small business today is highly complicated. Chapter 6 provides detailed information about managing in small businesses and entrepreneurial start-ups.

One interesting finding is that managers in small businesses tend to emphasize roles different from those of managers in large corporations. Managers in small companies often see their most important role as that of spokesperson because they must promote the small, growing company to the outside world. The entrepreneur role is also critical in small businesses because managers must be innovative and help their organizations develop new ideas to remain competitive. For example, Zach Schau, his younger brother Jordan, and two of their childhood friends founded Pure Fix Cycles. After finding a way to build fixed-gear bikes, or "fixies," that could be sold for less than half what they were selling for at the time, the founders hired a top manager so they could focus on further innovations. Pure Fix then became a pioneer in the business of glow-in-the-dark bikes.[49] Small-business managers tend to rate lower on the leader role and on information-processing roles compared with their counterparts in large corporations.

FRANCK FIFE/Getty Images

Concept Connection

Despite having launched and sold several successful start-ups already, San Francisco–based **small business** owner Loïc Le Meur is still a hands-on kind of manager. His daily blog about the blogosphere and the Web in general is read by hundreds of thousands of people worldwide, and he is the chief organizer behind Europe's largest annual tech conference, LeWeb.

Nonprofit organizations also represent a major application of management talent.[50] Organizations such as the Salvation Army, Nature Conservancy, Greater Chicago Food Depository, Girl Scouts, and Cleveland Orchestra all require excellent management. The functions of planning, organizing, leading, and controlling apply to nonprofits just as they do to business organizations, and managers in nonprofit organizations use similar skills and perform similar activities. The primary difference is that managers in businesses direct their activities toward earning money for the company and its owners, whereas managers in nonprofits direct their efforts toward generating some kind of social impact. The characteristics and needs of nonprofit organizations created by this distinction present unique challenges for managers.[51]

Financial resources for government and charity nonprofit organizations typically come from taxes, appropriations, grants, and donations rather than from the sale of products or services to customers. In businesses, managers focus on improving the organization's products and services to increase sales revenues. In nonprofits, however, services are typically provided to nonpaying clients, and a major problem for many organizations is securing a steady stream of funds to continue operating. Nonprofit managers, committed to serving clients with limited resources, must focus on keeping organizational costs as low as possible.[52] Donors generally want their money to go directly to helping clients rather than for overhead costs. If nonprofit managers can't demonstrate a highly efficient use of resources, they might have a hard time securing additional donations or government appropriations.

The roles defined by Mintzberg also apply to nonprofit managers, but they may differ somewhat. We might expect managers in nonprofit organizations to place more emphasis on the roles of spokesperson (to "sell" the organization to donors and the public), leader (to build a mission-driven community of employees and volunteers), and resource allocator (to distribute government resources or grant funds that are often assigned top-down).

Managers in all organizations—large corporations, small businesses, and nonprofit organizations—carefully integrate and adjust the management functions and roles to meet challenges within their own circumstances and keep their organizations healthy.

Remember This

- Good management is just as important for small businesses and nonprofit organizations as it is for large corporations.

- Managers in these organizations adjust and integrate the various management functions, activities, and roles to meet the unique challenges they face.

- Managers in small businesses often see their most important roles as being a *spokesperson* for the business and acting as an *entrepreneur*.

- Managers in nonprofit organizations direct their efforts toward generating some kind of social impact rather than toward making money for the organization.

- Managers in nonprofit organizations often struggle with what constitutes effectiveness.

1-7 The Evolution of Management Thinking

John Bunch used to be a technical adviser at online retailer Zappos. Today, Bunch doesn't have a title. No one at Zappos does. In the spring of 2015, Zappos did away with all job titles and abolished the organizational hierarchy in favor of a radical system of self-management called *holocracy*. No one has a supervisor, and employees voluntarily join various impermanent groups called *circles*, where they come up with their own job descriptions and decide what projects they will undertake.[53] Managers are watching to see how this extreme Theory Y approach will work at Zappos (Theory Y will be explained in detail later in the chapter). Managers at a number of companies are embracing the trend toward less hierarchical, even bossless, organizations. At least 18 organizations around the world, including French automotive components manufacturer FAVI; tomato processor Morning Star, based in Woodland, California; and Spain's diversified Mondragon Corporation, are operated as primarily bossless workplaces.[54] Although some management and HR professionals and scholars question whether the bossless trend will last for long,[55] it is interesting to note that some of these companies have been operating without traditional bosses for decades. When Jean-François Zobrist took over as CEO of FAVI in 1983, he eliminated two things: the personnel department and the bosses. "I have no idea what people are doing," Zobrist told *Fast Company* magazine. He believes that since the people on the front lines are the ones with the expertise to do the work, they are capable of working without someone looking over their shoulders.[56]

Some organizations will continue to operate with little or no hierarchy, and others will move toward a more hierarchical structure. Managers are always on the lookout for fresh ideas, innovative management approaches, and new tools and techniques. Management philosophies and organizational forms change over time to meet new needs and respond to current challenges. The workplace of today is different from what it was 50 years ago—indeed, from what it was even 10 years ago—yet historical concepts form the backbone of management education.[57] In addition, some management practices that seem modern have actually been around for a long time. Techniques can gain and lose popularity because of shifting historical forces and the persistent need to balance human needs with the needs of production activities.[58]

1-8 The Historical Struggle: The Things of Production versus the Humanity of Production

Studying history doesn't mean merely arranging events in chronological order; it means developing an understanding of the impact of societal forces on organizations. Studying history is a way to achieve strategic thinking, see the big picture, and improve conceptual skills.

Exhibit 1.9 Management Perspectives over Time

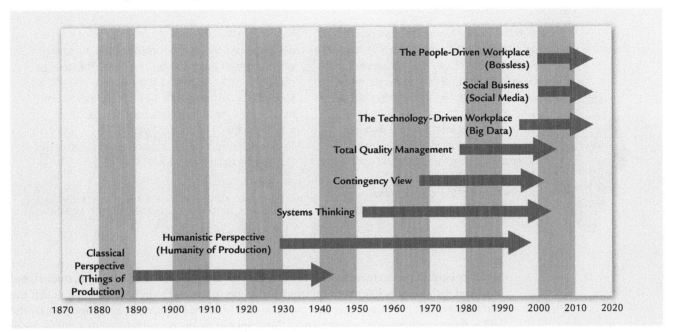

Management practices and perspectives vary in response to social, political, and economic changes in the larger society.[59] Exhibit 1.9 illustrates the evolution of significant management perspectives over time. The timeline reflects the dominant time period for each approach, but elements of each are still used in organizations today.[60]

One observation from looking at the timeline in Exhibit 1.9 is that the earliest focus of management (the classical perspective), well over a century ago, was on the things of production. In other words, the needs of people were often ignored in the interest of higher production efficiency and profit. By the 1920s and 1930s, the needs of and positive treatment of employees were discovered as another path to efficiency and profit. Since then, there has been a struggle of sorts within management to balance a management preference toward "the things of production" versus a preference toward "the humanity of production."[61] Exhibit 1.10 illustrates the management struggle between the desire for efficient production and the desire to meet human needs for greater motivation. When forces either outside or within the organization suggest a need for change to improve efficiency or effectiveness, managers have often responded with a technology- or numbers-oriented solution that makes people little more than cogs in a big machine. For instance, as the United States shifted from a world of small towns and small businesses to an industrialized network of cities and factories in the late nineteenth century, people

Exhibit 1.10 The Tension between Historical Forces in Management Thinking

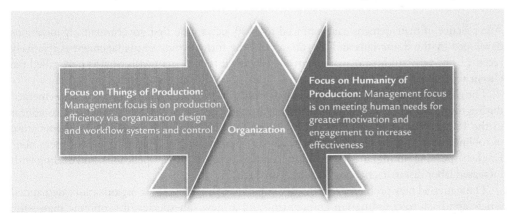

Green Power

Drop Back and Punt Glenn Rink's innovative product—popcorn-like sponges for absorbing oil spills—received a cool reception in the 1990s. Corporate skeptics said that traditional skimming of oil off water remained the preferred choice for disaster cleanup. Blocked by resistance to his product, Rink, founder of Abtech Industries, followed the historic and time-honored tradition of football teams, which sometimes need to drop back and punt before they can go on offense again.

Rink decided to focus on smaller-scale disasters instead. For more than a decade, Abtech

Industries built a reputation for offering low-cost alternatives to address the cleanup needs of cities struggling with a variety of water pollution problems. The strategy paid off. In 2011, a revitalized Abtech, maker of the Smart Sponge Plus, partnered with the huge company Waste Management Inc. as its exclusive North American distributor to cities, and oil cleanup orders began pouring in. To date, Smart Sponge Plus has been used in more than 15,000 spill locations worldwide.

SOURCE: "Innovation #71: Glenn Rink, Founder of Abtech Industries," *Fast Company* (June 2012): 136 (part of "The 100 Most Creative People in Business 2012," pp. 78–156).

began looking at management as a set of scientific practices that could be measured, studied, and improved with machinelike precision (the classical perspective). Frederick Taylor wrote that the best management is a true science, resting upon clearly defined laws, rules, and principles. By the 1920s, there was a minor rebellion against this emphasis on the quantifiable with a call for more attention to human and social needs (the humanistic perspective). In the first issue of the *Harvard Business Review* (1922), Dean Wallace B. Donham wrote that "the development, strengthening, and multiplication of socially-minded business men is the central problem of business."[62] This dilemma—the scientific numbers-driven push for greater productivity and profitability and the call for more humanistic, people-oriented management—has continued to the present day.

Remember This

- Managers are always on the lookout for new techniques and approaches to meet shifting organizational needs.
- Looking at history gives managers a broader perspective for interpreting and responding to current opportunities and problems.

- Management and organizations are shaped by forces in the larger society.
- The struggle to balance "the things of production" with the "humanity of production" has continued from the nineteenth century to today.

1-9 Classical Perspective

The practice of management can be traced to 3000 B.C., to the first government organizations developed by the Sumerians and Egyptians, but the formal study of management is relatively recent.[63] The early study of management as we know it today began with what is now called the **classical perspective**.

The classical perspective on management (primary focus on the things of production) emerged during the nineteenth and early twentieth centuries. The factory system that began to appear in the 1800s posed challenges that earlier organizations had not encountered. Problems arose in tooling the plants, organizing managerial structure, training employees (many of them non-English-speaking immigrants), scheduling complex manufacturing operations, and dealing with increased labor dissatisfaction and resulting strikes.

These myriad new problems and the development of large, complex organizations demanded a new approach to coordination and control, and a "new sub-species of economic man—the salaried manager"[64]—was born. Between 1880 and 1920, the number of professional managers in the United States increased from 161,000 to more than 1 million.[65] These professional managers began developing and testing solutions to the mounting challenges of organizing, coordinating, and controlling large numbers of people and increasing worker productivity. Thus began the evolution of modern management with the classical perspective.

This perspective contains four subfields, each with a slightly different emphasis: scientific management, bureaucratic organizations, administrative principles, and management science.[66]

1-9a Scientific Management

Scientific management emphasizes scientifically determined jobs and management practices as the way to improve efficiency and labor productivity. In the late 1800s, a young engineer, Frederick Winslow Taylor (1856–1915), proposed that workers "could be retooled like machines, their physical and mental gears recalibrated for better productivity."[67] Taylor insisted that improving productivity meant that management itself would have to change and, further, that the manner of change could be determined only by scientific study; hence, the label *scientific management* emerged. Taylor suggested that decisions based on rules of thumb and tradition be replaced with precise procedures developed after careful study of individual situations.[68]

Concept Connection

Automaker Henry Ford made extensive use of Frederick Taylor's **scientific management** techniques, as illustrated by this automobile assembly line at a Ford plant circa 1930. Ford replaced workers with machines for heavy lifting and moving autos from one worker to the next. This reduced worker hours and improved efficiency and productivity. Under this system, a Ford car rolled off the assembly line every 10 seconds.

The scientific management approach is illustrated by the unloading of iron from rail cars and reloading finished steel for the Bethlehem Steel plant in 1898. Taylor calculated that with the correct movements, tools, and sequencing, each man was capable of loading 47.5 tons per day instead of the typical 12.5 tons. He also worked out an incentive system that paid each man $1.85 a day for meeting the new standard, an increase from the previous rate of $1.15. Productivity at Bethlehem Steel shot up overnight.

Although known as the *father of scientific management*, Taylor was not alone in this area. Henry Gantt, an associate of Taylor's, developed the *Gantt chart*, a bar graph that measures planned and completed work along each stage of production by time elapsed. Two other important pioneers in this area were the husband-and-wife team of Frank B. and Lillian M. Gilbreth. Frank B. Gilbreth (1868–1924) pioneered *time and motion study* and arrived at many of his management techniques independently of Taylor. Gilbreth stressed efficiency and was known for his quest for the one best way to do work. Although he is known for his early work with bricklayers, his work had great impact on medical surgery by drastically reducing the time that patients spent on the operating table. Surgeons were able to save countless lives through the application of time and motion study. Lillian M. Gilbreth (1878–1972) was more interested in the human aspect of work. When her husband died at the age of 56, she had 12 children ages 2 to 19. The undaunted "first lady of management" went right on with her work. She presented a paper in place of her late husband, continued their seminars and consulting, lectured, and eventually became a professor at Purdue University.[69] She pioneered in the field of industrial psychology and made substantial contributions to human resource management.

Exhibit 1.11 shows the basic ideas of scientific management. To use this approach, managers should develop standard methods for doing each job, select workers with the appropriate abilities, train workers in the standard methods, support workers and eliminate interruptions, and provide wage incentives.

The ideas of scientific management that began with Taylor dramatically increased productivity across all industries, and they are still important today. Indeed, the idea of engineering work for greater productivity has enjoyed a renaissance in the retail industry. Supermarket chains such as Meijer Inc. and Hannaford, for example, use computerized labor waste elimination systems based on scientific management principles. The system breaks down tasks such as greeting a customer,

Exhibit 1.11 Characteristics of Scientific Management

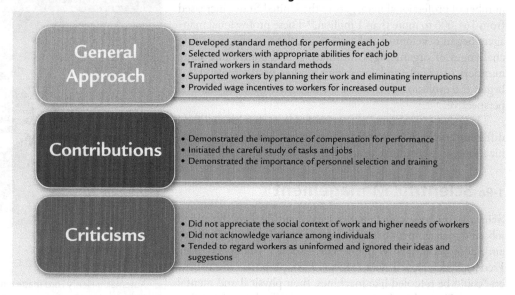

General Approach
- Developed standard method for performing each job
- Selected workers with appropriate abilities for each job
- Trained workers in standard methods
- Supported workers by planning their work and eliminating interruptions
- Provided wage incentives to workers for increased output

Contributions
- Demonstrated the importance of compensation for performance
- Initiated the careful study of tasks and jobs
- Demonstrated the importance of personnel selection and training

Criticisms
- Did not appreciate the social context of work and higher needs of workers
- Did not acknowledge variance among individuals
- Tended to regard workers as uninformed and ignored their ideas and suggestions

working the register, scanning items, and so forth into quantifiable units and devises standard times for completing each task. Executives say the computerized system has allowed supermarket managers to staff stores more efficiently because people are routinely monitored by computer and are expected to meet strict standards.[70]

A *Harvard Business Review* article discussing innovations that shaped modern management puts scientific management at the top of its list of 12 influential innovations. Indeed, the ideas of creating a system for maximum efficiency and organizing work for maximum productivity are deeply embedded in our organizations.[71] However, because scientific management ignores the social context and workers' needs, it can lead to increased conflict and clashes between managers and employees. The United Food and Commercial Workers Union, for instance, filed a grievance against Meijer in connection with its cashier-performance system. Under such performance management systems, workers often feel exploited—a sharp contrast from the harmony and cooperation that Taylor and his followers had envisioned.

1-9b Bureaucratic Organizations

A systematic approach developed in Europe that looks at the organization as a whole is the **bureaucratic organizations approach**, a subfield within the classical perspective. Max Weber (1864–1920), a German theorist, introduced most of the concepts on bureaucratic organizations.[72]

During the late 1800s, many European organizations were managed on a personal, family-like basis. Employees were loyal to a single individual rather than to the organization or its mission. The dysfunctional consequence of this management practice was that resources were used to realize individual desires rather than organizational goals. Employees in effect owned the organization and used resources for their own gain rather than to serve customers. Weber envisioned organizations that would be managed on an impersonal, rational basis. This form of organization was called a *bureaucracy*. Exhibit 1.12 summarizes the six characteristics of bureaucracy as specified by Weber.

Weber believed that an organization based on rational authority would be more efficient and adaptable to change because continuity is related to formal structure and positions rather than to a particular person, who may leave or die. To Weber, rationality in organizations meant employee selection and advancement based not on whom you know, but rather on competence and technical qualifications, which are assessed by examination or according to specific training and experience. The organization relies on rules and written records for continuity. In addition,

"Students would be more likely to have a positive impact on the future of management if they were more engaged with the history and traditions of management— particularly that of a German sociologist [Weber] who died nearly 100 years ago."

—STEPHEN CUMMINGS AND TODD BRIDGMAN, VICTORIA UNIVERSITY OF WELLINGTON, NEW ZEALAND

Exhibit 1.12 **Characteristics of Weberian Bureaucracy**

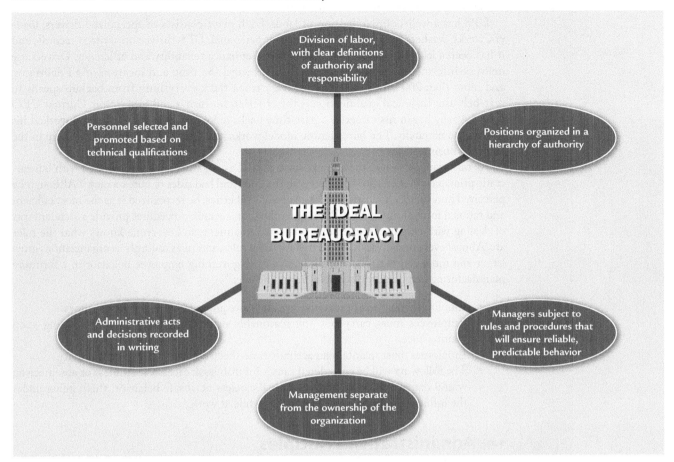

SOURCE: Adapted from Max Weber, The *Theory of Social and Economic Organizations*, ed. and trans. A. M. Henderson and Talcott Parsons (New York: Free Press, 1947), pp. 328–337.

rules and procedures are impersonal and applied uniformly to all employees. Distinct definitions of authority and responsibility and clearly defined duties create a clear division of labor. Positions are organized in a hierarchy, with each position under the authority of a higher one. The manager gives orders successfully not on the basis of his or her personality, but on the legal power invested in the managerial position.

The term *bureaucracy* has taken on a negative meaning in today's organizations and is associated with endless rules and red tape. We have all been frustrated by waiting in long lines or following seemingly silly procedures. However, the value of bureaucratic principles is still evident in many organizations, such as United Parcel Service (UPS), sometimes nicknamed *Big Brown*.

UPS UPS is the largest package delivery company in the world and a leading global provider of specialized transportation and logistics services. The company operates in more than 200 countries and territories worldwide.

Why has UPS been so successful? One important factor is the concept of bureaucracy. UPS operates according to strict rules and regulations. New drivers attend intensive training courses and have to memorize the company's more than 600 mandatory "methods," which include guidelines such as checking the mirrors every five to eight seconds and leaving one full car length in front when stopping. These employees learn precise steps for how to deliver a package correctly, such as how to load the truck, how to fasten their seat belts, how to walk, and how to carry their keys. Specific safety rules apply to drivers, loaders, clerks, and managers. Strict dress codes are enforced—clean uniforms (called *browns*), every day, black or brown polished shoes with nonslip soles, no beards, no hair below the collar, no tattoos visible during deliveries, and so on. Managers are given copies of policy books with the expectation that they will use them regularly, and memos on various policies and rules circulate by the hundreds every day.

UPS has a well-defined division of labor. Each plant consists of specialized drivers, loaders, clerks, washers, sorters, and maintenance personnel. UPS thrives on written records, and it has been a leader in using new technology to enhance reliability and efficiency. Drivers use delivery-information acquisition devices that record the time and location of all deliveries, and more than 200 sensors on each delivery truck track everything from backup speeds to seat-belt use. Technical qualification is the criterion for hiring and promotion. Current CEO David Abney began his career as a part-time package loader while in college and worked his way up the hierarchy. The bureaucratic model works just fine at UPS, "the tightest ship in the shipping business."[73]

As this example shows, there are positive as well as negative aspects associated with bureaucratic principles. Weber also struggled with the good and bad sides of bureaucracy.[74] Although he perceived bureaucracy as a threat to basic personal liberties, he recognized it as the most efficient and rational form of organizing. Rules and other bureaucratic procedures provide a standard way of dealing with employees. Everyone gets equal treatment, and everyone knows what the rules are. Almost every organization needs to have some rules, and rules multiply as organizations grow larger and more complex. Some examples of rules governing employee behavior in a furniture manufacturing company, for example, might include:[75]

- Employees must wear protective eye and ear equipment when using machines.
- Employees must carry out any reasonable duty assigned to them, including shop maintenance.
- Employees must maintain an accurate time sheet, which shows job and activity.
- The following will be considered causes for dismissal: excessive tardiness or absenteeism; willful damage to equipment; continual careless or unsafe behavior; theft; being under the influence of alcohol or illegal drugs while at work.

1-9c Administrative Principles

Another major subfield within the classical perspective is known as the *administrative principles* approach. Whereas scientific management focuses on the productivity of the individual worker, the **administrative principles approach** focuses on the total organization. A major contributor to this approach was Henri Fayol (1841–1925), a French mining engineer who worked his way up to become head of a large mining group known as Comambault. Pieces of Comambault survive today as part of ArcelorMittal, the world's largest steel and mining company. In his later years, Fayol wrote about his concepts on administration, based largely on his own management experiences.[76]

In his most significant work, *General and Industrial Management*, Fayol discussed 14 general principles of management, several of which are part of management philosophy today. For example:

- *Unity of command.* Each subordinate receives orders from one—and only one—superior.
- *Division of work.* Managerial work and technical work are amenable to specialization to produce more and better work with the same amount of effort.
- *Unity of direction.* Similar activities in an organization should be grouped together under one manager.
- *Scalar chain.* A chain of authority extends from the top to the bottom of the organization and should include every employee.

Fayol felt that these principles could be applied in any organizational setting. He also identified five basic functions or elements of management: *planning, organizing, commanding, coordinating,* and *controlling.* These functions underlie much of the general approach to today's management theory.

Remember This

- The study of modern management began in the late nineteenth century with the **classical perspective**, which took a rational, scientific approach to management and sought to turn organizations into efficient operating machines.

- **Scientific management** is a subfield of the classical perspective that emphasizes scientifically determined changes in management practices as the solution to improving labor productivity.

- Frederick Winslow Taylor is known as "the father of scientific management."

- Scientific management is considered one of the most significant innovations influencing modern management.

- Some supermarket chains are using computerized systems based on scientific management principles to schedule employees for maximum efficiency.

- Another subfield of the classical perspective is the **bureaucratic organizations approach**, which emphasizes management on an impersonal, rational basis through elements such as clearly defined authority and responsibility, formal recordkeeping, and separation of management and ownership.

- Max Weber introduced most of the concepts about bureaucratic organizations.

- The **administrative principles approach** is a subfield of the classical perspective that focuses on the total organization rather than the individual worker and delineates the management functions of planning, organizing, commanding, coordinating, and controlling.

- Henri Fayol was a major contributor to the administrative principles approach. Fayol outlined 14 general principles of management, several of which are a part of management philosophy today.

1-9d Management Science

Another, more recent, management approach that falls within the classical perspective is *management science*. World War II caused many management changes. To handle the massive and complicated problems associated with modern global warfare, managerial decision makers needed more sophisticated tools than ever before. **Management science**, also referred to as the *quantitative perspective*, provided a way to address those problems. This view is distinguished for its application of mathematics, statistics, and other quantitative techniques to management decision making and problem solving. During World War II, groups of mathematicians, physicists, and other scientists were formed to solve military problems that frequently involved moving massive amounts of materials and large numbers of people quickly and efficiently. Managers soon saw how quantitative techniques could be applied to large-scale business firms.[77]

Picking up on techniques developed for the military, scholars began cranking out numerous mathematical tools for corporate managers, such as the application of linear programming for optimizing operations, statistical process control for quality management, and the capital asset pricing model.[78]

These efforts were enhanced with the development and perfection of the computer. Coupled with the growing body of statistical techniques, computers made it possible for managers to collect, store, and process large volumes of data for quantitative decision making, and the quantitative approach is widely used today by managers in a variety of industries. The Walt Disney Company used **quantitative techniques** to develop FastPass, a sophisticated computerized system that spares people the ordeal of standing in

Concept Connection

At Catholic Health Partners, a nonprofit hospital, hospice, and wellness center system that spans a number of Midwestern states, **information technology (IT)** is a top priority. IT is critical to the efficient running of all aspects of the health care system, as well as to maintaining up-to-the-minute, completely accurate patient records.

Kaspars Grinvalds/Shutterstock.com

long lines for the most popular rides. Disney theme parks have machines that issue coupons with a return time that's been calculated based on the number of people standing in the actual line, the number who have already obtained passes, and each ride's capacity. The next generation of technology, FastPass+, lets visitors book times for rides before they even leave home for their Disney vacation.[79] Let's look at three subsets of management science:

Operations research grew directly out of the World War II military groups (called *operational research teams* in Great Britain and *operations research teams* in the United States).[80] It consists of mathematical model building and other applications of quantitative techniques to managerial problems.

However, as events in the mortgage and finance industries show, relying too heavily on quantitative techniques can cause problems for managers. Mortgage companies used quantitative models that showed that their investments in subprime mortgages would be okay even if default rates hit historically high proportions. However, the models didn't take into account that no one before in history had thought it made sense to give $500,000 loans to people making minimum wage![81] "Quants" also came to dominate organizational decisions in other financial firms. The term **quants** refers to financial managers and others who base their decisions on complex quantitative analysis under the assumption that using advanced mathematics and sophisticated computer technology can accurately predict how the market works and help them reap huge profits. The virtually exclusive use of these quantitative models led aggressive traders and managers to take enormous risks. When the market began to go haywire as doubts about subprime mortgages grew, the models went haywire as well. Stocks predicted to go up went down, and vice versa. Events that were predicted to happen only once every 10,000 years happened three days in a row in the market madness. Scott Patterson, a *Wall Street Journal* reporter and author of *The Quants: How a New Breed of Math Whizzes Conquered Wall Street and Nearly Destroyed It*, suggests that the financial crisis that began in 2008 is partly due to the quants' failure to observe market fundamentals, pay attention to human factors, and heed their own intuition.[82]

The overall classical perspective as an approach to management was very powerful and gave companies fundamental new skills for establishing high productivity and effective treatment of employees. Indeed, the United States surged ahead of the world in management techniques, and other countries, especially Japan, borrowed heavily from American ideas.

Remember This

- Management science became popular based on its successful application in solving military problems during World War II.
- **Management science**, also called the *quantitative perspective,* uses mathematics, statistical techniques, and computer technology to facilitate management decision making, particularly for complex problems.
- The Walt Disney Company uses management science to solve the problem of long lines for popular rides and attractions at its theme parks.

- Three subsets of management science are operations research, operations management, and information technology (IT).
- **Quants** have come to dominate decision making in financial firms, and the Wall Street meltdown in 2007–2008 shows the danger of relying too heavily on a quantitative approach.

1-10 Humanistic Perspective

The **humanistic perspective** on management (the primary focus on the humanity of production) emphasizes the importance of understanding human behaviors, needs, and attitudes in the workplace, as well as social interactions and group processes.[83] There are three primary subfields based on the humanistic perspective: the human relations movement, the human resources perspective, and the behavioral sciences approach.

1-10a Early Advocates

Two early advocates of a more humanistic approach were Mary Parker Follett and Chester I. Barnard. Mary Parker Follett (1868–1933) was trained in philosophy and political science, but she applied herself in many fields, including social psychology and management. She wrote of the importance of common superordinate goals for reducing conflict in organizations.[84] Her work was popular with businesspeople of her day but was often overlooked by management scholars.[85] Follett's ideas served as a contrast to scientific management and are re-emerging as applicable for modern managers dealing with rapid changes in today's global environment. Her approach to leadership stressed the importance of people rather than engineering techniques. She offered the pithy admonition, "Don't hug your blueprints," and analyzed the dynamics of management–organization interactions. Follett addressed issues that are timely today, such as ethics, power, and leading in a way that encourages employees to give their best. The concepts of *empowering*, facilitating rather than controlling employees, and allowing employees to act depending on the authority of the situation opened new areas for theoretical study by Chester Barnard and others.[86]

Chester I. Barnard (1886–1961) studied economics at Harvard but failed to receive a degree because he did not take a course in laboratory science. He went to work in the statistical department of AT&T, and in 1927, he became president of New Jersey Bell. One of Barnard's significant contributions was the concept of the informal organization. The *informal organization* occurs in all formal organizations and includes cliques, informal networks, and naturally occurring social groupings. Barnard argued that organizations are not machines and stressed that informal relationships are powerful forces that can help the organization if properly managed. Another significant contribution was the *acceptance theory of authority*, which states that people have free will and can choose whether to follow management orders. People typically follow orders because they perceive positive benefit to themselves, but they do have a choice. Managers should treat employees properly because their acceptance of authority may be critical to organization success in important situations.[87]

National Archives

Concept Connection

This 1914 photograph shows the initiation of a new arrival at a Nebraska planting camp. This initiation was not part of the formal rules and illustrates the significance of the **informal organization** described by Barnard. Social values and behaviors were powerful forces that could help or hurt the planting organization, depending on how they were managed.

1-10b Human Relations Movement

The **human relations movement** was based on the idea that truly effective control comes from within the individual worker rather than from strict, authoritarian control.[88] This school of thought recognized and directly responded to social pressures for enlightened treatment of employees. The early work on industrial psychology and personnel selection received little attention because of the prominence of scientific management. Then a series of studies at a Chicago electric company, which came to be known as the **Hawthorne studies**, changed all that.

Beginning about 1895, a struggle developed between manufacturers of gas and electric lighting fixtures for control of the residential and industrial market.[89] By 1909, electric lighting had begun to win, but the increasingly efficient electric fixtures used less total power, which was less profitable for the electric companies. The electric companies began a campaign to convince industrial users that they needed more light to get more productivity. When advertising did not work, the industry began using experimental tests to demonstrate their argument. Managers were skeptical about the results, so the Committee on Industrial Lighting (CIL) was set up to run the tests. To further add to the tests' credibility, Thomas Edison was made honorary chairman of the CIL. In one test location—the Hawthorne plant of the Western Electric Company—some interesting events occurred.

The major part of this work involved four experimental and three control groups. So many factors were changed and so many unforeseen factors uncontrolled that scholars disagree on the factors that truly contributed to the general increase in performance over that time period. Most early interpretations, however, agreed on one point: Money was not the cause of the increased output.[90] It was believed that the factor that best explained increased output was *human relations*.

Western Electric Photographic Services

Concept Connection

This is the Relay Room of the Western Electric Hawthorne, Illinois, plant in 1927. Six women worked in this relay assembly test room during the controversial experiments on employee productivity. Professors Mayo and Roethlisberger evaluated conditions such as rest breaks and workday length, physical health, amount of sleep, and diet. Experimental changes were fully discussed with the women and were abandoned if they disapproved. Gradually, the researchers began to realize they had created a change in supervisory style and **human relations**, which they believed was the true cause of the increased productivity.

Before reading on, Visit MindTap for "Self-Assessment: What Is Your Manager Frame?" This test will give you feedback about how your personal manager frame of reference relates to the perspectives described in this chapter.

Employees performed better when managers treated them in a positive manner. Recent reanalyses of the experiments have revealed that a number of factors were different for the workers involved, and some suggest that money may well have been the single most important factor.[91] An interview with one of the original participants revealed that just getting into the experimental group meant a huge increase in income.[92]

From a historical perspective, whether the studies were academically sound is less important than the fact that they stimulated an increased interest in looking at employees as more than extensions of production machinery. The interpretation that employees' output increased when managers treated them in a positive manner started a revolution in worker treatment aimed at improving organizational productivity. Despite flawed methodology or inaccurate conclusions, the findings provided the impetus for the human relations movement. This approach shaped management theory and practice for well over a quarter-century, and the belief that human relations is the best area of focus for increasing productivity persists today.

1-10c Human Resources Perspective

The human relations movement initially espoused a *dairy farm* view of management—just as contented cows give more milk, satisfied workers will produce more work. Gradually, views with deeper content that elevated the "humanity of production" began to emerge. The **human resources perspective** maintained an interest in worker participation and considerate leadership but shifted the emphasis to considering the daily tasks that people perform. The human resources perspective combines prescriptions for design of job tasks with theories of motivation.[93] In the human resources view, jobs should be designed so that tasks are not perceived as dehumanizing or demeaning but instead allow workers to use their full potential. Two of the best-known contributors to the human resources perspective were Abraham Maslow and Douglas McGregor.

Abraham Maslow (1908–1970), a practicing psychologist, observed that his patients' problems usually stemmed from an inability to satisfy their needs. Thus, he generalized his work and suggested a hierarchy of needs. Maslow's hierarchy started with physiological needs and progressed to safety, belongingness, esteem, and, finally, self-actualization needs. Chapter 12 discusses his ideas in more detail.

Douglas McGregor (1906–1964) had become frustrated with the early, simplistic human relations notions while president of Antioch College in Ohio. He challenged both the classical perspective and the early human relations assumptions about human behavior. Based on his experiences as a manager and consultant, his training as a psychologist, and the work of Maslow, McGregor formulated Theory X and Theory Y, which are explained in Exhibit 1.13.[94] McGregor believed that the classical perspective was based on Theory X assumptions about workers. He also felt that a slightly modified version of Theory X fit early human relations ideas. In other words, human relations ideas did not go far enough. McGregor proposed Theory Y as a more realistic view of workers for guiding management thinking.

The point of Theory Y is that organizations can take advantage of the imagination and intellect of all their employees. Employees will exercise self-direction and self-control to contribute to organizational goals when given the opportunity. A few companies today still use Theory X management, but many are using Theory Y techniques. Some are doing away with bosses altogether, such as Zappos Shoe Company. Another company that provides a good illustration of applying Theory Y assumptions to tap into employee creativity and mind power is the Netherlands-based health care organization Buurtzorg.

For managers like Jos de Blok, command and control is a thing of the past, with the future belonging to those companies that build leadership throughout the organization. The Theory Y

Sunny Side Up · Buurtzorg

When Buurtzorg, a Netherlands-based health care organization, needs to rent new office space, the decision isn't made by administrators or consultants. Teams of nurses decide where the offices will be located. The same goes for deciding which patients to serve, how to allocate resources and tasks, which doctors to work with, and how to coordinate with local hospitals.

The Netherlands has a long history, since the nineteenth century, of local nurses providing neighborhood care for the sick and elderly, and nurses worked largely autonomously for much of that history. However, in the 1990s, care-giving agencies began merging into larger organizations and implementing greater hierarchy and strict standards for care to improve efficiency and cut costs. Nurses as well as clients began to suffer. Jos de Blok founded Buurtzorg in 2006 after working for 10 years as a nurse and then as a manager and experiencing first-hand how degrading and demoralizing it could be to work in a system where there was little time to provide proper care. At Buurtzorg, nurses work in completely self-managed teams of 10 to 12, with a purpose of helping people live a rich and autonomous life rather than a goal of providing care as efficiently as possible. Management tasks are spread across team members, with teams even monitoring their own performance and taking corrective action when needed.

Buurtzorg grew from four nurses to 9,000 and captured 60 percent of market share within eight years. Some studies have found that under the self-management system, nurses are also more efficient and effective. Buurtzorg requires on average about 40 percent of the care hours per patient compared to a more traditional approach because clients become self-sufficient much faster. Hospital admissions have been cut by a third, and the average length of stay of a Buurtzorg patient is shorter.[95]

Exhibit 1.13 Theory X and Theory Y

Assumptions of Theory X

- The average human being has an inherent dislike of works and will avoid it if possible.
- Because of the human characteristics of dislike for work, most people must be coerced, controlled, directed, or threatened with punishment to get them to put forth adequate effort toward the achievement of organizational objectives.
- The average human being prefers to be directed, wishes to avoid responsibility, has relatively little ambition, and wants security above all.

Assumptions of Theory Y

- The expenditure of physical and mental effort in work is as natural as play or rest. The average human being does not inherently dislike work.
- External control and the threat of punishment are not the only means for bringing about effort toward organizational objectives. A person will exercise self-direction and self-control in the service of objectives to which he or she is committed.
- The average human being learns, under proper conditions, not only to accept but to seek responsibility.
- The capacity to exercise a relatively high degree of imagination, ingenuity, and creativity in the solution of organizational problems is widely, not narrowly, distributed in the population.
- Under the conditions of modern industrial life, the intellectual potentialities of the average human being are only partially utilized.

SOURCE: Douglas McGregor, *The Human Side of Enterprise* (New York: McGraw-Hill, 1960), pp. 33–48. © McGraw-Hill Companies, Inc. Reprinted by permission.

approach has helped Buurtzorg grow and succeed and has enabled nurses to provide better care. As described at the beginning of this chapter, a number of companies are using less hierarchical management systems that rely on Theory Y principles, which are more in line with today's emphasis on employee engagement and involvement.

1-10d Behavioral Sciences Approach

The **behavioral sciences approach** uses scientific methods and draws from sociology, psychology, anthropology, economics, and other disciplines to develop theories about human behavior and interaction in an organizational setting. This approach can be seen in practically every

Visit MindTap to *look back at your scores on your "Self-Assessment: Are You a New-Style Manager?" related to Theory X and Theory Y. How will your management assumptions about people fit into an organization today?*

organization. When a company such as Snapchat conducts research to determine the best set of tests, interviews, and employee profiles to use when selecting new employees, it is using behavioral science techniques. When Best Buy electronics stores train new managers in the techniques of employee motivation, most of the theories and findings are rooted in behavioral science research.

One specific set of management techniques based in the behavioral sciences approach is *organization development (OD)*. In the 1970s, OD evolved as a separate field that applied the behavioral sciences to improve the organization's health and effectiveness through its ability to cope with change, improve internal relationships, and increase problem-solving capabilities.[96] The techniques and concepts of OD have since been broadened and expanded to address the increasing complexity of organizations and the environment, and OD is still a vital approach for managers. OD will be discussed in detail in Chapter 8. Other concepts that grew out of the behavioral sciences approach include matrix organizations, self-managed teams, ideas about corporate culture, and management by wandering around. Indeed, the behavioral sciences approach has influenced the majority of tools, techniques, and approaches that managers have applied to organizations since the 1970s.

Remember This

- The **humanistic perspective** emphasizes understanding human behavior, needs, and attitudes in the workplace.
- Mary Parker Follett and Chester I. Barnard were early advocates of a more humanistic approach to management.
- Follett emphasized worker participation and empowerment, shared goals, and facilitating rather than controlling employees. Barnard's contributions include the acceptance theory of authority.
- The **human relations movement** stresses the satisfaction of employees' basic needs as the key to increased productivity.

- The **Hawthorne studies** were important in shaping ideas concerning how managers should treat workers.
- The **human resources perspective** suggests that jobs should be designed to meet people's higher-level needs by allowing employees to use their full potential.
- The **behavioral sciences approach** draws from psychology, sociology, and other social sciences to develop theories about human behavior and interaction in an organizational setting.
- Many current management ideas and practices can be traced to the behavioral sciences approach.

1-11 Recent Historical Trends

Among the approaches discussed so far, the humanistic perspective has been strongest from the 1950s until today. Peter Drucker's books *Concept of the Corporation* (1946) and *The Practice of Management* (1954) emphasized the corporation as a *social* and *human* institution. Drucker revived interest in the work of Mary Parker Follett from the 1920s in his call for managers to involve and respect employees.[97] The post-World War II period saw the rise of new concepts, along with a continued strong interest in the human aspect of managing, such as team and group dynamics and other ideas that relate to the humanistic perspective. Two new concepts that appeared were systems thinking and the contingency view.

1-11a Systems Thinking

Systems thinking is the ability to see both the distinct elements of a system or situation and the complex and changing interaction among those elements. A **system** is a set of interrelated parts that function as a whole to achieve a common purpose.[98] **Subsystems** are parts of a system, such as an organization, that depend on one another. Changes in one part of the system (the organization) affect other parts. Managers need to understand the synergy of the whole organization, rather

Recipe for Success } **McDonald's**

McDonald's is the world's largest hamburger chain, but sales and earnings have been slipping in recent years and managers are struggling to find the right approach to keep the chain growing.

McDonald's recent problems can be partly explained by subsystem interdependence. With a weak economy, people are eating out less often, so McDonald's managers have added new menu items, such as Premium McWraps, mozzarella sticks, and various types of smoothies, designed to lure in new customers. However, employees have been struggling to prepare the multitude of new products quickly and efficiently, which means customers aren't getting served as quickly as before. For instance, a recent study by *QSR* magazine of how long it took the average customer to make it through the drive-through at various fast-food restaurants found that McDonald's experienced its slowest average speed of service in the history of the study. When many customers see a long line at the drive-through or a long line waiting for service at the counter, they leave and go somewhere else. Thus, a change designed to bring in more customers (new menu items) has actually driven some customers away by slowing service.

"We overcomplicated the restaurants and didn't give restaurants an opportunity to breathe," said Tim Fenton, McDonald's chief operating officer. "We need to do fewer products with better execution." Managers are currently expanding prep tables and considering other changes to help employees efficiently handle the more complicated menu.[99]

than just the separate elements, and to learn to reinforce or change whole system patterns.[100] **Synergy** means that the whole is greater than the sum of its parts. The organization must be managed as a coordinated whole. Managers who understand subsystem interdependence and synergy are reluctant to make changes that do not recognize the impact of subsystems on the organization as a whole.

Many people have been trained to solve problems by breaking a complex system, such as an organization, into discrete parts and working to make each part perform as well as possible. However, the success of each piece does not add up to the success of the whole. In fact, sometimes changing one part to make it better actually makes the whole system function less effectively. Managers at McDonald's are currently experiencing this problem.

As another example of subsystem interdependence, consider the small city that embarked on a road-building program to solve traffic congestion without whole-systems thinking. With new roads available, more people began moving to the suburbs. Rather than reduce congestion, the solution actually increased traffic congestion, delays, and pollution by enabling suburban sprawl.[101]

It is the *relationship* among the parts that form a whole system—whether a community, an automobile, a nonprofit agency, a human being, or a business organization—that matters. Systems thinking enables managers to look for patterns of movement over time and focus on the qualities of rhythm, flow, direction, shape, and networks of relationships that accomplish the performance of the whole. When managers can see the structures that underlie complex situations, they can facilitate improvement. But doing that requires a focus on the big picture.

An important element of systems thinking is to discern circles of causality. Peter Senge, author of *The Fifth Discipline*, argues that reality is made up of circles rather than straight lines. For example, Exhibit 1.14 shows circles of influence for increasing a retail firm's profits. The events in the circle on the left are caused by the decision to increase advertising; hence, the retail firm adds to the advertising budget to aggressively promote its products. The advertising promotions increase sales, which increase profits, which provide money to further increase the advertising budget.

But another circle of causality is being influenced as well. The decision by marketing managers will have consequences for the operations department. As sales and profits increase, operations will be forced to stock up with greater inventory. Additional inventory will create a need for additional warehouse space. Building a new warehouse will cause a delay in stocking up. After the warehouse is built, new people will be hired, all of which add to company costs, which will have a negative impact on profits. Thus, understanding all the consequences of their decisions via circles of causality enables company leaders to plan and allocate resources to warehousing as well as to advertising to ensure stable increases in sales and profits. Without understanding system causality, top managers would fail to understand why increasing advertising budgets could cause inventory delays and temporarily reduce profits.

Exhibit 1.14 Systems Thinking and Circles of Causality

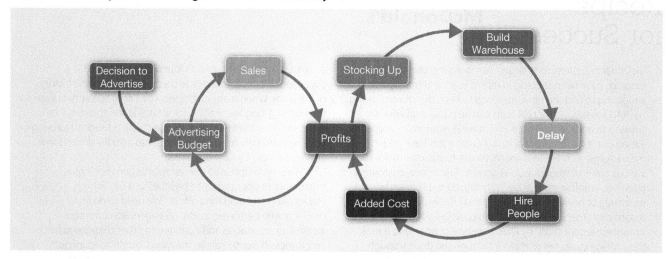

SOURCE: Based on concepts presented in Peter M. Senge, *The Fifth Discipline: The Art and Practice of the Learning Organization* (New York: Doubleday/Currency, 1990).

1-11b Contingency View

A second recent extension to management thinking is the **contingency view**. The classical perspective assumed a *universalist* view. Management concepts were thought to be universal; that is, whatever worked in one organization in terms of management style, bureaucratic structure, and so on would work in any other one. In business education, however, an alternative view exists. In this *case* view, each situation is believed to be unique. Principles are not universal, and one learns about management by experiencing a large number of case problem situations. Managers face the task of determining what methods will work in every new situation.

To integrate these views, the contingency view emerged, as illustrated in Exhibit 1.15.[102] Here, neither of the other views is seen as entirely correct. Instead, certain contingencies, or variables, exist for helping managers identify and understand situations. The contingency view tells us that what works in one setting might not work in another. *Contingency* means that one thing depends on other things, and a manager's response to a situation depends on identifying key contingencies in an organizational situation.

One important contingency, for example, is the industry in which the organization operates. The organizational structure that is effective for an online company, such as the microblogging services Twitter and China's Sina Weibo, would not be successful for a large auto manufacturer, such as Toyota or Ford. A management-by-objectives (MBO) system that works well in a manufacturing firm, in turn, might not be right for a school system. When managers learn to identify important patterns and characteristics of their organizations, they can fit solutions to those characteristics.

Exhibit 1.15 Contingency View of Management

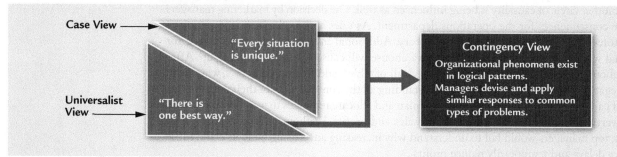

Remember This

- A **system** is a set of interrelated parts that function as a whole to achieve a common purpose. An organization is a system.
- **Systems thinking** means looking not just at discrete parts of an organizational situation, but also at the continually changing interactions among the parts.
- When managers think systemically and understand subsystem interdependence and synergy, they can get a better handle on managing in a complex environment.

- **Subsystems** are parts of a system that depend on one another for their functioning.
- The concept of **synergy** says that the whole is greater than the sum of its parts. The organization must be managed as a whole.
- The **contingency view** tells managers that what works in one organizational situation might not work in others. Managers can identify important *contingencies* that help guide their decisions regarding the organization.

1-12 Innovative Management Thinking into the Future

Many of the ideas and approaches discussed so far go into the mix that makes up modern management. Dozens of ideas and techniques in current use can trace their roots to these historical perspectives.[103] In addition, innovative concepts continue to emerge to address new management challenges. Wise managers heed the past but know that they and their organizations must change with the times.

Managers are always looking for new techniques and approaches that more adequately respond to customer needs and the demands of the environment. The following is a list of a wide variety of ideas and techniques used by today's managers, as revealed by the "2015 Management Tools and Trends" survey by Bain & Company.

Current Use of Management Tools and Trends   Over the history of management, many fashions and fads have appeared. Critics argue that new techniques may not represent permanent solutions. Others feel that managers must adopt new techniques for continuous improvement in a fast-changing world. In 1993, Bain & Company started a large research project to interview and survey thousands of corporate executives about the 25 most popular management tools and techniques.

The Top Ten.   The list of the top 10 tools for 2014–2015 is shown here and indicates how each tool is ranked globally and in North America. How many of the tools are you familiar with? For more information on specific tools, see Bain's *Management Tools 2015: An Executive's Guide* at http://www.bain.com/Images/BAIN_GUIDE_Management_Tools_2015_executives_guide.pdf.

Tool or Technique	Global Ranking	North America Ranking
Customer Relationship Management	1	4
Employee Engagement Surveys	2 (tie)	1
Benchmarking	2 (tie)	2 (tie)
Strategic Planning	2 (tie)	2 (tie)
Outsourcing	5	6
Balanced Scorecard	6 (tie)	7 (tie)
Mission and Vision Statements	6 (tie)	5
Supply Chain Management	8	7 (tie)

Change Management Programs	9	9
Core Competencies	10 (tie)	10
Big Data Analytics	10 (tie)	—
Total Quality Management	10 (tie)	—

In the Bain survey, most executives said they are optimistic about the economic recovery, but a majority also said excessive complexity is increasing their costs and slowing growth. Thus, managers are looking for new and creative approaches that can help them reduce and cope with complexity, cut costs, and invest in innovation for the future. Other top concerns of managers as revealed in the survey include the threat of cyber attacks, decreasing customer loyalty, and the pace of change brought about by digital technologies.[104] Responding to these and other concerns, the tools most used by today's managers tend to fall into the same dual categories of managing the "things of production" and managing the "humanity of production," discussed at the beginning of this chapter. The following sections discuss current approaches in these dual categories by looking at the technology-driven workplace and the people-driven workplace. New technology, for example, may ignore the needs of people and often has the potential to return them to cogs in the organizational machine. Social media and bossless management, on the other hand, focus more on meeting human needs to advance organizational performance.

1-12a Managing the New Technology-Driven Workplace

Managers see IT as presenting both opportunities and threats to their organizations. A total of 64 percent of managers surveyed said that their company's spending on IT must increase over the next three years to keep pace with evolving needs and technology. Two popular new uses of this technology are big data analytics and supply chain management.

Big Data Analytics   The newest business technology is big data analytics. In the Bain survey, big data analytics ranked relatively low in usage but was ranked No. 1 in satisfaction.[105] **Big data analytics** refers to technologies, skills, and processes for searching and examining massive, complex sets of data that traditional data processing applications cannot handle to uncover hidden patterns and correlations.[106] Facebook, for example, uses the personal data that you put on your page and tracks and monitors your online behavior, then searches through all that data to identify and suggest potential "friends."[107] This caused a great scandal in 2018 regarding privacy issues and problems with fake news. Amazon.com collects tons of data on customers, including what they buy, what else they look at, how they navigate through the Web site, how much they are influenced by promotions and reviews, and so forth. The company uses algorithms that predict and suggest what a customer might be interested in buying next. Moreover, the predictions get better every time a customer responds to or ignores a recommendation.[108] Another example of the power of big data analytics comes from the world of online dating Web sites such as eHarmony and Match.com, which sift through huge amounts of data to compare millions of people across hundreds of different variables and make matches for users in a matter of minutes, sending new matches out on a daily basis. The professional networking site LinkedIn applies a similar idea with its "People You May Want to Hire" recruiting feature. The company will plumb the depths of its huge data mines and provide a list of perfect candidates for a company's job openings.[109]

Popularity.   In the most recent survey, managers ranked customer relationship management (CRM) at the top of the list for the second time in a row. Across all geographical areas and industries, CRM emerged as managers' most important investment priority, reflecting a concern with the decline in customer loyalty. Managers also put a priority on investing in employee engagement based on evidence of a link between highly motivated employees and customer loyalty. Over a 10-year period, strategic planning, benchmarking, mission and vision statements, and outsourcing have consistently remained in the top 10. The tools with the greatest forecasted increase in use were scenario and contingency planning and complexity reduction, reflecting managers' concern with the turbulence of the environment.

Global Trends.   The most recent survey shows a distinct split between North America, where managers prefer to use more traditional tools such as strategic planning and benchmarking, and Asia-Pacific firms (China and India), where managers report a much higher usage of new tools such as disruptive innovation labs. In North America, the most widely used tool was the employee engagement survey, which aims to measure and improve employee motivation and by extension productivity, whereas in Latin America and Europe, the Middle East, and Africa (EMEA), CRM and benchmarking topped the list in terms of usage. Asia-Pacific region firms use big data analytics more than any other tool, while managers in Latin America rank strategic planning at the top of the list.

Source: Darrell Rigby and Barbara Bilodeau, "Management Tools and Trends 2015," Copyright © 2015, Bain & Company, Inc., http://www.bain.com/publications/articles /management-tools-and-trends-2015.aspx (accessed January 20, 2016). Reprinted by permission.

However, big data is not just for online companies. Big data analytics can be thought of as a direct descendant of Frederick Winslow Taylor's scientific management and the most recent iteration of the quantitative approach to management.[110] Caesars Entertainment uses data analytics not only to understand customers and create a richer customer experience at each resort and casino, but also to improve operations—everything from food and beverage services to human resources.[111] FedEx can reportedly use big data to identify with 65 to 90 percent accuracy which customers are likely to move to a competitor, then offer those customers incentives to stay.[112]

Supply Chain Management   **Supply chain management** refers to managing the sequence of suppliers and purchasers and covers all stages of processing, from obtaining raw materials to distributing finished goods to consumers.[113] Exhibit 1.16 illustrates a basic supply chain model. A *supply chain* is a network of multiple businesses and individuals that are connected through the flow of products or services.[114] Many organizations manage the supply chain with sophisticated electronic technology. In India, for example, Walmart managers have invested in an efficient supply chain that electronically links farmers and small manufacturers directly to the stores, maximizing value for both ends.[115] However, today's global supply chains create many challenges for managers. Several garment factory fires in Bangladesh and the collapse of another apparel plant that killed 1,100 workers put the spotlight on poor working conditions in that country. The problem for retailers such as Walmart, H&M, Target, and other big companies is that similar poor working conditions exist in other low-wage countries such as Pakistan, Cambodia, Indonesia, and Vietnam, which produce most of the world's clothing. Both European and U.S. retailers have announced plans aimed at improving safety in overseas factories, but the challenge of monitoring contractors and subcontractors in low-wage countries is a massive one. Even when managers in an organization such as H&M think they are hiring a responsible supplier, that company might subcontract or obtain materials from less responsible ones.[116]

Exhibit 1.16 **Supply Chain for a Retail Organization**

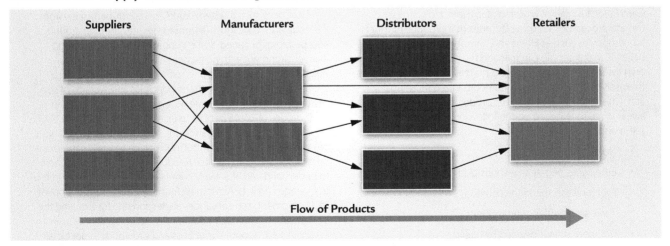

SOURCE: Adapted from an exhibit from the Global Supply Chain Games Project, Delft University and the University of Maryland, R. H. Smith School of Business, www.gscg.org:8080/opencms/export/sites/default/gscg/images /supplychain_simple.gif (accessed February 6, 2008).

1-12b Managing the New People-Driven Workplace

Organizations are undergoing tremendous changes. Some of these changes are related to new technology, whereas others are brought about primarily because of shifting needs of people. For example, younger employees are seeking more purpose in their work, which often brings changes in workplace cultures and practices. Barry Schwartz, professor of psychology at Swarthmore College and author of *Why We Work*, says that as "the Millennials ascend, they will change organizations" because "meaning is an important part of their agenda."[117] Two responses to these issues are the bossless workplace and a renewed emphasis on employee engagement.

The Bossless Workplace   As described at the beginning of this chapter, a few bossless work environments have existed for decades, but this has become a real trend in recent years. For one thing, how and where work gets done has shifted in major ways because new technology enables many people to work from home or other locations outside a regular office. At Symantec, for example, most employees used to work in cubicles, but now many of them work from home or other remote locations scattered all over the world.[118] When everyone has access to the information they need and the training to make good decisions, having layers of managers just eats up costs and slows down response time.[119]

Many bossless companies, such as Valve Software (Web platform for video games), Netflix (video streaming and rentals), and Atlassian (enterprise software), operate in technology-related industries, but companies as diverse as GE Aviation (aviation manufacturing), W. L. Gore & Associates (best known for Gore-Tex fabrics), Whole Foods Market (supermarkets), and Semco (diversified manufacturing) have succeeded for years with bossless structures. One of the most interesting examples of a bossless work environment is a tomato processor.

In a bossless work environment such as that at Morning Star, nobody gives orders, and nobody takes them. Accountability is to the customer and the team rather than to a manager. There can be many advantages to a bossless work environment, including increased flexibility, greater employee initiative and commitment, and better and faster decision making.[120] However, bossless work environments also present new challenges. Costs may be lower because of reduced overhead, but money must be invested in ongoing training and development for employees so that they can work effectively within a bossless system. The culture also must engage employees and support the nonhierarchical environment. Employee engagement is essential for a successful bossless workplace.

Recipe for Success } Morning Star

Chris Rufer, founder of Morning Star, the world's largest tomato processor with three factories that produce products for companies such as Heinz and Campbell Soup Company, believes that if people can manage the complexities of their own lives without a boss, there is no reason they can't manage themselves in the workplace. Rufer organized Morning Star, where 400 or so employees produce over $700 million a year in revenue, based on the following principles of self-management:

- No one has a boss.
- Employees negotiate responsibilities with their peers.
- Everyone can spend the company's money.
- There are no titles or promotions.
- Compensation is decided by peers.

How does such a system work? As the company grew from the original 24 colleagues (as employees are called) to around 400, problems occurred. Some people had trouble working in an environment with no bosses and no hierarchy. Thus, Rufer created the Morning Star Self-Management Institute to provide training for people in the principles and systems of self-management. Every colleague now goes through training, in small groups of 10–15 people, to learn how to work effectively as part of a team; how to handle the responsibilities of "planning, organizing, leading, and controlling" that are typically carried out by managers; how to balance freedom and accountability; how to understand and effectively communicate with others; and how to manage conflicts. At Morning Star, anyone can order supplies and equipment, and colleagues are responsible for initiating the hiring process when they need more help. "Around here," one associate said, "nobody's your boss and everybody's your boss."[121]

Using Engagement to Manage Millennials Employee **engagement** means that people are emotionally involved in their jobs and are satisfied with their work conditions, contribute enthusiastically to meeting team and organizational goals, and feel a sense of belonging and commitment to the organization and its mission.[122] To engage employees, managers unite people around a compelling purpose that encourages them to give their best. Millennial employees, the most educated generation in the history of the United States, grew up technologically adept and globally conscious. Unlike many workers in the past, they typically are not hesitant to question their superiors and challenge the status quo. They want a flexible, collaborative work environment that is challenging and supportive, with access to cutting-edge technology, opportunities to learn and further their careers and personal goals, and the power to make substantive decisions in the workplace. Meeting the shifting needs of this generation is one reason managers put employee engagement surveys high on the list of tools and techniques they are using.[123]

Meanwhile, savvy managers are looking ahead to the next generation after the Millennials that will soon be flooding into the workforce, bringing their own changes and challenges to the practice and evolution of management. Some observers predict that a sense or meaning and commitment, especially environmental responsibility, will be high on their list of priorities.[124]

Emil Matveyev/ITAR-TASS Photo Agency/Alamy Stock Photo

Concept Connection

Research has shown that organizations can deliberately create a culture that engages employees and encourages greater job satisfaction. At international shipping company Deutsche Post DHL Group (DHL), for example, the company is big on thanking employees for their contributions through thank-you notes, monetary rewards, and more. Other **engagement** tactics include communicating honestly with employees, supporting career development, and enabling employees to serve their communities.

1-13 The Historical Struggle: Is Social Business the Answer?

One current answer to the historical struggle within management to balance the things of production and the humanity of production is social business. **Social business** refers to using social media technologies for interacting with and facilitating communication and collaboration among employees, customers, and other stakeholders. **Social media programs** include company online community pages, wikis for virtual collaboration, social media sites such as Facebook or LinkedIn, video channels such as YouTube, microblogging platforms such as Twitter, and company online forums.

For the first time, a new technology (*thing* of production) adds directly to the *humanity* of production. Social media technology can improve efficiency, increase productivity, and facilitate faster and smoother operations by improving communication and collaboration within and across firms.[125] Social media can also improve the human aspect of organizations by enabling a sense of community and facilitating communication, collaboration, and knowledge sharing. Kaiser Permanente uses an internal social media platform called IdeaBook that supports blogs, wikis, online videos, and chat rooms and provides a way for people to meet and carry on conversations in virtual workspaces.[126] In addition, social media technology is being used by companies to build trusting relationships with customers.[127] An early leader in this realm was Morgan Stanley Wealth Management. As director of digital strategy, Lauren Boyman worked closely with the company's sales manager and investment advisors to use Twitter and other social media for communicating with clients.[128] Some companies have launched social media command centers to monitor what is being said about the company on social media platforms.[129]

Just as important, social media can build stronger, more authentic relationships between managers and employees. Mark Reuss left General Motors (GM) in Australia to run GM's operations in North America just after the company filed for bankruptcy in 2009 and was implementing plans to eliminate more than 2,000 U.S. dealerships. Reuss chose to communicate with the dealer network through a "get to know you" messaging part of Facebook rather than through e-mails or other corporate communications. The strategy helped build trust and credibility because Reuss made

"Social media is no longer the wave of the future. It is already a state-of-the-art leadership tool that surpasses many traditional approaches to listening and communicating with stakeholders."

—LESLIE GAINES-ROSS, CHIEF REPUTATION STRATEGIST AT WEBER SHANDWICK AND AUTHOR OF *CEO CAPITAL: A GUIDE TO BUILDING CEO REPUTATION AND COMPANY SUCCESS*

HOT TOPIC

himself accessible and was willing to engage others authentically. "No matter what happened," Reuss said, "they knew that I was listening and that they had . . . someone to talk to in the company and they could do it instantly. And if you look at how we got through that period and the dealers that we have and the trust that I have built . . . it's because of that conversation on Facebook." [130]

Social business is one of the most recent approaches in the evolution of management thinking and practice, as shown in Exhibit 1.9 earlier in this chapter. As managers confront new challenges and shifting environmental conditions and technology, management continues to evolve, incorporating ideas from the past with new concepts for changing times.

Remember This

- Modern management is a lively mix of ideas and techniques from varied historical perspectives, but new concepts continue to emerge.

- Managers tend to look for innovative ideas and approaches, particularly during turbulent times.

- Two recent trends are the transition to a more technology-driven workplace and a corresponding emphasis on a people-driven workplace.

- **Supply chain management** refers to managing the sequence of suppliers and purchasers and covers all stages of processing, from obtaining raw materials to distributing finished goods to consumers.

- Two ideas related to a people-driven workplace are the bossless work environment and employee engagement.

- **Engagement** means that people are involved in their jobs and are satisfied with their work conditions,

contribute enthusiastically to meeting team and organizational goals, and feel a sense of belonging and commitment to the organization and its mission.

- Managers are looking ahead to the next generation of employees to try to predict what changes and challenges they may bring to the evolution of management thinking.

- **Social business**, which refers to using social media technologies for interacting with and facilitating communication and collaboration among employees, customers, and other stakeholders, is one current answer to the historical struggle.

- **Social media programs** include company online community pages, wikis for virtual collaboration, social media sites such as Facebook or LinkedIn, video channels such as YouTube, microblogging platforms such as Twitter, and company online forums.

DISCUSSION QUESTIONS

1. How do you feel about having management responsibilities in today's world, which is characterized by uncertainty, ambiguity, and sudden changes or threats from the environment? Describe some skills and competencies that you think are important to managers working in these conditions.

2. Assume that you are a project manager at a biotechnology company and that you work with managers from research, production, and marketing on a major product modification. You notice that every memo you receive from the marketing manager has been copied to senior management. At every company function, she spends time talking to the big shots. You are also aware that sometimes when you and the other project members are slaving away over the project, she is playing golf with senior managers.

What is your evaluation of her behavior? As project manager, what do you do?

3. Jeff Immelt, CEO of GE, tweeted for the first time in September 2012, prompting this response: "@JeffImmelt how come my grandfather got on twitter before you?" Do you think managers should use Twitter and other social media? Can you be an effective manager today without using new media? Why?

4. Think about the highly publicized safety recall at General Motors (GM) for defective ignition systems. One observer said that a goal of efficiency had taken precedence over a goal of quality within this company. Do you think managers can improve both efficiency and effectiveness simultaneously? Discuss.

5. You are a bright, hard-working, entry-level manager who fully intends to rise up through the ranks. Your performance evaluation gives you high marks for your technical skills but low marks when it comes to people skills. Do you think people skills can be learned, or do you need to rethink your career path? If people skills can be learned, how would you go about learning them?

6. A college professor told her students, "The purpose of a management course is to teach students about management, not to teach them to be managers." Do you agree or disagree with this statement? Discuss.

7. How would you feel about working in a boss-less organization? What might be your role as a "manager" in such an environment? Do you think this is a trend that will continue to grow or fade away? Why?

8. Big data analytics programs (which analyze massive data sets to make decisions) use gigantic computing power to quantify trends that would be beyond the grasp of human observers. As the use of this quantitative analysis increases, do you think it may decrease the "humanity of production" in organizations? Why?

9. A management professor once said that for successful management, studying the present was most important, studying the past was next, and studying the future should come last. Do you agree? Why?

10. Why do you think Mary Parker Follett's ideas tended to be popular with businesspeople of her day but were ignored by management scholars? Why are her ideas appreciated more today?

APPLY YOUR SKILLS: SELF-LEARNING

Aptitude Questionnaire

Rate each of the following statements according to the following scale:

① I am never like this.
② I am rarely like this.
③ I am sometimes like this.
④ I am often like this.
⑤ I am always like this.

1. When I have a number of tasks or homework to do, I set priorities and organize the work around deadlines.

   1 2 3 4 5

2. Most people would describe me as a good listener.

   1 2 3 4 5

3. When I am deciding on a particular course of action for myself (such as hobbies to pursue, languages to study, which job to take, or special projects to be involved in), I typically consider the long-term (three years or more) implications of what I would choose to do.

   1 2 3 4 5

4. I prefer technical or quantitative courses rather than those involving literature, psychology, or sociology.

   1 2 3 4 5

5. When I have a serious disagreement with someone, I hang in there and talk it out until it is completely resolved.

   1 2 3 4 5

6. When I have a project or assignment, I really get into the details rather than the "big picture" issues.

   1 2 3 4 5

7. I would rather sit in front of my computer than spend a lot of time with people.

   1 2 3 4 5

8. I try to include others in activities or discussions.

   1 2 3 4 5

9. When I take a course, I relate what I am learning to other courses I took or concepts I learned elsewhere.

   1 2 3 4 5

10. When somebody makes a mistake, I want to correct the person and let her or him know the proper answer or approach.

    1 2 3 4 5

11. I think it is better to be efficient with my time when talking with someone, rather than worry about the other person's needs, so that I can get on with my real work.

    1 2 3 4 5

12. I have a long-term vision of career, family, and other activities and have thought it over carefully.

    1 2 3 4 5

13. When solving problems, I would much rather analyze some data or statistics than meet with a group of people.

    1   2   3   4   5

14. When I am working on a group project and someone doesn't pull a fair share of the load, I am more likely to complain to my friends than to confront the slacker.

    1   2   3   4   5

15. Talking about ideas or concepts can get me really enthusiastic or excited.

    1   2   3   4   5

16. The type of management course for which this book is used is really a waste of time.

    1   2   3   4   5

17. I think it is better to be polite and not hurt people's feelings.

    1   2   3   4   5

18. Data and things interest me more than people.

    1   2   3   4   5

Scoring and Interpretation Subtract your scores for statements 6, 10, 14, and 17 from the number 6, and then add the total points for the following sections:

1, 3, 6, 9, 12, 15 Conceptual skills total score _____
2, 5, 8, 10, 14, 17 Human skills total score _____
4, 7, 11, 13, 16, 18 Technical skills total score _____

These skills are three of the skills needed to be a good manager. Ideally, a manager should be strong (though not necessarily equal) in all three. Anyone noticeably weaker in any of these skills should take courses and read to build up that skill. For further background on the three skills, please refer to the explanation in the Management Skills section.

APPLY YOUR SKILLS: GROUP LEARNING

Your Best and Worst Managers

Step 1. On your own, think of two managers that you have had—the best and the worst. The managers could be anyone who served as an authority figure over you, including an instructor, a boss at work, a manager of a student organization, a leader of a student group, a coach, a volunteer committee in a nonprofit organization, and so on. Think carefully about the specific behaviors that made each manager the best or the worst and write down what that manager did.

The best manager I ever had did the following:

_____

_____

_____

_____

The worst manager I ever had did the following:

_____

_____

_____

_____

Step 2. Divide into groups of four to six members. Each person should share his or her experiences, one at a time. On a sheet of paper or on a whiteboard, write separate lists of best-manager and worst-manager behaviors.

Step 3. Analyze the two lists. What themes or patterns characterize "best" and "worst" manager behaviors? What are the key differences between the two sets of behaviors?

Step 4. What lessons does your group learn from its analysis? What advice or "words of wisdom" would you give managers to help them be more effective?

APPLY YOUR SKILLS: ACTION LEARNING

1. Think about some time in your life where you were a leader or had some authority over others. It could have been on a school committee, as a camp counselor, as a youth coordinator in church/synagogue, as a yearbook/prom organizer, etc.

2. Either individually, or in a group of two to four, ask yourself the following questions. If you are in a group, someone else can ask you the questions:

    a. Describe some incidents that went really well when you handled a problem in a satisfying manner.

    b. List some examples when you did not handle problems in a positive manner.

c. What were the differences between those two types of situations? Was it the type of person you dealt with, the level of your own supervision, the difficulty of the problem, etc.?

d. What can you learn about your own strengths and weaknesses and a manager from these situations?

e. What is your best strength as a manager? Can you find a theory in this chapter that refers to that strength?

f. What would you do differently in any of the situations you described, if you had it to do over again?

3. Write a short (two- to three-page) paper comparing situations you encountered. What are the deeper insights you have gained from reflection?

4. Your instructor may ask you to discuss your conclusions in groups; be prepared to share with them the whole class.

APPLY YOUR SKILLS: ETHICAL DILEMMA

The New Test[131]

The Civil Service Board in a midsize city in Indiana decided that a written exam should be given to all candidates for promotion to supervisor. A written test would assess mental skills and would open access to all personnel who wanted to apply for the position. The board believed a written exam for promotion would be completely fair and objective because it eliminated subjective judgments and personal favoritism regarding a candidate's qualifications.

Maxine Othman, manager of a social service agency, loved to see her employees learn and grow to their full potential. When a rare opening for a supervising clerk occurred, Maxine quickly decided to give Sheryl Hines a shot at the job. Sheryl had been with the agency for 17 years and had shown herself to be a true leader. In her new position, Sheryl worked hard at becoming a good supervisor, just as she had always worked hard at being a top-notch clerk. She paid attention to the human aspects of employee problems and introduced modern management techniques that strengthened the entire agency. Because of the board's new ruling, however, Sheryl would have to complete the exam in an open competition—anyone could sign up and take it, even a new employee. The board wanted the candidate with the highest score to get the job but allowed Maxine, as manager of the agency, to have the final say.

Because Sheryl had accepted the provisional opening and proved herself on the job, Maxine was upset that the entire clerical force was deemed qualified to

take the test. When the results came back, she was devastated. Sheryl placed twelfth in the field of candidates, while one of her newly hired clerks placed first. The Civil Service Board, impressed by this person's high score, urged Maxine to give the new clerk the permanent supervisory job over Sheryl; however, it was still Maxine's choice. Maxine wondered whether it was fair to base her decision only on the results of a written test. The board was pushing her to honor the objective written test, but could the test really assess fairly who was the right person for the job?

What Would You Do?

1. Ignore the test. Sheryl has proven herself via work experience and deserves the job.

2. Give the job to the candidate with the highest score. You don't need to make enemies on the Civil Service Board, and, although it is a bureaucratic procedure, the test is an objective way to select a permanent placement.

3. Press the board to devise a more comprehensive set of selection criteria—including test results, but also taking into account supervisory experience, ability to motivate employees, and knowledge of agency procedures—that can be explained and justified to the board and to employees.

APPLY YOUR SKILLS: CASE FOR CRITICAL ANALYSIS

SmartStyle Salons

Jamika Westbrook takes pride in her position as salon manager for SmartStyle Salon, one of six local hair salons associated with a large retail store chain located in the Southeast and one of five chain store groups under the Gold Group umbrella. She oversees a staff of 30, including hairdressers, a nail technician, receptionists, shampoo assistants, and a custodian. She enjoys

a reputation as a manager who works very hard and takes care of her people. Hairdressers want to work for her.

Following the salon's new-hire policy, Jamika began as a shampoo assistant and quickly became a top hairdresser in the company through a combination of skill, a large and loyal client base, and long hours at work. In 2007, retiring manager Carla Weems hand-picked Jamika as her successor, and the board quickly approved.

Initially, the salon, located in a suburban mall, managed a strong, steady increase, holding its position as one of the corporation's top performers. But economic woes hit the area hard, with increases in unemployment, mortgage woes, and foreclosures among current and potential customers. As families sought ways to save, the luxury of regular visits to the hair salon was among the first logical budget cuts. The past year has reflected this economic reality, and Jamika's salon saw a sharp decrease in profits.

Jamika's stomach is in knots as she arrives at the salon on Monday. Scheduled to fly to Atlanta the next morning for a meeting at corporate, she fears potential staffing cuts, but more important, she fears the loss of opportunity to secure her dream job: replacing the retiring manager at the Riverwood Mall location, which is the top-performing salon and is located in an upscale area of the city.

Distracted, Jamika walks past the receptionist, Marianne, who is busily answering the phones. Hanging up the phone, Marianne tells Jamika that Holly and Carol Jean, two popular hairdressers, called in sick, and Jamika now has to reschedule their clients. Jamika had denied their earlier request to travel out of town to attend a concert, and her irritation is obvious. She orders Marianne to call both women and instruct them that, when they return to work, they are to bring a doctor's statement and a copy of any prescriptions that they were given. "They had better be sick!" Jamika shouts as she enters her office, slamming the door more forcefully than she intended. Startled employees and early-morning customers hear the outburst, and, after a momentary pause, they resume their activities and quiet conversation, surprised by the show of managerial anger. Jamika knows she has let Holly and Carol Jean get away with unwarranted absences before and worries that she will do it again. She needs every head of hair that they can style to help the salon's profit.

Jamika takes a deep breath and sits at her desk, turning on the computer and checking e-mails, including one from the group manager reminding her to send the salon's status report in advance of tomorrow's meeting. She buzzes Marianne on the intercom to request final figures for the report on her desk by 1:00 p.m.

Picking up the phone, she calls Sharon, a manager at another SmartStyle salon. "I really lost my cool in front of everyone, but I'm not apologizing," Jamika admits, adding that she wished she had the guts to fire both stylists. "But this is not the day for that drama. I've got that report hanging over my head. I have no idea how to make things look better than they are, but I have to come up with something. Things look pretty dismal."

Sharon assures her that she did the best she could dealing with two "irresponsible" employees. "What will you do if they show up tomorrow with no doctor's statement?"

"I don't know. I hope I scared them enough so that they'll come in with something."

"I know you're worried about the report and the effect it might have on the Riverwood job," Sharon says. "But everyone knows you can't control the economy and its effect on the business. Just focus on the positive. You'll be fine."

At 10:30, as Jamika struggles to put the best possible spin on the report, she is paged to the receptionist desk to speak to an angry customer. "Another interruption," Jamika fumes to herself. Just then, the door opens and top stylist/assistant manager Victoria Boone sticks her head into the office.

"I know you're busy with the report. I'll handle this," she says enthusiastically.

"Thanks," Jamika replies.

No sooner has she handed off the irate client to Victoria than she second-guesses the decision. In addition to her talents as a hairdresser, Victoria had experience as the manager of a successful salon in another city before moving to the area. Recognizing her organizational and people skills, Jamika promoted Victoria to assistant manager soon after her arrival. Now each "I'll handle this" remark by Victoria convinces Jamika that her assistant manager is positioning herself as a potential rival for the Riverwood job. Jamika appreciates her enthusiastic attitude, but she's also trying to limit her opportunities to lead or appear too competent before staff, customers, and company officials. Jamika finds herself wanting to hide Victoria's competence, and she has condescendingly reminded management that Victoria is a "great help to me."

Now, thinking of Victoria's cheerful "I'll handle this," Jamika rises from her desk and marches to the door. *No*, Jamika thinks, *I'll take care of this personally.*

Questions

1. What positive and negative managerial characteristics does Jamika possess?

2. How do these traits help or hinder her potential to get the top position at the Riverwood Mall salon?

3. How do you think Jamika should have handled each of the incidents with Marianne? Holly and Carol Jean? Victoria?

ENDNOTES

1. Steven Hyden, "The Winners' History of Rock and Roll, Part 3: Bon Jovi," *Grantland* (January 21, 2013), http://www.grantland.com/story/_/id/8860424/the-winners-history-rock-roll-part-3-bon-jovi (accessed August 15, 2013); Colin Stutz, "Dr. Dre Tops Forbes' World's Highest Paid Musicians, Beats Beyoncé by $500M," *Billboard* (December 10, 2014), http:// www.billboard.com/articles/news/6398493/dr-dre-forbes-worlds-highest-paid-musicians-beyonce-eagles (accessed January 11, 2016); and "Bon Jovi to Release New Album," *BestClassicBands.com* (January 10, 2016), http://bestclassicbands.com/bon-jovi-to-release-new-album-1-10-16/ (accessed January 11, 2016).

2. Quoted in Zach O'Malley Greenburg, "Jon Bon Jovi: Still Rockin, and Making a Killing," *Forbes.com* (May 18, 2011), http://www.forbes.com/2011/05/17/celebrity-100-11-jon-bon-jovi-kanye-west-bieber-still-rocking .html (accessed August 13, 2013).

3. This example is based on John Jurgensen, "A Rocker Tunes Up," *Wall Street Journal Online* (February 7, 2013), http://online.wsj.com/article/SB10001424127887 32395190457828821383431386.2html (accessed August 14, 2013); Greenburg, "Jon Bon Jovi: Still Rockin, and Making a Killing"; and Hyden, "The Winners' History of Rock and Roll, Part 3: Bon Jovi." (The quote from Bon Jovi is from the Greenburg article.)

4. John Dowdy and John Van Reenen, "Why Management Matters for Productivity," *McKinsey Quarterly* (September 2014), http://www.mckinsey.com/insights/economic_studies/why_management_matters_for_productivity (accessed January 11, 2016).

5. This discussion is based on ideas in Paul J. H. Schoemaker, Steve Krupp, and Samantha Howland, "Strategic Leadership: The Essential Skills," *Harvard Business Review* (January–February 2013): 131–134; Stephen Denning, "Masterclass: The Reinvention of Management," *Strategy & Leadership* 39, no. 2 (2011): 9–17; Julian Birkinshaw and Jules Goddard, "What Is Your Management Model?" *MIT Sloan Management Review* (Winter 2009): 81–90; Paul McDonald, "It's Time for Management Version 2.0: Six Forces Redefining the Future of Modern Management," *Futures* (October 2011): 797ff; and Jeanne C. Meister and Karie Willyerd, "Leadership 2020: Start Preparing People Now," *Leadership Excellence* (July 2010): 5.

6. Nicolai J. Foss and Peter G. Klein, "Why Managers Still Matter," *MIT Sloan Management Review* 56, no. 1 (Fall 2014): 73–80.

7. See Joshua C. Ramo, *The Age of the Unthinkable: Why the New World Disorder Constantly Surprises Us and What We Can Do About It* (New York: Little Brown, 2009); and Richard Florida, *The Great Reset: How New Ways of Living and Working Drive Post-Crash Prosperity* (New York: HarperCollins, 2010).

8. Schoemaker, Krupp, and Howland, "Strategic Leadership: The Essential Skills."

9. Based on Jonathan Clegg, "Why the Oregon Ducks Don't Believe in Yelling," *The Wall Street Journal* (January 7, 2015), http://www.wsj.com/articles/oregon-college-footballs-kinder-gentler-team-1420663969 (accessed January 12, 2016); Isaac Rosenthal, "For Oregon Football, Even Leadership Is 'By Committee,'" *Eugene Daily News,* http://eugenedailynews.com/2013 /08/for-oregon-football-even-leadership-is-by-committee/ (accessed January 12, 2016); and Jena McGregor, "For the Fashionable Oregon Ducks, a Different Coaching Style," *The Washington Post* (January 12, 2015), https://www .washingtonpost .com/news/on-leadership/wp/2015/01/12/for-the-fashionable-oregon-ducks-a-different-coaching-style/ (accessed January 12, 2016).

10. Ibid.

11. "What Do Managers Do?" *The Wall Street Journal Online,* http://guides.wsj.com/management/developing-a-leadership-style/what-do-managers-do/ (accessed August 11, 2010); article adapted from Alan Murray, *The Wall Street Journal Essential Guide to Management* (New York: Harper Business, 2010).

12. David A. Graham, "A Timeline of Secret Service Scandals," *Government Executive* (March 13, 2015), http://www.govexec.com/management/2015/03/timeline-secret-service-scandals/107475/ (accessed January 12, 2016); Ed O'Keefe, "Lieberman Calls for Wider Inquiry into Secret Service Scandal," *The Washington Post* (April 23, 2012); Laurie Kellman and Alicia A. Caldwell, "Inquiry Hears of Wider Secret Service Misbehavior," *The Salt Lake Tribune* (May 25, 2012); and "Secret Service Toughens Agent Conduct Rules After Prostitution Scandal: Political Notebook," *The Boston Globe* (April 28, 2012).

13. Anton Troianovski, "Apps: The New Corporate Cost-Cutting Tool," *The Wall Street Journal Online* (March 5, 2013), http://online.wsj.com/article/SB100014241278873 24678604578342690461080894.html (accessed August 14, 2013).

14. Mike Hughlett, "Changing Consumer Tastes Forcing Companies Like General Mills to Change—Fast," *Star Tribune* (December 19, 2015), http://www.startribune .com/changing-consumer-tastes-forcing-companies-like-general-mills-to-change-fast/363037901/ (accessed January 12, 2016); and Annie Gasparro and Chelsey Dulaney, "General Mills Profit Jumps 24%; Cheerios Maker Reaps Benefits of Cost-Cutting in Latest Quarter," *The Wall Street Journal* (September 22, 2015), http://www.wsj.com/articles/general-mills-profit-jumps-24-1442921143 (accessed January 12, 2016).

15. Eilene Zimmerman, "Your True Calling Could Suit a Nonprofit" (interview, Career Couch column), *The New York Times,* April 6, 2008, http://www.nytimes .com/2008/04/06/jobs/06career.html?_r=0 (accessed May 11, 2014).

16. Aaron O. Patrick, "EMI Deal Hits a Sour Note," *The Wall Street Journal,* August 15, 2009; and Alex Pham, "EMI Group Sold As Two Separate Pieces to Universal Music and Sony," *Los Angeles Times* (November 12, 2011), http://articles.latimes.com/2011/nov/12/business/la-fi-ct-emi-sold-20111112-68 (accessed January 13, 2016).

17. Robert L. Katz, "Skills of an Effective Administrator," *Harvard Business Review* 52 (September–October 1974): 90–102.

18. Linda A. Hill and Kent Lineback, "Being the Leader: Observe Three Imperatives," *Leadership Excellence* (November 2012): 15–16; Boris Groysberg, L. Kevin Kelly, and Bryan MacDonald, "The New Path to the C-Suite," *Harvard Business Review* (March 2011): 60–68; Jeanne C. Meister and Karie Willyerd, "Leadership 2020: Start Preparing People Now," *Leadership Excellence* (July 2010): 5; Neena Sinha, N. K. Kakkar, and Vikas Gupta, "Uncovering the Secrets of the Twenty-First-Century Organization," *Global Business and Organizational Excellence* (January–February 2012): 49–63; and Rowena Crosbie, "Learning the Soft Skills of Leadership," *Industrial and Commercial Training* 37, no. 1 (2005).

19. Adam Bryant, "The Quest to Build a Better Boss," *The New York Times* (March 13, 2011).

20. Scott Tonidandel, Phillip W. Braddy, and John W. Fleenor, "Relative Importance of Managerial Skills for Predicting Effectiveness," *Journal of Managerial Psychology* 27, no. 6 (2012): 636–655.

21. William A. Gentry, Lauren S. Harris, Becca A. Baker, and Jean Brittain Leslie, "Managerial Skills: What Has Changed Since the Late 1980s?" *Leadership and Organization Development Journal* 29, no. 2 (2008): 167–181.

22. Clinton O. Longenecker, Mitchell J. Neubert, and Laurence S. Fink, "Causes and Consequences of Managerial Failure in Rapidly Changing Organizations," *Business Horizons* 50 (2007): 145–155.

23. Nicola Clark and Melissa Eddy, "In the Vortex of the Storm," *The New York Times* (September 23, 2015); Andreas Cremer and Tom Bergin, "Fear and Respect: VW's Culture Under Winterkorn," *Reuters* (October 10, 2015), http://www.reuters.com/article/us-volkswagen-emissions-culture-idUSKCN0S40MT20151010 (accessed January 13, 2016); and Danny Hakim, Aaron M. Kessler, and Jack Ewing, "As VW Pushed to Be No. 1, Ambitions Fueled a Scandal" (September 27, 2015), p. A1.

24. Sydney Finkelstein, "The Five Worst CEOs of 2012," *The Washington Post*, December 18, 2012, http://articles.washingtonpost.com/2012-12-18/national/35907884 _1_ bankia-spanish-banks-rodrigo-rato (accessed December 20, 2012); Thomas Lee, "Mark Pincus Is Back as CEO, Because No One Could Stop Him," *SFGate* (April 14, 2015), http://www.sfgate.com/business/article/Mark-Pincus-is-back-as-CEO-because-no-one-could-6197313.php (accessed November 30, 2015); and Matthew Lynley, "Mark Pincus Is Back—And His Vintage Management Style Might Be, Too," *TechCrunch* (May 16, 2015), http://techcrunch.com/2015/05/06/mark-pincus-is-back-and-his-vintage-management-style-might-be-too/ (accessed November 30, 2015).

25. Longenecker, Neubert, and Fink, "Causes and Consequences of Managerial Failure in Rapidly Changing Organizations."

26. Fisman, "In Defense of Middle Management."

27. Henry Mintzberg, *Managing* (San Francisco: Berrett-Kohler Publishers, 2009); Mintzberg, *The Nature of Managerial Work* (New York: Harper & Row, 1973); and Mintzberg, "Rounding Out the Manager's Job," *Sloan Management Review* (Fall 1994): 11–26.

28. Robert E. Kaplan, "Trade Routes: The Manager's Network of Relationships," *Organizational Dynamics* (Spring 1984): 37–52; Rosemary Stewart, "The Nature of Management: A Problem for Management Education," *Journal of Management Studies* 21 (1984): 323–330; John P. Kotter, "What Effective General Managers Really Do," *Harvard Business Review* (November–December 1982): 156–167; and Morgan W. McCall, Jr., Ann M. Morrison, and Robert L. Hannan, "Studies of Managerial Work: Results and Methods," Technical Report No. 9, Center for Creative Leadership, Greensboro, NC, 1978.

29. Alison M. Konrad, Roger Kashlak, Izumi Yoshioka, Robert Waryszak, and Nina Toren, "What Do Managers *Like* to Do? A Five-Country Study," *Group and Organizational Management* 26, no. 4 (December 2001): 401–433.

30. For a review of the problems faced by first-time managers, see Linda A. Hill and Kent Lineback, "Being the Leader: Observe Three Imperatives," *Leadership Excellence* (November 2012): 15–16; Linda A. Hill, "Becoming the Boss," *Harvard Business Review* (January 2007): 49–56; Loren B. Belker and Gary S. Topchik, *The First-Time Manager: A Practical Guide to the Management of People*, 5th ed. (New York: AMACOM, 2005); J. W. Lorsch and P. F. Mathias, "When Professionals Have to Manage," *Harvard Business Review* (July–August 1987): 78–83; R. A. Webber, Becoming a Courageous Manager: Overcoming Career Problems of New Managers (Englewood Cliffs, NJ: Prentice Hall, 1991); D. E. Dougherty, *From Technical Professional to Corporate Manager: A Guide to Career Transition* (New York: Wiley, 1984); J. Falvey, "The Making of a Manager," *Sales and Marketing Management* (March 1989): 42–83; M. K. Badawy, *Developing Managerial Skills in Engineers and Scientists: Succeeding as a Technical Manager* (New York: Van Nostrand Reinhold, 1982); and M. London, *Developing Managers: A Guide to Motivating and Preparing People for Successful Managerial Careers* (San Francisco, CA: Jossey-Bass, 1985).

31. Based on Evelyn Rusli, Nicole Perlroth, and Nick Bilton, "The Hoodie amid the Pinstripes: As Facebook IPO Nears, Is Its Chief up to Running a Public Company?" *International Herald Tribune*, May 14, 2012, 17.

32. This discussion is based on Linda A. Hill, *Becoming a Manager: How New Managers Master the Challenges of Leadership*, 2d ed. (Boston: Harvard Business School Press, 2003), 6–8; and Hill, "Becoming the Boss."

33. See also the "Boss's First Steps" sidebar in Erin White, "Learning to Be the Boss," *The Wall Street Journal*, November 21, 2005, http://online.wsj.com/news /articles/SB113252950779302595 (accessed May 11, 2014); and Belker and Topchik, *The First-Time Manager*.

34. Quoted in Eileen Zimmerman, "Are You Cut Out for Management?" (Career Couch column), *The New York Times*, January 15 2011, www.nytimes.com/2011/01 /16/jobs/16career.html (accessed June 14, 2012).

35. Hill and Lineback, "Being the Leader."

36. Mintzberg, *Managing*, pp. 17–41.

37. Study reported in Rachel Emma Silverman, "Where's The Boss? Trapped in a Meeting," *The Wall Street Journal*, February 14, 2012, http://online.wsj.com /article/SB100014 24052970204642604577215013504567548.html (accessed June 14, 2012).

38. Mintzberg, *Managing*, pp. 17–41.

39. Based on Allan Halcrow, "A Day in the Life of Kathy Davis: Just Another Day in HR," *Workforce Management* 77, no. 6 (June 1998): 56–62.

40. Mintzberg, *Managing*, pp. 17–41.

41. Carol Hymowitz, "Packed Calendars Rule," *The Asian Wall Street Journal*, June 16, 2009; and "The 18-Hour Day," *The Conference Board Review* (March–April 2008): 20.

42. Adam Shell, "CEO Profile: Casting a Giant (New Jersey) Net," *USA TODAY*, August 25, 2008; Matthew Boyle and Jia Lynn Yang, "All in a Day's Work," *Fortune* (March 20, 2006): 97–104.

43. Korn, "What It's Like Being a Middle Manager Today."

44. Frankki Bevins and Aaron De Smet, "Making Time Management the Organization's Priority," *McKinsey Quarterly* (January 2013), http://www.mckinsey.com /insights/organization/making_time_management_the_organizations_priority (accessed August 19, 2013).

45. "Four CEOs' Tips on Managing Your Time," *The Wall Street Journal*, February 14, 2012, http://online.wsj.com/article/SB100014240529702048833045772215571714492724.html (accessed June 14, 2012).

46. Bevins and De Smet, "Making Time Management the Organization's Priority"; A. Garrett, "Buying Time to Do the Things That Really Matter," *Management Today* (July 2000): 75; and Robert S. Kaplan, "What to Ask the Person in the Mirror," *Harvard Business Review* (January 2007): 86–95.

47. Mintzberg, *Managing*; Lance B. Kurke and Howard E. Aldrich, "Mintzberg Was Right! A Replication and Extension of *The Nature of Managerial Work*," *Management Science* 29 (1983): 975–984; Cynthia M. Pavett and Alan W. Lau, "Managerial Work: The Influence of Hierarchical Level and Functional Specialty," *Academy of Management Journal* 26 (1983): 170–177; and Colin P. Hales, "What Do Managers Do? A Critical Review of the Evidence," *Journal of Management Studies* 23 (1986): 88–115.

48. Erica E. Phillips, "Technology Helps Food Banks Handle Holiday Surge," *The Wall Street Journal* (December 2, 2015), http://www.wsj.com/articles/technology-helps-food-banks-handle-holiday-surge-1449101555 (accessed January 14, 2016).

49. Claire Martin, "How a Bicycle Maker Saw the Light, and Found Its Balance," *The New York Times* (April 12, 2014), http://www.nytimes.com/2014/04/13/business/how-a-bicycle-maker-saw-the-light-and-found-its-balance.html?ref=business (accessed January 12, 2016).

50. Jean Crawford, "Profiling the Non-Profit Leader of Tomorrow," *Ivey Business Journal* (May–June 2010), www.iveybusinessjournal.com/topics/leadership/-profiling-the-non-profit-leader-of-tomorrow (accessed June 14, 2012).

51. The following discussion is based on Peter F. Drucker, *Managing the Non-Profit Organization: Principles and Practices* (New York: HarperBusiness, 1992); and Thomas Wolf, *Managing a Nonprofit Organization* (New York: Fireside/Simon & Schuster, 1990).

52. Christine W. Letts, William P. Ryan, and Allen Grossman, *High Performance Nonprofit Organizations* (New York: Wiley & Sons, 1999), pp. 30–35.

53. Jerry Useem, "Are Bosses Necessary?" *The Atlantic* (October 2015): 28–32.

54. Lisa Thorell, "How Many Bossless Companies Exist Today?" *Innovatini* (April 1, 2013), http://www.innovatini.com/how-many-bossless-companies-are-there/ (accessed August 20, 2013).

55. See John Hollon, "The Bossless Office Trend: Don't Be Surprised If It Doesn't Last Long," HR Management, *TLNT.com* (July 2, 2012), http://www.tlnt.com/2012/07/02/the-bossless-office-trend-dont-be-surprised-if-it-doesnt-last-long/ (accessed August 20, 2013).

56. Matthew E. May, "Mastering the Art of Bosslessness," *Fast Company* (September 26, 2012), http://www.fastcompany.com/3001574/mastering-art-bosslessness (accessed August 20, 2013).

57. M. S. S. el Namaki, "Does the Thinking of Yesterday's Management Gurus Imperil Today's Companies?" *Ivey Business Journal* (March–April 2012), www.iveybusinessjournal.com/topics/strategy/does-the-thinking-of-yesterdays-management-gurus-imperil-todays-companies (accessed June 19, 2012).

58. Walter Kiechel III, "The Management Century," *Harvard Business Review* (November 2012): 62–75; Eric Abrahamson, "Management Fashion," *Academy of Management Review* 21, no. 1 (January 1996): 254–285.

59. Daniel A. Wren, *The Evolution of Management Thought*, 4th ed. (New York: Wiley, 1994); and Morgen Witzel and Malcolm Warner, "Introduction," in M. Witzel and M. Warner, eds., *Oxford Handbook of Management Theorists* (Oxford and New York: Oxford University Press, 2013), pp. 1–10.

60. Robert Tell and Brian Kleiner, "Organizational Change Can Rescue Industry," *Industrial Management* (March–April

2009): 20–24; Witzel and Warner, *Oxford Handbook of Management Theorists*; and Morgen Witzel and Malcolm Warner, "Taylorism Revisited: Culture, Management Theory and Paradigm-Shift," *Journal of General Management* 40, no. 3 (Spring 2015): 55–70.

61. This discussion is based on Kieche, "The Management Century," *Harvard Business Review* (November 2012): 62–75.

62. These quotes are from Kiechel, "The Management Century."

63. Daniel A. Wren, "Management History: Issues and Ideas for Teaching and Research," *Journal of Management* 13 (1987): 339–350.

64. Business historian Alfred D. Chandler, Jr., quoted in Jerry Useem, "Entrepreneur of the Century," *Inc.* (20th Anniversary Issue, 1999): 159–174.

65. Useem, "Entrepreneur of the Century."

66. The following is based on Wren, *Evolution of Management Thought*, Chapters 4 and 5; and Claude S. George, Jr., *The History of Management Thought* (Englewood Cliffs, NJ: Prentice-Hall, 1968), Chapter 4.

67. Cynthia Crossen, "Early Industry Expert Soon Realized a Staff Has Its Own Efficiency," *The Wall Street Journal*, November 6, 2006.

68. Alan Farnham, "The Man Who Changed Work Forever," *Fortune* (July 21, 1997): 114; Charles D. Wrege and Ann Marie Stoka, "Cooke Creates a Classic: The Story Behind F. W. Taylor's Principles of Scientific Management," *Academy of Management Review* (October 1978): 736–749; Robert Kanigel, *The One Best Way: Frederick Winslow Taylor and the Enigma of Efficiency* (New York: Viking, 1997); and "The X and Y Factors: What Goes Around Comes Around," special section in "The New Organisation: A Survey of the Company," *The Economist* (January 21–27, 2006): 17–18.

69. Wren, *Evolution of Management Thought*, 171; and George, *The History of Management Thought*, 103–104.

70. Vanessa O'Connell, "Stores Count Seconds to Trim Labor Costs," *The Wall Street Journal*, November 17, 2008; and Vanessa O'Connell, "Retailers Reprogram Workers in Efficiency Push," *The Wall Street Journal*, September 10, 2008.

71. Gary Hamel, "The Why, What, and How of Management Innovation," *Harvard Business Review* (February 2006): 72-84; Peter Coy, "Cog or CoWorker?" *BusinessWeek* (August 20 and 27, 2007): 58–60.

72. Max Weber, *General Economic History*, trans. Frank H. Knight (London: Allen & Unwin, 1927); Max Weber, *The Protestant Ethic and the Spirit of Capitalism*, trans. Talcott Parsons (New York: Scribner, 1930); and Max Weber, *The Theory of Social and Economic Organizations*, ed. and trans. A. M. Henderson and Talcott-Parsons (New York: Free Press, 1947).

73. Laura Stevens, "UPS Drivers Who Avoid Accidents for 25 Years Get Arm Patch and Bomber Jacket," *The Wall Street Journal* (June 4, 2014), http://www.wsj.com/articles/ups-drivers-who-avoid-accidents-for-25-years-get-arm-patch-and-bomber-jacket-1401933961 (accessed November 27, 2015); Nadira A. Hira, "The Making of a UPS Driver," *Fortune* (November 12, 2007): 118–129; Kelly Barron, "Logistics in Brown," *Forbes* (January 10, 2000): 78-83; Scott Kirsner, "Venture Vérité: United Parcel Service," *Wired* (September 1999): 83-96; and Esther Kaplan, "The Spy Who Fired Me," *Harper's Magazine* (March 2015): 31–40.

74. Stephen Cummings and Todd Bridgman, "The Relevant Past: Why the History of Management Should Be Critical to Our Future," *Academy of Management Learning & Education* 10, no. 1 (2011): 77–93.

75. These are based on Paul Downs, "How I Fire People," You're the Boss blog, *The New York Times*, June 4, 2012, http://boss.blogs.nytimes.com/2012/06/04 /how-i-fire-people/ (accessed June 20, 2012).

76. Henri Fayol, *Industrial and General Administration*, trans. J. A. Coubrough (Geneva: International Management Institute, 1930); Henri Fayol, *General and Industrial Management, trans. Constance Storrs* (London: Pitman and Sons, 1949); and W. J. Arnold et al., *Business Week, Milestones in Management* (New York: McGraw-Hill, vol. I, 1965; vol. II, 1966).

77. Mansel G. Blackford and K. Austin Kerr, *Business Enterprise in American History* (Boston: Houghton Mifflin, 1986), Chapters 10 and 11; Alex Groner and the editors of *American Heritage* and *BusinessWeek, The American Heritage History of American Business and Industry* (New York: American Heritage Publishing, 1972), Chapter 9; and Justin Fox, "From 'Economic Man' to Behavioral Economics," *Harvard Business Review* (May 2015): 79–85.

78. Geoffrey Colvin, "How Alfred P. Sloan, Michael Porter, and Peter Drucker Taught Us All the Art of Management," *Fortune* (March 21, 2005): 83–86.

79. Brooks Barnes, "Disney Technology Tackles a Theme-Park Headache: Lines," *The New York Times*, December 28, 2010; and "Disney Cracks Down on FastPass Enforcement," *Tampa Bay Times*, March 9, 2012.

80. Larry M. Austin and James R. Burns, *Management Science* (New York: Macmillan, 1985).

81. Dan Heath and Chip Heath, "In Defense of Feelings: Why Your Gut Is More Ethical Than Your Brain," *Fast Company* (July–August 2009): 58–59.

82. Scott Patterson, *The Quants: How a New Breed of Math Whizzes Conquered Wall Street and Nearly Destroyed It* (New York: Crown Business, 2010); and Harry Hurt III, "In Practice, Stock Formulas Weren't Perfect," *The New York Times*, February 21, 2010.

83. Gregory M. Bounds, Gregory H. Dobbins, and Oscar S. Fowler, *Management: A Total Quality Perspective* (Cincinnati, OH: South-Western Publishing, 1995), pp. 52–53.

84. Mary Parker Follett, *The New State: Group Organization: The Solution of Popular Government* (London: Longmans, Green, 1918); and Mary Parker Follett, *Creative Experience* (London: Longmans, Green, 1924).

85. Henry C. Metcalf and Lyndall Urwick, eds., *Dynamic Administration: The Collected Papers of Mary Parker Follett* (New York: Harper & Row, 1940); Arnold, et al., *Business-Week, Milestones in Management*.

86. Follett, *The New State*; Henry C. Metcalf and Lyndall Urwick, *Dynamic Administration* (London: Sir Isaac Pitman, 1941).

87. William B. Wolf, *How to Understand Management: An Introduction to Chester I. Barnard* (Los Angeles: Lucas Brothers, 1968); and David D. Van Fleet, "The Need-Hierarchy and Theories of Authority," *Human Relations* 9 (Spring 1982): 111–118.

88. Curt Tausky, *Work Organizations: Major Theoretical Perspectives* (Itasca, IL: F. E. Peacock, 1978), p. 42.

89. Charles D. Wrege, "Solving Mayo's Mystery: The First Complete Account of the Origin of the Hawthorne Studies—The Forgotten Contributions of Charles E. Snow and Homer Hibarger," paper presented to the Management History Division of the Academy of Management (August 1976).

90. F. J. Roethlisberger and W. J. Dickson, *Management and the Worker* (Cambridge, MA: Harvard University Press, 1939).

91. H. M. Parson, "What Happened at Hawthorne?" *Science* 183 (1974): 922–932; John G. Adair, "The Hawthorne Effect: A Reconsideration of the Methodological Artifact," *Journal of Applied Psychology* 69, no. 2 (1984): 334–345; and Gordon Diaper, "The Hawthorne Effect: A Fresh Examination," *Educational Studies* 16, no. 3 (1990): 261–268.

92. Greenwood Bolton, and Greenwood "Hawthorne a Half Century Later," 219–221.

93. Tausky, *Work Organizations: Major Theoretical Perspectives*, p. 55.

94. Douglas McGregor, *The Human Side of Enterprise* (New York: McGraw-Hill, 1960), pp. 16-18; Robert A. Cunningham, "Douglas McGregor: A Lasting Impression," *Ivey Business Journal* (October 2011): 5–7.

95. Frederic Laloux, "The Future of Management Is Teal," *Strategy + Business* (July 6, 2015), http://www.strategy -business.com/article/00344?gko=10921 (accessed January 18, 2016).

96. Wendell L. French and Cecil H. Jr. Bell, "A History of Organizational Development," in Wendell L. French, Cecil H. Jr. Bell, and Robert A. Zawacki, *Organization Development and Transformation: Managing Effective Change* (Burr Ridge, IL: Irwin McGraw-Hill, 2000), pp. 20–42.

97. Discussed in Kiechel, "The Management Century."

98. Ludwig von Bertalanffy et al., "General Systems Theory: A New Approach to Unity of Science," *Human Biology* 23 (December 1951): 302-361; and Kenneth E. Boulding, "General Systems Theory—The Skeleton of Science," *Management Science* 2 (April 1956): 197–208.

99. This example is cited in Sterman, "Systems Dynamics Modeling."

100. This section is based on Peter M. Senge, *The Fifth Discipline: The Art and Practice of the Learning Organization* (New York: Doubleday, 1990); John D. Sterman, "Systems Dynamics Modeling: Tools for Learning in a Complex World," *California Management Review* 43, no. 4 (Summer 2001): 8–25; Andrea Gabor, "Seeing Your Company as a System," *Strategy + Business* (Summer 2010), www.strategy-business.com/article/10210?gko=20cca (accessed June 20, 2012); and Ron Zemke, "Systems Thinking," *Training* (February 2001): 40–46.

101. Christopher Matthews, "3 Reasons Wendy's Is Eating McDonald's Lunch," *Time* (January 23, 2014), http:// business.time.com/2014/01/23/mcdonalds-and-wendys -battle-in-fast-food-wars/ (accessed January 20, 2016); and Julie Jargon, "McDonald's Seeks Relevance Amid Tepid Results, Fast-Food Chain Says Its Restaurants Are Too Complicated," *The Wall Street Journal* (January 24, 2014), http://online.wsj.com/news/articles/SB20001424052702303 94790457933833760745934 (accessed January 24, 2014).

102. Fred Luthans, "The Contingency Theory of Management: A Path Out of the Jungle," *Business Horizons* 16 (June 1973): 62-72; and Fremont E. Kast and James E. Rosenzweig, *Contingency Views of Organization and Management* (Chicago: Science Research Associates, 1973).

103. Thomas H. Davenport and Laurence Prusak, with Jim Wilson, *What's the Big Idea? Creating and Capitalizing on the Best Management Thinking* (Boston, MA: Harvard Business School Press, 2003); Theodore Kinni, "Have We Run out of Big Ideas?" *Across the Board* (March–April 2003): 16–21; Hamel, "The Why, What, and How of Management Innovation"; and Joyce Thompson Heames and Michael Harvey, "The Evolution of the Concept of the Executive from the 20th–Century Manager to the 21st–Century Global Leader," *Journal of Leadership and Organizational Studies* 13, no. 2 (2006): 29–41.

104. Darrell Rigby and Barbara Bilodeau, *Management Tools and Trends 2015* (Bain & Company, June 5, 2015), http://www.bain.com/publications/articles/management-tools-and-trends-2015.aspx (accessed January 20, 2016).

105. Ibid.

106. Darrell K. Rigby, *Management Tools 2013: An Executive's Guide* (Bain & Company 2013), http://www.bain.com/Images/MANAGEMENT_TOOLS_2013_An_Executives_guide.pdf (accessed August 27, 2013); Margaret Rouse, "Big Data Analytics," *TechTarget.com* (January 10, 2012), http://searchbusinessanalytics.techtarget.com/definition /big-data-analytics (accessed August 27, 2013); and David Kiron, Renee Boucher Ferguson, and Pamela Kirk Prentice, "From Value to Vision: Reimagining the Possible with Data Analytics," *MIT Sloan Management Review Special Report* (March 5, 2013), http://sloanreview.mit.edu/reports/analytics-innovation/ (accessed August 27, 2013).

107. Steve Lohr, "Sure, Big Data Is Great. But So Is Intuition," *The New York Times*, December 29, 2012.

108. Andrew McAfee and Erik Brynjolfsson, "Big Data: The Management Revolution," *Harvard Business Review* (October 2012): 61–68.

109. Spandas Lui, "eHarmony Translates Big Data into Love and Cash," ZDNet.com (November 6, 2012), http://www.zdnet.com/eharmony-translates-big-data-into-love-and-cash-7000006884/ (accessed August 27, 2013); and Jeff Russell, "LinkedIn's eHarmony-Style Recruiting: Big Data Meets HR," *HR.com* (April 16, 2013), http://www.hr.com/en/app/blog/2013/04/linkedin%E2%80%99s-eharmony-style-recruiting-big-data-meet_hfl6zpzd.html (accessed August 27, 2013).

110. Lohr, "Sure, Big Data Is Great."

111. Ruben Sigala, interviewed by Renee Boucher Ferguson, "A Process of Continuous Innovation: Centralizing Analytics at Caesars," *MIT Sloan Management Review* (Fall 2013): 1–6.

112. Alden M. Hayashi, "Thriving in a Big Data World," *MIT Sloan Management Review* (Winter 2014): 35–39.

113. This definition is based on Steven A. Melnyk and David R. Denzler, *Operations Management: A Value-Driven Approach* (Burr Ridge, IL: Richard D. Irwin, 1996): p. 613.

114. The Global Supply Chain Games project, www.gscg.org (accessed July 16, 2008).

115. Eric Bellman and Cecilie Rohwedder, "Western Grocer Modernizes Passage to India's Markets," *The Wall Street Journal*, November 28, 2007.

116. Steven Greenhouse and Stephanie Clifford, "U.S. Retailers Offer Safety Plan for Bangladeshi Factories" *The New York Times* (July 10, 2013), http://www.nytimes.com/2013/07/11/business/global/us-retailers-offer-safety-plan-for-bangladeshi-factories.html?pagewanted=all&_r=0 (accessed August 21, 2013); and Kate O'Keeffe and Sun Narin, "H&M Clothes Made in Collapsed Cambodian Factory," *The Wall Street Journal* (May 21, 2013), http://online.wsj.com/article/SB10001424127887324787004578497091806922254.html (accessed August 21, 2013).

117. Susan Cramm, "Paychecks with a Purpose," *Strategy + Business* (November 18, 2015), http://www.strategy-business.com/blog/Paychecks-with-a-Purpose?gko=24b5c (accessed January 21, 2016).

118. Roxane Divol and Thomas Fleming, "The Evolution of Work: One Company's Story," *McKinsey Quarterly*, Issue 4 (2012): 111–115.

119. Tom Ashbrook, "The Bossless Office," *On Point with Tom Ashbrook* (June 20, 2013), http://onpoint.wbur.org.

120. Hamel, "First, Let's Fire All the Managers."

121. Doug Kirkpatrick, "Self-Management's Success at Morning Star," *T+D* (October 2012): 25–27; and Gary Hamel, "First, Let's Fire All the Managers," *Harvard Business Review* (December 2011): 48–60.

122. This definition is based on Mercer Human Resource Consulting's Employee Engagement Model, as described in Paul Sanchez and Dan McCauley, "Measuring and Managing Engagement in a Cross-Cultural Workforce: New Insights for Global Companies," *Global Business and Organizational Excellence* (November–December 2006): 41–50.

123. Rigby and Bilodeau, "Management Tools and Trends 2015."

124. Max Mihelich, "Another Generation Rises: Looking Beyond the Millennials," *Workforce* (April 12, 2013), http://www.workforce.com/articles/108-another-generation-rises-looking-beyond-the-millennials (accessed August 22, 2013).

125. Jacques Bughin, Michael Chui, and James Manyika, "Capturing Business Value with Social Technologies," *McKinsey Quarterly* (November 2012), http://www.mckinsey.com/insights/high_tech_telecoms_internet/capturing_business_value_with_social_technologies (accessed September 27, 2013).

126. Vince Golla, interviewed by David Kiron, "Social Business at Kaiser Permanente: Using Social Tools to Improve Customer Service, Research and Internal Collaboration," *MIT Sloan Management Review* (March 6, 2012), http://sloanreview.mit.edu/article/social-tools-improve-service-research-collaboration/ (accessed April 30, 2013).

127. Roland Deiser and Sylvain Newton, "Six Social-Media Skills Every Leader Needs," *McKinsey Quarterly*, Issue 1 (February 2013), http://www.mckinsey.com/insights/high_tech_telecoms_internet/six_social-media_skills_every_leader_needs (accessed August 21, 2013).

128. David Kiron, Douglas Palmer, and Robert Berkman, "The Executive's Role in Social Business," *MIT Sloan Management Review* (Summer 2013): 83–89.

129. Ibid.; and Leslie Gaines-Ross, "Get Social: A Mandate for New CEOs," *MIT Sloan Management Review* (March 7, 2013), http://sloanreview.mit.edu/article/get-social-a-mandate-for-new-ceos/ (accessed August 21, 2013).

130. Gaines-Ross, "Get Social: A Mandate for New CEOs."

131. Based on Betty Harrigan, "Career Advice," *Working Woman* (July 1986): 22–24.

Chapter 2
The Environment and Corporate Culture

Chapter Outline

Learning Outcomes

After studying this chapter, you should be able to:

2.1 Define an organizational ecosystem and how the general and task environments affect an organization's ability to thrive.

2.2 Explain the strategies managers use to help organizations adapt to an uncertain or turbulent environment.

2.3 Define *corporate culture*.

2.4 Provide organizational examples of symbols, stories, heroes, slogans, and ceremonies and explain how they relate to corporate culture.

2.5 Describe four types of corporate culture.

2.6 Examine the relationship among culture, corporate values, and business performance.

2.7 Define a cultural leader and explain the tools that a cultural leader uses to create a high-performance culture.

Discover Your Management Approach

Are You Fit for Managerial Uncertainty?[a]

Instructions: Do you approach uncertainty with an open mind? Think back to how you thought or behaved during a time of uncertainty when you were in a formal or informal leadership position. Please answer whether each of the following items was Mostly True or Mostly False in that circumstance.

	Mostly True	Mostly False
1. Enjoyed hearing about new ideas even when trying to meet a deadline.	_____	_____
2. Welcomed unusual viewpoints of others, even if we were working under pressure.	_____	_____
3. Made it a point to attend industry trade shows and company events.	_____	_____

To complete and score the entire assessment, visit MindTap.

[a] These questions are based on ideas from R. L. Daft and R. M. Lengel, *Fusion Leadership* (San Francisco: Berrett Koehler, 2000), Chapter 4; B. Bass and B. Avolio, *Multifactor Leadership Questionnaire*, 2d ed. (Menlo Park, CA: Mind Garden, 2004); and Karl E. Weick and Kathleen M. Sutcliffe, *Managing the Unexpected: Assuring High Performance in an Age of Complexity* (San Francisco: Jossey-Bass, 2001).

At a McDonald's restaurant outside of Rochester, New York, about 30 demonstrators recently shouted "Hold the burgers, hold the fries, we want our wages supersized!" It was one of thousands of protests around the United States at McDonald's, Burger King, Wendy's, and other fast-food restaurants organized by advocacy group "Fight for $15" to argue for an increase in the minimum wage. Numerous other low-paid service workers joined the fast-food demonstrations, fighting to gain greater attention for the cause of raising the $7.25 minimum wage. "It's not just the financial piece, it's also about the dignity," said Kheila Cox, who works as a baggage handler at Logan Airport in Boston.[1]

The November 2015 fast-food workers' action took place just as the issue of minimum wage was taking center stage in the run-up to the 2016 U.S. presidential election. An increase in the federal minimum wage would affect managers and organizations not only in fast-food but also in numerous other industries. Managers face many challenges from both the external and internal environments every day. This chapter explores in detail components of the external environment and how they affect the organization. The chapter also examines a major part of the organization's internal environment—corporate culture. Corporate culture is both shaped by the external environment and shapes how managers respond to changes in the external environment.

2-1 The External Environment

The external **organizational environment** includes all elements existing outside the boundary of the organization that have the potential to affect it.[2] The environment includes competitors, resources, technology, and economic conditions that influence the organization. It does not include those events so far removed from the organization that their impact is not perceived.

The organization's external environment can be conceptualized further as having two components: task and general environments, as illustrated in Exhibit 2.1.[3] The **task environment** is closer to the organization and includes the sectors that conduct day-to-day transactions with the organization and directly influence its basic operations and performance. It is generally considered to include competitors, suppliers, customers, and the labor market. The **general environment** affects organizations indirectly. It includes social, economic, legal–political, international, natural, and technological factors that influence all organizations about equally. Changes in federal regulations or an economic recession are part of the organization's general environment, as are shifting social attitudes toward matters such as how and where the products we use are made. These events do not directly change day-to-day operations, but they do affect all organizations eventually.

A new view of the environment argues that organizations are now evolving into business ecosystems. An **organizational ecosystem** is a system formed by the interaction among a community of organizations in the environment. An ecosystem includes organizations in all the sectors of the task and general environments that provide the resource and information transactions, flows, and linkages necessary for an organization to thrive.[4] For example, Apple's ecosystem includes hundreds of suppliers and millions of customers for the products that it produces across several industries, including consumer electronics, Internet services, mobile phones, personal computers, and entertainment.[5]

The organization also has an **internal environment**, which includes the elements within the organization's boundaries. The internal environment is composed of current employees, management, and especially corporate culture, which defines employee behavior in the internal environment and how well the organization will adapt to the external environment.

Exhibit 2.1 illustrates the relationship among the task, general, and internal environments. As an open system, the organization draws resources from the external environment and releases goods and services back to it. We will first discuss the two components of the external environment in more detail. Later in the chapter, we examine corporate culture, the key element in the internal environment. Other aspects of the internal environment, such as structure and technology, are covered in later chapters of this book.

> "It is not the strongest of the species that survives, nor the most intelligent that survives. It is the one that is the most adaptable to change."
> —CHARLES DARWIN
>   (1809–1882), NATURALIST

2-1a Task Environment

The task environment includes those sectors that have a direct working relationship with the organization, among them customers, competitors, suppliers, and the labor market.

Customers   Those people and organizations in the environment that acquire goods or services from the organization are **customers**. As recipients of the organization's output, customers are important because they determine the organization's success. Organizations have to be responsive

Exhibit 2.1 Dimensions of the Organization's General, Task, and Internal Environments

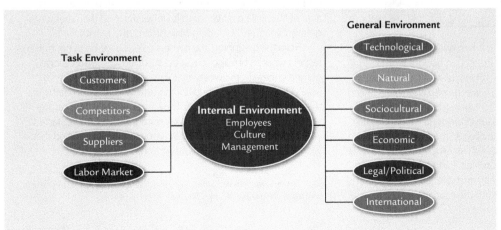

to marketplace changes. For example, as Millennials (people born in the 1980s and 1990s) make up a growing part of the customer base at retail chain Target, new CEO Brian Cornell is implementing changes to better serve that demographic. A big part of the transformation concerns making over Target's grocery offerings to add more natural and organic foods to the mix and provide fewer processed foods.[6]

Competitors   Organizations in the same industry or type of business that provide goods or services to the same set of customers are referred to as **competitors**. Competitors are constantly battling for loyalty from the same group of customers. For example, Samsung and Apple have been fighting for years for the top spot in the smartphone market. Samsung became the world leader in smartphone sales in 2013, Apple briefly emerged as the leader in the final quarter of 2014 based on strong sales of the iPhone 6, and then Samsung quickly regained the lead in the following quarter. Apple's iPhone still has strong brand loyalty, but overall Samsung has retained a strong number one position.[7] Being the first company to offer a product is a huge advantage because the company enters essentially without any competition. That was the strategy and a primary asset to Grilled Cheeserie, when it introduced the first movable food truck in Nashville, as described in the Recipe for Success box.

Suppliers   **Suppliers** provide the raw materials that the organization uses to produce its output. A candy manufacturer, for example, may use suppliers from around the globe for ingredients such as cocoa beans, sugar, and cream. A **supply chain** is a network of multiple businesses and individuals that are connected through the flow of products or services. For Toyota, the supply chain includes over 500 global parts suppliers organized by a production strategy called *just-in-time*

Recipe for Success } **Grilled Cheeserie**

B Christopher/Alamy Stock Photo

Food trucks are so cool. Now. But when twenty-somethings Joseph Bogan and Crystal De Luna-Bogan bought a truck and started sending it out in 2010, replete with the childhood favorite of gooey grilled cheese, it was new to Nashville. Having recently moved from Los Angeles, where food trucks were common, they saw this as a golden opportunity, to be the first "site-to-site" mobile truck in Nashville. On the menu were seven specialty comfort foods, from Spinach & Artichoke Melt, to B&B of Tennessee to the French Onion Melt. Part of their work was educating the public on the health and safety of truck food and how much the owners cared about the sourcing.

Eventually, the couple had a hit. But not an easy one. Health permits, hiring brilliant chefs, training staff, paying a living wage, and providing health insurance—these are not all on the lists of budding entrepreneurs who are just trying to get their business off the ground. But the partners knew they had to have an excellent, desirable product made by a good staff that is treated well and respected.

Being on the Food Network's hit show "Diners, Drive-ins and Dives" in 2013 helped with the legitimacy of their concept. Now there are food trucks everywhere in Nashville from various companies. But Bogan and Luna-Bogan were the innovators in a changing marketplace. They did so well that they added a second truck, and in 2017 opened a sit-down restaurant in a busy area of Nashville near Vanderbilt University. And their menu has greatly expanded, including Milkshake of the Month.

From the beginning, the owners' values have been not only to respect workers but also to respect the food. They source locally, getting cheese from Sweetwater Valley Farm and breads from Silke's Old World breads, and finding other ingredients nearby, so they can support local farmers. They also worked with local artisans to help design and build their restaurant space. "We started with simple comfort food that everyone could relate to and then we would blow their minds, said Joseph. "I guess we did."

SOURCES: Joseph Bogan, personal communication, February 2018; Lizzy Alfs, "Grilled Cheeserie Set to Open Friday," *The Tennessean*, January 4, 2017, D2.

(JIT).[8] JIT improves an organization's return on investment, quality, and efficiency because much less money is invested in idle inventory. In the 1970s, the Japanese taught U.S. companies how to boost profit by keeping inventories lean through JIT. "Instead of months' worth of inventory, there are now days and even hours of inventory," says Jim Lawton, head of supply management solutions at consultant Dun & Bradstreet. Lawton points out that there is a downside, however—one that became dramatically clear after a March 2011 earthquake in Japan: "If supply is disrupted, as in this situation, there's nowhere to get product."[9]

The quake, which triggered massive tsunami waves and caused the second-worst nuclear disaster in history at the Fukushima power plant along the Pacific coastline, revealed the fragility of today's JIT supply chains. Japanese parts suppliers for the global auto industry were shut down, disrupting production at auto factories around the world. "Even a missing $5 part can stop an assembly line," said a Morgan Stanley representative. Because of this natural disaster, Toyota's production fell by 800,000 vehicles—10 percent of its annual output. Despite the potential for such disruptions, most companies aren't willing to boost inventories to provide a cushion. Even a slight increase in inventory can cost companies millions of dollars.[10]

Labor Market   The **labor market** represents people in the environment who can be hired to work for the organization. Every organization needs a supply of trained, qualified personnel. Unions, employee associations, and the availability of certain classes of employees can influence the organization's labor market. Labor market forces affecting organizations right now include (1) the growing need for computer-literate knowledge workers; (2) the necessity for continuous investment in human resources through recruitment, education, and training to meet the competitive demands of the borderless world; and (3) the effects of international trading blocs, automation, outsourcing, and shifting facility locations on labor dislocations, all of which create unused labor pools in some areas and labor shortages in others.

Changes in the various sectors of the general and task environments can create tremendous challenges, especially for organizations operating in complex, rapidly changing industries. Costco Wholesale Corporation, with warehouses throughout the world, is an example of an organization operating in a highly complex environment.

2-1b General Environment

The dimensions of the general environment include international, technological, sociocultural, economic, legal–political, and natural.

International   In his book *The World Is Flat*, Thomas Friedman challenges managers to view global markets as having a level playing field where geographical divisions are irrelevant.[11] A flat world, Friedman argues, creates opportunities for companies to expand into global markets and build a global supply chain. As managers expand into global markets, they have to consider the **international dimension** of the external environment, which includes events originating in foreign countries, as well as new opportunities for U.S. companies in other countries. The international environment provides new competitors, customers, and suppliers and shapes social, technological, and economic trends as well.

Consider the mixed results Starbucks experienced as it expanded into European markets. Starbucks fans packed stores in Germany and the United Kingdom, for example, but sales and profits in the company's French stores were disappointing. In fact, after eight years operating 63 stores, Starbucks never turned a profit in France. What international factors could be hindering the company's success in France? First, a sluggish economy and Europe's debt crisis hurt sales. Plus, Starbucks faced high rent

Concept Connection

Finding employees with the skills needed to apply new information technology is a top concern for today's managers. The **labor market** is a key segment of every organization's **task environment.** All companies need a supply of well-qualified people to accomplish goals and meet customer needs.

Westend61/Getty Images

Sunny Side Up } Costco Wholesale Corporation

AP Images/Damian Dovarganes

Costco Wholesale Corporation, a no-frills, self-service warehouse club, operates an international chain of membership warehouses offering a limited selection of products at reduced prices. Costco's complex environment is illustrated in Exhibit 2.2.

Costco's business model focuses on maintaining its image as a pricing authority, consistently providing the most competitive prices. "Everything we do is to provide goods and services to the customer at a lower price," said Jim Sinegal, co-founder and former CEO. Current CEO Craig Jelinek has vowed that a low-price philosophy will continue to guide the company. Costco warehouses are designed to operate efficiently and to communicate value to members. The warehouse decor—high ceilings, metal

roofs, exposed trusses—keeps costs low and contributes to the perception that Costco is for serious shoppers seeking serious bargains. Other strategies for keeping prices low include offering only around 4,000 unique products at a time (by contrast, Walmart offers more than 100,000) and negotiating low prices with suppliers. Only about 28 percent of sales come from outside the United States, but same store sales in overseas markets have been growing about four times faster than those in the United States. The biggest part of Jelinek's plan is to increase Costco's international presence. The company recently opened stores in Spain and signed a purchase agreement for a location in Iceland. Jelinek has said in an interview that two-thirds of Costco's expansion over the next five years would be international, with a focus on Japan, Taiwan, and South Korea.

Costco's biggest competitive advantage is its loyal workforce. "Costco compensates employees very well—well above the industry in terms of wages and benefits," says R. J. Hottovy, a retail analyst at Morningstar. When the economic downturn worsened in late 2009 and many retailers cut wages and issued layoffs, Costco handed out raises. The happiness and morale of employees is often overlooked in the retail industry, but not at Costco. Thanks to its positive treatment of workers, Costco has one of the lowest turnovers in the retail industry (around 5 percent), and since 2009, sales have grown 39 percent and the stock price has doubled.[12]

Remember This

- The **organizational environment**, consisting of both task and general environments, includes all elements existing outside the boundary of the organization that have the potential to affect the organization.

- An **organizational ecosystem** includes organizations in all the sectors of the task and general environments that provide the resource and information transactions, flows, and linkages necessary for an organization to thrive.

- The **general environment** indirectly influences all organizations within an industry and includes five dimensions.

- The **task environment** includes the sectors that conduct day-to-day transactions with the organization

and directly influence its basic operations and performance.

- The **internal environment** includes elements within the organization's boundaries, such as employees, management, and corporate culture.

- **Customers** are part of the task environment and include people and organizations that acquire goods or services from the organization.

- **Competitors** are organizations within the same industry or type of business that vie for the same set of customers.

- **Suppliers** provide the raw materials the organization uses to produce its output.

- The **labor market** represents the people available for hire by the organization.

Exhibit 2.2 The External Environment of Costco Wholesale Corporation

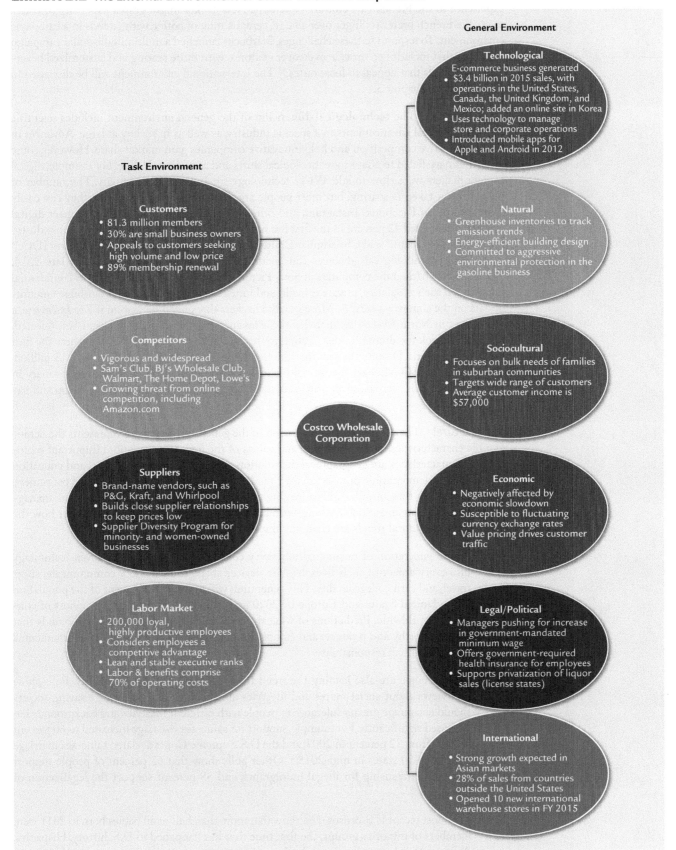

General Environment

Technological
- E-commerce business generated $3.4 billion in 2015 sales, with operations in the United States, Canada, the United Kingdom, and Mexico; added an online site in Korea
- Uses technology to manage store and corporate operations
- Introduced mobile apps for Apple and Android in 2012

Natural
- Greenhouse inventories to track emission trends
- Energy-efficient building design
- Committed to aggressive environmental protection in the gasoline business

Sociocultural
- Focuses on bulk needs of families in suburban communities
- Targets wide range of customers
- Average customer income is $57,000

Economic
- Negatively affected by economic slowdown
- Susceptible to fluctuating currency exchange rates
- Value pricing drives customer traffic

Legal/Political
- Managers pushing for increase in government-mandated minimum wage
- Offers government-required health insurance for employees
- Supports privatization of liquor sales (license states)

International
- Strong growth expected in Asian markets
- 28% of sales from countries outside the United States
- Opened 10 new international warehouse stores in FY 2015

Task Environment

Customers
- 81.3 million members
- 30% are small business owners
- Appeals to customers seeking high volume and low price
- 89% membership renewal

Competitors
- Vigorous and widespread
- Sam's Club, BJ's Wholesale Club, Walmart, The Home Depot, Lowe's
- Growing threat from online competition, including Amazon.com

Suppliers
- Brand-name vendors, such as P&G, Kraft, and Whirlpool
- Builds close supplier relationships to keep prices low
- Supplier Diversity Program for minority- and women-owned businesses

Labor Market
- 200,000 loyal, highly productive employees
- Considers employees a competitive advantage
- Lean and stable executive ranks
- Labor & benefits comprise 70% of operating costs

Costco Wholesale Corporation

SOURCES: Costco Wholesale Corporation Investor Relations Web site, http://phx.corporate-ir.net/phoenix.zhtml?c=83830&p=irol-reportsannual (accessed January 26, 2016); Brad Stone, "Costco CEO Craig Jelinek Leads the Cheapest, Happiest Company in the World" (June 6, 2013), http://www.businessweek.com/articles/2013-06-06/costco-ceo-craig-jelinek-leads-the-cheapest-happiest-company-in-the-world (accessed August 26, 2013); "Costco Whole-sale Corporation," *Marketline* (April 30, 2012): 3–9; Alaric DeArment, "Costco's Lobbying Changes WA's Liquor Laws: Who Is Next?" *Drug Store News* (December 12, 2011): 12; and Sharon Edelson, "Costco Keeps Formula as It Expands," *Women's Wear Daily* (January 30, 2012): 1.

and labor costs in France, which eroded profits. The company was also slow to tailor the Starbucks experience to the French café culture. Whereas a New Yorker might grab a paper cup of coffee to go, the French prefer to linger over a large, ceramic mug of coffee with friends in a café-style environment. To respond to these challenges, Starbucks launched a multimillion-dollar campaign in France that includes an upscale makeover of stores, with more seating and customized beverages and blends that appeal to local tastes.[13] The international environment will be discussed in more detail in Chapter 3.

Technological   The **technological dimension** of the general environment includes scientific and technological advancements in a specific industry, as well as in society at large. Advances in technology drive competition and help innovative companies gain market share. However, some industries have failed to adapt to technological shifts and are facing decline. For example, digital camera makers were slow to add Wi-Fi technology for Internet connectivity. The number of photos being taken is soaring, but most people are using their smartphones so they can easily share photos on Facebook, Instagram, and other social media. Shipments of compact digital cameras plummeted 42 percent in the first five months of 2013. "It's the classic case of an industry that is unable to adapt," said Christopher Chute, a digital imaging analyst at research firm IDC.[14] In addition, technological advances can create new threats to organizations. In late 2014, cybercriminals hacked the computers of Sony Pictures Entertainment, leaking highly confidential information such as salaries, private e-mails, and unreleased films and wiping out huge amounts of data on the company's servers. Moreover, the hackers threatened retaliation if *The Interview*, a comedy set in North Korea that included the assassination of leader Kim Jong-un, was released. Sony had to look for alternative distribution routes after many theaters declined to show the film for fear of reprisals. Despite the fact that the hacking episode cost Sony more than $15 million, Sony Pictures CEO Michael Lynton said it was a "relatively inexpensive, very noisy, canary in the coal mine. So if there's a silver lining, it's that this was a call for [people] to wake up and pay attention."[15]

Sociocultural   The **sociocultural dimension** of the general environment represents the demographic characteristics, norms, customs, and values of the general population. Important sociocultural characteristics are geographical distribution and population density, age, and education levels. Today's demographic profiles are the foundation of tomorrow's workforce and consumers. By understanding these profiles and addressing them in the organization's business plans, managers prepare their organizations for long-term success. Managers may want to consider how the following sociocultural trends are changing the consumer and business landscape:

1. A new generation of technologically savvy consumers has intimately woven technology into every aspect of their lives. Mobile devices shape the way they communicate, shop, travel, and earn college credits. This generation will make up 40 percent of the population in the United States and Europe by 2020 and will constitute the largest cohort of consumers worldwide. Predictions of what they will value as consumers include brands that are trustworthy and products and companies that show a commitment to environmental, social, and fiscal responsibility.[16]

2. Young people are also leading the trend toward widespread social equality. Polls show that views about social mores and lifestyles are shifting. The percentage saying society should encourage greater tolerance of people with different lifestyles and backgrounds has increased significantly. For example, support for same-sex marriage increased to 60 percent in 2015 from 32 percent in 2003, and the U.S. Supreme Court declared same-sex marriage legal in all 50 states in mid-2015.[17] Other polls show that 65 percent of people support a path to citizenship for illegal immigrants, and 58 percent support the legalization of marijuana.[18]

3. The most recent U.S. census data show that more than half of all babies born in 2011 were members of minority groups, the first time that has happened in U.S. history. Hispanics, African Americans, Asians, and other minorities represented 50.4 percent of births in 2011. The nation's growing diversity has huge implications for business.[19]

Economic The **economic dimension** represents the general economic health of the country or region in which the organization operates. Consumer purchasing power, the unemployment rate, and interest rates are part of an organization's economic environment. Because organizations today are operating in a global environment, the economic dimension has become exceedingly complex and creates enormous uncertainty for managers.

In the United States, many industries, such as banking, are finding it difficult to make a comeback despite the rebounding economy. KeyCorp, one of the nation's largest banking-based financial services organizations, reports an uneven turnaround, with a mix of both good and bad news. While KeyCorp faces a reduction in total assets, a drop in revenue, and a decline in the profit margin in the lending business, it also reports fewer delinquent loans and strong demand from corporate customers for new loans. With banks stretching from Alaska to Maine, KeyCorp has benefited from geographic diversity because some regions of the United States rebounded faster than others. "As we are in economic recovery . . . our business model, our size, our geographic diversity is an advantage," said Beth Mooney, KeyCorp's CEO. "Conventional wisdom five years ago would have said differently."[20]

Legal–Political The **legal–political dimension** includes government regulations at the local, state, and federal levels, as well as political activities designed to influence company behavior. The U.S. political system encourages capitalism, and the government tries not to overregulate business. However, government laws do specify rules of the game. The federal government influences organizations through the Occupational Safety and Health Administration (OSHA), Environmental Protection Agency (EPA), fair trade practices, libel statutes allowing lawsuits against business, consumer protection and privacy legislation, product safety requirements, import and export restrictions, and information and labeling requirements. One of the most prominent and far-reaching challenges in the legal–political dimension in recent years was the 2010 Dodd-Frank Act (financial regulatory reform). As one of the numerous federal regulations included in the Dodd-Frank Act, the Securities and Exchange Commission (SEC) in 2015 approved a rule requiring that large public companies disclose the pay gap between their CEOs and rank-and-file employees. The pay-ratio measure means companies will have to explain large pay disparities to shareholders and face public scrutiny of their pay practices. The SEC's action creates uncertainty for companies over how the requirement, which started with compensation paid in 2017, will influence not only shareholders and public opinion but also their own managers and employees.[21] Executive pay practices became a concern particularly during the recent mortgage crisis, and as mentioned at the beginning of this chapter, the issue of income inequality has also become a topic of divisive political debates.

Managers in many companies work closely with national lawmakers, educating them about products and services and legislation's impact on their business strategies. Long before its NASDAQ debut in May 2012, for example, Facebook had been quietly

pixelfit/Getty Images

Concept Connection

Successful organizations respond to shifts in the **sociocultural dimension**. Millennials, people born in the 1980s and 1990s, are reshaping shopping trends, social mores, and communication patterns. Smart managers are paying attention and supporting the use of social media and mobile commerce.

Ariel Skelley/Blend Images/Getty Images

Concept Connection

Whether they are motivated by a desire to preserve natural resources, to impress their customers with their social responsibility, or to comply with new legislation, many companies are looking for ways to treat the **natural environment** better. Some are doing it by switching to renewable energy sources, while others are trying to reduce pollution. Promoting the use of cloth carrying bags like these is just one example of how retailers can help minimize the amount of trash going into the world's landfills.

Green Power

There Is No Finish Line for Sustainability

In Greek mythology, Nike was the winged goddess of victory. With headquarters in Portland, Oregon—considered one of the world's "greenest" cities—Nike, Inc. has a corporate culture centered around a commitment to victory, both on the athletic field and as one of the top 100 most sustainable corporations. Some companies give a nod to sustainability by reducing toxins, but Nike goes further with a comprehensive integration of sustainability into company operations. Nike's Considered Design Index allows the company to monitor the total environmental impact of each running shoe or other product. A recently launched app lets engineers gauge the environmental effects of their material and design choices on water, chemistry, energy, and waste.

Victory in sustainability also means influencing other companies. Nike openly shares innovations, such as the technology for making water-based adhesives, that don't threaten its competitive advantage. As Nike's sustainability influence grows, its cultural mantra reflects the winged deity. "We've made significant progress," said Nike's CEO. "But as we all know at Nike, there is no finish line."

SOURCES: Ginger Christ-Martin, "Sustainability: Just Do It," *Industry Week* (February 2014): 22–23; and Marc J. Epstein, Adriana Rejc Buhovac, and Kristi Yuthas, "Why Nike Kicks Butt in Sustainability," *Organizational Dynamics* 39 (2010): 353–356.

---

befriending the nation's top lawmakers. Managers hired former political aides with access to top leaders in both parties and had them lead training sessions on using Facebook to communicate with voters. In addition, Facebook stepped up its lobbying efforts and set up a political action committee. "It's smart advocacy 101," said Rey Ramsey, CEO of TechNet, an industry group that includes Facebook. "What you ultimately want is for a legislator to understand the consequences of their actions."[22]

Natural In response to pressure from environmental advocates, organizations have become increasingly sensitive to the Earth's diminishing natural resources and the environmental impact of their products and business practices. As a result, the natural dimension of the external environment is growing in importance. The **natural dimension** includes all elements that occur naturally on Earth, including plants, animals, rocks, and resources such as air, water, and climate. Protection of the natural environment is emerging as a critical policy focus around the world. Governments are increasingly under pressure to explain their performance on pollution control and natural resource management. Nations with the best environmental performance, along with some comparison countries, are listed in Exhibit 2.3.[23]

The natural dimension is different from other sectors of the general environment because it has no voice of its own. Influence on managers to meet needs in the natural environment may come from other sectors, such as government regulation, consumer concerns, the media, competitors' actions, or even employees.[24] For example, environmental groups advocate various action and policy goals that include reduction and cleanup of pollution, development of renewable energy resources, reduction of greenhouse gases such as carbon dioxide, ethical treatment of animals, and sustainable use of scarce resources such as water, land, and air. In 2015, SeaWorld announced that it would replace its killer whale performance in San Diego with an "informative" experience that has a "conservation message inspiring people to act." The company came under growing scrutiny after the documentary *Blackfish* criticized its treatment of orca whales. The decision doesn't affect orca whale shows at SeaWorld's Orlando, Florida, and San Antonio, Texas, parks, but pressure from activist groups will continue. Jared Goodman, the director of animal law for People for the Ethical Treatment of Animals, said he and others are calling for the company to build sea sanctuaries and stop breeding orcas. In addition, Representative Adam Schiff of California has said he will introduce a bill in Congress that will stop the breeding of captive orcas, end the capture of wild ones, and stop the import and export of the whales.[25]

Exhibit 2.3 2016 Environmental Performance Index

Rank	Country	Score
1	Finland	90.68
2	Iceland	90.51
3	Sweden	90.43
4	Denmark	89.21
5	Slovenia	88.98
6	Spain	88.91
7	Portugal	88.63
8	Estonia	88.59
9	Malta	88.48
10	France	88.20
11	New Zealand	88.00
12	United Kingdom	87.38
13	Australia	87.22
14	Singapore	87.04
15	Croatia	86.98
25	Canada	85.06
26	United States	84.72
109	China	65.10
116	Iraq	63.97
141	India	53.58

Note: The scores for each country are based on 20 performance indicators covering both protection of public health and protection of ecosystems.

SOURCES: *2016 Environmental Performance Index,* Yale Center for Environmental Law and Policy and Yale Data-Driven Environmental Solutions Group, Yale University, http://epi.yale.edu/country-rankings (accessed January 27, 2016); and Center for International Earth Science Information Network, Columbia University.

Remember This

- The **international dimension** of the external environment represents events originating in foreign countries, as well as opportunities for U.S. companies in other countries.
- The **technological dimension** of the general environment includes scientific and technological advances in society.
- The **sociocultural dimension** includes demographic characteristics, norms, customs, and values of a population within which the organization operates.
- The **economic dimension** represents the general economic health of the country or region in which the organization operates.
- The **legal–political dimension** includes government regulations at the local, state, and federal levels, as well as political activities designed to influence company behavior.
- The **natural dimension** includes all elements that occur naturally on Earth, including plants, animals, rocks, and natural resources such as air, water, and climate.

2-2 The Organization–Environment Relationship

Why do organizations care so much about factors in the external environment? The reason is that the environment creates uncertainty for organization managers, and they must respond by designing the organization to adapt to the environment.

2-2a Environmental Uncertainty

Visit MindTap for "Self-Assessment: Are You Suited for Managerial Uncertainty?" to see how well you might adapt as a new manager in an uncertain environment.

Uncertainty means that managers do not have sufficient information about environmental factors to understand and predict environmental needs and changes.[26] As indicated in Exhibit 2.4, environmental characteristics that influence uncertainty are the number of factors that affect the organization and the extent to which those factors change. Managers at a large multinational like Costco must deal with thousands of factors in the external environment that create uncertainty. When external factors change rapidly, the organization experiences high uncertainty; examples of companies that often face such problems are telecommunications and aerospace firms, computer and electronics companies, and Internet organizations. Entertainment companies are also experiencing tremendous uncertainty as consumer behavior shifts rapidly. For example, Walt Disney Company had great success with the 2015 movie *Star Wars: The Force Awakens*, but its cable network division is suffering as viewers cancel their cable subscriptions or never sign up at all. Viewers can now access programming from HBO and other companies for a monthly fee that costs much less than a bundled cable bill, and it is likely Disney's ESPN will have to follow suit. Yet analysts say it will be hard for Disney to sign up enough subscribers to cover the huge cost of licensing live sports coverage.[27]

When an organization deals with only a few external factors and these factors are relatively stable, such as those affecting soft-drink bottlers or food processors, managers experience low uncertainty and can devote less attention to external issues.

2-2b Adapting to the Environment

Environmental changes may evolve unexpectedly, such as shifting customer tastes for video and computer games or social media sites, or they may occur violently, such as the devastating Japanese earthquake and tsunami in 2011. The level of turbulence created by an environmental shift will

Exhibit 2.4 The External Environment and Uncertainty

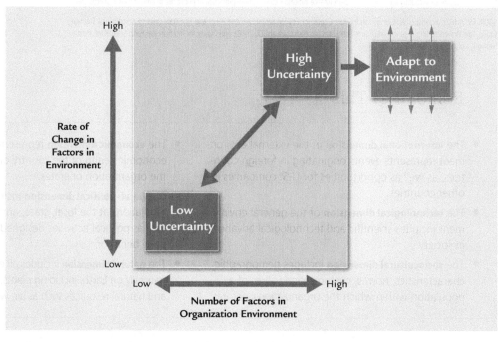

determine the type of response that managers must make in order for the organization to survive. Managers continuously scan the business horizon for both subtle and dramatic environmental changes, also called *strategic issues*, and identify those that require strategic responses. **Strategic issues** are "events or forces either inside or outside an organization that are likely to alter its ability to achieve its objectives." As environmental turbulence increases, strategic issues emerge more frequently.[28] Managers use several strategies to adapt to these strategic issues, including business intelligence applications, attempts to influence the environment, and mergers or joint ventures.

Business Intelligence   Organizations depend on information, and companies that most effectively acquire, interpret, disseminate, and use information come out as winners. Managers have learned the importance of not only being aware of what's going on inside the organization but also of getting a handle on what's going on in the external environment. **Boundary spanning** links to and coordinates the organization with key elements in the external environment.[29]

One area of boundary spanning is the use of *business intelligence*, which results from using sophisticated software to search through internal and external data to spot patterns, trends, and relationships that might be significant. The fastest-growing segment of business intelligence is big data analytics. As described in Chapter 1, *big data analytics* refers to searching and examining massive, complex sets of data to uncover hidden patterns and correlations and make better decisions.[30]

Big data analytics is becoming a driving force in many organizations.[31] One of the best-known examples of the use of data analytics among the general population is in the sports world. The popular book *Moneyball: The Art of Winning an Unfair Game*, later made into a movie starring Brad Pitt, tells the story of how the Oakland Athletics general manager Billy Beane built a winning team by analyzing previously ignored player statistics.[32] Today, most sports teams use sophisticated data analytics programs to analyze player statistics. Similarly, businesses use big data analytics to gain insights that can improve performance. PASSUR Aerospace, for instance, provides decision support technologies for the aviation industry, such as helping eliminate gaps between estimated and actual flight arrival times. PASSUR collects a wide range of multidimensional data and can analyze patterns spanning more than a decade to understand what happens under specific conditions. Enabling airlines to know when planes are going to land and plan accordingly can save several million dollars a year. According to PASSUR, 53 percent of U.S. domestic commercial flights are now managed with the company's predictive analytics.[33] Banks such as Capital One analyze customers based on credit risk, usage, and multiple other criteria to match customer characteristics with appropriate product offerings. Kaiser Permanente collects petabytes of health data on its 8 million members. Some of that data was used in a study sponsored by the U.S. Food and Drug Administration (FDA) that identified a greater risk of heart attacks among users of the pain medication Vioxx.[34]

Business intelligence and big data analytics are also related to the growing area of boundary spanning known as *competitive intelligence (CI)*, which refers to activities to get as much information as possible about one's rivals.[35]

Influence the Environment   Boundary spanning is an increasingly important task in organizations because environmental shifts can happen quickly in today's world. Managers need good information about their customers, competitors, and other elements to make good decisions. Boundary spanning also includes activities that represent the organization's interest in the environment and attempt to influence elements of the external environment.[36] General Electric (GE) spends more than $39 million a year on political lobbying to influence government officials to take actions that positively affect the company's business performance. GE's political lobbyists span the boundary between the organization and the government, a critical aspect of the external environment.[37]

JUSTIN TALLIS/Getty Images

Concept Connection

Anheuser-Busch InBev, the world's largest beer brewing company, was formed through successive mergers of three international brewing groups: Interbrew from Belgium, AmBev from Brazil, and Anheuser-Busch from the United States. In October 2015, the giant announced plans to acquire competitor SABMiller. **Mergers and acquisitions** are one way organizations adapt to an uncertain environment.

Another company that invests heavily in political lobbying to influence the environment is the ride service company Uber, which has one of the most powerful and effective lobbying forces in the United States. The company has 250 lobbyists and 29 lobbying firms registered in state capitols, at least a third more than Wal-Mart Stores, Inc. Many more work as lobbyists at the municipal level. One business writer said Uber has "made a name for itself by barging into cities and forcing politicians to respond."[38]

Mergers and Joint Ventures   Companies may also become involved in mergers or joint ventures to reduce environmental uncertainty. A frenzy of merger and acquisition activity, both in the United States and internationally, in recent years is an attempt by organizations to cope with the tremendous volatility of the environment.[39] In Bain's 2015 Management Tools and Trends survey described in Chapter 1, 57 percent of managers said mergers are critical to success in their industry, and 2015 was the biggest year on record for mergers and acquisitions, with nearly $5 trillion worth of deals announced.[40] Look at the health care industry, where a sweeping national trend toward joint operating agreements and mergers reflects the tremendous uncertainty in the industry. Gary Ahlquist, a senior partner with Booz & Company, predicts that of the 5,724 hospitals in the United States in 2013, about 1,000 will have new owners by 2020.[41]

A **merger** occurs when two or more organizations combine to become one. For example, Charter Communications acquired Time Warner Cable and Bright House Networks in 2016 to form the second-largest cable company in the United States, and AB InBev bought SABMiller to create a $104 billion beverage company.[42] A **joint venture** involves a strategic alliance or program by two or more organizations. A joint venture typically occurs when a project is too complex, expensive, or uncertain for one firm to handle alone. Sikorsky Aircraft and Lockheed Martin, for example, teamed up to bid on a new contract for a fleet of Marine One helicopters. The joint venture would have Sikorsky building the helicopters and Lockheed Martin providing the vast array of specialized systems that go into each one. Although the two companies have previously competed to build presidential helicopters, they joined together to be more competitive against rivals such as Boeing, Bell Helicopters, and Finmeccanica SpA's Agusta Westland.[43] Joint ventures are on the rise as companies strive to keep pace with rapid technological change and compete in the global economy.

Remember This

- When external factors change rapidly, the organization experiences high uncertainty.
- **Strategic issues** are events and forces that alter an organization's ability to achieve its goals. As environmental turbulence increases, strategic issues emerge more frequently.
- **Boundary spanning** links to and coordinates the organization with key elements in the external environment.
- Big data analytics uses powerful computer technology to search and examine massive, complex sets of data to uncover hidden patterns and correlations so managers can make better decisions.

- A **merger** occurs when two or more organizations combine to become one.
- The Charter Communications acquisition of Time Warner Cable and AB InBev's purchase of SABMiller are two recent mergers.
- A **joint venture** is a strategic alliance or program by two or more organizations.
- Sikorsky Aircraft and Lockheed Martin teamed up to bid on a new contract for Marine One helicopters.

2-3 The Internal Environment: Corporate Culture

The internal environment within which managers work includes corporate culture, production technology, organization structure, and physical facilities. Of these, corporate culture surfaces as being extremely important to competitive advantage. The internal culture must fit the needs of the external environment and company strategy. When this fit occurs, highly committed employees create a high-performance organization that is tough to beat.[44]

Most people don't think about culture; it's just "how we do things around here" or "the way things are here." However, managers have to think about culture. Culture guides how people within the organization interact with one another and how the organization interacts with the external environment; thus, culture plays a significant role in organizational success. Organizational culture has been defined and studied in many and varied ways. For the purposes of this chapter, we define **culture** as the set of key values, beliefs, understandings, and norms shared by members of an organization.[45] The concept of culture helps managers understand the hidden, complex aspects of organizational life. Culture is a pattern of shared values and assumptions about how things are done within the organization. This pattern is learned by members as they cope with external and internal problems and taught to new members as the correct way to perceive, think, and feel.

Although strong corporate cultures are important, they can also sometimes promote negative values and behaviors. For example, John Shaw, former city manager of Ferguson, Missouri, resigned after a Department of Justice report blamed him for the damaging policies that affected "nearly every aspect of Ferguson police and court operations" and led to routine bias against African Americans. The Justice Department study came after widespread protests following the deadly shooting of Michael Brown, an unarmed black 18-year-old resident, in 2014. The Ferguson city government was accused of creating an unhealthy culture that allowed the discrimination and misconduct to take root. For example, an emphasis on the need for increasing fees and fines to fund the city budget put pressure on police and court officials to meet targets for ticketing and arrests. Although Shaw didn't tell anyone to violate people's constitutional rights or target African Americans, as the city's top leader and most powerful official, he was held responsible for the culture and policies that allowed the abuse to occur.[46]

Culture can be analyzed at two levels, as illustrated in Exhibit 2.5.[47] At the surface level are visible artifacts, which include things such as manner of dress, patterns of behavior, physical symbols, organizational ceremonies, and office layout. Visible artifacts are all the things one can see, hear, and observe by watching members of the organization. At a deeper, less obvious level are values and beliefs, which are not observable but can be discerned from how people explain and justify what they do. Members of the organization hold some values at a conscious level. These values can be interpreted from the stories, language, and symbols that organization members use to represent them.

Some values become so deeply embedded in a culture that members are no longer consciously aware of them. These basic, underlying assumptions and beliefs are the essence of culture and

Exhibit 2.5 Levels of Corporate Culture

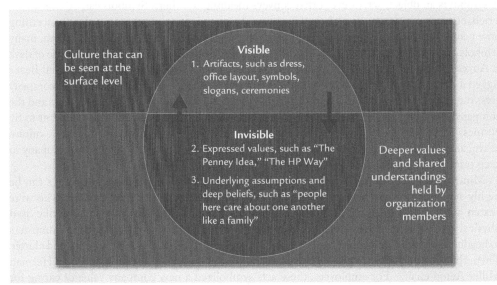

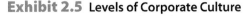

Sunny Side Up } Facebook

"You get zero credit for your title," said Don Faul, a former Marines Special Forces commander who joined Facebook as a manager in 2008. "It's all about the quality of the work, the power of your conviction, and the ability to influence people."

Facebook wants people to be working in areas that cater to their natural interests and abilities, so employees have an extraordinary degree of freedom to choose and change their assignments, rather than having them dictated by managers. People can even work on projects outside their area of expertise. Paddy Underwood came to Facebook as a lawyer working on the privacy team. Two years later, he decided he wanted to build products instead. Managers at Facebook also sometimes encourage people to shift roles based on what they do well. Mike

Welsh joined Facebook from PricewaterhouseCoopers as a risk-management accountant, but a manager noticed that he had a knack for helping people learn new concepts. Now, Welsh is a "People Engineer" for Facebook.

A majority of Facebook's 8,000 employees are young (the median age is 28), and leaders know younger workers don't respond well to command-and-control management. At Facebook, even low-level employees are encouraged to question and criticize managers. Peter Yewell, who worked for several years on the sales team, said the role of managers at Facebook is different from that in other companies where he had worked. Rather than telling people what to do, at Facebook "their role is to help you get the resources you need and to move things out of your way," he said.[48]

subconsciously guide behavior and decisions. In some organizations, a basic assumption might be that people are essentially lazy and will shirk their duties whenever possible; thus, employees are closely supervised and given little freedom, and colleagues are frequently suspicious of one another. More enlightened organizations operate on the basic assumption that people want to do a good job; in these organizations, employees are given more freedom and responsibility, and colleagues trust one another and work cooperatively. At social networking company Facebook, for example, employees often choose their own assignments.

Facebook doesn't give employees free rein, but the company's management practices are in line with the trend toward bossless organizations, which we discussed in Chapter 1. The "Sunny Side Up" box further describes the bossless trend and some of the values that exist in bossless organizations. An organization's fundamental values are demonstrated through symbols, stories, heroes, slogans, and ceremonies.

2-3a Symbols

A **symbol** is an object, act, or event that conveys meaning to others. Symbols can be considered a rich, nonverbal language that vibrantly conveys the organization's important values concerning how people relate to one another and interact with the environment.[49] At Amazon.com, many symbols convey an emphasis on frugality, one of the company's core values. A popular style of desk at Amazon is the "door desk," for instance, harkening back to Amazon's founding when Jeff Bezos rigged a desk out of a door. The door desk became such a symbol of frugality that the company gives out door desk awards for exceptional employee ideas that save money for customers and the company. Amazon pays only for economy air travel, even for top managers; if people want to fly business or first class, they have to pay for the upgrade on their own. Amazon believes a culture of frugality leads to resourcefulness, self-sufficiency, and innovation and enables the company to keep prices low for customers.[50]

Mindy Grossman, CEO of HSN Inc., found that sometimes even mundane things can be highly symbolic. When she became CEO, Grossman found a group of employees who were beaten down and uninspired. To fix the situation, she needed to change the culture. She used physical symbols to give people hope and motivation. One day, Grossman brought in dumpsters to headquarters and told people to start throwing away all the broken-down furniture and clutter. Then, she had the buildings pressure washed and painted and bought everyone a new Herman Miller Aeron chair.[51] For employees, these acts symbolized a new company value of caring for employees.

2-3b Stories

A **story** is a narrative based on true events that is repeated frequently and shared among organizational employees. Stories paint pictures that help symbolize the firm's vision and values and help employees personalize and absorb them.[52] A frequently told story at UPS concerns an employee who, without authorization, ordered an extra Boeing 737 to ensure timely delivery of a load of Christmas packages that had been left behind in the holiday rush. As the story goes, rather than punishing the worker, UPS rewarded his initiative. By telling this story, UPS workers communicate that the company stands behind its commitment to worker autonomy and customer service.[53]

2-3c Heroes

A **hero** is a figure who exemplifies the deeds, character, and attributes of a strong culture. Heroes are role models for employees to follow. Heroes with strong legacies may continue to influence a culture even after they are gone. Many people have wondered if the culture that Steve Jobs created

Sunny Side Up · The Bossless Workplace

The organizational hierarchy with formal bosses worked well in the past. Then a few leaders began to realize that all the bosses were actually slowing down productivity and stifling employee creativity, thus prompting experiments with the "bossless" workplace.

What are the key success factors of a bossless company?

- **Reduce hierarchies starting from the top down.** Dov Seidman, head of LRN (formerly Legal Research Network), stood in front of 300 employees and ripped up the organization chart, proclaiming that "none of us would report to a boss anymore." Seidman says, "This has to start at the top of any organization." Everyone now reports to the company's mission rather than to other people. The only control is shared values. Twenty teams from around the globe spent six months imagining what a self-governing LRN would look like. Employee councils handle recruiting, performance management, resource allocation, and conflict resolution. People can take as much vacation as they like, so long as it doesn't interfere with their work.

- **Develop a bossless environment that "fits" the organization**. Basecamp, a Chicago software firm formerly known as 37signals, got its start in 1999 and appointed a manager in 2013. Jason Zimdars, the reluctant manager appointee, said that he would rather write code and make things. Disdain for management is true at many newer companies with young employees who need to be creative. "We want people who are doing the work, not managing the work," said Zimdars. Employees at Basecamp are free to overrule the new boss if they feel strongly about green-lighting a creative project.

- **Recruit and hire employees who can adapt to a bossless culture.** Menlo Innovations, founded in 2001, became one of *Inc.* 500's fastest-growing privately held firms in the United States. Menlo's bossless hiring process is called "extreme interviewing," and it bears a striking resemblance to speed-dating. Applicants—sometimes as many as five for each open position—are brought into the offices for a series of rapid-fire interviews with a range of current employees. The emphasis is on "kindergarten skills": geniality, curiosity, generosity. Technical proficiency is less important than a candidate's "ability to make [his or her] partner look good." (Sample interview question: "What is the most challenging bug that you helped someone else fix?")

- **Expect bumps in the road with a flat organizational structure.** Retaining highly motivated workers is vital to making a boss-free system work. Most employees take anywhere from six months to a year to adapt, and some leave for more traditional settings. "It's absolutely less efficient upfront," says Terri Kelly, chief executive of W. L. Gore, the maker of Gore-Tex and other materials. "[But] once you have the organization behind it … the buy in and execution happens quickly." One study found that when teams of factory workers learned to "encourage and support each other. … They collectively perform the role of a good manager."

SOURCES: Matthew Shaer, "The Boss Stops Here," *New York Magazine* (June 24–July 1, 2013): 26–34; Rachel Emma Silverman, "Who's the Boss? There Isn't One," *The Wall Street Journal Online*, June 19, 2012, http://online.wsj.com/article/SB10001424052702303337920457747 4953586383604.html (accessed September 26, 2013); John Southerst, "First We Dump the Bosses," *Canadian Business* (April 1992): 46–51; Rachel Emma Silverman, "Some Tech Firms Ask: Who Needs Managers?" *The Wall Street Journal Online*, August 6, 2013, http://online.wsj.com/article/SB10001424127887323420604578652051466314748.html (accessed August 6, 2013); Dov Seidman, "Letting the Mission Govern a Company," *The New York Times*, June 23, 2012, http://www.nytimes.com/2012/06/24/jobs/a-company-lrn-adopts-collaborative-management.html (accessed June 23, 2012).

at Apple would be sustained after his death in 2011. Jobs exemplified the creativity, innovation, risk-taking, and boundary-breaking thinking that made the company famous.[54] When Jobs's health began to fail, Apple's board began considering replacements who could sustain the fertile culture that Jobs created. They chose Tim Cook, who long had served as second-in-command. Cook is trying to nurture a culture that reflects the values and behaviors of Apple's hero, Steve Jobs. "Apple has a culture of excellence that is, I think, so unique and so special. I'm not going to witness or permit the change of it," he said.[55]

Chris Rock has been greatly influenced by some comedians' style and work ethic, as shown in the **"Sunny Side Up"** box.

2-3d Slogans

A **slogan** is a phrase or sentence that succinctly expresses a key corporate value. Many companies use slogans or sayings to convey special meaning to employees. For example, Disney uses the slogan "The happiest place on earth." The Ritz-Carlton adopted the slogan "We are Ladies and Gentlemen serving Ladies and Gentlemen" to demonstrate its cultural commitment to take

Sunny Side Up } Chris Rock

Nigel Waldron/Redferns/Getty Images

Developing a successful comedy routine is no different than inventing and producing a new product, at least if you see how Chris Rock works. He has developed his own process that has become his own organizational "culture." Before a new global tour, Rock starts out by visiting at least 40 small comedy clubs with a yellow note pad that has ideas scribbled on it. He calls it a boxing training camp. Making sure there is an audience of about 50, he sits quietly until people start to notice him and ask him onstage. Up there, he doesn't do his full "preacher effect" performance, but rather talks and tells jokes in a more conversational style, with his notepad right next to him. In a typical 45-minute set, most of his jokes fall flat and watching it can be awfully painful, as sometimes he rambles, loses his train of thought, and keeps referring to his notes. Many audience members sit on their hands, unimpressed. In business, such people are referred to as "active users" and provide the kind of constant criticism needed to improve the material. Rock admits to audiences that

some jokes need work and writes on his pad. But during that less-than-an-hour time period, there might be 5 to 10 lines that bring the house down. He buildings on these "lightning bolts."

When he's finished, he's gone through thousands of ideas, and only a few make it in to the final routine. Comedians know that a successful joke has six to seven parts. With such complexity, even stars like Jerry Seinfeld or Rock don't know which combination of ideas is going to work in front of an audience. Even with the amazingly successful *Onion*, the writers propose 600 possibilities for 18 ultimate headlines, or a 3 percent rate.

By the time Rock is ready for an HBO special, he's spent 6–12 months testing and retesting his material, including opening, jokes, and transitions. He'll be on stage every night, five to seven nights a week, grinding through every sentence, until the routine is perfectly honed. Rock knows that good ideas don't spring into anyone's mind perfectly formed but take lots of work. Rock doesn't see the thousands of failed jokes in the clubs as failures but rather an information in a learning process that ultimately yields gold.

Rock's most recent Netflix act is even more searing that his previous one. He admits to cheating on his wife, of having an addiction to certain things on the Internet, getting divorced, and going through a horrible custody battle. When people in the audience start to clap, probably at what they think is courage, he tells them to stop, unless they are lawyers. "You don't want to get divorced," he says. "Let me tell you right now. I'm talking from hell."

SOURCES: Elahe Izadi, "What Makes Chris Rock's New Netflix Stand-up Special So Different?" *The Times*, February 26, 2018, B3; Kelefa Sanneh, "The Duke of Doubt," *The New Yorker*, November 10, 2014;

care of both employees and customers. "We're in the service business, and service comes only from people. Our promise is to take care of them, and provide a happy place for them to work," said general manager Mark DeCocinis, who manages the Portman Hotel in Shanghai, recipient of the "Best Employer in Asia" award for three consecutive years.[56] Cultural values can also be discerned in written public statements, such as corporate mission statements or other formal statements that express the core values of the organization. At DreamHost, a Web-hosting company where the culture reflects a serious commitment to democracy, the CEO (who was elected by employees) asked a team of workers to draft a mission statement and constitution to guide how the company makes decisions.[57]

2-3e Ceremonies

A **ceremony** is a planned activity at a special event that is conducted for the benefit of an audience. Managers hold ceremonies to provide dramatic examples of company values. Ceremonies are special occasions that reinforce valued accomplishments, create a bond among people by allowing them to share an important event, and anoint and celebrate heroes.[58] In a ceremony to mark its 20th anniversary, Southwest Airlines rolled out a specialty plane called the "Lone Star One," which had the Texas state flag painted on it to signify the company's start in Texas. Later, when the National Basketball Association (NBA) chose Southwest Airlines as the league's official airline, Southwest launched another specialty plane, the "Slam Dunk One," colored blue and orange with a large basketball painted on the nose of the plane. Today, 10 specialty planes celebrate significant milestones in Southwest's history and demonstrate key cultural values.[59]

2-4 Types of Culture

A big influence on internal corporate culture is the external environment. Cultures can vary widely across organizations; however, organizations within the same industry often reveal similar cultural characteristics because they are operating in similar environments.[60] The internal culture should embody what it takes to succeed in the environment. If the external environment requires extraordinary customer service, the culture should encourage good service; if it calls for careful technical decision making, cultural values should reinforce managerial decision making.

FashionStock.com/Shutterstock.com

Concept Connection

Around the offices of Tradesy, the high-fashion consignment e-commerce site that blossomed into a $10 million business in just about three years, employees like to tell the **story** of how Tracy DiNunzio started her business. Desperate for start-up capital, she sold many of her belongings, but when she still didn't have enough to pay the Web developers she was working with, Tracy started renting out her bedroom through the hotel-alternative Web site Airbnb while she slept on her own couch. The story is important to Tradesy because it demonstrates the passion and commitment that is part of the **corporate culture**.

Exhibit 2.6 Four Types of Corporate Culture

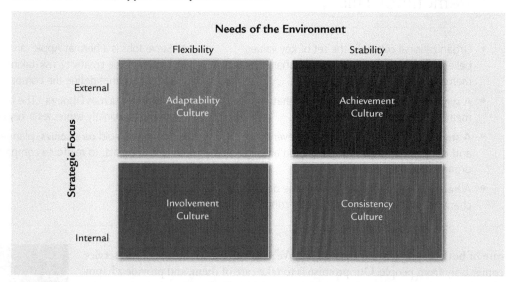

SOURCES: Based on D. R. Denison and A. K. Mishra, "Toward a Theory of Organizational Culture and Effectiveness," *Organization Science* 6, no. 2 (March–April 1995): 204–223; R. Hooijberg and F. Petrock, "On Cultural Change: Using the Competing Values Framework to Help Leaders Execute a Transformational Strategy," *Human Resource Management* 32, no. 1 (1993): 29–50; and R. E. Quinn, *Beyond Rational Management: Mastering the Paradoxes and Competing Demands of High Performance* (San Francisco: Jossey-Bass, 1988).

In considering what cultural values are important for the organization, managers consider the external environment, as well as the company's strategy and goals. Studies suggest that the right fit among culture, strategy, and the environment is associated with four categories or types of culture, as illustrated in Exhibit 2.6. These categories are based on two dimensions: (1) the extent to which the external environment requires flexibility or stability and (2) the extent to which a company's strategic focus is internal or external. The four categories associated with these differences are adaptability, achievement, involvement, and consistency.[61]

2-4a Adaptability Culture

The **adaptability culture** emerges in an environment that requires fast response and high-risk decision making. Managers encourage values that support the company's ability to rapidly detect, interpret, and translate signals from the environment into new behaviors. Employees have the

Sunny Side Up } **TubeMogul**

Brett Wilson and John Hughes founded TubeMogul while they were MBA students at the UC Berkeley Haas School of Business. From the beginning, they wanted the company to be guided by values of being fast and flexible. All new employees attend a class led by Wilson called "Culture and Values," where they learn about the principles that guide the organization. At TubeMogul, values are the basis for hiring, firing, and promoting people.

"Culture and people are everything," says Wilson, who serves as CEO of TubeMogul. "We were determined to build a company that had a certain culture, and that was just as important to us . . . as the software we were

building." The first cultural value at TubeMogul is that people shouldn't be afraid to make mistakes. If people aren't making mistakes, managers know they're not moving fast enough to keep pace with a fast-changing industry. Managers encourage people to take risks, be creative, make mistakes, and figure things out. The company also values people who have a high "do-to-say ratio," meaning they have a bias for action and follow through on what they commit to doing. Everyone from the CEO on down is expected to acknowledge mistakes and make quick course corrections as needed.[62]

autonomy to make decisions and act freely to meet new needs, and responsiveness to customers is highly valued. Managers also actively create change by encouraging and rewarding creativity, experimentation, and risk-taking. TubeMogul, a successful digital advertising software company, provides an example of the adaptability culture.

Many technology and Internet-based companies, like TubeMogul, use the adaptability type of culture, as do many companies in the marketing, electronics, and cosmetics industries because they must move quickly to respond to rapid changes in the environment.

2-4b Achievement Culture

The **achievement culture** is suited to organizations concerned with serving specific customers in the external environment but without the intense need for flexibility and rapid change. This results-oriented culture values competitiveness, aggressiveness, personal initiative, cost cutting, and willingness to work long and hard to achieve results. An emphasis on winning and achieving specific ambitious goals is the glue that holds the organization together.[63] Both Oracle and EMC Corporation have been criticized for having aggressive, take-no-prisoners cultures, but leaders at the companies make no apologies. Jack Mollen, executive vice president for human resources at EMC, says "Some people might feel it's aggressive, but our people want to be put in jobs where they can work hard, take risks, and get recognized." As for the critics, he adds, "I ask the search firms to name the three hardest companies to recruit [management talent] from, and they say 'Intel, Oracle, and EMC.'"[64]

Desire for achievement without ethics can be a problem, as Wells Fargo discovered, described in this chapter's Half-Baked Management box.

2-4c Involvement Culture

The **involvement culture** emphasizes an internal focus on the participation of employees to adapt rapidly to changing needs from the environment. This culture places a high value on meeting the needs of employees, and the organization may be characterized by a caring, family-like atmosphere. Managers emphasize values such as cooperation, consideration of both employees and customers, and avoiding status differences. Four Seasons Hotels and Resorts, for example, has been named one of the "100 Best Companies to Work For" by *Fortune* magazine every year since the survey's inception in 1998. With 96 luxury properties in 41 countries, Four Seasons managers have built a corporate culture that values employees above all other assets. Every location has a committee made up of people from all departments that meets with the general manager each month to discuss workplace concerns. The relentless commitment to employees sustained Four Seasons during the recent economic recession that battered many companies in the hospitality industry. Four Seasons clarified its corporate vision to include both being a first-choice ranking among guests and being the best employer.[65]

Half-Baked Management ⟩ Wells Fargo

Even though evidence had surfaced since 2005 that Wells Fargo managers were creating false accounts using customers' private information (managers were threatened with job loss if they did not have enough new accounts), the financial world was surprised in late 2016 when it was disclosed that a million new accounts had been fraudulently created. This means up to 3.5 million sham accounts were started using customer names, and this was 70 percent more than the company initially suspected. Wells Fargo agreed in September 2016 to pay $185 million to settle associated claims. Also not surprising is the fact that The Federal Reserve Bank replaced 4 of 16 Well Fargo board members. So much for Pony Express.

SOURCES: Emily Flitter et al., "Fed Shackles Wells Fargo Growth with Severe Penalties for Abuses," *The New York Times*, February 3, 2018, A1; Stacy Cowley and Michael Corkery, "After Scandal, Wells Fargo Board Faces a Contentious Re-Election," *The New York Times*, April 25, 2017, B1.

Discover Your Management Approach

Culture Preference

Instructions: The fit between a new manager and organizational culture can determine success and satisfaction. To understand your culture preference, rank the items here from 1 to 8 based on the strength of your preference (1 = strongest).

1. The organization is very personal, much like an extended family.

2. The organization is dynamic and changing, where people take risks.

3. The organization is achievement-oriented, with the focus on competition and getting jobs done.

4. The organization is stable and structured, with clarity and established procedures.

For the rest of the test, go to MindTap.

Would you rather work in an organization with an adaptability, achievement, involvement, or consistency culture? Visit MindTap for "Self-Assessment: What Is Your Culture Preference?" to get an idea of what type of culture you would be most comfortable working in.

2-4d Consistency Culture

The final category of culture, the **consistency culture**, uses an internal focus and a consistency orientation for a stable environment. Following the rules and being thrifty are valued, and the culture supports and rewards a methodical, rational, and orderly way of doing things. In today's fast-changing world, few companies operate in a stable environment, and most managers are shifting toward cultures that are more flexible and in tune with changes in the environment. However, Pacific Edge Software (now part of Serena Software) successfully implemented elements of a consistency culture to ensure that all its projects stayed on time and under budget. The husband-and-wife team of Lisa Hjorten and Scott Fuller implanted a culture of order, discipline, and control from the moment they founded the company. The emphasis on order and focus meant that employees could generally go home by 6 p.m. rather than working all night to finish an important project. Although sometimes being careful means being slow, Pacific Edge managed to keep pace with the demands of the external environment.[66]

Each of these four categories of culture can be successful. In addition, organizations usually have values that fall into more than one category. The relative emphasis on various cultural values depends on the needs of the environment and the organization's focus. Managers are responsible for instilling the cultural values the organization needs to be successful in its environment.

Remember This

- For an organization to be effective, corporate culture should be aligned with organizational strategy and the needs of the external environment.

- Organizations within the same industry often reveal similar cultural characteristics because they are operating in similar environments.

- The **adaptability culture** is characterized by values that support the company's ability to interpret and translate signals from the environment into new behavior responses.

- An **achievement culture** is a results-oriented culture that values competitiveness, personal initiative, and achievement.

- A culture that places high value on meeting the needs of employees and values cooperation and equality is an **involvement culture**.

- A **consistency culture** values and rewards a methodical, rational, orderly way of doing things.

2-5 Shaping Corporate Culture for Innovative Response

Many top leaders cite organizational culture as their most important mechanism for attracting, motivating, and retaining talented employees, a capability considered the single best predictor of overall organizational excellence.[67] In a survey of Canada's top 500 companies, 82 percent of leaders said that culture has a strong impact on their company's performance.[68] A recent study by Stanford University professor Charles A. O'Reilly III and his colleagues also found that cultures tend to reflect the characteristics of top leaders, and culture in turn influences a broad range of outcomes, including financial performance, company reputation, and employee attitudes.[69] For example, at Southwest Airlines, founder and former CEO Herb Kelleher created an "employees first" corporate culture that top leaders have kept strong for more than four decades. Kelleher believed that how a company treats employees determines how employees treat customers—and happy customers create and sustain shareholder value. The Southwest culture is based on cultivating collaborative and fun interactions among employees, making every customer feel valued and following through on every customer concern, and doing everything as frugally as possible. Southwest has been profitable every year since 1972 and has the lowest ratio of complaints per passengers in the industry.[70]

Corporate culture plays a key role in creating an organizational climate that enables learning and innovative responses to threats from the external environment, challenging new opportunities, or organizational crises. However, managers realize that they can't focus all their effort on values; they also need a commitment to solid business performance.

2-5a Managing the High-Performance Culture

Companies that succeed in a turbulent world are those in which managers are evaluated and rewarded for paying careful attention to both cultural values *and* business performance. Exhibit 2.7 illustrates four organizational outcomes based on the relative attention that managers pay to cultural values and business results.[71] For example, a company in Quadrant C pays little attention to either values or business results and is unlikely to survive for long. Managers in Quadrant D organizations are highly focused on creating a strong cohesive culture, but they don't tie organizational values directly to goals and desired business results.

When cultural values aren't connected to business performance, they aren't likely to benefit the organization during hard times. The corporate culture at the LEGO Group, with headquarters in Billund, Denmark, nearly doomed the toymaker in the 1990s when sales plummeted as children turned from traditional toys to video games. At that time, LEGO reflected the characteristics found in Quadrant D of Exhibit 2.7. Imagination and creativity, not business performance, were what guided the company. The attitude among employees was, "We're doing great stuff for kids— don't bother us with financial goals." When he became CEO in 2004, Jørgen Vig Knudstorp upended the corporate culture with a new employee motto: "I am here to make money for the company." The shift to bottom-line results had a profound impact, and LEGO has become one of the most successful companies in the toy industry.[72]

Quadrant A represents organizations that focus primarily on bottom-line results and pay little attention to organizational values. This approach may be profitable in the short run, but the success is difficult to sustain over the long term because the "glue" that holds the organization together—that is, shared cultural values—is missing. Consider how a bottom-line focus at social games company Zynga damaged the organization. Zynga, led by founder and CEO Mark Pincus, recorded a phenomenal $828 million in revenue in the first nine months of 2011, more than double the period a year earlier. Zynga also met ambitious profitability goals, rare among Internet start-ups. However, employee teams for each game, like FarmVille and CityVille, worked under aggressive deadlines and were continuously challenged to meet lofty goals. Managers emphasized performance reports, and they relentlessly aggregated data and used the data to demote or fire weak employees. Little attention was paid to cultural values that bind people into a unified

Exhibit 2.7 Combining Culture and Performance

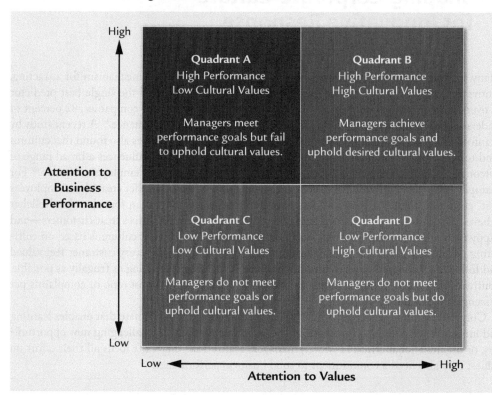

Attention to Business Performance (vertical axis: High → Low)

Quadrant A
High Performance
Low Cultural Values

Managers meet performance goals but fail to uphold cultural values.

Quadrant B
High Performance
High Cultural Values

Managers achieve performance goals and uphold desired cultural values.

Quadrant C
Low Performance
Low Cultural Values

Managers do not meet performance goals or uphold cultural values.

Quadrant D
Low Performance
High Cultural Values

Managers do not meet performance goals but do uphold cultural values.

Attention to Values (horizontal axis: Low ← → High)

SOURCES: Adapted from Jeff Rosenthal and Mary Ann Masarech, "High-Performance Cultures: How Values Can Drive Business Results," *Journal of Organizational Excellence* (Spring 2003): 3–18; and Dave Ulrich, Steve Kerr, and Ron Ashkenas, Figure 11-2, GE Leadership Decision Matrix, *The GE Work-Out: How to Implement GE's Revolutionary Method for Busting Bureaucracy and Attacking Organizational Problems—Fast!* (New York: McGraw-Hill, 2002), p. 230.

whole. Employees began voicing their frustration, complaining about long hours and aggressive deadlines, threats from top managers, and moments when colleagues broke down in tears. Many valued employees were lured away by competitors. The company's success could not be sustained without some attention to building a positive and responsive culture. It remains to be seen if Zynga's leadership will bring a greater focus on building a positive culture that can help to renew the company.[73]

Finally, companies in Quadrant B put high emphasis on both culture and solid business performance as drivers of organizational success. Managers in these organizations align values with the company's day-to-day operations—hiring practices, performance management, budgeting, criteria for promotions and rewards, and so forth. Consider the approach that GE took to accountability and performance management. When he was CEO, Jack Welch helped GE become one of the world's most successful and admired companies. He achieved this by creating a culture in which risk was rewarded and accountability and measurable goals were keys to individual success and company profitability.[74] The company's traditional approach had achieved stellar financial results, but managers motivated people to perform primarily through control, intimidation, and reliance on a small circle of staff. Welch was interested in more than just financial results—he wanted managers to exhibit the following cultural values in addition to "making their numbers":[75]

- Have a passion for excellence and hate bureaucracy
- Be open to ideas from anywhere
- "Live" quality, and drive cost and speed for competitive advantage

Welch knew that for the company to succeed in a rapidly changing world, managers needed to pay careful attention to both cultural values and business performance. Quadrant B organizations represent the **high-performance culture**, a culture that (1) is based on a solid organizational mission or purpose, (2) embodies shared adaptive values that guide decisions and business

"Leaders often treat culture as a happy accident—something that develops organically, driven by personalities. What a mistake. Culture is a critical building block of success."

—HIROSHI MIKITANI, CO-FOUNDER AND CEO OF RAKUTEN

practices, and (3) encourages individual employee ownership of both bottom-line results and the organization's cultural backbone.[76]

One of the most important things that managers do is create and influence organizational culture to meet strategic goals because culture has a significant impact on performance. In *Corporate Culture and Performance*, John Kotter and James Heskett provided evidence that companies that intentionally managed cultural values outperformed similar companies that did not. Recent research validates that elements of corporate culture are positively correlated with higher financial performance.[77]

2-5b Cultural Leadership

A primary way in which managers shape cultural norms and values to build a high-performance culture is through *cultural leadership*. Managers must *overcommunicate* to ensure that employees understand the new culture values, and they signal these values in actions as well as words.

A **cultural leader** defines and uses signals and symbols to influence corporate culture. The leader clarifies what the new culture should be and crafts a story that inspires people to change. A cultural leader is the "chief marketing officer" for the desired cultural values.[78]

Cultural leaders influence culture in two key areas:

1. ***The cultural leader articulates a vision for the organizational culture that employees can believe in.*** The leader defines and communicates central values that employees believe in and will rally around. Values are tied to a clear and compelling mission, or core purpose.

2. ***The cultural leader heeds the day-to-day activities that reinforce the cultural vision.*** The leader makes sure that work procedures and reward systems match and reinforce the values. Actions speak louder than words, so cultural leaders "walk their talk."[79]

When the culture needs to change, cultural leaders make sure people understand that the old way of doing things is no longer acceptable. For example, when he was corporate ombudsman at KeySpan Corporation (now part of National Grid), Kenny Moore held a "funeral" for everyone to say goodbye to the company as it once was.[80] Then, managers widely communicated the new cultural values through both words and actions to make sure the desired values took root. Values statements that aren't reinforced by management behavior are meaningless, or even harmful, for employees and the organization. Whole Foods founder and co-CEO John Mackey wants his managers to place more value on creating "a better person, company, and world" than on pursuing personal financial gain. To demonstrate his commitment to this belief, he asked the board of directors to donate all his future stock options to the company's two foundations, the Animal Compassion Foundation and the Whole Planet Foundation.[81]

iStock.com/Avava

Concept Connection

Johnson & Johnson, which makes a wide range of consumer, health, and prescription products, is considered a **high-performance** workplace. The company has a rich heritage of shared corporate values, and employees are focused on winning by serving their customers. The corporate culture encourages employees to work in teams, think like owners, and remain open to action and change.

SOURCES: Adapted from Jeff Rosenthal and Mary Ann Masarech, "High-Performance Cultures: How Values Can Drive Business Results," *Journal of Organizational Excellence* (Spring 2003): 3–18; and Dave Ulrich, Steve Kerr, and Ron Ashkenas, Figure 11–2, GE Leadership Decision Matrix, *The GE Work-Out: How to Implement GE's Revolutionary Method for Busting Bureaucracy and Attacking Organizational Problems—Fast!* (New York: McGraw-Hill, 2002), p. 230.

Remember This

-   Managers emphasize both values and business results to create a **high-performance culture**.
-   Culture enables solid business performance through the alignment of motivated employees with the mission and goals of the company.

-   Managers create and sustain adaptive high-performance cultures through cultural leadership.
-   **Cultural leaders** define and articulate important values that are tied to a clear and compelling mission, which they communicate widely and uphold through their actions.

Cultural leaders also uphold their commitment to values during difficult times or crises. Upholding the cultural values helps organizations weather a crisis and come out stronger on the other side. Creating and maintaining a high-performance culture is not easy in today's turbulent environment and changing workplace, but through their words—and particularly their actions—cultural leaders let everyone in the organization know what really counts.

DISCUSSION QUESTIONS

1. Surveys reveal dramatic shifts in social attitudes toward issues such as same-sex marriage and citizenship for illegal immigrants. How do you think these changing attitudes might affect the manager's job over the next few years?

2. Would the task environment for a wireless provider such as Verizon Wireless contain the same elements as that for a government welfare agency? Discuss the similarities and differences.

3. What strategic issues have the potential to create environmental uncertainty in the following four industries: (a) automobile; (b) social media; (c) newspaper; and (d) medical services?

4. Contemporary best-selling management books often argue that customers are the most important element in the external environment. Do you agree? In what company situations might this statement be untrue?

5. What do you see as the primary advantage of using big data analytics—understanding the environment or influencing the environment? Why?

6. Why do you think 2015 was the biggest year ever for mergers and acquisitions? What elements in the current environment might contribute to either an increase or a decrease in mergers? Discuss.

7. Consider the factors that influence environmental uncertainty (rate of change in factors and number of factors in the environment) that are presented in Exhibit 2.4. Classify each of the following organizations as operating in either (a) a low-uncertainty environment or (b) a high-uncertainty environment: Hyundai, Facebook, a local Subway franchise, FedEx, a cattle ranch in Oklahoma, and McDonald's. Explain your reasoning.

8. Distribution center managers for Anheuser-Busch InBev frequently start the day with a sort of pep rally, reviewing the day's sales targets and motivating people to get out and sell more beer. What does this suggest about the type of culture the company's managers promote?

9. As a manager, how would you use symbols to build an adaptability culture that encourages teamwork and risk-taking? What kinds of symbols could you use to promote the values of an involvement culture?

10. Do you think it is wise for a top executive to fire a manager who is bringing in big sales and profits for the company but not living up to a cultural value of "showing respect for employees"? Explain.

APPLY YOUR SKILLS: SELF-LEARNING

Working in an Adaptability Culture[82]

Think of a specific full-time job that you have held. Please answer the following questions according to your perception of the *managers above you* in that job. Circle a number on the 1–5 scale based on the extent to which you agree with each statement about the managers above you:

⑤ Strongly agree
④ Agree
③ Neither agree nor disagree
② Disagree
① Strongly disagree

1. Good ideas got serious consideration from management above me.

   1 2 3 4 5

2. Management above me was interested in ideas and suggestions from people at my level in the organization.

   1 2 3 4 5

3. When suggestions were made to management above me, they received a fair evaluation.

   1 2 3 4 5

4. Management did not expect me to challenge or change the status quo.

   1 2 3 4 5

5. Management specifically encouraged me to bring about improvements in my workplace.

   1 2 3 4 5

6. Management above me took action on recommendations made from people at my level.

   1 2 3 4 5

7. Management rewarded me for correcting problems.

   1 2 3 4 5

8. Management clearly expected me to improve work unit procedures and practices.

   1 2 3 4 5

9. I felt free to make recommendations to management above me to change existing practices.

   1 2 3 4 5

10. Good ideas did not get communicated upward because management above me was not very approachable.

    1 2 3 4 5

Scoring and Interpretation Subtract each of your scores for questions 4 and 10 from the number 6. Using your adjusted scores, add the numbers for all 10 questions to give you the total score. Divide that number by 10 to get your average score: _____.

An adaptability culture is shaped by the values and actions of top and middle managers. When managers actively encourage and welcome change initiatives from below, the organization will be infused with values for change. These 10 questions measure your management's openness to change. A typical average score for management openness to change is about 3. If your average score was 4 or higher, you worked in an organization that expressed strong cultural values of adaptation. If your average score was 2 or below, the company probably did not have an adaptability culture.

Think about this job. Was the level of management openness to change correct for the organization? Why? Compare your scores to those of another student, and take turns describing what it was like working for the managers above you in your jobs. Do you sense a relationship between job satisfaction and your management's openness to change? What specific management characteristics and corporate values explain the openness scores in the two jobs?

APPLY YOUR SKILLS: GROUP LEARNING

Organizational Culture in the Classroom and Beyond

Step 1. Write on the following table the norms that you believe to be operating in these places: (1) in most of your courses, (2) in formal social groups such as fraternities and sororities, and (3) in student clubs or school-sponsored organizations. Use your personal experience in each place and consider the norms. Some norms are implicit, so you may have to think carefully to identify them. Other norms may be explicit. Make sure you list *norms* but not *practices*. The difference is that when a norm is broken, there is some negative reaction, or even punishment, while violating a practice carries no negative result.

List norm	Which group or organization is identified with this norm?	What is a negative result if a norm is violated?

Step 2. After you have developed your lists, divide into groups of four to six students to discuss norms. Each student should share with the group the norms identified for each of the assigned places. Make a list of norms for each place and brainstorm any additional norms that you and your group members can think of.

Step 3. Try to group the norms by common themes, and give each group of norms a title. Decide as a group which norms are most important for regulating student behavior in each location. Use the following table.

Name of norm category	List norms in that category.	Rate each norm from 1–5, with 1 being least important for regulating behavior and 5 most important.	Where does each norm originate, from environment, leader, or other?

Step 4. As a group, analyze the source or origin of each of the more important norms. Does the norm originate in the environment, from a leader, or elsewhere? Can you find any examples of norms that are expressed but not followed, which means that people do not "walk the talk" of the norms?

Step 5. What did you learn about cultural norms that exist in organizations and social groups? How is it helpful to make explicit those aspects of organization culture that are typically implicit? Who should be responsible for setting norms in your courses or in student social groups and organizations?

APPLY YOUR SKILLS: ACTION LEARNING

Answer the following questions yourself.

1. Think of a really good work situation you've had (or as member of a student organization) and a really bad one.

2. Consider the types of organization cultures listed in pages 71–74. Which culture was your best and which was your worst?

3. List aspects of culture that fit you or did not fit.

4. Can you learn anything from this about what you need in a workplace in order for you to operate at your best?

What was the name of company or organization?	What type of culture was it? Refer to pages 71–74.	Which aspects fit you the best? Or which aspects were the worst fit?
Best:		
Worst:		

As a group, discuss the following:

1. Were there similarities or differences in what the members found in terms of ideal cultures?

2. If you could design the very ideal culture for your group members, what would it look like?

3. What would the ideal culture look like for people who have different, even opposite, qualities?

APPLY YOUR SKILLS: ETHICAL DILEMMA

CI Predicament[83]

Miquel Vasquez was proud of his job as a new product manager for a biotechnology start-up, and he loved the high stakes and tough decisions that went along with the job. But as he sat in his living room after a long day, he was troubled, struggling over what had happened earlier that day and the information that he now possessed.

Just before lunch, Miquel's boss had handed him a stack of private strategic documents from the company's closest competitor. The information was a confidential information gold mine—product plans, pricing strategies, partnership agreements, and other documents, most of them clearly marked "proprietary and confidential." When Miquel asked where the documents came from, his boss told him with a touch of pride that he had taken them right off the competing firm's server. "I got into a private section of their intranet and downloaded everything that looked interesting," he said. Later, realizing that Miquel was suspicious, the boss would say only that he had obtained "electronic access" via a colleague and had not personally broken into any passwords. Maybe not, Miquel thought to himself, but this situation wouldn't pass the *60 Minutes* test. If word of this acquisition of a competitor's confidential data ever got out to the press, the company's reputation would be ruined.

Miquel didn't feel good about using these materials. He spent the afternoon searching for answers to his dilemma, but found no clear company policies or regulations that offered any guidance. His sense of fair play told him that using the information was unethical, if not downright illegal. What bothered him even more was the knowledge that this kind of thing might happen again. Using this confidential information would certainly give him and his company a competitive advantage, but Miquel wasn't sure that he wanted to work for a firm that would stoop to such tactics.

What Would You Do?

1. Go ahead and use the documents to the company's benefit, but make clear to your boss that you don't want him passing confidential information to you in the future. If he threatens to fire you, threaten to leak the news to the press.

2. Confront your boss privately and let him know that you're uncomfortable with how the documents were obtained and what possession of them says about your company's culture. In addition to the question of the legality of using the information, point out that it is a public relations nightmare waiting to happen.

3. Talk to the company's legal counsel and contact the Strategic and Competitive Intelligence Professionals for guidance. Then, with their opinions and facts to back you up, go to your boss.

APPLY YOUR SKILLS: CASE FOR CRITICAL ANALYSIS

Not Measuring Up

"I must admit, I'm completely baffled by these scoring results for Cam Leslie," Carole Wheeling said as she and company CEO Ronald Zeitland scrolled through the latest employee surveys for middle management.

For the second year, RTZ Corporation used Wheeling's consulting firm to survey and score managers. An increasingly younger workforce, changing consumer tastes, and technology changes in the industry had caused Zeitland to look more closely at culture and employee satisfaction. The goal of this process was to provide feedback in order to ensure continuous improvement across a variety of criteria. The surveys could be used to highlight areas for improvement by showing manager and company strengths and weaknesses, anticipating potential problem areas, providing a barometer for individual job performance, and serving as a road map for transforming the culture as the company expanded.

From the outset, Zeitland insisted on employee honesty in scoring managers and providing additional comments for the surveys. "We can't change what we don't know," Zeitland instructed employees in meetings two years ago. "This is your opportunity to speak up. We're not looking for gripe sessions. We're looking for constructive analysis and grading for what we do and how we do it. This method ensures that everyone is heard. Every survey carries equal weight. Changes are coming to this organization. We want to make those changes as easy and equally beneficial as possible for everyone."

Now, two years into the process, the culture was showing signs of changing and improving.

"The results from last year to this year show overall improvement," Wheeling said. "But for the second year, Cam's survey results are disappointing. In fact, there appears to be a little slippage in some areas."

Zeitland leaned back in his chair, paused, and looked at the survey results on the screen.

"I don't really understand it," Wheeling remarked. "I've talked to Cam. He seems like a nice guy—a hard worker, intelligent, dedicated. He pushes his crew, but he's not a control freak."

"He actually implemented several of the suggestions from last year's survey," Zeitland said. "From all reports and my own observations, Cam has more presence in the department and has increased the number of meetings. He appears to have at least attempted to open up communications. I'm sure he will be as baffled as we are by these new results because he *has* put forth effort."

"Employees mentioned some of these improvements, but it's not altering the scores. Could it merely be a reflection of his personality?" Wheeling asked.

"Well, we have all kinds of personalities throughout management. He's very knowledgeable and very task oriented. I admit he has a way of relating to people that can be a little standoffish, but I don't think it's always necessary to be slapping everyone on the back and buying them beers at the local pub in order to be liked and respected and . . ."

". . . in order to get high scores?" Wheeling finished his sentence. "Still, the low percentage of 'favorable' scores in relation to 'unfavorable' and even 'neutral'. . ." her voice trailed off momentarily. "That's the one that gets me. There are so many 'neutral' scores. That's really strange. Don't they have an opinion? I'd love to flesh that one out more. It seems that in a sea of vivid colors, he's beige."

"It's like he's not there," Zeitland said. "The response doesn't tell me that they dislike Cam; they just don't *see* him as their manager."

Wheeling laughed. "Maybe we can wrap him in gauze like the 'Invisible Man,'" she joked.

The joke appeared lost on Zeitland. "That invisibility leaves him disengaged. Look at the comments."

He scrolled down. "Here's a follow-up comment: **Employee Engagement:** *Are you kidding?* And here's another: **Advocacy:** *I don't think and I don't believe anyone here thinks he would go to bat for us.*"

"I know," Wheeling said. "On the other hand, many of their remarks indicate they consider him fair in areas like distribution of workload, and they score him decently in the area of follow-through in achieving company goals. But overall satisfaction and morale levels are low."

"That's what I don't understand," Zeitland commented. "Morale and productivity are normally so strongly linked. Morale in this case is blah, blah, blah, and yet these guys manage to perform right up there with every other division in the company. So they're *doing* it. They just don't like it or find any sense of fulfillment."

"Does Cam?"

"Interesting question," Zeitland agreed.

"So, how do we help Cam improve these scores in the coming year?" Wheeling asked. "What positive steps can he take? I'd at least like to see an up-or-down vote—not all of this neutrality—on his management skills and job performance."

Questions

1. Do you think Zeitland's desire for changes in culture are related to changes in the external environment? Explain.

2. What additional investigation might Wheeling and Zeitland undertake before settling on a plan of action?

3. In which quadrant of Exhibit 2.7 would you place Cam? What are some steps that you would recommend Cam consider to better connect with the employees who report to him?

ENDNOTES

1. Paul Davidson, "Fast-Food Workers Strike, Seeking $15 Wage, Political Muscle," *USAToday* (November 10, 2015), http://www.usatoday.com/story/money/2015/11/10/fast-food-strikes-begin/75482782/ (accessed January 25, 2016); and Clare O'Connor, "Fast Food Workers Plan Tuesday Strikes in 270 Cities, Vow to Take $15 Wage to Voting Booth," *Forbes* (November 9, 2015), http://www.forbes.com/sites/clareoconnor/2015/11/09/fast-food-workers-plan-tuesday-strikes-in-270-cities-vow-to-take-15-wage-to-voting-booth/#2f518f6f247d (accessed January 25, 2016).

2. This section is based on Richard L. Daft, *Organization Theory and Design*, 10th ed. (Mason, OH: South-Western, 2010), pp. 140–143.

3. L. J. Bourgeois, "Strategy and Environment: A Conceptual Integration," *Academy of Management Review* 5 (1980): 25–39.

4. James Moore, *The Death of Competition: Leadership and Strategy in the Age of Business Ecosystems* (New York: HarperCollins, 1996).

5. David J. Teece, "Dynamic Capabilities: A Guide for Managers," *Ivey Business Journal* (March/April, 2011), www.iveybusinessjournal.com/topics/strategy/dynamic-capabilities-a-guide-for-managers (accessed June 12, 2012).

6. Paul Ziobro, "Target Revamps Groceries for Millennials," *The Wall Street Journal* (March 2, 2015), http://www.wsj.com/articles/target-to-focus-on-seven-food-categories-in-grocery-revamp-1425327752 (accessed January 26, 2016).

7. Lance Whitney, "Samsung Continues to Rule Over Apple in Smartphone Market," *CNET* (July 23, 2015), http://www.cnet.com/news/samsung-continues-to-rule-over-apple-in-smartphone-market/ (accessed January 26, 2016); and

"Smartphone Vendor Market Share," *IDC.com*, http://www
.idc.com/prodserv/smartphone-market-share.jsp (accessed
January 26, 2016).

8. Geoff Colvin, "Toyota's Comeback Kid," *Fortune* (February 2,
2012): 73.

9. "Downsides of Just-in-Time Inventory," *Bloomberg Businessweek* (March 28–April 3, 2011): 17–18.

10. Peter Valdes-Dapena, "Japan Earthquake Impact Hits U.S.
Auto Plants," *CNNMoney* (March 30, 2011), http://money
.cnn.com/2011/03/28/autos/japan_earthquake_autos_
outlook/index.htm# (accessed June 13, 2012); and Maxwell
Murphy, "Reinforcing the Supply Chain," *The Wall Street
Journal*, January 11, 2012, B6.

11. Thomas L. Friedman, *The World Is Flat: A Brief History of the
Twenty-First Century* (New York: Farrar, Straus, and Giroux,
2005), pp. 3–23.

12. Brad Stone, "Costco CEO Craig Jelinek Leads the Cheapest,
Happiest Company in the World," *Bloomberg Businessweek*
(June 6, 2013), http://www.businessweek.com/articles
/2013-06-06/costco-ceo-craig-jelinek-leads-the-cheapest
-happiest-company-in-the-world (accessed August 26,
2013); Sharon Edelson, "Costco Keeps Formula as It
Expands," *Women's Wear Daily*, Issue 19 (January 30, 2012):
1; Andria Cheng, "Costco Cracks Taiwan Market," *The Wall
Street Journal*, April 2, 2010; and *Costco Wholesale Annual
Report 2012*, Costco Wholesale Corporation Investor
Relations Web site, http://phx.corporate-ir.net/phoenix.
zhtml?c=83830&p=irol-reportsannual (accessed August 26,
2013).

13. Liz Alderman, "In Europe, Starbucks Adjusts to a Café
Culture," *The New York Times*, March 30, 2012.

14. Daisuke Wakabayashi, "The Point-and-Shoot Camera Faces
Its Existential Moment," *The Wall Street Journal*, July 30,
2013, http://online.wsj.com/article/SB1000142412788732
4251504578580263719432252.html (accessed August 26,
2013).

15. Adi Ignatius, "They Burned the House Down," (an interview
with Michael Lynton), *Harvard Business Review* (July–
August 2015): 107–113.

16. "Naming the Next Generation—Speaker Q&A" Tyrus
Cukavac, *YPulse* (May 28, 2013), http://www.ypulse.com
/post/view/naming-the-next-generation-qa-tyrus-cukavac
(accessed August 27, 2013); Roman Friedrich, Michael
Peterson, and Alex Koster, "The Rise of Generation C,"
Strategy + Business, Issue 62 (Spring 2011), www.strategy
-business.com/article /11110?gko=64e54 (accessed June 25,
2012); and Max Mihelich, "Another Generation Rises:
Looking Beyond the Millennials," *Workforce* (April 12, 2013),
http://www.workforce.com/articles/108-another-generation
-rises-looking-beyond-the-millennials (accessed August 22,
2013).

17. *Wall Street Journal* poll, reported in Colleen McCain Nelson,
"Poll: Most Women See Bias in the Workplace," *The Wall
Street Journal* (April 12, 2013), A4; and Eric Schulzke,
"Behind the Rapid Shift in Public Opinion on Same-Sex
Marriage," *Deseret News* (June 30, 2015), http://national
.deseretnews.com/article/5013/behind-the-rapid-shift
-in-public-opinion-on-same-sex-marriage.html (accessed
January 26, 2016).

18. Jeffrey M. Jones, "In U.S., 58% Back Legal Marijuana Use,"
Gallup.com (October 21, 2015), http://www.gallup.com
/poll/186260/back-legal-marijuana.aspx (accessed January
26, 2016); and Jeffrey M. Jones, "In U.S., 65% Favor Path to
Citizenship for Illegal Immigrants," *Gallup.com* (August 12,
2015), http://www.gallup.com/poll/184577

/favor-path-citizenship-illegal-immigrants.aspx (accessed
January 26, 2016).

19. Dennis Cauchon and Paul Overberg, "Census Data Shows
Minorities Now a Majority of U.S. Births," *USA TODAY*
(May 17, 2012), www.usatoday.com/news/nation/story/2012
-05-17/minority-births-census/55029100/1 (accessed June
12, 2012).

20. Matthias Rieker, "Uneven Economy Hits Banks," *The Wall
Street Journal Online* (January 25, 2012), http://online.wsj
.com/article/SB100014240529702037185045771806725161
74122.html (accessed June 22, 2012).

21. Victoria McGrane and Joann S. Lublin, "SEC Approval of
Pay-Gap Rule Sparks Concerns," *The Wall Street Journal*
(August 5, 2015), http://www.wsj.com/articles/sec-set-to
-approve-final-ceo-pay-ratio-rule-1438783961 (accessed
January 27, 2016).

22. Somini Sengupta, "Facebook Builds Network of Friends in
Washington," *The New York Times* (May 18, 2012), www
.nytimes.com/2012/05/19/technology/facebook-builds
-network-of-friends-in-washington.html?_r=1&emc=eta1
(accessed June 12, 2012).

23. A. Hsu et al., 2016 Environmental Performance Index, Yale
University (New Haven, CT: 2016). Available at www.epi
.yale.edu.

24. Dror Etzion, "Research on Organizations and the Natural
Environment," *Journal of Management* 33 (August 2007):
637–654.

25. Daniel Victor, "SeaWorld Ends Show with Orcas in San
Diego," *The New York Times*, November 10, 2015.

26. Robert B. Duncan, "Characteristics of Organizational
Environment and Perceived Environmental Uncertainty,"
Administrative Science Quarterly 17 (1972): 313–327; and
Daft, *Organization Theory and Design*, pp. 144–148.

27. Andrew Ross Sorkin, "At Disney, a Dark Force Looms
Large: Unbundling," *The New York Times* (December 22,
2015).

28. Bruce E. Perrott, "Strategic Issue Management as Change
Catalyst," *Strategy & Leadership* 39, no. 5 (2011): 20–29.

29. Patricia M. Buhler, "Business Intelligence: An Oppor-
tunity for Competitive Advantage," *Supervision* 74, no. 3
(March 2013): 8–11; David B. Jemison, "The Importance of
Boundary Spanning Roles in Strategic Decision-Making,"
Journal of Management Studies 21 (1984): 131–152; and
Marc J. Dollinger, "Environmental Boundary Spanning
and Information Processing Effects on Organizational
Performance," *Academy of Management Journal* 27 (1984):
351–368.

30. Darrell K. Rigby, *Management Tools 2013: An Executive's
Guide* (Bain & Company 2013), http://www.bain
.com/Images/MANAGEMENT_TOOLS_2013_An_
Executives_guide.pdf (accessed August 27, 2013); Margaret
Rouse, "Big Data Analytics," *TechTarget.com* (January 10,
2012), http://searchbusinessanalytics.techtarget.com/
definition/big-data-analytics (accessed August 27, 2013);
and David Kiron, Renee Boucher Ferguson, and Pamela Kirk
Prentice, "From Value to Vision: Reimagining the Possible
with Data Analytics," *MIT Sloan Management Review Special
Report* (March 5, 2013), http://sloanreview.mit.edu/reports
/analytics-innovation/ (accessed August 27, 2013).

31. R. Bean and D. Kiron, "Organizational Alignment Is Key
to Big Data Success," *MIT Sloan Management Review*
(January 28, 2013), http://sloanreview.mit.edu/article
/organizational-alignment-is-key-to-big-data-success/
(accessed August 27, 2013).

32. Michael Lewis, *Moneyball: The Art of Winning an Unfair Game* (New York: W.W. Norton, 2003).

33. Example described in Andrew McAfee and Erik Brynjolfsson, "Big Data: The Management Revolution," *Harvard Business Review* (October 2012): 61–68; and "Who We Are: Overview," PASSUR Aerospace, http://www.passur.com/who-we-are/ (accessed January 27, 2016).

34. Examples reported in Thomas H. Davenport and Jeanne G. Harris, *Competing on Analytics: The New Science of Winning* (Boston: Harvard Business School Press, 2007); and Kiron et al., "From Value to Vision: Reimagining the Possible."

35. Alexander Garrett, "Crash Course in Competitive Intelligence," *Management Today* (May 1, 2011): 18.

36. Jemison, "The Importance of Boundary Spanning Roles in Strategic Decision-Making"; and Dollinger, "Environmental Boundary Spanning and Information Processing Effects on Organizational Performance."

37. Sean Lux, T. Russell Crook, and Terry Leap, "Corporate Political Activity: The Good, the Bad, and the Ugly," *Business Horizons* 55, no. 3 (May–June 2012): 307–312.

38. Karen Weise, "How Uber Rolls," *BusinessWeek* (June 29–July 5, 2015): 54–59.

39. Richard L. Daft, "After the Deal: The Art of Fusing Diverse Corporate Cultures into One," paper presented at the Conference on International Corporate Restructuring, Institute of Business Research and Education, Korea University, Seoul, Korea (June 16, 1998).

40. Darrell Rigby and Barbara Bilodeau, *Management Tools and Trends 2015* (Bain & Company, June 5, 2015), http://www.bain.com/publications/articles/management-tools-and-trends-2015.aspx (accessed January 20, 2016); and Bourree Lam, "2015: A Merger Bonanza," *The Atlantic* (January 9, 2016), http://www.theatlantic.com/business/archive/2016/01/2015-mergers-acquisitions/423096/ (accessed January 28, 2016).

41. Marsha Mercer, "Merger Mania," *AARP Bulletin* (June 2013): 10–14.

42. Alex Sherman, "So Long Time Warner Cable: Charter to Retire Maligned Brand," *Bloomberg*, May 17, 2016, http://www.bloomberg.com/news/articles/2016-05-17/so-long-time-warner-cable-charter-to-retire-much-maligned-brand (accessed May 27, 2016); and Lam, "2015: A Merger Bonanza."

43. Peter Sanders, "Sikorsky's Business Heads Up," *The Wall Street Journal Online* (April 19, 2010), http://online.wsj.com/article/SB10001424052702304180804575188821353177134.html (accessed April 19, 2010).

44. Yoash Wiener, "Forms of Value Systems: A Focus on Organizational Effectiveness and Culture Change and Maintenance," *Academy of Management Review* 13 (1988): 534–545; V. Lynne Meek, "Organizational Culture: Origins and Weaknesses," *Organization Studies* 9 (1988): 453–473; John J. Sherwood, "Creating Work Cultures with Competitive Advantage," *Organizational Dynamics* (Winter 1988): 5–27; and Andrew D. Brown and Ken Starkey, "The Effect of Organizational Culture on Communication and Information," *Journal of Management Studies* 31, no. 6 (November 1994): 807–828.

45. Joanne Martin, *Organizational Culture: Mapping the Terrain* (Thousand Oaks, CA: Sage Publications, 2002); Ralph H. Kilmann, Mary J. Saxton, and Roy Serpa, "Issues in Understanding and Changing Culture," *California Management Review* 28 (Winter 1986): 87–94; and Linda Smircich, "Concepts of Culture and Organizational Analysis," *Administrative Science Quarterly* 28 (1983): 339–358.

46. John Eligon, "Ferguson City Manager Cited in Justice Department Report Resigns," *The New York Times* (March 10, 2015), http://www.nytimes.com/2015/03/11/us/ferguson-city-manager-resigns.html?_r=0 (accessed January 28, 2016); and Andrew Grossman, "Ferguson Police, Courts Accused of Racial Bias by Justice Department Probe," *The Wall Street Journal* (March 3, 2015), http://www.wsj.com/articles/ferguson-police-accused-of-racial-bias-by-federal-investigation-1425411657 (accessed January 28, 2016).

47. Based on Edgar H. Schein, *Organizational Culture and Leadership*, 2d ed. (San Francisco: Jossey-Bass, 1992): pp. 3–27.

48. Reed Albergotti, "At Facebook, Boss Is a Dirty Word," *The Wall Street Journal* (December 25, 2014), http://www.wsj.com/articles/facebooks-millennials-arent-entitled-they-are-empowered-1419537468 (accessed October 27, 2015).

49. Michael G. Pratt and Anat Rafaeli, "Symbols as a Language of Organizational Relationships," *Research in Organizational Behavior* 23 (2001): 93–132.

50. Julie Bort, "Here's a Peek Inside Amazon's Culture of 'Frugality,'" *Slate.com* (April 14, 2014), http://www.businessinsider.com/a-peek-at-amazons-culture-of-frugality-2014-4 (accessed January 28, 2016); J. P. Mangalindan, "Amazon's Core? Frugality," *Fortune* (March 26, 2012), http://fortune.com/2012/03/26/amazons-core-frugality/ (accessed February 16, 2016).

51. Mindy Grossman, "HSN's CEO on Fixing the Shopping Network's Culture," *Harvard Business Review* (December 2011): 43–46.

52. Chip Jarnagin and John W. Slocum, Jr., "Creating Corporate Cultures Through Mythopoetic Leadership," *Organizational Dynamics* 36, no. 3 (2007): 288–302.

53. Robert E. Quinn and Gretchen M. Spreitzer, "The Road to Empowerment: Seven Questions Every Leader Should Consider," *Organizational Dynamics* (Autumn 1997): 37–49.

54. Yukari Iwatani Kane and Jessica E. Vascellaro, "Successor Faces Tough Job at Apple," *The Wall Street Journal Online* (August 26, 2011), http://allthingsd.com/20110826/successor-faces-tough-job-at-apple/ (accessed June 13, 2012).

55. Based on an interview with Tim Cook conducted by *The Wall Street Journal*'s Walt Mossberg and Kara Swisher (June 4, 2012), http://online.wsj.com/article/SB10001424052702303552104577436952829794614.html?KEYWORDS=steve+jobs+apple+culture (accessed June 16, 2012).

56. Arthur Yeung, "Setting People Up for Success: How the Portman Ritz-Carlton Hotel Gets the Best from Its People," *Human Resource Management* 45, no. 2 (Summer 2006): 267–275.

57. Leigh Buchanan, "Reelect the Boss! Or Not," in the "Culture" segment of "The Audacious 25: Meet the Scrappiest, Smartest, Most Disruptive Companies of the Year," *Inc.* (May 2013): 54–76 (DreamHost profile is on page 76).

58. Harrison M. Trice and Janice M. Beyer, "Studying Organizational Cultures Through Rites and Ceremonials," *Academy of Management Review* 9 (1984): 653–669.

59. PRWeb, "Southwest Airlines Launches New NBA-Themed Specialty Airplane; Slam Dunk One Marks First Southwest Specialty Plane with a Partner in 17 Years," November 3, 2005, www.prweb.com/releases/2005/11/prweb306461.php (accessed February 7, 2008).

60. Jennifer A. Chatman and Karen A. Jehn, "Assessing the Relationship Between Industry Characteristics and

Organizational Culture: How Different Can You Be?" *Academy of Management Journal* 37, no. 3 (1994): 522–553.

61. This discussion is based on Paul McDonald and Jeffrey Gandz, "Getting Value from Shared Values," *Organizational Dynamics* 21, no. 3 (Winter 1992): 64–76; and Daniel R. Denison and Aneil K. Mishra, "Toward a Theory of Organizational Culture and Effectiveness," *Organization Science* 6, no. 2 (March–April 1995): 204–223.

62. Adam Bryant, "For Brett Wilson of TubeMogul, It's All in the Follow-Through," *The New York Times* (May 24, 2014), http://www.nytimes.com/2014/05/25/business/corner-office-for-brett-wilson-of-tubemogul-its-all-in-the-follow-through.html?ref=business (accessed November 30, 2015); and "Guiding Principles," *TubeMogul.com*, https://www.tubemogul.com/guiding-principles/ (accessed November 30, 2015).

63. Robert Hooijberg and Frank Petrock, "On Cultural Change: Using the Competing Values Framework to Help Leaders Execute a Transformational Strategy," *Human Resource Management* 32, no. 1 (1993): 29–50.

64. Dean Foust, "Where Headhunters Fear to Tread," *BusinessWeek* (September 4, 2009): 42–44.

65. "Four Seasons Hotels and Resorts Named to FORTUNE List of the '100 Best Companies to Work For': Employees Name Company an Employer of Choice for 18th Consecutive Year," *Four Seasons Press Release* (March 5, 2015), http://press.fourseasons.com/news-releases/2015/fortune-100-best-companies-to-work-for/ (accessed January 28, 2016); and Douglas A. Ready and Emily Truelove, "The Power of Collective Ambition," *Harvard Business Review* (December 2011): 94–102.

66. Rekha Balu, "Pacific Edge Projects Itself," *Fast Company* (October 2000): 371–381.

67. Sanam Islam, "Execs See Link to Bottom Line; Gap Is Closing; More Firms Keen to Be Seen as Best Corporate Culture," *National Post* (November 19, 2008); Jeremy Kahn, "What Makes a Company Great?" *Fortune* (October 26, 1998): 218; James C. Collins and Jerry I. Porras, *Built to Last: Successful Habits of Visionary Companies* (New York: HarperBusiness, 1994); and James C. Collins, "Change Is Good—But First Know What Should Never Change," *Fortune* (May 29, 1995): 141.

68. Islam, "Execs See Link to Bottom Line."

69. Charles A. O'Reilly III, David F. Caldwell, Jennifer A. Chatman, and Bernadette Doerr, "The Promise and Problems of Organizational Culture: CEO Personality, Culture, and Firm Performance," *Group and Organization Management* 39, no. 6 (2014): 595–625.

70. Based on information in Alison Beard and Richard Hornik, "It's Hard to Be Good," *Harvard Business Review* (November 2011): 88–96; and Jon Katzenbach, Rutger von Post, and James Thomas, "The Critical Few: Components of a Truly Effective Culture," *Strategy + Business* (Spring 2014), http://www.strategy-business.com/article/00237?gko=f5031 (accessed February 1, 2016).

71. This section is based on Jeff Rosenthal and Mary Ann Masarech, "High-Performance Cultures: How Values Can Drive Business Results," *Journal of Organizational Excellence* (Spring 2003): 3–18.

72. Nelson D. Schwartz, "One Brick at a Time," *Fortune* (June 12, 2006): 45–46; and Nelson D. Schwartz, "Lego's Rebuilds Legacy," *International Herald Tribune* (September 5, 2009).

73. Evelyn M. Ruslie, "Zynga's Tough Culture Risks a Talent Drain," *The New York Times Online* (November 27, 2011), http://dealbook.nytimes.com/2011/11/27/zyngas-tough-culture-risks-a-talent-drain/ (accessed June 18, 2012); Thomas Lee, "Mark Pincus Is Back as CEO, Because No One Could Stop Him," *SFGate* (April 14, 2015), http://www.sfgate.com/business/article/Mark-Pincus-is-back-as-CEO-because-no-one-could-6197313.php (accessed November 30, 2015); and Matthew Lynley, "Mark Pincus Is Back—And His Vintage Management Style Might Be, Too," *TechCrunch* (May 16, 2015), http://techcrunch.com/2015/05/06/mark-pincus-is-back-and-his-vintage-management-style-might-be-too/ (accessed November 30, 2015).

74. This example is based on Dave Ulrich, Steve Kerr, and Ron Ashkenas, *The GE Work-Out* (New York: McGraw-Hill, 2002), pp. 238–230.

75. From Ulrich, Kerr, and Ashkenas, "GE Values," in *The GE Work-Out*, Figure 11–2.

76. Rosenthal and Masarech, "High-Performance Cultures."

77. John P. Kotter and James L. Heskett, *Corporate Culture and Performance* (New York: The Free Press, 1992); O'Reilly III et al., "The Promise and Problems of Organizational Culture"; Eric Flamholtz and Rangapriya Kannan Narasimhan, "Differential Impact of Cultural Elements on Financial Performance," *European Management Journal* 23, no. 1 (2005): 50–64. Also see J. M. Kouzes and B. Z. Posner, *The Leadership Challenge: How to Keep Getting Extraordinary Things Done in Organizations*, 3d ed. (San Francisco: Jossey-Bass, 2002).

78. Susanne Biro, "Change the Culture," *Leadership Excellence* (April 2013): 4.

79. Rosenthal and Masarech, "High-Performance Cultures"; Katzenbach et al., "The Critical Few: Components of a Truly Effective Culture"; Patrick Lencioni, "Make Your Values Mean Something," *Harvard Business Review* (July 2002): 113–117; and Thomas J. Peters and Robert H. Waterman, Jr., *In Search of Excellence* (New York: Warner, 1988).

80. Biro, "Change the Culture"; and Linda Tischler, "Kenny Moore Held a Funeral and Everyone Came," *Fast Company* (February 2004), http://www.fastcompany.com/48491/kenny-moore-held-funeral-and-everyone-came (accessed August 28, 2013).

81. Jarnagin and Slocum, "Creating Corporate Cultures Through Mythopoetic Leadership."

82. Based on S. J. Ashford et al., "Out on a Limb: The Role of Context and Impression Management in Issue Selling," *Administrative Science Quarterly* 43 (1998): 23–57; and E. W. Morrison and C. C. Phelps, "Taking Charge at Work: Extrarole Efforts to Initiate Workplace Change," *Academy of Management Journal* 42 (1999): 403–419.

83. Adapted from Kent Weber, "Gold Mine or Fool's Gold?" *Business Ethics* (January–February 2001): 18.

iStock.com/oscarhdez

Chapter 3
Managing in a Global Environment

Chapter Outline

Learning Outcomes

After studying this chapter, you should be able to:

3.1 Define *globalization* and explain how it is creating a borderless world for today's managers.

3.2 Describe a global mindset and why it has become imperative for companies operating internationally.

3.3 Discuss how the international landscape is changing, and include in your discussion the growing power of China and India.

3.4 Describe the characteristics of a multinational corporation.

3.5 Explain the bottom of the pyramid concept.

3.6 Define outsourcing and the market entry strategies of exporting and partnerships.

3.7 Indicate how dissimilarities in the sociocultural and legal–political environments throughout the world can affect business operations.

3.8 Explain the communication challenges managers face in a global environment and why it is important for managers to develop their cultural intelligence.

Are You Ready To Be a Manager?

Before reading this chapter, please circle either "Mostly True" or "Mostly False" for each of the following five statements.

1 I have an ability to understand people from other cultures and to appreciate the differences.

Mostly True ◄·····················► Mostly False

[page 91]

2 I'm good at outsourcing (getting my little sister to do my chores, for example) and partnerships, both skills important in international business.

Mostly True ◄·····················► Mostly False

[page 99]

3 I work well individually and as part of a group.

Mostly True ◄·····················► Mostly False

[pages 102–103]

4 When I am solving problems or developing plans, I can think both in short-term and long-term goals.

Mostly True ◄·····················► Mostly False

[page 103]

5 I can easily move within other cultures and adapt to different behavioral norms.

Mostly True ◄·····················► Mostly False

[page 107]

Discover your
Management Approach

Are You Ready to Work Internationally?[a]

Instructions: Are you ready to negotiate a sales contract with someone from another country? Companies large and small deal on a global basis. To what extent are you guilty of the behaviors listed here? Please answer each item as Mostly True or Mostly False for you.

Are You Typically:	Mostly True	Mostly False
1. Impatient? Do you have a short attention span? Do you want to keep moving to the next topic?	_____	_____
2. A poor listener? Are you uncomfortable with silence? Does your mind think about what you want to say next?	_____	_____
3. Argumentative? Do you enjoy arguing for its own sake?	_____	_____

To complete and score entire assessment, visit MindTap.

[a]Adapted from Cynthia Barnum and Natasha Wolniansky, "Why Americans Fail at Overseas Negotiations," *Management Review* (October 1989): 54–57.

Canada has been nicknamed the "fifty-first state of retailing" by U.S. companies because of the similarities between the two markets, and Target Corporation made its first foray into the international environment by opening 124 stores in Canada in one fell swoop in early 2013. Two years later, Target CEO Brian Cornell pulled the plug after the company had spent the equivalent of about $4 billion setting up Canadian operations. Target lost $2.5 billion in Canada over a two-year period, and managers determined the red ink couldn't be stopped for at least six more years. "Target's experience offers some valuable lessons," wrote a Fortune magazine reporter, "perhaps the overriding one being that Canada is not as simple a market as many U.S. retailers believe it to be."[1]

Target isn't the first company to learn that doing business internationally presents enormous challenges. Consider the following blunders:

- It took McDonald's more than a year to figure out that Hindus in India do not eat beef because they consider the cow sacred. The company's sales took off only after McDonald's started making burgers out of lamb to sell in India.[2]
- When IKEA launched a superstore in Bangkok, managers learned that some of its Swedish product names sound like crude terms for sex when pronounced in Thai.[3]
- In Africa, the labels on bottles show pictures of what is inside so illiterate shoppers can know what they're buying. When a baby-food company showed a picture of an infant on its label, the product didn't sell very well.[4]
- United Airlines discovered that even colors can doom a product. The airline handed out white carnations when it started flying from Hong Kong, only to discover that, to many Asians, such flowers represent death and bad luck.[5]

Some of these examples might seem humorous, but there's nothing funny about them to managers trying to operate in a highly competitive global environment. **International management** is the management of business operations conducted in more than one country. The fundamental tasks of business management do not change in any substantive way when a firm is transacting business across international borders. The basic management functions of planning, organizing, leading, and controlling are the same whether a company operates domestically or internationally.

However, managers will experience greater difficulties and risks when performing these management functions on an international scale.

The international dimension is an increasingly important part of the external environment, discussed in Chapter 2. This chapter introduces basic concepts about the global environment and international management, such as a manager's global mindset, multinational corporations (MNCs), bottom of the pyramid (BOP), and multicountry trade agreements.

3-1 A Borderless World

Every manager today needs to think globally because the whole world is a source of business threats and opportunities. Even managers who spend their entire careers working in their home-towns must be aware of the international environment and will probably interact with people from other cultures. In addition, the reality facing most managers is that isolation from international forces is no longer possible. Organizations in all fields are being reordered around the goal of addressing needs and desires that transcend national boundaries. Consider that the Federal Bureau of Investigation (FBI) now ranks international cyber crime as one of its top priorities because electronic boundaries between countries are virtually nonexistent.[6] "The whole boundary mindset has been obliterated," says John Hering, co-founder and executive chairman of Lookout, a mobile security company that has customers in 170 countries and uses a global network of more than 100 million sensors for mobile phone malware detection. "For many people, this is the only computer they have," he says. "The thought of something bad happening to your phone is untenable."[7]

3-1a Globalization

Business, just like crime, has become a unified, global field. Events, ideas, and trends that influence organizations in one country are likely to influence them in other countries as well. The "Sunny Side Up" box describes how experiments with bosslessness are occurring in companies in multiple countries.

Globalization refers to the extent to which trade and investments, information, social and cultural ideas, and political cooperation flow between countries. One result is that countries, businesses, and people become increasingly interdependent. Japan's Nissan automaker has headquarters

Sunny Side Up ⟩ Bosslessness Emerges Around the Globe

Experimenting with less hierarchy and no bosses is not limited to the United States. Different national cultures create different challenges, but a bossless organization can succeed anywhere.

• **The organization must have a strong values-driven culture.** Semco S.A. is a 3,000-employee industrial equipment manufacturer in São Paulo, Brazil. Ricardo Semler decided to establish a culture built on extreme employee participation and involvement. Employees run the show. Semco has no official structure, no human resources or IT department, not even a fixed CEO (the job rotates). Salaries are public knowledge. Employees elect managers by vote. No promotion is given without letting coworkers have their say. Subordinates anonymously evaluate managers and can vote them out of office. There is no dress code.

Employees can change work areas anytime according to their tastes and desires.

• **Bossless environments are especially effective where creativity is essential.** Yoplait, jointly owned by French dairy cooperative Sodiaal and U.S.-based General Mills, has franchises all over the world and a history of relying on self-managing teams to create and launch new flavors and products. In the United States, a group of employees called the Culinary Community of Practice translates emerging ethnic tastes and cuisines into innovative foods made available in stores.

• **Bossless environments increase customer satisfaction.** When CEO Jean-François Zobrist took over FAVI, a 600-person French company that designs and manufactures automotive components, he eliminated the traditional hierarchy. There is no personnel department, no middle management, and there are no time clocks, no employee handbooks. "I told them, 'tomorrow when you come to work, you do not work for me or for a boss. You work for your customer. I don't pay you. They do.'" FAVI hasn't been late with a customer order in 10 years. In the United States, Southwest Airlines allows baggage clerks the freedom to decide how to solve a customer's complaint on the spot, without having to say, "Wait while I consult my boss."

- **Bossless designs may reflect national culture**. Mondragon Corporation in Spain uses a cooperative form of bosslessness. Made up as a collective of many smaller enterprises, the 85,000 employees actually own and direct their respective businesses. Workers choose a managing director and retain power to make all decisions about what to produce and what to do with profits. Top members can earn no more than 6.5 times the lowest-paid member, compared to about 350 times in large U.S. corporations. When times are hard, top people at Mondragon also take the biggest reductions in pay.

SOURCES: Fiona Smith, "Could Your Office Go Lord of the Flies?" *Business Review Weekly*, April 10, 2013, http://www.brw.com.au/p/blogs/fiona_smith/could_your_office_go_lord_of_the (accessed April 10, 2013); "Going Boss-free: Utopia or 'Lord of the Flies'?" Knowledge@Wharton, August 1, 2012, http://knowledge.wharton.upenn.edu/article/going-boss-free-utopia-or-lord-of-the-flies/ (accessed September 30, 2013); Peter A. Maresco and Christopher C. York, "Ricardo Semler: Creating Organizational Change Through Employee-Empowered Leadership," Sacred Heart University, http://www.newunionism.net/library/case%20studies/SEMCO%20-%20Employee-Powered%20Leadership%20-%20Brazil%20-%202005.pdf (accessed September 30, 2013); Polly LaBarre, "What Does Fulfillment at Work Really Look Like?" *Fortune* (May 1, 2012), http://management.fortune.cnn.com/2012/05/01/happiness-at-work-fulfillment/ (accessed September 30, 2013); Richard Wolff, "Yes, There Is an Alternative to Capitalism: Mondragon Shows the Way," *The Guardian*, June 24, 2012, http://www.theguardian.com/commentisfree/2012/jun/24/alternative-capitalism-mondragon; and Giles Tremlett, "Mondragon: Spain's Giant Cooperative Where Times Are Hard but Few Go Bust," *The Guardian*, March 7, 2013, http://www.theguardian.com/world/2013/mar/07/mondragon-spains-giant-cooperative (accessed September 30, 2013).

in Yokohama, but the chief executive of its luxury Infiniti division has his office in Hong Kong. The skin, cosmetics, and personal care business of Procter & Gamble (P&G) is based in Singapore.[8] The United States is the largest market for India-based Tata Consultancy Services (TCS) and other Indian information technology (IT) firms, while the U.S. firm IBM gets most of its tech services revenue from overseas, with sales in India growing 41 percent in one recent quarter.[9]

Globalization and increasing interdependence have dramatically shifted the environment for managers, with a decreasing number of large international corporations located in the United States. *Fortune* magazine editor Alan Murray recently wrote that the world is in the early stages of a new Industrial Revolution that is based on a model where "everyone is connected, everywhere and all the time, in a vast web of interactive data."[10] Success requires building companies on a truly global scale. Exhibit 3.1 provides a glimpse of how the business environment has changed by looking at the shifting geography of the *Fortune* Global 500 companies. Note that the number of Global 500 companies in the Americas (including the United States and Canada) and Europe (including the United Kingdom, France, and Germany) has declined. The number of Global 500 companies in Asia (including China, Japan, and South Korea), in contrast, has grown from 129 in 2005 to 201 in 2015.[11]

Exhibit 3.1 The Shifting Geography of Global 500 Companies

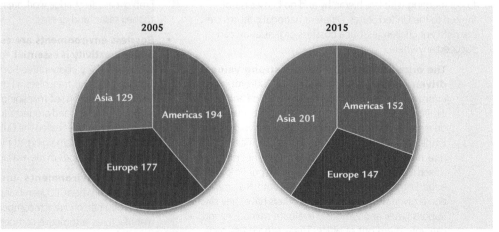

SOURCE: Based on "The New Geography of the Global 500 Companies," figure in Alan Murray, "The 21st-Century Club," *Fortune* (November 1, 2015): 9–12.

3-1b Developing a Global Mindset

Succeeding on a global level requires more than a desire to go global and a new set of skills and techniques; it requires that managers and organizations develop a *global mindset*. Managers who can help their companies develop a global perspective, such as Carlos Ghosn, the Brazilian-Lebanese-French CEO of Nissan, or Medtronic CEO Omar Ishrak, a Bangladesh native who was educated in the United Kingdom and worked in the United States for nearly two decades, are in high demand.[12] As more managers find themselves working in foreign countries or working with foreign firms within their own country, they need a mindset that enables them to navigate through ambiguities and complexities that far exceed anything they encounter within their traditional management responsibilities.[13] A **global mindset** can be defined as the ability of managers to appreciate and influence individuals, groups, organizations, and systems that represent different social, cultural, political, institutional, intellectual, and psychological characteristics.[14]

A manager with a global mindset can perceive and respond to many different perspectives at the same time rather than being stuck in a domestic mindset that sees everything from one's own cultural perspective. Reliance Industries, the largest private-sector company in India, specifically lists "global mindset" as one of the core competencies for its managers.[15] As illustrated in Exhibit 3.2, a global mindset requires skills, understanding, and competencies in three dimensions. The *cognitive dimension* means knowing about the global environment and global business, mentally understanding how cultures differ, and having the ability to interpret complex global changes. The *psychological dimension* is the emotional and affective aspect. This includes a liking for diverse ways of thinking and acting, a willingness to take risks, and the energy and self-confidence to deal with the unpredictable and uncertain. The *social dimension* concerns the ability to behave in ways that build trusting relationships with people who are different from oneself.[16] Thinking beyond borders is what the Ecuadorians who were suing Chevron had to do, as shown in this chapter's "Half-Baked Management" box.

Half-Baked Management } Chevron Ecuador

When Texaco—now Chevron—ceased oil drilling in Ecuador in 1992, it had produced enough oil to become the second largest exporter in Latin America and helped make today's Chevron the third largest U.S. corporation with annual revenues of $200 billion. During the time the company operated in Ecuador, it is alleged that it dumped 18 billion gallons of toxic waste and left hundreds of open pits of "malignant black sludge." In 1993 a group of Indigenous Ecuadorians filed a lawsuit, claiming damages to what is seen as "rain-forest Chernobyl," with high rates of disease and birth defects. Chevron claims it has no responsibility for the damage, saying Texaco's operations were "completely in line with standards of the day." The case has endured on for almost 20 years, with plaintiffs in 2013 being awarded $9.5 billion by the Ecuadorian courts (after U.S. courts said they owed $18 billion). But Chevron is fighting, spending millions of dollars on lawyers, and more millions on improving its PR image, such as images of smiling African women with the caption, "Oil companies should support the communities they're part of." The lead lawyer for Ecuador is not daunted and says this lawsuit is historic, as it is "the first time that a small developing country has had power over a multinational American company." Even so, Chevron won't give up soon. A lobbyist told Newsweek, "We can't let little countries screw around with big companies like this." Another Chevron spokesperson said, "We're going to fight this until hell freezes over—and then we'll fight it on the ice." Maybe that's why Greenpeace Switzerland gave Chevron a "Lifetime Award" for the most irresponsible business in the past 10 years. Then in 2017, Chevron tried to get the Ecuadorian Indigenous peoples to put up a bond of almost $1 million, to pay legal fees in case Chevron wins. Luckily, a judge threw that one out.

SOURCES: "Assembly of First Nations Lends Support," *Canada NewsWire*. February 6, 2017, https://search-proquest-com.proxy.library.vanderbilt.edu/central/docview/1973109246/3436 6E5705784EB5PQ/13?accountid=14816; "French President Links Economics and Security," *Telegraph-Journal*, January 2015: D3; and Patrick Radden Keefe, "Reversal of Fortune," *The New Yorker Magazine* (January 9, 2012: 38–49). (Vol.87:43), pp. 38–49.

"Being outside the United States makes you smarter about global issues. It lets you see the world through a different lens."
—JOHN RICE, VICE CHAIRMAN OF GENERAL ELECTRIC (GE), AND PRESIDENT AND CEO OF GLOBAL GROWTH AND OPERATIONS

People who have had exposure to different cultures and speak different languages develop a global mindset more easily. Global leaders often speak multiple languages and have extensive experience interacting with people different from themselves. People in the United States who have grown up without language and cultural diversity typically have more difficulties with foreign assignments, but willing managers from any country can cultivate a global mindset.

How do people expand their global mindset? Managers expand globally in two ways—by both thinking and doing.[17] Learning by thinking requires a genuine curiosity about other people and cultures, an interest in and study of world affairs and international business, and the ability to open your mind and appreciate different viewpoints. Learning by doing means cultivating relationships with people across cultural and national boundaries. Grace Hightower De Niro wanted to reach out to the people of Rwanda, to make a difference in their lives, as described in the "Recipe for Success" box.

The rise of social media has opened new opportunities for students as well as managers to create networks of relationships that cross-cultural divides. In addition, international travel, foreign study, and learning a foreign language are key activities for developing a global mindset. For example, Michael Zink, who grew up in the United States, joined the Peace Corps and went to Kenya in 1983. Then, after graduating from business school, he eagerly accepted a job working in Africa for Citigroup. Over a 27-year career with Citi, Zink has worked in Ivory Coast, Gabon, Tunisia, Russia, Australia, Indonesia, South Korea, China, and Singapore. Zink says he learned early on that global managers must immerse themselves in different environments and adapt to different ways of doing things if they want to be effective.[18] In the past, many managers who were sent on overseas assignments lived an insular lifestyle that kept them from truly becoming immersed in the foreign culture. "You can lead a true-blue German lifestyle in China," says Siegfried Russwurm, chief technology officer and a member of the managing board at Siemens AG. "You can live in a gated community with German neighbors. They will tell you where you can find a German baker and butcher."[19] Today, though, the goal for managers who want to succeed is to globalize their thinking.

Recipe for Success } Coffee of Grace

Grace Hightower DeNiro met Rwanda's president, Paul Kagame, who told her, "We need trade, not aid." She then visited the country in 2011 and was inspired by the spirit of the Rwandan people's will and spirit to succeed, and also by their culture, their generosity, and their intelligence. Rwanda's 11 million inhabitants are mostly subsistence farmers, trying to create a sustainable future. Because coffee is one of their main exports, she started the New York city-based company Coffee of Grace in 2013 that would import coffee beans, which have a unique flavor because of the amount of volcanic ash in the soil. She met with the farmers and fell more in love with the people and the community and developed a business model where the farmers were equal partners in the exchange.

Hightower DeNiro makes sure that Coffee of Grace works closely with farmers, developing relationships, supervising the growing, harvesting, and roasting. No third parties are trusted to give information back. All processes are organic and without pesticides or added chemicals. The company wants to help the farmers create livable wages and valued products, to go beyond merely invisible peasants in the food chain.

Jake Leonti is Director of Coffee for the company and he visits every one of the 80–100 farmers it works with each year.

Some of the farmers are in co-ops and some not. The company more recently started working with a small farm, a husband and wife with no one else, who have what is called a Nano-lot. In 2017, Coffee of Grace purchased their entire crop of 200 pounds of green coffee. Leonti meets each farmer, looks at the crops, inspects the beans, tastes the brewed coffee, and discusses prices and volume to purchase. After beans are shipped to the United States, they are roasted locally, under strict quality standards. Though they started in Rwanda, they have added farms in Guatemala, Peru, Costa Rica, and Columbia.

Everyone in the company is dedicated to its mission of Trade not Aid and helping local farmers around the world. And they love the business. Sales & Marketing Director Leila Benabid came from a family steeped in the coffee business. Her father sold espresso machines and her uncle is a roaster.

Coffee of Grace is proud to use Direct Trade, which means 100 percent of the money paid for the crops goes to the farmers, nothing to middlemen. Director of Operations Sandra Doussin was very inspired from the beginning with Hightower DeNiro's zeal to help the farms create a sustainable lifestyle. "Grace's passion is our role-model," she says.

SOURCES: Sandra Doussin and Leila Benabid, personal communications, March 2018.

Exhibit 3.2 Three Dimensions of Global Mindset

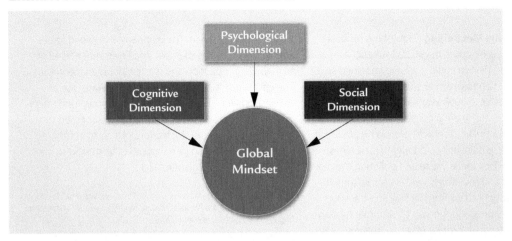

SOURCES: Based on Mansour Javidan and Jennie L. Walker, "A Whole New Global Mindset for Leadership," *People & Strategy* 35, no. 2 (2012): 36–41; and Mansour Javidan and David Bowen, "The 'Global Mindset' of Managers: What It Is, Why It Matters, and How To Develop It," *Organizational Dynamics* 42 (2013): 145–155.

Remember This

- The basic management functions are the same in either a domestic or an international subsidiary, but managers will experience greater difficulties and risks when performing these functions internationally.
- **International management** means managing business operations in more than one country.
- Today's companies and managers operate in a borderless world that provides both risks and opportunities.
- **Globalization** refers to the extent to which trade and investments, information, ideas, and political cooperation flow between countries.
- To succeed on a global level requires managers at all levels to have a **global mindset**, which is the ability to appreciate and influence individuals, groups, organizations, and systems that represent different social, cultural, political, institutional, intellectual, and psychological characteristics.

3-2 The Changing International Landscape

Many companies today are going straight to China or India as a first step into international business. At the same time, companies in these countries are growing rapidly as providers of both products and services to the United States, Canada, Europe, and other developed nations. China had only 16 companies on the *Fortune* Global 500 in 2005, but that number had shot up to 98 by 2015.[20]

3-2a China, Inc.

For the past several years, foreign companies have invested more in business in China than they spent anywhere else in the world. A market that was of little interest a decade ago has become the one place that nearly every manager is thinking about. With the fastest-growing middle class in history, China is the largest or second-largest market for a variety of products and services, including mobile phones, automobiles, consumer electronics, luxury goods, and Internet use.[21]

When Bentonville Met Beijing Establishing his business in Bentonville, Arkansas, in 1962, all-American entrepreneur Sam Walton could not have imagined an eventual expansion to over 430 stores and 7,000 local suppliers in China. In 2008, Walmart's CEO publicly addressed environmental concerns in China and put Walmart's vast resources behind his pledge to make sustainability a priority in the Chinese market. To address waste and pollution, Walmart trained and monitored workers across the Chinese supply chain, from factory and transport to retail stores, and then set environmental standards as a *requirement* for other companies to do business with Walmart. The company also joined forces with China's Institute of Public and Environmental Affairs to map water pollution and wastewater management. The efforts resulted in dramatic drops in water use at many supplier factories. To address mounting food safety concerns among the Chinese, Walmart established the Direct Farm Program, which offers local farmers higher incomes for providing safe supplies of fresh food to consumers through the giant retailer.

SOURCES: Orville Schell, "How Walmart Is Changing China—and Vice Versa," *The Atlantic* (December 2011): 80–98; and "Walmart China Fact Sheet," http://www.wal-martchina.com /english/walmart/ (accessed February 17, 2016).

In 2010, top managers of U.S.-based Ford Motor Company announced an ambitious $5 billion plan for China, and by 2015 the company had doubled its share of China's auto market. Ford was late getting into China, and despite some success, managers are looking for new ways to grow. One recent plan is to invest nearly $2 billion in research for a new generation of smartcars for the Chinese market.[22] The shift toward putting China at the center of decision making is reflected in a change in meeting times at the U.S. headquarters. "We get up really early, we stay really late," said Mark Fields, Ford's current CEO, referring to the practice of holding meetings early in the morning or late in the evening to accommodate managers in China, who are 12 hours ahead.[23]

However, doing business in China has never been smooth, and it appears to be getting even tougher. New regulations and government policies are making life hard for foreign companies in all industries. The Coca-Cola Company is training managers at its 40 bottling plants so they can double as public relations ambassadors. Managers in China are encouraged to build relationships with local food-safety regulators and other local officials. Walmart is adding social media staff to spot brewing online controversies in its China business.[24] For Internet companies such as Facebook, Twitter, eBay, and Google, China has sometimes seemed like more a source of trouble and frustration than of new customers.[25] Google closed its Chinese site, Google.cn, in early 2010 because of government restrictions and censorship, although the company later renewed its license to provide limited services in China. Some multinational firms doing business with Chinese organizations, particularly with big state-owned companies, have also had problems getting payments on their contracts. "A contract is not an unchangeable bible for Chinese companies," said Beijing-based lawyer Jingzhou Tao. Chinese managers frequently withhold payments as a tactic in price negotiations. Part of the reason is that these organizations are not just companies but also political entities. But another reason involves cultural differences. "Chinese culture will build a relationship before the contract," said Arthur Bowring, managing director of the Hong Kong Shipowners Association. "The relationship is always something that can be talked about. The contract is just a set of papers that you keep in your bottom drawer."[26]

Despite the problems, China is a market that foreign managers can't afford to ignore. Executives at heavy construction equipment maker Caterpillar say that unless the company can win in China, it risks losing its status as the industry's biggest player. Yet China's fast-growing machinery makers have already begun stealing market share.[27] Competition from domestic companies in other industries is also growing fast. In some industries, local companies have already become market leaders. Consider what has happened in the market for smartphones.

Companies such as Xiaomi and Shenzhen-based ZTE are now actively expanding beyond China's borders. Xiaomi is investing heavily in India, and ZTE has announced plans to double its share of the U.S. market in three years. For years, Chinese phone makers worked primarily as suppliers for

Sunny Side Up ⟩ Xiaomi

Apple and Samsung are the global leaders in mobile phones, and managers in both companies would love to capture the world's largest smartphone market. The trouble is, as demand in China grew, a multitude of local companies sprang up and quickly took over the market. In 2011 just 2 of the top 10 smartphone makers in China were Chinese (Huawei and Lenovo). Three years later, 8 of the top 10 smartphone makers in China were Chinese (Apple and Samsung were the only foreign holdouts), and 6 of the top 10 smartphone brands worldwide were Chinese.

Xiaomi, which ended 2014 as the top smartphone maker in China, was founded in Beijing in 2010 by entrepreneur Lei Jun, who began studying the smartphone business in the early 2000s. He carried a dozen or so phones around in his backpack and studied every detail of their design and operation. Jun was convinced that there was an opportunity to produce stylish, innovative phones at lower cost. Xiaomi's first phone went on sale in October 2011 for the equivalent of $330. The Chinese press often refers to Xiaomi as "the Apple of China" because of the rush of excitement that accompanies each new phone release. In January 2015, for example, the first shipment of Xiaomi's $370 Mi Note, the company's competitor to the $975 iPhone 6 Plus, sold out in three minutes.[28]

companies such as Nokia and others that outsourced manufacturing to lower-wage countries. Now, however, they are racing "to become the next Nokia of the '90s: affordable, high tech, global."[29]

One Chinese company that has rapidly become a global leader is Lenovo, which bought IBM's personal computer business, including the ThinkPad brand, in 2005. Lenovo is the world's largest PC maker and the third-largest smartphone maker, behind Samsung and Apple.[30] With its emphasis on quality (its PCs and laptops rank tops for reliability), Lenovo is redefining the perception of the phrase "made in China." Moreover, it is redefining the meaning of a Chinese company by blending the best of Eastern philosophy and culture with the best of Western business and management thinking. The company has headquarters in Beijing, but CEO Yang Yuanqing, who started as a salesperson and once delivered computers by bicycle, spends a third of his time at Lenovo's offices in Raleigh, North Carolina. Lenovo's top managers, once almost all Chinese with no international experience, now come from 14 different nations and live and work in six different cities.[31]

3-2b India, The Service Giant

India, second only to China in population, has taken a different path toward economic development. Whereas China is strong in manufacturing, India is a rising power in software design, services, and precision engineering. Numerous companies see India as a major source of technological and scientific brainpower, and the country's large English-speaking population makes it a natural for U.S. companies wanting to outsource services. India is the industry leader in IT (Information Technology) outsourcing, for example.[32] In addition, numerous multinational corporations, including Unilever, Expedia, Panasonic, and Ricoh, have established more than 1,000 research and development (R&D) centers in India to take advantage of highly skilled talent.[33] At least five Chinese handset manufacturers have said they plan to establish R&D centers in India.[34] Some of the fastest-growing industries in India are pharmaceuticals, medical devices, and diagnostics. Mitra Biotech, a start-up company with locations in Boston and Bangalore, India, is applying data analytics to rethink conventional cancer therapies. The company uses technology that re-creates an artificial environment for a patient's tumor sample and tests various drugs on it directly, enabling a physician to come up with

Zhang Peng/LightRocket/Getty Images

Concept Connection

Managers try to make sure their organizations benefit from the opportunities brought about by a **changing international landscape**. Unilever, which has headquarters in Rotterdam, Netherlands, and in London, has long struggled to gain a foothold in China. In 2015, the company established a partnership with JD.com, China's largest online direct sales company, that will enable Unilever to bypass some red tape and directly import its products into China. Unilever has also opened an R&D center in Shanghai to "deliver even bigger 'Made in China' innovations and faster roll-outs to Unilever's key growth markets around the world."

an optimal personalized treatment plan in less than a week.[35] Mitra has partnerships with several Indian hospitals, as well as with Cancer Treatment Centers of America.[36] India has a large number of highly trained scientists, doctors, and researchers, and U.S. pharmaceutical and health care firms, such as Abbott Laboratories and Bristol-Myers Squibb, have opened R&D centers there. India is also a growing manufacturer of pharmaceuticals and is the world's largest exporter of generic drugs. By 2020, India's pharmaceuticals industry will likely be a global leader, according to a report by PricewaterhouseCoopers (PwC).[37]

Remember This

- Many companies are going straight to China or India as a first step into international business.

- China is strong in manufacturing, whereas India is a major provider of services.

- The Chinese company Lenovo has emerged as the country's first global corporation, with managers coming from 14 different nations, living and working in six cities on three continents.

- Managers also look to China and India as sources of lower-cost technological and scientific brainpower.

3-3 Multinational Corporations

A large volume of international business is being carried out by large international businesses that can be thought of as *global corporations, stateless corporations,* or *transnational corporations.* In the business world, these large international firms typically are called *multinational corporations (MNCs),* and they have been the subject of enormous attention. In the past 40 years, both the number and the influence of MNCs have grown dramatically. MNCs can move a wealth of assets from country to country and influence national economies, politics, and cultures.

Agence France Presse /Douglas E. Curran/Hulton Archive/Getty Images

Concept Connection

The Maharaja Mac and Vegetable Burger served at this McDonald's in New Delhi, India, represent how this **multinational corporation (MNC)** changed its business model by decentralizing its operations. When McDonald's initiated international units, it copied what it did and sold in the United States. Today, however, the fast-food giant seeks local managers who understand the culture and laws of each country. Country managers have the freedom to use different furnishings and develop new products to suit local tastes.

3-3a Characteristics of Multinational Corporations

Although the term has no precise definition, a **multinational corporation (MNC)** typically receives more than 25 percent of its total sales revenues from operations outside the parent's home country. During the recent economic slump, the percentage of revenue from foreign operations increased for many multinationals because of stronger sales in developing markets such as China and India. An MNC also has the following distinctive managerial characteristics:

1. An MNC is managed as an integrated worldwide business system in which foreign affiliates act in close alliance and cooperation with one another. Capital, technology, and people are transferred among country affiliates. The MNC can acquire materials and manufacture parts wherever in the world it is most advantageous to do so.

2. An MNC is ultimately controlled by a single management authority that makes key strategic decisions relating to the parent and all affiliates. Although some headquarters are *binational,* such as the Royal Dutch/Shell Group, some centralization of management is required to maintain worldwide integration and profit maximization for the enterprise as a whole.

3. MNC top managers are presumed to exercise a global perspective. They regard the entire world as one market for strategic decisions, resource acquisition, and location of production, advertising, and marketing efficiency.

In a few cases, the MNC management philosophy may differ from that just described. For example, some researchers have distinguished among *ethnocentric* companies, which place emphasis on their home countries; *polycentric companies*, which are oriented toward the markets of individual foreign host countries; and *geocentric companies*, which are truly world-oriented and favor no specific country.[38] The truly global companies that transcend national boundaries are growing in number. These companies no longer see themselves as American, Chinese, or German; they operate globally and serve a global market. Nestlé SA provides a good example. The company gets most of its sales from outside its "home" country of Switzerland, more than half of the company's managers are non-Swiss, and its 333,000 employees are spread all over the world. Nestlé has hundreds of brands and has production facilities or other operations in almost every country in the world.[39]

3-3b Serving the Bottom of the Pyramid

Large multinational organizations are accused of many negative contributions to society, but they also have the resources needed to do good things in the world. One approach that combines business with social responsibility is referred to as *serving the bottom of the pyramid*.

The **bottom of the pyramid (BOP) concept** proposes that corporations can alleviate poverty and other social ills, as well as make significant profits, by selling to the world's poorest people. The term *bottom of the pyramid* refers to the more than 4 billion people who make up the lowest level of the world's economic "pyramid," as defined by per-capita income. These people earn less than US$1,500 a year, with about one-fourth of them earning less than a dollar a day.[40] Traditionally, these people haven't been served by most large businesses because products and services are too expensive, are inaccessible, and are not suited to

AP Images/Pavel Rahman

Concept Connection

New York investment banker and Bangladesh native Iqbal Quadir knew his impoverished homeland was one of the least connected places on Earth. That prompted him to collaborate with countryman Muhammad Yunus, Grameen Bank founder and 2006 Nobel Peace Prize winner, to create Village Phone, a program in line with the **bottom of the pyramid (BOP) concept**. Entrepreneurs (mostly women) use Grameen Bank microloans to purchase cell phones. "Telephone ladies," such as Monwara Begum (pictured here), then earn the money needed to repay the debt by providing phone service to fellow villagers.

Recipe for Success ⎬ Godrej & Boyce

By one estimate, a third of India's food is lost to spoilage, but in 2007, refrigerator market penetration was just 18 percent. Many lower-income people couldn't afford even a basic refrigerator. Another problem, particularly in rural areas, was that electric service was usually unreliable. Godrej & Boyce managers decided it was time to do something about this.

"As a company that made refrigerators for more than 50 years, we asked ourselves why it was that refrigerator penetration was just 18 percent," said G. Sunderraman, vice president of corporate development. The first major insight was that many people not only couldn't afford a refrigerator, but they didn't *need* a large refrigerator that took up too much space in a small house and used a lot of electricity. What they needed was the chotuKool ("The Little Cool"), an innovative appliance introduced by Godrej & Boyce in 2010. The chotuKool, a mini-fridge designed to cool five or six bottles of water and store a few pounds of food, was portable, ran on batteries, and sold for about 3,250 rupees (US$69), about 35 percent less than the cheapest refrigerator on the market.

To sell the new product, Godrej & Boyce trained rural villagers as salespeople. The villagers earn a commission of about US$3 for each refrigerator sold, and the system reduces Godrej's distribution costs. When asked how many chotuKools the company expected to sell, George Menezes, COO of Godrej Appliances, said, "In three years, probably millions." Godrej & Boyce managers spend a lot of time working directly with consumers and are now testing ideas for other low-cost products aimed at rural markets. "Currently, the rural market accounts for only 10 percent, but it is all set to expand in a huge way," said Menezes.[41]

their needs; therefore, in many countries, the poor end up paying significantly more than their wealthier counterparts for some basic needs.

A number of leading companies are changing that by adopting BOP business models geared to serving the poorest of the world's consumers. Consider this example from India's Godrej & Boyce.

U.S. companies are getting in on the BOP act too. S.C. Johnson Company has partnered with youth groups in a Nairobi slum since 2005 to create a community-based waste management and cleaning company that provides home cleaning, insect treatment, and waste disposal services for residents.[42] General Electric worked with doctors and nurses in the field to develop an affordable baby warmer for India's small, private hospitals.[43] P&G researchers are visiting homes in China, Brazil, India, and other developing countries to see how the company can come up with entirely new products and services for consumers living at the bottom of the pyramid. However, P&G is late getting into marketing to the poor. Rival Unilever, for instance, introduced Lifebuoy soap to India more than a century ago, promoting it as the enemy of dirt and disease.[44] Unilever gets about 58 percent of its sales from developing markets, up from just 20 percent in 1990.[45] "P&G is still very U.S.-centric," says Unilever's CEO, Paul Polman, a Dutchman who is a P&G veteran. "Emerging markets are in the DNA of our company." To try to catch up, P&G's CEO is focusing employees on the mission of "touching and improving more lives, in more parts of the world, more completely." When people feel they are changing lives, "it's almost like you don't have to pay us to do this," said one R&D scientist.[46] Proponents of BOP thinking believe multinational firms can contribute to positive lasting change when the profit motive goes hand in hand with the desire to make a contribution to humankind as TechSharks does, shown in the "Sunny Side Up" box.

Sunny Side Up } Social Entrepreneurship

At age 28, Ahmad Reza Zahedi started TechSharks, a Web site design business, the fulfillment of a longtime dream after falling in love with computing as a teen, something common among tech entrepreneurs. The best gift he ever got was from his older brother who got him a book about learning the computer language Pascal, and he couldn't stop reading it. When he first started TechSharks, Zahedi had to educate his clients about the difference between e-mails and Web sites, between hosting and domains. In 2011, he almost broke even and then doubled his revenue, to $50,000, in 2012. Not sound like much? Consider that Zahedi operates out of Kabul, in a system constantly battling against the Taliban, in a place where the war destroyed the educational system, where adult literacy is 25 percent and one of the world's poorest countries with annual GDP at $600 per capita.

Zahedi is part of a worldwide movement of people using business, nonprofits, and technology to create a better, more sustainable world built on peace and justice, and studies confirm that more money is being channeled into such organizations. One of the earliest and largest ventures in this area is Ashoka, started in 1980 by Bill Drayton, who set his sights on identifying leaders around the planet to help them address local problems through helping with leadership skills, resources, and ideas, so they could become capable ethical change-makers. Back in the 80s Drayon started by identifying change agents in various countries such as Brazil, India, and Indonesia. He looked for people who went beyond the political activism role and were using innovative ideas and building

structures to solve important issues, such as poverty elimination (like Grameen Bank), health care, educational models, or ingenious ideas to improve the environment. Ashoka funds these people and gives them the title of Fellow.

Since then, other organizations are doing similar work. Skoll Foundation funds projects and operates on the principle that "social entrepreneurs excel at togetherness" and that they pursue their goals in a communal way. Echoing Green supports early-stage social entrepreneurs and organizes itself around a core idea that resonates in the whole field: "Social entrepreneurship [has an] inherently hopeful message of individual engagement and efficacy."

Perhaps because of the explosion of refugees around the world, more organizations have been created. Yara Said was a young girl when she first heard the word "war" in her native Syria. Now in Amsterdam, she helps artists create work, has built a company that sells the art, and works hard to build artist networks. After Amnesty International commissioned her group to design a refugee flag, her work went viral. Said traces her good fortune back to being in a refugee camp and being offered the chance by Fleur Bakker to move to Amsterdam and work in social enterprise. "I never went back to the camp," says the award-winning 20-something. She embodies the potential of refugees everywhere.

SOURCES: Meabh Mahon, "A Space for Refugees," *Stanford Social Innovation Review* 16, no. 2 (Spring 2018): 13–14; and Stephen Mckay et al., *The Marketization of Charities in England and Wales* 26, no. 1 (2015): 336–54.

Remember This

- A **multinational corporation (MNC)** is an organization that receives more than 25 percent of its total sales revenues from operations outside the parent company's home country and has a number of distinctive managerial characteristics.

- Nestlé SA is a good example of a multinational corporation.

- Some researchers distinguish among *ethnocentric companies*, which place emphasis on their home countries; *polycentric companies*, which are oriented toward the markets of individual host countries; and *geocentric companies*, which are truly world-oriented.

- Multinational corporations have the resources to reach and serve the world's poorest people who cannot afford the typical products and services offered by big companies.

- The **bottom of the pyramid (BOP) concept** proposes that corporations can alleviate poverty and other social ills, as well as make significant profits, by selling to the world's poor.

- Godrej & Boyce created an innovative battery-powered refrigerator called the chotuKool for rural markets in India.

3-4 Getting Started Internationally

Organizations have a couple of ways to become involved internationally. One is to seek cheaper resources, such as materials or labor, offshore, which is called *offshoring* or *global outsourcing*. Another is to develop markets for finished products or services outside their home countries through strategies such as exporting and partnerships. Exhibit 3.3 shows three approaches that companies often use to engage in the international arena, either to acquire resources or to enter new markets.

- **Exporting.** Many companies first get involved internationally by exporting. With **exporting**, the company maintains its production facilities within the home nation and transfers its products for sale in foreign countries. Exporting enables a company to market its products in other countries at modest resource cost and with limited risk. Exporting does entail numerous problems based on physical distances, government regulations, foreign currencies, and cultural differences, but it is less expensive than committing the firm's own capital to build plants in host countries.

- **Outsourcing.** **Global outsourcing**, also called *offshoring*, means engaging in the international division of labor so that work activities can be done in countries with the cheapest sources of labor and supplies. Millions of low-level jobs, such as textile manufacturing, call center operations, and credit card processing, have been outsourced to low-wage countries in recent years. The Internet and plunging telecommunications costs have enabled companies to outsource more and higher-level work as well, such as software development, accounting, and medical services.

- **Partnerships.** Partnerships represent a higher level of involvement in international trade. One popular type of partnership is a joint venture. In a **joint venture**, a company shares costs and risks with another firm, typically in the host country, to develop new products, build a manufacturing facility, or set up a sales and distribution network.[47] A partnership is often the fastest, cheapest, and least

RosaIreneBetancourt 14/Alamy Stock Photo

Concept Connection

Tony the Tiger, who has been advertising Kellogg's Frosted Flakes since 1951, joined managers in announcing a **joint venture** between U.S.-based Kellogg Company and Singapore-based Wilmar International Limited for the manufacture, sale, and distribution of breakfast cereals and snacks in China. Kellogg brings deep expertise in cereal and snacks and a portfolio of globally recognized brands. Wilmar contributes infrastructure, an extensive sales and distribution network in China, and knowledge of the local market. The joint venture company has its headquarters in Shanghai.

Exhibit 3.3 **Three Strategies for Entering the International Arena**

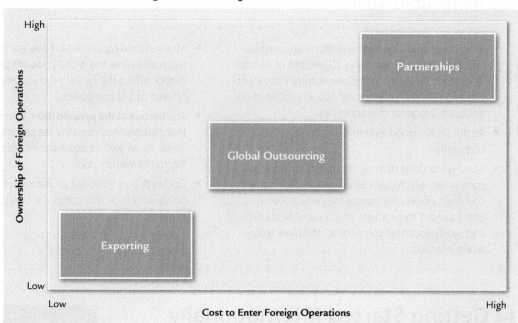

risky way to get into the global game. In addition to joint ventures, the complexity of today's global business environment is spurring managers at many companies to develop alliance networks, which are collections of partnerships with various other firms, often across international boundaries.[48]

Companies may use any or all of these approaches to get started or to grow internationally. Joint ventures have been an effective partnership approach to international expansion for Starbucks.

Recipe for Success ⎱ **Starbucks**

Howard Schultz, CEO of Starbucks, looks forward to "a day in the not-too-distant future when India takes its place alongside China as one of our two largest markets outside North America." Starbucks has had great success expanding in China with partnerships, and managers are using the same approach in India.

Because local cultures vary widely in China, Starbucks established partnerships with three different companies, working with Beijing Mei Da coffee company in the north, with Taiwan-based Uni-President in the east, and with Hong Kong–based Maxim's Caterers in the south. The first Starbucks opened in Beijing in 1999, and by 2015 there were well over 1,000 company-operated Starbucks stores and nearly 800 licensed stores in China. In India, Starbucks has entered into a joint venture with Tata Global Beverages Unlimited, a division of the largest business group in India. By mid-2015, Tata Starbucks Limited had nearly 80 stores and was growing rapidly.

Starbucks relies on local partners to help overcome the many legal and logistical problems associated with operating in another country, as well as to get store design and product offerings right. Stores in India, for example, have tandoori paneer rolls and cardamom-flavored croissants on the menu. A unique aspect of the joint venture with Tata in India is that Starbucks can obtain and roast coffee beans locally. Tata owns both large coffee farms and roasting facilities, so Starbucks and Tata worked together to develop an espresso roast designed specifically for India. "We created a unique blend for India, and it's not roasted by our team, which is something we had never done before," Schultz said. Starbucks has been able to grow and prosper in two rapidly growing international markets by establishing trusting relationships with carefully chosen local partners.[49]

Remember This

- Two major alternatives for engaging in the international arena are to seek cheaper resources via outsourcing and to develop markets outside the home country.

- **Global outsourcing**, sometimes called *offshoring*, means engaging in the international division of labor so as to obtain the cheapest sources of labor and supplies, regardless of country.

- **Exporting** is a market-entry strategy in which a company maintains production facilities within its

home country and transfers products for sale in foreign countries.

- With a **joint venture**, an organization shares costs and risks with another firm in a foreign country to build a facility, develop new products, or set up a sales and distribution network.

- Starbucks has used joint ventures to expand in China and India.

3-5 Legal–Political Challenges

Differing laws and regulations make doing business a challenge for international firms. Host governments have myriad laws concerning libel statutes, consumer protection, information and labeling, employment and safety, and wages. International managers must learn these rules and regulations and abide by them. In addition, managers must deal with unfamiliar political systems when they go international, as well as with increased government supervision and regulation. Government officials and the general public often view foreign companies as outsiders (or even intruders) and are suspicious of their impact on economic independence and political sovereignty.

Political risk is defined as the risk of loss of assets, earning power, or managerial control due to politically based events or actions by host governments. Although many developing countries today welcome and support foreign firms, political risk is a major concern for international companies, which face a broader and more complex array of threats than ever.[50] In Indonesia, state-owned PT Telekomunikasi Indonesia Tbk. (Telkom) dealt a blow to Netflix's newly launched operations in that country when it banned the U.S.-based firm's video streaming service. Telkom said Netflix didn't have the proper permit to operate as a content provider. Telkom, along with the Indonesian Film Censorship Board and others, has also objected to violent and adult content on Netflix. Citing a law stating that all films should be approved by Indonesia's censor board, Arif Prabowo, Telkom's vice president for corporate communications, said "Netflix's content should adjust to regulations in Indonesia."[51]

Another frequently cited problem for international companies is **political instability**, which includes riots, revolutions, civil disorders, and frequent changes in government. Political turmoil in Syria, for example, which has occurred off and on ever since the country came into existence following its independence from France in 1946, re-ignited as part of the Arab Spring, a revolutionary wave of protests in the Arab world that began in late 2010. By 2013, Syria was embroiled in a bloody civil war, and by 2016 more than 4 million refugees had left the country, many to neighboring countries such as Turkey, Jordan, and Egypt, and others fleeing to Europe. The overwhelming numbers of refugees created a crisis for those countries. The wave of protests in the Arab region, which affected not only Syria, but also Tunisia, Egypt, Libya, Yemen, and Bahrain, has created a tumultuous environment for businesses operating in the region. "No president, no government, no police," said Jalila Mezni, owner of Société d'Articles Hygiéniques in Tunisia. "Only complete disorder."[52] Political

Goh Chai Hin/AFP/Getty Images

Concept Connection

Amway, the U.S.-based network marketing company, spent years patiently negotiating China's **legal–political environment**. In 1998, the Chinese government closed down Amway operations in China because it suspected that the company was either an illegal pyramid scheme or a sinister cult. Amway survived by cultivating relationships with government officials and by departing from its business model. For example, it opened more than 200 retail stores like this one to demonstrate its commitment. In 2006, the Chinese government once again allowed Amway to sell directly to consumers, and the company now earns billions in annual revenue in China.

risk and political instability remain elevated throughout the Arab world, causing problems for both local and foreign organizations. For example, the Syrian Electronic Army (SEA), a group of progovernment computer hackers, disrupted several Western Web sites, including Twitter, *The Washington Post*, and *The New York Times*, which went down twice within a period of two weeks.[53] Zaid Qadoumi, the CEO of Canada's BroadGrain, which has been delivering agricultural commodities to emerging markets and political hot spots since the company was founded, offered extra pay for a crew to deliver a load of wheat to Libya, but advised workers to "cut the ropes and leave" if they believed the situation was too dangerous.[54]

Remember This

- Complicated legal and political forces can create huge risks for international managers and organizations.
- **Political risk** refers to a company's risk of loss of assets, earning power, or managerial control due to politically based events or actions by host governments.
- **Political instability** includes events such as riots, revolutions, or government upheavals that can affect the operations of an international company.

- A revolutionary wave of protests in the Arab world that began in late 2010, known as the *Arab Spring*, has created a tumultuous environment for businesses operating in the region. Millions of refugees fleeing the civil war in Syria have created a crisis in Middle Eastern and European countries.
- Managers must understand and follow the differing laws and regulations in the various countries where they do business.

3-6 Sociocultural Challenges

A nation's culture includes the shared knowledge, beliefs, and values, as well as the common modes of behavior and ways of thinking, among members of a society. Cultural factors sometimes can be more perplexing than political and economic factors when working or living in a foreign country.

3-6a Social Values

Many managers fail to realize that the values and behaviors that typically govern how business is done in their own country don't always translate to the rest of the world. U.S. managers in particular are regularly accused of an ethnocentric attitude that assumes their way is the best way. **Ethnocentrism** refers to a natural tendency of people to regard their own culture as superior and to downgrade or dismiss other cultural values. Ethnocentrism can be found in all countries, and strong ethnocentric attitudes within a country make it difficult for foreign firms to operate there.

One way that managers can fight their own ethnocentric tendencies is to understand and appreciate differences in social values.

Hofstede's Value Dimensions   In research that included 116,000 IBM employees in 40 countries, Dutch scientist Geert Hofstede identified four dimensions of national value systems that influence organizational and employee working relationships.[55] Examples of how countries rate on the four dimensions are shown in Exhibit 3.4.

1. *Power distance.* High **power distance** means that people accept inequality in power among institutions, organizations, and people. Low power distance means that people expect equality in power. Countries that value high power distance include Malaysia, India, and the Philippines. Countries that value low power distance include Denmark, Israel, and New Zealand.

Exhibit 3.4 Rank Orderings of Ten Countries Along Four Dimensions of National Value Systems

Country	Power Distance[a]	Uncertainty Avoidance[b]	Individualism[c]	Masculinity[d]
Australia	7	7	2	5
Costa Rica	8 (tie)	2 (tie)	10	9
France	3	2 (tie)	4	7
West Germany	8 (tie)	5	5	3
India	2	9	6	6
Japan	5	1	7	1
Mexico	1	4	8	2
Sweden	10	10	3	10
Thailand	4	6	9	8
United States	6	8	1	4

[a] 1 = Highest power distance
10 = Lowest power distance
[c] 1 = Highest individualism
10 = Lowest individualism

[b] 1 = Highest uncertainty avoidance
10 = Lowest uncertainty avoidance
[d] 1 = Highest masculinity
10 = Lowest masculinity

SOURCES: Dorothy Marcic, *Organizational Behavior and Cases*, 4th ed. (St. Paul, MN: West, 1995). Based on two books by Geert Hofstede: *Culture's Consequences* (London: Sage Publications, 1984) and *Cultures and Organizations: Software of the Mind* (New York: McGraw-Hill, 1991).

2. *Uncertainty avoidance.* High **uncertainty avoidance** means that members of a society feel uncomfortable with uncertainty and ambiguity and thus support beliefs that promise certainty and conformity. Low uncertainty avoidance means that people have great tolerance for the unstructured, the unclear, and the unpredictable. High uncertainty avoidance countries include Greece, Portugal, and Uruguay. Countries with low uncertainty avoidance values include Sweden, Singapore, and Jamaica.

3. *Individualism and collectivism.* **Individualism** reflects a value for a loosely knit social framework in which individuals are expected to take care of themselves. **Collectivism** means a preference for a tightly knit social framework in which individuals look after one another and organizations protect their members' interests. Countries with individualist values include the United States, Canada, and Great Britain. Countries with collectivist values include China, Mexico, and Brazil.

4. *Masculinity–femininity.* **Masculinity** stands for preference for achievement, heroism, assertiveness, work centrality (with resultant high stress), and material success. **Femininity** reflects the values of relationships, cooperation, group decision making, and quality of life. Societies with strong masculine values include Japan, Germany, Italy, and Mexico. Countries with feminine values include Sweden, Costa Rica, Norway, and France. Both men and women subscribe to the dominant value in masculine and feminine cultures.

Hofstede and his colleagues later identified a fifth dimension: long-term orientation versus short-term orientation. **Long-term orientation**, found in China and other Asian countries, includes a greater concern for the future and highly values thrift and perseverance. A **short-term orientation**, found in Russia and West Africa, is more concerned with the past and the present and places a high value on tradition and meeting social obligations.[56] Researchers continue to explore and expand on Hofstede's findings.[57] For example, in the last 30 years, more than 1,400 articles and numerous books were published on individualism and collectivism alone.[58]

GLOBE Project Value Dimensions   Recent research by the Global Leadership and Organizational Behavior Effectiveness (GLOBE) Project extends Hofstede's assessment and offers a broader understanding for today's managers. The GLOBE Project used data collected from 18,000 managers in 62 countries to identify nine dimensions that explain cultural differences. In addition to the ones identified by Hofstede, the GLOBE project identifies the following characteristics:[59]

> "Because management deals with the integration of people in a common venture, it is deeply embedded in culture. What managers do in Germany, in the United Kingdom, in the United States, in Japan, or in Brazil is exactly the same. How they do it may be quite different."
> —PETER DRUCKER, MANAGEMENT EXPERT

1. *Assertiveness.* A high value on assertiveness means that a society encourages toughness, assertiveness, and competitiveness. Low assertiveness means that people value tenderness and concern for others over being competitive.

2. *Future orientation.* Similar to Hofstede's time orientation, this dimension refers to the extent to which a society encourages and rewards planning for the future over short-term results and quick gratification.

3. *Gender differentiation.* This dimension refers to the extent to which a society maximizes gender role differences. In countries with low gender differentiation, such as Denmark, women typically have a high status and play a large role in decision making. Countries with high gender differentiation accord men higher social, political, and economic status.

4. *Performance orientation.* A society with a high performance orientation places great emphasis on performance and rewards people for performance improvements and excellence. A low performance orientation means that people pay less attention to performance and more attention to loyalty, belonging, and background.

5. *Humane orientation.* The final dimension refers to the degree to which a society encourages and rewards people for being fair, altruistic, generous, and caring. A country high on humane orientation places great value on helping others and being kind. A country low on this orientation expects people to take care of themselves. Self-enhancement and gratification have high importance.

Exhibit 3.5 gives examples of how some countries rank on these GLOBE dimensions. These dimensions give managers an added tool for identifying and managing cultural differences. Social values greatly influence organizational functioning and management styles. Consider the difficulty that Emerson Electric managers had when Emerson opened a new manufacturing facility in Suzhou, China. One area in which the U.S. view and the Chinese view differed widely was in terms of time orientation. The U.S. managers favored a short time horizon and quick results, and they viewed their assignments as stepping stones to future career advancement. The Chinese managers, on the other hand, favored a long-term approach, building a system, and setting a proper course of action to enable long-term success.[60] Other companies have encountered similar cultural differences. Consider the U.S. concept of self-directed teams, which emphasizes shared power and authority, with team members working on a variety of problems without formal guidelines, rules, and structure. Managers trying to implement teams have had trouble in areas where cultural values support high power distance and a low tolerance for uncertainty, such as Mexico. Many workers in Mexico, as well as in France and Mediterranean countries, expect organizations to be hierarchical. In Russia, people are good at working in groups and like competing as a team rather than on an individual basis. Organizations in Germany and other central European countries typically strive to be impersonal, well-oiled machines. Effective management styles differ in each country, depending on cultural characteristics.[61]

3-6b **Communication Challenges**

We all know that miscommunication can occur even among close friends, coworkers, or family members, so it is no wonder that the potential for miscommunication dramatically increases when managers are interacting with people from different countries and varied cultural backgrounds. In organizations where everyone shares the same culture, a great deal of successful communication can take place implicitly. **Implicit communication** means that people send and receive unspoken

Exhibit 3.5 **Examples of Country Rankings on Selected GLOBE Value Dimensions**

Dimension	Low	Medium	High
Assertiveness	Sweden Switzerland Japan	Egypt Iceland France	Spain United States Germany
Future orientation	Russia Italy Kuwait	Slovenia Australia India	Denmark Canada Singapore
Gender differentiation	Sweden Denmark Poland	Italy Brazil Netherlands	South Korea Egypt China
Performance orientation	Russia Greece Venezuela	Israel England Japan	United States Taiwan Hong Kong
Humane orientation	Germany France Singapore	New Zealand Sweden United States	Indonesia Egypt Iceland

SOURCE: Mansour Javidan and Robert J. House, "Cultural Acumen for the Global Manager: Lessons from Project GLOBE," *Organizational Dynamics* 29, no. 4 (2001): 289–305.

Remember This

- Managers working internationally should guard against **ethnocentrism**, which is the natural tendency among people to regard their own culture as superior to others.
- Hofstede's sociocultural value dimensions measure power distance, uncertainty avoidance, individualism–collectivism, and masculinity–femininity.
- **Power distance** is the degree to which people accept inequality in power among institutions, organizations, and people.
- **Uncertainty avoidance** is characterized by people's intolerance for uncertainty and ambiguity and resulting support for beliefs that promise certainty and conformity.
- **Individualism** refers to a preference for a loosely knit social framework in which individuals are expected to take care of themselves.
- **Collectivism** refers to a preference for a tightly knit social framework in which individuals look after one

another and organizations protect their members' interests.
- **Masculinity** is a cultural preference for achievement, heroism, assertiveness, work centrality, and material success.
- **Femininity** is a cultural preference for relationships, cooperation, group decision making, and quality of life.
- Hofstede later identified another dimension: **long-term orientation**, which reflects a greater concern for the future and a high value on thrift and perseverance versus **short-term orientation**, which reflects a concern with the past and present and a high value on meeting current obligations.
- Additional value dimensions recently identified by the GLOBE Project are assertiveness, future orientation, gender differentiation, performance orientation, and humane orientation.

cues, such as tone of voice or body language, in addition to the explicit spoken words when talking with others.[62] For example, you might know from facial expression and body language that a colleague who says "Yes" when asked if she can meet a deadline really means "I doubt it." One executive said managers at Louis Vuitton sometimes didn't even finish their sentences. "Instead, they would begin to make a point and then say something like, 'OK, you get it?' And for us, that said it all."[63] When managers are working with colleagues, subordinates, and customers who are from different cultural backgrounds, however, this implicit communication breaks down because unspoken cues are difficult to interpret.

In addition, people from some cultures tend to use implicit communication more than others do. That is, some cultures pay more attention to the social context (social setting, nonverbal behavior, social status, etc.) of their verbal communication. For example, Ian Bickley, now president of the international group of Coach, worked for many years with Coach in Japan, where he learned that it was extremely important to suppress impatience and devote the necessary time to build personal relationships. "You have to spend a lot of time actively listening and you have to learn how to read between the lines," Bickley advises. "It's almost more important to listen to what is not being said than what is said."[64]

Exhibit 3.6 indicates how the emphasis on social context varies among countries. In a **high-context culture**, people are sensitive to circumstances surrounding social exchanges. People use communication primarily to build personal social relationships; meaning is derived from context—setting, status, and nonverbal behavior—more than from explicit words; relationships and trust are more important than business; and the welfare and harmony of the group are valued. In a **low-context culture**, people use communication primarily to exchange facts and information; meaning is derived primarily from words; business transactions are more important than building relationships and trust; and individual welfare and achievement are more important than the group.[65]

To understand how differences in cultural context affect communications, consider the American expression, "The squeaky wheel gets the grease." It means that the loudest person will get the most attention, and attention is assumed to be favorable. Equivalent sayings in China and Japan are "Quacking ducks get shot," and "The nail that sticks up gets hammered down," respectively. In these latter two cultures, standing out as an individual earns *unfavorable* attention. Consider the culture gap when China's Lenovo Group acquired IBM's PC business. In meetings and conference calls, Western executives were frustrated by their Chinese counterparts' reluctance to speak up, while the Chinese managers were irritated by the Americans' propensity to "just talk and talk," as one vice president of human resources put it.[66]

High-context cultures include Asian and Arab countries. Low-context cultures tend to be North American and Northern European. Even within North America, cultural subgroups vary in the extent to which context counts, which explains why differences among groups can hinder successful communication. White females, Native Americans, and African Americans all tend to prefer higher-context communication than do white males. A high-context interaction requires more time because a relationship has to be developed, and trust and friendship must be established. Furthermore, most male managers and most people doing the hiring in organizations are from low-context cultures, which conflicts with people entering the organization from a background in a higher-context culture.

Visit MindTap to refer your score on the opening activity, "Self-Assessment: Are You Ready to Manage Internationally?" which will give you some insight into whether you lean toward low-context or high-context communications. A higher score indicates low-context behavior, which would be jarring when trying to do business in a high-context culture.

Exhibit 3.6 High-Context and Low-Context Cultures

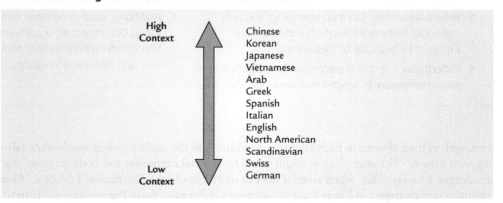

SOURCES: Edward T. Hall, *Beyond Culture* (Garden City, NY: Anchor Press/Doubleday, 1976); and J. Kennedy and A. Everest, "Put Diversity in Context," *Personnel Journal* (September 1991): 50–54.

Understanding the subtle contextual differences among cultures requires high **cultural intelligence (CQ)**, a person's ability to use reasoning and observation skills to interpret unfamiliar gestures and situations and devise appropriate behavioral responses.[67] Cultural intelligence includes three components that work together: cognitive, emotional, and physical.[68] The cognitive component involves a person's observational and learning skills and the ability to pick up on clues to understanding. The emotional aspect concerns one's self-confidence and self-motivation. A manager must believe in his or her ability to understand and assimilate into a different culture. Difficulties and setbacks are triggers to work harder, not causes to give up. The third component of cultural intelligence, the physical, refers to a person's ability to shift his or her speech patterns, expressions, and body language to be in tune with people from a different culture. Most managers aren't equally strong in all three areas, but maximizing cultural intelligence requires that they draw upon all three facets.

Visit MindTap for "Self-Assessment: Are You Culturally Intelligent?" to see if your level of CQ reflects a global mindset, as described earlier in the chapter.

Remember This

- The potential for communication breakdowns increases when managers are interacting with people from different countries and varied cultural backgrounds.

- **Implicit communication** refers to sending and receiving unspoken cues such as tone of voice or body language as well as spoken words.

- A **high-context culture** is one in which people use communication to build personal relationships.

- In a **low-context culture**, people use communication primarily to exchange facts and information.

- The United States exemplifies a low-context culture. China is an example of a high-context culture.

- Managers who develop cultural intelligence are more successful in international assignments.

- **Cultural intelligence (CQ)** refers to a person's ability to use reasoning and observation to interpret culturally unfamiliar situations and know how to respond appropriately. The three aspects of CQ are cognitive CQ, emotional CQ, and physical CQ.

3-7 International Trade Alliances

Another highly visible change in the international business environment in recent years has been the development of regional trading alliances and international trade agreements.

3-7a GATT and the WTO

The General Agreement on Tariffs and Trade (GATT), signed by 23 nations in 1947, started as a set of rules to ensure nondiscrimination, clear procedures, the negotiation of disputes, and the participation of lesser-developed countries in international trade.[69] GATT sponsored eight rounds of international trade negotiations aimed at reducing trade restrictions. The 1986 to 1994 Uruguay Round (the first to be named for a developing country) involved 125 countries and cut more tariffs than ever before. In addition to lowering tariffs 30 percent from the previous level, it boldly moved the world closer to global free trade by calling for the establishment of the World Trade Organization (WTO) in 1995.

The WTO represents the maturation of GATT into a permanent global institution that can monitor international trade and has legal authority to arbitrate disputes on some 400 trade issues. As of February 2016, 162 countries, including China, Vietnam, and Ukraine, were members of the organization. As a permanent membership organization, the WTO is bringing increased trade liberalization in goods, information, technological developments, and services; strong enforcement of rules and regulations; and great power to resolve disputes among trading partners.

3-7b European Union

An alliance begun in 1957 to improve economic and social conditions among its members, the European Economic Community has evolved into the 28-nation European Union (EU), which is illustrated in Exhibit 3.7. The biggest expansion came in 2004, when the EU welcomed 10 new members from central and eastern Europe.[70]

The goal of the EU is to create a powerful single-market system for Europe's millions of consumers, allowing people, goods, and services to move freely. The increased competition and economies of scale within Europe enable companies to grow large and efficient and to become more competitive in the United States and other world markets. Another aspect of European unification is the introduction of the euro. Several member states of the EU have adopted the **euro**, a single European currency that replaced national currencies in Austria, Belgium, Cyprus, Estonia, Finland, France, Germany, Greece, Ireland, Italy, Latvia, Lithuania, Luxembourg, Malta, the Netherlands, Portugal, Slovakia, Slovenia, and Spain.[71]

However, not all has gone smoothly for the integration, particularly since the global recession began. Small but vocal factions in several countries are arguing that companies and citizens would be better off withdrawing from the eurozone. The United Kingdom, which never adopted the euro, voted in June 2016 to withdraw from the European Union entirely. Its withdrawal will take about two years to complete and will have major political and economic consequences. Continuing economic problems in the eurozone were already creating uncertainty for European businesses. As economic stability varied from country to country, pitting winners against losers, the economic crisis that started in 2008 revived national loyalties and cross-border resentments and slowed the move toward a unified and cohesive "European identity." Spain, Ireland, Portugal,

Exhibit 3.7 The Nations of the European Union

and particularly Greece all have had trouble paying their debts, which put the entire eurozone at risk and led to a possible breakup of the euro system. Government and industries in many of these countries have reversed the downward slide and renewed their competitiveness by cutting spending, raising taxes, and laying off millions of employees, but economic uncertainties remain, and social unrest is growing. Even though debt is declining in many countries, unemployment is soaring. Unemployment in the single currency bloc remained stuck at 10.2 percent in mid-2016, with youth unemployment as high as 50 percent in parts of the eurozone. Moreover, conflicts over how to solve the chronic crisis continue. Resistance to changes in France, the eurozone's second-largest economy, for example, led to violent protests and crippling worker strikes.[72] Some analysts think a broad breakup of the eurozone is unlikely, but its economies are at a crossroads. Managers are rethinking what they would do in the event that a return to national currencies required a rethinking of everything from how to expand operations to how to pick suppliers and pay employees.[73]

3-7c North American Free Trade Agreement (NAFTA)

The North American Free Trade Agreement (NAFTA), which went into effect on January 1, 1994, merged the United States, Canada, and Mexico into a single market. Intended to spur growth and investment, increase exports, and expand jobs in all three nations, NAFTA broke down tariffs and trade restrictions over a 15-year period in a number of key areas. Thus, by 2008, virtually all U.S. industrial exports into Canada and Mexico were duty free.

Over the first decade of NAFTA, U.S. trade with Mexico increased more than threefold, while trade with Canada also rose dramatically.[74] Significantly, NAFTA spurred the entry of small businesses into the global arena. Jeff Victor, general manager of Treatment Products, Ltd., which makes car cleaners and waxes, credits NAFTA for his surging export volume. Prior to the pact, Mexican tariffs as high as 20 percent made it impossible for the Chicago-based company to expand its presence south of the border.[75]

However, opinions over the benefits of NAFTA appear to be as divided as they were when talks began, with some people calling it a spectacular success and others referring to it as a dismal failure.[76] Although NAFTA has not lived up to its grand expectations, experts stress that it increased trade, investment, and income and continues to enable companies in all three countries to compete more effectively with rival Asian and European firms.[77]

3-7d Trans-Pacific Partnership

A recent proposed trade alliance is the Trans-Pacific Partnership, a trade agreement among 12 countries, including the United States, Canada, Japan, and Malaysia. The agreement is designed to reduce trade barriers, promote economic growth and job creation, promote transparency, and enhance labor and environmental protections in the participating countries.

The Trans-Pacific Partnership (TPP) is an expansion of the Trans-Pacific Strategic Economic Partnership Agreement signed by Brunei, Chile, New Zealand, and Singapore in 2005. Beginning in 2008, eight additional countries (Australia, Canada, Japan, Malaysia, Mexico, Peru, the United States, and Vietnam) joined discussions for a broader agreement, which was signed in February 2016 but is subject to approval by each member country. The TPP is the largest regional agreement in history. Together the countries of the TPP represent about 40 percent of the world's economic power.

U.S. President Barack Obama made a strong push for the TPP, saying it would bolster the U.S. economy and increase national security in a fast-growing region, but the agreement has come under fire from both Republican and Democratic members of Congress, as well as 2016 presidential candidates Hilary Clinton, Donald Trump, and Bernie Sanders. The agreement has not yet received final approval by the U.S. Congress. A primary concern is the loss of U.S. jobs to low-wage countries. Others say the agreement doesn't go far enough to enforce high labor and environmental standards overseas.[78]

Remember This

- Regional trading alliances and international trade agreements are reshaping global business.
- The World Trade Organization (WTO) is a permanent membership organization that monitors trade and has authority to arbitrate disputes among 159 member countries.
- Two important, yet sometimes controversial, regional alliances are the European Union (EU) and the North American Free Trade Agreement (NAFTA).

- The **euro** is a single European currency that has replaced the currencies of 19 EU member nations.
- The Trans-Pacific Partnership is a proposed trade agreement among 12 countries, including the United States, Canada, Japan, Malaysia, and Vietnam.

DISCUSSION QUESTIONS

1. What specifically would the experience of living and working in another country contribute to your skills and effectiveness as a manager in your own country?

2. Both China and India are rising economic powers. How might your approach to doing business with China, a communist country, be different from your approach to doing business with India, the world's most populous democracy? In which country would you expect to encounter the most rules? The most bureaucracy?

3. Do you think it is realistic that BOP business practices can have a positive effect on poverty and other social problems in developing countries? Discuss.

4. Somnio, a start-up running shoe company in California, decided to start selling its products around the world from the very beginning. In general terms, name some of the challenges that a start-up company such as Somnio might face internationally.

5. Do you think that it's possible for individuals to develop a global mindset if they never live outside their native country? How might they do that?

6. Should a multinational organization operate as a tightly integrated, worldwide business system, or would it be more effective to let each national subsidiary operate autonomously? Why?

7. If you were to interview someone for an international business executive position, what are three questions you think it would be important to ask? Explain your reasoning.

8. Two U.S. companies are competing to take over a large factory in the Czech Republic. One delegation tours the facility and asks questions about how the plant might be run more efficiently. The other delegation focuses on ways to improve working conditions and produce a better product. Which delegation do you think is more likely to succeed with the plant? Why? What information would you want to collect to decide whether to acquire the plant for your company?

9. Which style of communicating do you think would be most beneficial to the long-term success of a U.S. company operating internationally—high-context or low-context communications? Why?

10. How might the social value of low versus high power distance influence how you would lead and motivate employees? What about the value of low versus high performance orientation?

APPLY YOUR SKILLS: SELF-LEARNING

Rate Your Global Management Potential[79]

A global environment requires that managers learn to deal effectively with people and ideas from a variety of cultures. How well prepared are you to be a global manager? Read the following statements and circle the number on the response scale that most closely reflects how well the statement describes you.

Good Description 10 9 8 7 6 5 4 3 2 1 Poor Description

1. I reach out to people from different cultures.

   10 9 8 7 6 5 4 3 2 1

2. I frequently attend seminars and lectures about other cultures or international topics.

   10 9 8 7 6 5 4 3 2 1

3. I believe female expatriates can be equally as effective as male expatriates.

   10 9 8 7 6 5 4 3 2 1

4. I have a basic knowledge about several countries in addition to my native country.

   10 9 8 7 6 5 4 3 2 1

5. I have good listening and empathy skills.

   10 9 8 7 6 5 4 3 2 1

6. I have spent more than two weeks traveling or working in another country.

   10 9 8 7 6 5 4 3 2 1

7. I easily adapt to the different work ethics of students from other cultures when we are involved in a team project.

   10 9 8 7 6 5 4 3 2 1

8. I can speak at least one foreign language.

   10 9 8 7 6 5 4 3 2 1

9. I know which countries tend to cluster into similar sociocultural and economic groupings.

   10 9 8 7 6 5 4 3 2 1

10. I feel capable of assessing different cultures on the basis of power distance, uncertainty avoidance, individualism, and masculinity.

    10 9 8 7 6 5 4 3 2 1

Total Score: _____

Scoring and Interpretation Add up the total points for the 10 questions. If you scored 81–100 points, you have a great capacity for developing good global management skills. A score of 61–80 points indicates that you have potential but may lack skills in certain areas, such as language or foreign experience. A score of 60 or less means you need to do some serious work to improve your potential for global management. Regardless of your total score, go back over each item and make a plan of action to increase scores of less than 5 on any question.

APPLY YOUR SKILLS: GROUP LEARNING

Global Entrepreneurship IQ

1. Which country is the best place to launch a new business?
   a. New Zealand
   b. United States
   c. Canada
   d. Denmark
   e. Singapore

2. Which country improved the most in terms of making it easier for companies to do business?
   a. France
   b. Burundi
   c. Brunei Darussalam
   d. Poland
   e. Serbia

3. Which country implemented the fewest reforms that would help business operate?
   a. Surinam
   b. Columbia
   c. Vietnam
   d. Rwanda
   e. Croatia

4. Which country or countries has a "one-stop shop" for clearance on construction permits and/or custom, duties, etc.?
   a. Venezuela
   b. Nigeria
   c. Tanzania
   d. Cote d'Ivoire
   e. Brunei Darussalam

5. Which country in the Middle East has strength
    of legal institutions and inexpensive procedures
    for doing business?
    a. Iraq
    b. Iran
    c. Algeria
    d. Saudi Arabia
    e. Lebanon

6. Which country in Latin America has sustained
    the most business-friendly reforms over time?
    a. Bolivia
    b. Panama
    c. Columbia
    d. Costa Rica
    e. Nicaragua

SOURCE: The World Bank, *Doing Business 2013*, World Bank and International Finance Corporation (Washington DC, 2018).

APPLY YOUR SKILLS: ACTION LEARNING

Try Being a Minority

1. Singly, or in groups of no more than two, find
    a place to be a minority, such as a Korean wedding (as long as you are not Korean), an Indian
    cultural fare, a Black church, a retirement home,
    etc. Do NOT choose something dangerous like a
    biker bar or unknown neighborhood club.

2. Go to the place or event and make an effort to
    talk to at least five people.

3. Write up your experiences in a short paper,
    answering the following questions:
    a. How did it feel to be the different one?
    b. How did people treat you? Is that how you
        react to someone who is in a minority situation where you are?
    c. What are the difficulties in being a
        minority?
    d. What skills do you need in such a situation?
    e. Do you see minorities any different now
        than you did before this Action Learning?

4. Be prepared to discuss your experiences and conclusions in class.

Adapted from Renate R. Mai-Dalton. From *Exchange: Organizational Behavior Teaching Review*, Vol. 9(3), 1984–85.

APPLY YOUR SKILLS: ETHICAL DILEMMA

AH Biotech[80]

Dr. Abraham Hassan knew that he couldn't put off the decision any longer. AH Biotech, the Bound Brook, New Jersey–based company started by this psychiatrist-turned-entrepreneur, had developed a novel drug that seemed to promise long-term relief from panic attacks. If it gained approval from the Food and Drug Administration (FDA), it would be the company's first product. It was now time for large-scale clinical trials. But where should AH Biotech conduct those tests?

David Berger, who headed up research and development, was certain he already knew the answer to that question: Albania. "Look, doing these trials in Albania will be quicker, easier, and a lot cheaper than doing them in the States," he pointed out. "What's not to like?"

Dr. Hassan had to concede that Berger's arguments were sound. If it did trials in the United States, AH Biotech would spend considerable time and money advertising for patients and then finding physicians who'd be willing to serve as clinical trial investigators. Rounding up U.S. doctors prepared to take on that job was getting increasingly difficult. They just didn't want to take time out of their busy practices to do the testing, not to mention all the recordkeeping that such a study entailed.

In Albania, it was an entirely different story. There were few legal or political barriers to testing drugs. And it was one of the poorest Eastern European countries—if not *the* poorest—with a just barely functioning health care system. Albanian physicians and patients would practically line up at AH Biotech's doorstep begging to take part. Physicians there could earn much better money as clinical investigators for a U.S. company than they could actually practicing medicine, and patients saw signing up as test subjects as their best chance for receiving any treatment at all, let alone cutting-edge Western medicine. All these factors meant that the company could count on realizing at least a 25 percent savings (maybe even more) by running the tests overseas.

So, what's not to like? As the Egyptian-born CEO of a start-up biotech company with investors and employees hoping for its first marketable drug, there was absolutely nothing not to like. It was when he thought like a U.S.-trained physician that Dr. Hassan felt qualms. If he used U.S. test subjects, he knew they'd likely continue to receive the drug until it was approved. At that point, most would have insurance that covered most of the cost of their prescriptions. But he already knew that it wasn't going to make any sense to market the drug in a poor country like Albania, so when the study was over, he'd have to cut off treatment. Sure, he conceded, panic attacks weren't usually fatal. But he knew how debilitating these sudden bouts of feeling completely terrified were—the pounding heart, chest pain, choking sensation, and nausea. The severity and unpredictability of these attacks often made a normal life all but impossible. How could he offer people dramatic relief and then snatch it away?

What Would You Do?

1. Do the clinical trials in Albania. You'll be able to bring the drug to market faster and cheaper, which will be good for AH Biotech's employees and investors and good for the millions of people who suffer from anxiety attacks.

2. Do the clinical trials in the United States. Even though it will certainly be more expensive and time consuming, you'll feel as if you're living up to the part of the Hippocratic oath that instructs you to "prescribe regimens for the good of my patients according to my ability and my judgment and never do harm to anyone."

3. Do the clinical trials in Albania, and if the drug is approved, use part of the profits to set up a compassionate use program in Albania, even though setting up a distribution system and training doctors to administer the drug, monitor patients for adverse effects, and track results will entail considerable expense.

APPLY YOUR SKILLS: CASE FOR CRITICAL ANALYSIS

We Want More Guitars!

Adam Wainwright's early-morning phone call from Valencia, Spain, initially startled his boss, Vincent Fletcher. Adam, a true slave to the latest techno-gadgetry, *never* called. Yet here he was, at 8 a.m. Pacific time, on the phone to the CEO of Fletcher Guitars in Los Angeles.

"What did they do—lose your luggage with all of your toys inside?" Fletcher joked. "Did the plant burn down?"

"No, I just decided to call you on this one. I've been here for a week, looking over operations. Forget the idea of getting any substantial increase in productivity. I don't think these guys are capable of upping production by *10* guitars per year," Adam complained.

"Isn't that an exaggeration?" Fletcher asked.

There was a momentary silence on the other end of the line. "Adam, did I lose you?"

"No."

"Look, part of our reputation is based on the quality and craftsmanship of the acoustic guitars produced by Dominguez and his workers. This is all high-end stuff," Fletcher said in a voice that always reminded Adam of actor Jason Robards. "Now, with the tremendous rise in the popularity of Latin music, we want to encourage increased production. That's your task, Adam. I shouldn't have to tell you that your success with this assignment could lead to some great opportunities for you."

"I know." Adam paused, carefully weighing his next words. "Salvador and his people do a fabulous job. Just walking through his operation, I have been blown away by the craftsmanship. But the slow pace of work is unbelievably frustrating. These guys act like they are birthing a baby. Everything is so precise, so touchy-feely with every guitar. I used my iPad to create some workflow specs for increased production. Salvador took one look, laughed, and said 'You Americans.'"

Poor Adam, Fletcher thought. *That had to be a major stab in his high-tech heart. Maybe I sent the wrong guy. Nope. He has great potential in management and he has to learn to work through this and deliver.* Fletcher's thoughts were interrupted by Adam's voice, flustered and increasing in volume.

"They go off to lunch and come wandering back in here hours later—*hours*, Fletcher."

"They're Spanish!" Fletcher replied. "So they take two-hour lunches. They work their schedule. It's just not *our* schedule. You may be a lot younger than I am, Adam. But you need to lighten up. Listen, talk to Salvador and see what works for them. They've increased output before and they can do it again. Get this done, Adam. And *e-mail* me."

The international rise in Latin music over the past decade, punctuated by the clear sound and dazzling rhythms of the acoustic guitar, created a sense of urgency for guitar makers around the globe to increase the availability of these classical instruments. Wanting to ride the crest of this musical trend, increase his product offerings, and tap into high-end market sales, Fletcher discovered master craftsman Salvador Dominguez and his Spanish company, Guitarra Dominguez, while attending the prestigious Frankfurt International Fair in 1980.

Salvador liked to tell that among the first sounds he heard following his birth were the words of his father's lullaby, accompanied by an acoustic guitar. As an adult, Salvador combined his lifelong passion for guitars with brilliant craftsmanship, and he started his own company in 1976. Located in the Poligono Industrial Fuente del Jarro—Paterna, Valencia, Spain, the company now employed more than 30 craftspeople in the production of acoustic and flamenco instruments. A thin, wiry bundle of energy with graying wavy hair and large eyes with that surprised "Salvador Dalí look," the guitar maker could grasp a piece of wood and, running his hand over the surface, be suddenly transformed into a patient, tender sculptor of sound. To watch this luthier work was almost mesmerizing. Salvador's total silence and habit of leaning his right ear close to the wood as he worked suggested that he was actually *hearing* the music of the instrument as he created it.

Following the phone call to Fletcher, Adam returned to the plant, determined that Salvador would now hear from him.

"Salvador, you do beautiful work. Latin music is one of the hottest trends in music, and musicians are clamoring for the instruments you make. But we can be doing so much more here. There's plenty of room for expansion in this place, and we could nearly double production within the next few years. I have visited companies all over the United States and analyzed their operations. If you will take time to look at the plan I've drawn up, you will clearly see the potential for cranking out more product and meeting the needs of more customers."

"Señor Wainwright. Here in Spain, we do not *crank out product*. We take pride in each creation, and it is important that our methods of craftsmanship remain the same. No two of these instruments are alike."

"Wait. Wait. I'm just saying that there are changes that can be made here that will make this operation more productive. In the States, I see a flow to their operations. Here, we have starts and stops. The Nato mahogany used in many of your acoustic guitar bodies provides a beautiful and unrestricted wood. But Carlos has been off in a corner most of the week, wearing protective gear and experimenting with his notions about the potential tonal qualities of Wenge in acoustic bodies. The bottom line is this: We simply must streamline this operation in order to increase your production."

"No, Señor. *My bottom line* is this: Guitarras Dominguez will not lower *our* standards of craftsmanship to meet *your* plan."

Questions

1. How accurate is Adam Wainwright's analysis of the situation at Guitarras Dominguez? Do you think craftsmanship is incompatible with increasing productivity in this company? Why or why not?

2. What social values are present in Guitarras Dominguez that seem different from U.S. social values (see Exhibit 3.4 and Exhibit 3.5)? Explain.

3. What do you recommend Adam do to increase production in a business setting that does not seem to value high production?

ENDNOTES

1. Caroline Fairchild, "In Canada, U.S. Retailers Can Be Their Own Worst Enemy," *Fortune* (March 13, 2014), http://fortune.com/2014/03/13/in-canada-u-s-retailers-can-be-their-own-worst-enemy/ (accessed February 1, 2016); Paul Ziobro and Rita Trichur, "Target to Exit Canada After Failed Expansion," *The Wall Street Journal*, January 15, 2015, http://www.wsj.com/articles/target-to-exit-canada-1421328919 (accessed February 1, 2016); and Phil Wahba, "Why Target Failed in Canada," *Fortune* (January 15, 2015), http://fortune.com/2015/01/15/target-canada-fail/ (accessed February 1, 2016).

2. Jim Holt, "Gone Global?" *Management Review* (March 2000): 13.

3. James Hookway, "IKEA's Products Make Shoppers Blush in Thailand," *The Wall Street Journal*, June 5, 2012.

4. Holt, "Gone Global?"

5. "Slogans Often Lose Something in Translation," *The New Mexican*, July 3, 1994.

6. Lolita C. Baldor, "FBI Sends More Agents Abroad to Shield U.S. from Cybercrime; Foreign Hackers Stepping up Their Attacks," *South Florida Sun-Sentinel*, December 10, 2009;

and Cassell Bryan-Low, "Criminal Network: To Catch Crooks in Cyberspace, FBI Goes Global," *The Wall Street Journal*, November 21, 2006.

7. Quoted in Ryan Underwood, "Going Global," *Inc.* (March 2011): 96–98.

8. Bettina Wassener, "Living in Asia Appeals to More Company Leaders," *The New York Times*, June 21, 2012; and Emily Glazer, "P&G Unit Bids Goodbye to Cincinnati, Hello to Asia." *The Wall Street Journal*, May 10, 2012.

9. "TCS Can Become India's First Company to Reach $100 Billion in Market Cap: CLSA," *The Economic Times*, August 31, 2013, http://articles.economictimes.indiatimes.com/2013-08-31/news/41619991_1_tcs-market-capitalisation-lakh-crore (accessed September 2, 2013); and Steve Hamm, "IBM vs. Tata: Which Is More American?" *BusinessWeek* (May 5, 2008): 28.

10. Alan Murray, "The 21st-Century Club," *Fortune* (November 1, 2015): 9–12.

11. "The New Geography of the Global 500 Companies," figure in Murray, "The 21st-Century Club," *Fortune* (November 1, 2015): 9–12.

12. Gregory C. Unruh and Ángel Cabrera, "Join the Global Elite," *Harvard Business Review* (May 2013): 135–139.

13. This section is based on Unruh and Cabrera, "Join the Global Elite"; Mansour Javidan and David Bowen, "The 'Global Mindset' of Managers: What It Is, Why It Matters, and How To Develop It," *Organizational Dynamics* 42 (2013): 145–155; and Schon Beechler and Dennis Baltzley, "Creating a Global Mindset," *Chief Learning Officer* (May 29, 2008), http://clomedia.com/articles/view/creating_a_global_mindset/1 (accessed June 26, 2012); Joana S. P. Story and John E. Barbuto, Jr., "Global Mindset: A Construct Clarification and Framework," *Journal of Leadership and Organizational Studies* 18, no. 3 (2011): 377–384; and Stephen L. Cohen, "Effective Global Leadership Requires a Global Mindset," *Industrial and Commercial Training* 42, no. 1 (2010): 3–10.

14. Definition based on Mansour Javidan and Jennie L. Walker, "A Whole New Global Mindset for Leadership," *People & Strategy* 35, no. 2 (2012): 36–41; Mansour Javidan and Mary B. Teagarden, "Conceptualizing and Measuring Global Mindset," *Advances in Global Leadership* 6 (2011): 13–39; and Beechler and Baltzley, "Creating a Global Mindset."

15. Amol Titus, "Competency of Intercultural Management," *The Jakarta Post*, March 11, 2009, www.thejakartapost.com/news/2009/03/11/competency-intercultural-management.html (accessed June 30, 2012).

16. Based on Javidan and Walker, "A Whole New Global Mindset for Leadership," 36–41; and Javidan and Bowen, "The 'Global Mindset' of Managers."

17. This is based on Unruh and Cabrera, "Join the Global Elite."

18. Sonia Kolesnikov-Jessop, "Adapt and Take on Challenges Around the World," *The New York Times*, December 20, 2015, http://www.nytimes.com/2015/12/21/business/international/adapt-and-take-on-challenges-around-the-world.html?_r=0 (accessed February 2, 2016).

19. Siegfried Russwurm et al., "Developing Your Global Know-How," *Harvard Business Review* (March 2011): 70–75.

20. "The New Geography of the Global 500 Companies."

21. George Stalk and David Michael, "What the West Doesn't Get About China," *Harvard Business Review* (June 2011): 25–27; Zoe McKay, "Consumer Spending in China: To Buy or Not to Buy," *Forbes.com*, June 15, 2012, www.forbes.com/sites/insead/2012/06/15/consumer-spending-in-china-to-buy-or-not-to-buy/ (accessed June 29, 2012); and Adam Davidson, "Come On, China, Buy Our Stuff!" *The New York Times*, January 25, 2012, www.nytimes.com/2012/01/29/magazine/come-on-china-buy-our-stuff.html?pagewanted=all (accessed June 29, 2012).

22. "Ford to Pour $1.8 Billion into Smartcars for China," *The Wall Street Journal*, October 12, 2015, http://www.wsj.com/articles/ford-to-focus-1-8-billion-on-china-smart-cars-1444642178 (accessed February 2, 2016).

23. Mike Ramsey, "Ford's CEO Revs up Auto Maker's China Role," *The Wall Street Journal*, April 16, 2013.

24. Laurie Burkitt and Paul Mozur, "Foreign Firms Brace for More Pressure in China," *The Wall Street Journal Online*, April 4, 2013, http://online.wsj.com/news/articles/SB10001424127887323916304578400463208890042 (accessed July 30, 2014).

25. David Barboza and Brad Stone, "A Nation That Trips Up Many," *The New York Times*, January 16, 2010.

26. Andrew Galbraith and Jason Dean, "In China, Some Firms Defy Business Norms," *The Wall Street Journal Online*, September 6, 2011, http://online.wsj.com/article/

SB10001424053111903895904576546381512015722.html (accessed June 29, 2012).

27. Colum Murphy, James T. Areddy, and James R. Hagerty, "Deal Gone Wrong Adds to Caterpillar's Troubles in China," *The Wall Street Journal*, January 21, 2013, http://online.wsj.com/article/SB10001424127887323301104578255740261180404.html (accessed August 29, 2013).

28. Scott Cendrowski, "Enter the Dragons," *Fortune* (March 1, 2015): 108–114.

29. Ibid.

30. "Lenovo Widens Lead as the World's Biggest PC Maker" *Irish Times*, May 21, 2015, http://www.irishtimes.com/business/technology/lenovo-widens-lead-as-the-worlds-biggest-pc-maker-1.2220862 (accessed February 3, 2016).

31. Chuck Salter, "Lenovo: Protect and Attack," *Fast Company* (December 2011–January 2012): 116–121, 154–155; and William J. Holstein, "Lenovo Goes Global," *Strategy + Business* (August 8, 2014), http://www.strategy-business.com/article/00274?pg=all (accessed February 3, 2014).

32. Reported in "2016 Global Services Location Index," A. T. Kearney, https://www.atkearney.com/strategic-it/global-services-location-index (accessed February 10, 2016).

33. Sujit John, "25 Global Companies Set Up R&D Centres in India in Last 18 Months," *The Times of India*, September 22, 2013, http://timesofindia.indiatimes.com/business/india-business/25-global-companies-set-up-RD-centres-in-India-in-last-18-months/articleshow/22846741.cms (accessed February 10, 2016).

34. "2016 Global Services Location Index," A. T. Kearney.

35. "The Top 10 Most Innovative Companies in India," *Fast Company* (February 10, 2014), http://www.fastcompany.com/most-innovative-companies/2014/industry/india (accessed February 9, 2016).

36. Ibid.; and "About Mitra," http://www.mitrabiotech.com/aboutus.php (accessed February 9, 2016).

37. "Pharmaceuticals," India Brand Equity Foundation, IBEF.org, May 2012, www.ibef.org/industry/pharmaceuticals.aspx (accessed June 29, 2012); and Sushmi Dey, "Indian Pharma Eyes US Generic Gold Rush," *Business Standard*, June 27, 2012, www.business-standard.com/india/news/indian-pharma-eyes-us-generic-gold-rush/478593/ (accessed June 29, 2012).

38. Howard V. Perlmutter, "The Tortuous Evolution of the Multinational Corporation," *Columbia Journal of World Business* (January–February 1969): 9–18; and Youram Wind, Susan P. Douglas, and Howard V. Perlmutter, "Guidelines for Developing International Marketing Strategies," *Journal of Marketing* (April 1973): 14–23.

39. Deborah Ball, "Boss Talk: Nestlé Focuses on Long Term," *The Wall Street Journal*, November 2, 2009; Transnationale Web site, www.transnationale.org/companies/nestle.php (accessed March 17, 2010); Company Analytics Web site, www.company-analytics.org/company/nestle.php (accessed March 17, 2010); and "Facts and Figures," Nestlé SA Web site, http://www.nestle.com/media/facts-figures (accessed February 10, 2016).

40. This discussion is based on C. K. Prahalad, "The Fortune at the Bottom of the Pyramid," *Fast Company* (April 13, 2011), www.fastcompany.com/1746818/fortune-at-the-bottom-of-the-pyramid-ck-prahalad (accessed June 30, 2012); C. K. Prahalad and S. L. Hart, "The Fortune at the Bottom of the Pyramid," *Strategy + Business* 26 (2002): 54–67; Jakki Mohr, Sanjit Sengupta, and Stanley F. Slater, "Serving Base-of-the-Pyramid Markets: Meeting Real Needs Through a

Customized Approach," *Journal of Business Strategy* 33, no. 6 (2012): 4–14; and Scott Johnson, "SC Johnson Builds Business at the Base of the Pyramid," *Global Business and Organizational Excellence* (September-October, 2007): 6–17.

41. Based on Bala Chakravarthy and Sophie Coughlan, "Emerging Market Strategy: Innovating Both Products and Delivery Systems," *Strategy & Leadership* 40, 1 (2012): 27–32; T. V. Mahalingam, "Godrej's Rediscovery of India: They Say They Touch More Consumers than Any Other Indian Company," *Business Today* (July 25, 2010): 58–64; and "Godrej Eyes Youth to Expand Portfolio," *Mail Today*, July 12, 2009.

42. Reported in Mohr, Sengupta, and Slater "Serving Base-of-the-Pyramid Markets."

43. Stephanie Strom, "Multinational Companies Court Lower-Income Consumers," (September 17, 2014), http://www.nytimes.com/2014/09/18/business/international/multinational-companies-court-lower-income-consumers.html?_r=0 (accessed February 3, 2016).

44. Rob Walker, "Cleaning Up," *New York Times Magazine* (June 10, 2007): 20.

45. Matthew Boyle, "Unilever: Taking on the World, One Stall at a Time," *Bloomberg Businessweek* (January 7–January 13, 2013): 18–20.

46. Ibid.; and Jennifer Reingold, "Can P&G Make Money in Places Where People Earn $2 a Day?" *Fortune* (January 17, 2011): 86–91.

47. Kathryn Rudie Harrigan, "Managing Joint Ventures," *Management Review* (February 1987): 24–41; and Therese R. Revesz and Mimi Cauley de Da La Sierra, "Competitive Alliances: Forging Ties Abroad," *Management Review* (March 1987): 57–59.

48. Anthony Goerzen, "Managing Alliance Networks: Emerging Practices of Multinational Corporations," *Academy of Management Executive* 19, no. 2 (2005): 94–107.

49. Howard Schultz, "The Power of Partnership (Starbucks)," *McKinsey Quarterly* 1st Quarter, Issue 1 (2014): 77–78; Howard Schultz, "A Tale of Two Countries: Starbucks in China and India," Starbucks Newsroom (March 27, 2014), https://news.starbucks.com/news/a-tale-of-two-countries-starbucks-growth-in-india-and-china (accessed February 5, 2016); and Helen H. Wang, "Five Things Starbucks Did to Get China Right," *Forbes* (August 10, 2012), http://www.forbes.com/sites/helenwang/2012/08/10/five-things-starbucks-did-to-get-china-right/#a894c0b48e35 (accessed February 5, 2016).

50. Ian Bremmer, "Managing Risk in an Unstable World," *Harvard Business Review* (June 2005): 51–60; Mark Fitzpatrick, "The Definition and Assessment of Political Risk in International Business: A Review of the Literature," *Academy of Management Review* 8 (1983): 249–254; and Jo Jakobsen, "Old Problems Remain, New Ones Crop Up: Political Risk in the 21st Century," *Business Horizons* 53 (2010): 481–490.

51. Resty Woro Yuniar, "Netflix Blocked by Indonesia's Top Telecom Provider," *The Wall Street Journal*, January 27, 2016, http://www.wsj.com/articles/netflix-blocked-by-indonesias-top-telecom-provider-1453896220 (accessed February 5, 2016).

52. Alisa Wiersema, "Everything You Need to Know About the Syrian Civil War," *ABC News*, August 31, 2013, http://abcnews.go.com/Politics/syrian-civil-war/story?id=20112311 (accessed September 2, 2013); and quote from Peter Wonacott, "An Entrepreneur Weathers a Tumultuous Arab Spring," *The Wall Street Journal*, January 17, 2012, http://online.wsj.com/article/SB10001424052970203436904577150690233235850.html (accessed June 27, 2012).

53. Suzanne Choney, "New York Times Hacked, Syrian Electronic Army Suspected," *NBC News*, August 28, 2013, http://www.nbcnews.com/technology/new-york-times-hacked-syrian-electronic-army-suspected-8C11016739 (accessed September 2, 2013).

54. Mary Gooderham, "Companies That Go Where Others Fear to Tread," *The Globe and Mail*, June 21, 2012.

55. Geert Hofstede, *Culture's Consequences: International Differences in Work-Related Values* (Beverly Hills, CA: Sage, 1980); G. Hofstede, "The Interaction Between National and Organizational Value Systems," *Journal of Management Studies* 22 (1985): 347–357; and G. Hofstede, *Cultures and Organizations: Software of the Mind*, revised and expanded 2d ed. (New York: McGraw-Hill, 2005).

56. Geert Hofstede, "Cultural Constraints in Management Theory," *Academy of Management Executive* 7 (1993): 81–94; and G. Hofstede and M. H. Bond, "The Confucian Connection: From Cultural Roots to Economic Growth," *Organizational Dynamics* 16 (1988): 4–21.

57. Vas Taras, Piers Steel, and Bradley L. Kirkman, "Three Decades of Research on National Culture in the Workplace: Do the Differences Still Make a Difference?" *Organizational Dynamics* 40 (2011): 189–198.

58. For an overview of the research and publications related to Hofstede's dimensions, see "Retrospective: *Culture's Consequences*," a collection of articles focusing on Hofstede's work, *The Academy of Management Executive* 18, no. 1 (February 2004): 72–93; and see also Michele J. Gelfand et al., "Individualism and Collectivism," *Culture, Leadership, and Organizations: The Globe Study of 62 Societies*, ed. R. J. House et al. (Thousand Oaks, CA: Sage, 2004).

59. Mansour Javidan et al., "In the Eye of the Beholder: Cross-Cultural Lessons from Project GLOBE," *Academy of Management Perspectives* (February 2006): 67–90; Robert J. House et al., eds., *Culture, Leadership, and Organizations: The GLOBE Study of 62 Societies* (Thousand Oaks, CA: Sage Publications, 2004); M. Javidan and R. J. House, "Cultural Acumen for the Global Manager: Lessons from Project GLOBE," *Organizational Dynamics* 29, no. 4 (2001): 289–305; and R. J. House et al., "Understanding Cultures and Implicit Leadership Theories Across the Globe: An Introduction to Project GLOBE," *Journal of World Business* 37 (2002): 3–10.

60. Carlos Sanchez-Runde et al., "Looking Beyond Western Leadership Models: Implications for Global Managers," *Organizational Dynamics* 40 (2011): 207–213.

61. Golnaz Sadri, "Managing Across Cultures," *Industrial Management* (July–August 2014): 16–19; Chantell E. Nicholls, Henry W. Lane, and Mauricio Brehm Brechu, "Taking Self-Managed Teams to Mexico," *Academy of Management Executive* 13, no. 2 (1999): 15–27; Carl F. Fey and Daniel R. Denison, "Organizational Culture and Effectiveness: Can American Theory Be Applied in Russia?" *Organization Science* 14, no. 6 (November–December 2003): 686–706; Ellen F. Jackofsky, John W. Slocum Jr., and Sara J. McQuaid, "Cultural Values and the CEO: Alluring Companions?" *Academy of Management Executive* 2 (1988): 39–49.

62. This discussion of implicit communication is based on Erin Meyer, "When Culture Doesn't Translate," *Harvard Business Review* (October 2015): 66–72.

63. Ibid.

64. Sonia Kolesnikov-Jessop, "The Value of Relationships" (an interview with Ian Bickley), *The New York Times*, October 2, 2015, http://www.nytimes.com/2015/09/28/business/international/the-value-of-relationships.html?_r=0 (accessed February 8, 2016).

65. J. Kennedy and A. Everest, "Put Diversity in Context," *Personnel Journal* (September 1991): 50–54; and Sadri, "Managing Across Cultures."

66. Jane Spencer, "Lenovo Goes Global, But Not Without Strife," *The Wall Street Journal*, November 4, 2008.

67. P. Christopher Earley and Elaine Mosakowski, "Cultural Intelligence," *Harvard Business Review* (October 2004): 139.

68. Ibid.

69. This discussion is based on "For Richer, for Poorer," *The Economist* (December 1993): 66; Richard Harmsen, "The Uruguay Round: A Boon for the World Economy," *Finance & Development* (March 1995): 24–26; Salil S. Pitroda, "From GATT to WTO: The Institutionalization of World Trade," *Harvard International Review* (Spring 1995): 46–47, 66–67; and the World Trade Organization Web site, http://www.wto.org/english/thewto_e/whatis_e /tif_e/org6_e.htm (accessed March 31, 2013).

70. EUROPA Web site, "The History of the European Union," http://europa.eu/about-eu/eu-history/index_en.htm (accessed July 14, 2010).

71. European Commission Economic and Financial Affairs Web site, http://ec.europa.eu/economy_finance/euro /index_en.htm (accessed March 18, 2010).

72. John Worthing, "France in 'Economic Emergency' as Strikes Threaten to Ruin Economic Recovery and Eurozone," *Express*, May 31, 2016, http://www.express.co.uk/finance/ city/675439/Eurozone-in-crisis-Rolling-strikes-threaten-to -ruin-France-economy-hitting-rest-of-EU (accessed June 1, 2016); "Eurozone Jobs Crisis Rumbles on as Unemployment Remains at 10.2%," *Daily Mail*, May 31, 2016, http://www. thisismoney.co.uk/money/news/article-3618824/Eurozone -jobs-crisis-rumbles-unemployment-remains-10-2.html (accessed June 1, 2016); Clive Crook, "Opening Remarks: Who Lost the Euro?" part of a "Special Euro Crisis" section, *Bloomberg BusinessWeek* (May 28–June 3, 2012): 10–12; and Dalibor Rohac, "The Never-Ending Greek Tragedy," *U.S. News and World Report* (August 30, 2013), http://www .usnews.com/opinion/articles/2013/08/30/greece -shows-the-eurozone-crisis-is-far-from-over (accessed

September 2, 2013); and Todd Buell, "Germans Believe Politicians Are Lying about Crisis, Says Study," *The Wall Street Journal*, August 15, 2013, http://blogs.wsj.com /eurocrisis/2013/08/15/germans-believe-politicians-are -lying-about-crisis-says-study/ (accessed September 2, 2013).

73. Vanessa Fuhrmans and Dana Cimilluca, "Business Braces for Europe's Worst—Multinationals Scramble to Protect Cash, Revise Contracts, Tighten Payment Terms," *The Wall Street Journal*, June 1, 2012.

74. Tapan Munroe, "NAFTA Still a Work in Progress," *Knight Ridder/Tribune News Service*, January 9, 2004; and J. S. McClenahan, "NAFTA Works," *IW* (January 10, 2000): 5–6.

75. Amy Barrett, "It's a Small (Business) World," *BusinessWeek* (April 17, 1995): 96–101.

76. Darrell Rigby and Barbara Bilodeau, "Management Tools and Trends 2011," Bain & Company, Inc., www.bain.com /publications/articles/Management-tools-trends-2011.aspx (accessed June 22, 2012).

77. Jeffrey Sparshott, "NAFTA Gets Mixed Reviews," *The Washington Times*, December 18, 2003; and Munroe, "NAFTA Still a Work in Progress"; and Amy Borrus, "A Free-Trade Milestone, with Many More Miles to Go," *BusinessWeek* (August 24, 1992): 30–31.

78. Peter Baker, "Obama Showcases Bipartisan Support, Past and Present, for Pacific Trade Pact," *The New York Times*, November 14, 2015; and Jackie Calmes, "Portman Will Oppose Trans-Pacific Trade Pact," *The New York Times*, February 5, 2016.

79. Based in part on "How Well Do You Exhibit Good Intercultural Management Skills?" in John W. Newstrom and Keith Davis, *Organizational Behavior: Human Behavior at Work* (Boston, MA: McGraw-Hill Irwin, 2002), pp. 415–416.

80. Based on Gina Kolata, "Companies Facing Ethical Issue as Drugs Are Tested Over-seas," *The New York Times*, March 5, 2004; and Julie Schmit, "Costs, Regulations Move More Drug Tests Outside USA," *USA TODAY*, June 16, 2005.

Chapter 4
Managing Ethics and Social Responsibility

iStock.com/oscarhdez

Chapter Outline

Learning Outcomes

After studying this chapter, you should be able to:

4.1 Define *ethics* and explain how ethical behavior relates to behavior governed by law and free choice.

4.2 Discuss why ethics is important for managers and identify recent events that call for a renewed commitment to ethical management.

4.3 Explain the utilitarian, individualism, moral rights, justice, and practical approaches for making ethical decisions.

4.4 Describe the factors that shape a manager's ethical decision making, including levels of moral development.

4.5 Identify important stakeholders for an organization and discuss how managers balance the interests of various stakeholders.

4.6 Explain the philosophy of sustainability, including the triple bottom line, and why organizations are embracing it.

4.7 Define *corporate social responsibility* and explain the concepts of conscious capitalism and benefit corporations.

4.8 Discuss how ethical organizations are created through ethical leadership and organizational structures and systems.

Are You Ready To Be a Manager?

Before reading this chapter, please circle either "Mostly True" or "Mostly False" for each of the following five statements.

1 I always strive to do the "right thing," even when it is difficult and I might suffer negative consequences.

Mostly True ◀ ···················· ▶ Mostly False

[page 140]

2 Even if something is legal, I still maintain it is important to make moral decisions.

Mostly True ◀ ···················· ▶ Mostly False

[page 121]

3 When I am faced with a difficult decision, I try to make sure all parties involved are dealt with fairly, rather than merely trying to "win" or gain the most.

Mostly True ◀ ···················· ▶ Mostly False

[page 126]

4 When there is a right and wrong moral dilemma, I don't just act based on what people will find out, or what they will think of me, but rather look to a moral or spiritual principle to follow.

Mostly True ◀ ···················· ▶ Mostly False

[pages 126–130]

5 I am a tireless recycler and I want to work with a company that values the environment.

Mostly True ◀ ···················· ▶ Mostly False

[page 134]

Discover Your
Management Approach

What Is Your Level of Ethical Maturity?

Instructions: It probably won't happen right away, but soon enough in your duties as a new manager, you will be confronted with a situation that will test the strength of your moral beliefs or your sense of justice. Are you ready? To find out, think about times when you were part of a student or work group. To what extent does each of the following statements characterize your behavior when working with others in a group? Please answer each of the following items as Mostly True or Mostly False for you.

	Mostly True	Mostly False
1. I can clearly state the principles and values that guide my actions.	_____	_____
2. I quickly acknowledge my mistakes and take responsibility for them.	_____	_____
3. I am able to quickly "forgive and forget" when someone has made a serious mistake that affected me.	_____	_____

To complete and score the entire assessment, visit MindTap.

A law professor told *The New York Times* he was "shocked and dismayed." An alumnus said it was "one of the lowest points in Harvard's recent history." Some people, both on campus and off, say the whole incident was blown out of proportion. The incident that they're referring to was the decision of Harvard University administrators to secretly search the e-mail accounts of resident deans to identify the source of media leaks about a cheating scandal on campus. In this scandal, more than 100 students were investigated, and many of them were punished for plagiarism or for copying one another's answers on a take-home test. Administrators said the perusal of resident deans' e-mail accounts, which was limited to a search of subject lines, was handled in a way that was designed to protect the students as well as the deans. "No one's e-mails were opened and the contents of no one's e-mails were searched by human or machine," a statement said. Administrators said they initiated the search because the leak of a confidential memo regarding the cheating scandal led to concerns that other material, including confidential student information, was at risk. The episode has raised privacy concerns and breached the sometimes fragile trust that exists among administrators and faculty and staff. It appears that no policies were broken, but the criticism motivated administrators to create a task force to develop recommendations for how to handle issues of e-mail privacy.[1]

What do you think? Did Harvard administrators do anything wrong? Most organizations allow the monitoring of official workplace e-mail. One faculty member said the search seemed out of character for Harvard but that it wasn't really surprising. "I subscribe to the [rule] that I never put anything in e-mail that I wouldn't want published in the *Harvard Crimson*," he said.[2] The dean who authorized the search at Harvard said that although no policies were broken, the way she handled the incident was a mistake. She referred to her 10-year-old son in stressing "how important it is to own up to your mistakes, to apologize, and to make amends. I have to model that behavior for him."[3]

This chapter expands on the ideas about environment, corporate culture, and the international environment discussed in Chapter 3 to explore the issues of ethical behavior and corporate social responsibility. We first discuss the topic of ethical values, which builds on the idea of corporate culture. We look at the current ethical climate in corporate America, consider the business case for ethics and social responsibility, and examine fundamental approaches that can help managers think through difficult ethical issues. Understanding these ideas will help you build a solid foundation on which to base future decision making. We also examine organizational relationships to the external environment as reflected in corporate social responsibility. The final section of the chapter describes how managers create an ethical organization using codes of ethics and other organizational policies, structures, and systems.

4-1 What Is Managerial Ethics?

Ethics is difficult to define in a precise way. In a general sense, **ethics** is the code of moral principles and values that governs the behaviors of a person or group with respect to what is right or wrong. Ethics sets standards as to what is good or bad in conduct and decision making.[4] An ethical issue is present in a situation when the actions of a person or organization may harm or benefit others.[5]

Ethics can be more clearly understood when compared with behaviors governed by law and by free choice. Exhibit 4.1 illustrates that human behavior falls into three categories. The first is codified law, in which values and standards are written into the legal system and enforceable in the courts. In this area, lawmakers set rules that people and corporations must follow in a certain way, such as obtaining licenses for driving, paying corporate taxes, and following other local, state, and national laws. For example, U.S. federal prosecutors uncovered a teacher-test cheating ring in which people paid others to take teacher certification exams for them using false identification. Several people have been indicted on conspiracy charges of wire, mail, and social security fraud, and some have already gone to prison for their participation in a scheme that spanned 15 years across three states.[6] Behaviors such as fraud and tax evasion are clearly against the law. The domain of free choice is at the opposite end of the scale and pertains to behavior about which the law has no say and for which an individual or organization enjoys complete freedom. Examples include a manager's choice of where to buy a new suit and an organization's choice of which of two well-qualified suppliers to use.

Between these domains lies the area of ethics. This domain has no specific laws, yet it does have standards of conduct based on shared principles and values about moral conduct that guide an individual or company. For example, it was not illegal for Facebook to use people as unwitting test subjects by manipulating over half a million people's news feeds to change the number of positive and negative posts they saw as part of a psychological study, or for ride service Uber to order and then cancel more than 5,000 fake rides to sabotage its main rival Lyft, but these actions tarnished the reputations of these successful companies. "No matter how disruptive or innovative your business is, there are still ethical values that are fundamental that businesses

Natee Meepian/Shutterstock.com

Concept Connection

Do you Uber? The ride-hailing app has been so successful that the company's brand has become a verb in many cities. However, critics question the company's **managerial ethics**. Uber has faced many legal battles in addition to a long list of ethical challenges. The controversy intensified after one Uber vice president was overheard suggesting that Uber launch a smear campaign against journalists who were critical of the company.

Exhibit 4.1   Three Domains of Human Action

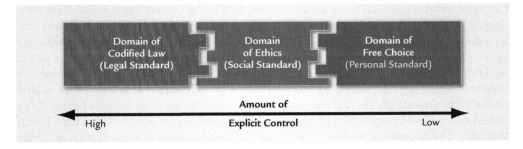

have to pay attention to," said Chris MacDonald, co-editor of the *Business Ethics Journal Review*. MacDonald and others say Silicon Valley companies are pushing the ethical boundaries, which could lead customers to take their business elsewhere. "There can be something after Facebook," MacDonald said. "And someone can eventually figure out how to beat Uber."[7] Numerous managers have gotten into trouble with the simplified view that decisions are governed by either law or free choice. This view leads people to mistakenly assume that if it's not illegal, it must be ethical, as if there were no third domain.[8] A better option is to recognize the domain of ethics and accept moral values as a powerful force for good that can regulate behaviors both inside and outside organizations.

4-1a Ethical Management Today

Every decade seems to experience its share of scoundrels, but the pervasiveness of ethical lapses during the early twenty-first century has been astounding. In a Gallup poll regarding the perception of business leaders, just 15 percent of respondents rated leaders' honesty and ethical standards as "high" or "very high."[9] More than 75 percent of people surveyed agreed with the statement that corporate America's moral compass is "pointing in the wrong direction"; 69 percent said that executives rarely consider the public good in making decisions; and a whopping 94 percent said that executives make decisions based primarily on advancing their own careers.[10]

Managers in U.S. companies aren't the only ones to experience ethical lapses. For example, former employees say managers at Japanese manufacturer Takata knew about defects in their airbags for four years before Takata said in regulatory filings that it first tested the airbags. Since that time, defective airbags have led to millions of vehicle recalls and been linked to several deaths.[11] The culture and business practices of industrial giant Toshiba have come under ethical and legal scrutiny after an independent accounting investigation found that the company overstated earnings by at least $1.2 billion over a seven-year period. Investigators say problems began during the economic slump brought about by the global financial crisis of 2008, when managers at all levels allegedly began using accounting gimmicks to appear to meet increasingly tough profit goals. The committee found that Toshiba's most senior executives were aware of the misleading accounting and that its accounting department "deliberately provided insufficient explanations to auditors, with the intention of carrying out a systematic cover-up."[12]

Managers and organizations engage in unethical behavior for any number of reasons, such as personal ego, greed, or pressures to increase profits or appear successful. Yet managers carry a tremendous responsibility for setting the ethical climate in an organization and can act as role models for ethical behavior.[13] Exhibit 4.2 details the findings from one study that boiled the range of ethical behaviors down to four primary ways in which managers can act to promote a climate in which everyone behaves in an ethical and socially responsible way. Ethical managers display honesty and integrity, communicate and enforce ethical standards through their behavior, are fair in their decisions and the distribution of rewards, and show kindness and concern for others.[14]

Unfortunately, in today's environment, an overemphasis on pleasing shareholders may cause some managers to behave unethically toward customers, employees, and the broader society. Managers are under enormous pressure to meet short-term earnings goals, and some even use accounting gimmicks or other techniques to show returns that meet market expectations rather than ones that reflect true performance. Moreover, most executive compensation plans include hefty stock-based incentives, a practice that sometimes encourages managers to do whatever will increase the share price, even if it hurts the company in the long run. When managers "fall prey to the siren call of shareholder value," all other stakeholders may suffer.[15]

Executive compensation has become a hot-button issue in the United States. In 2014, the average pay of CEOs at large U.S. corporations was 204 times what the average employee was paid, according to one estimate.[16] That's down from the high that was reached in the early 2000s, but by contrast, in 1980, CEO pay was only about 42 times that of the average worker. As part of the Dodd-Frank financial reform law, the Securities and Exchange Commission (SEC) recently approved a rule requiring public companies to disclose how CEO pay compares to their median pay for employees worldwide. "For any company out there, this number's going to be huge," said Steven Seelig, a senior regulatory adviser for executive compensation consultancy firm Towers Watson.[17] The question of whether it is ethical and socially responsible for managers to earn

"The bottom line is that when shareholder value capitalism is paramount, the rest of us suffer. CEOs will readily dupe customers, sack employees, and spoil the environment to meet expectations."

—ROGER MARTIN, AUTHOR AND FORMER DEAN AND PROFESSOR AT THE ROTMAN SCHOOL OF MANAGEMENT, TORONTO

Exhibit 4.2 **Four Types of Ethical Manager Behavior**

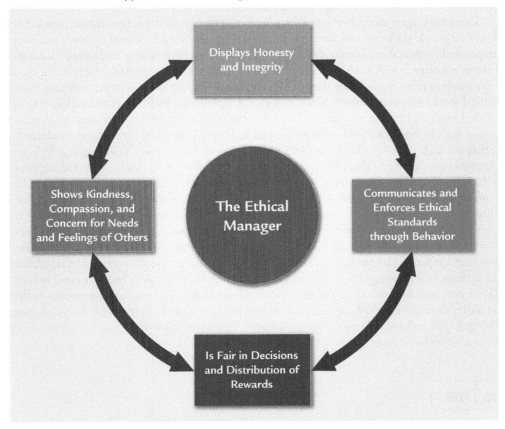

SOURCE: Based on Gary Yukl et al., "An Improved Measure of Ethical Leadership," *Journal of Leadership and Organizational Studies* 20, no. 1 (2013): 38–48.

huge sums of money compared to other employees is of growing concern, and in general, the widespread ethical lapses of the past decade have put managers under increasing scrutiny.

4-1b The Business Case for Ethics and Social Responsibility

Naturally, the relationship of ethics and social responsibility to an organization's financial performance concerns both managers and management scholars and has generated a lively debate.[18] Hundreds of studies have been undertaken to determine whether heightened ethical and social responsiveness increases or decreases a company's financial performance. Studies have provided varying results, but they have generally found a positive relationship between ethical and socially responsible behavior and a firm's financial performance.[19] For example, a study found that the top 100 global corporations that have made a commitment to *sustainability*, weaving environmental and social concerns into all their decisions, had significantly higher sales growth, return on assets, profits, and cash flow from operations in at least some areas of the business.[20] The philosophy of sustainability will be discussed later in this chapter. Another review of the financial performance of large U.S. corporations considered "best corporate citizens" found that they enjoy both superior reputations and superior financial performance.[21]

testing/Shutterstock.com

Concept Connection

Known for its **commitment to sustainability**, the German sports apparel manufacturer Adidas ranked fifth on a recent list of Top 100 Most Sustainable Corporations in the World. Kudos for the company's sustainability efforts may give Adidas a competitive edge over rivals like Nike and Puma because such recognition helps attract new customers and a better quality of employee.

Although results from these studies are not proof, they do provide an indication that using resources for ethics and social responsibility does not hurt companies.[22]

Shrewd managers also consider nonfinancial factors that create value. For example, researchers find that people prefer to work for companies that demonstrate a high level of ethics and social responsibility; thus, these organizations can attract and retain high-quality employees.[23] Customers pay attention, too. A study by Walker Research indicates that, price and quality being equal, two-thirds of customers say that they would switch brands to do business with a company that is ethical and socially responsible.[24] Another series of experiments by Remi Trudel and June Cotte of the University of Western Ontario's Ivey School of Business found that consumers were willing to pay slightly more for products they were told had been made using high ethical standards.[25]

There are high costs associated with ethical breakdowns. Think about Volkswagen, which was described in Chapter 1. The EPA said it would order VW to recall nearly half a million diesel vehicles, and the company would face fines that could reach as much as $37,500 per car. The company's share price plunged 30 percent within days after news broke that VW had sold cars that intentionally faked emissions testing. *Consumer Reports* suspended its "recommended" ratings on VW's Jetta and Passat diesel-engine models, and customers who thought they were buying environmentally friendly vehicles were left feeling angry and betrayed. A Seattle-based law firm has filed a class-action suit on behalf of owners that accuses Volkswagen of fraud, false advertising, and violating consumer rights, and there will almost certainly be many more lawsuits. "It's a new level of cynicism in the auto industry," said Jack R. Nerad, executive market analyst at Kelley Blue Book. "We have seen honest mistakes and lapses of judgment before, and tragic things happening, but this strikes me as different. The intent from the beginning seemed to be to evade standard norms."[26]

Remember This

- Managers face many pressures that can sometimes tempt them to engage in unethical behavior.
- **Ethics** is the code of moral principles and values that governs the behaviors of a person or group with respect to what is right or wrong.
- Just because managers aren't breaking the law doesn't necessarily mean that they are being ethical.
- Ethical managers display honesty and integrity, act in a way that communicates and enforces ethical standards, are fair in their decisions and the

- distribution of rewards, and show kindness and concern for others.
- Unethical managers seek to serve their own needs and interests at the expense of stakeholders.
- Confidence in business managers and leaders in all walks of life is at an all-time low.
- One hot-button ethical issue concerns excessive executive compensation.
- Companies that are ethical and socially responsible perform as well as—often even better than—those that are not socially responsible.

4-2 Ethical Dilemmas: What Would You Do?[27]

Being ethical is always about making decisions. An **ethical dilemma** arises in a situation concerning right or wrong when values are in conflict. Right and wrong cannot be clearly identified. Ethical issues can be exceedingly complex, and people may hold widely divergent views about the most ethically appropriate or inappropriate actions related to a situation.[28] Consider the issue of competitive intelligence (CI). Companies are increasingly using social media to learn more about their competitors, with some even going so far as to "friend" customers or employees of rivals and post seemingly innocuous questions to gather information that can provide the company with a competitive advantage.[29] The laws regarding information gathering aren't clear-cut, and neither are opinions regarding the ethics of such tactics. Whereas some people think that any form of corporate spying is wrong, others consider it an acceptable way of learning about the competition.[30]

The individual who must make an ethical choice in an organization is the *moral agent*.[31] Here are some dilemmas that a manager in an organization might face. Think about how you would handle them:

1. As top executive at a small, local bank, you have been asked to set up an account for a fledgling company involved in the emerging marijuana industry. You've read reports of the medical benefits of cannabis, and you know that banks in numerous states have opened their doors to marijuana-related businesses. However, you also know that public opinion in your area is highly divided over whether involvement with the cannabis industry is ethical or unethical.[32]

2. You work at a large corporation that requires a terrorist watch list screening for all new customers, which takes approximately 24 hours from the time an order is placed. You can close a lucrative deal with a potential long-term customer if you agree to ship the products overnight, even though that means the required watch list screening will have to be done after the fact.[33]

3. As a sales manager for a major pharmaceuticals company, you've been asked to promote a new drug that costs $2,500 per dose. You've read the reports saying that the drug is only 1 percent more effective than an alternative drug that costs less than $625 per dose. The vice president of sales wants you to promote the $2,500-per-dose drug aggressively. He reminds you that if you don't, lives could be lost that might have been saved with that 1 percent increase in the drug's effectiveness.

These kinds of dilemmas and issues fall squarely in the domain of ethics. How would you handle each of these situations?

> ### Remember This
>
> - Ethics is about making choices.
> - Most managers encounter ethical dilemmas that are tough to resolve.
>
> - An **ethical dilemma** is a situation in which all alternative choices or behaviors have potentially negative consequences. Right and wrong cannot be clearly distinguished.

4-3 Frameworks for Ethical Decision Making

Most ethical dilemmas involve a conflict between the needs of the part and of the whole—the individual versus the organization or the organization versus society as a whole. For example, should a company scrutinize job candidates' or employees' social media postings, which might benefit the organization as a whole but reduce the individual freedom of employees? Or should products that fail to meet tough Food and Drug Administration (FDA) standards be exported to other countries where government standards are lower, thereby benefiting the company but potentially harming world citizens? Sometimes ethical decisions entail a conflict between two groups. For example, should the potential for local health problems resulting from a company's effluents take precedence over the jobs the company creates as the town's leading employer?

Managers faced with these kinds of tough ethical choices often benefit from a normative strategy—one based on norms and values—to guide their decision making. Normative ethics uses several approaches to describe values for guiding ethical decision making. Five approaches that are relevant to managers are the utilitarian approach, individualism approach, moral rights approach, justice approach, and practical approach.[34]

4-3a Utilitarian Approach

The **utilitarian approach**, espoused by the nineteenth-century philosophers Jeremy Bentham and John Stuart Mill, holds that moral behavior produces the greatest good for the greatest number. Under this approach, a decision maker is expected to consider the effect of each decision alternative on all parties and select the one that optimizes the benefits for the greatest number of people. The utilitarian ethic is cited as the basis for the recent trend among companies to monitor employee use of the Internet and police personal habits such as alcohol and tobacco consumption because such behavior affects the entire workplace.[35]

4-3b Individualism Approach

The **individualism approach** contends that acts are moral when they promote the individual's best long-term interests.[36] In theory, with everyone pursuing self-direction, the greater good is ultimately served because people learn to accommodate each other in their own long-term interest. Individualism is believed to lead to honesty and integrity because that works best in the long run. Lying and cheating for immediate self-interest just causes business associates to lie and cheat in return. Thus, proponents say, individualism ultimately leads to behavior toward others that fits standards of behavior that people want toward themselves.[37] However, because individualism is easily misinterpreted to support immediate self-gain, it is not popular in the highly organized and group-oriented society of today.

4-3c Moral Rights Approach

The **moral rights approach** asserts that human beings have fundamental rights and liberties that cannot be taken away by an individual's decision. Thus, an ethically correct decision is one that best maintains the rights of those affected by it. To make ethical decisions, managers need to avoid interfering with the fundamental rights of others, such as the right to privacy, the right of free consent, or the right to freedom of speech. Performing experimental treatments on unconscious trauma patients, for example, might be construed to violate the right to free consent. A decision to monitor employees' nonwork activities violates the right to privacy. The right of free speech would support whistle-blowers who call attention to illegal or inappropriate actions within a company.

Jim West/Alamy Stock Photo

Concept Connection

Way back when labor unions first began to emerge, proponents took a **moral rights approach** to ethics in the workplace. They believed that workers had a right to earn a decent living wage and to have some time off from work each week. Some businesses tried to stop people from forming labor unions, so the moral rights support of the freedom of speech also became an important part of the movement. Union members today still share this same viewpoint.

4-3d Justice Approach

The **justice approach** holds that moral decisions must be based on standards of equity, fairness, and impartiality. Three types of justice are of concern to managers. **Distributive justice** requires that different treatment of people not be based on arbitrary characteristics. For example, men and women should not receive different salaries if they have the same qualifications and are performing the same job. **Procedural justice** requires that rules be administered fairly. Rules should be clearly stated and consistently and impartially enforced. **Compensatory justice** argues that individuals should be compensated for the cost of their injuries by the party responsible. The justice approach is closest to the thinking underlying the domain of law in Exhibit 4.1 because it assumes that justice is applied through rules and regulations. Managers are expected to define attributes on which different treatment of employees is acceptable.

4-3e Practical Approach

The approaches discussed so far presume to determine what is "right" or good in a moral sense. However, as has been mentioned, ethical issues are frequently not clear-cut, and there are disagreements over what is the ethical choice. The **practical approach** sidesteps debates about what is right, good, or just and bases decisions on prevailing standards of the profession and the larger society, taking the interests of all stakeholders into account.[38]

Sunny Side Up

Paula Reid, U.S. Secret Service

Put aside the issue of whether it is morally wrong to hire a prostitute, particularly in a country where prostitution is legal in certain areas. The bottom line for Paula Reid is that visits to strip clubs, heavy drinking, and payments to prostitutes are not acceptable behavior for Secret Service agents charged with protecting the President of the United States.

"If every boss was Paula Reid," said a former agent, "the Secret Service would never have a problem. It would be a lot more boring, but never a problem." Reid, the new supervising manager for the Miami office, a prestigious division that oversees the South American region, acted swiftly when she received a report of a disturbance at the hotel where agents preparing for President Barack

Obama's visit to Cartagena were staying. Based on information from the hotel manager, Reid swiftly rounded up a dozen agents, ordered them out of the country, and notified her superiors that she had found evidence of "egregious misconduct." She acted in spite of a potential internal backlash because she believed that the actions of the agents had both hurt the agency's reputation and damaged its ability to fulfill its protective and investigative missions.

For Reid and others, the "boys will be boys" mentality is not practical or acceptable. According to former director Ralph Basham, there are many former and current agents who are "deeply ashamed of what these people did."[39]

The action of Paula Reid, the manager who set the U.S. Secret Service prostitution scandal in motion by reporting the misconduct of agents in Cartagena, Colombia, was based largely on the practical approach.

With the practical approach, a decision would be considered ethical if it is one that would be considered acceptable by the professional community, one that the manager would not hesitate to publicize on the evening news, and one that a person would typically feel comfortable explaining to family and friends. Using the practical approach, managers may combine elements of the utilitarian, moral rights, and justice approaches in their thinking and decision making. For example, one expert on business ethics suggests that managers can ask themselves the following five questions to help resolve ethical dilemmas.[40] Note that these questions cover a variety of the approaches discussed previously.

1. What's in it for me?

2. What decision would lead to the greatest good for the greatest number?

3. What rules, policies, or social norms apply?

4. What are my obligations to others?

5. What will be the long-term impact for myself and important stakeholders?

Remember This

- Most ethical dilemmas involve a conflict between the interests of different groups or between the needs of the individual versus the needs of the organization.

- Managers can use various approaches based on norms and values to help them make ethical decisions.

- The **utilitarian approach** to ethical decision making says that the ethical choice is the one that produces the greatest good for the greatest number.

- The **individualism approach** suggests that actions are ethical when they promote the individual's best long-term interests because with everyone pursuing self-interest, the greater good is ultimately served. This concept is not considered appropriate today because it is easily misused to support one's personal gain at the expense of others.

- Some managers rely on a **moral rights approach**, which holds that ethical decisions are those that best maintain the fundamental rights of the people affected by them.

- The **justice approach** says that ethical decisions must be based on standards of equity, fairness, and impartiality.

- **Distributive justice** requires that different treatment of individuals not be based on arbitrary characteristics.

- **Procedural justice** holds that rules should be clearly stated and consistently and impartially enforced.

- **Compensatory justice** argues that individuals should be compensated for the cost of their injuries by the party responsible, and individuals should not be held responsible for matters over which they have no control.

- Many managers also use the **practical approach**, which sidesteps debates about what is right, good, or just and bases decisions on prevailing standards of the profession and the larger society and, in so doing, takes into account the interests of all stakeholders.

4-4 The Individual Manager and Ethical Choices

A recent study found that organizational factors such as an unethical corporate culture and pressure from superiors and colleagues can induce employees to behave unethically. Moreover, when people experience organizational pressure to go against their sense of what is right, they typically become frustrated and emotionally exhausted.[41] Yet there are also personal factors that influence a manager's ability to make ethical decisions. Individuals bring specific personality and behavioral traits to the job. Personal needs, family influence, and religious background all shape a manager's value system. Specific personality characteristics, such as ego strength, self-confidence, and a strong sense of independence, may enable managers to make more ethical choices despite outside pressures and personal risks.

For Robert Vito, his sense of entrepreneurship and fair play led to his designing equipment that would help prevent athletes' injuries, a kind of on-the-job safety issue that has caused the U.S. Occupational Safety and Health Administration to threaten the football league with shutdown, as described in the "Sunny Side Up" box.

4-4a The Stages of Moral Development

Visit MindTap for "Self-Assessment: What Is Your Level of Ethical Maturity?" which will give you some insight into your own level of ethical maturity. A high level of ethical maturity can help managers make ethical choices in the face of opposition or pressure from others.

One important personal factor is the stage of moral development.[42] A simplified version of one model of personal moral development is shown in Exhibit 4.3.

At the *preconventional level*, individuals are concerned with external rewards and punishments and obey authority to avoid detrimental personal consequences. In an organizational context, this level may be associated with managers who use an autocratic or coercive leadership style, with employees oriented toward dependable accomplishment of specific tasks.

At level 2, called the *conventional level*, people learn to conform to the expectations of good behavior as defined by colleagues, family, friends, and society. Meeting social and interpersonal obligations is important. Work-group collaboration is the preferred manner of accomplishing organizational goals, and managers use a leadership style that encourages interpersonal relationships and cooperation.

At the *postconventional*, or *principled*, level, individuals are guided by an internal set of values based on universal principles of justice and will even disobey rules or laws that violate these principles. Internal values become more important than the expectations of significant others. One example of the postconventional approach was the lifeguard in Hallandale Beach, Florida, who was fired for leaving his assigned zone to help a drowning man even though his supervisor ordered him not to leave his zone and to call 911 instead. "What he did was his own decision," said a manager for the company. "He knew the rules."[43]

Sunny Side Up

Unequal Technologies

In 2012 over 3,000 retired NFL players and their families sued the National Football League for allegedly covering up information about head injuries and brain disease. Though football is as popular as ever and about 100 million people watch the Super Bowl, football head injuries have been dominating the news.

Robert Vito founded Unequal technologies in 2008 to supply his patented lightweight bulletproof vests for soldiers and initially got a contract for 10,000 vests for NATO troops. Then in 2010 the company developed a modified vest for Philadelphia Eagles Michael Vick, who had a sternum injury. Vick wore the Exo Armour and led the Eagles to a strong victory. Before Vito could turn around, the Exo was being worn by NFL players from several teams. In 2011, Vita was asked to use the military technologies to make a helmet to prevent injuries, and the company created concussion-reduction-technology, which was a kind of peel-and-stick method of combining new padding with that already in the helmets. The composite material diffuses the impact throughout the whole helmet before it reaches the skull.

Building on successes, the 24 employees of Unequal were working with 27 of the 32 NFL teams by 2013, and the company is branching out to hockey, lacrosse, and baseball (re-engineering the bats). Its products sell for $40 to $150, and the company did $561 million in sales in 2011. By 2017, it was a leader in providing protection in girls' soccer.

Vito not only wants his business to thrive, but he wants to be part of the solution to head injuries. His next target is amateur sports. "My customer is the mom in Missouri who's buying our products for her kid," says Vito.

SOURCES: "Girls Soccer, not football, holds the highest risk of concussion," PR Newswire, Aug. 24, 2017 https://search-proquest-com.proxy.library.vanderbilt.edu/docview/1931593510 /5F8E635E297141A8PQ/3?accountid=14816; Alex Riley, Head gear or baseball still evolving, *Tribune business News*, April 19, 2014.

Research suggests that managers at higher stages of moral development have an influence on followers. The great majority of managers operate at level 2, meaning that their ethical thought and behavior is greatly influenced by their superiors and colleagues in the organization or industry. Only about 20 percent of U.S. adults reach the postconventional stage of moral development. People at level 3 are able to act in an independent, ethical manner regardless of expectations from

Exhibit 4.3 Three Levels of Personal Moral Development

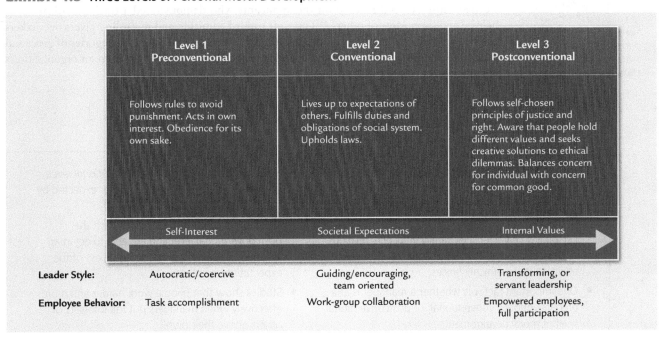

	Level 1 Preconventional	Level 2 Conventional	Level 3 Postconventional
	Follows rules to avoid punishment. Acts in own interest. Obedience for its own sake.	Lives up to expectations of others. Fulfills duties and obligations of social system. Upholds laws.	Follows self-chosen principles of justice and right. Aware that people hold different values and seeks creative solutions to ethical dilemmas. Balances concern for individual with concern for common good.
	Self-Interest	Societal Expectations	Internal Values
Leader Style:	Autocratic/coercive	Guiding/encouraging, team oriented	Transforming, or servant leadership
Employee Behavior:	Task accomplishment	Work-group collaboration	Empowered employees, full participation

SOURCES: Based on L. Kohlberg, "Moral Stages and Moralization: The Cognitive-Developmental Approach," in *Moral Development and Behavior: Theory, Research, and Social Issues*, ed. T. Lickona (New York: Holt, Rinehart, and Winston, 1976), pp. 31–53; and Jill W. Graham, "Leadership, Moral Development, and Citizenship Behavior," *Business Ethics Quarterly* 5, no. 1 (January 1995): 43–54.

Joerg Boethling/Alamy Stock Photo

Concept Connection

Ahmed Rahim, CEO of Numi Teas in Oakland, California, functions at a **postconventional level** of moral development. Rahim is committed to fair trade practices and to reducing the carbon footprint of his organization on the planet. But this leader has taken things a step further. Partnering with SCS Global Services and other third-party verifiers, Numi Teas has created a proprietary training program that teaches other business leaders how to adopt and verify fair labor practices on a global scale.

Visit MindTap for the "Self-Assessment: Are You a Giver or a Taker?" to see if you have the personal characteristics of a giver or a taker. What do you think your pattern means for your success and effectiveness as a manager?

others inside or outside the organization. More importantly, one study found that leaders at a level of high moral reasoning stood out as ethical role models whose behavior and communications attracted followers' attention.[44]

4-4b Giving versus Taking

When managers operate from a higher level of development, they may use a form of servant leadership, focusing on the needs of followers and encouraging others to think for themselves. Research has shown that people will work harder and more effectively for people who put others' interests and needs above their own.[45]

Organizations with giving cultures in which people help one another share information, collaborate, and also tend to be more effective. A study by Harvard psychologists of teams in the U.S. intelligence system found that the single biggest predictor of a team's effectiveness was the amount of help and support that members gave to one another. Other studies have discovered that giving and helping behavior influences effectiveness in organizations as diverse as pharmaceutical firms, banks, paper mills, and restaurants.[46] Adam Grant, an organizational psychologist at the Wharton School of the University of Pennsylvania, has been observing and studying the differences between "givers" and "takers" since he was an undergraduate student, and he says that changes in society and organizations make self-sacrifice for the sake of a larger purpose an increasingly beneficial characteristic.

Grant says that, in the past, takers (people who put their own interests first) could climb to the top over the backs of givers, but that is changing as the nature of work has shifted. Many companies, such as Berkshire Hathaway, Robert W. Baird, and IDEO, have official policies against hiring people who act like takers.[47] When Howard Lee was heading the South China office for Groupon, he received a flood of applications for sales jobs. By searching social media, he could identify that some candidates had a pattern of self-serving behavior. He quickly weeded those out and focused on the applicants who demonstrated a track record of being helpful and supportive of others.[48] The shift toward admiring and rewarding givers over takers can bring significant positive changes within organizations. The simple categories of *giver* and *taker* help people understand how they might contribute to or detract from an organization's ethical culture.

Remember This

- Organizational pressures can influence people to go against their own sense of right or wrong, and the resulting stress can lead to mental exhaustion and burnout.
- Personality characteristics, family influence, religious background, and other factors influence a manager's ability to make ethical choices.
- One important factor is whether a manager is at a preconventional, conventional, or postconventional level of moral development.

- Most managers operate at a *conventional level*, conforming to standards of behavior expected by society.
- Only about 20 percent of adults reach the *postconventional level* and are able to act in an independent, ethical manner regardless of the expectations of others.
- Studies show that people work harder and more effectively when managers put the interests of others above their own.

4-5 What Is Corporate Social Responsibility?

There has been an explosion of interest in recent years in the concept of corporate social responsibility.[49] In one sense, the concept of social responsibility, like ethics, is easy to understand: It means distinguishing right from wrong and doing right. It means being a good corporate citizen. The formal definition of **corporate social responsibility (CSR)** is management's obligation to make choices and take actions that will contribute to the welfare and interests of society, not just the organization.[50]

As straightforward as this definition seems, CSR can be a difficult concept to grasp because different people have different beliefs as to which actions improve society's welfare.[51] To make matters worse, social responsibility covers a range of issues, many of which are ambiguous with respect to right or wrong. If a bank deposits the money from a trust fund into a low-interest account for 90 days from which it makes a substantial profit, is it being a responsible corporate citizen? How about two companies engaging in intense competition? Is it socially responsible for the stronger corporation to drive the weaker one out of business or into a forced merger? Or consider General Motors (GM), Lehman Brothers, Hostess Brands, and the numerous other companies that have declared bankruptcy in recent years—which is perfectly legal—and thus avoided having to meet their mounting financial obligations to suppliers, labor unions, or competitors. These examples contain moral, legal, and economic complexities that make socially responsible behavior hard to define.

4-5a Organizational Stakeholders

One reason for the difficulty of understanding and applying CSR is that managers must confront the question, "Responsibility to whom?" Recall from Chapter 2 that the organization's environment consists of several sectors in both the task and the general environment. From a social responsibility perspective, enlightened organizations view the internal and external environment as a variety of stakeholders.

A **stakeholder** is any group or person within or outside the organization that has some type of investment or interest in the organization's performance and is affected by the organization's actions (employees, customers, shareholders, and so forth). Each stakeholder has a different criterion of responsiveness because it has a different interest in the organization.[52] There is growing interest in a technique called **stakeholder mapping**, which provides a systematic way to identify the expectations, needs, importance, and relative power of various stakeholders, which may change over time.[53] Stakeholder mapping helps managers identify or prioritize the key stakeholders related to a specific issue or project. For instance, when reports surfaced in the fall of 2009 that a contractor in Lesotho, Africa, that made clothing for Gap Inc. and other U.S. companies, was dumping toxic materials into local landfills and discharging chemicals into the Caledon River, managers at Gap were able to swing into action immediately. By using stakeholder mapping, Gap had identified key stakeholders and carefully cultivated open relationships with labor groups, human rights organizations, trade unions, nongovernmental organizations, and other groups. In the past, managers' approach would have been to deny responsibility and blame the subcontractor. With the Lesotho incident, however, Gap's top leaders immediately stepped forward to declare the company's commitment to fair and safe conditions and outline the steps Gap would take in dealing with this contractor. Because of the relationships Gap had developed with numerous stakeholder groups, the company had the support of labor and human rights organizations, which praised managers' commitment and actions.[54]

The global supply chain is a source of ongoing challenges for managers. As Dan Rees, former director of the Ethical Trading Initiative (ETI) said, "It is not a crime to find child labor in your supply chain. What is important is what you do about it when you find out."[55] Many companies retract their orders and stop doing business with companies that are found to use unsafe or unethical practices. A more recent approach some are taking is to work closely with overseas

HOT TOPIC

factories to improve their conditions, which managers say benefits both sides of the equation.[56] By using stakeholder mapping and cultivating open, trust-based relationships with key stakeholders, companies such as Gap are trying to ensure that managers are able to do the right thing swiftly, sometimes with the result that crises can become opportunities.

Exhibit 4.4 illustrates important stakeholders for a large organization such as Gap. Most organizations are influenced by a similar variety of stakeholder groups. Investors and shareholders, employees, customers, and suppliers are considered primary stakeholders without whom the organization cannot survive. Investors', shareholders', and suppliers' interests are served by managerial efficiency—that is, use of resources to achieve profits. Employees expect work satisfaction, pay, and good supervision. Customers are concerned with decisions about the quality, safety, and availability of goods and services. When any primary stakeholder group becomes seriously dissatisfied, the organization's viability is threatened.[57]

Other important stakeholders are the government and the community, which have become increasingly important in recent years. Corporations, for example, must operate within the limits of safety laws, environmental protection requirements, antitrust regulations, antibribery legislation, and other laws and regulations in the government sector. The community sector includes local governments, the natural environment, and the quality of life provided for residents. For many companies such as Gap, trade unions and human rights organizations are highly important stakeholders. Special interest groups may include trade associations, political action committees, professional associations, and consumerists.

Exhibit 4.4 **Major Stakeholders Relevant to Gap Inc.**

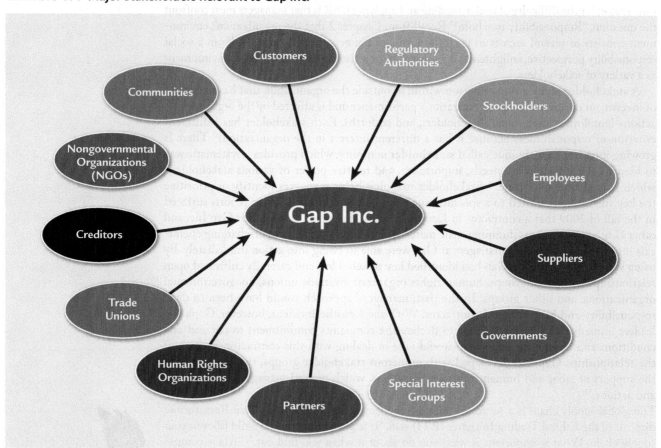

SOURCES: Based on information in D. Wheeler, B. Colbert, and R. E. Freeman, "Focusing on Value: Reconciling Corporate Social Responsibility, Sustainability, and a Stakeholder Approach in a Networked World," *Journal of General Management* 28, no. 3 (Spring 2003): 1–28; J. E. Post, L. E. Preston, and S. Sachs, "Managing the Extended Enterprise: The New Stakeholder View," *California Management Review* 45, no. 1 (Fall 2002): 6–28; and N. Craig Smith, Sean Ansett, and Lior Erex, "How Gap Inc. Engaged with Its Stakeholders," *MIT Sloan Management Review* 52, no. 4 (Summer 2011): 69–76.

- **Corporate social responsibility (CSR)** refers to the obligation of organizational managers to make choices and take actions that will enhance the welfare and interests of society as well as the organization.
- Different stakeholders have different interests in the organization and thus different criteria for social responsiveness.
- The term **stakeholder** refers to any group or person within or outside the organization that has some type of investment or interest in the organization's performance.
- Shareholders, employees, customers, and suppliers are considered primary stakeholders without whom the organization could not survive.
- **Stakeholder mapping** provides a systematic way to identify the expectations, needs, importance, and relative power of various stakeholders.

4-5b Conscious Capitalism

A number of both large and small companies are pursuing strategies and business opportunities that embrace a philosophy that has been called *conscious capitalism*. **Conscious capitalism**, which has also been referred to as a *shared value approach*, refers to following organizational policies and practices that both enhance the economic success of a company and advance the economic and social conditions of the communities in which the company operates.[58] Hindustan Unilever, for example, uses a direct-to-home distribution system for its hygiene products in parts of India, whereby women from low-income households in villages of less than 2,000 people are given micro loans and training to start their own small businesses. The system benefits communities by giving women skills and opportunities that sometimes double their household income, as well as by reducing the spread of disease by bringing hygiene products into isolated areas. It also benefits the company by extending its market and building its brand in hard-to-reach areas. The project now accounts for 5 percent of Hindustan Unilever's revenue in India.[59]

Conscious capitalism means having a higher purpose besides just making money by focusing on employees, customers, suppliers, and the community as well as on shareholders; seeking to bring out the best in people; and fostering trust and respect. One organization that reflects a conscious capitalism philosophy is The Container Store, as described in the following "Sunny Side Up" box.

Sunny Side Up   The Container Store

At The Container Store, CEO Kip Tindell renamed Valentine's Day "We Love Our Employees Day." Managers bring gifts and chocolates and make a point of telling employees they love them. It's just one symbol of the importance The Container Store puts on treating people and relationships with love and respect.

When Tindell co-founded The Container Store in 1978, he knew he wanted to build a different kind of company, one where employees were treated well and paid well and business was conducted to benefit all stakeholders. Tindell's approach, which he calls the Foundation Principles, is a key part of the corporate culture at The Container Store. It's a model "for conducting business without any trade-offs." Managers make clear what the company stands for, and everyone is expected to honor the values 100 percent of the time.

In addition to the We Love Our Employees Day, The Container Store has an annual chili cook-off and other special events. Whenever there's news to celebrate, people are gathered together for games and snacks and lots of confetti. Tindell believes it is important to recognize employees' efforts not only because it makes them happier and more fulfilled but also because the recognition trickles down and makes better, stronger families and communities. "I enjoy making money for myself and the people around me," Tindell says. "I'm not saying this is the only way to make money. I'm saying this is the best way."[60]

Other companies that embrace a conscious capitalism philosophy include Whole Foods Market, Costco, Pedigree, Medtronic, and Trader Joe's.

4-5c The Green Movement

When Jeffrey Immelt, CEO of General Electric (GE), first presented a plan for a "green" business initiative to 35 top GE executives in 2004, they voted it down. But Immelt, in a rare move, overruled them, and Ecomagination was born. Today, GE's Ecomagination is one of the world's most widely recognized corporate green programs. It has not only cut GE's greenhouse gas emissions by more than 30 percent but also added innovative products that are generating billions in annual revenue.[61]

Going green has become a new business imperative and is driven by shifting social attitudes, new governmental policies, climate changes, and information technology (IT), which quickly spreads any news of a corporation's negative impact on the environment. A survey found that 90 percent of Americans agree that there are important "green" issues and problems, and 82 percent think that businesses should implement environmentally friendly practices.[62] Entraprenuer Thomas McQuillan found a way to make Baldor more green with a new business opportunity, as described in the "Recipe for Success" box.

Since 2009, *Newsweek* has published a ranking that assesses the environmental performance of the 500 largest publicly traded companies in the United States and the 500 largest publicly traded global companies, which reflects the widespread interest in how companies are treating the environment. In 2015, the top five companies on *Newsweek*'s U.S. Green list were Biogen, Allergan, Adobe Systems, Broadcom Corporation, and Sigma Aldrich Corporation; this list shows the diversity of organizations embracing a green philosophy.[63] Each chapter of this text contains a "Green Power" example that highlights what companies are doing to improve their environmental performance.

Another indication of the growing consumer interest in environmentally friendly products, services, and business practices is the increasing practice of greenwashing. **Greenwashing** occurs when a company tries to portray itself as more environmentally minded than it actually is.[64] One of the most recent and most flagrant examples is Volkswagen, described in Chapter 1 and earlier in this chapter, which promoted its cars as being in the forefront of the clean energy trends even while rigging its "clean diesel" engines with software designed to trick emissions tests. Although most companies don't go as far as VW, the practice of greenwashing has intensified in recent

Recipe for Success ⟩ Urban Roots

Where someone sees waste, Thomas McQuillan, Baldor's director of food sales and sustainability, sees opportunity. Before he arrived, 150,000 pounds of waste each week were derived from the million pounds of produce delivered to Baldor's plant in the Bronx. What to do with the strawberry tops, carrot peels, onion skins, etc.? Previously, all went to the landfill. McQuillan realized it was food and should be treated as food.

Currently, nothing is hauled to the dump. Skins and other parts of veggies are bagged and sold to chefs for soups or sauces. Fruit leftovers are offered to juiceries, which use them in cold-pressed juices. Nonedible waste (such as rind from cantaloupes) is used for animal feed.

Baldor experimented and discovered it could blend scraps into completely new products and started a new line in organic food stores. Urban Roots sells items which derive from "dry vegetable blend," which contain 20 different veggies, dehydrated and crushed into a flourlike ingredient for gluten-free bakery and other foods.

The new venture saves money, because hauling scraps to the dump had cost 10 cents per pound. And it turns out, carrot scraps sell for 30 cents a pound. Who knew? Part of the challenge is getting the word out to food preparers, such as chef Adam Kaye. He uses the pale inner leaves of celery hearts for spice stocks, and he marinates the tough lettuce cores of lettuce heads. "We talk about the nose-to-tail approach in butchery," he says and we need to "apply that same approach to vegetables."

McQuillan isn't stopping there. He's experimenting re-using packaging and rethinking the unrecyclable produce containers in grocery stores. He is confident they'll find solutions. "We can do things differently."

SOURCE: Adele Peters, Peel Appeal, *INC Magazine*, August 2017, pp. 54–56.

Green Power

Riding the Wind Procter & Gamble (P&G) is in the forefront of an energy revolution, with plans to use 100 percent wind power to manufacture products such as Tide, Dawn, and Mr. Clean. A partnership with EDF Renewable Energy will build a Texas-based wind farm that will generate enough electricity each year to power all of P&G's North American Fabric & Home Care factories. P&G's North American Fabric Care president Shailesh Jejurikar said, "to put that in context: This is enough electricity to wash a million loads of laundry."

P&G announced the wind power partnership at the U.S. White House where P&G signed the "American Business Act on Climate Pledge," agreeing to achieve 30 percent renewable energy to power its plants globally by 2020, with a long-term vision of using 100 percent renewable energy. P&G has also committed to reduce absolute greenhouse gas emissions by 30 percent by 2020 as part of its mission to ride the wind.

SOURCE: Based on "Procter & Gamble to Make Iconic Brands Including Tide and Dawn with Wind Power," Procter & Gamble Press Release (October 19, 2015), http://news.pg.com/press-release/procter-gamble-make-iconic-brands-including-tide-and-dawn-wind-power (accessed February 15, 2016).

decades as companies try to capitalize on public interest in the green movement. The consulting firm TerraChoice, for example, found that almost all of the products marketed as eco-friendly contain at least some exaggeration.[65]

4-5d Sustainability and the Triple Bottom Line

Some corporations are embracing an idea called *sustainability* or *sustainable development*. **Sustainability** refers to the ability to generate wealth without compromising environmental responsibility and social stewardship, thus meeting the current and future needs of stakeholders while preserving the environment and society so that future generations can meet their needs as well.[66] With a philosophy of sustainability, managers weave environmental and social concerns into every strategic decision so that financial goals are achieved in a way that is socially and environmentally responsible. Managers in organizations that embrace sustainability measure their success in terms of a triple bottom line. The term **triple bottom line** refers to measuring an organization's social performance, its environmental performance, and its financial performance, as illustrated in Exhibit 4.5. This is sometimes called the three Ps: People, Planet, and Profit.[67]

Exhibit 4.5 **Sustainability and the Triple Bottom Line**

The "People" part of the triple bottom line looks at how socially responsible the organization is in terms of fair labor practices, diversity, supplier relationships, treatment of employees, contributions to the community, and so forth. The "Planet" aspect measures the organization's commitment to environmental sustainability. The third P, of course, looks at the organization's profit, the financial bottom line. Based on the principle that what you measure is what you strive for and achieve, using a triple-bottom-line approach to measuring performance ensures that managers take social and environmental factors into account rather than blindly pursuing profit no matter the cost to society and the natural environment.

4-5e Benefit Corporations and B Lab

> "For a long time, people believed that the only purpose of industry was to make a profit. They are wrong. Its purpose is to serve the general welfare."
>
> —HENRY FORD, SR. (1863–1947), AMERICAN INDUSTRIALIST

Businesses that focus on creating a better world have been around for some time, but this idea has really taken hold in the past few years.[68] By early 2016, 30 U.S. states and the District of Columbia had passed laws allowing mission-based businesses to incorporate as benefit corporations. A **benefit corporation** is a for-profit organization that has a stated purpose that includes creating a material that has a positive impact on society; is required to consider the impact of all decisions not only on shareholders but also on employees, the community, and the environment; and voluntarily holds itself to high standards of accountability and transparency.[69] This new form of corporation provides legal protection for managers to consider factors other than just making a profit. Managers have a legal authority to make decisions that are in the best interest of all stakeholders rather than maintaining a focus on short-term financial gains and shareholder returns. Thus, managers can choose to prioritize a social, moral, or environmental goal over financial goals without the risk of being sued by shareholders. Since the first benefit corporation law was passed by Maryland in 2010, numerous small and large companies, including Patagonia, Method, Plum Organics, King Arthur Flour, American Prison Data Systems, and Kickstarter, have been incorporated or reincorporated as benefit corporations.

One of the strongest proponents of benefit corporation legislation is B Lab, which is a nonprofit organization founded in 2006 by three friends who had extensive experience in the business world and who believed "the interests of business and society were no longer aligned."[70] B Lab has its own nonlegal framework for certifying businesses as B Corporations. Being a Certified B Corporation means that a company meets B Lab's highest standards of verified, overall social and environmental performance, public transparency, and legal accountability.[71] Companies can incorporate as benefit corporations without getting B Lab certification, but many choose to do both to reflect their high commitment to environmental and social performance. For example, according to one of B Lab's co-founders, having their social and environmental performance assessed and verified by the independent nonprofit organization and making that verified performance transparent helps companies avoid unintentional greenwashing, as defined earlier.[72] More than 1,400 companies have already been certified as B Corporations.

Remember This

- **Conscious capitalism** refers to following organizational policies and practices that both enhance the economic success of a company and advance the economic and social conditions of the communities in which the company operates.

- Companies that embrace a conscious capitalism philosophy include The Container Store, Whole Foods Market, and Trader Joe's.

- The *green movement* is a special interest group of particular importance today.

- Volkswagen is a recent example of **greenwashing**, which occurs when a company tries to portray itself as more environmentally minded than it actually is.

- **Sustainability** refers to economic development that generates wealth and meets the needs of the current population while preserving society and the environment for the needs of future generations.

- Companies that embrace sustainability measure performance in terms of financial performance, social performance, and environmental

- performance, which are collectively referred to as the **triple bottom line**.
- A survey found that 90 percent of Americans agree that there are important "green" issues and problems, and 82 percent think that businesses should implement environmentally friendly practices.
- Thirty states and the District of Columbia have passed laws that allow companies to be incorporated as benefit corporations.

- A **benefit corporation** is a for-profit organization that has a stated purpose of creating a positive impact on society; is required to consider the impact of decisions on employees, the community, and the environment as well as shareholders; and voluntarily holds itself to high standards of accountability and transparency.
- Companies can also be certified as B Corporations by B Lab, a nonprofit organization that provides a nonlegal framework for meeting high standards of social and environmental performance, public transparency, and legal accountability.

4-6 Managing Company Ethics and Social Responsibility

An expert on the topic of ethics said, "Management is responsible for creating and sustaining conditions in which people are likely to behave themselves."[73] Exhibit 4.6 illustrates ways in which managers create and support an ethical organization. One of the most important steps managers can take is to practice ethical leadership.[74] *Ethical leadership* means that managers are honest and trustworthy, are fair in their dealings with employees and customers, and behave ethically in both their personal and professional lives.

Managers and first-line supervisors are important role models for ethical behavior, and they strongly influence the ethical climate in the organization by adhering to high ethical standards in their own behavior and decisions. Moreover, managers are proactive in influencing employees to embody and reflect ethical values.[75] The "Sunny Side Up" box describes an approach that some leading companies are taking to strengthen managers' ethical and socially responsible underpinning.

Exhibit 4.6 Building an Ethical Organization

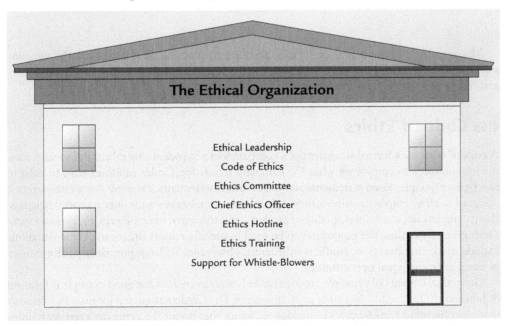

SOURCE: Adapted from Linda Klebe Treviño, Laura Pincus Hartman, and Michael Brown, "Moral Person and Moral Manager," *California Management Review* 42, no. 4 (Summer 2000): 128–142.

Sunny Side Up · Cultivating a Service Mind-Set

Some of today's best companies are taking a new approach to developing managers—global service programs that place employees with nonprofit organizations or small businesses, often in developing countries, to provide free or low-cost technical and managerial assistance. In line with the growing emphasis on sustainability and the triple bottom line, organizations want managers who have a service and sustainability mind-set rather than an attitude of getting all they can for themselves. In one survey, 88 percent of top executives said it was important that future managers have the mind-set and skills to address sustainability issues.

- **Global service programs benefit everyone.** Global service programs have been described as a "win-win-win." It might seem obvious that the nonprofit organizations served by these programs benefit, but the companies investing in them and the employees participating in them gain just as much. IBM credits its program with generating about $5 billion in new business. Companies gain greater knowledge of emerging markets, develop social capital and goodwill, and get more well-rounded managers who have adopted the service and sustainability mind-set needed in today's world. Participants benefit in numerous ways, including increased self-awareness, increased learning of new skills, and greater cross-cultural understanding.

- **Many managers view these opportunities as plum assignments.** Laura Benetti of Dow Corning spent four weeks working nine-hour days with rural women in India helping them learn how to price and market the garments they made. She and nine colleagues slept in a lodge with limited access to hot water and electricity. "It gives more meaning to your career," said Benetti. Participants in global service also appreciate the opportunity to expand their understanding of global issues. "We all *know* about things like poverty in Africa and corruption and bribery . . .," said one IBM participant who spent time in Nigeria. "This kind of experience really brings . . . things to life, you really feel it."

- **How widespread is the trend?** A recent survey by Deloitte indicates that the number of large corporations using corporate volunteering programs continues to rise steadily. Since 2008, IBM has sent more than 1,400 employees to work with projects such as reforming Kenya's postal system and developing ecotourism in Tanzania. Pfizer's program lends employees to nongovernmental organizations (NGOs) to address health care needs in Asia and Africa. The Accenture Development Partnership has been involved in more than 200 projects in 55 countries where Accenture's professionals work at 50 percent pay for up to six months with organizations such as UNICEF and Freedom from Hunger.

SOURCES: Based on Philip Mirvis, Kevin Thompson, and John Gohring, "Toward Next-Generation Leadership: Global Service," *Leader to Leader* (Spring 2012): 20–26; Matthew Gitsham, "Experiential Learning for Leadership and Sustainability at IBM and HSBC," *Journal of Management Development* 31, no. 3 (2012): 298–307; and Anne Tergesen, "Doing Good to Do Well," *The Wall Street Journal*, January 9, 2012.

Managers can also implement organizational mechanisms to help employees and the company stay on an ethical footing. Some of the primary mechanisms are codes of ethics, ethical structures, and measures to protect whistle-blowers.

4-6a Code of Ethics

A **code of ethics** is a formal statement of a company's values concerning ethics and social issues; it communicates to employees what the company stands for. Codes of ethics tend to exist in two types: principle-based statements and policy-based statements. *Principle-based statements* are designed to affect corporate culture; they define fundamental values and contain general language about company responsibilities, quality of products, and treatment of employees. *Policy-based statements* generally outline the procedures to be used in specific ethical situations. These situations include marketing practices, conflicts of interest, observance of laws, proprietary information, political gifts, and equal opportunities.

General statements of principle are often called *corporate credos*. One good example is Johnson & Johnson's "The Credo." Available in 36 languages, The Credo has guided Johnson & Johnson's managers for more than 60 years in making decisions that honor the company's responsibilities to employees, customers, the community, and stockholders. Another example is Google's *Code of Conduct*. Portions of the Google Code are shown in the "Sunny Side Up" box.

Sunny Side Up Google

Google is one of the best-known companies in the world, and managers take seriously its reputation for both technological superiority and a commitment to ethics and social responsibility. Google's Code of Conduct starts with these words: "Don't be evil. Googlers generally apply those words to how we serve our users. But 'Don't be evil' is much more than that."

Google uses a well-designed Code of Conduct to put the motto into practice. The code is divided into seven sections, with each subdivided into sections that describe specific values, policies, and expectations. The Code also clearly states that employees will be protected if they call attention to ethical violations or misconduct. Here are some excerpts from Google's Code:

Serve Our Users

Our users value Google not only because we deliver great products and services, but because we hold ourselves to a higher standard in how we treat users and operate more generally.

Respect Each Other

We are committed to a supportive work environment, where employees have the opportunity to reach their fullest potential. Each Googler is expected to do his or her utmost to create a respectful workplace culture that is free of harassment, intimidation, bias and unlawful discrimination of any kind.

Preserve Confidentiality

We get a lot of press attention around our innovations and our culture, and that's usually fine. However, company information that leaks prematurely into the press or to competitors can hurt our product launches, eliminate our competitive advantage and prove costly in other ways.

Ensure Financial Integrity and Responsibility

Financial integrity and fiscal responsibility are core aspects of corporate professionalism. . . . The money we spend on behalf of Google is not ours; it's the company's and, ultimately, our shareholders'.

Obey the Law

Google takes its responsibilities to comply with laws and regulations very seriously and each of us is expected to comply with applicable legal requirements and prohibitions.

Conclusion

Google aspires to be a different kind of company. It's impossible to spell out every possible ethical scenario we might face. Instead, we rely on one another's good judgment to uphold a high standard of integrity for ourselves and our company.

And remember . . . don't be evil, and if you see something that you think isn't right—speak up![76]

Having a strong code of conduct or code of ethics doesn't guarantee that companies won't get into ethical trouble or be challenged by stakeholders on ethical issues. Codes of ethics in and of themselves do little to influence and ensure ethical behavior among employees and managers.[77] However, they represent one key element of the organization's ethical framework. Codes of ethics state the values or behaviors expected and those that will not be tolerated. When top management supports and enforces these codes, including rewards for compliance and discipline for violation, ethics codes can boost a company's ethical climate.[78]

4-6b Ethical Structures

Ethical structures represent the various systems, positions, and programs that a company can undertake to encourage and support ethical behavior. An **ethics committee** is a group of executives (and sometimes lower-level employees as well) appointed to oversee company ethics. The committee provides rulings on questionable ethical issues and assumes responsibility for disciplining wrongdoers.

Many companies set up ethics offices with full-time staff to ensure that ethical standards are an integral part of company operations. These offices are headed by a **chief ethics officer**, sometimes called a *chief ethics and compliance officer*, a company executive who oversees all aspects of ethics and legal compliance, including establishing and broadly communicating standards, conducting ethics training programs, dealing with exceptions or problems, and advising senior managers in the ethical and compliance aspects of decisions.[79] Changing government regulations in the light of accounting irregularities require that large public firms have an individual who is responsible for the ethics and compliance program, and many experts are advising that to be effective, this person should have direct access to the board of directors.[80] Most ethics offices also serve as counseling centers to help employees resolve difficult ethical issues. A toll-free confidential *ethics hotline* allows employees to report questionable behavior as well as seek guidance concerning ethical dilemmas.

4-6c Whistle-Blowing

Employee disclosure of illegal, unethical, or illegitimate practices on the employer's part is called **whistle-blowing**.[81] But another name for this behavior is "conscience-seeking." No organization can rely exclusively on codes of conduct and ethical structures to prevent all unethical behavior. Holding organizations accountable depends to some degree on individuals who are willing to speak up if they detect illegal, dangerous, or unethical activities. Whistle-blowers often report wrongdoing to outsiders, such as regulatory agencies, senators, or newspaper reporters. Some firms have instituted innovative programs and confidential hotlines to encourage and support internal whistle-blowing. For this practice to be an effective ethical safeguard, however, companies must view whistle-blowing as a benefit to the company and make dedicated efforts to encourage and protect whistle-blowers.[82]

The following "Half-Baked Management" box illustrates what can happen when that isn't the case.

This example illustrates not only what can happen when companies don't have effective methods to support internal whistle-blowing but also how challenging it can be for managers in huge organizations to maintain oversight and control over far-flung offices and employees. JPMorgan Chase isn't the only case of managers trying to protect their organization, even at the risk of allowing unethical behavior to continue. The U.S. Office of Special Counsel recently found three Air Force officials guilty of retaliating against civilian employees who reported the mishandling of the remains of deceased soldiers at Dover Air Force Base, for example. A former executive at Countrywide Financial Corporation says he was bullied and eventually fired after he questioned the company's use of so-called "Ninja loans" (no income, no job, no assets) at the height of the subprime mortgage craze. And Matthew Lee, a former senior vice president in Lehman Brothers's accounting division, lost his job just weeks after he raised

Half-Baked Management ⟩ JPMorgan Chase

Johnny Burris was working as a broker at a JPMorgan Chase branch near Phoenix when he was promoted to work in the elite Chase Private Client division. Not long afterward, Burris was fired. His employer says Burris was fired because of poor performance and client complaints. Burris says he was fired because he blew the whistle on unethical practices.

Soon after his promotion, Burris began complaining that the company often pressured brokers to sell JP Morgan–branded mutual funds even when offerings from competitors were more suitable. After Burris started raising these concerns, his supervisors began voicing their own concerns about his job performance, and within a

few months, Burris was fired. When he sued for wrongful termination and went public with his allegations, letters of complaint from clients began showing up in Burris's disciplinary record, making it difficult for him to get another job and damaging his wrongful termination suit against JPMorgan. The trouble is, some clients have said they signed letters that were drafted by a JPMorgan employee without realizing the letters were critical of Burris. One client has even taken her money from JPMorgan because of the incident. Burris now has a whistle-blower case pending before the Occupational Safety and Health Administration (OSHA), and the SEC is investigating his allegations against his former employer.[83]

concerns about how the firm was masking risks by temporarily "parking" $50 billion in risky loan assets off its balance sheet.[84]

Unfortunately, many managers still look on whistle-blowers as disgruntled employees who aren't good team players. Yet to maintain high ethical standards, organizations need people who are willing to point out wrongdoing. Managers can be trained to view whistle-blowing as a benefit rather than a threat, and systems can be set up to protect employees who report illegal or unethical activities.

Remember This

- Managers are role models. One of the most important ways that managers create ethical and socially responsible organizations is by practicing ethical leadership.
- A **code of ethics** is a formal statement of the organization's values regarding ethics and social issues.
- An **ethics committee** is a group of executives (and sometimes lower-level employees) charged

with overseeing company ethics by ruling on questionable issues and disciplining violators.
- Some organizations have ethics offices headed by a **chief ethics officer**, a manager who oversees all aspects of ethics and legal compliance.
- Managers who want ethical organizations support **whistle-blowing**, the disclosure by employees of unethical, illegitimate, or illegal practices by the organization.

DISCUSSION QUESTIONS

1. Is it reasonable to expect that managers can measure their social and environmental performance on the same level as they measure financial performance with a triple bottom line? Discuss.

2. What is the difference between a benefit corporation and a B corporation?

3. Imagine yourself in a situation of being encouraged by colleagues to inflate your expense account. What factors do you think would influence your decision? Explain.

4. Is it ethical and socially responsible for large corporations to lobby against an SEC rule requiring that they report the ratio of their CEOs' pay compared to that of their average employee, as described in the chapter? Discuss.

5. Managers at some banks and mortgage companies have argued that providing subprime mortgages was based on their desire to give poor people a chance to participate in the American dream of home ownership. What is your opinion of this explanation in terms of ethics and social responsibility?

6. A survey found that 69 percent of MBA students view maximizing shareholder value as the primary responsibility of a company. Do you

agree? What do you think this finding suggests about the ethical and socially responsible stance of corporate managers over the next couple of decades?

7. Do you believe that it is ethical for organizational managers to try to get access to and scrutinize the Facebook pages of employees or job applicants? Discuss.

8. Which do you think would be more effective for shaping long-term ethical behavior in an organization: a written code of ethics combined with ethics training, or strong ethical leadership? Which would have more impact on you? Why?

9. The technique of stakeholder mapping lets managers classify which stakeholders they will consider more important and will invest more time to satisfy. Is it appropriate for management to define some stakeholders as more important than others? Should all stakeholders be considered as equally important?

10. This chapter described studies that show that people work harder and better for managers who put the interests of others above their own. Why might this happen? Do you believe being more of a "giver" than a "taker" will translate into greater career success for these managers? Discuss.

APPLY YOUR SKILLS: SELF-LEARNING

Ethical Work Climates[85]

Think of an organization for which you were employed. Respond to the following statements twice: The first time, circle the number that best describes the way things actually were. The second time, respond to the statements based on your beliefs about the ideal level that would meet the needs of both individuals and the organization.

Disagree ① ② ③ ④ ⑤ **Agree**

1. What was best for everyone in the company was the major consideration there.

   1   2   3   4   5

2. Our major concern was always what was best for the other person.

   1   2   3   4   5

3. People were expected to comply with the law and professional standards over and above other considerations.

   1   2   3   4   5

4. In the company, the first consideration was whether a decision violated any law.

   1   2   3   4   5

5. It was very important to follow the company's rules and procedures.

   1   2   3   4   5

6. People in the company strictly obeyed the company policies.

   1   2   3   4   5

7. In the company, people were mostly out for themselves.

   1   2   3   4   5

8. People were expected to do anything to further the company's interests, regardless of the consequences.

   1   2   3   4   5

9. In the company, people were guided by their own personal ethics.

   1   2   3   4   5

10. Each person in the company decided for himself or herself what was right and wrong.

    1   2   3   4   5

Scoring and Interpretation Subtract each of your scores for questions 7 and 8 from the number 6. Then, add up your score for all 10 questions: Actual = _____ Ideal = _____. These questions measure the dimensions of an organization's ethical climate. Questions 1 and 2 measure caring for people; questions 3 and 4 measure lawfulness; questions 5 and 6 measure adherence to rules; questions 7 and 8 measure emphasis on financial and company performance; and questions 9 and 10 measure individual independence. A total score above 40 indicates a highly positive ethical climate. A score from 30 to 40 indicates an above-average ethical climate. A score from 20 to 30 indicates a below-average ethical climate, and a score below 20 indicates a poor ethical climate. How far from your ideal score was the actual score for your organization? What does that difference mean to you?

Go back over the questions and think about changes that you could have made to improve the ethical climate in the organization. Discuss with other students what you could do as a manager to improve the ethics in future companies for which you work.

APPLY YOUR SKILLS: GROUP LEARNING

Current Events of an Unethical Type[86]

Step 1. Prior to meeting as a group, each person should find two newspaper or magazine articles from the past several months relating to someone violating business ethics or potentially breaking the law regarding business practices.

Step 2. Summarize the key points of the articles you found.

Step 3. Meet as a group. Have each person share key points from articles with group members.

Step 4. Identify similar themes across the unethical incidents reported in the articles. What was the source or underlying cause of the unethical behavior? What was the hoped-for outcome? Was an individual or a group involved? Can you identify similar conditions of any kind across incidents? Did the accused seem repentant or defensive? Write the common themes in a list on a sheet of paper or on whiteboard.

Step 5. What could you as a manager do to prevent such unethical behavior in your organization? What could you do to fix this kind of problem after it occurred in your organization?

Step 6. Report your findings to the class if asked to do so by your instructor.

Key points from articles	List theme from each article			
Article 1.				
2.				
3.				
4.				
5.				
6.				
7.				
8.				
9.				
10.				

Then fill in these boxes:

List similar themes
1.
2.
3.
4.
5.

Look at the underlying causes of the unethical behaviors

What were the sources of the underlying causes?
1.
2.
3.
4.

Why did they do it? What was the hoped for outcome?

How often was it a group?

How often an individual?

> What were the similar conditions among the various unethical scenarios?

APPLY YOUR SKILLS: ACTION LEARNING

1. Write at least three times when you were presented with an ethical dilemma, such as the opportunity to cheat on a test or a paper, being undercharged for something at a store or restaurant, being given "free" food by your friend who was an employee there, taking office supplies home from a workplace, using work time for personal activities, etc.

2. As a group of three to six people, choose three of the examples from the group to analyze.

Describe the ethical dilemma	What did you do?	What should you have done?	What ethical principle was involved?
1.			
2.			
3.			

3. Each person in the group should think of a time that someone behaved UNETHICALLY toward you. Fill out the following table.

Describe the unethical behavior	How did you react to the unethical behavior?	How did it impact your relationship with that person?	What would have been ethical behavior by the other person?

4. In your groups, discuss behaviors and consequences in your dilemmas and situations.

5. Why is it important to be ethical?

APPLY YOUR SKILLS: ETHICAL DILEMMA

Should We Go Beyond the Law?[87]

Nathan Rosillo stared out his office window at the lazy curves and lush, green, flower-lined banks of the Dutch Valley River. He'd grown up near here, and he envisioned the day that his children would enjoy the river as he had as a child. But now his own company might make that a risky proposition.

Nathan is a key product developer at Chem-Tech Corporation, an industry leader. Despite its competitive position, Chem-Tech experienced several quarters of dismal financial performance. Nathan and his team developed a new lubricant product that the company sees as the turning point in its declining fortunes.

Top executives are thrilled that they can produce the new product at a significant cost savings because of recent changes in environmental regulations. Regulatory agencies loosened requirements on reducing and recycling wastes, which means that Chem-Tech can now release waste directly into the Dutch Valley River.

Nathan is as eager as anyone to see Chem-Tech survive this economic downturn, but he doesn't think this route is the way to do it. He expressed his opposition regarding the waste dumping to both the plant manager and his direct supervisor, Martin Feldman. Martin has always supported Nathan, but this time was different. The plant manager, too, turned a deaf ear. "We're meeting government standards," he'd said. "It's up to them to protect the water. It's up to us to make a profit and stay in business."

Frustrated and confused, Nathan turned away from the window, his prime office view mocking his inability to protect the river he loved. He knew that the manufacturing vice president was visiting the plant next week. Maybe if he talked with her, she would agree that the decision to dump waste materials in the river was ethically and socially irresponsible. But if she didn't, he would be skating on thin ice. His supervisor had already accused him of not being a team player. Maybe he should just be a passive bystander—after all, the company isn't breaking any laws.

What Would You Do?

1. Talk to the manufacturing vice president and emphasize the responsibility that Chem-Tech has as an industry leader to set an example. Present her with a recommendation that Chem-Tech participate in voluntary pollution reduction as a marketing tool and as a way to position itself as the environmentally friendly choice.

2. Mind your own business and just do your job. The company isn't breaking any laws, and if Chem-Tech's economic situation doesn't improve, a lot of people will be thrown out of work.

3. Call the local environmental advocacy group and get the group to stage a protest of the company.

APPLY YOUR SKILLS: CASE FOR CRITICAL ANALYSIS

Too Much Intelligence?

The rapid growth of Pace Technologies was due in no small part to sales manager Ken Bodine and to the skills of the savvy young sales staff that he had assembled. Bodine prided himself on finding and hiring top grads from two major business schools in the area. In addition to the top salaries offered by Pace, the grads were attracted by Bodine's energy, innovative thinking, and can-do attitude. He was the embodiment of Pace culture—moving fast, ahead of the knowledge curve in high-tech. Pace's sales force consistently stunned the competition with their high performance level.

Among other things, Pace had the reputation for aggressive business intelligence. Competitors found both amusing and frustrating the company's ability to outmaneuver others and capture accounts. Bodine enjoyed the air of mystery surrounding the Pace organization. Awareness that some competitor sat on the verge of a big sale always stirred Bodine's passion for sales and ignited his desire to "one-up these guys" and grab the sale out from under them.

"If this was a poker game," one board member mused, "Pace would win every hand. It's like Bodine as well as his staff possess the uncanny ability to know the cards your company is holding. He keeps a straight face, a low profile throughout the game, and then suddenly he lays his cards on the table and you're sunk. Here at Pace, we all love it."

A former military intelligence officer, Bodine brought that "sneaky" air into the Pace culture, adding a bit of excitement to the day-to-day business of sales. "With a great product, great staff, and great business intelligence," Bodine was fond of saying, "you can dominate the market." He wanted everyone—customers, competitors, and the media—to see Pace everywhere. "Every time the competition holds a staff meeting," he said, "the first question should be, 'What's Pace doing?'"

The sales staff was a mirror image of Bodine—younger, but with the same air of invincibility, and very competitive with one another. This, too, Bodine encouraged. A chess player, he enjoyed observing and encouraging the competition within his own sales staff. And seeing the thrill it brought "the boss," ambitious salespeople worked vigorously to prove their competitive worth.

Bodine's latest competitive "match" pitted Cody Rudisell and Ali Sloan in an intellectual and strategic struggle for a coveted assignment to a potential major account with a company that had just expanded into the region. Bodine let it be known that Cody and Ali were being considered for the assignment, and that each could submit a proposal to lure the account to Pace and away from Pace's top rival, Raleigh-Tech.

Both Cody and Ali eagerly grabbed the opportunity to expand their influence within the company and to build their reputations. Putting together their presentations within a short time period meant working long days and late nights. On the evening before the presentations, Cody bounded into Ali's office and dropped a file on her desk. "Top that!" he said.

Ali began thumbing through the file, and as she looked up in startled amazement, Cody slammed his hand on the folder and jerked it from her desk.

"That's like a watershed of Raleigh-Tech's trade secrets," Ali said. "Where did you get that?"

"My secret, sweetie," Cody replied, taking a seat and noisily drumming his fingers on the folder. "With this information, R-T doesn't have a chance. And neither do you."

"You could get into all sorts of trouble," Ali said. "When you lay that on Bodine's . . . ."

"Bodine's espionage side will love it," Cody interrupted. "This is classic Bodine, classic Pace. You can't tell me that with all of the brilliant moves he's made over the years, Bodine hasn't done the same thing. This is business, cutthroat business, and I may have just topped the master. See you tomorrow."

As he left, Ali sat in stunned silence. "Cutthroat, indeed," she whispered, reaching for the phone. She held the phone for a moment, wondering whom she should call. *This is unethical, illegal*, she thought.

She hung up the phone. *Should I let him hang himself tomorrow? What if Bodine really does love it? If I call some manager tonight, will everyone see me as a sore loser and a crybaby? Is this really what it takes to win in the big leagues? Is this really the culture of this organization?*

Questions

1. How has Ken Bodine shaped the sales culture at Pace Technologies? Do you consider this culture to be at a preconventional, conventional, or post-conventional level of ethical development? Why?

2. What should Ali Sloan do? What would you actually do if you were in her place? Explain.

3. How might Cody Rudisell's decision differ if he based it on the utilitarian approach versus individualism approach versus practical approach to ethical decision making? Which approach does he appear to be using?

ENDNOTES

1. Jennifer Levitz, "Harvard Explains Secret Email Search," *The Wall Street Journal*, March 12, 2013; Jena McGregor, "The Harvard Email Controversy," *The Washington Post*, March 12, 2013, http://articles.washingtonpost.com/2013-03-11/national/37615752_1_emails-deans-search (accessed March 12, 2013); Rande Iaboni and Dana Ford, "Harvard College Dean Steps Down after E-mail Scandal," *CNN.com*, May 29, 2013, http://www.cnn.com/2013/05/28/us/massachusetts-harvard-dean (accessed September 3, 2013); and Mary Carmichael and Peter Schworm, "Harvard E-mail Searches Broader than First Described," *The Boston Globe*, April 2, 2013, http://www.bostonglobe.com/metro/2013/04/02/secret-mail-searches-harvard-cheating-scandal-broader-than-initially-described/uRRdtrde29hWtSSH5wujbO/story.html (accessed September 3, 2013).

2. Levitz, "Harvard Explains Secret Email Search."

3. Carmichael and Schworm, "Harvard E-mail Searches Broader than First Described."

4. Gordon F. Shea, *Practical Ethics* (New York: American Management Association, 1988); and Linda K. Treviño, "Ethical Decision Making in Organizations: A Person-Situation Interactionist Model," *Academy of Management Review* 11 (1986): 601–617.

5. Thomas M. Jones, "Ethical Decision Making by Individuals in Organizations: An Issue-Contingent Model," *Academy of Management Review* 16 (1991): 366–395.

6. Motoko Rich, "2 More Educators in the South Are Charged in Test Cheating," *The New York Times*, June 21, 2013, http://www.nytimes.com/2013/06/22/us/2-more-educators-in-the-south-are-charged-in-test-cheating.html?_r=0 (accessed June 29, 2013).

7. Nick Bilton, "Moral Issues Bedevil Silicon Valley," *The New York Times*, November 27, 2015.

8. Rushworth M. Kidder, "The Three Great Domains of Human Action," *Christian Science Monitor*, January 30, 1990.

9. Gallup Survey results reported in Roger Martin, "The CEO's Ethical Dilemma in the Era of Earnings Management," *Strategy & Leadership* 39, no. 6 (2011): 43–47.

10. Marist College Institute for Public Opinion and Knights of Columbus survey, results reported in Kevin Turner, "Corporate Execs: Nobody Trusts Us; U.S. Lacks Confidence in Business Ethics, Poll Says," *Florida Times Union*, February 27, 2009.

11. Hiroko Tabuchi, "Takata Saw and Hid Risk in Airbags in 2004, Former Workers Say," *The New York Times*, November 6, 2014, http://www.nytimes.com/2014/11/07/business/airbag-maker-takata-is-said-to-have-conducted-secret-tests.html?_r=0 (accessed February 9, 2016).

12. Jonathan Soble, "Panel Finds Accounting Irregularities at Toshiba," *The New York Times*, July 21, 2015.

13. Gary R. Weaver, Linda Klebe Treviño, and Bradley Agle, "'Somebody I Look Up To': Ethical Role Models in Organizations," *Organizational Dynamics* 34, no. 4 (2005): 313–330.

14. Gary Yukl et al., "An Improved Measure of Ethical Leadership," *Journal of Leadership and Organizational Studies* 20, no. 1 (2013): 38–48.

15. Martin, "The CEO's Ethical Dilemma in the Era of Earnings Management."

16. Andrew Chamberlain, "CEO to Worker Pay Ratios: Average CEO Earns 204 Times Median Worker Pay," *Glassdoor Economic Research Blog* (August 25, 2015), https://www.glassdoor.com/research/ceo-pay-ratio/ (accessed February 9, 2016).

17. Jennifer Liberto, "CEOs Earn 354 Times More than Average Worker," *CNNMoney.com*, April 15, 2013, http://money.cnn.com/2013/04/15/news/economy/ceo-pay-worker/index.html (accessed September 4, 2013); and Yuki Noguchi, "Comparing the Top Boss's Pay to Yours," *NPR.org* (August 31, 2015), http://www.npr.org/

2015/08/28/435245281/comparing-the-top-boss-pay-to-yours (accessed February 9, 2016).

18. Homer H. Johnson, "Does It Pay to Be Good? Social Responsibility and Financial Performance," *Business Horizons* (November–December 2003): 34–40; Jennifer J. Griffin and John F. Mahon, "The Corporate Social Performance and Corporate Financial Performance Debate: Twenty-Five Years of Incomparable Research," *Business and Society* 36, no. 1 (March 1997): 5–31; Bernadette M. Ruf et al., "An Empirical Investigation of the Relationship Between Change in Corporate Social Performance and Financial Performance: A Stakeholder Theory Perspective," *Journal of Business Ethics* 32, no. 2 (July 2001): 143ff; and Philip L. Cochran and Robert A. Wood, "Corporate Social Responsibility and Financial Performance," *Academy of Management Journal* 27 (1984): 42–56.

19. Heli Wang, Jaepil Choi, and Jiatao Li, "Too Little or Too Much? Untangling the Relationship Between Corporate Philanthropy and Firm Financial Performance," *Organization Science* 19, no. 1 (January–February 2008): 143–159; Philip L. Cochran, "The Evolution of Corporate Social Responsibility," *Business Horizons* 50 (2007): 449–454; Paul C. Godfrey, "The Relationship Between Corporate Philanthropy and Shareholder Wealth: A Risk Management Perspective," *Academy of Management Review* 30, no. 4 (2005): 777–798; Oliver Falck and Stephan Heblich, "Corporate Social Responsibility: Doing Well by Doing Good," *Business Horizons* 50 (2007): 247–254; J. A. Pearce II and J. P. Doh, "The High Impact of Collaborative Social Initiatives," *MIT Sloan Management Review* (Spring 2005): 31–39; Curtis C. Verschoor and Elizabeth A. Murphy, "The Financial Performance of Large U.S. Firms and Those with Global Prominence: How Do the Best Corporate Citizens Rate?" *Business and Society Review* 107, no. 3 (Fall 2002): 371–381; Johnson, "Does It Pay to Be Good?"; Dale Kurschner, "5 Ways Ethical Business Creates Fatter Profits," *Business Ethics* (March–April 1996): 20–23.

20. Rashid Ameer and Radiah Othman, "Sustainability Practices and Corporate Financial Performance: A Study Based on the Top Global Corporations," *Journal of Business Ethics* 108, no. 1 (June 2012): 61–79.

21. Verschoor and Murphy, "The Financial Performance of Large U.S. Firms."

22. Richard McGill Murphy, "Why Doing Good Is Good for Business," *Fortune* (February 8, 2010): 90–95; Jean B. McGuire, Alison Sundgren, and Thomas Schneeweis, "Corporate Social Responsibility and Firm Financial Performance," *Academy of Management Journal* 31 (1988): 854–872; and Falck and Heblich, "Corporate Social Responsibility: Doing Well by Doing Good."

23. Daniel W. Greening and Daniel B. Turban, "Corporate Social Performance as a Competitive Advantage in Attracting a Quality Workforce," *Business and Society* 39, no. 3 (September 2000): 254–280; and Kate O'Sullivan, "Virtue Rewarded," *CFO* (October 2006): 47–52.

24. "The Socially Correct Corporate Business," in Leslie Holstrom and Simon Brady, "The Changing Face of Global Business," a special advertising section, *Fortune* (July 24, 2000): S1–S38.

25. Remi Trudel and June Cotte, "Does Being Ethical Pay?" *The Wall Street Journal*, May 12, 2008.

26. Jack Ewing, "Volkswagen Stock Falls as Automaker Tries to Contain Fallout," *The New York Times*, September 21, 2015, http://www.nytimes.com/2015/09/22/business /international/volkswagen-shares-recall.html (accessed February 10, 2016); William Boston, Amy Harder, and Mike Spector, "Volkswagen Halts U.S. Sales of Certain Diesel Cars" *The Wall Street Journal*, September 20, 2015, http://www.wsj.com/articles/volkswagen-ceo-apologizes--after-epa-accusations-1442754877 (accessed June 2, 2016); and Jad Mouawad and Christopher Jensen, "The Wrath of Volkswagen's Drivers," *The New York Times*, September 21, 2015, http://www.nytimes.com/2015/09/22/business /the-wrath-of-volkswagens-drivers.html?_r=0 (accessed February 10, 2016).

27. Linda K. Treviño and Katherine A. Nelson, *Managing Business Ethics: Straight Talk About How to Do It Right* (New York: John Wiley & Sons, Inc. 1995), p. 4.

28. Shelby D. Hunt and Jared M. Hansen, "Understanding Ethical Diversity in Organizations," *Organizational Dynamics* 36, no. 2 (2007): 202–216.

29. "Socialising for Intelligence," *Computer News Middle East*, November 2, 2011.

30. Justin Scheck, "Accusations of Snooping in Ink-Cartridge Dispute," *The Wall Street Journal Online*, August 11, 2009, http://online.wsj.com/article/SB124995836273921661 .html?KEYWORDS=%22Accusations+of+Snooping+in+ Ink-Cartridge+Dispute%22 (accessed August 14, 2009).

31. Thomas M. Jones, "Ethical Decision Making by Individuals in Organizations: An Issue-Contingent Model," *Academy of Management Review* 16 (1991): 366–395.

32. Based on Andrew Ross Sorkin, "Ethical Questions of Investing in Pot," *The New York Times*, January 13, 2015; and Matt Ferner, "Some Banks Are Working With Marijuana Businesses, But They Remain Wary," *The Huffington Post*, April 13, 2015, http://www.huffingtonpost.com/2015/04/13/ banks-marijuana-businesses_n_7057138.html (accessed February 10, 2016).

33. Based on a question from a General Electric (GE) employee ethics guide, reported in Kathryn Kranhold, "U.S. Firms Raise Ethics Focus," *The Wall Street Journal*, November 28, 2005.

34. This discussion is based on Gerald F. Cavanagh, Dennis J. Moberg, and Manuel Velasquez, "The Ethics of Organizational Politics," *Academy of Management Review* 6 (1981): 363–374; Justin G. Longenecker, Joseph A. McKinney, and Carlos W. Moore, "Egoism and Independence: Entrepreneurial Ethics," *Organizational Dynamics* (Winter 1988): 64–72; Carolyn Wiley, "The ABCs of Business Ethics: Definitions, Philosophies, and Implementation," *Industrial Management* (February 1995): 22–27; and Mark Mallinger, "Decisive Decision Making: An Exercise Using Ethical Frameworks," *Journal of Management Education* (August 1997): 411–417.

35. Michael J. McCarthy, "Now the Boss Knows Where You're Clicking," and "Virtual Morality: A New Workplace Quandary," *The Wall Street Journal*, October 21, 1999; and Jeffrey L. Seglin, "Who's Snooping on You?" *Business 2.0* (August 8, 2000): 202–203.

36. John Kekes, "Self-Direction: The Core of Ethical Individualism," in *Organizations and Ethical Individualism*, ed. Konstanian Kolenda (New York: Praeger, 1988), pp. 1–18.

37. Tad Tulega, *Beyond the Bottom Line* (New York: Penguin Books, 1987).

38. Bill Lynn, *Ethics*, Practical Ethics Web site, www.practicalethics .net/ethics.html (accessed March 23, 2010); Richard E. Thompson, "So, Greed's Not Good After All," *Trustee* (January 2003): 28; and Dennis F. Thompson, *What Is Practical Ethics?* Harvard University Edmond J. Safra Foundation Center for Ethics Web site, www.ethics.harvard.edu/the-center /what-is -practical-ethics (accessed March 23, 2010).

39. Carol D. Leonnig and David Nakamura, "Official Quickly Corralled Agents," *The Washington Post*, April 22, 2012; David Nakamura, "Out of Public Eye, a Disgusted Secret Service Director," *The Washington Post*, April 26, 2012; and Carol D. Leonnig and David Nakamura, "Four in Secret Service Fight Back," *The Washington Post*, May 23, 2012.

40. Gerard L. Rossy, "Five Questions for Addressing Ethical Dilemmas," *Strategy & Leadership* 39, no. 6 (2011): 35–42.

41. John D. Kammeyer-Mueller, Lauren S. Simon, and Bruce L. Rich, "The Psychic Cost of Doing Wrong: Ethical Conflict, Divestiture Socialization, and Emotional Exhaustion," *Journal of Management* 38, no. 3 (May 2012): 784–808.

42. L. Kohlberg, "Moral Stages and Moralization: The Cognitive-Developmental Approach," in *Moral Development and Behavior: Theory, Research, and Social Issues*, ed. T. Lickona (New York: Holt, Rinehart and Winston, 1976), pp. 31–83; L. Kohlberg, "Stage and Sequence: The Cognitive-Developmental Approach to Socialization," in *Handbook of Socialization Theory and Research*, ed. D. A. Goslin (Chicago: Rand McNally, 1969); Linda K. Treviño, Gary R. Weaver, and Scott J. Reynolds, "Behavioral Ethics in Organizations: A Review," *Journal of Management* 32, no. 6 (December 2006): 951–990; and Jill W. Graham, "Leadership, Moral Development, and Citizenship Behavior," *Business Ethics Quarterly* 5, no. 1 (January 1995): 43–54.

43. Ihosvani Rodriguez, "Hallandale Beach Lifeguard Fired After Participating in Beach Rescue," *Sun Sentinel*, July 3, 2012, http://articles.sun-sentinel.com/2012-07-03/news/fl-hallandale-beach-lifeguards-20120703_1_lifeguard-services-jeff-ellis-beach-rescue (accessed July 9, 2012); and Gilma Avalos and Ari Odzer, "Hallandale Beach Lifeguard Fired For Leaving His Zone to Rescue Drowning Man," *NBCMiami.com*, July 5, 2012, www.nbcmiami.com/news/local/Hallandale-Beach-Lifeguard-Fired-For-Leaving-His-Zone-For-Rescue-161372785.html (accessed July 9, 2012).

44. Jennifer Jordan, Michael E. Brown, Linda K. Treviño, and Sydney Finkelstein, "Someone to Look Up To: Executive-Follower Ethical Reasoning and Perceptions of Ethical Leadership," *Journal of Management* 39, no. 3 (March 2013): 660–683.

45. Studies cited in Adam Grant, "Turning the Tables on Success," *Strategy + Business* (Summer 2013).

46. Studies reported in Adam Grant, "Givers Take All: The Hidden Dimension of Corporate Culture," *McKinsey Quarterly* (April 2013), http://www.mckinsey.com/insights/organization/givers_take_all_the_hidden_dimension_of_corporate_culture (accessed February 10, 2016).

47. Ibid.

48. Grant, "Givers Take All"; and Grant, "Turning the Tables on Success."

49. See Herman Aguinis and Ante Glavas, "What We Know and Don't Know About Corporate Social Responsibility: A Review and Research Agenda," *Journal of Management* 38, no. 4 (July 2012): 932–968; and Archie B. Carroll and Kareem M. Shabana, "The Business Case for Corporate Social Responsibility: A Review of Concepts, Research, and Practice," *International Journal of Management Reviews* 12, no. 1 (March 2010): 85–105.

50. Carroll and Shabana, "The Business Case for Corporate Social Responsibility"; Eugene W. Szwajkowski, "The Myths and Realities of Research on Organizational Misconduct," in *Research in Corporate Social Performance and Policy*, vol. 9, ed. James E. Post (Greenwich, CT: JAI Press, 1986): 103–122; and Keith Davis, William C. Frederick, and Robert L. Blostrom, *Business and Society: Concepts and Policy Issues* (New York: McGraw-Hill, 1979).

51. Douglas S. Sherwin, "The Ethical Roots of the Business System," *Harvard Business Review* 61 (November–December 1983): 183–192.

52. Nancy C. Roberts and Paula J. King, "The Stakeholder Audit Goes Public," *Organizational Dynamics* (Winter 1989): 63–79; Thomas Donaldson and Lee E. Preston, "The Stakeholder Theory of the Corporation: Concepts, Evidence, and Implications," *Academy of Management Review* 20, no. 1 (1995): 65–91; and Jeffrey S. Harrison and Caron H. St. John, "Managing and Partnering with External Stakeholders," *Academy of Management Executive* 10, no. 2 (1996): 46–60.

53. R. Mitchell, B. Agle, and D. J. Wood, "Toward a Theory of Stakeholder Identification and Salience: Defining the Principle of Who or What Really Counts," *Academy of Management Review* 22 (1997): 853–886; Virginie Vial, "Taking a Stakeholders' Approach to Corporate Social Responsibility," *Global Business and Organizational Excellence* (September–October 2011): 37–47; and Martijn Poel, Linda Kool, and Annelieke van der Giessen, "How to Decide on the Priorities and Coordination of Information Society Policy? Analytical Framework and Three Case Studies," *Info: The Journal of Policy, Regulation and Strategy for Telecommunications, Information, and Media* 12, no. 6 (2010): 21–39.

54. N. Craig Smith, Sean Ansett, and Lior Erex, "How Gap Inc. Engaged with Its Stakeholders," *MIT Sloan Management Review* 52, no. 4 (Summer 2011): 69–76.

55. Ibid.

56. Jens Hansegard, Tripti Lahiri, and Chritina Passariello, "Retailers' Dilemma: To Ax or Help Fix Bad Factories," *The Wall Street Journal*, May 28, 2011, http://online.wsj.com/article/SB10001424127887323336104578501143973731324.html (accessed September 5, 2013).

57. Max B. E. Clarkson, "A Stakeholder Framework for Analyzing and Evaluating Corporate Social Performance," *Academy of Management Review* 20, no. 1 (1995): 92–117.

58. Definition is based on John Mackey and Raj Sisodia, *Conscious Capitalism: Liberating the Heroic Spirit of Business* (Boston: Harvard Business Review Press, 2013); and Michael E. Porter and Mark R. Kramer, "Creating Shared Value: How to Reinvent Capitalism—and Unleash a Wave of Innovation and Growth," *Harvard Business Review* (January–February 2011): 62–77.

59. Porter and Kramer, "Creating Shared Value."

60. Based on Susan Berfield, "Will Investors Put the Lid on the Container Store's Generous Wages?" *Bloomberg Businessweek* (February 19, 2015), http://www.bloomberg.com/news/articles/2015-02-19/container-store-conscious-capitalism-and-the-perils-of-going-public (accessed October 20, 2015).

61. Rich Kauffeld, Abhishek Malhotra, and Susan Higgins, "Green Is a Strategy," *Strategy + Business* (December 21, 2009); and "GE Imagination at Work," General Electric Web site, http://www.ge.com/about-us/ecomagination (accessed February 10, 2016).

62. Reported in Dung K. Nguyen and Stanley F. Slater, "Hitting the Sustainability Sweet Spot: Having It All," *Journal of Business Strategy* 31, no. 3 (2010): 5–11.

63. "Top Green Companies in the U.S., 2015," *Newsweek*, http://www.newsweek.com/green-2015/top-green-companies-u.s.-2015 (accessed February 11, 2016).

64. David Gelles, "Social Responsibility That Rubs Right Off," *The New York Times*, October 17, 2015, http://www.nytimes.com/2015/10/18/business/energy-environment/social-responsibility-that-rubs-right-off.html?_r=0 (accessed February 11, 2016).

65. Ibid.

66. This definition is based on David The and Brian Corbitt, "Building Sustainability Strategy in Business," *Journal of Business Strategy* 36, no. 6 (2015): 39–46; Marc J. Epstein and Marie-Josée Roy, "Improving Sustainability Performance: Specifying, Implementing, and Measuring Key Principles," *Journal of General Management* 29, no. 1 (Autumn 2003): 15–31; World Commission on Economic Development, *Our Common Future* (Oxford, UK:Oxford University Press, 1987); and A. W. Savitz and K. Weber, *The Triple Bottom Line: How Today's Best-Run Companies Are Achieving Economic, Social, and Environmental Success* (San Francisco: Jossey-Bass, 2006).

67. This discussion is based on Nguyen and Slater, "Hitting the Sustainability Sweet Spot"; Savitz and Weber, *The Triple Bottom Line*; and "Triple Bottom Line," an article adapted from *The Economist Guide to Management Ideas and Gurus* by Tim Hindle (London:Profile Books, 2008), *The Economist* (November 17, 2009), www.economist.com/node/14301663 (accessed July 5, 2012). The "people, planet, profit" phrase was first coined in 1994 by John Elkington, founder of a British consulting firm called SustainAbility.

68. This discussion is based on Solange Hai and Richard L. Daft, "When Missions Collide: Lessons from Hybrid Organizations for a Sustaining Strong Social Mission," *Organizational Dynamics* 44, no. 4 (2016); and Kenrya Rankin, "Dawn of the Do-Gooders," *Fast Company* (December 2015–January 2016): 77.

69. Based on "What Is a Benefit Corporation?" Benefit Corporation Web site, http://benefitcorp.net/faq (accessed February 12, 2016).

70. Quote by B Lab co-founder Jay Coen Gilbert in Rankin, "Dawn of the Do-Gooders."

71. Hai and Daft, "When Missions Collide"; and Rankin, "Dawn of the Do-Gooders."

72. G. Benjamin Bingham, "Encountering Benefit Corporations," *Huffington Post*, June 22, 2015, http://www .huffingtonpost.com/g-benjamin-bingham/encountering-benefit-corp_b_7447466.html (accessed February 12, 2016).

73. Saul W. Gellerman, "Managing Ethics From the Top Down," *Sloan Management Review* (Winter 1989): 73–79.

74. This discussion is based on Linda Klebe Treviño, Laura Pincus Hartman, and Michael Brown, "Moral Person and Moral Manager," *California Management Review* 42, no. 4 (Summer 2000): 128–142; and Mark S. Schwartz, "Developing and Sustaining an Ethical Corporate Culture: The Core Elements," *Business Horizons* 56 (2013): 39–50.

75. Michael E. Brown and Linda K. Treviño, "Ethical Leadership: A Review and Future Directions," *The Leadership Quarterly* 17 (2006): 595–616; Weaver, Treviño, and Agle, "Somebody I Look Up To"; and L. K. Treviño et al., "Managing Ethics and Legal Compliance: What Works and What Hurts?" *California Management Review* 41, no. 2 (Winter 1999): 131–151.

76. "Code of Conduct," Google Investor Relations, April 25, 2012, http://investor.google.com/corporate/code-of-conduct. html (accessed September 28, 2012).

77. M. A. Cleek and S. L. Leonard, "Can Corporate Codes of Ethics Influence Behavior?" *Journal of Business Ethics* 17, no. 6 (1998): 619–630.

78. K. Matthew Gilley, Chris Robertson, and Tim Mazur, "The Bottom-Line Benefits of Ethics Code Commitment," *Business Horizons* 53 (January–February 2010): 31–37; Joseph L. Badaracco and Allen P. Webb, "Business Ethics: A View from the Trenches," *California Management Review* 37, no. 2 (Winter 1995): 8–28; and Ronald B. Morgan, "Self- and Co-Worker Perceptions of Ethics and Their Relationships to Leadership and Salary," *Academy of Management Journal* 36, no. 1 (February 1993): 200–214.

79. Alan Yuspeh, "Do the Right Thing," *CIO* (August 1, 2000): 56–58.

80. Mark S. Schwartz, "Developing and Sustaining an Ethical Corporate Culture: The Core Elements," *Business Horizons* 56 (2013): 39–50; and Gregory J. Millman and Ben DiPietro, "More Compliance Chiefs Get Direct Line to Boss; Companies Elevate Status of Head Watchdog, but Role Is Often Ambiguous," *The Wall Street Journal*, January 15, 2014, http://www.wsj.com/articles/SB100014240527023033302 04579250723925965180 (accessed February 12, 2016).

81. Marcia P. Miceli and Janet P. Near, "The Relationship Among Beliefs, Organizational Positions, and Whistle-Blowing Status: A Discriminant Analysis," *Academy of Management Journal* 27 (1984): 687–705; and Michael T. Rehg et al., "Antecedents and Outcomes of Retaliation Against Whistle-blowers: Gender Differences and Power Relationships," *Organization Science* 19, no. 2 (March–April 2008): 221–240.

82. Eugene Garaventa, "An Enemy of the People by Henrik Ibsen: The Politics of Whistle-Blowing," *Journal of Management Inquiry* 3, no. 4 (December 1994): 369–374; and Marcia P. Miceli and Janet P. Near, "Whistleblowing: Reaping the Benefits," *Academy of Management Executive* 8, no. 3 (1994): 65–74.

83. Nathaniel Popper, "Bank Wrote Grievances After Firing a Broker," *The New York Times*, December 4, 2015.

84. Nicole Gaudiano, "Report: Air Force Whistle-Blowers Targeted," *USA Today*, February 1, 2012; Gretchen Morgenson, "How a Whistle-Blower Conquered Country-wide," *The New York Times*, February 20, 2011; and Christine Seib and Alexandra Frean, "Lehman Whistleblower Lost Job a Month After Speaking Out," *The Times*, March 17, 2010.

85. Based on Bart Victor and John B. Cullen, "The Organizational Bases of Ethical Work Climates," *Administrative Science Quarterly* 33 (1988): 101–125.

86. Adapted from Richard L. Daft and Dorothy Marcic, *Understanding Management* (Mason, OH: South-Western, 2008), p. 134.

87. Adapted from Janet Q. Evans, "What Do You Do: What If Polluting Is Legal?" *Business Ethics* (Fall 2002): 20.

Chapter 5
Planning and Goal Setting

iStock.com/oscarhdez

Chapter Outline

Learning Outcomes

After studying this chapter, you should be able to:

5.1 Define *goals* and *plans* and explain the relationship between them.

5.2 Explain the concept of organizational mission and how it influences goal setting and planning.

5.3 Discuss the benefits and limitations of planning.

5.4 Describe and explain the importance of contingency planning, scenario building, and crisis planning for today's managers.

5.5 Identify innovative planning approaches that managers use in a fast-changing environment.

5.6 Define the components of strategic management and discuss the three levels of strategy.

5.7 Explain the strategic management process.

5.8 Summarize how SWOT analysis can be used to evaluate a company's strengths, weaknesses, opportunities, and threats.

5.9 Describe Michael Porter's competitive forces and strategies.

Are You Ready To Be a Manager?

Before reading this chapter, please circle either "Mostly True" or "Mostly False" for each of the following five statements.

1 I want to have a specific goal, or mission, that I can achieve in the next 5–10 years.

Mostly True ◄················► Mostly False

[page 155]

2 I wish I could figure out what I need to do to achieve the goal in 1. In other words, how do I come up with a workable strategy to help me reach my dreams?

Mostly True ◄················► Mostly False

[page 157]

3 I develop goals for my studying, my work, and my life. These goals help me stay focused and motivated and help me figure out how to allocate my time and money.

Mostly True ◄················► Mostly False

[page 163]

4 Trying new ways to develop strategy, such as crowdsourcing, appeals to me.

Mostly True ◄················► Mostly False

[page 173]

5 I have honestly assessed my strengths and weaknesses, and I have looked for ways to utilize my strengths in the most effective way possible.

Mostly True ◄················► Mostly False

[page 174]

Discover Your Management Approach

Does Goal Setting Fit Your Management Style?

Instructions: Are you a good planner? Do you set goals and identify ways to accomplish them? This questionnaire will help you understand how your work habits fit with making plans and setting goals. Answer the following questions as they apply to your work or study habits. Please indicate whether each item is Mostly True or Mostly False for you.

	Mostly True	Mostly False
1. I have clear, specific goals in several areas of my life.	_____	_____
2. I have a definite outcome in life that I want to achieve.	_____	_____
3. I prefer general to specific goals.	_____	_____

To complete and score the entire assessment, visit MindTap.

Steve Ells borrowed money from his parents and started a burrito stand in Denver in 1993. By 2015, Chipotle Mexican Grill had 2,000 locations and a market valuation of $23 billion. It sounds like an entrepreneur's dream come true, but the dream turned into a nightmare after five customers became ill with the *Escherichia coli* bacterium after eating at a Seattle Chipotle in mid-2015. Over the next several months, at least six more outbreaks of food-borne illness were connected with the restaurant chain. Chipotle managers kicked planning into high gear by hiring a noted food safety specialist, doing a comprehensive review of food safety practices, and developing a plan designed to "establish Chipotle as a leader in food safety." Chipotle has always emphasized providing food made from locally sourced, organic, fresh ingredients. Now, managers are scrambling to also make goals of food safety a top priority in all of Chipotle's restaurants. "There's nothing incompatible about being local, organic and fresh and also safe," said Bill Marler, a Seattle-based lawyer who specializes in representing victims of food-borne illnesses. He says Chipotle has to figure out how to embrace goals of food safety as effectively as it does the other goals the company strives for.[1]

One of the primary responsibilities of managers is to set goals for where the organization or department should go in the future and plan how to get it there. Managers in every organization work hard to decide what goals to pursue and how to achieve them. Lack of planning or poor planning can seriously hurt an organization. Managers cannot predict the future, nor can they prevent all problems that might occur, but proper planning can enable them to prioritize goals and respond swiftly and effectively to unexpected events.

Of the four management functions—planning, organizing, leading, and controlling—described in Chapter 1, planning is considered the most fundamental. Everything else stems from planning. Yet planning is also the most controversial management function. How do managers plan for the future in a constantly changing environment? The economic, political, and social turmoil of recent years has sparked a renewed interest in organizational planning, particularly planning for crises and unexpected events, yet it also has some managers questioning whether planning is even worthwhile in a world that is in constant flux. Planning cannot read an uncertain future. Planning cannot tame a turbulent environment. A statement by General Colin Powell, former U.S. secretary of state, offers a warning for managers: "No battle plan survives contact with the enemy."[2] Does that mean it is useless for managers to make plans? Of course not. No plan can be perfect, but without plans and goals, organizations and employees flounder. However, good managers understand that plans should grow and change to meet shifting conditions.

5-1 Goal Setting and Planning Overview

A **goal** is a desired future circumstance or condition that the organization attempts to realize.[3] Goals are important because organizations exist for a purpose, and goals define and state that purpose. A **plan** is a blueprint for goal achievement and specifies the necessary resource allocations, schedules, tasks, and other actions. Goals specify future ends; plans specify today's means. The concept of **planning** usually incorporates both ideas; it means determining the organization's goals and defining the means for achieving them.

5-1a Levels of Goals and Plans

Exhibit 5.1 illustrates the levels of goals and plans in an organization. The planning process starts with a formal mission that defines the basic purpose of the organization, especially for external audiences. The mission is the basis for the strategic (company) level of goals and plans, which in turn shapes the tactical (divisional) level and the operational (departmental) level.[4] That is, a broad higher-level mission, such as "improve the lives of families by providing consumer-preferred paper products for kitchen and bathroom," provides the framework for establishing more specific goals for top managers, such as "improve company profits by 5 percent next year." This might translate into "increase sales by 10 percent next year" as a goal for the manager of the Northwest sales division, and an individual salesperson might have a goal of calling on 10 percent more customers.[5] Top managers are typically responsible for establishing *strategic* goals and plans that reflect a commitment to both organizational efficiency and effectiveness, as described in Chapter 1. *Tactical* goals and plans are the responsibility of middle managers, such as the heads of major divisions or functional units. A division manager will formulate tactical plans that focus on the major actions that the division must take to fulfill its part in the strategic plan set by top management. *Operational* plans identify the specific procedures or processes needed at lower levels of the organization, such as individual departments and employees. Frontline managers and supervisors develop operational plans that focus on specific tasks and processes and that help meet tactical and strategic goals. Planning at each level supports the other levels.

Visit MindTap for the "Self-Assessment: Does Goal Setting Fit Your Management Style?" to see how your work and study habits align with goal setting and planning.

Exhibit 5.1 Levels of Goals and Plans

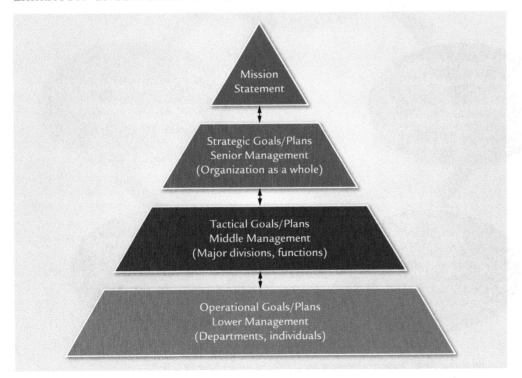

Concept Connection

From its beginning as a seven-cow farm in New England to its current status as a $350 million organic yogurt business, Stonyfield Farm has incorporated environmental responsibility into its **organizational planning**. Today, every operational plan encompasses Stonyfield's **goal** of carbon-neutral operations.

5-1b The Organizational Planning Process

The overall planning process, illustrated in Exhibit 5.2, prevents managers from thinking merely in terms of day-to-day activities. The process begins when managers develop the overall plan for the organization by clearly defining mission and strategic (company-level) goals. Second, they translate the plan into action, which includes defining tactical objectives and plans, developing a strategy map to align goals, formulating contingency and scenario plans, and applying flexible goal setting. Third, managers lay out the operational factors needed to achieve goals. This involves devising operational goals and plans, selecting the measures and targets that will be used to determine whether things are on track, and identifying stretch goals and crisis plans that might need to be put into action. Performance management tools for executing the plan include management by objectives (MBO), performance dashboards, single-use plans, and decentralized responsibility. Finally, managers periodically review plans to learn from results and shift plans as needed as they begin a new planning cycle.

Exhibit 5.2 The Organizational Planning Process

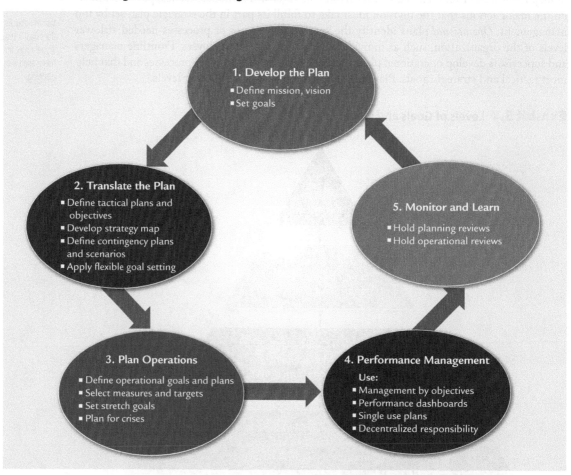

SOURCE: Based on Robert S. Kaplan and David P. Norton, "Mastering the Management System," *Harvard Business Review* (January 2008): 63–77.

Remember This

- Planning is the most fundamental of the four management functions.
- A **goal** is a desired future circumstance or condition that the organization wants to realize.
- **Planning** is the act of determining goals and defining the means of achieving them.
- A **plan** is a blueprint specifying the resource allocations, schedules, and other actions necessary for attaining goals.
- Planning helps managers think about the future rather than thinking merely in terms of day-to-day activities.

5-2 Goal Setting in Organizations

The overall planning process begins with a mission statement and goals for the organization as a whole. Goals don't just appear on their own in organizations. Goals are *socially constructed*, which means they are defined by an individual or a group. Managers typically have different ideas about what the goals should be. As A. G. Lafley, executive chairman and former CEO of Procter & Gamble, puts it, "Everyone selects and interprets data about the world and comes to a unique conclusion about the best course of action. Each person tends to embrace a single strategic choice as the right answer." Thus, the role of the top executive is to get people thinking as a team and negotiating about which goals are the important ones to pursue.[6] The "Sunny Side Up" describes the process of coalition building that often occurs during goal setting.

5-2a Organizational Mission

At the top of the goal hierarchy is the **mission**—the organization's reason for existence. The mission describes the organization's values, aspirations, and reason for being. A well-defined mission is the basis for development of all subsequent goals and plans. Without a clear mission, goals and plans may be developed haphazardly and not take the organization in the direction it needs to go. One of the defining attributes of successful companies is that they have a clear mission that guides decisions and actions. For example, CVS Caremark adopted a new name, CVS Health, and redefined its mission as "helping people on the path to better health."[7] In line with the new mission, CVS Health, which provides health clinics as well as pharmacy and retail sales, stopped selling cigarettes and other tobacco products in all its stores in late 2014. For a company involved in promoting health and wellness, managers say, selling tobacco products doesn't make sense and goes against the company's mission. CEO Larry J. Merlo says CVS is positioning itself "at the forefront of what we all see as a changing health care landscape."[8] When management actions and decisions go against the mission, organizations may get into trouble. "Think of it this way: Would you find . . . the gift shops in a hospital selling cigarettes? Of course not," said Nancy Copperman, the corporate director of public health initiatives for Northwell Health.[9]

The formal **mission statement** is a broadly stated definition of purpose that distinguishes the organization from others of a similar type. The founders of Holstee, a Brooklyn, New York–based company that sells inspirational posters, prints, greeting cards, and gift items, created a mission statement for their company that has inspired people around the world. Holstee's innovative mission statement is shown in Exhibit 5.3. The Holstee mission was written to remind the founders and employees that there is nothing more important than pursuing your passion.

Although most corporate mission statements aren't as broad or quite as inspiring as Holstee's, a well-designed mission statement can enhance employee motivation and organizational performance.[10] The content of a mission statement often describes the company's basic business activities and purpose, as well as the values that guide the company. Some mission statements also describe company characteristics, such as desired markets and customers, product quality, location of facilities, and attitude toward employees. An example of a short, straightforward mission statement comes from State Farm Insurance:

HOT TOPIC

"A real purpose can't just be words on paper. . . . If you get it right, people will feel great about what they're doing, clear about their goals, and excited to get to work every morning."

—ROY M. SPENCE JR. AUTHOR OF IT'S NOT WHAT YOU SELL, IT'S WHAT YOU STAND FOR

Sunny Side Up ⎬ Goal Conflict versus Manager Coalition

Organizations perform many activities and pursue many goals simultaneously to accomplish an overall mission. But how do managers decide what goals to strive for? Often there is a conflict between goals, and achieving one goal means another won't be accomplished. For example, Allegiant Air has achieved aggressive cost-control goals. However, pilots say the tight focus on reining in costs by purchasing older planes and outsourcing maintenance has thwarted safety goals. Another problem is that managers sometimes disagree about which goals to pursue. A new publisher of *The Los Angeles Times*, for example, disagreed with the goal of top executives at the newspaper's parent company, Tribune Publishing, to run its newspapers as a group, centralizing most operations and directing them from headquarters in Chicago. Austin Beutner, the *Los Angeles Times* publisher, believed the *Times* should pursue goals that made it a more independent, local newspaper. The conflict eventually led to Beutner being fired.

When goals are in conflict, or when managers disagree over which goals to pursue, coalitional management is crucial. *Coalitional management* involves building an alliance of people who support a manager's goals and can influence other people to accept and work toward them. Being an effective coalitional manager involves three key steps:

- **Talk to customers and other managers.** Building a coalition requires talking to many people both inside and outside the organization. Coalitional managers solicit the views of employees and key customers. They talk to other managers all across the organization to get a sense of what people care about and learn what challenges and opportunities they face. A manager can learn who believes in and supports a particular direction and goals as well as who is opposed to them and the reasons for their opposition.

- **Address conflicts.** Good managers don't let conflicts over goals simmer and detract from goal accomplishment or hurt the organization. At Nike, for example, the issue of manufacturing in Bangladesh created a conflict between the head of the production department, who had a goal of keeping manufacturing costs as low as possible, and Nike's head of sustainable business, who was worried about poor labor and safety practices in the Bangladesh factories. Rather than letting the conflict escalate, the two formed a committee made up of people from both sides of the debate. Committee members visited Bangladesh factories to see the conditions firsthand in order to reach agreement and make an informed decision.

- **Break down barriers and promote cross-silo cooperation.** A final step is to break down boundaries and get people to cooperate and collaborate across departments, divisions, and levels. When Colin Powell was chairman of the U.S. Joint Chiefs of Staff, he regularly brought together the heads of the Army, Air Force, Navy, and Marines so they could understand one another's viewpoints and come together around key goals. Understanding and cooperation across the enterprise is essential so that the entire organization will be aligned toward accomplishing desired goals.

As a manager, remember that you will accomplish more and be more effective as part of a coalition than as an individual actor. When there are goals that are highly important to you, take steps to build a coalition to support them. Throw your support behind other managers when appropriate. And remember that building positive relationships, discussing opposing viewpoints, and negotiating toward an informed agreement are key skills for good management.

SOURCES: Stephen Friedman and James K. Sebenius, "Organization Transformation: The Quiet Role of Coalitional Leadership," *Ivey Business Journal* (January–February 2009), www.iveybusinessjournal.com/topics/leadership/organizational-transformation-the-quiet-role-of-coalitional-leadership (accessed January 27, 2012); Gerald R. Ferris et al., "Political Skill in Organizations," *Journal of Management* (June 2007): 290–320; Jad Mouawad, "Pilots at Allegiant Air Question Safety Standards," *The New York Times*, April 20, 2015; Ravi Somaiya, "Firing at Los Angeles Times Focuses Discontent," *The New York Times*, September 21, 2015; and Shelly Banjo, "Inside Nike's Struggle to Balance Cost and Worker Safety in Bangladesh," *The Wall Street Journal*, April 21, 2014, http://www.wsj.com/articles/SB10001424052702303 87360457949350223139794 (accessed March 2, 2016).

The State Farm mission is to help people manage the risks of everyday life, recover from the unexpected, and realize their dreams.

We are people who make it our business to be like a good neighbor; who built a premier company by selling and keeping promises through our marketing partnership; who bring diverse talents and experiences to our work of serving the State Farm customer.

Our success is built on a foundation of shared values—quality service and relationships, mutual trust, integrity, and financial strength.

Our vision for the future is to be the customer's first and best choice in the products and services we provide. We will continue to be the leader in the insurance industry and we will become a leader in the financial services arena. Our customers' needs will determine our path. Our values will guide us.[11]

Exhibit 5.3 An Innovative Mission Statement: The Holstee Manifesto

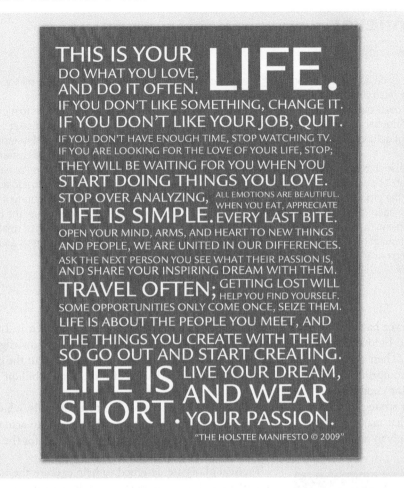

SOURCE: Holstee Web site, http://press.holstee.com/holstee-manifesto-poster © (accessed August 3, 2012).

Because of mission statements such as that of State Farm, employees as well as customers, suppliers, and stockholders know the company's stated purpose and values.

5-2b Goals and Plans

Strategic goals, sometimes called *official goals*, are broad statements describing where the organization wants to be in the future. These goals pertain to the organization as a whole rather than to specific divisions or departments. At Spirit Airlines, for example, new CEO Bob Fornaro has shifted from a strategic goal of growth to one focused on operational reliability and customer service. Spirit achieved aggressive growth goals, but the 30 percent annual growth rate came along with rising customer complaints about punctuality and other matters. Fornaro has reduced the emphasis on growth and put in place goals to improve service performance. For example, Spirit has goals for increasing staff, improving pricing transparency, improving on-time performance, and decreasing the number of customer complaints.[12]

Strategic plans define the action steps by which the company intends to attain strategic goals. The strategic plan is the blueprint that defines the organizational activities and resource allocations—in the form of cash, personnel, space, and facilities—required for meeting these targets. Strategic planning tends to be long term and may define organizational action steps from two to five years in the future. The purpose of strategic plans is to turn organizational goals into realities within that time period. At Unilever, CEO Paul Polman set a strategic goal of doubling the company's revenues by the year 2020.

Sunny Side Up } Unilever

"Our business is not rocket science," said Paul Polman, the first-ever company outsider to lead Unilever. "It's about being a little bit better every day." Polman's strategic plan to achieve the 2020 target of doubling revenues to €80 billion reflects that philosophy of getting a little better every day.

One of the biggest successes has been TRESemmé, which Unilever acquired when it bought Alberto Culver in 2010. To quickly introduce the product into the rapidly growing Brazilian market, managers implemented goals for a massive marketing campaign that involved reaching out to big retailers, courting fashion bloggers, establishing a Facebook page, and handing out 10 million free samples.

Sales of the product went from zero to €150 million in the space of a year.

Another part of Polman's strategic plan is to move Unilever into the higher-end personal care market. His initial goal was to send 80 percent of product development employees into the field to see what upscale customers want and to work closely with suppliers, who Polman says now contribute 7 of 10 new product ideas. In addition, the company has continued its goals for the "bottom of the pyramid (BOP)," as described in Chapter 3. Over the past three years, Unilever has accelerated its sales of small packets of Fair & Lovely skin cream, Sunsilk shampoo, and other products that cost about 35 cents a pop.[13]

Unilever has been operating in developing countries for decades (it's been in India since 1888 and Indonesia since 1933, for example), so managers have an intimate knowledge of these markets. There are two other components to Polman's new strategic plan—to cut the company's carbon footprint in half and to improve the hygiene habits of more than a billion people in developing countries.

After strategic goals are formulated, the next step is to define **tactical goals**, which are the results that major divisions and departments within the organization intend to achieve. These goals apply to middle management and describe what major subunits must do for the organization to achieve its overall goals.

Tactical plans are designed to help execute the major strategic plans and to accomplish a specific part of the company's strategy.[14] Tactical plans typically have a shorter time horizon than strategic plans—that is, over the next year or so. The word *tactical* originally comes from the military. In a business or nonprofit organization, tactical plans define what major departments and organizational subunits will do to implement the organization's strategic plan. For example, a tactical goal for Unilever's beauty products division is to develop personalized skin care treatments for the upscale market. Tactical goals and plans help top managers implement their overall strategic plan. Normally, it is the middle manager's job to take the broad strategic plan and identify specific tactical plans.

The results expected from departments, work groups, and individuals are the **operational goals**. They are precise and measurable. "Process 150 sales applications each week," "Achieve 90 percent of deliveries on time," "Reduce overtime by 10 percent next month," and "Develop two new online courses in accounting" are examples of operational goals. An operational goal for Unilever's distribution managers might be to improve on-shelf availability of products by five percentage points over the next two years. By keeping its products in stock, Unilever gets more sales and also cements strong relationships with merchants.[15] In the human resources department, an operational goal might be to keep turnover of product development personnel to less than 5 percent a year so that there are longtime employees who have close relationships with suppliers, who often contribute ideas for new products.

Pryzmat/Shutterstock.com

Concept Connection

Sustainability has been an ongoing **strategic goal** for NorthTec, a college in western New Zealand. Recently, school administrators and student volunteers worked together to set new tactical goals aimed at achieving greater sustainability. The group studied several specific areas in the school's operation, including electricity use and recycling, and discovered a surprising waste in the amount of photocopying performed on school grounds. The team has set a goal to reduce paper consumption by 15 percent.

Remember This

- Planning starts with the organization's purpose or reason for existence, which is called its **mission**.

- A **mission statement** is a broadly stated definition of the organization's basic business scope and operations that distinguishes it from similar types of organizations.

- Goals begin with broad strategic goals, followed by more specific tactical goals, and then operational goals.

- Plans are defined similarly, with strategic, tactical, and operational plans used to achieve the desired goals.

- **Strategic goals** are broad statements of where the organization wants to be in the future and pertain to the organization as a whole, rather than to specific divisions or departments.

- **Strategic plans** are the action steps by which an organization intends to attain strategic goals.

- The outcomes that major divisions and departments must achieve for the organization to reach its overall goals are called **tactical goals**.

- **Tactical plans** are designed to help execute major strategic plans and to accomplish a specific part of the company's strategy.

- **Operational goals** are specific, measurable results that are expected from departments, work groups, and individuals.

- **Operational plans** specify the action steps toward achieving operational goals and support tactical activities.

- Managers at Unilever set a strategic goal to double revenues, to €80 billion, by 2020.

- Goals and plans need to be in alignment so that they are consistent and mutually supportive.

5-3 Performance Management

Managers use operational goals to direct employees and resources toward achieving specific outcomes that enable the organization to perform efficiently and effectively. One consideration is how to establish effective goals. Then managers use a number of planning approaches, including MBO, single-use plans, and standing plans, for performance management.

5-3a Criteria for Effective Goals

Research has identified certain factors, shown in Exhibit 5.4, that characterize effective goals. First and foremost, goals need to be *specific and measurable*.[16] When possible, operational goals should be expressed in quantitative terms, such as increasing profits by 2 percent, having zero incomplete sales order forms, and increasing average teacher effectiveness ratings from 3.5 to 3.7. Not all goals can be expressed in numerical terms, but vague goals have little motivating power for employees. By necessity, goals are qualitative as well as quantitative. The important point is that the goals be precisely defined and allow for measurable progress. Effective goals also have a *defined time period* that specifies the date on which goal attainment will be measured. For instance, school administrators might set a deadline for improving teacher effectiveness ratings by the end of the 2018 school term. When a goal involves a two- to three-year time horizon, setting specific dates for achieving parts of the goal is a good way to keep people on track toward the goal.

Managers should design goals so that they can be translated into measurement of *key result areas*. Goals cannot be set for every aspect of employee behavior or organizational performance; if they were, their sheer number would render them meaningless. Instead, managers establish goals based on the idea of *measurement* and *clarity*. A few carefully chosen goals with clear measures of success can focus organizational attention, energy, and resources more powerfully.[17] The measurements are sometimes referred to as *key performance indicators*. **Key performance indicators (KPIs)** assess what is important to the organization and how well the organization is progressing toward attaining its strategic goal; these indicators help managers establish lower-level goals that

Exhibit 5.4   Characteristics of Effective Goals

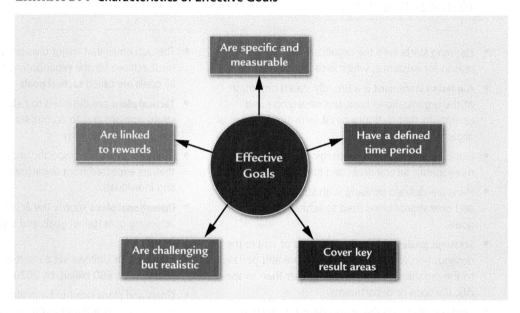

drive performance toward the overall strategic objective.[18] Managers should set goals that are *challenging but realistic*. When goals are unrealistic, they set up employees for failure and lead to a decrease in employee morale. However, if goals are too easy, employees may not feel motivated. Goals should also be *linked to rewards*. The ultimate impact of goals depends on the extent to which salary increases, promotions, and awards are based on goal achievement. Employees pay attention to what gets noticed and rewarded in the organization.[19]

5-3b Management by Objectives (MBO)

Described by famed management scholar Peter Drucker in his 1954 book *The Practice of Management*, management by objectives has remained a popular and compelling method for defining goals and monitoring progress toward achieving them. **Management by objectives (MBO)** is a system

Green Power

The Bees Buzz

Moving sustainability beyond fashionable "buzzwords" is a focus of North Carolina–based Burt's Bees—makers of personal care products made from natural substances (including, but not limited to, beeswax). Employees at Burt's Bees get down and dirty with the annual companywide Dumpster Dive, sorting through accumulated trash that reached monthly totals of up to 40 tons in one recent year. Employees recommitted to a zero-waste goal, which the company achieved in 2009. With 100 percent employee engagement, Burt's Bees has now focused on achieving a loftier "zero-waste, zero-carbon" goal by 2020.

Sustainability planning and goal setting at Burt's Bees engages employees in activities such as reducing water use by "steam-cleaning" containers (resulting in a 90 percent water use reduction) or extending the paper label on lip balm to eliminate shrink-wrapping (thereby eliminating 900 miles of shrink-wrap film). Managerial goals also extend to consumer education through the "Natural Vs." campaign (aimed at clarifying industry terms, such as *natural*). Through all its efforts, Burt's Bees works toward a goal of helping take the "sting" out of environmental problems.

SOURCE: Christopher Marquis and Bobbi Thomason, "Leadership and the First and Last Mile of Sustainability," *Ivey Business Journal*, September–October 2010, www.iveybusinessjournal.com/topics/leadership/leadership-and-the-first-and-last-mile-of-sustainability (accessed August 2, 2012).

whereby managers and employees define goals for every department, project, and person and use them to monitor subsequent performance.[20] A model of the essential steps of the MBO system is presented in Exhibit 5.5. Four major activities make MBO successful, as shown in the exhibit.[21]

Many companies have used MBO, and most managers think it is an effective management tool. Most managers believe that they are better oriented toward goal achievement when MBO is used. The "Sunny Side Up" describes how Google applies MBO-like thinking to goal setting and performance management.

Google has found that the OKR system provides a simple, easy-to-follow way to keep people focused on accomplishing important goals. In the language of the MBO model, objectives would be the goals, and key results might be thought of as the action plans and performance measures. People review their progress on a quarterly basis and make adjustments as needed to accomplish goals. OKRs are also used to align with and enable the attainment of goals at top management levels.

Exhibit 5.5 Model of the MBO Process

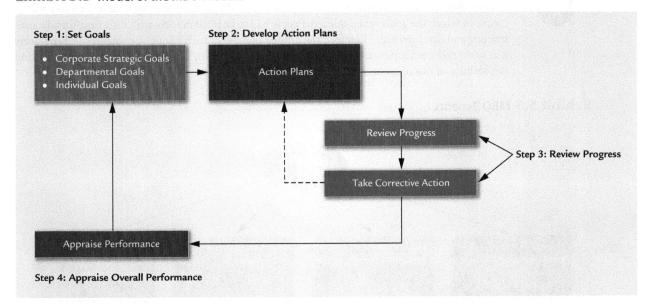

Companies have numerous goals and need effective methods for keeping people on track toward accomplishing them. Google uses a system called Objectives and Key Results, or OKRs.

Google has OKRs at the company level, at the team level, and at the individual level, which all work together to keep the entire company focused on goal outcomes. Here's how it works at the individual level: Each employee establishes several clearly defined and measurable objectives (goals) each quarter and then sets up a few "key results" for each objective. For example, one Google employee set an objective to "Improve Blogger's Reputation." Key results are things that will help achieve the objective, and they should be quantifiable, such as "Re-establish Blogger's leadership by speaking at three industry events" and "Identify and reach out to XX Blogger users." At the end of the quarter, people grade their key results to see how well they are progressing toward achieving the objective.

OKRs are done at Google on an annual basis and a quarterly basis. Quarterly OKRs do not change, but the annual OKR is a major goal that can change as the year evolves and circumstances shift. In addition, at Google OKRs are public, visible to everyone from the CEO on down. Everyone can see what everyone else is working on and what their objectives are.[22]

However, like any system, MBO can cause problems when used improperly. For example, an overemphasis on "meeting the goals" can obscure the means that people use to get there. People may cut corners, ignore potential problems, or behave unethically just to meet the targets. In addition, MBO cannot stand alone; it is only a part of effectively managing people to achieve goals. MBO is "like training wheels on a bicycle."[23] It gets you started, but it isn't all you need. In the United States, for example, the implementation of rigorous MBO-type systems in urban police departments and school systems has led to cheating on the numbers, with people lying about their work performance in order to score well on the metrics. The means for achieving goals is just as important as the outcomes. A new systematic approach that has recently emerged is called **management by means (MBM),** which focuses attention on the methods and processes used to achieve goals. A term coined by H. Thomas Johnson and his coauthors in the book *Profit Beyond Measures*, MBM is based on the idea that when managers pursue their activities in the right way, positive outcomes will result. MBM focuses people on considering the means rather than just on reaching the goals.[24]

At Toyota, the "sticky accelerator" problem that caused the automaker to recall millions of vehicles a few years ago has been blamed in part on a breakdown between goals and the methods used to achieve them. Years of aggressive growth goals eventually strained managers' ability to control the means by which the goals were achieved. People had to be hired quickly, with little time for adequate training and development. Therefore, the limited number of highly trained managers and engineers had to do more to keep pace toward the goals. Since the crisis, Toyota has refocused on improving the abilities of managers and employees to use the right means of achieving ambitious goals.[25]

Exhibit 5.6 MBO Benefits

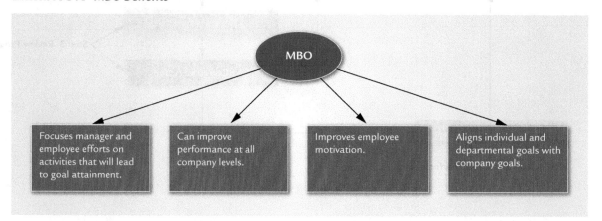

Remember This

- Managers formulate goals that are specific and measurable, cover key result areas, are challenging but realistic, have a defined time period, and are linked to rewards.
- **Key performance indicators (KPIs)** are measures that reflect how well lower-level goals are helping the organization progress toward attaining its strategic goal.
- Types of performance management systems include management by objectives, single-use plans, and standing plans.

- **Management by objectives (MBO)** is a method whereby managers and employees define goals for every department, project, and person and use them to monitor subsequent performance. MBO includes the steps of setting goals, developing action plans, reviewing progress, and appraising performance.
- A recent approach that focuses people on the methods and processes used to attain results, rather than on the results themselves, is called **management by means (MBM)**.

5-4 Benefits and Limitations of Planning

Some managers believe that planning ahead is necessary to accomplish anything, whereas others think planning limits personal and organizational performance. Both opinions have merit because planning can have both advantages and disadvantages.

Research indicates that planning generally positively affects a company's performance.[26] Here are some reasons why:[27]

- *Goals and plans provide a source of motivation and commitment.* Planning can reduce uncertainty for employees and clarify what they should accomplish. The lack of a clear goal hampers motivation because people don't understand what they're working toward.
- *Goals and plans guide resource allocation.* Planning helps managers decide where they need to allocate resources, such as employees, money, and equipment. At Netflix, for example, a goal of having more video offerings online rather than in DVD format means allocating more funds for Internet movie rights and spending more of managers' time developing alliances with other companies.[28]
- *Goals and plans are guides to action.* Planning focuses attention on specific targets and directs employee efforts toward important outcomes. It helps managers and other employees know what actions they need to take to achieve goals.
- *Goals and plans set a standard of performance.* Because planning and goal setting define desired outcomes, they also establish performance criteria so that managers can measure whether things are on- or off-track. Goals and plans provide a standard of assessment.

Despite these benefits, some researchers also think planning can hurt organizational performance in some ways.[29] Thus, managers should understand the limitations to planning, particularly when the organization is operating in a turbulent environment:

- *Goals and plans can create too much pressure.* If too much pressure is put on managers and employees to meet overly ambitious goals, they may resort to dysfunctional or unethical behavior in order to meet their targets. For example, the pressure to meet ambitious goals for U.S. sales may have contributed to Volkswagen's emissions scandal, when VW managers were found to have knowingly used software in diesel engines designed to cheat U.S. emissions tests, as we discussed in Chapter 1. In Chapter 3, we described how managers at all levels at Toshiba used misleading accounting to appear to meet high-profit goals. An investigation recently found that Toshiba overstated earnings by at least $1.2 billion over a seven-year period.[30]
- *Goals can create a false sense of certainty.* Having a plan can give managers a false sense that they know what the future will be like. However, all planning is based on assumptions, and managers can't know what the future holds for their industry or for their competitors, suppliers, and customers.
- *Goals and plans may cause rigidity in a turbulent environment.* A related problem is that planning can lock the organization into specific goals, plans, and time frames, which may no longer be appropriate. Managing under conditions of change and uncertainty requires a degree of flexibility. Managers who believe in "staying the course" will often stick with a faulty plan even when conditions change dramatically.
- *Goals and plans can get in the way of intuition and creativity.* Success often comes from creativity and intuition, which can be hampered by too much routine planning. For example, during the process of setting goals in the MBO process described previously, employees might play it safe to achieve objectives rather than offer creative ideas. Similarly, managers sometimes squelch creative ideas from employees that do not fit with predetermined action plans.[31]

HOT TOPIC

"In preparing for battle, I have always found that plans are useless, but planning is indispensable."

—DWIGHT D. EISENHOWER
(1890–1969), U.S. PRESIDENT

Remember This

- Benefits of planning and goal setting include serving as a source of motivation, determining resource allocation, providing a guide to action, and setting a standard for performance measurement.

- Limitations of planning and goal setting include the potential to create too much pressure to achieve targets, create a false sense of certainty, create rigidity that hinders response to a turbulent environment, and get in the way of creativity and intuition.

5-5 Planning for a Turbulent Environment

Considering the limitations to planning, what are managers to do? One way that managers can gain benefits from planning and control its limitations is by using innovative planning approaches that are in tune with today's turbulent environment. Three approaches that help brace the organization for unexpected—even unimaginable—events are contingency planning, scenario building, and crisis planning.

5-5a Contingency Planning

When organizations are operating in a highly uncertain environment or dealing with long time horizons, sometimes planning can seem like a waste of time. Indeed, inflexible plans may hinder rather than help an organization's performance in the face of rapid technological, social, economic, or other environmental change. In these cases, managers can develop multiple future alternatives to help them form more adaptive plans.

Contingency plans define company responses to be taken in the case of emergencies, setbacks, or unexpected conditions. To develop contingency plans, managers identify important factors in the environment, such as possible economic downturns, declining markets, increases in cost of supplies, new technological developments, or safety accidents. Managers then forecast a range of alternative responses to the most likely high-impact contingencies, focusing on the worst case.[32] For example, if sales fall 20 percent and prices drop 8 percent, what will the company do? Managers can develop contingency plans that might include layoffs, emergency budgets, new sales efforts, or new markets. A real-life example comes from the airlines, which had to scramble to develop contingency plans after problems in the electrical system of the new Boeing 787 led to the grounding of the entire fleet of 787s. Some routes that had been designed based on the 787, which offered fuel efficiency, long-range capability, and fewer seats to fill than other long-range jets, had to be closed or redesigned when the Federal Aviation Administration (FAA) grounded the new plane. As uncertainty over when the 787 would return to the skies lingered, airline managers began creating contingency plans for what to do if the 787 was out of commission due to this or other problems for months. Should the managers lease temporary aircraft? Should they substitute larger existing planes from their fleet and sell more seats at a discount to keep traffic moving or shut down routes altogether? What kind of alternative marketing plans were needed to reassure passengers that the plane would be safe once it was returned to service?[33] Theranos was too full of itself and its own impeccable model that it didn't even think about, much less plan for, any crises or setbacks, as described in this chapter's "Half-Baked Management" box.

5-5b Scenario Building

An extension of contingency planning is a forecasting technique known as *scenario building*.[34] **Scenario building** involves looking at current trends and discontinuities and visualizing future possibilities. Rather than looking only at history and thinking about what has been, managers think

Half-Baked Management

Theranos

Theranos sold the public on its new technology, which could do 200 diagnostic tests from one finger prick of blood. Other techniques could do only a few dozen tests. New ways of doing business and disruption were announced and celebrated.

Company founder Elizabeth Holmes, a 19-year-old Stanford student, launched her company in 2003 and got unbelievable media coverage, TED talks, and enough money and hype to have the company valued at $9 billion. Holmes had great plans for her company and got others to literally buy in, until *The Wall Street Journal* published a story showing how the Emperor had no clothes, that most of the blood tests were run on other companies' equipment rather than the Edison Technology that Theranos was touting. Later, Ralph Weissleder, of Massachusetts General

Hospital said, "They never shared their data with the scientific community. They were extremely evasive." The following month the ¨ß Centers for Medicare and Medicaid Research inspected Theranos' laboratories and found many deficiencies, posing "immediate jeopardy to patient health and safety."

In March 2018, Holmes was charged with widespread fraud by the Security and Exchange Commission. She agreed to a settlement to pay a fine of $500,000. In addition, she is barred by the Commission from serving with any public company as an officer or director for 10 years.

SOURCES: Katie Thomas and Reed Abelson, "CEO Who Promised Health in a Pinprick Is Charged with Fraud," *The New York Times*, March 15, 2018, A1, A21; and Emily Waltz, "After Theranos," *Nature Biotechnology* 35, no. 1 (January 2017), 11–15.

---

about what *could be*. The events that cause the most damage to companies are those that no one even conceived of. "Scenarios are meant to expand the range of future possibilities managers should consider and prepare for," says Stephen Millett, author of *Managing the Future*.[35] In today's tumultuous world, traditional planning can't help managers cope with the many shifting and complex variables that might affect their organizations. Lyndon Bird, technical development director at the Business Continuity Institute, emphasizes that broad plans are the answer. In a turbulent and interconnected world, he says, businesses "are going to be interrupted by something and they are probably not going to be able to predict what will happen except that they've got to be able to deal with the consequences."[36]

Managers can't predict the future, but they can rehearse a framework within which future events can be managed. Organizations can be disrupted by any number of events. A survey by the Chartered Management Institute and the Business Continuity Institute found that some of the top events that managers might need scenario plans for include extreme weather, loss of IT systems, loss of key employees, loss of access to offices or plants, failure of communications systems, and supply chain disruptions.[37] Some managers use published global scenarios, such as debt problems in Europe, a slowdown in Asia, or global warming, to analyze patterns and driving forces that might affect their industry as a starting point for scenario building. This *abbreviated scenario thinking* can give managers a head start on asking "What if . . .?" and lead to increased understanding even before any scenarios are written.[38] Then a broad base of managers mentally rehearses different scenarios based on anticipating the varied changes that could affect the organization. Scenarios are like stories that offer alternative vivid pictures of what the future will be like and how managers will respond. Typically, two to five scenarios are developed for each set of factors, ranging

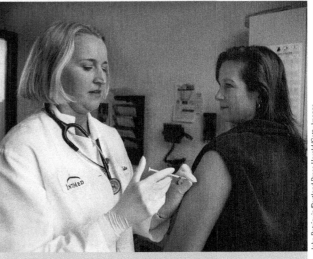

John Patriquin/Portland Press Herald/Getty Images

Concept Connection

After several outbreaks of the H1N1 flu revealed the dangers of widespread diseases, Mike Claver, State Farm insurance company's emergency management superintendent, oversaw the development of a thorough **contingency plan** designed to protect State Farm employees during any potential outbreaks in the future. In addition to coordinating with area agencies and encouraging employees to get vaccines, Claver tested the company's ability to function should managers have to ask employees to work at home during an outbreak. More than 1,000 people, about 10 percent of the workforce at the Bloomington, Illinois, headquarters, logged into the company computer network from their homes one August day. Managers used the results of the dry run to fine-tune contingency plans.

from the most optimistic to the most pessimistic view. For example, if the United States became involved in a military operation in Syria, leaders could create four broad scenarios of what might happen, as they did for Libya a few years ago—two that are positive for the United States and two that could have highly troublesome consequences—and develop plans for how to respond.[39] Similarly, in businesses and other organizations, scenario building forces managers to rehearse mentally what they would do if their best-laid plans collapse.

5-5c Crisis Planning

Many firms also engage in *crisis planning* to prepare the organization, its managers, and its employees to cope with sudden catastrophic events that could destroy the firm if a crisis-response plan were not in place. For example, weather events trigger crisis situations for organizations worldwide. Two of Western Digital's factories in Thailand that produce about a quarter of the world's hard drives were totally paralyzed after historic floods breached the dikes protecting the Bang Pa-In industrial estate in the fall of 2011.

Events like the floods in Thailand, Hurricane Sandy in the United States, and the massive earthquake and tsunami in Japan represent only one type of crisis organizations might face. Crises have become integral features of the organizational environment. Recent crises include the mass shooting at Inland Regional Center in San Bernardino, California, which killed 14 people and wounded 21; the shooting during a prayer meeting that killed nine people at The Emanuel African Methodist Episcopal Church in Charleston, South Carolina; an earthquake in Nepal that killed more than 8,000 people; the Ebola outbreak in West Africa; the "pink slime" YouTube video that led to closure of three plants owned by Beef Products, Inc.; the massive BP oil spill in the Gulf of Mexico; and a string of mishaps for the beleaguered Carnival Cruise Lines, including an engine fire on the *Triumph* that kept passengers stranded for nearly a week with no air conditioning, limited food and water, and few working restrooms.

Although crises may vary, a carefully thought-out and coordinated plan can be used to respond to any disaster. In addition, crisis planning reduces the incidence of trouble much like putting a good lock on a door reduces burglaries.[40] For example, Indiana State Fair officials have been sharply criticized for poor planning that probably contributed to a stage collapse disaster that killed seven people and injured dozens more. Because plans were so haphazard, no one seemed to

Sunny Side Up 〉 Western Digital Thailand

Like most large companies, Western Digital has emergency management plans, but the historic floods that inundated industrial areas of Thailand were well beyond what anyone expected. Western Digital managers had anticipated what would happen if the dikes protecting the area failed. A few days before the disaster, they pulled some inventory from the just-in-time (JIT) process at nearby warehouses and moved it to a safer location. The company also had a process in place for speeding up supplier qualification and assisting smaller suppliers that might need help after the disaster.

Ultimately, what helped the company most were its strong relationships with employees, customers, suppliers, and other stakeholders. Even though people's homes were flooded and power was out, more than 500 Western Digital employees, including all of its senior managers,

returned to work during the peak flood period. Within a week, operations to recover and restore equipment were underway. Company leaders worked alongside engineers and frontline employees, even taking personal risks by engaging in diving operations. Good relationships with customers meant some agreed to special provisions that deviated from normal contract agreements. Positive relationships with the Thai government meant Western Digital quickly got Thai navy divers dispatched to help with recovery and Royal Thai army soldiers to act as guards and haul heavy equipment.

Good decisions and the actions of managers both before and after the flooding helped Western Digital get up and running just 46 days after the factories were devastated, long before most other companies had reestablished normal operations.[41]

know who had the authority to delay or cancel the show or what procedures should be followed in case of severe weather. The Indiana Department of Labor fined the state fair commission, Mid-America Sound (which built the stage), and a stagehands union for faulty planning, insufficient inspections, and sloppy construction practices.[42]

Exhibit 5.7 outlines two essential stages of crisis planning.[43]

- ***Crisis prevention.*** The *crisis prevention* stage involves activities that managers undertake to try to prevent crises and to detect warning signs of potential crises. A critical part of the prevention stage is building open, trusting relationships with key stakeholders such as employees, customers, suppliers, governments, unions, and the community. By developing favorable relationships, managers can often prevent crises and respond more effectively to those that cannot be avoided.[44]

- For example, organizations that have open, trusting relationships with employees and unions may avoid crippling labor strikes. At the software firm Basecamp (formerly called 37 signals), managers prevented a crisis by responding quickly and openly when Campfire, a real-time chat tool for small businesses, kept turning off and on unexpectedly. Customers were furious because they used Campfire to run their organizations. Managers immediately began tweeting with customers and posting regular updates on the company's Web site to let people know what was going on and that they were working on the problem. If they didn't understand something, they admitted it. "We responded to every complaint and took the blame every time—even when people went overboard and launched into personal attacks," said CEO Jason Fried. Once the problem was fixed, they gave all customers a free month of service. Thanks to quick action, the company came out of the episode with stronger customer loyalty and goodwill than ever.[45]

- ***Crisis preparation.*** The *crisis preparation* stage includes all the detailed planning to handle a crisis when it occurs. Three steps in the preparation stage are (1) designating a crisis

Exhibit 5.7 **Essential Stages of Crisis Planning**

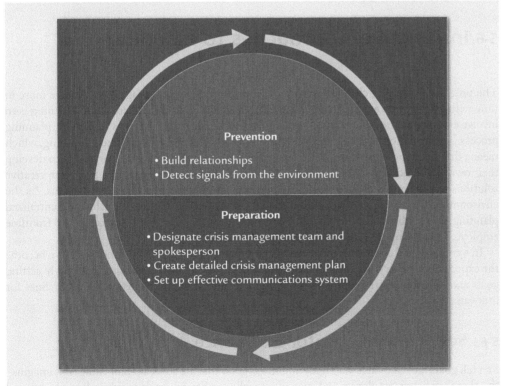

SOURCE: Based on information in W. Timothy Coombs, *Ongoing Crisis Communication: Planning, Managing, and Responding* (Thousand Oaks, CA: Sage Publications, 1999).

management team and spokesperson, (2) creating a detailed crisis management plan, and (3) setting up an effective communications system. The crisis management team, for example, is a cross-functional group of people who are designated to swing into action if a crisis occurs. The organization should also designate a spokesperson to be the voice of the company during the crisis.[46] The crisis management plan (CMP) is a detailed written plan that specifies the steps to be taken, and by whom, if a crisis occurs. The CMP should include the steps for dealing with various types of crises, such as natural disasters such as fires or earthquakes; normal accidents such as economic crises, industrial accidents, or product and service failures; and abnormal events such as product tampering or acts of terrorism.[47] A key point is that a CMP should be a living, changing document that is regularly reviewed, practiced, and updated as needed.

Remember This

- Managers use innovative planning approaches to cope with today's turbulent environment.
- **Contingency planning** identifies important factors in the environment and defines a range of alternative responses to be taken in the case of emergencies, setbacks, or unexpected conditions.
- With **scenario building**, managers look at trends and discontinuities and imagine possible alternative futures to build a framework within which unexpected future events can be managed.

- Scenarios are alternative vivid pictures of what the future might be like.
- Many companies increased their use of contingency and scenario planning because of the global financial crisis and volatile economic conditions.
- Crisis planning involves the two major stages of prevention and preparation.

5-6 Innovative Approaches to Planning

The process of planning changes over time, like other aspects of managing, to become more in tune with shifts in the environment and employee attitudes. A fresh approach to planning is to involve everyone in the organization, and sometimes outside stakeholders as well, in the planning process. The evolution to a new approach begins with a shift to **decentralized planning**, which means that planning experts work with managers in major divisions or departments to develop their own goals and plans. Managers throughout the company come up with their own creative solutions to problems and become more committed to following through on the plans. As the environment becomes even more volatile, top executives see the benefits of pushing decentralized planning even further by having planning experts work directly with line managers and frontline employees to develop dynamic plans that meet fast-changing needs.

In a complex and competitive business environment, strategic thinking and execution become the expectation of every employee.[48] Planning comes alive when employees are involved in setting goals and determining the means to reach them. The following sections provide guidelines for innovative planning.

5-6a Set Stretch Goals for Excellence

Stretch goals are reasonable yet highly ambitious goals that are so clear, compelling, and imaginative that they fire up employees and engender excellence. Stretch goals are typically so far beyond the current levels that people must innovate to find ways to reach them.

Remember This

- Approaches to planning change with the times. In many companies today, planning is decentralized.
- **Decentralized planning** means that top executives or planning experts work with managers in major divisions or departments to develop their own goals and plans.

- **Stretch goals** are reasonable yet highly ambitious and compelling goals that energize people and inspire excellence.
- At Amazon, a stretch goal was to build the first Kindle e-reader with built-in cellular access so people didn't have to connect to a PC.

Asking a group of engineers to create the first Amazon Kindle e-reader might be considered what James Collins and Jerry Porras have called a *big hairy audacious goal (BHAG)*. This phrase was first proposed by Collins and Porras in their 1996 article entitled "Building Your Company's Vision."[49] Since then, the phrase has evolved into a term used to describe any goal that is so big, inspiring, and outside the prevailing paradigm that it hits people in the gut and shifts their thinking. At the same time, however, goals must be seen as achievable or employees will be discouraged and demotivated, and some employees might resort to extreme or unethical measures to meet the targets.[50]

Stretch goals and BHAGs have become extremely important because things move fast. A company that focuses on gradual, incremental improvements in products, processes, or systems will be left behind. Managers can use these goals to compel employees to think in new ways that can lead to bold, innovative breakthroughs.[51]

Concept Connection

Many companies in the auto industry are setting aggressive, visionary goals that incorporate a social responsibility component. For example, Nissan managers have set a **stretch goal** called Vision Zero, which aims for "zero traffic accidents involving Nissan vehicles that inflict serious or fatal injuries." The goal requires everyone at Nissan to think differently about how they create, develop, and manufacture products. It also requires innovative ideas for marketing products and interacting with consumers. Nissan's Red Thumb campaign, for instance, encourages drivers to wear a red thumb band to remind themselves not to text and drive.

5-7 Strategy

In 2010, Uber Technologies Inc. launched a new kind of car service. People could use an app on their smartphones to quickly connect Uber with a white-gloved, professional driver in a Lincoln Town Car who would take them wherever they wanted to go. Then, along came Lyft, which offered a mobile app to facilitate peer-to-peer ride-sharing and connected people who needed a ride with drivers who had a car and were willing to take them. Uber quickly added a similar service to match passengers with amateur drivers. Since that day, the two companies have been battling it out to be the leader in this new mode of getting people—and now things—from one place to another. UberRush already offers delivery and courier services in three cities and will likely spur Lyft to add similar services. The two companies often announce changes in features, driver policies, or benefits within hours of one another. Traditional taxi companies and drivers are up in arms about lost business, but it is clear that the transportation industry has entered a phase of rapid transformation. Who will be the winner? The answer may depend on which company's leaders are best at strategic management.[52]

How important is strategic management? It largely determines which organizations succeed and which ones struggle. Differences in the strategies managers choose and how effectively they execute them help explain why a company like Amazon is thriving and Barnes & Noble is floundering, how Facebook all but killed MySpace in social networking, and why Apple is beating Microsoft in the world of mobile computing.

Strategic blunders can hurt a company. For instance, Kodak still hasn't recovered from its managers' failure to plan for the rapid rise of digital photography.[53] Blockbuster, which at its peak had 9,000 video stores and around 60,000 employees, is all but dead because managers failed to respond to changes in the industry. Sitting at the top of the video rental empire, Blockbuster managers turned down a chance to partner with fledgling company Netflix in 2000.[54] By 2015, Netflix had a market value of more than $30 billion, and Blockbuster was defunct, with only 51 franchise locations remaining.

Managers at Netflix, Kodak, Facebook, Uber, and Lyft are all involved in strategic management. They look for ways to respond to competitors, cope with difficult environmental challenges, meet changing customer needs, and effectively use available resources. Strategic management has taken on greater importance in today's environment because managers are responsible for positioning their organizations for success in a world that is constantly changing.

The first part of this chapter provided an overview of the types of goals and plans organizations use. In the next part we explore strategic management, which is one specific type of planning.

> "It's hard to outrun the future if you don't see it coming."
> —GARY HAMEL, MANAGEMENT SCHOLAR AND AUTHOR

5-7a Thinking Strategically

What does it mean to think strategically? *Strategic thinking* means to take the long-term view and to see the big picture, including the organization and the competitive environment, and consider how they fit together. Strategic thinking is important for both businesses and nonprofit organizations. In for-profit firms, strategic planning typically pertains to competitive actions in the marketplace. In nonprofit organizations such as the American Red Cross and the Salvation Army, strategic planning pertains to events in the external environment.

Research has shown that strategic thinking and planning positively affect a firm's performance and financial success.[55] Most managers are aware of the importance of strategic planning, as evidenced by a *McKinsey Quarterly* survey. Of responding executives whose companies had no formal strategic planning process, 51 percent said that they were dissatisfied with the company's development of strategy compared to only 20 percent of those at companies that had a formal planning process.[56] CEOs at successful companies make strategic thinking and planning a top management priority. For an organization to succeed, the CEO must be actively involved in making the tough choices and trade-offs that define and support strategy.[57] However, senior executives at today's leading companies want middle- and lower-level managers to think strategically as well. Understanding the strategy concept and the levels of strategy is an important start toward strategic thinking.

Visit MindTap for the "Self-Assessment: How Do You Study? Part 2" to evaluate your strategic thinking ability.

Remember This

- To think strategically means to take the long-term view and see the big picture.

- Managers in all types of organizations, including businesses, nonprofit organizations, and government agencies, must think about how the organization fits in the environment.

5-8 What Is Strategic Management?

Strategic management refers to the set of decisions and actions used to formulate and execute strategies that will provide a competitively superior fit between the organization and its environment to achieve organizational goals.[58] Managers ask questions such as the following: What changes and trends are occurring in the competitive environment? Who are our competitors, and what are their strengths and weaknesses? Who are our customers? What products or services should we offer, and how can we offer them most efficiently? What does the future hold for our industry, and how can we change the rules of the game? Answers to these questions help managers make choices about how to position their organizations in the environment with respect to rival companies.[59] Superior organizational performance is not a matter of luck. It is determined by the choices managers make.

5-8a Purpose of Strategy

The first step in strategic management is to define an explicit **strategy**, which is the plan of action that describes resource allocation and activities for dealing with the environment, achieving a competitive advantage, and attaining the organization's goals. **Competitive advantage** refers to what sets the organization apart from others and provides it with a distinctive edge for meeting customer or client needs in the marketplace. The essence of formulating strategy is choosing how the organization will be different.[60] Managers make decisions about whether the company will perform different activities or will execute similar activities differently than its rivals do. Strategy necessarily changes over time to fit environmental conditions, but to achieve competitive advantage, companies develop strategies that incorporate the elements illustrated in Exhibit 5.8: target specific customers, focus on core competencies, provide synergy, and create value.[61]

Target Customers   An effective strategy defines the customers and which of their needs are to be served by the company. Managers can define a target market geographically, such as serving people in a certain part of the country; demographically, such as aiming toward people in a certain income bracket or targeting preteen girls; or by a variety of other means. Some firms target people who purchase primarily over the Internet, whereas others aim to serve people who like to shop in small stores with a limited selection of high-quality merchandise. Zipcar managers identify their target customer as anyone who needs to occasionally rent a car by the hour, whereas Hertz identifies its target customer as the business or holiday traveler who needs to rent a car by the day or week while away from home.[62] In the paint and coatings industry, Sherwin Williams targets customers who prefer local, personalized service. The company sells paint only in its own stores and focuses on sales in North America, while competitor PPG Industries sells a large share of its paint through Walmart and other big box stores and targets a more global customer base, getting 54 percent of sales outside the United States and Canada.[63]

Exhibit 5.8 The Elements of Competitive Advantage

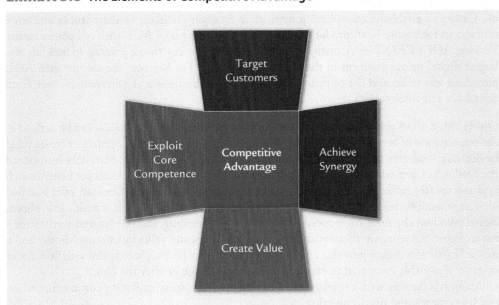

Concept Connection

When the U.S. Marines needed rugged motorcycles, they looked to manufacturers of on- and off-road bikes. But most motorcycles run on gasoline, which is the wrong fuel for military purposes. Hayes Diversified Technologies had the competitive advantage. After 20 years of building adapted motorcycles for the Marines and the Army Special Forces, Hayes had developed a **core competence** in technology that addresses the fuel limitations faced by the military. Most military machines run on JB8 fuel, a formulation of diesel and kerosene. Hayes Diversified's HDT M1030M1 motorcycle is designed for diesel service, so Hayes readily won the contract.

Exploit Core Competencies   A **core competence** is something that the organization does especially well in comparison to its competitors. A core competence represents a competitive advantage because the company acquires expertise that competitors do not have. A core competence may be in the area of superior research and development (R&D), expert technological know-how, process efficiency, or exceptional customer service.[64] Managers at companies such as Family Dollar and Southwest Airlines, for example, focus on a core competence of operational efficiency that enables them to keep costs low. Teekay Shipping Corporation, the world's largest tanker company and a leader in the transportation of crude oil and liquefied natural gas, thrives with core competencies of superior and reliable service, expertise with a broad range of shipping vessels to serve both major and niche markets, and strong relationships with stakeholders. Robinson Helicopter succeeds through superior technological know-how for building small, two-seater helicopters used for everything from police patrols in Los Angeles to herding cattle in Australia.[65] In each case, leaders identified what their company did especially well and built strategy around it.

Build Synergy   When organizational parts interact to produce a joint effect that is greater than the sum of the parts acting alone, **synergy** occurs. The organization may attain a special advantage with respect to cost, market power, technology, or management skill. When properly managed, synergy can create additional value with existing resources and provide a big boost to the bottom line.[66] Hostess Brands, maker of Twinkies and Ding Dongs, is hoping to attain synergy by adding products such as sliced bread and buns for hamburgers and hot dogs. By offering smaller convenience and drug stores a single source for fresh bread items and baked snack goods, Hostess can increase sales to stores that don't typically sell a lot of bread and might not get reliable deliveries from large bakeries.[67] Companies may also obtain synergy through acquisitions, mergers, and partnerships. Synergy was the motivation for food company Kraft to buy Cadbury and for Verizon Communications to acquire AOL, for example. Kraft can use Cadbury's established distribution network in emerging markets to share trucks and store contacts and sell more Kraft products. In explaining the merger of AOL with cell phone carrier Verizon, AOL's CEO Tim Armstrong said, "If there is one key to our journey to building the largest digital media platform in the world, it is mobile." For Verizon, the merger with AOL provides a way to expand the company's growing content business and gain more revenue from digital ads and wireless data.[68]

Create Value   Delivering value to the customer is at the heart of strategy. *Value* can be defined as the combination of benefits received and costs paid. Managers help their companies create value by devising strategies that exploit core competencies and attain synergy. Starbucks introduced the Starbucks Card, which works like a typical retail gift card except that users get benefits such as points for free coffee. Cable companies such as Charter Spectrum and Comcast offer bundled services, sometimes referred to as *value packages*, that provide a combination of basic cable, phone, digital premium channels, high-speed Internet, Wi-Fi, streaming, and on-demand services for a reduced cost. Some movie theaters are trying to provide greater value by offering "dinner and a movie." In-theater dining provides a more time-efficient way for people to spend a night out, and costs are reasonable compared to eating in a restaurant before or after the film.[69]

Amazon is thriving with a strategy based on targeting customers, exploiting core competencies, building synergy, and providing value.

Sunny Side Up ⟩ **Amazon**

It's hard to believe that Amazon was once a struggling online bookseller. In 2015, Amazon became one of the world's 10 largest companies by stock market value, far ahead of Walmart. Part of that success comes from the company's cloud computing business, but the core business of Amazon is selling stuff on Amazon.com. Over the past 20 or so years, founder and CEO Jeff Bezos has worked with other managers to patiently build an organization that is now "an existential threat" to every brick and mortar retailer, as Fiona Dias, executive vice president of GSI Commerce, put it.

Amazon targets customers who want to find good deals and purchase products conveniently over the Internet. Those customers can find just about anything they want on Amazon.com. They often pay less for it than they would anywhere else, and if they belong to Amazon Prime, they get free two-day shipping. Moreover, the new Prime Now service means a customer can place an order for a last-minute birthday gift, a quart of Ben & Jerry's ice cream, a bottle of wine, or practically anything else and get it within the hour if the customer lives in one of the 20 or so cities where Amazon is offering ultra-fast delivery.

The so-called "Prime effect" is a key to Amazon's long-term strategy because it means Amazon "keeps winning a larger share of customers' wallets." According to some estimates, people spend three to four times as much with Amazon after they sign up for Prime. Moreover, one analyst predicts that by 2020, 50 percent of U.S. households will have a Prime membership.[70]

Remember This

- **Strategic management** refers to the set of decisions and actions used to formulate and implement strategies that will provide a competitively superior fit between the organization and its environment so as to achieve organizational goals.
- A **strategy** is the plan of action that describes resource allocation and activities for dealing with the environment, achieving a competitive advantage, and attaining goals.
- **Competitive advantage** refers to what sets the organization apart from others and provides it with a distinctive edge in the marketplace.
- Four elements of competitive advantage are the company's target customer, core competencies, synergy, and value.

- A **core competence** is something that the organization does particularly well in comparison to others.
- Amazon has core competencies of operational efficiency and a superb distribution system.
- **Synergy** exists when the organization's parts interact to produce a joint effect that is greater than the sum of the parts acting alone.
- Kraft bought Cadbury to gain synergy by being able to sell products through Cadbury's established distribution network in emerging markets.
- The heart of strategy is to deliver value to customers.

5-9 Should You Crowdsource Your Strategy?

"Strategy, as we knew it, is dead," said Walt Shill, head of management consulting in North America for Accenture Ltd.[71] This might be an overstatement, but many managers have discovered that they need new approaches to strategy. For one thing, strategies developed by top leaders with little input from people on the front lines can be biased and fail to be embraced by the people who need to carry them out. One new approach that some pioneering companies are taking is to crowdsource their strategy. By opening up the process of strategy formulation to all employees, crowdsourcing adds diversity of thought, gets top executives closer to understanding the implications of their choices, and helps to avoid limited-perspective biases of top managers. Here are a few examples of how companies are using crowdsourcing:

- ***HCL Technologies' My Blueprint.*** Top managers at India's HCL Technologies turned the existing strategy planning process, a live meeting called Blueprint that involved a few hundred top executives, into an online platform open to 8,000 employees. Former CEO Vineet Nayar said managers did more thorough analysis and better planning because they knew that their plans would be reviewed and commented on by employees. One manager credited crowdsourcing for a fivefold increase in sales to an important client over a two-year period. Comments and insights had highlighted a need to reframe the plan away from commoditized applications support and toward new services where HCL had an edge over its larger competitors.
- ***Red Hat's Open-Source Strategy***. As the leading provider of open-source software, Red Hat Software wanted to try an open approach to strategy. Top managers defined an initial set of priorities for exploration and formed teams to explore each one. Teams used wikis and other online tools to generate and organize ideas and gave all employees the opportunity to comment and make suggestions for changes. Leaders say the fresh perspectives spurred "value-creating shifts in direction," including a change in the way the company offered virtualization services for enterprise data centers; this change led to the acquisition of an external technology provider.
- ***3M's "Innovation Live."*** 3M Company has long used a "Markets of the Future" process as a crucial aspect of its strategic planning. In the past, this involved a small group of analysts and managers researching megatrends and identifying markets of the future based on them. In 2009, the company reinvigorated the process by inviting all sales, marketing, and R&D employees to a Web-based forum called "Innovation Live." The forum attracted 1,200 participants from 40 countries and generated more than 700 ideas. "The end result was the identification of nine new future markets with an aggregate revenue potential in the tens of billions of dollars." 3M continues to hold "Innovation Live" events.

Crowdsourcing strategy, or "social strategy setting" as it is sometimes called, is a recent trend and creates opportunities for more meaningful participation by employees in strategy formulation and execution.[72]

5-9a Swot Analysis

Formulating strategy begins with understanding the circumstances, forces, events, and issues that shape the organization's competitive situation, which requires that managers conduct an audit of both internal and external factors that influence the company's ability to compete.[73] **SWOT analysis** (in which "SWOT" stands for "strengths, weaknesses, opportunities, and threats") includes a careful assessment of the strengths, weaknesses, opportunities, and threats that affect organizational performance. Managers obtain external information about opportunities and threats from a variety of sources, including customers, government reports, professional journals, suppliers, bankers, friends in other organizations, consultants, and association meetings. Many firms contract with special scanning organizations to provide the firms with news clippings, Internet research, and analyses of relevant domestic and global trends. Others hire competitive intelligence (CI) professionals to scope out competitors, as we discussed in Chapter 2.

Executives acquire information about internal strengths and weaknesses from a variety of reports, including budgets, financial ratios, profit and loss statements, and surveys of employee attitudes and satisfaction. In addition, managers build an understanding of the company's internal strengths and weaknesses by talking with people at all levels of the hierarchy in frequent face-to-face discussions and meetings.

Exhibit 5.9 shows a sample SWOT analysis from an international metals manufacturing company. Examples of strengths identified by managers include a highly competent workforce and a strong customer base, while a shortage of critical skills and the prevalence of aging technology are among the weaknesses. Opportunities include growing global demand and plant modernization while threats include the instability of the global market and low availability of key raw materials. Adam Lazar knew he had a strength with a new green product, but he also knew the opportunity wasn't quite there. So he waited a few years until it was, as described in the "Recipe for Success" box.

Internal Strengths and Weaknesses   *Strengths* are positive internal characteristics that the organization can exploit to achieve its strategic performance goals. One strength for interactive video game publisher Activision Blizzard Inc., for example, is a highly creative staff that consistently produces innovative and powerful video game franchises such as *World of Warcraft*, *Call of Duty*, and *Skylanders*.[74] *Weaknesses* are internal characteristics that might inhibit or restrict the organization's performance. Managers perform an internal audit of specific functions, such as marketing, finance, production, and research and development (R&D), to interpret strengths and weaknesses. Internal analysis also assesses overall organization structure, management

Recipe for Success } **Asarasi**

Adam Lazar took his two-year-old daughter, Lauren, out for a walk in the woods in the winter in Vermont and came across a maple house where people were turning maple sap into syrup. Traditionally, the sap has been boiled down for many hours, but newer technologies have changed that. What Lazar saw was a farmer with a new reverse osmosis machine, which separates the sugar from the water and saves between 8 and 20 hours in boiling time.

Lazar noticed a great deal of liquid, hundreds of gallons a minute, being spewed out. It seemed that there must be a fire hydrant somewhere because there was so much liquid thrown off. What was that? Water, said the farmer. Can't someone use it? No, it's just water, who needs that? Lazar thought a lot of people would want that water that was being thrown away. Sugar makes up only 3 percent of the sap, while water makes up the other 97 percent. Maple farmers have traditionally focused on the sugar being removed to make maple syrup and maple products. As a result, a billion gallons of incredibly pure, tree-filtered water are thrown away every year in the maple industry as a by-product of the syrup production process. Lazar went home and immediately wrote a business plan, something he'd learned studying for his MBA. But this was 2008, when alternative beverages were just beginning and specialty waters were barely being sold.

Lazar kept his job making ballistic equipment for the military and then was transferred to Los Angeles, where there was a drought in 2012. He remembered the unused source of water from the maple sap process and looked around. Now people were buying bottled waters, whether it was plain, coconut, or vitamin enhanced. So, he found that original business plan and submitted it to business competitions and kept winning awards, which motivated him more. Within two years he'd won over $60,000 in awards and raised an additional $235,000, enough to start his company, Asarasi.

By 2015, Asarasi was finally manufacturing water derived from maple syrup. Lazar ran 1,000 cases on a pilot run to see if people would care. Would they buy a pure, renewable plant-based water? Turns out they did care, both about the taste and the positive impact on the environment. Asarasi has been growing 300 percent a year and has managed to get on shelves in Tops Friendly Markets, Shaw's, Star Market, Shoprite, and Safeway along with many restaurants and food service accounts. Several international distributors have agreed to carry the brand, as well. Along the way, Asarasi won another $500,000 award from one of the largest business competitions in the world, 43 North. This has helped the company further expand its geographic reach and introduce flavors into the product lineup.

Lazar has budding entrepreneurs coming for advice and he says, "You don't have to have the best idea, just something incrementally better. People will adopt it, if it removes even a little pain in their lives."

His daughter Lauren? She doesn't remember that first visit to the maple house, but she is very proud of her dad and how he is helping the world.

SOURCE: Adam Lazar, personal communication, March 2018.

Exhibit 5.9 SWOT Analysis for a Global Metals Manufacturer

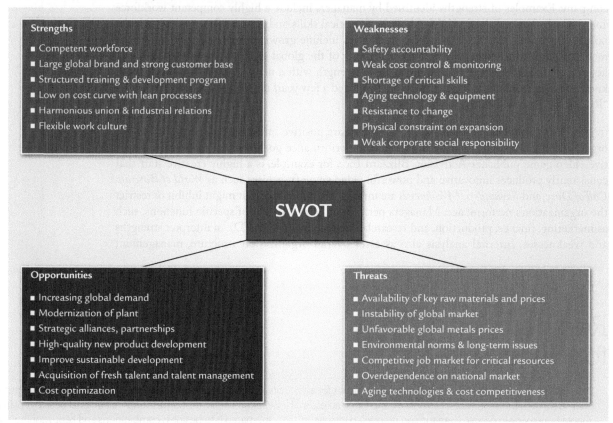

competence and quality, and human resource (HR) characteristics. Based on their understanding of these areas, managers can determine their strengths and weaknesses compared with those of other companies.

External Opportunities and Threats   *Threats* are characteristics of the external environment that may prevent the organization from achieving its strategic goals. One threat to Activision Blizzard is the growing criticism of violent video games in light of mass shootings in the United States by perpetrators who were said to play the games. For example, Adam Lanza, who killed 20 children and six adults at Sandy Hook Elementary School in Newtown, Connecticut, and Dylann Roof, who gunned down nine people at a Charleston, South Carolina, prayer meeting, were both said to be regular players of violent video games. Another event of this type occurred at the Washington Navy Yard in Washington, D.C., where Aaron Alexis, a former Navy reservist, killed 12 people at the secure military installation.[75] Alexis reportedly played games (including Activision's *Call of Duty*) for as many as 16 hours at a time. Although evidence suggests that there is no connection between violent video games and real-life violence, the media attention renews the debate with each new tragedy.[76] As another example of an external threat, Intel, whose microprocessors power most PCs, is being hurt by the decline in demand for personal computers as more people turn to tablets and smartphones.[77]

Opportunities are characteristics of the external environment that have the potential to help the organization achieve or exceed its strategic goals. For example, U.S. auto manufacturers have had an unprecedented opportunity to steal customers from Toyota because of the quality, safety, and public relations problems that Toyota has experienced in recent years.[78]

Managers evaluate the external environment based on the 10 sectors described in Chapter 2. The task environment sectors are the most relevant to strategic behavior and include the behavior of competitors, customers, suppliers, and the labor supply. The general environment contains

Sunny Side Up

InSinkErator, Emerson Electric Company

John Hammes invented the garbage disposal in 1927, but sales of the InSinkErator, now a division of Emerson Electric Company, didn't really take off until after World War II when housing construction boomed in the United States. Because it is so expensive to retrofit existing homes for garbage disposals, sales depend heavily on new construction. That's one reason InSinkErator managers see a big opportunity in China, which currently has more housing construction going on than any other country.

The U.S. market for garbage disposals is mature and slow growing, but China is a wide-open market.

InSinkErator has redesigned its disposals to handle tough food waste such as eel and bullfrog skin and to grind more finely so foods like leftover rice or noodles won't clog pipes. In the lab, workers are testing foods likely to be found in China, such as white radishes, duck heads, and mango pits (which have so far been found almost impossible to grind up). The company has also built its first factory outside the United States in Nanjing, China, and managers are heavily marketing the benefits of their products to consumers and home builders.[79]

those sectors that have an indirect influence on the organization but nevertheless must be understood and incorporated into strategic behavior. The general environment includes technological developments, the economy, legal–political and international events, the natural environment, and sociocultural changes. Additional areas that might reveal opportunities or threats include pressure groups, interest groups, creditors, and potentially competitive industries.

Managers at Emerson Electric Company's InSinkErator unit have spotted an opportunity to grow their business by redesigning garbage disposals for China.

Remember This

- **Strategy formulation** is the stage of strategic management that includes the planning and decision making that lead to the establishment of the organization's goals and a specific strategic plan.

- Managers often start with a **SWOT analysis**, an audit or careful examination of *strengths*, *weaknesses*, *opportunities*, and *threats* that affect organizational performance.

- The decline in demand for PCs is a *threat* to Intel. InSinkErator managers see China's booming housing market as an *opportunity* for growing sales of garbage disposals.

- **Strategy execution** is the stage of strategic management that involves the use of managerial and organizational tools to direct resources toward achieving strategic outcomes.

5-10 Formulating Corporate-Level Strategy

Two approaches to understanding corporate-level strategy are the Boston Consulting Group (BCG) matrix and diversification.

5-10a The BCG Matrix

One coherent way to think about portfolio strategy is the BCG matrix. The BCG matrix (named for the Boston Consulting Group, which developed it) is illustrated in Exhibit 5.10. The **BCG matrix** organizes businesses along two dimensions—business growth rate and market share.[80]

Green Power

A Transformation in Clean Power

The energy revolution isn't being led by tiny, innovative start-ups but by one of the giants. Italy's huge utility company, Enel, Number 69 on *Fortune*'s Global 500, is blasting through barriers with a growth strategy that focuses on increasing the access to renewable energy around the world. Enel, the world's largest producer of renewable energy, generates almost half of its total output from renewable energy sources such as hydro, wind, solar, and geothermal.

Managers have set a goal of becoming a completely carbon-free company by 2050. Enel is working with partners, including big corporations, small businesses and start-ups, universities, and research institutions, to develop new environmentally friendly technologies. Enel Green Power, the company's fastest growing division, produces energy at 708 plants in 16 countries and generated $3.9 billion in revenues in 2014.

SOURCES: "No. 5 Enel," segment in "Change the World List," *Fortune* (September 1, 2015), p. 63; and "New Era, New Energy," Enel Web site (January 26, 2016), https://www.enel.com/en-gb#/vision (accessed March 11, 2016).

Business growth rate pertains to how rapidly the entire industry is increasing. *Market share* defines whether a business unit has a larger or smaller share than competitors. The combinations of high and low market share and high and low business growth provide four categories for a corporate portfolio.

The *star* has a large market share in a rapidly growing industry. It is important because it has additional growth potential, and profits should be plowed into this business as investment for future growth and profits. The star is visible and attractive and will generate profits and a positive cash flow even as the industry matures and market growth slows.

The *cash cow* exists in a mature, slow-growth industry but is a dominant business in the industry with a large market share. Because heavy investments in advertising and plant expansion are no longer required, the corporation earns a positive cash flow. It can milk the cash cow to invest in other riskier businesses.

Exhibit 5.10 The BCG Matrix

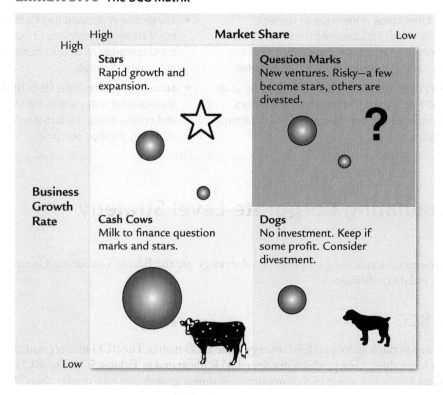

Sunny Side Up 〉 Procter & Gamble

Beauty is big business, but it turned out to be a dog for Procter & Gamble (P&G). P&G, with a *cash cow* of family and household products such as Tide laundry detergent, Pampers diapers, and Bounty paper towels, spent billions over the past couple of decades pushing hard into the beauty and fragrance business. P&G acquired companies such as Wella and Clairol, bought a chain of designer hair salons, and formed partnerships with designer brands to sell fragrances.

However, the beauty business turned out to be a poor fit for P&G. "P&G was looking to conquer the world of beauty but it went too far out of its comfort zone," said the vice president of consulting firm Kline & Co.'s consumer-products practice. Rather than attaining synergy, the addition of a wide range of beauty products took time, energy, and financial resources away from the core business and hurt performance and profits.

P&G is now divesting a number of its brands in the dog category to focus on its core business. In one recent deal, the company divested 43 beauty brands, including Wella, Clairol, and Cover Girl, into a separate company that will merge with cosmetics and fragrance company Coty.[81]

The *question mark* exists in a new, rapidly growing industry but has only a small market share. The question mark business is risky: It could become a star, or it could fail. The corporation can invest the cash earned from cash cows in question marks with the goal of nurturing them into future stars.

The *dog* is a poor performer. It has only a small share of a slow-growth market. The dog provides little profit for the corporation and may be targeted for divestment or liquidation if turnaround is not possible. Procter & Gamble has recently been rebalancing its portfolio and getting rid of some poor performers.

P&G isn't getting entirely out of the beauty business. The beauty division will retain Pantene and Olay, P&G's largest hair and skin care brands. P&G also has a number of other businesses. Most large organizations, like P&G, have businesses in more than one of the categories illustrated in Exhibit 5.5 (BCG Matrix) that represent different market shares and growth rates. The circles in Exhibit 5.5 show the business portfolio for a hypothetical corporation. Circle size represents the relative size of each business in the company's portfolio.

5-10b Diversification Strategy

The strategy of moving into new lines of business, as Amazon did by acquiring Twitch Interactive, or as UnitedHealth Group did by purchasing medical groups, is called **diversification**. Other examples of diversification include Facebook's move into text messaging technologies with the recent purchase of WhatsApp, Nestlé's entry into the pet food business with the purchase of Ralston Foods, and Microsoft's entry into the mobile phone business with the purchase of Nokia's handset and services units.[82]

Remember This

- The **BCG matrix** is a concept developed by the Boston Consulting Group that evaluates strategic business units (SBUs) with respect to two dimensions—business growth rate and market share—and classifies them as cash cows, stars, question marks, or dogs.

- The strategy of moving into new lines of business is called **diversification**.
- Amazon diversified when it purchased Twitch Interactive, and Facebook diversified by purchasing WhatsApp.

5-11 Formulating Business-Level Strategy

Now we turn to strategy formulation within the SBU in which the concern is how to compete. A popular and effective model for formulating strategy is Michael E. Porter's competitive strategies. Porter studied a number of business organizations and proposed that business-level strategies are the result of understanding competitive forces in the company's environment.[83]

5-11a Porter's Five Competitive Forces

Exhibit 5.11 illustrates the competitive forces that exist in a company's environment and indicates some ways that Internet technology is affecting each area. These five forces help determine a company's position vis-à-vis competitors in the industry environment. Although such a model might be used on a corporate level, most large companies have separate business lines and do an industry analysis for each line of business or SBU. Mars, Inc., for example, operates in six business segments: chocolate (e.g., Snickers), pet care (e.g., Pedigree), gum and confections (e.g., Juicy Fruit), food (e.g., Uncle Ben's rice), drinks (e.g., FLAVIA), and symbioscience (e.g., the Wilson Panel pet DNA kit, used for breed identification). Competitive forces for the chocolate division would be different from those for the symbioscience division, so managers would do a competitive analysis for each business segment, looking at Porter's five forces.

Exhibit 5.11 **Organizational Characteristics of Porter's Competitive Strategies**

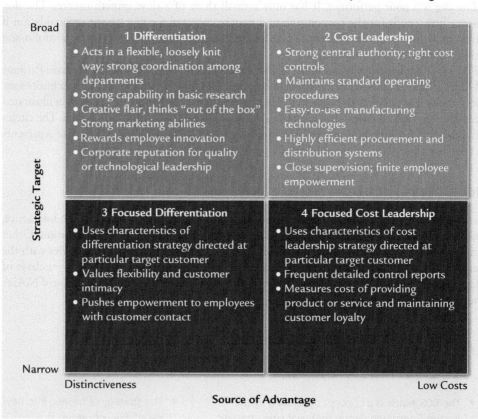

SOURCES: Based on Michael E. Porter, *Competitive Strategy: Techniques for Analyzing Industries and Competitors* (New York: Free Press, 1980); Michael Treacy and Fred Wiersema, "How Market Leaders Keep Their Edge," *Fortune* (February 6, 1995): 88–98; and Michael A. Hitt, R. Duane Ireland, and Robert E. Hoskisson, *Strategic Management* (St. Paul, MN: West, 1995), pp. 100–113.

To find a competitive edge within the specific business environment, Porter suggests that a company can adopt one of three strategies: differentiation, cost leadership, or focus. The organizational characteristics typically associated with each strategy are summarized in Exhibit 5.11.

Concept Connection

Rubber bands. Binders. Gum bands. Elastics. Whatever we call them, we all know what they are. With the benefits of lower labor costs, companies in China and Thailand have grabbed most of the market for rubber bands. One of the few remaining U.S. manufacturers, Alliance Rubber Company, is hoping to survive with a new **differentiation strategy**. Alliance is promoting new uses for its stretchy loops of rubber, including bands for stretching exercises, grips designed to help people hold tools more firmly, wristbands infused with fragrances to relieve stress, and wristbands that can be used as erasers. Employees earn bonuses by suggesting ideas that turn into new products, and Alliance has invested in sophisticated equipment to make customized products.

Mariusz Szczygiel/Shutterstock.com

Remember This

- A popular model for formulating business-level strategy is Porter's competitive strategies.

- Managers analyze the competitive environment and adopt one of three types of strategy: differentiation, cost leadership, or focus.

- A **differentiation strategy** is a strategy with which managers seek to distinguish the organization's products and services from those of others in the industry.

- A **cost leadership strategy** is a strategy with which managers aggressively seek efficient facilities, cut costs, and use tight cost controls to be more efficient than others in the industry.

- With a **focus strategy**, managers use either a differentiation or a cost leadership approach, but they concentrate on a specific regional market or buyer group.

DISCUSSION QUESTIONS

1. What strategic plans could the college or university at which you are taking this management course adopt to compete for students in the marketplace? Would these plans depend on the school's goals?

2. The MBO technique has been criticized for putting too much emphasis on achieving goals (ends) and not enough on the methods that people use to achieve them (means). Do you think this is a flaw in the technique or in the way managers apply it? How would you place a balanced emphasis on ends and means?

3. A new business venture must develop a comprehensive business plan if it hopes to acquire start-up funding. Companies such as FedEx and Nike say they did not follow the original plan closely. Does that mean that developing the plan was a waste of time for these eventually successful companies?

4. Assume that Southern University decides to do two things: (1) raise its admission standards and (2) initiate a small-business fair to which local townspeople will be invited. What types of plans might it use to carry out these two activities?

5. LivingSocial started with one "daily deal," a $25 voucher for $50 worth of food at a Washington, D.C., area restaurant. Since then, the company has grown at break-neck speed, has 46 million members in 25 countries, and has acquired a dozen companies that offer related deals and services. Why and how might a company such as LivingSocial want to use scenario building? Discuss.

6. Some people say an organization could never be "prepared" for a disaster such as the shooting at Inland Regional Center in San Bernardino, California; the Japan nuclear disaster; or the huge BP oil spill in the Gulf of Mexico. Discuss the potential value of crisis planning in situations like these, even if the situations are difficult to plan for.

7. Goals that are overly ambitious can discourage employees and decrease motivation, yet the idea of stretch goals is proposed as a way to get people fired up and motivated. As a manager, how might you decide where to draw the line between a "good" stretch goal and a "bad" one that is unrealistic?

8. Netflix has successfully adapted to a number of challenges in its industry. What do you see as some emerging opportunities and threats for the company?

9. *Fortune* magazine and the Hay Group found that a clear, stable strategy is one of the defining characteristics of companies on the list of "The World's Most Admired Companies." Why might this be the case?

10. Using Porter's competitive strategies, how would you describe the strategies of Walmart, Bergdorf Goodman, and T.J. Maxx?

APPLY YOUR SKILLS: SELF-LEARNING

Business School Ranking

The dean of the business school at a major university in your state has contacted students in your class to develop a plan for improving its national ranking among business schools. The school recently dropped 10 places in the rankings, and the dean wants to restore the school's perceived luster. The dean provided the following list of variables on which the national ranking is based.

- Written assessment by deans from peer institutions on a scale of 1 to 5
- Written assessment by corporate recruiters on a scale of 1 to 5
- Average grade point average (GPA) of incoming students
- Acceptance rate of student applications (a lower percentage is better)
- Average starting salary of the school's most recent graduates

- Percentage of graduates employed on the date of graduation
- Percentage of graduates employed three months after graduation
- Average Scholastic Aptitude Test (SAT; for the undergraduate program) and Graduate Management Admission Test (GMAT; for the MBA program) scores for entering students

The business school has a goal of improving its ranking by 10 places in two years. Brainstorm ideas and develop a 10-point action plan that will list the steps the dean can take to achieve this goal. To develop the plan, think carefully about actions the school might take to improve its ranking on any or all of the measured variables listed.

After writing your ideas to develop a plan, meet with a partner to share ideas and discuss the most helpful action steps that will be part of the action plan recommended to the business school dean.

APPLY YOUR SKILLS: GROUP LEARNING

SWOT Analysis[84]

Step 1. In a group of three to five students, select a local eating establishment for a SWOT analysis. This could be a restaurant, an ice cream store, or a bakery with which your group is familiar.

Step 2. Write a statement of what you perceive to be the business's current strategy.

Step 3. What do you perceive to be the key strengths and weaknesses of this business from a customer's perspective? Make one list for strengths and another list for weaknesses.

Step 4. What do you perceive to be potential opportunities and threats for this business? Make one list for opportunities and another for threats.

Step 5. If the store manager or owner is available, interview the person for his or her perception of strategy strengths, weaknesses, opportunities, and threats. Add new items to your lists.

Step 6. Use your SWOT analysis findings to set a goal of where this business could be in two

years in terms of growth, size, new offerings, and expanded customer base. What steps do you recommend to achieve this goal?

Step 7. How did your SWOT analysis help you determine the goal and how to accomplish it during the next two years? What did you learn from this exercise?

Questions to ask	Answers
Key strengths from customer point of view	
Key weaknesses from customer point of view	
Potential opportunities	
Potential threats	
Results of manager interview, if available	
Using your analysis, where do you think this business can be in two years?	
What steps would you recommend for the business to achieve what you have just proposed?	
What did you learn from this exercise?	

APPLY YOUR SKILLS: ACTION LEARNING

1. Think back to some of the courses you have taken in college or graduate school.

2. List the one you feel you did the best and got the best grade, and the one you did the worst.
   a. Best
   b. Worst

3. What did you do differently in the two classes? Fill out the table below:

	Study strategies and other behaviors that helped	Strategies and behaviors that did not help
Name of course		
Best:		
Worst:		

4. What were the differences in what you did in the best course versus the worst one?

5. List down lessons you can learn that will help you in future courses:
   a.   d.
   b.   e.
   c.   f.

APPLY YOUR SKILLS: ETHICAL DILEMMA

Inspire Learning Corporation[85]

When the idea first occurred to her, it seemed like such a win-win situation. Now she wasn't so sure.

Marge Brygay was a hardworking sales rep for Inspire Learning Corporation, a company intent on becoming the top educational software provider in five years. That newly adopted strategic goal translated into an ambitious, million-dollar sales target for each of Inspire's sales reps. At the beginning of the fiscal year, her share of the sales department's operational goal seemed entirely reasonable to Marge. She believed in Inspire's products. The company had developed innovative, highly regarded math, language, science, and social studies programs for the K–12 market. What set the software apart was a foundation in truly cutting-edge research. Marge had seen for herself how Inspire programs could engage whole classrooms of normally unmotivated kids; the significant rise in scores on those increasingly important standardized tests bore out her subjective impressions.

But now, just days before the end of the year, Marge's sales were $1,000 short of her million-dollar goal. The sale that would have put her comfortably over the top fell through due to last-minute cuts in one large school system's budget. At first, she was nearly overwhelmed with frustration, but then it occurred to her that if she contributed $1,000 to Central High, the inner-city high school in her territory probably most in need of what she had for sale, it could purchase the software and put her over the top.

Her scheme would certainly benefit Central High students. Achieving her sales goal would make Inspire happy, and it wouldn't do her any harm, either professionally or financially. Making the goal would earn her a $10,000 bonus check that would come in handy when the time came to write out that first tuition check for her oldest child, who had just been accepted to a well-known, private university.

Initially, it seemed like the perfect solution all the way around. The more she thought about it, however, the more it didn't quite sit well with her conscience. Time was running out. She needed to decide what to do.

What Would You Do?

1. Donate the $1,000 to Central High and consider the $10,000 bonus a good return on your investment.

2. Accept the fact that you didn't quite make your sales goal this year. Figure out ways to work smarter next year to increase the odds of achieving your target.

3. Don't make the donation, but investigate whether any other ways are available to help Central High raise the funds that would allow it to purchase the much-needed educational software.

APPLY YOUR SKILLS: CASE FOR CRITICAL ANALYSIS

Central City Museum

The recently completed new building to house the exhibits and staff of the Central City Museum was located adjacent to the campus of a private university. The new building was financed by the generosity of local donors. The university provided the land and would cover the annual operating expenses with the understanding that the museum would provide a resource for student education. The new governing board would be made up of key donors, as well as selected university administrators and faculty members.

The planning committee of the governing board hired two business students to interview various stakeholders about the future direction of the museum in its new relationship with the university. These interviews were conducted in person, and the interviewees seemed uniformly interested and eager to help. The major questions pertained to the future mission and goals of the museum. Some excerpts from the interviews are listed here:

A major donor: *I think the museum should be a major community resource. My wife and I gave money for the new building with the expectation that the museum would promote visits from the public schools in the area, and particularly serve the inner-city children who don't have access to art exhibits. We don't want the museum to be snobbish or elitist. The focus should definitely be local.*

A university administrator: *The important thing is to have lively contemporary exhibits that will attract both university students and community adults and provide new insight and dialogue about current events. We can bring attention to the museum by having an occasional controversial exhibit, such as an Islamic art, and exhibits that appeal to Hispanics and African Americans. This approach would entail bringing in traveling exhibitions from major museums, which would save the administrative costs and overhead of producing our own exhibits.*

Head of the art history department: *The key thing is that the museum will not have the artistic resources or the financial resources to serve the community at large. We have a wonderful opportunity to integrate the museum with the academic faculty and make it a teaching institution. It can be a major resource for both undergraduate and graduate students in art education and art history. We can also work with engineering students, architecture students, and liberal arts students. This is a unique opportunity that will distinguish our art history department's teaching mission from others in the country.*

A faculty member in the art history department: *The best use of the museum's relationship with the university is to concentrate on training Ph.D.-level students in art history and to support scholarly research. I strongly urge the museum to focus on graduate education, which would increase the stature of the university nationally. Graduate students would be involved in the design of exhibits that would fit their research. Trying to make the museum popular on campus or in the community will waste our limited resources. Our Ph.D. graduates will be sought after by art history departments throughout the country.*

The reason that you have been given this information from the interviews is that you have been invited to interview for the position of museum director. The previous director retired with the understanding that a new director would be hired upon the completion of fund-raising for and construction of the new building. You are thinking about what you would do if you took the job.

Questions

1. What goal or mission for the Central City Museum do you personally prefer? As director, would you try to implement your preferred direction? Explain.

2. How would you resolve the underlying conflicts among key stakeholders about museum direction and goals? What actions would you take?

Review the "Sunny Side Up" (Goal Conflict versus Manager Coalition) earlier in the chapter. Do you think that building a coalition and working out stakeholder differences in goal preferences is an important part of a manager's job? Why or why not?

ENDNOTES

1. James B. Stewart, "New Chipotle Mantra: Safe (and Fresh) Food," *The New York Times*, January 15, 2016.

2. Quoted in Oren Harari, "Good/Bad News About Strategy," *Management Review* (July 1995): 29–31.

3. Amitai Etzioni, *Modern Organizations* (Englewood Cliffs, NJ: Prentice Hall, 1984), p. 6.

4. Max D. Richards, *Setting Strategic Goals and Objectives*, 2d ed. (St. Paul, MN: West, 1986).

5. Based on A. G. Lafley and Roger Martin, "Instituting a Company-Wide Strategic Conversation at Procter & Gamble," *Strategy & Leadership* 41, no. 4 (2013): 4–9.

6. Ibid.

7. CVS Health, "About," http://www.cvshealth.com /about (accessed February 25, 2016).

8. Rachel Abrams, "CVS Stores Stop Selling All Tobacco Products," *The New York Times*, September 3, 2014.

9. Ibid.

10. Mary Klemm, Stuart Sanderson, and George Luffman, "Mission Statements: Selling Corporate Values to Employees," *Long-Range Planning* 24, no. 3 (1991): 73–78; John A. Pearce II and Fred David, "Corporate Mission Statements: The Bottom Line," *Academy of Management Executive* (1987): 109–116; Jerome H. Want, "Corporate Mission: The Intangible Contributor to Performance," *Management Review* (August 1986): 46–50; and Forest R. David and Fred R. David, "It's Time to Redraft Your Mission Statement," *Journal of Business Strategy* (January–February 2003): 11–14.

11. "Tennessee News and Notes from State Farm," *State Farm Mutual Automobile Insurance Company*, 2004; and "Our Mission, Our Vision, Our Shared Values," State Farm Web site, https://www.statefarm .com/about-us/company-over-view/company-profile /mission (accessed February 29, 2016).

12. Susan Carey, "Spirit Airlines New Boss Vows to Repair Image," *The Wall Street Journal*, February 12, 2016, http://www.wsj.com/articles/spirit-airlines-new-boss-vows-to-repair-image-1455319883 (accessed February 29, 2016).

13. Matthew Boyle, "Unilever: Taking on the World, One Stall at a Time," *Bloomberg Businessweek* (January 7–13, 2013): 18–20.

14. Paul Meising and Joseph Wolfe, "The Art and Science of Planning at the Business Unit Level," *Management Science* 31 (1985): 773–781.

15. Boyle, "Unilever: Taking on the World, One Stall at a Time."

16. Graham Kenny, "From the Stakeholder Viewpoint: Designing Measurable Objectives," *Journal of Business Strategy* 33, no. 6 (2012): 40–46.

17. Sayan Chatterjee, "Core Objectives: Clarity in Designing Strategy," *California Management Review* 47, no. 2 (Winter 2005): 33–49.

18. Jason Piatt, "5 Rules for Selecting the Best KPIs to Drive Operational Improvement," *Industry Week* (November 2012): 30.

19. Edwin A. Locke, Gary P. Latham, and Miriam Erez, "The Determinants of Goal Commitment," *Academy of Management Review* 13 (1988): 23–39.

20. Peter F. Drucker, *The Practice of Management* (New York: Harper & Row, 1954); George S. Odiorne, "MBO: A Backward Glance," *Business Horizons* 21 (October 1978): 14–24; and William F. Roth, "Is Management by Objectives Obsolete?" *Global Business and Organizational Excellence* (May–June 2009): 36–43.

21. Jan P. Muczyk and Bernard C. Reimann, "MBO as a Complement to Effective Leadership," The Academy of Management Executive 3 (1989): 131–138; and W. Giegold, Objective Setting and the MBO Process, vol.2 (New York: McGraw-Hill, 1978).

22. Jay Yarow, "This Is the Internal Grading System Google Uses for Its Employees, and You Should Use It Too," Business Insider (October 16, 2015), http://www.businessinsider.com/google-okr-employee-grading-system-2015–10 (accessed February 29, 2016).

23. This analogy is from Jeffrey K. Liker and Timothy N. Ogden, "The Toyota Recall: Missing the Forest for the Trees," Ivey Business Journal (November–December 2011), www.iveybusinessjournal.com/topics/marketing/the-toyota-recall-missing-the-forest-for-the-trees (accessed July 19, 2012).

24. Reylito A. H. Elbo, "MBM: Management by Means, Not Results," Manila Times, June 11, 2012, www.manilatimes.net/index.php/business/business-columnist/24633-mbm-management-by-means-not-results (accessed August 8, 2012); and Liker and Ogden, "The Toyota Recall."

25. Liker and Ogden, "The Toyota Recall."

26. C. Chet Miller and Laura B. Cardinal, "Strategic Planning and Firm Performance: A Synthesis of More than Two Decades of Research," Academy of Management Journal 37, no. 6 (1994): 1649–1685.

27. These are based on E. A. Locke and G. P. Latham, A Theory of Goal Setting & Task Performance (Englewood Cliffs, NJ: Prentice Hall, 1990); Richard L. Daft and Richard M. Steers, Organizations: A Micro/Macro Approach (Glenview, IL: Scott Foresman, 1986), pp. 319–321; Herbert A. Simon, "On the Concept of Organizational Goals," Administrative Science Quarterly 9 (1964): 1–22; and Charles B. Saunders and Francis D. Tuggel, "Corporate Goals," Journal of General Management 5 (1980): 3–13.

28. Nick Wingfield, "Netflix Boss Plots Life After the DVD," The Wall Street Journal, June 23, 2009.

29. These are based on Henry Mintzberg, The Rise and Fall of Strategic Planning (New York: Free Press, 1994); H. Mintzberg, "Rethinking Strategic Planning, Part I: Pitfalls and Fallacies," Long-Range Planning 27 (1994): 12–21; and H. Mintzberg, "The Pitfalls of Strategic Planning," California Management Review 36 (1993): 32–47.

30. Danny Hakim, Aaron M. Kessler, and Jack Ewing, "As VW Pushed to Be No. 1, Ambitions Fueled a Scandal (September 27, 2015); and Jonathan Soble, "Panel Finds Accounting Irregularities at Toshiba," The New York Times, July 21, 2015.

31. Roth, "Is Management by Objectives Obsolete?"

32. Curtis W. Roney, "Planning for Strategic Contingencies," Business Horizons (March–April 2003): 35–42; and "Corporate Planning: Drafting a Blueprint for Success," Small Business Report (August 1987): 40–44.

33. Doug Cameron, Jeffrey Ng, and Jack Nicas, "Post Jet Grounding, Airlines Scramble to Develop Plan Bs," The Wall Street Journal, January 18, 2013; and Gustav Sandstrom, "Norwegian Airlines Encounter Additional Dreamliner Tech Issues," The Wall Street Journal Online, September 9, 2013, http://online.wsj.com/article/BT-CO-20130909-701299.html (accessed September 12, 2013).

34. This section is based on Steven Schnaars and Paschalina Ziamou, "The Essentials of Scenario Writing," Business Horizons (July–August 2001): 25–31; Peter Cornelius, Alexander Van de Putte, and Mattia Romani, "Three Decades of Scenario Planning in Shell," California Management Review 48, no. 1 (Fall 2005): 92–109; Audrey Schriefer and Michael Sales, "Creating Strategic Advantage with Dynamic Scenarios," Strategy & Leadership 34, no. 3 (2006): 31–42; William J. Worthington, Jamie D. Collins, and Michael A. Hitt, "Beyond Risk Mitigation: Enhancing Corporate Innovation with Scenario Planning," Business Horizons 52 (2009): 441–450; Gill Ringland, "Innovation: Scenarios of Alternative Futures Can Discover New Opportunities for Creativity," Strategy & Leadership 36, no. 5 (2008): 22–27; and Stephen M. Millett, "Four Decades of Business Scenarios: What Can Experience Teach?" Strategy & Leadership 41, no 1 (1013): 29–33.

35. Millett, "Four Decades of Business Scenarios."

36. Quoted in Claire Churchard, "Tales of the Unexpected," People Management (February 2012).

37. Reported in Churchard, "Tales of the Unexpected."

38. Kathleen Wilburn and Ralph Wilburn, "Abbreviated Scenario Thinking," Business Horizons 54 (2011): 541–550.

39. Gerald F. Seib, "Four Scenarios for Libya—Some Good and Some Bad," The Wall Street Journal, March 29, 2011, http://online.wsj.com/article/SB10001424052748703739204576228620384027448.html (accessed July 20, 2012).

40. Ian Mitroff with Gus Anagnos, Managing Crises Before They Happen (New York: AMACOM, 2001); and Ian Mitroff and Murat C. Alpaslan, "Preparing for Evil," Harvard Business Review (April 2003): 109–115.

41. Lau Chee Wai and Winai Wongsurawat, "Crisis Management: Western Digital's 46-Day Recovery from the 2011 Flood Disaster in Thailand," Strategy & Leadership 41, no. 1 (2013): 34–38.

42. Jack Nicas, "Faulty Planning, Stage Cited in Fair Collapse," The Wall Street Journal, April 12, 2012, http://online.wsj.com/article/SB10001424052702304356604577339923897959492.html (accessed July 20, 2012).

43. The following discussion is based largely on W. Timothy Coombs, Ongoing Crisis Communication: Planning, Managing, and Responding (Thousand Oaks, CA: Sage Publications, 1999).

44. Ian I. Mitroff, "Crisis Leadership," Executive Excellence (August 2001): 19; and Andy Bowen, "Crisis Procedures That Stand the Test of Time," Public Relations Tactics (August 2001): 16.

45. Jason Fried, "How to Ride a Storm," Inc. (February 2011): 37–39.

46. Christine Pearson, "A Blueprint for Crisis Management," Ivey Business Journal (January–February 2002): 69–73.

47. See Mitroff and Alpaslan, "Preparing for Evil," for a discussion of the "wheel of crises" and the many different kinds of crises that organizations may face.

48. Harari, "Good/Bad News About Strategy."

49. James C. Collins and Jerry I. Porras, "Building Your Company's Vision," Harvard Business Review (September–October 1996): 65–77.

50. Steven Kerr and Steffan Landauer, "Using Stretch Goals to Promote Organizational Effectiveness and Personal Growth: General Electric and Goldman Sachs," Academy of Management Executive 18, no. 4 (November 2004): 134–138; and Lisa D. Ordóñez et al., "Goals Gone Wild: The Systematic Side Effects of Overprescribing Goal Setting," Academy of Management Perspectives (February 2009): 6–16.

51. See Kenneth R. Thompson, Wayne A. Hockwarter, and Nicholas J. Mathys, "Stretch Targets: What Makes Them Effective?" Academy of Management Executive 11, no. 3 (August 1997): 48.

52. Douglas MacMillan, "Tech's Fiercest Rivalry: Uber vs. Lyft," *The Wall Street Journal*, August 11, 2014, http://www.wsj.com/articles/two-tech-upstarts-plot-each-others-demise-1407800744 (accessed March 5, 2016).

53. John Bussey, "The Business: The Anti-Kodak: How a U.S. Firm Innovates," *The Wall Street Journal*, January 13, 2012.

54. Greg Satell, "A Look Back at Why Blockbuster Really Failed and Why It Didn't Have To," *Forbes* (September 5, 2014), http://www.forbes.com/sites/gregsatell/2014/09/05/a-look-back-at-why-blockbuster-really-failed-and-why-it-didnt-have-to/#32dffe04261a (accessed March 11, 2016).

55. Chet Miller and Laura B. Cardinal, "Strategic Planning and Firm Performance: A Synthesis of More than Two Decades of Research," *Academy of Management Journal* 37, no. 6 (1994): 1649–1665.

56. Renée Dye and Olivier Sibony, "How to Improve Strategic Planning," *McKinsey Quarterly*, no. 3 (2007), http://www.mckinsey.com/business-functions/strategy-and-corporate-finance/our-insights/how-to-improve-strategic-planning (accessed June 7, 2016).

57. Keith H. Hammonds, "Michael Porter's Big Ideas," *Fast Company* (March 2001): 150–156.

58. Cynthia A. Montgomery, "Strategist-in-Chief," *Leadership Excellence* (July 2012): 12; John E. Prescott, "Environments as Moderators of the Relationship Between Strategy and Performance," *Academy of Management Journal* 29 (1986): 329–346; John A. Pearce II and Richard B. Robinson, Jr., *Strategic Management: Strategy, Formulation, and Implementation*, 2d ed. (Homewood, IL: Irwin, 1985); and David J. Teece, "Economic Analysis and Strategic Management," *California Management Review* 26 (Spring 1984): 87–110.

59. Jack Welch, "It's All in the Sauce," excerpt from his book, *Winning*, published in *Fortune* (April 18, 2005): 138–144; and Constantinos Markides, "Strategic Innovation," *Sloan Management Review* (Spring 1997): 9–23.

60. Michael E. Porter, "What Is Strategy?" *Harvard Business Review* (November–December 1996): 61–78.

61. This discussion draws ideas from Ken Favaro, "The Two Levels of Strategy," *Strategy + Business*, April 27, 2012, http://www.strategy-business.com/article/cs00004?gko∇8d72a (accessed September 16, 2013); and Ken Favaro with Kasturi Rangan and Evan Hirsh, "Strategy: An Executive's Definition," *Strategy + Business*, March 5, 2012, www.strategy-business.com/article/cs00002?gko∇d59c2 (accessed July 24, 2012).

62. Brian Leavy, "Updating a Classic Formula for Strategic Success: Focus, Alignment, Repeatability, and Leadership," *Strategy & Leadership* 41, no. 1 (2013): 18–28.

63. James R. Hagerty, "Sherwin-Williams and PPG Tackle a Tough Paint Job," *The Wall Street Journal*, July 21, 2014, http://www.wsj.com/articles/sherwin-williams-and-ppg-tackle-a-tough-paint-job-1405971038 (accessed March 5, 2016).

64. Arthur A. Thompson, Jr., and A. J. Strickland III, *Strategic Management: Concepts and Cases*, 6th ed. (Homewood, IL: Irwin, 1992); and Briance Mascarenhas, Alok Baveja, and Mamnoon Jamil, "Dynamics of Core Competencies in Leading Multinational Companies," *California Management Review* 40, no. 4 (Summer 1998): 117–132.

65. "Angela Poulakidas, "Teekay Shipping Corporation Case Analysis," *Journal of Business Strategy* 35, no. 2 (2014): 26–35; and Chris Woodyard, "Big Dreams for Small Choppers Paid Off," *USA TODAY*, September 11, 2005.

66. Michael Goold and Andrew Campbell, "Desperately Seeking Synergy," *Harvard Business Review* (September–October 1998): 131–143.

67. Julie Jargon, "No Wonder: Twinkies Owner Adds Bread," *The Wall Street Journal*, September 17, 2015, http://www.wsj.com/articles/no-wonder-twinkies-owner-adds-bread-1442482200 (accessed March 5, 2016).

68. Anjali Cordeiro "Boss Talk: Tang in India and Other Kraft Synergies," *The Wall Street Journal Online*, April 19, 2010, http://online.wsj.com/article/SB10001424052702303348504575184103106388686.html (accessed October 8, 2012); and Farhad Manjoo, "Mobile Is Now a Magic Word," *The New York Times*, May 13, 2015.

69. Lauren A. E. Schuker, "Double Feature: Dinner and a Movie—To Upgrade from Dirty Carpets and Tubs of Popcorn, Theater Chains Try Full Menus, Seat-Side Service," *The Wall Street Journal*, January 5, 2011.

70. Farhad Manjoo, "How Amazon's Long Game Yielded a Retail Juggernaut," *The New York Times*, November 18, 2015, http://www.nytimes.com/2015/11/19/technology/how-amazons-long-game-yielded-a-retail-juggernaut.html?_r∇0 (accessed March 8, 2016); Lisa Eadicicco, "How Amazon Delivers Packages in Less than an Hour," *Time* (December 22, 2015), http://time.com/4159144/amazon-prime-warehouse-new-york-city-deliveries-christmas/ (accessed March 8, 2016); Brad Stone, "What's in the Box? Instant Gratification," *Bloomberg Businessweek* (November 29–December 5, 2010): 39–40; and S. Levy, "CEO of the Internet: Jeff Bezos Owns the Web in More Ways than You Think," *Wired*, December 2011, www.wired.com/magazine/2011/11/ff_bezos/ (accessed July 24, 2012).

71. Walt Shill, quoted in Joann S. Lublin and Dana Mattioli, "Theory & Practice: Strategic Plans Lose Favor," *The Wall Street Journal*, January 25, 2010.

72. Arne Gast and Michele Zanini, "The Social Side of Strategy," *McKinsey Quarterly*, Issue 2 (2012): 82–93.

73. Doug Reed, "SWOT Your Way to the Future," *Industrial Management* (March–April 2013): 23–26; and Christopher B. Bingham, Kathleen M. Eisenhardt, and Nathan R. Furr, "Which Strategy When?" *MIT Sloan Management Review* (Fall 2011): 71–78.

74. Activision Blizzard, "100 Best Companies to Work For 2016," *Fortune*, http://fortune.com/best-companies/activision-blizzard-77/ (accessed March 9, 2016); and John Kell, "Originality Helps Build Hit Toy Brands," *The Wall Street Journal*, February 10, 2013, http://online.wsj.com/article/SB10001424127887323696404578296301873193788.html (accessed September 16, 2013).

75. Lyndee Fletcher, "It's Time for Video Game Companies to Take Some Responsibility for These Shootings," *MovieGuide*, https://www.movieguide.org/news-articles/its-time-for-video-game-companies-to-take-some-responsibility-for-these-shootings.html (accessed March 9, 2016); and Nick Allen, "Aaron Alexis: Washington Navy Yard Gunman 'Obsessed with Violent Video Games,'" *The Telegraph*, September 18, 2013, http://www.telegraph.co.uk/news/worldnews/northamerica/usa/10314585/Aaron-Alexis-Washington-navy-yard-gunman-obsessed-with-violent-video-games.html (accessed September 18, 2013).

76. Jon M. Chang, "How Violent Video Games Fit In with Violent Behavior," *ABC News*, September 18, 2013, http://abcnews.go.com/Technology/navy-yard-shooter-played-military-style-videogames-relevant/story?id∇20285169 (accessed September 18, 2013); *Allen*, "Aaron Alexis: Washington Navy Yard Gunman 'Obsessed with Violent

Video Games'"; and Jonah Hicap, "Mass Killers in U.S. All
Found to Be Addicted to Playing Violent Video Games,"
Christian Today (October 18, 2015), http://www
.christiantoday.com/article/mass.killers.in.us.all.found.to.be.
addicted.to.playing.violent.video.games/67910.htm (accessed
March 9, 2016).

77. Don Clark, "Intel Hurt by PC Shift," *The Wall Street Journal*,
January 18, 2013.

78. David Welch, Keith Naughton, and Burt Helm, "Detroit's Big
Chance," *Bloomberg Businessweek* (February 22, 2010): 38–44.

79. James R. Hagerty, "How to Sell Garbage Disposals in China;
Emerson's InSinkErator Rejiggered to Munch Kitchen
Favorites Like Eel, Bullfrog Skin and Duck Heads," *The
Wall Street Journal*, March 26, 2014, http://www.wsj.com/
articles/SB1000142405270230354620457943500003153143
2 (accessed March 9, 2016).

80. Thompson and Strickland, *Strategic Management*; and
William L. Shanklin and John K. Ryans, Jr., "Is the International Cash Cow Really a Prize Heifer?" *Business Horizons* 24
(1981): 10–16.

81. Serena Ng and Ellen Byron, "P&G Faces Up to Mistakes in
Beauty Business," *The Wall Street Journal*, July 9, 2015, http://
www.wsj.com/articles/procter-gamble-agrees-to-sell-beauty-
businesses-1436444762 (accessed March 9, 2016).

82. Douglas MacMillan and Greg Bensinger, "Amazon to Buy
Video Site Twitch for $970 Million," *The Wall Street Journal*,
August 26, 2014, http://www.wsj.com/articles/amazon-to-
buy-video-site-twitch-for-more-than-1-billion-1408988885
(accessed March 9, 2016); David Gelles and Vindu Goel,
"Facebook Enters $16 Billion Deal," *The New York Times*,
February 20, 2014; and Nick Wingfield, "Microsoft Gets
Nokia Units, and Leader," *The New York Times*, September 3, 2013, http://www.nytimes.com/2013/09/03/
technology/microsoft-gets-nokia-units-and-leader.
html?pagewanted=all&_r=0 (accessed September 18, 2013).

83. The following discussion is based on Michael E. Porter, "The
Five Competitive Forces That Shape Strategy," *Harvard
Business Review* (January 2008): 79–93; Porter, *Competitive
Strategy* (New York: Free Press, 1980), pp. 36–46; Danny
Miller, "Relating Porter's Business Strategies to Environment
and Structure: Analysis and Performance Implementations,"
Academy of Management Journal 31 (1988): 280–308; and
Michael E. Porter, "From Competitive Advantage to Corporate
Strategy," *Harvard Business Review* (May–June 1987): 43–59.

84. Adapted from Richard L. Daft and Dorothy Marcic,
Understanding Management (Mason, OH: South-Western,
2008), pp. 177–178.

85. Based on Shel Horowitz, "Should Mary Buy Her Own
Bonus?" *Business Ethics* (Summer 2005): 34.

Chapter 6
Managerial Decision Making

iStock.com/oscarhdez

Chapter Outline

Learning Outcomes

After studying this chapter, you should be able to:

6.1 Explain why decision making is an important component of good management.

6.2 Compare and contrast programmed and nonprogrammed decisions, and describe the decision characteristics of certainty and uncertainty.

6.3 Compare the ideal, rational model of decision making to the political model of decision making.

6.4 Explain the process by which managers actually make decisions in the real world.

6.5 Summarize the six steps used in managerial decision making.

6.6 Describe four personal decision styles used by managers.

6.7 Identify the biases that frequently cause managers to make bad decisions.

6.8 Explain innovative techniques for decision making, including brainstorming, evidence-based management, and after-action reviews.

Are You Ready to Be a Manager?

Before reading this chapter, please circle either "Mostly True" or "Mostly False" for each of the following five statements.

1 I'm good at making decisions when there is certainty and need more help when there is uncertainty. I make both kinds of decisions, not automatically, but with thought and weighing of possible outcomes.

Mostly True ◄┄┄┄┄┄┄► Mostly False

[page 193]

2 When conditions are difficult and priorities conflicting, sometimes I have to make a decision based on "this is the best we can do" and I have to abandon the idea of getting all the needs met.

Mostly True ◄┄┄┄┄┄┄► Mostly False

[page 198]

3 I don't think gut instincts or intuition can help in the decision-making process.

Mostly True ◄┄┄┄┄┄┄► Mostly False

[page 199]

4 I'm good at building a coalitions or helping build consensus around a problem and its solution.

Mostly True ◄┄┄┄┄┄┄► Mostly False

[page 200]

5 I try to avoid making bad decisions through being aware that I should not let myself be influenced by (a) justifying past decisions I made, so that I now might look bad; (b) overconfidence; (c) trying to keep things the way they are or the status quo; (d) emotions; or (e) being swayed by initial impressions rather than digging deeper for more evidence.

Mostly True ◄┄┄┄┄┄┄► Mostly False

[page 209]

Discover Your Management Approach

How Do You Make Decisions?

Instructions: Most of us make decisions automatically without realizing that people have diverse decision-making behaviors, which they bring to management positions.[a] Think back to how you make decisions in your personal, student, or work life, especially where other people are involved. Please answer whether each of the following items is Mostly True or Mostly False for you.

	Mostly True	Mostly False
1. I like to decide quickly and move on to the next thing.	_____	_____
2. I would use my authority to make a decision if I'm certain I'm right.	_____	_____
3. I appreciate decisiveness.	_____	_____

To complete and score the entire assessment, visit MindTap.

[a]See Stephen J. Sauer, "Why Bossy Is Better for Rookie Managers," *Harvard Business Review* (May 2012): 30; and Kenneth R. Brousseau et al., "The Seasoned Executive's Decision-Making Style," *Harvard Business Review* (February 2006): 110–121, for a discussion of how decision-making behavior evolves as managers progress in their careers.

When the mayor of Flint, Michigan, stood before local news cameras and pushed a black button that connected the Flint River to the city's water treatment plant in April 2014, the ceremony was cheered as a symbol of efforts to save the financially strapped city millions of dollars. Eighteen months later, people learned that the water coming from their taps was contaminated with high levels of lead. City managers had chosen to temporarily use the Flint River as a cheaper source of water rather than buying high-priced water from Detroit. However, the decision brought even more turmoil to the struggling city. Under federal law, a corrosion-control plan to treat the river water should have been put in place, but no one involved in the decision making at the city, state, or federal level seemed to realize it. Then more bad decisions piled up. Officials dismissed complaints about the look, smell, and taste of the water, and response was slow as people began complaining about skin rashes. Now managers are struggling to control a full-blown crisis and provide safe drinking water, and Flint residents are facing the unknown effects of lead exposure. "They said it was safe to drink," said Marshall Green, who started buying bottled water after suffering rashes on his arms. Tracey Whepley, owner of the Lunch Studio sandwich shop, says, "I'm not sure I'm going to ever trust water again coming through pipes."[1]

Welcome to the world of managerial decision making. Every organization, whether it is General Motors (GM), Uber, the American Red Cross, or the city of Flint, Michigan, grows, prospers, or fails as a result of decisions made by its managers. Yet decision making, particularly in relation to complex problems, is not always easy. It is easy to look back and identify flawed decisions, but managers frequently make decisions amid ever-changing factors, unclear information, and conflicting points of view. Managers can sometimes make the wrong decision, even when their intentions are right.

The business world is full of evidence of both good and bad decisions. YouTube was once referred to as "Google's Folly," but decisions made by the video platform's managers have more than justified the $1.65 billion that Google paid for it and have turned YouTube into a highly admired company that is redefining the entertainment industry.[2] On the other hand, Caterpillar's decision to purchase China's ERA Mining Machinery Ltd. hasn't worked out so well. After paying $700 million for the deal, Caterpillar managers said less than a year later that they would write down ERA's value by $580 million. The company blamed deliberate accounting misconduct that was designed to overstate profits at the firm's mine-safety equipment unit.[3]

Good decision making is a vital part of good management because decisions determine how the organization solves problems, allocates resources, and accomplishes its goals. This chapter describes decision making in detail. We will look at several decision-making models and the steps managers should take when making important decisions. The chapter also explores some biases that can cause managers to make bad decisions and examines some specific techniques for innovative decision making in a fast-changing environment.

6-1 Types of Decisions and Problems

A **decision** is a choice made from available alternatives. For example, an accounting manager's selection among Colin, Tasha, and Carlos for the position of junior auditor is a decision. Many people assume that making a choice is the major part of decision making, but it is only a part of it.

Decision making is the process of identifying problems and opportunities and then resolving them. Decision making involves effort both before and after the actual choice. Thus, the decision of whether to select Colin, Tasha, or Carlos requires the accounting manager to ascertain whether a new junior auditor is needed, determine the availability of potential job candidates, interview candidates to acquire necessary information, select one candidate, and follow up with the socialization of the new employee into the organization to ensure the decision's success.

6-1a Programmed and Nonprogrammed Decisions

Management decisions typically fall into one of two categories: programmed and nonprogrammed. **Programmed decisions** involve situations that have occurred often enough to enable decision rules to be developed and applied in the future.[4] Programmed decisions are made in response to recurring organizational problems. The decision to reorder paper and other office supplies when inventories drop to a certain level is a programmed decision. Other programmed decisions concern the types of skills required to fill certain jobs, the reorder point for manufacturing inventory, and the selection of freight routes for product deliveries. Once managers formulate decision rules, subordinates and others can make the decision, thus freeing managers for other tasks. For example, when staffing banquets, many hotels use a rule that specifies having one server per 30 guests for a sit-down function and one server per 40 guests for a buffet.[5]

Nonprogrammed decisions are made in response to situations that are unique, are poorly defined and largely unstructured, and have important consequences for the organization. Perhaps one of the greatest nonprogrammed decisions of all time was Boeing's decision to build the 707. In the years following World War II, Boeing was primarily a maker of military aircraft. With its experience building bombers, the company had the technology for building jet aircraft, but no one had considered that the airlines would even be interested in buying jets. Converting to jet technology would be massively expensive for the airlines. Boeing's CEO, Bill Allen, had to decide whether to stick with the defense products that the company knew best or follow his conviction that the real growth would be in the civilian sector. In 1952, he asked Boeing's board to invest $16 million in building the world's first transatlantic commercial jetliner. By the

Darren Brode/Shutterstock.com

Concept Connection

A Ram 1500 pickup truck is proudly on display at the 2015 North American International Auto Show in Detroit. Managers at Chrysler, the U.S. subsidiary of Fiat Chrysler Automobiles N.V., created a standalone Ram Trucks division in 2010 so people could "come to work and do nothing but think about pickup trucks." The **nonprogrammed decision** to create a new division paid off. Ram is the fastest growing truck brand in America, and the Ram 1500 has been named the "Best Full Size Truck for the Money" two years in a row by *U. S. News and World Report*.

Revitalizing Small Farms PepsiCo executives discovered for themselves that sustainability decisions can be observed and measured in the lives of individuals. Management's decision to launch a pilot project cutting the intermediary from the supply chain for Sabritas, its Mexican line of snacks, by initiating direct purchase of corn from 300 small farmers in Mexico brought unimagined benefits.

The decision resulted in visible, measurable outcomes, including lower transportation costs and a stronger relationship with small farmers, who were able to develop pride and a businesslike approach to farming. The arrangement with PepsiCo gave farmers a financial edge in securing much-needed credit for purchasing equipment, fertilizer, and other necessities, which resulted in higher crop yields. New levels of financial security also reduced the once-rampant and highly dangerous treks back and forth across the U.S. border that farmers made at great personal risk as they sought ways to support their families. Within three years, PepsiCo's pilot program was expanded to 850 farmers.

SOURCE: Stephanie Strom, "For Pepsi, a Business Decision with Social Benefits," *The New York Times*, February 21, 2011, www.nytimes.com/2011/02/22/business/global/22pepsi.html?pagewanted=all (accessed August 2, 2012).

time the 707 rolled off the production line, Boeing had invested $185 million in it—that was $36 million more than Boeing's net worth the previous year. Essentially, Allen was betting the company's future, and it paid off. The 707 changed the course of history for Boeing and altered the course of the entire industry.[6]

Managers in every industry face nonprogrammed decisions every day. Consider the decision of managers at Chrysler to create a new division devoted to pickup trucks.

Many nonprogrammed decisions, such as the one at Chrysler to create a stand-alone Ram Trucks division, are related to strategic planning because uncertainty is great and decisions are complex. Decisions to develop a new product or service, acquire a company, create a new division, build a new factory, enter a new geographical market, or relocate headquarters to another city are all nonprogrammed decisions.

Sunny Side Up } **Ram Trucks**

In 2009, it was far from a sure thing that Chrysler would survive. After bankruptcy, a taxpayer bailout, and acquisition by Fiat, it did, but the decision of Sergio Marchionne, Chrysler Group's chairman and CEO, to create a stand-alone division for the Ram truck was a huge gamble. When the trend in the struggling auto industry was to consolidate, critics doubted the wisdom of creating a new brand, particularly one devoted to pickup trucks. "The skeptics, who were already predicting our company was going down the tubes, thought for sure that we'd been smoking something funny," Marchionne joked.

Five years later, though, the nonprogrammable gamble had paid off. Ram trucks were capturing a growing share of the full-size pickup market long dominated by Ford and GM's Chevrolet. The Chrysler truck plant in Warren, Michigan, was running 20 hours a day, six days a week to keep up with demand. Marchionne and other managers believed Chrysler could be more competitive by creating a separate division devoted to trucks. A conference room at Chrysler's headquarters was turned into a Ram war room where team members could brainstorm ideas to give truck buyers what they wanted. Engineers went to work adding features that increased the Ram's hauling capacity and at the same time topped the charts for fuel economy. Sean Kilmain, who test drove Chevys and Fords, says he bought a Ram because he thought it offered more features for less money than competitors. "I didn't want to get a gas guzzler, but also wanted something that could do pretty much anything I wanted," he said. "Haul some stuff, carry some people."

A Kelley Blue Book analyst says Ram could even seize the No. 2 spot in pickups, behind Ford, something that would have been unthinkable just a few years ago.[7]

6-1b Facing Uncertainty and Ambiguity

One primary difference between programmed and nonprogrammed decisions relates to the degree of uncertainty, risk, or ambiguity that managers deal with in making the decision. In a perfect world, managers would have all the information necessary for making decisions. In reality, however, some things are unknowable; thus, some decisions will fail to solve the problem or attain the desired outcome. Managers try to obtain information about decision alternatives that will reduce decision uncertainty. Every decision situation can be organized on a scale according to the availability of information and the possibility of failure. The four positions on the scale are certainty, risk, uncertainty, and ambiguity, as illustrated in Exhibit 6.1. Whereas programmed decisions can be made in situations involving certainty, many situations that managers deal with every day involve at least some degree of uncertainty and require nonprogrammed decision making.

Certainty   **Certainty** means that all the information the decision maker needs is fully available.[8] Managers have information on operating conditions, resource costs, and constraints and each course of action and possible outcome. For example, if a company considers a $10,000 investment in new equipment that it knows for certain will yield $4,000 in cost savings per year over the next five years, managers can calculate a before-tax rate of return of about 40 percent. If managers compare this investment with one that will yield only $3,000 per year in cost savings, they can confidently select the 40 percent return. However, few decisions are certain in the real world. Most contain risk or uncertainty.

Risk   **Risk** means that a decision has clear-cut goals and that good information is available, but the future outcomes associated with each alternative are subject to some chance of loss or failure. However, enough information is available to estimate the probability of a successful outcome versus failure.[9] For example, managers at Royal Dutch Shell PLC bet that the company could find enough oil in the Arctic Ocean to justify the risks of drilling there. The cost of drilling in the Arctic is huge, but so is the potential reward, as Alaska's portion of the Chukchi Sea where Shell began drilling could hold the equivalent of 29 billion barrels of oil and gas. So far, Shell is the only company taking the risk of drilling in the Arctic. "Everybody's watching to see if we're going to fail or succeed out there," said Ann Pickard, an executive vice president who runs Shell's Arctic division.[10] In late 2015, Shell pulled out of the Arctic drilling campaign at a loss of billions of dollars. The risk was too great.[11]

Exhibit 6.1 **Conditions That Affect the Possibility of Decision Failure**

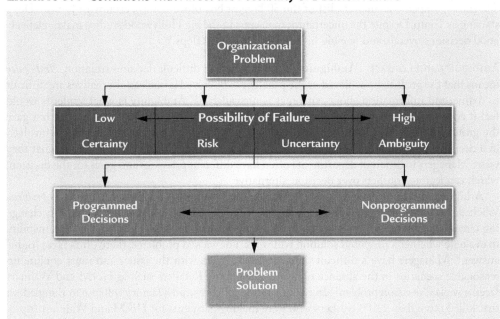

ghornephoto/Getty Images

Concept Connection

Uncertainty is a standard feature in the life of any farmer. Changing weather patterns and unexpected events, like droughts, floods, or unseasonable storms, can have devastating effects on crops that no amount of planning can prevent. Yet, despite these unforeseeable situations, farmers must make decisions and continue to operate based on assumptions and expectations.

Steve Krupp, CEO of Decision Strategies International, a consulting firm that helps managers and employees feel more comfortable taking balanced risks, says "You can't just avoid all risk, because it will lead to entropy."[12] For specific decisions, managers sometimes use computerized statistical analysis to calculate the probabilities of success or failure for each alternative. For example, executives at fast-food chains such as Subway, Wendy's, and McDonald's can analyze potential customer demographics, traffic patterns, supply logistics, and competition, and come up with a reasonably good idea of how successful a restaurant would be in each location being considered.[13]

Uncertainty Uncertainty means that managers know which goals they wish to achieve, but information about alternatives and future events is incomplete. Factors that may affect a decision, such as price, production costs, volume, or future interest rates, are difficult to analyze and predict. Managers may have to make assumptions from which to forge the decision, even though it will be wrong if the assumptions are incorrect. Former U.S. treasury secretary Robert Rubin defined *uncertainty* as a situation in which even a good decision might produce a bad outcome.[14] Managers face uncertainty every day. Many problems have no clear-cut solution, but managers rely on creativity, judgment, intuition, and experience to craft a response.

Consider the uncertainty faced by managers in the movie industry. Disney's *Oz the Great and Powerful* cost about $325 million to make and market, but the gamble in putting out a prequel to the beloved 1939 musical *The Wizard of Oz* paid off, bringing in $150 million in revenues on its opening weekend and eventually grossing $495 million. Even though Disney managers did a cost-benefit analysis, there was tremendous uncertainty about how viewers would feel about a new twist on such well-known material.[15] Many films made today don't even break even, which reflects the tremendous uncertainty in the industry. What do people want to see this summer? Will comic book heroes, vampires, or aliens be popular? Will animated films, disaster epics, classics, or romantic comedies attract larger audiences? The interests and preferences of moviegoers are extremely difficult to predict. Moreover, it is hard for managers to understand even after the fact what made a particular movie a hit: Was it because of the storyline, the actors in starring roles, the director, the release date? All of those things? Or none of them? *The Lone Ranger*, another Disney film on a familiar theme (based on a 1950s-era TV show), topped one analyst's list of the 50 biggest box office bombs, even with Johnny Depp starring as Tonto. Despite the uncertainty, managers in the big Hollywood studios make relatively good decisions overall, and one big hit can pay for a lot of flops.[16]

Ambiguity and Conflict **Ambiguity** is by far the most difficult decision situation. *Ambiguity* means that the goals to be achieved or the problem to be solved is unclear, alternatives are difficult to define, and information about outcomes is unavailable.[17] Ambiguity is what students would feel if an instructor created student groups and told each group to complete a project but gave the groups no topic, direction, or guidelines whatsoever. In some situations, managers involved in a decision create ambiguity because they see things differently and disagree about what they want. Managers in different departments often have different priorities and goals for the decision, which can lead to conflicts over decision alternatives.

A highly ambiguous situation can create what is sometimes called a *wicked decision problem*. Wicked decisions are associated with conflicts over goals and decision alternatives, rapidly changing circumstances, fuzzy information, unclear links among decision elements, and the inability to evaluate whether a proposed solution will work. For wicked problems, there often is no "right" answer.[18] Managers have a difficult time coming to grips with the issues and must conjure up reasonable scenarios in the absence of clear information. Retailers such as H&M and Walmart faced a wicked decision problem after a series of deadly fires and a factory collapse in Bangladesh that killed more than 1,100 workers who were making garments for H&M and Walmart stores.

HOT TOPIC

Remember This

- Good decision making is a vital part of good management, but decision making is not easy.
- **Decision making** is the process of identifying problems and opportunities and then resolving them.
- A **decision** is a choice made from available alternatives.
- A **programmed decision** is one made in response to a situation that has occurred often enough to enable managers to develop decision rules that can be applied in the future.
- A **nonprogrammed decision** is one made in response to a situation that is unique, is poorly defined and largely unstructured, and has important consequences for the organization.
- Decisions differ according to the amount of certainty, risk, uncertainty, or ambiguity in the situation.
- **Certainty** is a situation in which all the information the decision maker needs is fully available.
- **Risk** means that a decision has clear-cut goals and good information is available, but the future outcomes associated with each alternative are subject to chance.
- **Uncertainty** occurs when managers know which goals they want to achieve, but information about alternatives and future events is incomplete.
- **Ambiguity** is a condition in which the goals to be achieved or the problem to be solved is unclear, alternatives are difficult to define, and information about outcomes is unavailable.
- Highly ambiguous circumstances can create a wicked decision problem, the most difficult decision situation managers face.

The incidents set off public outrage, and retailers were compelled to respond. Walmart managers eventually decided to publicly blacklist about 250 Bangladesh suppliers found to have safety problems, while H&M managers decided they would stay with their suppliers and help them improve conditions. Neither decision will fix the deeper wicked problem. Almost all apparel and many other consumer goods are made in overseas factories in places like Bangladesh, Cambodia, and Thailand, and safety concerns and poor working conditions exist in many of them. Moreover, the global supply chain is so broad and diffuse that a single product might involve supplies and labor from several countries. Managers have a hard time even determining which factories and suppliers they are really using, and even when they do know, it is difficult to police every aspect of the suppliers' operations.[19]

6-2 Decision-Making Models

The approach managers use to make decisions usually falls into one of three types—the classical model, the administrative model, or the political model. The choice of model depends on the manager's personal preference, whether the decision is programmed or nonprogrammed, and the degree of uncertainty associated with the decision.

6-2a The Ideal, Rational Model

The **classical model** of decision making is based on rational economic assumptions and managers' beliefs about what ideal decision making should be. This model has arisen within the management literature because managers are expected to make decisions that are economically sensible and in the organization's best economic interests. The four assumptions underlying this model are as follows:

- The decision maker operates to accomplish goals that are known and agreed on. Problems are precisely formulated and defined.
- The decision maker strives for conditions of certainty and tries to gather complete information. All alternatives and the potential results of each are calculated.

- Criteria for evaluating alternatives are known. The decision maker selects the alternative that will maximize the economic return to the organization.
- The decision maker is rational and uses logic to assign values, order preferences, evaluate alternatives, and make the decision that will maximize the attainment of organizational goals.

The classical model of decision making is considered to be **normative,** which means that it defines how a decision maker *should* make decisions. It does not describe how managers actually make decisions so much as it provides guidelines on how to reach an ideal outcome for the organization. The ideal, rational approach of the classical model is often unattainable by real people in real organizations, but the model has value because it helps decision makers be more rational and not rely entirely on personal preference in making decisions. Indeed, a global survey by McKinsey & Company found that when managers incorporate thoughtful analysis into decision making, they get better results. Studying the responses of more than 2,000 executives regarding how their companies made a specific decision, McKinsey concluded that techniques such as detailed analysis, risk assessment, financial models, and consideration of comparable situations typically contribute to better financial and operational outcomes.[20]

The classical model is most useful when applied to programmed decisions and to decisions characterized by certainty or risk because relevant information is available and probabilities can be calculated. For example, new analytical software programs automate many programmed decisions, such as freezing the account of a customer who has failed to make payments, determining the cell phone service plan that is most appropriate for a particular customer, or sorting insurance claims so that cases are handled most efficiently.[21]

The growth of big data techniques, as described in Chapter 1, has expanded the use of the classical approach. The New York City Police Department uses computerized mapping and analysis of arrest patterns, paydays, sporting events, concerts, rainfall, holidays, and other variables to predict likely crime "hot spots" and decide where to assign officers. Retailers make decisions about what to stock and how to price it based on analysis of sales, economic and demographic data, and so forth. UPS is rolling out a sophisticated computer platform called Orion to optimize delivery routes for the company's drivers. Orion is designed to find the right balance between cost efficiency for the company and consistency for the customer. The system can consider billions of variables and alternatives and is projected to save UPS up to $400 million a year.[22]

6-2b How Managers Make Decisions

Another approach to decision making, called the **administrative model,** is considered to be **descriptive,** meaning that it describes how managers actually make decisions in complex situations rather than dictating how they *should* make decisions according to a theoretical ideal. The administrative model recognizes the human and environmental limitations that affect the degree to which managers can pursue a rational decision-making process. In difficult situations, such as those characterized by nonprogrammed decisions, uncertainty, and ambiguity, managers are typically unable to make economically rational decisions even if they want to.[23]

Bounded Rationality and Satisficing   The administrative model of decision making is based on the work of Herbert A. Simon. Simon proposed two concepts that were instrumental in shaping the administrative model: bounded rationality and satisficing. **Bounded rationality** means that people have limits, or boundaries, on how rational they can be. Organizations are incredibly complex, and managers have the time and ability to process only a limited amount of information with which to make decisions.[24] Because managers do not have the time or cognitive ability to process complete information about complex decisions, they must satisfice. **Satisficing** means that decision makers choose the first solution alternative that satisfies minimal decision criteria. Rather than pursuing all alternatives to identify the single solution that will maximize economic returns, managers will opt for the first solution that appears to solve the problem, even if better solutions are presumed to exist. The decision maker cannot justify the time and expense of obtaining complete information.[25]

Managers sometimes generate alternatives for complex problems only until they find one that they believe will work. For example, Liz Claiborne managers hired designer Isaac Mizrahi and targeted younger consumers in an effort to revive the flagging brand, but sales and profits continued to decline. Faced with the failure of the new youth-oriented line, a 90 percent cutback in orders from Macy's, high unemployment, a weak economy, and other complex and multifaceted problems, managers weren't sure how to stem the years-long tide of losses and get the company back in the black. They satisficed with a quick decision to form a licensing agreement to have the Liz Claiborne brand sold exclusively at JC Penney, which handles all manufacturing and marketing.[26]

The administrative model relies on assumptions that differ from those of the classical model and focuses on organizational factors that influence individual decisions. According to the administrative model:

- Decision goals often are vague, conflicting, and lack consensus among managers. Managers often are unaware of problems or opportunities that exist in the organization.
- Rational procedures are not always used, and when they are, they are confined to a simplistic view of the problem that does not capture the complexity of real organizational events.
- Managers' searches for alternatives are limited because of human, information, and resource constraints.
- Most managers settle for a satisficing rather than a maximizing solution, partly because they have limited information and partly because they have only vague criteria for what constitutes a maximizing solution.

James Leynse/Getty Images

Concept Connection

"Lots of people hear what I'm doing and think, 'That's a crazy idea!'" says Russell Simmons. The successful entrepreneur, who heads the New York–based media firm Rush Communications, has relied on his **intuition** to build a half-billion-dollar empire on one profitable "crazy idea" after another. It all began with his belief that he could go mainstream with the vibrant rap music he heard in African American neighborhoods. In 1983, he started the pioneering hip-hop Def Jam record label, which launched the careers of Beastie Boys, LL Cool J, and Run-DMC, among others. He's since moved on to successful ventures in fashion, media, consumer products, and finance.

Intuition and Quasirationality   Another aspect of administrative decision making is intuition. **Intuition** represents a quick apprehension of a decision situation based on past experience but without conscious thought.[27] Intuitive decision making is not arbitrary or irrational because it is based on years of practice and hands-on experience. A recent article on intuition cites the example of Formula One race car driver Juan Manuel Fangio. Fangio was leading in the 1950 Monaco Grand Prix as he came out of the tunnel on the second lap, yet instead of maintaining speed for an upcoming straight stretch, he inexplicably braked. It turned out to be a wise decision, as it allowed him to avoid crashing into a serious accident that had occurred around the next corner. Fangio said he just had a disturbing feeling as he came out of the tunnel. Reflecting back on the incident, he reasoned that his intuitive feeling was caused by a slight signal that he picked up unconsciously based on his racing experience: a change of color in the spectator stand. Spectators usually face toward the drivers as they come out of the tunnel, but this time they were facing further up the track. Although Fangio was focusing on the road, his peripheral vision was able to notice a shift in the light pattern from the stands that alerted his subconscious to a potential problem ahead.[28]

Psychologists and neuroscientists have studied how people make good decisions using their intuition under extreme time pressure and uncertainty.[29] Good intuitive decision making is based on an ability to recognize patterns at lightning speed, as in the case of Juan Manuel Fangio while racing at the Monaco Grand Prix. When people have a depth of experience and knowledge in a particular area, the right decision often comes quickly and effortlessly as a recognition of information that has been largely forgotten by the conscious mind. This ability could also be seen among soldiers in Iraq, who stopped many roadside bomb attacks based on gut feelings. High-tech gear designed to detect improvised explosive devices, or IEDs, was a supplement rather than a replacement for the ability of the human brain to sense danger and act on it. Soldiers with experience in Iraq subconsciously recognized when something didn't look or feel right. It might be a rock that wasn't there yesterday, a piece of concrete that looked too symmetrical, odd patterns of behavior, or

Half-Baked Management } Samsung Galaxy

Sometimes managers get too excited about a new product and don't think through consequences. The Samsung Galaxy had a new phone coming, the Note 7, and already engineers and consumers were salivating. So maybe they didn't take as much time to test the product as they normally did. Within weeks of the product launch, phones were catching fire, causing airlines to forbid carrying them

onboard. Analysts announced a $17 billion loss for the company. Fools rush in where wise men never go, and all of that.

SOURCE: How Samsung Moved Beyond Its Exploding Phones, *Gulf News* (Dubai), March 2018, https://search-proquest-com.proxy.library.vanderbilt.edu/docview/2009166502/455A970129 D84E54PQ/3?accountid=14816

just a different feeling of tension in the air.[30] Similarly, in the business world, managers continuously perceive and process information that they may not consciously be aware of, and their base of knowledge and experience helps them make decisions that may be characterized by uncertainty and ambiguity. However, managers need to remember to carefully check their assumptions when making decisions, something the Samsung executives apparently did not do with the Note 7 smartphone, as described in this chapter's "Half-Baked Management" box.

In today's rapidly moving business environment, intuition plays an increasingly important role in decision making. Numerous studies have found that effective managers use a combination of rational analysis and intuition in making complex decisions under time pressure.[31] A new trend in decision making is referred to as **quasirationality**, which basically means combining intuitive and analytical thought.[32] In many situations, neither analysis nor intuition is sufficient for making a good decision. However, managers may often walk a fine line between two extremes: on the one hand, making arbitrary decisions without careful study, and on the other, relying obsessively on rational analysis. One is not better than the other, and managers need to take a balanced approach by considering both rationality and intuition as important components of effective decision making.[33]

Do you tend to analyze things or rely on gut feelings when it comes to making an important decision? Visit MindTap for the "Self-Assessment: How Do You Make BIG Decisions?" to find out your predominant approach.

6-2c The Political Model

The third model of decision making is useful for making nonprogrammed decisions when conditions are uncertain, information is limited, and there are manager conflicts about what goals to pursue or what course of action to take. Most organizational decisions involve many managers who are pursuing different goals, and they must talk with one another to share information and reach an agreement. Managers often engage in coalition building for making complex organizational decisions.[34] A **coalition** is an informal alliance among managers who support a specific goal. *Coalition building* is the process of forming alliances among managers. In other words, a manager who supports a specific alternative, such as increasing the corporation's growth by acquiring another company, talks informally to other executives and tries to persuade them to support the decision. Without a coalition, a powerful individual or group could derail the decision-making process. Coalition building gives several managers an opportunity to contribute to decision making, enhancing their commitment to the alternative that is ultimately adopted. Results from the global survey by McKinsey & Company mentioned earlier suggest that coalition building is associated with faster implementation of decisions because managers have developed consensus about which action to pursue.[35] For example, an aerospace company that lost its supply of crucial parts due to the unexpected closing of a key supplier needed swift action to avoid a complete work stoppage. To make sure everyone would support any decisions that were made and implement them quickly, top managers set up a cross-functional team so members from various parts of the organization could identify, evaluate, and debate various options for ensuring that production

Half-Baked Management

U.S. Postal Service

Pity the poor Postal Service. Always in conflict with Congress. With the volume of traditional mail plummeting, the agency is running out of cash and struggling to stay in business. There are many reasons for the problems at the U.S. Postal Service, but managers have certainly tried over the past decade or more to find new ways to keep the nearly 250-year-old agency relevant for a new age.

For example, in 2000 (long before online bill paying became popular), the Postal Service began operating a secure system that would have enabled it to continue to be the primary way most Americans paid their monthly bills. The Internet industry, however, formed a coalition to oppose the service, and the U.S. Congress successfully shut it down. It's a pattern that has repeated itself over

and over, with Postal Service managers coming up with a new plan for coping with the decline in traditional mail, only to have powerful private companies lobby against it. In other countries, post offices double as banks or sell insurance or mobile phones. A recent report from the Postal Service's inspector general said that introducing new products like secure electronic bill payment could add $9.7 billion annually to the agency's revenue. Financial services firms, as well as companies such as United Parcel Service (UPS) and FedEx, however, have objected to the agency getting into nonpostal activities, and they have persuaded Congress to agree. Without building a political coalition in Congress, the Postal Service will continue to struggle.[37]

could continue. The team was ultimately awarded an International Team Excellence silver-level award from the American Society for Quality.[36]

Failing to build a coalition can allow conflict and disagreements to derail a decision, particularly if the opposition builds a powerful coalition of its own. Consider the inability of U.S. Postal Service managers to build an effective coalition among U.S. lawmakers to allow the organization to move into new lines of business. They try, but are stymied in many instances, as shown in the "Half-Baked Management" box.

As a government agency, the U.S. Postal Service is in a bind. Private companies are always lobbying Congress for legislation that supports their interests.

The political model closely resembles the real environment in which most managers and decision makers operate. Interviews with CEOs in high-tech industries found that they strived to use some type of rational decision-making process, but the way they actually decided things was through a complex interaction with other managers, subordinates, environmental factors, and organizational events.[38] Decisions are complex and involve many people, information is often ambiguous, and disagreement and conflict over problems and solutions are normal. The political model begins with four basic assumptions:

- Organizations are made up of groups with diverse interests, goals, and values. Managers disagree about problem priorities and may not understand or share the goals and interests of other managers.
- Information is ambiguous and incomplete. The attempt to be rational is limited by the complexity of many problems, as well as personal and organizational constraints.
- Managers do not have the time, resources, or mental capacity to identify all dimensions of the problem and process all relevant information. Managers talk to each other and exchange viewpoints to gather information and reduce ambiguity.
- Managers engage in the push and pull of debate to decide goals and discuss alternatives. Decisions are the result of bargaining and discussion among coalition members.

The key dimensions of the classical, administrative, and political models are listed in Exhibit 6.2. Research into decision-making procedures has found rational, classical procedures to be associated with high performance for organizations in stable environments. However, administrative and political decision-making procedures and intuition have been associated with high performance in unstable environments in which decisions must be made rapidly and under more difficult conditions.[39]

Exhibit 6.2 Characteristics of Classical, Administrative, and Political Decision-Making Models

Classical Model	Administrative Model	Political Model
Clear-cut problem and goals	Vague problem and goals	Pluralistic; conflicting goals
Condition of certainty	Condition of uncertainty	Condition of uncertainty or ambiguity
Full information about alternatives and their outcomes	Limited information about alternatives and their outcomes	Inconsistent viewpoints; ambiguous information
Rational choice by individual for maximizing outcomes	Satisficing choice for resolving problem using intuition	Bargaining and discussion among coalition members

Remember This

- The ideal, rational approach to decision making, called the **classical model**, is based on the assumption that managers should make logical decisions that are economically sensible and in the organization's best economic interest.

- The classical model is **normative**, meaning that it defines how a manager *should* make logical decisions and provides guidelines for reaching an ideal outcome.

- Software programs based on the classical model are being applied to programmed decisions, such as how to schedule airline crews or how to process insurance claims most efficiently.

- The **administrative model** includes the concepts of *bounded rationality* and *satisficing* and describes how managers make decisions in situations that are characterized by uncertainty and ambiguity.

- The administrative model is **descriptive**, an approach that describes how managers actually make decisions, rather than how they should make decisions according to a theoretical model.

- **Bounded rationality** means that people have the time and cognitive ability to process only a limited amount of information on which to base decisions.

- **Satisficing** means choosing the first alternative that satisfies minimal decision criteria, regardless of whether better solutions are presumed to exist.

- **Intuition** is an aspect of administrative decision making that refers to a quick comprehension of a decision situation based on past experience but without conscious thought.

- Soldiers in Iraq often detected roadside bombs using their intuition.

- A new trend in decision making, **quasirationality**, combines intuitive and analytical thought.

- The political model takes into consideration that many decisions require debate, discussion, and coalition building.

- A **coalition** is an informal alliance among managers who support a specific goal or solution.

6-3 Decision-Making Steps

Whether a decision is programmed or nonprogrammed, and regardless of whether managers choose the classical, administrative, or political model of decision making, six steps typically are associated with effective decision processes. These steps are summarized in Exhibit 6.3.

6-3a Recognition of Decision Requirement

Managers confront a decision requirement in the form of either a problem or an opportunity. A **problem** occurs when organizational accomplishment is less than established goals. Some aspect of performance is unsatisfactory. An **opportunity** exists when managers see a potential

Exhibit 6.3 **Six Steps in the Managerial Decision-Making Process**

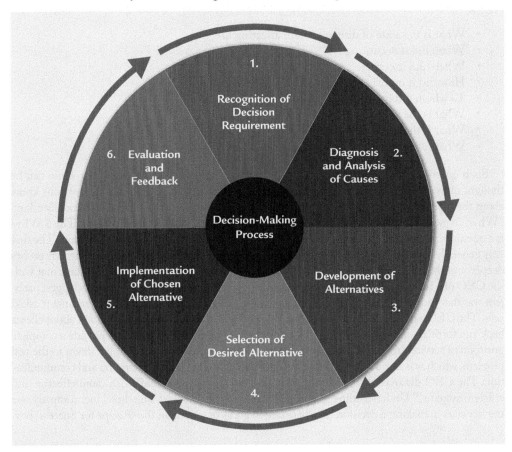

accomplishment that exceeds specified current goals. Managers see the possibility of enhancing performance beyond current levels.

Awareness of a problem or an opportunity is the first step in the decision-making sequence, and it requires surveillance of the internal and external environment for issues that merit executive attention.[40] Some information comes from periodic financial reports, performance reports, and other sources that are designed to discover problems before they become too serious. Managers also take advantage of informal sources. They talk to other managers, gather opinions on how things are going, and seek advice on which problems should be tackled or which opportunities embraced.[41] For example, at Google, some managers noticed that employees were eating too many of the free M&Ms scattered in bins around the company, which they thought might conflict with the company's goal of keeping employees not only happy but healthy as well.[42] The company decided to analyze the problem and experiment with ways to get people to eat healthier snacks and drink more water as well as consume the free candy. Recognizing decision requirements is sometimes difficult because it often means integrating bits and pieces of information in novel ways.

6-3b Diagnosis and Analysis of Causes

Once a problem or an opportunity comes to a manager's attention, the understanding of the situation should be refined. **Diagnosis** is the step in the decision-making process in which managers analyze underlying causal factors associated with the decision situation.

Many times, the real problem lies hidden behind the problem that managers *think* exists. By looking at a situation from different angles, managers can identify the true problem. In addition, they often discover opportunities that they didn't realize were there.[43] Charles Kepner and

"It isn't that they can't see the solution. It's that they can't see the problem."

—G. K. CHESTERTON, ENGLISH NOVELIST

Benjamin Tregoe, who conducted extensive studies of manager decision making, recommend that managers ask a series of questions to specify underlying causes, including the following:

- What is the state of disequilibrium affecting us?
- When did it occur?
- Where did it occur?
- How did it occur?
- To whom did it occur?
- What is the urgency of the problem?
- What is the interconnectedness of events?
- What result came from which activity?[44]

Such questions help specify what actually happened and why. Diagnosing a problem can be thought of as peeling an onion layer by layer. Managers cannot solve problems if they don't know about them or if they are addressing the wrong issues. Some experts recommend continually asking "Why?" to get to the root of a problem, a technique sometimes called "the 5 Whys." The **5 Whys** is a question-asking method used to explore the root cause underlying a particular problem. The first *why* generally produces a superficial explanation for the problem, and each subsequent *why* probes deeper into the causes of the problem and potential solutions. For example, a consultant met with the CEO of a large accounting and professional services firm, who said the company's biggest problem was that it didn't have enough qualified people to serve its global clients. The consultant asked *why*. The CEO said that staff members had to spend lots of time passing information about clients back and forth among themselves. *Why?* Because people must work together to provide a complete portfolio of services, the CEO said. *Why?* After a couple more *Whys*, the two got down to the real problem, which was not the lack of staff, but inefficiency in internal collaboration and communication. The CEO discovered that he might actually be able to *reduce* staff with more effective and efficient systems.[45] Understanding why Kevin Haight could not start a biodiesel fuel company was the key start in making a decision on where else to go, as described in the "Recipe for Success" box.

Recipe for Success } Hudson Valley Cold Pressed Oils

Kevin Haight did an internship in South Africa and worked with water treatment plans. He got interested in one of the client's customers who made avocado oil. Haight decided to come back to the United States and start a company based on biodiesel, and he turned to sunflowers, which are extremely drought resistant, easy to grow, and have one of the highest yields per acre.

Just when Kevin was ready to go, the market in diesel fuels collapsed. Kevin started talking to his brother Jeff and sister-in-law Allison, who were both experienced Culinary Institute of America grads, both having been in the restaurant business for years, with her in the kitchen and him in front of the house. But after they had their first child, that lifestyle did not work anymore. Jeff got a job in food distribution in Maryland. But he missed home, and working 80 hours a week, on the phone all night, was not conducive to a happy family life. So when Kevin called, Jeff and Allison gave up their lives in Maryland and moved to the Hudson Valley, near Poughkeepsie, to start a sunflower oil business. Early on, they figured out the best way to divide responsibility. Kevin is the farmer and his wife, Traci, is a registered dietician, who makes sure ingredients stay good. Jeff does sales and distribution while Allison handles marketing and PR.

Hudson Valley Cold Pressed Oils began in 2015 and had its first production run in 2016, and it is already being sold by

specialty grocers and some chains. When the company started, Kevin went to an old friend who has a farm-product sunflower oil business in Indiana, and he learned how to produce the oil. Then Kevin and Jeff met with a man who makes presses. Getting the press just right took a lot of trial and error. Getting the most from the seeds was not the company's main goal but rather a certain quality and taste. Other sunflower oil producers don't consider taste. Only with olive oil do people say, "Taste this oil," but the brothers' company is out to change that. Hudson Valley Cold Pressed Oils' product tastes earthier and is a healthier cooking oil than Canola or others. Other producers use hexane gas to get all the oil out, but not Hudson Valley.

What the Haights hope will keep the company growing is the flavor, non-GMO, family-farmed, and higher smoke point than olive oil, which gets smoky—and then unhealthy—at a much lower cooking temperature.

All four Haights like the new lifestyle. Instead of constant work and stress, they tend the farm and the business in normal work hours. "We all bottle the oil once a week, press five of seven days, and then we have togetherness by labeling the bottles at night while we watch TV."

SOURCE: Jeff Haight and Allison Haight, personal communications, March 2018.

6-3c Development of Alternatives

The next stage is to generate possible alternative solutions that will respond to the needs of the situation and correct the underlying causes.

For a programmed decision, feasible alternatives are easy to identify; in fact, they usually are already available within the organization's rules and procedures. Nonprogrammed decisions, however, require developing new courses of action that will meet the company's needs. For decisions made under conditions of high uncertainty, managers may develop only one or two custom solutions that will satisfice for handling the problem. However, studies find that limiting the search for alternatives is a primary cause of decision failure in organizations.[46]

Decision alternatives can be thought of as tools for reducing the difference between the organization's current and desired performance. Smart managers tap into the knowledge of people throughout the organization, and sometimes even outside the organization, for decision alternatives. Rob McEwen, the chairman and CEO of Canadian mining group Goldcorp, knew that the company's Red Lake site could be a huge moneymaker. A nearby mine was thriving. The problem was that no one could pinpoint where to find the high-grade ore at Red Lake. McEwen created the Goldcorp Challenge, putting Red Lake's closely guarded topographic data online and offering $575,000 in prize money to anyone who could identify rich drill sites. More than 1,400 technical experts in 50 countries offered alternatives to the problem, and two teams working together in Australia pinpointed locations that have made Red Lake one of the world's richest gold mines.[47]

6-3d Selection of the Desired Alternative

Once feasible alternatives are developed, one must be selected. In this stage, managers try to select the most promising of several alternative courses of action. The best alternative solution is the one that best fits the overall goals and values of the organization and achieves the desired results using the fewest resources.[48] Managers want to select the choice with the least amount of risk and uncertainty. Because some risk is inherent for most nonprogrammed decisions, managers try to gauge the prospects for success. They might rely on their intuition and experience to estimate whether a given course of action is likely to succeed. Basing choices on overall goals and values can also guide the selection of alternatives.

Choosing among alternatives also depends on managers' personality factors and willingness to accept risk and uncertainty. **Risk propensity** is the willingness to undertake risk with the opportunity of gaining an increased payoff. For example, Facebook would never have reached more than a billion users without Mark Zuckerberg's "move fast, break things" mind-set. Motivational posters with that slogan are papered all around the company to prevent delay from too much analysis of alternatives. Zuckerberg says, "If you're successful, most of the things you've done were wrong. What ends up mattering is the stuff you get right." Facebook runs a never-ending series of on-the-fly experiments with real users. Even employees who haven't finished their six-week training program are encouraged to work on the live site. That risky approach means that the whole site crashes occasionally, but Zuckerberg says, "The faster we learn, the better we're going to get to the model of where we should be."[49] The level of risk a manager is willing to accept will influence the analysis of the costs and benefits to be derived from any decision. Consider the situations in Exhibit 6.4. In each situation, which alternative would you choose? A person with a low risk propensity would tend to take ensured moderate returns by going for a tie score, building a domestic plant, or pursuing a career as a physician. A risk taker would go for the victory, build a plant in a foreign country, or embark on an acting career.

Courtesy of Red Door Interactive

Concept Connection

Reid Carr, founder and CEO of San Diego–based Red Door Interactive, Inc., a firm that manages clients' online presence, involves his staff throughout the decision-making process. Carr believes that when **developing, selecting, and implementing alternatives,** managers should "decide slowly and collaboratively so that you have the best plan produced by those who are tasked with execution. Then, let them execute." Red Door's annual "Start, Stop, and Keep" survey is one way that Carr gathers feedback. It asks employees to suggest which internal processes and practices should be introduced, continued, or discontinued.

Exhibit 6.4 Decision Alternatives with Different Levels of Risk

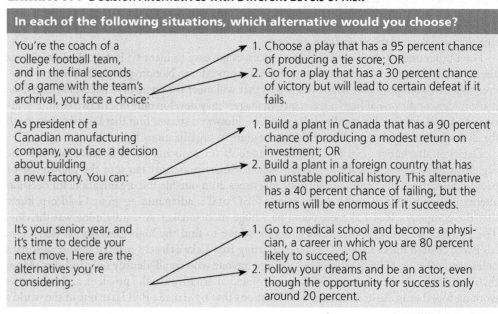

In each of the following situations, which alternative would you choose?

You're the coach of a college football team, and in the final seconds of a game with the team's archrival, you face a choice:

1. Choose a play that has a 95 percent chance of producing a tie score; OR
2. Go for a play that has a 30 percent chance of victory but will lead to certain defeat if it fails.

As president of a Canadian manufacturing company, you face a decision about building a new factory. You can:

1. Build a plant in Canada that has a 90 percent chance of producing a modest return on investment; OR
2. Build a plant in a foreign country that has an unstable political history. This alternative has a 40 percent chance of failing, but the returns will be enormous if it succeeds.

It's your senior year, and it's time to decide your next move. Here are the alternatives you're considering:

1. Go to medical school and become a physician, a career in which you are 80 percent likely to succeed; OR
2. Follow your dreams and be an actor, even though the opportunity for success is only around 20 percent.

6-3e Implementation of the Chosen Alternative

The **implementation** stage involves the use of managerial, administrative, and persuasive abilities to ensure that the chosen alternative is carried out. This step is similar to the idea of strategy execution described in Chapter 5. The ultimate success of the chosen alternative depends on whether it can be translated into action. Sometimes an alternative never becomes reality because managers lack the resources or energy needed to make things happen, or they have failed to involve people and achieve buy-in for the decision. Successful implementation may require discussion, trust building, and active engagement with people affected by the decision. Communication, motivation, and leadership skills must be used to see that the decision is carried out.[50] When employees see that managers follow up on their decisions by tracking implementation success, the employees are more committed to positive action.

6-3f Evaluation and Feedback

In the evaluation stage of the decision process, decision makers gather information that tells them how well the decision was implemented and whether it was effective in achieving its goals. The "move fast, break things" approach thrives at Facebook because of rapid feedback. Researchers have found that immediate and explicit feedback helps people significantly improve in activities as diverse as shooting basketball free throws, playing musical instruments, solving puzzles, and performing surgery.[51] Feedback also helps managers make better decisions. Decision making is an ongoing process that is not completed when a manager or board of directors votes yes or no. Feedback provides decision makers with information that can precipitate a new decision cycle. The decision may fail, thus generating a new analysis of the problem, evaluation of alternatives, and selection of a new alternative. Many big problems are solved by trying several alternatives in sequence, each providing modest improvement. Feedback is the part of monitoring that assesses whether a new decision needs to be made.

To illustrate the overall decision-making process, including evaluation and feedback, consider the decision at Rose Acre Farms, one of the largest egg producers in the United States, to shift to cage-free facilities for egg-laying hens, as shown in the "Recipe for Success" box.

Recipe for Success

Rose Acre Farms

The $9 billion U.S. egg industry is in turmoil. A number of states have passed new laws aimed at improving the well-being of the 300 million or so hens that lay the eggs we eat for our breakfast, dye for our Easter baskets, or use to bake our cakes. California, for example, recently began requiring that every shell egg sold in the state come from hens that have room to lie down, turn in a circle and extend their wings. Hen-cage laws are also in effect or pending in Washington, Oregon, Michigan, Ohio, and a number of other states

Along with other egg farmers, Marcus Rust, CEO of Rose Acre Farms, had to decide how to address the problem of meeting many different state rules and regulations as well as address the growing criticism from animal rights activists. The two primary alternatives for egg farmers are to build roomier cages or invest in cage-free facilities. Building cage-free facilities is much more expensive than building larger cages. Cage-free facilities also increase feeding costs because the birds are more active, and a higher percentage of birds die when they are free-roaming. However, even though larger cages meet most of the new rules, many animal rights activists aren't satisfied that it is enough. Moreover, companies such as Starbucks, Nestlé SA, Burger King, and McDonald's have pledged to phase out the use of eggs that come from caged hens. Cage-free eggs also command a higher price tag, and the market for cage-free eggs is growing.

Rust and his managers decided to bet that in the future, egg farming will succeed based on a cage-free strategy. They selected the more expensive choice that every facility Rose Acre builds or refurbishes will lack cages. Implementation of the decision has begun, and at the new Rose Acre facility in Frankfort, Indiana, 170,000 hens wander around a 550-foot long open barn, perch on metal rods, or run up and down ramps. They lay their eggs in covered nesting boxes and the eggs roll onto conveyor belts that carry them to the production plant.

Evaluation and feedback are ongoing, but managers have already discovered a need for adjustments. Rust says some birds have died from suffocation inside nest boxes when "hens have piled in on top of each other." Managers believe that problem can be solved with some relatively minor design changes.[52]

The decision to shift to cage-free facilities is a risky and expensive one for Rose Acre Farms, but Rust believes it will pay off. In addition, he said he often thinks about his wife's response when he showed her the hens in a cage-free facility while the team was evaluating alternatives. "She said, 'Why wouldn't you just do that for all of them?'" he says.[53] Strategic decisions always contain some risk, but feedback and follow-up can help keep companies on track. When decisions don't work out so well, managers can learn from their mistakes—and sometimes turn problems into opportunities.

Remember This

- Managers need to make a decision when they either confront a problem or see an opportunity.

- A **problem** is a situation in which organizational accomplishments have failed to meet established goals.

- An **opportunity** is a situation in which managers see potential organizational accomplishments that exceed current goals.

- The decision-making process typically involves six steps: recognizing the need for a decision, diagnosing causes, developing alternatives, selecting an alternative, implementing the alternative, and evaluating decision effectiveness.

- **Diagnosis** is the step in which managers analyze underlying causal factors associated with the decision situation.

- The **5 Whys** is a question-asking technique that can help diagnose the root cause of a specific problem.

- Selection of an alternative depends partly on managers' **risk propensity**, or their willingness to undertake risk with the opportunity of gaining an increased payoff.

- The **implementation** step involves using managerial, administrative, and persuasive abilities to translate the chosen alternative into action.

6-4 **Personal Decision Framework**

Imagine you are a manager at Snapchat, Twitter, *The New York Times*, an AMC movie theater, or the local public library. How would you go about making important decisions that might shape the future of your department or company? So far in this chapter, we have discussed a number of factors that affect how managers make decisions. For example, decisions may be programmed or nonprogrammed, situations are characterized by various levels of uncertainty, and managers may use the classical, administrative, or political model of decision making. In addition, the decision-making process follows six recognized steps.

However, not all managers go about making decisions in the same way. In fact, significant differences distinguish the ways in which individual managers may approach problems and make decisions concerning them. These differences can be explained by the concept of personal **decision styles**. Exhibit 6.5 illustrates the role of personal styles in the decision-making process. Personal decision styles refer to distinctions among people with respect to how they evaluate problems, generate alternatives, and make choices. Research has identified four major decision styles: directive, analytical, conceptual, and behavioral.[54]

1. The *directive style* is used by people who prefer simple, clear-cut solutions to problems. Managers who use this style often make decisions quickly because they do not like to deal with a lot of information and may consider only one or two alternatives. People who prefer the directive style generally are efficient and rational and prefer to rely on existing rules or procedures for making decisions.

2. Managers with an *analytical style* like to consider complex solutions based on as much data as they can gather. These individuals carefully consider alternatives and often base their decisions on objective, rational data from management control systems and other sources. They search for the best possible decision based on the information available.

3. People who tend toward a *conceptual style* also like to consider a broad amount of information. However, they are more socially oriented than those with an analytical style and like to talk to others about the problem and possible alternatives for solving it. Managers using a conceptual style consider many broad alternatives, rely on information from both people and systems, and like to solve problems creatively.

4. The *behavioral style* is often the style adopted by managers who have a deep concern for others as individuals. Managers using this style like to talk to people one on one, understand their feelings about the problem, and consider the effect of a given decision on them. People with a behavioral style usually are concerned with the personal development of others and may make decisions that help others achieve their goals.

Many managers have a dominant decision style. For example, Dawn M. Zier, CEO of Nutrisystem, reflects a primarily analytical decision style. Zier, who studied electrical engineering and computer science in undergraduate school, likes to "break down a complex issue and then build it back up." When she took over the CEO job, she told managers and employees that she liked dialogue and was willing to have any conversation, but she wanted information to be based on facts.[55]

However, managers frequently use several different styles or a combination of styles in making the varied decisions that they confront daily. A manager might use a directive style for determining which company to use for office supplies, yet shift to a more conceptual style when handling an interdepartmental conflict or considering a new product or service. The most effective managers are able to shift among styles as needed to meet the situation. Being aware of his or her dominant decision style can help a manager avoid making critical mistakes when the usual style may be inappropriate to the problem at hand.

Exhibit 6.5 Personal Decision Framework

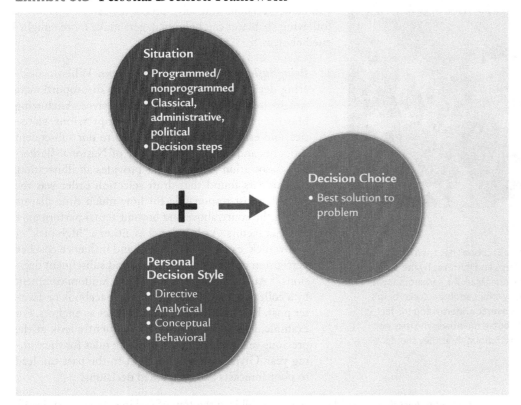

SOURCES: Based on A. J. Rowe, J. D. Boulgaides, and M. R. McGrath, *Managerial Decision Making* (Chicago: Science Research Associates, 1984); and Alan J. Rowe and Richard O. Mason, *Managing with Style: A Guide to Understanding, Assessing, and Improving Your Decision Making* (San Francisco: Jossey-Bass, 1987).

Remember This

- A manager's personal decision style influences how he or she makes decisions.
- **Decision styles** are differences among people with respect to how they perceive problems and make choices.
- Four major decision styles are directive, analytical, conceptual, and behavioral.
- Most experienced managers use a variety of styles depending on the decision situation.

6-5 Why Do Managers Make Bad Decisions?

Managers are faced with a relentless demand for decisions, from solving minor problems to implementing major strategic changes. Even the best manager will make mistakes, but managers can increase their percentage of good decisions by understanding some of the factors that cause people to make bad ones. A large body of research suggests that many bad decisions are the result of errors in judgment that originate in the human mind's limited capacity and in the natural biases managers unconsciously display during decision making.[56]

Frederic Legrand - COMEO/Shutterstock.com

Concept Connection

Despite its phenomenal success, Facebook has been soundly criticized for a number of missteps and mistakes by the organization's leaders, including founder Mark Zuckerberg, shown here at a press conference. Many critics attribute Zuckerberg's lapses in good judgment to his **overconfidence** and the fact that he surrounds himself with board members who may not always question his decisions as thoroughly as they should.

Are you aware of biases that cloud your judgment when you make decisions and solve problems? Awareness of the following six biases can help managers make more enlightened choices.[57]

1. ***Being influenced by initial impressions.*** When considering decisions, the mind often gives disproportionate weight to the first information it receives. **Anchoring bias** occurs when we allow initial impressions, statistics, and estimates to act as anchors to our subsequent thoughts and judgments. A study of National Basketball Association (NBA) teams provides an illustration. Researchers found that draft selection order was the variable most responsible for how much time players got on the court, above and beyond actual performance or other factors. A player's tag as either a "high pick" or a "low pick" can act as an anchor and influence coaches' perception of player performance and subsequent decisions.[58] Anchors can be as simple as a random comment by a colleague or a statistic read in a Facebook or Twitter post. Past events and trends also act as anchors. For example, in business, managers frequently look at the previous year's sales when estimating sales for the coming year. Giving too much weight to the past can lead to poor forecasts and misguided decisions.

2. ***Justifying past decisions.*** Many managers fall into the trap of making choices that justify their past decisions, even if those decisions no longer seem valid. One common example is when a manager continues to pour money into a failing project, hoping to turn things around. This is sometimes referred to as the **sunk cost effect**. Managers often stick with a decision because they've invested a lot of resources in it, even though they'd be better off cutting their losses and moving on.[59] One study of product development found that managers who initiate a new product are much more likely to continue funding it despite evidence that it is failing.[60] Behavioral science research by Daniel Kahneman and others shows that people typically respond more strongly to potential loss, referred to as *loss aversion*, than to expected gain. People hate to lose, so they continue to support a flawed decision in an effort to justify or correct the past.

3. ***Seeing what you want to see.*** People frequently look for information that supports their existing instinct or point of view. **Confirmation bias** occurs when a manager puts too much value on evidence that is consistent with a favored belief or viewpoint and discounts evidence that contradicts it.[61] Confirmation bias can affect where managers look for information, as well as how they interpret the information that they find. For example, managers at Tokyo Electric Power Company (Tepco) have been accused of delaying for too long the decision to use seawater to cool nuclear reactors at Fukushima Daiichi following the 2011 Japan earthquake and tsunami. Tepco managers knew that seawater would destroy the reactors, so they gave greater weight to information that supported their decision to delay its use, and they emphasized that they were "taking the safety of the whole plant into consideration" in judging the appropriate timing to use seawater in the cooldown efforts. Unfortunately, it took an explosion at the plant to convince managers that using seawater was essential to control the overheating of the reactors.[62]

4. **Perpetuating the status quo.** Managers may base decisions on what has worked in the past and may fail to explore new options, dig for additional information, or investigate new technologies. For example, GM stuck with its strategic decision to offer a multitude of brands long after there was clear evidence that trying to cover the whole range of the auto market was paving the way to disaster. The strategy started to fray in the 1970s with increased competition from Japanese automakers and spikes in oil prices. Yet, as late as February 2008, managers were saying that talk about killing brands was "not a thoughtful discussion." Only bankruptcy and a forced restructuring finally pushed managers to cut GM's brands from eight down to four.[63]

5. **Being influenced by emotions.** If you've ever made a decision when you were angry, upset, or extremely happy, you might already know the danger of being influenced by emotions. A recent study of traders in London investment banks found that effective regulation of emotions was a characteristic of higher-performing traders. Lower-performing traders were less effective in managing and modulating their emotional responses.[64] Another finding is that doctors make less effective decisions when they feel emotions of like or dislike for a patient. If they like a patient, they are less likely to prescribe a painful procedure. If they feel dislike, they may blame the patient for the condition and provide less treatment.[65] Unfortunately, some managers let their emotions influence their decisions on a regular basis. There is some evidence that when people make poor decisions under the influence of strong emotions (such as firing off an angry e-mail message), they tend to continue to make poor decisions because it becomes part of the mind's blueprint for how to behave.[66] Managers make better decisions when—to the extent possible—they take emotions out of the decision-making process.

6. **Being overconfident.** Most people overestimate their ability to predict uncertain outcomes. The managers at a fast-food chain were sure that low employee turnover was a key driver of customer satisfaction and store profitability, so they decided to invest in programs to keep employees happy. However, when they analyzed store data, they found that some locations with high turnover were highly profitable, while some with low turnover were struggling.[67] Overconfidence can be particularly dangerous when making risky decisions. Consider how overconfidence contributed to decisions at JPMorgan Chase's chief investment office, made by the so-called London Whale, that led to a multibillion-dollar loss. All banks take risks, but JPMorgan was praised for not taking the kind of outsized risks that many banks took during the mortgage boom and that contributed to the collapse of the U.S. economy. After the Wall Street crisis, JPMorgan's CEO, Jamie Dimon, was called "the world's most important banker," and his top executives were hailed as a management team that could seemingly do no wrong. The company's chief investment office in London, which was created to protect the bank from volatility caused by complex global financial transactions, gained a reputation for its trading prowess. The unit was a star performer and became a profit center for JPMorgan at a time when industry earnings were under pressure. But some managers got overconfident of their ability to spot and manage risks. They began taking larger and larger gambles, including involvement in a highly complicated trading strategy involving derivatives—similar in some ways to the risks that led to the Wall Street crisis. The strategy backfired, eventually causing a loss of almost $6 billion, which led to the firing of several key executives and damaged the reputation of both the bank and its CEO. Moreover, federal investigators were looking into potential fraud because they suspected that some traders improperly marked their trades to obscure the magnitude of the losses.[68]

Sunny Side Up

Do Biases Influence Your Decision Making?

All of us have biases, but most of us have a hard time seeing our own. What biases influence your decisions and solutions to problems? Answer the following questions to get an idea of the difficulties and mistakes that likely await you as a new manager.

1. A piece of paper is folded in half, in half again, etc. After 100 folds, how thick will it be? Take your best guess:_____. I am 90 percent sure that the correct answer lies between _____ and _____.

2. Which of the following figures is most different from the others?

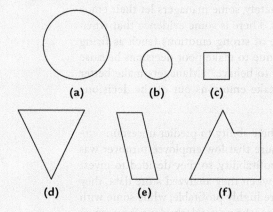

(a)   (b)   (c)

(d)   (e)   (f)

3. As owner and CEO of your company, you decided to invest $100 million to build pilotless drones that cannot be detected by enemy radar. When the project is 90 percent complete, a competing firm begins marketing a completed drone that cannot be detected by radar. In addition, the competitor's drone is much faster, smaller, cheaper, and more sophisticated than the drone that your company is developing. The question is: Should you invest the last 10 percent of the research funds to finish your drone? Check one of the following answers.

_____ No; there is no reason to continue spending money on the project.

_____ Yes; after investing $90 million, we might as well finish the project.

4. Give a quick (five-second) estimate of the following product without actually calculating it:

$8 \times 7 \times 6 \times 5 \times 4 \times 3 \times 2 \times 1 =$ _____.

5. Robert is envious, stubborn, critical, impulsive, industrious, and intelligent. In general, how emotional do you think Robert is? (Circle one number.)

Not emotional   1 2 3 4 5 6 7 8 9   Extremely
at all   emotional

6. Which would you choose between the following two alternatives?

_____ Alternative A: A 50 percent chance of gaining $1,000

_____ Alternative B: A sure gain of $500

Which would you choose between the following two alternatives?

_____ Alternative C: A 50 percent chance of losing $1,000

_____ Alternative D: A sure loss of $500

After you have specified an answer to each problem, you will find the answers and a description of the potential related bias at the end of this chapter.

SOURCES: Questions 1 and 3–6 are from research studies reviewed in Scott Plous, *The Psychology of Judgment and Decision Making* (Philadelphia: Temple University Press, 1993); question 2 is based on an item in the *Creativity in Action Newsletter*, as reported in Arthur B. VanGundy, *Idea Power: Techniques & Resources to Unleash the Creativity in Your Organization* (New York: AMACOM, 1992).

Remember This

- Being aware of biases that cloud judgment helps managers avoid decision traps and make better decisions.
- Biases to watch out for include being influenced by initial impressions, trying to correct or justify past flawed decisions, seeing only what you want to see, perpetuating the status quo, being influenced by emotions, and being overconfident.
- **Anchoring bias** occurs when a manager allows initial impressions, statistics, or estimates to act as anchors to subsequent thoughts and decisions.
- The tendency to continue investing in a failing project in the hope of turning it around is called the **sunk cost effect**.
- Some managers have a tendency to put too much value on evidence that is consistent with a favored belief or viewpoint and too little on evidence that contradicts their favored position; this is called **confirmation bias**.

6-6 Innovative Decision Making

The ability to make fast, widely supported, high-quality decisions on a frequent basis is a critical skill in today's fast-moving organizations.[69] Considering that managers are under pressure to decide quickly, and that biases creep in and cloud judgment, how do managers ever make good decisions? Some innovative techniques can help managers watch out for and avoid mistakes caused by cognitive biases. It is difficult for most managers to see their own biases, but they can build in mechanisms that neutralize or reduce bias-related decision errors at the organizational level.[70]

6-6a Start with Brainstorming

Brainstorming uses a face-to-face interactive group to spontaneously suggest as many ideas as possible for solving a problem. Brainstorming has been found to be highly effective for quickly generating a wide range of alternatives, but it does have some drawbacks.[71] For one thing, people in a group often want to conform to what others are saying. Others may be concerned about pleasing the boss or impressing colleagues. In addition, many creative people simply have social inhibitions that limit their participation or make it difficult to come up with ideas in a group setting. In fact, one study found that when four people are asked to "brainstorm" individually, they typically come up with twice as many ideas as a group of four brainstorming together.

Squaredpixels/Getty Images

Concept Connection

Brainstorming has its share of critics. Some say it prevents the quiet people from participating, and that a group can be too easily influenced by the ideas of some of the dominant players. In response, a number of brainstorming alternatives have been developed. In fact, some companies bring in certified trainers to teach employees how to use new methods such as the Six Thinking Hats, Lateral Thinking, Nominal Group Technique, Ideation, and more.

One recent approach, electronic brainstorming, takes advantage of the group approach while overcoming some disadvantages. **Electronic brainstorming** brings people together in an interactive group over a computer network.[72] One member writes an idea, another reads it and adds other ideas, and so on. Studies show that electronic brainstorming generates about 40 percent more ideas than individuals brainstorming alone, and 25 to 200 percent more ideas than regular brainstorming groups, depending on group size.[73] Because the approach is anonymous, it circumvents possible social inhibitions, so more people actively participate. Electronic brainstorming also allows people to write down their ideas immediately, thus avoiding the possibility that a good idea might slip away while the person is waiting for a chance to speak in a face-to-face group. Another advantage is that electronic brainstorming can be done with groups made up of employees from around the world, which further increases the diversity of alternatives.

6-6b Use Hard Evidence

Using hard evidence can help take emotion out of the decision-making process, keep people from relying on faulty assumptions, and help to limit confirmation bias, as described previously. **Evidence-based decision making** means a commitment to make more informed and intelligent decisions based on the best available facts and evidence. It means being alert to potential biases and seeking and examining the evidence with rigor. To keep emotion from clouding their judgment regarding patient care, for example, doctors in the Partners Health Care System incorporate the use of clinical decision support systems based on reams of data about what works and what doesn't.[74] Managers practice evidence-based decision making by being careful and thoughtful rather than carelessly relying on assumptions, past experience, rules of thumb, or intuition.[75] After catastrophic errors in the airline industry, where pilots relied solely on their personal experience, many airlines now use a process called Crew Resource Management (CRM), which has revolutionized safety practices. CRM teaches every member of the crew to conduct brief sessions during which they update each other about flight status, the current environment, and any impending challenges or safety concerns. Pilots are trained to act appropriately on issues raised by any crew member.[76]

A study by Erik Brynjolfsson, an economist at the Sloan School of Management at the Massachusetts Institute of Technology (MIT), supports the idea that organizational decisions can be improved with the use of evidence-based decision making. Brynjolfsson and his colleagues studied 179 large companies and found that the ones that have adopted data-driven decision making achieved productivity that was 5 to 6 percent higher than could be explained by any other factors.[77]

6-6c Engage in Rigorous Debate

Good managers recognize that constructive conflict based on divergent points of view can bring a problem into focus, clarify people's ideas, stimulate creative thinking, limit the role of bias, create a broader understanding of issues and alternatives, and improve decision quality.[78] Reed Hastings, CEO of Netflix, has built rigorous debate into the decision-making process to avoid another calamity such as the one the company experienced following a disastrous decision to both increase the price of the service and split Netflix into two separate businesses, the latter of which forced users to manage their accounts in two places. Hastings said later that he "slid into arrogance based upon past success." Although he still often uses a *directive style* of decision making, as described earlier in this chapter, Hastings has since tried to involve more people when making highly important nonprogrammed decisions.[79]

Stimulating rigorous debate can be done in several ways. One way is by ensuring that the group is diverse in terms of age and gender, functional area of expertise, hierarchical level, and experience with the business. Some groups assign a **devil's advocate**, who has the role of challenging the assumptions and assertions made by the group.[80] The devil's advocate may force the group to rethink its approach to the problem and avoid reaching premature conclusions. At Catholic Health Initiatives, someone is appointed to act as devil's advocate at senior management meetings, particularly if critical issues are being discussed. Jeffrey McKeever, CEO of MicroAge, often plays the devil's advocate, changing his position in the middle of a debate to ensure that other executives don't just go along with his opinions.[81] Still another way to encourage constructive conflict is to use a technique called **point–counterpoint**, which breaks a decision-making group into two subgroups and assigns them different, often competing, responsibilities.[82] The groups then develop and exchange proposals and discuss and debate the various options until they arrive at a common set of understandings and recommendations.

6-6d Avoid Groupthink

It is important for managers to remember that a certain amount of disagreement and conflict is much healthier than blind agreement. Pressures for conformity exist in almost any group, and particularly when people in a group like one another, they tend to avoid anything that might create disharmony. **Groupthink** refers to the tendency of people in groups to suppress contrary opinions. When people slip into groupthink, the desire for harmony outweighs concerns over decision quality. Group members emphasize maintaining unity rather than realistically challenging problems and alternatives. People censor their personal opinions and are reluctant to criticize the opinions of others.[83]

Author and scholar Jerry Harvey coined the related term *Abilene paradox* to illustrate the hidden pressures for conformity that can exist in groups.[84] Harvey tells the story of how members of his extended family sat sweltering on the porch in 104-degree heat in a small town about 50 miles from Abilene, Texas. When someone suggested driving to a café in Abilene, everyone went along with the idea, even though the car was not air conditioned. Everyone was miserable and returned home exhausted and irritable. Later, each person admitted that he or she hadn't wanted to make the trip, thought it was a ridiculous idea, and only went because of a belief that the others wanted to go. Because groupthink is such a natural and pervasive challenge to group decision making, some experts recommend using an expert *decision coach* to provide hands-on help and feedback so that people can learn and practice new behaviors rather than revert to the default behavior of suppressing opinions that are contrary to the group.[85]

> "The most dangerous thing is to be successful. You then think every decision is the right one."
> —WONG WAI MING, CFO OF LENOVO

6-6e Know When to Bail

In a fast-paced environment, good managers encourage risk-taking and learning from mistakes, but they also aren't hesitant to pull the plug on something that isn't working. Research has found that managers and organizations often continue to invest time and money in a solution even when there is strong evidence that it is not appropriate. This tendency is referred to as **escalating commitment**. Managers might block or distort negative information because they don't want to be responsible for a bad decision, or they might simply refuse to accept that their solution is wrong.[86] A study in Europe verified that even highly successful managers often miss or ignore warning signals because they become committed to a decision and believe that if they persevere, it will pay off.[87] As companies face increasing competition, complexity, and change, it is important that managers don't get so attached to their own ideas that they're unwilling to recognize when to move on. According to Stanford University professor Robert Sutton, the key to successful creative decision making is to "fail early, fail often, and pull the plug early."[88]

6-6f Do a Postmortem

To improve decision making, managers need to reflect on and learn from every decision they make. When people review the results of their decisions, they learn valuable lessons for how to do things better in the future. A technique that many companies have adopted from the U.S. army to encourage examination of the evidence and continuous learning is the **after-action review**, a disciplined procedure whereby managers invest time in reviewing the results of decisions on a regular basis and learn from them.[89] After implementation of any significant decision, managers meet to evaluate what worked, what didn't, and how to do things better. Many problems are solved by trial and error. For example, postmortem reviews of decisions regarding attacks from roadside bombs in Iraq led soldiers to suggest the implementation of an overall counterinsurgency strategy rather than relying so much on technology.[90] Numerous business organizations have adopted some form of after-action review. A similar technique emphasized by Lenovo founder Liu Chuanzhi is called *fu pan*, which means "replaying the chessboard." The idea is to review every move to improve the next one. Lenovo managers are trained to apply *fu pan* to everything from a small, quick review of a workday incident to a full, in-depth review of a major decision.[91] When managers get prompt feedback on decisions through after-action reviews, they can incorporate new information and greater understanding into their thinking and decision making.

Remember This

- Most decisions within organizations are made as part of a group, and whereas managers can't always see their own biases, they can build in mechanisms to prevent bias from influencing major decisions at the organizational level.
- **Brainstorming** is a technique that uses a face-to-face group to spontaneously suggest a broad range of alternatives for making a decision.
- **Electronic brainstorming** brings people together in an interactive group over a computer network rather than meeting face to face.
- **Evidence-based decision making** is founded on a commitment to examining potential biases, seeking and examining evidence with rigor, and making informed and intelligent decisions based on the best available facts and evidence.
- A **devil's advocate** is a person who is assigned the role of challenging the assumptions and assertions made by the group. This person's statements and questions can prevent premature consensus.

- A group decision-making technique that breaks people into subgroups and assigns them to express competing points of view regarding the decision is called **point–counterpoint**.
- **Groupthink** refers to the tendency of people in groups to suppress contrary opinions in a desire for harmony.
- **Escalating commitment** refers to continuing to invest time and money in a decision despite evidence that it is failing.
- A technique adopted from the U.S. army, the **after-action review** is a disciplined procedure whereby managers review the results of decisions to evaluate what worked, what didn't, and how to do things better.
- Managers at Lenovo apply a technique called *fu pan*, which means "replaying the chessboard," in which they review every move to improve the next one.

DISCUSSION QUESTIONS

1. Aaron Alexis, the former Navy reservist who went on a shooting rampage in September 2013 and killed 12 people at the Washington Navy Yard in Washington, D.C., had a history of mental instability, but he was carrying a valid security clearance. How would you suggest managers make decisions for issuing or revoking security clearances to prevent this kind of catastrophe?

2. Managers at Gap Inc., a once-popular retail chain, are reported to have made a series of decisions that hurt the company: They expanded so rapidly that the chain lost touch with customers; they tried to copy the successful approach of rivals rather than charting their own course; they cut quality to reduce costs; they shifted from one fashion approach to another they each one failed to appeal to customers, and so on. What techniques would you recommend Gap managers use to improve the quality of their decisions?

3. Explain the difference between risk and ambiguity. How might decision making differ for a risky versus an ambiguous situation?

4. Analyze three decisions you made over the past six months. Which of these were programmed and which were nonprogrammed? Which model—the classical, administrative, or political—best describes the approach you took to making each decision?

5. What opportunities and potential problems are posed by the formation of more than one coalition within an organization, each one advocating a different direction or alternative? What steps can you take as a manager to make sure that dueling coalitions result in constructive discussion rather than dissension?

6. Can you think of a bad decision from your own school or work experience, or from recent business or political news stories, that was made in an effort to correct or justify a past decision? As a new manager, how might you resist the urge to choose a decision alternative based on the idea that it might correct or validate a previous decision?

7. Experts advise that most catastrophes in organizations result from a series of small problems or mistakes. As a new, entry-level manager, how might you apply this understanding to help your organization avoid making major mistakes?

8. List some possible advantages and disadvantages to using computer technology for managerial decision making.

9. Can intuition and evidence-based decision making coexist as valid approaches within an organization? How might managers combine their intuition with a rational, data-driven, evidence-based approach?

10. What do you think is your dominant decision style? Is your style compatible with group techniques such as brainstorming and engaging in rigorous debate? Discuss.

APPLY YOUR SKILLS: SELF-LEARNING

What's Your Personal Decision Style?[92]

Read each of the following questions and circle the answer that best describes you. Think about how you typically act in a work or school situation and mark the answer that first comes to mind. There are no right or wrong answers.

1. In performing my job or class work, I look for
   a. Practical results
   b. The best solution
   c. Creative approaches or ideas
   d. Good working conditions

2. I enjoy jobs that
   a. Are technical and well defined
   b. Have a lot of variety
   c. Allow me to be independent and creative
   d. Involve working closely with others

3. The people I most enjoy working with are
   a. Energetic and ambitious
   b. Capable and organized
   c. Open to new ideas
   d. Agreeable and trusting

4. When I have a problem, I usually
   a. Rely on what has worked in the past
   b. Apply careful analysis
   c. Consider a variety of creative approaches
   d. Seek consensus with others

5. I am especially good at
   a. Remembering dates and facts
   b. Solving complex problems
   c. Seeing many possible solutions
   d. Getting along with others

6. When I don't have much time, I
   a. Make decisions and act quickly
   b. Follow established plans or priorities
   c. Take my time and refuse to be pressured
   d. Ask others for guidance and support

7. In social situations, I generally
   a. Talk to others
   b. Think about what's being discussed
   c. Observe
   d. Listen to the conversation

8. Other people consider me
   a. Aggressive
   b. Disciplined
   c. Creative
   d. Supportive

9. What I dislike most is
   a. Not being in control
   b. Doing boring work
   c. Following rules
   d. Being rejected by others

10. The decisions I make are usually
    a. Direct and practical
    b. Systematic or abstract
    c. Broad and flexible
    d. Sensitive to others' needs

Scoring and Interpretation These questions rate your personal decision style, as described in the text and listed in Exhibit 6.5.

Count the number of *a* answers. They provide your *directive* score.

Count the number of *b* answers for your *analytical* score.

The number of *c* answers is your *conceptual* score.

The number of *d* answers is your *behavioral* score.

What is your dominant decision style? Are you surprised, or does this result reflect the style that you thought you used most often?

APPLY YOUR SKILLS: GROUP LEARNING

A New Approach to Making Decisions[93]

Managers are typically effective at focusing on problems and diagnosing what is wrong and how to fix it when they have to make a decision. The typical questions that managers might ask themselves include: What is the problem here? What is the cause of this problem? Why is this problem happening to me? What alternatives do I have? What is the best alternative? How do I implement this alternative?

There is a novel approach to decision making, called *outcome-directed thinking*, that some managers have learned to use. It focuses on future outcomes and possibilities rather than on the causes of the problem. People tend to feel more positive emotions, have more creative ideas, and experience more optimism about solving a problem when they focus on desired future outcomes rather than on who or what caused the problem.

Step 1. Think of a problem that you have in your life right now, in which something is not what you would like it to be. It could be any problem that you are having at school, home, or work that you would like to solve. Summarize the problem here in a few words:

_____

_____

_____

_____

Step 2. Now write brief answers to the following questions:

1. What outcome do I really want with respect to this problem? (Your answer equals your desired result about the problem.)

    _____

    _____

    _____

    _____

2. How will I know when I have achieved this future outcome? (What will I see, hear, and feel?)

    _____

    _____

    _____

    _____

3. What resources do I need to pursue this future outcome?

    _____

    _____

    _____

    _____

4. What is the first step I can take to achieve this outcome?

    _____

    _____

    _____

    _____

Step 3. In a group of three to five students, take turns sharing your answers to these four questions. In addition, share what you are feeling about your desired outcome for the problem. For example, do you feel that you have created the beginning of a solution that you can implement? In addition, share whether your thinking is more creative and effective by focusing on achieving a desired outcome rather than on the cause of the problem.

APPLY YOUR SKILLS: ACTION LEARNING

1. Think about two times when you made decisions, one that had a positive outcome and one that did not turn out so well.

2. Fill out the following table.

What decision did you have to make?	Decision 1 (positive outcome)	Decision 1 (positive outcome)
Was the decision programmed or nonprogrammed		
Was there certainty or uncertainty?		
Did you use your intuition?		
Did you build a coalition?		
Did you engage in any bad decision behaviors, such as defending previous decisions, being too emotional or unduly influenced by initial impressions, etc.?		
Did you explore different alternatives?		
Did you use evidence-based thinking?		
Did you consult a devil's advocate?		

3. What differences do you see in the two decision-making situations?

4. What can you learn from this on how to more effectively make decisions in the future?

APPLY YOUR SKILLS: ETHICAL DILEMMA

The No-Show Consultant[94]

Jeffrey Moses was facing one of the toughest decisions of his short career as a manager with International Consulting. Andrew Carpenter, one of his best consultants, was clearly in trouble, and his problems were affecting his work. International Consulting designs, installs, and implements complex back-office software systems for companies all over the world. About half the consultants work out of the main office, while the rest, including Carpenter, work primarily from home.

This Monday morning, Moses had gotten an irate call from a major New York client saying that Carpenter never showed up at the company's headquarters, where the client had been expecting his new computer system to go live for the first time. In calling around to other customers on the East Coast in an effort to locate the missing consultant, Moses heard

other stories. Carpenter had also missed a few other appointments—all on Monday mornings—but no one had felt the need to report it because he had called to reschedule. In addition, he practically came to blows with an employee who challenged him about the capabilities of the new system, and he inexplicably walked out of one customer's office in the middle of the day, without a word to anyone. Another client reported that the last time he saw Carpenter, he appeared to have a serious hangover. Most of the clients liked Carpenter, but they were concerned that his behavior was increasingly erratic. One client suggested that she would prefer to work with someone else. As for the major New York customer, he preferred that Andrew rather than a new consultant finish the project, but he also demanded that International eat half the $250,000 consultant's fee.

After Moses finally located Carpenter by calling his next-door neighbor, Carpenter confessed that he'd had a "lost weekend" and been too drunk to get on the plane. He then told Moses that his wife had left and taken their two-year-old son with her. He admitted that he had been drinking a little more than usual lately, but insisted that he was getting himself under control and promised no more problems. "I'm really not an alcoholic or anything," he said. "I've just been upset about Brenda leaving, and I let it get out of hand this weekend." Moses told Carpenter that if he would get to New York and complete the project, all would be forgiven.

Now, however, he wondered whether he should really just let things slide. Moses talked to Carpenter's team leader about the situation and was told that the leader was aware of his recent problems but thought everything would smooth itself over. "Consultants with his knowledge, level of skill, and willingness to travel are hard to find. He's well liked among all the customers; he'll get his act together." However, when Moses discussed the problem with Carolyn Walter, vice president of operations, she argued that Carpenter should be dismissed. "You're under no obligation to keep him just because you said you would," she pointed out. "This was a major screw-up, and it's perfectly legal to fire someone for absenteeism. Your calls to customers should make it clear to you that this situation was not a one-time thing. Get rid of him now before things get worse. If you think eating half that $250,000 fee hurts now, just think what could happen if this behavior continues."

What Would You Do?

1. Give Carpenter a month's notice and terminate him. He's known as a good consultant, so he probably won't have any trouble finding a new job, and you'll avoid any further problems associated with his emotional difficulties and his possible alcohol problem.

2. Let it slide. Missing the New York appointment is Carpenter's first big mistake. He says he is getting things under control, and you believe that he should be given a chance to get himself back on track.

3. Let Carpenter know that you care about what he's going through, but insist that he take a short paid leave and get counseling to deal with his emotional difficulties and evaluate the seriousness of his problems with alcohol. If the alcohol abuse continues, require him to attend a treatment program or find another job.

APPLY YOUR SKILLS: CASE FOR CRITICAL ANALYSIS

The Office

Krista Acklen was the "golden girl" of metropolitan government in a large Midwestern city. The top graduate of a local high school, she studied in France and interned at *Vogue* in Paris before returning to the States to get an MBA, and she landed a position with a top New York PR firm. She knew *everyone*, and chatting with or "doing lunch" with the rich and famous was a normal day for Acklen.

The only child of a single mom, Acklen dropped it all and willingly returned to her Midwestern hometown when her mother's health declined suddenly. She had barely settled in and established home care for her mother when the mayor's office contacted her with a job proposal. Would Acklen consider a position developing and directing a public arts program for the city? She enthusiastically accepted the job. With her winning connections, drive, and abilities, she quickly expanded her mission to develop a range of arts programs. Donations and grant money poured into programs under her established nonprofit organization developed to support city parks. Headquarters for Acklen and her staff was a comfortable, unused third-floor space in the city library that used to hold books and magazines that were now stored digitally.

Then John Mitchell, director of parks and recreation, summoned her to a meeting "to learn of a decision I have made that will affect your group." Acklen was curious to find out what was going on. Knowing that budget factors recently forced reduction in staff and office space throughout city government, and aware of the importance of dealing carefully with public opinion, as well as the feelings of employees and other stakeholders, Acklen felt that she was prepared for any decision Mitchell might have reached.

She tried to get comfortable in the chair across from Mitchell, who seemed ill at ease. Avoiding small talk, Mitchell said that he intentionally did not discuss the decision in advance because he believed Acklen would object. He would not accept her objections anyway, he indicated, so the decision was final.

"What is the decision?" asked Acklen.

"The mayor wants half of your group's office space for the Greenways project," Mitchell replied, "and I see no alternative except for you to agree. Her idea makes sense, and you must go along."

Acklen felt fury rising in her chest as she stared at Mitchell while thinking, "This people-pleasing, brown-nosing jerk. He will do anything to win the mayor's favor."

The Greenways project, directed by Lisa Todd, had developed a number of beautiful areas throughout the city. In recent years, Greenways had received the bulk of new money and attention from the federal government, and Todd's staff had grown with the additional funding and development projects.

As Acklen regained her composure, she shot back at Mitchell, "Not consulting me on this is unacceptable. I should be part of any decision affecting my staff and program. I could have helped plan a solution that worked for everyone." Mitchell started to speak, but Acklen cut him off. "You have a responsibility to my group, as well as to Mayor Simpson and the other projects of this city. I think you are giving us the shaft as an easy way to please her."

The two argued a while longer, but Mitchell wouldn't budge. Finally, Acklen said, "John, since this was your decision, you should be the one to tell my people. You better come over soon before the word gets out."

"No," Mitchell said, "you are their immediate boss. You have to tell them. That's your job. Where is your team spirit, anyway?"

Acklen returned to her office, seething, and vented about the problem to Joanne Franklin, her most senior

employee. "Oh no," Joanne moaned. "We really need all this space. Our program is growing, too."

Acklen agreed, but she explained Mitchell's support of the suggestion from the mayor's office to make additional office space available to Lisa Todd and her staff. Joanne started brainstorming. "I suppose we could pair up in the offices."

Acklen shook her head. "We *are* team players. But John Mitchell and the mayor need to know that this was not handled in a way that shows respect for our employees." After a pause, she continued, "I'm too frazzled to think about it anymore today. Let's talk about this tomorrow."

Questions

1. What mistakes do you think John Mitchell made with the way he solved the problem of limited office space? Explain.

2. What approach would you have used if you were Mitchell? Why?

3. What are Krista Acklen's options for responding to Mitchell's decision? What should she do now? Why?

ENDNOTES

1. Kris Maher and Cameron McWhirter, "Series of Mistakes Tainted Flint Water," *The Wall Street Journal*, January 22, 2016, http://www.wsj.com/articles/flint-was-hit-by-a-perfect-storm-of-mistakes-1453499906 (accessed March 14, 2016); and Arthur Delaney, "How Flint's Water Got Poisonous," *The Huffington Post*, January 19, 2016, http://www.huffingtonpost.com/entry/how-flint-water-got-poisonous_us_569907f5e4b0b4eb759e1426 (accessed March 14, 2016).

2. Danielle Sacks, "Blown Away," *Fast Company* (February 2011): 58–65, 104.

3. Colum Murphy, James T. Areddy, and James R. Hagerty, "Deal Gone Wrong Adds to Caterpillar's Troubles in China," *The Wall Street Journal*, January 21, 2013, http://online.wsj.com/article/SB10001424127887323301104578255740261180404.html (accessed August 29, 2013).

4. Herbert A. Simon, *The New Science of Management Decision* (Englewood Cliffs, NJ: Prentice Hall, 1977), p. 47.

5. Paul J. H. Schoemaker and J. Edward Russo, "A Pyramid of Decision Approaches," *California Management Review* (Fall 1993): 9–31.

6. Adam Lashinsky, "Boeing Bets Big on the 707," segment of "The Greatest Business Decisions of All Time" book excerpt, *Fortune* (October 8, 2012): 178–184.

7. Aaron M. Kessler, "Five Years Later, Chrysler's Gamble on Ram Trucks Is Paying Off," *The New York Times*, September 17, 2014, http://www.nytimes.com/2014/09/18/business/ram-trucks-gain-on-their-detroit-rivals.html?_r=0 (accessed March 14, 2016).

8. Samuel Eilon, "Structuring Unstructured Decisions," *Omega* 13 (1985): 369–377; and Max H. Bazerman,

Judgment in Managerial Decision Making (New York: Wiley, 1986).

9. James G. March and Zur Shapira, "Managerial Perspectives on Risk and Risk Taking," *Management Science* 33 (1987): 1404–1418; and Inga Skromme Baird and Howard Thomas, "Toward a Contingency Model of Strategic Risk Taking," *Academy of Management Review* 10 (1985): 230–243.

10. Daniel Gilbert and Sarah Kent, "Shell Places Huge Bet on Arctic Oil Riches," *The Wall Street Journal*, July 7, 2015, http://www.wsj.com/articles/shell-places-huge-bet-on-arctic-oil-riches-1436311938 (accessed March 14, 2016).

11. Antonia Juhasz, "Shell Is Reeling after Pulling Out of the Arctic," *Newsweek* (October 13, 2015), http://www.newsweek.com/2015/10/23/shell-reeling-after-pulling-out-arctic-382551.html (accessed October 15, 2015).

12. Quoted in Leslie Kwoh, "Memo to Staff: Take More Risks" (Theory & Practice column), *The Wall Street Journal*, March 20, 2013.

13. Hugh Courtney, "Decision-Driven Scenarios for Assessing Four Levels of Uncertainty," *Strategy & Leadership* 31, no. 1 (2003): 14–22.

14. Reported in David Leonhardt, "This Fed Chief May Yet Get a Honeymoon," *The New York Times*, August 23, 2006.

15. Brooks Barnes, "'Oz the Great and Powerful' Has Big Opening," *The New York Times*, March 10, 2013, http://artsbeat.blogs.nytimes.com/2013/03/10/oz-the-great-and-powerful-has-big-opening/ (accessed September 20, 2013); and Barnes, "One More Trip to Land of Oz," *The New York Times*, March 3, 2013, http://www.nytimes.com/2013/03/04/business/media/disney-gambles-on-box-office-wizardry-of-oz.html?pagewanted=all (accessed March 4, 2013).

16. Angie Han, "Four of the 50 Biggest Box Office Bombs Are in Theaters Right Now," *Film* Web site, August 22, 2013, http://www.slashfilm.com/four-of-the-fifty-biggest-box-office-bombs-are-in-theaters-right-now/ (accessed September 20, 2013); and Adam Davidson, "When You Wish Upon 'Ishtar': How Does the Film Industry Actually Make Money?" *The New York Times Magazine* (July 1, 2012): 16–17.

17. Michael Masuch and Perry LaPotin, "Beyond Garbage Cans: An AI Model of Organizational Choice," *Administrative Science Quarterly* 34 (1989): 38–67; and Richard L. Daft and Robert H. Lengel, "Organizational Information Requirements, Media Richness and Structural Design," *Management Science* 32 (1986): 554–571.

18. Peter C. Cairo, David L. Dotlich, and Stephen H. Rhinesmith, "Embracing Ambiguity," *The Conference Board Review* (Summer 2009): 56–61; John C. Camillus, "Strategy as a Wicked Problem," *Harvard Business Review* (May 2008): 98–106; and Richard O. Mason and Ian I. Mitroff, *Challenging Strategic Planning Assumptions* (New York: Wiley Interscience, 1981).

19. Howard Schneider, "University Logos Become Weapons in Debate over Textile Factory Working Conditions," *The Washington Post*, May 27, 2013, http://articles.washingtonpost.com/2013-05-27/business/39558590_1_university-logos-nike-adidas (accessed August 26, 2013); and Jens Hansegard, Tripti Lahiri, and Christina Passariello, "Retailers' Dilemma: To Ax or Help Fix Bad Factories," *The Wall Street Journal*, May 28, 2013, http://online.wsj.com/article/SB10001424127887323336104578501143973731324.html (accessed May 30, 2013).

20. "How Companies Make Good Decisions: McKinsey Global Survey Results," *The McKinsey Quarterly* (January 2009), www.mckinseyquarterly.com (accessed February 3, 2009).

21. Thomas H. Davenport and Jeanne G. Harris, "Automated Decision Making Comes of Age," *MIT Sloan Management Review* (Summer 2005): 83–89; and Stacie McCullough, "On the Front Lines," *CIO* (October 15, 1999): 78–81.

22. These examples are from Steve Lohr, "The Age of Big Data," *The New York Times*, February 12, 2012, SR1; and Steven Rosenbush and Laura Stevens, "At UPS, the Algorithm Is the Driver," *The Wall Street Journal,* February 26, 2015, http://www.wsj.com/articles/at-ups-the-algorithm-is-the-driver-1424136536 (accessed March 16, 2016).

23. Simon, *The New Science of Management Decision*, pp. 5–6; and Amitai Etzioni, "Humble Decision Making," *Harvard Business Review* (July–August 1989): 122–126.

24. James G. March and Herbert A. Simon, *Organizations* (New York: Wiley, 1958).

25. Herbert A. Simon, *Models of Man* (New York: Wiley, 1957), pp. 196–205; and Simon, *Administrative Behavior*, 2d ed. (New York: Free Press, 1957).

26. Rachel Dodes, "Targeting Younger Buyers, Liz Claiborne Hits a Snag," *The Wall Street Journal*, August 16, 2010.

27. Weston H. Agor, "The Logic of Intuition: How Top Executives Make Important Decisions," *Organizational Dynamics* 14 (Winter 1986): 5–18; and Herbert A. Simon, "Making Management Decisions: The Role of Intuition and Emotion," *Academy of Management Executive* 1 (1987): 57–64. For recent reviews of research, see Eugene Sadler-Smith and Lisa A. Burke-Smalley, "What Do We Really Understand about How Managers Make Important Decisions?" *Organizational Dynamics* 44 (2015): 9–16; and Erik Dane and Michael G. Pratt, "Exploring Intuition and Its Role in Managerial Decision Making," *Academy of Management Review* 32, no. 1 (2007): 33–54.

28. Kurt Matzler, Borislav Uzelac, and Florian Bauer, "Intuition: The Missing Ingredient for Good Managerial Decision-Making," *Journal of Business Strategy* 35, no. 6 (2014): 31–40; and Eugene Sadler-Smith, *Inside Intuition* (New York: Routledge, 2008).

29. See Gary Klein, *Intuition at Work: Why Developing Your Gut Instincts Will Make You Better at What You Do* (New York: Doubleday, 2002); Kurt Matzler, Franz Bailom, and Todd A. Mooradian, "Intuitive Decision Making," *MIT Sloan Management Review* 49, no. 1 (Fall 2007): 13–15; Malcolm Gladwell, *Blink: The Power of Thinking Without Thinking* (New York: Little Brown, 2005); and Sharon Begley, "Follow Your Intuition: The Unconscious You May Be the Wiser Half," *The Wall Street Journal*, August 30, 2002.

30. Benedict Carey, "Hunches Prove to Be Valuable Assets in Battle," *The New York Times*, July 28, 2009.

31. Matzler, Uzelac, and Bauer, "Intuition: The Missing Ingredient for Good Managerial Decision-Making"; Jaana Woiceshyn, "Lessons from 'Good Minds': How CEOs Use Intuition, Analysis, and Guiding Principles to Make Strategic Decisions," *Long-Range Planning* 42 (2009): 298–319; Ann Hensman and Eugene Sadler-Smith, "Intuitive Decision Making in Banking and Finance," *European Management Journal* 29 (2011): 51–66; and Eugene Sadler-Smith and Erella Shefy, "The Intuitive Executive: Understanding and Applying 'Gut Feel' in Decision-Making," *Academy of Management Executive* 18, no. 4 (November 2004): 76–91.

32. Mandeep K. Dhami and Mary E. Thomson, "On the Relevance of Cognitive Continuum Theory and Quasirationality for Understanding Management Judgment and Decision Making," *European Management Journal* 30 (2012): 316–326.

33. Dhami and Thomson, "On the Relevance of Cognitive Continuum Theory"; C. Chet Miller and R. Duane Ireland, "Intuition in Strategic Decision Making: Friend or Foe in the Fast-Paced 21st Century?" *Academy of Management Executive* 19, no. 1 (2005): 19–30; Eric Bonabeau, "Don't Trust Your Gut," *Harvard Business Review* (May 2003): 116ff; Sadler-Smith and Shefy, "The Intuitive Executive"; Simon, "Making Management Decisions"; and Ann Langley, "Between 'Paralysis by Analysis' and 'Extinction by Instinct,'" *Sloan Management Review* (Spring 1995): 63–76.

34. This discussion is based on Stephen Friedman and James K. Sebenius, "Organizational Transformation: The Quiet Role of Coalitional Leadership," *Ivey Business Journal* (January–February 2009): 1ff; Gerald R. Ferris et al., "Political Skill in Organizations," *Journal of Management* (June 2007): 290–320; and William B. Stevenson, Jon L. Pierce, and Lyman W. Porter, "The Concept of 'Coalition' in Organization Theory and Research," *Academy of Management Review* 10 (1985): 256–268.

35. "How Companies Make Good Decisions."

36. Ronald A. Gill, "Quality-Oriented Teamwork Resolves Aerospace Manufacturer's Critical Path Tooling Crisis," *Global Business and Organizational Excellence* (September–October 2012): 34–41.

37. Ron Nixon, "Post Office Faces Hurdles in Efforts to Diversify," *The New York Times*, April 21, 2012.

38. George T. Doran and Jack Gunn, "Decision Making in High-Tech Firms: Perspectives of Three Executives," *Business Horizons* (November–December 2002): 7–16.

39. James W. Fredrickson, "Effects of Decision Motive and Organizational Performance Level on Strategic Decision Processes," *Academy of Management Journal* 28 (1985): 821–843; James W. Fredrickson, "The Comprehensiveness of Strategic Decision Processes: Extension, Observations, Future

Directions," *Academy of Management Journal* 27 (1984): 445–466; James W. Dean, Jr., and Mark P. Sharfman, "Procedural Rationality in the Strategic Decision-Making Process," *Journal of Management Studies* 30, no. 4 (July 1993): 587–610; Nandini Rajagopalan, Abdul M. A. Rasheed, and Deepak K. Datta, "Strategic Decision Processes: Critical Review and Future Directions," *Journal of Management* 19, no. 2 (1993): 349–384; and Paul J. H. Schoemaker, "Strategic Decisions in Organizations: Rational and Behavioral Views," *Journal of Management Studies* 30, no. 1 (January 1993): 107–129.

40. Marjorie A. Lyles and Howard Thomas, "Strategic Problem Formulation: Biases and Assumptions Embedded in Alternative Decision-Making Models," *Journal of Management Studies* 25 (1988): 131–145; and Susan E. Jackson and Jane E. Dutton, "Discerning Threats and Opportunities," *Administrative Science Quarterly* 33 (1988): 370–387.

41. Richard L. Daft, Juhani Sormumen, and Don Parks, "Chief Executive Scanning, Environmental Characteristics, and Company Performance: An Empirical Study" (unpublished manuscript, Texas A&M University, 1988).

42. Cecilia Kang, "Google Crunches Data on Munching in Office," *The Washington Post*, September 1, 2013, http://articles.washingtonpost.com/2013-09-01/business/41670762_1_laszlo-bock-last-year-google-data (accessed September 21, 2013).

43. Daniel Burrus and John David Mann, "Whatever Your Problem . . . That's Not Likely to Be Your Real Problem," *Leadership Excellence* (February 2011): 7–8.

44. Charles H. Kepner and Benjamin B. Tregoe, *The Rational Manager* (New York: McGraw-Hill, 1965).

45. Based on Burrus and Mann, "Whatever Your Problem . . ."; and Jonathan Taplin, "How to . . . Turn a Bad Idea into a Good Idea," *Fast Company* (February 2013): 20.

46. Paul C. Nutt, "Expanding the Search for Alternatives During Strategic Decision Making," *Academy of Management Executive* 18, no. 4 (2004): 13–28; and P. C. Nutt, "Surprising but True: Half the Decisions in Organizations Fail," *Academy of Management Executive* 13, no. 4 (1999): 75–90.

47. Olivier Leclerc and Mihnea Moldoveanu, "Five Routes to More Innovative Problem Solving," *McKinsey Quarterly* (April 2013), http://www.mckinsey.com/insights/strategy/five_routes_to_more_innovative_problem_solving (accessed May 14, 2013).

48. Peter Mayer, "A Surprisingly Simple Way to Make Better Decisions," *Executive Female* (March–April 1995): 13–14; and Ralph L. Keeney, "Creativity in Decision Making with Value-Focused Thinking," *Sloan Management Review* (Summer 1994): 33–41.

49. Vindu Goel, "Facebook Chief Says Secret of His Success Is Making Lots of Mistakes," *The New York Times*, December 11, 2014, http://bits.blogs.nytimes.com/2014/12/11/facebook-chief-says-secret-of-his-success-is-making-lots-of-mistakes/?_r=0 (accessed March 15, 2016); and Ashlee Vance, "The Making of 1 Billion Users," *Bloomberg Businessweek* (October 4, 2012), http://www.businessweek.com/articles/2012-10-04/facebook-the-making-of-1-billion-users (accessed September 21, 2013).

50. Paul J. H. Schoemaker, Steve Krupp, and Samantha Howland, "Strategic Leadership: The Essential Skills," *Harvard Business Review* (January–February 2013): 131–134; and Mark McNeilly, "Gathering Information for Strategic Decisions, Routinely," *Strategy & Leadership* 30, no. 5 (2002): 29–34.

51. Phil Rosenzweig, "Making Better Decisions over Time," *Strategy + Business* (January 6, 2014), http://www.strategy-business.com/article/00227?gko=12d89 (accessed March 15, 2016).

52. David Kesmodel, "Latest Flap on Egg Farms: Whether to Go 'Cage-Free,'" *The Wall Street Journal*, March 11, 2015, http://www.wsj.com/articles/latest-flap-on-egg-farms-going-whole-hog-on-cage-free-1426100062 (accessed March 16, 2016).

53. Ibid.

54. Based on A. J. Rowe, J. D. Boulgaides, and M. R. McGrath, *Managerial Decision Making* (Chicago: Science Research Associates, 1984); and Alan J. Rowe and Richard O. Mason, *Managing with Style: A Guide to Understanding, Assessing, and Improving Your Decision Making* (San Francisco: Jossey-Bass, 1987).

55. Adam Bryant, "Dawn Zier of Nutrisystem on When Your Company Is Adrift," *The New York Times,* January 30, 2014), http://www.nytimes.com/2014/01/31/business/corner-office-dawn-m-zier-chief-of-nutrisystem.html?_r=0 (accessed March 15, 2016).

56. Philip Meissner, Olivier Sibony, and Torsten Wulf, "Are You Ready to Decide?" *McKinsey Quarterly* (April 2015), http://www.mckinsey.com/business-functions/strategy-and-corporate-finance/our-insights/are-you-ready-to-decide (accessed March 16, 2016); and John Beshears and Francesca Gino, "Leaders as Decision Architects," *Harvard Business Review* (May 2015): 52–62.

57. This section is based on John S. Hammond, Ralph L. Keeney, and Howard Raiffa, *Smart Choices: A Practical Guide to Making Better Decisions* (Boston: Harvard Business School Press, 1999); Max H. Bazerman and Dolly Chugh, "Decisions Without Blinders," *Harvard Business Review* (January 2006): 88–97; J. S. Hammond, R. L. Keeney, and H. Raiffa, "The Hidden Traps in Decision Making," *Harvard Business Review* (September–October 1998): 47–58; Oren Harari, "The Thomas Lawson Syndrome," *Management Review* (February 1994): 58–61; Dan Ariely, "Q&A: Why Good CIOs Make Bad Decisions," *CIO* (May 1, 2003): 83–87; Leigh Buchanan, "How to Take Risks in a Time of Anxiety," *Inc.* (May 2003): 76–81; and Max H. Bazerman, *Judgment in Managerial Decision Making*, 5th ed. (New York: John Wiley & Sons, 2002).

58. This example is discussed in Matzler, Uzelac, and Bauer, "Intuition: The Missing Ingredient for Good Managerial Decision-Making."

59. James Surowiecki, "The Financial Page: That Sunk-Cost Feeling," *The New Yorker* (January 21, 2013): 24; and Dustin J. Sleesman et al., "Cleaning Up the Big Muddy: A Meta-Analytic Review of the Determinants of Escalation of Commitment," *Academy of Management Journal* 55, no. 3 (2012): 541–562.

60. J. B. Schmidt and R. J. Calantone, "Escalation of Commitment During New Product Development," *Journal of the Academy of Marketing Science* 30, no. 2 (2002): 103–118.

61. Beshears and Gino, "Leaders as Decision Architects."

62. Norihiko Shirouzu, Phred Dvorak, Yuka Hayashi, and Andrew Morse, "Bid to 'Protect Assets' Slowed Reactor Fight," *The Wall Street Journal*, March 19, 2011, http://online.wsj.com/article/SB10001424052748704608504576207912642629904.html (accessed August 6, 2012).

63. John D. Stoll, Kevin Helliker, and Neil E. Boudette, "A Saga of Decline and Denial," *The Wall Street Journal*, June 2, 2009.

64. Mark Fenton-O'Creevy et al., "Thinking, Feeling, and Deciding: The Influence of Emotions on the Decision Making and Performance of Traders," *Journal of Organizational Behavior* 32 (2011): 1044–1061.

65. Example from Jerome Groopman, *How Doctors Think* (New York: Houghton Mifflin, 2007).

66. Dan Ariely, "The Long-Term Effects of Short-Term Emotions," *Harvard Business Review* (January–February 2010): 38.

67. David Larcker and Brian Tayan study, reported in Michael J. Mauboussin, "The True Measures of Success," *Harvard Business Review* (October 2012): 46–56.

68. Jessica Silver-Greenberg, "New Fraud Inquiry as JPMorgan's Loss Mounts," *The New York Times*, July 13, 2012, http://dealbook.nytimes.com/2012/07/13/jpmorgan-says-traders-obscured-losses-in-first-quarter/ (accessed August 7, 2012); Ben Protess et al., "In JPMorgan Chase Trading Bet, Its Confidence Yields to Loss," *The New York Times*, May 11, 2012, http://dealbook.nytimes.com/2012/05/11/in-jpmorgan-chase-trading-bet-its-confidence-yields-to-loss/ (accessed May 15, 2012); Peter Eavis and Susanne Craig, "The Bet That Blew up for JPMorgan Chase," *The New York Times*, May 11, 2012, http://dealbook.nytimes.com/2012/05/11/the-bet-that-blew-up-for-jpmorgan-chase/ (accessed May 15, 2012); and Jessica Silver-Greenberg and Nelson D. Schwartz, "Red Flags Said to Go Unheeded by Bosses at JPMorgan," *The New York Times*, May 14, 2012, http://dealbook.nytimes.com/2012/05/14/warnings-said-to-go-unheeded-by-chase-bosses/ (accessed May 15, 2012).

69. Beshears and Gino, "Leaders as Decision Architects" Kathleen M. Eisenhardt, "Strategy as Strategic Decision Making," *Sloan Management Review* (Spring 1999): 65–72.

70. Daniel Kahneman, Dan Lovallo, and Olivier Sibony, "Before You Make That Big Decision," *Harvard Business Review* (June 2011): 50–60; and Meissner, Sibony, and Wulf, "Are You Ready to Decide?"

71. Josh Hyatt, "Where the Best—and Worst—Ideas Come From" (a brief synopsis of "Idea Generation and the Quality of the Best Idea," by Karen Girotra, Christian Terwiesch, and Karl T. Ulrich, *MIT Sloan Management Review* (Summer 2008): 11–12; and Robert C. Litchfield, "Brainstorming Reconsidered: A Goal-Based View," *Academy of Management Review* 33, no. 3 (2008): 649–668.

72. R. B. Gallupe et al., "Blocking Electronic Brainstorms," *Journal of Applied Psychology* 79 (1994): 77–86; R. B. Gallupe and W. H. Cooper, "Brainstorming Electronically," *Sloan Management Review* (Fall 1993): 27–36; and Alison Stein Wellner, "A Perfect Brainstorm," *Inc.* (October 2003): 31–35.

73. Wellner, "A Perfect Brainstorm"; Gallupe and Cooper, "Brainstorming Electronically."

74. Example from Thomas H. Davenport and Brook Manville, "From the Judgment of Leadership to the Leadership of Judgment: The Fallacy of Heroic Decision Making," *Leader to Leader* (Fall 2012): 26–31.

75. This section is based on Jeffrey Pfeffer and Robert I. Sutton, "Evidence-Based Management," *Harvard Business Review* (January 2006): 62–74; Rosemary Stewart, *Evidence-Based Decision Making* (Radcliffe Publishing, 2002); and Joshua Klayman, Richard P. Larrick, and Chip Heath, "Organizational Repairs," *Across the Board* (February 2000): 26–31.

76. Stephen H. Courtright, Greg L. Stewart, and Marcia M. Ward, "Applying Research to Save Lives: Learning from Team Training Approaches in Aviation and Health Care," *Organizational Dynamics* 41 (2012): 291–301.

77. Study by Erik Brynjolfsson, Lorin Hitt, and Heekyung Kim; results reported in Steve Lohr, "The Age of Big Data," *The New York Times*, February 12, 2012.

78. Sydney Finkelstein, "Think Again: Good Leaders, Bad Decisions," *Leadership Excellence* (June 2009): 7; "Flaws in Strategic Decision Making: McKinsey Global Survey Results," *The McKinsey Quarterly* (January 2009), www.mckinsey.com; Michael A. Roberto, "Making Difficult Decisions in Turbulent Times," *Ivey Business Journal* (May–June 2003): 1–7; Eisenhardt, "Strategy as Strategic Decision Making;" and David A. Garvin and Michael A. Roberto, "What You Don't Know About Making Decisions," *Harvard Business Review* (September 2001): 108–116.

79. Nick Wingfield and Brian Stelter, "A Juggernaut Stumbles," *The New York Times*, October 25, 2011; and James B. Stewart, "Netflix Looks Back on Its Near-Death Spiral," *The New York Times*, April 26, 2013, http://www.nytimes.com/2013/04/27/business/netflix-looks-back-on-its-near-death-spiral.html?pagewanted=all&_r=0 (accessed April 27, 2013).

80. David M. Schweiger and William R. Sandberg, "The Utilization of Individual Capabilities in Group Approaches to Strategic Decision Making," *Strategic Management Journal* 10 (1989): 31–43; "Avoiding Disasters," sidebar in Paul B. Carroll and Chunka Mui, "7 Ways to Fail Big," *Harvard Business Review* (September 2008): 82–91; and "The Devil's Advocate," *Small Business Report* (December 1987): 38–41.

81. Adam Bryant, "Kevin E. Lofton of Catholic Health Initiatives: Designate a Devil's Advocate," *The New York Times*, August 8, 2015, http://www.nytimes.com/2015/08/09/business/kevin-e-lofton-of-catholic-health-initiatives-designate-a-devils-advocate.html?_r=0 (accessed March 16, 2016); and Doran and Gunn, "Decision Making in High-Tech Firms."

82. Garvin and Roberto, "What You Don't Know About Making Decisions."

83. Irving L. Janis, *Groupthink: Psychological Studies of Policy Decisions and Fiascoes*, 2d ed. (Boston: Houghton Mifflin, 1982); and Shlomo Ben-Hur, Nikolas Kinley, and Karsten Jonsen, "Coaching Executive Teams to Better Decisions," *Journal of Management Development* 31, no. 7 (2012): 711–723.

84. Jerry B. Harvey, "The Abilene Paradox: The Management of Agreement," *Organizational Dynamics* (Summer 1988): 17–43.

85. Ben-Hur et al., "Coaching Executive Teams to Better Decisions."

86. B. M. Staw, "Escalation Research: An Update and Appraisal," in *Organizational Decision Making*, ed. Z. Shapira (Cambridge: Cambridge University Press, 1997), pp. 191–215; S. Trevis Certo, Brian L. Connelly, and Laszlo Tihanyi, "Managers and Their Not-So-Rational Decisions," *Business Horizons* 51 (2008): 113–119; and Sleesman et al., "Cleaning Up the Big Muddy."

87. Hans Wissema, "Driving Through Red Lights: How Warning Signals Are Missed or Ignored," *Long Range Planning* 35 (2002): 521–539.

88. Ibid.

89. Thomas E. Ricks, "Army Devises System to Decide What Does, Does Not Work," *The Wall Street Journal*, May 23, 1997; and David W. Cannon and Jeffrey McCollum, "Army Medical Department Lessons Learned Program Marks 25th Anniversary," *Military Medicine* (November 2011): 1212–1214.

90. Peter Eisler, Blake Morrison, and Tom Vanden Brook, "Strategy That's Making Iraq Safer Was Snubbed for Years," *USA TODAY*, December 19, 2007.

91. Chuck Salter, "Lenovo: Protect and Attack," *Fast Company* (December 2011–January 2012): 116–121, 154–155.

92. Adapted from Rowe and Mason, *Managing with Style*, pp. 40–41.

93. This approach to decision making was developed by Robert P. Bostrom and Victoria K. Clawson of Bostrom and Associates, Columbia, Missouri, and this exercise is based on a write-up appearing in *Inside USAA*, the company newsletter of the United Services Automobile Association (USAA) (September 11, 1996), pp. 8–10; and Victoria K. Clawson and Robert P. Bostrom, "Research-Driven Facilitation Training for Computer-Supported Environments," *Group Decision and Negotiation* 5 (1996): 7–29.

94. Based on information in Jeffrey L. Seglin, "The Savior Complex," *Inc.* (February 1999): 67–69; and Nora Johnson, "'He's Been Beating Me,' She Confided," *Business Ethics* (Summer 2001): 21.

Chapter 7
Designing Organization Structure

iStock.com/oscarhdez

Chapter Outline

Learning Outcomes

After studying this chapter, you should be able to:

7.1 Discuss the fundamental characteristics of organizing and explain division of labor, chain of command, span of management, and centralization versus decentralization.

7.2 Describe functional and divisional approaches to structure.

7.3 Explain the matrix approach to structure and its application to both domestic and international organizations.

7.4 Describe the contemporary team and virtual network structures and why they are being adopted by organizations.

7.5 Explain why organizations need coordination across departments and hierarchical levels, and describe mechanisms for achieving coordination.

7.6 Identify how structure can be used to achieve an organization's strategic goals.

7.7 Define *production technology* and explain how it influences organization structure.

Are You Ready to Be a Manager?

Before reading this chapter, please circle either "Mostly True" or "Mostly False" for each of the following five statements.

1 I'm comfortable taking on any authority that is given to me.

Mostly True ◀·····················▶ Mostly False

[page 232]

2 I'm able to delegate tasks to other people; in other words, I don't hold on with tight control or distrust of others.

Mostly True ◀·····················▶ Mostly False

[page 233]

3 I'm more capable of working in an organization that is decentralized with power and authority coming more from smaller units than from top management.

Mostly True ◀·····················▶ Mostly False

[page 235]

4 I think teams are a waste of time in organizations.

Mostly True ◀·····················▶ Mostly False

[page 244]

5 I believe all people would prefer to work out of their own home and be part of a virtual team.

Mostly True ◀·····················▶ Mostly False

[page 247]

Discover Your Management Approach

What Are Your Leadership Beliefs?[a]

Instructions: The fit between a new manager and the organization is often based on personal beliefs about the role of leaders. Things work best when organization design matches a new manager's beliefs about his or her leadership role.

Think about the extent to which each statement reflects your beliefs about a leader's role in an organization. Mark as Mostly True for the statements that are *most* true for you, and mark as Mostly False for that are *least* true for you.

	Mostly True	Mostly False
1. A leader should take charge of the group or organization.	_____	_____
2. The major tasks of a leader are to make and communicate decisions.	_____	_____
3. Group and organization members should be loyal to designated leaders.	_____	_____

To complete and score entire assessment, visit MindTap.

[a]This questionnaire is based on Richard M. Wielkiewicz, "The Leadership Attitudes and Beliefs Scale: An Instrument for Evaluating College Students' Thinking About Leadership and Organizations," *Journal of College Student Development* 41 (May–June 2000): 335–346.

In mid-2015, the business news was filled with speculation about the potential results of CEO Tony Hsieh's bold transformation of Zappos into a bossless company. Would Zappos continue to thrive, or would the lack of bosses lead to chaos and decline? To try to ensure that it's the former rather than the latter, managers at Zappos are likely still looking at how other companies have succeeded with a bossless approach to organization design. One of those companies is W. L. Gore and Associates, which was founded in 1958 by Bill Gore, who from the beginning wanted to "make sure that no one in his organization, including himself, would have the authority to kill a good idea or keep a bad idea alive." W. L. Gore, best known for Gore-Tex fabrics, has been operating without bosses ever since its founding. Gore designed the firm as a self-organizing network of teams rather than as a top-down hierarchy. People are accountable to their peers rather than to a supervisor. Today, Gore is a $3 billion company with 10,000 associates (as employees are called) in 30 countries. The company has made a profit every year since it began marketing its products and is one of only a handful of companies that have been on *Fortune* magazine's annual list of the "100 Best Companies to Work For" every year the list has been produced.[1]

Could you work in a company with no bosses, no permanent offices, and no clearly defined structure? As we've seen with examples in previous chapters, many companies are flattening their hierarchies and cutting out layers of management to improve efficiency and be more flexible. Some people thrive in less hierarchical, even bossless, organizations, whereas others have difficulty without a clearly defined vertical structure. Indeed, more than 200 people took severance pay and left Zappos rather than work in the new bossless structure at that company.[2] Research recently reported in *The Journal of Personality and Social Psychology* suggests that many people embrace hierarchies because they provide comfort in a chaotic world. In other words, people are naturally drawn to hierarchy because it lessens the stress of uncertainty.[3]

New managers in particular are typically more comfortable and more effective working in an organization system that is compatible with their leadership beliefs. In your career as a manager, you will have to understand and learn to work within a variety of structural configurations. All organizations wrestle with the question of structural design, and reorganization often is necessary to reflect a new strategy, changing market conditions, or innovative technology.

Visit MindTap for the "Self-Assessment: What Are Your Leadership Beliefs?" to see how your thinking aligns with different approaches to organization structure.

In recent years, many companies have realigned departmental groupings, chains of command, and horizontal coordination mechanisms to attain new strategic goals or to cope with a turbulent environment. For example, a new CEO at the British bank Standard Chartered restructured divisions from four to three and simplified reporting systems to cut costs, speed up decision making, and better respond to global customers in the shifting financial industry.[4] As sales of personal computers declined, managers at Dell created a separate division to focus specifically on products such as smartphones and other portable devices.[5] The giant oil company BP made significant structural changes after the disastrous 2010 explosion and oil spill in the Gulf of Mexico. To improve risk management and try to make sure a similar event never happens again, BP embarked on a major restructuring of its exploration, development, and production operations (referred to as "upstream") and appointed a dedicated chief executive for all of its upstream operations worldwide. In late 2012, following the appointment of H. Lamar McKay to oversee the operations, CEO Robert W. Dudley said, "During the past two years, we have successfully introduced a more centralized organization to our upstream, BP's largest organizational change for two decades."[6] Each of these organizations is using fundamental concepts of organizing.

HOT TOPIC

Organizing is the deployment of organizational resources to achieve strategic goals. The deployment of resources is reflected in the organization's division of labor into specific departments and jobs, formal lines of authority, and mechanisms for coordinating diverse organization tasks.

Organizing is important because it follows strategy—the topic of Part 3 of this book. Strategy defines *what* to do; organizing defines *how* to do it. Structure is a powerful tool for reaching strategic goals, and a strategy's success often is determined by its fit with organizational structure. Part 4 of this book explains the variety of organizing principles and concepts used by managers. This chapter covers fundamental concepts that apply to all organizations and departments, including organizing the vertical structure and using mechanisms for horizontal coordination. Later in this chapter, we discuss how organizations can be structured to facilitate innovation and change. Chapter 9 considers how to use human resources (HR) to the best advantage within the organization's structure.

7-1 Organizing the Vertical Structure

The organizing process leads to the creation of organization structure, which defines how tasks are divided and resources deployed. **Organization structure** is defined as (1) the set of formal tasks assigned to individuals and departments; (2) formal reporting relationships, including lines of authority, decision responsibility, number of hierarchical levels, and span of managers' control; and (3) the design of systems to ensure effective coordination of employees across departments.[7] Ensuring coordination across departments is just as critical as defining the departments to begin with. Without effective coordination systems, no structure is complete.

The set of formal tasks and formal reporting relationships provides a framework for vertical control of the organization. The characteristics of vertical structure are portrayed in the **organization chart**, which is the visual representation of an organization's structure.

A sample organization chart for a water bottling plant is illustrated in Exhibit 7.1. The plant has four major departments—accounting, HR, production, and marketing. The organization chart delineates the chain of command, indicates departmental tasks and how they fit together, and provides order and logic for the organization. Every employee has an appointed task, line of authority, and decision responsibility. The following sections discuss several important features of vertical structure in more detail.

7-1a Division of Labor

Organizations perform a wide variety of tasks. A fundamental principle is that work can be performed more efficiently if employees are allowed to specialize.[8] **Division of labor**, sometimes called *work specialization*, is the degree to which organizational tasks are subdivided into separate jobs. Division of labor in Exhibit 7.1 is illustrated by the separation of production tasks into bottling, quality control, and maintenance. Employees within each department perform only the tasks relevant to their specialized function. When organizations face new strategic issues, managers often create new positions or departments to deal with them. Sony added a new position of chief information security officer to its hierarchy after hackers accessed millions of customer files on the supposedly secure Sony network. However, that wasn't enough to prevent a massive 2014 hack of Sony Pictures Entertainment when a group calling itself the Guardians of Peace leaked confidential data about employees, embarrassing e-mail messages between executives and stars, copies of unreleased films, and other information and threatened retaliation unless Sony pulled its release of *The Interview*, a film that included a plot to assassinate North Korean leader Kim Jong-un. Managers at Sony and other studios are searching for mechanisms, including structural

Exhibit 7.1 Organization Chart for a Water Bottling Plant

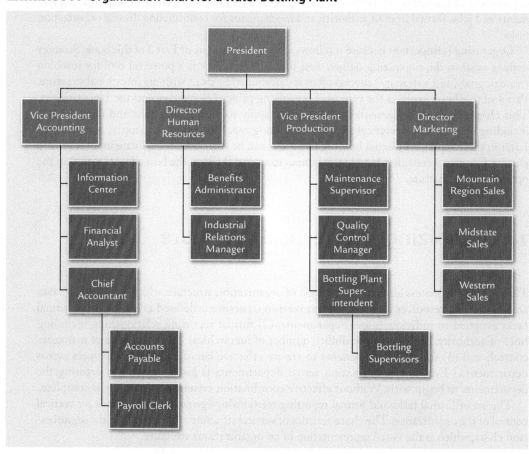

changes, that will beef up cybersecurity.[9] Many organizations, including Gannett, NBC, Simon & Schuster, Columbia University, and Starbucks, and cities, such as São Paolo, Brazil, and New York City, have created chief digital officer (CDO) positions to provide broad leadership for digital-based initiatives, including social business initiatives (as described in Chapter 2). Manufacturing companies have added chief technology officer (CTO) positions as digital technology becomes firmly implanted at the heart of today's sophisticated manufacturing operations. "We're no longer looking to operations for help," says Don Busiek, general manager of Operations Management, Manufacturing Software at General Electric (GE). "It's the CTO that has stepped up as the new hero on the plant floor."[10]

When division of labor is extensive, employees specialize in a single task. Jobs tend to be small, but they can be performed efficiently. Division of labor is readily visible on an automobile assembly line, where each employee performs the same task over and over again. It would not be efficient to have a single employee build the entire automobile, or even perform a large number of unrelated jobs.

Despite the apparent advantages of specialization, many organizations are moving away from this principle. With too much division of labor, employees are isolated and do only a single, boring job. In addition, too much specialization creates separation and hinders the coordination that is essential for organizations to be effective. Many companies are implementing teams and other mechanisms that enhance coordination and provide greater challenge for employees.

General Electric CEO Jeffrey Immelt evidently forgot he was supposed to be watching over resources, as described in this chapter's "Half-Baked Management" box.

Half-Baked Management

General Electric

When Jeffrey Immelt unexpectedly stepped down after 16 years as CEO of General Electric, *The Wall Street Journal* reported that GE had authorized an extra, a spare, company plane to follow Immelt's plane around on business trips, just in case that first plane (confusing, yes) had mechanical problems despite the fact GE was facing a stock slump with pressure to reduce costs.

Immelt claimed he did not know of the spare plane. Really? And you were CEO?

SOURCE: Thomas Gryta, "GE Board in Dark on CEO's Use of Extra Jet," *The Wall Street Journal*, October 30, 2017, B1.

Remember This

- Managers in every organization face the question about how to organize for maximum efficiency and effectiveness.
- **Organizing** refers to the deployment of organizational resources to achieve strategic goals.
- Organizations such as Simon & Schuster, Starbucks, and the City of New York have created CDO positions to meet changing needs.
- **Organization structure** is defined as the framework in which the organization defines how tasks are divided, resources are deployed, and departments are coordinated.
- An **organization chart** is the visual representation of an organization's structure.
- Fundamental characteristics of vertical organization structure include division of labor, span of management, and centralization and decentralization.
- **Division of labor**, sometimes called *work specialization*, is the degree to which organizational tasks are subdivided into individual jobs.

An organization's structure is based on authority. As a potential new manager, visit MindTap for the "Self-Assessment: What Kind of Authority Did Your Parents Use?" to check out your authority role models.

7-1b Chain of Command

The **chain of command** is an unbroken line of authority that links all employees in an organization and shows who reports to whom. It is associated with two underlying principles. *Unity of command* means that each employee is held accountable to only one supervisor. The *scalar principle* refers to a clearly defined line of authority in the organization that includes all employees. Authority and responsibility for different tasks should be distinct. All individuals in the organization should know to whom they report, as well as the successive management levels all the way to the top. For example, at Standard Chartered Bank, described earlier, managers of the business lines report directly to the CEO. Chief digital officers often report to a chief information officer, who in turn reports to the CEO.[11] In Exhibit 7.1, the payroll clerk reports to the chief accountant, who in turn reports to the vice president, who in turn reports to the company president.

Authority, Responsibility, and Delegation   The chain of command illustrates the authority structure of the organization. **Authority** is the formal and legitimate right of a manager to make decisions, issue orders, and allocate resources to achieve organizationally desired outcomes. Authority is distinguished by three characteristics:[12]

1.   *Authority is vested in organizational positions, not people*. Managers have authority because of the positions they hold, and other people in the same positions would have the same authority.

2.   *Authority flows down the vertical hierarchy*. Positions at the top of the hierarchy are vested with more formal authority than are positions at the bottom.

3.   *Authority is accepted by subordinates*. Although authority flows from the top down, subordinates comply because they believe managers have a legitimate right to issue orders. The *acceptance theory of authority* argues that a manager has authority only if subordinates choose to accept his or her commands. If subordinates refuse to obey because the order is outside their zone of acceptance, a manager's authority disappears.[13]

Responsibility is the flip side of the authority coin. **Responsibility** is the duty to perform the task or activity as assigned. Typically, managers are assigned authority commensurate with their responsibilities. When managers have responsibility for task outcomes but little authority, the job is possible but difficult. In this situation, managers rely on persuasion and luck. When managers have authority that exceeds responsibility, they may become tyrants and use authority to achieve frivolous outcomes.[14]

Accountability is the mechanism through which authority and responsibility are brought into alignment. **Accountability** means that the people with authority and responsibility are subject to reporting and justifying task outcomes to those above them in the chain of command.[15] For organizations to function well, everyone needs to know what they are accountable for and accept the responsibility and authority for performing it. Top executives at the British Broadcasting Corporation (BBC) undertook structural changes to clarify the chain of command and strengthen management accountability in the wake of a crisis that erupted after the BBC decided not to air a news report about former BBC television personality Jimmy Savile being accused of widespread sexual abuse of children. To make matters worse, the broadcaster got into trouble again by airing a false report that accused a former senior political official of similar offenses. The resulting scandal tarnished the image of the respected broadcaster and left the executive offices of the BBC in turmoil. The director-general resigned after just two months on the job, and two senior executives resigned under pressure while the organization sorted out what went wrong. New director-general Tony Hall emphasized the need to change the culture at the BBC, calling for "greater personal accountability" and a simpler, clearer management structure. Many problems contributed to the crisis, but one

HOT TOPIC

AP Images/Rich Schultz

Concept Connection

Cognizant Technology Solutions Corporation, a U.S.-based outsourcing firm, has an unusual **chain of command** referred to as "two in a box." Originally, project managers supervised company staff in India while living in the United States, where most customers were located. Because spanning that many time zones was difficult, CEO Francisco D'Souza implemented a solution: assign two managers to each project—one in India and one at the client's site. Each is equally responsible for the project's success. The model works because it enhances the company's customer responsiveness, even though it violates the principle of **unity of command**.

was a fuzzy chain of command without clear lines of authority for decision making. After the Savile crisis, the editorial leadership was under extreme pressure, and there was confusion over who had responsibility for the decision to run the story about the senior political official, for instance.[16]

Another important concept related to authority is delegation.[17] **Delegation** is the process that managers use to transfer authority and responsibility to positions below them in the hierarchy. Most organizations today encourage managers to delegate authority to the lowest possible level to provide maximum flexibility to meet customer needs and adapt to shifts in the environment. Delegating decision making to lower-level managers and employees can be highly motivating and improve speed, flexibility, and creativity. However, many managers find delegation difficult. When managers can't delegate, they undermine the role of their subordinates and prevent people from doing their jobs effectively.

An important distinction in many organizations is between line authority and staff authority, which reflects whether managers work in line departments or staff departments in the organization's structure. *Line departments* perform tasks that reflect the organization's primary goal and mission. In a software company, line departments make and sell the product. In an Internet-based company, line departments would be those that develop and manage online offerings and sales. *Staff departments* include all those that provide specialized skills in support of line departments. Staff departments have an advisory relationship with line departments and typically include marketing, labor relations, research, accounting, and HR.

Line authority means that people in management positions have the formal authority to direct and control immediate subordinates. **Staff authority** is narrower and includes the right to advise, recommend, and counsel in the staff specialists' area of expertise. Staff authority is a communication relationship; staff specialists advise managers in technical areas. For example, the finance department of a manufacturing firm would have staff authority to coordinate with line departments about which accounting forms to use to facilitate equipment purchases and standardize payroll services.

To understand the importance of the chain of command and clear lines of authority, responsibility, and delegation, consider the BP-Transocean *Deepwater Horizon* oil rig explosion that killed 11 crew members and set off an environmental disaster. Activities were so loosely organized that no one seemed to know who was in charge or what their level of authority and responsibility was. When the explosion occurred, confusion reigned. Twenty-three-year-old Andrea Fleytas issued a mayday (distress signal) over the radio when she realized that no one else had done so, but she was chastised for overstepping her authority. One manager said he didn't call for help because he wasn't sure he had authorization to do so. Still another said he tried to call to shore but was told that the order needed to come from someone else. Crew members knew that an emergency shutdown needed to be triggered, but there was confusion over who had the authority to give the OK. As fire spread, several minutes passed before people got directions to evacuate. Again, an alarmed Fleytas turned on the public address system and announced that the crew was abandoning the rig. "The scene was very chaotic," said worker Carlos Ramos. "There was no chain of command. Nobody in charge." In the aftermath of the explosion and oil spill, several federal agencies were also on the hot seat because of loose oversight and confusion over responsibility that led to delays and disagreements that prolonged the suffering of local communities.[18]

BP has a new safety department, created in the wake of the *Deepwater Horizon* disaster, that advises managers in line departments regarding risk management, agreements with contractors, and other safety-related issues. Unlike many staff departments, BP's safety unit has broad power to challenge line managers' decisions if it considers them too risky.[19]

7-1c Span of Management

The **span of management** is the number of employees reporting to a supervisor. Sometimes called the *span of control*, this characteristic of structure determines how closely a supervisor can monitor subordinates. Traditional views of organization design recommended a span of management of about 7 to 10 subordinates per manager. However, many lean organizations today have spans of management numbering 30, 40, and even higher. At PepsiCo, Inc.'s Gamesa cookie

> "I think the most difficult transition for anybody from being a worker bee to a manager is this issue of delegation. What do you give up? How can you have the team do what you would do yourself without you doing it?"
>
> —TACHI YAMADA, EXECUTIVE VICE PRESIDENT AND BOARD MEMBER, TAKEDA PHARMACEUTICALS LINE AND STAFF AUTHORITY

HOT TOPIC

operation in Mexico, for instance, employees are trained to keep production running smoothly and are rewarded for quality, teamwork, and productivity. Teams are so productive and efficient that Gamesa factories operate with around 56 subordinates per manager.[20] Research over the past 40 or so years shows that span of management varies widely and that several factors influence the span.[21] Generally, when supervisors must be closely involved with subordinates, the span should be small, and when supervisors need little involvement with subordinates, it can be large. The following list describes the factors that are associated with less supervisor involvement and thus larger spans of control:

- Work performed by subordinates is stable and routine.
- Subordinates perform similar work tasks.
- Subordinates are concentrated in a single location.
- Subordinates are highly trained and need little direction in performing tasks.
- Rules and procedures defining task activities are available.
- Support systems and personnel are available for the manager.
- Little time is required in nonsupervisory activities, such as coordination with other departments or planning.
- Managers' personal preferences and styles favor a large span.

The average span of control used in an organization determines whether the structure is tall or flat. A **tall structure** has an overall narrow span and more hierarchical levels. A **flat structure** has a wide span, is horizontally dispersed, and has fewer hierarchical levels.

Having too many hierarchical levels and narrow spans of control is a common structural problem for organizations. In a survey conducted for the Conference Board, 72 percent of managers surveyed said that they believed their organizations had too many levels of management.[22] At the British engineering group Rolls Royce, top executives recently cut a layer of management as part of a broad restructuring.

Reducing management levels is often a part of efforts to increase decision-making speed and efficiency. In addition, the trend in recent years has been toward wider spans of control as a way to facilitate delegation.[23] When organizations have too many management levels, routine decisions are made too high in the organization, which pulls higher-level executives away from important, long-range strategic issues and limits the creativity, innovativeness, and accountability of lower-level managers.[24]

Sunny Side Up   Rolls Royce

One of the first moves Warren East made after taking over as CEO of Rolls Royce was to reduce management levels as a way to speed decision making and cut costs. The engineering firm Rolls Royce was separated from the luxury car brand of the same name in the 1970s and became one of the most prominent engineering companies in Britain. It makes the reactors for Britain's fleet of nuclear submarines and currently holds a contract to develop a new generation of Trident submarines to be equipped with nuclear missiles. Profits were growing until 2013, but the company has recently struggled against increasing competition and weaker demand in some of its markets, along with cuts in British military spending.

When East took the CEO position in 2015, he quickly began making structural changes to try to turn the business around. He cut an entire level of senior management, saying that without the extra layer of management, a week would be saved for every month it took to make a decision. The heads of the five units—civil aero-engines, defense, nuclear, marine, and power systems—will now report directly to East. The restructuring also did away with the aerospace and land and sea divisions.

The structural changes are part of a broader plan aimed at cutting up to $300 million in annual operating costs. East believes Rolls Royce's world-class engineering capability, combined with lower costs, greater efficiency, and faster decision making, will mean a bright future for the company.[25]

One study found that the span of management for CEOs has doubled over the past two decades, rising from about 5 to around 10 managers who report directly to the top executive, with the span of management for those managers also increasing.[26] At the same time, the types of positions in the top team are shifting, with the position of chief operating officer (COO) declining and positions such as CIO, CTO, or chief marketing officer being added to the top team.[27] A number of factors may influence a top executive's optimum span of control. People who are new to their positions typically want a wider span of control to help them evaluate their executives and learn about more aspects of the business. A CEO who must spend a lot of time interacting directly with customers, partners, or regulators as part of his or her job will need a narrower span of control, allocating more responsibility to direct reports and freeing up more time for external activities, while a CEO involved in a major internal transformation may need a wider span of control to stay on top of what is happening all across the organization.[28] Exhibit 7.2 illustrates how an international metals company was reorganized. The multilevel set of managers shown in panel (a) was replaced with 10 operating managers and 9 staff specialists reporting directly to the CEO, as shown in panel (b). The CEO welcomed this wide span of 19 management subordinates because it fit his style, his management team was top notch and needed little supervision, and all members were all located on the same floor of an office building.

7-1d Centralization and Decentralization

Centralization and decentralization pertain to the hierarchical level at which decisions are made. **Centralization** means that decision authority is located near the top of the organization. With **decentralization**, decision authority is pushed downward to lower organization levels. Organizations may have to experiment to find the correct hierarchical level at which to make decisions. For example, most large school systems are highly centralized. However, a study by William Ouchi found that three large urban school systems that shifted to a decentralized structure (giving school principals and teachers more control over staffing, scheduling, and teaching methods and materials) performed better and more efficiently than centralized systems of similar size.[29] Government leaders in Great Britain hope the same thing will happen with decentralization of the country's National Health Service (NHS). The system is undergoing the most radical restructuring since it was founded in 1948, with a key part of the plan to shift control of the annual health care budget to doctors at the local level. Leaders believe decentralization will cut

Exhibit 7.2   **Reorganization to Increase the Span of Management for the President of an International Metals Company**

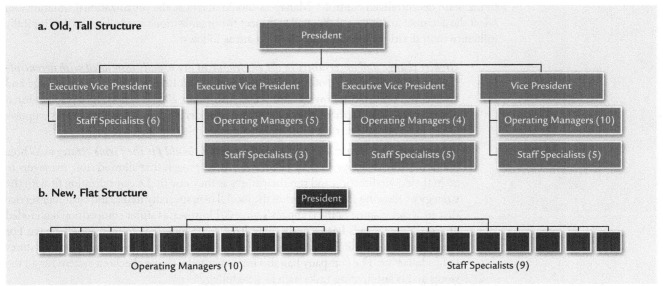

Green Power

Green-Rating the Produce As Whole Foods Market began centralizing the procurement of more of the items it sells in its stores, the upscale grocery chain also introduced a program that gives shoppers more information about what they're buying for their families. Through the "Responsibly Grown" program, Whole Foods will rate fruits, vegetables, and flowers as *good*, *better*, or *best*, depending on issues such as how the suppliers handle plastic waste, how farm workers are treated, and whether conservation areas are provided to foster bees, butterflies, and other pollinators. The program also looks at concerns such as water conservation, greenhouse gases, and soil health. Along with a program that rates the animal welfare practices of meat suppliers, the Responsibly Grown program is aimed at encouraging farmers to consider the effects of their growing and production activities on the environment and human health.

SOURCE: Stephanie Strom, "Whole Foods to Rate Its Produce and Flowers for Environmental Impact," *The New York Times*, October 15, 2014.

costs, simplify and streamline procedures, and reduce inefficiency by "putting power in the hands of patients and clinicians."[30]

In the United States and Canada, the trend over the past 30 years has been toward greater decentralization of organizations. Decentralization is believed to relieve the burden on top managers, make greater use of employees' skills and abilities, ensure that decisions are made close to the action by well-informed people, and permit more rapid response to external changes. Even Japanese companies such as Toyota, which have a strong tradition of centralization, are seeing the power of decentralization for promoting a sense of ownership among employees. "We didn't have to go back to Japan for approval on everything," said Randy Stephens, the chief engineer at the Toyota Technical Center near Ann Arbor, Michigan, where the new version of the Avalon was designed and engineered. "We might go back to review the status of the project, but there is a feeling of ownership of this car here." Toyota was strongly criticized for its need to coordinate with headquarters every decision regarding a spate of safety issues and recalls in 2009–2011. Executives have since overhauled the quality control process and decentralized more decision making to regional managers in charge of safety in North America, Europe, and Asia.[31]

However, not every organization should decentralize all decisions. Within many companies, there is often a "tug of war between centralization and decentralization," as top executives want to centralize some operations to eliminate duplication while business division managers want to maintain decentralized control.[32] Managers should diagnose the organizational situation and select the decision-making level that will best meet the organization's needs. Factors that typically influence centralization versus decentralization are as follows:

- *Greater change and uncertainty in the environment are usually associated with decentralization.* A good example of how decentralization can help cope with rapid change and uncertainty occurred following Hurricane Katrina in 2005. Mississippi Power restored power in just 12 days, thanks largely to a decentralized management system that empowered people at the electrical substations to make rapid, on-the-spot decisions.[33]

- *The amount of centralization or decentralization should fit the firm's strategy.* Whole Foods has thrived for years with a decentralized approach that allowed store managers to go in their own direction and run their stores as they saw fit. Decentralization fit with the strategy of allowing stores to provide the local flavor, specialty items, and customer service that are a cornerstone of the company's success. However, as stiffer competition has eroded profits, Whole Foods has recently centralized some functions to increase efficiency. For example, the responsibility for purchasing many items has been shifted from the stores to headquarters. The company has also implemented a single checkout system for all the stores and is automating tasks such as scheduling.[34]

- *In times of crisis or risk of company failure, authority may be centralized at the top.* Recall our example of how BP has centralized its exploration, development, and production operations so that a single executive is in charge of the upstream operations. Previously, three executives handled the upstream unit, but BP CEO Robert Dudley believed a strong centralized structure was needed to manage risk. After a rash of food-borne illnesses was linked to Chipotle Mexican Grill, managers have shifted to centralized purchase and production of some food items to maintain stronger control and show a commitment to new safety goals, as discussed in Chapter 5. CEO Steve Ells said products such as tomatoes, cilantro, and lettuce will now be tested for microbes and diced, sanitized, and hermetically sealed in a central kitchen and then shipped to restaurants.[35]

Remember This

- The **chain of command** is an unbroken line of authority that links all individuals in the organization and specifies who reports to whom.

- **Authority** is the formal and legitimate right of a manager to make decisions, issue orders, and allocate resources to achieve outcomes desired by the organization.

- **Responsibility** is the flip side of the authority coin; it refers to the duty to perform the task or activity that one has been assigned.

- **Accountability** means that people with authority and responsibility are subject to reporting and justifying task outcomes to those above them in the chain of command.

- When managers transfer authority and responsibility to positions below them in the hierarchy, it is called **delegation**.

- Managers may have **line authority**, which refers to the formal power to direct and control immediate

subordinates, or **staff authority**, which refers to the right to advise, counsel, and recommend in the manager's area of expertise.

- **Span of management**, sometimes called *span of control*, refers to the number of employees reporting to a supervisor.

- A **tall structure** is characterized by an overall narrow span of management and a relatively large number of hierarchical levels.

- A **flat structure** is characterized by an overall broad span of management and relatively few hierarchical levels.

- The trend is toward broader spans of management and greater decentralization.

- **Decentralization** means that decision authority is pushed down to lower organization levels.

- **Centralization** means that decision authority is located near top organization levels.

7-2 Departmentalization

Another fundamental characteristic of organization structure is **departmentalization**, which is the basis for grouping positions into departments and departments into the total organization. Managers make choices about how to use the chain of command to group people together to perform their work. Five approaches to structural design reflect different uses of the chain of command in departmentalization, as illustrated in Exhibit 7.3. The functional, divisional, and matrix are traditional approaches that rely on the chain of command to define departmental groupings and reporting relationships along the hierarchy. Two innovative approaches that have emerged to meet changing organizational needs in a turbulent global environment are the use of teams and virtual networks.

The basic difference among structures (illustrated in Exhibit 7.3) is the way in which employees are departmentalized and to whom they report.[36] Each structural approach is described in detail in the next sections.

Exhibit 7.3 Five Approaches to Structural Design

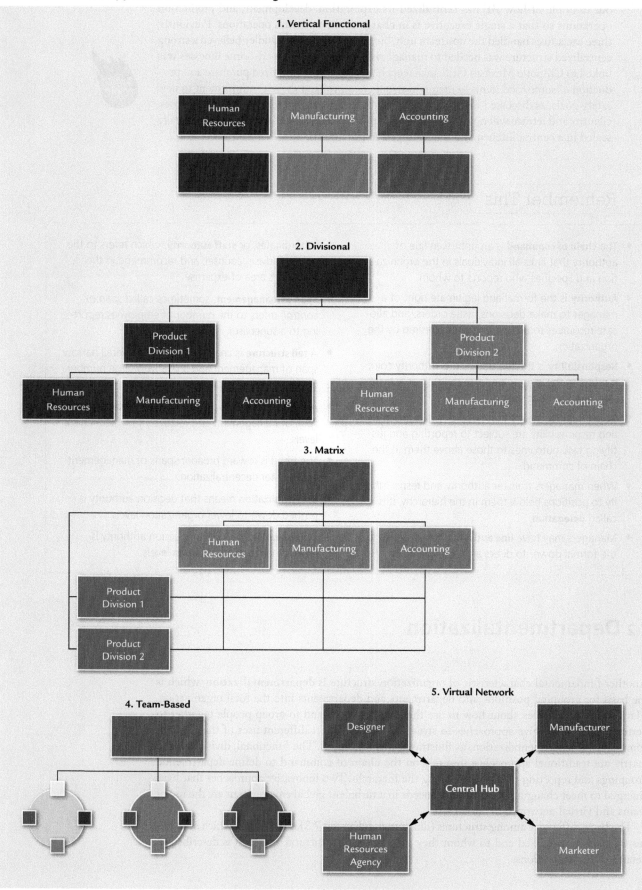

7-2a Vertical Functional Approach

In a **functional structure**, also called a *U-form* (*unitary structure*), activities are grouped together by common function from the bottom to the top of the organization.[37] The functional structure groups positions into departments based on similar skills, expertise, work activities, and resource use. A functional structure can be thought of as departmentalization by organizational resources because each type of functional activity—accounting, HR, engineering, and manufacturing—represents specific resources for performing the organization's task. People, facilities, and other resources representing a common function are grouped into a single department. One example is Blue Bell Creameries, which relies on in-depth expertise in its various functional departments to produce high-quality ice cream for a limited regional market. Blue Bell has functional departments such as sales, production, quality control, maintenance, distribution, research and development (R&D), and finance. The quality control department, for example, tests all incoming ingredients and also tests outgoing products. Because of their years of experience, quality inspectors can detect the slightest deviation from expected quality. However, after the Centers for Disease Control and Prevention (CDC) linked Blue Bell ice cream to a number of listeriosis cases, including three deaths, Blue Bell was forced to shut down production in April 2015 and recall all its products from 23 states. Managers have committed to stringent new safety procedures, including that all ice cream be sampled and found bacteria-free before being released for sale. Blue Bell is also dialing back on the number of states the company will serve, and it plans to expand slowly over the next several years to 15 states.[38]

How It Works   Refer to Exhibit 7.1 for an example of a functional structure. The major departments under the president are groupings of similar expertise and resources, such as accounting, HR, production, and marketing. Each of the functional departments is concerned with the organization as a whole. The marketing department is responsible for all sales and marketing, for example, and the accounting department handles financial issues for the entire company.

The functional structure is a strong vertical design. Information flows up and down the vertical hierarchy, and the chain of command converges at the top of the organization. In a functional structure, people within a department communicate primarily with others in the same department to coordinate work and accomplish tasks or implement decisions that are passed down the hierarchy. Managers and employees are compatible because of similar training and expertise. Typically, rules and procedures govern the duties and responsibilities of each employee, and employees at lower hierarchical levels accept the right of those higher in the hierarchy to make decisions and issue orders.

Functional Advantages and Disadvantages   Grouping employees by common task permits economies of scale and efficient resource use. For example, at AustralianSuper, a large superannuation (pension) firm, all employees who deal with legal, compliance, and financial matters work in the same Corporate Services department.[39] They have the expertise and skills to handle almost any issue related to legal and financial matters for the organization. Large, functionally based departments enhance the development of in-depth skills because people work on a variety of related problems and are associated with other experts within their own department. Because the chain of command converges at the top, the functional structure also offers a way to centralize decision making and provide unified direction from top managers. The primary disadvantages reflect barriers that exist across departments. Because people are separated into distinct departments, communication and

Concept Connection

The Internal Revenue Service (IRS) is the U.S. government agency we all love to hate. When managers set out to improve service to the nation's taxpayers, they undertook a massive reorganization into a customer-focused **divisional structure**. The IRS structure is strategically designed to provide better information and assistance to different taxpayer groups, such as large corporations, small businesses and self-employed individuals, and tax-exempt organizations.

Pgiam/Getty Images

coordination across functions are often poor, causing a slow response to environmental changes. Innovation and change require involvement of several departments. Another problem is that decisions involving more than one department may pile up at the top of the organization and be delayed. For example, the problems at Blue Bell Creamery described earlier could be partly due to poor coordination among departments and slow decision making regarding how to address the issue.

7-2b Divisional Approach

In contrast to the functional approach, in which people are grouped by common skills and resources, the **divisional structure** occurs when departments are grouped together based on similar organizational outputs. With a divisional structure, also called an *M-form* (*multidivisional*) or a *decentralized form*, separate divisions can be organized with responsibility for individual products, services, product groups, major projects or programs, divisions, businesses, or profit centers.[40] The divisional structure is also sometimes called a *product structure, program structure*, or *self-contained unit structure*. Each of these terms means essentially the same thing: Diverse departments are brought together to produce a single organizational output, whether it is a product, a program, or service to a single customer.

Most large corporations have separate divisions that perform different tasks, use different technologies, or serve different customers. When a large organization produces products or services for different markets, the divisional structure works because each division is an autonomous business. For example, Walmart uses three major divisions for Wal-Mart Stores, Sam's Club (U.S.), and International Stores. Each of these three large divisions is further subdivided into smaller geographical divisions to better serve customers in different regions.[41] The "Sunny Side Up" box describes a new divisional structure Google is using to make sure it keeps pace in the fast-moving technology industry.

Like Google, many companies shift to a divisional structure when they become so large that the disadvantages of a functional structure become too great. "There can be a lot of cross-company confusion when companies get too big, and this will allow people to build the right set of products for the right users without worrying about interference from other groups inside the company," said a veteran Google manager.[42]

Sunny Side Up } Google

Google is still best known for Internet search, but the company founded by Larry Page and Sergey Brin in 1998 does a lot more today, which is reflected in a new organization structure cofounder Larry Page initiated a couple of years ago.

Google is now a division of Alphabet, Inc., a new parent company Page created to separate the core businesses, such as Internet search, the Android operating system, and YouTube, from newer unrelated businesses such as Verily, a health and biotechnology company, and Nest Labs, which makes connected-home devices such as the Nest Internet-connected thermostat. Each of the new divisions has its own CEO and operates independently. For example, all functional managers at Nest report to CEO Tony Fadell, while all functional managers

in the Verily division (formerly Google Life Sciences) report to Verily CEO Andrew Conrad. Functional managers in the Google division report to CEO Sundar Pichai, who was appointed by Page as the new top leader of Google when Alphabet was created. Google is the largest division and includes search, Internet advertising, YouTube, and Android. Page serves as CEO of the parent company.

Page and other top managers see the new divisional structure as a way to make sure each smaller company can be more entrepreneurial and innovative and move more quickly. "It gets a little faster, more efficient, and a little more independent," said the CEO of Verily. "I act as a CEO of an independent company instead of a senior executive within a large company."[43]

How It Works   Functional and divisional structures are illustrated in Exhibit 7.4. In a divisional structure, divisions are created as self-contained units, with separate functional departments for each division. For example, in Exhibit 7.4, each functional department resource needed to produce the product is assigned to each division. Whereas in a functional structure, all R&D engineers are grouped together and work on all products, in a divisional structure, separate R&D departments are created within each division. Each department is smaller and focuses on a single product line or customer segment. Departments are duplicated across product lines.

The primary difference between divisional and functional structures is that in a divisional structure, the chain of command from each function converges lower in the hierarchy. In a divisional structure, differences of opinion among R&D, marketing, manufacturing, and finance would be resolved at the divisional level rather than by the top executive (president in Exhibit 7.4). Thus, the divisional structure encourages decentralization. Decision making is pushed down at least one level in the hierarchy, freeing the president and other top managers for strategic planning. Only if the divisions can't agree, fail to coordinate, or start making decisions that hurt the organization are some decisions pulled back up to the top.

Geographic- or Customer-Based Divisions   An alternative for assigning divisional responsibility is to group company activities by geographic region or customer group. A global geographic structure is illustrated in Exhibit 7.5. In a geographic-based structure, all functions in a specific country or region report to the same division manager. The structure focuses company activities on local market conditions. Competitive advantage may come from the production or sale of a product or service adapted to a given country or region. Walt Disney Company CEO Bob Iger reorganized the Disney Channel into geographic divisions because what appeals to people in different countries varies. Studio executives in Burbank, California, were miffed at the reorganization, but it has paid off. Iger learned that the No. 1 program on Italy's Disney Channel was one that he had never heard of—*Il Mondo di Patty*, an inexpensive, telenovela-style show about an Argentine girl. "It's important that Disney's products are presented in ways that are culturally relevant," Iger said about the geographic reorganization.[44] Large nonprofit organizations such as the National Council of YMCAs, Habitat for Humanity International, and the Girl Scouts of the USA also frequently use a type of geographic structure, with a central headquarters and semiautonomous local units.[45]

Divisional Advantages and Disadvantages   By dividing employees and resources along divisional lines, the organization will be flexible and responsive to change because each unit is small and tuned in to its environment. Because employees work on a single product line, their

Exhibit 7.4 Functional versus Divisional Structures

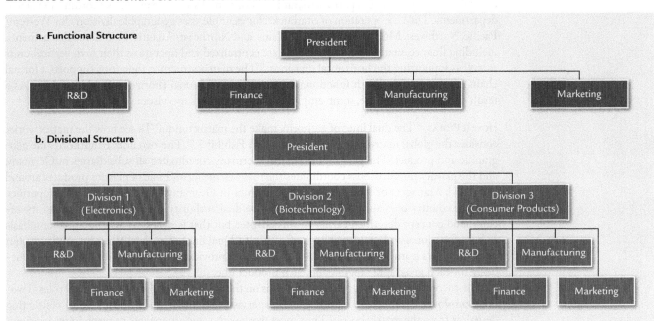

Exhibit 7.5 **Geographic-Based Global Organization Structure**

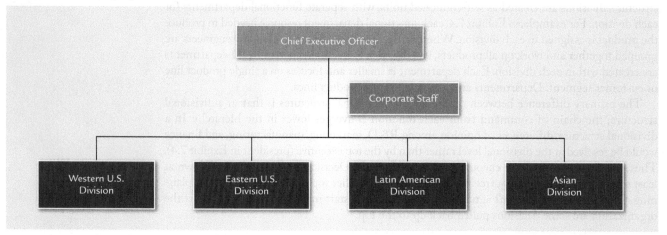

concern for customers' needs is high. Coordination across functional departments is better because employees are grouped together in a single location and committed to one product line. Great coordination exists within divisions; however, coordination *across* divisions is often poor. Problems can occur when autonomous divisions go in opposite directions. Another major disadvantage is duplication of resources and the high cost of running separate divisions. Instead of a single research department in which all research people use a single facility, each division could have its own research facility. The organization loses efficiency and economies of scale. In addition, the small size of departments within each division could result in a lack of technical specialization, expertise, and training.

7-2c Matrix Approach

The **matrix approach** combines aspects of both functional and divisional structures simultaneously, in the same part of the organization. The matrix structure evolved as a way to improve horizontal coordination and information sharing.[46] One unique feature of the matrix is that it has dual lines of authority. In Exhibit 7.6, the functional hierarchy of authority runs vertically, and the divisional hierarchy of authority runs horizontally. The vertical structure provides traditional control within functional departments, and the horizontal structure provides coordination across departments. The U.S. operation of Starbucks, for example, uses geographic divisions for Western/Pacific, Northwest/Mountain, Southeast/Plains, and Northeast/Atlantic. Functional departments, including finance, marketing, and so forth, are centralized and operate as their own vertical units as well as supporting the horizontal divisions.[47] The matrix structure, therefore, supports a formal chain of command for both functional (vertical) and divisional (horizontal) relationships. As a result of this dual structure, some employees report to two supervisors simultaneously.

How It Works   The dual lines of authority make the matrix unique. To see how the matrix works, consider the global matrix structure illustrated in Exhibit 7.7. The two lines of authority are geographic and product. The geographic boss in Germany coordinates all subsidiaries in Germany, and the plastics products boss coordinates the manufacturing and sale of plastics products around the world. Managers of local subsidiary companies in Germany would report to two superiors, both the country boss and the product boss. The dual authority structure violates the unity-of-command concept described earlier in this chapter, but that is necessary to give equal emphasis to both functional and divisional lines of authority. Dual lines of authority can be confusing, but after managers learn to use this structure, the matrix provides excellent coordination simultaneously for each geographic region and each product line.

The success of the matrix structure depends on the abilities of people in key matrix roles. **Two-boss employees**, those who report to two supervisors simultaneously, must resolve conflicting demands from the matrix bosses. They must work with senior managers to reach joint decisions.

Exhibit 7.6 Dual-Authority Structure in a Matrix Organization

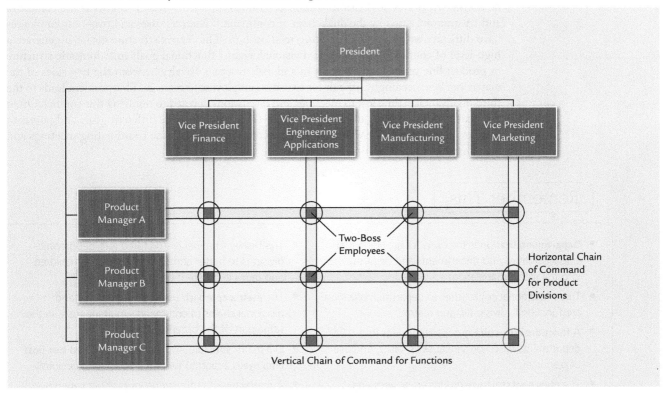

Exhibit 7.7 Global Matrix Structure

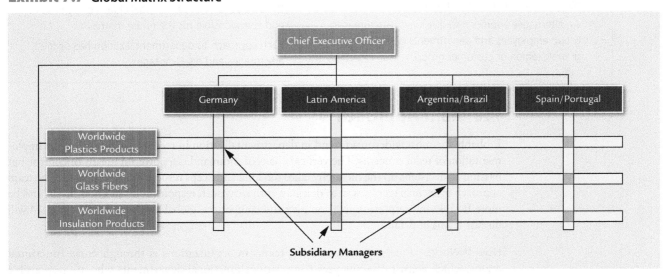

They need excellent human relations skills with which to confront managers and resolve conflicts. The **matrix boss** is the product or functional boss, who is responsible for one side of the matrix. The top leader is responsible for the entire matrix. The **top leader** oversees both the product and functional chains of command. His or her responsibility is to maintain a power balance between the two sides of the matrix. If disputes arise between them, the problem will be kicked upstairs to the top leader.

Matrix Advantages and Disadvantages The matrix can be highly effective in a complex, rapidly changing environment in which the organization needs to be flexible, innovative, and adaptable.[48] The conflict and frequent meetings generated by the matrix allow new issues to be raised and resolved. The matrix structure makes efficient use of HR because specialists can be transferred from one division to another. A major problem with the matrix is the confusion and frustration caused by the dual chain of command.[49] Matrix bosses and two-boss employees have difficulty with the dual reporting relationships. The matrix structure also can generate a high level of conflict because it pits divisional against functional goals in a domestic structure or product line versus country goals in a global structure. Rivalry between the two sides of the matrix can be exceedingly difficult for two-boss employees to manage. This problem leads to the third disadvantage: time lost to meetings and discussions devoted to resolving this conflict. Often the matrix structure leads to more discussion than action because different goals and points of view are being addressed. Managers may spend a great deal of time coordinating meetings and assignments, which takes time away from core work activities.

Remember This

- **Departmentalization** is the basis for grouping individual positions into departments and departments into the total organization.

- Three traditional approaches to departmentalization are functional, divisional, and matrix.

- A **functional structure** groups employees into departments based on similar skills, tasks, and use of resources.

- The **divisional structure** groups employees and departments based on similar organizational outputs (products or services), such that each division has a mix of functional skills and tasks.

- An alternative approach to divisional structure is to group employees and departments based on geographic region or customer group.

- The Disney Channel is structured into geographic divisions to better address the interests of children and teens in different parts of the world.

- The **matrix approach** uses both functional and divisional chains of command simultaneously, in the same part of the organization.

- In a matrix structure, some employees, called **two-boss employees**, report to two supervisors simultaneously.

- A **matrix boss** is a functional or product supervisor responsible for one side of the matrix.

- In a matrix structure, the **top leader** oversees both the product and the functional chains of command and is responsible for the entire matrix.

- Each approach to departmentalization has distinct advantages and disadvantages.

7-2d Team Approach

Probably the most widespread trend in departmentalization in recent years has been the implementation of team concepts. The vertical chain of command is a powerful means of control, but passing all decisions up the hierarchy takes too long and keeps responsibility at the top. The team approach gives managers a way to delegate authority, push responsibility to lower levels, and be more flexible and responsive in a complex and competitive global environment. Chapter 14 will discuss teams in detail.

How It Works   One approach to using teams in organizations is through **cross-functional teams**, which consist of employees from various functional departments who are responsible to meet as a team and resolve mutual problems. For example, at Total Attorneys, a Chicago-based company that provides cloud-based software and services to small law firms, founder and former CEO Ed Scanlan realized that the functional structure, which broke projects down into sequential stages that moved from one department to another, was slowing things down so much that clients' needs had sometimes changed by the time the product was completed. He solved this problem by creating small, cross-functional teams to increase horizontal coordination. Now, designers, coders, and quality-assurance testers work closely together on each project.[50] Cross-functional teams can provide needed horizontal coordination to complement an existing divisional or functional structure. A frequent use of cross-functional teams is for change projects, such as new product or service innovation. Team members typically still report to their functional departments, but they also report to the team, one member of whom may be the leader.

The second approach is to use **permanent teams**, groups of employees who are organized in a way similar to a formal department. Each team brings together employees from all functional areas focused on a specific task or project, such as parts supply and logistics for an automobile plant. Emphasis is on horizontal communication and information sharing because representatives from all functions are coordinating their work and skills to complete a specific organizational task. Authority is pushed down to lower levels, and frontline employees are often given the freedom to make decisions and take action on their own. Team members may share or rotate team leadership. With a **team-based structure**, the entire organization is made up of horizontal teams that coordinate their work and work directly with customers to accomplish the organization's goals. At Zappos, for example, the traditional hierarchy has been replaced with a series of overlapping, self-directed teams, which Zappos calls *circles*. At Zappos, employees don't have traditional bosses or job titles. They are assigned to several roles and may be a part of several different circles at any one time.[51]

Part 4 of Exhibit 7.3 illustrates a basic team-based structure. However, in addition to having close interactions among team members, organizations that fully implement a team-based structure also make sure the interactions among various teams are robust and frequent, as illustrated in Exhibit 7.8. China's Haier Group provides an excellent illustration of how multiple-function teams can interact in a team-based structure.

By decentralizing decision making; breaking down "the invisible walls," as Zhang calls the barriers between functions; and linking employees directly with customers, the team-based structure enables Haier to respond extremely quickly to changing consumer

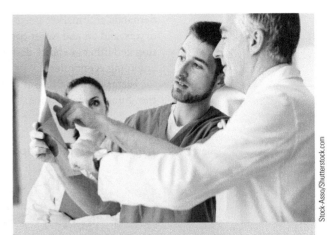

Stock-Asso/Shutterstock.com

Concept Connection

Hospitals and other health care providers face a great need for **horizontal coordination** because medical care needs to be integrated. For instance, collaborative care, like this **cross-functional team** of a nurse, doctor, and dietitian, helps patients with chronic illnesses require fewer emergency department visits. Rush University Medical Center in Chicago started its Virtual Integrated Practice (VIP) project to give physicians in private practice access to teams of physicians, dieticians, pharmacists, and social workers. VIP replicates the collaboration that can occur in a hospital setting by enabling members to share information via e-mail, phone, and fax.

Sunny Side Up   > Haier Group

When Zhang Ruimin took over as CEO of Haier Group, the company was in such dire straits that many of its products had to be repaired before they could be used for the first time, and the CEO once had to borrow money to pay employees' salaries. Today, Haier is a global innovation leader and the world's fastest-growing appliance manufacturer, with the largest market share of "white goods" worldwide. One important aspect of Zhang's stunning transformation of Haier has been a shift toward participative management and a fluid and flexible team-based structure.

In the early 2000s, Zhang turned the structure upside-down. Rather than a vertical hierarchy, Haier's structure is based on self-organizing work units called ZZJYTs (an abbreviation for *zi zhu jing ying ti*, which translates to *independent operating unit*). Each of these units, or teams, is made up of 10 to 20 people who come from various functional areas, such as research, manufacturing, procurement, and marketing, and each team is accountable for accomplishing a specific product or service mission.

Each team has profit and loss responsibility, its own accounting system, and the autonomy to hire and fire employees, make most operational decisions, and set its own rules for expenses, bonus distribution, and other issues. Everyone, no matter what functional area they represent, is expected to keep in close touch with customers. People apply to serve on projects that interest them, and an employee can propose an idea for a new ZZJYT and then must recruit others to work on it. The role of managers isn't to direct or supervise employees or teams but to provide them with the resources and guidance they need to serve customers. Linkages among the activities of various ZZJYTs are developed by the ZZJYTs as needed. For example, if a team needs market research about a specific region, it may consider proposals from several other teams, as well as from outside organizations, that provide those services.

Zhang and other managers believe the extreme team approach has helped Haier avoid being disrupted by rapid technological change.[52]

demands and market needs. In addition to selling products such as refrigerators, washers and dryers, and air and water conditioners, Haier also provides services such as water safety information and other guidance designed to improve the quality of life for consumers in China and other emerging economies.[53]

Teams such as those at Haier are related to the "bossless" trend, which is described further in the "Sunny Side Up" box.

Exhibit 7.8 Interactions Among Multiple-Function Teams

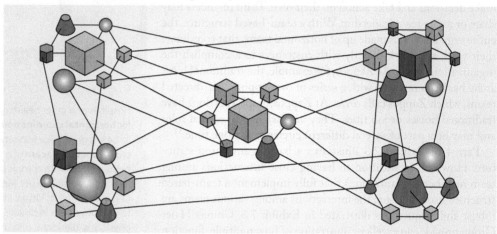

Sunny Side Up } The Bossless Upside-Down Structure

Some companies are finding that command-and-control structures of the past do not work with today's workforce. Young people are more demanding and are used to being involved via social media and the Internet. So the "bossless" structure is evolving from rigid organization charts to fluid operational and project teams, from narrow job descriptions to dynamic projects with multiple leadership roles, from top-down assignments to bottom-up initiatives by self-organizing teams.

- **How it works in a new company.** At Ciplex, a Web design company, there is no structure. There are no departments. There are no job titles like vice president, executive, or manager. The organization chart is upside down, with customers at the top, employees in the middle, and the higher-ups (called "team support") at the bottom. Flipping the structure promotes a culture where customer satisfaction is top priority. Employees, instead of sitting in department silos, are part of multifunctional teams, and they—not the bosses—solve problems to meet customers' needs.

- **How it works in an existing company.** One of the early bossless experiments was undertaken by Gerry Rich and his team at a Ciba-Geigy agricultural chemical plant in Cambridge, Ontario, Canada. Productivity

shot up 20 to 30 percent after they dumped the bosses. The sacred preserve of the bosses—setting schedules, managing costs, writing job descriptions, interviewing new hires, and making key decisions—was now in the purview of employees. "We've taken away the layers of bureaucracy that smothered incentive," said Rich. A big impact of the reorganization was on former managers, who were now called "advisors." They had to learn new roles of facilitating teamwork, leading training programs, and helping resolve conflicts. Many left rather than change. The hardest jolt was when a temporary supervisor was needed and former managers had to take their turn filling in along with other employees.

- **How do people progress?** At Valve, a video game developer, there are no promotions because there is no hierarchy. There is no corporate ladder to climb to advance one's career. But employees find it easy to progress in their careers anyway. There are new projects within which employees grow and learn. For pay increases, employees rank their peers, voting on who they think creates the most value. A flat structure works well for people involved in creative processes and innovation because it allows information to diffuse throughout so that people get exposed to more ideas and diverse thinking.

- **Focus on physical proximity.** At Valve, lawyers sit with engineers and other staff at neighboring desks so that they share knowledge and understand one another's challenges and skills. Valve's Web site says it has been bossless since its founding and has no managers or assigned projects. The 300 employees recruit colleagues to work on projects that they think are worthwhile. Employee desks are mounted on wheels, allowing them to shift quickly to new work areas.

SOURCES: Based on Ilya Pozin, "Why You Need to Flip Your Org Chart," *Inc.* (June 6, 2012), http://www.inc.com/ilya-pozin/why-you-need-to-flip-your-org-chart.html (accessed November 19, 2013); Rachel Emma Silverman, "Who's the Boss? There Isn't One," *The Wall Street Journal*, June 19, 2012, http://online.wsj.com/news/articles/SB100014240527 0230337920457747495358638360 (accessed June 20, 2012); Will Freeman, "Valve's Five Point Guide to 'Bossless Management,'" July 10, 2012, *DEVELOP* Web site: http://www.develop-online.net/news/valve-s-five-point-guide-to-bossless-management/0112454 (accessed July 11, 2012); and J. Southerst, "First We Dump the Bosses," *Canadian Business* 65, no. 4 (April 1992): 46–51.

Team Advantages and Disadvantages   The team approach breaks down barriers across departments and improves coordination and cooperation. Team members know one another's problems and compromise rather than blindly pursuing their own goals. The team concept also enables the organization to adapt more quickly to customer requests and environmental changes and speeds decision making because decisions need not go to the top of the hierarchy for approval. Another big advantage is the morale boost. Employees are typically enthusiastic about their involvement in bigger projects rather than in narrow departmental tasks.

Yet the team approach has disadvantages as well. Employees may be enthusiastic about team participation, but they may also experience conflicts and dual loyalties. A cross-functional team may make different work demands on members than do their department managers, and members who participate in more than one team must resolve these conflicts. A large amount of time is devoted to meetings, thus increasing coordination time. Unless the organization truly needs teams to coordinate complex projects and adapt to the environment, it will lose production efficiency with them. Finally, the team approach may cause too much decentralization. Senior department managers who traditionally made decisions might feel left out when a team moves ahead on its own. Team members often do not see the big picture of the corporation and may make decisions that are good for their group but bad for the organization as a whole.

7-2e Virtual Network Approach

sanjeri/Getty Images

Concept Connection

In today's environment of fast-moving science and tough access to funding, a slew of new bio technology companies are operating as **virtual network organizations**. Rather than having their own labs and research teams, startups such as Alkeus Pharmaceuticals and Rodin Therapeutics work with contract research organizations (CROs) that perform much of their lab and clinical work. Other functions are also outsourced. Alkeus, for example, which is working on finding treatments for "serious and untreatable diseases of the eye," operates with zero full-time employees. Co-founder and CEO Leonide Saad says the virtual approach offers numerous advantages, but he admits it can be challenging to work with contractors who might not be fully committed to the company's mission.

The most recent approach to departmentalization extends the idea of horizontal coordination and collaboration beyond the boundaries of the organization. In a variety of industries, vertically integrated, hierarchical organizations are giving way to loosely interconnected groups of companies with permeable boundaries.[54] *Outsourcing*, which means farming out certain activities, such as manufacturing or credit processing, has become a significant trend. British retailer J. Sainsbury, for example, lets Accenture handle its entire IT department. The Ohio State University outsourced its parking system. And the City of Maywood, California, decided to outsource everything from street maintenance to policing and public safety. The budget for the police department used to be nearly $8 million. Now the city pays about half that to the Los Angeles County Sheriff's Department, and residents say service has improved.[55]

Some organizations take this networking approach to the extreme to create an innovative structure. The **virtual network structure** means that the firm subcontracts most of its major functions to separate companies and coordinates their activities from a small organization at headquarters.[56] Philip Rosedale, the founder of Linden Labs, created and runs SendLove (formerly called LoveMachine) from his home and coffee shops around San Francisco. SendLove is a digital employee recognition system that lets managers or employees send Twitter-like messages to say "Thank you" or "Great job!" When the message is sent, everyone in the company gets a copy, which builds morale, and the basic software is free to companies. The firm has no full-time development staff; instead, it works with a network of freelancers who bid on jobs such as creating new features, fixing glitches, and so forth. Rosedale also contracts out payroll and other administrative tasks.[57]

Exhibit 7.9 Network Approach to Departmentalization

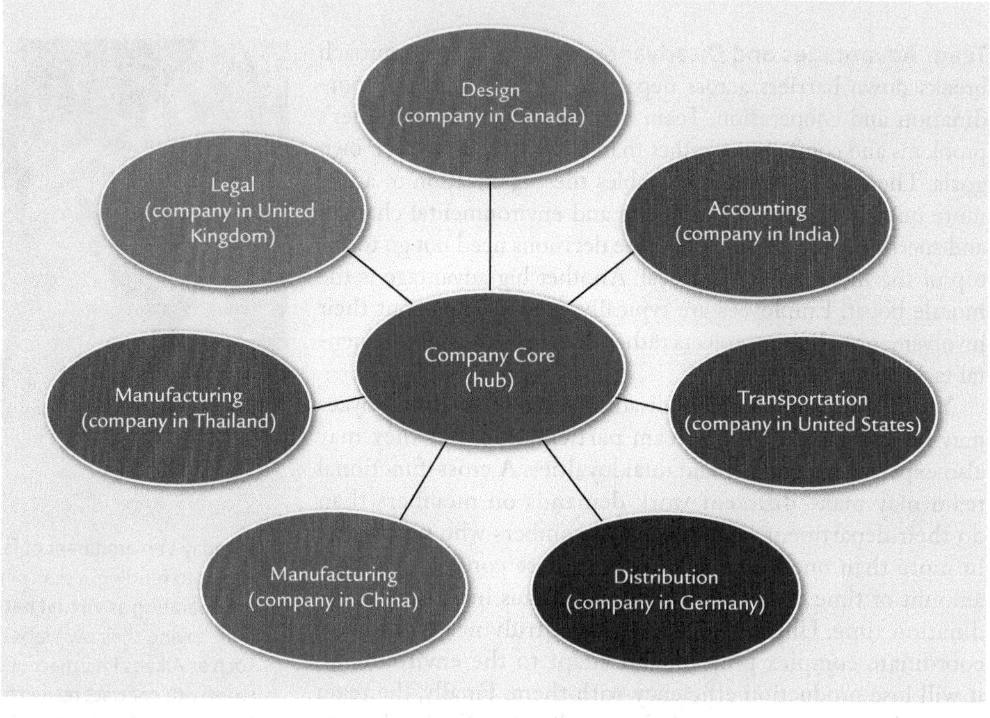

Recipe for Success } Smart Balance

Smart Balance has about 67 employees, but nearly 400 people are working for the company. Smart Balance started by making a buttery spread and now has a line of spreads, all-natural peanut butter, nutrient-enhanced milk, cheese, sour cream, popcorn, and other products. Managers credit the virtual network approach for helping the company innovate and expand rapidly.

Smart Balance keeps product development and marketing in-house but uses contractors to do just about everything else, including manufacturing, distribution, sales, IT services, and research and testing. The way the company got into the milk business shows how the network structure increases speed and flexibility. Peter Dray, vice president of product development, was able to get from contractors the help he needed to perfect the product.

Outside scientists and R&D consultants worked on the formula. The company contracted with a dairy processor to do tests and trial production runs. An outside laboratory assessed nutritional claims, and another company managed consumer taste tests.

Each morning, full-time employees and virtual workers exchange a flurry of e-mail messages and phone calls to update each other on what took place the day before and what needs to happen today. Executives spend much of their time managing relationships. Twice a year, they hold all-company meetings that include permanent staff and contractors. Information is shared widely, and managers make a point of recognizing the contributions of contractors to the company's success, which helps create a sense of unity and commitment.[58]

How It Works   The organization may be viewed as a central hub surrounded by a network of outside specialists, sometimes spread all over the world, as illustrated in Exhibit 7.9. Rather than being housed under one roof, services such as accounting, design, manufacturing, and distribution are outsourced to separate organizations that are connected electronically to a central office.[59] Networked computer systems, collaborative software, and the Internet enable organizations to exchange data and information so rapidly and smoothly that a loosely connected network of suppliers, manufacturers, assemblers, and distributors can look and act as one seamless company.

The idea behind networks is that a company can concentrate on what it does best and contract out other activities to companies with distinctive competence in those specific areas, which enables a company to do more with less.[60] The "heart-healthy" food company Smart Balance has been able to innovate and expand rapidly by using a virtual network approach.

With a network structure such as that used at Smart Balance, it is difficult to answer the question "Where is the organization?" in traditional terms. The different organizational parts in the virtual network structure are drawn together contractually and coordinated electronically, creating a new form of organization. Much like building blocks, parts of the network can be added or taken away to meet changing needs.[61]

Virtual Network Advantages and Disadvantages   The biggest advantages to a virtual network approach are flexibility and competitiveness on a global scale. The network structure provides extreme flexibility, enabling organizations to shift resources and respond quickly to changes in the environment and customer needs. A network organization can draw on resources and expertise worldwide to achieve the best quality and price and can sell its products and services worldwide. Flexibility comes from the ability to hire whatever services are needed and to change a few months later without constraints from owning plants, equipment, and facilities. The organization can redefine itself continually to fit new product and market opportunities. This structure is perhaps the leanest of all organization forms because little supervision is required. Large teams of staff specialists and administrators are not needed. A network organization may have only two or three levels of hierarchy, compared with 10 or more in traditional organizations.[62]

One of the major disadvantages is lack of hands-on control.[63] Managers do not have all operations under one roof and must rely on contracts, coordination, negotiation, and electronic linkages to hold things together. Each partner in the network necessarily acts in its own self-interest. The weak and ambiguous boundaries create higher uncertainty and greater demands on managers for defining shared goals, managing relationships, keeping people focused and motivated, and coordinating activities so that everything functions as intended. For instance, K'Nex Brands LP, a family-owned toy company near Philadelphia, brought most of the production of its plastic building toys back to its factory in the United States from subcontractors in China to maintain greater control over quality and materials. The safety of toys made in overseas factories has been a growing concern for parents. As wages and transportation costs rose in China, K'Nex managers saw a competitive advantage in bringing production back in-house. Ashley Furniture, the largest U.S. furniture maker, has its own warehouses and trucks, rather than outsourcing delivery to a third party, because managers believe maintaining control over distribution provides the company with a competitive advantage. Keith Koenig, who owns furniture stores in southern Florida and receives products from numerous suppliers, says Ashley is "unbeatable" in terms of reliability. Ashley's drivers also act as goodwill ambassadors, developing close customer relationships.[64]

Customer service and loyalty can suffer if outsourcing partners fail to perform as expected. Finally, in this type of organization, employee loyalty can weaken. Employees might feel that they can be replaced by contract services. A cohesive corporate culture is less likely to develop, and turnover tends to be higher because emotional commitment between organization and employee is fragile.

Exhibit 7.10 summarizes the major advantages and disadvantages of each type of structure that we have discussed.

Exhibit 7.10 Structural Advantages and Disadvantages

Structural Approach	Advantages	Disadvantages
Functional	Efficient use of resources; economies of scale In-depth skill specialization and development Top manager direction and control	Poor communication across functional departments Slow response to external changes; lagging innovation Decisions concentrated at the top of hierarchy, creating delay
Divisional	Fast response; flexibility in an unstable environment Fosters concern for customer needs Excellent coordination across functional departments	Duplication of resources across divisions Less technical depth and specialization Poor coordination across divisions
Matrix	More efficient use of resources than a single hierarchy Flexibility, adaptability to a changing environment Interdisciplinary cooperation; expertise available to all divisions	Frustration and confusion from a dual chain of command High conflict between two sides of the matrix Many meetings; more discussion than action
Team	Reduced barriers among departments; increased compromise Shorter response time; quicker decisions Better morale; enthusiasm from employee involvement	Dual loyalties and conflict Time and resources spent on meetings Unplanned decentralization
Virtual network	Can draw on expertise worldwide Highly flexible and responsive Reduced overhead costs	Lack of control; weak boundaries Greater demands on managers Weaker employee loyalty

Remember This

- Popular contemporary approaches to departmentalization include team and virtual network structures.

- A **cross-functional team** is a group of employees from various functional departments that meet as a team to resolve mutual problems.

- Total Attorneys uses cross-functional teams to improve coordination on software and services projects for small law firms.

- A **permanent team** is a group of employees from all functional areas permanently assigned to focus on a specific task or activity.

- A **team-based structure** is one in which the entire organization is made up of horizontal teams that coordinate their activities and work directly with customers to accomplish organizational goals.

- China's Haier Group uses a highly flexible team structure, with self-organizing work units called ZZJYTs (an abbreviation for *zi zhu jing ying ti*).

- With a **virtual network structure**, the organization subcontracts most of its major functions to separate companies and coordinates their activities from a small headquarters organization.

- Both the team and the network approach have distinct advantages and disadvantages.

7-3 Organizing for Horizontal Coordination

One reason for the growing use of teams and networks is that many managers recognize the limits of traditional vertical organization structures in a fast-shifting environment. In general, the trend is toward breaking down barriers between departments, and many companies are moving toward horizontal structures based on work processes rather than departmental functions.[65] However, regardless of the type of structure, every organization needs mechanisms for horizontal integration and coordination. The structure of an organization is not complete without designing the horizontal as well as the vertical dimensions of structure.[66]

7-3a The Need for Coordination

As organizations grow and evolve, two things happen. First, new positions and departments are added to deal with factors in the external environment or with new strategic needs, as described earlier in this chapter. As companies add positions and departments to meet changing needs, they grow more complex, with hundreds of positions and departments performing incredibly diverse activities.

Second, senior managers must find a way to tie all these departments together. The formal chain of command and the supervision it provides is effective, but it is not enough. The organization needs systems to process information and enable communication among people in different departments and at different levels. **Coordination** refers to the managerial task of adjusting and synchronizing the diverse activities among different individuals and departments. **Collaboration** means a joint effort between people from two or more departments to produce outcomes that meet a common goal or shared purpose and that are typically greater than what any of the individuals or departments could achieve working alone.[67] To understand the value of collaboration, consider the 2011 U.S. mission to raid Osama bin Laden's compound in Pakistan. The raid could not have succeeded without close collaboration between the Central Intelligence Agency (CIA) and the U.S. military. There has traditionally been little interaction between the nation's intelligence officers and its military officers, but the war on terrorism has changed that mind-set. During planning for the bin Laden mission, military officers spent every day for months working closely with the CIA team in a remote, secure facility on the CIA campus. "This is the kind of thing that, in the past, people who watched movies thought was possible, but no one in the government thought was possible," one official later said of the collaborative mission.[68]

Collaboration and coordination within business organizations is just as important. Without coordination, a company's left hand will not act in concert with the right, causing problems and conflicts. Coordination is required regardless of whether the organization has a functional, divisional, or team structure. Employees identify with their immediate department or team, taking its interest to heart, and they may not want to compromise and collaborate with other units even for the good of the organization as a whole. Poor coordination and collaboration among divisions are blamed for Microsoft's late entry into the profitable smartphone and tablet markets, for instance. Top managers have implemented structural changes to try to build in stronger horizontal coordination, moving toward a matrix structure.

It remains to be seen if Microsoft's long-feuding divisions can huddle and put the good of the whole above their individual goals. Achieving current CEO Satya Nadella's vision to make the

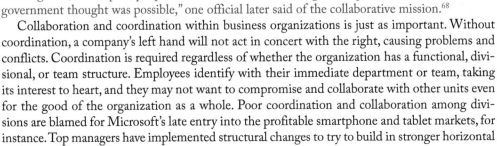

Sunny Side Up — Microsoft

Microsoft is having a hard time keeping pace with Apple and Google. One big reason is that the company's divisions have long been at war with one another. Steven A. Ballmer, the recently retired longtime CEO of Microsoft, said the company needed "to move from multiple Microsofts to one Microsoft."

Top executives dissolved the existing eight product divisions in favor of four units based on broad themes that will encourage greater collaboration and teamwork within the new units. Whereas each division once had its own finance and marketing departments, those functions have been centralized to force groups to work more closely together to create complete products where all the hardware, software, and services work together. In a telephone interview, Qi Lu, executive vice president of Microsoft's Applications and Services group, says the old structure was similar to baseball in that it gave individual players opportunities to perform. A better model for the new Microsoft, he says, is football: "You have to huddle before every play."[69]

company as dominant in the new technology environment as its software was in the PC world will require that people collaborate extensively both within the company and with partners.[70]

Microsoft is a huge organization, with more than 100,000 employees, which makes coordination even more challenging. The problem of coordination and collaboration is also amplified in the international arena because organizational units are differentiated not only by goals and work activities, but also by geographic distance, time differences, cultural values, and perhaps language. How can managers ensure that needed coordination and collaboration will take place in their company, both domestically and globally? Coordination is the outcome of information and cooperation. Managers can design systems and structures to promote horizontal coordination and collaboration.

Exhibit 7.11 illustrates the evolution of organizational structures; this evolution is characterized by a growing emphasis on horizontal coordination. Although the vertical functional structure is effective in stable environments, it does not provide the horizontal coordination that is needed in times of rapid change. Innovations such as cross-functional teams, task forces, and project managers work within the vertical structure but provide a means to increase horizontal communication and cooperation. The next stage involves re-engineering to structure the organization into teams working on horizontal processes. **Re-engineering** refers to the radical redesign of business processes to achieve dramatic improvements in cost, quality, service, and speed. Because the focus of re-engineering is on horizontal workflows rather than functions, re-engineering generally leads to a shift away from a strong vertical structure to one emphasizing stronger horizontal coordination. The vertical hierarchy is flattened, with perhaps only a few senior executives in traditional support functions such as finance and HR.

7-3b Task Forces, Teams, and Project Management

A **task force** is a temporary team or committee designed to solve a problem involving several departments.[71] Task force members represent their departments and share information that enables coordination. For example, at Irving Medical Center, a unit of Kaiser Permanente in California, a task force made up of operating room nurses, surgeons, technicians, housekeeping staff, and others came together to streamline the procedure for performing total-hip and knee-joint replacements, the hospital's costliest and most time-consuming surgeries. The resulting combination of enhanced coordination and reallocated resources meant that the number of these surgeries that could be performed increased from one or two a day up to four a day. Better coordination freed up 188 hours of operating room time a year, reflecting a significant cost savings.[72] In addition to creating task forces, companies also set up *cross-functional teams*, as described previously. A cross-functional team furthers horizontal coordination because participants from several departments meet regularly to solve ongoing problems of common interest.[73] This team is similar

Exhibit 7.11 Evolution of Organization Structures

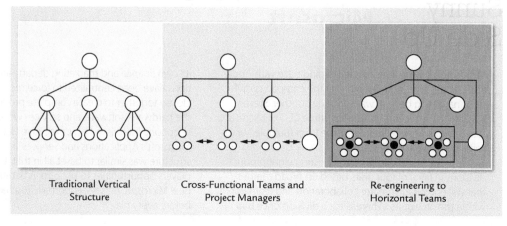

Traditional Vertical Structure

Cross-Functional Teams and Project Managers

Re-engineering to Horizontal Teams

to a task force except that it works with continuing rather than temporary problems and might exist for several years. Team members think in terms of working together for the good of the whole rather than just for their own departments.

Companies also use project managers to increase coordination. A **project manager** is a person who is responsible for coordinating the activities of several departments for the completion of a specific project.[74] Project managers might also have titles such as product manager, integrator, program manager, or process owner. The distinctive feature of the project manager position is that the person is not a member of one of the departments being coordinated. Project managers are located outside the departments and are responsible for coordinating several departments to achieve desired project outcomes. At General Mills, for example, a manager is assigned to each product line, such as Cheerios, Yoplait yogurt, and Annie's macaroni and cheese. Product managers set budget goals, marketing targets, and strategies and obtain the cooperation from advertising, production, and sales personnel needed for implementing product strategy.

In some organizations, project managers are included on the organization chart, as illustrated in Exhibit 7.12. The project manager is drawn to one side of the chart to indicate authority over the project but not over the people assigned to it. The *dashed lines* to the project manager indicate responsibility for coordination and communication with assigned team members, but department managers retain line authority over functional employees.

Concept Connection

Task forces are a common part of organizational life, from private industry to nonprofits to government operations. City and state officials likely used multiple task forces to help Rio de Janeiro prepare for the 2016 Summer Olympics. One issue of concern was preventing the spread of the mosquito *Aedes aegypti*, which is the carrier of the zika virus as well as other devastating diseases. Here a contractor sprays insecticide at the construction site where workers are expanding the city's subway, the MetrôRio, in early 2016.

7-3c Relational Coordination

The highest level of horizontal coordination is **relational coordination**, which refers to "frequent, timely, problem-solving communication carried out through [employee] relationships of shared goals, shared knowledge, and mutual respect."[75] Relational coordination isn't a structural device or mechanism such as a project manager, but rather is part of the very fabric and culture of the organization. In an organization with a high level of relational coordination, people share information freely across departmental boundaries, and people interact on a continuous basis to share knowledge and solve problems. Coordination is carried out through a web

Exhibit 7.12 **Example of Project Manager Relationships to Other Departments**

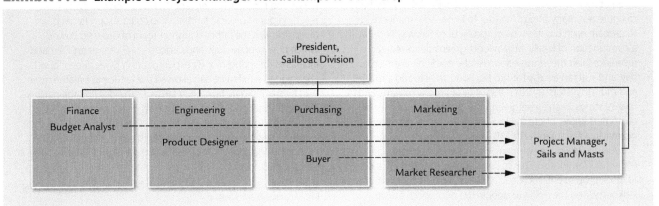

of ongoing positive relationships rather than because of formal coordination roles or mechanisms.[76] Employees coordinate directly with each other across units. The desire for relational coordination is reflected in the changing physical environment of many of today's offices. For example, Susan Goldberg, the new editor-in-chief at *National Geographic* magazine, required people to give up their individual offices and work in cubicles in a newsroom where print and digital writers, editors, and photo editors interact frequently and easily.[77] Goldberg is trying to encourage stronger coordination so the magazine can speed things up, attract younger readers, and provide better correlation between stories that get immediate coverage on the Web site and longer, more in-depth stories for print. Coordination is needed when companies expand their business and they need to garner support not only from internal employees, also from suppliers, as described in the "Recipe for Success" box.

Other companies are doing away with cubicles and using open offices with designated quiet spaces for conversation and impromptu problem solving. Companies including Campbell Soup and Microsoft have hired consultants from office furniture maker Herman Miller to help design common spaces that include "huddle rooms" for meetings of two to four people. Beth Jolly, a Campbell spokesperson, said, "People are collaborating much more" because they aren't "bound by walls or cubes."[78]

Studies have shown that having people work in close proximity to one another does increase collaboration.[79] However, changing the physical environment isn't enough. To build relational coordination into the fabric of the organization, managers invest in training people in the skills needed to interact with one another and resolve cross-departmental conflicts based on shared goals rather than emphasizing goals of their separate departments. People are given freedom from strict work rules so they have the flexibility to interact and contribute wherever they are needed, and rewards are based on team efforts and accomplishments. Frontline supervisors typically have smaller spans of control so they can develop close working relationships with subordinates and coach and mentor employees. Southwest Airlines provides a good illustration.

> "Management makes the assumption that after it calls you a team, you are a team. But in fact, collaboration requires leadership, commitment, resources, training, and constant reinforcement."
>
> —MICHAEL BEYERLEIN, PURDUE UNIVERSITY PROFESSOR AND CO-AUTHOR OF *BEYOND TEAMS: BUILDING THE COLLABORATIVE ORGANIZATION*

Recipe for Success } Sweetgreen

Three Georgetown college buddies got tired of fast food for lunch and realized that other students felt the same. Blessed with an entrepreneurial spirit they attribute to their immigrant parents, they raised $350,000 from family and friends, now saying it was Kickstarter before Kickstarter.

Starting close by, Nathaniel Ru, Nicolas Jammet, and Jonathan Neman opened their first restaurant in the D.C. neighborhood of their school. With no restaurant experience, they had to figure out many things. In order to know how many salads to prepare each day, they sat outside a busy Subway shop. With a combination of locally grown food, greens delivered each morning, salad dressings—and falafel—made on premise every day, and with an allergy toward Big Food, they found a market and more investors. By 2015, they'd raised many millions and had 39 stores. Each Sweetgreen location lists its suppliers, so customers know where the food comes from. None of this is normal in a restaurant with $10 salads.

As they build the company, they've moved headquarters from Washington, D.C., to Los Angeles, mostly, they say, to attract top talent, such as COO Karen Kelly, formerly of Pinkberry. And they plan to double the number of stores.

The biggest challenge as they move ahead is getting local farmers for each of the 100 stores they will have. Unlike McDonald's, they can't use the cheapest supplier for cheese for much of the country. Sweetgreen's appeal has been at least partly based on local sourcing. So how do you convince farmers in outlying regions to commit resources to grow for a restaurant that is new to the area and may or may not be around by harvesting time? Or is there another way? The company started reaching out to organic farmers who could supply larger quantities. One was the father-daughter team of Growing Power, which now supplies kale and cabbage to Sweetgreen. Demand increased for spring-mix. By experimenting, Sweetgreen found changing to a different bag allowed the lettuce to breathe more. And by sharing data from their farms, both sides find the partnership is stronger and can meet business needs more effectively.

The partners know it isn't all about food, but rather the total experience while getting and eating the food. They quote the founder of McDonald's, "We're not in the burger business, we're in show business."

SOURCES: Lindsay Blakely, "Green Machine," *Inc.* (October 2017): 60–62; and Mickey Rapkin, "Salad Days," *Inc.* (January 2017): 42–44.

Sunny Side Up

Southwest Airlines

Airlines face many challenges, but one they face hundreds of times on a daily basis is getting airplanes loaded and off the ground safely and on time. Flight departure is a highly complex process. It involves numerous employees from various departments—such as ticket agents, pilots, flight attendants, baggage handlers, gate agents, mechanics, ramp agents, and fuel attendants—performing multiple tasks within a limited time period, under uncertain and ever-changing conditions. If all these groups aren't tightly coordinated, a successful on-time departure is difficult to achieve.

Southwest Airlines has the shortest turnaround time in the business, partly because managers promote relational coordination to achieve superior on-time performance and a high level of customer satisfaction. In any airline, there can be serious disagreements among employees about who is to blame when a flight is

delayed, so Southwest managers created what they call *team delay*. Rather than searching for who is to blame when something goes wrong, the team delay is used to point out problems in coordination among various groups. The emphasis on the team focuses everyone on their shared goals of on-time departure, accurate baggage handling, and customer satisfaction. Because delay becomes a team problem, people are motivated to work closely together and coordinate their activities, rather than looking out for themselves and trying to avoid or shift blame. Supervisors work closely with employees, but their role is less "being the boss" as it is facilitating learning and helping people do their jobs. Southwest uses a small supervisory span of control—about one supervisor for every eight or nine frontline employees—so that supervisors have the time to coach and assist employees, who are viewed as internal customers.[80]

By using practices that facilitate relational coordination, Southwest managers ensure that all the departments involved in flight departure are tightly coordinated. When relational coordination is high, people share information and coordinate their activities without bosses or formal mechanisms telling them to do so.

Remember This

- In addition to the vertical structure, every organization needs mechanisms for horizontal integration and coordination.
- **Coordination** refers to the managerial task of adjusting and synchronizing the diverse activities among different individuals and departments.
- **Collaboration** means a joint effort between people from two or more departments to produce outcomes that meet a common goal or shared purpose.
- The successful U.S. mission to raid Osama bin Laden's compound in Pakistan was a result of collaboration between the nation's intelligence officers and its military officers.
- As organizations grow, they add new positions, departments, and hierarchical levels, which leads to greater coordination problems.
- Ways to increase horizontal coordination include task forces, teams, project managers, and relational coordination.

- A **task force** is a temporary team or committee formed to solve a specific short-term problem involving several departments.
- A **project manager** is a person responsible for coordinating the activities of several departments for the completion of a specific project.
- Companies often shift to a more horizontal approach after going through **re-engineering**, which refers to the radical redesign of business processes to achieve dramatic improvements in cost, quality, service, and speed.
- **Relational coordination** refers to frequent horizontal coordination and communication carried out through ongoing relationships of shared goals, shared knowledge, and mutual respect.
- Southwest Airlines achieves the shortest turnaround time in the airline industry because managers foster relational coordination among the varied people and departments involved in the flight departure process.

7-4 Factors Shaping Structure

Vertical hierarchies continue to thrive because they provide important benefits for organizations. Some degree of vertical hierarchy is often needed to organize a large number of people so they can effectively accomplish complex tasks within a coherent framework. Without a vertical structure, people in a large, global firm wouldn't know what to do. However, in today's environment, an organization's vertical structure often needs to be balanced with strong horizontal mechanisms to achieve peak performance.[81]

How do managers know whether to design a structure that emphasizes the formal, vertical hierarchy or one with an emphasis on horizontal communication and collaboration? An organization that is designed to fit the company's situation, considering factors such as organization size, strategy, and production technology, will achieve better performance. Two highly important factors managers consider are the organization's strategic goals and the nature of its workflow technology.[82] Exhibit 7.13 illustrates that forces affecting organization structure come from both outside and inside the organization. External strategic needs, such as environmental conditions, strategic direction, and organizational goals, create top-down pressure for designing the organization in such a way as to fit the environment and accomplish strategic goals. Structural decisions also take into consideration pressures from the bottom up—that is, from the technology and work processes that are performed to produce the organization's products and services.

7-4a Structure Follows Strategy

Studies demonstrate that business performance is strongly influenced by how well the company's structure is aligned with its strategic intent and the needs of the environment, so managers strive to pick strategies and structures that are congruent.[83] In Chapter 5, we discussed several strategies that business firms can adopt. Two strategies proposed by Michael E. Porter are differentiation and cost leadership.[84] With a differentiation strategy, the organization attempts to develop innovative products unique to the market. With a cost leadership strategy, the organization strives for internal efficiency.

Typically, strategic goals of cost efficiency occur in more stable environments while goals of innovation and flexibility occur in more uncertain environments. The terms *mechanistic* and *organic* can be used to explain structural responses to strategy and the environment.[85] Goals of efficiency and a stable environment are associated with a mechanistic system. This type of

Exhibit 7.13 Factors Affecting Organization Structure

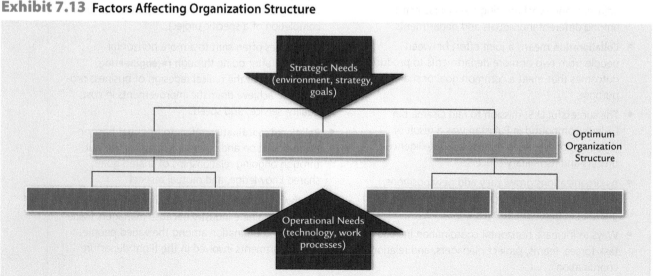

SOURCE: Based on David A. Nadler and Michael L. Tushman, with Mark B. Nadler, *Competing by Design: The Power of Organizational Architecture* (New York: Oxford University Press, 1997), p. 54.

organization typically has a rigid, vertical, centralized structure, with most decisions made at the top. The organization is highly specialized and characterized by rules, procedures, and a clear hierarchy of authority. With goals of innovation and a rapidly changing environment, however, the organization tends to be much looser, free-flowing, and adaptive, using an organic system. The structure is more horizontal, and decision-making authority is decentralized. People at lower levels have more responsibility and authority for solving problems, which enables the organization to be more fluid and adaptable to changes.[86]

Exhibit 7.14 shows a simplified continuum that illustrates how different structural approaches are associated with strategy and the environment. The pure functional structure is appropriate for achieving internal efficiency goals in a stable environment. The vertical functional structure uses task specialization and a strict chain of command to gain efficient use of scarce resources, but it does not enable the organization to be flexible or innovative. In contrast, horizontal teams are appropriate when the primary goal is innovation and the organization needs flexibility to cope with an uncertain environment. Each team is small, is able to be responsive, and has the people and resources necessary for performing its task. The flexible horizontal structure enables organizations to differentiate themselves and respond quickly to the demands of a shifting environment but at the expense of efficient resource use.

Exhibit 7.14 also illustrates how other forms of structure represent intermediate steps on the organization's path to efficiency or innovation. The functional structure with cross-functional teams and project managers provides greater coordination and flexibility than the pure functional structure. The divisional structure promotes differentiation because each division can focus on specific products and customers, although divisions tend to be larger and less flexible than small teams. Exhibit 7.14 does not include all possible structures, but it illustrates how structures can be used to facilitate the organization's strategic goals.

Exhibit 7.14 **Relationship of Structural Approach to Strategy and the Environment**

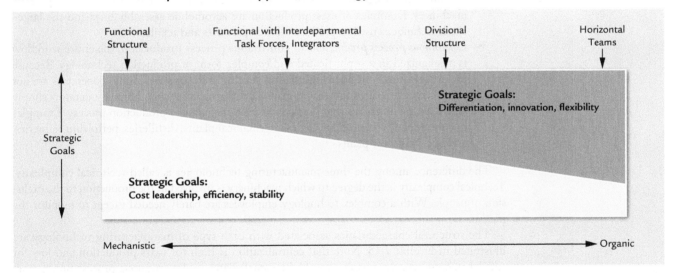

Remember This

- Contingency factors of strategic goals, environment, and technology influence the correct structural approach.

- A mechanistic, vertical structure is appropriate for a cost leadership strategy, which typically occurs in a stable environment.

- An organic, horizontal approach is needed for a differentiation strategy and when the organization needs flexibility to cope with an uncertain environment.

7-5 Structure Fits the Technology

Technology includes the knowledge, tools, techniques, and activities used to transform organizational inputs into outputs.[87] Technology includes machinery, employee skills, and work procedures. A useful way to think about technology is as "production activities." The production activities may be to produce Web site content, digital games, steel castings, television programs, or computer software. Technologies vary between manufacturing and service organizations.

Woodward's Manufacturing Technology   The most influential research into the relationship between manufacturing technology and organization structure was conducted by Joan Woodward, a British industrial sociologist.[88] She gathered data from 100 British firms to determine whether basic structural characteristics, such as administrative overhead, span of control, and centralization, were different across firms. She found that manufacturing firms could be categorized according to three basic types of production technology:

- *Small-batch and unit production.* **Small-batch production** firms produce goods in batches of one or a few products designed to customer specification. This technology also is used to make large, one-of-a-kind products, such as computer-controlled machines. Small-batch manufacturing is close to traditional skilled-craft work because human beings are a large part of the process. Examples of items produced through small-batch manufacturing include custom clothing, special-order machine tools, space capsules, satellites, and submarines.
- *Large-batch and mass production.* **Mass production** technology is distinguished by standardized production runs. A large volume of products is produced, and all customers receive the same product. Standard products go into inventory for sale as customers need them. This technology makes greater use of machines than does small-batch production. Machines are designed to do most of the physical work, and employees complement the machinery. Examples of mass production are automobile assembly lines and the large-batch techniques used to produce tobacco products and textiles.
- *Continuous process production.* In **continuous process production**, the entire workflow is mechanized in a sophisticated and complex form of production technology. Because the process runs continuously, it has no starting and stopping. Human operators are not part of actual production because machinery does all the work. Human operators simply read dials, fix machines that break down, and manage the production process. Examples of continuous process technologies are chemical plants, distilleries, petroleum refineries, and nuclear power plants.

The difference among the three manufacturing technologies is called **technical complexity**. Technical complexity is the degree to which machinery is involved in the production to the exclusion of people. With a complex technology, employees are barely needed except to monitor the machines.

The structural characteristics associated with each type of manufacturing technology are illustrated in Exhibit 7.15. Note that centralization is high for mass production and low for small-batch and continuous process. Unlike small-batch and continuous process production, standardized mass production machinery requires centralized decision making and well-defined rules and procedures. The administrative ratio and the percentage of indirect labor required also increase with technological complexity. Because the production process is nonroutine, close supervision is needed. More indirect labor, in the form of maintenance people, is required because of the machinery's complexity; thus, the indirect/direct labor ratio is high. Span of control for frontline supervisors is greatest for mass production. On an assembly line, jobs are so routine that a supervisor can handle an average of 48 employees. The number of employees per supervisor in small-batch and continuous process production is lower because closer supervision is needed. Overall, small-batch and continuous process firms have somewhat loose, flexible structures (organic), and mass production firms have tight vertical structures (mechanistic).

Woodward found that the relationship between structure and technology was directly related to company performance. Low-performing firms tended to deviate from the preferred structural

Exhibit 7.15 Relationship Between Manufacturing Technology and Organization Structure

	Manufacturing Technology		
	Small Batch	**Mass Production**	**Continuous Process**
Technical complexity of production technology	Low	Medium	High
Structural characteristics			
Centralization	Low	High	Low
Top administrator ratio	Low	Medium	High
Indirect/direct labor ratio	1/9	1/4	1/1
Supervisor span of control	23	48	15
Communication			
Written (vertical)	Low	High	Low
Verbal (horizontal)	High	Low	High
Overall structure	Organic	Mechanistic	Organic

SOURCE: Based on Joan Woodward, *Industrial Organizations: Theory and Practice* (London: Oxford University Press, 1965).

form, often adopting a structure appropriate for another type of technology. High-performing organizations had characteristics similar to those listed in Exhibit 7.15.

Service Technology   Examples of service organizations include consulting companies, law firms, brokerage houses, airlines, hotels, advertising companies, amusement parks, and educational organizations. In addition, service technology characterizes many departments in large corporations, even manufacturing firms. In a manufacturing company such as Ford Motor Company, the legal, HR, finance, and market research departments all provide service. Thus, the structure and design of these departments reflect their own service technology rather than the manufacturing plant's technology. **Service technology** can be defined as follows:

- *Intangible output.* The output of a service firm is intangible. Services are perishable and, unlike physical products, cannot be stored in inventory. The service is either consumed immediately or lost forever. Manufactured products are produced at one point in time and can be stored until sold at another time.
- *Direct contact with customers.* Employees and customers interact directly to provide and purchase the service. Production and consumption are simultaneous. Service firm employees have direct contact with customers. In a manufacturing firm, technical employees are separated from customers, and hence no direct interactions occur.[89]

One distinct feature of service technology that directly influences structure is the need for employees to be close to the customer.[90] Structural characteristics are similar to those for continuous manufacturing technology, shown in Exhibit 7.15. Service firms tend to be flexible, informal, and decentralized. Horizontal communication is high because employees must share information and resources to serve customers and solve problems. Services also are dispersed; hence, each unit is often small and located geographically close to customers. For example, banks, hotels, fast-food franchises, and doctors' offices disperse their facilities into regional and local offices to provide faster and better service to customers.

Some services can be broken down into explicit steps, so that employees can follow set rules and procedures. An interesting example comes from India, where Dr. Devi Shetty runs a hospital that performs open-heart surgery for about 10 percent of the cost charged by hospitals in the United States, without reduced quality, by applying standardized operating procedures and principles of mass production. His approach is in line with a trend toward *lean services*, which looks at how to design service work to improve both quality and efficiency. "In healthcare, you can't do one thing and reduce the price," Dr. Shetty says. "We have to do 1,000 small things."[91] When services can be standardized, a tight centralized structure can be effective, but service firms in general tend to be more organic, flexible, and decentralized.

Remember This

- Types of technologies include manufacturing and service.
- **Small-batch production** is a type of manufacturing technology that involves the production of goods in batches of one or a few products designed to customer specifications.
- **Mass production** is characterized by long production runs to manufacture a large volume of products with the same specifications.
- **Continuous process production** involves mechanization of the entire workflow and nonstop production, such as in chemical plants or petroleum refineries.
- Small-batch and continuous process technologies are associated with a more flexible horizontal

structure, whereas a tighter vertical structure is appropriate for mass production.

- Manufacturing technologies differ in terms of **technical complexity**, which refers to the degree to which complex machinery is involved in the production process to the exclusion of people.
- **Service technology** is characterized by intangible outputs and direct contact between employees and customers.
- Examples of service firms include banks, hotels, and law firms.
- Service technologies tend to have more flexible horizontal structures.

DISCUSSION QUESTIONS

1. If you wanted to add a group of big data scientists to a large organization such as PepsiCo, would you centralize the scientists in a central pool at headquarters or decentralize them to separate divisions? Discuss your reasons.

2. How does relational coordination differ from teams and task forces? Do you think relational coordination seems more valuable for a service technology or a manufacturing technology? Explain your answer.

3. An organizational consultant said, "Some aspect of functional structure appears in every organization." Do you agree? Explain.

4. Some people argue that the matrix structure should be adopted only as a last resort because the dual chains of command can create more problems than they solve. Discuss. Do you agree or disagree? Why?

5. What is the virtual network approach to structure? Is the use of authority and responsibility different compared to other forms of departmentalization? Explain.

6. A report published by Hay Group found that some managers have personalities suited to horizontal relationships, such as project management, and achieve results with little formal authority. Other managers are more suited to

operating roles with much formal authority in a vertical structure. What type of structure—functional, matrix, team, or virtual network—do you believe your personality would best fit? Which structure would be the most challenging for you? Give your reasons.

7. Describe the primary differences between manufacturing and service technology. How do these differences influence the type of structure that will be most effective?

8. Experts say that organizations are becoming increasingly decentralized, with authority, decision-making responsibility, and accountability being pushed farther down into the organization. How will this trend affect what will be asked of you as a new manager?

9. This chapter suggested that structure should be designed to fit strategy. Some theorists argue that strategy should be designed to fit the organization's structure. With which theory do you agree? Explain.

10. Would you expect the structure of a company such as Facebook, which operates almost entirely online, to differ from the structure of a bricks-and-mortar company, such as AT&T, which uses the Internet only for some things, such as customer service and business-to-business transactions? Why or why not?

APPLY YOUR SKILLS: SELF-LEARNING

Organic versus Mechanistic Organization Structure

Interview an employee at your university, such as a department head or secretary. Have the employee answer the following 13 questions about his or her job and organizational conditions. Then answer the same set of questions for a job that you have held.

Disagree Strongly ① ② ③ ④ ⑤ Agree Strongly

1. Your work would be considered routine.

   1   2   3   4   5

2. A clearly known way is established to do the major tasks that you encounter.

   1   2   3   4   5

3. Your work has high variety and frequent exceptions.

   1   2   3   4   5

4. Communications from above consist of information and advice rather than instructions and directions.

   1   2   3   4   5

5. You have the support of peers and your supervisor to do your job well.

   1   2   3   4   5

6. You seldom exchange ideas or information with people doing other kinds of jobs.

   1   2   3   4   5

7. Decisions relevant to your work are made above you and passed down.

   1   2   3   4   5

8. People at your level frequently have to figure out for themselves what their tasks are for each day.

   1   2   3   4   5

9. Lines of authority are clear and precisely defined.

   1   2   3   4   5

10. Leadership tends to be democratic rather than autocratic in style.

    1   2   3   4   5

11. Job descriptions are written and up to date for each job.

    1   2   3   4   5

12. People understand each other's jobs and often do different tasks.

    1   2   3   4   5

13. A manual of policies and procedures is available to use when a problem arises.

    1   2   3   4   5

Scoring and Interpretation To obtain the total score, subtract the scores for questions 1, 2, 6, 7, 9, 11, and 13 from the number 6 and add up the adjusted scores.

Total Score, Employee: _____

Total Score, You: _____

Compare the total score for a place that you have worked to the score of the university employee that you interviewed. A score of 52 or above suggests that you or the other respondent is working in an organic organization. The score reflects a loose, flexible structure that is often associated with uncertain environments and small-batch or service technology. People working in this structure feel empowered. Many organizations today are moving in the direction of flexible structures and empowerment.

A score of 26 or below suggests a mechanistic structure. This structure uses traditional control and functional specialization, which often occurs in a certain environment, a stable organization, and routine or mass production technology. People in this structure may feel controlled and constrained.

Discuss the pros and cons of organic versus mechanistic structure. Does the structure of the employee whom you interviewed fit the nature of the organization's environment, strategic goals, and technology? How about the structure for your own workplace? How might you redesign the structure to make the work organization more effective?

APPLY YOUR SKILLS: GROUP LEARNING

Family Business

Step 1. In groups of three to five students, assume that you are a consulting team to a family business. The family has used an inheritance to acquire a medium-sized pharmaceutical company. Last year, sales were down 10 percent from the previous year. Indeed, business has declined over the past three years, even though the pharmaceutical industry has been growing. The family that acquired the business has asked for your help.

Step 2. Your task as a group is to rank the priority of the departmental functions in the order of importance for assigning additional resources to improve business in the future.

Step 3. Individually, rank the following 10 functions in the order of importance, and make a note of your reasons:

Distribution
Manufacturing

Market research
New-product development
Human resources
Product promotion
Quality assurance
Sales
Legal and governmental affairs
Office of the comptroller

Step 4. As a group, discuss the order of importance for the 10 functions, sharing your reasons for how functional priority should relate to the company's strategic needs.

Step 5. How does the group's reasoning and ranking differ from your original thinking?

Step 6. What did you learn about organization structure and design from this exercise?

APPLY YOUR SKILLS: ACTION LEARNING

Team Skills

1. Think of three times you have been a member of a work team, with varying levels of success. Complete the following table.

	Team 1	Team 2	Team 3
Was there any formal authority in the team? How did that work?			
What was the informal structure?			
How was work divided? Was there specialization?			
Did anyone delegate? How did that work out?			
Over the course of time, did the team get better or did it deteriorate? Why?			

2. Can you see any patterns in the success of the team and some of the characteristics you have identified?

3. Based on what you have learned, how would you recommend structuring a work team?

APPLY YOUR SKILLS: ETHICAL DILEMMA

A Matter of Delegation[92]

Tom Harrington loved his job as an assistant quality control officer for Rockingham Toys. After six months of unemployment, he was anxious to make a good impression on his boss, Frank Golopolus. One of Harrington's responsibilities was ensuring that new product lines met federal safety guidelines. Rockingham had made several manufacturing changes over the past

year. Golopolus and the rest of the quality control team had been working 60-hour weeks to troubleshoot the new production process.

Harrington was aware of numerous changes in product safety guidelines that he knew would affect the new toys the company was producing. Golopolus was also aware of the guidelines, but he was taking no action to implement them. Harrington wasn't sure whether his boss expected him to implement the new procedures. The ultimate responsibility was his boss's, and Harrington was concerned about moving ahead on his own. To cover for his boss, he continued to avoid the questions that he received from the factory floor, but he was beginning to wonder whether Rockingham would have time to make changes with the Christmas season rapidly approaching.

Harrington felt loyalty to Golopolus for giving him a job and didn't want to alienate him by interfering. However, he was beginning to worry what might happen if he didn't act. Rockingham had a fine product safety reputation and was rarely challenged on matters of quality. Should he question Golopolus about implementing the new safety guidelines?

What Would You Do?

1. Prepare a memo to Golopolus summarizing the new safety guidelines that affect the Rockingham product line and requesting his authorization for implementation.

2. Mind your own business. Golopolus hasn't said anything about the new guidelines, and you don't want to overstep your authority. You've been unemployed and need this job.

3. Send copies of the reports anonymously to the operations manager, who is Golopolus's boss.

APPLY YOUR SKILLS: CASE FOR CRITICAL ANALYSIS

Abraham's Grocery Store

The first Abraham's Grocery Store was started in 1967 by Bill Abraham and his sister Doris. They used a small inheritance to start a small grocery store in a suburb of Atlanta, Georgia, and it was immediately successful. The location was good, and both Bill and Doris had winning personalities and a "serve the customer" attitude. Abraham's rapidly growing number of customers enjoyed an abundance of good meats and produce, for which Abraham's became well known.

By 2007, Abraham's had more than 200 stores. Company headquarters moved to downtown Atlanta to supervise stores throughout the southeastern United States. There were four regional managers responsible for about 50 stores each. Within each region, there were four districts of 12 to 13 stores each.

Because the stores specialized in excellent meats and produce, there was a separate meat department manager, grocery department manager, and produce department manager within each store. The grocery department manager also served as the store manager, but this person did not have direct authority over the meat department or the produce department. The store meat department manager reported directly to a district meat manager specialist, and the store produce department manager reported directly to a district produce manager specialist. The store manager (who is also the grocery department manager) reported directly to a district store supervisor. This direct line of authority for each store department provided excellent quality control over the meat, produce, and grocery departments within individual stores.

However, there was growing dissatisfaction within the stores. The turnover of store managers was high, mostly because they had no control over the meat and produce

departments within their stores. Coordination within stores was terrible, such as when a store manager decided to promote a sale on Coke products as a loss leader. Hundreds of cartons of Coke were brought into the store for the big sale, but the meat and produce department managers would not give up floor space to display Coke cartons. The frustrated store manager insisted that this was no way to run a business and quit on the spot. Many stores experienced conflict rather than cooperation among the meat, produce, and store managers because each was very protective of his or her separate responsibilities.

Doris Abraham asked a consultant for advice. The consultant recommended a reorganization within each store so that the meat, grocery, and produce departments would all report to the store manager. The store manager thus would have complete control over store activities and would be responsible for coordinating across the meat, produce, and grocery departments. The meat department manager in each store would report to the store manager and would also have a dashed-line relationship (communication, coordination) with the district meat specialist. Likewise, each store produce department manager would have a dashed-line relationship with the district produce specialist. The store manager would report directly to the district store supervisor. The district meat and produce specialists would visit individual stores periodically to provide advice and help the store department heads to ensure top quality in the meat, produce, and grocery areas.

The consultant was enthusiastic about the proposed structure. Store managers would have more freedom and responsibility. By assigning responsibility for all store departments to the store manager, the new structure would encourage coordination within stores and give managers the ability to adapt to local tastes and customer needs. The dashed-line relationships would ensure excellent meat, grocery, and produce departments across all stores.

Questions

1. Based on the information available in the case, sketch a picture of the original structure within an Abraham's store and the store managers' relationships with district specialist managers. What type of structure is this? Explain.

2. Based on the information available in the case, sketch a picture of the consultant's recommended structure within the store and the relationship of store department managers with district specialist managers. What type of structure is this? Explain.

3. What are some of the advantages and disadvantages you see for the two types of structures? Which structure do you think will work best for Abraham's? Why?

ENDNOTES

1. Rod Collins, "What's Happening at Zappos May Be All About the School Bus Test," *The Huffington Post*, July 3, 2015, http://www.huffingtonpost.com/great-work-cultures/whats-happening-at-zappos_b_7719650.html (accessed March 18, 2016).

2. Ibid.

3. Justin Friesen, Aaron C. Kay, Richard Eibach, and Adam Galinsky, "Seeking Structure in Social Organization: Compensatory Control and the Psychological Advantages of Hierarchy," *The Journal of Personality and Social Psychology* 106, no. 4 (April 2014): 590–609.

4. Chad Bray, "Standard Charter Shakes Up Management Structure," *The New York Times*, July 20, 2015, http://www.nytimes.com/2015/07/21/business/dealbook/standard-chartered-shakes-up-management-structure.html?_r=0 (accessed March 21, 2016).

5. Justin Scheck, "Dell Reorganizes, Creating New Mobile Device Division," *The Wall Street Journal*, December 5, 2009.

6. Julia Werdigier, "BP Appoints New Chief of Production," *The New York Times*, November 24, 2012.

7. John Child, *Organization: A Guide to Problems and Practice*, 2d ed. (London: Harper & Row, 1984).

8. Adam Smith, *The Wealth of Nations* (New York: Modern Library, 1937).

9. Julia Boorstin, "The Sony Hack: One Year Later," *CNBC* (November 24, 2015), http://www.cnbc.com/2015/11/24/the-sony-hack-one-year-later.html (accessed March 21, 2016).

10. David Kiron, Douglas Palmer, and Robert Berkman, "The Executive's Role in Social Business," *MIT Sloan Management Review* (Summer 2013): 83–89; Javier C. Hernandez, "A Digital Matchmaker for the City and Its Public," *The New York Times*, July 31, 2011; and Travis Hessman, "The Rise of the CTO," *IndustryWeek* (February 2014): 14–16.

11. John Bussey, "Has Time Come for More CIOs to Start Reporting to the Top?" *The Wall Street Journal*, May 17, 2011, http://online.wsj.com/article/SB10001424052748704281504576327510720752684.html (accessed August 14, 2012).

12. This discussion is based on A. J. Grimes, "Authority, Power, Influence, and Social Control: A Theoretical Synthesis," *Academy of Management Review* 3 (1978): 724–735; and W. Graham Astley and Paramjit S. Sachdeva, "Structural Sources of Intraorganizational Power: A Theoretical Synthesis," *Academy of Management Review* 9 (1984): 104–113.

13. C. I. Barnard, *The Functions of the Executive* (Cambridge, MA: Harvard University Press, 1938).

14. Thomas A. Stewart, "CEOs See Clout Shifting," *Fortune* (November 6, 1989): 66.

15. Michael G. O'Loughlin, "What Is Bureaucratic Accountability and How Can We Measure It?" *Administration & Society* 22, no. 3 (November 1990): 275–302; and Brian Dive, "When Is an Organization Too Flat?" *Across the Board* (July–August 2003): 20–23.

16. Jena McGregor, "The BBC and Crisis Management: Why the Second Mistake Can Be Worse than the First," *The Washington Post*, November 13, 2012, http://articles.washingtonpost.com/2012-11-13/national/35503757_1_jimmy-savile-george-entwistle-crisis-management (accessed November 14, 2012); and Matt Chorley and Alasdair Glennie, "BBC Savile Scandal Cost YOU £5 Million: Shocking Report Reveals How Probes into Corporation's Bungled Handling of Crisis Left Taxpayers with Huge Bill," *DailyMail*, July 16, 2013, http://www.dailymail.co.uk/news/article-2365251/BBCs-navel-gazing-Jimmy-Savile-crisis-cost-5million.html#ixzz2gTZOeOHj (accessed September 30, 2013).

17. Carrie R. Leana, "Predictors and Consequences of Delegation," *Academy of Management Journal* 29 (1986): 754–774.

18. Ian Urbina, "In Gulf, It Was Unclear Who Was in Charge of Oil Rig," *The New York Times*, June 5, 2010; and Douglas A. Blackmon et al., "There Was 'Nobody in Charge,'" *The Wall Street Journal*, May 27, 2010.

19. Clifford Kraus and Julia Werdigier, "BP's New Chief, Not Formally in the Role, Is Already Realigning Senior Managers," *The New York Times*, September 30, 2010; and Guy Chazan, "BP's New Chief Puts Emphasis on Safety," *The Wall Street Journal*, September 29, 2010.

20. George Anders, "Overseeing More Employees—With Fewer Managers" (Theory & Practice column), *The Wall Street Journal*, March 24, 2008.

21. Barbara Davison, "Management Span of Control: How Wide Is Too Wide?" *Journal of Business Strategy* 24, no. 4 (2003): 22–29; Paul D. Collins and Frank Hull, "Technology and Span of Control: Woodward Revisited," *Journal of Management Studies* 23 (March 1986): 143–164; David D. Van Fleet and Arthur G. Bedeian, "A History of the Span of Management," *Academy of Management Review* 2 (1977): 356–372; and C. W. Barkdull, "Span of Control—A Method of Evaluation," *Michigan Business Review* 15 (May 1963): 25–32.

22. Reported in Brian Dive, "Hierarchies for Flow and Profit," *Strategy + Business*, August 26, 2008, www.strategy-business.com/article/08315 (accessed May 25, 2010).

23. Anders, "Overseeing More Employees"; Davison, "Management Span of Control"; Dive, "When Is an Organization Too Flat?"; Brian Dumaine, "What the Leaders of Tomorrow See," *Fortune* (July 3, 1989): 48–62; and Raghuram G. Rajan and Julie Wulf, "The Flattening Firm: Evidence from Panel Data on the Changing Nature of Corporate Hierarchies," working paper, reported in Caroline Ellis, "The Flattening Corporation," *MIT Sloan Management Review* (Summer 2003): 5.

24. Dive, "Hierarchies for Flow and Profit"; and Gary Neilson, Bruce A. Pasternack, and Decio Mendes, "The Four Bases of Organizational DNA," *Strategy + Business* 33 (December 10, 2003): 48–57.

25. Nicola Clark, "Rolls-Royce to Restructure Management in Cost-Cutting Drive," *The New York Times*, December 16, 2015, http://www.nytimes.com/2015/12/17/business/international/rolls-royce-to-restructure-management-in-cost-cutting-drive.html?_r=0 (accessed March 21, 2016); and Sarah Young, "New CEO Cuts Management Layer at Struggling Rolls-Royce," *Reuters*, December 16, 2015, http://uk.reuters.com/article/uk-rolls-royce-hldg-restructuring-idUKKBN0TZ01V20151216 (accessed March 21, 2016).

26. Gary L. Neilson and Julie Wulf, "How Many Direct Reports?" *Harvard Business Review* (April 2012): 112–119; and Hessman, "The Rise of the CTO."

27. Bussey, "Has Time Come for More CIOs to Start Reporting to the Top?"

28. Gary L. Neilson, "Diagnosing Your Top Team's Span of Control," *Strategy + Business Online* (April 9, 2012), http://www.strategy-business.com/article/00107?gko=ce37c (accessed October 1, 2013).

29. William G. Ouchi, "Power to the Principals: Decentralization in Three Large School Districts," *Organization Science* 17, no. 2 (March–April 2006): 298–307.

30. Sarah Lyall, "Britain Plans to Decentralize Health Care," *The New York Times*, July 24, 2010, www.nytimes.com/2010/07/25/world/europe/25britain.html?pagewanted=all (accessed August 14, 2012).

31. Hiroko Tabuchi and Bill Vlasic, "Battered by Expensive Crises, Toyota Declares a Rebirth," *The New York Times*, January 3, 2013.

32. Andrew Campbell, Sven Kunisch, and Günter Müller-Stevens, "To Centralize or Not to Centralize?" *McKinsey Quarterly* (June 2011), www.mckinseyquarterly.com/To_centralize_or_not_to_centralize_2815 (accessed August 14, 2012).

33. Dennis Cauchon, "The Little Company That Could," *USA TODAY*, October 9, 2005, www.usatoday.com/money/companies/management/2005-10-09-mississippi-power-usat_x.htm.

34. Ilan Brat, "Whole Foods Works to Reduce Costs and Boost Clout with Suppliers," *The Wall Street Journal*, February 14, 2016, http://www.wsj.com/articles/whole-foods-works-to-reduce-costs-and-boost-clout-with-suppliers-1455445803 (accessed March 24, 2016).

35. Julie Jargon, "Chipotle Pulls Back on Local Ingredients," *The Wall Street Journal*, December 15, 2015, http://www.wsj.com/articles/chipotle-heads-back-to-the-test-kitchen-1450205438 (accessed March 21, 2016).

36. The following discussion of structural alternatives draws from Jay R. Galbraith, *Designing Complex Organizations* (Reading, MA: Addison-Wesley, 1973); Galbraith, *Organization Design* (Reading, MA: Addison-Wesley, 1977); Galbraith, *Designing Dynamic Organizations* (New York: AMACOM, 2002); Robert Duncan, "What Is the Right Organization Structure?" *Organizational Dynamics* (Winter 1979): 59–80; N. Anand and Richard L. Daft, "What Is the Right Organization Design?" *Organizational Dynamics* 36, no. 4 (2007): 329–344; and J. McCann and Jay R. Galbraith, "Interdepartmental Relations," in *Handbook of Organizational Design*, ed. P. Nystrom and W. Starbuck (New York: Oxford University Press, 1981), pp. 60–84.

37. Raymond E. Miles et al., "Designing Organizations to Meet 21st-Century Opportunities and Challenges," *Organizational Dynamics* 39, no. 2 (2010): 93–103.

38. Based on the story of Blue Bell Creameries in Richard L. Daft, *Organization Theory and Design*, 9th ed. (Mason, OH: South-Western, 2007), p. 103; and Peter Elkind, "How Blue Bell Blew It," *Fortune* (October 1, 2015): 122–126.

39. Lex Donaldson and Greg Joffe, "Fit—The Key to Organizational Design," *Journal of Organization Design* 3, no. 3 (2014): 38–45.

40. Miles et al., "Designing Organizations to Meet 21st-Century Opportunities and Challenges."

41. Jaimelynn Hitt, "The Organizational Structure of Starbucks, Unilever, and Wal-Mart" (May 28, 2008), http://voices.yahoo.com/the-organizational-structure-starbucks-unilever-1495147.html (accessed August 15, 2012); Mae Anderson, "Wal-Mart Reorganizes U.S. Operations to Help Spur Growth," *USA TODAY*, January 28, 2010, www.usatoday.com/money/industries/retail/2010-01-28-walmart-reorganization_N.htm (accessed August 15, 2012); and "Walmart," The Official Board Web site, www.theofficialboard.com/org-chart/wal-mart-stores (accessed August 15, 2012).

42. Dougherty, "Google Goal in Restructuring as Alphabet."

43. Conor Dougherty, "Google Goal in Restructuring as Alphabet: Autonomy," *The New York Times*, August 11, 2015, http://www.nytimes.com/2015/08/12/technology/autonomy-seen-as-goal-of-restructured-google.html?_r=0 (accessed March 22, 2016); and Alistair Barr, "At Google, Breathing Room for New Ideas," *The Wall Street Journal*, October 15, 2015, http://www.wsj.com/articles/at-google-breathing-room-for-new-ideas-1443729244 (accessed March 22, 2016).

44. Brooks Barnes, "Is Disney's Chief Having a Cinderella Moment?" *The New York Times*, April 11, 2010.

45. Maisie O'Flanagan and Lynn K. Taliento, "Nonprofits: Ensuring That Bigger Is Better," *McKinsey Quarterly*, no. 2 (2004): 112ff.

46. The discussion of matrix structure is based on Richard M. Burton, Børge Obel, and Dorthe Døjbak Håkonsson, "How to Get the Matrix Organization to Work," *Journal of Organization Design* 4, no. 3 (2015): 37–45; S. H. Appelbaum, D. Nadeau, and M. Cyr, "Performance Evaluation in a Matrix Organization: A Case Study," *Industrial and Commercial Training* 40, no. 5 (2008): 236–241; T. Sy and S. Cote, "Emotional Intelligence: A Key Ability to Succeed in the Matrix Organization," *Journal of Management Development* 23, no. 5 (2004): 439; and Carol Hymowitz, "Managers Suddenly Have to Answer to a Crowd of Bosses," *The Wall Street Journal*, August 12, 2003.

47. Howard Schultz, "Starbucks Makes Organizational Changes to Enhance Customer Experience," February 11, 2008, http://news.starbucks.com/article_display.cfm?article_id=66 (accessed August 15, 2012).

48. Robert C. Ford and W. Alan Randolph, "Cross-Functional Structures: A Review and Integration of Matrix Organization and Project Management," *Journal of Management* 18, no. 2 (1992): 267–294; Burton, Obel, and Håkonsson, "How to Get the Matrix Organization to Work"; and Thomas Sy and Laura Sue D'Annunzio, "Challenges and Strategies of Matrix Organizations: Top-Level and Mid-Level Managers' Perspectives," *Human Resources Planning* 28, no. 1 (2005): 39–48.

49. These disadvantages are based on Sy and D'Annunzio, "Challenges and Strategies of Matrix Organizations"; and Michael Goold and Andrew Campbell, "Making Matrix Structures Work: Creating Clarity on Unit Roles and Responsibilities," *European Management Journal* 21, no. 3 (June 2003): 351–363.

50. Darren Dahl, "Strategy: Managing Fast, Flexible, and Full of Team Spirit," *Inc.* (May 2009): 95–97.

51. Jena McGregor, " Zappos Says Goodbye to Bosses," *The Washington Post*, January 3, 2014, https://www.washingtonpost.com/news/on-leadership/wp/2014/01/03/zappos-gets-rid-of-all-managers/ (accessed March 22, 2016).

52. Bill Fischer, Umberto Lago, and Fang Liu, "The Haier Road to Growth," *Strategy + Business* (April 27, 2015), http://www.strategy-business.com/article/00323?gko=c8c2a (accessed March 23, 2016); and Art Kleiner, "China's Philosopher-CEO Zhang Ruimin," *Strategy + Business* (November 10, 2014), http://www.strategy-business.com/article/00296?gko=8155b (accessed March 23, 2016).

53. Ibid.

54. Melissa A. Schilling and H. Kevin Steensma, "The Use of Modular Organizational Forms: An Industry-Level Analysis," *Academy of Management Journal* 44, no. 6 (December 2001): 1149–1169.

55. Bob Sechler, "Colleges Shedding Non-Core Operations," *The Wall Street Journal*, April 2, 2012; and David Streitfeld, "A City Outsources Everything. California's Sky Doesn't Fall," *The New York Times*, July 20, 2010.

56. Raymond E. Miles and Charles C. Snow, "The New Network Firm: A Spherical Structure Built on a Human Investment Philosophy," *Organizational Dynamics* (Spring 1995): 5-18; and Raymond E. Miles et al., "Organizing in the Knowledge Age: Anticipating the Cellular Form," *Academy of Management Executive* 11, no. 4 (1997): 7-24.

57. Darren Dahl, "Want a Job? Let the Bidding Begin; A Radical Take on the Virtual Company," *Inc.* (March 2011): 93–96; and Eric Markowitz, "3 Weird, Game-Changing Ways to Make Employees Happy," *Inc.* (May 2012), http://www.inc.com/eric-markowitz/philip-rosedale-second-life-coffee-power-make-emloyees-happy.html (accessed October 2, 2013); and SendLove Web site, http://www.sendlove.us/trial/faq.php.

58. Joann S. Lublin, "Smart Balance Keeps Tight Focus on Creativity" (Theory & Practice column), *The Wall Street Journal*, June 8, 2009; and Rebecca Reisner, "A Smart Balance of Staff and Contractors," *BusinessWeek Online*, June 16, 2009, www.businessweek.com/managing/content/jun2009/ca20090616_217232.htm (accessed April 30, 2010).

59. Raymond E. Miles and Charles C. Snow, "Organizations: New Concepts for New Forms," *California Management Review* 28 (Spring 1986): 62–73; and John W. Wilson and Judith H. Dobrzynski, "And Now, the Post-Industrial Corporation," *BusinessWeek* (March 3, 1986): 64–74.

60. N. Anand, "Modular, Virtual, and Hollow Forms of Organization Design," working paper, London Business School (2000); and Don Tapscott, "Rethinking Strategy in a Networked World," *Strategy + Business* 24 (Third Quarter 2001): 34–41.

61. Gregory G. Dess et al., "The New Corporate Architecture," *Academy of Management Executive* 9, no. 3 (1995): 7-20.

62. Raymond E. Miles, "Adapting to Technology and Competition: A New Industrial Relations System for the Twenty-First Century," *California Management Review* (Winter 1989): 9-28; and Miles and Snow, "The New Network Firm."

63. These disadvantages are based on Cecily A. Raiborn, Janet B. Butler, and Marc F. Massoud, "Outsourcing Support Functions: Identifying and Managing the Good, the Bad, and the Ugly," *Business Horizons* 52 (2009): 347–356; Dess et al., "The New Corporate Architecture"; Anand and Daft, "What Is the Right Organization Design?"; Henry W. Chesbrough and David J. Teece, "Organizing for Innovation: When Is Virtual Virtuous?" *The Innovative Entrepreneur* (August 2002): 127–134; N. Anand, "Modular, Virtual, and Hollow Forms of Organization Design"; and M. Lynne Markus, Brook Manville, and Carole E. Agres, "What Makes a Virtual Organization Work?" *Sloan Management Review* (Fall 2000): 13–26.

64. James R. Hagerty, "A Toy Maker Comes Home to the U.S.A.," *The Wall Street Journal*, March 11, 2013; and James R. Hagerty, "A Radical Supply Chain Idea: Own Your Trucking Operation," *The Wall Street Journal*, April 29, 2015, http://www.wsj.com/articles/a-radical-idea-own-your-supply-chain-1430343217 (accessed March 23, 2016).

65. Laurie P. O'Leary, "Curing the Monday Blues: A U.S. Navy Guide for Structuring Cross-Functional Teams," *National Productivity Review* (Spring 1996): 43–51; and Alan Hurwitz, "Organizational Structures for the 'New World Order,'" *Business Horizons* (May–June 1996): 5–14.

66. Jay Galbraith, Diane Downey, and Amy Kates, "Processes and Lateral Capability," *Designing Dynamic Organizations* (New York: AMACOM, 2002), Chapter 4.

67. Thomas Kayser, "Six Ingredients for Collaborative Partnerships," *Leader to Leader* (Summer 2011): 48–54.

68. Siobhan Gorman and Julian E. Barnes, "Spy, Military Ties Aided bin Laden Raid," *The Wall Street Journal*, May 23, 2011, http://online.wsj.com/article/SB10001424052748704083904576334160172068344.html (accessed May 23, 2011).

69. Nick Wingfield, "Seeking Spark, Microsoft Revamps Its Structure," http://www.nytimes.com/2013/07/12/technology/microsoft-revamps-structure-and-management.html?pagewanted=all (accessed July 11, 2013).

70. Farhad Manjoo, "Microsoft's Rule-Breaking Vision of Myriad Devices," *The New York Times,* October 22, 2015; and Nick Wingfield, "Microsoft (Yes, Microsoft) Has a Far-Out Vision," *The New York Times,* April 30, 2015, http://www.nytimes.com/2015/05/03/technology/microsoft-yes-microsoft-has-a-far-out-vision.html?_r=0 (accessed November 25, 2015).

71. William J. Altier, "Task Forces: An Effective Management Tool," *Management Review* (February 1987): 52–57.

72. Example from Paul Adler and Laurence Prusak, "Building a Collaborative Enterprise," *Harvard Business Review* (July–August 2011): 95–101.

73. Henry Mintzberg, *The Structure of Organizations* (Englewood Cliffs, NJ: Prentice Hall, 1979).

74. Paul R. Lawrence and Jay W. Lorsch, "New Managerial Job: The Integrator," *Harvard Business Review* (November–December 1967): 142–151; and Ronald N. Ashkenas and

Suzanne C. Francis, "Integration Managers: Special Leaders for Special Times," *Harvard Business Review* (November–December 2000): 108–116.

75. Jody Hoffer Gittell, *The Southwest Airlines Way: Using the Power of Relationships to Achieve High Performance* (New York: McGraw-Hill, 2003).

76. This discussion is based on Jody Hoffer Gittell, "Coordinating Mechanisms in Care Provider Groups: Relational Coordination as a Mediator and Input Uncertainty as a Moderator of Performance Effects," *Management Science* 48, no. 11 (November 2002), 1408–1426; J. H. Gittell, "The Power of Relationships," *Sloan Management Review* (Winter 2004), 16–17; and Gittell, *The Southwest Airlines Way*.

77. Roger Yu, "A Faster Pace for National Geographic Magazine," *USA Today*, November 2, 2014, http://www.usatoday.com/story/money/business/2014/11/02/national-geographic-evolves-to-newsier-Source/18206349/ (accessed November 3, 2014).

78. Ben Kesling and James R. Hagerty, "Say Goodbye to the Office Cubicle," *The Wall Street Journal*, April 2, 2013.

79. University of Michigan study, reported in Rachel Emma Silverman, "The Science of Serendipity in the Workplace," *The Wall Street Journal*, May 1, 2013.

80. Jody Hoffer Gittell, "Paradox of Coordination and Control," *California Management Review* 42, no 3 (Spring 2000): 101–117.

81. Claudio Feser, "Long Live Bureaucracy," *Leader to Leader* (Summer 2012): 57–65; and Harold J. Leavitt, "Why Hierarchies Thrive," *Harvard Business Review* (March 2003): 96–102, discuss the benefits and problems of vertical hierarchies. See Timothy Galpin, Rod Hilpirt, and Bruce Evans, "The Connected Enterprise: Beyond Division of Labor," *Journal of Business Strategy* 28, no. 2 (2007): 38–47, for a discussion of the advantages of horizontal over vertical designs.

82. Lex Donaldson and Greg Joffe, "Fit—The Key to Organizational Design," *Journal of Organization Design* 3, no. 3 (2014): 38–45.

83. Ibid.; Eric M. Olson, Stanley F. Slater, and G. Tomas M. Hult, "The Importance of Structure and Process to Strategy Implementation," *Business Horizons* 48 (2005): 47–54; and Dale E. Zand, "Strategic Renewal: How an Organization Realigned Structure with Strategy," *Strategy & Leadership* 37, no. 3 (2009): 23–28.

84. Michael E. Porter, *Competitive Strategy* (New York: Free Press, 1980), pp. 36–46.

85. Tom Burns and G. M. Stalker, *The Management of Innovation* (London: Tavistock, 1961).

86. John A. Coutright, Gail T. Fairhurst, and L. Edna Rogers, "Interaction Patterns in Organic and Mechanistic Systems," *Academy of Management Journal* 32 (1989): 773–802.

87. For more on technology and structure, see Denise M. Rousseau and Robert A. Cooke, "Technology and Structure: The Concrete, Abstract, and Activity Systems of Organizations," *Journal of Management* 10 (1984): 345–361; Charles Perrow, "A Framework for the Comparative Analysis of Organizations," *American Sociological Review* 32 (1967): 194–208; and Denise M. Rousseau, "Assessment of Technology in Organizations: Closed versus Open Systems Approaches," *Academy of Management Review* 4 (1979): 531–542.

88. Joan Woodward, *Industrial Organizations: Theory and Practice* (London: Oxford University Press, 1965); and Woodward, *Management and Technology* (London: Her Majesty's Stationery Office, 1958).

89. Peter K. Mills and Thomas Kurk, "A Preliminary Investigation into the Influence of Customer-Firm Interface on Information Processing and Task Activity in Service Organizations," *Journal of Management* 12 (1986): 91–104; Peter K. Mills and Dennis J. Moberg, "Perspectives on the Technology of Service Operations," *Academy of Management Review* 7 (1982): 467–478; and Roger W. Schmenner, "How Can Service Businesses Survive and Prosper?" *Sloan Management Review* 27 (Spring 1986): 21–32.

90. Richard B. Chase and David A. Tansik, "The Customer Contact Model for Organization Design," *Management Science* 29 (1983): 1037–1050; and Gregory B. Northcraft and Richard B. Chase, "Managing Service Demand at the Point of Delivery," *Academy of Management Review* 10 (1985): 66–75.

91. Geeta Anand, "The Henry Ford of Heart Surgery," *The Wall Street Journal*, November 25, 2009.

92. Based on Doug Wallace, "The Man Who Knew Too Much," *Business Ethics* 2 (March–April 1993): 7–8.

PART 4

Chapter 8
Managing Change and Innovation

iStock.com/oscarhdez

Chapter Outline

Learning Outcomes

After studying this chapter, you should be able to:

8.1 Define *organizational change* and explain disruptive innovation and the ambidextrous approach as possible responses to the forces that drive innovation and change in today's organizations.

8.2 Describe the three innovation strategies that managers implement for changing products and technologies.

8.3 Explain the value of creativity, a bottom-up approach, internal contests, idea incubators, idea champions, and new-venture teams for innovation.

8.4 Describe the horizontal linkage model and how it contributes to successful product and service innovations.

8.5 Explain open innovation and how it is being used by today's organizations.

8.6 Discuss why changes in people and culture are critical to any change process.

8.7 Summarize the organization development (OD) stages of unfreezing, changing, and refreezing, and define *large-group interventions*.

8.8 Identify some reasons people frequently resist change.

8.9 Describe force-field analysis and implementation tactics that managers can use to overcome resistance.

Discover Your Management Approach

Do You Have True Grit?[a]

Instructions: Think about typical projects or hobbies that you initiate at home, school, or work. Respond to each of the following items as honestly as possible.

	Mostly True	Mostly False
1. I often set a goal but later choose to pursue a different one.	_____	_____
2. I have been obsessed with a certain idea or project for a short time but later lose interest.	_____	_____
3. I have difficulty maintaining my focus on projects that take more than a few months to complete.	_____	_____

To complete and score the entire assessment, visit MindTap.

[a]Angela Lee Duckworth and Patrick D. Quinn, "Development and Validation of the Short Grit Scale (Grit-S)," *Journal of Personality Assessment* 91, no. 2 (2009): 166–174. Used with permission.

The Kindle e-reader was a hit for Amazon in 2007, and CEO Jeff Bezos and other managers pushed hard into developing additional consumer products. A division called Lab126 has released a dozen or so devices over the past few years, including a television set-top box, a home barcode scanner, the Echo virtual assistant, and Amazon's first attempt at a smartphone. Some of those products haven't done so well. For instance, in 2015, Amazon pulled the plug on the Fire smartphone, laid off dozens of engineers at Lab126, and scrapped or scaled back plans for other projects. However, Lab126 is still developing some ambitious products, including a high-end computer for the kitchen that is being designed to serve as a hub for an Internet-connected home. In July 2015, Amazon began selling a $5 button that customers can press to order a single brand-name item, such as Brawny paper towels, All laundry detergent, or Huggies diapers, and offering a credit for the cost of the button after the first press. "The next logical step for them is a fully connected home," said Tom Mainelli, an IDC analyst. "With the data they have, they could soon be at the point where all the things you need just arrive at your home, without even asking."[1]

Even though Amazon's Fire smartphone was a flop, Jeff Bezos knows it is important to keep investing in developing innovative products and services. Innovation in products and services is what keeps companies thriving. In addition, all organizations need to regularly make changes in policies, practices, and operations to address shortcomings, respond to new challenges, or meet shifting needs. If organizations don't change and innovate successfully, they die. Consider that only a small number of large companies reach the age of 40, according to a study of more than 6 million firms. The ones that survive are ruthless about innovation and change.[2] Every organization sometimes faces the need to change swiftly and dramatically to cope with a changing environment. For example, one of the first things Mary T. Barra did after taking over the CEO job at GM in 2014 was to acknowledge the continuing need for change at the giant company to prevent problems such as the delayed recall of vehicles for an ignition flaw that has been blamed for more than 100 deaths. Barra said that "something went very wrong in our processes," and she vowed that GM would implement internal changes to make sure a similar situation never happens again.[3]

In this chapter, we look at how organizations can be designed to respond to the environment through internal change and development.[4] We examine two key aspects of change in organizations: changing organizational things—new products and technology—and changing organizational people and culture. The chapter also looks at some reasons people resist change and explores some techniques managers use to implement change.

8-1 Innovation and the Changing Workplace

Organizational change is defined as the adoption of a new idea or behavior by an organization.[5] Sometimes change and innovation are spurred by forces outside the organization, such as when a powerful customer demands annual price cuts, when a key supplier goes out of business, or when new government regulations go into effect. Other times, managers within the company see a need for product or service innovations, for creating greater efficiencies in operations, or for other alterations to keep the organization profitable. Two concepts that address the need for change in today's environment are disruptive innovation and the ambidextrous approach.

8-1a Disruptive Innovation

Disruptive innovation is becoming a goal for companies that want to remain competitive on a global basis. **Disruptive innovation** refers to innovations in products or services that typically start small and end up completely replacing an existing product or service technology for producers and consumers.[6] Companies that initiate a disruptive innovation typically win big; companies affected by a disruptive innovation may be put out of business. For example, when Netflix began, few people (including Blockbuster managers) saw it as a threat to Blockbuster (the giant firm renting videos and DVDs) because most of Blockbuster's customers didn't want to order a movie online and wait several days for it to arrive through the mail. However, as technology for streaming evolved, Netflix was able to attract more and more of Blockbuster's customers by offering a wide selection of on-demand content conveniently and at low cost. As described in Chapter 8, by failing to respond quickly and effectively to this disruptive innovation, Blockbuster was put out of business.[7] As another example, smartphones are disrupting the compact digital camera business because people can more easily take snapshots with their phones and quickly share the photos on social networks. Sales of point-and-shoot cameras continue to fall.[8] A company called Square developed the first credit card reader that plugs into a smartphone. This was a disruptive innovation in the trillion-dollar financial services system for credit card payments. Square enabled

Sunny Side Up ⟩ Elevate Packaging

Rich Cohen had a mission: to use innovative materials not well known to create sustainable packaging options. It had germinated during the year he took off work as a strategy and business developer to travel around the world. Thailand and the Philippines were two places he met paper makers and was intrigued. As he moved around the globe, he became more and more interested in the environment.

In 2000, he saw many people being interested in sustainability and very few packaging products that were recyclable. He decided to do something with paper that adds value to the world and started his Chicago-based company, Elevate Packaging. Its first product was a recyclable pressure-sensitive shipping label using the hemp plant with a recyclable adhesive. That product did well, especially in Europe. So the company came out with a compostable label, which launched in 2010. It's still the only compostable label in the entire world, even selling eight varieties, including ones you can print yourself (go to elevatepackaging.com). Then Cohen examined the packaging label materials. If the label is not compostable,

what difference does the label make? That's when he started thinking of packaging and used 90 percent wood pulp from Sustainable Forest Management (SFM) forests and bamboo to make bags and boxes. Why stop there? If he used invasive plants species, the kind that take over and kill other plants, he'd be helping the environment in other ways, so he began converting mulberry plants and water hyacinths to packaging goods. Cohen saw his path: Identify the best-of-class sustainable materials to create compostable packaging.

A newer innovation was developing cellophane bags that are bio-based and completely compostable. Then Elevate Packaging added stand-up pouches with zippers and coffee bags with valves, all of it compostable. The company has even gotten the fashion industry knocking on its doors.

Cohen's dream has been to create products that would not deplete the earth and would add value. It's about what we stand for. He says, "Packaging speaks to values."

SOURCE: Rich Cohen, personal communication, March 2018.

millions of small businesses that couldn't afford the transaction fees charged by financial companies to begin accepting credit cards.[9] Many disruptive innovations come from small entrepreneurial firms like Square, or such as Elevate Packaging, as described in the "Sunny Side Up" box.

Some observers think companies in emerging markets such as China and India will produce a great percentage of such innovations in the coming years.[10] Godrej & Boyce, for example, created a portable, low-cost, battery-powered refrigerator for India, called the chotuKool, as we described in Chapter 3.[11]

This is connected to the trend called **reverse innovation**. Rather than innovating in affluent countries and transferring products to emerging markets, companies such as Lenovo, General Electric (GE), John Deere, Nestlé, Procter & Gamble (P&G), and Xerox are creating innovative, low-cost products for emerging markets and then quickly and inexpensively repackaging them for sale in developed countries. GE Healthcare's team in China created a portable ultrasound machine that sold for less than 15 percent of the cost of the company's high-end machines. GE now sells the product around the world, and it grew to a $278-million global product line within six years. John Deere developed a high-quality, low-cost tractor for farmers in India that is increasingly in demand in the United States among farmers recovering from the recession.[12]

Concept Connection

Innovative companies use an **ambidextrous approach** by creating structures and processes that both encourage creative ideas and enable the efficient and effective implementation of innovations. Many organizations establish separate **creative departments** to give employees the freedom and flexibility to propose new ideas and work on innovative projects. An example of a creative department is the Google Engineering Center in Zurich, Switzerland, where historic cable car cabins serve as conference rooms. Implementation of innovations is carried out through the more structured systems of the regular organization.

8-1b The Ambidextrous Approach

Change—especially major change such as that associated with disruptive innovation—is not easy, and many organizations struggle with changing successfully. In some cases, employees don't have the desire or motivation to come up with new ideas, or their ideas never get heard by managers who could put them into practice. In other cases, managers learn about good ideas but have trouble getting cooperation from employees for implementation. Successful change requires that organizations be capable of both creating and implementing ideas, which means the organization must learn to be *ambidextrous*.

An **ambidextrous approach** means incorporating structures and processes that are appropriate for both the creative impulse and for the systematic implementation of innovations.[13] For example, a loose, flexible structure and greater employee freedom are excellent for the creation and initiation of ideas; however, these same conditions often make it difficult to implement a change because employees are less likely to comply. With an ambidextrous approach, managers encourage flexibility and freedom to innovate and propose new ideas with creative departments and other mechanisms that we will discuss in this chapter, but they use a more rigid, centralized, and standardized approach for implementing innovations.[14] Companies such as Home Depot, Target, and American Eagle have set up separate innovation labs in the San Francisco area in recent years to allow creative people the time, freedom, and resources to come up with innovative products and services. Many of these labs are designed to look and feel like start-up technology companies, including such elements as brightly colored furniture, ping pong tables, brainstorming pods, and catered meals. Implementation of the innovations for which routine and precision are important, takes place within the regular organization.[15] Twenty-eight year-old Nate Morris disrupted the way garbage is handled and has created a successful, growing company, as shown in the "Recipe for Success" box.v

Visa set up an innovation lab to encourage an ambidextrous approach and try to avoid being disrupted in the business of how people pay for purchases, as shown in the upcoming Sunny Side Up box.

Recipe for Success 〉 **Rubicon Global**

If you think Waste Management is run primarily by Tony Soprano & friends, think again. Nate Morris was 25 when he started Rubicon Global in Walton, KY, being inspired by fellow Kentuckian Colonel Sanders, who started the mega-company KFC from a single, roadside restaurant. Morris also dealt with food.

After graduating from George Washington University, he went to graduate school and hoped to go in to politics, but the 2008 crash came, and he knew his prospects were limited. So he did what he had avoided: go into the family waste management business, even though there was no company to take over. What he learned was that a large percentage of profits was from landfills, so companies were incentivized to create more garbage.

Morris decided it was time for a change and came up with a way to help customers and the environment. He borrowed against his credit cards, started a Web site, reached out to his network, and managed to get in front of the CEO of one of the largest pizza chains.

"I want your garbage contract," he said, stunning the CEO, who was used to loftier requests. Because of his forthrightness, he got the contract. He figured out that much of the leftover pizza dough could be reprocessed into ethanol. Innovative recycling became his thing. For a supermarket chain, he shredded 40,000 old uniforms for pet bedding; he repurposed used insulated cartons for a different purpose. One major recycling organization estimates that $11.4 billion worth of recyclable goods get wasted in landfills.

By 2018, Morris had managed to run waste management for a number of Fortune 500 companies, including 7-Eleven. He reduces their waste bills by up to 30 percent by not only recycling but also being a broker of waste-hauling services. The person he took longest to convince was his mother, who didn't imagine her son would end up as a garbageman. "You could have done that out of high school," she said. Maybe not, if he wanted to run a multi-million-dollar company. His mother has since come around.

SOURCE: Andy Kessler, "Inside View: Unicorns Need IPOs," *The Wall Street Journal*, January 8, 2018, A15; and David Zax, "Dividing and Conquering the Trash," *The New York Times*, October 26, 2014, BU1 & BU6.

Sunny Side Up 〉 **Visa**

Visa has been "pioneering payments from day one," says the company's Web site. The organization has its roots in the first credit card for middle-class consumers in the United States, launched by Bank of America in 1958 as the Bank Americard. Visa has changed a great deal since then, but the mission of the giant multinational company remains "to be the best way to pay and be paid, for everyone, everywhere."

When Google launched Google Wallet, an app that lets people pay for purchases in stores using their smartphones, Visa was caught off guard. Visa wants to be the company that defines the future of the payments industry, but managers realized that the future of payments is no longer a piece of plastic that you slip in your wallet. Google Wallet also created a problem for Visa (and other card companies) because purchases made through the app appeared to the card companies as if they were made at Google rather than at the merchant where the item was bought. That made it almost impossible for companies to resolve disputes or detect fraud.

Spurred by Google's surprise move, Visa managers thought a separate innovation center was the best way to give engineers the freedom to think creatively, solve problems, and develop innovative ideas. "We needed to become more willing to drive innovation rather than sit back and wait for things to break," said Jim McCarthy, Visa's global head of innovation and strategic partnerships. Visa's 12,000 square foot innovation center in downtown San Francisco is designed to facilitate interaction and collaboration. Employees have the freedom to experiment and make mistakes in the interest of coming up with new products and services.

One recent innovation from the center is a credit-card payment system that can be built directly into a car. It can alert drivers when they are low on gas, give them directions to the nearest place to fill up, and then allow them to make a payment through their dashboard. Another innovation in the works is a parking payment system developed in collaboration with ParkWhiz.[16]

Remember This

- Every organization must change and innovate to survive.
- **Organizational change** is defined as the adoption of a new idea or behavior by an organization.
- **Disruptive innovation** refers to innovations in products, services, or processes that radically change competition in an industry, such as the advent of streaming video or online college courses.

- An **ambidextrous approach** means incorporating structures and processes that are appropriate for both the creative impulse and the systematic implementation of innovations.
- Visa, Target, American Eagle, and other large companies have built separate innovation labs to promote an ambidextrous approach.

8-2 Changing Things: New Products and Technologies

The Visa example illustrates one vital area of change that organizations must embrace, which is the introduction of new products, services, and technologies. A **product change** is a change in the organization's product or service outputs. Product and service innovation is the primary way in which organizations adapt to changes in markets, technology, and competition.[17] One example of a service innovation is U.S.-based Robinhood, an app-based stock brokerage that offers commission-free trading and has helped open stock trading to young people, who are often put off by the various fees typically associated with trading stocks. Robinhood, founded in 2014, is the fastest-growing stock brokerage in history and is the first finance app to have won an Apple Design Award.[18] Examples of new products include Nike's Flyknit Racer running shoe, which weighs just 5.6 ounces; the Fitbit Blaze, an exercise-detecting smart fitness watch, which fitness tracking device company Fitbit introduced in 2016 to fend off competition from Apple and other rivals getting into the digital health and fitness tracking business; and the Nest home thermostat, which learns its user's patterns and adjusts to save energy.[19]

Product and service changes are related to changes in the technology of the organization. A **technology change** is a change in the organization's production process—how the organization does its work. Technology changes are designed to make the production of a product or service more efficient. Hammond's Candies saves hundreds of thousands of dollars a year by implementing technology changes suggested by employees. One example was tweaking a machine gear that reduced the number of employees needed on an assembly line from five to four.[20] Another example is How Khuram Mir used horticultural techniques new to Kashmir to bring about radical changes, as described below in the "Recipe for Success" box.

Other examples of technology change include the introduction of efficiency-boosting winglets on aircraft at Southwest Airlines, the adoption of automatic mail-sorting machines by the U.S. Postal Service, and the use of biosimulation software to run virtual tests on new drugs at Johnson & Johnson's pharmaceutical research and development department.

Three critical innovation strategies for changing products and technologies are illustrated in Exhibit 8.1.[21] The first strategy, *exploration*, involves designing the organization to encourage creativity and the initiation of new ideas. The strategy of *cooperation* refers to creating conditions and systems to facilitate internal and external coordination and knowledge sharing. Finally, the term *innovation roles* means that managers put in place processes and structures to ensure that new ideas are carried forward for acceptance and implementation.

Visit MindTap for the "Self-Assessment: How Creative Are You?"

8-2a Exploration

Exploration is the stage where ideas for new products and technologies are born. Managers design the organization for exploration by establishing conditions that encourage creativity and allow new ideas to spring forth. **Creativity** refers to the generation of novel ideas that might

Recipe for Success — HN Agri Serve

Starting a new business is difficult enough, without having to adjust to on-and-off war conditions. Coming from a long-line of farmers, Khuram Mir left India and the farm-life, got a masters in Industrial Systems Engineering and Operations Research at Purdue, where he developed supply-chain models. Then he worked in manufacturing processes in the semiconductor industry. Mir had education and money, but he needed more meaning in his life and decided to dedicate himself to making the world better. "Money never drove me," he said. "I wanted to make a difference."

Returning to his home state of Kashmir in India in 2008, he found himself in a war-weary zone (China, India and Pakistan all lay claim to Kashmir) and realized he need to create a business not dependent on the war. For example, tourism goes down as conflicts increase, whereas horticulture/agriculture continues despite political volatility. Because his father had owned and worked orchards, Mir knew enough to leverage his own experience with the education he'd gotten.

India has the second largest amount of land devoted to agriculture, behind China. Six percent of available land in India is devoted to apples, and the country is one of the top apple-producers in the world. Mir knew he could make a difference in Kashmir's horticulture of apples, where he saw many inefficiencies and waste. He used his supply-side mathematical models, dividing the processes into pre-harvest and post-harvest. Before harvest, he dramatically increased crop return by getting farmers to change to higher-yield trees, using drip irrigation rather

than flooding the fields, and making the grading and sorting more efficient. Post-harvest, he invested in a 2000-ton controlled atmosphere storage unit, so the fruit could sell for much of the year. Previously, farmers had loaded up all the fruit and flooded the market for a few weeks. Additional, Mir cut out the people who did not add value, which included middle-men sellers and money lenders. Mir got farmers and market sellers to work directly with one another, and he created a platform (F2UConnect) where the buyers and farmers could track the apples in the supply chain, and where the buyers could see exactly how much the farmer had been paid. HN Agri Serve makes money by providing such services to the farmers.

The company knew from the beginning women were major workers in the economy, from water-hauling, to planting, to harvesting, and so on. Therefore, they promoted women at a high rate. As a result, they'd had threats, but Mir pushes on with his company and his values to upraise Kashmir.

Mir started his business with $100,000 seed money, and he was offered $70 million for it in mid-2018. He turned down the offer, wanting to continue personally to be part of Kashmir's increasing prosperity. "I want this company to be even more successful," he said. "I want it to be the first billion dollar company that touches a million people in Kashmir."

SOURCES: Khuram Mir, personal communication, July 2018; Jose Alvaraez, Anjala Raina and Rachna Chawla, NH Agri Serve: Growing Prosperity, Harvard Business School Case Study, December 4, 2014.

Exhibit 8.1 Three Innovation Strategies for New Products and Technologies

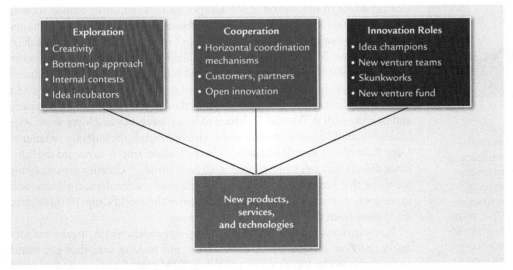

Exploration
- Creativity
- Bottom-up approach
- Internal contests
- Idea incubators

Cooperation
- Horizontal coordination mechanisms
- Customers, partners
- Open innovation

Innovation Roles
- Idea champions
- New venture teams
- Skunkworks
- New venture fund

New products, services, and technologies

SOURCE: Based on Patrick Reinmoeller and Nicole van Baardwijk, "The Link Between Diversity and Resilience," *MIT Sloan Management Review* (Summer 2005): 61–65.

meet perceived needs or respond to opportunities for the organization.[22] People noted for their creativity include Edwin Land, who invented the Polaroid camera, and Swiss engineer George de Mestral, who created Velcro after noticing the tiny hooks on some burrs caught on his wool socks. These people saw unique and creative opportunities in familiar situations.

Green Power

Adrian Sherratt/Alamy Stock Photo

Concept Connection

"People think of **creativity** as a mystical process," said Sir James Dyson, who founded the Dyson company and invented the Dual Cyclone bagless vacuum. "But this could not be more wrong." Wise managers know that everyone has creative potential. They encourage a **bottom-up approach** to creativity and innovation by creating organizational characteristics such as open communication, a playful culture, and freedom to take risks and make mistakes. The office walls at a business communication solutions provider in the United Kingdom have whiteboards where employees can flesh out ideas, contribute to projects, or just express their individuality.

Characteristics of highly creative people are illustrated in the left column of Exhibit 8.2. Creative people often are known for their originality, open-mindedness, curiosity, focused approach to problem solving, persistence, relaxed and playful attitude, and receptiveness to new ideas.[23] Creativity can also be designed into organizations. Most companies want more creative employees and often seek to hire creative individuals. However, the individual is only part of the story, and each of us has some potential for creativity. Managers are responsible for creating a work environment that allows creativity to flourish.[24]

The characteristics of creative organizations correspond to those of individuals, as illustrated in the right column of Exhibit 8.2. Creative organizations are loosely structured. People find themselves in a situation of ambiguity, assignments are vague, territories overlap, tasks are loosely defined, and much work is done by teams. Managers in creative companies embrace risk and experimentation. They involve employees in a varied range of projects, so that people are not stuck in the rhythm of routine jobs, and they drive out the fear of making mistakes that can inhibit creative thinking.[25] Research shows that successful innovations are often accompanied by a high rate of failure.[26] Soon Yu, global vice president of innovation at VF Corporation, which owns brands such as The North Face, SmartWool, and Timberlands, says he's a self-taught master of failure. Before coming to VF, Yu had five of his own start-ups that dissolved and more than 20 product launches that failed. At one point, his credit score was around 300. Top executives at VF hired him because they were convinced he could help employees overcome the fear of mistakes and failure so they could take creative risks. "My No. 1 job is to be the biggest failure in the company and be okay with it," Yu said. "It's hard to be a courageous employee when your leader is scared." Some companies even give out awards for mistakes or failures. Grey Advertising awards an annual "Heroic Failure" trophy to reward the "glorious defeats that can make success itself look timid."[27] Creative organizations are those that have an internal culture of playfulness, freedom, challenge, and grass-roots participation.[28] Exhibit 8.3 shows the world's top 10 innovative companies from the 2016 list in *Fast Company*.

Innovative companies use a **bottom-up approach**, which means encouraging the flow of ideas from lower levels and making sure they get heard and acted upon by top executives.[29] When RJMetrics faced a period of rapid customer growth, managers and employees alike felt that innovation was taking a back seat due to the pressure of just keeping pace with serving existing customer needs. To encourage bottom-up ideas, managers decided to set aside a 24-hour period each quarter for everyone to work on experimental projects, essentially shutting down the company for two days. Participation in the quarterly "hackathons" is voluntary, but most people like having the time to think creatively. At the end of the period, each team makes a five-minute presentation

Exhibit 8.2 Characteristics of Creative People and Organizations

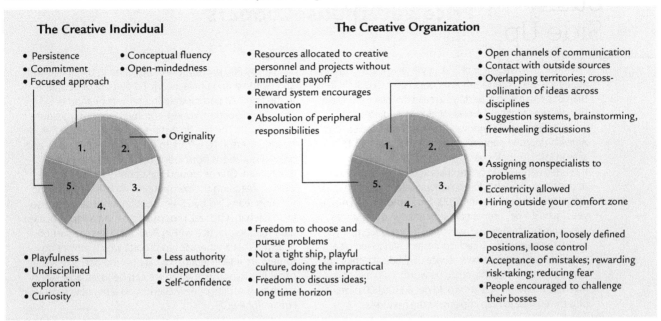

SOURCES: Based on Gary A. Steiner, ed., *The Creative Organization* (Chicago: University of Chicago Press, 1965), pp. 16–18; Rosabeth Moss Kanter, "The Middle Manager as Innovator," *Harvard Business Review* (July–August 1982): 104–105; James Brian Quinn, "Managing Innovation: Controlled Chaos," *Harvard Business Review* (May–June 1985): 73–84; Robert I. Sutton, "The Weird Rules of Creativity," *Harvard Business Review* (September 2001): 94–103; and Bridget Finn, "Playbook: Brainstorming for Better Brainstorming," *Business* 2.0 (April 2005), 109–114.

Exhibit 8.3 The World's Most Innovative Companies, 2016

Rank	Company	Reason
1	BuzzFeed	For shaking up media across the globe
2	Facebook	For not letting size get in the way of acting like a start-up
3	CVS Health	For becoming a one-stop health shop
4	Uber	For hustling corporate business
5	Netflix	For giving unexpected audiences exactly what they want
6	Amazon	For evolving from commerce to cool cloud services
7	Apple	For acing its China test
8	Alphabet	For finding a better way to bet big
9	Black Lives Matter	For turning the conversation about race into results
10	Taco Bell	For combining corn, meat, beans, and cheese into genius

SOURCE: "The World's 50 Most Innovative Companies," *Fast Company* (March 2016), http://www.fastcompany.com/most-innovative-companies (accessed March 31, 2016).

and everyone votes for the winning ideas. Today, founder and CEO Robert J. Moore says that at any given time, it's not uncommon for more than half of the work being done to have been initiated by hackathon projects.[30] Exhibit 8.3 describes a fun technique that some companies use to get people to come up with creative ideas for solving specific problems.

Some companies also use internal *innovation contests*, which are an increasingly popular way to realize product and service innovations.[31] Dow Chemical, for example, holds an annual innovation tournament that focuses on ideas for cutting waste and saving energy. Employees vote on the submissions, and the winners receive monetary rewards. Over a 10-year period, ideas from the innovation tournaments have led to nearly 600 projects that have produced an average return of 204 percent and saved Dow Chemical $100 million a year.[32] Managers at the accounting and consulting firm PricewaterhouseCoopers (PwC) challenged the stereotype that accountants are boring and unimaginative by sponsoring an *American Idol*–style contest to spur employees to come up with creative ideas.

Sunny Side Up } PricewaterhouseCoopers

"We have an average age of 27, but we have roots in tax and assurance," said PricewaterhouseCoopers (PwC) U.S. chairman Bob Moritz. "So how do you make this place feel like a Google or a Facebook? A place that feels leading edge?"

Mitra Best, PwC's "innovation leader" and a fan of *American Idol*, the popular television show that had its final season in 2016, took ideas from that show, plus ideas from the video game world of live chats and online discussions, to create PowerPitch, a fun, collaborative competition that would connect and inspire 30,000 PwC employees. Employees loved it. The competition, structured in three stages over a nine-month period, was open to any U.S. employee below the partner level. Each contestant had to recruit a team and pitch either a new service or a radical rethinking of an existing service that could be worth $100 million in revenue. The winning team would get a $100,000 prize, plus the chance to help implement the new idea.

Nearly 800 proposals were pitched in the first round, and by the grand finale, nearly 60 percent of people in the firm had participated in one way or another—direct participation, voting, comments and suggestions, and so forth. The five finalist teams were flown to PwC headquarters in New York to present their proposals and answer questions from judges in a packed corporate auditorium. Offices around the country held viewing parties, watching the competition via live Webcast. The winning team, led by 25-year-old financial services associate Zachary Capozzi, proposed creating a sophisticated data-mining practice within PwC that uses the sort of analytics that Netflix uses to predict which movies customers are interested in. For clients who don't have that capability in house, the service can be invaluable—and it can be a source of new clients and a big new revenue stream for PwC.[33]

Sunny Side Up } Use Six Thinking Hats for Better Ideas

A technique that can promote broader thinking is called *Six Thinking Hats*, which was developed by Edward de Bono. The model encourages people in a group to combine negative and critical thinking with positive and creative thinking. Participants either literally or figuratively wear a hat to represent a distinct perspective. The wearing of the hats helps individuals step out of their comfort zone and generate creative ideas in a risk-free way. The Six Thinking Hats technique can transform a typical nonproductive meeting into a highly creative problem-solving endeavor.

The Six Hats

- **White Hat:** This thinking hat is neutral and concerned with just the objective facts, figures, and information pertaining to a problem.

- **Red Hat:** This hat allows an emotional response to the subject. It is a perspective based on feelings, intuitions, instincts, and hunches.

- **Green Hat:** The green hat is the one that generates new ideas, possibilities, alternatives, and unique solutions for better problem solving.

- **Black Hat:** This is the negative, pessimistic, and critical hat, which focuses on why a suggestion will *not*

work. When people wear this hat, they point out the flaws and false assumptions in an idea.

- **Yellow Hat:** The yellow hat is the opposite of the black hat. It is optimistic and focuses on the values and benefits of an idea. Its focus is on what *will* work.

- **Blue Hat:** This hat is concerned with group facilitation. The group leader typically assumes the blue hat role, although any member can wear the blue hat from time to time.

Using the Technique

To apply the Six Thinking Hats technique, schedule a specific time during a creative problem-solving meeting when every person in the group wears the same color of hat—that is, takes the same perspective. A time is set aside when everyone uses rational, fact-based thinking (white hat), emotional thinking (red hat), creative thinking (green hat), and so forth. The result is that each perspective (hat) is heard in sequence, and negative views or arguments do not overwhelm creativity. Everyone together has a time to think of good ideas, as well as a time for finding weak points.

SOURCE: Based on Edward de Bono, *Serious Creativity: Using the Power of Lateral Thinking to Create New Ideas* (New York: HarperBusiness, 1992).

Just as important as creating ideas is turning them into action. Sadly, research indicates that, on average, a U.S. employee's ideas are implemented only once every six years.[34] "There's nothing worse for morale than when employees feel like their ideas go nowhere," says Larry Bennett, a professor of entrepreneurship.[35] At PwC, all of the final ideas were assigned to a senior "champion," who would help the teams further develop and implement their proposals. Other ideas from the top 20 semifinalists were assigned to an idea incubator group. An **idea incubator** is a mechanism that provides a safe harbor where ideas from employees throughout the company can be developed without interference from company bureaucracy or politics.[36]

Remember This

- A **product change** is a change in the organization's products or services, such as the Nike Flyknit Racer running shoe or Robinhood's app-based stock brokerage.
- **Technology change** refers to a change in production processes—how the organization does its work.
- *Exploration* involves designing the organization to encourage creativity and the initiation of new ideas.
- **Creativity** is the generation of novel ideas that may meet perceived needs or respond to opportunities for the organization.

- Using a **bottom-up approach** means encouraging the flow of ideas from lower levels and making sure they get heard and acted upon by top executives.
- Software start-up RJMetrics holds quarterly "hackathons," setting aside a 24-hour period each quarter for everyone to come up with innovative ideas and work on experimental projects.
- An **idea incubator** is an organizational program that provides a safe harbor where employees can generate and develop ideas without interference from company bureaucracy or politics.

8-2b Cooperation

Ideas for product and technology innovations typically originate at lower levels of the organization and need to flow horizontally across departments. In addition, people and organizations outside the firm can be rich sources of innovative ideas. Thus, many companies are undergoing a transformation in the way they find and use new ideas, focusing on improving both internal and external coordination and cooperation.

Internal Coordination   Successful innovation requires expertise from several departments simultaneously, and failed innovation is often the result of failed cooperation.[37] Studies at the Massachusetts Institute of Technology (MIT) suggest that keeping research and manufacturing close together helps companies be more innovative. For instance, GE custom-built a large manufacturing facility in upstate New York to be near its research campus, where a new secret battery technology was being invented. The idea was to knit together design, prototyping, manufacturing, testing, and production for uses of the new battery technology.[38]

Sony Electronics, once the epitome of Japanese innovation success, is literally fighting to stay alive because the company hasn't had a hit product in years. To be sure, Sony was battered by one after another disruptive new technology or unexpected competitor, but the biggest problem was that managers were unable to get high collaboration within the organization. The company had the technology to create a music player like the iPod long before Apple came out with it (cofounder Akio Morita actually envisioned such a device in the 1980s), but divisions couldn't cooperate to bring the idea to fruition.[39] "Innovation is a team sport," says Drew Boyd, a businessman who speaks about innovation to other companies.[40]

Companies that successfully innovate usually have the following characteristics:

- People in research and marketing actively work with customers to understand their needs and develop solutions.
- Technical specialists are aware of recent developments and make effective use of new technology.

- A shared new-product development process that is advocated and supported by top management cuts across organizational functions and units.
- Members from key departments—research, manufacturing, marketing—cooperate in the development of the new product or service.
- Each project is guided by a core cross-functional team from beginning to end.[41]

One approach to successful innovation is called the **horizontal linkage model**, which is illustrated in the center circle of Exhibit 8.4.[42] The model shows that the research, manufacturing, and sales and marketing departments within an organization simultaneously contribute to new products and technologies. People from these departments meet frequently in teams and task forces to share ideas and solve problems. Research people inform marketing of new technical developments to find out whether they will be useful to customers. Marketing people pass customer complaints to research to use in the design of new products and to manufacturing people to develop new ideas for improving production speed and quality. Manufacturing informs other departments whether a product idea can be manufactured within cost limits. Throughout the process, development teams keep in close touch with customers. A study by McKinsey found that 80 percent of successful innovators periodically test and validate customer preferences during development of new products and services.[43]

The horizontal linkage model is increasingly important in a high-pressure business environment that requires rapidly developing and commercializing products and services. Speed is a pivotal strategic weapon in the global marketplace.[44] Corning used a horizontal linkage model with people from research and development (R&D), manufacturing, and sales working together to quickly create Gorilla Glass, a thin, super-strong, flexible glass now used on most smartphone and tablet screens.[45] Even a traditional business such as manufacturing mattresses is continuously changing today, with each company touting the benefits of its new products. Sealy revived its high-end Stearns & Foster line of mattresses by pushing engineers, product designers, and sales and marketing people to work with one another as well as with customers and outside design firm IDEO. The result was that sales of the Stearns & Foster line broke records. Allen Platek, vice president of new-product development, said the new product revamp was "one of the most fun times of my career."[46] This kind of teamwork is similar to a rugby match, wherein players run together, passing the ball back and forth as they move downfield.[47] Famous innovation

Exhibit 8.4 Coordination Model for Innovation

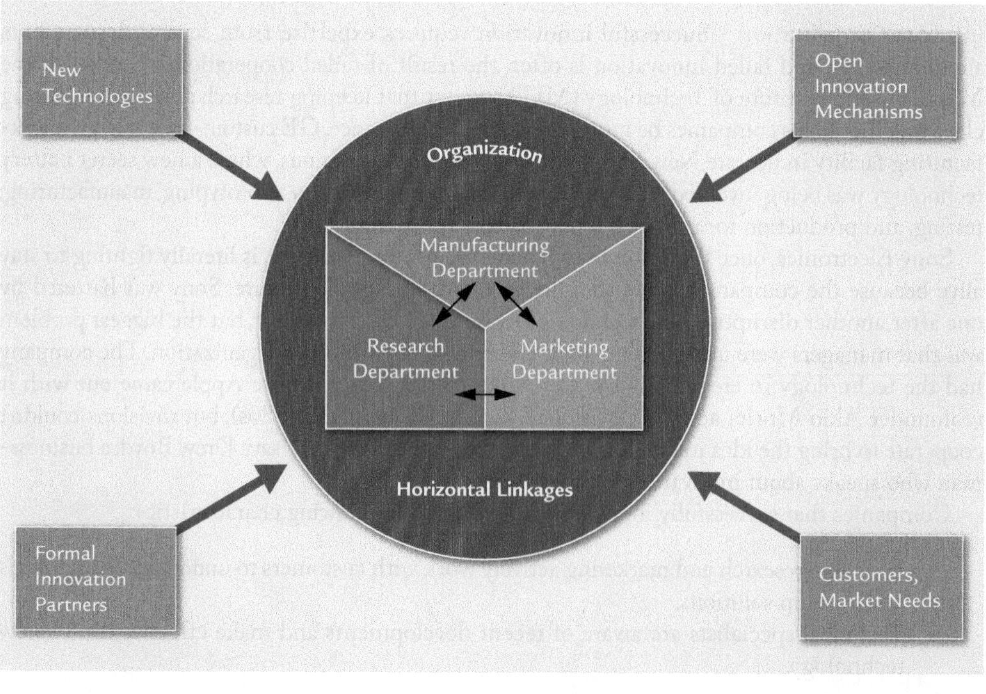

failures—such as Microsoft's Zune music player and the U.S. Mint's Susan B. Anthony dollar, perhaps the most unpopular coin in American history—usually violate the horizontal linkage model.

External Coordination   Exhibit 8.4 also illustrates that organizations look outside their boundaries to find and develop new ideas. Engineers and researchers stay aware of new technological developments. Marketing personnel pay attention to shifting market conditions and customer needs. Some organizations build formal strategic partnerships, such as alliances and joint ventures, to improve innovation success. Uber Ride-Sharing should have been more concerned about external coordination and cooperation, as shown in the "Half-Baked Management" box.

Successful companies often include customers, strategic partners, suppliers, and other outsiders directly in the product and service development process. One of the hottest trends is *open innovation*.[48] In the past, most businesses generated their own ideas in house and then developed, manufactured, marketed, and distributed them, which is a closed innovation approach. Today, however, forward-looking companies are trying a different method. **Open innovation** means extending the search for and commercialization of new ideas beyond the boundaries of the organization and even beyond the boundaries of the industry, sharing knowledge and resources with other organizations and individuals outside the firm. For example, game maker Rovio extended the commercialization of the Angry Birds brand into books, movies, and toys by letting outsiders license the popular gaming app.[49]

The Internet has made it possible for companies to tap into ideas from around the world and let hundreds of thousands of people contribute to the innovation process, which is why some approaches to open innovation are referred to as **crowdsourcing**. ModCloth, an online retailer of vintage-inspired clothing, lets customers weigh in on design trends and help decide which ideas to implement. Customers vote and express opinions on designs through the company's Web site. Fiat introduced the first crowdsourced car, the Mio, based on 11,000 ideas submitted by 17,000 customers from around the world.[50]

The most straightforward way to enlist the help of a crowd is with a contest.[51] Harvard Medical School used a worldwide contest to search for new ideas for treating and curing Type 1 diabetes. Within six weeks, researchers had received 190 submissions. The winners included an undergraduate chemistry student, a retired dentist, and a geophysicist.[52] Since September 2010, more than 250,000 people have participated in online competitions run by the U.S. government at Challenge.gov, and $220 million in prizes had been awarded by early 2016. Philips now sells a light-emitting diode (LED) bulb that won a $10-million Department of Energy contest.[53]

Organizations as diverse as BMW, GE, Zara, Netflix, and the National Eye Institute have used crowdsourcing. The New York–based start-up company Quirky has used the crowd from its beginning to determine what products it makes and sells.

Kaufman knows some products Quirky puts out will fail, but he says a crowd-based model makes the process of innovation much faster and the cost of failure much lower. Crowdsourcing is also being used to gather creative ideas for solving social problems. After Super Typhoon Haiyan devastated the Philippines, for example, relief agencies had trouble getting

> "Successful innovation requires rich cross-pollination both inside and outside the organization."
>
> —BRUCE BROWN AND SCOTT D. ANTHONY, IN "HOW P&G TRIPLED ITS INNOVATION SUCCESS RATE"

Half-Baked Management   Uber Ride-Sharing

It brought a new way to travel, but Uber can't stay out of the news, and most of it's not good. After firing its CEO, Antony Levandowski, Uber had to go through a difficult court battle with Alphabet Inc.'s Waymo Technologies (which grew out of Google) over Uber's alleged theft of Waymar's trade secrets. This on the heels of frequent articles about Uber's aggressive location policies, sometimes

breaking local laws. Uber even sent a letter of apology to the City of London as a result of the company's behaviors. Then a video went viral of the CEO berating a driver. The company seemed to still grow despite all the problems, but now there are some competitors, such as Lyft and VIA.

SOURCE: Greg Bensinger, *The Wall Street Journal* (Eastern ed.), February 10, 2018, B1.

Sunny Side Up > Quirky

Do you need a $79 gadget that lets you use your smartphone to see how many eggs you have left in the fridge or which egg has been there the longest? Not many people did, and Quirky pulled the plug on the Egg Minder. But other products from Quirky, the company founded by Ben Kaufman in 2009, have been more successful.

Quirky, which Kaufman calls a "modern invention machine," gets ideas from an online community of a million or so registered members and takes the most promising ideas for new products from concept to manufacturing to distribution. Young entrepreneur Jake Zien, for example, was frustrated with the standard power strip, where electric plugs often block the adjacent sockets, so he invented an adjustable power strip the year after he graduated from high school. Several years later, Zien sent the concept to Quirky, and within almost no time, the Pivot Power was on its way to store shelves. Zien gets a few cents on the dollar for every Pivot Power sold and has now earned more than $700,000 from sales of his innovative product. Community members who contribute ideas for enhancing a product, naming it, and so forth, also get a small percentage of the profits. Among the other 400 or so products Quirky has brought to the marketplace are the Pluck egg separator, the Pawcet drinking fountain, and the Aros smart air conditioner.

Quirky's ultimate mission is to create a crowd-based model that can accelerate the development of all kinds of innovative products, large and small. Quirky gets around 4,000 ideas a week, and about a quarter of them are for products that can connect to a smartphone or home Wi-Fi network. In addition, GE worked in partnership with Quirky on the development and manufacturing of the Aros smart air conditioner, an idea that originally came from Quirky community member Garthen Leslie.[54]

health care workers and supplies to some of the most distressed regions. A project called Open Street Map gave hundreds of people a chance to help remotely by identifying where roads and buildings are located and where best to deliver supplies. Having people physically check locations could have taken weeks or months. Similarly, crowdsourced maps were used to identify the location of clinics following a major earthquake in Haiti and to help relief workers set priorities for distribution of food, shelter, and sanitation services following the devastating earthquake and tsunami in Japan.[55]

Another approach to innovation in recent years has been to buy start-up companies in order to obtain the innovative products and services, and often the talent behind them as well. This **innovation by acquisition** strategy recognizes that the cutting edge of innovation often happens with young, small, entrepreneurial companies rather than inside the walls of established firms. Google bought Android, Facebook bought Instagram, and Amazon bought Twitch Interactive to cite just a few examples.[56] Look at almost any large, successful company today, particularly in fast-moving industries, and you will find examples of innovation by acquisition.

Remember This

- Successful product and service innovation depends on cooperation, both within the organization and with customers and others outside the organization.

- Using a **horizontal linkage model** means that several departments, such as marketing, research, and manufacturing, work closely together to develop new products.

- Corning created Gorilla Glass, used for most touch screens, using a horizontal linkage model.

- Many companies, including Rovio, creator of the Angry Birds games, extend the search for and commercialization of innovative ideas beyond the boundaries of the organization—a process called **open innovation**.

- **Crowdsourcing**, an open innovation approach used by Quirky, Netflix, ModCloth, General Electric, Fiat, and even the U.S. government, taps into ideas from around the world and lets thousands or hundreds of thousands of people participate in the innovation process, usually via the Internet.

- **Innovation by acquisition** means buying start-up companies to get innovative products and services, and usually the talent that created them.

8-2c Innovation Roles

The third aspect of product and technology innovation is creating structural mechanisms to make sure new ideas are carried forward, accepted, and implemented. Managers can directly influence whether entrepreneurship flourishes in the organization by expressing support of entrepreneurial activities, giving employees a degree of autonomy, and rewarding learning and risk-taking.[57] One important factor is fostering idea champions. The formal definition of an **idea champion** is a person who sees the need for and champions productive change within the organization.

Remember: Change does not occur by itself. Personal energy and effort are required to promote a new idea successfully. When Texas Instruments studied 50 of its new product introductions, a surprising fact emerged: Without exception, every one that failed lacked a zealous champion. By contrast, most of the new products that succeeded had such a champion. Managers made an immediate decision: No new product would be approved unless someone championed it. Similarly, at SRI International, a contract R&D firm, managers use the saying "No champion, no product, no exception."[58] Research confirms that successful new ideas are generally those that are backed by someone who believes in the idea wholeheartedly and is determined to convince others of its value.[59] Recall how the winning proposals at the PwC innovation contest discussed earlier in this chapter were all assigned to a senior champion so that they wouldn't get lost in the everyday shuffle.

Sometimes a new idea is rejected by top managers, but champions are passionately committed to a new idea or product despite rejection by others. For example, Robert Vincent was fired twice by two different division managers at a semiconductor company. Both times, he convinced the president and chairman of the board to reinstate him to continue working on his idea for an airbag sensor that measures acceleration and deceleration. He couldn't get approval for research funding, so Vincent pushed to finish another project in half the time and used the resulting savings to support the new-product development.[60]

Another way to facilitate entrepreneurship is through a **new-venture team**, which is a unit separate from the rest of the organization that is responsible for developing and initiating a major innovation.[61] New-venture teams give free rein to members' creativity because their separate facilities and location unleash people from the restrictions imposed by organizational rules and procedures. These teams typically are small, loosely structured, and flexible, reflecting the characteristics of creative organizations described in Exhibit 8.2. One good example is Niantic, which builds "augmented reality" mobile games such as Ingress. Niantic was founded by John Hanke as an internal start-up at Google in 2010 and was spun off as a separate company so the Niantic team could be more creative and nimble. As described in Chapter 7, Google is now part of Alphabet. The new structure gives small entrepreneurial teams working on projects such as self-driving cars and Internet-connected home devices greater freedom and flexibility by allowing them to operate as separate small companies.[62] At Nestlé, a team working to develop a line of high-quality coffees packaged in individual capsules for use in specially designed coffee machines, similar to Keurig's K-cup system, found itself hampered by the large company's rules, structures, and regulations. Top managers moved the Nespresso business outside the existing structure so that it could thrive with an entrepreneurial culture and promote innovative ideas.[63]

One variation of a new-venture team is called a **skunkworks**,[64] a separate, small, informal, highly autonomous, and often secretive group that focuses on breakthrough ideas for a business. The original skunkworks, which still exists, was created by Lockheed Martin more than 50 years ago. The essence of a skunkworks is that highly talented people are given the time and freedom to let creativity reign.[65] At GM, to protect creativity, the location of the skunkworks facility known as Studio X is kept secret even from the automaker's top executives.[66]

Idea champions often persevere through numerous challenges and setbacks, which requires perseverance and passion, sometimes called **grit**. To measure your grit, *Visit MindTap for the "Self-Assessment: Do You Have True Grit?"*

Benedict Evans/Redux

Concept Connection

When L'Oréal's R&D team presented new foundation shades in 2006 that were meant to be a breakthrough for women of color, L'Oréal chemist Balanda Atis bluntly told executives that the new range fell short. So, they challenged her to see what she could do. They didn't release Atis from her regular job working on mascara projects, but they allowed her to use the labs on the side. Atis worked for years as an **idea champion** for creating a broader range of shades for darker skin. L'Oréal eventually assigned her to work full time on the project and used her research to create a range of 30 new shades. Atis's team has grown into the Women of Color Lab, which has a goal of making sure that women in each of the 140 countries where L'Oréal products are sold can find makeup that matches the color and texture of their skin.

A related idea is the **new-venture fund**, which provides resources from which individuals and groups can draw to develop new ideas, products, or businesses. At Pitney Bowes, for example, the New Business Opportunity (NBO) program provides funding for teams to explore potentially lucrative but unproven ideas. The NBO program is intended to generate a pipeline of new businesses for the mail and document management services company. Similarly, Royal Dutch Shell puts 10 percent of its R&D budget into the GameChanger program, which provides seed money for innovation projects that are highly ambitious, radical, or long term and could get lost in the larger product development system.[67] With these programs, the support and assistance of senior managers are often just as important as the funding.[68]

Remember This

- To increase innovation, managers develop an internal culture, philosophy, and structure that encourage entrepreneurial activity.

- One structural mechanism that promotes entrepreneurship is the **new-venture team**, which is a unit separate from the mainstream organization that is responsible for initiating and developing innovations.

- A variation of the new-venture team is a **skunkworks**, a separate, informal, highly autonomous, and often secretive group that focuses on breakthrough ideas.

- The location of GM's skunkworks facility known as Studio X is kept secret even from the automaker's top executives.

- A **new-venture fund** provides financial resources from which individuals or teams can draw to develop new ideas, products, or businesses.

8-3 Changing People and Culture

All successful changes involve changes in people and culture as well. Changes in people and culture pertain to how employees think—changes in mind-set. **People change** concerns just a few employees, such as sending a handful of middle managers to a training course to improve their leadership skills. **Culture change** pertains to the organization as a whole, such as when the Internal Revenue Service (IRS) shifted its basic mind-set from an organization focused on collection and compliance to one dedicated to informing, educating, and serving customers (i.e., taxpayers).[69] Large-scale culture change is not easy. Indeed, managers routinely report that changing people and culture is their most difficult job.[70] Consider the situation at General Motors (GM).

Managers at GM have been praised for making tough decisions that led to impressive financial results, bringing out new models that connected with customers, and fixing a myriad of operational and systems issues. However, there is one area in which CEO Mary Barra and other executives admit significant challenges remain: changing the bureaucratic, tradition-bound culture that has crippled GM in the past.

Like managers in other companies, GM executives are finding that changing culture is the toughest part of leading a turnaround. Barra is attacking the "culture problem" head on. After the announcement of a $900 million settlement between GM and the U.S. Justice Department in connection with a case related to defective ignition switches in GM cars linked to over 100 deaths, Barra told employees at a town hall meeting: "I never want to put this behind us. I want to put this painful experience permanently in our collective memories." The old GM way would have been to deny mistakes and settle grudgingly, but Barra has apologized publicly and profusely, visited the families of victims, and set up a compensation fund for them even before any legal liability had been established.

"Defeating an entrenched, dysfunctional culture in a huge, old company is rare," wrote Geoff Colvin for *Fortune* magazine. "Barra is already ahead of any [previous GM CEO], but that's no assurance she'll succeed."[71]

Two specific tools that managers at GM and other companies can use to smooth the culture change process are training and development programs and organization development (OD).

8-3a Training and Development

Training is one of the most frequently used approaches to changing people's mind-sets. A company might offer training programs to large blocks of employees on subjects such as teamwork, diversity, emotional intelligence (EQ), quality circles, communication skills, or participative management.

Successful companies want to provide training and development opportunities for everyone, but they might particularly emphasize training and development for managers, with the idea that the behavior and attitudes of managers will influence people throughout the organization and lead to culture change. For example, by the time that Stephen Hemsley took over as CEO of UnitedHealth Group, the nation's largest health insurer and one of the most powerful companies in the health care industry, the atmosphere within the company was toxic. "We had lots of IQ but not nearly enough EQ," Hemsley said. To encourage more civil, emotionally intelligent, and collaborative behavior, Hemsley sent 8,000 managers to three-day sensitivity training programs to become more aware of their own biases and impact and be more sensitive to other people.[72]

8-3b Organization Development (OD)

Organization development (OD) is a planned, systematic process of change that uses behavioral science knowledge and techniques to improve an organization's health and effectiveness through its ability to adapt to the environment, improve internal relationships, and increase learning and problem-solving capabilities.[73] OD focuses on the human and social aspects of the organization and works to change attitudes and relationships among employees, helping to strengthen the organization's capacity for adaptation and renewal.[74]

OD can help managers address at least three types of current problems:[75]

- *Mergers/acquisitions.* The disappointing financial results of many mergers and acquisitions are caused by the failure of executives to determine whether the administrative style and corporate culture of the two companies fit. Executives may concentrate on potential synergies in technology, products, marketing, and control systems but fail to recognize that two firms may have widely different values, beliefs, and practices. These differences create stress and anxiety for employees, and these negative emotions affect future performance. Cultural differences should be evaluated during the acquisition process, and OD experts can be used to smooth the integration of two firms.

- *Organizational decline/revitalization.* Organizations undergoing a period of decline and revitalization experience a variety of problems, including a low level of trust, lack of innovation, high turnover, and high levels of conflict and stress. The period of transition requires the opposite, including confronting stress, creating open communication, and fostering creative innovation to emerge with high levels of productivity. OD techniques can contribute greatly to cultural revitalization by managing conflicts, fostering commitment, and facilitating communication.

- *Conflict management.* Conflict can occur at any time and place within a healthy organization. For example, a product team for the introduction of a new software package was formed at a software company. Made of strong-willed individuals, the team made little progress because members could not agree on project goals. At a manufacturing firm, salespeople promised delivery dates to customers that were in conflict with shop supervisor priorities for assembling customer orders. In a publishing company, two managers disliked each other intensely. They argued at meetings, lobbied politically against each other, and hurt the achievement of both departments. OD efforts can help resolve these kinds of conflicts, as well as conflicts that are related to growing diversity and the global nature of today's organizations.

OD can be used to solve the types of problems just described, as well as many others. However, to be truly valuable to companies and employees, OD practitioners go beyond looking at ways to settle specific problems. Instead, they become involved in broader issues that contribute to improving organizational life, such as encouraging a sense of community, pushing for an organizational climate of openness and trust, and making sure that the company provides employees with opportunities for personal growth and development.[76] One study looked at the results of an OD project in a large metropolitan sheriff's department that was plagued by extremely high turnover, low morale, ineffective leadership, and internal conflicts. OD consultants used a variety of activities over a period of four years to solve the crisis threatening the department. It was a long and sometimes difficult process; however, the study found not only that the OD interventions had highly beneficial results, but also that the positive impact lasted over a period of 30 years, right up to the present day.[77]

OD Activities   OD consultants use a variety of specialized techniques to help meet their goals. Three of the most popular and effective are the following:

- *Team-building activities.* **Team building** enhances the cohesiveness and success of organizational groups and teams. For example, a series of OD exercises can be used with members of cross-departmental teams to help them learn to act and function as a team. An OD expert can work with team members to increase their communication skills, facilitate their ability to confront one another, and help them accept common goals. A major team-building experience at UnitedHealth is the annual broomball tournament held at headquarters in Minnesota. Inaugurated in 2010, the tournament is now a prized tradition held every winter, with 90 teams representing every area of the company participating.[78]

- *Survey-feedback activities.* **Survey feedback** begins with a questionnaire distributed to employees on values, climate, participation, leadership, and group cohesion within their organization. After the survey is completed, an OD consultant meets with groups of employees to provide feedback about their responses and the problems identified. Employees are engaged in problem solving based on the data.

- *Large-group interventions.* In recent years, the need for bringing about fundamental organizational change in today's complex, fast-changing world has prompted a growing interest in applications of OD techniques to large-group settings.[79] The **large-group intervention** approach brings together participants from all parts of the organization—often including key stakeholders from outside the organization as well—to discuss problems or opportunities and plan for change. A large-group intervention might involve 50 to 500 people and last for several days. The idea is to include everyone who has a stake in the change, gather perspectives from all parts of the system, and enable people to create a collective future through sustained, guided dialogue. At Lenovo, for example, the company that acquired IBM's PC business in 2005, a large-group intervention helped to create a new manufacturing and supply chain culture in which the best ideas of all nationalities and backgrounds are blended. When Gerry P. Smith arrived at Lenovo a year after the acquisition, he found that people were going in different directions. Smith started bringing everyone who would be affected by a tough decision together for discussion and debate until they agreed on a solution. In some cases, the large-group approach led to doubling the productivity of a manufacturing line. Moreover, it created a more cohesive culture, rather than having people competing about the best way to do things. "The beauty of our culture is that we all moved to a new common ground," says Smith.[80]

Large-group interventions are among the most popular and fastest-growing OD activities and reflect a significant shift in the approach to organizational change from earlier OD concepts and approaches.[81] Exhibit 8.5 lists the primary differences between the traditional OD model and the large-scale intervention model of organizational change.[82] In the newer approach, the focus is on the entire system, which takes into account the organization's interaction with its environment.

The sources of information for discussion are expanded to include customers, suppliers, community members, and even competitors, and this information is shared widely so that everyone has the same picture of the organization and its environment. The acceleration of change when the entire system is involved can be remarkable. In addition, learning occurs across all parts of the organization simultaneously rather than by individuals, small groups, or business units alone. The result is that the large-group approach offers greater possibilities for fundamental, radical transformation of the entire culture, whereas the traditional approach creates incremental change in a few individuals or small groups at a time.

Exhibit 8.5 **OD Approaches to Culture Change**

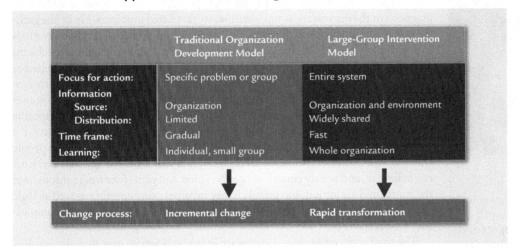

	Traditional Organization Development Model	Large-Group Intervention Model
Focus for action:	Specific problem or group	Entire system
Information Source:	Organization	Organization and environment
Distribution:	Limited	Widely shared
Time frame:	Gradual	Fast
Learning:	Individual, small group	Whole organization
Change process:	Incremental change	Rapid transformation

SOURCE: Adapted from Barbara Benedict Bunker and Billie T. Alban, "Conclusion: What Makes Large Group Interventions Effective?" *Journal of Applied Behavioral Science* 28, no. 4 (December 1992): 579–591.

Remember This

- Often, a manager's toughest job is changing people and culture.

- **People change** refers to a change in the attitudes and behaviors of a few employees.

- **Culture change** is a major shift in the norms, values, and mind-set of the entire organization.

- UnitedHealth Group sent 8,000 managers to sensitivity training sessions to help them learn to be more emotionally intelligent and create a less toxic work environment.

- **Organization development (OD)** is a planned, systematic process of change that uses behavioral science techniques to improve an organization's health and effectiveness through its ability to cope with environmental changes, improve internal relationships, and increase learning and problem-solving capabilities.

- OD can help managers with the task of blending corporate cultures following mergers and acquisitions, as well as with many other people-related problems.

- **Team building** is an OD intervention that enhances cohesiveness by helping groups of people learn to work together as a team.

- With **survey feedback**, OD change agents survey employees to gather their opinions regarding corporate values, leadership, participation, cohesiveness, and other aspects of the organization, and then meet with small groups to share the results and brainstorm solutions to problems identified by the results.

- **Large-group intervention** is an OD approach that brings together people from different parts of the organization (and often including outside stakeholders) to discuss problems or opportunities and plan for change.

Fabrice Dimier/Bloomberg/Getty Images

Concept Connection

One may not think of GE as an innovative leadership company at the forefront of **organization development (OD)**. At first glance, this multinational corporation may seem quite traditional. However, GE is well known for placing a premium on selecting, developing, and retaining strong leaders at every level of the organization. Along with the company's extensive training and development program, there are many activities at each worksite that provide opportunities for mentoring, volunteering, sports, and social interaction.

OD Steps   OD experts acknowledge that changes in corporate culture and human behavior are tough to accomplish and require major effort. The theory underlying OD proposes three distinct stages for achieving behavioral and attitudinal change: (1) unfreezing, (2) changing, and (3) refreezing.[83]

The first stage, **unfreezing**, makes people throughout the organization aware of problems and the need for change. This stage creates the motivation for people to change their attitudes and behaviors. Unfreezing may begin when managers present information that shows discrepancies between desired behaviors or performance and the current state of affairs. In addition, managers need to establish a sense of urgency to unfreeze people and create an openness and willingness to change. The unfreezing stage is often associated with *diagnosis*, which uses an outside expert called a *change agent*. The **change agent** is an OD specialist who performs a systematic diagnosis of the organization and identifies work-related problems. He or she gathers and analyzes data through personal interviews, questionnaires, and observations of meetings. The diagnosis helps determine the extent of organizational problems and helps unfreeze managers by making them aware of problems in their behavior.

The second stage, **changing**, occurs when individuals experiment with new behavior and learn new skills to be used in the workplace. This process is sometimes known as *intervention*, during which the change agent implements a specific plan for training managers and employees. The changing stage might involve a number of specific steps.[84] For example, managers put together a coalition of people with the will and power to guide change, create a vision for change that everyone can believe in, and widely communicate the vision and plans for change throughout the company. In addition, successful change involves using emotion as well as logic to persuade people and empowering employees to act on the plan and accomplish the desired changes.

The third stage, **refreezing**, occurs when individuals acquire new attitudes or values and are rewarded for them by the organization. The impact of new behaviors is evaluated and reinforced. The change agent supplies new data that show positive changes in performance. Managers may provide updated data to employees that demonstrate positive changes in individual and organizational performance. Top executives celebrate successes and reward positive behavioral changes. At this stage, changes are institutionalized in the organizational culture, so that employees begin to view the changes as a normal, integral part of how the organization operates. Employees may also participate in refresher courses to maintain and reinforce the new behaviors.

The process of unfreezing-changing-refreezing can be illustrated by efforts of managers at ENSR to create a high-performance, employee-focused culture.

Sunny Side Up } ENSR

When top executives at ENSR began hearing that high employee turnover was hurting the company's relationships with clients, they knew something had to be done. ENSR is a full-service environmental services firm with thousands of employees in locations around the world. Long-term relationships with clients are the key to ENSR's success.

To attack the turnover problem, managers embarked on a process of changing the culture. To make people aware of the need for change (unfreezing), ENSR's president and CEO traveled with the senior vice president of HR to the largest 50 or so of ENSR's global locations. They held town hall–style meetings with employees and leadership workshops with ENSR managers. The changing

stage included training. Surveys were conducted to find out what employees considered their primary needs. For example, supervisors were trained in how to help lower-performing employees improve their performance and how to provide greater challenges and rewards to employees who showed high potential for leadership.

Within a few years, new behaviors became the norm. Turnover dropped from 22 percent to only 9 percent, one of the lowest rates in the industry, and employees were recognized and rewarded for meeting high individual and collective goals (refreezing). ENSR continues to attract high-quality employees to fill job openings, which helps to keep the high-performance culture alive.[85]

Remember This

- OD practitioners recommend a three-stage approach for changing people's attitudes and behavior.
- **Unfreezing** is the stage in which people are made aware of problems and the need for change.
- Unfreezing requires diagnosing problems, which uses a **change agent**, an OD specialist who contracts with an organization to help managers facilitate change.

- **Changing** is the "intervention" stage of OD when change agents teach people new behaviors and skills and guide them in using them in the workplace.
- At the **refreezing** stage, people have incorporated new values, attitudes, and behaviors into their everyday work, and the changes become institutionalized in the culture.

8-4 Implementing Change

The final step in the change process is *implementation*. A new, creative idea will not benefit the organization until it is in place and being used. Managers are often frustrated because employees may seem to resist change for no apparent reason. To effectively implement change, it is important to be aware of the reasons people resist change and to use techniques that can overcome resistance and enlist employee buy-in.

8-4a Why Do People Resist Change?

Resistance to change is one explanation for why implementing change is so difficult. People resist change for several reasons, and understanding the reasons is a good start toward knowing how to bring about needed change in organizations.

Self-Interest   People typically resist a change that they believe conflicts with their self-interests. A proposed change in job design, structure, or technology may increase employees' workload, for example, or cause a real or perceived loss of power, prestige, pay, or benefits. Recall our discussion of loss aversion from Chapter 6 *The fear of personal loss is perhaps the biggest obstacle to organizational change.*[86] Many people will do whatever they can to avoid loss. For example, managers at Houston-based power producer Dynergy resisted the change to an open floor plan for their offices because they viewed their private offices as symbols of their power and prestige in the organization.[87] In addition, they saw the change as a loss of control over their own lives and circumstances, which provoked a strong emotional reaction.

Lack of Understanding and Trust   Employees often distrust the intentions behind a change or do not understand the intended purpose of a change. If previous working relationships with a manager or promoter of an idea have been negative, resistance may occur. At CareFusion Corporation (now part of Becton Dickinson), former CEO David L. Schlotterbeck and other top executives wanted to implement new values of collaboration and teamwork, but lower-level managers were initially suspicious of their intentions. Only when they saw that top leaders were fully committed to the values and honored them in their own behavior did others begin to support the changes.[88]

Uncertainty   *Uncertainty* is the lack of information about future events. It represents a fear of the unknown. It is especially threatening for employees who have a low tolerance for change and fear anything out of the ordinary. They do not know how a change will affect them, and they worry about whether they will be able to meet the demands of a new procedure or technology.[89] Hospitals that have spent millions of dollars adopting electronic medical records are having a hard time getting some doctors to use them. One reason is the uncertainty about how electronic records will change how doctors go about their daily work.[90] Most people have at least some fear of the unknown and are more comfortable dealing with the tried and true.[91]

> "Change hurts. It makes people insecure, confused, and angry. People want things to be the same as they've always been, because that makes life easier. But if you're a leader, you can't let your people hang on to the past."
>
> —RICHARD MARCINKO, FORMER U.S. NAVY SEAL, AUTHOR, AND CHAIRMAN OF RED CELL INTERNATIONAL CORPORATION

Different Assessments and Goals   Another reason for resistance to change is that people who will be affected by a change or innovation may assess the situation differently than managers or promoters of a new idea do. Critics frequently voice legitimate disagreements over the proposed benefits of a change. Managers in each department pursue different goals, and an innovation may detract from performance and goal achievement for some departments. At pharmaceuticals company Pfizer, top executives wanted to implement a computerized system for collecting and processing research trial data, which could cut the cost of new drug development by 40 percent. R&D managers resisted, citing their concern that the automation and standardization of case report forms would hamper their flexibility and creativity.[92]

These reasons for resistance are legitimate in the eyes of employees affected by the change. Managers should not ignore resistance; instead, they should diagnose the reasons for it and design strategies to gain acceptance by users.[93] Strategies for overcoming resistance and implementing change typically involve three approaches: making people aware of the need for change by creating a sense of urgency, analyzing resistance through the force-field technique, and using selective implementation tactics.

8-4b Create a Sense of Urgency

Many people are not willing to change unless they perceive a problem or a crisis. A crisis or strong need for change lowers resistance. To effectively lead change, managers help people *feel* the need for change rather than just giving them facts and figures. Managers should remember that implementing change requires speaking to people's hearts as well as to their heads. Emotion is a key component in persuading and influencing others. People are much more likely to change their behavior when they both understand the rational reasons for doing so and see a picture of change that influences their feelings.[94] Peter Löscher, the previous CEO of Siemens, said, "Never miss the opportunities that come from a good crisis." Löscher stepped in at a very difficult time for Siemens and needed to make massive changes in the structure and culture. He spent his first 100 days traveling around the world talking with employees and enlisting their support for change.[95] Sometimes, though, there is no obvious crisis. Many organizational problems are subtle, so managers have to recognize and then make others aware of the need for change.[96] A **need for change** is a disparity between existing and desired performance levels.

8-4c Apply Force-Field Analysis

One effective approach to overcoming resistance and implementing change is called force-field analysis. **Force-field analysis** grew from the work of Kurt Lewin, who proposed that change was a result of the competition between *driving* and *restraining forces*.[97] Driving forces can be thought of as problems or opportunities that provide motivation for change within the organization. Restraining forces are the various barriers to change, such as a lack of resources, resistance from middle managers, or inadequate employee skills. When a change is introduced, managers should analyze both the forces that drive change (problems and opportunities) and the forces that resist it (barriers to change). By selectively removing forces that restrain change, the driving forces will be strong enough to enable implementation, as illustrated by the move from A to B in Exhibit 8.6. As barriers are reduced or removed, behavior will shift to incorporate the desired changes.

Just-in-time (JIT) inventory control systems schedule materials to arrive at a company just as they are needed on the production line. In an Ohio manufacturing company, management's analysis showed that the driving forces (opportunities) associated with the implementation of JIT were (1) the large cost savings from reduced inventories; (2) labor/personnel savings from needing fewer workers to handle inventory; and (3) a quicker, more competitive market response for the company. Restraining forces (barriers) that managers discovered were (1) a freight system that was too slow to deliver inventory on time, (2) a facility layout that emphasized inventory maintenance over new deliveries, (3) worker skills that were inappropriate for handling rapid inventory deployment, and (4) union resistance to loss of jobs. The driving forces were not sufficient to overcome the restraining forces.

Exhibit 8.6 Using Force-Field Analysis to Change from Traditional to Just-in-Time Inventory Systems

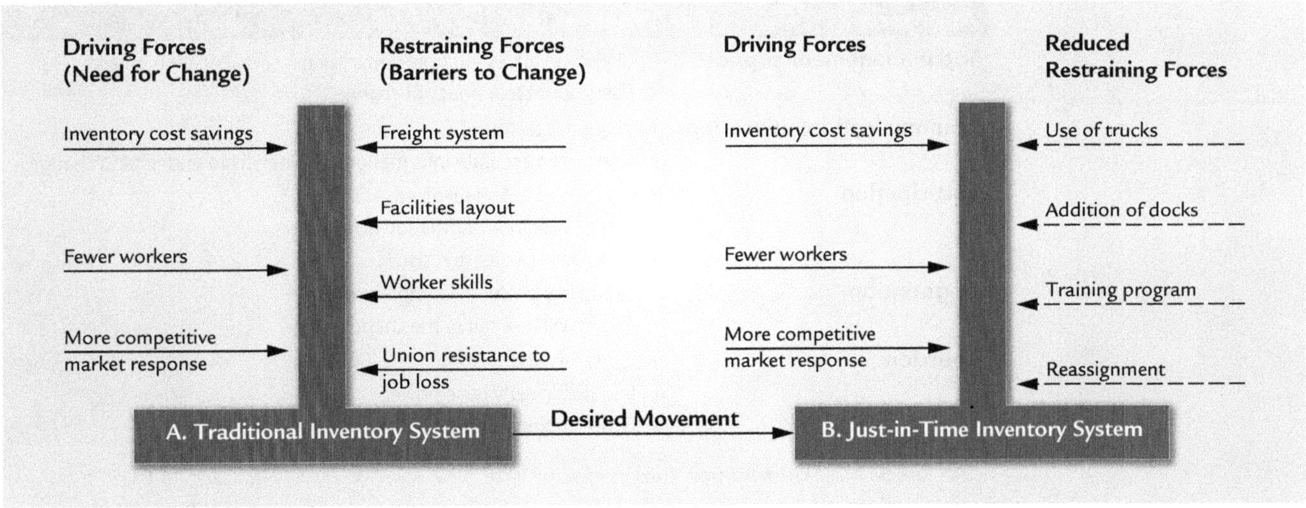

To shift the behavior to JIT, managers attacked the barriers. An analysis of the freight system showed that delivery by truck provided the flexibility and quickness needed to schedule inventory arrival at a specific time each day. The problem with the facility layout was met by adding four new loading docks. Inappropriate worker skills were improved with a training program to instruct workers in JIT methods and in assembling products with uninspected parts. Union resistance was overcome by agreeing to reassign workers no longer needed for maintaining inventory to jobs in another plant. With the restraining forces reduced, the driving forces were sufficient to allow the JIT system to be implemented.

8-4d Use Implementation Tactics

Another approach to implementing change is to use specific tactics to overcome resistance and more smoothly put changes into action. Researchers have studied various methods for dealing with resistance to change. The following five tactics, summarized in Exhibit 8.7, have proven successful.[98]

Top Management Support   One survey found that 80 percent of companies that are successful innovators have top executives who frequently reinforce the importance of innovation both verbally and symbolically.[99] The visible support of top management makes people aware of the importance of a change and gives the change project legitimacy. For instance, one of the primary correlates of the success of new business ventures is the strong support of top managers, and top management support and involvement has been shown to play a crucial role in successful new-product development.[100] *Top management support* is especially important when a change involves multiple departments or when resources are being reallocated among departments. Without top management support, changes can get bogged down in squabbling among departments or contradictory orders from lower-level managers.

Communication and Education   *Communication* and *education* are used when solid information about the change is needed by users and others who may resist implementation. When Gina Raimondo, the first female governor of the state of Rhode Island and Providence Plantations, was Rhode Island's state treasurer, she spent most of a year traveling all over the state to educate the public, union leaders, and legislators about the need for a radical overhaul of the state's pension system. Raimondo "conducted a long, relentless, public-education campaign" because she believed reform was essential to keep the state from going broke.[101] Within organizations, education can be especially important when the change involves new technical knowledge or users are unfamiliar with the idea.

Exhibit 8.7 Tactics for Implementing Change

Approach	When to Use
Top management support	• Change involves multiple departments or reallocation of resources. • Users doubt legitimacy of change.
Communication, education	• Change is technical. • Users need accurate information and analysis to understand change.
Participation	• Users need to feel involved. • Design requires information from others. • Users have power to resist.
Negotiation	• Group has power over implementation. • Group will lose out in the change.
Coercion	• A crisis exists. • Initiators clearly have power. • Other implementation techniques have failed.

SOURCE: Based on J. P. Kotter and L. A. Schlesinger, "Choosing Strategies for Change," *Harvard Business Review* 57 (March–April 1979): 106–114.

Participation   *Participation* involves users and potential resisters in designing the change. This approach is time consuming, but it pays off because users understand and become committed to the change. At Learning Point Associates, which needed to change dramatically to meet new challenges, the change team drew up a comprehensive road map for transformation but had trouble getting the support of most managers. The managers argued that they hadn't been consulted about the plans and didn't feel compelled to participate in implementing them.[102] Research studies have shown that proactively engaging people in up-front planning and decision making about changes that affect their work results in much smoother implementation.[103] Participation also helps managers determine potential problems and understand the differences in perceptions of change among employees.

Negotiation   Negotiation is a more formal means of achieving cooperation. *Negotiation* uses formal bargaining to win acceptance and approval of a desired change. For example, if the marketing department fears losing power if a new management structure is implemented, top managers may work with marketing to reach a resolution. Companies that have strong unions frequently must formally negotiate change with the unions. The change may become part of the union contract, reflecting the agreement of both parties.

Coercion   *Coercion* means that managers use their formal power to force employees to change. Resisters are told to accept the change or lose rewards (or even their jobs). In most cases, this approach should not be used because employees feel like victims, are angry at change managers, and may even sabotage the changes. However, coercion may be necessary in crisis situations when a rapid response is urgent.

Remember This

- Many people prefer the status quo and tend to resist change. The biggest obstacle to organizational change is the fear of personal loss.

- Other reasons why people resist change are lack of understanding and trust, uncertainty, and different assessments and goals.

- A **need for change** is a disparity between actual and desired performance.

- Many people aren't willing to change unless they perceive a crisis, so managers need to create a sense of urgency that change is really needed.

- **Force-field analysis** is a technique for determining which forces drive a proposed change and which forces restrain it.

- Driving forces are problems or opportunities that provide motivation to change. Restraining forces are barriers such as a lack of resources or inadequate employee skills.

- The support of top executives is crucial to the successful implementation of a change. In addition, managers use a variety of techniques to smooth the implementation process, including communicating with employees, providing training, and closely involving employees in the change process.

DISCUSSION QUESTIONS

1. Microsoft and Intel are giants of the computer industry. Why do you think these large companies have had such a hard time competing against disruptive innovations such as mobile computing?

2. A manager of an international chemical company says that few new products in her company have been successful. What would you advise the manager to do to help increase the company's success rate?

3. As a manager, how would you deal with resistance to change when you suspect that employees' fears of job loss are well founded?

4. If you were a manager responsible for floor-cleaning products at a consumer products company, how might you apply crowdsourcing to identify a new product that would meet customer needs?

5. To tap into the experience of battle-tested soldiers, the U.S. Army began encouraging personnel from all ranks to go online and collaboratively rewrite some of the Army's field manuals in a Wikipedia-like fashion. When the rank and file showed little interest, one retired colonel suggested that top leaders should make soldiers participate. Does coercion seem like a good way to implement this type of change? Discuss.

6. Analyze the driving and restraining forces of a change that you would like to make in your life. Do you believe understanding force-field analysis can help you more effectively implement a significant change in your own behavior?

7. Why do you think research has shown that idea champions are so essential to the initiation of change? Could they be equally important for implementation?

8. You are a manager, and you believe that the expense reimbursement system for salespeople is far too slow, taking weeks instead of days. How would you go about convincing other managers that this problem needs to be addressed?

9. Do the underlying values of OD differ from assumptions associated with other types of change? Discuss.

10. What do you see as the major advantages and disadvantages of a company moving to open innovation?

APPLY YOUR SKILLS: SELF-LEARNING

Is Your Company Creative?[104]

An effective way to assess the creative climate of an organization for which you have worked is to fill out the following questionnaire. Answer each question based on your work experience in that firm. Discuss the results with members of your group, and talk about whether changing the firm along the dimensions in the questions would make it more creative.

   Instructions: Answer each of the following questions using the five-point scale (*Note:* No rating of 4 is used):

   (0) We never do this.

   (1) We rarely do this.

   (2) We sometimes do this.

   (3) We frequently do this.

   (5) We always do this.

1. We are encouraged to seek help anywhere inside or outside the organization with new ideas for our work unit.

   0   1   2   3   5

2. Assistance is provided to develop ideas into proposals for management review.

   0   1   2   3   5

3. Our performance reviews encourage risky, creative efforts, ideas, and actions.

   0   1   2   3   5

4. We are encouraged to fill our minds with new information by attending professional meetings and trade fairs, visiting customers, and so on.

   0   1   2   3   5

5. Our meetings are designed to allow people to freewheel, brainstorm, and generate ideas.

   0   1   2   3   5

6. All members contribute ideas during meetings.

   0   1   2   3   5

7.   Meetings often involve much spontaneity and humor.

0   1   2   3   5

8.   We discuss how company structure and our actions help or spoil creativity within our work unit.

0   1   2   3   5

9.   During meetings, the chair is rotated among members.

0   1   2   3   5

10. Everyone in the work unit receives training in creativity techniques and maintaining a creative climate.

0   1   2   3   5

Scoring and Interpretation Add up your total score for all 10 questions: _____

To measure how effectively your organization fosters creativity, use the following scale:

Highly effective: 35–50, moderately effective: 20–34, moderately ineffective: 10–19, ineffective: 0–9

APPLY YOUR SKILLS: GROUP LEARNING

An Ancient Tale

Step 1. Read the introduction and case study and answer the questions.

Step 2. In groups of three to four, discuss your answers.

Step 3. Groups report to the whole class and the instructor leads a discussion on the issues raised.

Introduction

To understand, analyze, and improve organizations, we must carefully think through the issue of who is responsible for what activities in different organizational settings. Often we hold responsible someone who has no control over the outcome, or we fail to teach or train someone who could make the vital difference.

To explore this issue, the following exercise could be conducted on either an individual or a group basis. It provides an opportunity to see how different individuals assign responsibility for an event. It is also a good opportunity to discuss the concept of organizational boundaries (what is the organization, who is in or out, etc.)

Case Study

You should read the short story and respond quickly to the first three questions. Then take a little more time on questions four through six. The results, criteria, and implications could then be discussed in groups.

Long ago in an ancient kingdom there lived a princess who was very young and very beautiful. The princess, recently married, lived in a large and luxurious castle with her husband, a powerful and wealthy lord. The young princess was not content, however, to sit and eat strawberries by herself while her husband took frequent and long journeys to neighboring kingdoms. She felt neglected and soon became quite unhappy. One day, while she was alone in the castle gardens, a handsome vagabond rode out of the forest bordering the castle. He spied the beautiful princess, quickly won her heart, and carried her away with him.

Following a day of dalliance, the young princess found herself ruthlessly abandoned by the vagabond. She then discovered that the only way back to the castle led through the bewitched forest of the wicked sorcerer. Fearing to venture into the forest alone, she sought out her kind and wise godfather. She explained her plight, begged forgiveness of the godfather, and asked his assistance in returning home before her husband returned. The godfather, however, surprised and shocked at her behavior, refused forgiveness and denied her any assistance. Discouraged but still determined, the princess disguised her identity and sought the help of the most noble of all the kingdom's knights. After hearing the sad story, the knight pledged his unfailing aid—for a modest fee. But alas, the princess had no money and the knight rode away to save other damsels.

The beautiful princess had no one else from whom she might seek help and decided to brave the great peril alone. She followed the safest path she knew, but when she was almost through the forest, the wicked sorcerer spied her and caused her to be devoured by the fire-breathing dragon.

1.   Who was inside the organization and who was outside? Where were the boundaries?

2.   Who is most responsible for the death of the beautiful princess?

3.   Who is next most responsible? Least responsible?

4.   What is your criterion for the decisions made?

5.   What interventions would you suggest to prevent a recurrence?

6.   What are the implications for *organizational development and change?*

Character	Most Responsible	Next Most Responsible	Least Responsible
Princess			
Husband			
Vagabond			
Godfather			
Knight			
Sorcerer			

Check one character in each column.

Adapted from J. B. Ritchie and Paul Thompson. Reprinted with permission from *Organization and People: Readings, Cases and Exercises in Organizational Behavior*. Copyright 1980 by West Publishing, pp. 68–70. All rights reserved in Dorothy Marcic, *Organizational Behavior: Experiences and Cases*, 4: 378–379.

APPLY YOUR SKILLS: ACTION LEARNING

1. Think about two times you had to go through a change. It might have been in your worklife, as a student, in your family, with friends. Try to choose two situations that ended differently. In other words, one had a positive outcome, in the long term, and the other one did not have a positive outcome. Fill in the table below.

	Situation One (positive outcome):	Situation Two (not positive outcome):
Factors in the situation		
Were you happy with the way things were before the change?		
What was the cause of the change?		
What was your initial reaction to the change?		
Did you find any ways to cope with the change or find something positive? Explain.		
How did authority figures communicate with you?		
How did authority figures handle the situation in general?		
Was there support from other people?		
What was the long-term outcome?		

2. Can you see differences in the way the two situations unfolded in terms of other people's behaviors?

3. Were there differences in your behaviors in the two situations? Why?

4. What would you do differently, if you could go back?

5. What new insights do you now have about going through change?

APPLY YOUR SKILLS: ETHICAL DILEMMA

Crowdsourcing[105]

Last year, when Ai-Lan Nguyen told her friend Greg Barnwell that Off the Hook Tees, based in Asheville, North Carolina, was going to experiment with crowdsourcing, he warned her that she wouldn't like the results. Now, as she was about to walk into a meeting to decide whether to adopt this new business model, she was afraid her friend had been right.

Crowdsourcing uses the Internet to invite anyone—professionals and amateurs alike—to perform tasks such as product design that employees usually perform. In exchange, contributors receive recognition—but little or no pay. Ai-Lan, as vice president of operations for Off the Hook, a company specializing in witty T-shirts aimed at young adults, upheld the values of founder Chris Woodhouse, who, like Ai-Lan, was a graphic artist. Before he sold the company, the founder always insisted that T-shirts be well designed by top-notch graphic artists to make sure that each screen print was a work of art. Those graphic artists reported to Ai-Lan.

Over the past 18 months, Off the Hook's sales had been stagnating for the first time in its history. The crowdsourcing experiment was the latest in a series of attempts to jump-start sales growth. Last spring, Off the Hook issued its first open call for T-shirt designs and then posted the entries on the Web so people could vote for their favorites. The top five vote-getters were handed over to the in-house designers, who tweaked the submissions until they met the company's usual quality standards.

When CEO Rob Taylor first announced the company's foray into crowdsourcing, Ai-Lan found herself reassuring the designers that their positions were not in jeopardy. Now Ai-Lan was all but certain she would have to go back on her word. Not only had the crowdsourced shirts sold well, but Rob had put a handful of winning designs directly into production, bypassing the design department altogether. Customers didn't notice the difference.

Ai-Lan concluded that Rob was ready to adopt some form of this Web-based crowdsourcing because it made T-shirt design more responsive to consumer desires. In practical terms, it reduced the uncertainty that surrounded new designs, and it dramatically lowered costs. The people who won the competitions were delighted with the exposure that it gave them.

However, when Ai-Lan looked at the crowdsourced shirts with her graphic artist's eye, she felt that the designs were competent, but none achieved the aesthetic standards attained by her in-house designers. Crowdsourcing essentially replaced training and expertise with public opinion. That made the artist in her uncomfortable.

More distressing, it was beginning to look as if Greg had been right when he'd told her that his working definition of crowdsourcing was "a billion amateurs want your job." It was easy to see that if Off the Hook adopted crowdsourcing, she would be handing out pink slips to most of her design people, longtime employees whose work she admired. "Sure, crowdsourcing costs the company less, but what about the human cost?" Greg asked.

What future course should Ai-Lan argue for at the meeting? And what personal decisions does she face if Off the Hook decides to put the crowd completely in charge when it comes to T-shirt design?

What Would You Do?

1. Go to the meeting and argue for abandoning crowdsourcing for now in favor of maintaining the artistic integrity and values that Off the Hook has always stood for.

2. Accept the reality that because Rob strongly favors crowdsourcing; it's a *fait accompli*. Be a team player and help work out the details of the new design approach. Prepare to lay off graphic designers as needed.

3. Accept the fact that converting Off the Hook to a crowdsourcing business model is inevitable, but because it violates your own personal values, start looking for a new job elsewhere.

APPLY YOUR SKILLS: CASE FOR CRITICAL ANALYSIS

Cleaver's Sausage House

Allison Elam, vice president of operations for Cleaver's Sausage House, a maker of fine sausages in Minnesota, was stunned. She felt numb. Just 30 minutes ago, she had been happy and excited about the upcoming meeting, which would decide whether to launch the new material requirements planning (MRP) software system that her department had been planning. Now the meeting was over, and Cleaver's executive committee had not agreed to launch the system.

She thought the go/no-go decision would be just a formality. But David Martin, CFO, expressed a doubt about implementing the system, and things went downhill from there. "I *so* thought he was on board," Elam hissed to herself. Other senior staff then pushed back hard. They warned that the change could be a

costly disaster. The vice president of sales doubted whether the MRP system could provide the solid sales forecasts that Cleaver needed. He called MRP "just big corporate BS." He also feared it would result in shortages of raw materials. The director of logistics, Susan Frisch, warned about problems that had erupted at one of her previous employers when a similar system was installed. She related a horror story about customers not getting orders and trucks leaving the plant half-full. Her final comment was, "We're successful. Why upset the apple cart?"

Cleaver CEO Jayden Anderson had hired Elam to take the position vacated by his ailing brother Stefan, who died in late 2015. Elam has been on the job for 10 months, spending much of her time working alone on the

MRP project. Stefan had purchased the MRP software prior to his illness, but it had sat unused since then. Elam sometimes wondered if Stefan would have had an easier time with implementation had he lived to see the project through. Elam was a veteran of big companies such as Heinz and Coca-Cola, and Anderson wanted an outsider like her to bring in new technology to help operations get to the next level. Elam had worked with successful MRP systems in the past, and she had assured Anderson that the new system would overhaul procurement, production, and shipping and would impose much-needed discipline on operations. She estimated that the system would increase annual cash flow by $600,000 and save up to $200,000 annually by reducing waste. This was serious money for a company with only 350 employees.

Elam wondered if the real problem was that implementing the MRP idea would require a radical overhaul of every facet of Cleaver's operations. Making the system work would require at least 25 Cleaver managers and employees to change how they did their jobs. Still angry, Elam thought, "What are the VPs and department heads so scared of?"

Prior to the executive committee meeting, Elam had encountered plenty of obstacles. She was unable to get data from several people to create a mock-up of how the system would work. Some key managers or their direct reports came late to the first and second meetings or simply skipped them, and she had complained to the CEO about the lack of cooperation. It was obvious to Elam that the topic was not a priority for the other VPs and department heads. Anderson's response was to suggest forming a cross-departmental task force to help her. Elam told him, "I believe in this technology, and I will get it done. A task force will just slow me down."

Allison Elam was a pleasant, reserved individual who did not like conflict. She had been mentally unprepared for the executive committee's no-go decision, and she shuddered at the thought that the MRP system might not be adopted at all. She decided to sleep on it for a night or two and then plan a course of action to get this system implemented, both for Cleaver's benefit and for her own conscience.

Questions

1. What do you think are the reasons for people's resistance to the MRP implementation? Explain.

2. What is the value of the task force idea suggested by the CEO as a way to facilitate implementation? Explain.

3. Which implementation tactics do you think Elam should follow? Why?

ENDNOTES

1. Greg Bensinger, "Amazon Curtails Development of Consumer Devices," *The Wall Street Journal*, August 26, 2015, http://www.wsj.com/articles/amazon-curtails-development-of-consumer-devices-1440632203 (accessed March 29, 2016).

2. Study by Charles I. Stubbart and Michael B. Knight, reported in Spencer E. Ante, "Avoiding Innovation's Terrible Toll," *The Wall Street Journal*, January 7, 2012, http://online.wsj.com/article/SB1000142405297020433130457714498024749346.html (accessed August 21, 2012).

3. Alex Taylor III, "The New GM: A Report Card," *Fortune* (September 5, 2011): 38–46; and Bill Vlasic, "Something 'Very Wrong' in G.M. Processes, Chief Says," *The New York Times*, March 17, 2014, http://www.nytimes.com/2014/03/18/business/gm-chief-barra-releases-video-on-recalls.html?ref=business (accessed March 17, 2014).

4. For a recent review of the extensive literature related to creativity and innovation in organizations, see Neil Anderson, Kristina Potočnik, and Jing Zhou, "Innovation and Creativity in Organizations: A State-of-the-Science Review, Prospective Commentary, and Guiding Framework," *Journal of Management* 40, no. 5 (July 2014): 1297–1333.

5. Richard L. Daft, "Bureaucratic vs. Nonbureaucratic Structure in the Process of Innovation and Change," in *Perspectives in Organizational Sociology: Theory and Research*, ed. Samuel B. Bacharach (Greenwich, CT: JAI Press, 1982), pp. 129–166.

6. Juan Pablo Vázques Sampere, Martin J. Bienenstock, and Ezra W. Zuckerman, "Debating Disruptive Innovation," *MIT Sloan Management Review* 57, no. 3 (Spring 2016): 26–30; and Clayton M. Christenson, Michael Raynor, and Rory McDonald, "What Is Disruptive Innovation?" *Harvard Business Review* (December 2015): 44–53.

7. Christenson et al., "What Is Disruptive Innovation?"

8. Daisuke Wakabayashi, "The Point-and-Shoot Camera Faces Its Existential Moment," *The Wall Street Journal*, July 30, 2013, http://online.wsj.com/article/SB10001424127887324251504578580263719432252.html (accessed August 26, 2013).

9. "05: Square, For Making Magic Out of the Mercantile," in "The World's 50 Most Innovative Companies," *Fast Company* (March 2012): 83–85, 146.

10. David W. Norton and B. Joseph Pine II, "Unique Experiences: Disruptive Innovations Offer Customers More 'Time Well Spent,'" *Strategy & Leadership* 37, no. 6 (2009): 4; "The Power to Disrupt," *The Economist* (April 17, 2010): 16; and Constantinos C. Markides, "How Disruptive Will Innovations from Emerging Markets Be?" *MIT Sloan Management Review* (Fall 2012): 23–25.

11. Markides, "How Disruptive Will Innovations from Emerging Markets Be?"

12. Jeffrey R. Immelt, Vijay Govindarajan, and Chris Trimble, "How GE Is Disrupting Itself," *Harvard Business Review* (October 2009): 3–11; and Navi Radjou, "Polycentric Innovation: A New Mandate for Multinationals," *The Wall Street Journal Online*, November 9, 2009, http://online.wsj.com/article/SB125774328035737917.html (accessed November 13, 2009).

13. See Julian Birkinshaw and Kamini Gupta, "Clarifying the Distinctive Contribution of Ambidexterity to the Field of Organization Studies," *The Academy of Management Perspectives* 27, no. 4 (November 2013): 287–298, for a recent review of research and a comprehensive discussion of the concept of ambidexterity in organizations.

14. For more information on the ambidextrous approach, see R. Duncan, "The Ambidextrous Organization: Designing Dual Structures for Innovation," in R. H. Killman, L. R. Pondy, and D. Sleven, eds., *The Management of Organization* (New York: North Holland, 1976), pp. 167–188; S. Raisch et al., "Organizational Ambidexterity: Balancing Exploitation and Exploration for Sustained Performance," *Organization Science* 20, no. 4 (July–August 2009): 685–695; Charles A. O'Reilly III and Michael L. Tushman, "The Ambidextrous Organization," *Harvard Business Review* (April 2004): 74–81; and Duane Ireland and Justin W. Webb, "Crossing the Great Divide of Strategic Entrepreneurship: Transitioning Between Exploration and Exploitation," *Business Horizons* 52 (2009): 469–479.

15. Elizabeth Dwoskin, "How Nontechnology Companies Are Trying to Mimic Startups," *The Wall Street Journal*, October 13, 2015, http://www.wsj.com/articles/nontech-companies-launch-innovation-labs-1444734539 (accessed March 30, 2016).

16. Ibid.; "History of Visa," Visa Web site, https://usa.visa.com/about-visa/our_business/history-of-visa.html (accessed March 30, 2016); Arjun Kharpal, "Visa Wants Your Car to Become Your New Credit Card," *CNBC* (February 26, 2016), http://www .cnbc.com/2016/02/22/ (accessed March 31, 2016); and "Peek Inside 7 of The Banking World's Coolest Innovation Labs," *The Financial Brand* (July 8, 2015), http://thefinancialbrand.com/52177/7-of-the-coolest-innovation-labs-in-banking/ (accessed March 31, 2016).

17. Glenn Rifkin, "Competing Through Innovation: The Case of Broderbund," *Strategy + Business* 11 (Second Quarter 1998): 48–58; and Deborah Dougherty and Cynthia Hardy, "Sustained Product Innovation in Large, Mature Organizations: Overcoming Innovation-to-Organization Problems," *Academy of Management Journal* 39, no. 5 (1996): 1120–1153.

18. Example from "The World's 50 Most Innovative Companies," *Fast Company* (March 2016), http://www.fastcompany.com/company/robinhood (accessed March 31, 2016).

19. "The World's 50 Most Innovative Companies," *Fast Company* (March 2013): 86–156; and "Fitbit," segment from "The World's 50 Most Innovative Companies," *Fast Company* (March 2016), http://www.fastcompany.com/company/fitbit (accessed March 31, 2016).

20. Example from Teri Evans, "Entrepreneurs Seek to Elicit Workers' Ideas—Contests with Cash Prizes and Other Rewards Stimulate Innovation in Hard Times," *The Wall Street Journal*, December 22, 2009.

21. Adapted from Patrick Reinmoeller and Nicole van Baardwijk, "The Link Between Diversity and Resilience," *MIT Sloan Management Review* (Summer 2005): 61–65.

22. Teresa M. Amabile, "Motivating Creativity in Organizations: On Doing What You Love and Loving What You Do," *California Management Review* 40, no. 1 (Fall 1997): 39–58; Brian Leavy, "Creativity: The New Imperative," *Journal of General Management* 28, no. 1 (Autumn 2002): 70–85; and Timothy A. Matherly and Ronald E. Goldsmith, "The Two Faces of Creativity," *Business Horizons* (September–October 1985): 8.

23. Gordon Vessels, "The Creative Process: An Open-Systems Conceptualization," *Journal of Creative Behavior* 16 (1982): 185–196.

24. Robert J. Sternberg, Linda A. O'Hara, and Todd I. Lubart, "Creativity as Investment," *California Management Review* 40, no. 1 (Fall 1997): 8–21; Amabile, "Motivating Creativity in Organizations"; Leavy, "Creativity: The New Imperative"; and Ken Lizotte, "A Creative State of Mind," *Management Review* (May 1998): 15–17.

25. James Brian Quinn, "Managing Innovation: Controlled Chaos," *Harvard Business Review* 63 (May–June 1985): 73–84; Howard H. Stevenson and David E. Gumpert, "The Heart of Entrepreneurship," *Harvard Business Review* 63 (March–April 1985): 85–94; Marsha Sinetar, "Entrepreneurs, Chaos, and Creativity—Can Creative People Really Survive Large Company Structure?" *Sloan Management Review* 6 (Winter 1985): 57–62; Constantine Andriopoulos, "Six Paradoxes in Managing Creativity: An Embracing Act," *Long Range Planning* 36 (2003): 375–388; and Justin Brady, "How Removing Fear Can Be Your Innovation Trump Card," *The Washington Post*, May 15, 2015, https://www.washingtonpost.com/news/innovations/wp/2015/05/15/how-removing-fear-can-be-your-innovation-trump-card/ (accessed April 7, 2016).

26. Research studies reported in Sue Shellenbarger, "Better Ideas Through Failure," *The Wall Street Journal*, September 27, 2011.

27. Brady, "How Removing Fear Can Be Your Innovation Trump Card"; and "Culture of Creativity," Grey Advertising Web site, http://grey.com/us/culture (accessed May 19, 2014).

28. Cynthia Browne, "Jest for Success," *Moonbeams* (August 1989): 3–5; and Rosabeth Moss Kanter, *The Change Masters* (New York: Simon and Schuster, 1983).

29. Adam Grant, "How to Build a Culture of Originality," *Harvard Business Review* (March 2016): 86–94; Jen Swetzoff, "Linda A. Hill on the Creative Power of the Many," *Strategy + Business* (March 16, 2015); J. C. Spender and Bruce Strong, "Who Has Innovative Ideas? Employees." *The Wall Street Journal*, August 23, 2010; and Roger L. Martin, "The Innovation Catalysts," *Harvard Business Review* (June 2011): 82–87.

30. Robert J. Moore, "How We Use 'Hackathons' to Generate Big Ideas," *The New York Times*, December 12, 2014, http://boss.blogs.nytimes.com/2014/12/12/how-we-use-hackathons-to-generate-big-ideas/?_r=0 (accessed April 4, 2016).

31. Sabrina Adamczyk, Angelika C. Bullinger, and Kathrin M. Möslein, "Innovation Contests: A Review, Classification, and Outlook," *Creativity and Innovation Management* 21, no. 4 (2012): 335–355.

32. Grant, "How to Build a Culture of Originality."

33. Alison Overholt, "American Idol: Accounting Edition," *Fortune* (October 17, 2011): 100–106.

34. Reported in Rachel Emma Silverman, "For Bright Ideas, Ask the Staff," *The Wall Street Journal*, October 17, 2011.

35. Quoted in Darren Dahl, "Technology: Pipe Up, People! Rounding Up Staff Ideas," *Inc.* (February 2010): 80–81.

36. Sherry Eng, "Hatching Schemes," *The Industry Standard* (November 27–December 4, 2000): 174–175.

37. James I. Cash, Jr., Michael J. Earl, and Robert Morison, "Teaming Up to Crack Innovation and Enterprise Integration," *Harvard Business Review* (November 2008): 90–100; Barry Jaruzelski, Kevin Dehoff, and Rakesh Bordia, "Money Isn't Everything," *Strategy + Business*, no. 41 (December 5, 2005): 54–67; William L. Shanklin and John K. Ryans, Jr., "Organizing for High-Tech Marketing," *Harvard Business Review* 62 (November–December 1984): 164–171; Arnold O. Putnam, "A Redesign for Engineering," *Harvard Business Review* 63 (May–June 1985): 139–144; and Joan Schneider and Julie Hall, "Why Most Product Launches Fail," *Harvard Business Review* (April 2011): 21–23.

38. Annie Lowrey, "Ideas on an Assembly Line," *The New York Times*, December 14, 2012.

39. Hiroko Tabuchi, "How the Parade Passed Sony By," *The New York Times*, April 15, 2012.

40. Quoted in Janet Rae-DuPree, "Teamwork, the True Mother of Invention," *The New York Times*, December 7, 2008.

41. Based on Gloria Barczak and Kenneth B. Kahn, "Identifying New Product Development Best Practice," *Business Horizons* 55 (2012): 293–305; Andrew H. Van de Ven, "Central Problems in the Management of Innovation," *Management Science* 32 (1986): 590–607; Richard L. Daft, *Organization Theory and Design* (Mason, OH: South-Western, 2010), pp. 424–425; and Science Policy Research Unit, University of Sussex, *Success and Failure in Industrial Innovation* (London: Centre for the Study of Industrial Innovation, 1972).

42. Based on Daft, *Organization Theory and Design*; and Lee Norris Miller, "Debugging Dysfunctional Development," *Industrial Management* (November–December 2011): 10–15.

43. Mike Gordon et al., "The Path to Successful New Products," *McKinsey Quarterly*, January 2010, www.mckinseyquarterly.com/the_path_to_successful_new_products_2489 (accessed February 10, 2012).

44. Erik Brynjolfsson and Michael Schrage, "The New, Faster Face of Innovation," *The Wall Street Journal Online*, August 17, 2009, http://online.wsj.com/article/SB10001424052970 2048303045741308201842 60340.html (accessed August 21, 2009).

45. William J. Holstein, "Five Gates to Innovation," *Strategy + Business* (March 1, 2010), www.strategy-business.com/article/00021?gko=0bd39 (accessed September 16, 2011); and "Corning: For Becoming the 800-Pound Gorilla of the Touch Screen Business," segment of "The World's 50 Most Innovative Companies," *Fast Company* (March 2013): 86–156.

46. Daniel Roberts, "Going to the Mattresses," *Fortune* (September 24, 2012): 28–29.

47. Brian Dumaine, "How Managers Can Succeed Through Speed," *Fortune* (February 13, 1989): 54–59; and George Stalk, Jr., "Time—The Next Source of Competitive Advantage," *Harvard Business Review* (July–August 1988): 41–51.

48. This discussion of open innovation is based on Henry Chesbrough, "The Era of Open Innovation," *MIT Sloan Management Review* (Spring 2003): 35–41; Ulrich Lichtenthaler, "Open Innovation: Past Research, Current Debates, and Future Directions," *Academy of Management Perspectives* (February 2011): 75–92; Julian Birkinshaw and Susan A. Hill, "Corporate Venturing Units: Vehicles for Strategic Success in the New Europe," *Organizational Dynamics* 34, no. 3 (2005): 247–257; Amy Muller and Liisa Välikangas, "Extending the Boundary of Corporate Innovation," *Strategy & Leadership* 30, no. 3 (2002): 4–9; Navi Radjou, "Networked Innovation Drives Profits," *Industrial Management* (January–February 2005): 14–21; and Henry Chesbrough, "The Logic of Open Innovation: Managing Intellectual Property," *California Management Review* 45, no. 3 (Spring 2003): 33–58.

49. Amy Muller, Nate Hutchins, and Miguel Cardoso Pinto, "Applying Open Innovation Where Your Company Needs It Most," *Strategy & Leadership* 40, no. 2 (2012): 35–42.

50. Andrew King and Karim R. Lakhani, "Using Open Innovation to Identify the Best Ideas," *MIT Sloan Management Review* (Fall 2013): 41–43; and Muller, Hutchins, and Cardoso Pinto, "Applying Open Innovation."

51. Kevin J. Boudreau and Karim R. Lakhani, "Using the Crowd as an Innovation Partner," *Harvard Business Review* (April 2013): 61–67; and King and Lakhani, "Using Open Innovation to Identify the Best Ideas."

52. King and Lakhani, "Using Open Innovation to Identify the Best Ideas."

53. Karen Weise, "Solve a Washington Problem, Win a Prize," *Bloomberg BusinessWeek* (June 10, 2013): 34–35; and "Introduction to Challenge.gov," https://www.challenge.gov/about/ (accessed April 5, 2016).

54. Steve Lohr, "The Invention Mob Brought to You by Quirky," *The New York Times*, February 14, 2015, http://www.nytimes.com/2015/02/15/technology/quirky-tests-the-crowd-based-creative-process.html?_r=0 (accessed April 6, 2016); and Ruth Simon, "One Week, 3,000 Product Ideas," *The Wall Street Journal*, July 3, 2014, http://www.wsj.com/articles/one-week-3-000-product-ideas-1404332942 (accessed April 6, 2016).

55. "Crowdsource Mapping Helps Recovery Efforts in Philippines," *Here & Now*, WBUR, November 15, 2013, http://hereandnow.wbur.org/2013/11/15/mapping-effort-philippines (accessed November 18, 2013); Declan Butler, "Crowdsourcing Goes Mainstream in Typhoon Haiyan Response," *Scientific American*, November 20, 2013, http://www.scientificamerican.com/article.cfm?id=crowdsourcing-goes-mainstream-in-typhoon-haiyan-response (accessed November 12, 2013); Steve Lohr, "Online Mapping Shows Potential to Transform Relief Efforts," *The New York Times*, March 28, 2011, www.nytimes.com/2011/03/28/business/28map.html?_r=1 (accessed August 22, 2012); and Tina Rosenberg, "Crowdsourcing a Better World," *The New York Times*, March 28, 2011, http://opinionator.blogs.nytimes.com/2011/03/28/crowdsourcing-a-better-world/ (accessed March 29, 2011).

56. "Innovation Through Acquisition," *The Wall Street Journal*, January 21, 2013, http://online.wsj.com/article/SB10001424127887323468604578245 620735086626.html (accessed October 7, 2013); and "Innovation by Acquisition," Royal Pingdom Web site, March 10, 2010, http://royal.pingdom.com/2010/03/10/innovation-by-acquisition/ (accessed October 7, 2013).

57. Daniel T. Holt, Matthew W. Rutherford, and Gretchen R. Clohessy, "Corporate Entrepreneurship: An Empirical Look at Individual Characteristics, Context, and Process," *Journal of Leadership and Organizational Studies* 13, no. 4 (2007): 40–54.

58. Curtis R. Carlson and William W. Wilmot, *Innovation: The Five Disciplines for Creating What Customers Want* (New York: Crown Business, 2006).

59. Robert I. Sutton, "The Weird Rules of Creativity," *Harvard Business Review* (September 2001): 94–103; and Julian Birkinshaw and Michael Mol, "How Management Innovation Happens," *MIT Sloan Management Review* (Summer 2006): 81–88.

60. Jane M. Howell, "The Right Stuff: Identifying and Developing Effective Champions of Innovation," *Academy of Management Executive* 19, no. 2 (2005): 108–119.

61. C. K. Bart, "New Venture Units: Use Them Wisely to Manage Innovation," *Sloan Management Review* (Summer 1988): 35–43; Michael Tushman and David Nadler, "Organizing for Innovation," *California Management Review* 28 (Spring 1986): 74–92; Peter F. Drucker, *Innovation and Entrepreneurship* (New York: Harper & Row, 1985); and Henry W. Chesbrough, "Making Sense of Corporate Venture Capital," *Harvard Business Review* 80, no. 3 (March 2002): 90–99.

62. Conor Dougherty, "Alphabet Trying to Mix Heft with Start-Up Agility," *The New York Times*, November 24, 2015, http://bits.blogs.nytimes.com/2015/11/24/alphabet-trying-to-mix-heft-with-start-up-agility/?_r=0 (accessed April 6, 2016).

63. Sebastian Raisch, "Balanced Structures: Designing Organizations for Profitable Growth," *Long Range Planning* 41 (2008): 483–508.

64. Christopher Hoenig, "Skunk Works Secrets," *CIO* (July 1, 2000): 74–76; and Tom Peters and Nancy Austin, *A Passion for Excellence: The Leadership Difference* (New York: Random House, 1985).

65. Hoenig, "Skunk Works Secrets."

66. Taylor, "The New GM."

67. David Dobson, "Integrated Innovation at Pitney Bowes," *Strategy + Business Online*, October 26, 2009, www.strategy-business.com/article/09404b?gko=f9661 (accessed December 30, 2009); and Cash et al., "Teaming Up to Crack Innovation and Enterprise Integration."

68. Robert C. Wolcott and Michael J. Lippitz, "The Four Models of Corporate Entrepreneurship," *MIT Sloan Management Review* (Fall 2007): 75–82.

69. E. H. Schein, "Organizational Culture," *American Psychologist* 45 (February 1990): 109–119; and Eliza Newlin Carney, "Calm in the Storm," *Government Executive* (October 2003): 57–63.

70. Rosabeth Moss Kanter, "Execution: The Un-Idea," sidebar in Art Kleiner, "Our 10 Most Enduring Ideas," *Strategy + Business*, no. 41 (December 12, 2005): 36–41.

71. Alex Taylor III, "The New GM: A Report Card," *Fortune* (September 5, 2011): 38–46; and Geoff Colvin, "How CEO Mary Barra Is Using the Ignition-Switch Scandal to Change GM's Culture," *Fortune* (September 18, 2015), http://fortune.com/2015/09/18/mary-barra-gm-culture/ (accessed April 6, 2016).

72. Shawn Tully, "Can UnitedHealth Really Fix the System?" *Fortune* (May 29, 2013): 187–194.

73. M. Sashkin and W. W. Burke, "Organization Development in the 1980s," *General Management* 13 (1987): 393–417; and Richard Beckhard, "What Is Organization Development?" in Wendell L. French, Cecil H. Bell, Jr., and Robert A. Zawacki, eds., *Organization Development and Transformation: Managing Effective Change*, (Burr Ridge, IL: Irwin McGraw-Hill, 2000), pp. 16–19.

74. Wendell L. French and Cecil H. Bell, Jr., "A History of Organization Development," in French, Bell, and Zawacki, *Organization Development and Transformation*, pp. 20–42; and Christopher G. Worley and Ann E. Feyerherm, "Reflections on the Future of Organization Development," *The Journal of Applied Behavioral Science* 39, no. 1 (March 2003): 97–115.

75. Paul F. Buller, "For Successful Strategic Change: Blend OD Practices with Strategic Management," *Organizational Dynamics* (Winter 1988): 42–55; Robert M. Fulmer and Roderick Gilkey, "Blending Corporate Families: Management and Organization Development in a Postmerger Environment," *The Academy of Management Executive* 2 (1988): 275–283; and Worley and Feyerherm, "Reflections on the Future of Organization Development."

76. W. Warner Burke, "The New Agenda for Organization Development," *Organizational Dynamics* (Summer 1997): 7–19.

77. R. Wayne Bass et al., "Sustainable Change in the Public Sector: The Longitudinal Benefits of Organization Development," *The Journal of Applied Behavioral Science* 46, no. 4 (2010): 436–472.

78. Tully, "Can UnitedHealth Really Fix the System?"

79. This discussion is based on Kathleen D. Dannemiller and Robert W. Jacobs, "Changing the Way Organizations Change: A Revolution of Common Sense," *The Journal of Applied Behavioral Science* 28, no. 4 (December 1992): 480–498; and Barbara Benedict Bunker and Billie T. Alban, "Conclusion: What Makes Large Group Interventions Effective?" *Journal of Applied Behavioral Science* 28, no. 4 (December 1992): 570–591.

80. William J. Holstein, "Lenovo Goes Global," *Strategy + Business* (Autumn 2014): 1–10.

81. For a recent review of the literature related to large-group interventions, see Christopher G. Worley, Susan A. Mohrman, and Jennifer A. Nevitt, "Large Group Interventions: An Empirical Study of Their Composition, Process, and Outcomes," *The Journal of Applied Behavioral Science* 47, no. 4 (2011): 404–431.

82. Bunker and Alban, "Conclusion: What Makes Large Group Interventions Effective?"

83. Kurt Lewin, "Frontiers in Group Dynamics: Concepts, Method, and Reality in Social Science," *Human Relations* 1 (1947): 5–41; and E. F. Huse and T. G. Cummings, *Organization Development and Change*, 3d ed. (St. Paul, MN: West, 1985).

84. Based on John Kotter's eight-step model of planned change, which is described in John P. Kotter, *Leading Change* (Boston: Business School Press, 1996), pp. 20–25, and John Kotter, "Leading Change: Why Transformation Efforts Fail," *Harvard Business Review* (March–April, 1995): 59–67.

85. Based on Bob Kelleher, "Employee Engagement Carries ENSR Through Organizational Challenges and Economic Turmoil," *Global Business and Organizational Excellence* 28, no. 3 (March–April 2009): 6–19.

86. J. P. Kotter and L. A. Schlesinger, "Choosing Strategies for Change," *Harvard Business Review* 57 (March–April 1979): 106–114.

87. Joann S. Lublin, "Can a New Culture Fix Troubled Companies?" *The Wall Street Journal*, March 13, 2013.

88. Joann S. Lublin, "Theory & Practice: Firm Offers Blueprint for Makeover in a Spinoff," *The Wall Street Journal*, June 29, 2009.

89. G. Zaltman and Robert B. Duncan, *Strategies for Planned Change* (New York: Wiley Interscience, 1977).

90. Katherine Hobson, "Getting Docs to Use PCs," *The New York Times*, March 15, 2011.

91. Brian J. Hurn, "Management of Change in a Multinational Company," *Industrial and Commercial Training* 44, no. 2 (2012): 41–46.

92. Todd Datz, "No Small Change," *CIO* (February 15, 2004): 66–72.

93. Dorothy Leonard-Barton and Isabelle Deschamps, "Managerial Influence in the Implementation of New Technology," *Management Science* 34 (1988): 1252–1265.

94. Gerard H. Seijts and Grace O'Farrell, "Engage the Heart: Appealing to the Emotions Facilitates Change," *Ivey Business Journal* (January–February 2003): 1–5; John P. Kotter and Dan S. Cohen, *The Heart of Change: Real-Life Stories of How People Change Their Organizations* (Boston: Harvard Business School Press, 2002); and Shaul Fox and Yair Amichai-Hamburger, "The Power of Emotional Appeals in Promoting Organizational Change Programs," *Academy of Management Executive* 15, no. 4 (2001): 84–95.

95. Peter Löscher, "How I Did It. . . . The CEO of Siemens on Using a Scandal to Drive Change," *Harvard Business Review* (November 2012): 39–42.

96. Kotter, *Leading Change*, pp. 20–25; and "Leading Change: Why Transformation Efforts Fail."

97. Kurt Lewin, *Field Theory in Social Science: Selected Theoretical Papers* (New York: Harper & Brothers, 1951).

98. Paul C. Nutt, "Tactics of Implementation," *Academy of Management Journal* 29 (1986): 230–261; Kotter and Schlesinger, "Choosing Strategies for Change"; R. L. Daft and S. Becker, *Innovation in Organizations: Innovation Adoption in School Organizations* (New York: Elsevier, 1978); and R. Beckhard, *Organization Development: Strategies and Models* (Reading, MA: Addison-Wesley, 1969).

99. Strategos survey results, reported in Pierre Loewe and Jennifer Dominiquini, "Overcoming the Barriers to Effective Innovation," *Strategy & Leadership* 34, no. 1 (2006): 24–31.

100. Donald F. Kuratko, Jeffrey G. Covin, and Robert P. Garrett, "Corporate Venturing: Insights from Actual Performance," *Business Horizons* 52 (2009): 459–467; and Burcu Felekoglu and James Moultrie, "Top Management Involvement in New Product Development: A Review and Synthesis," *Journal of Product Innovation Management* 31, no. 1 (2014): 159–175.

101. Allysia Finley, "The Democrat Who Took On the Unions," *The Wall Street Journal*, March 24, 2012.

102. Gina Burkhardt and Diane Gerard, "People: The Lever for Changing the Business Model at Learning Point Associates," *Journal of Organizational Excellence* (Autumn 2006): 31–43.

103. Henry Hornstein, "Using a Change Management Approach to Implement IT Programs," *Ivey Business Journal* (January–February 2008); Philip H. Mirvis, Amy L. Sales, and Edward J. Hackett, "The Implementation and Adoption of New Technology in Organizations: The Impact on Work, People, and Culture," *Human Resource Management* 30 (Spring 1991): 113–139; Arthur E. Wallach, "System Changes Begin in the Training Department," *Personnel Journal* 58 (1979): 846–848, 872; and Paul R. Lawrence, "How to Deal with Resistance to Change," *Harvard Business Review* 47 (January–February 1969): 4–12, 166–176.

104. Adapted from Edward Glassman, *Creativity Handbook: Idea Triggers and Sparks That Work* (Chapel Hill, NC: LCS Press, 1990).

105. Based on Paul Boutin, "Crowdsourcing: Consumers as Creators," *BusinessWeek Online*, July 13, 2006, www.business-week.com/innovate/content/jul2006/id20060713_755844.htm (accessed August 30, 2010); Jeff Howe, "The Rise of Crowdsourcing," *Wired*, June 2006, www.wired.com/wired/archive/14.06/crowds.html (accessed August 30, 2010); and Jeff Howe, Crowdsourcing blog, www.crowdsourcing.com (accessed August 30, 2010).

Chapter 9
Managing Human Talent and Diversity

iStock.com/oscarhdez

Chapter Outline

Learning Outcomes

After studying this chapter, you should be able to:

9.1 Explain the strategic role of human resource management.

9.2 Describe federal legislation and societal trends that influence human resource management.

9.3 Explain what the changing social contract between organizations and employees means for workers and human resource managers.

9.4 Show how organizations determine their future staffing needs through human resource planning.

9.5 Describe the tools that managers use to recruit and select employees.

9.6 Describe some of the diversity challenges that managers face in the United States and globally.

9.7 Summarize the factors that affect women's opportunities, including the glass ceiling, the opt-out trend, the female advantage, and sexual harassment.

Are You Ready to Be a Manager?

Before reading this chapter, please circle either "Mostly True" or "Mostly False" for each of the following five statements.

1 Employees who learn and grow are more valuable to their company.

| Mostly True | ◄ · · · · · · · · · · · · · · · · · · · ► | Mostly False |

[page 307]

2 I know that the kind of job security my parents or grandparents had is gone.

| Mostly True | ◄ · · · · · · · · · · · · · · · · · · · ► | Mostly False |

[page 311]

3 I know how important it is to behave professionally and do my homework for a job interview.

| Mostly True | ◄ · · · · · · · · · · · · · · · · · · · ► | Mostly False |

[page 318]

4 It is easy for me to relate to people from different ethic backgrounds, social classes, or religions.

| Mostly True | ◄ · · · · · · · · · · · · · · · · · · · ► | Mostly False |

[page 330]

5 In some ways, women make better managers than men.

| Mostly True | ◄ · · · · · · · · · · · · · · · · · · · ► | Mostly False |

[page 344]

Discover Your Management Approach

When was the last time you called in sick to work? What was your reason? According to CareerBuilder's annual survey, the percentage of employees admitting that they called in sick when they actually felt fine increased to 38 percent in 2015, up 10 percentage points from the previous year. The excuse given to supervisors most often was a doctor's appointment, but CareerBuilder also found some much more interesting reasons people gave for why they couldn't come to work. One employee said she was stuck under the bed, for example. Another told her manager that she had to go to the beach because her doctor said she needed more Vitamin D. How about the employee who said he broke his arm while trying to catch a falling sandwich, or the one who poked herself in the eye while combing her hair? Perhaps they were a bit luckier than the guy who claimed his grandmother had poisoned him with ham.[1]

As these humorous examples show, there can be some interesting challenges in the area of managing human resources. All managers, no matter their hierarchical level or functional area, deal with human resource issues, such as finding and training the right people, evaluating performance fairly, and sometimes firing people for the good of the team or organization.

This chapter explores the topic of human resource management in detail. The term **human resource management (HRM)** refers to the design and application of formal systems in an organization to ensure the effective and efficient use of human talent to accomplish organizational goals.[2] This includes activities undertaken to attract, develop, and maintain an effective workforce. Managers have to find the right people, place them in positions where they can be most effective, and develop them so that they contribute to company success. Hot-button issues such as executive compensation, changing government regulations, and the frequency of mergers and acquisitions make HRM a critical skill for both business and nonprofit organizations.[3]

9-1 The Strategic Role of HRM Is to Drive Organizational Performance

Managers around the world often cite *human capital* as the top factor in maintaining competitive success, which reflects the critical role of managing talent. *Talent management* has emerged as a central topic of concern not only for human resource managers but for all managers searching for ways to keep their organizations thriving in the fast-changing, competitive environment of the early twenty-first century.[4] Smart managers know that employees *are* the company—if they don't perform well, the company doesn't stand a chance of succeeding. **Human capital** refers to the economic value of the combined knowledge, experience, skills, and capabilities of employees.[5] Exhibit 9.1 shows the top three factors cited by CEOs as contributing to organizational success based on a survey of more than 1,700 top executives from around the world. Human capital ranked far higher than assets such as technology, physical resources, and access to raw materials.[6]

9-1a The Strategic Approach

HRM has shed its old "personnel" image and gained recognition as a vital player in corporate strategy.[7] The best HR departments not only support strategic objectives but also actively pursue an ongoing, integrated plan for furthering the organization's performance.[8] Research has found that effective HRM and the alignment of HR strategies with the organization's strategic direction have a positive impact on performance, including higher employee productivity and stronger financial results.[9]

Tesla Motors has been on a hiring spree to help the car company meet its strategic goals.

Exhibit 9.1 **Top Three Factors for Maintaining Competitive Success**

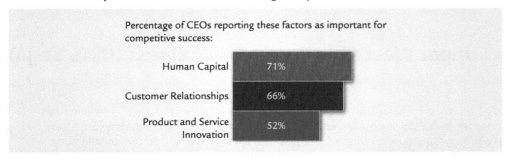

SOURCE: "Leading Through Connections: The IBM 2012 Chief Executive Officer Study," reported in Eric Lesser and Carl Hoffman, "Workforce Analytics: Making the Most of a Critical Asset," *Ivey Business Journal* (July–August 2012), www.iveybusinessjournal.com/topics/strategy/workforce-analytics-making-the-most-of-a-critical-asset (accessed August 27, 2012).

Sunny Side Up ⟩ Tesla Motors Inc.

In late 2015, Tesla Motors CEO Elon Musk put out an urgent call on Twitter for "hard-core software engineers" to work on Tesla's autonomous car project, known as Autopilot. "This is a super-high priority," Musk tweeted.

The need is intense as Tesla's strategy is based on large-scale growth through the end of the decade. Tesla is competing for engineering talent with a growing number of companies working to develop electric and self-driving vehicles. Start-ups such as China's Faraday Future Inc., Karma Automotive Inc., and Atieva Inc. have been luring employees away from Tesla for their car projects. Traditional automakers such as Ford and Toyota are fighting for talent

in Silicon Valley to help them create the software and other components of electric and autonomous vehicles and fend off the threat from Apple and Alphabet's Google as those companies work to create a self-driving car.

To meet its ambitious growth goals, Tesla needs to add people faster than smaller start-ups do. The company expanded from only 899 employees at the end of 2010 to more 14,000 by the end of 2015, and Musk has plans to add 4,500 more in California alone over the next four years. He personally interviews engineers for Autopilot, reflecting the importance of each new hire for meeting the company's long-term goals.[10]

Tesla Motors and other automakers aren't the only firms fighting for talent. Airlines, for example, are facing a severe pilot shortage as the retirement of thousands of airline pilots collides with an increase in air travel and new FAA rules requiring expanded training for new pilots and longer rest times for pilots of passenger airlines. The problem isn't going away anytime soon, as analysts predict more than 2,600 pilot retirements at major airlines in 2020 compared with 560 retirements in 2012.[11] Hiring and keeping high-quality employees with the right set of skills is one of the most urgent concerns for today's organizations.

The strategic approach to HRM recognizes three key elements. First, all managers are involved in managing human resources. Second, employees are viewed as assets. No strategy can be implemented effectively without the right people to put it into action. Employees, not buildings and machinery, give a company its competitive edge. Third, HRM is a matching process, integrating the organization's strategy and goals with the correct approach to managing human capital.[12] Some current strategic issues of particular concern to managers include the following:

- Hiring the right people to become more competitive on a global basis
- Hiring the right people for improving quality, innovation, and customer service
- Knowing the right people to retain after mergers, acquisitions, or downsizing
- Hiring the right people to apply new information technology (IT) for mobile business

Hiring the right people is important for smaller businesses as well, even Yoga studios, as described in the "Sunny Side Up" box.

> "If each of us hires people who are smaller than we are, we shall become a company of dwarfs. But if each of us hires people who are bigger than we are, we shall become a company of giants."
>
> —DAVID OGILVY (1911–1999), FOUNDER OF THE OGILVY & MATHER ADVERTISING AGENCY

Sunny Side Up — Upper West Side Yoga and Wellness (UWS Yoga)

"Running a Yoga studio is a business not unlike managing a dance or even a martial-arts studio," said Stephan Kolbert, who owns UWS Yoga with his wife and business partner, Ingrid Marcroft. Their goal is to offer high-quality classes to students and support their overall health and wellness. Along with their teaching responsibilities, they also have to manage the studio well to make ends meet. Currently, they have 21 teachers, though fewer than 70 percent are active in any single pay period, as well as their four part-time front desk staff.

Students choose Yoga classes largely based on teachers, according to a multiyear industry study, so the reputation of the teacher is a magnet to healthy class sizes. When choosing a new teacher, Kolbert and Marcroft look for a high-quality teacher who is sensitive to students' varying needs, someone who gets along with people in the studio, and someone who is reliable. Because UWS Yoga is considered a small-to-medium size studio, the owners rely on subcontractor teachers to do about two-thirds of the teaching, while Marcroft and Kolbert do the rest. They strictly adhere to Department of Labor Standards regarding the way they work with independent contractor teachers and their desk staff. According to Kolbert, some studios blur this boundary of labor and have teachers greet students, take cash, or clean up, but UWS Yoga asks them only to teach because the desk staff (or Marcroft and Kolbert) do those other tasks.

Most Yoga studios do teacher-training programs as a way of increasing their income, and this gives them a healthy stream of new people to choose from when a teacher position opens. UWS Yoga does not have a teacher-training program, so Kolbert says the studio finds teachers through word of mouth, and if he and Marcroft hear of a really good teacher, they'll attend that person's class. "We used to get to know someone personally and then have that person teach for us, but we've learned we need to see someone sample teach a regular class first." Some studios hold an "open call" to look for new teachers, not unlike the audition in *A Chorus Line*, but Kolbert said he and Marcroft had found that too competitive and dispiriting and prefer a more personal approach to recruitment. They also often ask regular students to provide them with feedback on substitute teachers to see if they are a good fit for the studio.

As for retaining good teachers and desk staff, both Marcroft and Kolbert practice bringing the principles of Yoga into their business. Yoga is about balancing physical energy and mental clarity. "We treat our teachers and staff with a lot of respect, compassion, and professionalism, and don't look to micromanage them. We hear other studio owners complain about teachers or staffing issues but, overall, we've had excellent experiences with the human resources side of the business. Teachers and staff have also told us that they love working with us because we 'walk the talk.'"

SOURCE: Stephan Kolbert, personal communication, March 2018.

All of these strategic decisions determine a company's need for skills and employees.

This chapter examines the three primary goals of HRM, as illustrated in Exhibit 9.2. HRM activities and goals do not take place inside a vacuum, but within the context of issues and factors affecting the entire organization, such as globalization, changing technology, the need for rapid innovation, quick shifts in markets and the external environment, societal trends, government regulations, and changes in the organization's culture, structure, strategy, and goals.

The three broad HRM activities outlined in Exhibit 9.2 are to find the right people, manage talent so that people achieve their potential, and maintain the workforce over the long term.[13]

9-1b Building Human Capital to Drive Performance

In many companies, especially those that rely more on employee information, creativity, knowledge, and service rather than on production machinery, success depends on the ability to manage human capital, as described earlier. To build human capital, HRM develops strategies for finding the best people, enhancing their skills and knowledge with training programs and opportunities for personal and professional development, and providing compensation and benefits that support the sharing of knowledge and appropriately reward people for their contributions to the organization.[14]

The importance of human capital for business results is illustrated in Exhibit 9.3, which shows a portion of a framework developed by Accenture and used by software and services company SAP. Managers at SAP needed a way to evaluate and revise human capital processes

Concept Connection

Lowe's 265,000 employees help customers with remodeling, building, and gardening ideas at its 1,840 stores. They cut lumber, blinds, pipe, and chains; thread pipes; assemble items; provide computer project design and landscape garden design; match paint colors; teach how-to clinics; and offer many other services. Managers know that providing superior customer service depends on **human capital**, so they invest in finding the best people and helping them develop and apply their combined knowledge, skills, experience, and talent.

Kevork Djansezian/Getty Images

Exhibit 9.2 Strategic Human Resource Management

to shift to a new strategy that called for stronger customer focus and greater individual employee accountability. The idea is to show how investments in human capital contribute to stronger organizational performance and better financial results. The framework begins at the bottom (level 3) by assessing internal processes such as workforce planning, career development, performance appraisal, and so forth. Managers use these activities to increase human capital capabilities that drive higher performance in key areas such as innovation or customer service (level 2). Improvements in key performance areas, in turn, lead to improved business results (level 1).[15]

Exhibit 9.3 The Role and Value of Human Capital Investments

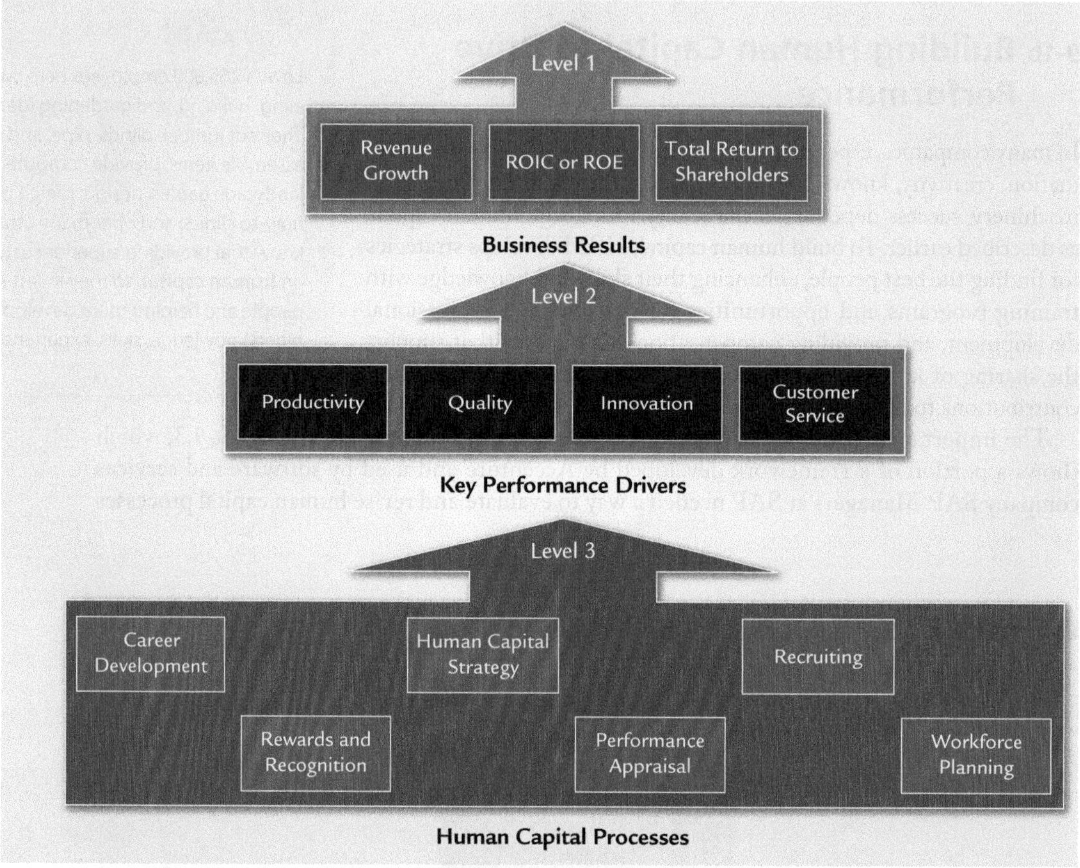

SOURCE: Adapted from Susan Cantrell et al., "Measuring the Value of Human Capital Investments: The SAP Case," *Strategy & Leadership* 34, no. 2 (2006): 43–52.

Remember This

- **Human resource management (HRM)** refers to the design and application of formal systems to ensure the effective and efficient use of human talent to accomplish organizational goals.
- HRM includes activities undertaken to attract, select, develop, and maintain an effective workforce.

- HR managers are vital players in corporate strategy because no strategy can be effective without the right people to put it into action.
- **Human capital** refers to the economic value of the combined knowledge, experience, skills, and capabilities of employees.

Green Power

The "You" in Sustainability *"You* are our sustainability edge!" is the new slogan to bring employees on board for sustainability. HSBC bank carried employee involvement to a new level by promoting individual projects and action plans through its Climate Champions Program. HSBC paved the way by partnering with powerful environmental organizations, including the Smithsonian Institution, Earthwatch, and the Climate Group. Participants go through an application process for a 12-month residential program. Working alongside Earthwatch scientists, HSBC employees complete climate-related business projects, gaining skills and developing methods that can be transferred to the workplace. HSBC's Climate Champions program has ignited employee curiosity and excitement. The program tells participants, "You have a voice in sustainability. You *own* this project. *You* are our sustainability edge."

SOURCE: Matthew Gitsham, "Experiential Learning for Leadership and Sustainability at IBM and HSBC," *Journal of Management Development* 31, no. 3 (2012): 298–307.

9-2 The Impact of Federal Legislation on HRM

Managing HR effectively is a complex challenge for managers. For one thing, the legal and regulatory environment is constantly changing, and HR managers have to stay on top of issues that might have legal consequences. It is critically important that managers know and apply a variety of federal laws that have been passed to ensure equal employment opportunity (EEO). Some of the most significant legislation and executive orders are summarized in Exhibit 9.4. The point of the laws is to stop discriminatory practices that are unfair to specific groups and to define enforcement agencies for these laws. EEO legislation attempts to balance the pay given to men and women; provide employment opportunities without regard to race, religion, national origin, and gender; ensure fair treatment for employees of all ages; and avoid discrimination against disabled individuals.

The Equal Employment Opportunity Commission (EEOC) created by the Civil Rights Act of 1964 initiates investigations in response to complaints concerning discrimination. **Discrimination** occurs when hiring and promotion decisions are made based on criteria that are not job relevant; for example, refusing to hire a black applicant for a job that he is qualified to fill and paying a woman a lower wage than a man for the same work are discriminatory acts. When discrimination is found, remedies include providing back pay and taking affirmative action. **Affirmative action** requires that an employer take positive steps to guarantee equal employment opportunities for people within protected groups.

Are you suited to work as an HR manager, which often requires following routine procedures and keeping detailed records to document compliance with federal laws and regulations? Visit MindTap for the "Self-Assessment: What Is Your Focus?" to get an idea of your natural orientation toward systematic recordkeeping.

Exhibit 9.4 Major Federal Laws Related to Human Resource Management

Federal Law	Year	Provisions
Equal Opportunity/ Discrimination Laws		
Civil Rights Act	1991	Provides for possible compensatory and punitive damages, plus traditional back pay, for cases of intentional discrimination brought under Title VII of the 1964 Civil Rights Act. Shifts the burden of proof to the employer.
Americans with Disabilities Act	1990	Prohibits discrimination against qualified individuals by employers on the basis of disability and demands that "reasonable accommodations" be provided for disabled people to allow them to perform their duties.
Vocational Rehabilitation Act	1973	Prohibits discrimination based on physical or mental disability and requires that employees be informed about affirmative action plans.

CONTINUED

Federal Law	Year	Provisions
Age Discrimination in Employment Act (ADEA)	1967 (amended in 1978 and 1986)	Prohibits age discrimination and restricts mandatory retirement.
Civil Rights Act, Title VII	1964	Prohibits discrimination in employment on the basis of race, religion, skin color, sex, or national origin.
Compensation/Benefits Laws		
Health Insurance Portability and Accountability Act (HIPAA)	1996	Allows employees to switch health insurance plans when changing jobs and get the new coverage regardless of preexisting health conditions; prohibits group plans from dropping a sick employee.
Family and Medical Leave Act	1993	Requires employers to provide up to 12 weeks unpaid leave for childbirth, adoption, or family emergencies.
Equal Pay Act	1963	Prohibits sex differences in pay for substantially equal work.
Health/Safety Laws		
Patient Protection and Affordable Care Act (PPACA)	2010	Imposes a fee on firms with 50 or more employees if the government subsidizes their employees' health care coverage; prevents insurers from denying coverage based on preexisting conditions or charging women more than men.
Consolidated Omnibus Budget Reconciliation Act (COBRA)	1985	Requires continued health insurance coverage (paid by employee) following termination.
Occupational Safety and Health Act (OSHA)	1970	Establishes mandatory safety and health standards in organizations.

Failure to comply with EEO legislation can result in substantial fines and penalties for employers. Suits for discriminatory practices can cover a broad range of employee complaints. One issue of growing concern is *sexual harassment,* which is also a violation of Title VII of the Civil Rights Act. The EEOC guidelines specify that behavior such as unwelcome advances, requests for sexual favors, and other verbal and physical conduct of a sexual nature becomes sexual harassment when submission to the conduct is tied to continued employment or advancement or when the behavior creates an intimidating, hostile, or offensive work environment.[16] Changes in the workplace have brought about shifts in the types of complaints being seen. Complaints of sexual harassment by men against both male and female bosses, for example, have increased in recent years. In addition, fewer complaints are related to blatant harassment and more are related to bosses who make sexually charged comments and send inappropriate e-mail or text messages.[17] Sexual harassment will be discussed later in the chapter.

Exhibit 9.4 also lists major federal laws related to compensation and benefits and health and safety issues. This is only a sampling of the federal laws that HR managers must know and understand. In addition, many states and municipalities have their own laws that relate to HR issues. California, for example, requires that companies with 50 or more employees provide sexual harassment training for all employees every two years.[18] Businesses and managers may agree or disagree with these laws depending on how the laws affect the recruitment and treatment of their employees. In 2016, the governor of Mississippi signed a controversial "religious freedom bill" that would allow religious groups and some private businesses to refuse to serve gay customers based on personal faith. The Mississippi Religious Freedom Restoration Act was set to become law on July 1, 2016. In the case of this state law, many corporations disagreed. Companies such as Nissan, Tyson Foods, MGM Resorts, and Toyota, which employ large numbers of people in the state, have denounced the new bill, as have the Mississippi Manufacturers Association, the Mississippi Economic Council, and other groups that represent smaller businesses.[19]

The scope of HR legislation is increasing at federal, state, and municipal levels. Companies operating internationally also have to be aware of laws related to HRM in the various countries in which they do business. In addition, social and technological changes bring new legal challenges. In 2011, the National Labor Relations Board (NLRB) filed its first lawsuit related to social media when it filed suit on behalf of Dawnmarie Souza, who was fired because of a comment she made on Facebook. Since then, the NLRB has been involved in a steady stream of similar cases.[20]

Remember This

- HR managers have to understand and apply a variety of federal laws that prohibit discrimination, establish safety standards, or require organizations to provide certain benefits.
- **Discrimination** means making hiring and promotion decisions based on criteria that are not job relevant.

- **Affirmative action** requires that employers take positive steps to guarantee equal employment opportunities for people within protected groups.
- The National Labor Relations Board (NLRB) filed its first suit related to social media in 2011 and has been involved in a steady stream of social media–related cases since then.

9-3 The Changing Social Contract

Another current issue is the changing nature of careers and a shift in the relationship between employers and employees.

9-3a The End of Lifetime Employment

In the old social contract between organization and employee, the employee could contribute ability, education, loyalty, and commitment and expect in return that the company would provide wages and benefits, work, advancement, and training throughout the employee's working life. Then along came globalization, outsourcing, hypercompetition, and other volatile changes in the environment. Consider the following list found on a bulletin board at a company undergoing major restructuring:

- We can't promise how long we'll be in business.
- We can't promise that we won't be acquired.
- We can't promise that there'll be room for promotion.
- We can't promise that your job will exist when you reach retirement age.
- We can't promise that the money will be available for your pension.
- We can't expect your undying loyalty, and we aren't even sure we want it.[21]

This list reflects a somewhat negative view of the new employer–employee relationship, but there are positive aspects as well. In a sense, companies and employees become allies helping one another grow stronger. Companies today expect and encourage employees to take control of their own careers, but in successful organizations, managers and employees work together to actively create opportunities that meet the needs of the organization at the same time managers give employees the chance to develop their skills and advance their careers. Employees help the company become more adaptable, while the company helps the employee become more employable.[22] Many young people don't have any desire to stay with one company throughout their careers. They like the expectations of responsibility, learning, growth, and mobility embedded in the new social contract. CEO Reed Hastings of Netflix says of his company: "We're a team; not a family."[23] Workplace expert Lynda Gratton says that building trust is more important than loyalty today, when "serial career monogamy" is the order for many young employees who are continually evaluating whether their work is meaningful and challenging and fits with their lives.[24]

Exhibit 9.5 lists some elements of the new social contract. The new contract is based on the concept of employability rather than lifetime employment. Individuals are responsible for developing their own skills and abilities and demonstrating their value to the organization. The employer, in turn, invests in creative training and development opportunities so that people will be more employable when the company no longer needs their services. This means offering challenging work assignments, opportunities to participate in decision making, and access to information and resources. In addition, an important challenge for HRM is revising performance evaluation, compensation, and other practices to be compatible with the new social contract. Many organizations, including KPMG International, IBM, Microsoft, and Lockheed Martin, have set up "alumni social networks" so that people who have left the organization can keep in touch with former colleagues and the industry.[25] McKinsey & Company has operated an alumni network since the 1960s.[26]

9-3b Innovative HR Practices

The field of HRM is constantly changing. Some important HR issues today are blind hiring, branding the company as an employer of choice, fast track hiring, and acquiring companies to obtain talent.

Exhibit 9.5 The Changing Social Contract

	New Contract	Old Contract
Employee	• Employability; personal responsibility • Partner in business improvement • Learning; skill development	• Job security • A cog in the machine • Knowing
Employer	• Creative development opportunities • Lateral career moves; incentive compensation • Challenging assignments • Information and resources; decision-making authority	• Standard training programs • Traditional compensation package • Routine jobs • Limited information and authority

SOURCES: Based on Louisa Wah, "The New Workplace Paradox," *Management Review* (January 1998): 7; and Douglas T. Hall and Jonathan E. Moss, "The New Protean Career Contract: Helping Organizations and Employees Adapt," *Organizational Dynamics* (Winter 1998): 22–37.

Blind Hiring   When symphony orchestras began using anonymous auditions, employing a curtain to shield auditioning musicians from the view of the evaluating committee, some interesting results occurred. With the use of curtains, the likelihood that female musicians advanced to further tryout rounds increased by 50 percent. Today, almost 40 percent of musicians at major U.S. orchestras are women, a dramatic increase from the days before curtains were used.[27] Corporations, small businesses, and other types of organizations have picked up on the concept of anonymous auditions with a trend called **blind hiring** that focuses managers on an applicant's job skills and performance rather than educational credentials, appearance, or prior experience. Some companies, such as Compose Inc., a cloud storage company recently acquired by IBM, don't ask for résumés, which may contain cues that bias readers. Others redact information such as an applicant's name, alma mater, or other identifying data, so managers won't be subconsciously influenced. With blind hiring, people are usually asked to complete a project or assignment that relates to the type of work they'll be doing if hired. Proponents of blind hiring say it contributes to better, more diverse hiring.[28] Levenson Group, a Dallas-based advertising firm, used blind hiring to bring in a new junior copywriter. After asking the 50 or so applicants to create an Instagram campaign for a specific product, Levenson hired a young woman just out of college who hadn't studied marketing and had no experience. Paul McEnany, Levenson's chief product officer, says that, based on her résumé, he's "not even certain we would have interviewed her in the first place."[29]

Branding the Company as an Employer of Choice   Managers in many industries often find that the most skilled and knowledgeable employees are in short supply and great demand.[30] Both small and large companies are using employer branding to attract desirable job candidates. An **employer brand** is similar to a product brand, except that rather than promoting a specific product, its aim is to make the organization seem like a highly desirable place to work. Employer-branding campaigns are like marketing campaigns to "sell" the company and attract the best job candidates. At Risk Management Solutions (RMS), HR executive Amelia Merrill used employer branding after she discovered that few people in Silicon Valley, where the firm is based, had a clue what RMS was. To attract the kind of high-quality technology professionals that RMS needed, Merrill's team began selling the company in the same way that its salespeople sold its services. One step was to rent San Francisco's popular "Bacon Bacon" food truck for a day and set it up at a local cloud-computing exposition. Merrill says employer branding is having a slow but sure effect on recruiting efforts, as people in the IT industry become more familiar with the company name.[31] However, many large, well-known companies, including PepsiCo, General Electric (GE), Nokia, AT&T, and Credit Suisse Group, are also using employer branding as companies fight for talent.[32]

Fast Track Hiring In 2015, the average time it took for companies to hire reached an all-time high of almost 29 days. However, with the fast pace of today's business environment and the growing need for employees, some managers are experimenting with a fast track approach, filling open jobs in a matter of days or even hours. Chipotle, for example, hired 1,800 entry-level employees in a single day. Return Path Inc., a global data solutions company, uses a single-day hiring process for entry-level marketers, salespeople, and account managers. At AppDynamics, a San Francisco–based software company, applicants typically go from application to acceptance or rejection in less than a week. Each promising candidate is interviewed twice by phone within a few days of applying. Those who pass that round come into the office for six to seven hours of back-to-back interviews with AppDynamics employees. The interviewers and the hiring manager meet for 15 minutes after the final interview and decide whether to offer the candidate a position. Fast track hiring is being used particularly in high-tech industries. "The best candidates get snagged quickly," says John Sullivan, a professor of management at San Francisco State University who has helped companies implement one-day hiring.[33]

Acquiring Start-Ups to Get the Talent Another approach companies use to get talented employees quickly is to acquire start-ups. Andrea Vaccari created Glancee as a mobile app to help people find others with similar interests. But just as the company was taking off, he and his cofounders faced a tough decision—accept an acquisition bid from Facebook or go for broke? The problem was that Vaccari was already almost broke, living in a closet at a friend's apartment. The co-founders decided to accept Facebook's offer, even though they knew that it was made primarily to recruit them to work at the larger company.[34] So-called **acqui-hiring** has become common in the tech world. Established companies such as Facebook, Google, Yahoo, LinkedIn, and Salesforce.com buy early-stage start-ups, often shutting them down, simply to acquire their engineering talent. Yahoo bought 52 start-ups in less than three years, partly to acquire the talent.

Sunny Side Up ⟩ Yahoo

Nick D'Aloisio wasn't even born when Yahoo was founded, but he sold his news aggregation service Summly to the company for $30 million in 2013 when he was 17 years old, making him one of the richest high school students in Great Britain. D'Aloisio then tested out of his last year of high school and went to work in Yahoo's London office (he left Yahoo in late 2015 to focus on his schoolwork at Oxford). Summly is one of 52 start-ups Yahoo CEO Marissa Mayer has acquired for around $2.1 billion to replenish and reinvigorate Yahoo's workforce and gain the talent needed to try to keep Yahoo relevant as the technology world changes.

Among the numerous acqui-hires still at Yahoo in early 2016 were Jeff Bonforte, who now runs mail and messaging products; Simon Khalaf, who oversees Yahoo's home page; and Arjun Sethi, who works with a team building a new mobile-messaging product. Yahoo has added about 3,000 employees through acquisitions since 2012. Jacqueline Reses, Yahoo's chief development officer who oversees acquisitions, says, "If you actually look at the achievements of some of the people who have been acquired at Yahoo, you would argue [this strategy] has been wildly successful in order to help change the products."[35]

The acqui-hiring strategy makes sense for companies such as Yahoo, Google, and Facebook because the larger companies get teams of talented engineers who are accustomed to working together. However, working in a larger, bureaucratic company rather than a nimble start-up can be difficult for some acqui-hires. To try to retain these valuable employees, Yahoo holds dinners a few times each year for the entrepreneurs who have sold their start-ups to the larger company and still work there. The dinners give them a chance to share tips with one another, as well as the opportunity to voice their frustration directly with the CEO.[36]

Remember This

- The new social contract between employers and employees is based on the notion of employability and personal responsibility rather than lifelong employment at an organization.

- Some companies are using **blind hiring** by doing without résumés or by redacting some information on résumés and asking applicants to complete assignments, focusing on the applicant's job skills and performance rather than educational credentials or prior experience.

- An **employer brand** is similar to a product brand except that it promotes the organization as a great place to work rather than promoting a specific product or service.

- Rather than spending weeks making hiring decisions, companies such as Return Path Inc., Chipotle, and AppDynamics are using fast track hiring to bring on new employees in a matter of days or even hours.

- **Acqui-hiring** means buying an early-stage start-up (and usually shutting it down) in order to obtain its creative talent.

- Yahoo acquired 52 start-ups in less than three years, adding about 3,000 acqui-hires.

9-4 Finding the Right People

Now let's turn to the three broad goals of HRM: finding, developing, and maintaining an effective workforce. The first step in finding the right people is human resource planning, in which managers or HRM professionals predict the need for new employees based on the types of vacancies that exist, as illustrated in Exhibit 9.6. The second step is to use recruiting procedures to communicate with potential applicants. The third step is to select from the applicants those persons believed to be the best potential contributors to the organization. Finally, the new employees are welcomed into the organization.

Underlying the organization's effort to attract employees is a matching model. With the **matching model**, the organization and the individual attempt to match the needs, interests, and values that they offer each other.[37] For example, a small software developer might require long hours from creative, technically skilled employees. In return, it can offer freedom from bureaucracy, tolerance of idiosyncrasies, and potentially high pay. A large manufacturer can offer employment security and stability, but it might have more rules and regulations and require a greater ability to "get approval from the higher-ups." The individual who would thrive working for the software developer might feel stymied and unhappy working for a large manufacturer. Both the company and the employee are interested in finding a good match.

9-4a Human Resource Planning

Human resource planning is the forecasting of HR needs and the projected matching of individuals with expected vacancies. Human resource planning begins with several big-picture questions:

- What new technologies are emerging, and how will these affect the work system?
- How much is the volume of the business likely to change in the next 5 to 10 years?
- What is the turnover rate, and how much, if any, is avoidable?

Exhibit 9.6 Attracting an Effective Workforce

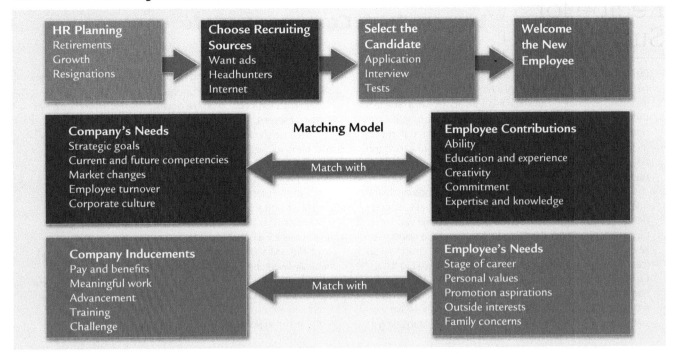

The responses to these questions are used to formulate specific questions pertaining to HR activities, such as the following:

- What types of engineers will we need, and how many?
- How many administrative personnel will we need to support the additional engineers?
- Can we use temporary, part-time, or virtual workers to handle some tasks?[38]

By anticipating future HR needs, the organization can prepare itself to meet competitive challenges more effectively than organizations that react to problems only as they arise.

9-4b Recruiting

Recruiting is defined as performing "activities or practices that define the characteristics of applicants to whom selection procedures are ultimately applied."[39] Today, recruiting is sometimes referred to as *talent acquisition* to reflect the importance of the human factor in the organization's success.[40] Faith Holmes uses competencies, including emotional intelligence, when she hired employees for her café, as shown in the "Recipe for Success" box.

Although we frequently think of campus recruiting as a typical recruiting activity, many organizations use *internal recruiting,* or *promote-from-within* policies, to fill their high-level positions.[41] Internal recruiting has two major advantages: It is less costly than an external search, and it generates higher employee commitment, development, and satisfaction because it offers opportunities for career advancement to employees rather than outsiders. Frequently, however, *external recruiting*—recruiting newcomers from outside the organization—is advantageous. Applicants are provided by a variety of outside sources, including advertising, state employment services, online job boards and social media, private employment agencies (headhunters), job fairs, and employee referrals.

Assessing Jobs Basic building blocks of HRM include job analysis, job descriptions, and job specifications. **Job analysis** is a systematic process of gathering and interpreting information about the essential duties, tasks, and responsibilities of a job, as well as about the context within which the job is performed.[42] To perform job analysis, managers or specialists ask about work activities and work flow, the degree of supervision given and received in the job, knowledge

Recipe for Success

Love 'n Faith Community Café

Faith Holmes got a job in Chicago right out of high school, but her desire to learn led her to take night courses on many topics, including psychology and race relations about which she felt the need to learn more. Later on she started a nonprofit, Oneness, hoping to help the elimination of racism through music, arts, and education. It got top hit makers to record a song (not unlike "Heal the World") to use in a national campaign until the nonprofit hit legal issues with some of the record labels.

Enough of that already, thought Holmes, who was thankfully offered a job in Washington, D.C. Her plan was to spend all her spare time experimenting with food. Since she was six years old, Holmes had been a passionate baker and she wanted to keep learning and creating. Her first project was creating a tasty ice-cream made from liquid nitrogen, which was a big hit at the District of Columbia Convention Center in 2011. Though a few had tried this before, Holmes's liquid nitrogen ice cream had a custard base and actually tasted delicious, all the while the smokiness of the liquid nitrogen made it visually appealing as

well. Then she started creating naturally sweetened desserts. Her sales were doing so well, she opened Love 'n Faith Community Café in the District of Columbia downtown in 2014 and now has nine employees.

Because she feels she is selling and serving delicious foods that bring joy and happiness, Holmes is careful in hiring staff to make sure they are honest, filled with integrity, and have a happy personality. She can teach them everything else: the cooking, the presentation. But only they can bring their personality filled with a desire to show love to the customers.

Holmes is branching out. One of her new products is "Pie in a Jar," for which all you need is two eggs, two minutes, and a pie crust. Her goal sheet includes selling liquid nitrogen ice cream and naturally sweetened desserts in grocery stores. Another one is TV, where she has already done numerous TV news segments. "I have a dream," she says, "to have a culinary show about cooking with love."

SOURCE: Faith Holmes, personal communication, May 2018.

and skills needed, performance standards, working conditions, and so forth. The manager then prepares a written **job description**, which is a clear and concise summary of the specific tasks, duties, and responsibilities, and **job specification**, which outlines the knowledge, skills, education, physical abilities, and other characteristics needed to perform the job adequately.

Job analysis helps organizations recruit the right kind of people and match them to appropriate jobs. For example, to enhance internal recruiting, Sara Lee Corporation (now Hillshire Brands) identified six functional areas and 24 significant skills that it wanted its finance executives to develop, such as communication (and under that, credibility and presentation style) and planning (which includes profitability analysis and managing budget processes).[43]

Realistic Job Previews   Job analysis also enhances recruiting effectiveness by enabling the creation of **realistic job previews (RJPs)**, which give applicants all pertinent and realistic information—positive and negative—about the job and the organization.[44] RJPs contribute to higher employee satisfaction and lower turnover because they facilitate matching individuals, jobs, and organizations. People have a better basis on which to determine their suitability to the organization and "self-select" into or out of positions based on full information.

Social Media   Managers do much of their recruiting today via the Internet, including social media sites such as LinkedIn, Facebook, and Twitter. Interestingly, a survey by staffing services firm Spherion found that high-achieving young professionals deem a company's social media reputation as important as the job offer when considering which company they want to work for.[45] Retailers who must quickly find thousands of seasonal workers for the holiday rush have found social media to be an effective approach. Crate & Barrel and children's clothing chain Carter's consider tweeting to be a good way to reach prospective hires. At Beverages and More, online applications

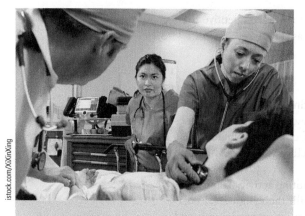

istock.com/XiXinXing

Concept Connection

For people just entering the medical field, working in a hospital's emergency room (ER) where you can save lives every day may sound exciting and meaningful, but not everyone is cut out to deal with the hectic pace of a typical ER. That's why this hospital asks job applicants to work a shift or two as part of a **realistic job preview (RJP)**. The trial run allows both the applicant and the hospital's staff to determine whether the job candidate is a good fit for this challenging work environment.

for seasonal jobs increased 66 percent after the California-based chain began posting job ads on social media alongside cocktail recipes and product promotions. Even the British army is using social media, launching a campaign to recruit 10,000 new soldiers.[46] Companies in China have become particularly adept at using social media for recruiting because traditional online recruiting boards in China attract far too many unqualified candidates to make them valuable. Therefore, managers turn to social media such as Weibo, a Twitter-like messaging service, to build a community of potential candidates. China's Lenovo Group reports finding 70 good candidates during a three-month recruiting surge via social media, including LinkedIn, Weibo, and Tianji, a Chinese professional social networking site.[47]

A recent *Global Recruiting Trends Report* from LinkedIn surveyed 3,300 talent acquisition managers around the globe and found that HR recruiters are becoming more social, mobile, and data driven. Recruiters have historically had little data on external candidates, but professional social media can provide recruiters with an immense amount of data, such as work experience, skills, certifications, achievements, connections, and education. The report indicates that 39 percent of recruiters list social and professional networks as their number-one long-lasting recruiting trend.[48]

Internships   Another popular use of social media is to find people to serve as either paid or unpaid interns at the organization. An **internship** is an arrangement whereby an intern (usually a high school or college student) exchanges free or low-cost labor for the opportunity to explore whether a particular career is appealing or to gain valuable work experience in a particular field.[49] Companies are increasingly viewing internships as a valuable recruiting tool because they provide a way to "test-drive" a potential employee, as well as allow the intern to evaluate whether the job and the company make a good fit. The old image of the intern as the "gopher" who makes coffee and photocopies has given way to the budding professional who performs meaningful tasks and learns valuable skills. Nationwide sends teams of executives to events such as the National Black MBA Association conference and the National Society of Hispanic MBA conference, where Nationwide executives conduct interviews and often hire full-time employees as well as interns on the spot. Nearly half of all interns at Nationwide join the company full time at the end of their internships.[50] Interns aren't always offered a job with the company, but one career development expert says that internships are more closely tied to permanent hiring today than ever before.[51] Media and online entertainment company IGN takes an innovative approach to recruiting via internships.

Sunny Side Up   IGN's Code Foo

"Flipping burgers to scrape together enough cash to buy *Portal 2*? Blow our minds while you're here and we'll hire you." That was the recruitment ad for IGN's first Code Foo challenge—a no-résumés-allowed program designed to find exceptional "hackers," the term that IGN's director of engineering prefers when referring to computer programmers and coders. "For serious engineers who really care about their craft, it's a good thing to be a hacker," Tony Ford says.

For the first Code Foo challenge in 2011, 75,000 people viewed the application, 104 applied, and 30 were selected to participate. Only half of those had college degrees in a technical field, and some didn't have degrees at all. Applicants to the Code Foo challenge complete an online form in which they submit a statement of passion for IGN and answer questions that test their coding ability. The 2016 challenge application states: "We don't care about your official credentials. In fact, we won't even accept a resume. You do need to be able to code—and be passionate about IGN." Once accepted to the program, the Code Fooers spend six weeks working at IGN, getting paid a small amount while learning coding languages and working on real engineering projects. Adam Passey, for example, spent his summer coding unique features for a hub for mobile games. IGN's engineers were impressed, and Passey was offered a job.

Although managers hoped the Code Foo experiment would lead to one or two good hires, the company actually extended job offers to eight people the first time around. It was so successful that IGN has held the Code Foo challenge every year since. As the market for programmers and coders grows more competitive, it's a "guerilla recruitment strategy" that is paying off.[52]

Remember This

- Finding the right people starts with **human resource planning**, which refers to the forecasting of HR needs and the projected matching of individuals with anticipated job vacancies.

- The **matching model** is an HR approach in which the organization and the individual attempt to match each other's needs, interests, and values.

- **Recruiting** refers to activities or practices that define the desired characteristics of applicants for specific jobs.

- Many of today's organizations use social media, including Twitter, Weibo, LinkedIn, Tianji, and Facebook, for recruiting.

- **Job analysis** is the systematic process of gathering and interpreting information about the essential duties, tasks, and responsibilities of a job.

- Managers prepare a **job description** for each open position, which is a concise summary of the specific tasks and responsibilities of that job.

- A **job specification** outlines the knowledge, skills, education, physical abilities, and other characteristics needed to perform a specific job adequately.

- Managers use **realistic job previews (RJPs)** in recruiting to give applicants all pertinent and realistic information—both positive and negative—about a job and the organization.

- Internships are an increasingly popular approach to recruiting because they provide a way to "test-drive" a potential employee.

- An **internship** is an arrangement whereby an intern (usually a high school or college student) exchanges his or her services for the opportunity to gain work experience and see whether a particular career is appealing.

Visit MindTap for the "Self-Assessment: Will You Get the Right People on the Bus?" to test your own preparation as a new manager for recruiting and selecting the right people for your team. Do you have what it takes?

9-4c Selecting

In the **selection** process, employers assess applicants' characteristics in an attempt to determine the "fit" between the job and applicant characteristics. The most frequently used selection devices are the application form, interview, and employment test. In general, the more the skill requirements and work demands of an open position, the higher the number and variety of selection tools the organization will use.[53]

Application Form   The **application form** is used to collect information about the applicant's education, previous job experience, and other background characteristics. Research shows that biographical information inventories can validly predict future job success.[54]

One pitfall to be avoided is the inclusion of questions that are irrelevant to job success. In line with EEO guidelines, the application form should not ask questions that will create an adverse impact on protected groups unless the questions are clearly related to the job.[55] For example, employers should not ask whether the applicant rents or owns his or her own home because (1) an applicant's response might adversely affect his or her chances at the job, (2) minorities and women may be less likely to own a home, and (3) home ownership is probably unrelated to job performance. By contrast, passing the CPA exam is relevant to job performance in a CPA firm; thus, it is appropriate to ask whether an applicant for employment has passed the CPA exam, even if only one-half of all female or minority applicants have done so, versus nine-tenths of white male applicants.

Interview   Some type of *interview* is used as a selection technique in almost every job category in nearly every organization. This is another area where the organization can get into legal trouble if the interviewer asks questions that violate EEO guidelines. Exhibit 9.7 lists some examples of appropriate and inappropriate interview questions.

There is some evidence that the typical interview is not generally a good predictor of job performance. Many companies are bringing in coaches or using training programs to boost managers' interviewing skills because bad hires are costly. Researchers at Harvard Business School found that interviewers who let their own insecurities or biases subconsciously drive the interviewing process can have a worse effect on hiring decisions than if a candidate were simply chosen at random.[56] Managers can improve their interviewing skills, and candidates can improve their chances of having a successful interview, by understanding some do's and don't's related to the interview, as outlined in the "Sunny Side Up" box.

Exhibit 9.7 Employment Applications and Interviews: What Can You Ask?

Category	Okay to Ask	Inappropriate or Illegal to Ask
National origin	• The applicant's name • If the applicant has ever worked under a different name	• The origin of the applicant's name • The applicant's ancestry/ethnicity
Race	• Nothing	• Race or color of skin
Disabilities	• Whether the applicant has any disabilities that might inhibit performance on the job	• If the applicant has any physical or mental defects • If the applicant has ever filed a workers' compensation claim
Age	• If the applicant is over 18	• Applicant's specific age • When the applicant graduated from high school
Religion	• Nothing	• The applicant's religious affiliation • What religious holidays the applicant observes
Criminal record	• If applicant has ever been convicted of a crime	• If the applicant has ever been arrested
Marital/family status	• Nothing	• Marital status; number of children or planned children • Childcare arrangements
Education and experience	• Where the applicant went to school • Prior work experience	• When the applicant graduated • Hobbies
Citizenship	• If the applicant has a legal right to work in the United States	• If the applicant is a citizen of another country

SOURCES: Based on "Appropriate and Inappropriate Interview Questions," in George Bohlander, Scott Snell, and Arthur Sherman, *Managing Human Resources*, 12th ed. (Cincinnati, OH: South-Western, 2001), p. 207; and "Guidelines to Lawful and Unlawful Preemployment Inquiries," Appendix E, in Robert L. Mathis and John H. Jackson, *Human Resource Management*, 2nd ed. (Cincinnati, OH: South-Western, 2002), pp. 189–190.

Sunny Side Up ⟩ Ace the Interview

Many of us have experienced job interviews where everything seems to be going well, but then things take a drastic turn for the worse. Here are some suggestions that can help you ace your next interview—and improve your interviewing skills as a manager.

The Big Three Questions

No matter what questions you are asked in an interview, you can be more effective if you remember that there are really only three essential things that the hiring manager and company want to know:

• **Can you do the job?** The company wants to know your strengths, not just in terms of technical ability, but also your leadership, teamwork, and interpersonal skills. Can you not only handle the tasks and activities of the job exceptionally well but also interact effectively with your colleagues and contribute to a positive organizational atmosphere?

• **Will you love the job?** Organizations want people who bring enthusiasm and positive energy with them into the workplace every day. The hiring manager wants to be convinced that you're excited about the particular position you're interviewing for, as well as the overall industry, and that you'll thrive on embracing the challenges associated with the job.

• **Can we tolerate working with you?** Believing that you'll be a good fit with the culture is a huge part of the equation when most managers are deciding among job candidates. At LivingSocial, every job candidate is interviewed by a member of the "culture police," a team of people who have a knack for spotting what works and doesn't work with the company's culture. No one gets hired unless the culture police give the okay.

CONTINUED

Killer Interview Strategies

- **Do your research.** To answer the Big Three Questions, you have to understand the job you're applying for, know something about the overall industry the company operates in, and have some feeling for the organizational culture. Learn all you can. Find out how the company is structured and managed by looking at its Web site. Tap into your social networking connections, see if there are videos on YouTube, read stories in blogs, and so forth.

- **Turn questions into conversations.** If you've done your research, you'll be able to converse with the interviewer on a peer-to-peer level. If asked, for example, how you would restructure a division, you might politely say something like: "Do you mind if I ask you a couple of questions first? I know there's a plant in Greece. Has the business been affected by the country's economic troubles?" Also, think of a few stories

and examples ahead of time that illustrate your skills and strengths, show off your commitment and motivation, and demonstrate how you will fit with the organization. Use them judiciously when you get the chance.

- **Think the way they do.** Again, if you've done your research, you should have some idea of the issues and problems the company faces and the type of questions you might be asked. A company such as Zappos.com will interview in a different way than a company like GE. Imagine that you were a manager with the company, and think of 10 or so questions that *you* would ask a candidate.

SOURCES: George Brandt, "Top Executive Recruiters Agree There Are Only Three True Job Interview Questions," *Forbes* (April 27, 2011), www.forbes.com/sites/georgebradt/2011/04/27/top-executive-recruiters-agree-there-are-only-three-key-job-interview-questions/ (accessed August 29, 2012); Jennifer Alsever, "How to Get a Job: Show, Don't Tell," *Fortune* (March 19, 2012): 29–31; and LivingSocial example from Darren Dahl, "Hiring: You Get a Job, and You, and You . . . How to Staff Up in a Hurry," *Inc.* (November 2010): 128–129.

Concept Connection

Employment tests range from personality profiles to proficiency testing in specific skills required for a position. For a 911 operator position, an applicant should expect to take tests such as data entry for speed and accuracy, 911 address checking, 911 grid map reading and direction accuracy, 911 memorization, customer service assessment, and a personal characteristics profile. Rick Bias, 911 communications director for Morgan County, Missouri, oversees operations in the Public Service Answer Point Area.

Managers use a variety of interview approaches to get a more reliable picture of a candidate's suitability for the job. **Structured interviews** use a set of standardized questions that are asked of every applicant so comparisons can easily be made. These may include *biographical questions*, which ask about the person's previous life and work experiences; *behavioral questions*, which ask people to describe how they have performed a certain task or handled a particular problem; and *situational or case questions*, which require people to describe how they might handle a hypothetical situation. With a **nondirective interview**, the interviewer asks broad, open-ended questions and permits the applicant to talk freely, with minimal interruption. For example, Marla Malcolm Beck, CEO of Bluemercury, a beauty products and spa services retailer, calls herself the queen of the seven-minute interview and says she interviews for "skill, will, and fit." Beck asks each applicant questions such as, "What's the biggest impact you had at your past organization?" and "What do you want to do in 5 or 10 years?" Nondirective interviews may bring to light information, attitudes, and behavioral characteristics that might not come through when someone is answering structured questions. Beck says asking about aspirations is important, for example, because it shows if someone is creative and "hungry to get somewhere," which means the person wants to learn. "And if you want to learn," she says, "you can do any job."[57]

Some organizations put candidates through a series of interviews, each one conducted by a different person and each one probing a different aspect of the candidate. Others use **panel interviews** in which the candidate meets with several interviewers who take turns asking questions.[58] In addition, some firms are using offbeat approaches, sometimes referred to as *extreme interviewing*, to test job candidates' ability to handle problems, cope with change, think on their feet, and work well with others. Danielle Bemoras found herself in a joint interview with a rival candidate when she applied for a job with *SceneTap,* a digital nightlife guide. Rather than trying to upstage her competitor, Bemoras was respectful and helpful, an approach that won her an internship, followed by a full-time job offer.[59]

Employment Test   **Employment tests** may include cognitive ability tests, physical ability tests, personality inventories, and other assessments. *Cognitive ability tests* measure an applicant's thinking, reasoning, verbal, and mathematical abilities. IQ tests, for example, have been found to be the most consistent predictor of good performance across a variety of jobs because a high IQ shows a candidate's ability to learn.[60] Many companies also use various types of *personality tests* to assess such characteristics as openness to learning, agreeableness, conscientiousness, creativity, and emotional stability. In addition, companies look for personality characteristics that match the needs of the particular job so that there is a good fit. One company found that people who score well in traits such as assertiveness and extroversion typically make good salespeople, so that company looked for those traits in testing candidates for new positions.[61] Interestingly, numerous studies show that personality tests are better predictors of future career success than job interviews, letters of recommendation, and educational credentials.[62]

Pre-hire testing is a billion-dollar industry today. Managers can measure and analyze the personality and behavioral characteristics of their top performers and use customized assessments to see how applicants compare to the ideal employee. Using computers and data analysis software, a single customized assessment can appraise a wide range of characteristics, such as personality traits, technical ability, and communication skills.[63] Most pre-hire assessments, such as those used by Delaware North Companies, are administered online.

> "In my final assessment, I always think about whether they are willing to take out the garbage. I don't mean that literally. Taking out the garbage means, 'Are they willing to do what it takes?'"
> —SALLY J. SMITH, CEO OF BUFFALO WILD WINGS INC.

Sunny Side Up > Delaware North

Delaware North has plenty of applicants for open jobs at its call center in Fresno, California, where customer service representatives help people plan vacations at national parks. The problem managers had was that many of the people they hired didn't work out so well and were either fired or quit after a short time.

Delaware North decided to work with the firm FurstPerson to see if pre-hire testing could lead to a better match between the job and the person hired. Now, to get a job at the call center, applicants complete a customized assessment online so managers can see how they stack up against top call-center employees in such characteristics as friendliness, curiosity, and willingness to learn. The questions are designed so people can't figure out the best answers. For instance, they might have to agree or disagree with statements such as, "I dislike yelling, but sometimes a little yelling is necessary" or "I have never understood why some people find abstract art appealing."

Delaware North managers say the pre-hire assessments have enabled them to find better employees. The company used to hire 15 people for every 12 jobs, since about three employees would quit even before their training period ended. Now, it hires only candidates who are a good match, and managers say the customized assessment has cut turnover and created a happier workplace.[64]

Many other companies are also using customized assessments for selecting people to hire. In 2013, 57 percent of large U.S. employers said they were using pre-hire assessments, up from only 21 percent in 2001. With good online tools and inexpensive software, even small companies can analyze their best employees and search for candidates who match those characteristics. Although there is plenty of criticism of this trend in hiring, one of the first academic studies of pre-hire testing found that managers who ignored the test results hired employees who were more likely to quit or be fired.[65]

Another unusual type of test, called a *brain teaser,* is being used by companies that put a premium on innovativeness and problem solving. The answers aren't as important as how the applicant goes about solving the problem. See how you do answering the brain teasers in Exhibit 9.8.

Exhibit 9.8 **Try Your Hand at Some Interview Brain Teasers**

How would you answer the following questions in a job interview?

1. How would you fit a stack of pennies as high as the Empire State Building in one room?
2. Why are manhole covers round?
3. How much should you charge to wash all the windows in Seattle?
4. You're shrunk and trapped in a blender that will turn on in 60 seconds. What do you do?
5. A man pushed his car to a hotel and lost his fortune. What happened?

Answers: There might be many solutions to these questions. Here are some that interviewers consider good answers:

1. The Empire State Building has about 110 floors. To fit the stack into one room, break it into one hundred shorter, floor-to-ceiling stacks.
2. A square cover might fall into its hole. If you hold a square manhole cover vertically and turn it a little, it will fall easily into the hole. In contrast, a round cover with a slight recess in the center can never fall in, no matter how it is held.
3. Assuming 10,000 city blocks, 600 windows per block, five minutes per window, and a rate of $20 per hour, about $10 million.
4. Use the measurement marks on the side of the container to climb out.
5. This is an oddball question more than a brain teaser, but one good answer would be: The man was playing Monopoly.

SOURCES: Similar questions have been used at companies such as Microsoft, Google, and eBay. Reported in William Poundstone, "The Google Cheat Sheet," *Bloomberg BusinessWeek* (January 9–15, 2012): 79; Michael Kaplan, "Job Interview Brainteasers," *Business 2.0* (September 2007): 35–37; and William Poundstone, "Impossible Questions," *Across the Board* (September–October 2003): 44–48.

Online Checks   The Internet also gives recruiters and hiring managers a new way to search for a candidate's criminal record, credit history, and other indications of honesty, integrity, and stability. Moreover, many companies want to see what a candidate has to say about himself or herself on blogs and social networking sites to gauge whether the person would be a good fit with the organization. In a survey by Adecco Staffing, inappropriate content on social media was the number-two reason hiring managers gave for why applicants ages 18 to 32 didn't get jobs (wearing inappropriate attire to job interviews was the top reason).[66] However, online checks are an increasingly murky area for companies. Many states have passed or are considering laws to make it illegal for employers to ask job candidates for their social media passwords.[67] Using social media as a background check without disclosing the investigation to the candidate can also open organizations to lawsuits. Moreover, because an online search often reveals information such as race, gender, sexual orientation, and so forth, HR managers have to be sure this information isn't used in a way that could be construed as discriminatory.

Remember This

- **Selection** is the process of assessing the skills, abilities, and other attributes of applicants in an attempt to determine the fit between the job and each applicant's characteristics.
- The **application form** is a selection device that collects information about the applicant's education, previous work experience, and other background characteristics.
- A **structured interview** uses a set of standardized questions that are asked of every applicant so that comparisons can be made easily. Types of questions include biographical questions, behavioral questions, and situational or case questions.
- In a **nondirective interview**, the interviewer asks broad, open-ended questions and permits the applicant to talk freely with minimal interruption in an attempt to bring to light information, attitudes, and behavioral characteristics that might not come out in a structured interview.
- A **panel interview** is an interview in which the candidate meets with several interviewers who take turns asking questions.
- Some companies are using offbeat approaches, called *extreme interviewing*, to test job candidates' ability to handle problems, cope with change, and work well with others.
- **Employment tests** assess candidates on various factors considered important for the job to be performed; they include cognitive ability tests, physical ability tests, and personality tests.
- One way in which HR managers gauge an applicant's suitability for an open position is by checking what the applicant says on social media sites.
- Many states have passed laws making it illegal to ask job applicants for their social media passwords.

9-5 Developing Talent

Following selection, the next goal of HRM is to develop employees into an effective workforce. Key development activities include training and performance appraisal.

9-5a Training and Development

Training and development programs represent a planned effort by an organization to facilitate employees' learning of job-related skills and behaviors. *Training* magazine's most recent "Industry Report" shows that organizations spent some $70.6 billion on formal training and development programs in 2015, but not all training is equally effective in keeping employees motivated and productive.[68] Exhibit 9.9 shows how high-achieving young professionals view various development practices, according to a recent study. The practice these employees considered most important to their career development was working on high-stakes projects, while working on an inherited problem ranked the lowest.[69]

Exhibit 9.9 Ranking of Training and Development Practices by Young Professionals

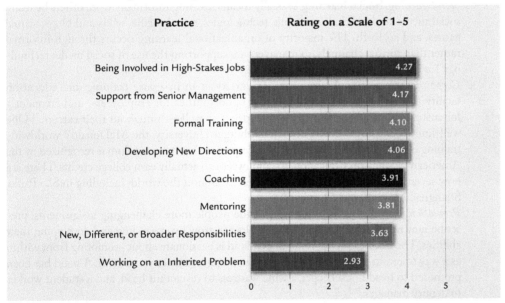

Practice	Rating on a Scale of 1–5
Being Involved in High-Stakes Jobs	4.27
Support from Senior Management	4.17
Formal Training	4.10
Developing New Directions	4.06
Coaching	3.91
Mentoring	3.81
New, Different, or Broader Responsibilities	3.63
Working on an Inherited Problem	2.93

SOURCE: "Which Development Practices Matter Most," exhibit in Monika Hamori, Burak Koyuncu, Jie Cao, and Thomas Graf, "What High-Potential Young Managers Want," *MIT Sloan Management Review* (Fall 2015): 61–68.

To understand the importance of training, consider the following extreme example from the Taj Mahal Palace in Mumbai (Taj Mumbai).

When terrorists stormed the Taj Mumbai at the end of a dinner hosted by Hindustan Lever, banquet staff quickly swung into action, locking the doors and turning off the lights. As the group huddled in the banquet room overnight, staff constantly went around offering water and calming the guests. The next morning, a fire broke out, forcing the group to climb out the windows. Again, the staff calmly evacuated all the guests first. "It was my responsibility," said 24-year-old Mallika Jagad. "I may have been the youngest person in the room, but I was still doing my job." Elsewhere in the hotel, similar acts of heroism were going on. At least 11 Taj Mumbai employees died while helping guests escape.

The Taj Mumbai staff gave the term *customer service* a whole new meaning that night. The actions of the staff were a result of unique hiring, training, and incentive systems that create a culture in which employees always put guests first, even if it means risking their own lives. All Taj employees go through 18 months of training, which includes both classroom and on-the-job training. People are taught to think and be creative rather than rely on strict rules and procedures, and they learn to be customer ambassadors who place guests' interests ahead of the company's interests.[70]

The Taj Group expects managers to lead by example, and every manager goes through 18 months of training similar to that for lower-level employees. In addition, the company hires an external coach to support each manager's development.

Development is sometimes distinguished from training. The general term *training* is typically used to refer to teaching people how to perform tasks related to their present jobs, while *development* means teaching people broader skills that not only are useful in their present jobs but also prepare them for greater responsibilities in future jobs. At farming equipment manufacturer Deere, rising managers get coaching from influential board members, for example, to develop their leadership skills.[71] Types of training and development include on-the-job training, social learning, corporate universities, and promotion from within.

- *On-the-job training.* The most common type of training is **on-the-job training (OJT)**, where an experienced employee is asked to take a new employee "under his or her wing" and show the newcomer how to perform job duties. When implemented well, OJT is considered the fastest and most effective means of facilitating learning in the workplace.[72]

- *Social learning.* **Social learning** basically means learning informally from others by using social media tools, including mobile technologies, social media, wikis and blogs, virtual games, and so forth. The majority of organizational learning occurs through informal rather than formal channels, so managers are supporting the use of social media technology for learning in day-to-day work.[73]

- *Corporate universities.* A **corporate university** is an in-house training and education facility that offers broad-based learning opportunities for employees—and frequently for customers, suppliers, and strategic partners as well—throughout their careers.[74] One well-known corporate university is Hamburger University, the McDonald's worldwide training center. This institution is so well respected that its curriculum is recognized by the American Council on Education, so employees can actually earn college credits. There are now seven locations of Hamburger University around the world, including in São Paulo, Shanghai, Munich, and Mumbai.[75]

- *Promotion from within.* Promotions provide people more challenging assignments, prescribe new responsibilities, and help employees grow by expanding and developing their abilities. The Peebles Hydro hotel in Scotland is passionate about promoting from within as a way to retain good people and give them opportunities for growth. A maid has been promoted to head housekeeper, a wine waitress to restaurant head, and a student worker to deputy manager.[76]

9-5b Performance Appraisal

Performance appraisal refers to observing and assessing employee performance, recording the assessment, and providing feedback to the employee. Managers give feedback and praise concerning the acceptable elements of the employee's performance and describe performance areas that need improvement. One of the biggest talent management mistakes, according to management expert Ram Charan, is the failure to provide candid performance assessments that focus on development needs.[77] When employees get this feedback, they can use it to improve their performance. Exhibit 9.10 provides an interesting look at how people in different countries give positive and negative feedback. Unfortunately, only 3 in 10 employees surveyed believe that their companies' performance review system actually helps to improve performance; this finding indicates a need for improved methods of appraisal and feedback.[78] Current thinking is that performance appraisal should be ongoing, not something that is done only once a year as part of a consideration of raises. Sometimes performance appraisal gets done quickly, as in professional football, where much is at stake on assessing whether a particular player should be out on the field, as shown in the "Half-Baked Management" box.

Half-Baked Management Patriots Super Bowl 52

Super Bowl 51, New England Patriots versus Philadelphia Eagles. Many people expected a win by the Patriots as they'd already bested in five Super Bowls while the Eagles had never won even a single Super Bowl.

Not only did star Patriot Tom Brady run amok that night, but the coaches decided to bench strong player Malcolm Butler, which sportswriter David Steele called "boneheaded," particularly because another strong player, Brandin Cooks, was removed from most of the game because of a concussion.

Whom you hire and put on your team is vitally important. And how you assess them in the moment is crucial in many organizations.

SOURCE: David Steele, "Patriots Benching Malcolm Butler Among Worst Coaching Mistakes in Super Bowl History," *Sporting News*, February 5, 2008, http://www.sportingnews.com/nfl/news/patriots-malcolm-butler-benched-super-bowl-bill-belichick/r7lwi42z8rqu14t9k6516rt9w

Assessing Performance Accurately Jobs are multidimensional, and therefore performance may be multidimensional as well. Two popular approaches used in recent years are 360-degree feedback and the performance review ranking system.

- **360-degree feedback:** A recent trend in performance appraisal is called **360-degree feedback**, a process that uses multiple raters, including self-rating, as a way to increase awareness of strengths and weaknesses and guide employee development.[79] Members of the appraisal group may include supervisors, coworkers, and customers, as well as the individual, thus providing a holistic view of the employee's performance. When used appropriately, 360-degree feedback can lead to a more valid assessment of performance as well as identify greater development opportunities for employees. Some companies use social networking–style systems to make 360-degree performance feedback a dynamic, ongoing process. For example, people can post short, Twitter-style questions about their performance of a particular task and get feedback from managers, peers, or anyone else the user selects.[80]
- **Performance review ranking system:** Another alternative performance evaluation method is the *performance review ranking system*, which is sometimes referred to as a forced ranking system, stack ranking, or "rank and yank."[81] This method is increasingly controversial because it essentially evaluates employees by pitting them against one another. As most commonly used, these systems rank employees according to their relative performance: 20 percent would be placed in the top group of performers; 70 percent have to be ranked in the middle; and 10 percent are ranked at the bottom. The bottom tier are given a set period of time to improve their performance, and if they don't improve, they are fired. The idea behind the forced ranking of employees is that everyone will be motivated to improve performance. A performance ranking system forces reluctant managers to make difficult decisions and identify the best and worst performers, and proponents say it can create and sustain a high-performance culture in which people continuously improve. However, critics say the system often increases cutthroat competition among employees, discourages collaboration and teamwork, and harms morale. One HR manager at Intel, for example,

said morale typically declined significantly in a big portion of employees who fell into the 70 percent ranking (the second lowest). "We'd call them the walking wounded," she said.[82] Many companies have dropped the ranking system or modified it so that it doesn't insist on quotas for underperformers.[83]

Exhibit 9.10 How People in Different Countries Give Feedback

SOURCE: "How These Countries Critique," visual based on Erin Meyer, *The Culture Map: Breaking Through the Invisible Boundaries of Global Business,* in Aaron Taube and Skye Gould, "Here Are the Wildly Different Ways People Give Feedback Around the World," *Business Insider,* http://www.businessinsider.com/how-people-give-criticism-all-over-the-world-2014-11 (accessed August 18, 2016).

Performance Evaluation Errors   Although we would like to believe that every manager assesses employees' performance in a careful and bias-free manner, researchers have identified several rating problems.[84] One of the most dangerous is **stereotyping**, which occurs when a rater places an employee into a class or category based on one or a few traits or characteristics—for example, stereotyping an older worker as slower and more difficult to train. Another rating error is the **halo effect**, in which a manager gives an employee the same rating on all dimensions, even if his or her performance is good on some dimensions and poor on others.

Exhibit 9.11 illustrates the **behaviorally anchored rating scale (BARS)** method for evaluating a production line supervisor. The production supervisor's job can be broken down into several dimensions, such as equipment maintenance, employee training, and work scheduling. A BARS should be developed for each dimension. The dimension in Exhibit 9.11 is work scheduling. Good performance is represented by a 4 or 5 on the scale, and unacceptable performance by a 1 or 2. If a production supervisor's job has eight dimensions, the total performance evaluation will be the sum of the scores for each of eight scales.[85]

Exhibit 9.11 Example of a Behaviorally Anchored Rating Scale

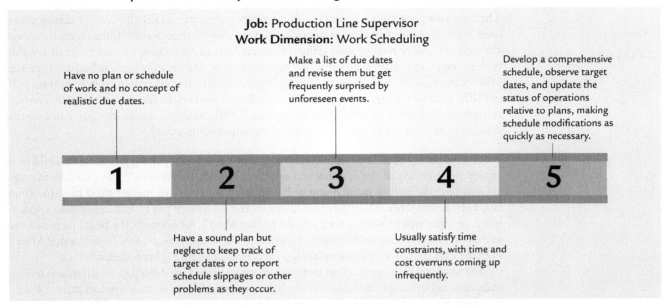

SOURCES: Based on J. P. Campbell et al., "The Development and Evaluation of Behaviorally Based Rating Scales," *Journal of Applied Psychology* 57 (1973): 15–22; and Francine Alexander, "Performance Appraisals," *Small Business Reports* (March 1989): 20–29.

Remember This

- Training typically refers to teaching people skills needed in their current job, whereas development refers to teaching people broader career skills.
- The most common method of training is **on-the-job-training (OJT)** in which an experienced employee is asked to teach a new employee how to perform job duties.
- **Social learning** refers to using social media tools to network and learn informally.
- A **corporate university** is an in-house training and development facility that offers broad-based learning opportunities for employees.
- McDonald's Hamburger University has seven management training centers around the world, including one in Shanghai and one in São Paulo.
- **Performance appraisal** is the process of observing and evaluating an employee's performance, recording the assessment, and providing feedback.

- A recent trend is **360-degree feedback**, which uses multiple raters, including self-rating, to appraise employee performance and guide development.
- Performance review ranking systems, sometimes called "rank and yank," are increasingly being criticized because they tend to pit employees against one another rather than promoting cooperation and teamwork.
- **Stereotyping** is a performance evaluation error that occurs when a manager places an employee into a class or category based on one or a few traits or characteristics.
- The **halo effect** occurs when a manager gives an employee the same rating on all dimensions of the job, even though performance may be good on some dimensions and poor on others.
- One way to overcome evaluation errors is to use a **behaviorally anchored rating scale (BARS)**, which is a performance evaluation technique that relates an employee's performance to specific job-related incidents.

9-6 Maintaining an Effective Workforce

Now we turn to the topic of how managers and HRM professionals maintain a workforce that has been recruited and developed. Maintenance of the current workforce involves compensation, wage and salary systems, benefits, and (occasionally) termination.

9-6a **Rewards**

The term **compensation** refers to (1) all monetary payments and (2) all goods or commodities used in lieu of money to reward employees. Over the past 15 years, most HR managers have used the term *rewards* or *total rewards* rather than *compensation*, to include a broad range of rewards such as wages and salaries, incentive payments, bonuses, and benefits such as health insurance, paid vacations, or other benefits.[86] Developing an effective reward system is an important part of HRM because it helps to attract and retain talented workers. In addition, a company's reward system has an impact on strategic performance.[87] HR managers design the pay and benefits systems to fit company strategy and to provide compensation equity.

Wage and Salary Systems   Ideally, management's strategy for the organization should be a critical determinant of the features and operations of the pay system.[88] For example, managers may have the goal of maintaining or improving profitability or market share by stimulating employee performance. Thus, they should design and use a merit pay system rather than a system based on other criteria such as seniority. At retailer Macy's, for example, the board increased the sales component of bonuses for senior executives to encourage sales growth. In addition, if Macy's sales increase above the company plan, top executives can earn higher bonuses.[89]

The most common approach to employee compensation is *job-based pay,* which means linking compensation to the specific tasks and employee performs. However, these systems present several problems. For one thing, job-based pay may fail to reward the type of learning behavior needed for the organization to adapt and survive in a turbulent environment. In addition, these systems reinforce an emphasis on organizational hierarchy and centralized decision making and control, which are inconsistent with the growing emphasis on employee participation and increased responsibility.[90]

Skill-based pay systems are increasingly popular in both large and small companies. Employees with higher skill levels receive higher pay than those with lower skill levels.[91] Also called *competency-based pay,* skill-based pay systems encourage people to develop their skills and competencies, thus making them more valuable to the organization, as well as more employable if they leave their current jobs.

As with other aspects of management, big data analytics programs are now being used to make decisions about rewards. A company wondering how to cut attrition can gather data on turnover, promotions, job changes, benefits, work–life balance, and other factors for hundreds of thousands of workers and use predictive analytics to see what truly makes a difference. Does increasing pay keep people from leaving, or do other factors play a larger role? A large regional bank, for example, found that increasing pay shaved only half a point off the turnover rate for customer service representatives. People felt dissatisfied, not underpaid.[92]

Compensation Equity   Whether the organization uses job-based pay or skill-based pay, good managers strive to maintain a sense of fairness and equity within the pay structure and thereby fortify employee morale. **Job evaluation** refers to the process of determining the value or worth of jobs within an organization through an examination of job content. Job evaluation techniques enable managers to compare similar and dissimilar jobs and to determine internally equitable pay rates—that is, pay rates that employees believe are fair compared to those for other jobs in the organization.

Organizations also want to make sure that their pay rates are fair compared to other companies. HR managers may obtain **wage and salary surveys** that show what other organizations pay incumbents in jobs that match a sample of "key" jobs selected by the organization. These surveys are available from a number of sources, including the U.S. Bureau of Labor Statistics National Compensation Survey.

Pay-for-Performance   Many of today's organizations develop compensation plans based on a *pay-for-performance standard* to raise productivity and cut labor costs in a competitive global environment. **Pay-for-performance,** also called *incentive pay,* means tying at least part of compensation to employee effort and performance, whether it be through merit-based pay, bonuses, team incentives, or various gain-sharing or profit-sharing plans. With pay-for-performance, incentives are aligned with the behaviors needed to help the organization achieve its strategic goals. Employees have an incentive to make the company more efficient and profitable because if goals are not met, no bonuses are paid.

However, recent years have shown the potential dangers of misdirected pay-for-performance plans. Alan Blinder, Princeton professor of economics and public affairs, points out that a fundamental cause of the 2008–2009 financial crisis in the United States was the "perverse go-for-broke incentives" that rewarded people for taking excessive risks with other people's money.[93] During the financial meltdown, it became clear that people at every level of the financial system were getting rewarded for short-term performance—if things went wrong down the line, it was someone else's problem. Then it all came crashing down. Managers can take care to create pay-for-performance plans that align with the long-term interests of the organization, shareholders, and the broader society.

9-6b Benefits

An effective rewards package requires more than money. Although salary is an important component, benefits are equally important.

Organizations are required by law to provide some benefits, such as Social Security, unemployment compensation, and workers' compensation. Other types of benefits, such as vacations and things such as onsite fitness centers or educational reimbursements, are not required by law but are provided by organizations to attract and maintain an effective workforce. Companies such as PricewaterhouseCoopers, Natixis Global Asset Management, and Fidelity Investments are offering help paying off student loan debt to attract and keep talented young employees. The benefits packages provided by large companies attempt to meet the needs of all employees. Some companies, particularly in the technology industry where skilled employees are hard to find, offer extremely generous benefits packages. Today, even nontechnology companies, such as Alterra, based in Provo, Utah, are offering innovative benefits to recruit and retain top talent.

Alterra isn't the only "low-tech" company adding perks typically found primarily in high-tech firms like Google or Facebook as a way to attract and retain top performers. For example, the Society for Human Resource Management reports that 16 percent of insurance companies offer free dry cleaning for employees, and more than 11 percent of waste management companies give employees free food and drinks.[94]

9-6c Termination

Despite the best efforts of line managers and HRM professionals, the organization will lose employees. Some will retire, others will depart voluntarily for other jobs, and still others will be forced out through mergers and cutbacks or for poor performance.

The value of termination for maintaining an effective workforce is twofold. First, employees who are poor performers can be dismissed. Productive employees often resent disruptive, low-performing employees who are allowed to stay with the company and receive pay and benefits comparable to theirs. Second, managers can use exit interviews as a valuable HRM tool, regardless of whether the employee leaves voluntarily or is forced out. An **exit interview** is an interview conducted with departing employees to determine why they are leaving the company. The value of the exit interview is to provide an inexpensive way to learn about pockets of dissatisfaction within the organization and hence find ways to reduce future turnover.[95] The oil services giant Schlumberger includes an exit interview as part of a full-scale investigation of every departure, with the results posted online so that managers all around the company can get insight into problems.[96]

Marvin Joseph/The Washington Post/Getty Images

Concept Connection

Many students have heard about perks such as onsite fitness centers and free snacks at Silicon Valley companies such as Google and Facebook. Today, even nontechnology companies are offering **generous rewards** and **innovative benefits** to retain quality employees. At outdoor retailer REI, people take home an extra 5 percent to 15 percent of their base pay thanks to a profit-sharing plan. REI also pays most of the health insurance costs for employees working at least 20 hours a week and offers tuition reimbursement so people can continue their education. All employees get two "Yay Days" each year to go out and play. They can use the paid time off to "try something new, challenge themselves in a favorite activity, or work on an outdoor stewardship project."

Sunny Side Up ⟩ Alterra LLC

It doesn't make software, provide social media services, or create high-tech products in Silicon Valley, but you'd never know it. The office of Alterra LLC, a pest services company in Provo, Utah, has an NCAA regulation-size basketball court, a TruGolf simulator, and a 90-inch television. Food trucks come by regularly and treat the staff to free food. "It makes me feel like I am at the most elite pest company there is," says sales manager Garret Swenson.

Alterra invests more than 10 percent of its profits in lavish perks for its employees. CEO David Royce says he was inspired to focus on employee happiness after reading articles by Zappos founder Tony Hsieh. He began looking at various high-tech offices online and decided "it's not fair that they have all the fun." Royce says the benefits are paying off because it's easier to recruit good people and the ones he hires produce better results and stay around a lot longer.[97]

However, in some cases, employees who leave voluntarily are reluctant to air uncomfortable complaints or discuss their real reasons for leaving. Companies such as T-Mobile, Campbell Soup, and Conair found that having people complete an online exit questionnaire yields more open and honest information. When people have negative things to say about managers or the company, the online format is a chance to speak their mind without having to do it in a face-to-face meeting.[98]

Remember This

- **Compensation** refers to all monetary payments and all nonmonetary goods or benefits used to reward employees.

- Most companies use the term *rewards* or *total rewards* rather than *compensation* to include a broad range of rewards such as wages and salaries, incentive payments, bonuses, and benefits.

- Managers strive to maintain fairness and equity in the pay system.

- **Job evaluation** is the process of determining the value of jobs within an organization through an examination of job content.

- **Wage and salary surveys** show what other organizations pay incumbents in jobs that match a sample of key jobs selected by the organization.

- **Pay-for-performance**, also called *incentive pay,* means tying at least a portion of compensation to employee effort and performance.

- Benefits make up a large portion of labor costs in the United States.

- Pest services company Alterra and many other low-tech companies are offering lavish perks once found only in high-term firms such as Google and Facebook.

- An **exit interview** is an interview conducted with departing employees to determine reasons for their departure and learn about potential problems in the organization.

- Campbell Soup Company and some other organizations let people complete an online exit questionnaire so they can express their complaints or ideas freely, without having to talk face to face with a manager.

9-7 Diversity in the Workplace

Pinterest CEO Ben Silbermann and cofounder Evan Sharp recently gathered employees of the successful and rapidly growing company together in the cafeteria to have a little chat about diversity. Pinterest had been trying for two years to add more women, African Americans, and Hispanics to its programming teams. But when Sharp and Silbermann looked at the numbers in

2015, they found that the percentage of women in tech roles was still only 21 percent, the same as the previous year. Statistics for African Americans (1 percent) and Hispanics (2 percent) were even more dismal. Even after announcing an ambitious plan for increasing diversity; recruiting at events for female, African American, and Hispanic engineers; mentoring minority students; and other efforts, Sharp had to admit, "We just hadn't made any progress." Sharp and Silbermann realized that they hadn't given employees enough reason to care about diversifying, nor had they explicitly defined their goals for diversity. The chat in the Pinterest cafeteria was the first step in changing that, but the problem of bringing greater diversity to the company won't be easily solved.[99]

Managers at many companies, as at Pinterest, have found that saying you want a more diverse workforce isn't enough. Pinterest and other technology companies face a particularly tough challenge because there are fewer female and minority programmers and engineers, but all companies struggle with diversity issues. For example, managers at most companies strive to avoid discriminatory policies and practices, but a *Harvard Business Review* survey found that 93 percent of female respondents and 92 percent of non-Caucasian respondents felt that they had been treated unfairly at work because of someone else's bias.[100]

Forward-thinking managers in all industries are taking steps to attract and retain a workforce that reflects the cultural diversity of the population. They take seriously the fact that there is a link between the diversity of the workforce and financial success in the marketplace. At Pinterest, cofounder Evan Sharp is passionate about the ethical and societal value of greater workforce diversity, but he realizes that diversity also leads to better results. "This is not a charity; it's a business," Sharp said.[101] Exhibit 9.12 lists some corporations that are considered leaders in diversity and shows the top 10 companies for African Americans, Asian Americans, and Hispanics and Latinos from *Fortune* magazine's 2015 ranking. These companies actively pursue a corporate culture that values equality and reflects today's diverse consumer base.

This section describes how the domestic and global workforce is becoming increasingly diverse and how corporations are responding to the challenges and opportunities this presents. We look at the myriad complex issues that managers and employees face in a diverse workplace and present an overview of initiatives taken by corporations to create a more inclusive work environment.

When Brenda Thompson, the director of diversity and leadership education at MGM Resorts International, steps into one of the company's hotel lobbies, she closes her eyes and listens. "It's amazing all the different languages I can hear just standing in the lobbies of any of our hotels," she says. "Our guests come from all over the world, and it really makes us realize the importance of reflecting that diversity in our workplace."[102] The diversity that Thompson notices in the lobbies of the MGM Mirage hotels is a small reflection of the cultural diversity in the larger domestic and global workplaces.

"If we don't reflect the global nature of our business in our employees, how can we possibly hope to understand our customers?"

—MARK PALMER-EDGECUMBE, CEO, GLOBAL DIVERSITY LIST AND FORMER HEAD OF DIVERSITY AT GOOGLE

9-7a Diversity Challenges in Corporate America

The previous example described the diversity challenge managers at Pinterest are facing. The company first began looking at the problem when one of Pinterest's female Asian American programmers, Tracy Chou, disclosed in a blog post that almost 90 percent of her engineering colleagues were male. Her post sparked a call for similar disclosures of diversity (or the lack of it) at other technology companies. The numbers show that other big technology companies are also overwhelmingly male and white or Asian. In 2015, 30 percent of employees at both Google and Twitter were women, only 2 percent were African American, and 3 percent were Hispanic or Latino. Facebook reported that 32 percent of its employees were women, 2 percent were African American, and 4 percent were Hispanic or Latino. Managers in these and other tech companies are trying new approaches to bring in more diverse employees, but executives say they find themselves fighting over the same small pool of nonwhite, nonmale candidates, particularly for higher-level positions. "You can imagine how in demand these candidates are," said Morgan Missen, a recruiter who has worked at both Google and Twitter.[103]

Exhibit 9.12 Examples of Leaders in Corporate Diversity

Company	Percent of Race or Ethnicity
Top 10 for African Americans	
1. Quicken Loans	16
2. Credit Acceptance	43
3. Ultimate Software	12
4. Alliance Data	14
5. Navy Federal Credit Union	20
6. Carmax	22
7. Hyatt Hotels	17
8. QuikTrip	18
9. JM Family Enterprises	16
10. St. Jude Children's Research Hospital	25
U.S. Average	12
Top 10 for Asian Americans	
1. Workday	26
2. St. Jude Children's Research Hospital	12
3. Hyatt Hotels	16
4. FactSet Research Systems Inc.	23
5. Salesforce	23
6. Genentech	31
7. American Savings Bank	54
8. Intuit	20
9. Cadence	45
10. Navy Federal Credit Union	11
U.S. Average	6
Top 10 for Hispanics and/or Latinos	
1. Ultimate Software	17
2. Camden Property Trust	35
3. Hyatt Hotels	28
4. NuStar Energy	20
5. Baptist Health South Florida	53
6. USAA	31
7. Scripps Health	19
8. Nugget Market	24
9. Carmax	16
10. The Cheesecake Factory	37
U.S. Average	16

NOTE: Rankings are based on surveys of nearly 70,000 minority employees at 600 organizations and take into consideration the representation of employees by race, ethnicity, and gender as well as the percentage of minorities and women in management positions.

SOURCE: Christopher Tkaczyk, "Best Workplaces for Diversity," *Fortune* (December 1, 2015): 24.

Managers in all industries are searching for ways to set their organizations apart from the competition and create breakthrough innovations, and creating a more diverse workplace is an important part of that. Managers who cultivate a diverse workforce have been shown to improve their organization's chances of success. Diverse teams that perform efficiently add value by combining individuals' strengths, making the whole greater than the sum of its parts.[104]

In the past, when managers thought of diversity, they focused on the "problems" associated with diversity, such as discrimination, bias, affirmative action, and tokenism. Now managers recognize that the differences people bring to the workplace are valuable.[105] Rather than expecting all employees to adopt similar attitudes and values, managers are learning that these differences enable their companies to compete globally and tap into rich sources of new talent. Although diversity in North America has been a reality for some time, genuine efforts to accept and *manage* diverse people began only in recent years. Exhibit 9.13 lists some interesting milestones in the history of corporate diversity.

Diversity in corporate America has become a key topic in part because of the vast changes occurring in today's environment. Consider the uproar that surrounded the Academy Awards in early 2016. For the second year in a row, every Oscar nominee and almost every nominated producer and director were white. The hottest topic besieging Hollywood, reflected in the social media label #oscarssowhite, became not who would win Best Actress or Best Picture but instead why nonwhite moviegoers, who buy 46 percent of movie tickets, were so underrepresented in both films and the studios that make them. A study from the University of Southern California (USC) released in the midst of the hubbub, for example, showed that Hispanics represented just 2.7 percent of onscreen characters in 2014 and less than 5 percent of production executives at major studios. During the same year, Hispanics represented 17 percent of the U.S. population and bought 23 percent of movie tickets in the United States.[106]

The furor over the Oscars reflects trends in the larger society. Just as movie studios are under growing pressure to change as audiences become increasingly diverse, so are managers in other types of organizations. Two specific issues that illustrate how the environment and the workplace are changing are an increase in foreign-born employees and the rise of female employees:

- *Increased diversity.* Today's workplace is becoming more diverse as the number of foreign-born workers increases. In 2014, there were 25.7 million foreign-born workers in the U.S. workforce, making up 16.5 percent of all U.S. workers. Of the total number of foreign-born employees, nearly half are Hispanic and 24 percent are Asian.[107] Looking ahead, the number of Hispanic employees is projected to grow the most.[108] Exhibit 9.14 shows the projected changes in employment among different racial and ethnic groups in the United States.
- *More women workers.* Women outnumber men in the workplace, and their numbers are projected to grow slightly faster, at 7.4 percent compared to 6.3 percent for men. The good news is that nearly 73 percent of *Fortune* 500 companies now have at least one female executive officer, but women hold just 17 percent of board seats in the United States.[109] In addition, the United States has fallen behind in a ranking of gender equality in 148 countries by the World Economic Forum. In the Forum's 2015 Global Gender Gap report, the United States fell to 28th place, 8 places down from the previous year and behind countries such as Iceland (which ranked number 1), Rwanda, and Germany.[110]

These trends underscore the complex nature of today's workforce and the potential pitfalls managers face as they lead diverse teams toward common goals. While many managers recognize the value of diversity, some simply haven't kept pace with changes in the workforce and the larger society. In fact, as diversity has increased, so have the number of discrimination complaints with the EEOC, which investigates employee claims and sometimes brings lawsuits on behalf of workers. One recent complaint, for example, is against Bass Pro Shops, accused of repeatedly refusing to hire nonwhite workers as clerks, cashiers, or managers, and using discriminatory language to explain their reasons. Among other charges in the lawsuit is the allegation that a senior worker in Indiana was seen discarding employment applications, explaining that he could tell by the job seekers' names that they were black. The suit also alleges that the general manager of a Houston store regularly referred to those of Hispanic origin as "Pedro" or "Mexican."[111]

Exhibit 9.13   Milestones in the History of Corporate Diversity

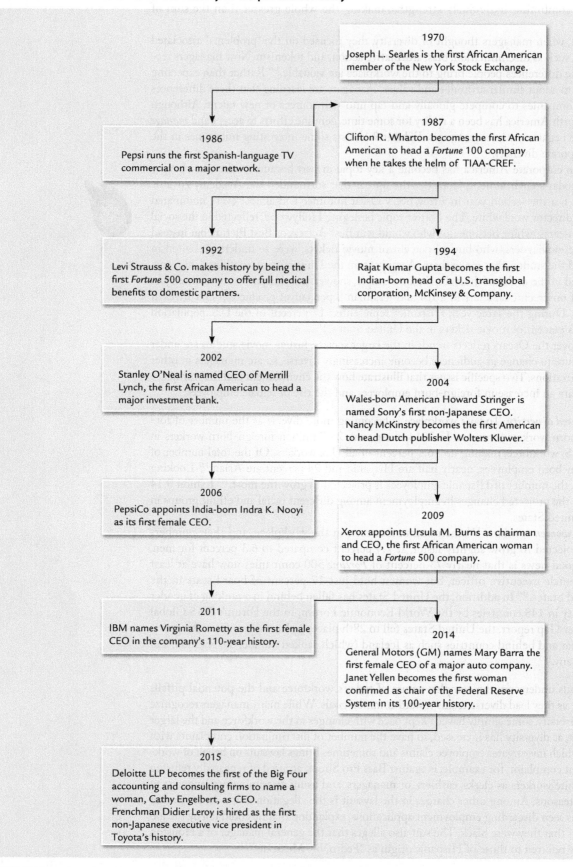

1970
Joseph L. Searles is the first African American member of the New York Stock Exchange.

1986
Pepsi runs the first Spanish-language TV commercial on a major network.

1987
Clifton R. Wharton becomes the first African American to head a *Fortune* 100 company when he takes the helm of TIAA-CREF.

1992
Levi Strauss & Co. makes history by being the first *Fortune* 500 company to offer full medical benefits to domestic partners.

1994
Rajat Kumar Gupta becomes the first Indian-born head of a U.S. transglobal corporation, McKinsey & Company.

2002
Stanley O'Neal is named CEO of Merrill Lynch, the first African American to head a major investment bank.

2004
Wales-born American Howard Stringer is named Sony's first non-Japanese CEO. Nancy McKinstry becomes the first American to head Dutch publisher Wolters Kluwer.

2006
PepsiCo appoints India-born Indra K. Nooyi as its first female CEO.

2009
Xerox appoints Ursula M. Burns as chairman and CEO, the first African American woman to head a *Fortune* 500 company.

2011
IBM names Virginia Rometty as the first female CEO in the company's 110-year history.

2014
General Motors (GM) names Mary Barra the first female CEO of a major auto company. Janet Yellen becomes the first woman confirmed as chair of the Federal Reserve System in its 100-year history.

2015
Deloitte LLP becomes the first of the Big Four accounting and consulting firms to name a woman, Cathy Engelbert, as CEO. Frenchman Didier Leroy is hired as the first non-Japanese executive vice president in Toyota's history.

SOURCES: "Spotlight on Diversity," special advertising section, *MBA Jungle* (March–April 2003): 58–61; Xerox corporate Web site, www.news.xerox.com; Michael Rapoport and Julie Steinberg, "Deloitte Taps Woman, a First, for CEO Post," *The Wall Street Journal,* February 9, 2015, http://www.wsj.com/articles/deloitte-taps-cathy-engelbert-as-chief-executive-1423492486 (accessed April 19, 2016); and Yoko Kubota, "Toyota Opts to Diversify Senior Posts," *The Wall Street Journal,* March 4, 2015, http://www.wsj.com/articles/toyota-taps-first-foreign-vice-president-1425451312 (accessed April 20, 2016).

Exhibit 9.14 Projected Changes in U.S. Labor Force, 2012–2022

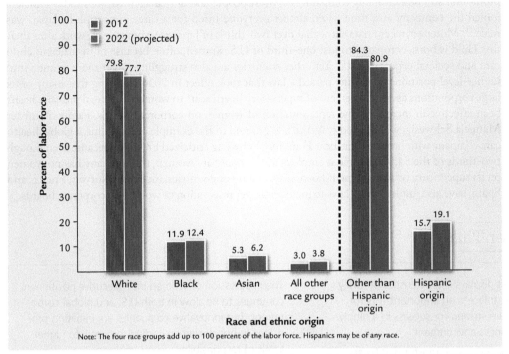

Note: The four race groups add up to 100 percent of the labor force. Hispanics may be of any race.

SOURCE: *Employment Projections: Civilian Labor Force by Age, Sex, Race, and Ethnicity,* Bureau of Labor Statistics, U.S. Department of Labor, Table 3.1, Civilian Labor Force by Age, Sex, Race, and Ethnicity, 1992, 2002, 2012, and Projected 2022, http://www.bls.gov/emp/ep_table_301.htm (accessed May 22, 2014).

9-7b Diversity Challenges on a Global Scale

Managers across the globe wrestle with many of the same diversity challenges as U.S. managers, especially concerning the progression of women into upper management positions. Companies in Japan, for example, have made a strong push to hire more women, and in 2015 a higher percentage of working-age women were employed in Japan than in the United States and Europe. However, in a ranking of the percentage of women in business leadership roles in 34 major countries, Japan placed last, with only 8 percent of women holding leadership roles. Managers at some Japanese companies are changing their policies and practices to try to improve the chances for women to move into management positions.

Sunny Side Up ⟩ Yokohama Nursery Company, Yamato Holdings

Yokohama Nursery has been innovating since it was founded more than 120 years ago to export unique Japanese plants to the West. Today, some of those innovations relate to getting more women into management. The city of Yokohama recently gave the company an award for its child-care and nursing-care leave policies, which make it easier for women to work and advance in their careers. But President Kazuo Ariyoshi says when he realized how few women were in management positions, he felt guilty about getting the award. Soon afterward, he asked Michiru Tomabechi to be in charge of the gardening trade show. Tomabechi thought it was a joke. Running the trade show was a job no woman had ever done in the company's history.

Another company that is making changes to try to move women higher up the career ladder is Yamato

Holdings, Japan's largest package delivery company. Yamato has aggressively hired women, but only 3 percent are managers. The company recently created a diversity division, led by Mio Yamauchi. "There are so few role models, so it's hard for women to imagine what it's like," she says. Yamauchi is working with top managers to try to change the culture and make it easier for both male and female employees to balance work and family life. "At some companies, saying 'I'm going home early' is the same as saying 'I'm giving up,'" said Fumie Yui, a management consultant who works with companies on women's issues. By creating a better work–life balance for all employees, companies such as Yamato and Yokohama Nursery hope to recruit more women, as well as move more of them into management jobs.[112]

Japan faces a particularly tough task because the practices of lifetime employment and age-based promotion still hold at many companies, so most people taking management jobs today typically joined the company at a time when almost everyone hired for a career-track job in Japan was male.[113] Moreover, recent data show that over two-thirds of Japanese women leave work after their first child is born, compared to just one-third of U.S. women, often because of insufficient child care and societal expectations.[114] Yet other countries are also struggling to get more women into higher-level positions. Germany passed a law that took effect in 2016 requiring that many of its large corporations assign 30 percent of supervisory board seats to women. Informal pressure hasn't been effective in increasing the representation of women on corporate boards. Family Minister Manuela Schwesig, who helped craft the law, pointed to the example of Fresenius, a global health care company with headquarters near Frankfurt. Schwesig criticized Fresenius because even though two-thirds of the 54,000 people it employs in Germany are women, the company has no women on its supervisory or management boards. Several other countries, including Norway, France, and Spain, have also implemented laws to increase the representation of women on corporate boards.[115]

Remember This

- A workforce that displays characteristics of today's diversified marketplace is an important tool for managers who are striving for success in a highly competitive business environment.

- The U.S. workforce is being transformed by an increase in foreign-born employees and an increasing number of women employees.

- The progression of women into executive positions continues to be slow in both U.S. and global corporations, but innovative companies are initiating programs to boost women's advancement into higher levels of responsibility.

- Germany passed a law requiring some companies to give 30 percent of supervisory board seats to women beginning in 2016.

Green Power

Diversity and Biodiversity When we were children running up against differing opinions, our grandmothers reminded us, "It takes all kinds to make a world." The preservation of diverse plant and animal life forms also echoes Grandma's words. To promote biodiversity preservation, managers at beverage maker Bean and Body use proceeds from the sale of the company's healthy coffees to sponsor The Bean and Body Protected Grounds Initiative, which works in collaboration with the World Land Trust to buy, protect, and preserve the most threatened areas of the world's rain forests, wetlands, and coastlines. The award-winning effort meets corporate goals to promote a healthy lifestyle while taking intentional steps to promote ecological, economic, and social preservation. The Bean and Body initiative works to solve biodiversity problems by helping the farmers whose cultivation of coffee beans affects the environment through groundwater runoff and incursions into rain forests.

SOURCES: Andrew J. Hoffman, "Climate Change as a Cultural and Behavioral Issue: Addressing Barriers and Implementing Solutions," *Organizational Dynamics* 39 (2010): 295–305; and Erin Legg, "Coffee Re-imagined: Bean and Body Emerge as Global Leaders," *Healthy New Age* Web site, July 2010, www.healthynewage.com/blog/bean-and-body-wins-award/ (accessed August 1, 2012).

9-8 Managing Diversity

Managers who want to boost performance and jumpstart innovation agree that diverse teams produce the best results. In one survey of department heads and executives, 84 percent stated that they prefer heterogeneous teams because they lead to multiple viewpoints and more prolific ideas.[116] The following sections describe the characteristics of a diverse workforce and the dividends of cultivating one.

9-8a Diversity and Inclusion

Diversity is defined as all the ways in which people differ.[117] Diversity wasn't always defined this broadly. Decades ago, many companies defined *diversity* in terms of race, gender, age, lifestyle, and disability. That focus helped create awareness, change mind-sets, and create new opportunities for many. Today, companies are embracing a more inclusive definition of *diversity* that recognizes a spectrum of differences that influence how employees approach work, interact with each other, derive satisfaction from their work, and define who they are as people in the workplace.[118]

Exhibit 9.15 illustrates the difference between the traditional model and the inclusive model of diversity. The dimensions of diversity shown in the traditional model include inborn differences that are immediately observable such as race, gender, age, and physical ability. However, the inclusive model of diversity includes *all* the ways in which employees differ, including aspects of diversity that can be acquired or changed throughout one's lifetime. These dimensions may have less impact than those included only in the traditional model, but they nevertheless affect a person's self-definition and worldview and the way the person is viewed by others. Many organizational leaders embrace this more inclusive definition of *diversity*. "Diversity has to be looked at in its broadest sense," said Wally Parker, former CEO of KeySpan Energy (now National Grid). "To me, it's all about recognizing, respecting, and supporting individuals regardless of what makes up that individuality. So, yes, that's race, gender, and sexual orientation. But it's also introverted and extroverted, ethnic backgrounds, cultural upbringing, all those things."[119]

One of the challenges of managing a diverse workforce is creating an environment where all employees feel accepted as members of the team and where their unique talents are appreciated. When managers create a feeling of inclusiveness, employees display more loyalty, cooperation, and trustworthiness. **Inclusion** is the degree to which an employee feels like an esteemed member of a group in which his or her uniqueness is highly appreciated. Inclusion creates a strong sense of belonging and a trust that all people can have their voices heard and appreciated.[120] Consider how a manager of a retail store embraced an employee's unique perspective with positive results. Raj, the manager, supervised an employee, Olivia, who was quiet and seemed to have few innovative ideas. But as Raj discussed marketing strategies for the store with Olivia, he was surprised to learn that she was a highly creative thinker, consistently interjecting novel ideas into the discussion. Over time, he realized that this seemingly quiet employee was one of the most creative marketing thinkers he had ever met, and together they created a very successful line of children's outerwear. Raj has become a strong supporter of inclusion and a champion for individuals who operate differently from the norm.[121]

In creating a culture of inclusion, managers may experience times of tension and discord as people with different backgrounds bring different opinions and ideas. Conflicts, anxiety, and misunderstandings may increase. Embracing these differences and using them to improve company performance can be challenging. **Managing diversity**, a key management skill in

Paul Morigi/Getty Images

Concept Connection

"Diversity is a driver of innovation," says Ursula Burns, who began working at Xerox Corporation as an intern in 1980 and over the course of her career held various management positions in corporate services, manufacturing, and product development. In 2009, Burns became the first African American woman to head a *Fortune* 500 company when she was appointed chairman and CEO of Xerox. Successful organizations seek a **diverse and inclusive workforce**. Minorities represent 42 percent of Xerox employees and 13 percent of executives and senior-level managers in the United States. Women hold 27 percent of top jobs in the company.

Exhibit 9.15 Traditional Versus Inclusive Models of Diversity

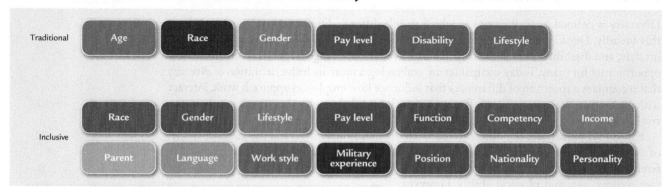

SOURCE: Based on Anthony Oshiotse and Richard O'Leary, "Corning Creates an Inclusive Culture to Drive Technology Innovation and Performance," *Global Business and Organizational Excellence* 26, no. 3 (March/April 2007): 7–21.

today's global economy, means creating a climate in which the potential advantages of diversity for organizational or group performance are maximized, while the potential disadvantages are minimized.[122]

9-8b Diversity of Thought

You may have heard the expression, "Great minds think alike." But when it comes to achieving breakthrough levels of innovation and performance, the best minds are those that *don't* think alike. Over a 10-year-period, for example, DiversityInc.'s top 50 companies for any given year outperformed the Dow Jones Industrial Average by 22 percent and NASDAQ by 28 percent, according to Catalyst. Other studies by McKinsey & Company of executive board diversity in the United States, France, Germany, and the United Kingdom show that companies that rank in the top quartile for diversity had returns on equity that were 53 percent higher, on average, than those for the least diverse companies.[123]

Heterogeneous teams and organizations, made up of individuals with different backgrounds and skill sets, increase the chances of getting a **diversity of thought**, which provides a broader and deeper base of ideas, opinions, and experiences for problem solving, creativity, and innovation. Managers who cultivate a diversity of thought significantly increase the chance of creating hard-to-replicate competitive advantage. By tapping into the strengths of diversity, teams are more likely to experience higher efficiency, better quality, less duplication of effort among team members, and increased innovation and creativity.[124] Hala Moddelmog, former president of Arby's Restaurant Group and currently serving as the first female president and CEO of the Metro Atlanta Chamber of Commerce, surrounds herself with colleagues of different races, socioeconomic classes, and personality styles. "You really don't need another you," Moddelmog says. Cindy Holland, vice president for original content at Netflix, also says she tries to hire for diversity of thought and diversity of experience on her team because it leads to better ideas and solutions.[125]

According to the results of one study, companies that rate high on creativity and innovation have a higher percentage of women and nonwhite male employees than less innovative companies. Another recent study showed that a team's collective intelligence increases when there are more women members on the team.[126] Moreover, companies with more diverse top management teams outperform their peers financially. Researchers analyzed return on equity (ROE) and margins for earnings before interest and taxes (EBIT) for 180 corporations in the United States, France, Germany, and the United Kingdom and found that those with a higher percentage of women and foreign nationals performed significantly better than their peers with less-diverse top teams.[127] At Reckitt Benckiser, a U.K.-based producer of home, health, and personal care products, no nationality dominates management. The executive committee, led by CEO Rakesh Kapoor, is made up of seven nationalities, the top 400 senior executives include 47 nationalities, and 69 percent of the company's general managers, marketing managers, and sales managers work outside of their native country.[128] Reckitt Benckiser managers believe the diversity of the company's workforce is one reason income increased 17 percent annually, on average, from 1999 to 2010.[129]

9-8c Dividends of Workplace Diversity

Managers who build strong, diverse organizations reap numerous dividends, as described here and shown in Exhibit 9.16.[130] The dividends of diversity include the following:

Rawpixel.com/Shutterstock.com

- **Better use of employee talent.** Companies with the best talent are the ones with the best competitive advantage. Attracting a diverse workforce is not enough; companies must also provide career opportunities and advancement for minorities and women to retain them.

- **Increased understanding of the marketplace.** A diverse workforce is better able to anticipate and respond to changing consumer needs. Ford Motor Company realized it could reach its business objectives only if it created a workforce that reflected the multicultural face of the country. So it assembled a workforce made up of 25 percent minorities to foster a culture of inclusion; as a result, the company won a spot on *Black Enterprise's* "40 Best Companies for Diversity."[131]

- **Enhanced breadth of understanding in leadership positions.** Homogeneous top management teams tend to be myopic in their perspectives. According to Niall FitzGerald of Unilever, "It is important for any business operating in an increasingly complex and rapidly changing environment to deploy a broad range of talents. That provides a breadth of understanding of the world and environment and a fusion of the very best values and different perspectives which make up that world."[132]

Concept Connection

One important dividend of workplace diversity is **diversity of thought**. Teams such as this one made up of diverse participants typically produce more innovative solutions. Bart Becht, former CEO of Reckitt Benckiser, said, "It doesn't matter whether I have a Pakistani, a Chinese person, a Brit, or a Turk, man or woman, sitting in the same room, or whether I have people from sales or something else, so long as I have people with different experiences—because the chance for new ideas is much greater when you have people with different backgrounds."

- **Increased quality of team problem solving.** Teams with diverse backgrounds bring different perspectives to a discussion that result in more creative ideas and better solutions.[133] A recent research project found that when people participated in diverse teams, their answers to problems were 58 percent more accurate than those of people participating in homogeneous teams. Moreover, performance improved over time as people worked within a diverse group, while performance of the homogeneous groups tended to go in the opposite direction as people began to copy one another or agree to solutions without debate.[134]

- **Reduced costs associated with high turnover, absenteeism, and lawsuits.** Companies that foster a diverse workforce reduce turnover, absenteeism, and the risk of lawsuits. Because family responsibilities contribute to turnover and absenteeism, many companies now offer child-care and elder-care benefits, flexible work arrangements, telecommuting, and part-time employment to accommodate employee responsibilities at home. Discrimination lawsuits are also a costly side effect of a discriminatory work environment. A racial harassment suit against Lockheed Martin Corporation cost the company $2.5 million, the largest individual racial-discrimination payment obtained by the EEOC.[135]

Exhibit 9.16 Dividends of Workplace Diversity

Better use of employee talent

Increased understanding of marketplace

Diversity Dividends

Lower costs related to turnover, absenteeism, lawsuits

Better team problem solving

Enhanced breadth of understanding among managers

SOURCE: Based on Gail Robinson and Kathleen Dechant, "Building a Business Case for Diversity," *Academy of Management Executive* 11, no. 3 (1997): 21–31.

- **Diversity** is defined as all the ways in which employees differ.

- **Inclusion** is the degree to which an employee feels like an esteemed member of a group in which his or her uniqueness is highly appreciated.

- **Diversity of thought** is achieved when a manager creates a heterogeneous team made up of individuals with diverse backgrounds and skill sets.

- **Managing diversity**, which means creating a climate in which the potential advantages of diversity for organizational performance are maximized while the potential disadvantages are minimized, is a key management skill today.

- Corporations that recruit and retain a diverse workforce reap numerous benefits, including improved team problem solving and increased understanding of the marketplace.

- Reckitt Benckiser attributes an increase in sales and income to the diversity of its top management team and workforce.

9-9 Factors Shaping Personal Bias

Recent research by Harvard psychology professor Mahzarin Banaji indicates that the human brain seems to be wired to categorize people by race in the first one-fifth of a second after seeing a face. Banaji's studies suggest that all people have an ingrained propensity to racial bias, even if they are unaware of and even disapprove of such bias. Other studies by social psychologists also suggest that there is a natural tendency among humans to identify themselves with a particular group and to feel somewhat antagonistic and discriminatory toward other groups.[136] This natural force toward separation, combined with other factors such as unconscious bias, prejudice, discrimination, stereotypes, and ethnocentrism, creates a number of challenges for minority managers and employees.

9-9a Unconscious Bias

What judgmental beliefs or attitudes do you have that influence your feelings about diversity in the workplace? Visit MindTap for the "Self-Assessment: What Are Your Workplace Diversity Values?" to see how prepared you are to put stereotypes aside so you can manage effectively.

The deaths of African Americans at the hands of police in Ferguson, Missouri, and other states in recent years have brought the debate about racial bias in the United States to the forefront. Blatant and active discrimination in the workplace is not as big a problem as in the past, but subtle, and often unconscious, bias is still a big problem in organizations. **Unconscious bias** occurs when a person is not aware of the bias in his or her favorable and unfavorable assessments, actions, and decisions toward members of specific groups. As noted, some sociologists and psychologists have proposed that people have innate biases and, left to their own devices, they will automatically discriminate. *Unconscious bias theory* suggests that white males, for example, will inevitably slight women and minorities because people's decisions are influenced by unconscious bias.[137] Consider the following findings related to unconscious bias:[138]

- When researchers mailed thousands of similar résumés, some with stereotypically black names (such as Jamal or Lakisha) and some with stereotypically white names (such as Greg or Emily), to companies with job openings, the résumés with white-sounding names were 50 percent more likely to result in a request for an interview.
- Research has found that women who come to the emergency room with a stroke wait 15 percent longer than men to get brain imaging, even when they have similar symptoms, and severely injured women are 15 percent less likely than severely injured men to be sent from a nontrauma hospital to a trauma center.
- Doctors who were shown patient histories and asked to make decisions about heart disease were much less likely to recommend cardiac catheterization (a helpful procedure) to black patients, even when their medical histories were statistically identical to those of white patients. After a stroke diagnosis, women are up to 30 percent less likely than men to be given one of the main treatment drugs.

- Several studies have found that e-mail messages with stereotypically black names sent in response to apartment rental ads on Craigslist get fewer responses than ones with white-sounding names.
- Studies of state legislators have found that white legislators in both political parties are less likely to respond to constituents with African American–sounding names.

In many cases, these are not acts of conscious discrimination. For example, human resource managers were stunned when shown the results of the résumé study because they truly believed they were making a commitment to valuing diversity in their organizations. Most doctors certainly have no intention to treat women or African American patients less effectively than they do white men. Dozens of researchers have studied and documented bias that occurs outside of our awareness and despite good intentions.[139] You can assess your own unconscious bias toward various groups at https://implicit.harvard.edu/implicit/takeatest.html

Some companies are beginning to address the problem of unconscious or hidden bias. For example, BAE Systems, a large defense contractor, provides unconscious bias training to all employees so that people are aware that their hidden biases may affect decisions. About 20 percent of large corporations now provide unconscious bias training, and diversity consultants say that figure could swell to 50 percent within a few years.[140]

9-9b Workplace Prejudice, Discrimination, and Stereotypes

Beyond hidden or unconscious bias, there are still examples of open and blatant prejudice and discrimination in organizations. **Prejudice** is the tendency to view people who are different as being deficient. If someone acts out their prejudicial attitudes toward people who are the targets of their prejudice, discrimination has occurred.[141] Paying a woman less than a man for the same work is gender discrimination. Mistreating people because they have a different ethnicity is ethnic discrimination. Although blatant discrimination is not as widespread as in the past, bias in the workplace often shows up in subtle ways. "I could go to a meeting and offer an opinion, and it was like I didn't even say a word," said Christine Dale. "A guy can offer the same opinion and it's like, 'Oh, that's brilliant.'"[142] A survey by Korn Ferry International found that 59 percent of minority managers surveyed had observed a racially motivated double standard in the delegation of assignments.[143] One interesting recent study found that while talkative men tend to be seen as powerful and competent, talkative women tend to be perceived as less competent and pushy.[144]

A major component of prejudice is **stereotypes**, which are rigid, exaggerated, irrational beliefs associated with a particular group of people.[145] To be successful managing diversity, managers need to eliminate harmful stereotypes from their thinking, shedding any biases that negatively affect the workplace. For example, old stereotypes often bubble up and block women's rise to higher-level positions. These silent but potent beliefs include the perception that women pose a greater risk in senior positions or that working mothers are unable to hold positions requiring extensive travel and stress. Stereotypes also may block the honest feedback women need for improving their performance.[146]

KEVIN HAGEN/The New York Times/Redux

Concept Connection

Age discrimination makes the challenge of looking for a job even more trying for older workers. While searching for work after he was let go from his job as director of corporate communications at Time Warner, James Kunen says he "was interviewed by 30-year-olds who totally didn't 'get' me." Kunen continues, "You can sense it immediately; it's like being on a bad blind date." **Stereotypes** that plague older job seekers include the beliefs that they are more expensive, harder to train, more likely to leave, and less productive, adaptable, and technologically adept.

Managers can learn to *value differences*, which means that they recognize individual differences and see these differences with an appreciative attitude. To facilitate this attitude, managers can learn about cultural patterns and typical beliefs of groups to help understand why people act the way they do. It helps to understand the difference between these two ways of thinking—most notably that stereotyping is a barrier to diversity, but valuing cultural differences facilitates diversity. These two different ways of thinking are listed in Exhibit 9.17 and described here.[147]

- *Stereotypes are often based on folklore, media portrayals, and other unreliable sources of information.* For example, studies have shown that the traditional stereotype of a "good" manager is masculine and reflects characteristics such as assertiveness and competitiveness. Interestingly, however, for people who have worked in organizations with a high percentage of female managers, that stereotype no longer exists. Those employees often show a stronger preference for feminine characteristics such as caring and compassion.[148] Legitimate cultural differences are backed up by systematic research of real differences, not folklore and supposition.
- *Stereotypes contain negative connotations.* On the other hand, managers who value diversity view differences as potentially positive or neutral. For example, the observation that Asian males are typically less aggressive does not imply they are inferior or superior to white males—it simply means that there is a difference.

Exhibit 9.17 **Difference Between Stereotyping and Valuing Cultural Differences**

Stereotyping	Valuing Cultural Differences
Is based on false assumptions, anecdotal evidence, or impressions without any direct experience with a group	Is based on cultural differences verified by scientific research methods
Assigns negative traits to members of a group	Views cultural differences as positive or neutral
Assumes that all members of a group have the same characteristics	Does not assume that all individuals within a group have the same characteristics
Example: Suzuko Akoi is Asian and is therefore not aggressive by white, male standards.	*Example: As a group, Asians tend to be less aggressive than white, male Americans.*

SOURCE: Adapted from Taylor Cox, Jr., and Ruby L. Beale, *Developing Competency to Manage Diversity: Readings, Cases and Activities* (San Francisco: Berrett-Koehler Publishers, 1997).

- *Stereotypes assume that all members of a group have the same characteristics.* Managers who value diversity recognize that individuals within a group of people may or may not share the same characteristics.[149]

9-9c Challenges Minorities Face

Research shows that it takes longer for people of color to move into their first management job, and minority managers also struggle to move up the hierarchy.[150] Data from the Bureau of Labor Statistics, for example, show that African Americans hold less than 7 percent of the management jobs in the United States, although they account for twice that share of the working-age population. African Americans who have made it into management positions often feel that they have two jobs: one job managing a team, department, or division, and another "representing" people of color for their organization at diversity fairs or other events.[151] The frustration many minority managers feel is reflected in the experiences of two former Twitter managers. As discussed earlier in the chapter, technology companies such as Google, Facebook, and Twitter have recently published reports that show a serious lack of diversity in large technology companies, where African Americans make up about 1 percent of employees. Two former Twitter executives gave a glimpse into what it was like to be African American at Twitter.

Top executives at Twitter, as at other technology companies, are struggling to find ways to diversify their organizations. One dilemma that gets in the way of minority managers is

Sunny Side Up

Mark Luckie and Leslie Miley, Twitter

Mark Luckie, previously Twitter's manager of journalism and media, and Leslie Miley, who was Twitter's highest-ranking black engineer, say they left the company partly because they felt a lack of commitment by top leadership to recruit, hire, develop, and promote racially diverse employees in any meaningful way. Luckie worked from the company's New York office and noted a lack of advancement potential for African Americans. "People who were promoted looked just like their manager," he says, which means they were mostly white.

Miley says that whenever he presented diverse candidates for engineering positions who didn't have typical Silicon Valley educations or backgrounds, he got a laundry list of reasons why they weren't suitable. He claims the numerous talks he had with his boss about ways to improve recruitment and retention of diverse employees went nowhere, and he says at one point the boss told him, "Diversity is fine, but we don't want to lower the bar."[152]

ethnocentrism. **Ethnocentrism** is the belief that one's own group and culture are inherently superior to other groups and cultures. Ethnocentrism makes it difficult for managers to value diversity. Viewing one's own culture as the best culture is a natural tendency among most people. Moreover, the business world still tends to reflect the values, behaviors, and assumptions based on the experiences of a rather homogeneous, white, middle-class male workforce. Ethnocentric viewpoints and a standard set of cultural practices produce a **monoculture**, a culture that accepts only one way of doing things and one set of values and beliefs, which can cause problems for minority employees. People of color, women, people who are gay and transgender, disabled individuals, elderly persons, and other diverse employees may feel undue pressure to conform, may be victims of stereotyping attitudes, and may be presumed deficient because they are different.

The goal for organizations seeking diversity is pluralism rather than a monoculture and ethnorelativism rather than ethnocentrism. **Ethnorelativism** is the belief that groups and subcultures are inherently equal. **Pluralism** means that an organization accommodates several subcultures. Movement toward pluralism seeks to integrate fully into the organization the employees who otherwise would feel isolated and ignored.

Remember This

- **Unconscious bias** occurs when a person is not aware of the bias in his or her favorable and unfavorable assessments, actions, and decisions toward members of specific groups.
- Many researchers have documented unconscious bias in education, government, and the workplace, and companies are beginning to provide unconscious bias training to employees.
- The tendency to view people who are different as being deficient is called **prejudice.**
- **Discrimination** occurs when people act out their negative attitudes toward people who are the targets of their prejudice.
- A rigid, exaggerated, irrational belief associated with a particular group of people is called a **stereotype**.

- One stereotype is that talkative women are less capable and pushy, whereas talkative men are viewed as competent and powerful.
- Minority employees and managers face many challenges because of unconscious bias, prejudice, and stereotypes.
- **Ethnocentrism** is the belief that one's own group is inherently superior to other groups.
- A culture that accepts only one way of doing things and one set of values and beliefs is called a **monoculture**.
- **Ethnorelativism** is the belief that groups and subcultures are inherently equal.
- **Pluralism** describes an environment in which the organization accommodates several subcultures, including employees who would otherwise feel isolated and ignored.

9-10 Factors Affecting Women's Careers

Research shows that companies with several senior-level women outperform those without senior-level women both financially and organizationally. One survey of 58,000 employees in more than 100 global companies revealed that companies with three or more women in top management are perceived to be more capable, have stronger leadership, and inspire higher employee motivation, among other important organizational characteristics.[153] However, there is evidence that women are stalling at the middle-management level.[154] In addition, men as a group still have the benefit of higher wages and faster promotions.

Both the glass ceiling and the decision to "opt out" of a high-pressure career have an impact on women's advancement opportunities and pay. Yet women are sometimes favored in leadership roles for demonstrating behaviors and attitudes that help them succeed in the workplace, a factor called "the female advantage."

9-10a The Glass Ceiling

For the first time in U.S. history, women hold a majority of the nation's jobs.[155] As they move up the career ladder, the numbers of men and women are comparable, with women holding 51 percent of all lower- and mid-level managerial and professional jobs.[156] But very few women break through the glass ceiling to reach senior management positions. In fact, only 4.4 percent of *Fortune* 500 companies had a woman CEO in early 2016. The **glass ceiling** is an invisible barrier that exists for women and minorities that limits their upward mobility in organizations. They can look up through the ceiling and see top management, but prevailing attitudes and stereotypes are invisible obstacles to their own advancement. As described in the Hot Topic on page 345, in addition to societal and institutional barriers, some women believe that mistakes women make in their patterns of communication and power relationships have held them back from achieving higher-level positions.

The glass ceiling also impedes the career progress of minorities. The previous section discussed challenges African American managers face in trying to move up the hierarchy. Asian managers bump up against the *bamboo ceiling*, a combination of cultural and organizational barriers that impede Asians' career progress. Many Asian managers have found themselves stereotyped as "not top manager material" because they are too quiet and unassertive. Today, while Asians make up a good share of the entry-level workforce in certain industries, they make up only 1.5 percent of corporate board members in the United States.[157]

To break through the glass ceiling into senior management roles, top executives suggest female and minority managers follow this advice:

- *Be assertive and ask for what you want.* Women in general are uncomfortable asking for what they want for fear of being perceived as too aggressive or too selfish. Self-doubt and lack of confidence can also hold women back, as Leyla Seka discovered after she almost quit her job at Salesforce because she didn't think she could compete for the promotion she wanted.

Janet Kimber/The Image Bank/Getty Images

Concept Connection

A number of studies conducted around the world in recent years confirm that weight discrimination adds to the **glass ceiling** effect for women. While overweight males are disproportionately represented among CEOs, overweight women are underrepresented. Several years ago, ABC News sent a woman out to interview twice—once appearing to be an individual of normal weight and the second time in padded clothing to appear overweight. She received more job offers as a thin person despite the fact that she handed prospective employers a stronger résumé in her overweight incarnation.

Top executives at Salesforce now actively encourage all managers to talk openly about their career ambitions and to ask for what they want. Seka still fights to overcome what psychologists call "imposter fear," which refers to a fear that she got the job by luck or chance rather than because she deserved it. The "Recipe for Success" further describes how women may hold themselves back because of insecurity or lack of confidence.

- **_Highlight your achievements._** Women tend to downplay their accomplishments and insights. One study found that in a group of men and women who scored the same on a science exam, the women underestimated their performance and refused to enter a science fair, while the men did the opposite.[158] Men, particularly from nonminority groups, typically self-promote their successes. Some women and minority managers are learning to do the same so that they receive recognition and credit.[159] For example, Maggie Wilderotter, former CEO and chairman of Frontier Communications, recalls making points in boardrooms, then watching the group actively take notes when a man later said the same thing. "When that happened, I'd stop the conversation and say, 'Do you realize I said that 10 minutes ago?'"[160]

9-10b The Opt-Out Trend

Some women never hit the glass ceiling because they choose to get off the fast track long before it comes into view. In recent years, an ongoing discussion concerns something referred to as the *opt-out trend*. Research conducted by LeanIn.org and McKinsey & Co. shows that about equal percentages of women and men want to be promoted early in their careers (75 percent and 78 percent, respectively), but only 43 percent of women say they want to be top executives compared to 53 percent of men.[161]

> "The most important factor in determining whether you will succeed isn't your gender, it's you. Be open to opportunity and take risks. In fact, take the worst, the messiest, the most challenging assignment you can find, and then take control."
>
> —ANGELA BRALY, FORMER WELLPOINT CEO

Sunny Side Up   Leyla Seka, Salesforce

Leyla Seka came to Salesforce in 2008 to run its AppExchange unit. After earning three promotions in six years, Seka thought that was as high as she could go. Although Seka wanted to run a business, she didn't think she could compete to become general manager of a Salesforce division. "I assumed I'd never get that job," Seka says. "So I did something I see many women doing. I didn't ask. . . . I just assumed I'd always be 'the AppExchange lady.'"

Rather than talking to top Salesforce executives about her desire for more challenge and responsibility, Seka began applying for jobs outside the company. After she got an offer to head sales and marketing at another firm, Seka decided to express her frustration to her bosses at Salesforce. Cofounder Parker Harris was surprised to learn that Seka was thinking about quitting and told her he'd been in discussions with CEO Marc Benioff about promoting her. Harris encouraged her to consider becoming a general manager at Salesforce. Seka says she "felt kind of giddy" at the idea and realized that it was her own insecurities that were limiting her.

She turned down the other job offer, and today, Seka is a Salesforce senior vice president and general manager of Desk.com, a division that serves small business. "I've never had more fun at work, and I've never felt more challenged and engaged," Seka says. "I almost missed this opportunity, by shutting the doors on myself."[161]

Quite a debate rages over the reasons for the large number of women who drop out of striving for higher management levels. Opt-out proponents say women are deciding that corporate success isn't worth the price in terms of reduced family and personal time, increased stress, and negative health effects.[163] Anne-Marie Slaughter, a Princeton professor and a former top aide to Hillary Clinton when Clinton was U.S. Secretary of State, left her prestigious position to spend more time at home with a rebellious teenager. Unable to balance work and family with success, Slaughter challenged the concept that women can "have it all" in a controversial article in *The*

Atlantic. In the piece, Slaughter said that today's workplace needs to adapt, and women who opt out have no need to apologize. "Women of my generation have clung to the feminist credo we were raised with . . . because we are determined not to drop the flag for the next generation," Ms. Slaughter wrote. "But when many members of the younger generation have stopped listening, on the grounds that glibly repeating 'you can have it all' is simply airbrushing reality, it is time to talk."[164]

One school of thought says that women don't want corporate power and status in the same way that men do, and clawing one's way up the corporate ladder has become less appealing. Yet critics argue that this view is just another way to blame women themselves for the dearth of female managers at higher levels.[165] The LeanIn.org and McKinsey & Company research cited earlier found that 25 percent of women felt that their gender had hindered their career progress, particularly as they reached higher organizational levels.[166] Vanessa Castagna says she left JCPenney after decades with the company not because she wanted more family or personal time, but because she kept getting passed over for top jobs.[167] Although some women are voluntarily leaving the fast track, many more genuinely want to move up the corporate ladder but find their paths blocked.[168] A survey of women voluntarily leaving executive jobs in *Fortune* 1000 companies found that corporate culture was cited as the number-one reason for leaving.[169] The greatest disadvantages of women leaders stem largely from prejudicial attitudes and a heavily male-oriented corporate culture.[170] Consider, for example, that men with children are perceived as more stable and more committed to their work, which is reflected in higher pay, while women with children are less likely to be hired and less likely to be perceived as competent at work or to be paid as much as their male colleagues with the same qualifications. Michelle Budig, a sociology professor at the University of Massachusetts, Amherst, found that men's pay increased an average of 6 percent once they had children, but women's decreased 4 percent for each child they had. In other research, Shelley J. Correll, a sociology professor at Stanford University and director of the school's Clayman Institute for Gender Research, found that employers rate fathers as the most desirable employees, while mothers are rated the least desirable. Correll's research also shows that companies hold mothers to harsher performance standards.[171]

9-10c The Female Advantage

Are you guilty of gender bias when it comes to your attitudes toward authority? Visit MindTap for the Self-Assessment: "Do You Have a Gender and Authority Bias?" to see if your biases are creating a stumbling block in your ability to embrace diversity.

Some people think women might actually be better managers, partly because of a more collaborative, less hierarchical, more relationship-oriented approach that is in tune with today's global and multicultural environment.[172] The movement of more women into management positions has coincided with a transition in many organizations to a preference for a nonhierarchical, collaborative, and inclusive style of management that women seem particularly suited for.[173] As attitudes and values change with changing generations, the qualities that women seem to possess naturally may lead to a gradual role reversal in organizations. For example, a stunning gender reversal is taking place in U.S. education with girls taking over almost every leadership role from kindergarten to graduate school. In addition, women of all races and ethnic groups are outpacing men in earning bachelor's and master's degrees.[174] Women are rapidly closing the M.D. and Ph.D. gap, and they make up about half of all U.S. law students, half of all undergraduate business majors, and about 30 percent of MBA candidates. Overall, women's participation in both the labor force and civic affairs has steadily increased since the mid-1950s, while men's participation has slowly but steadily declined.[175]

According to James Gabarino, an author and professor of human development at Cornell University, women are "better able to deliver in terms of what modern society requires of people— paying attention, abiding by rules, being verbally competent, and dealing with interpersonal relationships in offices."[176] His observation is supported by the fact that female managers are typically rated higher by subordinates on interpersonal skills, as well as on factors such as task behavior, communication, ability to motivate others, and goal accomplishment.[177] In one study of 16,000 male and female leaders, women were rated higher than men on 12 of 16 competencies.[178] Research has found a correlation between balanced gender composition in companies (i.e., roughly equal male and female representation) and higher organizational performance. Moreover, a study by Catalyst indicates that organizations with the highest percentage of women in top management financially outperform, by about 35 percent, those with the lowest percentage of women in higher-level jobs.[179]

Remember This

- Companies that promote women to senior-level positions outperform those without women in these positions, both financially and organizationally.
- The **glass ceiling** is an invisible barrier that separates women and minorities from senior management positions.
- Proponents of the opt-out trend say that some women choose to leave the workforce because they decide success isn't worth it in terms of reduced family and personal time, increased stress, and negative health effects.

- Critics say that this opinion is just a way to blame women for the scarcity of female top managers and argue that organizations must change.
- One study found that fathers are rated as the most desirable employees, while mothers are rated the least desirable.
- Women are likely to be more collaborative, less hierarchical, and more relationship-oriented than men, qualities that prepare them to succeed in today's multicultural work environment.

9-11 Diversity Initiatives and Programs

In responding to a survey by the Society for Human Resource Management, 91 percent of company executives said they believe diversity initiatives and programs help maintain a competitive advantage. Some specific benefits they cited include improving employee morale, decreasing interpersonal conflict, facilitating progress in new markets, and increasing the organization's creativity.[180]

9-11a Enhancing Structures and Policies

Many policies within organizations originally were designed to fit the stereotypical male employee. Now leading companies are changing structures and policies to facilitate and support diversity. For example, the U.K. telecommunications company Vodafone recently adopted a new global policy that gives women 16 weeks of maternity leave and then lets new moms work 30-hour work weeks at full-time salaries for six months after they return to work. Vodafone executives believe giving new mothers the flexibility they need is one way the company can keep more women and move them up the hierarchy.[181] Most large organizations have formal policies against racial and gender discrimination, as well as structured grievance procedures and complaint review processes. Companies are also developing policies to support the recruitment and career advancement of diverse employees. Many have added a new senior management position called *chief diversity officer*, whose role is to create working environments where women and minorities can flourish. About 60 percent of *Fortune* 500 companies have chief diversity officers. Among them, 65 percent are women and 37 percent are African American.[182] Increasingly, organizations such as Proctor & Gamble (P&G), Ernst & Young, and Allstate Insurance are tying managers' bonuses and promotions to how well they diversify the workforce. Exhibit 9.18 illustrates some of the most common diversity initiatives.

Exhibit 9.18 The Most Common Diversity Initiatives: Percentage of *Fortune* 1000 Respondents

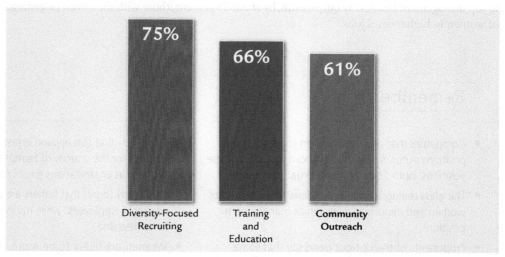

SOURCE: Adapted from data in "Impact of Diversity Initiatives on the Bottom Line: A SHRM Survey of the *Fortune* 1000," pp. S12–S14, in *Fortune*, special advertising section, "Keeping Your Edge: Managing a Diverse Corporate Culture," produced in association with the Society for Human Resource Management, www.fortune.com/sections

Managers at Google and Intel are implementing new programs to address the problem of unconscious bias, as defined earlier, and try to bring more diversity into technology companies.

Sunny Side Up } Google and Intel

Laszlo Bock, Google's senior vice president for people operations, says that "you don't usually see outright manifestations of bias" at the company. "Occasionally you'll have some idiot do something stupid and hurtful, and I like to fire those people." But Bock and other Google executives know it's the hidden and often unconscious biases that can be the real problem. Google began diversity training workshops for all employees in 2013 to help people confront and overcome the bias hidden within themselves, with particular focus on how unconscious biases affect hiring and promotion decisions. Although there are few explicit results yet, Google leaders say just acknowledging the problem is starting to shift Google to a more inclusive culture.

At Intel, leaders are taking more concrete steps. In early 2015, the company announced a goal of increasing the number of women, African Americans, Hispanics, and other minority groups by at least 14 percent within five years. "This is the right time to make a bold statement," said Intel CEO Brian M. Krzanich. Intel also set up a $300 million fund to be used to improve diversity in its workforce, attract more women and minorities to the technology field, and make the industry more open to minorities. The Rev. Jesse L. Jackson, Sr., who led a campaign to pressure technology companies on diversity, welcomed Intel's bold move and believes it will compel other companies to follow their lead.[183]

Managers at Google and Intel hope bringing the problem into the open is a start toward a more diverse technology industry. Leaders in other industries are also struggling to increase diversity and inclusiveness.

9-11b Expanding Recruitment Efforts

For many organizations, a new approach to recruitment means making better use of formal recruiting strategies, offering internship programs to give people opportunities, and developing creative ways to draw on previously unused labor markets. Nationwide sends recruiters, including top executives and board members, to conferences run by groups such as the National Black MBA Association, the Anita Borg Institute (an advocate for women in technology), and the National Society of Hispanic MBAs to hire full-time employees as well as interns.[184] At Change.org, a start-up company that offers online petition software to create social change, women make up 51 percent of the employees, 40 percent of the management team, and 27 percent of the engineering team. CEO Jennifer Dulski says the company's success in hiring and promoting women comes from actively working with programs that train female engineers, hosting speaking and networking events, and using mentoring programs and other innovative recruiting and development strategies.[185]

Concept Connection

A counselor for CAMBA, a social services group in New York City, directs a role-playing session during a course to help immigrants apply for jobs at Whole Foods Market. The grocer helped CAMBA develop the course to support its **diversity recruiting goals**. The classes include instruction on organic foods, customer service, and tours of Whole Foods Markets.

Ruby Washington/The New York Times/Redux

9-11c Establishing Mentor Relationships

The successful advancement of diverse employees means that organizations must find ways to eliminate the glass ceiling. One of the most successful structures to accomplish this goal is the mentoring relationship. A **mentor** is a higher-ranking organizational member who is committed to providing upward mobility and support to a protégé's professional career.[186] Mentoring provides minorities and women with direct training and inside information on the norms and expectations of the organization. A mentor also acts as a friend or counselor, enabling the employee to feel more confident and capable. Companies are also using *reverse mentoring*. Rather than having an older, more experienced manager mentor a younger employee, reverse mentoring has younger managers and employees helping older workers navigate the challenges they face with new technology. Some companies, such as Cisco, have been using reverse mentoring for years, and its use is likely to grow as organizations face increasing generational diversity, with people of widely varying ages and experience working side by side.[187]

One researcher who studied the career progress of high-potential minorities found that those who advance the most all share one characteristic—a strong mentor or network of mentors who nurtured their professional development.[188] However, research also indicates that minorities, as well as women, are much less likely than white men to develop mentoring relationships.[189] The solution is for organizations to overcome some of the barriers to mentoring relationships between white males and minorities. When organizations can institutionalize the value of white males actively seeking women and minority protégés, the benefits will mean that women and minorities will be steered into pivotal jobs and positions critical to advancement. Mentoring programs also are consistent with the Civil Rights Act of 1991, which requires the diversification of middle and upper management.

9-11d Increasing Awareness of Sexual Harassment

Although psychological closeness between men and women in the workplace may be a positive experience, sexual harassment is not. It is illegal. As a form of sexual discrimination, sexual harassment in the workplace is a violation of Title VII of the 1964 Civil Rights Act. Sexual harassment in the classroom is a violation of Title VIII of the Education Amendment of 1972. Many companies offer sexual harassment awareness programs that create awareness of what defines sexual harassment and the legal ramifications of violations. The following list categorizes various forms of sexual harassment as defined by one university:

- *Generalized.* This form involves sexual remarks and actions that are not intended to lead to sexual activity but that are directed toward a coworker based solely on gender and reflect on the entire group.
- *Inappropriate/offensive.* Although it is not sexually threatening, the behavior causes discomfort in a coworker, whose reaction in avoiding the harasser may limit his or her freedom and ability to function in the workplace.
- *Solicitation with promise of reward.* This action treads a fine line as an attempt to "purchase" sex, with the potential for criminal prosecution.
- *Coercion with threat of punishment.* The harasser coerces a coworker into sexual activity by using the threat of power (through recommendations, grades, promotions, and so on) to jeopardize the victim's career.
- *Sexual crimes and misdemeanors.* The highest level of sexual harassment, these acts would, if reported to the police, be considered felonies or misdemeanors.[190]

A recent example comes from the city of San Diego, where more than a dozen women accused former mayor Bob Filner of making unwanted sexual advances, including groping, kissing, and making lewd comments. One woman says that Filner asked her to work without panties, told her he wanted to see her naked, and dragged her in a headlock while whispering in her ear. Filner continued to proclaim his innocence and refused for months to resign, agreeing to step down only after the city agreed to pick up some of his legal costs in order to avoid the time and expense of a recall. The scandal left the city in turmoil.[191]

9-11e Encouraging Employee Affinity Groups

Employee affinity groups are based on social identity, such as gender or race, and are organized within companies to focus on concerns of employees from that group.[192] For example, about 100 women participate in Change.org's WHOA (Women Helping Others Achieve) affinity group. Members meet monthly to talk about issues of interest or concern.[193] Affinity groups pursue a variety of activities, such as meetings to educate top managers, mentoring programs, networking events, training sessions and skills seminars, minority intern programs, and community volunteer activities. These activities give people a chance to meet, interact with, and develop social and professional ties to others throughout the organization, which may include key decision makers. Affinity groups provide a powerful way to reduce social isolation for women and minorities, help these employees be more effective, and enable members to achieve greater career advancement. Research confirms that affinity groups can be important tools for helping organizations retain managerial-level minority employees.[194] For example, when she was a senior vice president at Best Buy, Julie Gilbert launched a women's leadership forum, known as WOLF, to get more women involved in solving core business problems and to pull frontline employees into the top ranks. As a result of these "WOLF packs," recruitment of female regional sales managers increased 100 percent over the previous year, and turnover among women managers dropped almost 10 percentage points.[195]

Affinity groups for minorities who have faced barriers to advancement in organizations, including African Americans, Hispanics, Native Americans, Asian Americans, women, gays and lesbians, and disabled employees, are growing in number. Even managers who once thought

Concept Connection

Caterpillar's commitment to diversity and to the development of leaders from diverse backgrounds is supported by the number of affinity groups within the company. Employees can participate in **support networks and affinity groups** for African Americans, Chinese, Asian Indians, Koreans, and Latinos, as well as young professionals, women, armed forces veterans, experienced professionals, and gay, lesbian, bisexual, and transgendered employees.

Stockbyte/Photos.com

of these as "gripe groups" are now seeing them as essential to organizational success because they help to retain minority employees, enhance diversity efforts, and spark new ideas that can benefit the organization.[196] When people feel that they are making genuine contributions and have a chance to advance in their careers because of it, engagement soars. "At some of our events, the buzz in the room is magnificent," said Shakrat Alli, chairwoman of Britain's Crown Prosecution Service's affinity group for African Americans (the National Black Crown Prosecution Association). "People return to the workplace with the sense that everything is possible."[197] In general, female and minority employees who participate in an affinity group feel more pride about their work and are more optimistic about their careers than those who do not have the support of a group.[198]

Remember This

- Many organizations have added a new senior management position called *chief diversity officer* whose role is to spearhead diversity efforts and cultivate working environments that help women and minorities flourish.

- A **mentor** is a higher-ranking senior member of the organization who is committed to providing upward mobility and support to a protégé's professional career.

- Some companies are using *reverse mentoring*, in which younger managers and employees help older workers navigate the challenges they face with new technology.

- To eliminate sexual harassment, companies may offer sexual harassment awareness programs that define harassment and the legal ramifications of it.

- **Employee affinity groups** are based on social identity, such as gender or race, and are organized to focus on the concerns of employees from that group.

- The National Black Crown Prosecution Association is an employee affinity group for African Americans at Britain's Crown Prosecution Service.

DISCUSSION QUESTIONS

1. Does it seem like a good idea to let a big data computer program make hiring decisions, as some companies like Xerox are doing? What types of positions do you think this might be suitable for? What might be some drawbacks to this approach?

2. Assume that it is the year 2027. In your company, central planning has given way to frontline decision making, and bureaucracy has given way to teamwork. Shop floor workers use handheld devices and robots. A labor shortage currently affects many job openings, and the few applicants that you do attract lack skills to work in teams, make their own production decisions, or use sophisticated technology. As vice president of HRM since 2015, what might you have done to prepare for this situation?

3. Is it wise for managers to evaluate a promising candidate's tweets or postings on social media sites as grounds for rejection before even interviewing him or her? What might be some ethical and legal issues for managers to consider? Discuss.

4. One HR manager recently got a thank-you note on her iPhone that said "Thx 4 the Iview!" The manager had liked the candidate in the interview, but after getting this note, she put him in the reject pile. Why do you think she rejected the candidate? Was that fair? Should "textspeak" be considered acceptable workplace communication? Discuss.

5. How do you think feedback based on a 360-degree feedback system would be received by employees in Germany or China (see Exhibit 9.10) compared to employees in America? How about feedback from a forced ranking system? Which system—360 or forced ranking—would be more suitable for each country? Discuss.

6. How would you go about deciding whether to use a job-based, skills-based, or pay-for-performance compensation plan for employees in a textile manufacturing plant? For waitstaff in a restaurant? For salespeople in an insurance company?

7. Evaluate your own personal experiences with people from other cultural backgrounds. How well do you think those experiences have prepared you to understand the unique needs and dilemmas of a diverse workforce?

8. Until Sheryl Sandberg was promoted to chief operating officer of Facebook in 2012, its board was composed of only men. Yet a majority of Facebook's 845 million users are women. Given this demographic, explain how Facebook might benefit from increasing the presence of women on its corporate board.

9. If talkative men are viewed as powerful and competent, why do you think talkative women are seen as less capable and pushy? Do you think this perception would be different in an organization with a large percentage of female managers at top levels?

10. Describe how diversity of thought boosts creativity and innovation in the workplace. Why do managers consider diversity of thought a competitive advantage?

11. How might organizations strike a balance between respecting and meeting the needs of a diverse workforce and shaping a high-performance corporate culture where shared values contribute to the accomplishment of strategic goals?

APPLY YOUR SKILLS: SELF-LEARNING

How Tolerant Are You?[199]

For each of the following questions, circle the answer that best describes you.

1. Most of your friends:
   a. Are very similar to you
   b. Are very different from you and from each other
   c. Are like you in some respects but different in others

2. When someone does something you disapprove of, you:
   a. Break off the relationship
   b. Tell how you feel but keep in touch
   c. Tell yourself that it doesn't really matter and behave as you always have

3. Which virtue is most important to you?
   a. Kindness
   b. Objectivity
   c. Obedience

4. When it comes to beliefs, you:
   a. Do all you can to make others see things the same way you do
   b. Advance your point of view actively, but stop short of argument
   c. Keep your feelings to yourself

5. Would you hire a person who has had emotional problems?
   a. No
   b. Yes, provided that the person shows evidence of complete recovery
   c. Yes, if the person is suitable for the job

6. Do you voluntarily read material that supports views different from your own?
   a. Never
   b. Sometimes
   c. Often

7. You react to elderly people with:
   a. Patience
   b. Annoyance
   c. Sometimes *a*, sometimes *b*

8. Do you agree with the statement, "What is right and wrong depends upon the time, place, and circumstance"?
   a. Strongly agree
   b. Agree to a point
   c. Strongly disagree

9. Would you marry someone from a different race?
   a. Yes
   b. No
   c. Probably not

10. If someone in your family were homosexual, you would:
    a. View this as a problem and try to change the person to a heterosexual orientation
    b. Accept the person as a homosexual with no change in feelings or treatment
    c. Avoid or reject the person

11. You react to little children with:
    a. Patience
    b. Annoyance
    c. Sometimes *a*, sometimes *b*

12. Other people's personal habits annoy you:
    a. Often
    b. Not at all
    c. Only if extreme

13. If you stay in a household run differently from yours (in terms of cleanliness, manners, meals, and other customs), you:
    a. Adapt readily
    b. Quickly become uncomfortable and irritated
    c. Adjust for a while, but not for long

14. Which statement do you agree with most?
    a. We should avoid judging others because no one can fully understand the motives of another person.
    b. People are responsible for their actions and must accept the consequences of their actions.
    c. Both motives and actions are important when considering questions of right and wrong.

Scoring and Interpretation Circle your score for each of the answers and total the scores:

1. a = 4; b = 0; c = 2

2. a = 4; b = 2; c = 0

3. a = 0; b = 2; c = 4

4. a = 4; b = 2; c = 0

5. a = 4; b = 2; c = 0

6. a = 4; b = 2; c = 0

7. a = 0; b = 4; c = 2

8. a = 0; b = 2; c = 4

9. a = 0; b = 4; c = 2

10. a = 2; b = 0; c = 4

11. a = 0; b = 4; c = 2

12. a = 4; b = 0; c = 2

13. a = 0; b = 4; c = 2

14. a = 0; b = 4; c = 2

Total Score

0–14: If you score 14 or below, you are a very tolerant person, and dealing with diversity comes easily to you.

15–28: You are basically a tolerant person, and others think of you that way. In general, diversity presents few problems for you; you may be broad-minded in some areas and have less-tolerant ideas in other areas of life, such as attitudes toward older people or male–female social roles.

29–42: You are less tolerant than most people and should work on developing greater tolerance of people different from you. Your low tolerance level could affect your business or personal relationships.

43–56: You have a very low tolerance for diversity. The only people that you are likely to respect are those with beliefs similar to your own. You reflect a level of intolerance that could cause difficulties in today's multicultural business environment.

APPLY YOUR SKILLS: GROUP LEARNING

Management Competencies[200]

Step 1. An important responsibility of the HR department at many companies is to develop a list of managerial competencies and then to provide training to help managers improve on those competencies. The following list includes desired manager competencies from IBM. Make notes to the right of each competency describing the management behaviors that you think would be covered.

Desired Competencies	Management Behaviors
Having collaborative influence	
Developing IBM people and communities	
Earning trust	
Embracing challenge	

Enabling growth	
Having passion for IBM's future	
Using strategic risk taking	
Thinking horizontally	

Step 2. In groups of three to five students, compare, discuss, and agree upon the expected behaviors for each competency. One student should be the recorder and be prepared to report the behaviors to the class.

Step 3. After agreeing upon competency behaviors, students should take turns stating the competencies they believe will be easiest and hardest for them to master.

Step 4. Why do you think IBM arrived at this set of competencies? How do you think it might differ from management or leadership competencies for other companies?

Step 5. Outside of class, go online and look up information on IBM's competencies. (Search for "IBM Leadership Competencies.") Are the competencies defined as you expected? Look up competencies for a company as well. Why do you think HR departments in this company puts so much energy into developing a list of desired manager competencies?

APPLY YOUR SKILLS: ACTION LEARNING

Gender and Management

This exercise will help you to examine the differences in career and family life of male versus female managers.

1. Divide into groups of two. It would be good if you can have a male and a female paired up, but that won't be possible for the whole class. Each of you will interview two managers.

2. Choose two managers to interview personally, one male, one female. They must have been managers at least 15 years and they should be roughly in the same level of position in their own organizations. And they should be close to the same age. The questions to ask follow.

3. After your interviews, get together with your partner and discuss similarities and differences between the male and female managers.

4. Write a report to give to your instructor.

5. Be prepared to talk about your findings in class without giving any managers' names.

Questions to ask in interview. You may ask other ones, as well. Let the managers know that you are doing a study on gender issues and management for a course. Answers will be kept confidential. No identifying information will be given to the teacher.

Question	Female Manager's Answer	Male Manager's Answer
1. What education do you have?		
2. How did you start your career?		
3. What were your career aspirations when you started out?		
4. What were the obstacles in your career advancement?		

Question	Female Manager's Answer	Male Manager's Answer
5. Are you married? Have children? What ages?		
6. Do women and men make different types of managers?		
7. Is it different now for women than it used to be?		
8. What would you do differently than you did in your career?		
9. What do you wish had been different for you?		

APPLY YOUR SKILLS: ETHICAL DILEMMA

Sunset Prayers[201]

Frank Piechowski, plant manager for a Minnesota North Woods Appliance Corporation refrigerator plant, just received his instructions from the vice president for manufacturing. He was to hire 40 more temporary workers through Twin Cities Staffing, the local labor agency that North Woods used. Frank already knew from past experience that most, if not all, of the new hires available to work the assembly line would be Muslim Somali refugees, people who had immigrated to Minnesota from their war-torn native country en masse over the past 15 years.

North Woods, like all appliance manufacturers, was trying to survive in a highly competitive, mature industry. Appliance companies were competing mainly on price. The entrance of large chains such as Best Buy and Home Depot only intensified the price wars, not to mention that consumers could easily do comparison shopping before leaving home by logging on to the Internet. The pressure to keep production costs low was considerable.

That's where the Somali workers came in. In an effort to keep labor costs low, North Woods was relying more and more on temporary workers rather than increasing the ranks of permanent employees. Frank was quite pleased with the Somalis already at work on the assembly line. Although few in number, they were responsible, hardworking, and willing to work for the wages that he could afford to pay.

It was the first time this son of Polish immigrants had ever come into contact with Muslims, but so far, it had gone well. Frank had established a good working relationship with the Somalis' spokesperson, Halima Adan, who explained that unlike most Western faiths, Islamic religious practices were inextricably woven into everyday life. As a result of the good rapport they had, together they had worked out ways to accommodate Muslim customs. Frank authorized changes in the plant's cafeteria menu so that the Somali workers had more options that conformed to their dietary restrictions, and he allowed women to wear traditional clothing, so long as they weren't violating safety standards.

After learning that the Somalis would need to perform at least some of the ceremonial washing and prayers they were required to do five times a day during work hours, the plant manager set aside a quiet, clean room where they could observe their 15-minute rituals during their breaks and at sunset. The Maghrib sunset prayers that second-shift workers had to perform were disruptive to a smooth workflow. Compared to their midday and afternoon rituals, the Muslim faithful had considerably less leeway as to when they said the sunset prayers, and, of course, the sun set at a slightly different time each day. But so far, they'd all coped.

But what was Frank going to do about the sunset prayers with an influx of 40 Somali workers that would dramatically increase the number of people who would need to leave the line to pray? Was it time to modify his policy? He knew that Title VII of the Civil Rights Act required that he make "reasonable" accommodations to his employees' religious practices unless doing so would impose an "undue hardship" on the employer. Had he reached the point where the accommodations that Halima Adan would probably request crossed the line from reasonable to unreasonable? But if he changed his policy, did he risk alienating his workforce?

What Would You Do?

1. Continue the current policy that leaves it up to the Muslim workers as to when they leave the assembly line to perform their sunset rituals.

2. Try to hire the fewest possible Muslim workers so the work line will be efficient on second shift.

3. Ask the Muslim workers to delay their sunset prayers until a regularly scheduled break occurs, pointing out that North Woods is primarily a place of business, not a house of worship.

APPLY YOUR SKILLS: CASE FOR CRITICAL ANALYSIS

The Right Way with Employees?

As a senior manager for a global player in automobile production and sales, Kirby Ellis had joined thousands of fellow employees in the excitement surrounding production of the company's new hybrid vehicles.

But barely two years into production, embarrassing component shortages, delivery delays, and a recall of the first models had a ripple effect, presenting the company with mounting concerns. In the confusion, many customers canceled orders and turned to competitors for purchase of the eco-friendly vehicles. Ellis's company was facing a financial downturn.

With three decades of service to the company, Kirby led a contingent of managers' intent upon keeping together as much of the company and as many employees as possible.

"We know there will be some necessary cuts," Kirby admitted. "But this company has a long history of sticking by its people. Our first priority should be internal streamlining of how we do things and making sure we have the right people on board."

Many managers liked what they heard from Kirby. He was well respected and had an unequaled reputation for his leadership and collaborative skills and his ability to work with managers as well as line workers on the factory floors. People marveled at the number of individuals he knew on a personal level throughout the company.

Drew Cunningham influenced a second contingent within the management group. A brash go-getter with a reputation for *fixing* companies in crisis, he proposed across-the-board cuts in employees in order to implement a solution as quickly as possible. He proposed the immediate creation of a forced ranking system in order to identify and get rid of lower-ranking employees.

Kirby raised his hand and rose to his feet in objection. "So we're going to create a system to *fire* . . ."

"I didn't say *fire* . . ."

"OK, *cut* our own hard-working people? It sounds like some lame government commission," Kirby said. "We've got bright people. This thing simply got worse faster than we thought. We can work with the people we have in setting up more efficient workflow, establishing reasonable deadlines to increase output and . . . ."

"Kirby, these are not the days of knowing everyone in the plant," Drew said. "You're not throwing out your wife's uncle Harry. We are taking a serious look at what we do, how we do it, and streamlining everything by keeping the right people in the organization and cutting the rest."

Questions

1. What kind of employee social contract is assumed by Kirby and by Drew? Explain.

2. If you were an HR manager at the company, which view would you support? Why?

3. HR departments hire and develop human capital to serve the organization's strategy and drive performance. Which approach—Kirby's or Drew's—is more likely to have a greater positive impact on performance? Discuss.

ENDNOTES

1. Kevin McCoy, "Study Finds Absurd Excuses for Calling in Sick to Work," *USA Today*, October 16, 2015, http://www.usatoday.com/story/money/business/2015/10/16/study-finds-absurd-excuses-calling-sick-work/74044732/ (accessed April 17, 2016).

2. Robert L. Mathis and John H. Jackson, *Human Resource Management: Essential Perspectives*, 2d ed. (Cincinnati, OH: South-Western Publishing, 2002), p. 1.

3. Joann S. Lublin, "HR Executives Suddenly Get Hot" (Theory & Practice column), *The Wall Street Journal*, December 14, 2009.

4. Ram Charan, Dominic Barton, and Dennis Carey, "People Before Strategy: A New Role for the CHRO," *Harvard Business Review* (July–August 2015): 63–71; and Peter Cappelli and J. R. Keller, "Talent Management: Conceptual Approaches and Practical Challenges," *Annual Review of Organization Psychology and Organizational Behavior* 1 (2014): 305–331.

5. This definition is based on George Bohlander, Scott Snell, and Arthur Sherman, *Managing Human Resources*, 12th ed. (Cincinnati, OH: South-Western, 2001), pp. 13–15.

6. "Leading Through Connections: The IBM 2012 Chief Executive Officer Study," reported in Eric Lesser and Carl Hoffman, "Workforce Analytics: Making the Most of a Critical Asset," *Ivey Business Journal* (July–August 2012), www.iveybusinessjournal.com/topics/strategy/workforce-analytics-making-the-most-of-a-critical-asset (accessed August 27, 2012).

7. Charan, Barton, and Carey, "People Before Strategy: A New Role for the CHRO"; James C. Wimbush, "Spotlight on Human Resource Management," *Business Horizons* 48 (2005): 463–467; Jonathan Tompkins, "Strategic Human Resources Management in Government: Unresolved Issues," *Public Personnel Management* (Spring 2002): 95–110; Cynthia A. Lengnick-Hall and Mark L. Lengnick-Hall, "Strategic Human Resources Management: A Review of the Literature and a Proposed Typology," *Academy of Management Review* 13 (July 1988): 454–470.

8. P. Wright, G. McMahan, and A. McWilliams, "Human Resources and Sustained Competitive Advantage: A Resource-Based Perspective," *International Journal of Human Resource Management* 5 (1994): 301–326; Tompkins, "Strategic Human Resource Management in Government."

9. Liza Castro Christiansen and Malcolm Higgs, "How the Alignment of Business Strategy and HR Strategy Can Impact Performance," *Journal of General Management* 33, no. 4 (Summer 2008): 13–33; Seema Sanghi, "Building Competencies," *Industrial Management* (May–June 2009): 14–17; B. Becker and M. Huselid, "High Performance Work Systems and Firm Performance: A Synthesis of Research and Managerial Implications," *Research in Personnel and Human Resources Management* 16 (1998): 53–101; S. Ramlall, "Measuring Human Resource Management's Effectiveness in Improving Performance," *Human Resource Planning* 26 (2003): 51; Mark A. Huselid, Susan E. Jackson, and Randall S. Schuler, "Technical and Strategic Human Resource Management Effectiveness as Determinants of Firm Performance," *Academy of Management Journal* 40, no. 1 (1997): 171–188; and John T. Delaney and Mark A. Huselid, "The Impact of Human Resource Management Practices on Perceptions of Organizational Performance," *Academy of Management Journal* 39, no. 4 (1996): 949–969.

10. Mike Ramsey, "Tesla Ramps Up Hiring as Rivals Loom," *The Wall Street Journal*, December 28, 2015, http://www.wsj.com/articles/tesla-ramps-up-hiring-as-rivals-loom-1451350702 (accessed April 11, 2016).

11. Susan Carey and Jack Nicas, "Airline-Pilot Shortage Arrives Ahead of Schedule," *The Wall Street Journal*, February 3, 2014, http://www.wsj.com/articles/SB10001424052702304851104579361320202756500 (accessed April 11, 2016).

12. James N. Baron and David M. Kreps, "Consistent Human Resource Practices," *California Management Review* 41, no. 3 (Spring 1999): 29–53.

13. Cynthia D. Fisher, "Current and Recurrent Challenges in HRM," *Journal of Management* 15 (1989): 157–180.

14. This discussion is based in part on Bohlander, Snell, and Sherman, *Managing Human Resources*, pp. 13–15; and Harry Scarbrough, "Recipe for Success," *People Management* (January 23, 2003): 22–25.

15. Susan Cantrell et al., "Measuring the Value of Human Capital Investments: The SAP Case," *Strategy & Leadership* 34, no. 2 (2006): 43–52.

16. Section 1604.1 of the EEOC Guidelines based on the Civil Rights Act of 1964, Title VII.

17. Reported in Jeff Green, "The Silencing of Sexual Harassment," *Bloomberg BusinessWeek* (November 21–27, 2011): 27–28.

18. Ibid.

19. Melissa Chan, "Bryan Adams Cancels Mississippi Show Over New Religious Freedom Law," *Time* (April 11, 2016), http://time.com/4288369/bryan-adams-mississippi-cancels-show/ (accessed April 11, 2016); and Bracey Harris, "Coca-Cola Latest to Seek 'Religious Freedom' Law Repeal," *The Clarion-Ledger*, April 8, 2016, http://www.clarionledger.com/story/news/2016/04/08/coca-cola-latest-ask-religious-freedom-repeal/82804246/ (accessed April 11, 2016).

20. Melanie Trottman, "For Angry Employees, Legal Cover for Rants," *The Wall Street Journal*, December 2, 2011, http://online.wsj.com/article/SB10001424052970203710704577049822809710332.html (accessed August 27, 2012); and Adriana Gardella, "Here's Why Employees Can Trash Their Bosses on Social Media," *Forbes*, May 21, 2015, http://www.forbes.com/sites/adrianagardella/2015/05/21/can-your-employees-trash-you-on-social-media/#66e26a8e36b6 (accessed April 11, 2016).

21. Reported in D. T. Hall and P. H. Mirvis, "The New Protean Career: Psychological Success and the Path with a Heart," in D. T. Hall & Associates, *The Career Is Dead—Long Live the Career: A Relational Approach to Careers* (San Francisco: Jossey-Bass, 1995), pp. 15–45.

22. Cappelli and Keller, "Talent Management: Conceptual Approaches and Practical Challenges"; and Reid Hoffman, Ben Casnocha, and Chris Yeh, "Tours of Duty: The New Employer-Employee Compact," *Harvard Business Review* (June 2013): 49–58.

23. Hoffman, Casnocha, and Yeh, "Tours of Duty: The New Employer-Employee Compact."

24. Lynda Gratton, as reported in Phyllis Korkki, "The Shifting Definition of Worker Loyalty," *The New York Times*, April 23, 2011, www.nytimes.com/2011/04/24/jobs/24search.html (accessed August 27, 2012).

25. Stephen Baker, "You're Fired—But Stay in Touch," *BusinessWeek* (May 4, 2009): 54–55.

26. Hoffman, Casnocha, and Yeh, "Tours of Duty: The New Employer-Employee Compact."

27. Studies reported in Iris Bohnet, "Real Fixes for Workplace Bias," *The Wall Street Journal*, March 11, 2016, http://www.wsj.com/articles/real-fixes-for-workplace-bias-1457713338 (accessed April 12, 2016).

28. Rachel Feintzeig, "The Boss Doesn't Want Your Résumé," *The Wall Street Journal*, January 5, 2016, http://www.wsj.com/articles/the-boss-doesnt-want-your-resume-1452025908 (accessed April 12, 2016); and Marianne Bertrand and Sendhil Mullainathan, *Are Emily and Greg More Employable than Lakisha and Jamal?* (National Bureau of Economic Research Report), as reported in L. A. Johnson, "What's in a Name: When Emily Gets the Job over Lakisha," *The Tennessean*, January 4, 2004.

29. Feintzeig, "The Boss Doesn't Want Your Résumé."

30. This discussion is based on Joe Light, "In Hiring, Firms Shine Images," *The Wall Street Journal*, May 16, 2011; and Lauren Weber, "On the Hunt for Tech Hires," *The Wall Street Journal*, April 11, 2012.

31. Weber, "On the Hunt for Tech Hires."

32. Ibid.; and Light, "In Hiring, Firms Shine Images."

33. Rachel Feintzeig, "Companies Fast Track Hiring," *The Wall Street Journal*, September 16, 2015, http://www.wsj.com/articles/companies-fast-track-hiring-1442395981 (accessed April 12, 2016).

34. This example and the discussion are based on Sarah E. Needleman, "Start-Ups Get Snapped Up for Their Talent," *The Wall Street Journal*, September 13, 2012.

35. Douglas MacMillan, "Yahoo's Other Challenge: Retaining Acquired Talent," *The Wall Street Journal*, April 30, 2015, http://www.wsj.com/article_email/yahoos-other-challenge-retaining-acquired-talent-1430424735-lMyQjAxMTE1NzMwMDUzNjA1Wj (accessed April 12, 2016); and Brian Stelter, "He Has Millions and a New Job at Yahoo. Soon, He'll Be 18," *The New York Times*, March 25, 2013, http://www.nytimes.com/2013/03/26/business/media/nick-daloisio-17-sells-summly-app-to-yahoo.html?_r0 (accessed March 26, 2013).

36. MacMillan, "Yahoo's Other Challenge."

37. James G. March and Herbert A. Simon, *Organizations* (New York: Wiley, 1958).

38. Dennis J. Kravetz, *The Human Resources Revolution* (San Francisco: Jossey-Bass, 1989).

39. J. W. Boudreau and S. L. Rynes, "Role of Recruitment in Staffing Utility Analysis," *Journal of Applied Psychology* 70 (1985): 354–366.

40. Megan Santosus, "The Human Capital Factor," *CFO-IT* (Fall 2005): 26–27.

41. Brian Dumaine, "The New Art of Hiring Smart," *Fortune* (August 17, 1987): 78–81.

42. This discussion is based on Mathis and Jackson, *Human Resource Management*, Chapter 4, pp. 49–60.

43. Victoria Griffith, "When Only Internal Expertise Will Do," *CFO* (October 1998): 95–96, 102.

44. J. P. Wanous, *Organizational Entry* (Reading, MA: Addison-Wesley, 1980).

45. Paul Shread, "Your Social Media Reputation Can Attract Employees," *Time* (March 1, 2013), http://business.time.com/2013/03/01/your-social-media-reputation-can-attract-employees/ (accessed October 10, 2013).

46. Eric Morath, "To Fill Holiday Jobs, Retailers Reach Out through Social Media," *The Wall Street Journal*, October 26, 2014, http://www.wsj.com/articles/to-fill-holiday-jobs-retailers-reach-out-through-social-media–1414352103 (accessed April 13, 2016); and Kate Burrows, "British Army Launches Social Media Recruitment Campaign," *Chartered Management Institute*, May 22, 2013, http://www.managers.org.uk/news/british-army-launches-social-media-recruitment-campaign (accessed October 10, 2013).

47. Juro Osawa and Paul Mozur, "In China, Recruiting Gets Social," *The Wall Street Journal*, August 1, 2012.

48. Kristin Burnham, "4 Recruiting Trends for Job Hunters, via LinkedIn," *Information-Week* (July 17, 2013), http://www.informationweek.com/global-cio/recruiting/4-recruiting-trends-for-job-hunters-via/240158373 (accessed October 10, 2013); and George Anders, "Who Should You Hire? LinkedIn Says: Try Our Algorithm," *Forbes* (April 10, 2013), http://www.forbes.com/sites/georgeanders/2013/04/10/who-should-you-hire-linkedin-says-try-our-algorithm/ (accessed October 10, 2013).

49. Based on "United Nations New York Headquarters Internship Programme," www.un.org/depts/OHRM/sds/internsh/index.htm (accessed August 29, 2012); and Phyllis Korkki, "The Internship as Inside Track," *The New York Times*, March 25, 2011, www.nytimes.com/2011/03/27/jobs/27searches.html (accessed March 27, 2011).

50. Katherine Reynolds Lewis, "Nationwide's On-the-Spot Hiring," *Fortune* (October 1, 2015): 22.

51. Trudy Steinfeld, as reported in Korkki, "The Internship as Inside Track."

52. "Silicon Valley's New Hiring Strategy," *Fast Company* (October 20, 2011), www.fastcompany.com/1784737/silicon-valleys-new-hiring-strategy (accessed August 29, 2012); Andrea Siedsma, "Alternative Recruiting Strategies Employed by Companies Vying for Top Tech Talent," *Workforce Management* *(May 18, 2012), www.workforce.com/article/20120518/NEWS02/120519953/alternative-recruiting-strategies-employed-by-companies-vying-for-top (accessed August 27, 2012); and "Code Foo 6," IGN Web site, http://www.ign.com/code-foo/2016/ (accessed April 13, 2016).

53. Wimbush, "Spotlight on Human Resource Management."

54. Paul W. Thayer, "Somethings Old, Somethings New," *Personnel Psychology* 30, no. 4 (Winter 1977): 513–524.

55. J. Ledvinka, *Federal Regulation of Personnel and Human Resource Management* (Boston: Kent, 1982); and *Civil Rights Act*, Title VII, Section 2000e *et seq.*, U.S. Code 42 (1964).

56. Research reported in Lauren Weber, "Tips on Acing Job Interviews—For Managers," *The Wall Street Journal*, December 5, 2012.

57. Adam Bryant, "Marla Malcolm Beck's Three Keys to Hiring: Skill, Will and Fit" (Corner Office column), *The New York Times*, January 10, 2015, http://www.nytimes.com/2015/01/11/business/corner-office-marla-malcolm-becks-three-keys-to-hiring-skill-will-and-fit.html?_r=0 (accessed April 13, 2016).

58. Bohlander, Snell, and Sherman, *Managing Human Resource*, p. 202.

59. Tiffany Hsu, "Job Interviewing, to the Extreme," *Los Angeles Times*, February 19, 2012, http://articles.latimes.com/2012/feb/19/business/la-fi-extreme-interviewing-20120219 (accessed February 19, 2012).

60. Reported in Tomas Chamorro-Premuzic and Christopher Steinmetz, "The Perfect Hire," *Scientific American Mind* (July–August 2013): 43–47.

61. Susan Greco, "Sales & Marketing: He Can Close, but How Is His Interpersonal Sensitivity? Testing Sales Recruits," *Inc.* (March 2009): 96–98.

62. Reported in Chamorro-Premuzic and Steinmetz, "The Perfect Hire."

63. Lauren Weber, "Today's Personality Tests Raise the Bar for Job Seekers," *The Wall Street Journal*, April 14, 2015, http://www.wsj.com/articles/a-personality-test-could-stand-in-the-way-of-your-next-job-1429065001 (accessed April 14, 2016).

64. Ibid.

65. Reported in Weber, "Today's Personality Tests Raise the Bar."

66. Adecco survey, reported in Jenna Goudreau, "Top 5 Interview Mistakes Millennials Make," *Forbes* (September 26, 2012), http://www.forbes.com/sites/jennagoudreau/2012/09/26/top-5-interview-mistakes-millennials-make/ (accessed October 10, 2013).

67. "Access to Social Media Names and Passwords," National Conference of State Legislatures, April 6, 2016, http://www.ncsl.org/research/telecommunications-and-information-technology/employer-access-to-social-media-passwords-2013.aspx (accessed April 13, 2016).

68. "2015 Training Industry Report," *Training*, https://trainingmag.com/trgmag-article/2o15-training-industry-report (accessed April 14, 2016); and Monika Hamori, Burak Koyuncu, Jie Cao, and Thomas Graf, "What High-Potential Young Managers Want," *MIT Sloan Management Review* (Fall, 2015): 61–68.

69. Hamori et al., "What High-Potential Young Managers Want."

70. Rohit Deshpandé and Anjali Raina, "The Ordinary Heroes of the Taj," *Harvard Business Review* (December 2011): 119–123; and "Building an Institution Through Human Values," *Shanmugam's Blog*, January 22, 2012, http://cgshanmugam.wordpress.com/2012/01/22/building-an-institution-through-human-values/ (accessed October 10, 2013).

71. How Do Great Companies Groom Talent?" *Fortune* (November 21, 2011): 166.

72. William J. Rothwell and H. C. Kazanas, *Improving On-the-Job Training: How to Establish and Operate a Comprehensive OJT Program* (San Francisco: Jossey-Bass, 1994).

73. Matt Allen and Jennifer Naughton, "Social Learning: A Call to Action for Learning Professionals," *T+D* (August 2011): 50–55; and Margaret Schweer et al., "Building a Well-Networked Organization," *MIT Sloan Management Review* (Winter 2012): 35–42.

74. Jeanne C. Meister, "The Brave New World of Corporate Education," *The Chronicle of Higher Education* (February 9, 2001): B10; and Meryl Davids Landau, "Corporate Universities Crack Open Their Doors," *The Journal of Business Strategy* (May–June 2000): 18–23.

75. Janet Wiscombe, "McDonald's Corp." *Workforce Management* (November 2010): 38–40.

76. Jim Dow, "Spa Attraction," *People Management* (May 29, 2003): 34–35.

77. "Talent Tutor: Ram Charan's List of Biggest Corporate Talent-Management Mistakes," sidebar in Joann S. Lublin, "Managing & Careers—Boss Talk; Ram Charan: Message to CEOs: Do More to Keep Your Key Employees," *The Wall Street Journal*, December 27, 2010.

78. Survey by HR consulting firm Watson Wyatt, reported in Kelley Holland, "Performance Reviews: Many Need Improvement," *The New York Times*, September 10, 2006.

79. David W. Bracken and Allan H. Church, "The 'New' Performance Management Paradigm: Capitalizing on the Unrealized Potential of 360 Degree Feedback," *People & Strategy* 36, no. 2 (2013): 34–40; Kyle Couch, "Talent Management: Build on Four Key Components," *Leadership Excellence* (February 2012): 18; and Walter W. Tornow, "Editor's Note: Introduction to Special Issue on 360-Degree Feedback," *Human Resource Management* 32, no. 2–3 (Summer–Fall 1993): 211–219.

80. Jena McGregor, "Job Review in 140 Keystrokes," *BusinessWeek* (March 23 & 30, 2009): 58.

81. This discussion is based on Dick Grote, "Forced Ranking: Behind the Scenes," *Across the Board* (November–December 2002): 40–45; Matthew Boyle, "Performance Reviews: Perilous Curves Ahead," *Fortune* (May 28, 2001): 187–188; Rachel Feintzeig, "The Trouble with Grading Employees," *The Wall Street Journal*, April 21, 2015; and Phyllis Korkki, "Invasion of the Annual Reviews," *The New York Times*, November 23, 2013.

82. Feintzeig, "The Trouble with Grading Employees."

83. Ibid; Korkki, "Invasion of the Annual Reviews"; "Forced Ranking (Forced Distribution)," *HR Management Web site*, www.humanresources.hrvinet.com/forced-ranking-forced-distribution/ (accessed January 21, 2012); and Leslie Kwoh, "'Rank and Yank' Retains Vocal Fans," *The Wall Street Journal*, January 31, 2012.

84. V. R. Buzzotta, "Improve Your Performance Appraisals," *Management Review* (August 1988): 40–43; and H. J. Bernardin and R. W. Beatty, *Performance Appraisal: Assessing Human Behavior at Work* (Boston: Kent, 1984).

85. Bernardin and Beatty, *Performance Appraisal*.

86. Gerald E. Ledford Jr., "The Changing Landscape of Employee Rewards: Observations and Prescriptions," *Organizational Dynamics* 43 (2014): 168–179; and Richard I. Henderson, *Compensation Management: Rewarding Performance*, 4th ed. (Reston, VA: Reston, 1985).

87. L. R. Gomez-Mejia, "Structure and Process Diversification, Compensation Strategy, and Firm Performance," *Strategic Management Journal* 13 (1992): 381–397; and E. Montemayor, "Congruence Between Pay Policy and Competitive Strategy in High-Performing Firms," *Journal of Management* 22, no. 6 (1996): 889–908.

88. Renée F. Broderick and George T. Milkovich, "Pay Planning, Organization Strategy, Structure and 'Fit': A Prescriptive Model of Pay," paper presented at the 45th Annual Meeting of the Academy of Management, San Diego (August 1985).

89. Rachel Dodes and Dana Mattioli, "Theory & Practice: Retailers Try on New Sales Tactics," *The Wall Street Journal*, April 19, 2010.

90. E. F. Lawler, III, *Strategic Pay: Aligning Organizational Strategies and Pay Systems* (San Francisco: Jossey-Bass, 1990); and R. J. Greene, "Person-Focused Pay: Should It Replace Job-Based Pay?" *Compensation and Benefits Management* 9, no. 4 (1993): 46–55.

91. L. Wiener, "No New Skills? No Raise," *U.S. News and World Report* (October 26, 1992): 78; and Ledford, "The Changing Landscape of Employee Rewards."

92. Reported in Rachel Emma Silverman, "Big Data Upends the Way Workers Are Paid," *The Wall Street Journal*, September 19, 2012, http://online.wsj.com/news/articles/SB100008723 96390444433504577651741900453730 (accessed September 20, 2012).

93. Alan S. Blinder, "Crazy Compensation and the Crisis," *The Wall Street Journal*, May 28, 2009.

94. Ibid.

95. Scott Westcott, "Goodbye and Good Luck," *Inc.* (April 2006): 40–42.

96. Nanette Byrnes, "Star Search," *BusinessWeek* (October 10, 2005): 68–78.

97. Rachel Feintzeig, "Google Style Office Perks Go Mainstream," *The Wall Street Journal*, August 4, 2015.

98. Mike Brewster, "No Exit," *Fast Company* (April 2005): 93.

99. Vauhini Vara, "Pinterest's Great Expectations," *Fast Company* (November 2015): 33–36.

100. Harvard Business Review Staff, "HBR Survey: Were You Ever Treated Unfairly at Work Because of Someone Else's Bias?" *Harvard Business Review* (May 2015): 19.

101. Vara, "Pinterest's Great Expectations."

102. Quoted in Susan Caminiti, "The Diversity Factor," *Fortune* (October 19, 2007): 95–105.

103. Vara, "Pinterest's Great Expectations"; Nick Wingfield, "Intel Budgets $300 Million for Diversity," *The New York Times*, January 6, 2015; and Jena McGregor, "Google Admits It Has a Diversity Problem," *The Washington Post*, May 29, 2014, https://www.washingtonpost.com/news/on-leadership /wp/2014/05/29/google-admits-it-has-a-diversity-problem / (accessed November 17, 2015).

104. Yair Holtzman and Johan Anderberg, "Diversify Your Teams and Collaborate: Because Great Minds Don't Think Alike," *Journal of Management Development* 30, no. 1 (2011): 75–92.

105. Lynn M. Shore et al., "Inclusion and Diversity in Work Groups," *Journal of Management* 37, no. 4 (July 2011): 1262–1289; Taylor H. Cox, "Managing Cultural Diversity: Implications for Organizational Competitiveness," *Academy of Management Executive* 5, no. 3 (1991): 45–56; and Faye Rice, "How to Make Diversity Pay," *Fortune* (August 8, 1994): 78–86.

106. Ben Fritz, "Hollywood Wrestles with Diversity," *The Wall Street Journal*, February 24, 2016, http://www.wsj.com/ articles/hollywood-wrestles-with-diversity-1456354526 (accessed May 9, 2016).

107. "Labor Force Characteristics of Foreign Born Workers Summary: 2014," *United States Labor Department Bureau of Labor Statistics*, http://www.bls.gov/news.release/forbrn.nr0.htm (accessed April 19, 2016).

108. *Occupational Outlook Handbook*, Bureau of Labor Statistics, www.bls.gov/ooh/about/projections-overview.htm#laborforce (accessed June 29, 2012).

109. Joann S. Lublin and Kelly Eggers, "More Women Are Primed to Land CEO Roles," *The Wall Street Journal Online*, April 30, 2012, http://online.wsj.com/article/SB100014240 52702303990604577368344256435440.html (accessed June 29, 2012); and Alison Smale and Claire Cain Miller, "Germany Sets Gender Quotas in Boardrooms," *The New York Times*, March 6, 2015, http://www.nytimes.com/2015/03/07 /world/europe/german-law-requires-more-women-on-corporate-boards.html?_r=0 (accessed April 20, 2016).

110. Elizabeth Weise, "U.S. Falls to 28th on Global Gender Equality List," *USA Today*, November 19, 2015, http://www.usatoday.com/story/money/2015/11/19/us-falls-28th-global-gender-equality-list/76018174/ (accessed April 20, 2016).

111. Ann Zimmerman, "U.S. Charges Bass Pro Shops with Racial Bias," *The Wall Street Journal*, September 22, 2011.

112. Eleanor Warnock, "Japan Inc. Hires More Women, but Men Still Hold Top Jobs," *The Wall Street Journal*, November 10, 2015, http://www.wsj.com/articles/japan-inc-hires-more-women-but-men-still-hold-top-jobs-1447136380 (accessed April 20, 2016).

113. Ibid.

114. Hiroka Tabuchi, "Leading in 3-D TV, Breaking Japan's Glass Ceiling," *The New York Times Online*, January 17, 2011, www.nytimes.com/2011/01/18/business/global/18screen.html?pagewanted=all (accessed July 3, 2012).

115. Smale and Miller, "Germany Sets Gender Quotas in Boardrooms."

116. Holtzman and Anderberg, "Diversify Your Teams and Collaborate."

117. Michael L. Wheeler, "Diversity: Business Rationale and Strategies," The Conference Board, Report No. 1130–95–RR (1995), p. 25.

118. Anthony Oshiotse and Richard O'Leary, "Corning Creates an Inclusive Culture to Drive Technology Innovation and Performance," Wiley InterScience, *Global Business and Organizational Excellence* 26, no. 3 (March/April 2007): 7–21.

119. "When CEOs Drive Diversity, Everybody Wins," *Chief Executive* (July 2005), www.chiefexecutive.net/ME2/dirmod.asp?sid=&nm=&type=Publishing&mod=Publications%3A%3AArticle&mid=8F3A7027421841978F18BE895F87F791&tier=4&id=201D3B11B9D4419893E78DDA4-B7ACDC8 (accessed September 21, 2010).

120. Shore et al., "Inclusion and Diversity in Work Groups."

121. Martin N. Davidson, "The End of Diversity: How Leaders Make Differences Really Matter," *Leader to Leader* (Spring 2012): 51–55.

122. Taylor Cox, Jr., and Ruby L. Beale, *Developing Competency to Manage Diversity* (San Francisco: Berrett-Koehler, 1997), p. 2.

123. Reported in Marjorie Derven, "The Competitive Advantage of Diverse Perspectives," *T+D* (August 2013): 45–48.

124. Holtzman and Anderberg, "Diversify Your Teams and Collaborate"; Thomas E. Poulin, "The Other Diversity," *PA Times, American Society for Public Administration* (March 2009): 8; and Clayton H. Osborne and Vincent M. Cramer, "Fueling High Performance Through Diversity," *Chief Learning Officer* (November 2005): 22.

125. Paul J. H. Schoemaker and Steven Krupp, "The Power of Asking Pivotal Questions," *MIT Sloan Management Review* 56, no. 2 (Winter 2015): 39–47; and Adam Bryant, "Cindy Holland of Netflix: Learning to Lead on a Pair of Water Skis," *The New York Times*, November 19, 2015, http://www.nytimes.com/2015/11/22/business/cindy-holland-of-netflix-learning-to-lead-on-a-pair-of-water-skis.html?_r=0 (accessed April 20, 2016).

126. Anita Woolley and Thomas Malone, "What Makes a Team Smarter? More Women," *Harvard Business Review* (June 2011): 32–33; and Peter Gwynne, "Group Intelligence, Teamwork, and Productivity," *Research-Technology Management* 55, no. 2 (March–April 2012): 7–8.

127. Thomas Barta, Markus Kleiner, and Tilo Neumann, "Is There a Payoff from Top-Team Diversity?" *McKinsey Quarterly*, Issue 2 (April 2012): 13–15.

128. "A Diverse and Global Workforce," Reckitt Benckiser Website, http://www.rb.com/responsibility/workplace/diversity/ (accessed April 20, 2016).

129. Herminia Ibarra and Morten T. Hansen, "Are You a Collaborative Leader?" *Harvard Business Review* (July–August 2011): 69–74.

130. Gail Robinson and Kathleen Dechant, "Building a Business Case for Diversity," *Academy of Management Executive* 11, no. 3 (1997): 21–31.

131. Sonie Alleyne and Nicole Marie Richardson, "The 40 Best Companies for Diversity," *Black Enterprise* 36, no. 12 (July 2006): 15.

132. Robinson and Dechant, "Building a Business Case for Diversity."

133. Ibid.; and Sheen S. Levine and David Stark, "Diversity Makes You Brighter," *The New York Times*, December 9, 2015.

134. Research reported in Levine and Stark, "Diversity Makes You Brighter."

135. Kris Maher, "Lockheed Settles Racial-Discrimination Suit," *The Wall Street Journal*, January 3, 2008.

136. Mahzarin Banaji's research as discussed in Nicholas Kristof, "Our Biased Brains," *The New York Times*, May 7, 2015; and Atul Gawande, "Manning the Hospital Barricades: Why Do Groups—Even Groups of Doctors—Hate Each Other?" *Slate* (June 26, 1998), http://www.slate.com/articles/health_and_science/medical_examiner/1998/06/manning_the_hospital_barricades.html (accessed July 10, 2013).

137. Reported in Michael Orey, "White Men Can't Help It," *BusinessWeek* (May 15, 2006), pp. 54, 57.

138. Marianne Bertrand and Sendhil Mullainathan, "Are Emily and Greg More Employable Than Lakisha and Jamal? A Field Experiment on Labor Market Discrimination," *American Economic Review* 94, no. 4 (September 2004): 991–1013; research findings reported in Sendhil Mullainathan, "Racial Bias, Even When We Have Good Intentions," *The New York Times*, January 3, 2015, http://www.nytimes.com/2015/01/04/upshot/the-measuring-sticks-of-racial-bias-.html?_r=0 (accessed April 21, 2016); and Tula Karras, "Crisis in the E.R.: Why Women Are at Risk," *Woman's Day* (May 2016): 120–125.

139. Mullainathan, "Racial Bias, Even When We Have Good Intentions."

140. Joann S. Lublin, "Bringing Hidden Biases Into the Light," *The Wall Street Journal*, January 9, 2014, http://online.wsj.com/news/articles/SB10001424052702303754404579308562690896896?mod∇Business_newsreel_3 (accessed January 9, 2014).

141. Norma Carr-Ruffino, *Managing Diversity: People Skills for a Multicultural Workplace* (Tucson, AZ: Thomson Executive Press, 1996), p. 92.

142. Quoted in Colleen McCain Nelson, "Poll: Most Women See Bias in the Workplace," *The Wall Street Journal*, April 12, 2013.

143. Reported in Roy Harris, "The Illusion of Inclusion," *CFO* (May 2001): 42–50.

144. Studies by Victoria Brescoll, reported in Leslie Kwoh, "News & Trends: Talkative Women Lose at Work, Study Says," *The Wall Street Journal*, May 16, 2012; and in Selena Rezvani, "What's Wrong with Research About Female Bosses," *The Washington Post*, June 4, 2013, http://www.washingtonpost.com/blogs/on-leadership/wp/2013/06/04/whats-wrong-with-research-about-female-bosses/ (accessed October 15, 2013).

145. Carr-Ruffino, *Managing Diversity*, pp. 98–99.

146. Based on an interview with PepsiCo chairman and CEO Indra Nooyi, in Rebecca Blumenstein, "View from the Top," *The Wall Street Journal*, April 11, 2011.

147. Cox and Beale, "Developing Competency to Manage Diversity," p. 79.

148. Ibid., pp. 80–81.

149. Ibid.

150. This discussion is based on Ellen McGirt, "Leading While Black," *Fortune* (February 1, 2016): 76–84.

151. Ibid.

152. Ibid.

153. Georges Desvaux, Sandrine Devillard-Hoellinger, and Mary C. Meaney, "A Business Case for Women," *The McKinsey Quarterly: The Online Journal of McKinsey & Co.*, September 2008, www.mckinseyquarterly.com/A_business_case_for_women_2192 (accessed June 17, 2010).

154. Joanna Barsh and Lareina Yee, "Changing Companies' Minds About Women," *McKinsey Quarterly Online*, September 2011, www.mckinsey.com/careers/women/~/media/Reports/Women/Changing_companies_minds_about_women.ashx (accessed June 29, 2012).

155. Hanna Rosin, "The End of Men," *The Atlantic* (July/August 2010), www.theatlantic.com/magazine/print/2010/07/the-end-of-men/8135/ (accessed July 9, 2012).

156. Jenny M. Hoobler, Grace Lemmon, and Sandy J. Wayne, "Women's Underrepresentation in Upper Management: New Insights on a Persistent Problem," *Organizational Dynamics* 40 (2011): 151–156.

157. Jane Hyun, "Leadership Principles for Capitalizing on Culturally Diverse Teams: The Bamboo Ceiling Revisited," *Leader to Leader* (Spring 2012): 14–19.

158. Reported in Claire Cain Miller, "The Kleiner Perkins Lawsuit, and Rethinking the Confidence-Driven Workplace," *The New York Times*, March 12, 2015, http://www.nytimes.com/2015/03/13/upshot/the-kleiner-perkins-lawsuit-and-rethinking-the-confidence-driven-workplace.html?_r=0 (accessed April 23, 2016).

159. Marie-Helene Budworth and Sara L. Mann, "Becoming a Leader: The Challenge of Modesty for Women," *Journal of Management Development* 29, no. 2 (2010): 177–186.

160. Quoted in John Bussey, "How Women Can Get Ahead: Advice from Female CEOs," *The Wall Street Journal Online*, May 18, 2012, http://online.wsj.com/article/SB10001424052702303879604577410520511235252.html (accessed July 8, 2012).

161. Reported in Nikki Waller and Joann S. Lublin, "What's Holding Women Back in the Workplace?" *The Wall Street Journal*, September 30, 2015, http://www.wsj.com/articles/whats-holding-women-back-in-the-workplace-1443600242 (accessed April 23, 2016).

162. Sue Shellenbarger, "One Way to Get Unstuck and Move Up? All You Have to Do Is Ask," *The Wall Street Journal*, April 14, 2015, http://www.wsj.com/articles/one-way-to-get-unstuck-and-move-up-all-you-have-to-do-is-ask-1429037179 (accessed April 23, 2016).

163. Lisa Belkin, "The Opt-Out Revolution," *The New York Times Magazine* (October 26, 2002): 43–47, 58.

164. Jodi Kantor, "Elite Women Put a New Spin on an Old Debate," *The New York Times*, June 21, 2012, www.nytimes.com/2012/06/22/us/elite-women-put-a-new-spin-on-work-life-debate.html (accessed July 9, 2012); and Anne-Marie Slaughter, "Why Women Still Can't Have It All," *The Atlantic* (July–August 2012), www.theatlantic.com/magazine/archive/2012/07/why-women-still-cant-have-it-all/309020/ (accessed October 15, 2012).

165. C. J. Prince, "Media Myths: The Truth About the Opt-Out Hype," *NAFE Magazine* (Second Quarter 2004): 14–18; Patricia Sellers, "Power: Do Women Really Want It?" *Fortune* (October 13, 2003): 80–100.

166. Waller and Lublin, "What's Holding Women Back in the Workplace?"

167. Jia Lynn Yang, "Goodbye to All That," *Fortune* (November 14, 2005): 169–170.

168. Sheila Wellington, Marcia Brumit Kropf, and Paulette R. Gerkovich, "What's Holding Women Back?" *Harvard Business Review* (June 2003): 18–19.

169. The Leader's Edge/Executive Women Research 2002 survey, reported in "Why Women Leave," *Executive Female* (Summer 2003): 4.

170. Barbara Reinhold, "Smashing Glass Ceilings: Why Women Still Find It Tough to Advance to the Executive Suite," *Journal of Organizational Excellence* (Summer 2005): 43–55; Jory Des Jardins, "I Am Woman (I Think)," *Fast Company* (May 2005): 25–26; and Alice H. Eagly and Linda L. Carli, "The Female Leadership Advantage: An Evaluation of the Evidence," *The Leadership Quarterly* 14 (2003): 807–834.

171. Reported in Claire Cain Miller, "The Motherhood Penalty vs. the Fatherhood Bonus; A Child Helps Your Career, If You're a Man," *The New York Times*, September 6, 2014, http://www.nytimes.com/2014/09/07/upshot/a-child-helps-your-career-if-youre-a-man.html?_r=0 (accessed April 23, 2016).

172. Sally Helgesen, "How Women Leaders Have Transformed Management," *Strategy + Business* (March 17, 2014), http://www.strategy-business.com/blog/How-Women-Leaders-Have-Transformed-Management?gko=9e1ad (accessed April 24, 2016); Corinne Post, "When Is Female Leadership an Advantage?" *Journal of Organizational Behavior* 36, no. 8 (November 2015): 1153–1175; Eagly and Carli, "The Female Leadership Advantage"; and Sally Helgesen, *The Female Advantage: Women's Ways of Leadership* (New York: Doubleday Currency, 1990).

173. Helgesen, "How Women Leaders Have Transformed Management."

174. Tamar Lewin, "At Colleges, Women Are Leaving Men in the Dust," *The New York Times Online*, July 9, 2006, www.nytimes.com/2006/07/09/education/09college.html?_r=1&scp=1&sq=at%20colleges%20women%20are%20leaving%20men%20in%20the%20dust&st=cse&oref=slogin (accessed March 13, 2008).

175. Michelle Conlin, "The New Gender Gap," *BusinessWeek* (May 26, 2003): 74–82.

176. Quoted in Conlin, "The New Gender Gap."

177. Kathryn M. Bartol, David C. Martin, and Julie A. Kromkowski, "Leadership and the Glass Ceiling: Gender and Ethnic Group Influences on Leader Behaviors at Middle and Executive Managerial Levels," *Journal of Leadership and Organizational Studies* 9, no. 3 (2003): 8–19; Bernard M. Bass and Bruce J. Avolio, "Shatter the Glass Ceiling: Women May Make Better Managers," *Human Resource Management* 33, no. 4 (Winter 1994): 549–560; and Rochelle Sharpe, "As Leaders, Women Rule: New Studies Find that Female Managers Outshine Their Male Counterparts in Almost Every Measure," *BusinessWeek* (November 20, 2000): 5ff.

178. Zenger Folkman study reported in Tony Schwartz, "Overcoming the Confidence Gap in Women," *The New York Times*, June 12, 2015, http://www.nytimes.com/2015/06/13/business/dealbook/overcoming-the-confidence-gap-for-women.html?_r=0 (accessed April 25, 2016).

179. Dwight D. Frink et al., "Gender Demography and Organization Performance: A Two-Study Investigation with Convergence," *Group & Organization Management* 28, no. 1 (March 2003): 127–147; Catalyst research project cited in Reinhold, "Smashing Glass Ceilings."

180. "Impact of Diversity Initiatives on the Bottom Line: A SHRM Survey of the *Fortune* 1000," in "Keeping Your Edge: Managing a Diverse Corporate Culture," special advertising section produced in association with the Society for Human Resource Management, *Fortune* (June 3, 2001): S12–S14.

181. Lauren Weber, "A Company Is Making Life Easier for New Moms (and Why That's News)," *The Wall Street Journal*, March 6, 2015, http://blogs.wsj.com/atwork/2015/03/06/vodafone-full-pay-for-part-time-new-moms/ (accessed April 25, 2016).

182. Leslie Kwoh, "Firms Hail New Chiefs (of Diversity)," *The Wall Street Journal Online*, January 5, 2012, http://online.wsj.com/article/SB10001424052970203899504577129261732884578.html (accessed July 9, 2012).

183. Farhad Manjoosept, "Exposing Hidden Bias at Google," *The New York Times*, September 25, 2014; Nick Wingfield, "Intel Budgets $300 Million for Diversity," *The New York Times*, January 6, 2015; and McGregor, "Google Admits It Has a Diversity Problem."

184. Katherine Reynolds Lewis, "Nationwide's On-the-Spot Hiring," *Fortune* (October 1, 2015): 22.

185. Eileen Zimmerman, "How One Technology Company Managed to Hire a More Diverse Workforce," *The New York Times*, December 19, 2014, http://boss.blogs.nytimes.com/2014/12/19/how-one-technology-company-managed-to-hire-a-more-diverse-workforce/ (accessed April 25, 2016).

186. Terry Morehead Dworkin, Virginia Maurer, and Cindy A. Schipani, "Career Mentoring for Women: New Horizons /Expanded Methods," *Business Horizons* 55 (2012): 363–372; Melanie Trottman, "A Helping Hand," *The Wall Street Journal*, November 14, 2005; B. Ragins, "Barriers to Mentoring: The Female Manager's Dilemma," *Human Relations* 42, no. 1 (1989): 1–22; and Belle Rose Ragins, Bickley Townsend, and Mary Mattis, "Gender Gap in the Executive Suite: CEOs and Female Executives Report on Breaking the Glass Ceiling," *Academy of Management Executive* 12, no. 1 (1998): 28–42.

187. Theodore Kinny, "Stop Managing Generational Diversity," *Strategy + Business* (January 21, 2015), http://www.strategy-business.com/blog/Stop-Managing-Generational-Diversity?gko=a346a (accessed April 25, 2016).

188. David A. Thomas, "The Truth About Mentoring Minorities—Race Matters," *Harvard Business Review* (April 2001): 99–107.

189. Mary Zey, "A Mentor for All," *Personnel Journal* (January 1988): 46–51.

190. "Sexual Harassment: Vanderbilt University Policy" (Nashville, TN: Vanderbilt University, 1993).

191. Julie Watson and Elliot Spagat, "Bob Filner Resigns: San Diego Mayor Agrees to Step Down Amid Sexual Harassment Scandal," *Associated Press*, August 23, 2013, http://www.huffingtonpost.com/2013/08/23/san-diego-mayor-bob-filner-resigns-sexual-harass_n_3807073.html (accessed October 17, 2013); and Tamara Audi, "San Diego Mayor Bob Filner to Resign amid Sexual-Harassment Scandal," *The Wall Street Journal*, August 23, 2013, http://online.wsj.com/news/articles/SB100014241278873236655045790314239525222220 (accessed October 17, 2013).

192. This definition and discussion are based on Raymond A. Friedman, "Employee Network Groups: Self-Help Strategy for Women and Minorities," *Performance Improvement Quarterly* 12, no. 1 (1999): 148–163.

193. Zimmerman, "How One Technology Company Managed to Hire a More Diverse Workforce."

194. Raymond A. Friedman and Brooks Holtom, "The Effects of Network Groups on Minority Employee Turnover Intentions," *Human Resource Management* 41, no. 4 (Winter 2002): 405–421.

195. Diane Brady and Jena McGregor, "What Works in Women's Networks," *BusinessWeek* (June 18, 2007): 58.

196. Elizabeth Wasserman, "A Race for Profits," *MBA Jungle* (March–April 2003): 40–41.

197. Hashi Syedain, "Premium Bonds," *People Management* (September 2012): 23–26.

198. Raymond A. Friedman, Melinda Kane, and Daniel B. Cornfield, "Social Support and Career Optimism: Examining the Effectiveness of Network Groups Among Black Managers," *Human Relations* 51, no. 9 (1998): 1155–1177.

199. Adapted from the Tolerance Scale by Maria Heiselman, Naomi Miller, and Bob Schlorman, Northern Kentucky University, 1982. In George Manning, Kent Curtis, and Steve McMillen, *Building Community: The Human Side of Work* (Cincinnati, OH: Thomson Executive Press, 1996), pp. 272–277.

200. Based on Linda Tischler, "IBM's Management Makeover," *Fast Company* (November 1, 2004), www.fastcompany.com/51673/ibms-management-makeover (accessed November 26, 2012); and www.zurich.ibm.com/employment/environment.html (accessed September 13, 2010).

201. Based on Rob Johnson, "30 Muslim Workers Fired for Praying on Job at Dell," *The Tennessean*, March 10, 2005; Anayat Durrani, "Religious Accommodation for Muslim Employees," *Workforce.com*, www.workforce.com/archive/feature/religious-accommodation-muslim-employees/index.php (accessed September 21, 2010); "Questions and Answers About Employer Responsibilities Concerning the Employment of Muslims, Arabs, South Asians, and Sikhs," the U.S. Equal Employment Opportunity Commission, www.eeoc.gov/facts/backlash-employer.html (accessed September 20, 2010); and "2006 Household Appliance Industry Outlook," U.S. Department of Commerce, International Trade Administration, www.ita.doc.gov/td/ocg/outlook06_appliances.pdf (accessed September 21, 2010).

Chapter 10
Understanding Individual Behavior

iStock.com/oscarhdez

Learning Outcomes

After studying this chapter, you should be able to:

10.1 Explain why understanding yourself is essential for being a good manager, and describe two methods for enhancing self-awareness.

10.2 Discuss the importance of job satisfaction and trust for effective employee performance.

10.3 Describe the perception process and explain internal and external attributions.

10.4 Identify and define major personality traits and describe how personality can influence workplace behaviors.

10.5 Identify positive and negative emotions and describe how emotions affect behavior.

10.6 Identify and define the four components of emotional intelligence and explain why they are important for today's managers.

10.7 Outline a step-by-step system for managing yourself and your time.

10.8 Explain the difference between challenge stress and threat stress.

10.9 Identify ways individuals and organizations can manage stress to improve employee health, satisfaction, and productivity.

Are You Ready to Be a Manager?

Before reading this chapter, please circle either "Mostly True" or "Mostly False" for each of the following five statements.

1 If I try something and it fails, I don't give up but instead keep trying.

Mostly True ◄···············► Mostly False

[page 366]

2 If I have to make a choice between a high-paying job and one I desperately love, I'd pick the one I love.

Mostly True ◄···············► Mostly False

[page 369]

3 I try to make a distinction between fact and opinion when I'm making decisions.

Mostly True ◄···············► Mostly False

[page 372]

4 I'm aware of my personality strengths and I try not to judge people's "goodness" as being similar to my own personality.

Mostly True ◄···············► Mostly False

[page 375]

5 If I fail a test, I often think that the teacher was unfair in the grading.

Mostly True ◄···············► Mostly False

[page 378]

Discover Your Management Approach

Do You Have a Gender and Authority Bias?[a]

Instructions: Indicate whether each of the following statements is Mostly True or Mostly False for you.

	Mostly True	Mostly False
1. I would feel more comfortable if the pilot of an airplane I was traveling on were male.	_____	_____
1. In general, I would rather work for a man than for a woman.	_____	_____
2. If I were being sentenced in court, I would prefer that the judge be a woman.	_____	_____

To complete and score the entire assessment, visit MindTap.

[a]Laurie A. Rudman and Stephan E. Killanski, "Implicit and Explicit Attitudes Toward Female Authority," *Personality and Social Psychology Bulletin* 26 (November 2000): 1315–1328.

After a decade working at SAP North America, Thomas Lynch felt that he was ready to move into management. Yet Lynch, an engineer who also has an MBA, kept getting passed over for promotions. His bosses knew he was smart. They knew he was good at solving problems and that he often earned top performer ratings. They knew he was well respected and got along well with almost everyone. So, what was the problem? The feedback Lynch got was that his bosses felt he lacked ambition and drive because of his naturally quiet, shy, introverted style. Lynch started working with a coach to find ways to make sure people knew what he could do and what he wanted for himself and the company. "I realized I needed to stop flying under the radar and take more risks," he says. Lynch began speaking up in meetings, even when his thoughts weren't fully formed. He began talking more with other managers and asking to participate in projects. He called one of his bosses who he knew saw him as lacking in ambition to describe what he felt were his strengths and ask how he could get more responsibility. On a recent team project, the change in Lynch's self-confidence and leadership was so marked that "I barely recognized him," says that boss, Michael Nixon. Asked how he perceives Lynch now, Nixon says, "I would label him a difference-maker."[1]

Lynch first began working with a coach because he believed he needed to become more extroverted, but the coach helped him see that what he really needed was to understand his own strengths and abilities and make sure other people recognized them as well. By realizing his strengths, Lynch was able to develop the self-confidence to take risks.

Naturally, when people take risks, they sometimes fail, but many people who have accomplished great outcomes give credit to their previous failures for driving them to succeed. Consider billionaire author J. K. Rowling, whose first *Harry Potter* book was rejected by 12 publishers before Bloomsbury bought it for the equivalent of $4,000. In her 2008 commencement speech to the graduating class at Harvard University, Rowling recounted how setbacks and rejection had not discouraged her, but simply made her stronger.[2] Unlike J. K. Rowling, however, there are many talented individuals who experience one defeat or discouragement and never try again.[3]

What makes the difference? Psychologists suggest it comes down to a characteristic called *self-efficacy*. It is one of the many ways in which individuals differ, along with their personality traits, attitudes, emotions, and values. **Self-efficacy** is an individual's strong belief that he or she can accomplish a specific task or outcome successfully.[4] Self-efficacy is one dimension of **self-confidence**, which can be defined as general assurance in one's own ideas, judgment, and capabilities. Personality traits, emotions, and characteristics such as self-confidence and self-efficacy influence how people behave, including how they handle work situations and relate to others.

10-1 Understanding Yourself and Others

Having insight into why people behave the way they do is a part of good management. People bring their individual differences to work each day, and these differences influence how they interpret assignments, whether they like to be told what to do, how they handle challenges, and how they interact with others. By increasing their understanding of individual differences, as described throughout this chapter, managers can learn how to get the best out of each employee and more effectively lead people through workplace challenges. However, the first requirement for being a good manager is understanding oneself. Managers' characteristics and behavior can profoundly affect the workplace and influence employee motivation, morale, and job performance.

10-1a The Value and Difficulty of Knowing Yourself

A survey of 75 members of the Stanford Graduate School of Business's Advisory Council revealed the nearly unanimous answer to a question about the most important capability for leaders to develop: self-awareness.[5] **Self-awareness** means being aware of the internal aspects of one's nature, such as personality traits, beliefs, emotions, and perceptions, and appreciating how your patterns affect other people. Most management experts agree that a primary characteristic of effective leaders is that they know who they are and what they stand for.[6] When managers deeply understand themselves, they remain grounded and constant. People know what to expect from them. As one employee put it, "it's like they have a stick down through the center of them that's rooted in the ground."[7]

Yet developing self-awareness is easier said than done. Consider Charlotte Beers, former chairwoman and CEO of Ogilvy & Mather Worldwide, who now conducts seminars for women leaders. When Beers first became a management supervisor, she considered herself to be a friendly, approachable, easygoing leader. She was shocked when a friend told her that one of her colleagues described her management style as "menacing." That comment was devastating to Beers because it was the exact opposite of the way she thought of herself.[8] Many of us, like Beers, might be surprised to find out what others honestly think about us. Most of us don't take the time to think about who we really are or the effect our patterns of thought and behavior have on others. To be a good manager, such self-reflection is essential.

10-1b Enhancing Your Self-Awareness

There are a number of ways by which people can increase their understanding of themselves. Two important approaches to enhancing self-awareness, as shown in Exhibit 10.1, are soliciting feedback from others and using self-assessments.

Soliciting Feedback   Just as we use a mirror in the mornings to shave or fix our hair, we can use other people as a mirror to see ourselves more clearly.[9] A manager might consider himself to be patient and understanding, but his employees may see that he is easily irritated and unsympathetic. Francisco D'Souza, CEO of Cognizant Technology Solutions Corporation, worked with a coach who talked to people who worked with and for him. "It was difficult feedback," D'Souza says, "but very enlightening. That helped me identify a couple of my blind spots." Many people have **blind spots**—attributes about themselves that they are not aware of or don't recognize as problems—that limit their effectiveness and hinder their career success.[10] D'Souza learned that people had confidence in his ability but felt that he was harsh in his criticism. "It made me understand that the weight of my words was a lot heavier than I gave myself credit for, and it led

Exhibit 10.1 Two Keys to Self-Awareness

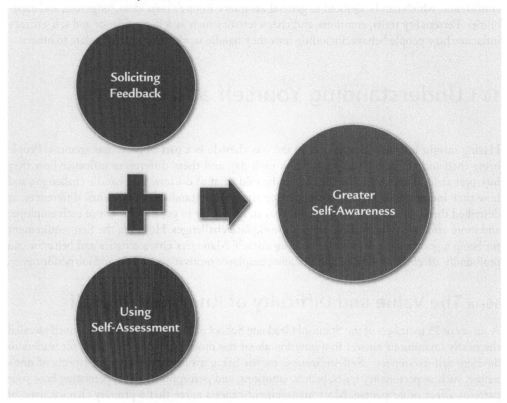

me to be much more thoughtful and measured in how I give feedback," he said.[11] When we go through life without feedback, we're like the balding man who sweeps thin strands of hair across his scalp and thinks no one notices. Seeking feedback to enhance self-awareness can improve performance and job satisfaction for both managers and employees.[12] We all have illusions about ourselves, so we need help from others to get a clear picture of who we are.

Lois Braverman uses her background as a psychotherapist to help people in her organization develop greater self-awareness.

Sunny Side Up   Lois Braverman, Ackerman Institute for the Family

"In the psychotherapy world, we call [it] being 'loaded,'" says Lois Braverman, currently the CEO of the Ackerman Institute for the Family. Braverman was the oldest daughter in the family; her mother was the oldest daughter in her family; and her grandmother was the oldest daughter in her family. "You're kind of loaded to be domineering," Braverman says, admitting that she's had to work to keep from thinking her way of doing things is always right.

Braverman was trained in psychotherapy, and she also learned a lot about herself in her work with couples and families. As she moved into management roles, Braverman examined what the "first-born 'right' disease" meant for working in organizations. There were good things about it, because it gave her the courage to make difficult decisions and take risks. Yet always thinking she was right could create

problems in interpersonal relationships and limit creativity and innovation. Now, even if she thinks she knows the answer, she accepts that there may be other, even better answers. Braverman says she learned that "I have to make room for the legitimacy of your point of view, and not let my righteousness make me think my perception is more meaningful than yours." Braverman also tries to help others in the organization be aware of their personality traits, values, perceptions, and other characteristics that affect working relationships. She believes when people understand that everyone has different characteristics and that incorporating different ideas and perceptions can lead to better results, organizations work more creatively and overcome some of the discord that occurs when people argue over who is right or wrong.[13]

By helping people "make room for the differences," Braverman helps to prevent the conflicts that inevitably arise in organizations from escalating out of control. Everyone, she says, needs to feel that "[his or her] perception of reality at least has a chance to be heard."

Self-Assessment Another highly valuable way to increase self-awareness is *self-assessment*, which uses self-inquiry and reflection to gain insights into oneself from the results of scores on self-assessment instruments such as those discussed throughout this text. By completing these assessments as honestly as possible, you can analyze your scores and increase your understanding of various aspects of yourself. Some managers, including Stuart McClure, who left a job as chief technology officer at McAfee to start information security company Cylance, go through assessment exercises administered by Development Dimensions International (DDI) and other consulting firms to learn about aspects of themselves. McClure learned that he has great strengths in getting things done, but that he tends to take on too much and be impatient when interrupted by people or ideas outside his immediate interest. "I have to slow myself down," he says.[14]

Self-assessment also means regularly reflecting on our thoughts and feelings. Introspection—reflecting on our experiences, examining the effects of our actions and behavior, looking at the consequences for ourselves and others, and asking, "What can I learn?" is a valuable use of time that too many managers overlook. Some people keep a journal, meditate, or just sit quietly and think through their day.[15] A manager who understands himself or herself is better able to understand and interact effectively with others.

Remember This

- Individual differences among people, including personality traits, emotions, and characteristics such as self-confidence and self-efficacy, influence how people relate to others and behave at work.
- **Self-efficacy** is an individual's strong belief that he or she can successfully accomplish a specific task or outcome.
- J. K. Rowling demonstrated self-efficacy with her belief that she could publish her first book about Harry Potter despite repeated rejections.
- Self-efficacy is related to **self-confidence**, which means general assurance in one's own ideas, judgment, and capabilities.

- Thomas Lynch developed greater self-confidence and found ways to work around his naturally shy and introverted style when he learned that his bosses didn't think he had any ambition for career advancement.
- Understanding oneself is essential for being a good manager, but self-awareness is not easy to achieve. **Self-awareness** means being conscious of the internal aspects of one's nature, such as personality traits, beliefs, emotions, attitudes, and perceptions, and appreciating how your patterns affect other people.
- Two valuable ways to enhance self-awareness are soliciting feedback and self-assessment, including introspection.

10-2 Job Satisfaction and Trust

Most managers strive to develop and reinforce positive attitudes among all employees because people are healthier and more effective when they have positive feelings about their jobs, their coworkers, the company, and the work environment.[16] Two important elements of happy and productive employees are job satisfaction and trust.

10-2a Job Satisfaction

Job satisfaction reflects the degree to which a person finds fulfillment in his or her job. In general, people experience job satisfaction when their work matches their needs and interests, when working conditions and rewards (such as pay) are satisfactory, when they like their coworkers, and

Luke Sharrett/Bloomberg/Getty Images

Concept Connection

Surveys indicate that competitive pay is one of the top contributors to **job satisfaction,** but how people feel about their jobs also has a lot to do with other factors, such as a feeling of purpose and good working conditions. Two areas in which satisfaction has declined significantly since the late 1980s are job security and health care benefits.

when they have positive relationships with supervisors. Take the quiz in Exhibit 10.2 to better understand some of the factors that contribute to job satisfaction.

Managers, particularly for today's knowledge workers, often rely on job satisfaction to keep motivation and enthusiasm high. They can't afford to lose talented, highly skilled employees. Regrettably, a recent survey by the Conference Board found that less than 50 percent of U.S. employees say they are satisfied at work. The two categories where satisfaction has declined the most since the survey began in 1987 are job security and health care benefits, reflecting growing dissatisfaction with the changing social contract between employers and employees, as discussed in Chapter 9.[17]

Managers create the environment that determines whether employees have positive or negative feelings toward their jobs.[18] For example, in a survey of more than 20,000 employees worldwide by *The New York Times* and the *Harvard Business Review*, people with a manager who created a clear and inspiring vision were 70 percent more satisfied with their jobs and 100 percent more likely to stay with the company. Those who felt that they were treated with respect were 55 percent more satisfied and engaged and 200 percent more likely to stay with the company.[19]

10-2b Trust

"Organizations are no longer built on force. They are increasingly built on trust."

—PETER DRUCKER,
MANAGEMENT SCHOLAR AND
AUTHOR OF *MANAGEMENT
CHALLENGES FOR THE 21ST
CENTURY*

Considering how important trust is in any relationship, it is surprising how little attention many managers devote to building and maintaining trust in the workplace. Trust can make all the difference between an employee who is emotionally committed to the organization and one who is not.[20] **Organizational commitment** refers to an employee's loyalty to and engagement with the organization. An employee with a high degree of organizational commitment is likely to say *we* when talking about the company. Such a person likes being a part of the organization and tries to contribute to its success. Sadly, the most recent Gallup workforce survey found that 68.5 percent of employees in the United States were *disengaged* in 2018 with the highest level of disengagement among younger employees.[21] Other surveys suggest that commitment and engagement levels around the world are also relatively low.[22]

These results reflect a low level of trust in management, which is an essential component for success in today's chaotic environment. Companies cannot prevent major catastrophes or crises, but by

Green Power

Make It Meaningful The success of a sustainability program often depends on the ability of managers to engage employees. Canada's LoyaltyOne management team believes the secret to employee satisfaction lies in doing small things that transform employee thinking and behavior over time. LoyaltyOne's sustainability efforts, including regular town hall meetings, annual environmental fairs, contests, and giveaways, create a participatory culture of fun as the organization moves to fulfill its sustainability goals. Employees are encouraged to build initiatives based on their own concerns. LoyaltyOne provided people with take-home meters to measure their personal power usage, which had greater impact

on individual social responsibility than any lecture or position paper. Recognized in 2016 by global consulting firm Aon Hewitt as one of the Best Employers in Canada for the seventh time, LoyaltyOne successfully injects challenge, empowerment, creativity, fun, and "making a difference" into the workplace sustainability experience of each employee.

SOURCES: "Environmental Sustainability and Top Talents," *Cool Choices*, August 4, 2011, www.coolchoicesnetwork.org/2011/08/04/environmental-sustainability-and-top-talents/(accessed August 1, 2012); Derek Wong, "Top Talents Attracted to Socially Responsible Companies," *Environmental Leaders: Environmental and Energy Management News*, July 11, 2011, http://www.environmentalleader.com/2011/07/11/top-talents-attracted-to-socially-responsible-companies (accessed August 1, 2012); and "2016 Aon Best Employers in Canada," http://www.aon.com/canada/products-services/human-capital-consulting/consulting/best_employers/ (accessed April 26, 2016).

Exhibit 10.2 Rate Your Job Satisfaction

Instructions: Think of a job—either a current or previous job—that was important to you, and then answer the following questions with respect to how satisfied you were with that job. Please answer the six questions with a number (1–5) that reflects the extent of your satisfaction.

| 1 = Very dissatisfied | 3 = Neutral | 5 = Very satisfied |
| 2 = Dissatisfied | 4 = Satisfied | |

	1	2	3	4	5
1. Overall, how satisfied are you with your job?	1	2	3	4	5
2. How satisfied are you with the opportunities to learn new things?	1	2	3	4	5
3. How satisfied are you with your boss?	1	2	3	4	5
4. How satisfied are you with the people in your work group?	1	2	3	4	5
5. How satisfied are you with the amount of pay you receive?	1	2	3	4	5
6. How satisfied are you with the advancement that you are making in the organization?	1	2	3	4	5

Scoring and Interpretation: Add up your responses to the six questions to obtain your total score: _____. The questions represent various aspects of satisfaction that an employee may experience on a job. If your score is 24 or above, you probably feel satisfied with the job. If your score is 12 or below, you probably do not feel satisfied. What is your level of performance in your job, and is your performance related to your level of satisfaction?

SOURCES: These questions were adapted from Daniel R. Denison, *Corporate Culture and Organizational Effectiveness* (New York: John Wiley, 1990); and John D. Cook et al., *The Experience of Work: A Compendium and Review of 249 Measures and Their Use* (San Diego, CA: Academic Press, 1981).

building organizations based on trust, they can be "battle-ready" when crises and catastrophes hit. When Irene Rosenfeld, CEO of Mondelez International, talked about the restructuring of Kraft (the predecessor of Mondelez) at the World Business Forum, she emphasized the effort that managers had made to be "straightforward, open, and honest," even in the midst of plant closings and job cuts. The trust that this fostered, Rosenfeld said, was "a critical part" of the company's ability to move forward.[23] Various polls in recent years have found that a majority of people don't trust what senior management is telling them. Most people think managers try to hide things or "spin" them.[24] Only 20 percent of people surveyed by Leadership IQ, a leadership training organization, said that they strongly trust their top management, with 36 percent reporting a moderate trust level and 44 percent saying that they either distrust or strongly distrust their bosses.[25] In addition, the survey confirms that trust relates to organizational commitment. According to the study, about 32 percent of an employee's desire to stay with a company or leave depends on trust in management. Most of us don't need a poll to tell us that the level of trust in business and government leaders is dismal. From the Enron debacle early in the century, to the scads of Wall Street managers and traders rewarded for unethical behavior with large bonuses during the 2008 financial crisis, to the recent efforts of VW managers to deceive U.S regulators regarding diesel emissions, there are numerous reasons why people mistrust organizational leadership.

HOT TOPIC

Once trust is undermined, everything else tends to unravel. Managers promote trust by being open and honest in their business dealings, keeping employees informed, giving them a say in decisions, providing the necessary training and other resources that enable them to succeed, treating them fairly, and offering rewards that they value. "People in leadership positions simply have not done a good job of earning trust," says Doug Harward, president of Training Industry, Inc. "Employees have a right to expect that their managers are trustworthy and that they will create stable organizations. Too many of our leaders have violated that trust."[26]

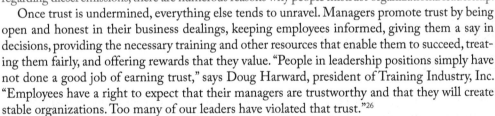

Remember This

- A positive feeling about one's job is called **job satisfaction**.
- Surveys suggest that less than half of employees in the United States are satisfied with their jobs.
- In one global survey, people with managers who created a clear and inspiring vision were 70 percent more satisfied with their jobs, and those who felt respected at work were 55 percent more satisfied and engaged.

- **Organizational commitment** refers to loyalty to and engagement with one's work organization.
- Trust is an important component of organizational commitment.
- A survey found that 32 percent of an employee's desire to stay with a company or leave depends on the employee's trust in management.

10-3 Perception and Attributions

Other critical aspects of understanding behavior are perception and attributions, which are special kinds of perception.

10-3a Perception and Perceptual Distortions

Perception is the cognitive process that people use to make sense out of the environment by selecting, organizing, and interpreting information from the environment. Because of individual differences in personality, values, interests, and so forth, people often "see" the same thing in different ways. A class that is boring to one student might be fascinating to another. One student might perceive an assignment to be challenging and stimulating, whereas another might find it a silly waste of time.

We can think of perception as a step-by-step process, as shown in Exhibit 10.3. First, we observe information (sensory data) from the environment through our senses: taste, smell, hearing, sight, and touch. Next, our mind screens the data and will select only the items that we will process further. Third, we organize the selected data into meaningful patterns for interpretation and response. Most differences in perception among people at work are related to how they select and organize sensory data. You can experience differences in perceptual organization by looking at the visuals in Exhibit 10.4. What do you see in part a. of Exhibit 10.4? Most people see this image as a dog, but others see only a series of unrelated ink blots. Some people will see the figure in part b. as a beautiful young woman while others will see an old one. Now look at part c. How many blocks do you see—six or seven? Some people have to turn the figure upside down before they can see seven blocks. These visuals illustrate the complexity of perception.

Of particular concern in the work environment are **perceptual distortions**, errors in perceptual judgment that arise from inaccuracies in any part of the perception process. The CEO of Pershing Square Capital Management had a very costly perceptual distortion, as described in the "Half-Baked Management" box.

One common perceptual error is **stereotyping**, the tendency to assign an individual to a group or broad category (e.g., female, black, elderly; or male, white, disabled) and then to attribute widely held generalizations about the group to the individual. As an example, someone meets a new colleague, sees that he is in a wheelchair, assigns him to the category "physically disabled," and attributes to this colleague generalizations that she believes about people with disabilities,

Half-Baked Management ⎱ Valeant

William A. Ackman of the hedge fund Pershing Square Capital Management and Valeant Pharmaceuticals International is an in-your-face activist investor, someone who boldly speaks his mind and never seemed to think he made a mistake, and certainly has never apologized for anything. He has made billions of dollars with that style and fancies himself in the mold of the more measured Warren E. Buffett.

Ackman always supported whatever Valeant did and even staked his own reputation on that support. In the face of criticism and scrutiny from regulators on Valeant's aggressive pricing moves, Ackman faced down even the Senate in a hearing about the pharma company's aggressive practice of buying up drugs and jacking up the prices.

But in March 2017, Ackman conceded that his push for Pershing to take on Valeant Pharmaceuticals was "a huge mistake" and cost the firm $4 billion. Stock prices of the Pershing Square went from $257 per share to $12.11. "I personally assume 100 percent of the responsibility on behalf of the firm," he said—Yeah, but did he use his own money to pay back the investors who lost so much?

SOURCE: Alexandra Stevenson, "Valeant Bet Was a 'Huge Mistake,'" *The New York Times*, March 29, 2017, https://www.nytimes.com/2017/03/29/business/dealbook/valeant-bet-was-a-huge-mistake-hedge-fund-chief-ackman-says.html

Exhibit 10.3 The Perception Process

Exhibit 10.4 Perception—What Do You See?

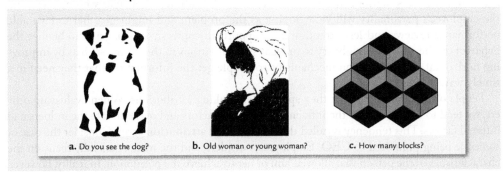

a. Do you see the dog?   **b.** Old woman or young woman?   **c.** How many blocks?

which may include a belief that he is less able than other coworkers. However, his inability to walk should not be seen as indicative of lesser abilities in other areas. Stereotyping prevents people from truly knowing those whom they classify in this way. In addition, negative stereotypes prevent talented people from advancing in an organization and fully contributing their talents to the organization's success.

The **halo effect** occurs when the perceiver develops an overall impression of a person or situation based on one characteristic, either favorable or unfavorable. In other words, a halo blinds the perceiver to other characteristics that should be used in generating a more complete assessment. The halo effect can play a significant role in performance appraisal, as we discussed in Chapter 9. For example, a person with an outstanding attendance record may be assessed as responsible, industrious, and highly productive; another person with less-than-average attendance may be assessed as a poor performer. Either assessment may be true, but it is the manager's job to be sure that the assessment is based on complete information about all job-related characteristics, not just the employee's attendance record. How accurate is your perception? Answering the questions in Exhibit 10.5 will give you an idea of whether you allow perceptual distortions to cloud your judgment.

Exhibit 10.5 How Accurate Is Your Perception?

Instructions: Think about a job that you have held or a project that you have worked on in class or a volunteer organization. With respect to data or information coming to you, rate whether each statement below is Mostly True or Mostly False for you.

	Mostly True	Mostly False
1. I look for inconsistencies and seek explanations for them.	_____	_____
2. I generate multiple explanations for available information.	_____	_____
3. I check for omissions, distortions, or exaggerations in available information.	_____	_____
4. I make it a point to distinguish facts from opinions.	_____	_____
5. I stay conscious of my own style of approaching problems and how this might affect the way that I process information.	_____	_____
6. I am well aware of my own biases and values that influence the way I see people.	_____	_____

Scoring and Interpretation: Your total score is the number of Mostly True answers to all six questions. A score of 5 or 6 suggests that you are conscious of and make attempts to remove distortions from your perception. A score of 3 or 4 indicates that you make a solid effort, and a score of 1 or 2 suggests that you take perception for granted. Look at any individual items where you have marked Mostly False to get an idea of where you might have perceptual weaknesses. What can you do to improve your perception?

SOURCE: Adapted from Patricia M. Fandt, *Management Skills: Practice and Experience* (Minneapolis: West Publishing, 1994), pp. 210–211.

10-3b Attributions: A Special Case of Perception

Among the assessments that people make as part of the perception process are attributions.[27] **Attributions** are judgments about what caused a person's behavior—something about the person or something about the situation. People make attributions as an attempt to understand why others behave as they do. An *internal attribution* says that characteristics of the person led to the behavior. ("Sophia missed the deadline because she's careless and lazy.") An *external attribution* says that something about the situation caused the person's behavior. ("Sophia missed the deadline because she couldn't get the information she needed in a timely manner.") Understanding attributions is important because attributions influence how a manager will handle a situation. In the case of the missed deadline, a manager who blames it on the employee's personality will view Sophia as the problem and might give her unfavorable performance reviews and less attention and support. In contrast, a manager who blames the behavior on the situation might try to prevent such situations in the future, such as by improving horizontal communication mechanisms so people get the information that they need in a timely way.

People often have biases that they apply when making attributions. When evaluating others, we tend to underestimate the influence of external factors and overestimate the influence of internal factors. This tendency is called the **fundamental attribution error.** Consider the case of someone being promoted to CEO. Employees, outsiders, and the media generally focus on the characteristics of the person that allowed him or her to achieve the promotion. In reality, however, the selection of that person might have been heavily influenced by external factors, such as business conditions creating a need for someone with a strong financial or marketing background at that particular time.

Another bias that distorts attributions involves those that we make about our own behavior. People tend to overestimate the contribution of internal factors to their successes and overestimate the contribution of external factors to their failures. This tendency, called the **self-serving bias,** means that people give themselves too much credit when they do well and give external forces too much blame when they fail. Laszlo Bock, the senior vice president of people operations at Google, says humility is an important characteristic that the company looks for when hiring because highly intelligent, successful people can tend to have a self-serving bias. That is, they think "if something good happens, it's because I'm a genius. If something bad happens, it's because someone's an idiot or I didn't get the resources or the market moved," he says. Bock says the most successful people at Google are those who will argue vehemently for their position but are also able to admit to their mistakes and can step back and say, "Oh well, that changes things. You're right."[28]

Remember This

- **Perception** is the cognitive process that people use to make sense out of the environment by selecting, organizing, and interpreting information.
- People often see the same thing in different ways.
- **Perceptual distortions** are errors in perceptual judgment that result from inaccuracies in any part of the perception process.
- **Stereotyping** refers to the tendency to assign an individual to a group or broad category and then attribute generalizations about the group to the individual.
- The **halo effect** occurs when a perceiver develops an overall impression of a person or situation based on one characteristic, either favorable or unfavorable.

- **Attributions** are judgments about what caused a person's behavior—either characteristics of the person or of the situation.
- An internal attribution says that characteristics of the individual caused the person to behave in a certain way, whereas an external attribution places the cause on aspects of the situation.
- The **fundamental attribution error** is a tendency to underestimate the influence of external factors on another person's behavior and to overestimate the influence of internal factors.
- The **self-serving bias** is the tendency to overestimate the contribution of internal factors to one's successes and the contribution of external factors to one's failures.

10-4 Personality and Behavior

In recent years, many employers have shown a heightened interest in matching people's personalities to the needs of the job and the organization. An individual's **personality** is the set of characteristics that underlie a relatively stable pattern of behavior in response to ideas, objects, or people in the environment. Interestingly, although 71 percent of human resource (HR) professionals surveyed say personality tests can be useful for predicting job-related behavior and organizational fit, the use of such tests has actually declined in recent years. Only 18 percent reported that their companies use personality tests in hiring and promotion decisions. Part of the reason is that more companies are relying on social media to assess candidates based on what they have to say and show about themselves.[29]

10-4a Personality Traits

In common use, people think of personality in terms of traits, the fairly consistent characteristics that a person exhibits. Researchers investigated whether any traits stand up to scientific scrutiny. Although investigators examined thousands of traits over the years, their findings fit into five general dimensions that describe personality. These dimensions, often called the "Big Five" personality factors, are illustrated in Exhibit 10.6.[30] Each factor may contain a wide range of specific traits. The **Big Five personality factors** describe an individual's extroversion, agreeableness, conscientiousness, emotional stability, and openness to experience:

1. *Extroversion.* The degree to which a person is outgoing, sociable, assertive, and comfortable with interpersonal relationships.

2. *Agreeableness.* The degree to which a person is able to get along with others by being good natured, likable, cooperative, forgiving, understanding, and trusting.

3. *Conscientiousness.* The degree to which a person is focused on a few goals, thus behaving in ways that are responsible, dependable, persistent, and achievement-oriented.

4. *Emotional stability.* The degree to which a person is calm, enthusiastic, and self-confident, rather than tense, depressed, moody, or insecure.

5. *Openness to experience.* The degree to which a person has a broad range of interests and is imaginative, creative, artistically sensitive, and willing to consider new ideas.

Exhibit 10.6 The Big Five Personality Factors

Instructions: Each individual's collection of personality traits is different; it is what makes us unique. But although each *collection* of traits varies, we all share many common traits. The following phrases describe various traits and behaviors. Rate how accurately each statement describes you on a scale of 1 to 5, with 1 being very inaccurate and 5 very accurate. Describe yourself as you are now, not as you wish to be. There are no right or wrong answers.

Very Inaccurate   1   2   3   4   5   Very Accurate

__ Extroversion __
I am usually the life of the party.	1	2	3	4	5
I feel comfortable around people.	1	2	3	4	5
I am talkative.	1	2	3	4	5

__ Neuroticism (Low Emotional Stability) __
I often feel critical of myself.	1	2	3	4	5
I often envy others.	1	2	3	4	5
I am temperamental.	1	2	3	4	5

__ Agreeableness __
I am kind and sympathetic.	1	2	3	4	5
I have a good word for everyone.	1	2	3	4	5
I never insult people.	1	2	3	4	5

__ Openness to New Experiences __
I am imaginative.	1	2	3	4	5
I prefer to vote for liberal political candidates.	1	2	3	4	5
I really like art.	1	2	3	4	5

__ Conscientiousness __
I am systematic and efficient.	1	2	3	4	5
I pay attention to details.	1	2	3	4	5
I am always prepared for class.	1	2	3	4	5

Which are your most prominent traits? For fun and discussion, compare your responses with those of classmates.

stefanolunardi/Shutterstock.com

Concept Connection

Marriott carefully screens candidates for critical customer service positions, such as this housekeeper at a Marriott Residence Inn in Cleveland, Ohio. One important way managers determine whether people have the "right stuff" is through **personality testing**. During the application process, candidates answer a series of questions about their beliefs, attitudes, work habits, and how they might handle situations; this enables Marriott to identify people with interests and motivations that are compatible with company values. As managers reevaluate Marriott's mission and goals, the test evolves.

HOT TOPIC

As illustrated in the exhibit, these factors represent a continuum. That is, a person may have a low, moderate, or high degree of each quality. Answer the questions in Exhibit 10.6 to see where you fall on the Big Five scale for each of the factors. A company called Five Labs gave people a chance to test their Big Five profile based on their Facebook postings. The tool analyzed people's Facebook posts to come up with how they rate on the Big Five attributes. Then, the company showed the people how they compare to famous people as well as to their Facebook friends. Five Labs cofounder Nikita Bier says the point of the exercise was to give people an idea of what social media companies are doing. Facebook, Google, Twitter, and others look at the queries, updates, and so forth that people put on their sites to help decide what ads might be most persuasive. "The predictive qualities of the five types are good for advertising," Bier said. "People who are more open go to coffee shops and have interesting apartments. You might want to give them an ad for Ikea. Neurotic people worry about their health, so you might pitch them vitamins."[31]

Having a moderate-to-high degree of each of the Big Five personality factors is considered desirable for a wide range of employees, but this isn't always a key to success. For example, having an outgoing, sociable personality (extroversion) is considered desirable for managers, but many successful leaders, including Larry Page of Google, Apple CEO Tim Cook, 2016 presidential candidate Hillary Clinton, and screenwriter and director Steven Spielberg, are introverts, people who may become drained by social encounters and need time alone to reflect and recharge their batteries. One study found that 4 in 10 top executives test out to be introverts.[32] Two other introverts who have found success in high-profile positions are Marisa Mayer and Richard Branson.

Sunny Side Up ⟩ Marissa Mayer, Yahoo, and Richard Branson, Virgin Group

If you ever watched the YouTube video of Marissa Mayer interviewing Lady Gaga, or saw *Vogue*'s take on her 2009 wedding to Zack Bogue, you probably wouldn't think of her as an introvert, but Mayer describes herself as a very shy person by nature. She says that in high school, she was the student who knew all the answers but waited to be called on. Like many introverts, Mayer can overcome her natural tendencies to do things that are important to her.

Another leader who understands that is Richard Branson, who dresses up in silly costumes to publicize the Virgin Group. Branson says that his flamboyant public persona bears little resemblance to his innate personality. "I was a shy and retiring individual who couldn't make speeches and get out there," Branson says of himself prior to founding Virgin. "I had to train myself into becoming more of an extrovert" in order to promote the new company.

Nancy Ancowitz wrote a book called *Self-Promotion for Introverts* because she knew from experience that it is easy for introverted people to get overlooked in the corporate world. Ancowitz worked for years on Wall Street, but she found so draining the days filled with meetings, constant jockeying for attention, and the lack of quiet time to reflect and recharge that she eventually left. However, she learned some valuable lessons before doing so, such as the importance of speaking up more frequently at meetings, making sure her accomplishments were noticed, and building a strong professional network. Ancowitz says that she could have thrived on Wall Street, even as an introvert, if she had wanted it badly enough, but today she works as a consultant helping other introverts learn to raise their visibility so they can succeed in the business world.[33]

In recent years, there has been a growing awareness that introverted people have some qualities that actually might make them better leaders.[34] The following "Sunny Side Up" box describes some benefits of the introverted personality for managers and offers some tips for introverted managers on how to shine despite their lack of natural gregariousness. Introversion or extroversion is simply one aspect of an individual's personality, and each style has both strengths and weaknesses.

Although the quality of extroversion is not as significant as is often presumed, traits of agreeableness seem to be particularly important in today's collaborative organizations. Studies show that people who score high on agreeableness are more likely to get jobs and keep them than are less agreeable people.[35] Although there is also some evidence that people who are *overly* agreeable tend to be promoted less often, the days are over when a hard-driving manager can run roughshod over others to earn a promotion. Executive search firm Korn Ferry International examined data from millions of manager profiles and found that the most successful executives are team-oriented leaders who gather information and work collaboratively with many different people.[36] Recent research also suggests that traits of conscientiousness are more important than those of extroversion for effective management. A study at the Stanford Graduate School of Business found a link between how guilty people feel when they make serious mistakes and how well they perform as leaders. Guilt can be a positive emotion for a manager because it is associated with a heightened sense of responsibility to others.[37]

10-4b Attitudes and Behaviors Influenced by Personality

An individual's personality influences his or her work-related attitudes and behaviors. As a new manager, you will have to manage people with a wide variety of personality characteristics. Four areas related to personality that are of particular interest to managers are locus of control, authoritarianism, Machiavellianism, and problem-solving styles.

Sunny Side Up ⟩ The Rise of the Introverted Manager

In today's world of open offices and collaborative work arrangements, being an introverted manager is a challenge, especially in the United States and other cultures that reward people for being outgoing and sociable. Yet experts are beginning to tout the virtues of the introverted manager, as well as offer tips for how introverts can make sure that they don't get lost amid the gregarious leaders around them.

The Upside of Being an Introvert

Some benefits of an introverted personality include the following:

- **They are more cautious and deliberate.** Introverts tend to make more thoughtful decisions. They can become excited by opportunities and potential rewards, but they seem to have a keener awareness of risks than do extroverts, which can help to prevent train wrecks such as those that felled Bear Stearns and Lehmann Brothers.

- **They have a greater ability to listen and take suggestions.** We've all been charmed by charismatic, talkative people who are "working the room" while the introverts are huddled in a corner. Yet new research confirms what many of us suspect: Extroverts tend to be poor listeners! Adam M. Grant, who studies this subject, says that introverted managers can be better bosses in dynamic and unpredictable environments because of their ability to listen, empathize with others, and empower employees to think for themselves.

- **They are more creative.** The most stunningly innovative people in many fields are introverts. Why? Because creativity thrives on solitude. "Without great solitude, no serious work is possible," Picasso said. Steve Jobs was the extrovert behind Apple, but the company would never have come into being without the hard work put in by introverted cofounder Steve Wozniak, who spent long hours working alone to create the company's first computer. "Most inventors and engineers I've met are like me . . . they live in their heads," Wozniak said.

Succeeding as an Introverted Manager

Introverted managers can get overlooked, particularly in large organizations. In addition, introverts are often,

CONTINUED

although not always, shy, which makes it harder for them to feel comfortable in the role of a manager. Here are some tips that can help introverts succeed as managers:

- **Stretch your personality.** If you want something badly enough, you can stretch the limits of a naturally introverted personality. Like Richard Branson, who had to train himself to act more extroverted to promote Virgin, managers can stretch beyond their natural tendency toward introversion to achieve an important goal.

- **Focus on what you're good at.** Many introverts have trouble with large events, but as managers they may attend a lot of them. Rebekah Campbell, CEO of Posse, says it pays for introverts to focus on their greater ability to engage people one-on-one rather than trying to work the room. Successful introverts also try to quickly chat with people they want to meet, getting contact information so they can follow up later in a more comfortable situation.

- **Mix with people, speak up, and get out there.** If you want to be a manager, and particularly if you want to advance to higher levels, there is no denying that you need to push yourself to get out there and connect with people both within and outside the organization. You will have to speak up at meetings, make presentations, and be more sociable at conferences and other professional events. You can behave in more extroverted ways when you need to. Just remember to find alone time to recharge your batteries.

SOURCES: Based on Adam M.Grant, Francesca Gino, and David A. Hoffmann, "The Hidden Advantages of Quiet Bosses," *Harvard Business Review* (December 2010): 28; Susan Cain, "The Rise of the New Groupthink," *The New York Times*, January 15, 2012; Bryan Walsh, "The Upside of Being an Introvert (and Why Extroverts Are Overrated)," *Time* (February 6, 2012): 40–45; Joann S. Lublin, "Introverted Execs Find Ways to Shine," *The Wall Street Journal Asia*, April 18, 2011; Jack and Suzy Welch, "The Welchway: Release Your Inner Extrovert," *BusinessWeek* (December 8, 2008): 92; and Rebekah Campbell, "An Introvert's Guide to Networking," *The New York Times*, October 15, 2014.

iStock.com/monkeybusinessimages

Concept Connection

Teach for America sends recent college graduates to teach for two years in low-income schools throughout the United States. What does Teach for America look for when reviewing approximately 45,000 applications for only about 5,000 positions? Founder and former CEO Wendy Kopp says a high **internal locus of control** is at the top of her list. Those are the candidates who, when faced with a challenge, respond with optimism and resolve. Says Kopp, "They have the instinct to figure out what they can control and to own it, rather than to blame everyone else in the system."

Locus of Control   Individuals differ in terms of what they tend to accredit as the cause of their success or failure. **Locus of control** refers to how people perceive the cause of life events—whether they place the primary responsibility within themselves or on outside forces.[38] Some people believe that their own actions strongly influence what happens to them. They feel in control of their own fate. These individuals have a high *internal* locus of control. Other people believe that events in their lives occur because of chance, luck, or outside people and events. They feel more like pawns of their fate. These individuals have a high *external* locus of control.

Research on locus of control shows real differences in behavior across a wide range of settings. People with an internal locus of control are easier to motivate because they believe that rewards are the result of their behavior. They are better able to handle complex information and problem solving, and are more achievement-oriented but are also more independent and therefore more difficult to manage. By contrast, people with an external locus of control are harder to motivate, less involved in their jobs, and more likely to blame others when faced with a poor performance evaluation, but they are also more compliant and conforming and, therefore, easier to manage.[39]

Do you believe luck plays an important role in your life, or do you feel that you control your own fate? To find out more about your locus of control, read the instructions and complete the questionnaire in Exhibit 10.7. Having an internal locus of control would be a plus for anyone going into farming, as shown in the "Recipe for Success" box.

Recipe for Success } **Frank's Little Farm**

"It's a way of life, not an occupation," said Sean McCoy in describing farming. He and his partner, Prairie Wolfe, share the land (and two children) of their urban, Missoula-based "Frank's Little Farm," which is named after Frank Little, an early labor organizer in Montana. McCoy went into farming as an extension of his previous work as an activist, though his college degree was in English. Farming is a way to help the world be more sustainable, he said.

Farming is a huge responsibility and a great deal of work, which is why McCoy recommends people volunteer or intern early to see if that's the kind of life they want. The farmer has to take responsibility for everything, or it doesn't get done. Planning begins in January, when it is determined how many and what kinds of seeds to buy. It's a complicated system that involves figuring out how many of each seed is needed. Farmers have to consider how many sales there will be of each of their almost 20 kinds of vegetables and then order seeds. For example, lettuce heads are planted in either a 30- or 50-foot bed, eight inches apart in four rows. Because farmers sell them every week, they have to have enough head lettuce beds to get through May through early July. Salad mix, on the other hand, is sold the entire season. About half the produce starts out in the greenhouse and is then transplanted to the ground. Part of the planning process is called "mapping," showing where each row of every plant is located. McCoy said larger farms use complex spreadsheets to keep track of seeds, mapping them and planning when to harvest, but his farm is small enough that he is able to keep all of it in his head. Sustainable farming entails crop rotation, which reduces pests (and therefore is a natural pesticide) and many types of plant disease.

Wolfe and McCoy now own their farm after having worked the land owned by several others. "We learned pretty early that it was hard to make a living unless you own the land." This is their third farm and the eighth year on the current one. And when future farmers get their farm, it takes them a while to get it ready and have everything they need. On Frank's Little Farm, for example, Wolfe and McCoy have wash stations to clean vegetables that will be harvested and sold that day. They also need coolers.

What advice does McCoy have for aspiring farmers? They should volunteer and intern at a farm to understand what farming is all about and the amount of work required. They need to be the right kind of person, he said.

"You need to be honest if this is the life you want," said McCoy. "If so, it is very satisfying."

SOURCE: Sean McCoy, personal communication.

Authoritarianism   **Authoritarianism** is the belief that power and status differences should exist within the organization.[40] Individuals high in authoritarianism tend to be concerned with power and toughness, obey recognized authority above them, stick to conventional values, critically judge others, and oppose the use of subjective feelings. The degree to which managers possess authoritarianism will influence how they wield and share power. The degree to which employees possess authoritarianism will influence how they react to their managers. If a manager and employees differ in their degree of authoritarianism, the manager may have difficulty leading effectively. The trend toward empowerment and shifts in expectations among younger employees for more equitable relationships contribute to a decline in strict authoritarianism in many organizations.

Machiavellianism   Another personality dimension that is helpful in understanding work behavior is **Machiavellianism**, which is characterized by the acquisition of power and the manipulation of other people for purely personal gain. Machiavellianism is named after Niccolò Machiavelli, a sixteenth-century Italian political philosopher who wrote *The Prince*, a book for noblemen of the day on how to acquire and use power, in 1513.[41] Psychologists have developed instruments to measure a person's Machiavellianism (Mach) orientation.[42] The short quiz in Exhibit 10.8 will give you an idea of how you rate on Machiavellian tendencies. Research shows that high Machs are predisposed to being pragmatic, capable of lying to achieve personal goals, more likely to win in win-lose situations, and more likely to persuade than be persuaded.[43]

Exhibit 10.7 Measuring Locus of Control

Your Locus of Control

Instructions: For each of these ten questions, indicate the extent to which you agree or disagree using the following scale:

1. = Strongly disagree   4. = Neither disagree nor agree   7. = Strongly agree
2. = Disagree   5. = Slightly agree
3. = Slightly disagree   6. = Agree

	1	2	3	4	5	6	7
1. When I get what I want, it is usually because I worked hard for it.	1	2	3	4	5	6	7
2. When I make plans, I am almost certain to make them work.	1	2	3	4	5	6	7
3. I prefer games involving some luck over games requiring pure skill.	1	2	3	4	5	6	7
4. I can learn almost anything if I set my mind to it.	1	2	3	4	5	6	7
5. My major accomplishments are entirely due to my hard work and ability.	1	2	3	4	5	6	7
6. I usually don't set goals because I have a hard time following through on them.	1	2	3	4	5	6	7
7. Competition discourages excellence.	1	2	3	4	5	6	7
8. Often people get ahead just by being lucky.	1	2	3	4	5	6	7
9. On any sort of exam or competition, I like to know how well I do relative to everyone else.	1	2	3	4	5	6	7
10. It's pointless to keep working on something that's too difficult for me.	1	2	3	4	5	6	7

Scoring and Interpretation: To determine your score, reverse the values that you selected for questions 3, 6, 7, 8, and 10 (1 = 7, 2 = 6, 3 = 5, 4 = 4, 5 = 3, 6 = 2, 7 = 1). For example, if you strongly disagree with the statement in question 3, you would have given it a value of 1. Change this value to a 7. Reverse the scores in a similar manner for questions 6, 7, 8, and 10. Now add the point values for all ten questions together.

Your score _____

Researchers using this questionnaire in a study of college students found a mean of 51.8 for men and 52.2 for women, with a standard deviation of 6 for each. The higher your score on this questionnaire, the more you tend to believe that you are generally responsible for what happens to you; in other words, higher scores are associated with internal locus of control. Lower scores are associated with external locus of control. Scoring low indicates that you tend to believe that forces beyond your control, such as powerful people, fate, or chance, are responsible for what happens to you.

SOURCES: Adapted from J. M. Burger, *Personality: Theory and Research* (Belmont, CA: Wadsworth, 1986), pp. 400–401, cited in D. Hellriegel, J. W. Slocum, Jr., and R. W. Woodman, *Organizational Behavior*, 6th ed. (St. Paul, MN: West, 1992), pp. 97–100. Original source: D. L. Paulhus, "Sphere-Specific Measures of Perceived Control," *Journal of Personality and Social Psychology*, 44, no. 6 (1983): 1253–1265.

Exhibit 10.8 What's Your Mach?

Instructions: Managers differ in how they view human nature and the tactics that they use to get things done through others. Answer the questions below based on how you view others. Think carefully about each question and be honest about what you feel inside. Please answer based on whether each item below is Mostly True or Mostly False for you.

	Mostly True	Mostly False
1. Overall, it is better to be humble and honest than to be successful and dishonest.	_____	_____
2. If you trust someone completely, you are asking for trouble.	_____	_____
3. A leader should take action only when it is morally right.	_____	_____
4. A good way to handle people is to tell them what they like to hear.	_____	_____
5. There is no excuse for telling a white lie to someone.	_____	_____
6. It makes sense to flatter important people.	_____	_____
7. Most people who get ahead as leaders have led very moral lives.	_____	_____
8. It is better not to tell people the real reason that you did something unless it benefits you to do so.	_____	_____
9. The vast majority of people are brave, good, and kind.	_____	_____
10. It is hard to get to the top without sometimes cutting corners.	_____	_____

Scoring and Interpretation: To compute your Mach score, give yourself one point for each Mostly False answer to items 1, 3, 5, 7, and 9, and one point for each Mostly True answer to items 2, 4, 6, 8, and 10. These items were drawn from the works of Machiavelli. Successful management intrigue at the time of Machiavelli was believed to require behaviors that today would be considered ego centered and manipulative, which is almost the opposite of more enlightened management. A score of 8–10 points suggests that you have a high Mach score; 4–7 points indicate a moderate score; and 0–3 points indicate a low Mach score. Having a high Mach score does not mean that the individual is a sinister or vicious person, but it probably means that he or she has a cool detachment, sees life as a game, and is not personally engaged with other people. Discuss your results with other students, and talk about whether you think politicians and top executives would have a high or a low Mach score.

SOURCE: Adapted from R. Christie and F. L. Geis, *Studies in Machiavellianism* (New York: Academic Press, 1970).

Different situations may require people who demonstrate one or the other type of behavior. In loosely structured situations, high Machs actively take control, while low Machs accept the direction given by others. Low Machs thrive in highly structured situations while high Machs perform in a detached, disinterested way. High Machs are particularly good in jobs that require bargaining skills or that involve substantial rewards for winning.[44]

Remember This

- **Personality** is the set of characteristics that underlie a relatively stable pattern of behavior in response to ideas, objects, or people in the environment.

- The **Big Five personality factors** are dimensions that describe an individual's extroversion, agreeableness, conscientiousness, emotional stability, and openness to experience.

- Marissa Mayer, Tim Cook, Steven Spielberg, and Hillary Clinton are examples of leaders with introverted personalities who succeeded in high-profile positions.

- **Locus of control** defines whether an individual places the primary responsibility for her or his successes and failures within herself or himself or on outside forces.

- **Authoritarianism** is the belief that power and status differences should exist within an organization.

- A person high in authoritarianism is typically concerned with power and status, obeys established authority, and sticks to conventional values.

- **Machiavellianism** refers to a tendency to direct one's behavior toward the acquisition of power and the manipulation of other people for personal gain.

10-4c Problem-Solving Styles and the Myers-Briggs Type Indicator™

Managers also need to realize that individuals solve problems and make decisions in different ways. One approach to understanding problem-solving styles grew out of the work of psychologist Carl Jung. Jung believed that differences resulted from our preferences in how we go about gathering and evaluating information.[45] According to Jung, gathering information and evaluating information are separate activities. People gather information either by *sensation* or *intuition*, but not by both simultaneously. Sensation-type people would rather work with known facts and hard data and prefer routine and order in gathering information. Intuitive-type people would rather look for possibilities than work with facts and prefer solving new problems and using abstract concepts.

Evaluating information involves making judgments about the information that a person has gathered. People evaluate information by *thinking* or *feeling*. These represent the extremes in orientation. Thinking-type individuals base their judgments on impersonal analysis, using reason and logic rather than personal values or emotional aspects of the situation. Feeling-type individuals base their judgments more on personal feelings such as harmony and tend to make decisions that result in approval from others.

According to Jung, only one of the four functions—sensation, intuition, thinking, or feeling—is dominant in an individual. However, the dominant function usually is backed up by one of the functions from the other set of paired opposites. Exhibit 10.9 shows the four problem-solving styles that result from these matchups, as well as occupations that people with each style tend to prefer.

Two additional sets of paired opposites not directly related to problem solving are *introversion-extroversion* and *judging-perceiving*. Introverts gain energy by focusing on personal thoughts and feelings, whereas extroverts gain energy from being around others and interacting with others. On the judging versus perceiving dimension, people with a judging preference favor certainty and closure and tend to make decisions quickly based on available data. Perceiving people, on the other hand, enjoy ambiguity, dislike deadlines, and may change their minds several times as they gather large amounts of data and information to make decisions.

"Each of us is meant to have a character all our own, to be what no other can exactly be, and do what no other can exactly do."
—WILLIAM ELLERY CHANNING (1780–1842), AMERICAN WRITER AND CLERGYMAN

Exhibit 10.9 Four Problem-Solving Styles

Personal Style	Action Tendencies	Likely Occupations
Sensation-Thinking	• Emphasizes details, facts, certainty • Is a decisive, applied thinker • Focuses on short-term, realistic goals • Develops rules and regulations for judging performance	• Accounting • Production • Software engineers • Market research • Engineering
Intuitive-Thinking	• Prefers dealing with theoretical or technical problems • Is a creative, progressive, perceptive thinker • Focuses on possibilities using impersonal analysis • Is able to consider a number of options and problems simultaneously	• Systems design • Internet security • Law • Middle/top management • Teaching business, economics
Sensation-Feeling	• Shows concern for current, real-life human problems • Is pragmatic, analytical, methodical, and conscientious • Emphasizes detailed facts about people rather than tasks • Focuses on structuring organizations for the benefit of people	• Directing supervisor • Counseling • Negotiating • Selling • Interviewing
Intuitive-Feeling	• Avoids specifics • Is charismatic, participative, people-oriented, and helpful • Focuses on general views, broad themes, and feelings • Decentralizes decision making, develops few rules and regulations	• Public relations • Advertising • Human Resources • Politics • Customer service

A widely used test that measures how people differ on all four of Jung's sets of paired opposites is the **Myers-Briggs Type Indicator (MBTI™)** assessment. The MBTI™ assessment measures a person's preferences for introversion versus extroversion, sensation versus intuition, thinking versus feeling, and judging versus perceiving. The various combinations of these four preferences result in 16 unique personality types.

Each of these types can have positive and negative consequences for behavior. Based on the limited research that has been done, the two preferences that seem to be most strongly associated with effective management in a variety of organizations and industries are thinking and judging.[46] However, people with other preferences can also be good managers. One advantage of understanding your natural preferences is to maximize your innate strengths and abilities and minimize your weaknesses.

Nearly 200 agencies of the U.S. government, including the Environmental Protection Agency (EPA), the Central Intelligence Agency (CIA), and the Department of Veterans Affairs (VA), have been reported to use the MBTI™ instrument as part of their training programs. Brian Twillman of the EPA says that at least a quarter of the agency's 17,000 federal employees have taken the test, and that without it, "there would be a lot of blind spots within the agency."[47] Many corporations have used the MBTI™ to help people better understand themselves and improve their interactions. Hallmark Cards, for example, used the assessment to give managers greater self-awareness and insight into how their patterns of thought and behavior affect others. "We tend to place people into 'files' according to our perceptions of them, which are often skewed," said Mary Beth Ebmeyer, HR manager for corporate development at Hallmark.[48]

Some organizations also use the MBTI™ assessment to help put people in the right jobs, where they will be happiest and make their best contribution to the organization. In one survey, 89 of the *Fortune* 100 companies reported that they have used the test in hiring and promotion decisions.[49]

Remember This

- Four problem-solving styles are sensation-thinking, intuitive-thinking, sensation-feeling, and intuitive-feeling.
- The **Myers-Briggs Type Indicator (MBTI™)** assessment measures a person's preferences for introversion versus extroversion, sensation versus

intuition, thinking versus feeling, and judging versus perceiving.

- Hallmark Cards used the MBTI™ assessment to increase managers' self-awareness and enable them to understand how their patterns of behavior affect others.

10-5 Emotions

Managers might like to think that people come to work and conduct their jobs in a logical and rational manner, leaving their emotions at home or tucked safely in the car until it's time to go home for the day. Yet people cannot be separated from their emotions, and organizations suffer when managers fail to pay attention to how employees' emotions affect productivity and the work environment.[50] Managers can increase their effectiveness by understanding positive and negative emotions and developing emotional intelligence.

10-5a Positive and Negative Emotions

Although the term is somewhat difficult to define in a precise way, an **emotion** can be thought of as a mental state that arises spontaneously within a person based on interaction with the environment rather than through conscious effort and is often accompanied by physiological changes or sensations. People can experience a wide range of emotions at work, such as happiness, anger, fear, or relief, and these affect their workplace attitudes and behaviors. Researchers have been attempting to understand emotions for thousands of years, and scientific debate continues about how to categorize emotions.[51] One model that is useful for managers, shown in Exhibit 10.10, distinguishes the major positive and negative emotions. Negative emotions are sparked when a person becomes frustrated in trying to achieve his or her goals, while positive emotions are triggered when people are on track toward achieving goals.

Thus, emotions can be understood as being determined by whether people are getting their needs and goals met. An employee who fails to get a pay raise or is reprimanded by a supervisor would likely experience negative emotions such as sadness, anger, or anxiety, whereas a person who gets a promotion would experience feelings of pride and happiness. Managers can influence whether people experience primarily positive or negative emotions at work. For one thing, the emotional state of the manager influences the entire team or department. Most of us realize that we can "catch" emotions from others. **Emotional contagion** is the tendency of people to absorb and express the emotions, moods, and attitudes of those around them.[52] If we're around someone who is happy and enthusiastic, the positive emotions rub off on us. On the other hand, someone who is sad and angry can bring us down. Managers who express positive emotions such as happiness, enthusiasm, and appreciation trigger positive emotions and behavior in employees. Research suggests that nearly all human beings are subject to emotional contagion and will automatically and unconsciously start feeling and displaying the same emotions as those around them.[53] A recent study by researchers at the University of Florida, for example, found that rudeness in the workplace "can spread as easily as a common cold." Researchers found that when people witnessed or experienced incidents of rude behavior, they were likely to be rude to the next person they interacted with. "It is an automatic cognitive process and occurs deep in our brains," said lead researcher Trevor Foulk. The study indicates that 98 percent of people have experienced workplace rudeness, with about half of those experiencing it on a weekly basis.[54] Research by organization behavior scientists suggests that negative emotions might spread more easily than positive ones. Psychologists have also found that negative people and events have a disproportionately large effect on our emotions and moods.[55]

Exhibit 10.10 Positive and Negative Emotions

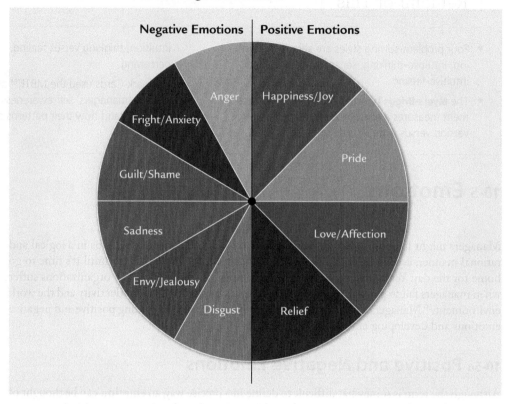

Good managers pay attention to people's emotions because positive emotions are typically linked to higher productivity and greater effectiveness. A *Gallup Management Journal* survey found that managers, especially frontline supervisors, have a lot to do with whether employees have positive or negative emotions associated with their work lives.[56]

10-5b Emotional Intelligence

In recent years, research in the area of *emotional intelligence* has shown that managers who are in touch with their own feelings and the feelings of others can enhance employee and organizational performance. Chade-Meng Tan, a software engineer who was one of Google's early employees and led the team that developed the company's first mobile search service, developed a program to help people strengthen their emotional intelligence.

Sunny Side Up } Chade-Meng Tan, Google

Chade-Meng Tan was employee number 107 at Google. He also held the title of Jolly Good Fellow, a position that included the task to "enlighten minds, open hearts, create world peace." Tan got the appointment to Jolly Good Fellow after he developed an influential course called "Search Inside Yourself."

Tan worked with a team that included outside consultants, a Stanford scientist, and Marc Lesser, a Zen teacher with an MBA and experience as an entrepreneur. Lesser explains that the course is based on the components of emotional intelligence, "or, as we call them, leadership skills." Everyone at Google is expected to be a leader, and at Google, leadership is equated with mindfulness and emotional intelligence. In 2015, approximately 1,500 Googlers went through the training and thousands were on a waiting list for future open seats. The goal of the program is to help people become more aware of their emotions, develop greater empathy and compassion toward others, and be more able to build enduring relationships. Greater emotional intelligence, Lesser says, also improves communication and collaboration by enabling people to think calmly and clearly, listen more closely to others, and be more mindful.[57]

Google offered the first Search Inside Yourself course in 2007, and five years later, Tan and his team made the course available to organizations outside of Google. Today, Lesser serves as CEO of the nonprofit Search Inside Yourself Leadership Institute (SIYLI) and Tan's book, also called *Search Inside Yourself*, has been endorsed by the Dalai Lama and former U.S. President Jimmy Carter.

Emotional intelligence includes four basic components:[58]

- **Self-awareness.** Being aware of what you are feeling; the basis for all the other components. People who are in touch with their feelings are better able to guide their own lives and actions. A high degree of self-awareness means you can accurately assess your own strengths and limitations and have a healthy sense of self-confidence.
- **Self-management.** The ability to control disruptive or harmful emotions and balance one's moods so that worry, anxiety, fear, and anger do not cloud thinking and get in the way of what needs to be done. People who are skilled at self-management remain optimistic and hopeful despite setbacks and obstacles. This ability is crucial for pursuing long-term goals. MetLife found that applicants who failed the regular sales aptitude test but scored high on optimism made 21 percent more sales in their first year and 57 percent more in their second year than those who passed the sales test but scored high on pessimism.[59] Sandy Khorrami knows how to balance her dreams with reality, as described in the "Recipe for Success" box.

Recipe for Success } Something Good to Eat

Sandy Khorrami always loved to cook, and people couldn't stop talking about how delicious her recipes where. "Start a restaurant," they told her. But she knew it was too much to take on when she was married with small children. A food business consultant confirmed her decision and asked her what she was most proud of in her cooking. "My soups," she replied, and the consultant told her that getting her product on a shelf would match her lifestyle better than opening and running a cafe.

Narrowing it down to four soups, Khorrami decided she wanted high quality and chose glass jars rather than metal cans, so people could see what they are getting, and she wouldn't use preservatives. Her goal was to see if there was even any interest. People seemed to especially like her pomegranate beet soup.

Khorrami started her business in 2016 and is already in a number of grocery stores and restaurants, even though it generally takes three to five years to get a product on a store shelf.

Khorrami is living her dream because she not only gets to see her food out in the world, but also she loves to speak to vendors and customers to see that her products have satiated people, have brought some positive outcome. What has she learned? The product stands on its own, but it is also helpful to have the right connections to move your business forward. She's had a crash course in manufacturing and business slotting fees, for shelf space, eye-level product placement—all important concepts that she had never thought about before.

She was even featured in *The New York Times* as a trendsetter in glass jars. "I was so naïve. But I learned," says Khorrami. "It's like having a baby. Once you have it [the company], you're committed and need to take care of it."

SOURCE: Sandy Khorrami, personal communication, March 2018.

- **Social awareness.** The ability to understand others and practice *empathy*, which means being able to put yourself in someone else's shoes, to recognize what others are feeling without them needing to tell you. People with social awareness are capable of understanding divergent points of view and interacting effectively with many different types of people.
- **Relationship management.** The ability to connect to others, build positive relationships, respond to the emotions of others, and influence others. People with relationship management skills know how to listen and communicate clearly, and they treat others with compassion and respect.

Studies show a positive relationship between job performance and a high emotional intelligence quotient (EQ) in a variety of jobs. Numerous organizations, including the U.S. Air Force

Visit MindTap for "Self-Assessment: Can You Express Emotions?" to assess your level of positive emotional expression.

and Canada Life, use EQ tests to measure things such as self-awareness, ability to empathize, and capacity to build positive relationships.[60] A high EQ seems to be particularly important for jobs such as sales, which require a high degree of social interaction. It is also critical for managers, who are responsible for influencing others and building positive attitudes and relationships in the organization.

Managers with low EQ can undermine employee morale and harm the organization. Nearly 45 percent of people surveyed by the Employment Law Alliance say they have worked for a manager that they considered an abusive bully.[61] "It's usually the manager or senior executive who's just a complete out-of-control jerk," said Margaret Fiester, operations manager at the Society for Human Resource Management, where she often fields questions about the growing problem of workplace bullying. In Massachusetts, the National Association of Government Executives Local 282 became one of the first unions in the country to include in collective bargaining agreements an antibullying clause calling for "mutual respect." A recent survey found that 56 percent of companies have some kind of antibullying policy, usually as part of an employee handbook or code of conduct.[62] Growing concerns over workplace bullying have prompted enlightened companies to take action that helps managers develop greater emotional intelligence, such as by honing their self-awareness and empathy and enhancing their self-management skills.

Remember This

- An **emotion** is a mental state that arises spontaneously, rather than through conscious effort, and is often accompanied by physiological changes.

- People experience both positive emotions of happiness, pride, love, and relief, as well as negative emotions of anger, anxiety, sadness, envy, and disgust.

- The concept of **emotional contagion** refers to the tendency of people to absorb and express the emotions, moods, and attitudes of those around them.

- Recent research suggests that rudeness at work can be as contagious as the common cold and that negative emotions spread more quickly than positive ones.

- About 98 percent of people say they have experienced rudeness at work, with 50 percent saying they experience it on a weekly basis.

- Emotional intelligence includes the components of self-awareness, self-management, social awareness, and relationship management.

- Chade-Meng Tan, who held the title of Jolly Good Fellow at Google, developed a course called Search Inside Yourself to teach people to be more emotionally intelligent.

- The National Association of Government Executives Local 282 became one of the first unions in the country to include an antibullying clause in collective bargaining agreements.

10-6 Managing Yourself

Now let's turn to another topic that every manager needs to know about—time management. We introduced the topic of time management in Chapter 1, and a "Sunny Side Up" box outlined some specific time management tips. In this chapter, we talk about a broader self-management system that people can apply to gain control over their hectic schedules. **Self-management** is the ability to engage in self-regulating thoughts and behavior to accomplish all your tasks and handle difficult or challenging situations. Yet all of us have patterns of habit and behavior that may make it hard to manage ourselves toward more efficient behavior. Even the best managers can find themselves feeling overwhelmed. Many people get stuck and can't take action when they have too much on their minds or too many competing demands on their time. One approach for "getting a grip" when you have too much to do and can't seem to get any of it done is to apply a bottom-up strategy that starts by analyzing the details of what you are actually doing right now and then building a system to manage all your activities.

10-6a Basic Principles for Self-Management

Three basic principles define how to manage your many big and small commitments effectively so that you can get them accomplished:[63]

1. *Clarity of mind.* The first principle is that, if you're carrying too much around in your head, your mind can't be clear. If your mind isn't clear, you can't focus. If you can't focus, you can't get anything done. Thus, anything you consider unfinished needs to be placed in some kind of trusted system outside your head.

2. *Clarity of objectives.* Next, you have to be clear about exactly what you need to do and decide the steps to take toward accomplishing it.

3. *An organized system.* Finally, once you've decided the actions that you need to take, you need to keep reminders in a well-organized system.

By building a self-management approach based on these three principles—clarity of mind, clarity of objectives, and a system of organized reminders—you can get unstuck and make measurable progress toward achieving all the things that you need to do.

10-6b A Step-By-Step Guide for Managing Your Time

Many people don't realize that they waste at least an hour of a typical workday simply because they are disorganized.[64] You can gain better control of your life and the many things that you have to do by mastering some simple but powerful steps.[65] Exhibit 10.11 summarizes these five steps, and each is described next.

1. *Empty your head.* In order to clear your mind, you first have to see all the many things weighing on it. The first step, therefore, is to write down on separate scraps of paper all the activities, duties, tasks, or commitments that are demanding part of your attention. The idea is to get everything out of your head and down on paper.

    To organize all this "stuff," combine similar items into various "buckets." There are numerous tools that can serve as your buckets, including computer and wireless devices for electronic note-taking; physical in-baskets for holding mail, memos, and phone slips; notebooks or legal pads for writing down things to do; or digital recorders for recording things you need to remember. Keep a notepad or handheld device with you so that you can add new projects or commitments at any time and get them out of your head. Remember to keep the number of buckets to a minimum; otherwise, you'll still feel scattered and overwhelmed.

2. *Decide the next action.* For each item in your buckets, decide the real, specific, physical action that you need to take next. If you have a team meeting on Friday to discuss a class project, your next action might be to draft thoughts and ideas that you want to share with the team. Then, you have three options:

    - *Do it.* Follow the two-minute rule: If something can be done in less than two minutes, do it now. In some cases, you'll find items in your bucket that require no action and are of no importance. These should be trashed immediately. For items that are of potential use in the future, file in a system for reference material.
    - *Delegate it.* Ask yourself if you're the right person to handle a task. If something can be done as well by someone else, delegate it.
    - *Defer it.* If something will take longer than two minutes but cannot be delegated to someone else, you'll have to defer it. These things go into an incubation or tickler file, such as an organized "To Do" list, which you will review regularly and perhaps schedule a specific time for their completion.

Exhibit 10.11 **Follow These Steps to Get Organized**

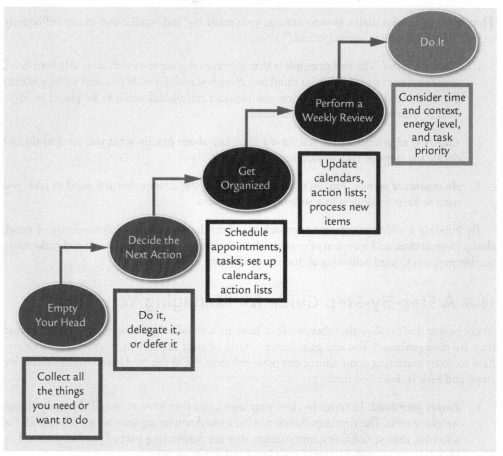

SOURCE: Based on David Allen, *Getting Things Done: The Art of Stress-Free Productivity* (New York: Viking, 2001).

3. ***Get organized.*** The third step is to organize all the items that you've deferred. At this stage, schedule any appointments that you identified as "next actions" and record them on whatever calendar you check daily. Also record on your calendar any items that have to be done on a specific day or at a specific time. You can assign yourself a definite date in the future to perform certain tasks that are in your incubation or tickler file.

     For all other items, keep a list of "Next Actions," either on paper on in a portable device that you will have with you at all times so that you can take action when and where you have the time to do so. This can be either on a single list or in categories.

4. ***Perform a weekly review.*** Once a week, review your complete Next Actions list and your calendar for the coming week. Scan the entire list of outstanding projects and actions needed so that you can make efficient choices about using your time. This weekly review is critical because it keeps your mind from taking back the job of trying to hold and remember everything. The weekly review is also the time to "put your house in order" by collecting, processing, and organizing new items. Thus, during the weekly review, you'll take four actions: (1) collect and process all the new stuff; (2) review your entire system; (3) revise your lists; and (4) get clear, up to date, and complete about what needs to be done next.

5. ***Now do it.*** Once you have collected, processed, organized, and reviewed your current commitments, you'll have a better sense of what needs to be done, which will enable you to make better choices about how to use your time. Your intuition and your understanding of yourself can help you in deciding what to do when.

     This approach to self-management can help you get a handle on all the various things that you have to do and approach them in a systematic way with a clear mind. If you follow it, you'll find yourself getting more accomplished with less stress—and with fewer things falling between the cracks. Refer to the time management tips in the "Sunny Side Up" box in Chapter 1. You can pick and choose the techniques that work for you and combine them with this overall self-management approach.

> ## Remember This
>
> - **Self-management** is the ability to engage in self-regulating thoughts and behavior to accomplish all your tasks and handle difficult or challenging situations.
> - Three basic principles for self-management are clarity of mind, clarity of objectives, and an organized system.
>
> - One self-management system is based on five steps: Empty your head; decide the next action; get organized; perform a weekly review; then do what needs to be done.

10-7 Stress and Stress Management

No matter how organized you are, as a manager you will likely experience stress—your own and that of others—at some time in your career. Formally defined, **stress** is an individual's physiological and emotional response to external stimuli that place physical or psychological demands on the individual and create uncertainty and lack of personal control when important outcomes are at stake.[66] These stimuli, called *stressors*, produce some combination of frustration (the inability to achieve a goal, such as the inability to meet a deadline because of inadequate resources) and anxiety (such as the fear of being disciplined for not meeting deadlines).

Stress levels have gone up in many organizations in recent years. The number of employees who are irritable, insulting, or discourteous has grown, as people are coping with the stress of job uncertainty, overwhelming debt, tighter access to credit, and increased workloads due to downsizing. In one survey, nearly half of U.S. workers reported experiencing yelling and verbal abuse on the job, and another study found that 2 to 3 percent of people admit to pushing, slapping, or hitting someone at work.[67] "People are trapped; they don't have the same alternative jobs to jump to," said Gary Namie, a social psychologist who cofounded the Workplace Bullying Institute. People "are staying longer in these pressured, stress-filled toxic work environments."[68]

10-7a Challenge Stress and Threat Stress

Stress isn't always negative. Without a certain amount of stress, we would be complacent and accomplish little. Psychologists have long noted this "dual face of stress," and they distinguish between *challenge stress* and *threat stress*. Challenge stress fires you up, whereas threat stress burns you out.[69] As originally proposed by two Harvard researchers, Robert Yerkes and John Dodson, and illustrated in Exhibit 10.12, a certain level of stress challenges you and increases your focus, alertness, efficiency, and productivity.[70] After that point, however, things go downhill quickly, and stress compromises your job performance, your relationships, and even your health. Another interesting finding is that too much stress inhibits learning and flexibility.[71]

The point at which things tip over from challenge stress (good) to threat stress (bad) may vary with each individual. Most of us can easily tell when we've gone over the top of the stress curve. We stop feeling productive; experience emotions of anxiety, fear, depression, anger, or a combination of them; are easily irritated; and may have trouble making decisions. Many people also have physical symptoms, such as headaches, insomnia, or stomach problems. In the United States, an estimated 1 million people each day don't show up for work because of stress.[72] Similarly, a survey in the United Kingdom found that 68 percent of nonmanual workers and 42 percent of manual workers reported missing work because of stress-related illness.[73] Just as big a problem for organizations as absenteeism is *presenteeism*, which refers to people who go to work but are too stressed and distracted to be productive.[74]

Exhibit 10.12 The Yerkes-Dodson Stress Curve

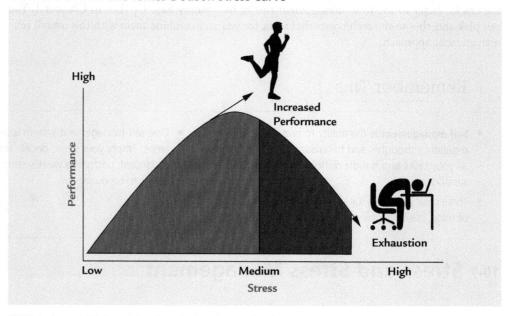

SOURCE: Based on an exhibit by Emeran A. Mayer, M.D., UCLA Center for Neurobiology of Stress.

10-7b Type A and Type B Behavior Patterns

Researchers have observed that some people seem to be more vulnerable than others to the ill effects of stress. From studies of stress-related heart disease, researchers categorized people as having behavior patterns called Type A and Type B.[75] The **Type A behavior** pattern includes extreme competitiveness, impatience, aggressiveness, and devotion to work. For example, David Sacks, founder of Yammer and current CEO of Zenefits, says he is "in a perpetual state of frustration over the product. I want it to be perfect and it's not." He adds, "I think about work constantly, I wish I had an On/Off switch."[76] In contrast, people with a **Type B behavior** pattern exhibit fewer of these behaviors. They consequently experience less conflict with other people and a more balanced, relaxed lifestyle. Type A people tend to experience more stress-related illness than Type B people.

Most Type A individuals, like David Sacks, are high-energy people and may seek positions of power and responsibility. By pacing themselves and learning the control and intelligent use of their natural high-energy tendencies, Type A individuals can be powerful forces for innovation and leadership within their organizations. However, many Type A personalities cause stress-related problems for themselves, and sometimes for those around them. Sacks says he has consciously changed some of his behaviors so that his impatience doesn't cause stress for others. Type B individuals typically live with less stress unless they are in high-stress situations. A number of factors can cause stress in the workplace, even for people who are not naturally prone to high stress.

10-7c Causes of Work Stress

Workplace stress has been skyrocketing worldwide for some years. In the 2013 Work Stress survey conducted by Harris Interactive and Everest College, 83 percent of people surveyed in the United States said they experienced stress at work, an increase of 10 percentage points from the previous year's survey. Poor compensation and unreasonable workloads were cited as the top causes of harmful workplace stress.[77] Surveys in Canada consistently cite work as the top source of stress for people in that country. In India, growing numbers of young software professionals and call center workers are falling prey to depression, anxiety, and other mental illnesses because of increasing workplace stress.[78] And the long hours and stressful conditions that have led to suicides among contract manufacturing workers in China have prompted managers at technology firms such as Apple, IBM, Hewlett-Packard, and Toshiba to do some serious soul-searching.[79] "Work conditions can cause mental illness," says psychologist Rodney L. Lowman. "If we put healthy, well-adjusted people in the right foxhole with guns blaring at them, the likelihood of them experiencing depression and anxiety is very high."[80]

Managers can better cope with their own stress and establish ways for the organization to help employees cope if they understand the conditions that tend to produce work stress. Unethical environments and unsafe working conditions, such as those at some contract manufacturers, are major stressors, of course. In terms of more typical everyday work stressors, one approach is to think about the stress caused by the demands of job tasks and stress caused by interpersonal pressures and conflicts:

- *Task demands* are stressors arising from the tasks required of a person holding a particular job. Some kinds of decisions are inherently stressful: those made under time pressure, those that have serious consequences, and those that must be made with incomplete information. For example, emergency room doctors are under tremendous stress as a result of the task demands of their jobs. They regularly have to make quick decisions based on limited information that may determine whether a patient lives or dies. Jobs in which people have to deal with irate customers can also be highly stressful. Turnover among customer service employees can be as high as 300 percent a year in some industries.[81] Almost all jobs, especially those of managers, have some level of stress associated with task demands. Task demands also sometimes cause stress because of **role ambiguity**, which means that people are unclear about what task behaviors are expected of them. In a survey by the American Psychological Association (APA), 35 percent of respondents cited unclear job expectations as a cause of their workplace stress.[82]
- *Interpersonal demands* are stressors associated with relationships in the organization. Although interpersonal relationships can alleviate stress in some cases, they also can be a source of stress when the group puts pressure on an individual or when conflicts arise between individuals. Managers can resolve many conflicts using techniques that will be discussed in Chapter 14. **Role conflict** occurs when an individual perceives incompatible demands from others. Managers often feel role conflict because the demands of their superiors conflict with those of the employees in their department. They may be expected to support employees and provide them with opportunities to experiment and be creative, while at the same time top executives are demanding a consistent level of output that leaves little time for creativity and experimentation.

10-7d Innovative Responses to Stress

Organizations that want to challenge their employees and stay competitive will never be stress free, but healthy workplaces promote the physical and emotional well-being of their employees. Even simple things can change how people feel about their work. John Weaver, a psychologist at Psychology for Business, a management consultancy firm, advised managers at a long-term care facility in Wisconsin that had been flooded. Because of the water damage, the residents and employees had to move into an already occupied facility, and everyone was feeling cramped and annoyed. Pettiness was getting out of hand. Weaver and managers began asking each employee a simple question: *Why do you do this work?* "As they thought about the question," Weaver says, "you could see their attitude change. They could see the reasons why they needed to work together to put aside difficulties and compromise, and residents were treated better."[83]

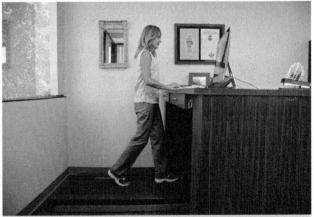

Melissa Lyttle/Redux

Concept Connection

Many companies help employees **manage stress** by offering discounts to local gyms, although a fairly recent workplace trend enables people to work out while they work. Treadmill desks have shelves where employees can park their laptops and plug in their smartphones so they can review documents, do online research, and hold meetings as they rack up the miles. Employees who've made use of these multitasking opportunities report that they have more energy, feel less stressed, and have lost weight thanks to these treadmill desks.

What You Can Do to Combat Stress   Scientist and stress researcher Hans Selye said, "It's not stress that kills us, it is our reaction to it." Exhibit 10.13 lists 10 ways to stress-proof your day. A variety of techniques can help individuals avoid or manage the harmful effects of stress.

- ***Seek and destroy key sources of stress.*** A recent study found that the most beneficial stress management competency is *prevention.*[84] None of us can eliminate all the potential sources of stress from our lives, but we can avoid some of them and manage others. Take some time each day to identify stressors in your life and find ways to eliminate or reduce them. Being well organized, planning ahead, and using the various time management techniques we've discussed in this chapter are highly effective ways to manage and prevent stress. One source of stress for some workers, especially freelancers, has been lack of health insurance. Sara Horowitz is on a mission to help prevent this type of stress, as described in the "Sunny Side Up" box.

- ***Find meaning and support.*** You are much more likely to experience ill effects from stress if you're working in a job that has no meaning for you and if you feel alone in life. The *buffering hypothesis* says that a perceived high degree of social support from family and friends protects one from the potentially adverse effects of stressful events.[85] That is, if you feel like you have a lot of support, you're less susceptible to the negative effects of bad stress.

- ***Meditate and manage your energy.*** Meditation is a way to both prevent and alleviate harmful stress responses. Some people meditate every morning or evening as a routine

Sunny Side Up } Freelancers Union

Being an independent worker has the advantages of being able to set our own hours, to take off for a yoga class, and schedule your own vacation time, but it also usually means you don't have health insurance. Sara Horowitz is on a mission to change that. After being hired by a law firm as an "independent contractor," she faced the realities of work with no benefits. Considering that her father was a labor attorney and her grandfather a leader in the International Ladies' Garment Workers Union, it's not surprising she started her own organization, The Freelancers Union. But whereas her paterfamilias organized strikes, she realized times have changed. Independent employees now number 20 million. Their most burning issue, Horowitz found, was lack of health insurance (though that had eased since The Affordable Care Act, and now faces some uncertainty). So she provided it to what are now more than 200,000 members including graphic designers, accountants, lawyers, consultants, writers, Web designers, and sellers on Etsy. That might not sound like much until you consider that the United Auto Workers currently has 380,000 members.

Another problem is how to get work. Horowitz thinks Work Market and others like it are part of the solution, for they offer leads without cost to freelancers and help with one of the big frustrations: getting paid. Work Market kicks companies off their site if they don't follow through with the money. And there is a growing need. From 2005 to 2015, the number of independent workers increased from 10 to 15 percent of the entire workforce.

On a typical day, Horowitz meets in the health clinic's Yoga and Meditation Studio with a group of union members to talk about the clinic . People like the on-site nutritionist and acupuncturist and the fact that the average wait to see a doctor is just 10 minutes. The clinic is free to anyone who has signed up for the insurance whose premiums range from $225 to $603 per month. Running on an unusual team structure, the clinic pairs doctors with full-time "health coaches" who follow up on diet and medications, often helping patients avoid costly hospital stays. Because they operate more like a co-op than a for-profit, the clinic is able to put all the profits back in to the company, to provide even better services. About 2,300 members have signed up for clinics, while others see doctors through plans such as Blue Cross Blue Shield.

Horowitz operates more like an entrepreneur than an old-time union organizer. She identified the gaping hole of no health insurance and found investors to back up her plan to address it. And she knows that she brings more independence to workers who feel trapped in jobs that offer benefits. One such person is Jo-Ann Mort, who left corporate America to start her own fund-raising firm. "I was scared to go out on my own because I was worried I couldn't find affordable insurance," she said. "Sara made that possible."

SOURCES: Chris Dunn, "The Economy's Latest Gig," *York Daily Record*, February 18, 2018, A6; and Lydia DePillis, "Freelancing Can Be the Future," *The Plain Dealer*, February 8, 2015, 3.

Exhibit 10.13 Ten Ways to Stress-Proof Your Day

Most people can find plenty of ways at work to get stressed out. Here are ten steps that can help you depressurize:

1. Reframe a negative experience. If you left your laptop for a meeting in the car, for example, interpret it as a chance to compose your thoughts on the walk to retrieve it.
2. Attend a meeting in another department, just out of interest, to see what people in that department are doing.
3. Notice at least one good thing about someone you don't like very well.
4. Find a quiet place where you can sit undisturbed and be alone, even if it's just for a few minutes.
5. Do something nice for someone—studies show that it can make you happier and calmer.
6. If you encounter a problem in your work or personal life, think of it as a challenge and an opportunity to learn.
7. Notice at least one good thing that you experience each day.
8. Make a list of achievable goals for the week and aim to mark one off your list each day.
9. Every day when you wake up, express gratitude for the new day and another chance to make a difference in the world.
10. Get enough sleep each night. If you don't, take a nap!

SOURCES: Based on "8 Steps to Stress-Proof Your Day," sidebar in Thea Singer, "The Perfect Amount of Stress," *Psychology Today* (March–April 2012): 78–85; "A New Kind of 'To Do' List," sidebar in Betty Shotton, "Awe: A Doorway to Breakthroughs, Insight, and Innovation," *Leader to Leader* (Spring 2013): 7–12; and Ruth Mantell, "How to Lower Your Workplace Stress," *The Wall Street Journal*, January 15, 2012, http://online.wsj.com/news/articles/SB10001424052970204257504577152502470874464 (accessed October 18, 2013).

practice. Others find that short breaks to meditate for a few minutes several times a day are just as effective.[86] Any time during the day when you're feeling overwhelmed, you can close your eyes, focus on an image or a phrase that you find calming, and breathe deeply. Meditation can be an important part of an overall healthy lifestyle, such as eating right, getting enough rest, and exercising regularly, that helps you better cope with stress.

- *Find a work–life balance.* One study found that a lack of work–life balance was the number 1 predictor of high levels of unhealthy stress.[87] Innovative organizations offer options to help people lead more balanced lives. But you, as an individual, are also responsible for finding work–life balance. A survey by the Society for Human Resource Management found that 70 percent of employees said that they work beyond scheduled time and on weekends, but more than half of those admitted that it is because of *self-imposed pressure.* People who live balanced lives typically accomplish more than those who push themselves.

What Managers and Organizations Can Do   Helping employees manage stress can sometimes be as simple as encouraging people to take regular breaks and vacations. Consider that more than a third of U.S. employees surveyed by the Families and Work Institute don't take their full allotment of vacation time.[88] Here are some proactive approaches that managers can take to combat the growing stress level in today's workplace:

- *Create a psychologically healthy workplace.* The number 1 way to lessen employee stress is to create a healthy corporate culture that makes people feel valued.[89] This includes making sure that people don't have unreasonable workloads, providing opportunities for growth and advancement, and offering suitable salaries and benefits. It also means setting an example for employees to live balanced lives. Paul English, cofounder and CEO of Blade LLC and cofounder of the travel search firm Kayak, sometimes takes his children on business trips so that he and his children can have new experiences together. At night, he reads murder mysteries or books about global health rather than reading about business or technology.[90]
- *Make sure people have some fun at work.* Particularly for jobs that have a high degree of task-related stress, allowing people to blow off steam by having fun can make all the difference in the stress level. At one Tampa-based software company help desk, Zane Bond is the "go-to guy for angry callers," but the stress doesn't get to him. One reason is that he loves solving problems. Another is that he has fun with his team members, such as breaking out the foam-dart guns and launching into battle with the soundtrack from *Top Gun* playing in the background.[91]

Managers should always remember that employees are *human* resources, with human needs. By acknowledging the personal aspects of employees' lives, these various initiatives communicate that managers and the organization care about employees. In addition, managers' attitudes make a tremendous difference in whether employees are stressed out and unhappy or relaxed, energetic, and productive.

Remember This

- **Stress** is a physiological and emotional response to stimuli that place physical or psychological demands on an individual and create uncertainty and lack of personal control when important outcomes are at stake.

- Stress can sometimes be a positive force, but too much stress is harmful to individuals and the organizations where they work.

- The behavior pattern referred to as **Type A behavior** is characterized by extreme competitiveness, impatience, aggressiveness, and devotion to work.

- **Type B behavior** is a behavior pattern that reflects few of the Type A characteristics and includes a more balanced, relaxed approach to life.

- Type A managers can be powerful forces for innovation and change, but they can also create great stress for themselves and others.

- Work stress can be caused by both task demands and interpersonal demands.

- **Role ambiguity** refers to uncertainty about what behaviors are expected of a person in a particular role.

- **Role conflict** refers to incompatible demands of different roles, such as the demands of a manager's superiors conflicting with those of the manager's subordinates.

- Individuals can apply a variety of techniques to alleviate the ill effects of stress, and managers can implement initiatives in the workplace to help solve the problem of skyrocketing workplace stress.

DISCUSSION QUESTIONS

1. Why is self-awareness important for being a good manager? Can you think of some specific negative consequences that might result from a manager with low self-awareness?

2. As a manager, how might you deal with an employee who is always displaying negative emotions that affect the rest of the team? How might you use an understanding of attributions and emotional contagion to help you decide what to do?

3. What are some specific tips that you would give a new manager for building trust with subordinates? With other managers?

4. The chapter suggests that optimism is an important characteristic for a manager, yet some employees complain that optimistic managers cause them significant stress because they expect their subordinates to meet unreasonable goals or expectations. How might an employee deal with a perpetually optimistic manager?

5. Studies have suggested that extroverts contribute less to teams and are poor listeners, yet other studies suggest that they are more likely to earn six-figure incomes, even in today's collaborative, team-oriented workplaces. Discuss why you think this might be the case.

6. Surveys by the Conference Board show that job satisfaction has declined from 61 percent of people surveyed in 1987 to 50 percent in 2013, and one workplace analyst has said a high level of dissatisfaction is "the new normal." What are some factors that might explain this decline in satisfaction levels? Do you think it is possible for managers to reverse the trend? Discuss.

7. Which of the four components of emotional intelligence do you consider most important to an effective manager in today's world? Why?

8. How might understanding whether an employee has an internal or an external locus of control help a manager better communicate with, motivate, and lead the employee?

9. How do you think a system for self-management such as the five-step system described in this chapter could benefit you as a student? What parts of the system seem particularly useful to you? Explain.

10. Why do you think workplace stress is skyrocketing? Do you think it is a trend that will continue? Explain the reasons for your answer. Do you think it is the responsibility of managers and organizations to help employees manage stress? Why or why not?

APPLY YOUR SKILLS: SELF-LEARNING

Personality Assessment: Jung's Typology[92]

For each of the following items, circle either a. or b. In some cases, both a. and b. may apply to you. You should decide which is more like you, even if it is only slightly more so.

1. I would rather:
   a. Solve a new and complicated problem
   b. Work on something that I have done before

2. I like to:
   a. Work alone in a quiet place
   b. Be where "the action" is

3. I want a boss who:
   a. Establishes and applies criteria in making decisions
   b. Considers individual needs and makes exceptions

4. When I work on a project, I:
   a. Like to finish it and get some closure
   b. Often leave it open for possible change

5. When making a decision, the most important considerations are:
   a. Rational thoughts, ideas, and data
   b. People's feelings and values

6. On a project, I tend to:
   a. Think it over and over before deciding how to proceed
   b. Start working on it right away, thinking about it as I go along

7. When working on a project, I prefer to:
   a. Maintain as much control as possible
   b. Explore various options

8. In my work, I prefer to:
   a. Work on several projects at a time, and learn as much as possible about each one
   b. Have one project that is challenging and keeps me busy

9. I often:
   a. Make lists and plans whenever I start something and may hate to alter my plans significantly
   b. Avoid plans and just let things progress as I work on them

10. When discussing a problem with colleagues, it is easy for me:
    a. To see "the big picture"
    b. To grasp the specifics of the situation

11. When the phone rings in my office or at home, I usually:
    a. Consider it an interruption
    b. Don't mind answering it

12. The word that describes me better is:
    a. Analytical
    b. Empathetic

13. When I am working on an assignment, I tend to:
    a. Work steadily and consistently
    b. Work in bursts of energy with "down time" in between

14. When I listen to someone talk on a subject, I usually try to:
    a. Relate it to my own experience and see whether it fits
    b. Assess and analyze the message

15. When I come up with new ideas, I generally:
    a. "Go for it"
    b. Like to contemplate the ideas more thoroughly before implementing them

16. When working on a project, I prefer to:
    a. Narrow the scope so it is clearly defined
    b. Broaden the scope to include related aspects

17. When I read something, I usually:
    a. Confine my thoughts to what is written there
    b. Read between the lines and relate the words to other ideas

18. When I have to make a decision in a hurry, I often:
    a. Feel uncomfortable and wish I had more information
    b. Am able to do so with available data

19. In a meeting, I tend to:
   a. Continue formulating my ideas as I talk about them
   b. Speak out only after I have carefully thought the issue through

20. In work, I prefer spending a great deal of time on issues of:
   a. Ideas
   b. People

21. In meetings, I am most often annoyed with people who:
   a. Come up with many sketchy ideas
   b. Lengthen the meeting with many practical details

22. I tend to be:
   a. A morning person
   b. A night owl

23. My style in preparing for a meeting is:
   a. To be willing to go in and be responsive
   b. To be fully prepared and sketch an outline of the meeting

24. In meetings, I would prefer for people to:
   a. Display a full range of emotions
   b. Be more task-oriented

25. I would rather work for an organization where:
   a. My job was intellectually stimulating
   b. I was committed to its goals and mission

26. On weekends, I tend to:
   a. Plan what I will do
   b. Just see what happens and decide as I go along

27. I am more:
   a. Outgoing
   b. Contemplative

28. I would rather work for a boss who is:
   a. Full of new ideas
   b. Practical

29. The word in each of the following pairs that appeals to you more is:
   a. Social
   b. Theoretical

30. a. Ingenuity
    b. Practicality

31. a. Organized
    b. Adaptable

32. a. Active
    b. Concentration

Scoring and Interpretation Count one point for each of the following items that you circled in the inventory.

	Score for I (Introversion)	Score for E (Extroversion)	Score for S (Sensing)	Score for N (Intuition)
	2a	2b	1b	1a
	6a	6b	10b	10a
	11a	11b	13a	13b
	15b	15a	16a	16b
	19b	19a	17a	17b
	22a	22b	21a	21b
	27b	27a	28b	28a
	32b	32a	30b	30a
Totals	_____	_____	_____	_____

Circle the one with more points: Circle the one with more points:
I or E   S or N
(If tied on I/E, don't count #11)   *(If tied on S/N, don't count #16)*

	Score for T (Thinking)	Score for F (Feeling)	Score for J (Judging)	Score for P (Perceiving)
	3a	3b	4a	4b
	5a	5b	7a	7b
	12a	12b	8b	8a
	14b	14a	9a	9b
	20a	20b	18b	18a
	24b	24a	23b	23a
	25a	25b	26a	26b
	29b	29a	31a	31b
Totals	_____	_____	_____	_____

Circle the one with more points:
T or F
(*If tied on T/F, don't count #24*)

Circle the one with more points:
J or P
(*If tied on J/P, don't count #23*)

Your score is: I or E _____ S or N _____ T or F _____ J or P _____
Your type is _____ (example: INTJ, ESFP, etc.)

Characteristics Frequently Associated with Each Type

The preceding scores measure variables similar to those of the MBTI™ assessment based on the work of psychologist Carl Jung. The MBTI ™ assessment, which was described in the chapter text, identifies four dimensions and 16 different "types." The dominant characteristics associated with each type are shown in the following chart. Remember that no one is a pure type; however, each individual has preferences for introversion versus extroversion, sensing versus intuition, thinking versus feeling, and judging versus perceiving. Read the description of your type as determined by your scores in the survey. Do you believe the description fits your personality?

Characteristics for Each Type

ISTJ: Organizer, trustworthy, responsible; good trustee or inspector

ISFJ: Quiet, conscientious, devoted, handles detail; good conservator

INFJ: Perseveres, inspirational, quiet, caring for others; good counselor

INTJ: Independent thinker, skeptical, theory, competence; good scientist

ISTP: Cool, observant, easygoing; good craftsperson

ISFP: Warm, sensitive, team player, avoids conflict; good artist

INFP: Idealistic, strong values, likes learning; good at noble service

INTP: Designer, logical, conceptual, likes challenges; good architect

ESTP: Spontaneous, gregarious; good at problem solving and promoting

ESFP: Sociable, generous, makes things fun; good entertainer

ENFP: Imaginative, enthusiastic, starts projects; good champion

ENTP: Resourceful, stimulating, dislikes routine, tests limits; good inventor

ESTJ: Order, structure, practical; good administrator or supervisor

ESFJ: People skills, harmonizer, popular, does things for people; good host

ENFJ: Charismatic, persuasive, fluent presenter, sociable, active; good teacher

ENTJ: Visionary planner, takes charge, hearty speaker; natural leader

APPLY YOUR SKILLS: GROUP LEARNING

Personality Role-Play[93]

Step 1. Read the following background information: You are the new distribution manager for French Grains Bakery. Five drivers who deliver French Grains baked goods to grocery stores in the metropolitan area report to you. The drivers are expected to complete a Delivery Report to keep track of actual deliveries and any changes that occur. The Delivery Report is a key element in inventory control and provides the data for the company's invoicing of grocery stores. Errors become excessive when drivers fail to complete the report each day, especially when store managers request additional or different breads and baked goods when the driver arrives. As a result, French Grains may not be paid for several loaves of bread a day for each mistake in the Delivery Report. The result is lost revenue and poor inventory control.

One of the drivers accounts for about 60 percent of the errors in the Delivery Reports. This driver is a nice person and is generally reliable, but he is sometimes late for work. His major problem is that he falls behind in his paperwork. A second driver accounts for about 30 percent of the errors, and a third driver for about 10 percent of the errors. The other two drivers turn in virtually error-free Delivery Reports.

Step 2. Divide into groups of four to six students. As a group, discuss why you think one driver makes so many mistakes.
List the reasons here:

1.

2.

3.

4.

Then, one person volunteers to play the role of the new distribution manager and another person plays the role of the driver who accounts for 60 percent of the errors in the Delivery Reports.

Step 3. The new distribution manager should act the role as if his or her personality is high on "thinking" and low on "feeling," (on the MBTI) or as if he or she is high on "authoritarianism."

You have called the driver into your office to talk to him about doing a more complete and accurate job with the Delivery Report. Make some notes about how you will go about correcting this problem as a thinking-oriented or authoritarian leader. Exactly what will you say, and how will you get the driver to listen and change his behavior?

_____

_____

_____

Step 4. Now, start the role-play between the distribution manager and the driver. Other group members should act as observers.

Step 5. After the role-play is completed, the observers should give feedback on what worked and did not work with respect to the thinking or authoritarian personality style of giving feedback. How effective was it?

_____

_____

_____

Step 6. Repeat steps 3 through 5, with other students volunteering to be the distribution manager and driver. This time, the manager should act as if his or her personality is strongly "feeling" or nonauthoritarian. Was this personality style more or less effective for correcting the problem?

Step 7. The instructor can ask students to volunteer to play the role of the distribution manager and the driver in front of the class. Different students might take turns playing the role of distribution manager, emphasizing a different personality trait each time. The instructor can ask other students for feedback on the leader's effectiveness and about which approach seems more effective for correcting this situation and why.

Step 8. The instructor will lead a discussion on attribution theory and personality types and how these relate to effective work behaviors.

APPLY YOUR SKILLS: ACTION LEARNING

1. On your own, complete the following table, making assessments of your family members according to the Myers-Briggs Type Indicator™. Include some notes on why you have chosen each type for each person.

2. Talk over these assessments with at least one person in your family and try to listen to that person's opinions, changing any of your own assessments as you think is necessary.

3. In class in groups of three to four, share your results and talk about why you think each person is a certain type and whether you changed any assessments after the discussion with a family member. Also talk about how the combination of personality types has impacted your family.

4. Your instructor may choose to have you write a paper on your assessments.

	Introvert or Extravert?	Sensing or Intuition?	Thinking or Feeling?	Perceptive or Judging?
Mother				
Father				
Sibling				
Sibling				
Other				
Other				
Other				

APPLY YOUR SKILLS: ETHICAL DILEMMA

Should I Fudge the Numbers?[94]

Sara MacIntosh recently joined MicroPhone, a large telecommunications company, to take over the implementation of a massive customer service training project. The program was created by Kristin Cole, head of HR and Sara's new boss. According to the grapevine, Kristin is hoping this project alone will give her the "star quality" that she needs to earn a coveted promotion. Industry competition is heating up, and MicroPhone's strategy calls for being the best at customer service, which means having the most highly trained people in the industry, especially those who work directly with customers. Kristin's new training program includes an average of one full week of intense customer service training for each of 3,000 people and has a price tag of about $40 million.

Kristin put together a team of overworked staffers to develop the training program, but she needed someone well qualified and dedicated to manage and implement the project. Sara, with eight years of experience, a long list of accomplishments, and advanced degrees in finance and organizational behavior, seemed perfect for the job.

During a thorough review of the proposal, Sara discovered some assumptions built into the formulas that raised red flags. She approached Dan Sotal, the team's coordinator, about her concerns, but the more that Dan tried to explain how the financial projections were derived, the more Sara realized that Kristin's proposal was seriously flawed. No matter how she tried to work them out, the most that could be squeezed out of the $40 million budget was 20 hours of training per person, not the 40 hours everyone expected for such a high price tag.

Sara knew that although the proposal had been largely developed before she came on board, it would bear her signature. As she carefully described the problems with the proposal to Kristin and outlined the potentially devastating consequences, Kristin impatiently tapped her pencil. Finally, she stood up, leaned forward, and interrupted Sara, quietly saying, "Sara, make the numbers work so that it adds up to 40 hours and stays within the $40 million budget."

Sara glanced up and replied, "I don't think it can be done unless we either change the number of employees who are to be trained or the cost figure. . . ."

Kristin's smile froze on her face as she again interrupted. "I don't think you understand what I'm saying. We have too much at stake here. *Make the previous numbers work.*" Stunned, Sara belatedly began to realize that Kristin was ordering her to fudge the numbers. She felt an anxiety attack coming on as she wondered what she should do.

What Would You Do?

1. Make the previous numbers work. Kristin and the entire team have put massive amounts of time into the project, and they all expect you to be a team player. You don't want to let them down. Besides, this project is a great opportunity for you in a highly visible position.

2. Stick to your principles and refuse to fudge the numbers. Tell Kristin that you will work overtime to help develop an alternative proposal that stays within the budget by providing more training to employees who work directly with customers and fewer training hours for those who don't have direct customer contact.

3. Go to the team and tell its members what you've been asked to do. If they refuse to support you, threaten to reveal the true numbers to the CEO and board members.

APPLY YOUR SKILLS: CASE FOR CRITICAL ANALYSIS

A Nice Manager

The management promotion process at Chisum Industries was a benchmark for providing lateral moves, as well as promotion to the next level within the company. With offices, plants, and warehouses located in seven Texas cities, opportunities for the best and brightest at Chisum were extensive for middle management employees. The process invited candidates to explore their goals, strengths, and weaknesses, and to recount real-life scenarios and accomplishments. The selection team also visited the work sites of candidates for on-the-job observations and talks with fellow workers before bringing the final candidates to Dallas for interviews. The process offered personal insight and growth opportunities to all candidates for promotion. In March 2011, top management, including Marcus Chisum, Karl Jacobson, Mitch Ivey, Wayne Hughes, and Barbara Kennedy, was midway through a meeting to consider which of four middle management candidates to promote to the top position in the San Antonio office.

Marcus: "Who do we have next?"

Barbara: "Harry Creighton."

Scanning the group, Marcus saw a few nods and a shrug.

Marcus: "Feedback?"

Karl and Wayne, simultaneously: "Great guy."

Karl: "We all know that Harry came into a situation in which that particular location was suffering a drop in performance. Morale was low, and there were rumors of layoffs. He came in and calmed employee fears and has done a good job of raising performance levels."

Wayne: "He has a great relationship with employees. As we went around and talked to people, it was obvious that he has developed a level of trust and a vision that workers buy into."

Barbara: "The word that kept coming up among the workers was 'nice.'"

As was his habit during meetings, Mitch leaned back in his chair, tapping his pencil on the table. Initially annoyed by the habit, the team had gotten used to the sound over time.

Marcus: "Mitch, your initial reaction to his name was a shrug. What are you thinking?"

Mitch: "Just wondering if *nice* is what we're looking for here."

The remark was met with laughter.

Mitch: "Tell me, how does a manager achieve an across-the-board reputation as a *nice* guy? I've worked for and with a number of managers during my life. I respected them, thought many of them were fair and up-front in their treatment of us, thought some were jerks who should be canned. . . ."

Marcus: "I hope I don't fall into that last category." (Laughter)

Mitch: "I don't recall any consensus about a manager being *nice*."

Karl: "Several people mentioned that Harry always has their back."

Barbara: "I got the impression that Harry covers for them."

Marcus: "Meaning what?"

Wayne: "Meaning, giving them some slack when it comes to things like overlooking their weaknesses, a little sloppiness with deadlines or taking time off."

Barbara: "Several mentioned that he's always willing to . . . let me look at my notes . . . '*Always willing to step in and help out.*' The phrase came up more than a few times and when I pressed them, they didn't elaborate. But I wondered. . . ."

Karl: "... Is he managing or taking on some of their responsibilities?"

Barbara: "Exactly."

Mitch: "It's bothering me that he comes across as the parent who does his kid's project for the science fair."

Wayne: "I don't think it's that bad, but when you look at him in comparison with the other candidates, it makes me question whether he can take on the tough part of top management. There is nothing distinctive about him or his style."

Karl: "There's no *edge* here. No sense of boundaries. Does he want to manage employees or be popular with them? Can he say 'No' and mean it?"

Barbara: "Does Harry have the capability to walk that fine line that separates leaders; that distinguishes respect versus popularity or encouragement and support over *stepping in and helping out*?"

Marcus: "So, we see some good things about Harry. He has a lot of potential. But we also see that he hasn't

yet reached a level where we can entrust him with this top management position. Our task here, then, is to move on with the selection process, but over the next weeks, I would like for us to consider ways to help Harry reach that potential for future opportunities."

Questions

1. What does *nice* mean to you? Is being considered nice a good trait for managers to have, or is it the kiss of death?

2. Is *nice* related to any concepts in the chapter, such as agreeableness, conscientiousness, or emotional intelligence? Discuss.

3. If Harry is passed over for promotion, what feedback and advice should he be given about how to improve his management skills for possible future promotion?

ENDNOTES

1. Sue Shellenbarger, "Shaking Off a Shy Reputation at Work; How Office Introverts Can Get Ahead While Staying True to Themselves," *The Wall Street Journal*, January 14, 2014, http://www.wsj.com/articles/SB10001424052702304049704579320683598535824 (accessed April 25, 2016).

2. "There's Life (and a Living) After Rejection," *The Independent on Sunday*, January 6, 2008; Amy Ellis Nutt, "Harry Potter's Disappearing Act," *Newhouse News Service*, April 23, 2007, 1; and Tom Muha, "Achieving Happiness: Setbacks Can Make Us Stronger," *The Capital*, May 31, 2009.

3. Muha, "Achieving Happiness"; and Melinda Beck, "If at First You Don't Succeed, You're in Excellent Company," *The Wall Street Journal*, April 29, 2008.

4. M. E. Gist, "Self-Efficacy: Implications for Organizational Behavior and Human Resource Management," *Academy of Management Review* (July 1987): 47; and Arthur Bandura, "Self-efficacy," in V. S. Ramachaudran, ed., *Encyclopedia of Human Behavior*, vol. 4 (New York: Academic Press, 1994), pp. 71–81.

5. Reported in William W. George et al., "Discovering Your Authentic Leadership," *Harvard Business Review* (February 2007): 129–138.

6. Bill George, "Leadership Skills: It Starts with Self-Awareness," *Leadership Excellence* (June 2011): 13; Tricia Bisoux, "What Makes Leaders Great" (interviews with leadership experts), *BizEd* (September–October 2005): 40–45; Warren Bennis, *Why Leaders Can't Lead* (San Francisco: Jossey-Bass, 1989); Daniel Goleman, "What Makes a Leader?" *Harvard Business Review* (November–December 1998): 93ff; and Richard E. Boyatzis, *The Competent Manager: A Model for Effective Performance* (New York: Wiley, 1982).

7. Employee quoted in Stratford Sherman, "How Tomorrow's Best Leaders Are Learning Their Stuff," *Fortune* (November 27, 1995): 90–102.

8. Charlotte Beers, interviewed by Adam Bryant, "The Best Scorecard Is the One You Keep for Yourself," *The New York Times*, March 31, 2012, www.nytimes.com/2012/04/01/business/charlotte-beers-on-the-importance-of-self-assessment.html?pagewanted5all (accessed April 1, 2012).

9. Thanks to Scott Williams, "Self-Awareness and Personal Development," *LeaderLetter* Web site, www.wright.edu/~scott.williams/LeaderLetter/selfawareness.htm (accessed August 21, 2007), for this image.

10. Steven Snyder, "Leadership Struggle: It's an Art to Be Mastered," *Leadership Excellence* (January 2013): 11; and Ira Chaleff, "Avoid Fatal Crashes: Leaders and Their Blind Spots," *Leadership Excellence* (May 2012): 13.

11. Adam Bryant, "Francisco D'Souza of Cognizant, on Finding Company Heroes" (Corner Office column), *The New York Times*, September 1, 2013.

12. C. Fletcher and C. Baldry, "A Study of Individual Differences and Self-Awareness in the Context of Multi-Source Feedback," *Journal of Occupational and Organizational Behavior* 73, no. 3 (2000): 303–319.

13. Adam Bryant, "Making Room for Differences" (Corner Office column), *The New York Times*, February 7, 2015, http://www.nytimes.com/2015/02/08/business/corner-office-making-room-for-differences.html?_r=0 (accessed October 13, 2015).

14. Ellen McGirt, "Do You Pass the Leadership Test?" *Fast Company* (December 2012–January 2013): 63–67.

15. George, "Leadership Skills"; and Beers, "The Best Scorecard Is the One You Keep for Yourself."

16. Jerry Krueger and Emily Killham, "At Work, Feeling Good Matters," *Gallup Management Journal* (December 8, 2005), http://gmj.gallup.com/content/20311/work-feeling-good-matters.aspx (accessed September 17, 2010).

17. Conference Board survey, reported in Susan Adams, "Most Americans Are Unhappy at Work," *Forbes* (June 20, 2014), http://www.forbes.com/sites/susanadams/2014/06/20/most-americans-are-unhappy-at-work/#64c5f9d5862a (accessed April 26, 2016).

18. Tony Schwartz, "The Greatest Sources of Satisfaction in the Workplace Are Internal and Emotional," *Fast Company* (November 2000): 398–402.

19. Tony Schwartz, "The Secret to Sustaining High Job Performance," *The New York Times*, November 13, 2015, http://www.nytimes.com/2015/11/14/business/dealbook/the-secret-to-sustaining-high-job-performance.html?_r=0 (accessed April 26, 2016).

20. Victor Lipman, "The Foundational Importance of Trust in Management," *Forbes* (October 7, 2013), http://www.forbes.com/sites/victorlipman/2013/10/07/the-foundational-importance-of-trust-in-management/ (accessed October 17, 2013).

21. Ryan Rendall, "Millenials are burning Out," *Gallup workplace*, July 13, 2018.

22. "Closing the Engagement Gap: A Road Map for Driving Superior Business Performance," *Towers Perrin Global Workforce Study* 2007–2008, www.towersperrin.com/tp/getwebcachedoc?webc=HRS/USA/2008/200803/GWS_Global_Report20072008 _31208.pdf (accessed September 20, 2010).

23. Example in Rick Wartzman, "Trust: Effective Managers Make It a Priority," *Bloomberg BusinessWeek*, October 16, 2009, http://www.businessweek.com/managing/content/oct2009/ca20091019_333718.htm (accessed October 17, 2013).

24. Lipman, "The Foundational Importance of Trust in Management"; and Wartzman, "Trust: Effective Managers Make It a Priority."

25. Leadership IQ survey, reported in "Many Employees Don't Trust Their Boss," *Machine Design* (September 2007): 2.

26. Quoted in Paul Harris, "Leadership: Role Models Earn Trust and Profits," *T&D* (March 2010): 47.

27. This is a very brief introduction to the subject of attributions and their role in organizations. For recent overviews of the research on attribution theory and a special issue devoted to the topic, see Paul Harvey, Kristin Madison, Mark Martinko et al., "Attribution Theory in the Organizational Sciences: The Road Less Traveled and the Path Ahead," *The Academy of Management Perspectives* 28, no. 2 (2014): 128–146; and Marie Dasborough, Paul Harvey, and Mark J. Martinko, "An Introduction to Attributional Influences in Organizations," *Group & Organization Management* 36, no. 4 (2011): 419–426.

28. Thomas L. Friedman, "How to Get a Job at Google," *The New York Times*, February 22, 2014, http://www.nytimes.com/2014/02/23/opinion/sunday/friedman-how-to-get-a-job-at-google.html?_r=0 (accessed April 26, 2016).

29. "Poll: Most Organizations Don't Use Personality Tests," *HR Magazine* 57, no. 2 (February 2012): 88; and Stephen T. Watson, "Job Hunting in the Virtual Age: Recruiters Can Be Overwhelmed by the Flood of Resumes," *Buffalo News*, August 19, 2012.

30. See J. M. Digman, "Personality Structure: Emergence of the Five-Factor Model," *Annual Review of Psychology* 41 (1990): 417–440; M. R. Barrick and M. K. Mount, "Autonomy as a Moderator of the Relationships Between the Big Five Personality Dimensions and Job Performance," *Journal of Applied Psychology* (February 1993): 111–118; and J. S. Wiggins and A. L. Pincus, "Personality: Structure and Assessment," *Annual Review of Psychology* 43 (1992): 473–504.

31. Quentin Hardy, "Your Personality Type, Defined by the Internet," *The New York Times*, June 11, 2014, http://bits.blogs.nytimes.com/2014/06/11/your-personality-type-defined-by-the-internet/?_r=0 (accessed April 26, 2016); and Caitlin Dewey, "Can We Guess Who You Are Based on the Pages You've Liked on Facebook?" *The Washington Post*, September 2, 2015, https://www.washingtonpost.com/news/the-intersect/wp/2015/09/02/can-we-guess-who-you-are-based-on-the-pages-youve-liked-on-facebook/ (accessed April 26, 2016).

32. Del Jones, "Not All Successful CEOs Are Extroverts," *USA TODAY*, June 6, 2006, www.usatoday.com/money/companies/management/2006-06-06-shy-ceo-usat_x.htm (accessed September 20, 2010).

33. Patricia Sellers, "Marissa Mayer: Ready to Rumble at Yahoo," *Fortune* (October 29, 2012): 118–128; Ginka Toegel and Jean-Louis Barsoux, "How to Become a Better Leader," *MIT Sloan Management Review* (Spring 2012): 51–60; and Nancy Ancowitz, "Success Isn't Only for the Extroverts," *The New York Times*, November 1, 2009.

34. Susan Cain, "Hire Introverts," *The Atlantic* (July–August 2012): 68ff; Adam M. Grant, Francesca Gino, and David A. Hofmann, "The Hidden Advantages of Quiet Bosses," *Harvard Business Review* (December 2010): 28ff; Susan Cain, "Must Great Leaders Be Gregarious?" *The New York Times*, September 16, 2012; and Bryan Walsh, "The Upside of Being an Introvert (and Why Extroverts Are Overrated)," *Time* (February 6, 2012): 40–45.

35. Reported in Daisy Grewal, "When Nice Guys Finish First," *Scientific American Mind* (July–August 2012): 62–65.

36. Reported in Christopher Palmeri, "Putting Managers to the Test," *BusinessWeek* (November 20, 2006): 82.

37. Research reported in J. J. McCorvey, "Research Corner: Feeling Guilty? Good. Why Guilt Makes You a Better Leader," *Inc.* (July–August 2012): 26; and Rachel Emma Silverman, "Plagued by Guilt? You May Be Management Material," *The Wall Street Journal*, May 29, 2012, http://blogs.wsj.com/atwork/2012/05/29/plagued-by-guilt-you-may-be-management-material/ (accessed June 3, 2012).

38. Julian B. Rotter, "Generalized Expectancies for Internal versus External Control of Reinforcement," *Psychological Monographs* 80, no. 609 (1966); and J. B. Rotter, "Internal Versus External Control of Reinforcement: A Case History," *American Psychologist* 45, no. 4 (April 1990): 489–493.

39. See P. E. Spector, "Behavior in Organizations as a Function of Employees' Locus of Control," *Psychological Bulletin* (May 1982): 482–497.

40. T. W. Adorno et al., *The Authoritarian Personality* (New York: Harper & Row, 1950).

41. Niccolò Machiavelli, *The Prince*, trans. George Bull (Middlesex: Penguin, 1961); James O'Toole, "After 500 Years, Why Does Machiavelli Still Hold Such Sway?" *Strategy + Business* (January 27, 2014), http://www.strategy-business.com/blog/After-500-Years-Why-Does-Machiavelli-Still-Hold-Such-Sway?gko=986c4 (accessed April 26, 2016).

42. Richard Christie and Florence Geis, *Studies in Machiavellianism* (New York: Academic Press, 1970).

43. R. G. Vleeming, "Machiavellianism: A Preliminary Review," *Psychological Reports* (February 1979): 295–310.

44. Christie and Geis, *Studies in Machiavellianism*.

45. Carl Jung, *Psychological Types* (London: Routledge and Kegan Paul, 1923).

46. Mary H. McCaulley, "Research on the MBTI and Leadership: Taking the Critical First Step," keynote address, The Myers-Briggs Type Indicator and Leadership: An International Research Conference (January 12–14, 1994).

47. Reported in Lillian Cunningham, "Does It Pay to Know Your Type?" *The Washington Post*, December 14, 2012, http://articles.washingtonpost.com/2012-12-14/national/35847528_1_personality-types-myers-briggs-type-indicator-financial-success (accessed March 20, 2013).

48. Jennifer Overbo, "Using Myers-Briggs Personality Type to Create a Culture Adapted to the New Century," *T+D* (February 2010): 70–72.

49. Reported in Lisa Takeuchi Cullen, "SATs for J-O-B-S," *Time* (April 3,2006): 89.

50. Michael Kinsman, "Businesses Can Suffer If Workers' Emotions Not Dealt With" (an interview with Mel Fugate), *San Diego Union-Tribune*, December 17, 2006; and Mel Fugate, Angelo J. Kinicki, and Gregory E. Prussia, "Employee Coping with Organizational Change: An Examination of Alternative Theoretical Perspectives and Models," *Personnel Psychology* 61, no. 1 (Spring 2008): 1–36.

51. "Emotion," *The Free Dictionary*, www.thefreedictionary.com/ Emotions (accessed June 15, 2010); and "Motivation and Emotion," *Psychology 101* (AllPsych Online), http://allpsych. com/psychology101/emotion.html (accessed June 15, 2010).

52. E. Hatfield, J. T. Cacioppo, and R. L. Rapson, *Emotional Contagion* (New York: Cambridge University Press, 1994); G. Schoenewolf, "Emotional Contagion: Behavioral Induction in Individuals and Groups," *Modern Psychoanalysis* 15 (1990): 49–61.

53. Hatfield et al., *Emotional Contagion*; Schoenewolf, "Emotional Contagion; and studies reported in Robert I. Sutton, "Are You Being a Jerk? Again?" *BusinessWeek* (August 25, 2008): 52.

54. Trevor Foulk, Andrew Woolum, and Amir Erez, "Catching Rudeness Is Like Catching a Cold: The Contagion Effects of Low-Intensity Negative Behaviors," *Journal of Applied Psychology* 101, no. 1 (January 2016): 50–67; Rachel Emma Silverman, "Workplace Rudeness Is as Contagious as a Cold," *The Wall Street Journal*, August 11, 2015, http://www. wsj.com/articles/at-work-1439335893 (accessed April 27, 2016); and Lindsey Murray, "Study: Workplace Rudeness Is Like a Virus," *CNN*, August 19, 2015, http://www.cnn. com/2015/08/19/health/rude-workplace-study-health/ (accessed April 27, 2016).

55. Research by NoahEisenkraft and Hillary Anger Elfenbein, reported in Nicole Branan, "The 'Me' Effect," *Scientific American Mind* (November–December 2010): 14–15; Noah Eisenkraft and Hillary Anger Elfenbein, "The Way You Make Me Feel," *Psychological Science* 21 (April 2010): 505–510; Robert I.Sutton, "How Bad Apples Infect the Tree," *The New York Times*, November 28, 2010; and Roy Baumeister et al., "Bad Is Stronger Than Good," *Review of General Psychology* 5, no. 4 (2001): 323–370.

56. Krueger and Killham, "At Work, Feeling Good Matters."

57. Based on Vivian Giang, "Inside Google's Insanely Popular Emotional-Intelligence Course," *Fast Company* (March 25, 2015), http://www.fastcompany.com/3044157/the-future-of-work/inside-googles-insanely-popular-emotional-intelligence-course (accessed October 19, 2015); and Julie Bort, "This Google Engineer's Title Is 'Jolly Good Fellow' and He's Solving Unhappiness and War," *Business Insider* (September 18, 2015), http://www.businessinsider.com/ google-jolly-good-fellow-chade-meng-tan-2015-9 (accessed April 27, 2016).

58. DanielGoleman, "Leadership That Gets Results," *Harvard Business Review* (March–April 2000): 79–90; Daniel Goleman, "Emotional Mastery: Seek to Excel in Four Dimensions," *Leadership Excellence* (June 2011): 12–13; and DanielGoleman, *Emotional Intelligence: Why It Can Matter More Than IQ* (New York: Bantam Books, 1995).

59. Alan Farnham, "Are You Smart Enough to Keep Your Job?" *Fortune* (January 15, 1996): 34–47.

60. Hendrie Weisinger, *Emotional Intelligence at Work* (San Francisco: Jossey-Bass, 2000); D. C. McClelland, "Identifying Competencies with Behavioral-Event Interviews," *Psychological Science* (Spring 1999): 331–339; Goleman, "Leadership That Gets Results"; D. Goleman, *Working with Emotional Intelligence* (New York: Bantam Books, 1999); and Lorie Parch, "Testing … 1, 2, 3," *Working Woman* (October 1997): 74–78.

61. Reported in Cari Tuna, "Lawyers and Employers Take the Fight to 'Workplace Bullies'" (Theory & Practice column), *The Wall Street Journal*, August 4, 2008.

62. These examples and statistics are from Sam Hananel, "Workplace Bullying Gets Higher Profile as Movement Grows to Limit Worker Abuse," Associated Press, at *Yahoo News*, March 1, 2013, http://news.yahoo.com/growing-push-halt-workplace-bullying-091201526.html (accessed October 18, 2013).

63. This section on self-management is based heavily on David Allen, *Getting Things Done: The Art of Stress-Free Productivity* (New York: Viking Penguin, 2001).

64. Reported in "One of These Days," *The Wall Street Journal*, March 11, 1997.

65. Based on Allen, *Getting Things Done*; and Francis Heylighen and Clément Vidal, "Getting Things Done: The Science Behind Stress-Free Productivity," *Long Range Planning* 41 (2008): 585–605.

66. T. A. Beehr and R. S. Bhagat, *Human Stress and Cognition in Organizations: An Integrated Perspective* (New York: Wiley, 1985); and Bruce Cryer, Rollin McCraty, and Doc Childre, "Pull the Plug on Stress," *Harvard Business Review* (July 2003): 102–107.

67. "Desk Rage Rising," *Office Solutions* (January 2009): 9; and Carol Hymowitz, "Bosses Have to Learn How to Confront Troubled Employees," *The Wall Street Journal*, April 23, 2007.

68. Hananel, "Workplace Bullying Gets Higher Profile."

69. Discussed in Alice Park, "The Two Faces of Anxiety," *Time* (December 5, 2011): 54–65; Alina Tugend, "The Contrarians on Stress: It Can Be Good for You," *The New York Times*, October 4, 2014; and Melinda Beck, "Anxiety Can Bring Out the Best," *The Wall Street Journal*, June 18, 2012, http://online.wsj.com/article/SB1000142405270230383640 4577474451463041994.html (accessed June 20, 2012).

70. "Are You Working Too Hard? A Conversation with Mind-Body Researcher Herbert Benson," *Harvard Business Review* (November 2005): 53–58; and R. M. Yerkes and J. D. Dodson, "The Relation of Strength of Stimulus to Rapidity of Habit Formation," *Journal of Comparative Neurology and Psychology* 18 (1908): 459–482.

71. Mathias V. Schmidt and Lars Schwabe, "Splintered by Stress," *Scientific American Mind* (September–October 2011): 22–29.

72. Reported in Brian Nadel, "The Price of Pressure," special advertising feature, *Fortune* (December 11, 2006): 143–146.

73. Health and Safety Authority survey, reported in Joe Humphreys, "Stress Will Be Main Cause of Workplace Illness by 2020," *Irish Times*, July 27, 2005.

74. Don Mills, "Running on High Octane or Burning Out Big Time? Stress Flunkies," *National Post*, April 8, 2006.

75. M. Friedman and R. Rosenman, *Type A Behavior and Your Heart* (New York: Knopf, 1974).

76. David Sacks, "The Way I Work: Yammer," *Inc.* (November 2011): 123–124.

77. "Work Stress on the Rise: 8 in 10 Americans Are Stressed About Their Jobs, Survey Finds," *The Huffington Post*, April 10, 2013, http://www.huffingtonpost.com/2013/04/10/

work-stress-jobs-americans_n_3053428.html (accessed April 27, 2016).

78. Mills, "Running on High Octane or Burning Out Big Time?"; and Vani Doraisamy, "Young Techies Swell the Ranks of the Depressed," *The Hindu*, October 11, 2005.

79. Charles Duhigg and David Barboza, "In China, Human Costs Are Built into an iPad," *The New York Times*, January 25, 2012, www.nytimes.com/2012/01/26/business/ieconomy-apples-ipad-and-the-human-costs-for-workers-in-china.html?pagewanted=all (accessed January 26, 2012); and Nick Wingfield and Charles Duhigg, "Apple Asks Outside Groups to Inspect Factories," *The New York Times*, February 13, 2012, http://bits.blogs.nytimes.com/2012/02/13/apple-announces-independent-factory-inspections/ (accessed February 13, 2012).

80. Quoted in Elizabeth Bernstein, "When a Co-Worker Is Stressed Out," *The Wall Street Journal*, August 26, 2008.

81. Reported in Sue Shellenbarger, "Health & Fitness: How to Keep Your Cool in Angry Times," *The Wall Street Journal Asia*, September 27, 2010.

82. American Psychological Association, "APA Survey Finds Feeling Valued at Work Linked to Well-Being and Performance," March 12, 2012, www.apa.org/news/press/releases/2012/03/well-being.aspx (accessed September 5, 2012).

83. Reported in Ruth Mantell, "How to Lower Your Workplace Stress," *The Wall Street Journal*, January 15, 2012, http://online.wsj.com/news/articles/SB10001424052970204257504577152502470874464 (accessed October 18, 2013).

84. Robert Epstein, "Fight the Frazzled Mind," *Scientific American Mind* (September-October 2011): 30–35.

85. Sheldon Cohen and Thomas Ashby Wills, "Stress, Social Support, and the Buffering Hypothesis," *Psychological Bulletin* 85, no. 2 (1985): 310–357.

86. Eilene Zimmerman, "When Stress Flirts with Burnout," *The New York Times*, January 17, 2010; and Joanna Barsh, J. Mogelof, and C. Webb, "How Centered Leaders Achieve Extraordinary Results," *McKinsey Quarterly* (October 2010), www.mckinseyquarterly.com/How_centered_leaders_achieve_extraordinary_results_2678 (accessed January 16, 2011).

87. Kenexa High Performance Institute study, reported in Ann Pace, "Stressed Out?" *T + D* (October 2012): 14.

88. Rosabeth Moss Kanter, "Balancing Work and Life," *Knight-Ridder Tribune News Service*, April 8, 2005.

89. "APA Survey Finds Feeling Valued at Work Linked to Well-Being and Performance."

90. "The Way I Work: Paul English, Kayak," *Inc.* (February 2010): 98–101.

91. Shellenbarger, "Health & Fitness: How to Keep Your Cool in Angry Times."

92. From Dorothy Marcic, *Organizational Behavior*, 4th ed. (Mason, OH: South-Western, Cengage Learning, 1995). Reproduced by permission.

93. Based on K. J. Keleman, J. E. Garcia, and K. J. Lovelace, *Management Incidents: Role Plays for Management Development* (Dubuque, IA: Kendall-Hunt Publishing, 1990): 69–72.

94. Adapted from Doug Wallace, "Fudge the Numbers or Leave," *Business Ethics* (May–June 1996): 58–59. Copyright © 1996 by New Mountain Media LLC. Reproduced with permission of New Mountain Media LLC.

Chapter 11
Leadership

iStock.com/oscarhdez

Chapter Outline

Learning Outcomes

After studying this chapter, you should be able to:

11.1 Define *leadership* and explain its importance for organizations.

11.2 Describe the leadership trends emerging in today's organizations, including Level 5 leadership, servant leadership, and authentic leadership.

11.3 Discuss how women's style of leading is typically different from men's.

11.4 Identify personal characteristics associated with effective leaders.

11.5 Define *task-oriented behavior* and *people-oriented behavior* and explain how these categories are used to evaluate and adapt leadership style.

11.6 Describe the situational model of leadership and its application to subordinate participation.

11.7 Discuss how leadership fits the organizational situation and how organizational characteristics can substitute for leadership behaviors.

11.8 Describe transformational leadership and when it should be used.

11.9 Explain how followership is related to effective leadership.

11.10 Identify sources of leader power and the tactics that leaders use to influence others.

Are You Ready to Be a Manager?

Before reading this chapter, please circle either "Mostly True" or "Mostly False" for each of the following five statements.

1 I'm able to get people enthused about an idea and to take action.

Mostly True ◄ ················· ► Mostly False

[page 409]

2 I think a leader who is humble will not gain the respect of subordinates. Servant leadership is an oxymoron.

Mostly True ◄ ················· ► Mostly False

[pages 411–412]

3 Leaders need to be strong and hard-nosed and I'm not sure women are up to that part of the job.

Mostly True ◄ ················· ► Mostly False

[page 415]

4 When I'm working with a leader, I make sure I bring my critical thinking skills so that I'm not merely a passive follower.

Mostly True ◄ ················· ► Mostly False

[page 428]

5 When I'm working with a group, I'm able to get things done through the strength of the relationships and my expertise, rather than relying on authoritarian methods.

Mostly True ◄ ················· ► Mostly False

[page 432]

Discover Your Management Approach

What Is Your Leadership Orientation?

Instructions: Responding to the following statements can help you diagnose your approach to dealing with others when you are in a leadership role. If you have been a leader at work with people reporting to you, think back to that experience. Or you can think about how you usually behave as a formal or informal leader in a group to complete an assignment. Please answer honestly about how frequently you display each behavior.

	Mostly True	Mostly False
1. I intentionally try to make people's work on the job more pleasant.	_____	_____
2. I focus more on execution than on being pleasant with people.	_____	_____
3. I go out of my way to help others.	_____	_____

To complete and score the entire assessment, visit MindTap.

General Stanley A. McChrystal founded the McChrystal Group to "bring lessons from the battlefield to the boardroom." McChrystal, who is best known for leading the covert Joint Special Operations Command during the Persian Gulf Wars and commanding all U.S. and coalition forces in Afghanistan, retired from the U.S. Army in 2010 as a four-star general after more than 34 years of service. What lessons does the man former U.S. Secretary of Defense Robert Gates called "one of America's greatest warriors" have for corporate leaders? One of the most important lessons is that leaders must challenge the hierarchical, command-and-control approach to organizational management. McChrystal bases much of his leadership philosophy on advice that came from his mentor, Lieutenant General John Vines, whom McChrystal describes as the perfect model of a servant leader. McChrystal believes that good leadership, whether in the military or in today's businesses, schools, and other organizations, comes from committing to and investing in followers, who are the ones doing the hard work on the front lines. McChrystal says his greatest fear was "not fear of getting shot at, or worrying that you're going to crash the airplane, or something like that," but rather the fear of failing his soldiers. "I think of the young private on a checkpoint in Baghdad ... who has almost no control [over what happens] and lots of time on his hands to think," McChrystal says. "When I look at courage, I look at the 18-year-old kid ... standing out there doing that. ... That's pretty humbling."[1]

In most situations, a military unit, team, department, or volunteer group is only as good as its leader. As described by General McChrystal in the chapter opening example, a humble approach to leadership that puts followers and the organization ahead of one's own ego and self-interest is highly effective in today's chaotic environment. Yet there are as many variations among leaders as there are among other people, and many styles of leadership can be effective. In Chapter 10, we explored differences in personality, perception, and emotions that affect behavior. Some of the most important personality differences for the organization's success are those of its leaders because leader behaviors play a critical role in shaping employee performance. In this chapter, we define *leadership* and explore how managers develop leadership qualities. We examine various leadership theories, look at some important leadership approaches for contemporary organizations, and explore the role of followership. Chapters 12 through 14 will look in detail at many of the functions of leadership, including employee motivation, communication, and encouraging teamwork.

11-1 The Nature of Leadership

What does it mean to be a leader? Among all the ideas and writings about leadership, three aspects stand out—people, influence, and goals. Leadership occurs among people, involves the use of influence, and is used to attain goals.[2] *Influence* means that the relationship among people is not passive. Moreover, influence is designed to achieve some end or goal. Thus, **leadership**, as defined here, is the ability to influence people toward the attainment of goals. This definition captures the idea that leaders are involved with other people in the achievement of goals. Leadership is reciprocal, occurring *among* people.[3] Leadership is a "people" activity, distinct from administrative paperwork or problem-solving activities. Throughout this text, we have looked at various organizations that are experimenting with bosslessness. But every team and organization needs leadership. As described in the "Sunny Side Up" box being a "leader" can be more powerful than being a "boss."

As the "Sunny Side Up" box indicates, taking calculated risks is part of good leadership. Connie McDonald and Pam Weeks left their well-paying jobs, hiring their first employee, then going into store fronts—and it paid off, as they now have arguably the best-tasting cookie in New York City, as shown in the "Recipe for Success" box.

Source: Inc. Magazine

Concept Connection

Chris Zane, founder and owner of Zane's Cycles in Branford, Connecticut, is an expert at turning first-time customers into lifetime customers. In fact, he wrote the book on it—*Reinventing the Wheel*. The book is a reflection of his enduring goal, which is to provide the ultimate shopping experience that makes customers feel great about his products and services. Zane actually started his business at age 16 with a $23,000 loan from his grandfather. Under his **leadership**, Zane's Cycles has become one of the largest independent bicycle distributors in the United States.

Remember This

- The attitudes and behaviors of leaders shape the conditions that determine how well employees can do their jobs; thus, leaders play a tremendous role in the organization's success.

- **Leadership** is the ability to influence people toward the attainment of organizational goals.
- Many different styles of leadership can be effective.

Sunny Side Up ⟩ Bossless Does Not Mean Leaderless

Conventional management states that organizations need to be highly ordered, with well-defined roles, rules, and regulations, and led by a strong boss. This has always been the standard in the U.S. military. But what if bosslessness and self-organization give rise to an effective order far more powerful than what traditional management might carry out?

The story of Captain Michael Abrashoff and his command of the USS *Benfold* is legendary inside and outside the Navy. Within months, he transformed a crew of demoralized sailors into confident and inspired problem solvers eager to take the initiative. To do this, Captain Abrashoff had to change his traditional management style to a more "bossless" leadership style. Some of Captain Abrashoff's methods for becoming less of a boss and more of a leader include:

- **Lead by example.** Real leadership is done by example. Whenever he could not get the results he wanted, Captain Abrashoff asked himself three questions: Did I clearly articulate the goals? Did I give people enough time and resources to accomplish the task? Did I give them enough training? He discovered that many times, he was as much a part of the problem as his people were.

- **Communicate purpose and meaning.** Give employees a compelling vision of their work and a good reason to believe that it is important. Tell people personally what's in it for them. Abrashoff found that the more people knew what the goals were, the better buy-in he got—and the better results they achieved together.

CONTINUED

- **Create a climate of trust.** The best way to get a ship—or any organization—to improve dramatically is to give the troops all the responsibility they can handle and then stand back.

- **Look for results, not salutes.** You need to have people in your organization who can tap you on your shoulder and say, "Is this the best way?" or "Slow down," or "Think about this." When managers announce decisions after little or no consultation, and when they make it clear that their orders aren't to be questioned, then conditions are ripe for disaster.

- **Take calculated risks.** An organization that aims to stay alive and strong should make sure to praise and promote risk takers, even when they fail once in a while. As Abrashoff states, "Show me someone who has never

made a mistake, and I will show you someone who is not doing anything to improve your organization. If all you give are orders, then all you will get are order takers."

- **Generate unity.** Abrashoff says organizations can always hire smart people, but he found that what works best are staff members who work together and support one another. Treating people with dignity and respect is not only morally right but also highly practical and productive.

SOURCES: D. Michael Abrashoff, "Retention Through Redemption," *Harvard Business Review* (February 2001): 136–141; Abrashoff, *It's Your Ship: Management Techniques from the Best Damn Ship in the Navy* (New York: Business Plus, 2002); and Mike Abrashoff, "The Bossless, Not Leaderless Office," Leadership Blog, *GLS Worldwide*, June 25, 2013, http://www.glsworld.com/thought-leadership/leadership-blog/2013/06/the-bossless-not-leaderless-office/(accessed November 23, 2013.)

Recipe for Success } **Levain Bakery**

What happens when two high-powered and successful 22-ish-year-old women decide to create the best-tasting chocolate chip cookie in all of New York City? They end up with three bakeries and waiting lines so long they've installed cameras so customers can go online and gauge how long they'd have to stand and linger.

But it wasn't always like that. Connie McDonald started working all over the country in resorts and restaurants, teaching tennis, and even dressing like a pirate at Long John Silver's. Then at her father's suggestion, she got into Wall Street as a broker's assistant. But McDonald discovered she loved swimming and doing triathlons much more. To make ends meet, she started catering and discovered she enjoyed making food. So when her Wall Street job ended (she got fired), she enrolled in what now is the Institute of Culinary Education and got an internship at Amy's bread. She found her mission as a baker.

By coincidence, McDonald ended up with a roommate, Pam Weeks, who was working in the fashion business for Norma Kamali. Weeks also loved swimming and triathlons, and the two women connected as athletes. When the restaurant McDonald was working for was declining and she met a celebrity chef, she asked Weeks if she wanted to go into the bakery business. They

started with bread. One would bake and the other deliver, and then they'd switch off. Finally there were enough orders to hire a delivery person—an employee!

The famous 6-ounce cookie that made their business came from their triathlon days, when they'd be so exhausted and hungry after training that they were looking for something to sustain them but found the power bars on the market then were horrible. Therefore, they made their original cookies substantial enough to be placed in pockets of bike shirts, provide a few bites, and then be put back. And they couldn't crumble. By this time, McDonald and Weeks were baking in a subterranean store and the bread customers went crazy for the cookie. Somehow Oprah found them, as did TripAdvisor. McDonald and Weeks wanted to grow the business and they have, through smart decisions and a lot of hard work—and knowing who should do what. McDonald has more patience, so she trains new staff—there are more than 40 now. Weeks is quieter and happy to let her business partner take the limelight. Weeks is detail oriented and minds most of the organizing parts. It works: just go and see the lines outside their bakeries.

SOURCE: Ina Yalof, *Food and the City* New York (GP Putnam's, 2016, pp. 262–271.)

11-2 Contemporary Leadership

The concept of leadership evolves as the needs of organizations change. That is, the environmental context in which leadership is practiced influences which approach might be most effective as well as what kinds of leaders are most admired by society. The technology, economic conditions, labor conditions, and social and cultural mores of the times all play a role. A significant influence on leadership styles in recent years is the turbulence and uncertainty of the environment. Ethical and economic difficulties, **corporate governance** concerns, globalization, changes in technology, new ways of working, shifting employee expectations, and significant social transitions have contributed to a shift in how we think about and practice leadership. Four approaches that are in tune with leadership for today's turbulent times are Level 5 leadership, servant leadership, authentic leadership, and interactive leadership, which has been associated with women's style of leading.

11-2a Level 5 Leadership

A study conducted by Jim Collins and his research associates identified the critical importance of what Collins calls *Level 5 leadership* in transforming companies from merely good to truly great organizations.[4] As described in his book *Good to Great: Why Some Companies Make the Leap . . . and Others Don't*, Level 5 leadership refers to the highest level in a hierarchy of manager capabilities, as illustrated in Exhibit 11.1.

As the exhibit reflects, a key characteristic of Level 5 leaders is an almost complete lack of ego (humility) coupled with a fierce resolve to do what is best for the organization (will). **Humility** means being unpretentious and modest rather than arrogant and prideful. In contrast to the view of great leaders as larger-than-life personalities with strong egos and big ambitions, Level 5 leaders often seem shy and self-effacing. Although they accept full responsibility for mistakes, poor results, or failures, Level 5 leaders give credit for successes to other people. Level 5 leaders build organizations based on solid values that go far beyond just making money, with an unwavering resolve to do whatever is needed to make the company successful over the long term.[5]

An example of a leader who demonstrates Level 5 leadership qualities is Sir Terry Leahy, who recently retired after more than a decade leading Britain's Tesco chain of supermarkets. That's a long and successful tenure for a leader that most people know little about. Leahy didn't court personal publicity, much to the chagrin of journalists, and he put his energies into promoting Tesco and its employees rather than himself.[6] Or consider Qi Lu of Microsoft, who grew up in a rural village in China with no electricity or running water. Today, he is executive vice president of Microsoft's Applications and Services Group. How did he get there? Not from personal ambition, say former colleagues at Yahoo. "He shunned the limelight," said Tim Cadogan, now CEO of OpenX, "but he was considered one of the stars." Lu rose through the ranks at Yahoo, and he got the job at Microsoft based not on aggressiveness and pursuit of personal advancement, but rather because of his sheer intellectual abilities and his commitment to go above and beyond the call of

Exhibit 11.1 Level 5 Hierarchy

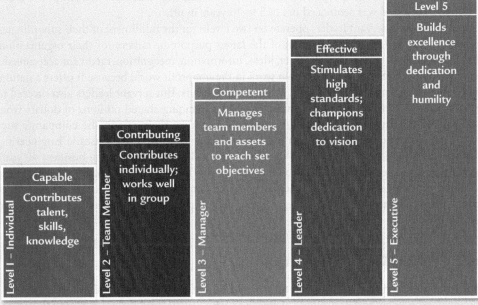

SOURCE: Based on Jim Collins, *Good to Great: Why Some Companies Make the Leap . . . and Others Don't* (New York: HarperCollins, 2001), p. 20.

duty to accomplish organizational goals. Lu feels a strong sense of duty and loyalty, pouring his heart and soul into the mission rather than spending his energies promoting himself.[7]

Level 5 leaders like Sir Terry Leahy and Qi Lu are extremely ambitious for their companies rather than for themselves. This attitude becomes highly evident in the area of succession planning. Level 5 leaders develop a solid corps of leaders throughout the organization so that when they leave, the company can continue to thrive and grow even stronger. Egocentric leaders, by contrast, often set their successors up for failure because it will be a testament to their own greatness if the company doesn't perform well without them. Rather than building an organization around "a genius with a thousand helpers," Level 5 leaders want everyone to develop to their fullest potential.

11-2b Servant Leadership

Jack Welch spent 20 years as chairman and CEO of General Electric (GE), and during his tenure with GE, the company's value increased 4,000 percent. Known for his forceful personality, Welch was also known to tell his managers that he loved them. When Welch speaks to MBA students, he reminds them that "any time you are managing people, your job is not about you, it's about them. It starts out about you as . . . an individual in a company," Welch says. "But once you get a leadership job, it moves very quickly to being about them."[8] Some leaders operate from the assumption that work exists for the development of the worker as much as the worker exists to do the work.[9] The concept of servant leadership, first described by Robert Greenleaf in 1970, has gained renewed interest in recent years as companies recover from ethical scandals and compete to attract and retain the best human talent.[10]

A **servant leader** transcends self-interest to serve others, the organization, and society.[11] Marilyn Carlson Nelson, former chairman and CEO of the Carlson Companies (Radisson Hotels, TGI Fridays, Regent Seven Seas Cruises), says being a true leader means that you "have to subordinate your own emotions, your own desires, even make decisions on behalf of the whole that might conflict with what you would do on an individual basis."[12] A stunning example of this occurred when a U.S.-flagged cargo ship, the *Maersk Alabama*, was seized and raided by Somali pirates. Captain Richard Phillips ordered crew members of the unarmed ship not to fight and gave himself up as a hostage to free the ship and crew. The story of the captain's dilemma and rescue is told in a 2013 movie starring Tom Hanks, *Captain Phillips*. Contrast his behavior with that of Captain Francesco Schettino, who allegedly abandoned his ship while passengers were still aboard after the luxury cruise liner *Costa Concordia* hit a rock and sank off the coast of Italy in 2012, killing at least 30 people. Schettino was charged with manslaughter, shipwreck, and abandoning ship, and was sentenced in 2015 to 16 years in prison.[13]

In organizations, servant leaders operate on two levels: for the fulfillment of their subordinates' goals and needs and for the realization of the larger purpose or mission of their organization. Servant leaders give things away—power, ideas, information, recognition, credit for accomplishments, even money. Servant leaders often work in the nonprofit world because it offers a natural way to apply their leadership drive and skills to serve others. But servant leaders also succeed in business. For two years in a row, Lenovo CEO Yang Yuanqing shared millions of dollars from his bonus with hourly manufacturing workers to recognize their role in the company's success.[14] Fred Keller built a $250 million plastics manufacturing company, Cascade Engineering, by continuously asking one question: *What good can we do?* Keller started the business 40 years ago with six employees. Today, it has 1,000 employees in 15 business divisions. Keller has made social responsibility a cornerstone of the business. The company offers jobs to welfare recipients. Keller has also donated large amounts to various philanthropic causes, both as an individual and through Cascade.[15]

11-2c Authentic Leadership

Another popular concept in leadership today is the idea of **authentic leadership**, which refers to individuals who know and understand themselves, who espouse and act consistent with higher-order ethical values, and who empower and inspire others with their openness and authenticity.[16]

To be authentic means being *real*, staying true to one's values and beliefs, and acting based on one's true self rather than emulating what others do. Authentic leaders inspire trust and commitment because they respect diverse viewpoints, encourage collaboration, and help others learn, grow, and develop as leaders. Nike went through a period recently when it was difficult to feel that some leaders were authentic, as shown in the "Half-Baked Management" box.

Exhibit 11.2 outlines the key characteristics of authentic leaders, and each is discussed next.[17]

- **Authentic leaders pursue their purpose with passion.** Leaders who lead without a purpose can fall prey to greed and the desires of the ego. When leaders demonstrate a high level of passion and commitment to a purpose, they inspire commitment from followers.
- **Authentic leaders practice solid values.** Authentic leaders have values that are shaped by their personal beliefs, and they stay true to them even under pressure. People come to know what the leader stands for, which inspires trust.

Half-Baked Management 〉 Nike

Trevor Edwards was on the succession list to take over Nike when CEO Mark Parker retired. In early March 2018, Parker sent a message to all employees about workplace behaviors that did not reflect the company's values of respect, empowerment, and inclusivity. Parker said all of this "disturbs and saddens me." Then he went on to say he was going to restructure the leadership team and that Edwards was resigning. A spokesman later said (without naming anyone) that conduct inconsistent with Nike's principles had occurred and appropriate actions had been taken. By March 20, a meeting with hundreds of employees explained the changes needed. Employees reported that a boys-club atmosphere had prevailed, that those close to Edwards (more often males) were promoted more quickly, and talk about FOT (friends of Trevor) had started. Some employees said culture problems had existed for years, such as taking managers to strip clubs. At least the company apparently decided to handle it,

SOURCE: Sara Germano and Joann S. Lublin, "Inside Nike, A Boy-Club Culture," *The Wall Street Journal*, Eastern ed, April 2, 2018, B!.

Exhibit 11.2 Components of Authentic Leadership

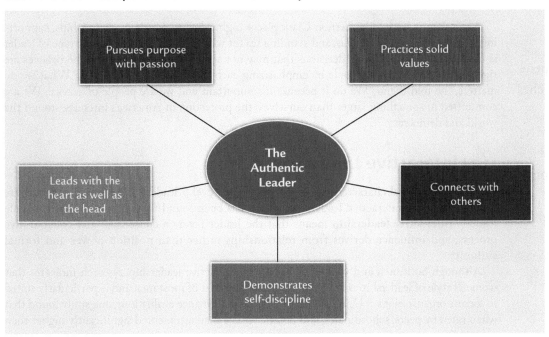

SOURCE: Based on Bill George, *Authentic Leadership: Rediscovering the Secrets to Lasting Value* (San Francisco: Jossey-Bass, 2003).

- *Authentic leaders lead with their hearts as well as their heads.* All leaders sometimes have to make tough choices, but authentic leaders maintain a compassion for others as well as the courage to make difficult decisions.
- *Authentic leaders establish connected relationships.* Authentic leaders build positive and enduring relationships, which makes followers want to do their best. In addition, authentic leaders surround themselves with good people and work to help others grow and develop.
- *Authentic leaders demonstrate self-discipline.* A high degree of self-control and self-discipline keeps leaders from taking excessive or unethical risks that could harm others and the organization. When authentic leaders make mistakes, they openly admit them.

One leader who demonstrates many of the characteristics of authentic leadership is Admiral Vernon Clark, who retired in 2005 after a 37-year Navy career.

Sunny Side Up } Admiral Vernon E. Clark, U.S. Chief of Naval Operations, 2000–2005

Admiral Vernon E. Clark was the second-longest-serving U.S. Chief of Naval Operations (CNO). The job of the CNO is to advise the president on the conduct of war.

When Clark was named CNO in July 2000, the Navy was losing too many good sailors who didn't want to reenlist. For Clark, getting and keeping good sailors who could protect the national security was a top priority, and all his decisions were based on connecting with and valuing the people on the front lines. When Navy officials proposed budget cuts in training and development, Clark rebelled. Instead he *increased* the training budget, strongly supported an increase in pay for sailors, and established the Naval Education and Training Command to increase training. Clark also revised the performance appraisal system to

provide constructive feedback for people at all levels. Clark made it a priority to blur the lines between enlisted sailors and officers and revised the job assignment process so that people didn't get forced into jobs and locations they didn't want. Always more concerned about doing things right than *being* right, Clark encouraged everyone to challenge assumptions, ask questions, and express conflicting views.

Thanks to Admiral Clark's emphasis on treating sailors right, first-term reenlistment soared from 38 percent to 56.7 percent within his first 18 months as CNO. Moreover, as the Navy retained more sailors, its ability to respond more quickly to protect the nation increased.[18]

An authentic leader like Vernon Clark places high value on personal relationships, supporting followers, being courageous, and standing up for what one believes. Thus, this type of leader is much more likely to make decisions that may not always be popular but that he believes are right. Clark also engaged people by emphasizing each individual's personal role. "What we do matters," he told them. "We do it because it's important and we are people of service. We are committed to something larger than ourselves: the protection of America's interests around the world and democracy."[19]

11-2d Interactive Leadership

Some of the general characteristics associated with Level 5 leaders and authentic leaders are also hallmarks of interactive leadership, which has been found to be associated with female leaders. **Interactive leadership** means that the leader favors a consensual and collaborative process, and influence derives from relationships rather than position power and formal authority.[20]

Although both men and women can practice interactive leadership, research indicates that women's style of leadership is typically different from that of most men and is particularly suited to today's organizations.[21] Using data from actual performance evaluations, one study found that when rated by peers, subordinates, and bosses, female managers scored significantly higher than

"The boss drives people; the leader coaches them. The boss depends on authority; the leader on good will. The boss inspires fear; the leader inspires enthusiasm."

—H. GORDON SELFRIDGE, FOUNDER OF SELFRIDGES

men on abilities such as motivating others, fostering communication, and listening.[22] Another study of leaders and their followers in businesses, universities, and government agencies found that women were rated higher on social and emotional skills, which are crucial for interactive leadership.[23] Indeed, studies by leadership development firm Zenger Folkman have found that women outshone men in almost every leadership dimension measured, even some considered typically masculine qualities, such as driving for results.[24] Exhibit 11.3 shows results for 6 of the 16 dimensions measured by the Zenger Folkman studies.

One good example of an interactive leader is Cindy Szadokierski, who started as a reservations agent for United Airlines and today is vice president in charge of operations for United's largest hub at O'Hare International Airport. As she oversees 4,000 employees and 600 flights a day, her favorite times are her weekly afternoon walkabouts on the O'Hare ramp and weekly morning strolls through the terminal, where she can connect with employees and customers. Pete McDonald, chief operating officer of United's parent, UAL Corporation, says there were serious operations problems at O'Hare, so they put "the most communicative person" in the job. Szadokierski's approach to leadership is more about collaboration than command and control.[25]

Men can be interactive leaders as well, and the characteristics associated with interactive leadership are emerging as valuable qualities for both male and female leaders in today's workplace. John Gerzema, author of *The Athena Doctrine* and a fellow with the Athena Center for Leadership at Barnard College, asked 32,000 people to classify 125 traits as masculine, feminine, or neutral, and another 32,000 to rate the importance of the traits in effective leadership. The results showed that traits considered feminine and often associated with interactive leadership, such as empathy, personal humility, inclusiveness, vulnerability, generosity, patience, and flexibility, topped the list of qualities most desirable for leaders.[26]

Jin Lee/Bloomberg /Getty Images

Concept Connection

The 2008 financial collapse put Debra Cafaro's leadership skills to the test. The CEO of Ventas Inc. saw the housing crisis approaching and insisted the Louisville-based health care real estate investment trust build cash reserves. Although she wanted to project calmness and certainty when the economic downturn hit, Cafaro says that "in order to be authentic, I also had to acknowledge, 'I'm scared, too.'" Throughout the crisis, Cafaro operated as an **interactive leader**, one who, in her words, makes sure "we're working together, collaborating—marching in the same direction." She succeeded. Ventas not only survived the recession but also is flourishing.

Exhibit 11.3 Gender Differences in Leadership Behaviors

Leadership Ability	Who Does It Best
Developing Others	(Women rated higher)
Driving for Results	(Women rated higher)
Inspiring and Motivating Others	(Women rated higher)
Solving Problems	(Women and men rated about equality)
Building Relationships	(Women rated higher)
Analyzing Issues	(Women and men rated about equality)

SOURCE: Data from Zenger Folkman, Inc., reported in Tony Schwartz, "Overcoming the Confidence Gap in Women," *The New York Times*, June 12, 2015, http://www.nytimes.com/2015/06/13/business/dealbook/overcoming-the-confidence-gap-for-women.html (accessed April 25, 2016).

Remember This

- A significant influence on leadership styles in recent years is the turbulence and uncertainty of the environment.

- One effective approach in today's environment is Level 5 leadership, which is characterized by an almost complete lack of ego (humility), coupled with a fierce resolve to do what is best for the organization (will).

- **Humility** means being unpretentious and modest rather than arrogant and prideful.

- A **servant leader** is a leader who serves others by working to fulfill followers' needs and goals, as well as to achieve the organization's larger mission.

- **Authentic leadership** refers to leadership by individuals who know and understand themselves, who espouse and act consistent with higher-order ethical values, and who empower and inspire others with their openness and authenticity.

- Women leaders typically score higher than men on abilities such as motivating others, building relationships, and developing others—skills that are based on humility and authenticity and are particularly suited to today's organizations.

- **Interactive leadership** is a leadership style characterized by values such as inclusion, collaboration, relationship building, and caring.

- Although interactive leadership is associated with women's style of leading, both men and women can be effective interactive leaders.

11-3 From Management to Leadership

Hundreds of books and articles have been written in recent years about the differences between management and leadership. Good management is essential in organizations, yet managers must be leaders too because distinctive qualities are associated with management and leadership that provide different strengths for the organization. A good way to think of the distinction between management and leadership is that management organizes the production and supply of fish to people, whereas leadership teaches and motivates people to fish. Organizations need both types of skills.[27]

As shown in Exhibit 11.4, management and leadership reflect two different sets of qualities and skills that frequently overlap within a single individual. A person might have more of one set of qualities than the other, but ideally, a manager develops a balance of both manager and leader qualities.[28] A primary distinction between management and leadership is that management promotes stability and order within the existing organizational structure and systems. This ensures that suppliers are paid, customers invoiced, products and services produced on time, and so forth. Leadership, on the other hand, promotes vision and change. Leadership means questioning the status quo and being willing to take reasonable risks so that outdated, unproductive, or socially irresponsible norms can be replaced to meet new challenges.

For example, when Google's founders needed more structured management at their small and rapidly growing company, they hired Eric Schmidt as CEO to provide operational expertise and oversight. Schmidt was not a heavy take-charge manager, which suited the founders just fine, but coming from a corporate background, Schmidt knew how to plan and organize and keep things focused. More important, it turned out that Schmidt also had leadership qualities that fit well with Google's need for innovation and change to keep the company thriving. His leadership principles can be summarized in the following five precepts:

1. Get to know your employees.

2. Create new ways to reward and promote high performers.

3. Let employees own the problems that you want them to solve.

4. Allow people to function outside the hierarchy.

5. Have employees' performance reviewed by someone whom they respect for their objectivity.[29]

Exhibit 11.4 Leader and Manager Qualities

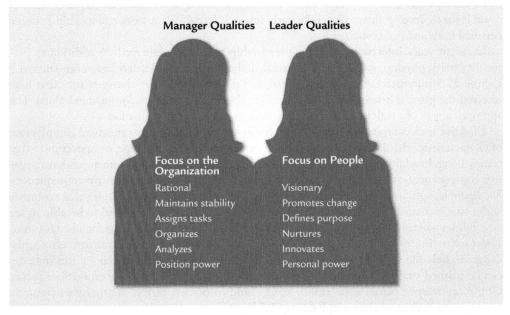

Manager Qualities   Leader Qualities

Focus on the Organization

Rational
Maintains stability
Assigns tasks
Organizes
Analyzes
Position power

Focus on People

Visionary
Promotes change
Defines purpose
Nurtures
Innovates
Personal power

SOURCES: Based on "What Is the Difference Between Management and Leadership?" *The Wall Street Journal Online*, http://guides.wsj.com/management/developing-a -leadership-style/what-is-the-difference-between-management-and-leadership (accessed June 28, 2009); and Genevieve Capowski, "Anatomy of a Leader: Where Are the Leaders of Tomorrow?" *Management Review* (March 1994): 12.

When he was CEO, Schmidt used to make a list of his best employees so that he could interact with them personally, encourage them to implement their innovative ideas, and protect them from unwanted interference by other managers. He made employees the owners of their work by allowing them a great deal of latitude in how they accomplished goals. He believed in structure, but he also allowed people to work outside the company hierarchy when necessary to solve problems and be creative.[30] Schmidt used a combination of skillful management and good leadership to take Google to the next stage of growth.

Leadership cannot replace management; it should be in addition to management. Good management is needed to help the organization meet current commitments, while good leadership is needed to move the organization into the future. Leadership's power comes from being built on the foundation of a well-managed organization.

Remember This

- Leadership and management reflect two different sets of qualities and skills that provide different benefits for the organization.

- Management promotes stability and efficient organizing to meet current commitments, whereas leadership often inspires engagement and organizational change to meet new conditions.

- Both leadership and management are important to organizations, and people can learn to be good leaders as well as good managers.

- When he was CEO of Google, Eric Schmidt applied both skilled management and good leadership to take the start-up to the next stage of growth.

11-4 Leadership Traits

Early efforts to understand leadership success focused on the leader's traits. **Traits** are the distinguishing personal characteristics of a leader, such as intelligence, honesty, self-confidence, and even appearance. The early research looked at leaders who had achieved a level of greatness, which

"The good news: these [leadership] traits are not genetic. It's not as if you have to be tall or left-handed. These qualities are developed through attitude, habit, and discipline—factors that are within your control."

—ADAM BRYANT, SENIOR EDITOR FOR FEATURES AT *THE NEW YORK TIMES*

referred to their style as the "Great Man" approach. The idea was relatively simple: Find out what made these people great, and select future leaders who already have exhibited the same traits or could learn to develop them. Generally, early research found only a weak relationship between personal traits and leader success.[31]

In recent years, interest in examining leadership traits has reemerged. In addition to personality traits, physical, social, and work-related characteristics of leaders have been studied.[32] Exhibit 11.5 summarizes the physical, social, and personal leadership characteristics that have received the greatest research support. However, these characteristics do not stand alone. The appropriateness of a trait or set of traits depends on the leadership situation.

Effective leaders typically possess varied traits, and no single leader can have a complete set of characteristics that is appropriate for handling any problem, challenge, or opportunity that comes along. In addition, traits that are typically considered positive can sometimes have negative consequences, and traits sometimes considered negative can have positive consequences. For example, optimism is a highly desirable trait for a leader. Studies have shown that optimism is the single characteristic most common to top executives.[33] Leaders need to be able to see possibilities where others see problems and to instill in others a sense of hope for a better future. However, optimism can also lull leaders into laziness and overconfidence, causing them to miss danger signals and underestimate risks. The 2007–2008 crisis in the financial services industry can be blamed partly on leaders who grew overconfident and led their organizations astray. Optimism must be paired with "reality testing" and conscientiousness, another trait common to successful leaders, as shown in Exhibit 11.5.[34]

Therefore, rather than just understanding their *traits*, the best leaders recognize and hone their *strengths*.[35] **Strengths** are natural talents and abilities that have been supported and reinforced with learned knowledge and skills and provide each individual with his or her best tools for accomplishment and satisfaction.[36] Every manager has a limited capacity; those who become good leaders are the ones who tap into their key strengths that can make a difference. Effective leadership isn't about having the "right" traits, but rather about finding the strengths that one can best exemplify and apply as a leader. Nancy Dubec, CEO of A&E Networks, believes that people have natural strengths that fall into the categories of "thinker, doer, or feeler." The right balance, she says, is essential for any team or organization to perform well. Dubec realizes that her strengths place her in the *doer* category, so she is careful to make sure she has thinkers and feelers on her management team and to respect their strengths and leadership approaches.[37]

Exhibit 11.5   Personal Characteristics of Leaders

Physical Characteristics	Personality Characteristics	Work-Related Characteristics
Energy Physical stamina	Self-confidence Honesty and integrity Optimism Desire to lead Independence	Achievement drive, desire to excel Conscientiousness in pursuit of goals Persistence against obstacles, tenacity
Intelligence and Ability	**Social Characteristics**	**Social Background**
Intelligence, cognitive ability Knowledge Judgment, decisiveness	Sociability, interpersonal skills Cooperativeness Ability to enlist cooperation Tact, diplomacy	Education Mobility

SOURCES: Based on Bernard M. Bass, *Bass & Stogdill's Handbook of Leadership: Theory, Research, and Managerial Applications*, 3rd ed. (New York: Free Press, 1990), pp. 80–81; and S. A. Kirkpatrick and E. A. Locke, "Leadership: Do Traits Matter?" *Academy of Management Executive* 5, no. 2 (1991): 48–60.

Remember This

- **Traits** are distinguishing personal characteristics, such as intelligence, self-confidence, energy, and independence.

- **Strengths** are natural talents and abilities that have been supported and reinforced with learned knowledge and skills.

11-5 Behavioral Approaches

The inability to define effective leadership based solely on traits led to an interest in looking at the behavior of leaders and how it might contribute to leadership success or failure. Two basic leadership behaviors identified as important for leadership are attention to tasks and attention to people.

11-5a Task versus People

Two types of behavior that have been identified as applicable to effective leadership in a variety of situations and time periods are *task-oriented behavior* and *people-oriented behavior*.[38] Although they are not the only important leadership behaviors, concern for tasks and concern for people must be shown at some reasonable level. Thus, many approaches to understanding leadership use these *metacategories*, or broadly defined behavior categories, as a basis for study and comparison.

Important early research programs on leadership were conducted at The Ohio State University and the University of Michigan.[39] Ohio State researchers identified two major behaviors they called *consideration* and *initiating structure*. **Consideration** falls in the category of people-oriented behavior and is the extent to which the leader is mindful of subordinates, respects their ideas and feelings, and establishes mutual trust. **Initiating structure** is the degree of task behavior, that is, the extent to which the leader is task-oriented and directs subordinate work activities toward goal attainment. Studies suggest that effective leaders may be high on consideration and low on initiating structure or low on consideration and high on initiating structure, depending on the situation.[40]

Concept Connection

Satya Nadella worked at Microsoft for more than two decades before being named only the third CEO in the giant software firm's history. Nadella's ability to focus on both people and production results reflects his **team management** leadership style. He has shifted Microsoft to a culture of cooperation rather than internal competition, enabling people to innovate more quickly and keep Microsoft competitive as the industry shifts. Since taking over the top job, Nadella has set tough goals, but he has also shown that he cares about people's needs and feelings. He once said in an interview that he believed the top thing leaders must do is "to bolster the confidence of the people you're leading."

Research at the University of Michigan at about the same time also considered task- and people-oriented behaviors by comparing the behavior of effective and ineffective supervisors.[41] The most effective supervisors were those who established high performance goals and displayed supportive behavior toward subordinates. These were referred to as *employee-centered leaders*. The less effective leaders were called *job-centered leaders*; they tended to be less concerned with goal achievement and human needs in favor of meeting schedules, keeping costs low, and achieving production efficiency.

11-5b The Leadership Grid®

Building on the work of the Ohio State and Michigan studies, Robert R. Blake and Jane S. Mouton of the University of Texas proposed a two-dimensional theory called the Managerial Grid®, which was later restated by Robert R. Blake and Anne Adams McCanse as the **Leadership Grid®**.[42] The model and five of its major management styles are depicted in Exhibit 11.6. Each axis on the grid is a nine-point scale, with 1 meaning low concern and 9 meaning high concern.

Team management (9, 9) often is considered the most effective style and is recommended for leaders because organization members work together to accomplish tasks. *Country club management* (1, 9) occurs when the primary emphasis is given to people rather than to work outputs. *Authority-compliance management* (9, 1) occurs when efficiency in operations is the dominant orientation. *Middle-of-the-road management* (5, 5) reflects a moderate amount of concern for both people and production. *Impoverished management* (1, 1) means the absence of a management philosophy; managers exert little effort toward interpersonal relationships or work accomplishment.

As a new manager, realize that both task-oriented behavior and people-oriented behavior are important, although some situations call for a greater degree of one over the other. Visit MindTap for Self-Assessment: "What Is Your Leadership Orientation?" to measure your degree of task orientation and people orientation.

Lucas Jackson/Reuters

Exhibit 11.6 The Leadership Grid® Figure

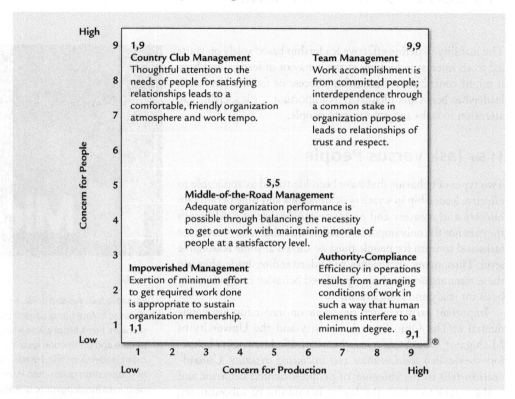

SOURCE: The Leadership Grid® figure, Paternalism figure, and Opportunism figure from Robert R. Blake and Anne Adams McCanse, *Leadership Dilemmas-Grid Solutions* (formerly *The Managerial Grid* by Robert R. Blake and Jane S. Mouton) (Houston: Gulf Publishing Company, 1991), Grid figure, p. 29; Paternalism figure, p. 30; Opportunism figure, p. 31. Copyright © 1991 by Blake and Mouton, and Scientific Methods, Inc. Reproduced by permission of the owners.

Remember This

- Two basic leadership behaviors identified as important for leadership are attention to tasks and attention to people.
- **Consideration** is the term used by researchers at The Ohio State University to describe the extent to which a leader is sensitive to subordinates, respects their ideas and feelings, and establishes mutual trust.
- **Initiating structure** is the term that describes the extent to which a leader is task-oriented and directs subordinates' work activities toward goal accomplishment.
- Researchers at the University of Michigan used the terms *employee-centered leaders* and *job-centered leaders* to describe the same two basic leadership behaviors.
- The **Leadership Grid®** is a two-dimensional leadership model that measures the leader's concern for people and concern for production to categorize the leader in one of five different leadership styles.

11-6 Contingency Approaches

Satya Nadella, the current CEO of Microsoft, is known as a quiet, humble leader who emphasizes listening, helpfulness, and collaboration. Previous CEO Steve Ballmer, in contrast, had a forceful, driven approach to leadership and was known for his competitiveness and exuberant displays of emotion. Yet both have been successful leading the same company.[43]

How can two people with widely different styles both be effective leaders? The answer lies in understanding **contingency approaches** to leadership, which explore how the organizational situation influences leader effectiveness. Contingency approaches include the situational model based on the work of Paul Hersey and Kenneth Blanchard, the leadership model developed by Fred Fiedler and his associates, and the substitutes-for-leadership concept.

11-6a The Situational Model of Leadership

The **situational model** of leadership, which originated with Hersey and Blanchard, is an interesting extension of the behavioral theories summarized in the Leadership Grid® (see Exhibit 11.6). This approach focuses a great deal of attention on the characteristics of followers in determining appropriate leadership behavior. The point of the situational model is that subordinates vary in readiness, which is determined by the degree of willingness and ability that a subordinate demonstrates while performing a specific task. *Willingness* refers to a combination of confidence, commitment, and motivation, and a follower may be high or low on any of the three variables. *Ability* refers to the amount of knowledge, experience, and demonstrated skill that a subordinate brings to the task. Effective leaders adapt their style according to the readiness level of the people they are managing. People low in readiness—because of little ability or training or insecurity—need a different leadership style than those who are high in readiness and have good ability, skills, confidence, and willingness to work.[44]

Exhibit 11.7 summarizes the relationship between leader style and follower readiness. The upper part of the exhibit indicates the style of the leader, which is based on a combination of concern for people and concern for production tasks. The bell-shaped curve is called a *prescriptive curve* because it indicates when each style should be used. The *telling style (S1)* is a highly directive style and involves giving explicit instructions about how tasks should be accomplished. The *selling style (S2)* is one in which the leader explains decisions and gives subordinates a chance to ask questions and gain clarity and understanding about work tasks. The *participating style (S3)* is one in which

Exhibit 11.7 Hersey and Blanchard's Situational Model of Leadership

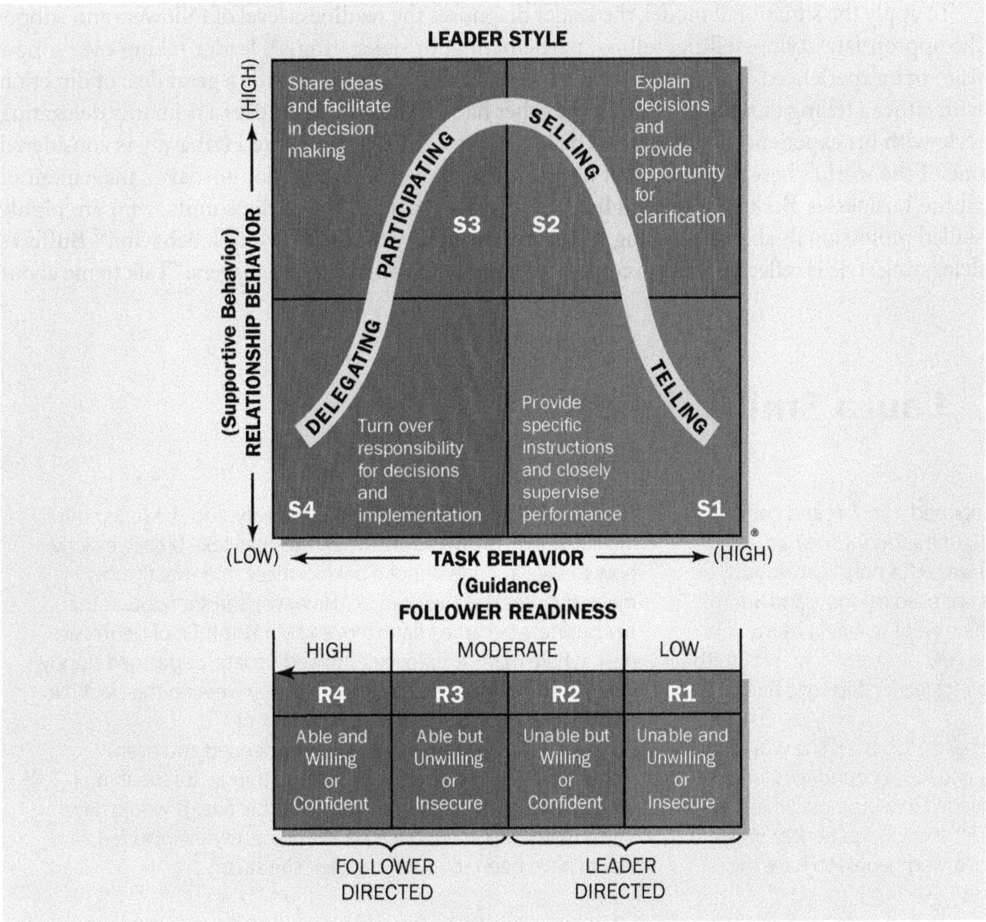

SOURCE: Adapted from The Hersey and Blanchard Situational Leadership Model/The Center for Leadership Studies, Inc.

the leader shares ideas with subordinates, gives them a chance to participate, and facilitates decision making. The fourth style, the *delegating style (S4)*, provides little direction and little support because the leader turns over responsibility for decisions and their implementation to subordinates.

The appropriate leader style depends on the readiness level of followers, shown in the lower part of Exhibit 11.7. R1 represents low readiness and R4 represents high follower readiness. The S1 telling style has the highest probability of successfully influencing low-readiness followers who are unable or unwilling—because of poor ability and skills, lack of experience, or insecurity—to take responsibility for their own task behavior. The leader is specific, telling people exactly what to do, how to do it, and when. The S2 selling and S3 participating styles work for followers at moderate-to-high readiness levels. For example, followers might lack some education and experience for the job but have high confidence, interest, and willingness to learn. The S2 selling style is effective in this situation because it involves giving direction, but it also includes seeking input from others and clarifying tasks rather than simply instructing that they be performed. When followers have the necessary skills and experience but are somewhat insecure in their abilities or lack high willingness, the S3 participating style enables the leader to guide followers' development and act as a resource for advice and assistance. When followers demonstrate very high readiness (i.e., they have high levels of education, experience, and readiness to accept responsibility for their own task behavior), the S4 delegating style can effectively be used. Because of the high readiness level of followers, the leader can delegate responsibility for decisions and their implementation to subordinates who have the skills, abilities, and positive attitudes to follow through. The leader provides a general goal and sufficient authority to do the task as followers see fit. Using an incorrect style can damage employee morale as well as hurt organizational performance, as Laura Smith learned in her first entrepreneurial venture.

At Yola, Laura Smith tried to use a selling or a participating style because these approaches fit with her idea of what a good leader should be. She failed to realize that many of her employees were at a low readiness level and needed a telling style, with the leader providing clear instructions and specific rules regarding work activities and behavior.

To apply the situational model, the leader diagnoses the readiness level of followers and adopts the appropriate style—telling, selling, participating, or delegating. A leader taking over a new team of inexperienced or uncertain members would likely have to provide a great deal of direction with either a telling or selling style. On the other hand, Warren Buffett uses a primarily delegating style with his experienced managers. The legendary CEO of Berkshire Hathaway is considered one of the world's best managers, but he isn't closely involved in the day-to-day management of all the businesses Berkshire owns. He trusts the managers of the various units, who are highly skilled professionals able and willing to take responsibility for their own task behavior.[45] Buffett's delegating style is reflected in an excerpt from a memo he sent to top managers: "Talk to me about

Recipe for Success } Laura Smith, Yola

When 26-year-old Laura Smith opened a yogurt and coffee shop in Washington, D.C. in 2010, she thought she had a winning formula because her shop was D.C.'s only fresh yogurt bar. Less than two years later, Yola closed its doors and Smith was looking for a new career. There were several reasons Yola didn't make it, not least of all the very high rent cost. Yet Smith also acknowledges that an incorrect leadership style hurt the business.

Smith says that if she could have a "do-over," she would provide more structure, more rules, and more boundaries for her employees, something that is needed in a business where most employees are young and have little work experience. Smith wanted to run her business by allowing people to have the freedom to express their personal creativity, and she hated the idea of "telling grown adults when they can take breaks, exactly how to slice a scone out of a baking sheet, and exactly how many minutes late they can be." However, she soon found that her business became characterized by an attitude of permissiveness, where many employees showed up late, performed sloppy work, or did as little as possible while they were on the clock. No one was happy with the work environment.

Smith realized that her employees needed and even wanted to be told what and how to do things. "It's the thing I wish I could go back and do over—not because it would have saved my business but because everyone, myself included, would have been so much happier," she says.[46]

what is going on as little or as much as you wish. Each of you does a first-class job of running your operation with your own individual style and you don't need me to help."[47] A delegating leader style is not always appropriate, but all managers need to be able to delegate some tasks and decisions for the organization to work smoothly.

11-6b Fiedler's Contingency Theory

Whereas the situational model focused on the characteristics of followers, Fiedler and his associates looked at some other elements of the organizational situation to assess when one leadership style is more effective than another.[48] The starting point for Fiedler's theory is the extent to which the leader's style is task-oriented or relationship-(people) oriented. Fiedler considered a person's leadership style to be relatively fixed and difficult to change; therefore, the basic idea is to match the leader's style with the situation most favorable for his or her effectiveness. By diagnosing leadership style and the organizational situation, the correct fit can be arranged.

Situation: Favorable or Unfavorable? The suitability of a person's leadership style is determined by whether the situation is favorable or unfavorable to the leader. The favorability of a leadership situation can be analyzed in terms of three elements: the quality of relationships between leader and followers, the degree of task structure, and the extent to which the leader has formal authority over followers.[49]

As illustrated in the lower portion of Exhibit 11.8, a situation would be considered *highly favorable* to the leader when leader–member relationships are positive, tasks are highly structured, and the leader has formal authority over followers. In this situation, followers trust, respect, and have confidence in the leader. The group's tasks are clearly defined, involve specific procedures, and have clear, explicit goals. In addition, the leader has formal authority to direct and evaluate followers, along with the power to reward or punish. In a highly unfavorable situation, followers have little respect for or confidence and trust in the leader. Tasks are vague and ill-defined and lack clear-cut procedures and guidelines. The leader has little formal authority to direct subordinates and does not have the power to issue rewards or punishments.

Matching Leader Style to the Situation When Fiedler examined the relationships among leadership style and situational favorability, he found the pattern shown in the upper portion of Exhibit 11.8. Task-oriented leaders are more effective when the situation is either highly favorable or highly unfavorable. Relationship-oriented leaders are more effective in situations of moderate favorability.

Exhibit 11.8 How Leader Style Fits the Situation

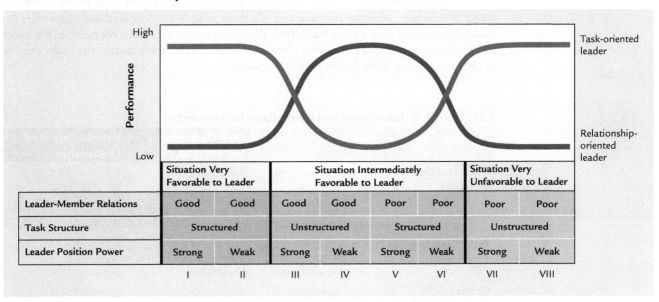

	Situation Very Favorable to Leader		Situation Intermediately Favorable to Leader				Situation Very Unfavorable to Leader	
Leader-Member Relations	Good	Good	Good	Good	Poor	Poor	Poor	Poor
Task Structure	Structured		Unstructured		Structured		Unstructured	
Leader Position Power	Strong	Weak	Strong	Weak	Strong	Weak	Strong	Weak
	I	II	III	IV	V	VI	VII	VIII

The task-oriented leader excels in the favorable situation because everyone gets along, the task is clear, and the leader has power; all that is needed is for someone to lead the charge and provide direction. Similarly, if the situation is highly unfavorable to the leader, a great deal of structure and task direction is needed. A strong leader will define task structure and establish strong authority. Because leader–member relations are poor anyway, a strong task orientation will make no difference in the leader's popularity.

Researchers at the University of Chicago who looked at CEOs in turnaround situations—where companies typically have high debt loads and a need to improve results in a hurry—found that tough-minded, task-focused characteristics such as analytical skills, a focus on efficiency, and setting high standards were more valuable leader qualities than were relationship skills such as good communication, listening, and teamwork.[50]

The relationship-oriented leader performs better in situations of intermediate favorability because human relations skills are important in achieving high group performance. In these situations, the leader may be moderately well liked, have some power, and supervise jobs that contain some ambiguity. A leader with good interpersonal skills can create a positive group atmosphere that will improve relationships, clarify task structure, and establish position power.

A leader, then, needs to know two things to use Fiedler's contingency theory. First, the leader should know whether he or she has a relationship- or task-oriented style. Second, the leader should diagnose the situation and determine whether leader–member relations, task structure, and position power are favorable or unfavorable.

Fiedler believed that fitting leader style to the situation can yield big dividends in profits and efficiency.[51] On the other hand, the model has also been criticized.[52] For one thing, some researchers have challenged the idea that leaders cannot adjust their styles as situational characteristics change. Despite criticisms, Fiedler's model has continued to influence leadership studies. Fiedler's research called attention to the importance of finding the correct fit between leadership style and situation.

11-6c Situational Substitutes for Leadership

The contingency leadership approaches considered so far focus on the leader's style, the subordinates' nature, and the situation's characteristics. The final contingency approach suggests that situational variables can be so powerful that they actually substitute for or neutralize the need for leadership.[53] This approach outlines those organizational settings in which a leadership style is unimportant or unnecessary.

Exhibit 11.9 shows the situational variables that tend to substitute for or neutralize leadership characteristics. A **substitute for leadership** makes the leadership style unnecessary or redundant. For example, highly professional subordinates who know how to do their tasks do not need a leader who initiates structure for them and tells them what to do. A **neutralizer** counteracts the leadership style and prevents the leader from displaying certain behaviors. For example, if a leader has absolutely no position power or is physically removed from subordinates, the leader's ability to give directions to subordinates is greatly reduced.

Exhibit 11.9 Substitutes and Neutralizers for Leadership

	Variable	Task-Oriented Leadership	People-Oriented Leadership
Organizational variables	Group cohesiveness	Substitutes for	Substitutes for
	Formalization	Substitutes for	No effect on
	Inflexibility	Neutralizes	No effect on
	Low position power	Neutralizes	Neutralizes
	Physical separation	Neutralizes	Neutralizes
Task characteristics	Highly structured task	Substitutes for	No effect on
	Automatic feedback	Substitutes for	No effect on
	Intrinsic satisfaction	No effect on	Substitutes for
Group characteristics	Professionalism	Substitutes for	Substitutes for
	Training/experience	Substitutes for	No effect on

Situational variables in Exhibit 11.9 include characteristics of the group, the task, and the organization itself. When followers are highly professional and experienced, both leadership styles are less important. People do not need much direction or consideration. With respect to task characteristics, highly structured tasks substitute for a task-oriented style, and satisfying task substitutes for a people-oriented style. With respect to the organization itself, group cohesiveness substitutes for both leader styles. Formalized rules and procedures substitute for leader task orientation. Physical separation of leader and subordinate neutralizes both leadership styles.

The value of the situations described in Exhibit 11.9 is that they help leaders avoid leadership overkill. Leaders should adopt a style with which to complement the organizational situation. Consider the work situation for bank tellers. A bank teller performs highly structured tasks, follows clearly written rules and procedures, and has little flexibility in terms of how to do the work. The head teller should not adopt a task-oriented style because the organization already provides structure and direction. The head teller should concentrate on a people-oriented style to provide a more pleasant work environment. In other organizations, if group cohesiveness or intrinsic satisfaction meets employees' social needs, the leader is free to concentrate on task-oriented behaviors. The leader can adopt a style complementary to the organizational situation to ensure that both the task needs and people needs of the work group will be met.

Remember This

- **Contingency approach** is a model of leadership that describes the relationship between leadership styles and specific situations.

- One contingency approach is the **situational model**, which links the leader's behavioral style with the readiness level of followers.

- In general, a task-oriented leader style fits a low-readiness follower, and a relationship-oriented leader style fits a higher-readiness follower.

- In Fiedler's contingency theory, the suitability of a leader's style is determined by whether the situation is considered favorable or unfavorable to the leader.

- Task-oriented leaders are considered to perform better in either highly favorable or highly unfavorable situations.

- Relationship-oriented leaders are considered to perform better in situations of intermediate favorability.

- A **substitute for leadership** is a situational variable that makes a leadership style redundant or unnecessary.

- A **neutralizer** is a situational variable that counteracts a leadership style and prevents the leader from displaying certain behaviors.

11-7 Charismatic and Transformational Leadership

Research has also looked at how leadership can inspire and motivate people beyond their normal levels of performance. Some leadership approaches are more effective than others for bringing about high levels of commitment and enthusiasm. Two types with a substantial impact are charismatic and transformational.

11-7a Charismatic Leadership

Charisma has been referred to as "a fire that ignites followers' energy and commitment, producing results above and beyond the call of duty."[54] The **charismatic leader** has the ability to inspire and motivate people to do more than they would normally do, despite obstacles and personal sacrifice. Followers are willing to put aside their own interests for the sake of the team, department, or organization. The impact of charismatic leaders normally comes from (1) stating a lofty vision of an imagined future with which employees identify, (2) displaying an ability to understand and empathize with followers, and (3) empowering and trusting subordinates to accomplish results.[55] Charismatic leaders tend to be less predictable because they create an atmosphere of change, and they may be obsessed by visionary ideas that excite, stimulate, and drive other people to work hard.

One of the best-known charismatic leaders in the business world in recent years was Apple's late cofounder and CEO Steve Jobs.[56] Jobs commanded a rock star–like following. The tale of how he dropped out of college, cofounded Apple, got fired from his own company, returned years later to save it, and then transformed it by creating a whole new business with the iPod and iPhone is the stuff of legend. Yet Jobs could be immature, impatient, and downright cruel at times. Despite this, many people—even some he mistreated—admired and respected (some have even said *worshiped*) Steve Jobs. They tell their "Steve-Jobs-yelled-in-my-face" stories with pride. His energizing personality and his refusal to "sell out" made people want to be around him and want to be *like* him.[57]

As the example of Steve Jobs illustrates, there can be both positive and negative aspects of charisma. Other charismatic leaders include Mother Teresa, Adolf Hitler, Sam Walton, Aung San Suu Kyi, Alexander the Great, Oprah Winfrey, Martin Luther King, Jr., and Osama bin Laden. Charisma can be used for positive outcomes that benefit the group, but it can also be used for self-serving purposes that lead to the deception, manipulation, and exploitation (and even deaths) of others. When charismatic leaders respond to organizational problems in terms of the needs of the entire group rather than their own emotional needs, they can have a powerful, positive influence on organizational performance.[58] As with the Level 5 and authentic leadership approaches that we discussed earlier in the chapter, *humility* typically plays an important part in distinguishing whether a charismatic leader will work to benefit primarily the larger organization or use his or her gifts for ego-building and personal gain.[59]

Charismatic leaders are skilled in the art of *visionary leadership*. A **vision** is an attractive, ideal future that is credible yet not readily attainable. Vision is an important component of both charismatic and transformational leadership. Visionary leaders speak to the hearts of employees, letting them be part of something bigger than themselves. Where others see obstacles or failures, visionary leaders see possibility and hope.

Charismatic leaders typically have a strong vision for the future, almost an obsession, and they can motivate others to help realize it.[60] These leaders have an emotional impact on subordinates because they strongly believe in the vision and can communicate it to others in a way that makes the vision real, personal, and meaningful.

11-7b Transformational versus Transactional Leadership

Transformational leaders are similar to charismatic leaders, but they are distinguished by their special ability to bring about innovation and change by recognizing followers' needs and concerns, providing meaning, challenging people to look at old problems in new ways, and acting as role models for the new values and behaviors. Transformational leaders inspire followers not just to believe in the leader personally, but also to believe in their own potential to imagine and create a better future for the organization. Transformational leaders create significant change in both followers and the organization.[61]

Green Power

In the Hands of a Matador It was, by any standard, a bold move. Taking the leadership reins in 2004 as CEO and president of Spain-based Acciona, one of Europe's most profitable real estate and construction businesses, José Manuel Entrecanales envisioned a future in which businesses would balance economic gain with environmental standards. Entrecanales convinced his board to address climate change and promote renewable energy development. The company wasted no time making a public announcement of its long-term sustainability plans and undertaking new strategies led by a Sustainability Committee. Over the next several years, Acciona managers invested heavily in sustainability, including wind, solar, and other forms of renewable energy. Acciona established a green reputation in less than a decade, and it was the leadership of Entrecanales, with the precise timing and calculated moves of a great matador, that envisioned the new spheres of action.

SOURCES: Daniel Arenas, Jeremie Fosse, and Matthew Murphy, "Acciona: A Process of Transformation Towards Sustainability," *Journal of Management Development* 30, no. 10 (2011): 1027–1048; and Sarah Gordon and Tobias Buck, "José Manuel Entrecanales Acciona CEO: Establishment Eco-Warrior," *Financial Times*, November 16, 2014, http://www.ft.com/intl/cms/s/0/ce7baf8c-6065-11e4-833b-00144feabdc0.html#axzz47V4QhBWJ (accessed May 2, 2016).

Transformational leadership can be better understood in comparison to *transactional leadership*.[62] **Transactional leaders** clarify the role and task requirements of subordinates, initiate structure, provide appropriate rewards, and try to be considerate and meet the social needs of subordinates. The transactional leader's ability to satisfy subordinates may improve productivity. Transactional leaders excel at management functions. They are hardworking, tolerant, and fair-minded. They take pride in keeping things running smoothly and efficiently. Transactional leaders often stress the impersonal aspects of performance, such as plans, schedules, and budgets. They have a sense of commitment to the organization and conform to organizational norms and values. Transactional leadership is important to all organizations, but leading change requires a different approach.

Transformational leaders have the ability to lead changes in the organization's mission, strategy, structure, and culture, as well as to promote innovation in products and technologies. Transformational leaders do not rely solely on tangible rules and incentives to control specific transactions with followers. They focus on intangible qualities, such as vision, shared values, and ideas, to build relationships, give larger meaning to diverse activities, and find common ground that will encourage followers to enlist in the change process.[63] For example, Michelle Rhee, former chancellor of the District of Columbia public schools, acted as a transformational leader to revamp one of the most expensive, lowest-performing school systems in the country.

Rhee served as chancellor of the D.C. public school system from 2007 to 2010 and then founded StudentsFirst, a nonprofit organization that works on education reform. She stepped down as CEO of StudentsFirst in 2014 but continues to drive change in the educational system. "Some people think she is a transformative leader, and some people think she is a controversial figure, but everyone agrees she gets people talking," said one organizer of a recent conference in Michigan.[64]

Studies show that transformational leadership has a positive impact on follower development and follower performance.[65] Moreover, transformational leadership skills can be learned and are not ingrained personality characteristics. However, some personality traits may make it easier for a leader to display transformational leadership behaviors. For example, studies of transformational leadership have found that the trait of agreeableness, as discussed in Chapter 10, is often associated with transformational leaders.[66] In addition, transformational

Sunny Side Up > Michelle Rhee

Michelle Rhee, former chancellor of Washington, D.C., public schools and founder of StudentsFirst, is one of the most controversial figures in U.S. education—but love her or hate her, you can't say that she's afraid of change. A daughter of Korean immigrants, Rhee wanted to quit halfway through her first year in Teach for America, an organization that sends new college graduates into some of the toughest schools in the United States, but her father made her go back and finish the job. That's where she first embarked on a personal mission to change the system for the country's poorest students. Rhee noticed that students responded to teachers who pushed them hard and kept them interested.

A couple of decades later, Rhee had the chance to put some of her ideas into action on a large scale as she tried to revamp one of the most expensive, lowest-performing school systems in the country. As chancellor of the D.C. public schools, Rhee attacked the dysfunctional culture that rewarded teachers for seniority rather than performance, revised systems and structures to slash bureaucracy, held school principals accountable for improving student performance, and focused people on a mission of putting the best interests of students first.

Her vision of making D.C. schools "the highest-performing urban school district in the nation" brought new energy and movement to a long-stagnant system. Rhee becomes angry when people say that "teachers cannot make up for what parents and students will not do," emphasizing that each teacher *can* make a difference. She didn't hesitate to cut administrative positions that weren't contributing value, fire teachers and principals who didn't meet performance standards, and close underperforming schools. She instituted new procedures to handsomely reward high-performing teachers and give principals more control over hiring, promoting, and firing. New evaluation procedures put people on alert that low performance and complacency would not be tolerated.[67]

leaders are typically emotionally stable and positively engaged with the world around them, and they have a strong ability to recognize and understand others' emotions.[68] These characteristics are not surprising, considering that these leaders accomplish change by building networks of positive relationships.

Remember This

- A **charismatic leader** is a leader who has the ability to inspire and motivate people to transcend their expected performance, even to the point of personal sacrifice.
- Both charismatic and transformational leaders provide followers with an inspiring **vision**, an attractive, ideal future that is credible yet not readily attainable.

- A **transformational leader** is distinguished by a special ability to bring about innovation and change by creating an inspiring vision, shaping values, building relationships, and providing meaning for followers.
- A **transactional leader** clarifies subordinates' roles and task requirements, initiates structure, provides rewards, and displays consideration for followers.

11-8 Followership

No discussion of leadership is complete without a consideration of followership. Indeed, despite the focus on leadership, everyone in an organization is both a follower and a leader.[69] Leadership matters, but without effective followers, no organization can survive. People have different expectations of what constitutes a good follower versus a good leader, as illustrated by the results of studies asking people to rank the desired characteristics of leaders and followers. The top five qualities desired in each are as follows:[70]

Leader	Follower
Honest	Honest
Competent	Competent
Forward-looking	Dependable
Inspiring	Cooperative
Intelligent	Loyal

There may be some differences, but overall, many of the qualities that define a good follower are the same qualities as those possessed by a good leader. Leaders can develop an understanding of their followers and create the conditions that help them be most effective.[71]

One model of followership is illustrated in Exhibit 11.10. Robert E. Kelley conducted extensive interviews with managers and their subordinates and came up with five *follower styles*, which are categorized according to two dimensions, as shown in the exhibit.[72]

The first dimension is the quality of independent, **critical thinking** versus dependent, **uncritical thinking**. Independent, critical thinkers are mindful of the effects of their own and others' behavior on achieving organizational goals. They can weigh the impact of their boss's and their own decisions and offer constructive criticism, creativity, and innovation. Conversely, a dependent, uncritical thinker does not consider possibilities beyond what he or she is told, does not contribute to the cultivation of the organization, and accepts the supervisor's ideas without thinking.

The second dimension of follower style is active versus passive behavior. An active follower participates fully in the organization, engages in behavior that is beyond the limits of the job, demonstrates a sense of ownership, and initiates problem solving and decision making. A passive follower, by contrast, is characterized by a need for constant supervision and prodding by superiors. Passivity is often regarded as laziness; a passive person does nothing that is not required and avoids added responsibility.

Exhibit 11.10 Styles of Followership

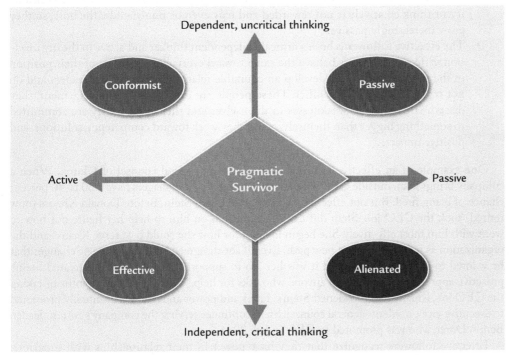

SOURCE: Based on Robert E. Kelley, *The Power of Followership* (New York: Doubleday, 1992).

The extent to which an individual is active or passive and is an independent, critical thinker or a dependent, uncritical thinker determines whether the person will be an alienated follower, a passive follower, a conformist, a pragmatic survivor, or an effective follower, as illustrated in Exhibit 11.10.

- The **alienated follower** is a passive, yet independent, critical thinker. Alienated employees are often effective followers who have experienced setbacks and obstacles—perhaps promises broken by their superiors. Thus, they are capable, but they focus exclusively on the shortcomings of their bosses. Often cynical, alienated followers are able to think independently, but they do not participate in developing solutions to the problems or deficiencies that they see. These people waste valuable time complaining about their boss without offering constructive feedback.

- The **conformist** participates actively in a relationship with the boss but doesn't use critical thinking skills. In other words, a conformist participates willingly, but without considering the consequences of what he or she is being asked to do—even at the risk of contributing to a harmful endeavor. In his book *The Foreclosure of America*, which examined problems that led to the crisis in the mortgage industry, former Countrywide executive Adam Michaelson writes of the groupthink and blind conformity that squelched resistance and led people to go along with company actions even if they thought they were wrong.[73] A conformist is concerned only with avoiding conflict. This follower style might reflect an individual's overdependent attitude toward authority, yet it can also result from rigid rules and authoritarian environments that create a culture of conformity.

- The **pragmatic survivor** has qualities of all four extremes—depending on which style fits with the prevalent situation. This type of person uses whatever style best benefits his or her own position and minimizes risk. Pragmatic survivors often emerge when an organization is going through desperate times and individuals find themselves doing whatever is needed to get through the difficulty. Within any given company, some 25 to 35 percent of people tend to be pragmatic survivors, avoiding risks and fostering the status quo.[74]

- The **passive follower** exhibits neither critical, independent thinking nor active participation. Being passive and uncritical, these people show neither initiative nor a sense of responsibility. Their activity is limited to what they are told to do, and they accomplish things only with a great deal of supervision. Passive followers leave the thinking to the boss. Often, this style is the result of a micromanaging boss who encourages passive behavior. People learn that to show initiative, accept responsibility, or think creatively is not rewarded and may even be punished by the boss, so they grow increasingly passive.

- The **effective follower** is both a critical, independent thinker and active in the organization. Effective followers behave the same toward everyone, regardless of their position in the organization. They develop an equitable relationship with their leaders and do not try to avoid risk or conflict. These people are capable of self-management, they discern strengths and weaknesses in themselves and their bosses, they are committed to something bigger than themselves, and they work toward competency, solutions, and positive impact.

Are you an effective follower, or do you tend to be alienated, passive, conforming, or a pragmatic survivor? To find out, visit MindTap for the Self-Assessment: "What Is Your Follower Style?"

One example of an effective follower is Laura Stein, general counsel of Clorox. When a company brings in an outside CEO, one expert estimates that managers have a 30 to 40 percent chance of being fired. But not effective followers like Laura Stein. Before Donald Knauss (now retired) took the CEO job, Stein did extensive research on him to help her figure out how to work with him most effectively. She began looking for how she could best serve Knauss and the organization as it embarked on a new path. Even if she disagreed with any strategic changes that he wanted to make, Stein believed it was her job to support them. Knauss appreciated Stein's proactive approach. "She will help anyone who asks for help," he says. Within months of taking the CEO job, Knauss had broadened Stein's duties and power and she was eventually promoted to executive vice president–general counsel. Stein continues serving the company's current leader, Benno Dorer, who was promoted to CEO in late 2014.[75]

Effective followers recognize that they have power in their relationships with superiors; thus, they have the courage to manage upward, to initiate change, and even to put themselves at risk or in conflict with the boss if they believe it serves the best interest of the team or organization.

Remember This

- Leaders can accomplish nothing without effective followers.
- **Critical thinking** means thinking independently and being mindful of the effect of one's behavior on achieving goals.
- **Uncritical thinking** means failing to consider the possibilities beyond what one is told and accepting others' ideas without thinking.
- An **effective follower** is a critical, independent thinker who actively participates in the organization.

- An **alienated follower** is a person who is an independent, critical thinker but is passive in the organization.
- A **conformist** is a follower who participates actively in the organization but does not use critical thinking skills.
- A **passive follower** is one who exhibits neither critical, independent thinking nor active participation.
- A follower who has qualities of all four follower styles, depending on which fits the prevalent situation, is called a **pragmatic survivor**.

11-9 Power and Influence

Both followers and leaders use power and influence to get things done in organizations. Sometimes the terms *power* and *influence* are used synonymously, but there are distinctions between the two. **Power** is the potential ability to influence the behavior of others.[76] **Influence** is the effect that a person's actions have on the attitudes, values, beliefs, or behavior of others. Whereas power is the capacity to cause a change in a person, influence may be thought of as the degree of actual change.

Most discussions of power include five types that are available to leaders,[77] and these can be categorized as either *hard power* or *soft power*. Hard power is power that stems largely from a person's position of authority and includes legitimate, reward, and coercive power. Soft power includes expert power and referent power, which are based on personal characteristics and interpersonal relationships more than on a position of authority.

11-9a Hard Position Power

The traditional manager's power comes from the organization (hard power). The manager's position gives him or her the ability to reward or punish subordinates to influence their behavior. Legitimate power, reward power, and coercive power are all forms of position power used by managers to change employee behavior.

Legitimate Power Power coming from a formal management position in an organization and the authority granted to it is called **legitimate power**. Once a person has been selected as a supervisor, most employees understand that they are obligated to follow his or her direction with respect to work activities. Subordinates accept this source of power as legitimate, which is why they comply.

Reward Power Another kind of power, **reward power**, stems from the authority to bestow rewards on other people. Managers may have access to formal rewards, such as pay increases or promotions. They also have at their disposal rewards such as praise, attention, and recognition. Managers can use rewards to influence subordinates' behavior.

Coercive Power The opposite of reward power is **coercive power**. It refers to the authority to punish or recommend punishment. Managers have coercive power when they have the right to fire or demote employees, criticize them, or withhold pay increases. If an employee does not perform as expected, the manager has the coercive power to reprimand him, put a negative letter in his file, deny him a raise, and hurt his chances for a promotion.

stevecoleimages/Getty Images

Concept Connection

The coaches of many of today's sports teams are using a softer, collaborative style rather than a "drill sergeant approach" to influence players. Instead of using only hard position power and formal authority, effective coaches also stimulate high performance by relying on **expert power**, which stems from their knowledge of the game, and **referent power**, which comes from treating people in a way that earns players' respect and admiration.

11-9b Personal Soft Power

Effective leaders don't rely solely on the hard power of their formal position to influence others. Jeff Immelt, CEO of GE, considers himself a failure if he exercises his formal authority more than seven or eight times a year. The rest of the time, he is using softer means to persuade and influence others and to resolve conflicting ideas and opinions.[78] Ron Rivera, head coach of the Carolina Panthers, also uses soft referent power as well as hard power.

Having closer personal relationships with his players has enabled Ron Rivera to influence players using soft, personal power as well as the hard authority of his position.

In contrast to the external sources of position power, personal power most often comes from internal sources, such as an individual's special knowledge or personal characteristics. Personal power is the primary tool of the leader, and it is becoming increasingly important as more businesses are run by teams of workers who are less tolerant of authoritarian management.[79] Two types of personal power are expert power and referent power.

Expert Power Power resulting from a person's special knowledge or skill regarding the tasks being performed is referred to as **expert power**. When someone is a true expert, others go along

Sunny Side Up 〉 Ron Rivera, Carolina Panthers

A respected advisor told Ron Rivera he could have greater influence if he learned to "remove rank" when talking to subordinates. Rivera wanted to create a culture of total honesty and trust, where players felt they could ask him or tell him anything. Rather than maintaining distance from players, Rivera decided to get to know and understand his players at a deep personal level.

Most NFL coaches keep their time in the locker room to a minimum, but Rivera is in the locker room interacting with players all the time. "Unless you are exposed to them [in the locker room], when they let their hair down, you won't get to know them," he says. Rivera set up a second office closer to the locker room and he regularly visits the training room and cafeteria to interact informally with players as well. "I have answered questions in the locker room about whether a player should get puppies," Rivera said. "I told them having a puppy is just like having a baby, there's a lot of responsibility."[80]

with recommendations because of his or her superior knowledge. Both followers and leaders can possess expert power. For example, some managers lead teams in which members have expertise that the leader lacks. Some leaders at top management levels may lack expert power because subordinates know more about technical details than they do.

Referent Power   **Referent power** comes from an individual's personal characteristics that command others' identification, respect, and admiration so that they wish to emulate that individual. Referent power does not depend on a formal title or position. When employees admire a supervisor because of the way that she deals with them, the influence is based on referent power. Referent power is most visible in the area of charismatic leadership. In social and religious movements, we often see charismatic leaders who emerge and gain a tremendous following based solely on their personal power.

11-9c Other Sources of Power

There are additional sources of power that are not linked to a particular person or position, but rather to the role that an individual plays in the overall functioning of the organization. These important sources include personal effort, relationships with others, and information.

Personal Effort   People who show initiative, work beyond what is expected of them, take on undesirable but important projects, and show interest in learning about the organization and industry often gain power as a result. Stephen Holmes says that he began his journey toward the CEO's office at Wyndham Worldwide because of personal effort. As a young internal auditor at a private equity firm in the early 1980s, Holmes was spending his evenings trying to learn a new spreadsheet program. Noted investor Henry Silverman saw him night after night and, intrigued by the young auditor's efforts, stopped by to see what he was doing. Silverman asked Holmes to move with him to future companies, including Blackstone, HMS, and eventually Wyndham. "I was a kid," Holmes says, "[but he] put me into positions that no one else my age was getting to do."[81]

Network of Relationships   People who are enmeshed in a network of relationships have greater power. A leader or employee with many relationships knows what's going on in the organization and industry, whereas one who has few interpersonal connections is often in the dark about important activities or changes. Networks of relationships are crucial in the political arena, for instance. Abraham Lincoln is considered by historians to be one of the greatest U.S. presidents partly because he built relationships and listened carefully to a broad range of people both inside and outside of his immediate circle when the nation was so bitterly divided over the Civil War. He included people who didn't agree with him and were critical of his goals and plans.[82]

Information Information is a primary business resource, and people who have access to information and control over how and to whom it is distributed are typically powerful. To some extent, access to information is determined by a person's position in the organization. Top managers typically have access to more information than middle managers, who in turn have access to more information than lower-level supervisors or frontline employees.

Both leaders and followers can tap into these additional sources of power. Leaders succeed when they take the time to build relationships both inside and outside the organization and to talk informally about important projects and priorities. Jack Griffin was forced out as CEO of Time Inc. after less than six months on the job, largely because he failed to develop positive relationships. Griffin tried to use the hard power of his position to make needed changes at Time without building the soft-power connections needed to implement the changes. Board members began to realize that Griffin had become so unpopular that the company was likely to lose valuable employees if he stayed on as CEO.[83]

11-9d Interpersonal Influence Tactics

Leaders often use a combination of influence strategies, and people who are perceived as having greater power and influence typically are those who use a wide variety of tactics. One survey of a few hundred leaders identified more than 4,000 different techniques that these people used to influence others.[84]

However, these tactics fall into basic categories that rely on understanding the principles that cause people to change their behavior and attitudes. Exhibit 11.11 lists six principles for asserting influence. Notice that most of these involve the use of personal power rather than relying solely on position power or the use of rewards and punishments.[85]

1. ***Use rational persuasion.*** The most frequently used influence strategy is to apply facts, data, and logical argument to persuade others that a proposed idea, request, or decision is appropriate. Using rational persuasion can often be highly effective because most people have faith in facts and analysis.[86] Rational persuasion is most successful when a leader has technical knowledge and expertise related to the issue at hand (expert power), although referent power is also used. That is, in addition to facts and figures, people must believe in the leader's credibility.

2. ***Help people to like you.*** People would rather say yes to someone they like than to someone they don't. Effective leaders strive to create goodwill and favorable impressions. When a leader shows consideration and respect, treats people fairly, and demonstrates trust in others, people are more likely to want to help and support this person by doing what he or she

Exhibit 11.11 Six Interpersonal Influence Tactics for Leaders

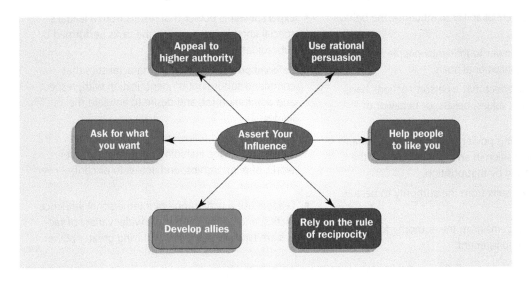

asks. In addition, most people like a leader who makes them feel good about themselves, so leaders should never underestimate the power of praise.

3. ***Rely on the rule of reciprocity.*** Leaders can influence others through the exchange of benefits and favors. Leaders share what they have—whether it is time, resources, services, or emotional support. The feeling among people is nearly universal that others should be paid back for what they do, in one form or another. This unwritten "rule of reciprocity" means that leaders who do favors for others can expect that others will do favors for them in return.[87]

4. ***Develop allies.*** Effective leaders develop networks of allies—people who can help the leader accomplish his or her goals. Leaders talk with followers and others outside formal meetings to understand their needs and concerns, as well as to explain problems and describe the leader's point of view. Leaders strive to reach a meeting of minds with others about the best approach to a problem or decision.[88]

5. ***Ask for what you want.*** Another way to influence others is to make a direct and personal request. Leaders must be explicit about what they want or they aren't likely to get it. An explicit proposal is sometimes accepted simply because others have no better alternative. Also, a clear proposal or alternative will often receive support if other options are less well-defined.

6. ***Appeal to higher authority.*** Sometimes, to get things done, leaders must use their formal authority as well as gain the support of people at higher levels to back them up. However, research has found that the key to successful use of formal authority is to be knowledgeable, credible, and trustworthy—that is, to demonstrate expert and referent power as well as legitimate power. Managers who become known for their expertise, who are honest and straightforward with others, and who inspire trust can exert greater influence than those who simply issue orders.[89]

Research indicates that people rate leaders as "more effective" when they are perceived to use a variety of influence tactics. But not all managers use influence in the same way. Studies have found that leaders in human resources, for example, tend to use softer, more subtle approaches, such as building goodwill, using favors, and developing allies, whereas those in finance are inclined to use harder, more direct tactics, such as formal authority and assertiveness.[90]

Remember This

- **Power** is the potential ability to influence the behavior of others.
- All leaders use power to influence people and accomplish organizational goals.
- **Influence** is the effect that a person's actions have on the attitudes, values, beliefs, or behavior of others.
- **Legitimate power** is power that stems from a manager's formal position in an organization and the authority granted by that position.
- **Reward power** results from the authority to bestow rewards.
- **Coercive power** stems from the authority to punish or recommend punishment.

- **Expert power** is power that results from a leader's special knowledge or skill in the tasks performed by subordinates.
- **Referent power** results from characteristics that command subordinates' identification with, respect and admiration for, and desire to emulate the leader.
- Both leaders and followers can tap into other sources of power, including personal effort, networks of relationships, and access to or control over information.
- Leaders use a wide range of interpersonal influence tactics, and people who use a wider variety of tactics are typically perceived as having greater power.

DISCUSSION QUESTIONS

1. Suggest some personal traits that you believe would be useful to a business leader today. Are these traits more valuable in some situations than in others? How do you think traits differ from strengths?

2. In a study asking what people wanted from leaders versus followers, people ranked *maturity* number 8 for followers but number 15 for leaders. What might account for people wanting a higher maturity level from followers?

3. If a male manager changes his behaviors to incorporate elements of interactive leadership more common to female managers, can he still be an "authentic" leader? Discuss.

4. Studies of women leaders suggest that many of them view power differently than men do and prefer a collaborative, relationship-oriented use of power. If this is the case, what does it suggest about women leaders' abilities to accomplish goals? What does it suggest about women's ability to rise to higher organizational levels? Discuss.

5. What skills and abilities does a manager need to lead effectively in a virtual environment? Do you believe a leader with a consideration style or an initiating-structure style would be more successful as a virtual leader? Explain your answer.

6. What is transformational leadership? Give examples of organizational situations that would call for transformational, transactional, or charismatic leadership.

7. How does Level 5 leadership differ from the concept of servant leadership? Do you believe that anyone has the potential to become a Level 5 leader? Discuss.

8. Why do you think so little attention is given to followership compared to leadership in organizations? Discuss how the role of an effective follower is similar to the role of a leader.

9. Do you think leadership is more important or less important in today's flatter, team-based organizations? Are some leadership styles better suited to such organizations as opposed to traditional hierarchical organizations? Explain.

10. Consider the leadership position of a senior partner in a law firm. What task, subordinate, and organizational factors might serve as substitutes for leadership in this situation?

APPLY YOUR SKILLS: SELF-LEARNING

What Is the Impact of Leadership?[91]

What are your beliefs and understandings about how top leaders influence organizational performance? To learn about your beliefs, please answer whether each of the following items is Mostly True or Mostly False based on your personal beliefs.

	Mostly True	Mostly False
1. The quality of leadership is the most important influence on the performance of an organization.		
2. People in top-level leadership positions have the power to make or break an organization.		
3. Most activities in an organization have little to do with the decisions or activities of the top leaders.		
4. Even in a bad economy, a good leader can prevent a company from doing poorly.		
5. A company cannot do well unless it has high-quality leadership at the top.		
6. High-quality versus low-quality leadership has a bigger impact on a firm's performance than does the business environment.		
7. Poor organizational performance is often due to factors beyond the control of even the best leaders.		

	Mostly True	Mostly False
8. Eventually, bad leadership at the top will trigger poor organizational performance.		
9. Leaders typically should not be held responsible for a firm's poor performance.		

Interpretation This scale is about the "romance" of leadership, which is the romantic view that leaders are very responsible for organizational performance as opposed to other factors such as economic conditions. Company performance is difficult to control and is an outcome of complex forces. Attributing too much responsibility to leaders is a simplification shaped more by our own mental construction than by the reality and complexity of organizational performance. Top leaders are not heroes, but they are important as one of several key factors that can shape organizational performance.

Scoring Give yourself 1 point for each item 1, 2, 4, 5, 6, and 8 marked as Mostly True and each item 3, 7, and 9 marked as Mostly False. A score of 7 or higher suggests a belief in the romance of leadership—that leaders have more control over performance outcomes than is actually the case. If you scored 3 or less, you may underestimate the impact of top leaders—a somewhat skeptical view. A score of 4 to 6 suggests a balanced view of leadership.

In Class Sit with a student partner and explain your scores to each other. What are your beliefs about leadership? What is the basis for your beliefs? The instructor can ask for a show of hands concerning the number of high, medium, and low scores on the questionnaire. Discuss the following questions: Do you believe that presidents, top executives, and heads of nonprofit organizations act alone and hence are largely responsible for performance? What is the evidence for this belief? What other forces will affect an organization? What is a realistic view of top leader influence in a large organization?

APPLY YOUR SKILLS: GROUP LEARNING

Assumptions About Leaders

Individually complete the following sentences.

1. A leader must always...

2. Leaders should never...

3. The best leader I ever had did...

4. The worst leader I ever had did...

5. When I am doing a good job as a leader, I...

6. I am afraid of leaders who...

7. I would follow a leader who...

8. I am repelled by leaders who...

9. Some people think they are good leaders, but they are not because they...

10. I want to be the kind of leader who...

In groups of four to six, discuss the following:

A. What did you learn about your own assumptions about leadership?

B. Trace those assumptions back to theories on leadership in this chapter.

C. What were common themes in your group?

APPLY YOUR SKILLS: ACTION LEARNING

1. Find three people who have had bosses or CEOs who were either charismatic or transformational.

2. Ask these people to describe what the leader was like and what his or her values and behaviors were.

3. Ask these people to contrast those charismatic/transformational leaders with an ineffective boss or CEO with whom they have worked.

4. What were the differences in behavior mentioned? How did the behavior of the ineffective leaders impact the organization?

5. Ask these people to give a few sentences on how they would compare the transformational/charismatic leader to the ineffective one.

6. Your instructor may ask you to write a paper on Assumptions About Leaders or bring this information to class and be prepared to discuss it.

7. What did you learn about transformational and charismatic leadership from this assignment? Did it agree with what the textbook described?

APPLY YOUR SKILLS: ETHICAL DILEMMA

Too Much of a Good Thing?

Not long ago, Jessica Armstrong, vice president of administration for Delaware Valley Chemical Inc., a New Jersey–based multinational company, made a point of stopping by department head Darius Harris's office and lavishly praising him for his volunteer work with an after-school program for disadvantaged children in a nearby urban neighborhood. Now she was about to summon him to her office so she could take him to task for his dedication to the same volunteer work.

It was Carolyn Clark, Harris's secretary, who'd alerted her to the problem. "Darius told the community center he'd take responsibility for a fund-raising mass mailing. And then he asked me to edit the letter he'd drafted, make all the copies, stuff the envelopes, and get it into the mail—most of this on my own time," she reported, still obviously indignant. "When I told him, 'I'm sorry, but that's not my job,' he looked me straight in the eye and asked when I'd like to schedule my upcoming performance appraisal."

Several of Harris's subordinates also volunteered with the program. After chatting with them, Armstrong concluded most were volunteering out of a desire to stay on the boss's good side. It was time to talk to Harris.

"Oh, come on," responded Harris impatiently when Armstrong confronted him. "Yes, I asked for her help as a personal favor to me. But I only brought up the appraisal because I was going out of town, and we needed to set some time aside to do the evaluation." Harris went on to talk about how important working for the after-school program was to him personally. "I grew up in that neighborhood, and if it hadn't been for the people at the center, I wouldn't be here today," he said. Besides, even if he had pressured employees to help out—and he wasn't saying he had—didn't all the emphasis the company was putting on employee volunteerism make it okay to use employees' time and company resources?

After Harris left, Armstrong thought about the conversation. There was no question that Delaware Valley actively encouraged employee volunteerism—and not just because it was the right thing to do. The chemical company had suffered a couple of unfortunate accidental spills in its recent past that caused environmental damage and sparked community anger.

Volunteering had the potential to help employees acquire new skills, create a sense of camaraderie, and play a role in recruiting and retaining talented people. But most of all, it gave a badly needed boost to the company's public image. Recently, Delaware Valley took every opportunity to publicize its employees' extracurricular community work on its Web site and in company publications. And the company created the annual Delaware Prize, which granted cash awards ranging from $1,000 to $5,000 to outstanding volunteers.

So now that Armstrong had talked with everyone concerned, just what was she going to do about the dispute between Darius Harris and Carolyn Clark?

What Would You Do?

1. Tell Carolyn Clark that employee volunteerism is important to the company and that while her performance evaluation will not be affected by her decision, she should consider helping Harris because it is an opportunity to help a worthy community project.

2. Tell Darius Harris that the employee volunteer program is just that: a volunteer program. Even though the company sees volunteerism as an important piece of its campaign to repair its tarnished image, employees must be free to choose whether to volunteer. Harris should not ask for the help of his direct employees with the after-school program.

3. Discipline Darius Harris for coercing his subordinates to spend their own time on his volunteer work at the community after-school program. This action will send a signal that coercing employees is a clear violation of leadership authority.

APPLY YOUR SKILLS: CASE FOR CRITICAL ANALYSIS

"What's Wrong with the Team?"

What's wrong with the team? What's wrong with the team? Nichole Dyer's words repeated over and over in Henry Rankin's head as he boarded the plane from Los Angeles to Chicago.

Rankin is responsible for the technical implementation of the new customer relationship management (CRM) software being installed for the sales offices in both cities. The software is badly needed to improve follow-up sales for Rankin's company, Reflex Systems. Reflex sells exercise equipment to high schools and colleges, as well as to small to mid-sized businesses for recreation centers, through a national force of 310 salespeople. The company's low prices have won a lot of sales; however, follow-up service is uneven, and the new CRM system promises to resolve those problems, with historical data, inquiries, reminders, and updates going to sales reps daily. The CEO of Reflex has ordered the CRM system be installed with all possible haste.

Rankin pulled a yellow pad and pen from the side pocket of his carry-on bag and tossed them on the seat beside the window, stashed the bag in the overhead compartment, and sat down as other passengers filed past. In an effort to shut out his thoughts, he closed his eyes and concentrated on the muffled voices and low whooshing sound of the air vents. He wrote "What's wrong with the team?" three times and began drawing arrows to circles bearing the names of his team members: Barry Livingston and Max Wojohowski in Los Angeles, and Bob Finley, Lynne Johnston, and Sally Phillips in Chicago.

He marked through Sally's name. She had jumped ship recently, taking her less-than-stellar but still-much-needed talents with her to another company. It was on a previous LA-to-Chicago flight that Sally had pumped him for feedback on her future with Reflex. She had informed him that she had another job offer. She admitted it was for less money, but she was feeling under pressure as a member of the team and she wanted more "quality of life." Rankin told Sally bluntly that her technical expertise, on which he placed top importance, was slightly below her peers, so future promotion was less likely despite her impressive people and team skills.

He wrote "quality of life," circled it, and then crossed it out and wrote "what the hell?" "Why should she get quality of life?" he mused. "I've barely seen my wife and kids since this project started." Rankin's team was under a great deal of pressure, and he had needed Sally to stick it out. He told her so, but the plane had barely touched down when she went directly to the office and quit, leaving the team shorthanded and too close to deadline to add another body.

What's wrong with the team? Rankin furiously scribbled as his thoughts raced:

1. *The deadline is ridiculously short.* Dyer had scheduled a 10-week completion deadline for the new CRM software, including installation and training for both cities.

   Rankin suddenly stopped writing and drew a rider and horse, then returned to his list.

2. *I feel like some frazzled pony-express rider running back and forth across the country, trying to develop, build, set up, and work the kinks out of a new system that everyone at Reflex is eager to see NOW.*

   He was interrupted by the flight attendant. "Would you care for a drink, sir?" "Yes. Make it a scotch and water. And be light on the water." Rankin took his drink and continued to write.

3. *Thank God for LA.* From the outset, Barry and Max had worked feverishly while avoiding the whining and complaining that seemed to overwhelm members of the Chicago team. The atmosphere was different. Although the project moved forward, meeting deadlines, there appeared to be less stress. The LA guys focused tirelessly on work, with no families to consider, alternating intense work with joking around. *Those are my kind of people, he thought.*

4. *But there is Chicago*, he wrote. Earlier in the day, Sam Matheny from sales had e-mailed, and then called, Rankin to tell him that the two remaining members of the Chicago team appeared to be alternating between bickering and avoiding one another. Apparently, this had been going on for some time. "What's with that?" Rankin wondered. "And why did Sam know and I didn't?"

So that morning, before his flight, Rankin had to make time to call and text both Finley and Johnston. Finley admitted that he had overreacted to Johnston.

"Look, man. I'm tired and stressed out," Finley said. "We've been working nonstop. My wife is not happy."

"Just get along until this project is completed," Rankin ordered.

"When will *that* be?" Finley asked before hanging up.

Rankin thought about Nichole Dyer's persistent complaints to him that the team appeared to have a lack of passion, and she admonished him to "get your people to understand the urgency of this project." Her complaints only added to his own stress level. He had long considered himself the front-runner for Dyer's job when she retired in two years. But had his team ruined that opportunity? The sense of urgency could be measured now in the level of stress and the long hours that they had all endured. He admitted his team members were unenthusiastic, but they seemed committed.

Rankin wondered, "Is it too late to turn around and restore the level of teamwork?" He tore off the sheet from the pad, crumpled it in his hand, and stared out the window.

Questions

1. How would you characterize Rankin's leadership style? What approach do you think is correct for this situation? Why?

2. What would you do now if you were Rankin? How might you awaken more enthusiasm in your team for completing this project on time? Suggest specific steps.

3. How would you suggest that Rankin modify his leadership style if he wants to succeed Dyer in two years? Be specific.

ENDNOTES

1. General Stanley McChrystal, as told to Kris Frieswick, "How I Deal with My Biggest Fear," *Inc.* (July–August 2015): 90–91; Dan Schawbel, "Stanley McChrystal: What the Army Can Teach You About Leadership," *Forbes* (July 13, 2015), http://www.forbes.com/sites/danschawbel/2015/07/13/stanley-mcchrystal-what-the-army-can-teach-you-about-leadership/ (accessed October 20, 2015); and "Our Team," McChrystalGroup.com, http://mcchrystalgroup.com/about-mcchrystal-group/our-team/ (accessed April 28, 2016).

2. Gary Yukl, "Managerial Leadership: A Review of Theory and Research," *Journal of Management* 15 (1989): 251–289.

3. James M. Kouzes and Barry Z. Posner, "The Credibility Factor: What Followers Expect from Their Leaders," *Management Review* (January 1990): 29–33.

4. Jim Collins, "Level 5 Leadership: The Triumph of Humility and Fierce Resolve," *Harvard Business Review* (January 2001): 67–76; Jim Collins, "Good to Great," *Fast Company* (October 2001): 90–104; A. J. Vogl, "Onward and Upward" (an interview with Jim Collins), *Across the Board* (September–October 2001): 29–34; and Jerry Useem, "Conquering Vertical Limits," *Fortune* (February 19, 2001): 84–96.

5. Jim Collins, "Enduring Greatness," *Leadership Excellence* (January 2011): 8.

6. As described in Stefan Stern, "A New Leadership Blueprint," *Management Today* (October 1, 2010): 38.

7. Miguel Helft, "A Hired Gun for Microsoft, in Dogged Pursuit of Google," *The New York Times*, August 31, 2009, www.nytimes.com/2009/08/31/technology/internet/31search.html (accessed August 31, 2009); and Brian R. Fitzgerald, "Who Will Be the Next Microsoft CEO?" *The Wall Street Journal*, August 23, 2013, http://blogs.wsj.com/digits/2013/08/23/who-will-be-the-next-microsoft-ceo/ (accessed October 21, 2013).

8. Quoted in William J. Holstein, "The View's Still Great from the Corner Office," *The New York Times*, May 8, 2005; and "12. Jack Welch," from "The List: CNBC First 25; Rebels, Icons and Leaders," CNBC, http://www.cnbc.com/2014/04/29/ (accessed April 28, 2016).

9. Richard L. Daft and Robert H. Lengel, *Fusion Leadership: Unlocking the Subtle Forces That Change People and Organizations* (San Francisco: Berrett-Koehler, 1998).

10. Leigh Buchanan, "In Praise of Selflessness: Why the Best Leaders Are Servants," *Inc.* (May 2007): 33–35.

11. Robert K. Greenleaf, *Servant Leadership: A Journey into the Nature of Legitimate Power and Greatness* (Mahwah, NJ: Paulist Press, 1977).

12. "Not Her Father's Chief Executive" (an interview with Marilyn Carlson Nelson), *U.S. News & World Report* (October 30, 2006): 64–65.

13. "*Maersk Alabama* Crew Recalls Pirate Attack," *USA TODAY*, April 16, 2009, www.usatoday.com/news/nation/2009-04-16-pirates_N.htm (accessed April 30, 2009); Stacy Meichtry, Arian Campo-Flores, and Leslie Scism, "Cruise Company Blames Captain," *The Wall Street Journal*, January 17, 2012, http://online.wsj.com/article/SB100014240529702037 35304577165290656739300.html (accessed January 20, 2012); and "Costa Concordia Captain Found Guilty in Fatal Shipwreck, Sentenced to 16 Years," *ABC News*, February 11, 2015, http://abcnews.go.com/International/costa-concordia-captain-francesco-schettino-found-guilty-fatal/story?id=28894507 (accessed April 28, 2016).

14. Jena McGregor, "Lenovo CEO Hands over His Bonus to Hourly Workers—Again," *The Washington Post*, September 5, 2013, http://www.washingtonpost.com/blogs/on-leadership/wp/2013/09/05/lenovo-ceo-hands-over-his-bonus-to-hourly-workers-again/ (accessed October 21, 2013).

15. Adam Bluestein, "Start a Company. Change the World," *Inc.* (May 2011): 71–80.

16. Bill George et al., "Discovering Your Authentic Leadership," *Harvard Business Review* (February 2007): 129–138; and Bill George, *Authentic Leadership: Rediscovering the Secrets to Lasting Value* (San Francisco: Jossey-Bass, 2003). For a review of the literature on authentic leadership, see William L. Gardner et al., "Authentic Leadership: A Review of the Literature and Research Agenda," *The Leadership Quarterly* 22 (2011): 1120–1145.

17. George, *Authentic Leadership*; and Bill George, "Truly Authentic Leadership," Special Report: America's Best Leaders, *U.S. News & World Report* (October 22, 2006), www.usnews.com/usnews/news/articles/061022/30authentic.htm (accessed October 5, 2010).

18. Example from Michael Lee Stallard, "Great Leaders Connect: Using Their Vision, Values, and Voice," *Leadership Excellence* (August 2012): 19.

19. Vernon Clark, quoted in Michael Lee Stallard and Jason Pankau, "To Boost Performance, Connect with the Core," *Leader to Leader* (Summer 2010): 51–57.

20. Judy B. Rosener, *America's Competitive Secret: Utilizing Women as a Management Strategy* (New York: Oxford University Press, 1995), pp. 129–135.

21. Alice H. Eagly and Linda L. Carli, "The Female Leadership Advantage: An Evaluation of the Evidence," *Leadership Quarterly* 14 (2003): 807–834; Rosener, *America's Competitive Secret*; Judy B. Rosener, "Ways Women Lead," *Harvard Business Review* (November–December 1990): 119–125; Sally Helgesen, *The Female Advantage: Women's Ways of Leadership* (New York: Currency/Doubleday, 1990); Bernard M. Bass and Bruce J. Avolio, "Shatter the Glass Ceiling: Women May Make Better Managers," *Human Resource Management* 33, no. 4 (Winter 1994): 549–560; and Carol Kinsey Goman, "What Men Can Learn from Women about Leadership in the 21st Century," *The Washington Post*, August 10, 2011, www.washingtonpost.com/national/on-leadership/what-men-can-learn-from-women-about-leadership/2011/08/10/gIQA4J9n6I_story.html (accessed September 12, 2012).

22. Rochelle Sharpe, "As Leaders, Women Rule," *BusinessWeek* (November 20, 2000): 75–84.

23. Kevin S. Groves, "Gender Differences in Social and Emotional Skills and Charismatic Leadership," *Journal of Leadership and Organizational Studies* 11, no. 3 (2005): 30ff.

24. Jack Zenger and Joseph Folkman, "Are Women Better Leaders Than Men?" HBR Blog Network, *Harvard Business Review* (March 11, 2012), http://blogs.hbr.org/cs/2012/03/a_study_in_leadership_women_do.html (accessed September 12, 2012); Zenger Folkman study reported in Tony Schwartz, "Over-coming the Confidence Gap in Women," *The New York Times*, June 12, 2015, http://www.nytimes.com/2015/06/13/business/dealbook/overcoming-the-confidence-gap-for-women.html?_r=0 (accessed April 25, 2016); and Herminia Ibarra and Otilia Obodaru, "Women and the Vision Thing," *Harvard Business Review* (January 2009): 62–70.

25. Susan Carey, "More Women Take Flight in Airline Operations," *The Wall Street Journal*, August 14, 2007; and Ann Therese Palmer, "Teacher Learns All About Airline; United VP Began as Reservations Clerk, Rose Through Ranks," *Chicago Tribune*, December 24, 2006.

26. Reported in Leigh Buchanan, "Between Venus and Mars," *Inc.* (June 2013): 64–74, 130.

27. This analogy is from Gordon P. Rabey, "Leadership Is Response: A Paper for Discussion," *Industrial and Commercial Training* 42, no. 2 (2010): 87–92.

28. This discussion is based on Philip A. Dover and Udo Dierk, "The Ambidextrous Organization: Integrating Managers, Entrepreneurs, and Leaders," *Journal of Business Strategy* 31, no. 5 (2010): 49–58; Gary Yukl and Richard Lepsinger, "Why Integrating the Leading and Managing Roles Is Essential for Organizational Effectiveness," *Organizational Dynamics* 34, no. 4 (2005): 361–375; and Henry Mintzberg, *Managing* (San Francisco: Berrett-Kohler Publishers, 2009).

29. Mathew J. Manimala and Kishinchand Poornima Wasdani, "Distributed Leadership at Google: Lessons from the Billion-Dollar Brand," *Ivey Business Journal* (May–June 2013), http://iveybusinessjournal.com/topics/leadership/distributed-leadership-at-google-lessons-from-the-billion-dollar-brand#.UmalkSbD91s (accessed October 22, 2013).

30. Ibid.

31. G. A. Yukl, *Leadership in Organizations* (Englewood Cliffs, NJ: Prentice Hall, 1981); and S. C. Kohs and K. W. Irle, "Prophesying Army Promotion," *Journal of Applied Psychology* 4 (1920): 73–87.

32. R. Albanese and D. D. Van Fleet, *Organizational Behavior: A Managerial View-point* (Hinsdale, IL: The Dryden Press, 1983); and S. A. Kirkpatrick and E. A. Locke, "Leadership: Do Traits Matter?" *Academy of Management Executive* 5, no. 2 (1991): 48–60.

33. A summary of various studies and surveys is reported in Del Jones, "Optimism Puts Rose-Colored Tint in Glasses of Top Execs," *USA TODAY*, December 15, 2005.

34. Annie Murphy Paul, "The Uses and Abuses of Optimism (and Pessimism)," *Psychology Today* (November–December 2011): 56–63.

35. Tom Rath and Barry Conchie, *Strengths Based Leadership* (Gallup Press, Gallup, New Mexico, 2009); Marcus Buckingham and Donald O. Clifton, *Now, Discover Your Strengths* (New York: Free Press, 2001).

36. Buckingham and Clifton, *Now, Discover Your Strengths*.

37. Adam Bryant, "Nancy Dubuc of A&E: Mixing Doers, Thinkers and Feelers" (Corner Office column), *The New York Times*, March 19, 2015, http://www.nytimes.com/2015/03/22/business/nancy-dubuc-of-ae-mixing-doers-thinkers-and-feelers.html?_r=0 (accessed October 13, 2015).

38. Gary Yukl, Angela Gordon, and Tom Taber, "A Hierarchical Taxonomy of Leader-ship Behavior: Integrating a Half-Century of Behavior Research," *Journal of Leadership and Organizational Studies* 9, no. 1 (2002): 13–32.

39. C. A. Schriesheim and B. J. Bird, "Contributions of the Ohio State Studies to the Field of Leadership," *Journal of Management* 5 (1979): 135–145; C. L. Shartle, "Early Years of the Ohio State University Leadership Studies," *Journal of Management* 5 (1979): 126–134; and R. Likert, "From Production- and Employee-Centeredness to Systems 1-4," *Journal of Management* 5 (1979): 147–156.

40. P. C. Nystrom, "Managers and the High-High Leader Myth," *Academy of Management Journal* 21 (1978): 325–331; and L. L. Larson, J. G. Hunt, and Richard N. Osborn, "The Great High-High Leader Behavior Myth: A Lesson from Occam's Razor," *Academy of Management Journal* 19 (1976): 628–641.

41. Likert, "From Production- and Employee-Centeredness to Systems 1–4."

42. Robert R. Blake and Jane S. Mouton, *The Managerial Grid III* (Houston: Gulf Publishing Company, 1985).

43. Ryan Nakashima, "New Microsoft CEO's Collegial Style Sparks Hope," *USA Today*, February 9, 2014, http://www.usatoday.com/story/tech/2014/02/09/new-microsoft-ceo-hope/5340519/ (accessed October 12, 2015).

44. This discussion is based on Paul Hersey and Ken Blanchard, "Revisiting the Life-Cycle Theory of Leadership," in "Great Ideas Revisited," *Training & Development* (January 1996): 42–47; Blanchard and Hersey, "Life-Cycle Theory of Leadership," in "Great Ideas Revisited," *Training & Development* (January 1996): 42–47; Paul Hersey, "Situational Leaders: Use the Model in Your Work," *Leadership Excellence* (February 2009): 12; and Paul Hersey and Kenneth H. Blanchard, *Management of Organizational Behavior: Utilizing Human Resources*, 4th ed. (Englewood Cliffs, NJ: Prentice Hall, 1982). The concept of *readiness* comes from Hersey, "Situational Leaders."

45. Andrew Ross Sorkin, "Warren Buffett, Delegator in Chief," *The New York Times*, April 23, 2011, www.nytimes.com/2011/04/24/weekinreview/24buffett.html (accessed September 14, 2012); and Eileen Newman Rubin, "Assessing Your Leader-ship Style to Achieve Organizational Objectives," *Global Business and Organizational Excellence* (September–October 2013): 55–66.

46. Laura Smith, "Why I Regret Being a Nice Boss," *Slate.com* (October 2, 2014), http://www.slate.com/articles/business/building_a_better_workplace/2014/10/why_i_regret_being_a_nice_boss_setting_boundaries_with_employees.html (accessed October 12, 2015); and Jessica Sigman, "Closing Time: On Its Last Day, Yola Opens Up About Shutting Down," *Washington City Paper* (October 3, 2012), http://www.washingtoncitypaper.com/blogs/youngandhungry/2012/10/03/closing-time-on-its-last-day-yola-opens-up-about-shutting-down/ (accessed October 12, 2015).

47. Rubin, "Assessing Your Leadership Style to Achieve Organizational Objectives."

48. Fred E. Fiedler, "Assumed Similarity Measures as Predictors of Team Effectiveness," *Journal of Abnormal and Social Psychology* 49 (1954): 381–388; F. E. Fiedler, *Leader Attitudes and Group Effectiveness* (Urbana, IL: University of Illinois Press, 1958); and F. E. Fiedler, *A Theory of Leadership Effectiveness* (New York: McGraw-Hill, 1967).

49. Fred E. Fiedler and M. M. Chemers, *Leadership and Effective Management* (Glen-view, IL: Scott Foresman, 1974).

50. Reported in George Anders, "Theory & Practice: Tough CEOs Often Most Successful, a Study Finds," *The Wall Street Journal*, November 19, 2007.

51. Fred E. Fiedler, "Engineer the Job to Fit the Manager," *Harvard Business Review* 43 (1965): 115–122; and Fiedler, M. M. Chemers, and L. Mahar, *Improving Leadership Effectiveness: The Leader Match Concept* (New York: Wiley, 1976).

52. R. Singh, "Leadership Style and Reward Allocation: Does Least Preferred Coworker Scale Measure Tasks and Relation Orientation?" *Organizational Behavior and Human Performance* 27 (1983): 178–197; and D. Hosking, "A Critical Evaluation of Fiedler's Contingency Hypotheses," *Progress in Applied Psychology* 1 (1981): 103–154.

53. S. Kerr and J. M. Jermier, "Substitutes for Leadership: Their Meaning and Measurement," *Organizational Behavior and Human Performance* 22 (1978): 375–403; and Jon P. Howell and Peter W. Dorfman, "Leadership and Substitutes for Leadership Among Professional and Nonprofessional Workers," *Journal of Applied Behavioral Science* 22 (1986): 29–46.

54. Katherine J. Klein and Robert J. House, "On Fire: Charismatic Leadership and Levels of Analysis," *Leadership Quarterly* 6, no. 2 (1995): 183–198.

55. Jay A. Conger and Rabindra N. Kanungo, "Toward a Behavioral Theory of Charismatic Leadership in Organizational Settings," *Academy of Management Review* 12 (1987): 637–647; Jaepil Choi, "A Motivational Theory of Charismatic Leader-ship: Envisioning, Empathy, and Empowerment," *Journal of Leadership and Organizational Studies* 13, no. 1 (2006): 24ff; and William L. Gardner and Bruce J. Avolio, "The Charismatic Relationship: A Dramaturgical Perspective," *Academy of Management Review* 23, no. 1 (1998): 32–58.

56. Loizos Heracleous and Laura Alexa Klaering, "Charismatic Leadership and Rhetorical Competence: An Analysis of Steve Jobs's Rhetoric," *Group and Organization Management* 39, no. 2 (April 2014): 131–161; and "Why Steve Jobs Was Such a Charismatic Leader," Warwick University, WBS.com, November 11, 2015, http://www.wbs.ac.uk/news/why-steve-jobs-was-such-a-charismatic-leader1/ (accessed April 29, 2016).

57. Jon Katzenbach, "The Steve Jobs Way," *Strategy + Business* (Summer 2012), www.strategy-business.com/article/00109?gko=d331b (accessed June 11, 2012); Steve Moore, "Not Bad for a Hippie Dropout," *Management Today* (March 2009): 27; and Leslie Kwoh and Emma Silverman, "Bio as Bible: Managers Imitate Steve Jobs," *The Wall Street Journal*, March 31, 2012.

58. Robert J. House and Jane M. Howell, "Personality and Charismatic Leadership," *Leadership Quarterly* 3, no. 2 (1992): 81–108; and Jennifer O'Connor et al., "Charismatic Leaders and Destructiveness: A Historiometric Study," *Leadership Quarterly* 6, no. 4 (1995): 529–555.

59. Rob Nielsen, Jennifer A. Marrone, and Holly S. Slay, "A New Look at Humility: Exploring the Humility Concept and Its Role in Socialized Charismatic Leadership," *Journal of Leadership and Organizational Studies* 17, no. 1 (February 2010): 33–44.

60. Robert J. House, "Research Contrasting the Behavior and Effects of Reputed Charismatic vs. Reputed Non-Charismatic Leaders," paper presented as part of a symposium, "Charismatic Leadership: Theory and Evidence," Academy of Management, San Diego, 1985.

61. Bernard M. Bass, "Theory of Transformational Leadership Redux," *Leadership Quarterly* 6, no. 4 (1995): 463–478; Noel M. Tichy and Mary Anne Devanna, *The Transformational Leader* (New York: John Wiley, 1986); James C. Sarros, Brian K. Cooper, and Joseph C. Santora, "Building a Climate for Innovation Through Transformational Leadership and Organizational Culture," *Journal of Leadership and Organizational Studies* 15, no. 2 (November 2008): 145–158; and P. D. Harms and Marcus Crede, "Emotional Intelligence and Transformational and Transactional Leadership: A Meta-Analysis," *Journal of Leadership and Organizational Studies* 17, no. 1 (February 2010): 5–17.

62. The terms *transactional* and *transformational* come from James M. Burns, *Leadership* (New York: Harper & Row, 1978); and Bernard M. Bass, "Leadership: Good, Better, Best," *Organizational Dynamics* 13 (Winter 1985): 26–40.

63. Daft and Lengel, *Fusion Leadership*.

64. Jonathan Oosting, "StudentsFirst's Michelle Rhee Returns to Michigan as Education Reform Group Makes Mark," *MLive*, May 26, 2013, http://www.mlive.com/politics/index.ssf/2013/05/studentsfirst_spotlight_michel.html (accessed June 11, 2013).

65. Gang Wang et al., "Transformational Leadership and Performance Across Criteria and Levels: A Meta-Analytic Review of 25 Years of Research," *Group & Organization Management* 36, no. 2 (2011): 223–270; and Taly Dvir et al., "Impact of Transformational Leadership on Follower Development and Performance: A Field Experiment," *Academy of Management Journal* 45, no. 4 (2002): 735–744.

66. Robert S. Rubin, David C. Munz, and William H. Bommer, "Leading from Within: The Effects of Emotion Recognition and Personality on Transformational Leadership Behavior," *Academy of Management Journal* 48, no. 5 (2005): 845–858; and Timothy A. Judge and Joyce E. Bono, "Five-Factor Model of Personality and Transformational Leadership," *Journal of Applied Psychology* 85, no. 5 (October 2000): 751ff.

67. Naomi Schaefer Riley, "Seeing Through the School Daze; Michelle Rhee Fired 241 Teachers, 36 Principals, and 22 Assistant Principals After Taking over the District's Schools," *The Wall Street Journal*, February 19, 2013; Michelle Rhee and Adrian Fenty, "Review—The Education Manifesto—Michelle Rhee and Adrian Fenty on What They Learned While Pushing to Reform D.C.'s Failing Public Schools," *The Wall Street Journal*, October 30, 2010; Jeff Chu, "The Iron Chancellor," *Fast Company* (September 2008): 112–143; Amanda Ripley, "Can She Save Our Schools?" *Time* (December 8, 2008): 36–44; and William McGurn, "Giving Lousy Teachers the Boot; Michelle Rhee Does the Once Unthinkable in Washington," *The Wall Street Journal*, July 27, 2010.

68. Rubin, Munz, and Bommer, "Leading from Within."

69. The discussion of followership is based in part on Marc and Samantha Hurwitz, *Leadership Is Half the Story: Rethinking Followership, Leadership, and Collaboration* (Toronto: University of Toronto Press, 2015); John S. McCallum, "Followership: The Other Side of Leadership," *Ivey Business Journal* (September–October 2013), http://iveybusinessjournal. com/topics/leadership/followership-the-other-side-of-leadership#.UmfUoybD91s (accessed October 23, 2013); Warren Bennis, "Art of Followership: Followers Engage in an Interdependent Dance," *Leadership Excellence* (January 2010): 3–4; and Robert E. Kelley, "In Praise of Followers," *Harvard Business Review* (November–December 1988): 142–148.

70. Augustine O. Agho, "Perspectives of Senior-Level Executives on Effective Followership and Leadership," *Journal of Leadership and Organizational Studies* 16, no. 2 (November 2009):159–166; and James M. Kouzes and Barry Z. Posner, *The Leadership Challenge: How to Get Extraordinary Things Done in Organizations* (San Francisco: Jossey-Bass, 1990).

71. Barbara Kellerman, "What Every Leader Needs to Know About Followers," *Harvard Business Review* (December 2007): 84–91.

72. Robert E. Kelley, *The Power of Followership* (New York: Doubleday, 1992).

73. Discussed in Michael G. Winston, "Say *No* to Yes Men," *Leadership Excellence* (November 2010): 15; Adam Michaelson, *The Foreclosure of America: The Inside Story of the Rise and Fall of Countrywide* (New York: Penguin/Berkley, 2009).

74. Kelley, *The Power of Followership*, pp. 117–118.

75. Joann S. Lublin, "How to Prove You're a Keeper to a New CEO," *The Wall Street Journal*, March 8, 2013.

76. Henry Mintzberg, *Power In and Around Organizations* (Englewood Cliffs, NJ: Prentice Hall, 1983); and Jeffrey Pfeffer, *Power in Organizations* (Marshfield, MA: Pitman, 1981).

77. John R. P. French, Jr., and Bertram Raven, "The Bases of Social Power," in D. Cartwright and A. F. Zander, eds., *Group Dynamics* (Evanston, IL: Row Peterson, 1960), pp. 607–623.

78. Reported in Vadim Liberman, "Mario Moussa Wants You to Win Your Next Argument" (Questioning Authority column), *Conference Board Review* (November–December 2007): 25–26.

79. Jay A. Conger, "The Necessary Art of Persuasion," *Harvard Business Review* (May–June 1998): 84–95.

80. Kevin Clark, "The Coach Who Won't Leave the Locker Room," *The Wall Street Journal*, October 13, 2015, http:// www.wsj.com/articles/the-coach-who-wont-leave-the-locker-room-1444755991 (accessed October 15, 2015).

81. Roger Yu, "Co-Workers Praise Wyndham CEO's Welcoming Demeanor," *USA TODAY*, November 22, 2010, www. usatoday.com/money/companies/management/profile/2010-11-22-wyndhamceo22_ST_N.htm (accessed September 14, 2012).

82. Nancy F. Koehn, "Lincoln's School of Management," *The New York Times*, January 26, 2013; Hitendra Wadhwa, "Lessons in Leadership: How Lincoln Became America's Greatest President," *Inc.com*, February 12, 2012, http:// www.inc.com/hitendra-wadhwa/lessons-in-leadership-how-abraham-lincoln-became-americas-greatest-president.html (accessed March 4, 2013); and Gil Troy and Karl Moore, "Leading from the Centre: What CEOs Can Learn from U.S. Presidents," *Ivey Business Journal* (September–October, 2010), http://www.iveybusinessjournal.com/topics/leadership/leading-from-the-centre-what-ceos-can-learn-from-u-s-presidents (accessed May 21, 2013).

83. Jeremy W. Peters, "Time Inc. Chief Executive Jack Griffin Out," *The New York Times*, February 17, 2011, http://mediadecoder. blogs.nytimes.com/2011/02/17/time-inc-chief-executive-jack-griffin-out/ (accessed February 18, 2011).

84. D. Kipnis et al., "Patterns of Managerial Influence: Shotgun Managers, Tacticians, and Politicians," *Organizational Dynamics* (Winter 1984): 58–67.

85. These tactics are based on "The Uses (and Abuses) of Influence (Spotlight: Interview with Robert Cialdini)," *Harvard Business Review* (July–August 2013): 76–81; Kipnis et al., "Patterns of Managerial Influence"; and Robert B. Cialdini, "Harnessing the Science of Persuasion," *Harvard Business Review* (October 2001): 72–79.

86. Ibid.; and Jeffrey Pfeffer, *Managing with Power: Politics and Influence in Organizations* (Boston: Harvard Business School Press, 1992), Chapter 13.

87. Cialdini, "Harnessing the Science of Persuasion."

88. V. Dallas Merrell, *Huddling: The Informal Way to Management Success* (New York: AMACOM, 1979).

89. Robert B. Cialdini, *Influence: Science and Practice*, 4th ed. (Boston: Pearson Allyn & Bacon, 2000).

90. Harvey G. Enns and Dean B. McFarlin, "When Executives Influence Peers, Does Function Matter?" *Human Resource Management* 4, no. 2 (Summer 2003): 125–142.

91. Adapted from Birgit Schyns, James R. Meindl, and Marcel A. Croon, "The Romance of Leadership Scale: Cross-Cultural Testing and Refinement," *Leadership* 3, no. 1 (2007): 29–46.

Chapter 12
Motivating Employees

iStock.com/oscarhdez

Chapter Outline

Learning Outcomes

After studying this chapter, you should be able to:

12.1 Define *motivation* and explain the difference between intrinsic and extrinsic rewards.

12.2 Identify and describe content theories of motivation based on employee needs.

12.3 Identify and explain process theories of motivation.

12.4 Describe the reinforcement perspective and social learning theory and how they can be used to motivate employees.

12.5 Discuss major approaches to job design and how job design influences motivation.

12.6 Explain how empowerment heightens employee motivation.

12.7 Identify three elements of employee engagement and describe some ways that managers can create a work environment that promotes engagement.

12.8 Describe how managers give people a sense of making progress toward meaningful goals to build a thriving workforce and create a high-performing organization.

Are You Ready to Be a Manager?

Before reading this chapter, please circle either "Mostly True" or "Mostly False" for each of the following five statements.

1 Everyone knows that people are mostly motivated by money at work.

Mostly True ◄·················· ► Mostly False

[page 447]

2 The need for power seems to dominate every workplace I've seen.

Mostly True ◄·················· ► Mostly False

[page 454]

3 I wish I worked somewhere that encourages people to set goals and then gives feedback on how well they achieved those targets.

Mostly True ◄·················· ► Mostly False

[page 456]

4 I like learning new skills and behaviors when I have a positive role model, someone I work with who easily does the skills I'm trying to learn.

Mostly True ◄·················· ► Mostly False

[Page 462]

5 I'd find it very motivating for me if I were empowered to do a more difficult job; this would include having information on the company's performance, to be given enough power to carry out the assignment, and then to be rewarded on my performance.

Mostly True ◄·················· ► Mostly False

[page 467]

Discover Your Management Approach

What Motivates You?

Instructions: Think of a specific recent work or study task on which you worked alone. How important were each of the following as a reason for doing that activity?

	Mostly True	Mostly False
1. I received a reward for doing it.	_____	_____
2. I was supposed to do the activity.	_____	_____
3. It was something I felt that I had to do.	_____	_____

To complete and score the entire assessment, visit MindTap.

Rich Sheridan knows what it's like to work in a job where you're miserable. He was there in 1999, when he began exploring ideas for starting a business and searching for ways to organize a workplace where people could be happy as well as productive. Two years later, Sheridan and two colleagues founded Menlo Innovations with the goal of creating an organization "with joyful people achieving joyful outcomes." At Menlo, a custom software company located in Ann Arbor, Michigan, people have a great deal of autonomy in how they do their work, and managers involve employees in all important decisions. Software programmers work in pairs, often sharing a single computer and passing the keyboard and mouse back and forth. People are encouraged to experiment continually, and mistakes are accepted as a way to learn. A culture and environment that helps people feel engaged with their work and their colleagues has kept Menlo Innovations thriving. Thousands of businesspeople tour Menlo each year to learn what makes the company's "joyful" work environment so effective.[1]

Sheridan points out that being joyful is not just about having fun. Menlo is guided by the idea that "humans are wired to work on things bigger than themselves" and "to be in community with one another."[2] Managers in other companies are discovering that creating an environment where people feel valued, feel that their work is meaningful, have good relationships with their colleagues and managers, and feel that they have opportunities for growth and development can be a key to high employee motivation. A motivated workforce is an essential ingredient for organizational success. Most people begin a new job with energy and enthusiasm, but employees can lose their drive if managers fail in their role as motivators. Yet motivation is a challenge for many managers because motivation arises from within employees and may differ for each person. Some people are motivated primarily by money, others are motivated to perform well because managers make them feel appreciated for doing a good job, and still others find their primary motivation in the challenge of solving complex problems or making a contribution to society. With such diverse motivations among individuals, how do managers find the right way to motivate people toward common organizational goals?

This chapter reviews several approaches to employee motivation. First, we define *motivation* and the types of rewards that managers use. Then, we examine several models that describe the employee needs and processes associated with motivation. We also look at the use of reinforcement for motivation, explain social learning theory, and examine how job design—changing the structure of the work itself—can affect employee satisfaction and productivity.

12-1 Individual Needs and Motivation

Most of us get up in the morning, go to school or work, and behave in ways that are predictably our own. All these behaviors are motivated by something, but most of us don't think of why we do the things we do. **Motivation** refers to the forces either within or external to a person that arouse enthusiasm and persistence to pursue a certain course of action. Employee motivation affects productivity, and part of a manager's job is to channel motivation toward the accomplishment of organizational goals.[3] Studies have found that high employee motivation goes hand in hand with high organizational performance and profits.[4] It is the responsibility of managers to find the right combination of motivational techniques and rewards to satisfy employees' needs and simultaneously encourage great work performance. A simple model of human motivation is illustrated in Exhibit 12.1. People have *needs*—such as for recognition, achievement, or monetary gain—that translate into an internal tension that motivates specific behaviors with which to fulfill various needs. To the extent that the behavior is successful, the person is rewarded because the need is satisfied. The reward also informs the person that the behavior was appropriate and can be used again in the future.

Exhibit 12.1   **A Simple Model of Motivation**

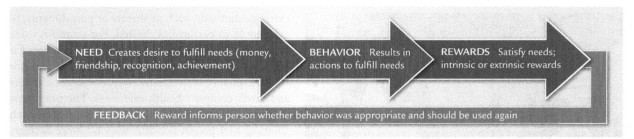

12-2 Intrinsic and Extrinsic Rewards

Managers who understand the motives that compel people to initiate, alter, or continue a desired behavior are more successful as motivators. Exhibit 12.2 illustrates four categories of motives based on two criteria. The vertical dimension contrasts intrinsic versus extrinsic rewards. The horizontal dimension contrasts behaviors that are driven by fear or pain versus those driven by growth or pleasure.

Intrinsic rewards are the satisfactions that a person receives in the process of performing a particular action. The completion of a complex task may bestow a pleasant feeling of accomplishment, or solving a problem that benefits others may fulfill a personal mission. For example, employees at Salesforce.com, which provides cloud computing services to organizations such as Bank of America, Cisco, Google, and the Japanese government, are motivated by being on the "cutting edge" of reinventing how companies handle ordinary but critical tasks like sales, customer relations, and internal communications.[5] **Extrinsic rewards** are given by another person, typically a manager, and include promotions, praise, and pay increases. They originate externally as a result of pleasing others. At the Alta Gracia factory in the Dominican Republic, owned by Knights Apparel, employees are motivated by the extrinsic reward of high pay because they need money to support their families and can't make nearly as much anywhere else.[6]

Effective managers want people to receive both extrinsic and intrinsic rewards to meet their needs. Researchers at the London School of Economics analyzed more than 50 studies to examine what gets people motivated at work. They concluded that people give their best effort when the work itself interests and excites them, when they feel that their work provides meaning and purpose, and when they feel appreciated for their work and contributions.[7]

The four quadrants in Exhibit 12.2 represent four differing approaches for motivating people.[8] Quadrants 1 and 2 are both negative approaches to motivating. Quadrant 1 uses negative,

Exhibit 12.2 Four Categories of Motives Managers Can Use

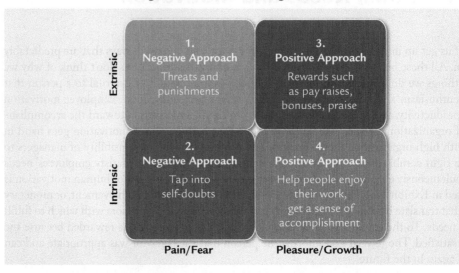

	Pain/Fear	**Pleasure/Growth**
Extrinsic	**1. Negative Approach** — Threats and punishments	**3. Positive Approach** — Rewards such as pay raises, bonuses, praise
Intrinsic	**2. Negative Approach** — Tap into self-doubts	**4. Positive Approach** — Help people enjoy their work, get a sense of accomplishment

SOURCE: Based on Bruce H. Jackson, "Influence Behavior; Become a Master Motivator," *Leadership Excellence* (April 2010): 14.

Daniel Acker/Bloomberg/Getty Images

Concept Connection

Why does Google (a division of Alphabet) regularly top *Fortune* magazine's list of "Best Places to Work"? One reason is that Google provides extraordinary **extrinsic rewards**, including good salaries, no-cost health and dental insurance, tuition reimbursement, onsite fitness centers, and free gourmet meals. But the real key to motivation may be the **intrinsic rewards** people get from working there. Most Google employees say the opportunity to work on projects they find meaningful and challenging is what keeps them satisfied and motivated.

extrinsic methods, such as threats or punishments, to get people to perform as desired. For example, some companies have found that penalizing employees for smoking or being overweight by charging extra for health insurance is an effective way to change behaviors and lower company health care costs. The practice is growing, with leaders citing behavioral science research showing that people typically respond more strongly to a potential loss (such as a financial penalty for not losing weight), a response referred to as *loss aversion*, than to an expected gain (such as a financial reward for losing weight). Participation in the health-risk assessment program at Mohawk Industries increased 97 percent after managers began penalizing employees $100 if they didn't participate. Previously, the company offered rewards for participation, but enrollment rates remained low, which sparked the shift to penalties.[9] Quadrant 2 methods attempt to motivate people by tapping into their self-doubts or anxieties. For example, a manager might motivate people to work hard by emphasizing the weak economy and high unemployment rate. Quadrants 1 and 2 methods can indeed be effective as fear is a powerful motivator.[10] However, using fear to motivate people in organizations almost always has negative consequences for employee development and long-term performance.

Quadrants 3 and 4 are positive motivational approaches. Quadrant 3 methods attempt to influence behavior by using extrinsic rewards that create pleasure. At Hilcorp Energy, for example, managers offered employees the chance to earn a bonus of $100,000 each if they helped the organization meet its growth goal.[11] A recent survey found that something as simple as giving employees free food and beverages makes them happier and more motivated. Public relations firm InkHouse installed a seltzer machine in the office and offers free fruit, chips, cookies, and popcorn. "It helps employees be more excited about coming to work," said InkHouse cofounder Beth Monaghan.[12] Many managers have learned that praise and expressions of appreciation are also powerful extrinsic motivators. Carmelyn P. Malalis, chairperson and commissioner of the

New York City Commission on Human Rights, makes a point to tell people when they're doing a good job, and she also tells others about the great work the people on their team are doing. Malalis says she learned early on that she didn't want to lead with fear or force because "it didn't make me inspired to do a good job when I worked with people who did that."[13]

This positive motivational approach is useful but limited. External rewards are important, but they can lose their power as motivational tools over time. The most effective managers also emphasize Quadrant 4 techniques that tap into deep-seated employee energy and commitment by helping people get intrinsic rewards from their work. For example, at Morrison Management Specialists, which provides food, nutrition, and dining services to the health care and senior living industries, managers provide training sessions under the title of "Our Great Partnership" and strive to help people see how their jobs make a difference in the lives of elderly or ill people. A "People First" recognition program gives employees a chance to recognize one another for exceptional service.[14] In organizations that have shifted to a bossless workplace, where no one is telling people what to do and keeping tabs on whether they do it, managers need people who can act based on their own motivation. The "Sunny Side Up" box describes motivation techniques managers use in a bossless environment.

Sunny Side Up } Motivating in a Bossless Environment

As companies flatten their hierarchies and eliminate managers, motivated employees become especially important. In a truly bossless organization, no one is taking attendance or monitoring work. People and teams act on their own. An organization that wants to go bossless should consider the following motivational methods:

- **Don't hide information.** At Menlo Innovations, information concerning motivational factors is so open that a new employee is likely to feel exposed. A chart displays the names, titles, and pay grades of all employees. In response to a question about what it felt like to have his salary visible to colleagues, an employee responded, "It's liberating."

- **Rely on intrinsic rewards.** People at the Web design firm DreamHost understand that the way employees are motivated is changing. "Twenty years ago, it was about higher pay. Now it's more about finding your work meaningful and interesting," said CEO Simon Anderson. Chris Rufer, founder of tomato-processor Morning Star, describes his company as deeply humane, something that buoys the spirits of workers because relationships among members are deep and substantive.

- **Let people own the goal.** At Morning Star, goals, not supervisors, are used for motivation. A tomato sorter pledges to sort a predetermined amount of tomatoes a day, for example. A person responsible for helping evaporate the water out of tomato pulp signs an agreement to evaporate a specific number of gallons of water every week. With a clear goal, people are left alone to do their work.

- **Reward the team**. In a bossless environment, achievement is usually tied to the team, so individual

work means nothing until it fits into a larger project that requires the assistance of peers. Individual rewards are replaced by shared achievement. Friendliness and helpfulness matter more than personal ladder-climbing and reward-seeking. At Menlo Innovations and other bossless companies, peer teams make hiring decisions as well as decide promotions, layoffs, and firings.

- **Hire attitude over aptitude.** Hiring workers who are self-starters and team players can be vital to making a boss-free system work. Technical wizards who are jerks will poison the culture. Cissy Pau of Clear HR Consulting says employees "need to know what to do, how to do it, when to do it."

- **Reinvent management.** Thomas Davenport, co-author of *Manager Redefined*, says managers must learn to motivate in a different way. "Nobody comes to work in the 21st century world and says, 'Please manage me.' They say, 'Create an environment where I can be successful.'" Managers must learn to see themselves as working among equals rather than being above others. Their new job is to support the people around them, remove obstacles, and encourage better work, which is similar to "servant leadership," as described in Chapter 11.

SOURCES: Matthew Shaer, "The Boss Stops Here," *New York Magazine* (June 24–July 1, 2013): 25–34; Knowledge@Wharton, "Going Boss-Free: Utopia or 'Lord of the Flies'?" August 1, 2012, http://knowledge.wharton.upenn.edu/article/going-boss-free-utopia-or-lord-of-the-flies/; Shelley White, "The Bossless Office: Motivational Experience or Invitation to Anarchy?" October 11, 2012,http://www.theglobeandmail.com/report-on-business/small-business/sb-managing/human-resources/the-bossless-office-motivational-experience-or-invitation-to-anarchy/article4601671/; and Ilya Pozin, "Want Happier Employees? Get Rid of the Bosses," *Inc.* (June 18, 2012), http://www.inc.com/ilya-pozin/want-happier-employees-get-rid-of-the-bosses.html.

Remember This

- **Motivation** is the arousal of enthusiasm and persistence to pursue a certain course of action.
- All behaviors are motivated by something, such as the desire to fulfill needs for money, recognition, friendship, or a sense of accomplishment.
- **Intrinsic rewards** are the satisfactions that a person receives in the process of performing a particular action.

- **Extrinsic rewards** are given by another person, such as a manager, and include pay increases, promotions, and praise.
- People can be driven to act by fear, but good managers avoid the use of fear tactics to motivate people because this approach damages employee commitment and performance in the long run.
- In addition to providing appropriate extrinsic rewards, effective managers try to help people achieve intrinsic rewards from their work.

12-3 Content Perspectives on Motivation

Content theories emphasize the needs that motivate people. At any point in time, people have a variety of needs. These needs translate into an internal drive that motivates specific behaviors in an attempt to fulfill the needs. In other words, our needs are like a hidden catalog of the things that we want and will work to get. To the extent that managers understand employees' needs, they can design reward systems to meet them and direct employees' energies and priorities toward attaining organizational goals.

12-3a The Hierarchy of Needs

Probably the most famous content theory was developed by Abraham Maslow.[15] Maslow's **hierarchy of needs theory** proposes that people are motivated by multiple needs and that these needs exist in a hierarchical order, as illustrated in Exhibit 12.3.

Maslow identified five general types of motivating needs, listed in order of ascendance:

1. *Physiological needs.* These most basic human physical needs include food, water, and oxygen. In the organizational setting, they are reflected in the needs for adequate heat, air, and base salary to ensure survival.

2. *Safety needs.* These needs include a safe and secure physical and emotional environment and freedom from threats—that is, for freedom from violence and for an orderly society. In the workplace, safety needs reflect the needs for safe jobs, fringe benefits, and job security. Because of the weak economy and high unemployment in recent years, safety needs have taken priority for many people. One job satisfaction survey indicated that job security was the most important element of job satisfaction, with good benefits being second most important.[16] When managers at Burgerville, a regional restaurant chain based in Vancouver, Washington, began paying at least 90 percent of health insurance premiums for hourly employees who worked at least 20 hours a week, turnover plunged, employees began working harder to get more hours (which are assigned based on performance), service improved, and sales increased.[17]

3. *Belongingness needs.* These needs reflect the desire to be accepted by one's peers, have friendships, be part of a group, and be loved. In the organization, these needs influence the desire for good relationships with coworkers, participation in a work group, and a positive relationship with supervisors. In some Chinese factories, leaders have gone beyond financial incentives to try to meet belongingness and esteem needs of employees with work

Exhibit 12.3 Maslow's Hierarchy of Needs

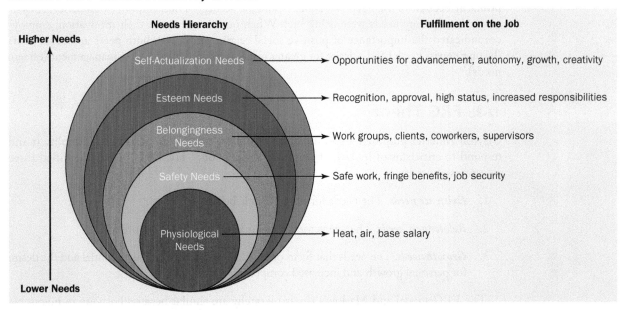

Needs Hierarchy	Fulfillment on the Job
Higher Needs	
Self-Actualization Needs	→ Opportunities for advancement, autonomy, growth, creativity
Esteem Needs	→ Recognition, approval, high status, increased responsibilities
Belongingness Needs	→ Work groups, clients, coworkers, supervisors
Safety Needs	→ Safe work, fringe benefits, job security
Physiological Needs	→ Heat, air, base salary
Lower Needs	

contests, American Idol–type singing contests, karaoke rooms, dinners with managers, and more communications about the greater purpose of employees' contributions.[18]

4. ***Esteem needs.*** These needs relate to the desire for a positive self-image and the desire to receive attention, recognition, and appreciation from others. Within organizations, esteem needs reflect a motivation for recognition, an increase in responsibility, high status, and credit for contributions to the organization. One example comes from Intuit, where Jennifer Lepird spent weeks working long, grueling hours on a big acquisition deal. After the deal closed, Lepird was delighted to get a thank-you note from her manager, along with a small gift certificate, because it met her need to feel appreciated. "The fact that somebody took the time to recognize the effort made the long hours just melt away," she says.[19]

5. ***Self-actualization needs.*** These needs include the need for self-fulfillment, which is the highest need category. They concern developing one's full potential, increasing one's competence, and becoming a better person. Self-actualization needs can be met in the organization by providing people with opportunities to grow, be creative, and acquire training for challenging assignments and advancement.

According to Maslow's theory, low-order needs take priority—they must be satisfied before higher-order needs are activated. The needs are satisfied in sequence: Physiological needs come before safety needs, safety needs before belongingness needs, and so on. A person desiring physical safety will devote his or her efforts to securing a safer environment and will not be concerned with esteem needs or self-actualization needs. Once a need is satisfied, it declines in importance, and the next higher need is activated.

A study of employees in the manufacturing department of a major health care company in the United Kingdom provides

imtmphoto/Shutterstock.com

Concept Connection

Millennial employees, who, according to their managers, report for work with self-esteem to spare, often proceed directly from **existence needs** to **growth needs**. Once they're satisfied that they're receiving fair pay, what younger employees want most is training. In fact, recent studies found that respondents chose training from a list of benefits three times more often than a cash bonus. There's a practical reason for this interest in personal growth. Millennials know they need to acquire skills that will make them attractive job candidates. Unlike many of their elders, they don't expect to work for a single employer throughout their careers.

some support for Maslow's theory. Most line workers said that they worked at the company primarily because of the good pay, benefits, and job security. Thus, employees' lower-level physiological and safety needs were being met. When questioned about their motivation, employees indicated the importance of positive social relationships with both peers and supervisors (belongingness needs) and a desire for greater respect and recognition from management (esteem needs).[20]

12-3b ERG Theory

Clayton Alderfer proposed a modification of Maslow's theory in an effort to simplify it and respond to criticisms of its lack of empirical verification.[21] His **ERG theory** identified three categories of needs:

1. *Existence needs.* The needs for physical well-being

2. *Relatedness needs.* The needs for satisfactory relationships with others

3. *Growth needs.* The needs that focus on the development of human potential and the desire for personal growth and increased competence

The ERG model and Maslow's needs hierarchy are similar because both are in hierarchical form and presume that individuals move up the hierarchy one step at a time. However, Alderfer reduced the number of need categories to three and proposed that movement up the hierarchy is more complex, reflecting a **frustration-regression principle**: namely, that failure to meet a high-order need may trigger a regression to an already fulfilled lower-order need. Thus, a worker who cannot fulfill a need for personal growth may revert to a lower-order need and redirect his or her efforts toward making a lot of money. The ERG model therefore is less rigid than Maslow's needs hierarchy, suggesting that individuals may move down as well as up the hierarchy, depending on their ability to satisfy needs. Needs hierarchy theories explain why organizations find ways to recognize employees, encourage their participation in decision making, and give them opportunities to make significant contributions to the organization and society. Ari Weinzweig and Paul Saginaw created an organization that enables all employees to meet higher-level growth needs.

Meeting employee needs helps keep motivation at Zingerman's high. In addition to sharing information at the weekly huddles, employees frequently send e-mail or text messages to

Recipe for Success } Zingerman's Community of Businesses

From the moment Ari Weinzweig and Paul Saginaw decided to start a business, they focused more on how they would run it than on what the business would be. Weinzweig and Saginaw "wanted to build an extraordinary organization . . . where decisions would not be based on who had the most authority but on whoever had the most relevant information." The partners opened a small delicatessen in Ann Arbor, Michigan, in 1982, and from the beginning, they wanted everyone to think like an owner and help run the business.

When the deli hit a plateau in the mid-1990s, the two wrote a vision statement for what would become the Zingerman's Community of Businesses (ZCoB). ZCoB is a group of distinct, local businesses that buy and sell to one another but stand on their own. Each business, such as Zingerman's Bakehouse,

Zingerman's Coffee Company, and Zingerman's Creamery, was founded and is run by a managing partner who shares the Zingerman's culture and values. ZCoB gives employees a chance not only to run the businesses but even to start a new one. One employee, who is running an Asian food cart near the deli, hopes to eventually open a Korean restaurant under the ZCoB umbrella.

Weinzweig and Saginaw share operating and financial data, such as sales, expenses, customer service metrics, and energy efficiency with employees at all levels and give them responsibility for improving the metrics, which are tracked on a scoreboard. Weekly huddles and regular training courses help people understand what the numbers mean and let them offer ideas for improvement.[22]

Weinzweig or Saginaw with tips and ideas for saving money, increasing sales, or generally doing things better. Krystal Walls, who works in the mail-order business, says, "I have never worked anywhere where I was trusted or respected like this."[23]

Some companies have also found that job flexibility is a great high-level motivator. At J. A. Counter, an insurance and investment advisory firm in New Richmond, Wisconsin, employees can come and go as they please without telling anyone where they are going or why, so long as they get their jobs done. Shannon Mehls, a financial services manager at the company, says employees now feel like "mini-entrepreneurs," managing their own schedules and focusing on results instead of just putting in 40 hours and getting a paycheck.[24] Although not all managers would be comfortable working in an environment where employees come and go as they please, there is some evidence that people who have greater control over their work schedules are significantly less likely to suffer job burnout and are more highly committed to their employers.[25]

12-3c A Two-Factor Approach to Motivation

Frederick Herzberg developed another popular theory of motivation called the *two-factor theory*.[26] Herzberg interviewed hundreds of workers about times when they were highly motivated to work and other times when they were dissatisfied and unmotivated. His findings suggested that the work characteristics associated with dissatisfaction were quite different from those pertaining to satisfaction, which prompted the notion that two factors influence work motivation.

The two-factor theory is illustrated in Exhibit 12.4. The center of the scale is neutral, meaning that workers are neither satisfied nor dissatisfied. Herzberg believed that two entirely separate dimensions contribute to an employee's behavior at work. The first, called **hygiene factors**, involves the presence or absence of job dissatisfiers, such as working conditions, pay, company policies, and interpersonal relationships. When hygiene factors are poor, work is dissatisfying. However, good hygiene factors simply remove the dissatisfaction; they do not in themselves cause people to become highly satisfied and motivated in their work.

Exhibit 12.4 Herzberg's Two-Factor Theory

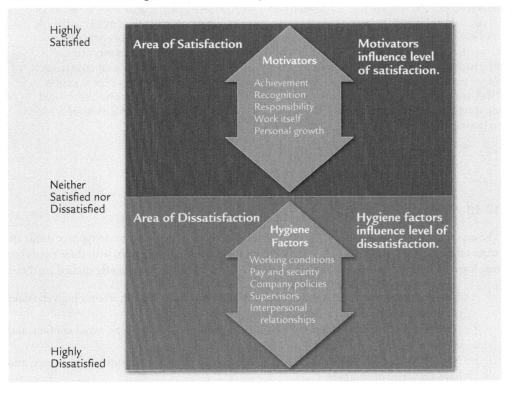

The second set of factors does influence job satisfaction. **Motivators** focus on high-level needs and include achievement, recognition, responsibility, and opportunity for growth. Herzberg believed that when motivators are absent, workers are neutral toward work, but when motivators are present, workers are highly motivated and satisfied. Thus, hygiene factors and motivators represent two distinct factors that influence motivation. Hygiene factors work only in the area of dissatisfaction. Unsafe working conditions or a noisy work environment will cause people to be dissatisfied, but correction of these conditions will not lead to a high level of motivation and satisfaction. Motivators such as challenge, responsibility, and recognition must be in place before employees will be highly motivated to excel at their work. There is a growing realization among managers of the importance of employee recognition, perhaps because tough economic conditions have made it more difficult for them to reward people with large pay increases. The most recent Globoforce MoodTracker Survey report indicates that 82 percent of employees surveyed say that being recognized for their efforts increased their motivation. "It made me work harder, want to come to work every day, and I was proud to work for my boss," said one respondent. Among job seekers, a lack of recognition was the number-two reason cited for leaving a job.[27]

The implication of the two-factor theory for managers is clear. On one hand, providing hygiene factors will eliminate employee dissatisfaction but will not motivate workers to high achievement levels. On the other hand, recognition, challenge, and opportunities for personal growth are powerful motivators and will promote high satisfaction and performance. The manager's role is to remove dissatisfiers—that is, to provide hygiene factors sufficient to meet basic needs—and then to use motivators to meet higher-level needs and propel employees toward greater achievement and satisfaction. The following example describes how managers at Mars Incorporated provide both hygiene factors and motivators.

Recipe for Success } **Mars Incorporated**

When people get a job at Mars Incorporated, they rarely leave. Managers at Mars, the maker of candy such as M&Ms and Snickers and pet food such as Pedigree and Whiskas, try to make sure employees are satisfied with their pay, working conditions, and other hygiene factors, but they also incorporate higher-level motivators.

Compensation at Mars is very good compared to similar companies, and many employees get bonuses from 10 percent to 100 percent of their salaries if their team performs well. Vending machines dispense free candy all day long, and employees in the pet food division can bring their dogs to work. These elements provide positive hygiene factors, but Mars also provides motivators. People at Mars are often paired with a mentor to learn new skills. Younger employees may serve as mentors for high-level executives, helping them develop social media skills. Development doesn't stop at the factory gates, either. People can take paid time off to volunteer for community activities such as cleaning parks, planting gardens, or assisting at medical clinics. A highly competitive program selects 80 or so people each year to spend up to six weeks working with Mars-related partners (such as growers of cocoa beans) in remote areas of other countries.[28]

12-3d Acquired Needs

The *acquired needs theory*, developed by David McClelland, proposes that certain types of needs are acquired during the individual's lifetime. In other words, people are not born with these needs but may learn them through their life experiences.[29] The three needs most frequently studied are these:

- *Need for achievement.* The desire to accomplish something difficult, attain a high standard of success, master complex tasks, and surpass others
- *Need for affiliation.* The desire to form close personal relationships, avoid conflict, and establish warm friendships
- *Need for power.* The desire to influence or control others, be responsible for others, and have authority over others

Early life experiences typically determine whether people acquire these needs. If children are encouraged to do things for themselves and receive reinforcement, they will acquire a need to achieve. If they are reinforced for forming warm human relationships, they will develop a need for affiliation. If they get satisfaction from controlling others, they will acquire a need for power.

For more than 20 years, McClelland studied human needs and their implications for management. People with a high need for *achievement* are frequently entrepreneurs. People who have a high need for *affiliation* are successful integrators, whose job is to coordinate the work of several departments in an organization. Integrators include brand managers and project managers who must have excellent people skills. A high need for power often is associated with successful attainment of top levels in the organizational hierarchy.[30] For example, McClelland studied managers at AT&T for 16 years and found that those with a high need for power were more likely to follow a path of continued promotion over time. More than half of the employees at the top levels had a high need for power. In contrast, managers with a high need for achievement but a low need for power tended to peak earlier in their careers and at a lower level. The reason is that achievement needs can be met through the task itself, but power needs can be met only by ascending to a level at which a person has power over others.

In summary, content theories focus on people's underlying needs and label those particular needs that motivate behavior. The hierarchy of needs theory, the ERG theory, the two-factor theory, and the acquired needs theory all help managers understand what motivates people. In this way, managers can design work to meet needs and hence elicit appropriate and successful work behaviors.

Visit MindTap for "Self-Assessment: Do You Have a Need for Achievement, Affiliation, or Power?" to learn more about which needs motivate you.

Remember This

- **Content theories** emphasize the needs that motivate people.
- The most well-known content theory is Maslow's **hierarchy of needs theory**, which proposes that people are motivated by five categories of needs—physiological, safety, belongingness, esteem, and self-actualization—that exist in a hierarchical order.
- **ERG theory** is a modification of the needs hierarchy and proposes three categories of needs: existence, relatedness, and growth.
- The **frustration-regression principle** is the idea that failure to meet a higher-order need may cause a regression to an already satisfied lower-order need; thus, people may move down as well as up the needs hierarchy.
- Giving people more control over their work schedules and opportunities to contribute ideas are two ways that managers meet people's higher-level needs.

- At J. A. Counter, employees can come and go as they please without telling anyone where they are going or why, as long as they get their jobs done.
- One element of Herzberg's two-factor theory, **hygiene factors**, focuses on lower-level needs and involves the presence or absence of job dissatisfiers, including working conditions, pay, and company policies.
- Herzberg's second factor, **motivators**, influences job satisfaction based on fulfilling higher-level needs such as achievement, recognition, responsibility, and opportunities for personal growth.
- The *acquired needs theory* proposes that certain types of needs, including the need for achievement, for affiliation, and for power, are acquired during an individual's lifetime of experiences.

12-4 Process Perspectives on Motivation

Process theories explain how people select behavioral actions to meet their needs and determine whether their choices were successful. Important perspectives in this area include goal setting, equity theory, and expectancy theory.

12-4a Goal Setting

Recall from Chapter 5 our discussion of the importance and purposes of goals. Numerous studies have shown that specific, challenging targets significantly enhance people's motivation and performance levels.[31] You have probably noticed in your own life that you are more motivated when you have a specific goal, such as making an A on a final exam, losing 10 pounds before spring break, or earning enough money during the summer to buy a used car.

Green Power

Making Sustainability Goals Count A lot of companies say they want to reduce their impact on the environment. Some, such as Intel, make sure they actually do. Intel was one of the earliest companies to tie sustainability goals directly to management's financial incentives. The company began incorporating environment-related goals into both its corporate vision and its compensation programs in 2008. Each year, managers determine a different environmental focus and employees receive bonuses for meeting specific targets. Intel's employee

grant program, Sustainability in Action, provides money for innovative employee projects that promote sustainability within the company and in the local communities where Intel operates. Examples of Sustainability in Action projects include using roofs to grow algae for biofuel in Arizona and implementing new water purification technologies in India.

SOURCE: Ellen Weinreg, "Motivating Employees, With or Without Money," GreenBiz.com, August 21, 2013, https://www.greenbiz.com/blog/2013/08/21/motivating-employees-and-without-money (accessed May 11, 2016).

Goal-setting theory, described by Edwin Locke and Gary Latham, proposes that managers can increase motivation and enhance performance by setting specific, challenging goals, and then helping people track their progress toward goal achievement by providing timely feedback. Exhibit 12.5 illustrates key components of goal-setting theory.[32]

- *Goal specificity* refers to the degree to which goals are concrete and unambiguous. Specific goals, such as "Visit one new customer each day" or "Sell $1,000 worth of merchandise a week," are more motivating than vague goals, such as "Keep in touch with new customers" or "Increase merchandise sales." A lack of clear, specific goals is cited as a major cause of the failure of pay-for-performance incentive plans in many organizations.[33] Vague goals can be frustrating for employees.

Exhibit 12.5 Criteria for Motivational Goals

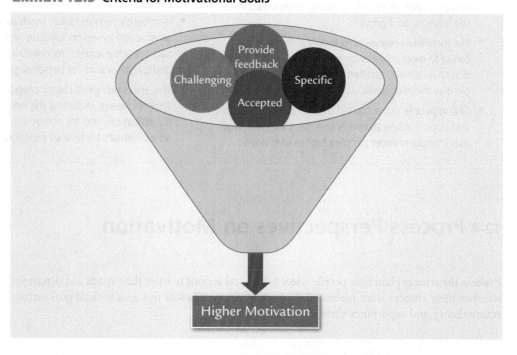

Challenging · Provide feedback · Specific · Accepted → Higher Motivation

- In terms of *goal difficulty*, hard goals are more motivating than easy ones. Easy goals provide little challenge for employees and don't require them to increase their output. Highly ambitious but achievable goals ask people to stretch their abilities and provide a basis for greater feelings of accomplishment and personal effectiveness. A study in Germany found that, over a three-year period, only employees who perceived their goals as difficult reported increases in positive emotions and feelings of job satisfaction and success.[34]
- *Goal acceptance* means that employees have to "buy into" the goals and be committed to them. Having people participate in setting goals is a good way to increase acceptance and commitment.
- Finally, the component of *feedback* means that people get information about how well they are doing in progressing toward goal achievement. It is important for managers to provide performance feedback on a regular, ongoing basis. However, self-feedback, by which people are able to monitor their own progress toward a goal, has been found to be an even stronger motivator than external feedback.[35]

Why does goal setting increase motivation? For one thing, it enables people to focus their energies in the right direction. People know what to work toward so they can direct their efforts toward the most important activities to accomplish the goals. Goals also energize behavior because people feel compelled to develop plans and strategies that keep them focused on achieving the targets. Specific, difficult goals provide a challenge and encourage people to put forth high levels of effort. In addition, when goals are achieved, pride and satisfaction increase, contributing to higher motivation and morale.[36] The motivational power of goal setting is illustrated by something that occurred when Advanced Circuits was having trouble with frequent stops and restarts on its production line, which was costing the company about $50,000 a month. Former CEO Ron Huston came up with a plan. He bought a junk car, placed it in the parking lot, and told employees they could take a sledgehammer to the car every day the production line didn't have a restart. Employees set a goal of flattening the car in 90 days. Everybody had fun, and they met the 90-day goal by solving production-line problems, which was the whole point of the exercise for Huston. He realized how motivating it could be for people to have a clear, specific goal, especially if achieving it was fun. He began setting goals for other aspects of the business and rewarding people when the goals were met.[37]

> "If you look at the modern workplace, I would say it's one of the most feedback-deprived places in American civilization."
> —DANIEL PINK, JOURNALIST AND AUTHOR OF *DRIVE: THE SURPRISING TRUTH ABOUT WHAT MOTIVATES US*

12-4b Equity Theory

Equity theory focuses on individuals' perceptions of how fairly they are treated compared with others. Developed by J. Stacy Adams, equity theory proposes that people are motivated to seek social equity in the rewards they receive for performance.[38]

According to equity theory, if people perceive their compensation as equal to what others receive for similar contributions, they will believe that their treatment is fair and equitable. People evaluate equity by a ratio of inputs to outcomes. Inputs to a job include education, experience, effort, and ability. Outcomes from a job include pay, recognition, benefits, and promotions. The input-to-outcome ratio may be compared to that of another person in the work group or to a perceived group average. A state of **equity** exists whenever the ratio of one person's outcomes to inputs equals the ratio of another's outcomes to inputs.

Inequity occurs when the input-to-outcome ratios are out of balance, such as when a new, inexperienced employee receives the same salary as a person with a high level of education or experience. Consider what happened when the founder and CEO of Gravity Payments increased the minimum wage at his company.

When Dan Price cut his own salary and announced that every employee at Gravity Payments, even the newly hired clerk or the lowest paid assistant, would earn at least $70,000 a year, he thought people would be happier and more motivated. Almost overnight, Price became a hero, touted in the media as the "world's nicest boss" and portrayed as a daring entrepreneur tackling the growing problem of income inequality. At first, employees at the Seattle-based credit card processing company celebrated. After all, who doesn't like a big pay raise?

HOT TOPIC

Then, the problems started. The toughest one for Price was that he started losing some of his best people. A Web developer quit, even though he had gotten a $9,000 raise. Why? He felt like he put 110 percent into his job and didn't like the fact that "people who were just clocking in and out were making the same as me." The financial manager also resigned, believing that the biggest raises were going to "the people with the least skills," rather than rewarding those who were making the greatest contribution. Even a couple of newly hired employees were unhappy, despite the fact that they were making a lot of money for an entry-level job. "Am I doing my job well enough to deserve this?" one asked. "I didn't earn it."[39]

The difficulties Dan Price has experienced at Gravity Payments show that motivation can falter if people feel that they aren't being treated fairly. Some long-term experienced employees lost their motivation when they saw that newly hired people were earning the same as they were. Others believed they put in more effort and should be rewarded for it rather than earning the same as people they believed weren't making similar contributions. The example also supports the idea that perceived inequity can occur in the other direction when people feel they are making too much money. Scientific studies indicate that the human brain seems programmed to dislike inequity, even when we benefit from it. Moreover, people get less satisfaction from money they receive without having to earn it than they do from money they work to receive.[40] Perceived inequity creates tensions within individuals that motivate them to bring equity into balance.[41]

The most common methods for reducing a perceived inequity are these:

Source: Berman Photos

Concept Connection

Dan Price, founder and CEO of Gravity Payments, bumped up the national debate over a $15 minimum wage when he announced that everyone at his payment processing company would make at least $70,000 a year. To help cover the cost, Price slashed his own $1.1 million annual salary to $70,000. Most employees celebrated, but some valued employees quit because of **perceived inequity**, believing that the pay increases rewarded some of the weakest performers and diminished their own value and contributions to the company.

- **Change work effort.** A person may choose to increase or decrease his or her inputs to the organization. Individuals who believe that they are underpaid may reduce their level of effort or increase their absenteeism. Overpaid people may increase their effort on the job.
- **Change outcomes.** A person may change his or her outcomes. An underpaid person may request a salary increase or a bigger office. A union may try to improve wages and working conditions to be consistent with a comparable union whose members make more money.
- **Change perceptions.** Research suggests that people may change perceptions of equity if they are unable to change inputs or outcomes. They may increase the status attached to their jobs artificially or distort others' perceived rewards to bring equity into balance.
- **Leave the job.** People who feel inequitably treated may decide to leave their jobs rather than suffer the inequity of being underpaid or overpaid. In their new jobs, they expect to find a more favorable balance of rewards.

The implication of equity theory for managers is that employees indeed evaluate the perceived equity of their rewards compared to the rewards of others. Many big law firms are reducing the compensation of 10 to 30 percent of their partners each year in order to free up money to hire and reward "star performers," rejecting the traditional practice of paying partners relatively similar amounts. The change fits with the strategy of rewarding people who generate more business, but it is having a damaging effect on the morale and motivation of other partners, who perceive the new compensation scheme as inequitable.[42] Inequitable pay puts pressure on employees that is sometimes almost too great to bear. They attempt to change their work habits, try to change the system, or leave the job.[43]

Equity theory explains why Hostess Brands, Inc. employees got riled up when the failing company paid its executives high bonuses, as shown in this chapter's "Half-Baked Management."

12-4c Expectancy Theory

Expectancy theory suggests that motivation depends on individuals' expectations about their ability to perform tasks and receive desired rewards. Expectancy theory is associated with the work of Victor Vroom, although a number of scholars have made contributions in this area.[44]

Expectancy theory is concerned not with identifying types of needs but with the thinking process that individuals use to achieve rewards. For example, one interesting study of expectancy theory looked at patrol officer drug arrests in the midwestern United States. The research found that officers who produced the most drug arrests were more likely to have perceived that such arrests were a management priority and were rewarded by their organization, received specialized training to hone their skills related to drug interdiction, and perceived that they had sufficient time and resources to investigate suspected drug activity properly.[45] Walmart is using expectancy theory by tying some senior executive compensation to an overhaul of its corporate compliance program (executives' compliance with antibribery laws and other policies for international behavior). By tying rewards directly to achieving specific compliance goals, top leaders are demonstrating that the compliance overhaul is a priority.[46]

Patti McConville/Alamy Stock Photo

Concept Connection

According to **expectancy theory**, a reward that effectively motivates one individual doesn't necessarily work for another. So how can employers create attractive rewards that motivate all their employees, especially when economic conditions necessitate cuts in salary and benefits budgets? Some managers are turning to gift cards. One advantage is that they can be issued in virtually any denomination. But even more important, many gift cards allow the recipient to tailor a reward to his or her individual preference. A person can choose to splurge on some small luxury or use the card for essentials such as groceries.

Half-Baked Management — Twinkies

Twinkies took a dive in 2012 when its manufacturer, Hostess Brands, Inc., went out of business. Evidently executives thought they better give themselves raises before they went in to Chapter 11, skirting federal law that prohibits bonuses during bankruptcy. The executives didn't seem to be thinking about the impact this would have on the workforce. Union representatives cried foul and led a strike. Poisoned relationships between management and labor didn't help the ailing company, which was liquidated in December 2012. More than 18,000 people lost their jobs. And the world was left—at least for the time being—Twinkie-less. That is, until turnaround billionaire—once the owner of Pabst Brewing Co.—bought Hostess and reintroduced Twinkies to an appreciative world in 2013, calling it "The sweetest comeback in the history of ever." Hostess Brands did become sweeter in 2018, when they gave employees a year's worth (whatever that means) of Twinkies and a $1,250 bonus after the 2018 tax reform bill.

SOURCE: Hostess Brands, Inc., *Food Weekly News* (February 15, 2018): 122; Darrell Hofheinz, "Billionaire Pays $7.4 Million for Midtown House—The Buyer, C. Dean Metropoulos Saved Twinkie Last Year," *Palm Beach Daily News*, December 20, 2014, A1.

Expectancy theory is based on the relationship among the individual's *effort*, the individual's *performance*, and the desirability of *outcomes* associated with high performance. These elements and the relationships among them are illustrated in Exhibit 12.6. The keys to expectancy theory are the expectancies for the relationships among effort, performance, and the value of the outcomes to the individual.

E → P expectancy involves determining whether putting effort into a task will lead to high performance. For this expectancy to be high, the individual must have the ability, previous experience, and necessary equipment, tools, and opportunity to perform. Let's consider a simple sales example. If Paloma, a salesperson at the Diamond Gift Shop, believes that increased selling effort will lead to higher personal sales, we can say that she has a high E → P expectancy. However, if Paloma believes that she has neither the ability nor the opportunity to achieve high performance, the expectancy will be low, and so will be her motivation.

P → O expectancy involves determining whether successful performance will lead to the desired outcome or reward. If the P → O expectancy is high, the individual will be more highly motivated. If the expectancy is that high performance will not produce the desired outcome, motivation will be lower. If Paloma believes that higher personal sales will lead to a pay increase, we can say that she has a high P → O expectancy. She might be aware that raises are coming up for consideration and talk with her supervisor or other employees to see whether increased sales will help her earn a better raise. If not, she will be less motivated to work hard.

Valence is the value of outcomes, or attraction to outcomes, for the individual. If the outcomes that are available from great effort and good performance are not valued by employees, motivation will be low. Likewise, if outcomes have a high value, motivation will be higher. If Paloma places a high value on the pay raise, valence is high, and she will have a high motivational force. On the other hand, if the money has low valence for Paloma, the overall motivational force will be low. For an employee to be highly motivated, all three factors in the expectancy model must be high.[47]

Expectancy theory attempts not to define specific types of needs or rewards but only to establish that they exist and may be different for every individual. One employee might want to be promoted to a position of increased responsibility, and another might have high valence for good relationships with peers. Consequently, the first person will be motivated to work hard for a promotion and the second for the opportunity of a team position that will keep him or her associated with a group. Studies substantiate the idea that rewards need to be individualized to be motivating. A recent finding from the U.S. Department of Labor shows that the top reason for people leaving their jobs is that they "don't feel appreciated." Yet Gallup's analysis of 10,000 work groups in 30 industries found that making people feel appreciated depends on finding the right kind of reward for each individual. Some people prefer tangible rewards such as bonuses, gifts, or luxury trips, while others place high value on words of appreciation and recognition. In addition, some want public recognition, while others prefer to be quietly praised by someone they admire and respect.[48]

Exhibit 12.6 Major Elements of Expectancy Theory

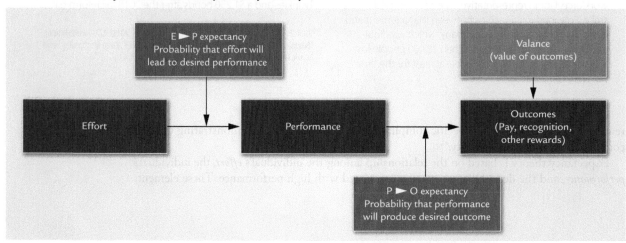

Remember This

- **Process theories**, including goal-setting theory, equity theory, and expectancy theory, explain how people select behaviors with which to meet their needs and determine whether their choices were successful.
- **Goal-setting theory** proposes that specific, challenging goals increase motivation and performance when the goals are accepted by subordinates and these subordinates receive feedback to indicate their progress toward goal achievement.
- **Equity theory** focuses on individuals' perceptions of how fairly they are treated relative to others.
- A situation of **equity** exists when the ratio of one person's outcomes to inputs equals that of another's.
- When Dan Price increased the minimum wage at Gravity Payments to $70,000 a year, some valuable employees left their jobs because they felt that the new pay system was inequitable.
- **Expectancy theory** proposes that motivation depends on individuals' expectations about their ability to perform tasks and receive desired rewards.
- A person's **E → P expectancy** is the expectancy that putting effort into a given task will lead to high performance.
- **P → O expectancy** is the expectancy that high performance of a task will lead to the desired outcome.
- **Valence** is the value of outcomes (rewards) to the individual.

12-5 Reinforcement Perspective on Motivation

The reinforcement approach to employee motivation sidesteps the issues of employee needs and thinking processes described in the content and process theories. **Reinforcement theory** simply looks at the relationship between behavior and its consequences. It focuses on changing or modifying employees' on-the-job behavior through the appropriate use of immediate rewards and punishments.

12-5a Direct Reinforcement

Behavior modification is the name given to the set of techniques by which reinforcement theory is used to modify human behavior.[49] The basic assumption underlying behavior modification is the **law of effect**, which states that behavior that is positively reinforced tends to be repeated, and behavior that is not reinforced tends not to be repeated. **Reinforcement** is defined as anything that causes a certain behavior to be repeated or inhibited. For example, Whole Foods gives employees a 30 percent discount on store purchases if they meet certain criteria for healthy habits, such as maintaining low cholesterol and blood pressure or quitting smoking. With health insurance costs on the rise, many companies are searching for ways to reinforce behaviors that create healthier employees.[50] The four reinforcement tools are positive reinforcement, avoidance learning, punishment, and extinction, as summarized in Exhibit 12.7 and described next:

- **Positive reinforcement** is the administration of a pleasant and rewarding consequence following a desired behavior. Research shows that positive reinforcement does help motivate desired behaviors. Moreover, nonfinancial reinforcements such as positive feedback, social recognition, and attention are just as effective as financial incentives.[51] As mentioned earlier, expressions of appreciation have been found to be highly effective motivators. In one recent study, researchers asked professionals to advise students about cover letters they were using to apply for jobs. After receiving the feedback, the students then sent notes requesting help with a second letter. About 32 percent of people agreed to help with a second letter, but when the students added a line to their notes saying "Thank you so much! I am really grateful," the number of people agreeing to help a second time increased to 66 percent. Similarly, a recent survey of employees in the United States found that 80 percent say receiving gratitude makes them more motivated to work harder.[52] Manager attention, appreciation, and feedback provide a psychological boost to motivation that has nothing to do with financial rewards.

Exhibit 12.7 Changing Behavior with Reinforcement

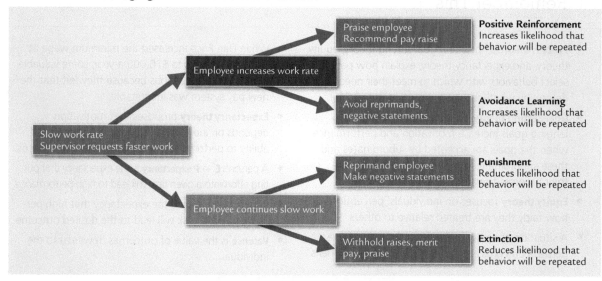

SOURCE: Based on Richard L. Daft and Richard M. Steers, *Organizations: A Micro/Macro Approach* (Glenview, IL: Scott Foresman, 1986), p. 109.

- **Avoidance learning** is the removal of an unpleasant consequence once a behavior is improved, thereby encouraging and strengthening the desired behavior. Avoidance learning is sometimes called *negative reinforcement*. The idea is that people will change a specific behavior to avoid the undesired result that the behavior provokes. As a simple example, a supervisor who constantly reminds or nags an employee who is goofing off on the factory floor and stops the nagging when the employee stops goofing off is applying avoidance learning.
- **Punishment** is the imposition of unpleasant outcomes on an employee. Punishment typically occurs following undesirable behavior. An example of punishment is the board of JPMorgan Chase cutting CEO Jamie Dimon's bonus by 50 percent because of oversight failures that led to a multibillion-dollar trading loss related to the so-called London Whale fiasco, described in Chapter 6.[53] The use of punishment in organizations is controversial and often criticized because it fails to indicate the correct behavior. However, almost all managers report that they find it necessary to occasionally impose forms of punishment ranging from verbal reprimands to employee suspensions or firings.[54]

Concept Connection

The Seattle Seahawks and their "Legion of Boom" have consistently led the NFL in numerous defensive categories and ranked first in fewest points allowed for four straight years. The Seahawks defensive backs have an unofficial **punishment** system that fines players $100 for every time they drop an interception, miss a tackle, or otherwise commit an error or botch a play during a game. "You drop an interception, you do something stupid, you say something crazy—that's going to cost you," said cornerback DeShawn Shead. "It's not a nice feeling."

- **Extinction** is the withholding of a positive reward. Whereas with punishment, the supervisor imposes an unpleasant outcome such as a reprimand, extinction involves withholding praise or other positive outcomes. With extinction, undesirable behavior is essentially ignored. The idea is that behavior that is not positively reinforced will gradually disappear. A *New York Times* reporter wrote a humorous article about how she learned to stop nagging and instead use reinforcement theory to shape her husband's behavior after studying how professionals train animals.[55] When her husband did something she liked, such as throw a dirty shirt in the hamper, she would use *positive reinforcement*, thanking him or giving him a hug and a kiss. Undesirable behaviors, such as throwing dirty clothes on the floor, on the other hand, were simply ignored, applying the principle of *extinction*.

12-5b Social Learning Theory

Social learning theory is related to the reinforcement perspective, but it proposes that an individual's motivation can result not just from direct experience of rewards and punishments, but also from the person's observations of other people's behavior.[56]

Vicarious learning, or *observational learning*, occurs when an individual sees others perform certain behaviors and get rewarded for them. Young children often learn to behave well in school because they see that well-behaved children get more positive attention from the teacher, for example. Managers can enhance an individual's motivation to perform desired behaviors by ensuring that the individual (1) has a chance to observe the desirable behaviors, (2) accurately perceives the behaviors, (3) remembers the behaviors, (4) has the necessary skills to perform the behaviors, and (5) sees that the behaviors are rewarded by the organization.[57] Recall the discussion from Chapter 9 of on-the-job training. Managers typically pair a new employee with someone who models the type of behavior that the organization wants. Managers also promote social learning by highlighting top performers' strengths and grooming them as examples for others.[58] A key to vicarious motivation, though, is to make sure that the learner knows that the desired behaviors are rewarded.

Remember This

- **Reinforcement theory** is based on the relationship between a given behavior and its consequences.
- **Behavior modification** refers to the set of techniques by which reinforcement theory is used to modify human behavior.
- The **law of effect** asserts that positively reinforced behavior tends to be repeated, and unreinforced or negatively reinforced behavior tends to be inhibited.
- **Reinforcement** is anything that causes a certain behavior to be repeated or inhibited.
- **Positive reinforcement** is the administration of a pleasant and rewarding consequence following a desired behavior.
- Managers apply **avoidance learning**, also called *negative reinforcement*, when they remove an unpleasant consequence once a behavior is improved.

- **Punishment** refers to the imposition of an unpleasant outcome following an undesirable behavior.
- The Seattle Seahawks defensive backs unofficially use punishment by fining players $100 for every time they commit an error or botch a play during a game.
- **Extinction** refers to withholding positive rewards and essentially ignoring undesirable behavior.
- **Social learning theory** proposes that an individual's motivation can result not just from direct experience of rewards and punishments, but also from thoughts, beliefs, and observations of other people's behavior.
- **Vicarious learning** occurs when an individual sees others perform certain behaviors and get rewarded for them.

12-6 Job Design for Motivation

A *job* in an organization is a unit of work that a single employee is responsible for performing. A job could include writing tickets for parking violators in New York City, performing magnetic resonance imaging (MRI) at Salt Lake Regional Medical Center, or doing long-range planning for Netflix. Jobs are important considerations for motivation because performing their components may provide rewards that meet employees' needs. Managers need to know what aspects of a job provide motivation as well as how to compensate for routine tasks that have little inherent satisfaction. **Job design** is the application of motivational theories to the structure of work for improving productivity and satisfaction.

12-6a Job Enrichment

Recall from Chapter 1 the principles of scientific management in which tasks are designed to be simple, repetitive, and standardized. This contributes to efficiency, but simplified jobs aren't typically effective as a motivational technique because they can be boring and routine. Thus, managers in many companies are redesigning simplified jobs into jobs that provide greater variety and satisfaction. One technique, called *job rotation*, is to move employees systematically from one job to another to provide variety and stimulation. Another approach is to combine a series of small tasks into one new, broader job so that people perform a variety of activities, which is referred to as *job enlargement*.

Overall, the trend is toward **job enrichment**, which means incorporating high-level motivators into the work, including responsibility, recognition, and opportunities for growth, learning, and achievement. In an enriched job, employees have control over the resources necessary for performing tasks, make decisions on how to do the work, experience personal growth, and set their own work pace. Research shows that when jobs are designed to be controlled more by employees than by managers, people typically feel a greater sense of involvement, commitment, and motivation, which in turn contributes to higher morale, lower turnover, and stronger organizational performance.[59]

12-6b Job Characteristics Model

One significant approach to job design is the job characteristics model developed by Richard Hackman and Greg Oldham.[60] Their research concerned **work redesign**, which is defined as altering jobs to increase both the quality of employees' work experience and their productivity. Hackman and Oldham's research into the design of hundreds of jobs yielded the **job characteristics model**, which is illustrated in Exhibit 12.8. The model consists of three major parts: core job dimensions, critical psychological states, and employee growth-need strength.

Core Job Dimensions Hackman and Oldham identified five dimensions that determine a job's motivational potential:

- *Skill variety.* This is the number of diverse activities that compose a job and the number of skills used to perform it. A routine, repetitious assembly-line job is low in variety, whereas an applied research position that involves working on new problems every day is high in variety.
- *Task identity.* This is the degree to which an employee performs a total job with a recognizable beginning and ending. A chef who prepares an entire meal has more task identity than a worker on a cafeteria line who ladles mashed potatoes.
- *Task significance.* This is the degree to which the job is perceived as important and having an impact on the company or consumers. People who distribute penicillin and other medical supplies during times of emergencies would feel that they have significant jobs.

Exhibit 12.8 The Job Characteristics Model

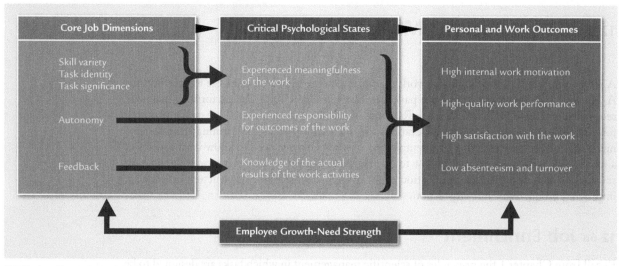

SOURCE: Adapted from J. Richard Hackman and G. R. Oldham, "Motivation Through the Design of Work: Test of a Theory," *Organizational Behavior and Human Performance* 16 (1976): 256.

Roya Shadravan and Kristy Lam had high-powered and high-paying jobs that had some impact, but the company they started together, Mulan Dumplings, gives them a greater feeling of impact, as well as autonomy, next on this list.

- *Autonomy.* This is the degree to which the worker has freedom, discretion, and self-determination in planning and carrying out tasks. A house painter can determine how to paint the house; a paint sprayer on an assembly line has little autonomy.
- *Feedback.* This is the extent to which doing the job provides feedback to the employee about his or her performance. Jobs vary in their ability to let workers see the outcomes of their efforts. A football coach knows whether the team won or lost, but a basic research scientist may have to wait years to learn whether his or her research project was successful.

The job characteristics model says that the more these five core characteristics can be designed into the job, the more the employees will be motivated and the higher will be the employees' performance, quality of work, and satisfaction.

Critical Psychological States   The job characteristics model posits that core job dimensions are more rewarding when individuals experience three psychological states in response to job design. In Exhibit 12.8, skill variety, task identity, and task significance tend to influence the employee's psychological state of *experienced meaningfulness of work.* The work itself is satisfying and provides intrinsic rewards for the worker. The job characteristic of autonomy influences the worker's *experienced responsibility.* The job characteristic of feedback provides the worker with

Recipe for Success } **Mulan Dumplings**

Roya Shadravan was a CNN journalist who worked in war zones. Kristy Lam graduated from London School of Economics and was a successful commodities trader. Yet they wanted more from life. Now they run a food truck in Northern Virginia.

The change was stimulated by Shadravan's brain tumor in May 2016. Surgery removed 99 percent of the tumor, but she was encouraged to eat healthy and as close to vegan as she could, adding items such as eggs, only if they were cage-free. She consulted with her good friend Lam, whom she had met in a gym in Hong Kong, where they both had worked years before. Lam had attended culinary school before she went in to finance.

Lam and Shadravan came up with a lot of really good recipes, but they realized how difficult it would be for most people to prepare high-quality, organic, and yummy foods. Working together gathering and preparing recipes, they both realized they weren't really satisfied in their high-flying careers. So they took huge risks and quit to start their own business, making and selling food.

Lam has the culinary background and is the chef of the two partners. Her dream was to create a selection of dumplings, which she grew up with and which are a kind of comfort food for Chinese and something Americans have also shown a taste for, so the partners called it "Mulan Dumplings." One thing they would not compromise was good-quality ingredients, organic and locally sourced when possible.

Lam and Shadravan thought why not operate a food truck, which has far less investment involved than opening a restaurant. So they sent a question out on social media. Who knew someone with a food truck in the area? Turns out a friend's cousin did, and they shadowed him for a week. Lam and Shadravan both learned a lot. In the following weeks, they staked out other food trucks to see when and where they got business and to figure out why some trucks did better than others.

In May 2017, they bought a truck and were open by June. Business started off briskly because they went to a new location every day. They always parked in front of big office buildings, letting the businesses know ahead of time when they'd be there and what the menu was. In addition, Instagram helped, and they really worked it. In the first two months, they had 100 followers, and less than a year later they had 1,000.

Both Lam and Shadravan had engaging and financially successful careers, living in China, Hong Kong, and other places. They were women on the move, women who were going somewhere. Turns out where they wanted to go was the food truck. "I never thought it would be so gratifying," says Shadravan. "Selling food, making people happy, even being cashier, it brings so much satisfaction."

SOURCE: Roya Shadravan, personal communication, March 2018.

knowledge of actual results. The employee thus knows how he or she is doing and can change work performance to increase desired outcomes.

Personal and Work Outcomes   The impact of the five job characteristics on the psychological states of experienced meaningfulness, responsibility, and knowledge of actual results leads to the personal and work outcomes of high work motivation, high work performance, high satisfaction, and low absenteeism and turnover.

Employee Growth-Need Strength   The final component of the job characteristics model is called *employee growth-need strength*, which means that people have different needs for growth and development. If a person wants to satisfy low-level needs, such as safety and belongingness, the job characteristics model has less effect. When a person has a high need for growth and development, including the desire for personal challenge, achievement, and challenging work, the model is especially effective. People with a high need to grow and expand their abilities respond favorably to the application of the model and to improvements in core job dimensions.

One interesting finding concerns the cross-cultural differences in the impact of job characteristics. Intrinsic factors such as autonomy, challenge, achievement, and recognition can be highly motivating in countries such as the United States. However, they may contribute little to motivation and satisfaction in a country such as Nigeria and might even lead to *demotivation*. A recent study indicates that the link between intrinsic characteristics and job motivation and satisfaction is weaker in economically disadvantaged countries with poor governmental social welfare systems, as well as in countries that value high power distance, as defined in Chapter 3.[61] Thus, the job characteristics model would be expected to be less effective in these countries.

Remember This

- Jobs are an important consideration for motivation because performing their components may provide intrinsic rewards that meet employees' needs.
- **Job design** refers to applying motivational theories to the structure of work to improve motivation, productivity, and satisfaction.
- Most companies are moving away from simplified jobs and are using job rotation, job enlargement, and job enrichment to provide employees with greater variety, stimulation, and satisfaction.

- **Job enrichment** refers to incorporating high-level motivators, such as achievement, recognition, and opportunities for growth, into the work.
- **Work redesign** means altering jobs to increase both the quality of employees' work experience and their productivity.
- The **job characteristics model** is a model of job design that considers core job dimensions, individuals' critical psychological states, and employee growth-need strength.

12-7 Innovative Ideas for Motivating

Organizations are increasingly using various types of incentive compensation as a way to motivate employees to higher levels of performance. Lump-sum bonuses, for example, reward employees with a one-time cash payment based on performance. When Elise Lelon, owner of the leadership consulting firm The You Business, couldn't give pay raises because of budget pressures, she created a generous lump-sum bonus program tied to the amount of revenue employees generated for the firm. "It gets their juices flowing and it helps the business grow," Lelon says.[62] Other popular methods of incentive pay include an employee stock ownership plan (ESOP), which gives employees part ownership of the company, enabling them to share in improved profits; gain sharing, which rewards all managers and employees in a business unit when predetermined performance targets are met; and pay for performance, which rewards individual employees in proportion to their performance contributions. Performance pay may also be called *merit pay*. Hamdi Ulukayahe, founder and CEO of yogurt company Chobani, recently created an ESOP that gave his 2,000 employees shares worth about 10 percent of the company. With Chobani valued at more than $3 billion, the average payout if Chobani goes public or is bought by another company would be around $150,000, and some long-time employees would become millionaires. "It's better than a bonus or a raise," said Rich Lake, one of the first employees at the company. "It's the best thing because you're getting a piece of this thing you helped build."[63]

Variable compensation and forms of "at risk" pay such as bonus plans are key motivational tools that are becoming more common than fixed salaries at many companies. However, unless they are carefully designed, incentive plans can backfire, as evidenced by problems in the mortgage and finance industries, where some people resorted to overly aggressive and even unethical behavior to earn huge bonuses. Numerous companies, including financial firms such as Morgan Stanley, Credit Suisse, and Goldman Sachs, as well as other organizations such as Home Depot, Verizon, and Aflac, have revised compensation plans to make sure incentives reward the desired behaviors.[64]

Incentive programs can be effective if they are used appropriately and combined with motivational ideas that also provide people with intrinsic rewards and meet higher-level needs. The most effective motivational programs typically involve much more than money or other extrinsic rewards in order to create an environment in which people thrive. Three important approaches are empowerment, engagement, and making progress, as described in the following sections.

12-7a Empowering People to Meet Higher Needs

One significant way that managers can meet higher motivational needs is to shift power down from the top of the organization and share it with employees to enable them to achieve goals. **Empowerment** is power sharing, the delegation of power and authority to subordinates in an organization.[65] Increasing employee power heightens motivation for task accomplishment because people improve their own effectiveness, choosing how to do a task and using their creativity.[66] At Ritz-Carlton hotels, employees have up to $1,000 to use at their discretion to create a great customer experience. When homes in the area near the Ritz in Laguna Niguel, California, were evacuated due to risk of fires, the hotel made an exception to its "no pets" rule. One employee anticipated the need for pet food and drove to the nearest grocery for dog and cat food, making life a little easier for harried guests who were temporarily homeless.[67] Empowering employees involves giving them four elements that enable them to act more freely to accomplish their jobs: information, knowledge, power, and rewards.[68]

1. *Employees receive information about company performance.* In companies where employees are fully empowered, all employees have access to all financial and operational information.

2. *Employees have knowledge and skills to contribute to company goals.* Companies use training programs and other development tools to help people acquire the knowledge and skills that they need to contribute to organizational performance.

3. *Employees have the power to make substantive decisions.* Empowered employees have the authority to influence work procedures and organizational performance directly, such as through quality circles or self-directed work teams.

4. *Employees are rewarded based on company performance.* Organizations that empower workers often reward them based on the results shown in the company's bottom line. Organizations may also use other motivational compensation programs that tie employee efforts to company performance.

The following example from Hilcorp Energy illustrates the four elements of empowerment.

At companies such as Hilcorp Energy, empowerment means giving employees almost complete freedom and power to make decisions and exercise initiative and imagination. However, organizations empower workers to varying degrees, from a situation where managers encourage employee ideas but retain final authority for decisions to a condition of full empowerment such as that at Hilcorp. Research shows that empowerment typically increases employee satisfaction, motivation, and productivity.[69]

"I think a lot of times it's not money that's the primary motivation factor; it's the passion for your job and the professional and personal satisfaction that you get out of doing what you do that motivates you."
—MARTIN YAN, CHINESE CHEF, AUTHOR, AND HOST OF COOKING SHOWS, INCLUDING *YAN CAN COOK* AND *MARTIN YAN'S CHINA*

Sunny Side Up ⟩ **Hilcorp Energy**

Hilcorp Energy, based in Houston, Texas, is one of the nation's largest private producers of onshore crude oil and natural gas. But Hilcorp is different from most energy companies. Hilcorp takes over holes abandoned by the big energy companies—and produces millions of barrels of oil and gas from them each year.

Hilcorp is different from most other energy companies in its approach to managing people, too. Managers attribute the company's success to the people on the front lines. All associates have access to all financial and operating information. Because managers put decision-making power in the hands of people on the front lines, those people need to have full information to make good choices.

"You want to know how we're doing? How your slice of the pie is performing? We share the good news and the bad," said a senior financial analyst. "We owe that to every employee whose work generates the numbers we report."

Associates at Hilcorp are always interested in how well the company is doing because they are rewarded based on company performance. In 2015, Hilcorp gave every employee a $100,000 bonus after they met a performance goal of increasing output to 150,000 barrels a day. At Hilcorp, employees truly do feel like owners. "Since we pull together, not competing against each other, and we all have skin in the game, it's amazing what we can accomplish," said founder Jeff Hildebrand.[70]

12-7b Giving Meaning to Work Through Engagement

Employee **engagement** means that people enjoy their jobs and are satisfied with their work conditions, contribute enthusiastically to meeting team and organizational goals, and feel a sense of belonging and commitment to the organization. Surveys by Gallup show that employee engagement in the United States has been steadily increasing since 2013, yet 49.5 percent of employees surveyed in early 2016 were identified as not engaged and 12.5 percent were actively *disengaged*.[71] Fully engaged employees care deeply about the organization and actively seek ways to serve the mission.[72] Active disengagement means that people are actively undermining their organization's success.

Managers can improve engagement by providing employees with three key elements: a sense of meaningfulness, a sense of connection, and a sense of growth.[73] When managers organize the workplace in such a way as to create these feelings, employee engagement grows, leading to high motivation and high organizational performance.

- *People feel that they are working toward something important.* When employees have a chance to accomplish something that provides real value, they feel a sense of *meaningfulness*. Good managers help people understand the purpose of their work, which contributes to feelings of pride and dignity. Research by Yale School of Management's Amy Wrzesniewski found that people who connect their work to a higher purpose are more satisfied with their jobs, tend to work longer hours, and are absent from work less often. When professional services firm KPMG surveyed employees, the company found that employees whose managers talked about KPMG's positive impact on society were 42.4 percent more likely to describe the firm as a great place to work.[74]
- *People feel connected to the company, to one another, and to their managers.* In a survey asking people what factors contribute to their engagement, 79 percent of people said that "good relationships with coworkers" drove engagement to a high or very high extent. Even more (91 percent) pointed to good relationships with their immediate supervisor as highly important.[75] The behavior of managers makes the biggest difference in whether or not people feel engaged at work.[76] Managers promote engagement when they listen to employees, genuinely care about their concerns, and help them develop positive relationships with colleagues.
- *People have the chance to learn, grow, and advance.* To be fully engaged, people need to feel not only that they are competent to handle what is asked of them but also that they have the chance to learn and expand their potential. Good managers help employees understand their own unique set of talents, skills, interests, attitudes, and needs;

put people in jobs where they can make their best contribution and receive intrinsic rewards every day; and make sure people have what they need to perform well. In addition, they give people the chance to work on challenging projects, offer high-quality training and learning programs, and provide opportunities for advancement within the organization.

Studies have identified a correlation between high levels of employee engagement and company performance, including less turnover, greater profitability, and stronger employee and customer loyalty.[77] Exhibit 12.9 shows a variety of factors that managers can evaluate to see how they are doing in creating an environment that promotes employee engagement.

Managers can use strategies to facilitate engagement and improve performance. Mary Laschinger, currently CEO of Veritiv Corporation, says one of the most important lessons she learned early in her management career was that she needed to engage people. When Laschinger became general manager of a division for International Paper, she thought she had "finally made it," but then she looked around and saw that "we weren't doing very well." Laschinger says she felt very alone for a while until she realized that she couldn't do anything by herself and that she had to engage people throughout the division in order to make things happen.[78]

12-7c The Making Progress Principle

Sometimes what makes the biggest difference is a relatively "small" thing. Recent research points to the importance of *making progress toward goals* as a key to high motivation. The **making**

Exhibit 12.9 What Makes an Employee Highly Engaged?

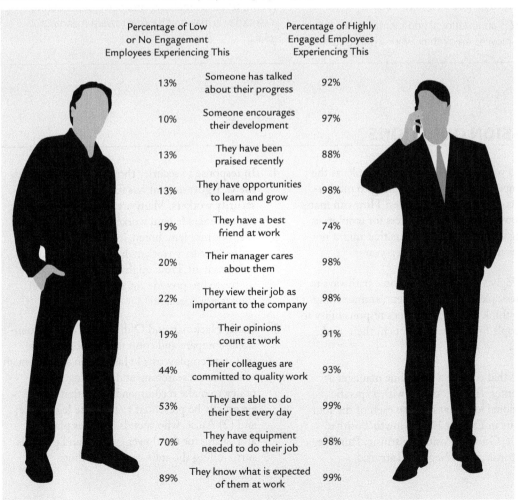

Percentage of Low or No Engagement Employees Experiencing This		Percentage of Highly Engaged Employees Experiencing This
13%	Someone has talked about their progress	92%
10%	Someone encourages their development	97%
13%	They have been praised recently	88%
13%	They have opportunities to learn and grow	98%
19%	They have a best friend at work	74%
20%	Their manager cares about them	98%
22%	They view their job as important to the company	98%
19%	Their opinions count at work	91%
44%	Their colleagues are committed to quality work	93%
53%	They are able to do their best every day	99%
70%	They have equipment needed to do their job	98%
89%	They know what is expected of them at work	99%

progress principle is the idea that the single most important factor that can boost motivation, positive emotions, and perceptions during a workday is making progress toward meaningful goals.[79] People are most motivated when they have the opportunity to experience achievement. Providing feedback on how well people are progressing and giving them a way to track their progress toward goals provides a renewable energy that fuels motivation. Knowing that they are making everyday progress, even in small steps, can make all the difference in how motivated people feel to continue pursuing a course of action.

Remember This

- Variable compensation and "at risk" pay have become key motivational tools, although these practices have been criticized in recent years for rewarding the wrong types of behavior.

- Employee empowerment and engagement are recent motivational trends that focus less on extrinsic rewards and more on creating a work environment that enables people to achieve intrinsic rewards and meet higher-level needs.

- **Empowerment** is the delegation of power and authority to subordinates in an organization.

- Empowering employees involves giving them information, knowledge, power, and rewards.

- **Engagement** is an emotional and mental state in which employees enjoy their work, contribute enthusiastically to meeting goals, and feel a sense of belonging and commitment to the organization.

- Managers create an environment that promotes engagement by providing employees with a sense of meaning, a sense of connection, and a sense of competence and growth.

- The behavior of managers is the biggest factor in determining whether people feel motivated and engaged at work.

- The **making progress principle** is the idea that the single most important factor that can boost motivation, positive emotions, and perceptions during a workday is making progress toward meaningful goals.

DISCUSSION QUESTIONS

1. Why do you think *making progress* ranks as the most important factor contributing to motivation, according to recent studies? How can managers provide a sense of progress for employees working on long-range projects that might not show results for months or even years?

2. Psychologists have identified three pathways to happiness: pleasure, engagement, and meaning. Do you think it is the manager's responsibility to help people find these elements in their work? Discuss.

3. Assume that you are a front-line manager at a call center. Try to come up with a specific motivational idea that fits into each of the four quadrants in Exhibit 12.2: Growth/Positive Extrinsic; Growth/Positive Intrinsic; Pain/Negative Extrinsic; Pain/Negative Intrinsic.

4. In response to security threats in today's world, the U.S. government has federalized airport security workers. Many argued that simply making screeners federal workers would not solve the root problem: bored, low-paid, and poorly trained security workers have little motivation to be vigilant. How might these employees be motivated to provide the security that travel threats now demand?

5. Using Hackman and Oldham's core job dimensions, compare and contrast the jobs of these two state employees: (1) Jared, who spends much of his time researching and debating energy policy to make recommendations that will eventually be presented to the state legislature; and (2) Anise, who spends her days planting and caring for the flower gardens and grounds surrounding the state capitol building.

6. If an experienced executive assistant discovered that she made the same amount of money as a newly hired janitor, how do you think she would react? What inputs and outcomes might she evaluate to make this comparison?

7. A survey of teachers found that two of the most important rewards were the belief that their work was important and a feeling of accomplishment. According to Maslow's theory, what needs do these rewards meet?

8. Use Herzberg's two-factor theory to explain why motivation seems to be high and turnover low at Zingerman's, based on the information provided in a "Recipe for Success" box in the chapter.

9. Why do you think empowerment increases motivation? Do you see any ways in which a manager's empowerment efforts might contribute to demotivation among employees? Discuss.

10. A recent Gallup survey shows that highly educated workers are significantly less likely to be engaged than are those with a high school diploma or less. What might be some reasons for this lower level of engagement among more well-educated employees?

APPLY YOUR SKILLS: SELF-LEARNING

What Motivates You?[80]

Indicate how important each characteristic is to you. Answer according to your feelings about the most recent job you had or about the job you currently hold. Circle the number on the scale that represents your feeling—ranging from 1 (very unimportant) to 7 (very important).

1. The feeling of self-esteem that a person gets from being in that job

   1 2 3 4 5 6 7

2. The opportunity for personal growth and development in that job

   1 2 3 4 5 6 7

3. The prestige of the job inside the company (i.e., regard received from others in the company)

   1 2 3 4 5 6 7

4. The opportunity for independent thought and action in that job

   1 2 3 4 5 6 7

5. The feeling of security in that job

   1 2 3 4 5 6 7

6. The feeling of self-fulfillment a person gets from being in that position (i.e., the feeling of being able to use one's own unique capabilities, realizing one's potential)

   1 2 3 4 5 6 7

7. The prestige of the job outside the company (i.e., the regard received from people not in the company)

   1 2 3 4 5 6 7

8. The feeling of worthwhile accomplishment in that job

   1 2 3 4 5 6 7

9. The opportunity in that job to give help to other people

   1 2 3 4 5 6 7

10. The opportunity in that job for participation in the setting of goals

    1 2 3 4 5 6 7

11. The opportunity in that job for participation in the determination of methods and procedures

    1 2 3 4 5 6 7

12. The authority connected with the job

    1 2 3 4 5 6 7

13. The opportunity to develop close friendships in the job

    1 2 3 4 5 6 7

Scoring and Interpretation Score the exercise as follows to determine what motivates you:

Rating for question 5 = _____.
Divide by 1 = _____ security.
Rating for questions 9 and 13 = _____.
Divide by 2 = _____ social.
Rating for questions 1, 3, and 7 = _____.
Divide by 3 = _____ esteem.
Rating for questions 4, 10, 11, and 12 = _____.
Divide by 4 = _____ autonomy.

Rating for questions 2, 6, and 8 = _____.
Divide by 3 = _____ self-actualization.

Your instructor has national norm scores for presidents, vice presidents, and upper-middle-level, lower-middle-level, and lower-level managers with which you can compare your mean importance scores. How do your scores compare with the scores of managers working in organizations? (Instructors: You can find this information in the Instructors Manual.)

APPLY YOUR SKILLS: GROUP LEARNING

Work versus Play

1. Form groups of three to four members.
   a. Answer these questions:
      i. What drives you to expend energy on a play activity?
      ii. For leisure, why do you choose the activities you do? (Don't discuss the particular activities, but rather *why* you choose them.)
      iii. Select one of your group members as presenter.

2. Each group presents its main points to the class. The instructor will draw on the board a table, similar to the following one, based on information from the class presentations.

Activities	Outcome 1	Outcome 2	Outcome 3	Outcome 4	Outcome 5	Outcome 6
Example: 1 Soccer	High energy	Team bonding	Fitness			
2						
3						
4						

3. Questions for class discussion:
   a. How can you build some of these motives for play into a work environment?
   b. What prevents you from making work more intrinsically motivating, as play is?
   c. Which motivation theories are relevant here?

SOURCE: Adapted from Phil Anderson, University of St. Thomas, Minneapolis.

APPLY YOUR SKILLS: ACTION LEARNING

1. Interview four people who've had at least three jobs (maybe part-time) in their lives.

2. Ask them which jobs they had liked the best and for which they had worked the hardest. Why did they like that job and why did they work harder? Fill out the following table:

Name of person	Job 1		Job 2		Job 3	
	What they liked about the job	What they didn't like about the job	What they liked about the job	What they didn't like about the job	What they liked about the job	What they didn't like about the job
1.						
2.						
3.						
4.						

3. Try to find patters in the answers of the four people. Compare your outcomes to the motivation theories in this chapter. Which theories are confirmed or disconfirmed based on your interviews? Did you see patterns of working hard and how much the people liked the job or particular tasks? Did you see any patterns in motivation?

4. Your instructor may ask you to write a report on your findings or meet in small groups to discuss the identified patterns among all the interviewees. You would then be asked to either present your findings in class or write a group report.

APPLY YOUR SKILLS: ETHICAL DILEMMA

To Renege or Not to Renege?[81]

Federico Garcia, vice president of sales for Puget Sound Building Materials, a company based in Tacoma, Washington, wasn't all that surprised by what company president Michael Otto and CFO James Wilson had to say during their meeting that morning.

Last year, launching a major expansion made sense to everyone at Puget, a well-established company that provided building materials as well as manufacturing and installation services to residential builders in the Washington and Oregon markets. Puget looked at the record new housing starts and decided that it was time to move into the California and Arizona markets, especially concentrating on San Diego and Phoenix, two of the hottest housing markets in the country. Federico carefully hired promising new sales representatives and offered them hefty bonuses if they reached the goals set for the new territory over the following 12 months. All the representatives had performed well, and three of them had exceeded Puget's goal—and then some. The incentive system he'd put in place had worked well. The sales reps were expecting handsome bonuses for their hard work.

Early on, however, it became all too clear that Puget had seriously underestimated the time required to build new business relationships and the costs associated with the expansion, a mistake that was already eating into profit margins. Even more distressing were the most recent figures for new housing starts, which were heading in the wrong direction. As Michael said, "Granted, it's too early to tell if this is just a pause or the start of a real long-term downturn. But I'm worried. If things get worse, Puget could be in real trouble."

James looked at Federico and said, "Our lawyers built enough contingency clauses into the sales reps' contracts that we're not really obligated to pay those bonuses you promised. What would you think about not paying them?" Federico turned to the president, who said, "Why don't you think about it, and get back to us with a recommendation?"

Federico felt torn. On the one hand, he knew that the CFO was correct. Puget wasn't, strictly speaking, under any legal obligation to pay out the bonuses, and the eroding profit margins were a genuine cause for concern. The president clearly did not want to pay the bonuses. But Federico had created a first-rate sales force that had done exactly what he'd asked it to do. He prided himself on being a man of his word—someone others could trust. Could he go back on his promises?

What Would You Do?

1. Recommend to the president that a meeting be arranged with the sales representatives entitled to a bonus and tell them that their checks were going to be delayed until Puget's financial picture clarified. The sales reps would be told that the company had a legal right to delay payment and that it may not be able to pay the bonuses if its financial situation continues to deteriorate.

2. Recommend a meeting with the sales representatives entitled to a bonus and tell them that the company's deteriorating financial situation triggers one of the contingency clauses in their contract, so the company won't be issuing their bonus checks. Puget will just have to deal with the negative impact on sales rep motivation.

3. Recommend strongly to the president that Puget pay the bonuses as promised. The legal contracts and financial situation don't matter. Be prepared to resign if the bonuses are not paid as you promised. Your word and a motivated sales team mean everything to you.

APPLY YOUR SKILLS: CASE FOR CRITICAL ANALYSIS

Lauren's Balancing Act

DeMarco's Department Store manager Lauren Brewster's "Wow" moment came when she observed a Chicago restaurant staff's gushing treatment of an international celebrity.

"Everyone dreams of that kind of star treatment," Lauren told her assistant, Jack Klein. "Think about it. People brag about their bank or the local bar where 'everybody knows your name,' or enjoy showing off a favorite restaurant where the hostess always remembers their favorite table."

DeMarco's, like other upscale department stores, suffered the double whammy of a slumping economy and increased competition from discount retailers and online shopping. How could the store, the "box," compete, retain its old customers, and build a strong future customer base?

"We've always known that it's all about customer service," Lauren said. "But what's so great about grabbing a giant plastic shopping cart and slogging through some giant warehouse in your shorts and flip-flops, and then joining the herd at the checkout? That is not a shopping *experience*."

"And what *isn't* great about being treated like Oprah from the moment you hit the door until the sales associate swipes your card and hands over something lovely that you just purchased?" Jack asked.

Lauren's idea was that store customers receive that personal, upscale, "you're somebody special here" treatment at DeMarco's. Sales associates would raise their own professional level, regard customers as worthy of personalized service, and build their own clientele. As added incentive, the entire DeMarco's sales team was changed over from hourly pay to straight commission. "Your pay is built through your own initiative and individualized service that makes customers return to you again and again," Lauren instructed the sales force at the outset of the experiment. The idea intrigued Corporate, which approved a two-year experiment.

As expected, the new plan created a minor exodus among those who wanted the assurance of a "regular paycheck." But as the program moved through its first year, both store and corporate management were pleased with the overall results. Marketing pushed the new image of elite, personalized customer service, and statements such as "Katherine at DeMarco's helped me select this outfit" or "Damien always lets me know when something new arrives at DeMarco's that he thinks is perfect for me" became the typical boast of savvy shoppers.

Now, two years into the experiment, Corporate urged Lauren to submit a full assessment of the program as a potential model for implementation throughout the department store chain. Sales numbers vouched for the overall success, particularly over the last two quarters of the second year. Certain associates, including Katherine Knowles in designer dresses and Damien Fotopolous in women's shoes, showed significant gains as a result of straight commissions, and sales associates and customers responded favorably

overall, urging a continuation of the program. Reliance on commissions inspired these and other sales associates to treat their individual department as if it were their own small business, becoming experts on nuances of merchandise, exploring designs and trends, finding ways to promote their expertise, and building an impressive number of loyal customers.

The satisfaction level of customers was apparent in the numbers—not only in sales numbers, but also in repeat business, customer referrals to friends, and customer comment cards, all of which had been tracked since the beginning of the program.

The downside of the experiment was that while some associates soared, others either veered toward an aggressive, pushy sales style or became intimidated by coworkers and teetered, monthly, on the verge of being replaced because they weren't making sales. The once-proud tradition of cooperation among sales staff was, in many instances, being eaten away by relentless competition. Work assignments away from the sales floor were resented. In addition, the managers and sales associates of certain departments, such as women's accessories, complained of lower wages because, as one sales associate pointed out, "My commission on a $50 belt is nothing compared to Katherine's commission on a $2,800 designer dress." Resentment was mounting among those who witnessed the extravagant wages of a few.

"If we change this program, if we keep straight commission for some and return to hourly pay for others, how does that fit with our new image?" Lauren said to Jack. "How does it deal with the difference in pay scale? How does it assure us that the attitudes of our sales team and the culture of this store will not return to what we were before—just another store?"

Questions

1. What do you see as the advantages and disadvantages of the incentive system that DeMarco's is using for sales associates? What impact do you think it's having on the DeMarco's culture? Explain.

2. Do you think the complaints of lower-paid sales associates are legitimate? Why or why not? How do you suggest that Lauren respond to these complaints, such as the gripe that the system offers few opportunities for large commissions in some departments?

3. Have the successes of sales associates such as Katherine or Damien created a situation in which customers' loyalty to particular salespeople is stronger than their loyalty to the store? For example, if a successful associate leaves DeMarco's, might the customer leave also?

ENDNOTES

1. Based on Rich Sheridan, *Joy, Inc.: How We Built a Workplace People Love* (New York: Portfolio/Penguin, 2013); and "Our Story," Menlo Innovations Website," https://www.menloinnovations.com/our-story/ (accessed May 3, 2016).

2. Sheridan, *Joy, Inc.*

3. Richard M. Steers and Lyman W. Porter, eds., *Motivation and Work Behavior*, 3rd ed. (New York: McGraw-Hill, 1983); Don Hellriegel, John W. Slocum, Jr., and Richard W. Woodman, *Organizational Behavior*, 7th ed. (St. Paul, MN: West, 1995), p. 170; and Jerry L. Gray and Frederick A. Starke, *Organizational Behavior: Concepts and Applications*, 4th ed. (New York: Macmillan, 1988), pp. 104–105.

4. See Linda Grant, "Happy Workers, High Returns," *Fortune* (January 12, 1998): 81; Elizabeth J. Hawk and Garrett J. Sheridan, "The Right Stuff," *Management Review* (June 1999): 43–48; Michael West and Malcolm Patterson, "Profitable Personnel," *People Management* (January 8, 1998): 28–31; Anne Fisher, "Why Passion Pays," *FSB* (September 2002): 58; and Curt Coffman and Gabriel Gonzalez-Molina, *Follow This Path: How the World's Great Organizations Drive Growth by Unleashing Human Potential* (New York: Warner Books, 2002).

5. David A. Kaplan, "Salesforce's Happy Workforce," *Fortune* (February 6, 2012): 100–112.

6. Greenhouse, "A Factory Defies Stereotypes, But Can It Thrive?"

7. Reported in Janice Kaplan, "It Pays to Give Thanks at the Office," *The Wall Street Journal*, August 7, 2015, http://www.wsj.com/articles/it-pays-to-give-thanks-at-the-office-1438959788 (accessed May 4, 2016).

8. Based on Bruce H. Jackson, "Influence Behavior; Become a Master Motivator," *Leadership Excellence* (April 2010): 14.

9. Leslie Kwoh, "Shape Up or Pay Up: Firms Put in New Health Penalties," *The Wall Street Journal*, April 6, 2013.

10. Ashley Halsey III, "Fines Lower Drivers' Use of Cellphones," *The Washington Post*, July 10, 2011, www.washingtonpost.com/local/fines-lower-drivers-use-of-cellphones/2011/07/08/gIQAMvX67H_story.html (accessed July 11, 2011).

11. Jack Stack, "Hilcorp Energy Shares the Wealth," *The New York Times*, July 6, 2010, http://boss.blogs.nytimes.com/2010/07/06/hilcorp-energy-shares-the-wealth/ (accessed July 7, 2010); and Hilcorp Energy Gives $100,000 Bonus to All 1,381 Employees," *Fox News*, December 12, 2015, http://www.foxnews.com/us/2015/12/12/hilcorp-energy-gives-100000-bonus-to-all-1381-employees.html (accessed May 15, 2016).

12. Hadley Malcolm, "Study: The Key to Happiness at Work Is Free Snacks," *USA Today*, September 16, 2015, http://www.usatoday.com/story/money/2015/09/16/study-says-snacks-affect-happiness-at-work/72259746/ (accessed May 3, 2016).

13. Adam Bryant, "Carmelyn P. Malalis: Leading Through Praise, Not Fear," *The New York Times*, November 5, 2015, http://www.nytimes.com/2015/11/08/business/carmelyn-p-malalis-leading-through-praise-not-fear.html?_r=0 (accessed May 3, 2016).

14. This example is from Maureen Soyars and Justin Brusino, "Essentials of Engagement: Contributions, Connections, Growth," *T+D* (March 2009): 62–65.

15. Abraham F. Maslow, "A Theory of Human Motivation," *Psychological Review* 50 (1943): 370–396.

16. Barbara Bowes, "More than Money: Make Your Employees Feel Secure, Satisfied in Job," *Winnipeg Free Press*, July 24, 2010.

17. Sarah E. Needleman, "Burger Chain's Health-Care Recipe," *The Wall Street Journal*, August 31, 2009.

18. Kathy Chu, "China Factories Try Karaoke, Speed Dating, to Keep Workers," *The Wall Street Journal*, May 2, 2013, http://online.wsj.com/article/SB100014241278873237981045784526340755192230.html?KEYWORDS=kathy+Chu (accessed May 13, 2013).

19. Telis Demos, "The Way We Work: Motivate Without Spending Millions," *Fortune* (April 12, 2010): 37–38.

20. Sarah Pass, "On the Line," *People Management* (September 15, 2005): 38.

21. Clayton Alderfer, *Existence, Relatedness, and Growth* (New York: Free Press, 1972).

22. Jennifer Conlin, "At Zingerman's, Pastrami and Partnership to Go," *The New York Times*, July 5, 2014, http://www.nytimes.com/2014/07/06/business/at-zingermans-pastrami-and-partnership-to-go.html?_r=0 (accessed May 2, 2016).

23. Ibid.

24. Scott Westcott, "Beyond Flextime; Trashing the Work Week," *Inc.* (August 2008): 30–31; and "Join Our Team," http://jacounter.com/about-us/career-opportunities/ (accessed May 3, 2016).

25. Studies and surveys reported in Karol Rose, "Work-Life Effectiveness," special advertising section, *Fortune* (September 29, 2003): S1–S17.

26. Frederick Herzberg, "One More Time: How Do You Motivate Employees?" *Harvard Business Review* (January 2003): 87–96.

27. "Workforce MoodTracker Summer 2013 Report: Empowering Employees to Improve Employee Performance" (Southborough, MA: Globoforce, 2013), http://go.globoforce.com/rs/globoforce/images/Summer2013Moodtracker.pdf (accessed October 28, 2013); and "Workforce MoodTracker Fall 2012 Report: Revealing Key Practices for Effective Recognition" (Southborough, MA: Globoforce, 2012), http://www.globoforce.com/resources/research-reports/mood-tracker-fall-2012-revealing-key-practices-for-effective-recognition/ (accessed October 28, 2013).

28. David A. Kaplan, "Inside Mars," *Fortune* (February 4, 2013): 72–82.

29. David C. McClelland, *Human Motivation* (Glenview, IL: Scott Foresman, 1985).

30. David C. McClelland, "The Two Faces of Power," in D. A. Colb, I. M. Rubin, and J. M. McIntyre, eds., *Organizational Psychology* (Englewood Cliffs, NJ: Prentice Hall, 1971), pp. 73–86.

31. See Gary P. Latham and Edwin A. Locke, "Enhancing the Benefits and Overcoming the Pitfalls of Goal Setting," *Organizational Dynamics* 35, no. 4 (2006): 332–338; Edwin A. Locke and Gary P. Latham, "Building a Practically Useful Theory of Goal Setting and Task Motivation: A 35-Year Odyssey," *American Psychologist* 57, no. 9 (September 2002): 705ff; Gary P. Latham and Edwin A. Locke, "Self-Regulation Through Goal Setting," *Organizational Behavior and Human Decision Processes* 50, no. 2 (December 1991): 212–247; G. P. Latham and G. H. Seijts, "The Effects of Proximal and Distal Goals on Performance of a Moderately Complex Task," *Journal of Organizational Behavior* 20, no. 4 (1999): 421–428; P. C. Earley,

T. Connolly, and G. Ekegren, "Goals, Strategy Development, and Task Performance: Some Limits on the Efficacy of Goal Setting," *Journal of Applied Psychology* 74 (1989): 24–33; E. A. Locke, "Toward a Theory of Task Motivation and Incentives," *Organizational Behavior and Human Performance* 3 (1968): 157–189; Gerard H. Seijts, Ree M. Meertens, and Gerjo Kok, "The Effects of Task Importance and Publicness on the Relation Between Goal Difficulty and Performance," *Canadian Journal of Behavioural Science* 29, no. 1 (1997): 54ff. See Gerard H. Seijts and Gary P. Latham, "Knowing When to Set Learning versus Performance Goals," *Organizational Dynamics* 41 (2012): 1–6, for a discussion of the importance of learning goals versus performance goals in turbulent environments.

32. Locke and Latham, "Building a Practically Useful Theory of Goal Setting and Task Motivation."

33. Edwin A. Locke, "Linking Goals to Monetary Incentives," *Academy of Management Executive* 18, no. 4 (2005): 130–133.

34. Latham and Locke, "Enhancing the Benefits and Overcoming the Pitfalls of Goal Setting."

35. J. M. Ivanecevich and J. T. McMahon, "The Effects of Goal Setting, External Feedback, and Self-Generated Feedback on Outcome Variables: A Field Experiment," *Academy of Management Journal* 25, no. 2 (June 1982): 359–372; G. P. Latham and E. A. Locke, "Self-Regulation Through Goal Setting," *Organizational Behavior and Human Decision Processes* 50, no. 2 (1991): 212–247.

36. Gary P. Latham, "The Motivational Benefits of Goal-Setting," *Academy of Management Executive* 18, no. 4 (2004): 126–129.

37. Julie Sloane, "The Number Cruncher," in Ellyn Spragins, "The Best Bosses," *Fortune Small Business* (October 2004): 39–57; and Maggie Rauch, "Great Expectations," *Incentive* (December 2004): 18–19.

38. J. Stacy Adams, "Injustice in Social Exchange," in *Advances in Experimental Social Psychology*, 2d ed., ed. L. Berkowitz (New York: Academic Press, 1965); and J. Stacy Adams, "Toward an Understanding of Inequity," *Journal of Abnormal and Social Psychology* (November 1963): 422–436.

39. Won-Yong Oh and Youngkyun Chang, "Gravity Payments: $70,000 Minimum Salary Company," *Ivey Publishing* (January 21, 2016), Ivey Cases Product Number 9B16C001, https://www.iveycases.com/ProductView.aspx?id=77081; Michael Wheeler, "Why Raising Employee Wages Sometimes Backfires," *Hospitality Business Development Web site*, August 7, 2015, http://www.hospitalitybusinessdevelopment.com/blog/why-raising-employee-wages-sometimes-backfires (accessed October 27, 2015); and Patricia Cohen, "One Firm's Annual Pay of $70,000 Stirs Debate," *The New York Times*, April 20, 2015.

40. Elizabeth Weise, "Our Brains Dislike Inequality, Even When It's in Our Favor," *USA TODAY*, February 25, 2010, http://content.usatoday.com/communities/sciencefair/post/2010/02/our-brains-dont-like-inequality-even-when-its-in-our-favor/1 (accessed March 21, 2011); Daniel Yee, "Brain Prefers Working over Money for Nothing," *Cincinnati Post*, May 14, 2004.

41. Ray V. Montagno, "The Effects of Comparison to Others and Primary Experience on Responses to Task Design," *Academy of Management Journal* 28 (1985): 491–498; and Robert P. Vecchio, "Predicting Worker Performance in Inequitable Settings," *Academy of Management Review* 7 (1982): 103–110.

42. Nathan Koppel and Vanessa O'Connell, "Pay Gap Widens at Big Law Firms as Partners Chase Star Attorneys," *The Wall Street Journal*, February 8, 2011, http://online.wsj.com/article/SB10001424052748704570104576124232780067002.html (accessed February 8, 2011).

43. James E. Martin and Melanie M. Peterson, "Two-Tier Wage Structures: Implications for Equity Theory," *Academy of Management Journal* 30 (1987): 297–315.

44. Victor H. Vroom, *Work and Motivation* (New York: Wiley, 1964); B. S. Gorgopoulos, G. M. Mahoney, and N. Jones, "A Path-Goal Approach to Productivity," *Journal of Applied Psychology* 41 (1957): 345–353; and E. E. Lawler III, *Pay and Organizational Effectiveness: A Psychological View* (New York: McGraw-Hill, 1981).

45. Richard R. Johnson, "Explaining Patrol Officer Drug Arrest Activity Through Expectancy Theory," *Policing* 32, no. 1 (2009): 6ff.

46. Shelly Banjo, "Wal-Mart Will Tie Executive Pay to Compliance Overhaul," *The Wall Street Journal*, April 22, 2013.

47. Richard L. Daft and Richard M. Steers, *Organizations: A Micro/Macro Approach* (Glenview, IL: Scott Foresman, 1986).

48. Studies reported in Tom Rath, "The Best Way to Recognize Employees," *Gallup Management Journal* (December 9, 2004): 1–5; and Erin White, "Theory & Practice: Praise from Peers Goes a Long Way—Recognition Programs Help Companies Retain Workers as Pay Raises Get Smaller," *The Wall Street Journal*, December 19, 2005.

49. Alexander D. Stajkovic and Fred Luthans, "A Meta-Analysis of the Effects of Organizational Behavior Modification on Task Performance, 1975–95," *Academy of Management Journal* (October 1997): 1122–1149; H. Richlin, *Modern Behaviorism* (San Francisco: Freeman, 1970); and B. F. Skinner, *Science and Human Behavior* (New York: Macmillan, 1953).

50. "100 Best Companies to Work For: Whole Foods Market," *Fortune* (May 23, 2011): 30; "Employees Earn Cash for Exercising More," *The Wall Street Journal*, June 2, 2010.

51. Stajkovic and Luthans, "A Meta-Analysis of the Effects of Organizational Behavior Modification on Task Performance"; and Fred Luthans and Alexander D. Stajkovic, "Reinforce for Performance: The Need to Go Beyond Pay and Even Rewards," *Academy of Management Executive* 13, no. 2 (1999): 49–57.

52. Studies reported in Janice Kaplan, "It Pays to Give Thanks at the Office," *The Wall Street Journal*, August 7, 2015, http://www.wsj.com/articles/it-pays-to-give-thanks-at-the-office-1438959788 (accessed May 4, 2016).

53. Jessica Silver-Greenberg, "JPMorgan Cuts Dimon's Pay, Even as Profit Surges," *The New York Times*, January 16, 2013, http://dealbook.nytimes.com/2013/01/16/jpmorgan-4th-quarter-profit-jumps-53-to-5-7-billion/ (accessed January 16, 2013).

54. Kenneth D. Butterfield and Linda Klebe Treviño, "Punishment from the Manager's Perspective: A Grounded Investigation and Inductive Model," *Academy of Management Journal* 39, no. 6 (December 1996): 1479–1512; and Andrea Casey, "Voices from the Firing Line: Managers Discuss Punishment in the Workplace," *Academy of Management Executive* 11, no. 3 (1997): 93–94.

55. Amy Sutherland, "What Shamu Taught Me About a Happy Marriage," *The New York Times*, June 25, 2006, www.nytimes.com/2006/06/25/fashion/25love.html?ex=1175659200&en=4c3d257c4d16e70d&ei=5070 (accessed April 2, 2007).

56. Arthur Bandura, *Social Learning Theory* (Englewood Cliffs, NJ: Prentice Hall, 1977); and T. R. V. Davis and F. Luthans, "A Social Learning Approach to Organizational Behavior," *Academy of Management Review* 5 (1980): 281–290.

57. Bandura, *Social Learning Theory*; and Davis and Luthans, "A Social Learning Approach to Organizational Behavior."

58. Ilya Pozin, "The Takeaway: Three Things That Motivate Employees More Than Money," *Inc.* (February 2012): 6.

59. Christine M. Riordan, Robert J. Vandenberg, and Hettie A. Richardson, "Employee Involvement Climate and Organizational Effectiveness," *Human Resource Management* 44, no. 4 (Winter 2005): 471–488.

60. J. Richard Hackman and Greg R. Oldham, *Work Redesign* (Reading, MA: Addison-Wesley, 1980); and J. Richard Hackman and Greg Oldham, "Motivation Through the Design of Work: Test of a Theory," *Organizational Behavior and Human Performance* 16 (1976): 250–279.

61. Xu Huang and Evert Van de Vliert, "Where Intrinsic Job Satisfaction Fails to Work: National Moderators of Intrinsic Motivation," *Journal of Organizational Behavior* 24 (2003): 157–179.

62. Sarah E. Needleman, "Business Owners Try to Motivate Employees; As Recession Lingers, Managers Hold Meetings and Change Hiring Practices to Alleviate Workers' Stress," *The Wall Street Journal*, January 14, 2010.

63. Stephanie Strom, "At Chobani, Now It's Not Just the Yogurt That's Rich," *The New York Times*, April 26, 2016, http://www.nytimes.com/2016/04/27/business/a-windfall-for-chobani-employees-stakes-in-the-company.html?_r=0 (accessed May 6, 2016).

64. Aaron Lucchetti, "Morgan Stanley to Overhaul Pay Plan," *The Wall Street Journal*, December 29, 2009; Graham Bowley, "Credit Suisse Overhauls Compensation," *The New York Times*, October 21, 2009; Liam Pleven and Susanne Craig, "Deal Fees Under Fire Amid Mortgage Crisis; Guaranteed Rewards of Bankers, Middlemen Are in the Spotlight," *The Wall Street Journal*, January 17, 2008; Phred Dvorak, "Companies Seek Shareholder Input on Pay Practices," *The Wall Street Journal*, April 6, 2009; and Carol Hymowitz, "Pay Gap Fuels Worker Woes," *The Wall Street Journal*, April 28, 2008.

65. Edwin P. Hollander and Lynn R. Offermann, "Power and Leadership in Organizations," *American Psychologist* 45 (February 1990): 179–189.

66. Jay A. Conger and Rabindra N. Kanungo, "The Empowerment Process: Integrating Theory and Practice," *Academy of Management Review* 13 (1988): 471–482.

67. John Izzo, "Step-Up Initiative: Create a Culture of Initiators," *Leadership Excellence* (June 2012): 13.

68. David E. Bowen and Edward E. Lawler III, "The Empowerment of Service Workers: What, Why, How, and When," *Sloan Management Review* (Spring 1992): 31–39; and Ray W. Coye and James A. Belohav, "An Exploratory Analysis of Employee Participation," *Group and Organization Management* 20, no. 1 (March 1995): 4–17.

69. Golnaz Sadri, "Empowerment for the Bottom Line," *Industrial Management* (May–June 2011): 8–13; and Robert C. Ford and Myron D. Fottler, "Empowerment: A Matter of Degree," *Academy of Management Executive* 9, no. 3 (1995): 21–31.

70. Stack, "Hilcorp Energy Shares the Wealth"; and "Hilcorp Energy Gives $100,000 Bonus to All 1,381 Employees."

71. Amy Adkins, "U.S. Employee Engagement Reaches New High in March," *Gallup.org*, April 13, 2016, http://www.gallup.com/poll/190622/employee-engagement-reaches-new-high-march.aspx?g_source=EMPLOYEE_ENGAGEMENT&g_medium=topic&g_campaign=tiles (accessed May 6, 2016).

72. This definition is based on Mercer Human Resource Consulting's Employee Engagement Model, as described in Paul Sanchez and Dan McCauley, "Measuring and Managing Engagement in a Cross-Cultural Workforce: New Insights for Global Companies," *Global Business and Organizational Excellence* (November–December 2006): 41–50.

73. This section is based on Soyars and Brusino, "Essentials of Engagement"; Kenneth W. Thomas, "The Four Intrinsic Rewards That Drive Employee Engagement," *Ivey Business Journal*, November–December 2009, www.iveybusinessjournal.com/article.asp?intArticle_id=867 (accessed November 24, 2009); and Cristina de Mello e Souza Wildermuth and Patrick David Pauken, "A Perfect Match: Decoding Employee Engagement—Part II: Engaging Jobs and Individuals," *Industrial and Commercial Training* 40, no. 4 (2008): 206–210.

74. Reported in Rachel Feintzeig, "I Don't Have a Job. I Have a Higher Calling," *The Wall Street Journal*, February 24, 2015, http://www.wsj.com/articles/corporate-mission-statements-talk-of-higher-purpose-1424824784 (accessed May 6, 2016).

75. Soyars and Brusino, "Essentials of Engagement."

76. Theresa M. Welbourne, "Employee Engagement: Beyond the Fad and into the Executive Suite," *Leader to Leader* (Spring 2007): 45–51.

77. See J. K. Harter, F. L. Schmidt, and T. L. Hayes, "Business-Unit-Level Relationship Between Employee Satisfaction, Employee Engagement, and Business Outcomes: A Meta-Analysis," *Journal of Applied Psychology* 87, no. 2 (2002): 268–279; Coffman and Gonzalez, *Follow This Path*; M. Buckingham and C. Coffman, *First, Break All the Rules: What the World's Greatest Managers Do Differently* (New York: Simon & Schuster, 1999); A. M. Saks, "Antecedents and Consequences of Employee Engagement," *Journal of Managerial Psychology* 21, no. 7 (2006): 600–619; J. Lee Whittington and Timothy J. Galpin, "The Engagement Factor: Building a High-Commitment Organization in a Low-Commitment World," *Journal of Business Strategy* 32, no. 5 (2010): 14–24; and Nikki Blacksmith and Jim Harter, "Majority of American Workers Not Engaged in Their Jobs," *Gallup.com*, October 28, 2011, www.gallup.com/poll/150383/majority-american-workers-not-engaged-jobs.aspx (accessed September 24, 2012).

78. Adam Bryant, "Mary Laschinger of Veritiv: Leadership with Its Roots on the Farm," *The New York Times*, October 31, 2015, http://www.nytimes.com/2015/11/01/business/mary-laschinger-of-veritiv-leadership-with-its-roots-on-the-farm.html?_r=0 (accessed May 6, 2016).

79. This definition and discussion is based on Teresa M. Amabile and Steven J. Kramer, "The Power of Small Wins," *Harvard Business Review* (May 2011): 71–80; and Teresa M. Amabile and Steven J. Kramer, "What Really Motivates Workers: Understanding the Power of Progress," *Harvard Business Review* (January–February 2010): 44–45.

80. Lyman W. Porter, *Organizational Patterns of Managerial Job Attitudes* (New York: American Foundation for Management Research, 1964), pp. 17, 19.

81. Based on Doug Wallace, "The Company Simply Refused to Pay," *Business Ethics* (March–April 2000): 18; and Adam Shell, "Overheated Housing Market Is Cooling," *USA TODAY*, November 2, 2005, http://usatoday30.usatoday.com/money/economy/housing/2005-11-01-real-estate-usat_x.htm?csp=34 (accessed May 22, 2014).

Chapter 13
Managing Communication

iStock.com/oscarhdez

Chapter Outline

Communication Is the Manager's Job
  What Is Communication?
  A Model of Communication

Communicating Among People
  Open Communication Climate
  Communication Channels

Communicating to Persuade and Influence Others
Communicating with Radical Candor
Asking Questions
Listening
Nonverbal Communication

Workplace Communication
  Social Media
  Personal Communication Channels
  Formal Communication Channels

Learning Outcomes

After studying this chapter, you should be able to:

13.1 Explain why communication is essential for effective management.

13.2 Describe the model of communication.

13.3 Explain how an open communication climate and the choice of a communication channel influence the quality of communication.

13.4 Clarify how communicating with candor, asking questions, listening, and paying attention to nonverbal communication affect communication between a manager and an employee.

13.5 Describe the manager's role in using social media to improve organizational communication.

13.6 Explain the role of personal communication channels, including networks and the grapevine, in enhancing organizational communication.

13.7 Compare and contrast formal and informal organizational communications

Are You Ready to Be a Manager?

Before reading this chapter, please circle either "Mostly True" or "Mostly False" for each of the following five statements.

1 If someone doesn't understand what I'm saying, it's important for me to make sure I'm using an effective means of communication for that particular person.

Mostly True ◀················▶ Mostly False

[page 484]

2 When I have a message to deliver with emotional content, I know better than to send it via e-mail. Face-to-face is the best, or if that's not possible, then telephone.

Mostly True ◀················▶ Mostly False

[page 486]

3 If I hope to persuade people, I know that I have to communicate with them often and easily.

Mostly True ◀················▶ Mostly False

[page 487]

4 I could learn a lot about good communication from listening to women interact.

Mostly True ◀················▶ Mostly False

[page 484]

5 When someone else is talking, I focus on what the person is saying, as well as trying to find the underlying meaning, rather than just prepare for my next air time.

Mostly True ◀················▶ Mostly False

[page 491]

Discover Your Management Approach

Do You Focus on What Others Say?[a]

Instructions: Think about how you communicate with other people during a typical day at work or school. Answer the following statements based on whether they are Mostly True or Mostly False for you. There are no right or wrong answers, so answer honestly.

	Mostly True	Mostly False
1. I'm extremely attentive to what others say.	_____	_____
2. I deliberately show people that I'm listening to them.	_____	_____
3. I really enjoy listening very carefully to people.	_____	_____

To complete and score entire assessment, visit MindTap.

[a]Based in part on William B. Snavely and John D. McNeill, "Communicator Style and Social Style: Testing a Theoretical Interface," *Journal of Leadership and Organizational Studies* 14, no. 1 (February 2008): 219–232.

"If you give someone a mask, they'll tell you the truth," says Aaron Bell, founder and CEO of AdRoll, an online advertising placement firm. Bell started working in software companies at the age of 14, so by the time he founded AdRoll in his late 20s, he already had a lot of experience seeing what can happen if problems and issues in a company don't get brought into the open. Bell holds weekly all-hands meetings as "a weekly flush to get the toxins out." Before each meeting, he sends a companywide e-mail message with an anonymous question and answer board. He also encourages people to post their fears, uncertainties, doubts, and anything else that is bothering them. Giving people a "mask" with the anonymous posting board is one way Bell gets problems into the open and keeps communication flowing. "The alternative, if you don't do that," he says, "is that you have people behind closed doors chatting about the company, gossiping, saying negative things."[1]

The most successful organizations are the ones whose managers, like Aaron Bell, keep the lines of communication open. They have the courage to listen to employees, to talk about what employees want to hear, and to explain difficult decisions. At AdRoll, Bell guarantees that he will address every question in the open meetings, unless it is something personal about a specific individual. Many managers know that good communication builds trust and enables people to do their jobs more effectively. One recent study found that companies with highly effective communication had 47 percent higher total returns to shareholders between 2004 and 2009 compared to companies with less effective communication practices.[2]

Knowing how to communicate effectively is a vital part of every manager's job. Good managers know which channels of communication to use for different types of messages, as well as why aspects of communication such as listening, asking questions, and giving candid feedback are so important to organizational success.

This chapter examines communication as a crucial part of the manager's job. We consider how the interpersonal aspects of communication, including open communication climates, communication channels, persuasion, communicating with candor, asking questions, and listening, affect managers' ability to communicate. Then we look at the workplace as a whole and consider the role of social media, personal communication networks, and formal communications.

13-1 Communication Is the Manager's Job

Managers spend at least 80 percent of every working day in direct communication with others. In other words, 48 minutes of every hour is spent in meetings, on the telephone, communicating online, or talking informally while walking around. The other 20 percent of a typical manager's time is spent doing desk work, most of which is also communication in the form of reading and writing.[3]

Exhibit 13.1 illustrates the crucial role of managers as communication champions. Managers gather important information from both inside and outside the organization and then distribute appropriate information to others who need it. Managers' communication is *purpose-directed* in that it directs everyone's attention toward the vision, values, and desired goals of the team or organization and influences people to act in a way that will help to achieve those goals. Managers facilitate *strategic conversations* by using open communication, actively listening to others, asking questions, and using feedback for learning and change. **Strategic conversation** refers to people talking across boundaries and hierarchical levels about the team or organization's vision, critical strategic themes, and the values that help achieve important goals.[4] At Procter & Gamble (P&G), for instance, former CEO A. G. Lafley created a process that opened a strategic conversation between top management and leaders in the business units to discuss five themes: What is your vision? Where will you play? How will you win? What capabilities must be in place? What

Exhibit 13.1 The Manager as Communication Champion

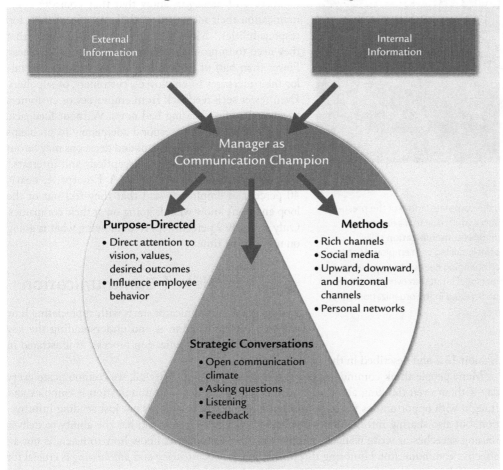

SOURCES: Adapted from Henry Mintzberg, *The Nature of Managerial Work* (New York: Harper and Row, 1973); and Richard L. Daft, *The Leadership Experience*, 3d ed. (Mason, OH: South-Western, 2005), p. 346.

management systems are needed? Rather than formal presentations by top leaders, strategy meetings became informal dialogues among small teams of people from all levels. The goal was to create strategic thinkers throughout the organization.[5]

Managers use different *methods* to communicate, depending on the purpose of the communication and the audience. Ginni Rometty, CEO of IBM, posted a video on the company's internal Web site to get the word out to hundreds of thousands of employees in 170 countries that IBM must move faster and do better at letting clients know the value that IBM can bring to them. Her "think fast, move faster" speech was part reprimand and part pep talk after a string of disappointing sales results.[6] Managers are increasingly using social media, which will be discussed later in the chapter, to communicate with employees.

13-1a What Is Communication?

Most of us think of spoken or written language when we think about communication, but words are only a small part of human communication. Managers are observed carefully by employees, so it's important to remember that everything a manager does *and* says will communicate something. In addition, communication is a two-way street that includes asking questions, seeking feedback, paying attention to nonverbal communication of others, and listening actively. **Communication** is the process by which information is exchanged and understood by two or more people, usually with the intent to influence or motivate behavior.

Surveys of managers show that they consider communication their most critical skill and one of their top responsibilities.[7] Most managers realize, however, that they need to improve their communication effectiveness. Fewer than half of responding managers bother to tailor their messages to employees, customers, or suppliers. Even fewer seek feedback from employees or customers because they fear hearing bad news. Without feedback, though, managers can't respond adequately to problems or opportunities, and their plans and decisions may be out of alignment with employee perceptions and interests.[8] In another recent survey by AMA Enterprise, nearly 40 percent of employees said that they feel out of the loop and don't know what is going on at their companies. Only a measly 9 percent reported knowing what is going on most of the time.[9]

E. O./Shutterstock.com

Concept Connection

Michael Newcombe has climbed the corporate ladder of the prestigious Four Seasons Hotel chain successfully due to his exceptional management capabilities, including his **communication** skills. Newcombe firmly believes in routinely talking with employees at all levels in order to understand their changing needs and to prevent problems before they occur. His personal interest in every employee also makes people feel valued and invested in the organization.

13-1b A Model of Communication

Being a good communicator starts with appreciating how complex communication is and understanding the key elements of the communication process, as illustrated in Exhibit 13.2 and described in the following text.

Many people think communication is simple and natural. After all, we communicate every day without even thinking about it. In reality, though, human communication is complex and fraught with opportunities for misunderstanding. Communication is not just sending information, but also sharing information in a planned way. A manager who has the ability to deliver rousing speeches or write brilliant commentary, but who doesn't know how to listen, is not an effective communicator. Honoring this distinction between *sharing* and *proclaiming* is crucial for successful management.

Knowing what communication entails helps you appreciate the complexity of it. As shown in Exhibit 13.2, a manager who wants to communicate with an employee **encodes** a thought or idea by selecting symbols (such as words) with which to compose a message. The **message** is the tangible formulation of the thought or idea sent to the employee, and the **channel** is the

Exhibit 13.2 A Model of Communication

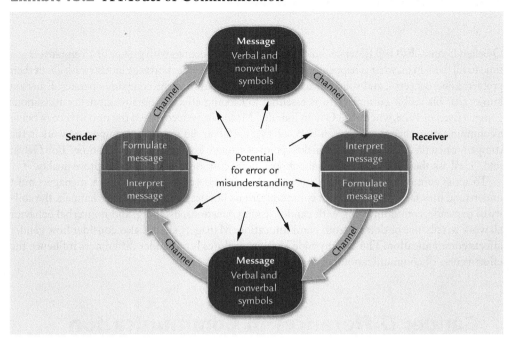

medium by which the message is sent. The channel might be a telephone call, an e-mail or a text message, a formal report, or a face-to-face conversation. The employee **decodes** the symbols to interpret the meaning of the message. **Feedback** occurs when the employee responds to a manager's communication with a return message. As illustrated in the exhibit, the nature of effective communication is cyclical in that a sender and receiver may exchange messages several times to achieve a mutual understanding.

Encoding and decoding sometimes can cause communication errors. Have you heard someone say, "But that's not what I meant!" or wasted time and energy on misunderstood instructions? Individual differences, knowledge, values, attitudes, and background act as filters and may create "noise" when translating from symbols to meanings. Feedback enables a manager to determine whether the employee correctly interpreted the message. The potential for communication errors is why feedback is so important. Without feedback, the communication cycle is incomplete. Effective communication involves both the transference and the mutual understanding of information.[10]

Remember This

- The manager's role as communication champion means to engage in purpose-driven strategic conversations via multiple channels.

- Social media is a method of communication that is growing in popularity as an effective way to communicate information within an organization.

- **Strategic conversation** refers to dialogue across boundaries and hierarchical levels about the team or organization's vision, critical strategic themes, and the values that help achieve important goals.

- **Communication** is the process by which information is exchanged and understood by two or more people.

- The sender **encodes** the idea by selecting symbols with which to compose a message and selecting a communication channel; the receiver **decodes** the symbols to interpret the meaning of the message.

- The **message** is the tangible formulation of an idea to be sent to the employee.

- The term **channel** refers to the medium by which a message is sent, such as a phone call, blog, or text message.

- **Feedback** occurs when the receiver responds to the sender's communication with a return message.

13-2 Communicating Among People

Quicken Loans CEO Bill Emerson holds two-hour lunch meetings with groups of 15 employees at a time to fill them in on what is happening with the company and the mortgage industry, ask about their problems and concerns, and solicit ideas and opinions about how the company operates. Emerson knows that his visible commitment is essential to keeping effective organizational conversations going.[11] Even in 1928, when Paul Galvin founded Motorola, he recognized the importance of being a communication champion. His son Bob said that his father did much of his important work in the company cafeteria. "He would always make a point of eating with employees at lunchtime," Bob Galvin said. "He'd ask them lots of questions about operations, customers, and how to improve quality."[12]

To act as communication champions and achieve the best possible outcomes, managers must understand how factors such as open communication climates, communication channels, the ability to persuade, communicating with candor, asking questions, listening, and nonverbal behavior all work to enhance or detract from communication. Managers should also consider how gender affects communication. The "Sunny Side Up" box explores how gender differences influence the effectiveness of communication between men and women.

Sunny Side Up } Gender Differences in Communication

To improve the effectiveness of workplace communication, managers should be aware of various factors that influence how people communicate. For example, according to Marianne Legato, founder of the Partnership for Gender-Specific Medicine at New York's Columbia University, there is evidence that men's and women's brains process language differently, which leads to real differences in communication. In addition, learned behaviors associated with being male or female influence communication patterns. Deborah Tannen, author of *You Just Don't Understand: Women and Men in Conversation*, has spent three decades studying gender differences in communication. Grasping the following different communication styles of men and women can help managers maximize every employee's talents and encourage both men and women to contribute more fully to the organization.

- **Purposes of conversations.** Men's conversations tend to focus on hierarchy—competition for relative power. To men, talk is primarily a means to preserve independence and negotiate and maintain status in a hierarchy. Men tend to use verbal language to exhibit knowledge and skill, such as by telling stories, joking, or passing on information. For most women, although certainly not all, conversation is primarily a language of rapport, a way to establish connections and negotiate relationships. Women use their unique conversational style to show involvement, connection, and participation, such as by seeking similarities and matching experiences with others.

- **Decision-making styles.** When women make decisions, they tend to process and think of options out loud. Men process internally until they come up with a solution. Men can sometimes misunderstand women's verbal brainstorming and assume that a woman is seeking approval rather than just thinking aloud.

- **Success in collaborative environments.** A report from McKinsey & Company, "Leadership Through the Crisis and After," notes that the kinds of behaviors that executives say will help their companies through difficult times are most often practiced by female managers. Women typically score higher than men on abilities such as motivating others, fostering communication, and listening, abilities that are more important than ever when organizations are going through tough times.

- **Interpretation of nonverbal messages.** About 70 percent of communication occurs nonverbally, but men and women interpret nonverbal communication differently. Women believe that good listening skills involve making eye contact and demonstrating understanding by nodding. To men, listening can take place with minimum eye contact and almost no nonverbal feedback. Further, when a man nods, it means that he agrees. When a woman nods, it means that she is listening. Women tend to be better at interpreting nonverbal communication. They are able to assess coalitions and alliances just by noting who is making eye contact during critical points in a meeting.

Interestingly, some male managers may be shifting to a more female-oriented communication style in today's challenging economic environment because women's approach to leadership and communication may be more suited to inspiring employees and helping people pull together toward goals during difficult times.

SOURCES: Based on Deborah Tannen, "He Said, She Said," *Scientific American Mind* (May–June 2010): 55–59; Carol Kinsey Goman, "Men and Women and Workplace Communication," *Business Analyst Times*, May 26, 2009, www.batimes.com/articles/men-and-women-and-workplace-communication.html (accessed September 20, 2012); and Elizabeth Bernstein, "She Talks a Lot, He Listens a Little," *The Wall Street Journal*, November 16, 2010, http://online.wsj.com/news/articles/SB10001424052748704658204575610921238173714 (accessed October 30, 2013).

13-2a Open Communication Climate

A survey of U.S. employees reveals that people genuinely want open and honest communication from their managers, including the bad news as well as the good.[13] Tom Szaky, CEO of TerraCycle, a waste-recycling business, learned the value of sharing both good and bad news. Szaky was hesitant to share bad news with his employees because he didn't want them worrying about something that didn't affect their jobs and becoming distracted and unproductive as a result. "The problem with hiding information," Szaky said, "was that when challenges came up, I felt pretty much alone on them, and the staff was left guessing what was happening. Predictably, the lack of information fueled rumors and damaged morale." Today, Szaky encourages transparency and promotes open, honest communication. Employees see everything in great detail, even the bad news. This new climate has fostered a feeling of ownership and trust. It also brings issues to the forefront faster than ever before.[14]

Open communication means sharing all types of information throughout the organization, across functional and hierarchical boundaries. People throughout the organization need to see the big picture, understand the decisions managers make, and know how their work contributes to the success of the company. Particularly in times of change, if people don't hear what's happening from managers, they rely on rumors and will often assume the worst.[15] In an open communication environment, people know where they stand and what rules they need to play by. Open communication helps people accept, understand, and commit to goals. People can see how their actions interact with and affect others in the organization. When people have access to complete information, they are more likely to come up with creative solutions to problems and make decisions that are good for the company.

Managers can build an open communication climate by breaking down conventional hierarchical and department boundaries that may be barriers to communication. Managers can take care to communicate honestly with subordinates, keep people posted when things change in either a positive or negative direction, and help people see the financial impact of their decisions and actions.[16]

To achieve the advantages of open communication, managers should use the type of communication network that maximizes employee performance and job satisfaction. Research into employee communication has focused on two characteristics of effective communication: the extent to which team communications are centralized and the nature of the team's task.[17] The relationship between these characteristics is illustrated in Exhibit 13.3. In a **centralized network**, team members must communicate through one individual to solve problems or make decisions. Centralized communication can be effective for large teams because it limits the number of people involved in decision making. The result is a faster decision that involves fewer people.[18] In a **decentralized network**, people can communicate freely with other team members. Members process information equally among themselves until all agree on a decision.[19] Decentralized communication is best for complex, difficult work environments where teams need a free flow of communication in all directions.[20]

AP Images/Wade Payne

13-2b Communication Channels

Managers have a choice of many channels through which to communicate. A manager may discuss a problem face-to-face, make a telephone call, use text messaging, send an e-mail, write a memo or letter, or use social media, depending on the nature of the message. Research has attempted to explain how managers select communication channels to enhance communication effectiveness.[21]

One important factor that shapes a manager's selection of a communication channel is the type and amount of information to be communicated. Research has shown that channels differ in their capacity to convey data. Just as a pipeline's physical characteristics limit the kind and amount of liquid that can be pumped through it, a communication channel's physical characteristics limit the kind and amount of information that can be conveyed through it. The channels available to managers can be classified into a hierarchy based on information richness.

The Hierarchy of Channel Richness   **Channel richness** is the amount of information that can be transmitted during a communication episode. The hierarchy of channel richness is illustrated in Exhibit 13.4. The capacity of an information channel is influenced by three characteristics: (1) the ability to handle multiple cues simultaneously; (2) the ability to facilitate rapid, two-way feedback; and (3) the ability to establish a personal focus for the communication. Face-to-face discussion is the richest medium because it permits direct experience, multiple information cues, immediate feedback, and personal focus. Because of its richness, it is the best channel when communicating to people who are exhibiting strong emotions, such as anxiety, fear, or defensiveness. Face-to-face discussions facilitate the assimilation of broad cues and deep, emotional understanding of the situation. Telephone conversations are next in the richness hierarchy. Although eye contact, posture, and other body language cues are missing, the human voice still can carry a tremendous amount of emotional information.

Exhibit 13.3 Communication Networks

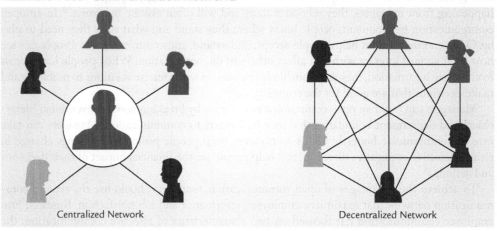

Centralized Network   Decentralized Network

SOURCE: Joel Spolsky, "A Little Less Conversation," *Inc.* (February 2010): 28–29. From Mansueto Ventures LLC, 2010.

Exhibit 13.4 A Continuum of Channel Richness

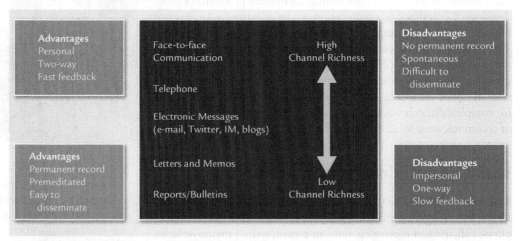

Electronic communication, such e-mail, instant messaging, and text messaging, is increasingly being used for messages that were once handled face-to-face or by telephone. However, in a survey by researchers at The Ohio State University, most respondents said that they preferred the telephone or face-to-face conversation for communicating difficult news, giving advice, or expressing affection.[22] Because e-mail messages lack both visual and verbal cues and don't allow for interaction and feedback, messages can sometimes be misunderstood. Using e-mail to discuss disputes, for example, can lead to escalation rather than resolution of conflict.[23] Too often, managers use e-mail or text messaging to avoid the emotional discomfort of a real-time conversation, hiding behind their computers to send rebukes or criticisms that they would never deliver in person. "Because we can't see their hurt, it doesn't matter as much," says business consultant Margie Warrell. She advises managers to never use e-mail in the following circumstances:

- ***When you are angry***. As our anger increases, so does our inability to communicate effectively. Wait at least two hours to cool off before sending an e-mail message. Then you will be more able to choose the most constructive way to convey that you are upset.
- ***When your message may be misunderstood***. Meet in person with someone who may be defensive about certain issues. A face-to-face conversation ensures that the other person hears your message in the most positive way.
- ***When you are canceling or apologizing***. To cancel an engagement, pick up the phone and call instead of e-mailing, to demonstrate that you care about the relationship. When an apology is called for, meet in person so that you can ask for and receive forgiveness, which goes a long way toward restoring a damaged relationship.
- ***When you are rebuking or criticizing***. While it is never easy to deliver negative feedback, it is better to communicate rebukes or criticisms in person so that you can read visual cues and address any issues that the other person might raise.[24]

Still lower on the hierarchy of channel richness are written letters and memos. Written communication can be personally focused, but it conveys only the cues written on paper and results in slower receipt of feedback. Impersonal written media, including flyers, bulletins, and standard computer reports, are the lowest in richness. These channels are not focused on a single receiver, use limited information cues, and do not permit feedback.

Selecting the Appropriate Channel   It is important for managers to understand that each communication channel has advantages and disadvantages and that each can be an effective means of communication in the appropriate circumstances.[25] Channel selection depends on whether the message is routine or nonroutine. *Nonroutine messages* typically are ambiguous, concern novel events, and involve great potential for misunderstanding. They often are characterized by time pressure and surprise. Managers can communicate nonroutine messages effectively by selecting rich channels. *Routine* messages are simple and straightforward. They convey data or statistics or simply put into words what managers already agree on and understand. Routine messages can be efficiently communicated through a channel lower in richness, such as a memo, e-mail, or text message. Written communications should be used when the communication is official and a permanent record is required.[26]

The key is to select a channel to fit the message. During a major acquisition, one firm decided to send top executives to all major work sites of the acquired company, where most of the workers met the managers in person, heard about their plans for the company, and had a chance to ask questions. The results were well worth the time and expense of the personal, face-to-face meetings because the acquired workforce saw their new managers as understanding, open, and willing to listen.[27] Communicating their nonroutine message about the acquisition in person prevented damaging rumors and misunderstandings. The choice of a communication channel can also convey a symbolic meaning to the receiver; in a sense, the medium becomes the message. The firm's decision to communicate face-to-face with the acquired workforce signaled to employees that managers cared about them as individuals.

13-2c Communicating to Persuade and Influence Others

Communication is not just for conveying information but also for persuading and influencing people. Although communication skills have always been important to managers, the ability to persuade and influence others is even more critical today. The command-and-control mind-set of managers telling workers what to do and how to do it is gone. Key points for practicing the art of persuasion include the following:[28]

> "Electric communication will never be a substitute for the face of someone who with their soul encourages another person to be brave and true."
> —CHARLES DICKENS (1812– 1870), ENGLISH NOVELIST

- ***Establish credibility.*** A manager's credibility is based on knowledge, expertise, and interpersonal skills. By demonstrating a consistent ability to make well-informed, sound decisions, managers inspire employees to have more confidence in the manager's leadership abilities.
- ***Build goals on common ground.*** To be persuasive, managers should describe the benefits that employees will experience by embracing a new policy or fulfilling a request. An example is the manager who wanted to persuade fast-food franchisees to support new pricing discounts desired by headquarters. The manager didn't just explain that headquarters wanted the policies implemented; he cited research showing that the revised pricing would increase franchisees' profits.[29] When the franchisees saw how they would benefit personally, they were eager to adopt the new policies. If a manager can't find common advantages, this is typically a signal that goals and plans need to be adjusted.
- ***Connect emotionally.*** The most effective persuaders are good listeners who establish an emotional connection with others and balance their competence and credibility with warmth and understanding.[30] They learn to understand others' emotions and needs and adjust their approach to match the audience's ability to receive their message. In addition, by looking at how people have interpreted and responded to past events, a manager can get a better grasp on how they might react to new ideas and proposals that the manager wants them to adopt. Robert Tolmach learned how to connect on an emotional and intellectual level when starting his nonprofit, Changing the Present, as described in the "Sunny Side Up" box.

Sunny Side Up } **Changing the Present**

Robert Tolmach had an idea for a nonprofit 10 years ago, but it really took off when he relaunched it in fall of 2017. He had been an architect, did real estate investing, and spent time in Asia. When he got back, he was ready to do something that would have a positive impact on people and the environment, so he returned his attention to his nonprofit, Changing the Present, which helps the country's 1.1 million nonprofits, most of which are always fund-raising and lamenting about how much more they could do with more money. His plan included capturing some of the $50 billion Americans spend each year on birthday, wedding, and holiday presents.

Tolmach was inspired by Heifer International, which pioneered and provided the opportunity to capture some of that gift money. It does so by making donations given in a friend's name feel like a rewarding gift and nice alternative to buying more "stuff." Heifer offers lovely greeting cards saying the person just provided a flock of ducks for a family in India (cost $20) or a cow for a family in Rwanda (cost $500), plus many other options. This is in contrast to what many nonprofits do, which is send an e-mail (or perhaps a generic letter) saying a donation was made in the person's name.

Changing the Present works with any nonprofit to make the experience of a donation, given a friend's name, feel like a memorable gift, with unique cards (which the donor designs online) to notify a loved one of the gift by the donor's choice. For example, someone can give $60 and restore eyesight to a person overseas, preserve an acre of rainforest, or fund an hour of cancer research. Changing the Present takes the donor's $60 and sends it with only a 5 percent surcharge to the charity and then helps the donor send a card to the recipient (with the donor's return address, so it is more likely to be opened by the recipient). Any nonprofit that is a 501 (c) (3) can sign up for free and be on the Changing the Present's Web site.

One of Tolmach's challenges is staffing. Because this is a huge undertaking and it hasn't yet found its own big donor, no one, including Tolmach, has a salary. He therefore relies on volunteers, interns, and pro bono consultants, which means recruiting is ongoing. Changing the Present needs people with skills such as sales, marketing, and design. In order to provide maximum experience for the volunteers, no one volunteering runs the copy machine or stuffs envelopes. Therefore, Tolmach has been able to recruit highly skilled volunteers who believe in the mission and want to make the greatest impact on the world for one or two days week.

Tolmach also spends a great deal of time communicating about the mission, how it is executed, what the nonprofit world needs, and so on. He ably talks to people at charities, potential donors, recruits, and everyone involved in the organization. You might say he is on a mission. "Save as many people as you can," he says. "Or the environment. Or both."

SOURCE: Robert Tolmach, personal communication, May 2018.

- *Use multiple media to send important messages*. When a message is highly important, managers often use *redundant communications*, sending the same message using different channels. For example, one manager explained a request to an employee in person, then immediately composed a follow-up e-mail to the same employee that summarized the request in writing. For companywide changes, managers might hold small-group sessions to talk with employees about a new policy, post an article in the company's newsletter, and use social media to make sure that everyone gets the information. By saying the same thing more than once via multiple channels, managers add weight to the message and keep the issue at the top of employees' minds.[31]

To persuade and influence, managers must communicate frequently and easily with others. Yet some people find interpersonal communication experiences unrewarding or difficult and thus tend to avoid situations in which communication is required. The term **communication apprehension** describes this avoidance behavior and is defined as an individual's level of fear or anxiety associated with either real or anticipated communication. With training and practice, managers can overcome their communication apprehension and become more effective communicators.

Green Power

Local Impact Logistics giant Deutsche Post DHL Group has 38 locations in Thailand where Buddhist teachings about caring for one another lend themselves to helping and teaching the local population. Deutsche Post DHL Group managers plan for corporate social responsibility with sustainability at the *local* level. DHL pinpointed local needs and issues and communicated site-specific strategies, such as efficient lighting and the reduction of air conditioner demand on Thailand's hot climate, and the installation of global positioning satellite (GPS) systems to minimize fuel consumption.

DHL's commitment to social responsibility is reflected in its three pillars: "Go Green" (climate protection), "Go Help" (disaster relief), and "Go Teach" (education). Each pillar in this corporate plan indicates broad goals—such as a 30 percent reduction in CO_2 emissions by 2020—that are customized to fit local needs and cultures. For example, managers at DHL Thailand communicate to potential business partners to gain buy-in to the company's "Go Green" philosophy, reflecting a giant leap in sustainability at the local level.

SOURCE: Based on David Ferguson, "CSR in Asian Logistics: Operationalisation within DHL (Thailand)," *Journal of Management Development* 30, no. 10 (2011): 985–999.

13-2d Communicating with Radical Candor

To influence and persuade, managers also must be frank and straightforward about what they want and need from others. Communicating with radical candor means providing feedback and being direct, honest, and clear about what employees need to do to meet objectives while also expressing care and respect and not making people feel slighted, controlled, or exploited.

Unfortunately, communicating with candor is a problem for many managers. Jack Welch, speaker, author, and former CEO of General Electric (GE), says that when he asks groups of managers how many of them have received candid performance appraisals, only about 10 percent of people raise their hands. When he asks how many have given candid appraisals to their employees, the results aren't much better.[32] Kim Scott, a coach who works with companies including Twitter, Shyp, and Qualtrics, recalls an experience she had when she worked at Google. After a successful presentation to Google's founders and the CEO, Scott's boss Sheryl Sandberg (now COO at Facebook) told Scott all the things she liked about the presentation and how impressed she was with the success the team was having. Then she added, "But you said *um* a lot." Sandberg suggested that the company could hire a speaking coach and offered other ideas. Since the presentation had gone over so well, Scott kept brushing aside the comments. Finally, Sandberg said, "You know, Kim, I can tell I'm not really getting through to you. I'm going to have to be clearer here. When you say *um* every third word, it makes you sound stupid." Scott says it took Sandberg's use of radical candor to get her attention.[33] Sandberg has become known as a straight talker who believes in giving and soliciting candid feedback broadly. Other managers have also learned that providing people with useful information sometimes means they have to communicate with radical candor.

Communicating with radical candor is a confident, positive approach that lets others know exactly where you stand and what you're asking of them. The Seattle Seahawks football team provides a good illustration of the power of radical candor.

Sunny Side Up ⟩ Seattle Seahawks

The Seattle Seahawks are known for having one of the best defenses in NFL football. Having talented players is only part of the formula. Another big reason the Seahawks are so good is the unusual degree of open and honest communication.

Earl Thomas, the team's star safety, says there are a lot of "hard talks," his term for candid conversations. Because of the blunt honesty players display with one another, a *Wall Street Journal* reporter said the Seahawks have "perhaps the most emotionally healthy locker room in the NFL." It's

an intentional strategy by coach Pete Carroll and general manager John Schneider. With the Seahawks, whoever sees a mistake or a problem says something about it. Players admit the brutal frankness can sometimes be difficult, but in the long run they say it helps them be better on and off the field. Many also prefer not having to worry about where they stand. "It lets you be at peace," one player said. "You are never worried about what guys are thinking about."[34]

When everyone in an organization feels free to open up and speak frankly, more people get involved in organizational conversations, which leads to more ideas and faster learning. In addition, candor allows ideas to be debated, adapted, and acted upon more quickly. "It's like being in a good marriage," said Seahawks defensive end Michael Bennett. "We're continuously learning about each other every day."[35]

Candid communication also limits common organizational problems such as meaningless meetings, workplace incivility, or rancorous silence. At Taunton Press, a special-interest publishing company, the lack of candor led to endless meetings and decreased productivity. In a small, close-knit company like Taunton, people naturally don't want to offend one another. Yet over time, the culture of "terminal niceness" that had evolved sabotaged teamwork. Executives hired consultants from Fierce Inc. to help Taunton managers and employees see that healthy relationships include both confrontation and appreciation. Over time, Taunton transformed to a culture of candor, collaboration, and accountability.[36]

The appropriate use of radical candor acknowledges another person's perspective and opinion yet is very specific about what the manager wants and why. Some valuable techniques for communicating with candor include:[37]

- *Use "I statements."* To communicate with candor, you should keep the focus on the specific perception that you have, how it makes you feel, and the effect that it is having on you rather than accusing or blaming the person with whom you are communicating. Suppose that you share office space with a sloppy colleague. Rather than saying, "You drive me crazy by leaving food wrappers scattered all over the place," you might say, "I'm finding it really hard to get our work done with all this clutter on the work table."
- *Stick to facts rather than judgments.* Don't tell your colleague that she's a disgusting slob; just let her know that the clutter she's leaving on the table is interfering with your ability to do your work.
- *Be clear, specific, and direct in your requests.* Say "I'd like for you to keep the worktable clean because we both have to use it to get our work done," rather than "Why don't you clean up the mess you leave around here?"

Communicating with radical candor is an important part of creating an open communication climate. When managers communicate with candor, they encourage others to do the same. In an organization where candid communication is the norm, everything works faster and better.

13-2e Asking Questions

The traditional top-down, command-and-control approach to organizational communication is no longer viable in today's global, technologically sophisticated workplace. This traditional model is giving way to a more dynamic form of communication that is characterized by *organizational conversations*, which involve a give-and-take exchange of information. Succeeding in today's environment means that managers need to learn to ask the right questions.[38] Most managers do 80 percent telling and 20 percent asking, while it should be the other way around. Glenn Kelman, CEO of online real estate site Redfin, says one of the most important things a manager can do is to "ask the most basic question, which is, 'What should [we] be doing better?'" Kelman says people will automatically respond that everything is great, but if you keep asking and show that you're sincere, they'll eventually come forward with thoughts and ideas for how to make things better.[39] Asking questions can benefit both managers and employees in numerous ways: [40]

- *Asking questions builds trust and openness between managers and employees*. Managers who ask questions encourage their employees to share ideas and offer feedback. James E. Rogers, former president and CEO of Duke Energy, held listening sessions with groups of 90–100 employees in which he would ask questions and respond to questions from employees. By engaging with employees in a format resembling ordinary person-to-person conversation, Rogers built a culture based on trust and authenticity.[41]
- *Asking questions builds critical thinking skills*. In one survey, 99 percent of top managers said critical thinking skills at all levels are crucial to the success of their organizations.[42] Asking questions stimulates critical, independent thinking, encourages people to use their creativity, and leads to deeper, more lasting learning.
- *Questions stimulate the mind and give people a chance to make a difference*. When a manager asks a question of someone, it puts the individual on alert in a way that making a statement does not. If a plant foreman says, "We have to increase production to fill this order," workers can listen to him and try to speed things up, or continue working as they have been. If, instead, the foreman asks employees, "What can we do to make sure we fill this order on time?" people can't ignore him; they have to start looking for solutions. Thus, asking questions gets people to accept responsibility for solving their own problems.

Asking questions is an important dimension of the organizational conversation. Just as important is listening to the answers.

13-2f Listening

Of all the competencies critical to successful managerial communication, listening is at the top of the list. Yet listening seems to be a rare skill among managers, and the inability to listen is one of the key reasons that managers fail. In fact, a startling 67 percent of new managers fail within 18 months, and it's often because they don't listen.[43]

Listening involves the skill of grasping both facts and feelings to interpret a message's genuine meaning. Only then can the manager provide the appropriate response. Listening requires attention, energy, and skill. Although about 75 percent of effective communication is listening, most people spend only 30 to 40 percent of their time listening, which leads to many communication errors.[44] One of the secrets of highly successful salespeople is that they spend 60 to 70 percent of a sales call letting the customer talk.[45] However, listening involves much more than just not talking. Many people don't know how to listen effectively. They concentrate on formulating what they are going to say next rather than on what is being said to them. *Harvard Business Review on Effective Communication* cites research indicating that within 48 hours, most people retain only 25 percent of what they've heard. [46]

Most managers now recognize that important information flows from the bottom up, not the top down, and managers had better be tuned in.[47] Some organizations use innovative techniques for finding out what's on employees' and customers' minds. Consider how managers at Earl's restaurants keep in touch with how employees are thinking and feeling.

Recipe for Success ⎫ Earl's Kitchen + Bar

Earl's, a Canadian-based chain of casual restaurants with as many as 8,000 workers at its seasonal peak, shows up regularly on lists of the best places to work in Canada. For example, in late 2015, Earl's was at the top of Glassdoor's list as the best employer in Canada based on its Employees Choice Awards ratings. Glassdoor's ratings are based entirely on anonymous employee feedback.

Earl's takes the engagement of employees seriously—so seriously that it places more emphasis on that measurement than it does on sales figures. Earl's formerly did do an annual survey to make sure all employees felt that they had a chance to be heard and that managers were listening to what they had to say. But new technology has given managers an easier way to find out what people are thinking. Earl's now sends out short surveys

at least every three months and people can say whatever they want, anonymously.

Using a software tool called Culture Amp, managers can push short surveys to employees' mobile devices at any time. Being able to remain anonymous helps employees overcome their reluctance to vent about little things or to ask tough questions of managers. The regular surveys also let people know that the company cares about what they're going through because managers follow-up on the information they receive. Importantly, the technology seems to be spurring more face-to-face conversations too. Managers say that since the company started using Culture Amp, employees seem to be talking more with their supervisors in person.[48]

Earl's uses electronic communication to supplement, not replace, a manager communication style that emphasizes listening to employees. Done correctly, listening is a vital link in the communication process, shown in the model of communication in Exhibit 13.2.

Concept Connection

Messages are conveyed not only by what is said but also by how it is said and the facial expressions and body language of the people involved. Face-to-face communication is the richest **communication channel** because it facilitates these **nonverbal cues** and allows for immediate feedback. Important issues should be discussed face-to-face.

What constitutes good listening? Exhibit 13.5 gives 10 keys to effective listening and illustrates a number of ways to distinguish a bad listener from a good listener. A good listener finds areas of interest, is flexible, works hard at listening, and uses thought speed to mentally summarize, weigh, and anticipate what the speaker says. Good listening means shifting from thinking about self to empathizing with the other person, which requires a high degree of emotional intelligence, as described in Chapter 10.

13-2g Nonverbal Communication

Managers should be aware that their body language—facial expressions, gestures, touch, and use of space—can communicate a range of messages, from enthusiasm, warmth, and confidence to arrogance, indifference, displeasure, and condescension.[49] For example, a manager who consistently delivers his or her verbal messages with a scowling expression or a sarcastic look will likely not develop positive interpersonal relationships, no matter how positive the verbal messages are.[50]

Nonverbal communication refers to messages sent through human actions and behavior rather than through words.[51] Managers should take care to align their facial expressions and body language to support an intended message. When nonverbal

Exhibit 13.5 Ten Keys to Effective Listening

Key	Poor Listener	Good Listener
1. Listen actively	Is minimally involved and unfocused	Shows interest; nods; asks questions; paraphrases what is said
2. Keep an open mind	Pays attention only to ideas that conform to his or her own opinions	Looks for opportunities and new learning
3. Resist distractions	Is easily distracted	Fights distractions; tolerates bad habits; knows how to concentrate
4. Capitalize on the fact that thought is faster than speech	Tends to daydream with slow speakers	Challenges assumptions, anticipates; summarizes; listens between lines to tone of voice
5. Seek understanding	Feigns agreement to bring the conversation to an end	Searches for common ground and new understanding
6. Judge content, not delivery	Tunes out if delivery is poor	Judges content; skips over delivery errors
7. Hold one's fire	Spouts solutions before understanding the problem or question	Does not judge or respond until comprehension is complete
8. Listen for ideas	Listens for facts	Listens to central themes
9. Work at listening	Provides no energy output; is passive and laid back	Works hard; exhibits active body state, eye contact
10. Show respect	Interrupts; talks over the other person when trying to get a point across	Learns to keep quiet and let the other person do most of the talking

SOURCES: Based on "A Field Guide to Identifying Bad Listeners," *McKinsey Quarterly*, Issue 2 (2012): 112; Bernard T. Ferrari, "The Executive's Guide to Better Listening," *McKinsey Quarterly*, Issue 2 (2012): 50–60; John Keyser, "Active Listening Leads to Business Success," *T+D* (July 2013): 26–28; Diann Daniel, "Seven Deadly Sins of (Not) Listening," *CIO*, September 7, 2004, www.cio.com /article/134801/Seven_Deadly_Sins_of_Not_Listening_ (accessed December 7, 2012); and Philip Morgan and Kent Baker, "Building a Professional Image: Improving Listening Behavior," *Supervisory Management* (November 1985): 34–38.

signals contradict a manager's words, people become confused and may discount what is being said and believe the body language instead. Managers are watched, and their behavior, appearance, actions, and attitudes are symbolic of what they value and expect of others.

Most of us have heard the saying, "Actions speak louder than words." Indeed, we communicate without words all the time, whether we realize it or not. Interesting new research shows that posture and body position have a tremendous impact both on how people are perceived as well as how they actually perform.[52] Katy Keim, chief marketing officer of Lithium, used to step back from listeners during presentations or conversations, resting her weight on her back foot with her hands clasped in front of her. She was often surprised when people asked if she was nervous. After working with a coach and watching herself on video, she realized that her posture "was slightly standoffish" and didn't project the strength that she wanted to show to clients.[53] Research from Harvard Business School and Columbia Business School shows that merely holding your body in a "high-power pose" for a few minutes in private—such as standing tall with shoulders pulled back, widening your stance, or leaning forward over a desk with hands planted firmly on the surface—leads to higher levels of testosterone and lower levels of stress. That is, these powerful body poses seem to boost as well as project confidence and assertiveness. Most people are totally unaware of the signals they send through their body language, and breaking old habits that project defensiveness, nervousness, or a lack of confidence, such as slumping, folding one's arms across the chest, and waving the hands when talking, can take concentrated effort and practice.

Most managers are astonished to learn that words themselves often carry little meaning. A significant portion of the shared understanding from communication comes from the nonverbal messages of facial expression, voice, mannerisms, posture, and dress. One researcher found three sources of communication cues during face-to-face communication: the *verbal*, actually spoken words; the *vocal*, which includes the pitch, tone, and timbre of a person's voice; and *facial expressions*. According to this study, the relative weights of these three factors in message interpretation are as follows: verbal impact, 7 percent; vocal impact, 38 percent; and facial impact, 55 percent.[54]

Remember This

- **Open communication** means sharing all types of information throughout the organization and across functional and hierarchical boundaries.

- A **centralized network** is a communication structure in which team members communicate through a single individual to solve problems or make decisions.

- A **decentralized network** is a communication structure in which team members freely communicate with one another and arrive at decisions together.

- **Channel richness** is the amount of information that can be transmitted during a communication episode.

- Although communication skills have always been important to managers, the ability to persuade and influence others is even more critical today.

- **Communication apprehension** is an individual's level of fear or anxiety associated with interpersonal communication.

- Communicating with radical candor means being direct, honest, and clear about what employees need to do to meet objectives while also expressing respect for others and not making people feel slighted, controlled, or exploited.

- To encourage a give-and-take exchange of information between managers and employees, managers need to learn to ask questions.

- **Listening** involves the skill of grasping both facts and feelings to interpret a message's genuine meaning.

- **Nonverbal communication** means communicating through actions, gestures, facial expressions, and behavior rather than through words.

- Practicing powerful body poses seems to boost as well as project confidence and assertiveness.

13-3 Workplace Communication

Another aspect of management communication concerns the organization as a whole. Three elements of workplace communication for managers to master are (1) using social media to improve internal and external communication; (2) using informal, personal communication channels; and (3) establishing formal communication channels.

13-3a Social Media

Social media refers to a group of Internet-based applications that allow the creation and exchange of user-generated content. The term *social media* covers a broad range of applications, including wikis, blogs, microblogs (e.g., Twitter and China's Sina Weibo), content communities (e.g., YouTube), social networking sites (e.g., Facebook), and virtual social worlds (e.g., Second Life).[55] Various forms of social media are reinventing how people in organizations communicate among themselves and with customers and other stakeholders. Dallas-based 7-Eleven Inc. has about 2,000 field consultants who use Yammer to share knowledge and learn best practices for how to help franchise owners improve their businesses.[56] Managers at Aquasana, a home water filtration company, mine the social media interactions of competitors' customers to find out what people like and don't like and create marketing campaigns that win business.[57]

Companies are embracing social media in a big way. So far, social media hasn't boosted U.S. productivity significantly, but economists such as MIT's Erik Brynjolfsson say it takes about five years for a new technology to show its full impact on companies that use it. Social media has been used for only two or three years in most companies, largely for communicating with customers and enhancing employee collaboration.[58]

Listening to Customers   Managers in organizations from small entrepreneurial firms and nonprofit agencies to huge corporations are using social media to listen to customers. Dr. Pepper, for example, uses social media to listen to customers by building an 8.5-million-strong fan base on Facebook. These loyal followers who "like" the soft drink help the brand hone its marketing message. The company sends out two messages daily on its Facebook fan page and then monitors the fans' reactions. Using tools from Facebook, Dr. Pepper measures how many times a message is viewed, how many times it is shared with other Facebook users, and what responses it gets. These data help managers adjust their brand messaging. "We mine data to understand what is appreciated, and what is not," says Robert Stone, director of interactive media services for Dr. Pepper Snapple Group Inc. "It helps us shape what we are."[59] The huge health care provider Kaiser Permanente has used social media tools so effectively to listen to customers and improve service that positive media mentions of the organization have increased close to 500 percent over the past five years.[60]

Communicating to Customers

Managers also use social media to communicate corporate news quickly to customers. O2, a popular mobile phone service company in the United Kingdom, uses its signature "Be More Dog" slogan on Instagram to broadcast behind-the-scenes looks at events or advertising campaigns the company has produced, helping customers feel like part of a special community. O2 also effectively used social media to turn a potential public relations disaster into a positive story when the company's digital network crashed, leaving many customers without mobile service for almost 24 hours. By quickly responding to angry complaints on Twitter and other social media platforms in a light-hearted and personal manner, O2 changed the tone of the conversation and won its customers back.[61] Another company that effectively used social media to calm a crisis is Domino's. After pranksters uploaded a damaging video to YouTube showing two employees defacing pizzas and sandwiches, Domino's managers responded with a viral video of their own. The company president apologized and thanked the online community for bringing the issue to his attention. He announced that the wrongdoers would be prosecuted and outlined the steps Domino's managers were taking to make sure a similar episode would never happen again. By engaging in an online conversation about the crisis, Domino's demonstrated concern for its customers and squelched further rumors and fears.[62]

Concept Connection

Poor customer service can quickly ruin a company's reputation, and bad news travels faster than ever in the age of social media. Successful companies such as Starbucks develop **social media** communication strategies that enable **listening** to customers **by managers, who then** and effectively handle customer service issues. Starbucks is quick to respond to customers on its Facebook page and Twitter account. The company also started a separate Twitter account, @MyStarbucksIdea, to gives customers a way to submit and discuss ideas for making Starbucks better.

Engaging Employees   Using social media can enable people to connect with one another easily across organizational and geographical boundaries based on professional relationships, shared interests, problems, or other criteria. Interacting through public sites and corporate networks gives employees opportunities to participate in an online community, sharing personal and professional information and photos, producing and sharing all sorts of ideas and opinions. Social media has also become an effective employee engagement tool for many companies.[63] GE's internal social network has been an astounding success, thanks partly to the efforts of Ron Utterbeck, CIO for GE Corporate, who first introduced the internal social network to GE's "power users" to encourage high levels of activity. "Our social media metrics focus largely on engagement [of both employees and customers] because that's where we connect with people and build the bond of

"Don't think of social media as just another check box on your list of things to do. . . . It's not just about putting information out there, but listening and engaging in conversation."

—LASANDRA BRILL, SENIOR MANAGER OF GLOBAL SOCIAL MEDIA, CISCO

emotional equity," said Linda Boff, GE's executive director of global digital marketing.[64] Another company that effectively uses social media for engagement is the Northern European branch of Tupperware, Tupperware Nordic.

13-3b Personal Communication Channels

Personal communication channels coexist with formal channels within an organization but may skip hierarchical levels, cutting across vertical chains of command to connect virtually anyone in the organization. In most organizations, these informal channels are the primary way information spreads and work gets accomplished. Three important types of personal communication channels are *personal networks*, the *grapevine*, and *written communication*.

Developing Personal Communication Networks   **Personal networking** refers to acquiring and cultivating personal relationships that cross departmental, hierarchical, and even organizational boundaries.[65] Successful managers consciously develop personal communication networks

Sunny Side Up } Tupperware Nordic

Tupperware may seem "old school," but it is cutting edge when it comes to using social media to engage people and build community. Steve Ove Fenne, former managing director at Tupperware Nordic, used social media to create a high level of employee engagement by building a connected community based on authenticity, pride, attachment, and fun.

To support authenticity, Fenne began building positive connections with distributors and consultants in the real world and then made sure the messages delivered through social media were consistent with actions in the real world. Previously, sales consultants and the people operating distribution warehouses were almost never invited to headquarters. Fenne didn't just invite them—he literally rolled out a long red carpet as a symbolic

gesture. He began regularly visiting all major centers of activity to establish personal relationships. He followed up with blogs, e-mails, podcasts, and other messages on social media. He also personally read every message sent to him by consultants rather than assigning the job to others, and would respond with one-liners such as "WOW! We are so proud of you" (adding the person's first name). When his time was limited, he posted messages on his social media page explaining the situation and reaffirming his support of and pride in each and every consultant.

By using social media to build a community, Fenne helped people who were often working in isolation feel more attached to one another and to the company as a whole.[66]

and encourage others to do so. Consider Nick Chen, who loved his job as a software engineer designing programs for mobile phones. Nick's team had recently designed a chipset that would revolutionize the way people communicate with their mobile phones. Nick's managers recognized his contributions with a year-end bonus, so he was feeling confident about his future with the company. However, Nick had become eager for more responsibility, so he began looking for a management position. During his one-hour commute to work every morning, he used LinkedIn to strengthen his professional network and explore job openings in the mobile technology industry. His efforts paid off. One morning, while updating his profile, Nick got a message from a former colleague who had recently taken a position at Qualcomm in San Diego. She recommended that Nick apply for a new position as product manager for the Android smartphone. Eager to learn more, Nick became one of the company's LinkedIn followers, and he found out that Qualcomm had earned a strong reputation as a great place to work and had been named to *Fortune* magazine's list of "100 Best Companies to Work For" 14 years in a row. Nick quickly updated his résumé and applied for the position.[67]

Personal networking enhanced through social and professional networking sites like LinkedIn is an important skill for managers because it enables them to get things done more smoothly and rapidly than they could do in isolation. People who have more contacts have greater influence in the organization and get more accomplished. Exhibit 13.6 illustrates a communication network within an organization. Some people are central to the network while others play only a peripheral role. The key is that relationships are built across functional and hierarchical boundaries. For example, in Exhibit 13.6, Sharon has a well-developed personal communication network, sharing information and assistance with many people across the marketing, manufacturing, and engineering departments. Contrast Sharon's contacts with those of Mike or Jasmine, who are on the periphery of the network. Who do you think is more likely to have greater access to resources and more influence in the organization?

Here are a few tips from one expert networker for building a personal communication network:[68]

Concept Connection

There are many opportunities for **personal networking**, both in the real world and online. Professional and trade associations, for example, often host after-work events where professionals from the same industry can meet and get to know one another. A city's chamber of commerce may also sponsor networking events that span industries and business types. And, of course, Web sites like LinkedIn provide excellent networking opportunities online. A savvy businessperson will pursue many of these options simultaneously in an ongoing manner.

- ***Build it before you need it.*** Smart managers don't wait until they need something to start building a network of personal relationships—by then, it's too late. Instead, they show genuine interest in others and develop honest connections.
- ***Never eat lunch alone.*** Master networkers make an effort to connect with as many people as possible, and they keep their social as well as business conference and event calendars full. Tim Gutwald created a service called Network Shuffle that randomly assigns members a new connection once a month to make sure that people's networks are constantly expanding.[69]

- ***Make it win-win.*** Successful networking isn't just about getting what *you* want; it's also about making sure other people in the network get what *they* want.

- ***Focus on diversity.*** The broader your base of contacts, the broader your range of influence. Build connections with people from as many different areas of interest as possible (both within and outside the organization).

Visit MindTap for "Self-Assessment: Are You Building a Personal Network?" It is essential to see whether as a new manager you have the skills to nurture a personal communication network effectively.

More than 200 years ago, Joseph Priestly, a young amateur scientist and minister, was performing experiments in isolation in a makeshift laboratory in the English countryside. Priestly was very intelligent, but he was isolated from other scientists until he traveled to London to attend a meeting of the Club of Honest Whigs, where a wide range of thinkers convened to talk about

Exhibit 13.6 An Organizational Communication Network

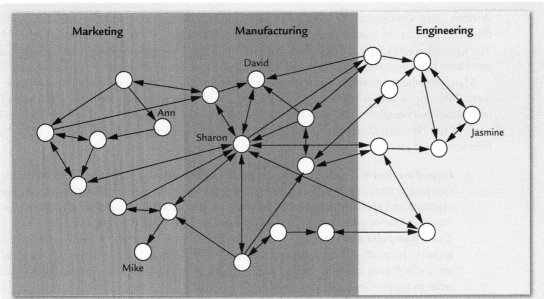

science, theology, politics, and other topics. The brainchild of Benjamin Franklin, the club was an early networking group that gave Priestly the chance to build a network of relationships and collaborations. He went on to have an illustrious scientific and writing career, famously discovering the existence of oxygen.[70] Like Priestly, by cultivating a broad network of contacts, managers can extend their influence significantly and accomplish greater results.

The Grapevine   Because 90 percent of employees engage in gossip, every manager eventually will have to contend with its effects in the workplace.[71] Although the word *gossip* has a negative connotation, it may actually be good for a company, especially during times of significant organizational change, such as layoffs or downsizing. In fact, gossip can be an invaluable tool for managers. Gossip provides an efficient channel to communicate information because it will move more rapidly than through a formal channel. Another advantage of gossip is that managers who tap into the gossip network may find it a useful "early warning system" that helps them learn about internal situations or events that might need their attention. Plus, gossip is one way employees relieve feelings of tension and anxiety, especially during periods of change. Another benefit is that gossip may give marginalized employees an opportunity to have a voice within the organization.[72]

Gossip typically travels along the **grapevine**, an informal, person-to-person communication network that is not officially sanctioned by the organization.[73] The grapevine links employees in all directions, ranging from the CEO through middle management, support staff, and line employees. The grapevine will always exist in an organization, but it can become a dominant force when formal channels are closed. In such cases, the grapevine is actually a service because the information that it provides helps make sense of an unclear or uncertain situation. Employees use grapevine rumors to fill in information gaps and clarify management decisions. One estimate is that as much as 70 percent of all communication in a firm is carried through its grapevine.[74] The grapevine tends to be more active during periods of change, excitement, anxiety, and sagging economic conditions. Managers often keep silent during times of change because they don't want to mislead employees by giving out incomplete information.[75] However, when people don't hear about what is going on from managers, the grapevine goes into overdrive. A survey by the professional employment services firm Randstad found that about half of all employees reported first hearing of major company changes through the grapevine.[76]

Surprising aspects of the grapevine are its accuracy and its relevance to the organization. About 80 percent of grapevine communications pertain to business-related topics rather than personal gossip. Moreover, from 70 to 90 percent of the details passed through a grapevine are accurate.[77] Managers should be aware that almost five of every six important messages are carried to some extent by the grapevine rather than through official channels. In a survey of 22,000 shift workers in varied industries, 55 percent said they get most of their information via the grapevine.[78] In all cases, but particularly in times of rapid change, uncertainty, or crisis, executives need to manage communications effectively so that the grapevine is not the only source of information.[79]

Written Communication   "With the fast pace of today's electronic communications, one might think that the value of fundamental writing skills has diminished in the workplace," said Joseph M. Tucci, president and CEO of EMC Corporation. "Actually, the need to write clearly and quickly has never been more important than in today's highly competitive, technology-driven global economy."[80]

Managers who are unable to communicate in writing will limit their opportunities for advancement. "Writing is both a 'marker' of high-skill, high-wage, professional work and a 'gatekeeper' with clear equity implications," says Bob Kerrey, president of The New School in New York and chair of the National Commission on Writing. Managers can improve their writing skills by following these guidelines:[81]

- *Respect the reader.* The reader's time is valuable; don't waste it with a rambling, confusing memo or e-mail that must be read several times to make sense of it. Pay attention to your grammar and spelling. Sloppy writing indicates that you think your time is more important than that of your readers. You'll lose their interest—and their respect.
- *Know your point and get to it.* What is the key piece of information that you want the reader to remember? Many people just sit and write, without clarifying in their own mind what it is they're trying to say. To write effectively, know what your central point is and write to support it.

- *Write clearly rather than impressively.* Don't use pretentious or inflated language, and avoid jargon. The goal of good writing for business is to be understood the first time through. State your message as simply and as clearly as possible.
- *Get a second opinion.* When the communication is very important, such as a formal memo to the department or organization, ask someone you consider to be a good writer to read it before you send it. Don't be too proud to take his or her advice. In all cases, read and revise the memo or e-mail a second and third time before you hit the Send button.
- Getting a second opinion and checking the data provided is what UC-Irvine should have done when it sent out acceptance letters to applications, as described in the "Half-Baked Management" box.

Half-Baked Management } University of California-Irvine

University of California-Irvine (UC-Irvine) has been rated as one of the top universities in the country. Then how could its administrators be so thoughtless? The university mistakenly sent out acceptance letters to 800 more students than it could accommodate on campus. Many of those students quickly had turned down other offers and accepted the more desirable UC-Irvine. Eventually, the university realized the error and thought it was solving the problem by rescinding the offers to the 800 students. Problem was, it was too late for those 800 to enroll in any other college that had accepted them. An 18-year-old who was the first in her family to ever go to college was devastated said, "I couldn't stop crying."

After days of explaining to the world why their solution was right, Irvine's administrators at last admitted they had made a mistake. They reinstated most of the students and the chancellor apologized publicly—at least there was that.

SOURCE: David Leonhardt, "A College Admits a Big Mistake. Imagine That," *The New York Times,* August 3, 2017. https://www.nytimes.com/2017/08/03/opinion/university-of-california-irvine.html

Remember This

- Three elements of workplace communication are using social media, using personal communication channels, and establishing formal communication channels.
- The term **social media** refers to a group of Internet-based applications that allow the creation and sharing of user-generated content.
- Companies are using social media for enabling employees to communicate among themselves and with managers, communicating with customers and other outsiders, and building employee engagement.
- **Personal communication channels** exist outside formally authorized workplace channels and include

personal networks, the grapevine, and written communication.

- **Personal networking** refers to acquiring and cultivating personal relationships that cross departmental, hierarchical, and even organizational boundaries.
- Benjamin Franklin established the Club of Honest Whigs in London more than 200 years ago as a networking group where a wide range of thinkers from various walks of life could establish relationships with others and advance their professional and personal interests.
- The **grapevine** carries workplace gossip, a dominant force in workplace communication when official channels are not functioning effectively.

A former manager of communication services at consulting firm Arthur D. Little Inc. has estimated that around 30 percent of all business memos and e-mails are written simply to get clarification about an earlier written communication that didn't make sense to the reader.[82] By following these guidelines, you can get your message across the first time.

13-3c Formal Communication Channels

Formal communication channels are those that flow within the chain of command or task responsibility defined by the organization. Each of the three formal channels and the types of information conveyed in is illustrated in Exhibit 13.7.[83] Downward and upward communications are the primary forms of communication used in most traditional, vertically organized companies. However, many of today's organizations emphasize horizontal communication, with people continuously sharing information across departments and levels. Electronic communication methods such as e-mail and social media, as described previously, have made it easier than ever for information to flow in all directions.

The most familiar and obvious flow of formal communication, **downward communication**, consists of the messages and information sent from top management to subordinates in a downward direction. Managers can communicate downward to employees in many ways. Some of the most common are through speeches, videos, blogs, social media, and company intranets. When Red Robin Gourmet Burgers introduced its new line of Tavern Burgers, top executives decided to use an internal social network to communicate the recipe and cooking methods to company managers. Instead of mailing out spiral-bound books, Red Robin successfully used social media as a method to train managers and encourage free wheeling discussions and feedback.[84] When Mary Darling and Clark Donnelly started their TV Series, *Little Mosque on the Prairie*, they were using formal communication channels to connect with six unions and various caterers, as well as informal channels to huddle with people between filming scenes, as described in the "Sunny Side Up" box.

Sunny Side Up ⟩ Little Mosque on the Prairie

How do you produce a weekly sitcom about Muslims in Canada six years after the 9/11 tragedy? With a lot of communication as executive producer Mary Darling found out. She and her husband, Clark Donnelly, who both founded WestWind Pictures, had produced documentaries and some television, and they wanted to create a fresh program that would help people understand one another better. Why not try to look at how Muslim immigrant families adjust to life in Canada? Why not, indeed?

Darling and Donnelly obtained some development money and started doing research and creating early script ideas. Then they traveled to different cities to do focus tests on scenes of the comedy show. Most people knew WestWind for its documentaries and news, so the assumption was that this new product would be documentary in nature. When the series aired in 2007, the fact that it was a scripted series surprised viewers, including the immigrants it was portraying. First generation Muslims looked at their children and asked, "Is this funny?" Their kids said yes, in between the guffaws. Darling and Donnelly are members of the Baha'i Faith and believe in the oneness of humanity, so it was very important for them to portray the Muslims as real people, with their own hopes and dreams—and conflicts, just like everyone else. Topics covered were issues such as conflicts between generations, women wearing the hijab, how to define modest dress for women, and many other real issues. Audiences loved the sitcom and it was picked up for six seasons.

Communicating and coordinating were vital to success. Part of Darling and Donnelly's budget required them to get tax credits in Saskatchewan and Toronto, which meant filming a certain number of days in each location and getting writers and directors from both sites. Such complications were in addition to working with the various tech unions for crew, writers union, actors unions, and so on. Coordinating with the requirements of each union, plus location requirements/differences meant frequent discussions and negotiations, as well as written communications on the logistics.

Broadcasting a TV show about Muslims when prejudices were high after 9/11 took a lot of courage—and the desire for positive change. Even many Muslims did not like their own religion after what had happened. But, as Darling said, "*Little Mosque on the Prairie* helped them to see the religious core of Islam." Many of the ideas in the show came from Zarqa Nawaz, born in Canada to Muslim parents from Pakistan. Her own assimilation, which included a move from big-city Toronto to a smaller one in Saskatchewan, provided much material for the comedy. Nawaz wanted to get the balance between representing her community correctly and being entertaining, said the mother of four. Getting that balance required a great deal of communication between writers, producers, directors, and actors, all of which increased the show's quality and the ability to offer insights. As Nawaz said, "You have to push the boundaries so you can grow and evolve as a community."

SOURCES: Mary Darling, personal communication, April 2018; Neil MacFarquhar, "Sitcom's Precarious Premise: Being Muslim Over Here," *The New York Times*, December 7, 2006, E-1.

It is impossible for managers to communicate with employees about everything that goes on in the organization, so they must make choices about the important information to communicate.[85] Typical topics used by downward communication include goals and strategies, job instructions and rationale, procedures, policies and practices, performance feedback, and motivation and indoctrination. For example, some managers use Twitter as a preferred channel of downward communication for time-sensitive job instructions. Reading and replying to a tweet is a lot faster than other forms of communication.[86]

Exhibit 13.7 **Downward, Upward, and Horizontal Communication in Organizations**

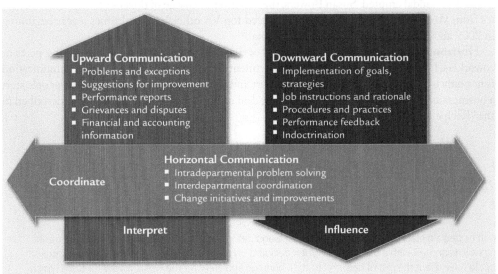

Many U.S. managers could do a better job of effective downward communication. As we reported earlier in this chapter, the results of one survey show that employees want open and honest communication about both the good and the bad aspects of the organization's performance. But when asked to rate their company's communication effectiveness on a scale of 0 to 100, the survey respondents' average score was 69. In addition, a study of 1,500 managers, mostly at first and second management levels, found that 84 percent of them perceive communication as one of their most important tasks, yet only 38 percent believe they have adequate communication skills.[87]

Formal **upward communication** includes messages that flow from the lower to the higher levels of the organization's hierarchy. Most organizations take pains to build in healthy channels for upward communication. Employees need to air grievances, report progress, and provide feedback on management initiatives. Coupling a healthy flow of upward and downward communication ensures that the communication circuit between managers and employees is complete.[88] Mike Hall, CEO of Borrego Solar Systems, found an effective way to encourage his introverted engineers to speak up and submit ideas for improving the business. To get his staff to offer feedback and suggestions, Hall organized an internal contest that he called the Innovation Challenge. All employees were encouraged to use the company intranet to submit ideas about improving the business. Once all of the ideas had been submitted, employees voted for their favorite idea, and the winner won $500 in cash. Nearly all of Borrego's employees participated in the contest.[89]

Typical areas of information communicated upward include problems and exceptions that need management's attention, ideas and

Gil C/Shutterstock.com

Concept Connection

When the world-famous Mayo Clinic formulated a new strategic plan for its medical center, the communications department experimented with a new way to facilitate **upward and downward communications**. They created "Let's Talk," an internal blog that allowed managers to use videos and blog posts to explain the plan. The clinic's employees found the blog to be so useful that it continues to be used years later as an ongoing, open communication channel. The Mayo Clinic has since added numerous external blogs to facilitate greater **horizontal communication** with customers and other stakeholders as well.

suggestions for improvement, performance reports, grievances and disputes, and financial and accounting information. It is also crucial that managers genuinely listen to upward communications and take appropriate action. For example, a nationwide scandal surrounding Veterans Administration (VA) hospitals erupted after whistle-blowers revealed in 2014 that some veterans seeking appointments at the VA Medical Center in Phoenix faced delays of up to a year and that as many as 40 veterans had died while waiting for care. One big problem in the VA hospital system is that top managers weren't listening or taking appropriate action on the upward communication they received. Documents and sworn statements indicate that top officials at the Department of Veterans Affairs had been warned of problems at the Phoenix hospital for years before the scandal erupted. Susan Bowers, the executive in charge of dozens of hospitals and clinics from West Texas to Arizona, says she briefed top VA officials several times a year beginning in 2009 about problems at the Phoenix hospital.[90]

Horizontal communication is the lateral or diagonal exchange of messages among peers or coworkers. It may occur within or across departments. The purpose of horizontal communication is not only to inform but also to request support and coordinate activities. When two people start a business as equal partners, they need a great deal of horizontal communication, as described in the "Recipe for Success" box.

Recipe for Success } Lazeez

Sisters Désirée and Céline Akhavan turned a dietary nightmare into a business plan. At 16, Céline was diagnosed with a digestive autoimmune disorder and could have spent the rest of her life on medications. Instead, she kept experimenting with various foods and ultimately discovered that the Paleo diet (consisting of lean meats, fish, fruit, nuts, seeds and vegetables) kept her the most healthy. As an avid baker and lover of all things sweet, she kept trying different recipes of her own and discovered she could live on food she actually loved. Désirée eventually adopted the Paleo lifestyle as well, and given the lack of tasty Paleo baked goods in the market, she and her sister decided to create Lazeez to make such products more accessible.

Before they founded Lazeez, Céline had followed a nonconventional career path, most recently working as the director of a co-retail marketplace, restaurant, and event space, while Désirée had spent almost a decade in law school and as an attorney and senior manager at a global company. Both craved more control and more creativity, so they strategized on starting a company that would leverage all the learning they had acquired about nutrition, food preparation, and business, as well as the intense networking the two had done in recent years to figure out which direction to take. They also relied on their support systems: parents and other family who had valuable knowledge about business and marketing, friends who had a whole range of competencies, and most of all, each other. Céline and Désirée share an apartment and talk constantly about ideas and plans. To start their company, they had to develop a logo and

a website and get Instagram and other social media accounts. When deciding on a name for their company, they were drawn to their heritage and went for the Persian word for tasty, which is Lazeez. And in developing their recipes, they are including flavors familiar to an Iranian palette that would also appeal to an American audience, such as their rose cardamom and orange blossom donuts.

Based on brainstorming sessions with friends and their own research, the sisters determined that their target market would be people (slightly more women) who love coffee and sweets and have enough disposable income to afford such treats. Because of the nature of the ingredients required for Paleo baking and the desire to provide high-quality baked goods, production is costly. Although they intended to focus initially on wholesaling to coffee shops and cafes within driving distance, the positive reaction to their social media posts has led them to think about shipping options, which introduces additional costs and a new set of questions regarding packaging. Ultimately, they want their own storefront café somewhere in New York City, probably in Brooklyn.

"You need passion," said Céline, to weather the ups and downs of the business. Her sister agreed. "It's really a lot of hard work," said Désirée, "but one thing we know. Our product surprises people. They're not used to baked goods tasting so delicious and also being really healthy."

SOURCES: Désirée and Céline Akhavan, person communication, May 2018.

Recall from Chapter 7 that many organizations build in horizontal communication in the form of task forces, committees, or even a matrix or horizontal structure to encourage coordination. At Chicago's Northwestern Memorial Hospital, two doctors created a horizontal task force to reduce the incidence of hospital-borne infections. The infection epidemic that kills nearly 100,000 people a year is growing worse worldwide, but Northwestern reversed the trend by breaking down communication barriers. Infectious-disease specialists Lance Peterson and Gary Noskin launched a regular Monday-morning meeting involving doctors and nurses, lab technicians, pharmacists, computer technicians, admissions representatives, and even the maintenance staff. The enhanced communication paid off. Over a three-year period, Northwestern's rate of hospital-borne infections plunged 22 percent and was roughly half the national average.[91]

Remember This

- A communication channel that flows within the chain of command is called a **formal communication channel**.

- **Downward communication** refers to messages sent from top management down to subordinates; **upward communication** includes messages that flow from the lower to the higher levels in the organization's hierarchy.

- **Horizontal communication** is the lateral or diagonal exchange of messages among peers or coworkers and includes team communication.

DISCUSSION QUESTIONS

1. What are the characteristics of an open communication climate? Describe the organizational benefits of managers cultivating an open communication climate.

2. Describe the elements of the communication model in Exhibit 13.2. Give an example of each part of the model as it exists in the classroom during communication between teacher and students.

3. Lana Lowery, a regional manager for a 100-person inside-sales team, notices that the team's best performer is struggling. Her sales are down 20 percent from a year ago, and she frequently arrives late for work, looking upset. Lowery needs to find out why her performance is suffering. What advice would you give Lowery for communicating with this employee? Which communication channel should she use? What would be the relative importance of candor, listening, and asking questions? Explain.

4. One small business owner said that he had to teach his young employees what a "dial tone" was. Do you have phone aversion? Do you think it is possible to build a solid business relationship with customers using only text messaging, e-mail, and social media?

5. Some senior managers believe they should rely on written information and computer reports because these yield more accurate data than do face-to-face communications. Do you agree? Why or why not?

6. During times of significant organizational change, such as downsizing and layoffs, the grapevine becomes more active as anxious employees share organizational news and rumors. As a manager, what communication strategies would you employ during a time of uncertainty in the workplace? What are the advantages and disadvantages of gossip during a time of uncertainty?

7. Assume that you manage a small online business that sells herbal supplements. Without your knowledge, a disgruntled employee has posted damaging information about your company on the company's public blog, including false information about dangerous ingredients in your best-selling supplement. What specific steps would you take to minimize the impact of this crisis?

8. If you were asked to design a training program to help managers become better communicators, what would you include in the program?

9. Suppose that you manage an employee who is spending too much time using social media at work. The result is that he has missed three important deadlines in one week. You are planning a face-to-face conversation to address this performance problem, and your goal is to communicate with radical candor. Using "I" statements as described in this chapter, how would you begin this conversation?

10. Describe specific ways that you might incorporate Twitter into an organization's communication with customers and with employees.

APPLY YOUR SKILLS: SELF-LEARNING

Personal Assessment of Communication Apprehension[92]

The following questions are about your feelings toward communication with other people. Indicate the degree to which each statement applies to you by circling one of the following: (5) Agree Strongly, (4) Agree, (3) Undecided, (2) Disagree, or (1) Disagree Strongly. There are no right or wrong answers. Many of the statements are similar to other statements. Do not be concerned about their similarities. Work quickly, recording just your first impressions.

Disagree Strongly ① ② ③ ④ ⑤ **Agree Strongly**

1. When talking in a small group of acquaintances, I'm tense and nervous.

    1 2 3 4 5

2. When presenting a talk to a group of strangers, I'm tense and nervous.

    1 2 3 4 5

3. When conversing with a friend or colleague, I'm calm and relaxed.

    1 2 3 4 5

4. When talking in a large meeting of acquaintances, I'm calm and relaxed.

    1 2 3 4 5

5. When presenting a talk to a group of friends or colleagues, I'm tense and nervous.

    1 2 3 4 5

6. When conversing with an acquaintance or colleague, I'm calm and relaxed.

    1 2 3 4 5

7. When talking in a large meeting of strangers, I'm tense and nervous.

    1 2 3 4 5

8. When talking in a small group of strangers, I'm tense and nervous.

    1 2 3 4 5

9. When talking in a small group of friends and colleagues, I'm calm and relaxed.

    1 2 3 4 5

10. When presenting a talk to a group of acquaintances, I'm calm and relaxed.

    1 2 3 4 5

11. When conversing with a stranger, I'm calm and relaxed.

    1 2 3 4 5

12. When talking in a large meeting of friends, I'm tense and nervous.

    1 2 3 4 5

13. When presenting a talk to a group of strangers, I'm calm and relaxed.

    1 2 3 4 5

14. When conversing with a friend or colleague, I'm tense and nervous.

    1 2 3 4 5

15. When talking in a large meeting of acquaintances, I'm tense and nervous.

    1 2 3 4 5

16. When talking in a small group of acquaintances, I'm calm and relaxed.

    1 2 3 4 5

17. When talking in a small group of strangers, I'm calm and relaxed.

    1 2 3 4 5

18. When presenting a talk to a group of friends, I'm calm and relaxed.

    1 2 3 4 5

19. When conversing with an acquaintance or colleague, I'm tense and nervous.

    1 2 3 4 5

20. When talking in a large meeting of strangers, I'm calm and relaxed.

    1 2 3 4 5

21. When presenting a talk to a group of acquaintances, I'm tense and nervous.

    1 2 3 4 5

22. When conversing with a stranger, I'm tense and nervous.

    1 2 3 4 5

23. When talking in a large meeting of friends or colleagues, I'm calm and relaxed.

    1 2 3 4 5

24. When talking in a small group of friends or colleagues, I'm tense and nervous.

    1 2 3 4 5

Scoring and Interpretation This questionnaire includes the computation of four subscores and one total score. Subscores relate to communication apprehension in four common situations—public speaking, meetings, group discussions, and interpersonal conversations. To compute your scores, add or subtract your scores for each item as indicated next.

Subscore/Scoring Formula For each subscore, start with 18 points, and then add the scores for the plus (+) items and subtract the scores for the minus (–) items.

Public Speaking 18 + scores for items 2, 5, and 21; – scores for items 10, 13, and 18. Score = _____

Meetings 18 + scores for items 7, 12, and 15; – scores for items 4, 20, and 23. Score = _____

Group Discussions 18 + scores for items 1, 8, and 24; – scores for items 9, 16, and 17. Score = _____

Interpersonal Conversations 18 + scores for items 14, 19, and 22; – scores for items 3, 6, and 11. Score = _____

Total Score Sum the four subscores to get the Total Score _____

This personal assessment provides an indication of how much apprehension (fear or anxiety) you feel in a variety of communication settings. Total scores may range from 24 to 120. Scores above 72 indicate that you are more apprehensive about communication than the average person. Scores above 85 indicate a high level of communication apprehension. Scores below 59 indicate a low level of apprehension. These extreme scores (below 59 and above 85) are generally outside the norm. They suggest that the degree of apprehension that you may experience in any given communication situation may not be associated with a realistic response to that situation.

Scores on the subscales can range from a low of 6 to a high of 30. Any score above 18 indicates some degree of apprehension. If you score above 18 for the public speaking context, you are like the overwhelming majority of people.

To be an effective communication champion, you should work to overcome your communication anxiety. Interpersonal conversations create the least apprehension for most people, followed by group discussions, larger meetings, and finally public speaking. Compare your scores with another student's. What aspect of communication creates the most apprehension for you? How do you plan to improve it?

APPLY YOUR SKILLS: GROUP LEARNING

Not Listening Exercise

Step 1. In small groups, identify one person as the speaker for each round. That person will talk about something important to her or him or something that happened recently that had a great impact on that person.

Step 2. Round one: ABC round. Listeners mark on a paper the number of times the speaker uses words that start with A, B, or C.

Step 3. Round two: Self-directed. Listeners try to direct attention to themselves. For example, if someone is talking about his or her planned trip to Europe, someone else may jump in with, "Oh, I went to Europe last year."

Step 4. Round four: Not listening. When the person is speaking, you should be as inattentive as possible. If she or he asks if you are listening, always say "yes." You must stay in your seat.

Not Listening Behaviors
The following are things often done that are part of poor listening habits:

1. *Not paying attention* or being distracted.

2. *Pseudolistening*: Pretending to be listening but thinking of other things.

3. Listening but *not really hearing*: Getting the words but not the meaning.

4. *Rehearsing*: Going over in your mind what you will say next.

5. *Interrupting*: Not giving the other person the chance to finish.

6. *Hearing only what you expect*: Sometimes listeners think they already know the other person's position and don't really hear what is being said.

7. *Defensiveness*: Expecting to be attacked and getting ready to explain your position.

8. *Listen for disagreement*: Only looking for something to argue about.

Good Listening Skills
Becoming conscious of the poor listening habits and working to change that can help anyone become a better listener. The following are good listening skills.

1. *Pay attention*: Even if the person speaking is dull or cantankerous, make an effort to really listen for all the points.

2. *Listen for the whole message*: Look for deeper meanings in the message and for consistency with verbal and nonverbal cues.

3. *Listening before evaluating*: Ask questions to get further clarification before making up your mind what the speaker is saying.

4. *Paraphrasing*: Try to reword the message (not merely parroting back words in a different order) to avoid misinterpretations.

Adapted from Joe Seltzer in Marcic and Seltzer, *Organizational Behavior: Experiences and Cases* (Cincinnati, OH, Southwestern Publishing, 1998).

APPLY YOUR SKILLS: ACTION LEARNING

1. Students should form pairs. You will be studying organizational communications at your university (or another company where one of you may or may not work).

2. Go to pages 500–502 in this chapter to the section on "Formal Communication Channels," especially referring to the sections on downward communication and upward communication. Become familiar with the two lists of communication channels in both upward and downward communication.

3. Go to the university's (or the company's) Web site and find places relevant to faculty and students. Find examples of upward and downward communication and list them.

4. What is the purpose of each of these communications? What, in reality, do you expect the actual consequence of each communication to be?

5. The instructor may ask you to either bring your findings to class for a discussion or to hand in a written report.

APPLY YOUR SKILLS: ETHICAL DILEMMA

On Trial[93]
When Werner and Thompson, a Los Angeles business and financial management firm, offered Iranian-born Firoz Bahmani a position as an accountant assistant one spring day in 2007, Bahmani felt a sense of genuine relief, but his relief was short-lived.

With his degree in accounting from a top-notch U.S. university, he knew he was more than a little overqualified for the job. But time after time, he'd been rejected for suitable positions. His language difficulties were the reason most often given for his unsuccessful candidacy.

Although the young man had grown up speaking both Farsi and French in his native land, he'd begun to pick up English only shortly before his arrival in the United States a few years ago. Impressed by his educational credentials and his quiet, courtly manner, managing partner Beatrice Werner overlooked his heavy accent and actively recruited him for the position, the only one available at the time. During his interview, she assured him that he would advance in time.

It was clear to Beatrice that Firoz was committed to succeeding at all costs. But it soon also became apparent that Firoz and his immediate supervisor, Cathy Putnam, were at odds. Cathy was a seasoned account manager who had just transferred to Los Angeles from the New York office. Saddled with an enormous workload, she had let Firoz know right from the start, speaking in her rapid-fire Brooklyn accent, that he'd need to get up to speed as quickly as possible.

Shortly before Cathy was to give Firoz his three-month probationary review, she came to Beatrice, expressed her frustration with Firoz's performance, and suggested that he be let go. "His bank reconciliations and financial report preparations are first-rate," Cathy admitted, "but his communication skills leave a lot to be desired. In the first place, I simply don't have the time to keep repeating the same directions over and over again when I'm trying to teach him his responsibilities. Then there's the fact that public contact is part of his written job description. Typically, he puts off making phone calls to dispute credit card charges or ask a client's staff for the information he needs. When he does finally pick up the phone . . . well, let's just say I've had more than one client mention how hard it is to understand what he's trying to say. Some of them are getting pretty exasperated."

"You know, some firms feel it's their corporate responsibility to help foreign-born employees learn English," Beatrice began. "Maybe we should help him find an English-as-a-second-language course and pay for it."

"With all due respect, I don't think that's our job," Cathy replied with barely concealed irritation. "If you come to the United States, you should learn our language. That's what my mom's parents did when they came over from Italy. They certainly didn't expect anyone to hold their hands."

Beatrice had mixed feelings. On the one hand, she recognized that Werner and Thompson had every right to expect someone in Firoz's position to be capable of carrying out his public contact duties. Perhaps she had made a mistake in hiring him. But as the daughter of German immigrants herself, she knew firsthand both how daunting language and cultural barriers can be and that they can be overcome in time. Perhaps in part because of her family background, she had a passionate commitment to the firm's stated goals of creating a diverse workforce and a caring, supportive culture. Besides, she felt a personal sense of obligation to help a hard-working, promising employee realize his potential. What will she advise Cathy to do now that Firoz's probationary period is drawing to a close?

What Would You Do?

1. Agree with Cathy Putnam. Despite your personal feelings, accept that Firoz Bahmani is not capable of carrying out the accountant assistant's responsibilities. Make the break now, and give him his notice on the grounds that he cannot carry out one of the key stated job requirements. Advise him that a position that primarily involves paperwork would be a better fit for him if he doesn't improve his speaking skills.

2. Place Firoz with a more sympathetic account manager who is open to finding ways to help him improve his English and has the time to help him develop his assertiveness and telephone skills. Send Cathy Putnam to diversity awareness training.

3. Create a new position at the firm that will allow Firoz to do the reports and reconciliations for several account managers, freeing the account assistants to concentrate on public contact work. Make it clear that he will have little chance of future promotion unless his English improves markedly.

APPLY YOUR SKILLS: CASE FOR CRITICAL ANALYSIS

E-mail Adventure

The toy industry is highly competitive and can be as cutthroat as any pirate adventure. *Yo-ho-ho*! Snooping, corporate espionage, and efforts to keep emerging ideas under wraps are all part of life in the toy industry. A certain level of managerial paranoia is expected. But when the private e-mail of an industry CEO was discovered and began making the rounds, it unleashed a firestorm and brought disastrous results on company morale, unwanted media attention, and public embarrassment.

Howard Tannenbaum is the longtime CEO of a major toy company. Over the past few years, his company worked to develop a new product line, called Brainchild, that he was passionate about and that all concerned believed would be a blockbuster. This new line of toys was so top secret that portions of the line were created and produced piecemeal among the various divisions. In the beginning, it was all very hush-hush. But as the line moved closer to completion with the expected Christmas season launch date more than a year away, press and industry rumors gained momentum.

At 8:00 a.m. on a June morning, Barry Paine, Tannenbaum's attorney and longtime friend and confidante, arrived at his office, opened his e-mail, and saw a flagged message from Howard:

Barry:

We have a disaster in the making here. Looks like I'm going to have to come down hard on all of my managers. Somebody will go—perhaps several people—before this situation is over. They're obviously getting EXTREMELY slack on design security. I won't say now how I discovered the breach or what was stolen with regard to the new product designs, but suffice it to say that at this point, EVERYONE is suspect. Needless to say, I am FURIOUS! When I find out who it is—and it could be anyone—believe me, heads will roll!!! I'll call you later this morning. WE NEED TO MEET. Thanks for letting me vent. Now, I can compose the REAL e-mail to managers.

Howard

Later that same morning, managers throughout the company received the following:

TO ALL MANAGERS:

We have a situation here in which product design information on the new line—information that should have been under the HIGHEST SECURITY—has been breached. Let me make it clear that each of you is responsible for investigating your division and finding the source of the leak. Please be thorough in your investigation and be TOTALLY HONEST with me in presenting your findings in this matter. Someone will pay for this. THIS IS TOP PRIORITY!
Howard Tannenbaum, CEO

Many recipients of the e-mail felt personally attacked and threatened. Before day's end, e-mails, phone calls, and rumors were flying. By the following day, Tannenbaum felt pressured into trying to defuse the anger by issuing a second, apologetic e-mail. However, events were already spiraling out of hand, as somehow the contents of the original e-mail to Barry Paine began circulating throughout management and beyond—to employees and at least one member of the press, who dubbed the debacle "*Toy-Gate.*" The perception of a CEO and a company out of control increased, and the stock price took a minor hit.

"The first e-mail left me stunned," one longtime manager said. "But when I saw the e-mail to Paine about how Howard *really* felt and the level of contempt he showed for all of us, making us *all* appear incompetent and dishonest—that, for me, is the last straw. Even if I stay, it has destroyed my relationship with Howard forever."

Now Tannenbaum sat, head in hands, in Paine's office. "Barry, I was simply trying to find the truth."

Paine walked over to a bookshelf and pulled an old, well-used volume. "Do you remember your Sophocles from school, Howard? In one Greek tragedy, Oedipus the King and his persistent search for truth in the murder of his predecessor, King Laius, followed a path that abandoned reason and led to his own undoing. My friend, in your case, it's not the search for truth, but it's the path you take—what you say, how you say it, and to whom you say it—that is important."

"OK—what do you think I should do next?"

Questions

1. What is the underlying communication mistake in this case? Why do you think Howard Tannenbaum sent those e-mails?

2. How do you think Tannenbaum should have communicated his concerns about the information link? Why?

3. What should Tannenbaum do now to try to recover from the negative impact of his e-mails? Suggest specific steps.

ENDNOTES

1. Adam Bryant, "Aaron Bell of AdRoll: The Truth May Hurt, but It Also Heals," *The New York Times*, March 18, 2016, http://www.nytimes.com/2016/03/20/business/aaron-bell-of-adroll-the-truth-may-hurt-but-it-also-heals.html?_r=0 (accessed May 9, 2016).

2. "Capitalizing on Effective Communication: How Courage, Innovation, and Discipline Drive Business Results in Challenging Times," Communication ROI Study Report by Watson Wyatt Worldwide, 2009/2010, www.towerswatson.com/assets/pdf/670/Capitalizing%20on%20Effective%20Communication.pdf (accessed September 5, 2012).

3. Henry Mintzberg, *The Nature of Managerial Work* (New York: Harper & Row, 1973).

4. Phillip G. Clampitt, Laurey Berk, and M. Lee Williams, "Leaders as Strategic Communicators," *Ivey Business Journal* (May–June 2002): 51–55.

5. A. G. Lafley and Roger Martin, "Instituting a Company-Wide Strategic Conversation at Procter & Gamble," *Strategy & Leadership* 41, no. 4 (2013): 4–9.

6. Spencer E. Ante, "IBM's Chief to Employees: Think Fast, Move Faster," *The Wall Street Journal*, April 25, 2013.

7. Eric Berkman, "Skills," *CIO* (March 1, 2002): 78–82; Louise van der Does and Stephen J. Caldeira, "Effective Leaders Champion Communication Skills," *Nation's Restaurant News* (March 27, 2006): 20; and Peter Lowy and Byron Reimus, "Ready, Aim, Communicate," *Management Review* (July 1996): 40ff.

8. Lowy and Reimus, "Ready, Aim, Communicate"; and Dennis Tourish, "Critical Upward Communication: Ten Commandments for Improving Strategy and Decision Making," *Long Range Planning* 38 (2005): 485–503.

9. AMA Enterprise, a division of American Management Association, reported in "Employees Are Clueless About What's Going on at Work," *T+D* (June 2012): 23.

10. Bernard M. Bass, *Bass & Stogdill's Handbook of Leadership*, 3rd ed. (New York: Free Press, 1990).

11. Dana Mattioli, "As Crisis Eases, CEOs Give Staff Some TLC," *The Wall Street Journal*, April 5, 2010, http://online.wsj.com/article/SB10001424052702303450705475159850647117086.html (accessed September 21, 2012).

12. Reported in Andrew Sobel, "Leading with Questions: Ask, Don't Tell," *Leader to Leader* (Winter 2013): 24–29.

13. Reported in van der Does and Caldeira, "Effective Leaders Champion Communication Skills."

14. Tom Szaky, "How Much Information Do You Share with Employees?" *The New York Times*, September 8, 2011, http://boss.blogs.nytimes.com/author/tom-szaky/page/2/ (accessed September 5, 2012).

15. Quint Studer, "Case for Transparency," *Leadership Excellence* (April 2010): 19.

16. Ibid.

17. E. M. Rogers and R. A. Rogers, *Communication in Organizations* (New York: Free Press, 1976); and A. Bavelas and D. Barrett, "An Experimental Approach to Organization Communication," *Personnel* 27 (1951): 366–371.

18. Joel Spolsky, "A Little Less Conversation," *Inc.* (February, 2010): 28–29.

19. This discussion is based on Richard L. Daft and Richard M. Steers, *Organizations: A Micro/Macro Approach* (New York: HarperCollins, 1986).

20. Richard L. Daft and Norman B. Macintosh, "A Tentative Exploration into the Amount and Equivocality of Information Processing in Organizational Work Units," *Administrative Science Quarterly* 26 (1981): 207–224.

21. Robert H. Lengel and Richard L. Daft, "The Selection of Communication Media as an Executive Skill," *Academy of Management Executive* 2 (August 1988): 225–232; Richard L. Daft and Robert H. Lengel, "Organizational Information Requirements, Media Richness, and Structural Design," *Managerial Science* 32 (May 1986): 554–572; and Jane Webster and Linda Klebe Treviño, "Rational and Social Theories as Complementary Explanations of Communication Media Choices: Two Policy-Capturing Studies," *Academy of Management Journal* 38, no. 6 (1995): 1544–1572.

22. Research reported in "E-mail Can't Mimic Phone Calls," *Johnson City Press*, September 17, 2000.

23. Ray Friedman and Steven C. Currall, "E-Mail Escalation: Dispute Exacerbating Elements of Electronic Communication," IACM 15th Annual Conference, Salt Lake City, Utah, http://papers.ssrn.com/sol3/papers.cfm?abstract_id=304966 (accessed August 9, 2016); Lauren Keller Johnson, "Does E-Mail Escalate Conflict?" *MIT Sloan Management Review* (Fall 2002): 14–15; and Alison Stein Wellner, "Lost in Translation," *Inc. Magazine* (September 2005): 37–38.

24. Margie Warrell, "Hiding Behind E-mail? Four Times You Should Never Use E-mail," *Forbes*, www.forbes.com/sites/margiewarrell/2012/08/27/do-you-hide-behind-email/ (accessed September 10, 2012).

25. Ronald E. Rice, "Task Analyzability, Use of New Media, and Effectiveness: A Multi-Site Exploration of Media Richness," *Organization Science* 3, no. 4 (November 1992): 475–500; and M. Lynne Markus, "Electronic Mail as the Medium of Managerial Choice," *Organizational Science* 5, no. 4 (November 1994): 502–527.

26. Richard L. Daft, Robert H. Lengel, and Linda Klebe Treviño, "Message Equivocality, Media Selection and Manager Performance: Implication for Information Systems," *MIS Quarterly* 11 (1987): 355–368.

27. Mary Young and James E. Post, "Managing to Communicate, Communicating to Manage: How Leading Companies Communicate with Employees," *Organizational Dynamics* (Summer 1993): 31–43.

28. This section is based on Jay A. Conger, "The Necessary Art of Persuasion," *Harvard Business Review* (May–June 1998): 84–95.

29. Conger, "The Necessary Art of Persuasion."

30. Amy J. C. Cuddy, Matthew Kohut, and John Neffinger, "Connect, Then Lead," *Harvard Business Review* (July–August 2013): 3–9; and Kevin Daum, "7 Things Really Persuasive People Do," *Inc.com*, August 2, 2013, http://www.inc.com/kevin-daum/7-things-really-persuasive-people-do.html (accessed October 31, 2013).

31. Paul M. Leonardi, Tsedal B. Neeley, and Elizabeth M. Gerber, "How Managers Use Multiple Media: Discrepant Events, Power, and Timing in Redundant Communication," *Organization Science* 23, no. 1 (January–February 2012): 98–117.

32. This discussion is based in part on Jack Welch with Suzy Welch, *Winning* (New York: HarperBusiness, 2005), Chapter 2.

33. "Former Googler Lets Us in on the Surprising Secret to Being a Good Boss," *Fast Company* (December 18, 2015), http://www.fastcompany.com/3054668/lessons-learned/former-googler-lets-us-in-on-the-surprising-secret-to-being-a-good-boss (accessed May 9, 2016).

34. Kevin Clark, "The Seattle Seahawks' Edge: Airing Their Grievances; Brutal Honesty Is the Seattle Defense's Policy," *The Wall Street Journal*, January 7, 2015, http://www.wsj.com/articles/the-seattle-seahawks-edge-airing-their-grievances-1420652292 (accessed November 4, 2015).

35. Ibid.

36. Halley Bock, "Fierce Communication," *T+D* (November 2012): 80.

37. These are based on E. Raudsepp, "Are You Properly Assertive?" *Supervision* (June 1992); and M. J. Smith, *When I Say No, I Feel Guilty* (New York: Bantam Books, 1975).

38. Boris Groysberg and Michael Slind, "Leadership Is a Conversation," *Harvard Business Review* (June 2012): 75–84; Elizabeth Doty, "Why Leaders Who Listen Achieve Breakthroughs," *Strategy + Business* (March 21, 2016), http://www.strategy-business.com/blog/Why-Leaders-Who-Listen-Achieve-Breakthroughs?gko=7282c (accessed May 10, 2016); and Paul J. H. Schoemaker and Steven Krupp, "The Power of Asking Pivotal Questions," *MIT Sloan Management Review* 56, no. 2 (Winter 2015): 39–47.

39. Adam Bryant, "Be Yourself, Even If You're a Little Goofy" (Corner Office column, an interview with Redfin's Glenn Kelman), *The New York Times*, August 25, 2013.

40. Many of these benefits are based on "The Power of Questions," *Leader to Leader* (Spring 2005): 59–60; Quinn Spitzer and Ron Evans, "The New Business Leader: Socrates with a Baton," *Strategy & Leadership* (September–October 1997): 32–38; and Gary B. Cohen, "Just Ask Leadership: Why Great Managers Always Ask the Right Questions," *Ivey Business Journal* (July–August 2010), www.iveybusinessjournal.com/topics/leadership/just-ask-leadership-why-great-managers-always-ask-the-right-questions (accessed March 7, 2011).

41. Groysberg and Slind, "Leadership Is a Conversation."

42. Reported in Spitzer and Evans, "The New Business Leader: Socrates with a Baton."

43. Kevin Cashman, "Powerful Pause: Listening Is Leadership," *Leadership Excellence* (January 2012): 5.

44. M. P. Nichols, The Lost Art of Listening (New York: Guilford Publishing, 1995).

45. "Benchmarking the Sales Function," a report based on a study of 100 salespeople from small, medium, and large businesses, conducted by the Ron Volper Group, White Plains, New York, as reported in "Nine Habits of Highly Effective Salespeople," *Inc.com*, June 1, 1997, www.inc.com/articles/1997/06/12054.html (accessed September 23, 2010).

46. Discussed in John Keyser, "Active Listening Leads to Business Success," *T+D* (July 2013): 26–28.

47. Rick Bommelje, "Listening Pays! Achieve Significance Through the Power of Listening," *Leader to Leader* (Fall 2013): 18–25; Keyser, "Active Listening Leads to Business Success"; C. Glenn Pearce, "Doing Something About Your Listening Ability," *Supervisory Management* (March 1989): 29–34; and Tom Peters, "Learning to Listen," *Hyatt Magazine* (Spring 1988): 16–21.

48. Christopher Mims, "Bosses Use Anonymous Networks to Learn What Workers Really Think," *The Wall Street Journal*, June 21, 2015, http://www.wsj.com/articles/bosses-use-anonymous-networks-to-learn-what-workers-really-think-1434930794 (accessed November 5, 2015); and Anita Sthankiya, "B.C. Based Restaurant Group Named Best Place to Work in Canada," *KelownaNow*, December 9, 2015, https://www.kelownanow.com/good_stuff/good_fun/news/Food_Wine/15/12/09/B_C_Based_Restaurant_Group_Named_Best_Place_to_Work_in_Canada/ (accessed May 10, 2016).

49. This discussion is based in part on Carol Kinsey Goman, "Body Language: Mastering the Silent Language of Leadership" (The Leadership Playlist column), *Washington Post Online*, July 17, 2009, http://views.washingtonpost.com/leadership/leadership_playlist/2009/07/body-language-mastering-the-silent-language-of-leadership.html (accessed July 17, 2009).

50. "Management Tip of the Day: Leaders, Stop These Behaviors Now," *Harvard Business Review* (August 30, 2013), http://hbr.org/tip/2013/08/30/leaders-stop-these-behaviors-now (accessed October 31, 2013).

51. Goman, "Body Language"; and I. Thomas Sheppard, "Silent Signals," *Supervisory Management* (March 1986): 31–33.

52. This research is reported in Carol Kinsey Goman, "10 Simple and Powerful Body Language Tips for 2013," *Forbes* (January 7, 2013), http://www.forbes.com/sites/carolkinseygoman/2013/01/07/10-simple-and-powerful-body-language-tips-for-2013/ (accessed November 4, 2013); and Sue Shellenbarger, "How 'Power Poses' Can Help Your Career," *The Wall Street Journal*, August 20, 2013, http://online.wsj.com/news/articles/SB10001424127887323360850 4579022942032641408 (accessed November 4, 2013).

53. Shellenbarger, "How 'Power Poses' Can Help Your Career."

54. Albert Mehrabian, *Silent Messages* (Belmont, CA: Wadsworth, 1971); and Albert Mehrabian, "Communicating Without Words," *Psychology Today* (September 1968): 53–55.

55. Andreas M. Kaplan and Michael Haenlein, "Social Media: Back to the Roots and Back to the Future," *Journal of Systems and Information Technology* 14, no. 2 (2012): 101–104.

56. Shayndi Raice, "Social Networking Heads to the Office," *The Wall Street Journal*, April 2, 2012, http://online.wsj.com/article/SB100014240527023044598045772853540466016 14.html (accessed September 18, 2012).

57. Scott Martin, "Small-Business Customer Service Tools: Social Media, Surveys," *USA TODAY*, August 26, 2012, http://usatoday30.usatoday.com/money/smallbusiness/story/2012-08-26/efficient-small-business-online-ecommerce/57291490/1 (accessed November 1, 2013).

58. Tim Mullaney, "Social Media Is Reinventing How Business Is Done," *USA TODAY*, August 31, 2012, www.usatoday.com/money/economy/story/2012-05-14/social-media-economy-companies/55029088/1 (accessed September 5, 2012).

59. Geoffrey A. Fowler, "Are You Talking to Me?" *The Wall Street Journal*, April 25, 2011, http://online.wsj.com/article/SB1000 1424052748704116404576263083970961862.html (accessed September 18, 2012).

60. Vince Golla, interviewed by David Kiron, "Social Business at Kaiser Permanente: Using Social Tools to Improve Customer Service, Research, and Internal Collaboration," *MIT Sloan Management Review* (March 6, 2012), http://sloanreview.mit.edu/article/kaiser-permanente-using-social-tools-to-improve-customer-service-research-and-internal-collaboration/ (accessed November 1, 2013).

61. Casey Fleischmann, "How Can O2 #BeMoreDog on Social Media? #SMLondon" *SocialMediaLondon*, October 26, 2015, http://socialmedialondon.co.uk/o2-be-more-dog/ (accessed May 11, 2016); and Connie Sklar, "How to Use Social Media to Understand and Engage Your Customers," *The Guardian*, March 13, 2013, http://www.theguardian.com/media-network/media-network-blog/2013/mar/13/social-media-customer-engagement (accessed May 11, 2016).

62. Richard S. Levick, "Domino's Discovers Social Media," *BusinessWeek* (April 21, 2009), www.businessweek.com/print/managing/content/apr2009/ca20090421_555468.htm (accessed April 21, 2009).

63. Ron Utterbeck, interviewed by Robert Berkman, "GE's Colab Brings Good Things to the Company," *MIT Sloan Management Review* (November 2012), http://sloanreview.mit.edu/article/ges-colab-brings-good-things-to-the-company/ (accessed November 1, 2013); Meenu Bhatnagar, "General Electric: Engaging Employees Through Social Media," Case Study 413-103-1, Amity Research Centers, Bangalore, India, Distributed by The Case Centre, 2013; and Giselle Abramovich, "Inside General Electric's Digital Strategy" (an interview with GE's Linda Boff), *Digiday*, May 21, 2012, http://digiday.com/brands/inside-general-electrics-digital-strategy/ (accessed November 1, 2013).

64. Quoted in Abramovich, "Inside General Electric's Digital Strategy." The relationship between internal social media and emotional capital is discussed in Quy Huy and Andrew Shipilov, "The Key to Social Media Success Within Organizations," *MIT Sloan Management Review* (Fall 2012), http://sloanreview.mit.edu/article/the-key-to-social-media-success-within-organizations/(accessed November 1, 2013).

65. This discussion of informal networks is based on Rob Cross, Nitin Nohria, and Andrew Parker, "Six Myths About

Informal Networks," *MIT Sloan Management Review* (Spring 2002): 67–75; and Rob Cross and Laurence Prusak, "The People Who Make Organizations Go—or Stop," *Harvard Business Review* (June 2002): 105–112.

66. The Tupperware example is discussed in Huy and Shipilov, "The Key to Social Media Success Within Organizations."

67. Careercast.com Web site, www.careercast.com/jobs-rated/10-best-jobs-2012 (accessed September 21, 2012); George Anders, "LinkedIn's Edge: The 7 Habits of a Well-Run Social Network," *Forbes* (August 3, 2012), www.forbes.com/sites/georgeanders/2012/08/03/linkedins-edge-the-7-habits-of-a-well-run-social-network/ (accessed September 3, 2012); and CNNmoney.com Web site, http://money.cnn.com/magazines/fortune/best-companies/2012/full_list/.

68. Tahl Raz, "The 10 Secrets of a Master Networker," *Inc.* (January 2003).

69. Laura Vanderkam, "What Successful People Do During Lunch," *Fast Company* (July 29, 2013), http://www.fastcompany.com/3014909/how-to-be-a-success-at-everything/what-successful-people-do-during-lunch (accessed November 1, 2013).

70. Reid Hoffman and Ben Casnocha, "The Start-up of You," *Leader to Leader* (Spring 2013): 41–45. Adapted from their book *The Start-up of You: Adapt to the Future, Invest in Yourself, and Transform Your Career* (New York: Crown Business, 2012).

71. Travis J. Grosser et al., "Hearing It Through the Grapevine: Positive and Negative Workplace Gossip," *Organizational Dynamics* 41 (2012): 52–61.

72. Grant Michelson, Ad van Iterson, and Kathryn Waddington, "Gossip in Organizations: Contexts, Consequences, and Controversies," *Group & Organizational Management* 35, no. 4 (2010): 371–390.

73. Keith Davis and John W. Newstrom, *Human Behavior at Work: Organizational Behavior*, 7th ed. (New York: McGraw-Hill, 1985).

74. Suzanne M. Crampton, John W. Hodge, and Jitendra M. Mishra, "The Informal Communication Network: Factors Influencing Grapevine Activity," *Public Personnel Management* 27, no. 4 (Winter 1998): 569–584.

75. N. DiFonzo and P. Bordia, "A Tale of Two Corporations: Managing Uncertainty During Organizational Change," *Human Resource Management* 37, no. 3–4 (1998): 295–303.

76. Survey results reported in Jared Sandberg, "Ruthless Rumors and the Managers Who Enable Them," *The Wall Street Journal*, October 29, 2003.

77. Donald B. Simmons, "The Nature of the Organizational Grapevine," *Supervisory Management* (November 1985): 39–42; and Davis and Newstrom, *Human Behavior at Work*.

78. Barbara Ettorre, "Hellooo. Anybody Listening?" *Management Review* (November 1997): 9.

79. Lisa A. Burke and Jessica Morris Wise, "The Effective Care, Handling, and Pruning of the Office Grapevine," *Business Horizons* (May–June 2003): 71–74; "They Hear It Through the Grapevine," cited in Michael Warshaw, "The Good Guy's Guide to Office Politics," *Fast Company* (April–May 1998):

157–178; and Carol Hildebrand, "Mapping the Invisible Workplace," *CIO Enterprise*, section 2 (July 15, 1998): 18–20.

80. National Commission on Writing, "Writing Skills Necessary for Employment, Says Big Business," September 14, 2004, www.writingcommission.org/pr/writing_for_employ.html (accessed April 8, 2008).

81. Based on Michael Fitzgerald, "How to Write a Memorable Memo," *CIO* (October 15, 2005): 85–87; and Jonathan Hershberg, "It's Not Just What You Say," *Training* (May 2005): 50.

82. Mary Anne Donovan, "E-Mail Exposes the Literacy Gap," *Workforce* (November 2002): 15.

83. Daft and Steers, *Organizations*; and Daniel Katz and Robert Kahn, *The Social Psychology of Organizations*, 2d ed. (New York: Wiley, 1978).

84. Mullaney, "Social Media Is Reinventing How Business Is Done."

85. Phillip G. Clampitt, Robert J. DeKoch, and Thomas Cashman, "A Strategy for Communicating About Uncertainty," *Academy of Management Executive* 14, no. 4 (2000): 41–57.

86. Alexandra Samuel, "Better Leadership Through Social Media," *The Wall Street Journal*, April 2, 2012, http://online.wsj.com/article/SB10001424052970203753704577255531558650636.html (accessed September 12, 2012).

87. Reported in van der Does and Caldeira, "Effective Leaders Champion Communication Skills."

88. Michael J. Glauser, "Upward Information Flow in Organizations: Review and Conceptual Analysis," *Human Relations* 37 (1984): 613–643; and "Upward/Downward Communication: Critical Information Channels," *Small Business Report* (October 1985): 85–88.

89. Darren Dahl, "Pipe up, People! Rounding up Staff," *Inc.* (February 2010): 80–81.

90. "3 More Phoenix VA Officials to Be Fired over Wait-Time Scandal," *Fox News*, March 16, 2016, http://www.foxnews.com/us/2016/03/16/3-more-phoenix-va-officials-to-be-fired-over-wait-time-scandal.html (accessed May 11, 2016); and Richard A. Oppel Jr., "Some Top Officials Knew of V.A. Woes, Before the Scandal," *The New York Times*, December 26, 2014.

91. Thomas Petzinger, "A Hospital Applies Teamwork to Thwart an Insidious Enemy," *The Wall Street Journal*, May 8, 1998.

92. J. C. McCroskey, "Measures of Communication-Bound Anxiety," *Speech Monographs* 37 (1970): 269–277; J. C. McCroskey and V. P. Richmond, "Validity of the PRCA as an Index of Oral Communication Apprehension," *Communication Monographs* 45 (1978): 192–203; J. C. McCroskey and V. P. Richmond, "The Impact of Communication Apprehension on Individuals in Organizations," *Communication Quarterly* 27 (1979): 55–61; and J. C. McCroskey, *An Introduction to Rhetorical Communication* (Englewood Cliffs, NJ: Prentice Hall, 1982).

93. Mary Gillis, "Iranian Americans," *Multicultural America*, www.everyculture.com/multi/Ha-La/Iranian-Americans.html (accessed September 19, 2006); and Charlene Marmer Solomon, "Managing Today's Immigrants," *Personnel Journal* 72, no. 3 (February 1993): 56–65.

Chapter 14
Leading Teams

iStock.com/oscarhdez

Chapter Outline

Learning Outcomes

After studying this chapter, you should be able to:

14.1 Explain contributions that teams make and how managers can help teams be more effective.

14.2 Identify the types of teams in organizations.

14.3 Summarize some of the problems and challenges of teamwork.

14.4 Identify ways in which team size and diversity of membership affect team performance.

14.5 Identify roles within teams and the type of role that you could play to help a team be effective.

14.6 Explain the general stages of team development.

14.7 Explain the concepts of team cohesiveness and team norms and their relationship to team performance.

14.8 Identify the causes of conflict within and among teams and explain how to reduce conflict.

14.9 Describe the different characteristics and consequences of task conflict versus relationship conflict.

Are You Ready to Be a Manager?

Before reading this chapter, please circle either "Mostly True" or "Mostly False" for each of the following five statements.

1 I'm energized when I work in a productive team.

Mostly True ◀·················▶ Mostly False

[page 515]

2 I find it difficult to have honest discussions with "free riders" on my team.

Mostly True ◀·················▶ Mostly False

[page 521]

3 I work to create accountability because I know its lack is hazardous to effective teams.

Mostly True ◀·················▶ Mostly False

[page 522]

4 When I join a new team, I spend time observing its norms before I take any actions or make comments.

Mostly True ◀·················▶ Mostly False

[page 531]

5 I know that some conflict is good in a team, to prevent "groupthink," and I'm able to help resolve conflicts by assertively and collaboratively addressing the issues.

Mostly True ◀·················▶ Mostly False

[page 534]

Discover Your Management Approach

How Do You Like to Work?[a]

Instructions: Your approach to your job or schoolwork may indicate whether you thrive on a team. For each of the following statements about your work preferences, indicate whether each item is Mostly True or Mostly False for you.

	Mostly True	Mostly False
1. I prefer to work on a team rather than do individual tasks.	_____	_____
2. Given a choice, I try to work by myself rather than face the hassles of group work.	_____	_____
3. I enjoy the personal interaction when working with others.	_____	_____

To complete and score entire assessment, visit MindTap.

[a]Based on Eric M. Stark, Jason D. Shaw, and Michelle K. Duffy, "Preference for Group Work, Winning Orientation, and Social Loafing Behavior in Groups," *Group & Organization Management* 32, no. 6 (December 2007): 699–723.

Changing your Facebook status and posting tons of photos when you're in a new relationship is exhilarating. But what happens when that relationship comes to an end? "Not 15 minutes after we broke up . . . he changed his status to 'single,'" said Kate Sokoloff. "There was no hiding or time to cry on my own." That "emotional sucker punch" was just the beginning, says Sokoloff, who recalls wishing for a Facebook vacuum cleaner that could remove all traces of the relationship, particularly photos, so she wouldn't have to keep experiencing the sting of the breakup all over again. Thanks to Facebook's Compassion Team, there now is such a tool, referred to as the "breakup flow," and millions of people have used some aspect of it to ease the pain of breaking up in the digital age. The Compassion Team has also created tools to help with bullying and online aggression. Another team at Facebook is working on how to manage profiles after someone has died, and still another is creating ways to help identify suicide ideation in a friend's posts and connect to suicide prevention resources.[1]

Teamwork is how everything gets done at Facebook, from designing new products and features such as the breakup flow to managing human resources and handling legal matters. Many other companies have discovered that teams have real advantages, but it can be tough to work in a team. You may have already experienced the challenges of teamwork as a student, where you've had to give up some of your independence and rely on a team to perform well in order to earn a good grade. Many people get their first management experience in a team setting, and you probably will have to work in a team from time to time in your position as a new manager.

Good teams can produce amazing results, but teams aren't always successful. In a survey of manufacturing organizations, about 80 percent of respondents reported using some kind of team, but only 14 percent of those companies rated their teaming efforts as highly effective. Just over half of the respondents said their efforts were only "somewhat effective," and 15 percent considered their efforts not effective at all.[2]

This chapter focuses on teams and their applications within organizations. We define what a team is, look at the contributions that teams can make, and define various types of teams. Then we discuss the dilemma of teamwork and present a model of work team effectiveness, explore the stages of team development, and examine how characteristics such as size, cohesiveness, diversity, and norms influence team effectiveness. The chapter also looks at the roles that individuals play in teams, discusses techniques for managing team conflict, and describes how negotiation can facilitate cooperation and teamwork. Teams are a central aspect of organizational life, and the ability to manage them is a vital component of manager and organization success.

14-1 The Value of Teams

Why aren't organizations just collections of individuals going their own way and doing their own thing? Clearly, teamwork provides benefits, or companies wouldn't continue to use this structural mechanism. One illustration of the value of teamwork comes from the military, where forward surgical teams made up of U.S. Navy surgeons, nurses, anesthesiologists, and technicians operated for the first time ever in combat during Operation Iraqi Freedom. These teams were scattered over Iraq and were able to move to new locations and be set up within an hour. With the goal of saving the lives of the 15–20 percent of wounded soldiers and civilians who would die unless they received critical care within 24 hours, members of these teams smoothly coordinated their activities to accomplish a vital shared mission.[3]

Although their missions might not involve life or death, all organizations are made of various individuals and groups that must work together and coordinate their activities to accomplish objectives. Much work in organizations is *interdependent*, which means that individuals and departments rely on other individuals and departments for information or resources to accomplish their work. When tasks are highly interdependent, a team can be the best approach to ensuring the level of coordination, information sharing, and exchange of materials necessary for successful task accomplishment.

14-1a What Is a Team?

A **team** is a unit of two or more people who interact and coordinate their work to accomplish a common goal to which they are committed and hold themselves mutually accountable.[4] The definition of a team has three components. First, two or more people are required. Second, people in a team interact regularly. People who do not interact (e.g., people standing in line at a lunch counter or riding in an elevator) do not compose a team. Third, people in a team share a performance goal, whether it is to design a new smartphone, build an engine, or complete a class project.

"Individual commitment to a group effort—that is what makes a team work, a company work, a society work, a civilization work."
—VINCE LOMBARDI (1913–1970), NFL FOOTBALL COACH

Green Power

The Team's the Thing Managers at Subaru Indiana Automotive (SIA) put the company's desire to reduce, reuse, and recycle waste squarely on the line with television ads boasting "zero-landfill." SIA was not hedging, maintaining that "zero means zero," and managers placed confidence in every member of every team in every manufacturing process to hit the target. And the teams proved to be up to the challenge. For example, shop floor initiatives within the stamping unit led to partnering agreements with suppliers for more precise steel sheeting that reduced 100 pounds of steel per vehicle.

Teams initiated efforts to use plant water flow to drive mini-hydraulic electric generators, and the company's Green Payback Curve recycled a variety of waste products. Assembly-line lights were turned down during breaks and shift changes to decrease the company's carbon footprint. Respect for and confidence in its teams has made SIA a recognized leader of sustainability in manufacturing.

SOURCES: Brad Kenney, "The Zero Effect: How to Green Your Facility," *Industry Week* (July 2008): 36–41; and Dean M. Schroeder and Alan G. Robinson, "Green Is Free: Creating Sustainable Competitive Advantage Through Green Excellence," *Organizational Dynamics* 39, no. 4 (2010): 345–352.

Putting together a *team* and building *teamwork* aren't the same thing. Exhibit 14.1 shows the elements of effective teamwork. Teamwork requires bringing together the right set of personalities, specialties, and skills; clearly defining roles and responsibilities; focusing everyone on a well-defined mission; establishing clear channels of communication and information sharing so that team members communicate their objectives and needs in all directions; and getting everyone to sublimate their individual egos and pull together in the same direction. Trust is a crucial aspect of teamwork. People must be willing to collaborate and sometimes sacrifice their individual objectives for the sake of the larger goal, which requires that they believe that others are willing to do the same thing. The Golden State Warriors NBA team demonstrates the power of effective teamwork as reported in the "Sunny Side Up" box.

Exhibit 14.1 Requirements of Teamwork

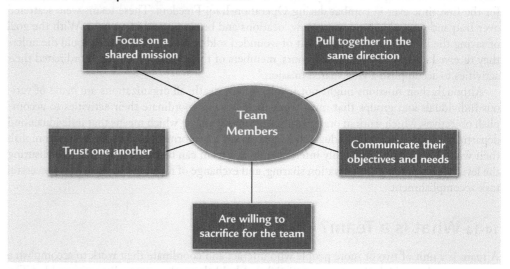

SOURCES: Based on Rick Wartzman, "Microsoft's New Mission: To Create Real Teamwork, Not Just Teams," *Time* (July 17, 2013), http://business.time.com/2013/07/17/microsofts-new-mission-to-create-real-teamwork-not-just-teams/ (accessed July 19, 2013); and Chuck Salter, "What LeBron James and the Miami Heat Teach Us About Teamwork," *Fast Company* (April 2011), http://www.fastcompany.com/magazine/155/the-worlds-greatest-chemistry-experiment.html (accessed April 25, 2011).

Sunny Side Up } Golden State Warriors

After winning the NBA Championship in June 2015, the Golden State Warriors and coach Steve Kerr kept things just as they were for the 2015–2016 season, while other teams were taking steps to strengthen their rosters. The key parts of the Warriors team had been together for about three years and had cultivated a camaraderie and cohesiveness that team members consider a competitive weapon.

The success of the Warriors can be attributed not to standout individual performances (although there have been some) but to outstanding teamwork. Team members say their success comes from the fact that they genuinely like one another, enjoy playing together, and have developed good communication and deep bonds of trust. "It's a brotherhood," says forward Marreese Speights. "We support every guy that steps on the court, whether it's 30 minutes or two minutes." When the Warriors are on the road, team members go out to eat together, "bonding like Little Leaguers at a pizza party," as a *Wall Street Journal* reporter put it. Most professional basketball players go off on their own, but the Warriors make a habit of huge communal meals, deciding when and where to eat with a teamwide group text message.

The camaraderie and teamwork of the Warriors have made it one of the best teams in the NBA. It has also made them one of the most pleasant teams to play for and one of the most enjoyable teams to watch. "Chemistry is something you can't fake," said Warriors forward David Lee. "You either have it or you don't."[5]

The Golden State Warriors know that individual stars don't necessarily make a great team, so players willingly put aside their personal quests for glory for the good of the whole. Effective teams in businesses and other organizations also are those in which members trust one another and are willing to forgo their individual objectives if necessary to accomplish a shared goal.

David Novak, the recently retired chairman and former CEO of Yum Brands, describes the role of teamwork in the success of the giant restaurant company. Novak spent nearly 30 years with Yum Brands (which includes KFC, Pizza Hut, and Taco Bell). When he was first put in charge of running KFC, the U.S. division hadn't met its profit target for ages. Headquarters blamed the franchisees; the franchisees blamed headquarters. After Novak embarked on a team-building crusade, KFC resumed growing and its profits nearly doubled in three years. "What really made the difference," Novak says, "was the idea that if we trusted each other, we could work together to make something happen that was bigger than our individual capabilities."[6]

14-1b Contributions of Teams

Effective teams can provide many advantages, as illustrated in Exhibit 14.2 and as described in the following list. These contributions of teams lead to stronger competitive advantage and higher overall organizational performance.

- *Creativity and innovation.* Because teams include people with diverse skills, strengths, experiences, and perspectives, they contribute to a higher level of creativity and innovation in the organization.[7] One factor that has been overlooked in the success of Apple, for instance, is that Steve Jobs built a top management team of superb technologists, marketers, designers, and others who kept the company's innovative juices flowing. Most of Jobs's top management team worked with him for a decade or more.[8]
- *Improved quality.* One criterion for organizational effectiveness is whether products and services meet customer requirements for quality. Perhaps nowhere is this more essential than in health care. The days when a lone physician could master all the skills, keep all the information in his or her head, and manage everything required to treat a patient are long gone. Organizations that provide the highest quality of patient care are those in which teams of closely coordinated professionals provide an integrated system of care.[9]
- *Speed of response.* Tightly integrated teams can maneuver incredibly fast. Apple again provides an example. Apple's close-knit team has changed pricing as late as 48 hours before the launch of a new product, which would be inconceivable at most companies.[10] In addition, teams can speed product development (as we discussed in Chapter 7), respond more quickly to changing customer needs, and solve cross-departmental problems more quickly.

Exhibit 14.2 Five Contributions Teams Make

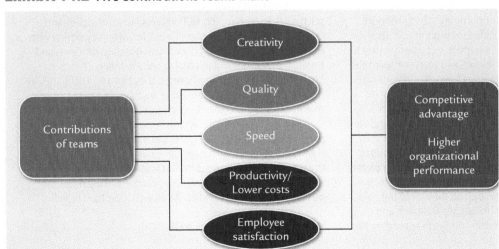

- *Higher productivity and lower costs.* Effective teams can unleash enormous energy from employees. **Social facilitation** refers to the tendency for the presence of others to enhance one's performance. Simply being around others has an energizing effect.[11] In addition, the blend of perspectives enables creative ideas to percolate. At Boeing, innovation teams made up of engineers, mechanics, and other workers have come up with time-saving ideas that have helped to boost production of the 737 jet to 47 a month as of 2017.[12]
- *Enhanced motivation and satisfaction.* As described in Chapter 12, people have needs for belongingness and affiliation. Working in teams can meet these needs and create greater camaraderie across the organization. Teams also reduce boredom, increase people's feelings of dignity and self-worth, and give people a chance to develop new skills. Individuals who work in an effective team cope better with stress, enjoy their jobs more, and have a higher level of motivation and commitment to the organization. Beth Gherlain and her husband David Tyson never set out to be a business team, but after they became one, they found it very satisfying, as described in the "Recipe for Success" box.

14-1c Types of Teams

Organizations use many types of teams to achieve the advantages discussed in the previous section. Two common types of teams in organizations are functional and cross-functional, as illustrated in Exhibit 14.3. Organizations also use self-managed teams to increase employee participation.

Recipe for Success ⎱ Tandem Bakery

When Beth Gherlein moved to Missoula, Montana, in 2011, her life changed. As a vegan living in Portland, Oregon, she had never had problems finding foods that fit her diet. But moving to Montana when her husband David Tyson started graduate school made her realize not every place has vegan options. One day Gherlain was hungry for her food favorite, donuts, and went to a health food store but couldn't find any vegan ones. A clerk told her there was nothing like that available in Missoula, but if someone started a vegan and gluten-free donut shop, it would be successful.

Gherlain had always been a foodie and loved to bake, even taking jobs as a night baker—but making it a career had never crossed her mind. Yet here was opportunity staring her right in the face, so she and Tyson decided to respond to it. They rented a shared commercial baking space, got a permit to sell goods at the Missoula Farmer's Market, and then she spent the winter experimenting with gluten-free/vegan recipes, using flours from white rice flour, chickpea-fava bean flour, potato starch, and arrowroot powder. When the first weekend of May 2012 arrived, she and Tyson stayed up all night baking and went to the farmer's market, hoping people would at least try their donuts with flavors of cinnamon and sugar, powdered sugar, and coconut and mocha. Within an hour, they were completely sold out. Because of the design of the farmer's market, their car was very far away, so Tyson walked all the way to the baking site, made another batch of donuts, walked back, and they sold old immediately again. Gherlain and Tyson knew they had

something. They realized they were (and still are) the only commercial baking company in Montana to offer vegan and gluten-free donuts. Within a year, they were in their own dedicated baking space.

The farmer's market continued as a success for Gherlain and Tyson, and it gave them confidence to start selling wholesale, which meant completing paperwork and meeting a new set of state requirements, which they completed by the end of 2014. The farmer's market became their product incubator. Gherlain said its lower regulations allowed them to experiment with different recipes and products so that they could determine what would be popular in the wholesale market. Now they sell breads, English muffin-stuffed breakfast sandwiches, and coconut-based bacon as part of a BLT. In 2018, they signed with a distributor that will bring their baked goods to groceries and restaurants across Montana, Idaho, and Wyoming. Their 5- to 10-year goal is to get a bank loan so they can add a café. They've managed so far without borrowing anything, but they know that to expand more, they'll need to get a bank involved.

Gherlain is grateful to be working with her husband on this project because they share goals and a sense of purpose. "The downside," she said, "is that we can easily just talk about work all the time, but we've learned to shut that off at home, especially when our daughter is around." She noted the many hours the business required, and added, "It's all worth the hard work."

SOURCE: Beth Gherlain, personal communication, May 2018.

Exhibit 14.3 Functional and Cross-Functional Teams in an Organization

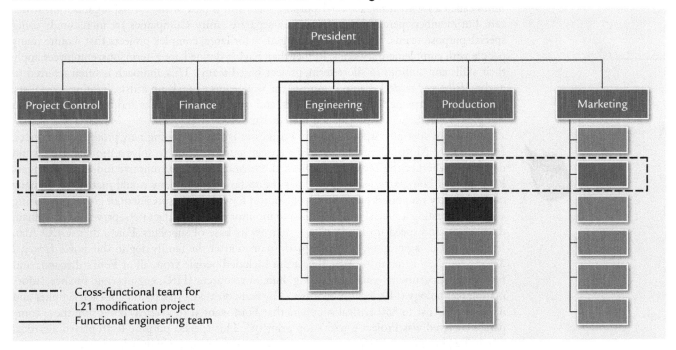

- - - - - Cross-functional team for L21 modification project
———— Functional engineering team

Functional Teams   A **functional team** is composed of a manager and his or her subordinates in the formal chain of command. Sometimes called a *command team*, the functional team in some cases may include three or four levels of hierarchy within a functional department. Typically, the team includes a single department in an organization. A financial analysis department, a quality control department, an engineering department, and a human resource department can all have functional teams. Each is created by the organization to attain specific goals through members' joint activities and interactions.

Cross-Functional Teams   A **cross-functional team** is composed of employees from about the same hierarchical level but from different areas of expertise. For example, Kohl's department store chain has teams of photographers, stylists, carpenters, models, art directors, production assistants, makeup artists, and other specialists who produce thousands of images each week for Kohl's to use for in-store posters, print advertising, and online product descriptions.[13] One type of cross-functional team is a *task force*, which is a group of employees from different departments formed to deal with a specific activity and existing only until the task is completed. For example, after one of its suppliers went out of business, an aerospace company created a task force to solve the problem of an unexpected loss of key parts needed to keep the aircraft assembly going.[14]

Another type of cross-functional team, the **special-purpose team**, is created outside the

Concept Connection

In recent years, hundreds of hospitals have been forming palliative care teams to address the unique needs of patients with terminal illnesses. These teams consist of doctors, nurses, social workers, and various types of spiritual advisors, who work together to treat each patient holistically—physically, mentally, emotionally, and spiritually. Dr. Diane Meier, a leader in the palliative care trend, notes, "Patients [typically] see a different person for every single part of their body or every problem. The patient as a whole person gets lost." Hospitals are adopting these **cross-functional teams** because they improve the quality of care provided to patients just when they need it most.

formal organization structure to undertake a project of special importance or creativity.[15] Sometimes called a *project team*, a special-purpose team still is part of the formal organization structure, but members perceive themselves as a separate entity. Companies are increasingly using special-purpose teams, bringing people together for large, complex projects that require many people with complementary skills. Rather than having defined, long-term jobs, employees apply their skills and abilities in short-term, project-based teams. This approach is often referred to as the *Hollywood model* because it mirrors the way teams of makeup artists, lighting specialists, set designers, carpenters, cinematographers, and others come together and blend their skills to complete a specific movie project and then disband.[16]

One use of special-purpose teams in businesses is for developing new products or services. In 2008, Ford Motor Company created a special-purpose team to solve a problem that could determine whether the company survived the turmoil in the automotive industry. Managers knew that without parts, nothing else they did to save the company would matter. With many of the industry's suppliers on the brink of bankruptcy, Ford's vice president of global purchasing suggested creating a special-purpose team to monitor parts manufacturers, prevent supply chain disruptions, and speed up Ford's plan to narrow its base of suppliers. Ford's then-CEO Alan Mulally quickly agreed, and Project Quark (named after the family dog in the movie *Honey, I Shrunk the Kids)* came into being. The team included people from all of Ford's divisions and functional departments—manufacturing, human resources (HR), engineering, finance, information technology (IT), legal, and others. The team created a risk profile for each supplier and narrowed the list to 850 critical suppliers that Ford wanted to keep. Making sure these companies survived was Project Quark's top priority.[17] This special-purpose team played a critical role in helping Ford prevent a supply breakdown—and ultimately in helping managers revive the company.

Self-Managed Teams   The third common type of team used in organizations is designed to increase the participation of workers in decision making and conducting their jobs, with the goal of improving performance. **Self-managed teams** typically consist of 5 to 20 multiskilled workers who rotate jobs to produce an entire product or service or at least one complete aspect or portion of a product or service (e.g., engine assembly or insurance claim processing). At the Chicago-based software firm Basecamp, for example, customer service is run by a self-managed team that handles everything associated with providing service and support. Customer service, support, and satisfaction have improved since the company started using the self-managed team. "We've measured the difference, and we know it works," says cofounder Jason Fried. Today, Basecamp is run almost entirely by self-managed teams.[18]

Self-managed teams are related to the trend toward the bossless organization. The central idea is that the teams themselves, rather than managers or supervisors, take responsibility for their work, make decisions, monitor their own performance, and alter their work behavior as needed to solve problems, meet goals, and adapt to changing conditions.[19] At Ciplex, a Web design and marketing company, founder Ilya Pozin did away with all the bosses and reorganized the whole company into self-managed teams who have full freedom to accomplish their goals. Pozin says employees are happier and more productive since he smashed the hierarchy.[20]

A self-managed team is a permanent team that typically includes the following elements:

- The team includes employees with several skills and functions, and its combined skills are sufficient to perform a major organizational task. For example, in a manufacturing plant, a team may include members from the foundry, machining, grinding, fabrication, and sales departments with members cross-trained to perform one another's jobs. The team eliminates barriers among departments, enabling excellent coordination to produce a product or service.
- The team is given access to the resources, such as information, equipment, machinery, and supplies, needed to perform the complete task.
- The team is empowered with decision-making authority, which means that members have the freedom to select new members, solve problems, spend money, monitor results, and plan for the future. Self-managed teams can enable employees to feel challenged, find their work meaningful, and develop a stronger sense of identity with the organization.

Remember This

- A **team** is a unit of two or more people who interact and coordinate their work to accomplish a goal to which they are committed and hold themselves mutually accountable.
- Organizations as diverse as Ford Motor Company, Facebook, and the U.S. Navy use teams to perform tasks that are highly interdependent and require a high level of coordination.
- Teams provide distinct advantages in the areas of innovation, quality, speed, productivity, and employee satisfaction.
- **Social facilitation** is the tendency for the presence of other people to influence an individual's motivation and performance.
- A **functional team** is composed of a manager and his or her subordinates in the formal chain of command.
- A **cross-functional team** is made up of employees from about the same hierarchical level, but from different areas of expertise.
- Cross-functional teams include task forces and special-purpose teams.
- A task force is a group of employees from different departments who deal with a specific activity and exist as a team only until the task is completed.
- A **special-purpose team** is a team created outside the formal structure to undertake a project of special importance, such as developing a new product.
- A **self-managed team** consists of multiskilled employees who rotate jobs to produce an entire product or service, often led by an elected team member.
- Self-managed teams are related to the trend toward bosslessness because team members take responsibility for their work, make decisions, monitor their own performance, and alter their work behavior as needed to solve problems and meet goals.

14-2 The Personal Dilemma of Teamwork

When David Ferrucci was trying to recruit scientists to participate on a team at IBM to build a computer smart enough to beat grand champions at the game of *Jeopardy!*, he learned firsthand that teamwork presents a dilemma for many people. To be sure, building "Watson" was an unusual project, and its results would be put to the test in a televised "human versus machine" competition. If it failed, it would be a public fiasco that would hurt the credibility of everyone involved. And if it succeeded, the hero would be the team, not any individual team member. Many of the scientists that Ferrucci approached preferred to work on their individual projects for which the success would be theirs alone. Eventually, however, he pulled together a core team of people willing to take the risk. "It was a proud moment, frankly, just to have the courage as a team to move forward," Ferrucci says.[21] In organizations all over the world, some people love the idea of teamwork, others hate it, and many people have both positive and negative emotions about being part of a team. There are three primary reasons that teams present a dilemma for many people:

- *We have to give up our independence.* When people become part of a team, their success depends on the team's success; therefore, they must depend on how well other people perform, not just on their own individual initiative and actions. Most people are comfortable with the idea of making sacrifices to achieve their own individual success, yet teamwork demands that they make sacrifices for *group* success.[22] The idea is that each person should put the team first, even if it hurts an individual at times. Some cultures, such as Japan, have had greater success with teams because traditional Japanese culture values the group over the individual.
- *We have to put up with free riders.* Teams are sometimes made up of people who have different work ethics. The term **free rider** refers to a team member who attains benefits

Half-Baked Management ⟩ Comcast

Low-functioning teams lead to poor performance, and, in the case of a company dealing with thousands of customers, to poor customer service. If you think your Internet and cable services are less than stellar, join the crowd. And if you have Comcast, you might want to know that Comcast remains at the bottom of the list (or near the bottom) of cable providers according to many surveys, including 24/7 Wall Street's Customer Hall of Shame. Where are the high-functioning teams at Comcast which would bring up the

ratings of the media giant? In 2017, Comcast finally got the message and is now revamping its customer service, with newly-trained teams of phone representatives.

SOURCE: Tamara Chuang, "How Has Comcast Improved Customer Service?" *Denver Post*, October 24, 2017, https://www.denverpost.com/2017/11/05/comcast-improved-customer-service/ed; Josh Beckerman, "Comcast to Add 5,500 Customer Service Jobs; Company to Beef up Performance After Faring Poorly in Customer-Satisfaction Surveys," *The Wall Street Journal*, May 5, 2015, https://search-proquest-com.proxy.library.vanderbilt.edu/docview/1678637733/161E81D0BC544755PQ/4?accountid=14816

from team membership but does not actively participate in and contribute to the team's work. You might have experienced this frustration in a student project team when one member put little effort into the group project but benefited from the hard work of others when grades were handed out. Free riding is sometimes called *social loafing* because some members don't exert equal effort.[23]

- *Teams are sometimes dysfunctional.* Some companies have had great success with teams, but there are also numerous examples of how teams in organizations have failed spectacularly.[24] Comcast has not done well developing its teams, as described in the "Half-Baked Management" box.

- "The best groups will be better than their individual members, and the worst groups will be worse than the worst individual," says organizational psychologist Robert Sutton.[25] A great deal of research and team experience over the past few decades has produced significant insights into what causes teams to succeed or fail. The evidence shows that the way teams are managed plays the most critical role in determining how well they function.[26] Exhibit 14.4 lists five dysfunctions that are common in teams and describes the contrasting desirable characteristics that effective team leaders develop.

Exhibit 14.4 Five Common Dysfunctions of Teams

Dysfunction	Effective Team Characteristics
Lack of trust—People don't feel safe to reveal mistakes, share concerns, or express ideas.	**Trust**—Members trust one another on a deep emotional level; feel comfortable being vulnerable with one another.
Fear of conflict—People go along with others for the sake of harmony; don't express conflicting opinions.	**Healthy conflict**—Members feel comfortable disagreeing and challenging one another in the interest of finding the best solution.
Lack of commitment—If people are afraid to express their true opinions, it's difficult to gain their true commitment to decisions.	**Commitment**—Because all ideas are put on the table, people can achieve genuine buy-in around important goals and decisions.
Avoidance of accountability—People don't accept responsibility for outcomes; engage in finger-pointing when things go wrong.	**Accountability**—Members hold one another accountable rather than relying on managers as the source of accountability.
Inattention to results—Members put personal ambition or the needs of their individual departments ahead of collective results.	**Results orientation**—Individual members set aside personal agendas; focus on what's best for the team. Collective results define success.

SOURCES: Based on Patrick Lencioni, *The Five Dysfunctions of a Team* (New York: John Wiley, 2002); and P. Lencioni, "Dissolve Dysfunction: Begin Building Your Dream Team," *Leadership Excellence* (October 2009): 20.

- Teams present a dilemma for most people because individual success depends on how well others perform, common dysfunctions afflict teams, and there is a potential for free riders.

- A **free rider** is a person who benefits from team membership but does not make a proportionate contribution to the team's work.

- Five common dysfunctions of teams are lack of trust, fear of conflict, lack of commitment, avoidance of accountability, and inattention to results.

14-3 Model of Team Effectiveness

Smoothly functioning teams don't just happen. Stanford University sociologist Elizabeth Cohen studied group work among young schoolchildren and found that only when teachers took the time to define roles, establish norms, and set goals did the groups function effectively as a team.[27] In organizations, effective teams are built by managers who take specific actions to help people come together and perform well as a team.

Some of the factors associated with team effectiveness are illustrated in Exhibit 14.5. Work team effectiveness is based on three outcomes—productive output, personal satisfaction, and the capacity to adapt and learn.[28] *Satisfaction* pertains to the team's ability to meet the personal needs of its members and hence maintain their membership and commitment. *Productive output* pertains to performance and the quality and quantity of task outputs as defined by team goals. *Capacity to adapt and learn* refers to the ability of teams to bring greater knowledge and skills to job tasks and enhance the potential of the organization to respond to new threats or opportunities in the environment.

The model of team effectiveness in Exhibit 14.5 provides a structure for this chapter. The factors that influence team effectiveness begin with the organizational context.[29] The organizational context in which the team operates is described throughout this book and includes such matters as overall leadership, strategy, environment, culture, and systems for controlling and rewarding employees. Within that context, managers define teams. Important team characteristics are its type and composition. Managers must decide when to create permanent self-managed teams and when to use a temporary task force or special-purpose team. The diversity of the team in terms of task-related knowledge and skills can have a tremendous impact on team processes and effectiveness. In addition, diversity in terms of gender and race can affect a team's performance.[30] Team size and roles also are important.

Exhibit 14.5 **Work Team Effectiveness Model**

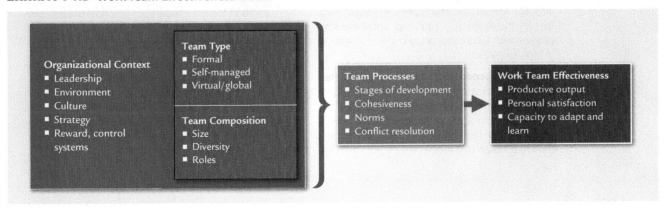

These team characteristics influence processes that are internal to the team, which, in turn, affect output, satisfaction, and the team's contribution to organizational adaptability. Good team leaders understand and manage stages of team development, cohesiveness, norms, and conflict to build an effective team. These processes are influenced by team and organizational characteristics and by the ability of members and leaders to direct these processes in a positive manner. Another requirement of the team leader is to know how to run a good meeting. The "Sunny Side Up" box gives some tips for running a dynamic, productive meeting.

14-4 Virtual Teams

An exciting new approach to teamwork has resulted from advances in IT, shifting employee expectations, and the globalization of business.[31] A **virtual team** is a group made up of geographically or organizationally dispersed members who are linked primarily through advanced information and telecommunications technologies.[32] A virtual team can be local, national, or global with members coming from one firm or many.

Sunny Side Up > How to Run a Great Meeting

A survey in the United States and Britain found that people spend an average of 5.6 hours a week in meetings, yet 69 percent of respondents considered most of that time wasted. Meetings can be excellent avenues to solving problems, sharing information, and achieving shared goals, but good meetings don't just happen. Here are some tips on how to make meetings worthwhile and productive.

Prepare in Advance

Advance preparation is the single most important tool for running an efficient, productive meeting:

- **Define the purpose.** Is the meeting's purpose to share information, draw on participants' expertise and skills, elicit their commitment to a project, or coordinate the efforts required to accomplish a specific task? The leader needs to be clear about what the purpose is. If a meeting isn't essential, don't have it.

- **Invite the right people.** Meetings fail when too many, too few, or the wrong people are involved. Don't let the meeting get too big, but make sure everyone with a contribution to make or a stake in the topic is represented.

- **Prepare an agenda and identify the expected outcome.** Distributing a simple list of the topics to be discussed lets people know what to expect. If the meeting is for exploration only, say so. A lack of decision making can be frustrating if participants expect action to be taken.

Bring Out the Best During the Meeting

During the meeting, certain techniques will bring out the best in people and ensure a productive session:

- **Start on time, state the purpose, and review the agenda.** Starting on time has symbolic value: It tells people that the topic is important and that the leader values their time. Begin by stating the meeting's explicit purpose and clarifying what should be accomplished by its conclusion.

- **Establish ground rules.** Banning the use of mobile phones, tablets, and laptops in meetings can make sure that people aren't distracted. Other rules concern how people should interact, such as emphasizing equal participation and respectful listening.

- **Create involvement.** Good leaders draw out the silent and control the talkative so that the meeting isn't dominated by one or two assertive people. In addition, leaders encourage a free flow of ideas, provoke discussion with open-ended questions, and make sure that everyone feels heard.

- **Keep it moving.** For virtual meetings, it can be a good idea to begin with a "warm-up" of informal, nonwork-related conversation. Otherwise, allowing people to waste time by getting into discussions of issues not on the agenda is a primary reason that people hate meetings. Move the meeting along as needed to meet time constraints.

Attend to the End as Much as the Beginning

Review and follow-up is important to summarize and implement agreed-upon points:

- **End with a call to action.** Summarize the discussion, review any decisions made, and make sure that each person understands his or her assignment.

- **Follow up swiftly.** Send a short e-mail or memo to summarize the meeting's key accomplishments, outline agreed-upon activities, and suggest schedules for implementation.

SOURCES: Based on Antony Jay, *How to Run a Meeting* (Boston: Harvard Business Review Classics, 2009); Beth Bratkovic, "Running an Effective Meeting," *Government Finance Review* (April 2007): 58–60; Phred Dvorak, "Corporate Meetings Go Through a Makeover," *The Wall Street Journal*, March 6, 2006; Richard Axelrod et al., "Creating Dynamic, Energy-Producing Meetings," *Leader to Leader* (Spring 2005): 53–58; Howard M. Guttman, "Leading Meetings 101: Transform Them from Dull to Dynamic," *Leadership Excellence* (July 2009): 18; and Darleen DeRosa, "Hello, Is Anybody Out There? Six Steps to High-Impact V-Meetings," *T+D* (August 2011): 28–29.

According to recent surveys, nearly half of all organizations use virtual teams, and about 80 percent of responding employees say they have worked in a virtual team at some time. Most managers expect that the use of virtual teams will continue to grow.[33] In a virtual team, members use groupware, e-mail, instant messaging, telephone and text messaging, wikis and blogs, videoconferencing, and other technology tools to collaborate and perform their work, although they also might meet face to face at times. Although some virtual teams are made up of only organizational members, virtual teams often include contingent workers, members of partner organizations, customers, suppliers, consultants, or other outsiders. Many virtual teams are also global teams. A **global team** is a cross-border team made up of members of different nationalities whose activities span multiple countries.[34]

One of the primary advantages of virtual teams is the ability to assemble the most talented group of people to complete a complex project, solve a particular problem, or exploit a specific strategic opportunity. The diverse mix of people can fuel creativity and innovation. On a practical level, organizations can save employees time and cut travel expenses when people meet in virtual rather than physical space. IBM reported that it saved more than $50 million in travel-related expenses in one recent year by using virtual teams.[35]

However, virtual teams also present unique challenges, particularly in terms of building rapport and trust. Exhibit 14.6 lists some critical areas that managers should address when leading virtual teams. Each of these areas is discussed in more detail in the following list:[36]

Rawpixel.com/Shutterstock.com

Concept Connection

Some managers have **virtual teams** meet face to face in the beginning to help establish a foundation for trusting relationships. "Trust is huge on a virtual team," says A. J. Paron-Wildes, national architectural and design manager for office furniture company Allsteel. "If you're interacting by phone you can't see their faces or read their body language." Paron-Wildes works with a team of designers spread across the country. The team uses a wide range of technology tools for interacting in virtual space, but Paron-Wildes also makes sure team members meet live at least twice a year.

- **Use virtual technology to build trust and relationships for effective teamwork.** Leaders first select people who have the right mix of technical, interpersonal, and communication skills to work in a virtual environment and then make sure that members have opportunities to know one another and establish trusting relationships. Encouraging online social networking, where people can share photos and personal biographies, can help team members get to know one another. One study suggests that high levels of online communication increase team cohesiveness and trust.[37] Leaders also build trust by making everyone's roles, responsibilities, and authority clear from the beginning; by shaping norms of full disclosure and

Exhibit 14.6 What Effective Virtual Team Leaders Do

Practice	How It's Done
Use virtual technology to build relationships.	• Bring attention to and appreciate diverse skills and opinions. • Use technology to enhance communication and trust. • Ensure timely responses online. • Manage online socialization.
Shape culture through virtual technology.	• Create a psychologically safe virtual culture. • Share members' special experience and strengths. • Engage members from cultures that may discourage people from sharing their ideas.
Monitor progress and rewards.	• Scrutinize electronic communication patterns. • Post targets and scorecards in virtual work space. • Reward people through online ceremonies and recognition.

SOURCES: Based on Table 1, "Practices of Effective Virtual Team Leaders," in Arvind Malhotra, Ann Majchrzak, and Benson Rosen, "Leading Virtual Teams," *Academy of Management Perspectives* 21, no. 1 (February 2007): 60–69; and Table 2, "'Best Practices' Solutions for Overcoming Barriers to Knowledge Sharing in Virtual Teams," in Benson Rosen, Stacie Furst, and Richard Blackburn, "Overcoming Barriers to Knowledge Sharing in Virtual Teams," *Organizational Dynamics* 36, no. 3 (2007): 259–273.

respectful interaction; and by providing a way for everyone to stay up to date. In a study of which technologies make virtual teams successful, researchers found that round-the-clock virtual workspaces where team members can access the latest versions of files, keep track of deadlines and timelines, monitor one another's progress, and carry on discussions between formal meetings, got top marks.[38]

- *Shape culture through virtual technology to reinforce productive norms.* This involves creating a virtual environment in which people feel safe to express concerns, admit mistakes, share ideas, acknowledge fears, or ask for help. Team leaders reinforce a norm of sharing all forms of knowledge, and they encourage people to express "off-the-wall" ideas and ask for help when it's needed. Leaders set the example by their own behavior. Leaders also make sure that they bring diversity issues into the open and educate members early on regarding possible cultural differences that could cause communication problems or misunderstandings in a virtual environment. Leaders address conflicts immediately because virtual conflicts can escalate quickly.

- *Monitor progress and reward members to keep the team progressing toward its goals.* Leaders stay on top of the project's development and make sure everyone knows how the team is progressing toward meeting its goals. Posting targets, measurements, and milestones in the virtual workspace can make progress explicit. Leaders also provide regular feedback, and they reward both individual and team accomplishments through avenues such as virtual award ceremonies and recognition at virtual meetings. They are liberal with praise and congratulations, but criticism or reprimands are handled individually, rather than in the virtual "presence" of the team.

As the use of virtual teams increases, understanding what makes them successful is also increasing. Many experts suggest that leaders bring people together face-to-face at the beginning of a project so people can begin building trusting relationships. Others suggest that managers solicit volunteers as much as possible for virtual teams, and interviews with virtual team members and leaders support the idea that members who truly want to work as a virtual team are more effective.[39] Andy Mattes leads an effective virtual top management team at Diebold, the largest manufacturer of ATMs in North America as discussed in the "Sunny Side Up" box.

Many of the executives Mattes recruited for his virtual executive team were people he had worked with before, so he was familiar with their abilities and working styles. Experts say that

Sunny Side Up ⟩ Diebold Inc.

When Andy Mattes took over as CEO of Diebold, he knew he needed to "change the company's mindset with new people." Diebold's sales and profits had been declining for several years, and the previous CEO had left under the cloud of a foreign bribery scandal. Getting the kind of talent Mattes needed to lead the company wasn't easy, though. With Diebold's headquarters in Canton, Ohio, he says, "We were fishing in a small pond."

Mattes decided there was no reason his top managers had to live and work in Canton, so he began reaching out to experienced executives who were comfortable working virtually. He replaced about 60 percent of the top 100 executives at Diebold, and two-thirds of them work far from headquarters. For example, the chief strategist works from San Jose, the vice president of global marketing from Boston, and the executive vice president

of software from Dallas. Many of those top executives are also managing people who work in scattered locations around the globe.

Mattes had some experience managing virtual teams in his previous jobs at Hewlett-Packard and Siemens. He says it requires "trust and discipline," so he builds in ways to promote those qualities. Every Monday morning, Mattes holds a teleconference with his direct reports and he talks with many of them daily by phone. Rather than sending long e-mail messages if they need to communicate a problem, question, or concern, Diebold's virtual managers send text messages and then connect by phone. Mattes also makes a point to see managers in person every few weeks. "As long as they live near an airport, where they work isn't nearly as important as what they can contribute," he says.[40]

including people in a virtual team who have worked together before provides a base for trusting relationships and typically makes teamwork run more smoothly.[41]

When virtual teams are global, team leaders face even greater challenges because they must bridge gaps of time, distance, and culture. Different cultural attitudes can affect work pacing, team communications, decision making, the perception of deadlines, and other issues, providing rich soil for misunderstandings and conflict. No wonder when the executive council of *CIO* magazine asked global chief information officers (CIOs) to rank their greatest challenges, managing virtual global teams ranked as the most pressing issue.[42]

Remember This

- A **virtual team** is a team made of members who are geographically or organizationally dispersed, rarely meet face to face, and interact to accomplish their work primarily using advanced information and telecommunications technologies.

- A **global team** is a group made of employees who come from, and whose activities span, multiple countries.

- Virtual teams provide many advantages, but they also present new challenges for leaders who must learn to build trusting relationships in a virtual environment.

14-5 Team Characteristics

After deciding the type of team to use, the next issue of concern to managers is designing the team for greatest effectiveness. Team characteristics of particular concern are size, diversity, and member roles.

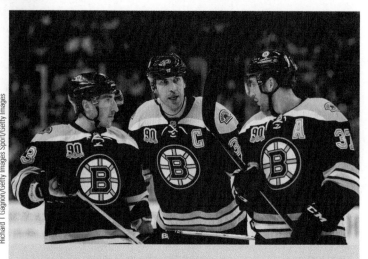

Concept Connection

At 6-foot-9, professional hockey player Zdeno Chara is a commanding presence, but as the captain of the Boston Bruins, he is all about making team members feel like equals who all contribute to the group's success. Chara plays a **socioemotional role** on the team and has established certain boundaries that help unite people. For example, team members cannot refer to new players as "rookies," nor are they allowed to engage in any kind of harmful bullying behavior that can be common on sports teams. And with this **diverse team** filled with players from a number of countries, Chara insists that all team meetings and conversations be conducted in English. Under his supportive leadership, the Bruins have advanced to the Stanley Cup finals several times in the last few seasons.

14-5a Size

More than 30 years ago, psychologist Ivan Steiner examined what happened each time the size of a team increased, and he proposed that a team's performance and productivity peaked when it had about five members. Steiner found that adding members beyond five caused a decrease in motivation, an increase in coordination problems, and a general decline in performance.[43] Since then, numerous studies have found that smaller teams perform better, although most researchers say that it's impossible to specify an optimal team size. One investigation of team size based on data from 58 software development teams found that the best-performing teams ranged in size from three to six members.[44]

Teams need to be large enough to incorporate the diverse skills needed to complete a task, enable members to express good and bad feelings, and aggressively solve problems. However, they also should be small enough to permit members to feel an intimate part of the team and to communicate effectively and efficiently. The ability of people to identify with the team is an important determinant of high performance.[45] At Amazon, CEO Jeff Bezos established a "two-pizza rule." If a team gets so large that members can't be fed with two pizzas, it should be split into smaller teams.[46] In general, as a team increases in size, it becomes harder for each member to interact with and influence the others. Subgroups often form in large teams, and conflicts among members can occur. Turnover and absenteeism are higher because members feel less like an important part of the team.[47]

Although the Internet and advanced technologies are enabling large groups of people to work more effectively in virtual teams, studies show that members of small virtual teams participate more actively, are more committed to the team, are more focused on team goals, and have higher levels of rapport than larger virtual teams.[48]

14-5b Diversity

Because teams require a variety of skills, knowledge, and experience, it seems likely that heterogeneous teams would be more effective than homogeneous ones. In general, research supports this idea, showing that diverse teams produce more innovative solutions to problems.[49] Diversity in terms of functional area and skills, thinking styles, and personal characteristics is often a source of creativity. In addition, diversity may contribute to a healthy level of disagreement that leads to better decision making.

Research studies have confirmed that both functional diversity and demographic diversity can have a positive impact on work team performance.[50] For example, recent research suggests that gender diversity, particularly with more women than men on a team, leads to better performance.[51] Ethnic, national, and racial diversity sometimes can hinder team interaction and performance in the short term, but with effective leadership, these problems fade over time.[52]

14-5c Member Roles

For a team to be successful over the long run, it must be structured in a way that both maintains its members' social well-being and accomplishes its task. To understand the importance of members fulfilling various roles on a team, consider the 33 miners who were trapped underground after a copper mine collapsed in San José, Chile, in August 2010. With little food, scant water, dusty conditions, and frayed nerves, the situation could have led to chaos. However, the miners organized into several teams in charge of critical activities such as communication with rescue workers, transport of supplies from above ground, rationing and distributing food, managing health concerns, and securing the mine to prevent further collapses. Some team members were clearly focused on helping the trapped miners meet their needs for physical survival; some focused on helping people coordinate their activities; and still others focused on the group's psychological and social needs, helping people maintain hope and a sense of solidarity as the ordeal stretched to a harrowing 69 days. Experts agree that teamwork and leadership were key to the miners' survival.[53]

With successful teams, the requirements for task performance and social satisfaction are met by the emergence of two role types: task specialist and socioemotional roles.[54]

People who play a **task specialist role** spend time and energy helping the team reach its goal. They often display the following behaviors:

- *Initiate ideas.* Propose new solutions to team problems.
- *Give opinions.* Offer judgments on task solutions; give candid feedback on others' suggestions.
- *Seek information.* Ask for task-relevant facts.
- *Summarize.* Relate various ideas to the problem at hand; pull ideas together into a brief overview.
- *Energize.* Stimulate the team into action when interest drops.[55]

People who adopt a **socioemotional role** support team members' emotional needs and help strengthen the social entity. They do the following:

- *Encourage.* Are warm and receptive to others' ideas; praise and encourage others to draw forth their contributions.
- *Harmonize.* Reconcile group conflicts; help disagreeing parties reach agreement.
- *Reduce tension.* Tell jokes or diffuse emotions in other ways when the group atmosphere is tense.
- *Follow.* Go along with the team; agree to other team members' ideas.
- *Compromise.* Shift their own opinions to maintain team harmony.[56]

Visit MindTap for "Self-Assessment: What Team Role Do You Play" to see how you contribute as a team member.

Teams with mostly socioemotional roles can be satisfying, but they also can be unproductive. At the other extreme, a team made up primarily of task specialists will tend to have a singular focus on task accomplishment. This team will be effective for a short period of time but will not be satisfying for members over the long run. Effective teams have people in both task specialist and socioemotional roles. A well-balanced team will do best over the long term because it will be personally satisfying for team members, and it will permit the accomplishment of team tasks.

Remember This

- Issues of particular concern to managers for team effectiveness are selecting the right type of team for the task, balancing the team's size and diversity, and ensuring that both task and social needs are met.
- Small teams are typically more productive and more satisfying to their members than are large teams.
- Jeff Bezos established a "two-pizza rule" at Amazon: If a team gets so large that members can't be fed with two pizzas, it is split into smaller teams.

- The **task specialist role** is a team role in which an individual devotes personal time and energy to helping the team accomplish its activities and reach its goal.
- The **socioemotional role** is a team role in which an individual provides support for team members' emotional needs and helps strengthen social unity.

14-6 Team Processes

Now we turn our attention to internal team processes. Team processes pertain to those dynamics that change over time and can be influenced by team leaders. In this section, we discuss stages of development, cohesiveness, and norms. The fourth type of team process, conflict, will be covered in the next section.

14-6a Stages of Team Development

After a team has been created, it develops by passing through distinct stages. New teams are different from mature teams. Recall a time when you were a member of a new team, such as a fraternity or sorority pledge class, a committee, or a small team formed to do a class assignment. Over time, the team changed. In the beginning, team members had to get to know one another, establish roles and norms, divide the labor, and clarify the team's task. In this way, each member became part of a smoothly operating team. The challenge for leaders is to understand the stages of development and take action that will lead to smooth functioning.

Research findings suggest that team development is not random but evolves over definitive stages. One useful model for describing these stages is shown in Exhibit 14.7. Each stage presents unique problems and challenges.[57]

Forming The **forming** stage of development is a period of orientation and getting acquainted. Members break the ice and test one another for friendship possibilities and task orientation.

Exhibit 14.7 Five Stages of Team Development

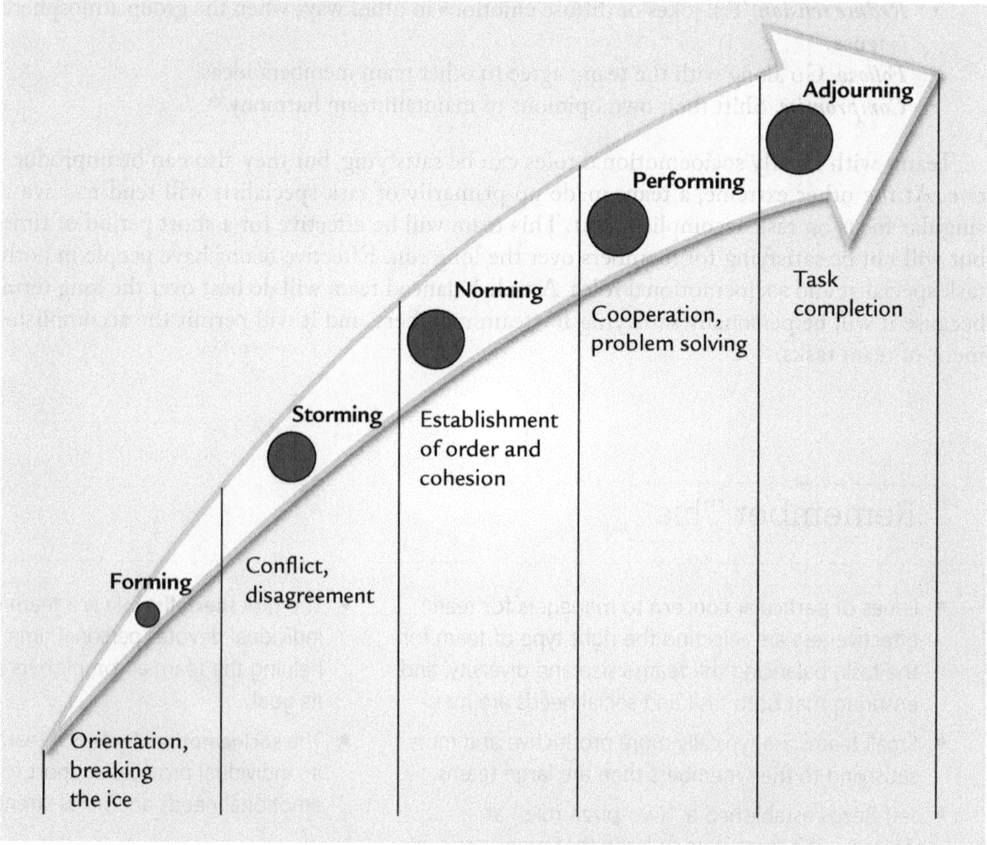

SOURCES: Based on the stages of small group development in Bruce W. Tuckman, "Developmental Sequence in Small Groups," *Psychological Bulletin* 63 (1965): 384–399; and B. W. Tuckman and M. A. Jensen, "Stages of Small Group Development Revisited," *Group and Organizational Studies* 2 (1977): 419–427.

Uncertainty is high during this stage, and members usually accept whatever power or authority is offered by either formal or informal leaders. During this initial stage, members are concerned about things such as "What is expected of me?" "What behavior is acceptable?" and "Will I fit in?" During the forming stage, the team leader should provide time for members to get acquainted with one another and encourage them to engage in informal social discussions.

Storming   During the **storming** stage, individual personalities emerge. People become more assertive in clarifying their roles and what is expected of them. This stage is marked by conflict and disagreement. People may disagree over their perceptions of the team's goals or how to achieve them. Members may jockey for position, and coalitions or subgroups based on common interests may form. Unless teams can successfully move beyond this stage, they may get bogged down and never achieve high performance. A recent experiment with student teams confirms the idea that teams that get stuck in the storming stage perform significantly less well than teams that progress to future stages of development.[58] During the storming stage, the team leader should encourage participation by each team member. Members should propose ideas, disagree with one another, and work through the uncertainties and conflicting perceptions about team tasks and goals. The expression of emotions, even negative ones, helps to build camaraderie and a shared understanding of goals and tasks.[59]

Norming   During the **norming** stage, conflict is resolved and team harmony and unity emerge. Consensus develops on who has the power, who the leaders are, and what the various members' roles are. Members come to accept and understand one another. Differences are resolved, and members develop a sense of team cohesion. During the norming stage, the team leader should emphasize unity within the team and help to clarify team norms and values.

Performing   During the **performing** stage, the major emphasis is on problem solving and accomplishing the assigned task. Members are committed to the team's mission. They are coordinated with one another and handle disagreements in a mature way. They confront and resolve problems in the interest of task accomplishment. They interact frequently and direct their discussions and influence toward achieving team goals. During this stage, the leader should concentrate on managing high task performance. Both socioemotional and task specialist roles contribute to the team's functioning.

Adjourning   The **adjourning** stage occurs in committees and teams that have a limited task to perform and are disbanded afterward. During this stage, the emphasis is on wrapping up and gearing down. Task performance is no longer a top priority. Members may feel heightened emotionality, strong cohesiveness, and depression or regret over the team's disbanding. At this point, the leader may wish to signify the team's disbanding with a ritual or ceremony, perhaps giving out plaques and awards to members to signify closure and completeness.

These five stages typically occur in sequence, but in teams that are under time pressure, they may occur quite rapidly. The stages may also be accelerated for virtual teams.

14-6b Building a Cohesive Team

Another important aspect of the team process is cohesiveness. **Team cohesiveness** is defined as the extent to which members are attracted to the team and motivated to remain in it.[60] Members of highly cohesive teams are committed to team activities, attend meetings, and are happy when the team succeeds. Members of less cohesive teams are less concerned about the team's welfare. High cohesiveness is normally considered an attractive feature of teams.

Determinants of Team Cohesiveness   Several characteristics of team structure and context influence cohesiveness. First is *team interaction*. When team members have frequent contact, they get to know one another, consider themselves a unit, and become more committed to the team.[61] Second is the concept of *shared goals*. If team members agree on purpose and direction, they will be more cohesive. Third is *personal attraction to the team*, meaning that members have similar attitudes and values and enjoy being together.

Two factors in the team's context also influence cohesiveness. The first is the *presence of competition*. When a team is in moderate competition with other teams, its cohesiveness increases as it strives to win. Finally, *team success* and the favorable evaluation of the team by outsiders add to cohesiveness. When a team succeeds in its task and others in the organization recognize the success, members feel good, and their commitment to the team will be high.

Consequences of Team Cohesiveness   The outcome of team cohesiveness can fall into two categories—morale and productivity. As a general rule, morale is higher in cohesive teams because of increased communication among members, a friendly team climate, maintenance of membership because of commitment to the team, loyalty, and member participation in team decisions and activities. High cohesiveness has almost uniformly good effects on the satisfaction and morale of team members.[62]

With respect to the productivity of the team as a whole, research findings suggest that teams in which members share strong feelings of connectedness and generally positive interactions tend to perform better.[63] Thus, a friendly, positive team environment contributes to productivity as well as member satisfaction. Among call center teams at Bank of America, for example, productivity rose 10 percent when leaders scheduled more face-to-face interaction time outside of formal meetings. Simply interacting with others in a positive way has an energizing effect. Alex "Sandy" Pentland, a professor at the Massachusetts Institute of Technology (MIT), and his colleagues at MIT's Human Dynamics Laboratory studied teams across diverse industries to identify what gives some teams the energy, creativity, and shared commitment that leads to high productivity. They found positive patterns of communication to be the most important predictor of a team's success—as significant as individual intelligence, personality, skill, and the substance of discussions combined.[64]

Other research indicates that the degree of productivity in cohesive teams may depend on the relationship between management and the work team. One study surveyed more than 200 work teams and correlated job performance with their cohesiveness.[65] Highly cohesive teams were more productive when team members felt management support and less productive when they sensed management hostility and negativism.

14-6c Establishing Team Norms

A **team norm** is an informal standard of conduct that is shared by team members and guides their behavior.[66] Norms are valuable because they provide a frame of reference for what is expected and acceptable.

Norms begin to develop in the first interactions among members of a new team. Exhibit 14.8 illustrates four common ways in which norms develop.[67] Sometimes the first behaviors that occur

Exhibit 14.8   Four Ways Team Norms Develop

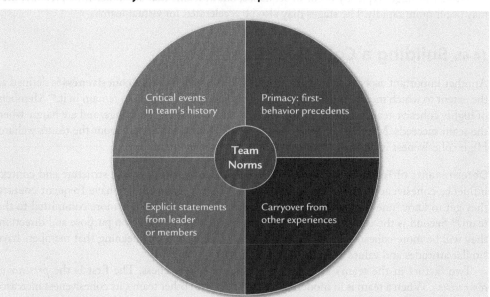

in a team set a precedent. For example, at one company, a team leader began his first meeting by raising an issue and then "leading" team members until he got the solution he wanted. The pattern became ingrained so quickly into an unproductive team norm that members dubbed meetings the "Guess What I Think" game.[68] Other influences on team norms include critical events in the team's history, explicit statements from leaders, and behaviors, attitudes, and norms that members bring with them from outside the team.

Norms can have a tremendous influence on how well teams perform. In studying what makes a team effective, researchers at Carnegie Mellon University and MIT found that the right norms increase a team's "collective intelligence" to perform well, whereas negative norms can hamper a team, even if all its members are highly intelligent.[69] In teams with unproductive or negative norms, people must work harder to accomplish goals, and team members may experience dissatisfaction. Research at Google into hundreds of team characteristics found that two norms were especially important to both positive team feelings and productive team output:

- *Psychological safety.* One of the most critical norms for an effective team is psychological safety. *Psychological safety* means a team climate characterized by mutual trust and respect in which team members are comfortable being themselves. Psychological safety is composed of both emotional expression and social sensitivity.
- *Emotional expression.* People in effective teams feel comfortable enough to express their emotions as well as their thoughts. Team members communicate freely and easily in a relaxed way and may joke around and share personal stories.
- *Social sensitivity.* A team's collective intelligence also increases when people are sensitive to and inquire into one another's moods and emotions. Team members pay attention to and ask about one another's facial expressions, body language, and other nonverbal cues.
- *Equal participation.* In effective teams, all team members participate in roughly equal proportion. No one member or subset of members dominates the conversation. Anita Woolley, the lead researcher in the Carnegie Mellon–MIT study, noted, "As long as everyone got a chance to talk, the team did well," whereas if one person or a small group did all the talking, the collective intelligence of the team declined.

A team at Google showed that applying norms of psychological safety was vital for the team's success as discussed in the "Sunny Side Up" box.

Sunny Side Up } Google

Several years ago, Google set out to determine what went into making the perfect team. Through an initiative code named Project Aristotle, a team of Google's statisticians, psychologists, sociologists, engineers, and others gathered data on hundreds of the company's teams to try to figure out why some struggled while others soared.

Google managers once thought that building the best teams meant putting the best people together, but after studying lots of data, Project Aristotle couldn't find any patterns showing that the "who" part of the equation made any difference to a team's effectiveness. So, Project Aristotle started searching through the data looking for norms. Although the researchers identified a variety of norms that seem important to high team performance, they determined that psychological safety, more than anything else, was vital to making a team effective. Moreover,

roughly equal participation among members also signaled an effective team.

Matt Sakaguchi was interested in the findings because he had previously led a team that hadn't come together so well and was hoping for a better outcome with his new team. He decided to try to establish a norm of psychological safety by gathering the team offsite and asking everyone to share something personal about themselves. Sakaguchi started things off by revealing that he had stage 4 cancer. Team members had no idea that their leader had been battling cancer for nearly half a decade while working at Google. After he spoke, other team members shared difficult personal experiences. This helped the team talk more easily about other issues, problems within the team, and everyday annoyances, and agree to adopt new norms for how they would work together.[70]

As this example shows, team leaders play an important role in shaping norms that will help the team be effective. For example, research shows that when leaders have high expectations for collaborative problem solving, teams develop strong collaborative norms.[71] Making explicit statements about desired team behaviors is a powerful way that leaders influence norms. When he was CEO of Ameritech, Bill Weiss established a norm of cooperation and mutual support among his top leadership team by telling them bluntly that if he caught anyone trying to undermine the others, the guilty party would be fired.[72]

Remember This

- The **forming** stage of team development is a period of orientation and getting acquainted.
- **Storming** is the stage of team development in which individual personalities and roles emerge along with resulting conflicts.
- **Norming** refers to the stage of development in which conflicts are resolved and team harmony and unity emerge.
- The **performing** stage is the stage in which members focus on problem solving and accomplishing the team's assigned task.
- **Adjourning** is the stage during which members of temporary teams prepare for the team's disbanding.

- **Team cohesiveness** refers to the extent to which team members are attracted to the team and motivated to remain a part of it.
- Morale is almost always higher in cohesive teams, and cohesiveness can also contribute to higher productivity.
- A **team norm** is an informal standard of conduct that is shared by team members and guides their behavior.
- Important norms for high team effectiveness include psychological safety and equal participation.

14-7 Managing Team Conflict

The final characteristic of team process is conflict. It can arise among members within a team or between one team and another. **Conflict** refers to an antagonistic interaction in which one party attempts to block the intentions or goals of another.[73] Whenever people work together in teams, some conflict is inevitable. Bringing conflicts into the open and effectively resolving them is one of the team leader's most challenging yet most important jobs. Effective conflict management has a positive impact on team cohesiveness and performance.[74]

14-7a Types of Conflict

Two basic types of conflict that occur in teams are task conflict and relationship conflict.[75] **Task conflict** refers to disagreements among people about the goals to be achieved or the content of the tasks to be performed. Two shop supervisors might disagree over whether to replace a valve or let it run despite the unusual noise that it is making. Alternatively, two members of a top management team might disagree about whether to acquire a company or enter into a joint venture as a way to expand globally. **Relationship conflict** refers to interpersonal incompatibility that creates tension and personal animosity among people. For example, in one team at a company that manufactures and sells upscale children's furniture, team members found their differing perspectives and working styles to be a significant source of conflict during crunch times. Members who needed peace and quiet were irked at those who wanted music playing in the background. Compulsively neat members found it almost impossible to work with those who liked working among stacks of clutter.[76]

"In great teams, conflict becomes productive. The free flow of ideas and feelings is critical for creative thinking, for discovering new solutions no one individual would have come to on his own."

—PETER SENGE, AUTHOR OF *THE FIFTH DISCIPLINE: THE ART AND PRACTICE OF THE LEARNING ORGANIZATION*

In general, research suggests that task conflict can be beneficial because it leads to better decision making and problem solving. On the other hand, relationship conflict is typically associated with negative consequences for team effectiveness.[77] One study of top management teams, for example, found that task conflict was associated with increased decision quality, commitment, and decision acceptance, while the presence of relationship conflict significantly reduced those same outcomes.[78]

14-7b Balancing Conflict and Cooperation

There is evidence that mild conflict can be beneficial to teams.[79] A healthy level of conflict helps to prevent *groupthink* (as discussed in Chapter 6) in which people are so committed to a cohesive team that they are reluctant to express contrary opinions. When people in work teams go along simply for the sake of harmony, problems typically result. Thus, a degree of conflict leads to better decision making because multiple viewpoints are expressed.

However, conflict that is too strong, that is focused on personal rather than work issues, or that is not managed appropriately can be damaging to the team's morale and productivity. Too much conflict can be destructive, tear relationships apart, and interfere with the healthy exchange of ideas and information.[80] Team leaders must find the right balance between conflict and cooperation, as illustrated in Exhibit 14.9. Too little conflict can decrease team performance because the team doesn't benefit from a mix of opinions and ideas—even disagreements—that might lead to better solutions or prevent the team from making mistakes. At the other end of the spectrum, too much conflict outweighs the team's cooperative efforts and leads to a decrease in employee satisfaction and commitment, hurting team performance. A moderate amount of conflict, when it is managed appropriately, typically results in the highest levels of team performance.

14-7c Causes of Conflict

Several factors can lead to conflict.[81] One of the primary causes is competition over resources, such as money, information, or supplies. When individuals or teams must compete for scarce or declining resources, conflict is almost inevitable. In addition, conflict often occurs simply because people are pursuing differing goals. Goal differences are natural in organizations.

Exhibit 14.9 Balancing Conflict and Cooperation

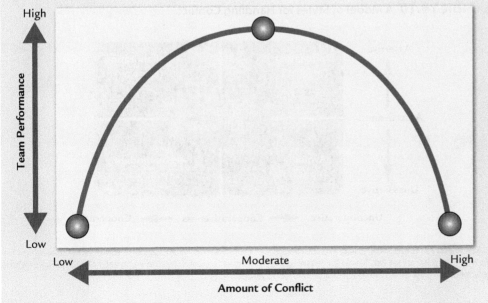

Targets of individual salespeople may put them in conflict with one another or with the sales manager. Moreover, the sales department's goals might conflict with those of manufacturing, and so forth.

Conflict may also arise from communication breakdowns. Poor communication can occur in any team, but virtual and global teams are particularly prone to communication breakdowns. In one virtual team developing a custom polymer for a Japanese manufacturer, the marketing team member in the United States was frustrated by a Japanese team member's failure to provide her with the manufacturer's marketing strategy. The Japanese team member, in turn, thought her teammate was overbearing and unsupportive. She knew that the manufacturer hadn't yet developed a clear marketing strategy, and that pushing for more information could damage the relationship by causing the customer to "lose face."[82] Trust issues can be a major source of conflict in virtual teams if members feel that they are being left out of important communication interactions.[83] In addition, the lack of nonverbal cues in virtual interactions leads to more misunderstandings.

14-7d Styles of Handling Conflict

Teams as well as individuals develop specific styles for dealing with conflict based on the desire to satisfy their own concern versus the other party's concern. A model that describes five styles of handling conflict is shown in Exhibit 14.10. The two major dimensions are the extent to which an individual is assertive versus unassertive and cooperative versus uncooperative in his or her approach to conflict:[84]

- The *dominating style* (my way) reflects assertiveness to get one's own way and should be used when quick, decisive action is vital on important issues or unpopular actions, such as during emergencies or urgent cost-cutting requirements.
- The *compromising style* (halfway) reflects a moderate amount of both assertiveness and cooperativeness. It is appropriate when the goals on both sides are equally important, when opponents have equal power and both sides want to split the difference, or when people need to arrive at temporary or expedient solutions under time pressure.
- The *accommodating style* (your way) reflects a high degree of cooperativeness, which works best when people realize that they are wrong, when an issue is more important to others than to oneself, when building social credits for use in later discussions, and when maintaining harmony is especially important.

Exhibit 14.10   A Model of Styles for Handling Conflict

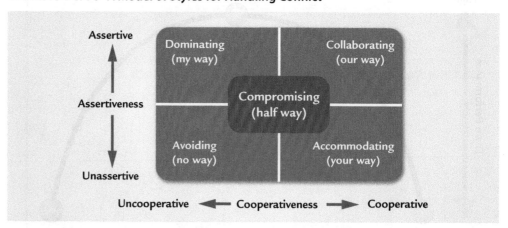

SOURCES: Adapted from Kenneth Thomas, "Conflict and Conflict Management," in *Handbook of Industrial and Organizational Behavior*, ed. M. D. Dunnette (New York: John Wiley, 1976), p. 900; and Nan Peck, "Conflict 101: Styles of Fighting," North Virginia Community College Web site, September 20, 2005, www.nvcc.edu/home/ npeck/conflicthome/conflict/Conflict101/conflictstyles.htm (accessed April 13, 2011).

- The *collaborating style* (our way) reflects a high degree of both assertiveness and cooperativeness. The collaborating style enables both parties to win, although it may require substantial bargaining and negotiation. The collaborating style is important when both sets of concerns are too important to be compromised, when insights from different people need to be merged into an overall solution, and when the commitment of both sides is needed for a consensus.
- The *avoiding style* (no way) reflects neither assertiveness nor cooperativeness. It is appropriate when an issue is trivial, when there is no chance of winning, when a delay to gather more information is needed, or when a disruption would be costly.

Caroline Lim, global head of human resources and corporate affairs at PSA International, provides an example of the collaborating style. Lim says to motivate her team, she always tries to reinforce the positives and show appreciation, but she doesn't "sweep things under the carpet." Lim addresses problems head on and talks with people about ways to learn and improve.[85] Each of the five styles of handling conflict is appropriate in certain cases, and effective team members and leaders vary their styles to fit the specific situation.

14-7e Ways of Expressing Conflict

Whether an interpersonal conflict has positive or negative effects may be largely determined by how the conflict is expressed.[86] One factor is the *intensity* with which a conflict is expressed. For example, if a teammate approaches you shouting forcefully that you failed to give her a report she needs, you are likely to become defensive and respond in a negative way. On the other hand, a teammate who approaches you and calmly asks why you haven't given her the report she needs to complete her work opens the door to discussion and positive resolution.

Four primary ways of expressing conflict are as follows:[87]

- *High directness–high intensity.* A person using this approach expresses a conflict unambiguously by using aggressive or antagonistic verbal and nonverbal communication, such as shouting, scowling, or eye rolling.
- *High directness–low intensity.* With this approach, communication is also unambiguous, but the person uses a low-voltage style, such as asking questions, listening, debating, and deliberating.
- *Low directness–high intensity.* A person using this approach expresses a conflict ambiguously but uses aggressive tactics. This may include behaviors such as ignoring another's viewpoint, mean-spirited teasing or bullying, backstabbing, or undermining the opponent to third parties.
- *Low directness–low intensity.* With this approach, a person expresses conflict in an ambiguous, low-key way. Behaviors might include withholding information an opponent needs or deliberately missing a deadline.

The most constructive way to express a conflict is high directness–low intensity. This approach enables people to take other viewpoints into consideration and work together toward a positive outcome. When conflicts are expressed with high intensity, others tend to respond

Concept Connection

The stunning Beijing National Aquatics Center, built for the 2008 Summer Olympics, resulted from a **collaborative style of handling conflict**. When designing the Aquatics Center (typically called the "Water Cube"), two architectural firms—one Chinese and the other Australian—developed designs that were totally different. Although this created some tension, instead of fighting for their own ideas, the two sides came up with a totally new concept that excited everyone. After the 2008 Olympics, the National Aquatics Center underwent a revamp to turn half of its interior into a water park. The Center is also slated to host the curling events during the 2022 Winter Olympics.

Songquan Deng/Shutterstock.com

with defensiveness. They may stop listening and hold fast to their own positions, making a positive resolution unlikely. Expressing conflict in an indirect way can hurt team performance because decisions may be made without complete information and the conflict will escalate without being resolved. Effective team leaders and members typically use a direct but low-key approach.

14-7f Negotiation

One distinctive type of conflict management is **negotiation** whereby people engage in give-and-take discussions and consider various alternatives to reach a joint decision that is acceptable to both parties. Negotiation is used when a conflict is formalized, such as between a union and management.

Types of Negotiation Conflicting parties may embark on negotiation from different perspectives and with different intentions, reflecting either an *integrative* approach or a *distributive* approach.

Integrative negotiation is based on a win-win assumption in that all parties want to come up with a creative solution that can benefit both sides. Rather than viewing the conflict as a win-lose situation, people look at the issues from multiple angles, consider trade-offs, and try to "expand the pie" rather than divide it. With integrative negotiation, conflicts are managed through cooperation and compromise, which fosters trust and positive long-term relationships. **Distributive negotiation**, on the other hand, assumes that the size of the "pie" is fixed, and each party attempts to get as much of it as possible. One side wants to win, which means the other side must lose. With this win-lose approach, distributive negotiation is competitive and adversarial, rather than collaborative, and does not typically lead to positive long-term relationships.[88]

Most experts emphasize the value of integrative negotiation for today's collaborative business environment. That is, the key to effectiveness is to see negotiation not as a zero-sum game but as a process for reaching a creative solution that benefits everyone.[89]

Rules for Reaching a Win-Win Solution Achieving a win-win solution through integrative negotiation is based on four key strategies:[90]

- *Separate the people from the problem.* For successful integrative negotiation, people stay focused on the problem and the source of conflict rather than attacking or attempting to discredit each other.
- *Focus on underlying interests, not current demands.* Demands are what each person wants from the negotiation whereas underlying interests represent the "why" behind the demands. Consider two sisters arguing over the last orange in the fruit bowl. Each insists that she should get the orange and refuses to give up (demands). If one sister had asked the other *why* she wanted the orange, the sisters would have discovered that one wanted to eat it, and the other wanted the peel to use for a project (interests). By focusing on interests, the sisters would have been able to arrive at a solution that gave each what she wanted.[91] *Demands* create yes-or-no obstacles to effective negotiation whereas *interests* present problems that can be solved creatively.
- *Listen and ask questions.* A good strategy for most negotiations is to listen and ask questions. You can learn more about your opponent's position, constraints, and needs by being quiet or asking questions. Smart negotiators want to learn the other side's constraints so that they can help overcome them. Don't dismiss the opposing party's limitation as unreasonable or think "that's your problem." You can take it on as your own problem and try to come up with a solution for your opponent so that you can get closer to an agreement.
- *Insist that results be based on objective standards.* Each party in a negotiation has its own interests and naturally would like to maximize its outcomes. Successful negotiation requires focusing on objective criteria and maintaining standards of fairness rather than using subjective judgments about the best solution.

Remember This

- **Conflict** refers to antagonistic interaction in which one party attempts to block the intentions or goals of another.
- Some conflict, particularly task conflict, can be beneficial to teams.
- **Task conflict** is conflict that results from disagreements about the goals to be achieved or the content of the tasks to be performed.
- **Relationship conflict** results from interpersonal incompatibility that creates tension and personal animosity among people.
- Causes of conflict include competition over resources, goal differences, and communication breakdowns.
- Teams and individuals use a variety of styles for dealing with conflict, including the dominating style, the avoiding style, the compromising style, the accommodating style, and the collaborating style, and each can be effective under certain circumstances.
- The way in which conflict is expressed may determine whether there is a positive or a negative outcome. The most constructive way to express conflict is with high directness but low intensity.
- **Negotiation** is a conflict management strategy whereby people engage in give-and-take discussions and consider various alternatives to reach a joint decision that is acceptable to both parties.
- **Integrative negotiation** is a collaborative approach that is based on a win-win assumption, whereby the parties want to come up with a creative solution that benefits both sides of the conflict.
- **Distributive negotiation** is a competitive and adversarial approach in which each party strives to get as much as it can, usually at the expense of the other party.

DISCUSSION QUESTIONS

1. One company had 40 percent of its workers and 20 percent of its managers resign during the first year after it reorganized from a vertical hierarchy into teams. What might account for this dramatic turnover? How might managers ensure a smooth transition to teams?

2. Have you experienced with a team that you have participated in any of the five contributions of teams shown in Exhibit 14.2? If so, describe your experience and why you think the team was able to make that specific contribution.

3. Suppose that you are the leader of a team that has just been created to develop a new registration process at your college or university. How can you use an understanding of the stages of team development to improve your team's effectiveness?

4. Research on team interactions indicates that when people eat lunch at 12-person tables, they are more productive and collaborative than when they eat at 4-person tables, even if they aren't eating with their own team members. What do you think would explain this finding?

5. Imagine yourself as a potential member of a team responsible for designing a new package for a breakfast cereal. Do you think interpersonal skills would be equally important if the team is organized as a face-to-face versus a virtual team? Why or why not? Might different types of interpersonal skills be required for the two types of teams? Be specific.

6. If you were the leader of a special-purpose team developing a new computer game and conflicts arose related to power and status differences among team members, what would you do? Of the conflict-handling styles described in this chapter, which do you think might be most effective? Explain your answer.

7. Experts say that for teams to function well, members must get to know one another in some depth. What specifically would you do to facilitate this in a co-located team? What about in a global, virtual team?

8. Some people argue that the presence of an outside threat correlates with a high degree of team cohesiveness. Would you agree or disagree? Explain your answer.

9. Discuss how the dilemma of teamwork versus individual work might be intensified in a virtual

team. What dilemmas do you encounter when you have to do class assignments as part of a team? Discuss.

10. If you were the leader of a newly formed team, what might you do to make sure the team developed norms of high performance?

APPLY YOUR SKILLS: SELF-LEARNING

This and That: Best Team–Worst Team[92]

Think of two teams of which you were a member—the best and the worst in terms of personal satisfaction and team performance. These teams could come from any area in your experience—for example, athletic team, student club, class team, work team, project team, church committee, or volunteer organization. List here the specific behaviors of the teams that made them the best and the worst for you.

Best team behaviors: _____

_____

Worst team behaviors: _____

_____

In class: (1) Sit in a small group of three to five students. Each student should tell the brief story of his or her best and worst team experiences. (2) After all the stories are heard, one team member writes on a flipchart (or blackboard/whiteboard) two headings—"More of This" and "Less of That." Under "This," write team member suggestions for positive behaviors that make for effective teamwork. Under "That," write team member suggestions for negative behaviors that prevent effective teamwork. (3) After brainstorming items, each group condenses each list to five key behaviors that the group considers most important. (4) After the lists are finalized, students can walk around the classroom and review all lists. (5) Discuss answers to the following questions, either in your group or as a class.

1. What are the most important behaviors for This and for That?

2. What factors influence the presence of This or That behaviors on a team?

3. What personal changes would you need to make as a team member to demonstrate more of This?

4. What personal changes would you need to make as a team member to demonstrate less of That?

5. How might a team leader be able to attain more of This on a team and less of That?

APPLY YOUR SKILLS: GROUP LEARNING

Teams on TV

Step 1. Form into groups of three to five members. As a group, choose a TV program where teams are central to the plot. Examples include *Modern Family, The Office, Law & Order* (any of the series), *CSI, New Girl, Third Rock from the Sun,* and *Silicon Valley.* Make sure the instructor agrees with your choice of TV program.

Step 2. Watch several programs (make sure group members watch the same ones) and study team behavior. Use the Member Roles on pages [528-529] of this textbook and the Stages of Team Development on pages [530-531, including Exhibit 14.7]. Take notes on which characters perform which role(s) and what stages of development the group is in during a particular program.

Step 3. As a group, come to an agreement on which roles and stages were present in those program.

Step 4. Your instructor will tell you whether to prepare either a group presentation or group paper on your findings.

Step 5. What did you learn about teams from this assignment? Were there some surprises?

APPLY YOUR SKILLS: ACTION LEARNING

Team Feedback Exercise

1. Divide into groups of three to four students. Think back to recent experiences working in a team, either at work or school. Write your answers to the following questions.

a. What behaviors by other team members did you most appreciate?

_____

_____

b. What behaviors of other team members did you least appreciate?

_____

_____

c. What do you think the team members appreciated about you?

_____

_____

d. What actions of yours might the team members have appreciated least?

_____

_____

2. Take turns sharing your answers with other members of your group. Make notes about common themes for answers to each of the lettered questions. What is the single most important theme for each of the answers?

3. What are the implications of the answers for you as a member of a future team? How might you change your behavior to make a larger contribution to a team?

APPLY YOUR SKILLS: ETHICAL DILEMMA

One for All and All for One?[93]

Melinda Asbel watched as three of her classmates filed out of the conference room. Then she turned back to the large wooden table and faced her fellow members (a student and three faculty members) of the university's judiciary committee.

The three students—Joe Eastridge, Brad Hamil, and Lisa Baghetti—had just concluded their appeal against a plagiarism conviction stemming from a group project for an international marketing course. Melinda, who happened to be in the class with the students on trial, remembered the day that the professor, Hank Zierden, had asked Joe, Brad, and Lisa, along with the group's leader, Paul Colgan, to stay after class. She happened to walk by the classroom a half hour later and saw four glum students emerge. Even though Paul had a chagrined expression on his face, Joe was the one who looked completely shattered. It didn't take long for word to spread along the ever-active grapevine that Paul had admitted to plagiarizing his part of the group paper.

At the hearing, the students recounted how they'd quickly and unanimously settled on Paul to lead the group. He was by far the most able student among them, someone who managed to maintain a stellar GPA even while handling a full course load and holding down a part-time job. After the group worked together for weeks analyzing the problem and devising a marketing plan, Paul assigned a section of the final paper to each member. With the pressure of all those end-of-the-semester deadlines bearing down on them, everyone was delighted when Paul volunteered to write the company and industry background, the section that typically took the most time to produce. He gathered everyone's contributions, assembled them into a paper, and handed the final draft to the other members. They each gave it a quick read. They liked what they saw and thought they had a good chance for an A.

Unfortunately, as Paul readily admitted when Professor Zierden confronted them, he had pulled the section that he'd contributed directly off the Internet. Pointing out the written policy that he had distributed at the beginning of the semester, which stated that each group member was equally responsible for the final product, the professor gave all four students a zero for the project. The group project and presentation counted for 30 percent of the course grade.

Joe, Brad, and Lisa maintained that they were completely unaware that Paul had cheated. "It just never occurred to us Paul would ever need to cheat," Brad said. They were innocent bystanders, the students argued. Why should they be penalized? Besides, the consequences weren't going to fall on each of them equally. Although Paul was suffering the embarrassment of public exposure, the failing group project grade would only put a dent in his solid GPA. Joe, on the other hand, was already on academic probation. A zero probably meant that he wouldn't make the 2.5 GPA that he needed to stay in the business program.

At least one of the faculty members of the judiciary committee supported Professor Zierden's actions. "We're assigning more and more group projects because increasingly that's the way these students are going to find themselves working when they get real jobs in the real world," he said. "And the fact of the matter is that if someone obtains information illegally while on the job, it's going to put the whole corporation at risk for being sued, or worse."

Even though she could see merit to both sides, Melinda was going to have to choose. If you were Melinda, how would you vote?

What Would You Do?

1. Vote to exonerate the three group project members who didn't cheat. You're convinced that they had no reason to suspect Paul Colgan of dishonesty. Exonerating them is the right thing to do.

2. Vote in support of Hank Zierden's decision to hold each individual member accountable for the entire project. The professor clearly stated his policy at the beginning of the semester, and the students should have been more vigilant.

The committee should not undercut a professor's explicit policy.

3. Vote to reduce each of the three students' penalties. Instead of a zero, each student will receive only half of the possible total points for the project, which would be an F. You're still holding students responsible for the group project but not imposing catastrophic punishment. This compromise both undercuts the professor's policy and punishes "innocent" team members to some extent but not as severely as Paul.

APPLY YOUR SKILLS: CASE FOR CRITICAL ANALYSIS

Are We a Team?

Hi. My name is Jenny McConnell. I am the newly appointed CIO of a medium-sized technology company. Our company recruits top graduates from schools of business and engineering. Talent, intellect, creativity—it's all there. If you lined up this crowd for a group photo, credentials in hand, the "wow" factor would be there.

Our company is spread over a dozen states, mostly in the Northwest. The talent pool is amazing across the board, both in IT and in the rest of the company. But when the CEO hired me, he said that we are performing nowhere near our potential. On the surface, the company is doing fine. But we should be a *Fortune* 500 organization. With this much talent, we should be growing at a much faster rate. The CEO also said that I was inheriting "a super team with disappointing performance." His task for me was to pull the IT stars into a cohesive team that would meet company needs for new IT systems and services much faster and more effectively.

Without making our superstars feel that they were being critiqued and second-guessed, or indicating "there's a real problem here," I wanted to gather as much information and feedback as possible from the 14 team members (regional CIOs and department heads) who report to me. I held one-on-one meetings in order to give a voice to each person, allowing each individual to provide an honest assessment of the team as well as areas for improvement and a vision for the future of team efforts.

I was surprised by the consistency of remarks and opinions. For example, a picture emerged of the previous CIO, who was obviously awed by the talent level of team members. Comments such as "Bob pretty much let us do what we wanted" and

"Bob would start the meeting and then just fade into the background, as if he found us intimidating" were typical. The most disturbing comment, "Bob always agreed with *me*," was expressed by most of the team members at some point in our conversation. It was as if the regional heads believed that the CIO wanted them to succeed by doing as they thought best for themselves.

I queried members about the level of cooperation during meetings and uncovered areas of concern, including the complaint that others at the table were constantly checking their iPads and smartphones during meetings. One department head told me, "You could turn off the sound while watching one of our meetings, and just by the body language and level of attention, tell who is aligned with whom and who wishes the speaker would just shut up. It would be comical if it weren't so distressing."

Such remarks indicated a lack of trust and respect and a breakdown of genuine communication. One team member told me, "I recently encountered a problem that a department head from another region had successfully solved, but the information was never shared, so here I am reinventing the wheel and wasting valuable time." It was apparent that these so-called high performers were territorial, and that the "each division for itself" attitude was becoming a cultural norm that, unchecked, was slowing our response to line departments and customers.

I was also struck by the similarity of the regional IT leaders in their backgrounds, comments, and attitudes, which presented a whole new dilemma: How do we create diversity, jump-start ideas, and reignite passion? This looks like a group of individualists who don't know how to play as a team.

I don't want to diminish the individual talent, but I am concerned by the lack of cohesion. I need to find a way to help people think less about themselves and more about sharing work and information and achieving collective results for the good of the company.

Team building is an art, anchored by trust and communication, and committed to mutual success. What I'm seeing looks like team dysfunction to me. Now I have to determine the steps necessary to build a cohesive, visionary team.

Questions

1. What type of team does the new CIO have? What do you see as the key problem with the team?

2. How do you think that the team evolved to this low level of cooperation and cohesiveness?

3. What suggestions do you have for the CIO to help her turn this collection of individual regional and department heads into a top-performing team? Explain.

ENDNOTES

1. Penelope Green, "The Facebook Breakup," *The New York Times*, March 12, 2016, http://www.nytimes.com/2016/03/13/fashion/facebook-breakup-compassion-team.html?_r=0 (accessed May 16, 2016).

2. Industry Week/Manufacturing Performance Institute's Census of Manufacturers for 2004, reported in Traci Purdum, "Teaming, Take 2," *Industry Week* (May 2005): 41–43.

3. "'Golden Hour' Crucial Time for Surgeons on Front Line," *Johnson City Press*, April 1, 2003.

4. Carl E. Larson and Frank M. J. LaFasto, *TeamWork* (Newbury Park, CA: Sage, 1989); J. R. Katzenbach and D. K. Smith, *The Wisdom of Teams* (Boston: Harvard Business School Press, 1993); and Dawn R. Utley and Stephanie E. Brown, "Establishing Characteristic Differences Between Team and Working Group Behaviors," *Institute of Industrial Engineers Annual Conference Proceedings*, Cancun, Mexico (June 5–9, 2010): 1–6.

5. Ben Cohen, "Golden State: The Team That Eats Together," *The Wall Street Journal*, February 11, 2015, http://www.wsj.com/articles/golden-state-the-team-that-eats-together-1423682960 (accessed November 9, 2015); Jared Stearne, "Warriors' Continuity Could Prove More Valuable than Change for the Rockets, Spurs," *Golden State of Mind*, November 8, 2015, http://www.goldenstateofmind.com/2015/11/8/9692794/golden-state-warriors-continuity-san-antonio-spurs-houston-rockets (accessed November 9, 2015); and Ed Frauenheim, "Lessons from Warriors," *Fortune* (January 1, 2016): 16.

6. Geoff Colvin, "Great Job! Or How Yum Brands Uses Recognition to Build Teams and Get Results," *Fortune* (August 12, 2013): 62–66.

7. Some of the advantages in this section are discussed in "The Rewards of Teaming" sidebar in Amy C. Edmondson, "Teamwork on the Fly," *Harvard Business Review* (April 2012): 72–80.

8. Geoff Colvin, "First: Team Players Trump All-Stars," *Fortune* (May 21, 2012): 46–47.

9. See the excellent discussion in Atul Gawande, "Cowboys and Pit Crews," 2011 Harvard Medical School commencement address, *The New Yorker* (May 26, 2011), www.newyorker.com/online/blogs/newsdesk/2011/05/atul-gawande-harvard-medical-school-commencement-address.html (accessed September 26, 2012).

10. Colvin, "First: Team Players Trump All-Stars."

11. R. B. Zajonc, "Social Facilitation," *Science* 145 (1969): 269–274.

12. Dominic Gates, Boeing Ramps up Automation, Seattle Times, Feb. 17, 2017, https://www.seattletimes.com/business/boeing-aerospace/boeing-ramps-up-automation-innovation-as-it-readies-737max/; David Kesmodel, "Boeing Teams Speed Up 737 Output," *The Wall Street Journal Online*, February 7, 2012, http://online.wsj.com/article/SB10001424052970203436904577155204034907744.html (accessed September 25, 2012); and Jeremy Dwyer-Lindgren, "Boeing Will Boost 737 Production, Slow 777 Rates," *USA Today*, January 28, 2016, http://www.usatoday.com/story/travel/flights/todayinthesky/2016/01/28/boeing-boost-737-production-but-slow-777-rates/79450198/ (accessed May 17, 2016).

13. "Teams of the 500," *Fortune* (June 15, 2015): 276–285.

14. Ronald A. Gill, "Quality-Oriented Teamwork Resolves Aerospace Manufacturer's Critical Path Tooling Crisis," *Global Business and Organizational Excellence* (September–October 2012): 34–41.

15. Susanne G. Scott and Walter O. Einstein, "Strategic Performance Appraisal in Team-Based Organizations: One Size Does Not Fit All," *Academy of Management Executive* 15, no. 2 (2001): 107–116.

16. Adam Davidson, "What Hollywood Can Teach Us about the Future of Work," *The New York Times Sunday Magazine*, May 10, 2015.

17. Bryce G. Hoffman, "Inside Ford's Fight to Avoid Disaster," *The Wall Street Journal*, March 9, 2012.

18. Jason Fried, "Get Real: When the Only Way Up Is Out," *Inc.* (April 2011): 35–36.

19. The discussion of self-managed teams is based on Ruth Wageman, "Critical Success Factors for Creating Superb Self-Managing Teams," *Organizational Dynamics* (Summer 1997): 49–61; James H. Shonk, *Team-Based Organizations* (Homewood, IL: Business One Irwin, 1992); and Thomas Owens, "The Self-Managing Work Team," *Small Business Report* (February 1991): 53–65.

20. Lindsay Blakely, "The Right Man for the Job (Sometimes)," *Inc.* (July 2, 2012), http://www.inc.com/30under30/lindsay-blakely/ilya-pozin-founder-of-ciplex.html (accessed November 5, 2013); and Ilya Pozin, "Want Happier Employees? Get Rid of the Bosses," *Inc.* (June 18, 2012), http://www.inc.com/ilya-pozin/want-happier-employees-get-rid-of-the-bosses.html/1 (accessed October 2, 2013).

21. David A. Ferrucci, "Building the Team That Built Watson," *The New York Times*, January 7, 2012, www.nytimes.com/2012/01/08/jobs/building-the-watson-team-of-scientists.html?_r=0 (accessed October 1, 2012).

22. Study by G. Clotaire Rapaille, reported in Karen Bernowski, "What Makes American Teams Tick?" *Quality Progress* 28, no. 1 (January 1995): 39–42.

23. Avan Jassawalla, Hemant Sashittal, and Avinash Malshe, "Students' Perceptions of Social Loafing: Its Antecedents and Consequences in Undergraduate Business Classroom Teams," *Academy of Management Learning and Education* 8, no. 1 (2009): 42–54; and Robert Albanese and David D. Van Fleet, "Rational Behavior in Groups: The Free-Riding Tendency," *Academy of Management Review* 10 (1985): 244–255.

24. See David H. Freedman, "The Idiocy of Crowds" ("What's Next" column), *Inc.* (September 2006): 61–62.

25. Quoted in Jason Zweig, "The Intelligent Investor: How Group Decisions End Up Wrong-Footed," *The Wall Street Journal*, April 25, 2009.

26. "Why Some Teams Succeed (and So Many Don't)," *Harvard Management Update* (October 2006): 3–4; Frederick P. Morgeson, D. Scott DeRue, and Elizabeth P. Karam, "Leadership in Teams: A Functional Approach to Understanding Leadership Structure and Processes," *Journal of Management* 36, no. 1 (January 2010): 5–39; and Patrick Lencioni, "Dissolve Dysfunction: Begin Building Your Dream Team," *Leadership Excellence* (October 2009): 20.

27. Reported in Jerry Useem, "What's That Spell? Teamwork!" *Fortune* (June 12, 2006): 65–66.

28. Eric Sundstrom, Kenneth P. DeMeuse, and David Futtrell, "Work Teams," *American Psychologist* 45 (February 1990): 120–133; María Isabel Delgado Piña, Ana María Romero Martínez, and Luis Gómez Martínez, "Teams in Organizations: A Review on Team Effectiveness," *Team Performance Management* 14, no. 1–2 (2008): 7–21; and Morgeson, DeRue, and Karam, "Leadership in Teams."

29. Deborah L. Gladstein, "Groups in Context: A Model of Task Group Effectiveness," *Administrative Science Quarterly* 29 (1984): 499–517. For an overview of research on team effectiveness, see John Mathieu et al., "Team Effectiveness 1997–2007: A Review of Recent Advancements and a Glimpse into the Future," *Journal of Management* 34, no. 3 (June 2008): 410–476.

30. Sujin K. Horwitz and Irwin B. Horwitz, "The Effects of Team Diversity on Team Outcomes: A Meta-Analytic Review of Team Demography," *Journal of Management* 33, no. 6 (December 2007): 987–1015; and Dora C. Lau and J. Keith Murnighan, "Demographic Diversity and Faultlines: The Compositional Dynamics of Organizational Groups," *Academy of Management Review* 23, no. 2 (1998): 325–340.

31. See Lucy L. Gilson, M. Travis Maynard, Nicole C. Jones Young et al., "Virtual Teams Research: 10 Years, 10 Themes, and 10 Opportunities," *Journal of Management* 41, no. 5 (July 2015): 1313–1337 for a recent review of research related to virtual teams.

32. The discussion of virtual teams is based on Andrea Lekushoff, "Lifestyle-Driven Virtual Teams: A New Paradigm for Professional Services Firms," *Ivey Business Journal* (September–October 2012): 24–27; Phillip L. Hunsaker and Johanna S. Hunsaker, "Virtual Teams: A Leader's Guide," *Team Performance Management* 14, no. 1–2 (2008): 86ff; Chris Kimble, "Building Effective Virtual Teams: How to Overcome the Problems of Trust and Identity in Virtual Teams," *Global Business and Organizational Excellence* (January–February 2011): 6–15; Wayne F. Cascio and Stan Shurygailo, "E-Leadership and Virtual Teams," *Organizational Dynamics* 31, no. 4 (2002): 362–376; Anthony M. Townsend, Samuel M. DeMarie, and Anthony R. Hendrickson, "Virtual Teams: Technology and the Workplace of the Future," *Academy of Management Executive*

12, no. 3 (August 1998): 17–29; and Deborah L. Duarte and Nancy Tennant Snyder, *Mastering Virtual Teams* (San Francisco: Jossey-Bass, 1999).

33. "Virtual Teams," Society for Human Resource Management, July 13, 2012, https://www.shrm.org/research/surveyfindings/articles/pages/virtualteams.aspx (accessed May 18, 2016); Richard Lepsinger and Darleen DeRosa, "How to Lead an Effective Virtual Team," *Ivey Business Journal* (May–June 2015), http://iveybusinessjournal.com/how-to-lead-an-effective-virtual-team/ (accessed November 9, 2015); and Gilson et al., "Virtual Teams Research."

34. Vijay Govindarajan and Anil K. Gupta, "Building an Effective Global Business Team," *MIT Sloan Management Review* 42, no. 4 (Summer 2001): 63–71.

35. Jessica Lipnack and Jeffrey Stamps, "Virtual Teams: The New Way to Work," *Strategy & Leadership* (January–February 1999): 14–19; and Sadri Golnaz and Condia John, "Managing the Virtual World," *Industrial Management* (Jan 2012), Vol. 54 Issue 1.

36. This discussion is based on Lepsinger and DeRosa, "How to Lead an Effective Virtual Team"; Lekushoff, "Lifestyle-Driven Virtual Teams"; Arvind Malhotra, Ann Majchrzak, and Benson Rosen, "Leading Virtual Teams," *Academy of Management Perspectives* 21, no. 1 (February 2007): 60–69; Benson Rosen, Stacie Furst, and Richard Blackburn, "Overcoming Barriers to Knowledge Sharing in Virtual Teams," *Organizational Dynamics* 36, no. 3 (2007): 259–273; Marshall Goldsmith, "Crossing the Cultural Chasm," *BusinessWeek Online*, May 31, 2007, www.businessweek.com/careers/content/may2007/ca20070530_521679.htm (accessed August 24, 2007); and Bradley L. Kirkman et al., "Five Challenges to Virtual Team Success: Lessons from Sabre, Inc.," *Academy of Management Executive* 16, no. 3 (2002): 67–79.

37. Darl G. Kolb, Greg Prussia, and Joline Francoeur, "Connectivity and Leadership: The Influence of Online Activity on Closeness and Effectiveness," *Journal of Leadership and Organizational Studies* 15, no. 4 (May 2009): 342–352.

38. Ann Majchrzak et al., "Can Absence Make a Team Grow Stronger?" *Harvard Business Review* 82, no. 5 (May 2004): 131.

39. Lynda Gratton, "Working Together . . . When Apart," *The Wall Street Journal*, June 18, 2007; and Kirkman et al., "Five Challenges to Virtual Team Success."

40. Carol Hymowitz, "Diebold's New Executive Suite," *Bloomberg Businessweek* (August 10–23, 2015): 21–23.

41. Pete Engardio, "A Guide for Multinationals: One of the Greatest Challenges for a Multinational Is Learning How to Build a Productive Global Team," *BusinessWeek* (August 20, 2007): 48–51; and Gratton, "Working Together . . . When Apart."

42. Ellen Sheng, "How to Manage Cultural Differences in Global Teams," *Fast Company*, January 12, 2016, http://www.fastcompany.com/3054879/the-future-of-work/how-to-manage-cultural-differences-in-global-teams (accessed May 30, 2016); and Richard Pastore, "Global Team Management: It's a Small World After All," *CIO* (January 23, 2008), www.cio.com/article/174750/Global_Team_Management_It_s_a_Small_World_After_All (accessed May 20, 2008).

43. Reported in Jia Lynn Yang, "The Power of Number 4.6," part of a special series, "Secrets of Greatness: Teamwork," *Fortune* (June 12, 2006): 122.

44. Martin Hoegl, "Smaller Teams–Better Teamwork: How to Keep Project Teams Small," *Business Horizons* 48 (2005): 209–214.

45. Stephanie T. Solansky, "Team Identification: A Determining Factor of Performance," *Journal of Managerial Psychology* 26, no. 3 (2011): 247–258.

46. Reported in Yang, "The Power of Number 4.6"; and Eric Schmidt and Jonathan Rosenberg, *How Google Works* (New York: Grand Central Publishing, 2014), p. 46.

47. For research findings on group size, see Erin Bradner, Gloria Mark, and Tammie D. Hertel, "Team Size and Technology Fit: Participation, Awareness, and Rapport in Distributed Teams," *IEEE Transactions on Professional Communication* 48, no. 1 (March 2005): 68–77; M. E. Shaw, *Group Dynamics*, 3rd ed. (New York: McGraw-Hill, 1981); G. Manners, "Another Look at Group Size, Group Problem-Solving, and Member Consensus," *Academy of Management Journal* 18 (1975): 715–724; and Martin Hoegl, "Smaller Teams—Better Teamwork."

48. Bradner, Mark, and Hertel, "Team Size and Technology Fit: Participation, Awareness, and Rapport in Distributed Teams"; and Sadri and Condia, "Managing the Virtual World."

49. Sheen S. Levine and David Stark, "Diversity Makes You Brighter," *The New York Times*, December 9, 2015; Warren E. Watson, Kamalesh Kumar, and Larry K. Michaelsen, "Cultural Diversity's Impact on Interaction Process and Performance: Comparing Homogeneous and Diverse Task Groups," *Academy of Management Journal* 36 (1993): 590–602; Gail Robinson and Kathleen Dechant, "Building a Business Case for Diversity," *Academy of Management Executive* 11, no. 3 (1997): 21–31; and David A. Thomas and Robin J. Ely, "Making Differences Matter: A New Paradigm for Managing Diversity," *Harvard Business Review* (September–October 1996): 79–90.

50. D. van Knippenberg and M. C. Schippers, "Work Group Diversity," *Annual Review of Psychology* 58 (2007): 515–541; J. N. Cummings, "Work Groups: Structural Diversity and Knowledge Sharing in a Global Organization," *Management Science* 50, no. 3 (2004): 352–364; J. Stuart Bunderson and Kathleen M. Sutcliffe, "Comparing Alternative Conceptualizations of Functional Diversity in Management Teams: Process and Performance Effects," *Academy of Management Journal* 45, no. 5 (2002): 875–893; and Marc Orlitzky and John D. Benjamin, "The Effects of Sex Composition on Small Group Performance in a Business School Case Competition," *Academy of Management Learning and Education* 2, no. 2 (2003): 128–138.

51. Anita Woolley and Thomas Malone, "Defend Your Research: What Makes a Team Smarter? More Women," *Harvard Business Review* (June 2011), http://hbr.org/2011/06/defend-your-research-what-makes-a-team-smarter-more-women/ar/1 (accessed October 1, 2012).

52. Watson et al., "Cultural Diversity's Impact on Interaction Process and Performance"; and D. C. Hambrick et al., "When Groups Consist of Multiple Nationalities: Towards a New Understanding of the Implications," *Organization Studies* 19, no. 2 (1998): 181–205.

53. Matt Moffett, "Trapped Miners Kept Focus, Shared Tuna—Foiled Escape, Bid to Organize Marked First Two Weeks Underground in Chile," *The Wall Street Journal*, August 25, 2010; and "Lessons on Leadership and Teamwork—From 700 Meters Below the Earth's Surface," Universia Knowledge @ Wharton, September 22, 2010, www.wharton.universia.net/index.cfm?fa=viewArticle&id=1943&language=english (accessed September 29, 2010).

54. R. M. Belbin, *Team Roles at Work* (Oxford, UK: Butterworth Heinemann, 1983); Tony Manning, R. Parker, and G. Pogson, "A Revised Model of Team Roles and Some Research Findings," *Industrial and Commercial Training* 38, no. 6 (2006): 287–296; George Prince, "Recognizing Genuine Teamwork," *Supervisory Management* (April 1989): 25–36; K. D. Benne and P. Sheats, "Functional Roles of Group Members," *Journal of Social Issues* 4 (1948): 41–49; and R. F. Bales, *SYMLOG Case Study Kit* (New York: Free Press, 1980).

55. Robert A. Baron, *Behavior in Organizations*, 2d ed. (Boston: Allyn & Bacon, 1986).

56. Ibid.

57. Bruce W. Tuckman and Mary Ann C. Jensen, "Stages of Small-Group Development Revisited," *Group and Organizational Studies* 2 (1977): 419–427; and Bruce W. Tuckman, "Developmental Sequences in Small Groups," *Psychological Bulletin* 63 (1965): 384–399. See also Linda N. Jewell and H. Joseph Reitz, *Group Effectiveness in Organizations* (Glenview, IL: Scott Foresman, 1981).

58. Oluremi B. Ayoko, Alison M. Konrad, and Maree V. Boyle, "Online Work: Managing Conflict and Emotions for Performance in Virtual Teams," *European Management Journal* 30 (2012): 156–174.

59. Ibid.

60. Shaw, *Group Dynamics*.

61. Daniel C. Feldman and Hugh J. Arnold, *Managing Individual and Group Behavior in Organizations* (New York: McGraw-Hill, 1983).

62. Amanuel G. Tekleab, Narda R. Quigley, and Paul E. Tesluk, "A Longitudinal Study of Team Conflict, Conflict Management, Cohesion, and Team Effectiveness," *Group & Organization Management* 34, no. 2 (April 2009): 170–205; Dorwin Cartwright and Alvin Zander, *Group Dynamics: Research and Theory*, 3d ed. (New York: Harper & Row, 1968); and Elliot Aronson, *The Social Animal* (San Francisco: W. H. Freeman, 1976).

63. Vishal K. Gupta, Rui Huang, and Suman Niranjan, "A Longitudinal Examination of the Relationship Between Team Leadership and Performance," *Journal of Leadership and Organizational Studies* 17, no. 4 (2010): 335–350; and Marcial Losada and Emily Heaphy, "The Role of Positivity and Connectivity in the Performance of Business Teams," *American Behavioral Scientist* 47, no. 6 (February 2004): 740–765.

64. Bank of America example from Rachel Emma Silverman, "Tracking Sensors Invade the Workplace; Devices on Workers, Furniture Offer Clues for Boosting Productivity," *The Wall Street Journal*, March 7, 2013, http://online.wsj.com/article/SB10001424127887324034804578344303429080678.html (accessed May 3, 2013); and Alex "Sandy" Pentland, "The New Science of Building Great Teams," *Harvard Business Review* (April 2012): 61–70.

65. Stanley E. Seashore, *Group Cohesiveness in the Industrial Work Group* (Ann Arbor, MI: Institute for Social Research, 1954).

66. J. Richard Hackman, "Group Influences on Individuals," in *Handbook of Industrial and Organizational Psychology*, ed. M. Dunnette (Chicago: Rand McNally, 1976).

67. These are based on Daniel C. Feldman, "The Development and Enforcement of Group Norms," *Academy of Management Review* 9 (1984): 47–53.

68. Jeanne M. Wilson et al., *Leadership Trapeze: Strategies for Leadership in Team-Based Organizations* (San Francisco: Jossey-Bass, 1994), p. 12.

69. This discussion is based on Charles Duhigg, "What Google Learned from Its Quest to Build the Perfect Team," *The New York Times Magazine*, February 25, 2016, http://www.nytimes.com/2016/02/28/magazine/what-google-learned-from-its-quest-to-build-the-perfect-team.html?_r=0 (accessed May 19, 2016).

70. Ibid.

71. Simon Taggar and Robert Ellis, "The Role of Leaders in Shaping Formal Team Norms," *The Leadership Quarterly* 18 (2007): 105–120.

72. Geoffrey Colvin, "Why Dream Teams Fail," *Fortune* (June 12, 2006): 87–92.

73. Stephen P. Robbins, *Managing Organizational Conflict: A Nontraditional Approach* (Englewood Cliffs, NJ: Prentice Hall, 1974).

74. Tekleab, Quigley, and Tesluk, "A Longitudinal Study of Team Conflict, Conflict Management, Cohesion, and Team Effectiveness."

75. Based on K. A. Jehn, "A Multimethod Examination of the Benefits and Determinants of Intragroup Conflict," *Administrative Science Quarterly* 40 (1995): 256–282; K. A. Jehn, "A Qualitative Analysis of Conflict Types and Dimensions in Organizational Groups," *Administrative Science Quarterly* 42 (1997): 530–557; and Mélanie Schaeffner and Hendrik Huettermann et al., "Swim or Sink Together: The Potential of Collective Team Identification and Team Member Alignment for Separating Task and Relationship Conflicts," *Group and Organization Management* 40, no. 4 (2015): 467–499.

76. Linda A. Hill, "A Note for Analyzing Work Groups," *Harvard Business School Cases*, August 28, 1995; revised April 3, 1998, Product # 9-496-026, ordered at http://hbr.org/search/linda+a+hill/4294934969/.

77. A. Amason, "Distinguishing the Effects of Functional and Dysfunctional Conflict on Strategic Decision Making: Resolving a Paradox for Top Management Teams," *Academy of Management Journal* 39, no. 1 (1996): 123–148; Jehn, "A Multimethod Examination of the Benefits and Determinants of Intragroup Conflict"; and K. A. Jehn and E. A. Mannix, "The Dynamic Nature of Conflict: A Longitudinal Study of Intragroup Conflict and Group Performance," *Academy of Management Journal* 44 (2001): 238–251.

78. Amason, "Distinguishing the Effects of Functional and Dysfunctional Conflict on Strategic Decision Making."

79. Dean Tjosvold et al., "Conflict Values and Team Relationships: Conflict's Contribution to Team Effectiveness and Citizenship in China," *Journal of Organizational Behavior* 24 (2003): 69–88; Matt Palmquist, "The Dangers of Too Much Workplace Cohesion," *Strategy + Business* (February 10, 2015), http://www.strategy-business.com/blog/The-Dangers-of-Too-Much-Workplace-Cohesion?gko=ef547 (accessed November 6, 2015); C. De Dreu and E. Van de Vliert, *Using Conflict in Organizations* (Beverly Hills, CA: Sage, 1997); and Kathleen M. Eisenhardt, Jean L. Kahwajy, and L. J. Bourgeois III, "Conflict and Strategic Choice: How Top Management Teams Disagree," *California Management Review* 39, no. 2 (Winter 1997): 42–62.

80. Kenneth G. Koehler, "Effective Team Management," *Small Business Report* (July 19, 1989): 14–16; and Dean Tjosvold, "Making Conflict Productive," *Personnel Administrator* 29 (June 1984): 121.

81. This discussion is based in part on Richard L. Daft, *Organization Theory and Design* (St. Paul, MN: West, 1992), Chapter 13; and Paul M. Terry, "Conflict Management," *Journal of Leadership Studies* 3, no. 2 (1996): 3–21.

82. Edmondson, "Teamwork on the Fly."

83. Yuhyung Shin, "Conflict Resolution in Virtual Teams," *Organizational Dynamics* 34, no. 4 (2005): 331–345.

84. This discussion is based on K. W. Thomas, "Towards Multidimensional Values in Teaching: The Example of Conflict Behaviors," *Academy of Management Review* 2 (1977): 487.

85. Sonia Kolesnikov-Jessop, "Building Teams by Winning Hearts and Minds," *The New York Times*, June 7, 2015, http://www.nytimes.com/2015/06/08/business/international/building-teams-by-winning-hearts-and-minds.html?_r=0 (accessed May 19, 2016).

86. This discussion is based on Laurie R. Weingart et al., "The Directness and Oppositional Intensity of Conflict Expression," *Academy of Management Review* 40, no. 2 (2015): 235–262; and Phyllis Korkki, "Be Direct and Low-Key to Defuse Discord at the Office," *The New York Times*, May 9, 2015, http://www.nytimes.com/2015/05/10/business/be-direct-and-low-key-to-defuse-discord-at-the-office.html?_r=0 (accessed May 20, 2016).

87. Weingart et al., "The Directness and Oppositional Intensity of Conflict Expression."

88. "Negotiation Types," The Negotiation Experts, June 9, 2010, www.negotiations.com/articles/negotiation-types/ (accessed September 28, 2010).

89. Rob Walker, "Take It or Leave It: The Only Guide to Negotiating You Will Ever Need," *Inc.* (August 2003): 75–82.

90. Based on Roger Fisher and William Ury, *Getting to Yes: Negotiating Agreement Without Giving In* (New York: Penguin, 1983); Walker, "Take It or Leave It"; Robb Mandelbaum, "How to Negotiate Effectively," *Inc.*, November 1, 2010, www.inc.com/magazine/20101101/how-to-negotiate-effectively.html (accessed April 12, 2011); and Deepak Malhotra and Max H. Bazerman, "Investigative Negotiation," *Harvard Business Review* (September 2007): 72–78.

91. This familiar story has been reported in many publications, including "The Six Best Questions to Ask Your Customers," Marketing and Distribution Company Limited, www.madisco.bz/articles/The%20Six%20Best%20Questions%20to%20Ask%20Your%20Customers.pdf (accessed September 28, 2010).

92. Based on James W. Kinneer, "This and That: Improving Team Performance," in *The 1997 Annual: Volume 2, Consulting* (San Francisco: Pfeiffer, 1997), pp. 55–58.

93. Based on Ellen R. Stapleton, "College to Expand Policy on Plagiarism," *The Itha-can Online*, April 12, 2001, www.ithaca.edu/ithacan/articles/0104/12/news/0college_to_e.htm (accessed April 12, 2001).

PART 6

Chapter 15
Managing Quality and Performance

iStock.com/oscarhdez

Chapter Outline

Learning Outcomes

After studying this chapter, you should be able to:

15.1 Explain the four steps in the control process.

15.2 Describe the benefits of using a balanced scorecard to track the performance and control of the organization.

15.3 Contrast the hierarchical and decentralized methods of control.

15.4 Explain the benefits of open-book management.

15.5 Describe the concept of total quality management (TQM) and major TQM techniques, including quality circles, benchmarking, Six Sigma principles, quality partnering, and continuous improvement.

15.6 Discuss the use of financial statements, financial analysis, and budgeting as management controls.

15.7 Identify current trends in quality and financial control, including ISO 9000 and electronic monitoring, and their impact on organizations.

Are You Ready to Be a Manager?

Before reading this chapter, please circle either "Mostly True" or "Mostly False" for each of the following five statements.

1 I set goals for myself each week and then look and see how well I met them.

Mostly True ◄····················► Mostly False

[page 554]

2 In my own life, I judge my success not only by how much money I do or can earn but also by how much I learn and the quality of my relationships.

Mostly True ◄····················► Mostly False

[page 555]

3 I enjoy keeping track of my own or my team's progress and like to keep statistics on how well we're doing.

Mostly True ◄····················► Mostly False

[page 561]

4 When I'm working on a project, I try to find someone who's done something similar very successfully and I try to learn from that person how I can be even more effective.

Mostly True ◄····················► Mostly False

[page 562]

5 I have a budget for myself and know this is a tool to help me make better decisions about how to use my resources.

Mostly True ◄····················► Mostly False

[page 567]

Discover Your Management Approach

What Is Your Attitude Toward Improvement?

Instructions: Respond to each of the following statements based on how you think and act in a typical situation of work accomplishment at school or on the job. Mark whether each statement is Mostly True or Mostly False for you. There are no right or wrong answers, so answer honestly.

	Mostly True	Mostly False
1. I spend time developing new ways to approach old problems.	_____	_____
2. So long as things are done correctly and efficiently, I prefer not to take on the hassle of changing them.	_____	_____
3. I believe the effort to improve something should be rewarded even if the final outcome is disappointing.	_____	_____

To complete and score entire assessment, visit MindTap.

Imagine taking a beloved family member to a hospital or clinic to receive an injection of pain medication only to have the person contract fungal meningitis, a rare but potentially deadly disease. That's exactly what happened for many families when tainted spinal steroid injections from the New England Compounding Center (NECC) caused one of the worst public health drug disasters in U.S. history. As many as 14,000 patients across 20 states were exposed to fungal meningitis in 2012, with 800 becoming ill and at least 64 dying. A federal inspection found mold and bacteria growing on surfaces, greenish-yellow residue on sterilization equipment, and air conditioning equipment that was shut off at night despite the importance of controlling temperature and humidity. Although U.S. Food and Drug Administration (FDA) inspectors found numerous instances of violations of federal standards, they also noted that surfaces in the clean rooms were contaminated with levels of bacteria or mold exceeding levels at which the company's own procedures called for remedial measures, yet there was no evidence that the company ever took such measures. Company managers, the Massachusetts Board of Pharmacy, and FDA officials all came under scrutiny in the wake of this breakdown of quality control. Fourteen owners, managers, employees, and others associated with the now-defunct NECC went on trial in late 2016 on 131 charges ranging from fraud to second-degree murder.[1]

What a tragic illustration of the need for quality and behavioral control. Control is a serious responsibility for every manager. It might not always be a matter of life or death, but as a manager, you'll use a variety of measures to monitor employee behavior and keep track of the organization's performance and finances. Many of these measures will involve control issues, including controlling work processes, regulating employee behavior, maintaining quality standards, setting up basic systems for allocating financial resources, developing human resources, analyzing financial performance, and evaluating overall profitability.

This chapter introduces basic mechanisms for controlling an organization. We begin by defining organizational control and summarizing the four steps in the control process. Then we discuss the use of the balanced scorecard to measure performance and examine the changing philosophy of control. We discuss today's approach to total quality management (TQM) and consider methods for controlling financial performance, including the use of budgets and financial statements.

15-1 The Meaning of Control

Before New York City buildings are demolished or renovated, licensed inspectors are required to inspect them for the presence of lead or asbestos. Both substances can cause severe, long-term health problems, including cancer. If either is found, it must first be either removed or contained using an expensive and time-consuming process. Given the serious health risks associated with these two substances, you could assume that the inspection process would be carefully regulated and controlled. Yet many law enforcement officials and industry experts say that New York City's inspection system is highly corrupt. As evidence, licensed safety inspector Saverio F. Todaro recently made a stunning confession in federal court. He revealed that although he had submitted clean asbestos and lead test results for more than 200 buildings and apartments, he had not performed a single one of the tests. Although shocking, the Department of Environmental Protection (DEP) claims that these crimes occur frequently and easily because of a lack of controls. The DEP audits only a tiny fraction of the roughly 28,400 projects that inspectors like Todaro certify each year as safe. "We can always look for new ways to improve our process," said a spokesman for the mayor. "DEP is going to start increasing audits, which is the right step to ensure inspections are being completed properly."[2]

Organizational control refers to the systematic process of regulating organizational activities to make them consistent with the expectations established in plans, targets, and standards of performance. In a classic article on the control function, Douglas S. Sherwin summarizes the concept as follows: "The essence of control is action which adjusts operations to predetermined standards, and its basis is information in the hands of managers."[3] Thus, effectively controlling an organization requires information about performance standards and actual performance, as well as actions taken to correct any deviations from the standards.

Managers must decide what information is essential, how they will obtain that information, and how they can and should respond to it. Having the correct data is essential. Managers decide which standards, measurements, and metrics are needed to monitor and control the organization effectively and set up systems for obtaining that information. The Fyre Festival evidently did not have goals, data gathering, or any metrics to determine level of success, as described in the "Half-Baked Management" box.

If a hospital, for example, carefully monitors and controls its health care services, patients should receive safe, high-quality health care. A pay-for-performance system built into President Barack Obama's health care overhaul for Medicare payments to hospitals prompted some hospitals to initiate broader initiatives to tie doctors' pay to patient outcomes and quality measures. New York City's Health and Hospitals Corporation, which runs the city's 11 public hospitals, for example, will monitor 13 performance indicators that are believed to be correlated with better quality care, including how quickly emergency room patients go from triage to beds, whether doctors get to the operating room on time, how well patients say their doctors communicate with them, and so forth. The idea is that tying doctors' raises to how well they perform on the benchmarks would improve patient care.[4] The "Sunny Side Up" box describes auto-analytics, an innovative reporting system for individuals that can provide information that may help people control their own personal and professional growth.

ndoeljindoel/Shutterstock.com

Concept Connection

The state of California has deep concerns about paint solvents, concrete slurry, and other pollutants entering the water supply through work done at construction sites. Thus, the state government now offers training programs for contractors and others in the construction industry to learn how to improve **organizational control**. In addition to using filters that keep the water supply clean, effective control means ensuring that builders comply with new state regulations.

Half-Baked Management 〉 Fyre Festival

Fyre Festival in the Bahamas was advertised as the "cultural experience of the decade," even better than Coachella, South by Southwest, or Bonnaroo. Scheduled for two weekends in April and May of 2017, people paid up to $12,000 for airfare, event admission, and rental fees for the supposedly hot event, which had been promoted by social influencers such as Kendall Jenner, who were paid for their "influence." Attendees arrived to find a festival ground only half built, cancelled music acts, and terrible food. More than 20 individuals had lent $4 million to the Festival, and many of those are suing it, which was started by Billy McFarland, who was arrested in July 2017 for wire fraud in connection with the festival. Lenders are hoping Fyre's bankruptcy will help them find out what happened to their money.

SOURCE: "Business News: Business Watch," *The Wall Street Journal*, July 10, 2017, B6.

Remember This

- **Organizational control** is the systematic process through which managers regulate organizational activities to meet planned goals and standards of performance.

- Most organizations measure and control performance using quantitative financial measures.

15-2 Feedback Control Model

Teams of researchers asked managers in thousands of organizations questions designed to determine how well they were implementing various management control practices, such as establishing standards and targets and measuring performance data, and they found that better control is strongly correlated with better organizational productivity and performance.[5] A feedback control model can help managers meet strategic goals by monitoring and regulating the organization's activities and using feedback to determine whether performance meets established standards.

15-2a Four Steps of Feedback Control

Managers set up control systems that consist of the four key steps illustrated in Exhibit 15.1: establish standards, measure performance, compare performance to standards, and make corrections as necessary.

Exhibit 15.1 Feedback Control Model

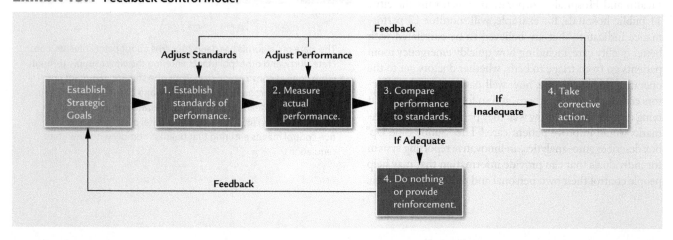

Sunny Side Up

Quantify Yourself

Imagine becoming better at your job and more satisfied with your life by tracking information that reveals exactly how you spend your day. For 22 years, entrepreneur and scientist Stephen Wolfram did just that. He mapped data about his time spent in meetings, his use of e-mail, and the number of keystrokes he logged so that he could analyze how he spent his time. Wolfram was able to identify work habits that squelched his creativity and stymied his productivity. So he started planning changes that would help him become more productive and happier.

New devices such as computer software and smartphone apps help people gather and analyze data about what they do at work so they can use it to do their jobs better. This interest in self-awareness is part of a growing discipline called *auto-analytics*, which is the practice of voluntarily collecting and analyzing data about oneself in order to improve. It consists of the following:

- *Tracking screen time.* While it may be unsettling to have our managers watching what's on our computer screens, it's much more acceptable when we do the watching. New technology called *knowledge workload tracking* records how you use your computer, such as measuring how long you have an open window, how often you switch between windows, and how long you're idle. The software turns all the measurements into charts so you can see where you're spending your time and how you can improve your productivity. One computer programmer thought his online chats were eating into his programming time, so he analyzed how much time he spent chatting during certain periods and then looked at how much code he wrote during those times. Surprisingly, he found that talking online with colleagues actually *improved* his productivity.

- *Measuring cognitive tasks.* Another set of tracking tools can help you gather data as you perform cognitive tasks, such as client research on your smartphone

or statistical analysis in Microsoft Excel. Bob Evans, a Google engineer, used an app called MeetGrinder to explore the relationship between his attention and his productivity. "As engineers, we load up our heads with all these variables, the intellectual pieces of the systems we are building. If we get distracted, we lose that thread in our heads," he said. MeetGrinder revealed to Evans that he needs about four straight hours to get anything challenging done, so he tackles those projects when he has that kind of time, not on days that are interrupted with meetings and phone calls.

- *Improving health.* Exercise, amount of sleep, and the stress levels of knowledge workers have been shown to affect productivity, creativity, and job performance. People can choose from a variety of mobile apps and wearable sensors that collect valuable data about their physical health. Sacha Chua wanted to better understand how her sleep schedule affected her professional priorities, so she monitored her bedtimes, wake-up times, and amount of sleep over several weeks using a tracker called Sleep On It. She changed her routine and started waking up at 5:40 a.m. instead of 8:30 a.m. She gave up late-night activities like browsing the Web and started going to bed earlier. With these adjustments, she discovered that her work productivity soared.

Tools used for auto-analytics will continue to become more sophisticated. The data they reveal can provide the hard evidence we sometimes need to adjust the way we use our time and nurture our minds and bodies to have more success in work and life.

SOURCES: Based on H. James Wilson, "Employees, Measure Yourselves," *The Wall Street Journal*, April 2, 2012, http://online.wsj.com/article/SB10001424052970204520204577249691204802060.html#articleTabs%3Darticle (accessed September 28, 2012); and H. James Wilson, "You, by the Numbers," *Harvard Business Review* (September, 2012): 2–5.

Establish Standards of Performance   Within the organization's overall strategic plan, managers define goals for organizational departments in specific operational terms that include a *standard of performance* against which to compare organizational activities. At H&M retail stores, for example, sales floor employees are guided by the standard that clothes should always be "easy to find, easy to buy." Pants, sweaters, and shirts are stacked neatly, with perfect folds; size stickers are placed with precision; and hangers are lined up uniformly. All that precision turns to chaos as soon as the doors open for business, of course, but employees are trained to restore order whenever they have moments to do so. "One thing to keep in mind," said Edwin Mercedes, a store visual manager who is responsible for the look of several stores in the eastern United States, "is standards. We want perfect folds." Basic standards for customer service are also followed precisely.[6] Managing Mary Darling's TV show *Little Mosque on the Prairie* required having goals relating to hot, delicious food for cast and crew and the ability to meet widely varying (and shifting) schedules of the unions on set, as described in the "Recipe for Success" box.

Recipe for Success

Little Mosque on the Prairie

"Shouldn't everyone everywhere be fed like this?" asked producer Mary Darling's daughter, Bre Vader, on the set of the hit Canadian TV series, *Little Mosque on the Prairie*. What she referred to was the breakfast truck rolling in at 5 a.m., making omelets, pancakes, or anything else on the griddle for everyone involved in the program. Inside the sound studio was a huge table with various breads, including gluten-free and vegan options, along with fruits and many, many toast toppings, coffee, tea, and just about everything else you could ask for. And that was only for *breakfast*. Vader continued, saying that lots of other people besides actors and crews—such as teachers, and students—work hard and should be fed accordingly.

How do you manage feeding 250 people for three meals and various snacks a day for months? Consider that you have to please people with very different palates and widely varying food allergies or vegan, Paleo, or gluten-free dietetic lifestyles. And you have to make sure people don't get bored with the food. Dinners for *Little Mosque on the Prairie* were catered by a company that does only weddings and film shoots, which meant that the quality of the food was higher than average. The caterer made the best filets, pastas, chicken cacciatore, and on and on. Every single dinner was the type of meal expected at a high-class wedding. Then each afternoon, the actors and crew would have a surprise. For example, baristas would make incredible coffees, there might be sundae heaven, or an ice cream truck might come. Such surprises had to be different *every* day.

Consider also that Darling's group had to work with more than six unions, each of which had different meal and break schedules, so groups ate one after the other, requiring food for each meal to be available and hot for a long time. Darling worked with her producer, Colin Brunton, and craft service manager, Mark DeNuzzo, to plan meals and the daily surprises. Then decisions had to be made. Generally, in the industry, extras are not fed, but Darling decided it wasn't good to have the extras waiting in their area, not far from where the food was served and to be denied access. So they also had to schedule when the extras would eat.

All of this required complicated scheduling with the various caterers, the different groups of cast and crew, the director, and the producers. Next time you watch a movie or TV show, think about all the food and logistics involved.

SOURCE: Mary Darling, personal communication, April 2018.

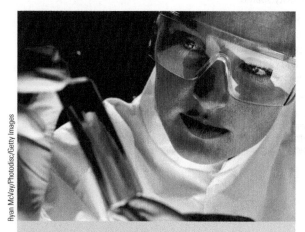

Ryan McVay/Photodisc/Getty Images

Concept Connection

When it comes to pharmaceutical drugs, accuracy is essential—human lives are at stake. Researchers like this one follow precise procedures to ensure that test results are both objective and accurate and that the testing processes meet research goals. Pharmaceutical firms establish **standards of performance** to measure research activities and results. For example, many companies set a standard for how many compounds should move forward at each stage of the drug development process.

Tracking such measures as customer service, product quality, or order accuracy is an important supplement to traditional financial and operational performance measurement, but many companies have a hard time identifying and defining nonfinancial measurements. To evaluate and reward employees effectively for the achievement of standards, managers need clear standards that reflect activities that contribute to the organization's overall strategy in a significant way. Standards should be defined clearly and precisely so that employees know what they need to do and can determine whether their activities are on target.[7]

Measure Actual Performance   Most organizations prepare formal reports of quantitative performance measurements that managers review daily, weekly, or monthly. Managers should take care, however, that they aren't generating reports just because they have data to do so.[8] These measurements should be related to the standards set in the first step of the control process, and the reports should be designed to help managers evaluate how well the organization is meeting its standards. For example, if sales growth is a target, the organization should have a means of gathering and reporting sales data. If the organization has identified appropriate measurements, regular review of these reports helps managers stay aware of whether or not the organization is doing what it should. Grady Memorial Hospital in Atlanta measures patient satisfaction based in part on the results of a government-mandated patient satisfaction survey that has been administered since 2006. Hospitals that receive Medicare payments must administer at least 100 patient surveys over a period of a year, and Grady's administrators use the results combined with other metrics to evaluate overall patient care.[9]

Recipe for Success } FreshDirect

It may be surprising that this successful organization stumbled through a series of missteps during its early days. Although FreshDirect was very successful attracting first-time customers with coupons and incentives, the majority of these customers dropped the service after placing one or two orders because of poor customer service. "We broke too many eggs," said former Richard S. Braddock. "We showed up with thawed ice cream. We bruised produce. We delivered late. We missed boxes."

Managers decided to create a system of continuous feedback, a real-time database that would follow every step—and misstep—of each business day, so that minor problems could be corrected before they erupted into big problems. FreshDirect developed performance standards designed to strengthen customer service and build loyal customers. For example, managers introduced a rating system to measure the quality of produce and seafood. Every morning, managers and buyers rate their products from one star (below average) to five (never better) and share that information with customers so they can simulate the in-store shopping experience and decide what to purchase. Other standards of performance included tracking on-time deliveries and the number of errors per order. FreshDirect has a warehouse on Long Island where workers are responsible for butchering, baking, and food preparation. Warehouse managers analyze numerous reports that track plant operations, including inventory levels, quality assurance, and freshness. Managers also monitor real-time data that show the popularity of certain products in specific delivery zones and time slots.

Analyzing performance data also showed other problems: FreshDirect was falling short of its revenue goals, and customers were complaining about sold-out items, limited delivery options, and mistakes in orders. The CEO took corrective action by remaking the company with a stronger focus on customer service. He upgraded the company's Web site to provide a customized online experience. Now the Web site can analyze order patterns, remind customers of their favorite products, and suggest other items that they might like.[10]

Compare Performance to Standards   The third step in the control process is comparing actual activities to performance standards. When managers read computer reports or walk through the plant, they identify whether actual performance meets, exceeds, or falls short of standards. Typically, performance reports simplify such comparisons by placing the performance standards for the reporting period alongside the actual performance for the same period and by computing the variance—that is, the difference between each actual amount and the associated standard. To correct the problems that most require attention, managers focus on variances.

When performance deviates from a standard, managers must interpret the deviation. They are expected to dig beneath the surface and find the cause of the problem. Assume that a grocer established a goal of increasing seafood sales by 10 percent during the month of July, but sales increased by only 8 percent. Managers must investigate the reasons behind the shortfall. They may discover that recent price increases for shrimp and three late shipments of salmon from Canada caused weaker sales during July, for instance. Managers should take an inquiring approach to deviations to gain a broad understanding of factors that influence performance. Effective management control involves subjective judgment and employee discussions, as well as objective analysis of performance data.

Take Corrective Action   The final step in the feedback control model is to determine what changes, if any, are needed. An example comes from FreshDirect, a premium online grocer in New York City, which used a feedback control model to improve the quality of its products and customer service.

15-2b The Balanced Scorecard

A current approach to organizational control is to take a balanced perspective on company performance, integrating various dimensions of control that focus on markets and customers, as well as employees and financials.[11] Managers recognize that relying exclusively on financial measures can result in short-term, dysfunctional behavior. Nonfinancial measures provide a healthy supplement to the traditional financial measures, and companies are investing significant sums in developing more balanced measurement systems as a result.[12] The **balanced scorecard** is a comprehensive management control system that balances traditional financial measures with operational measures relating to a company's critical success factors.[13]

"Not everything that counts can be counted, and not everything that can be counted counts."

—ALBERT EINSTEIN, THEORETICAL PHYSICIST

A balanced scorecard contains four major perspectives, as illustrated in Exhibit 15.2: financial performance, customer service, internal business processes, and the organization's potential for learning and growth.[14] Within these four areas, managers identify key performance metrics the organization will track:

- *Financial performance.* The *financial performance* perspective reflects a concern that the organization's activities contribute to improving short- and long-term financial performance. It includes traditional measures such as net income and return on investment.
- *Customer service.* *Customer service* indicators measure information such as how customers view the organization and customer retention and satisfaction. These data may be collected in many forms, including testimonials from customers describing superlative service or from customer surveys.[15] The Internal Revenue Service (IRS) became embroiled in a controversy that suggests poor attention to customer service. As a part of the government that many people already loathe, the IRS opened itself to scathing attack by selecting certain groups applying for tax-exempt status for extra scrutiny. The initial impression was that the IRS was targeting only conservative "tea party" organizations, but subsequent investigation revealed it was looking at both left- and right-leaning groups. The scandal particularly tarnished the image of the IRS's tax-exempt unit, which one critic described as "a bureaucratic mess, with some employees ignorant about tax laws, defiant of their supervisors, and blind to the appearance of impropriety."[16]

Exhibit 15.2 **The Balanced Scorecard**

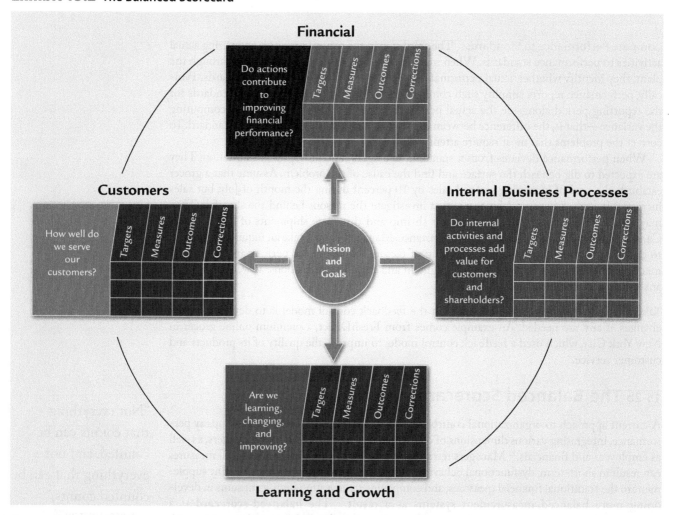

SOURCES: Based on Robert S. Kaplan and David P. Norton, "Using the Balanced Scorecard as a Strategic Management System," *Harvard Business Review* (January–February 1996): 75–85; and Chee W. Chow, Kamal M. Haddad, and James E. Williamson, "Applying the Balanced Scorecard to Small Companies," *Management Accounting* 79, no. 2 (August 1997): 21–27.

- *Internal business processes.* *Business process* indicators focus on production and operating statistics. For an airline, business process indicators may include on-time arrivals and adherence to safety guidelines. An event at Reagan National Airport in Washington, D.C., reflected weak adherence to safety standards, for instance. When a lone air traffic controller at this airport fell asleep while on duty and failed to respond to repeated radio transmissions, two pilots waiting to land jets carrying a total of 160 people decided to land without clearance, violating Federal Aviation Administration (FAA) safety regulations and damaging the reputations of both airlines involved, as well as the airport.[17]

- *Potential for learning and growth.* The final component of the balanced scorecard looks at the organization's *potential for learning and growth*, focusing on how well resources and human capital are being managed for the company's future. Metrics may include things such as employee retention and the introduction of new products. The components of the scorecard are designed in an integrative manner, as illustrated in Exhibit 15.2.

Managers record, analyze, and discuss these various metrics to determine how well the organization is achieving its strategic goals. The balanced scorecard is an effective tool for managing and improving performance, but only if it is clearly linked to a well-defined organizational strategy and goals.[18] At its best, use of the scorecard cascades down from the top levels of the organization so that everyone becomes involved in thinking about and discussing strategy. The scorecard has become the core management control system for many well-known organizations, such as Bell Emergis (a division of Bell Canada), Exxon Mobil Corporation, CIGNA (insurance), Hilton Hotels, and even some units of the U.S. federal government.[19] As with all management systems, the balanced scorecard is not right for every organization in every situation. The simplicity of the system causes some managers to underestimate the time and commitment that is needed for the approach to become a truly useful management control system. If managers implement the balanced scorecard using a *performance measurement* orientation rather than a *performance management* approach that links targets and measurements to corporate strategy, use of the scorecard can actually hinder or even decrease organizational performance.[20]

Remember This

- The feedback control model involves using feedback to determine whether performance meets established standards.

- Well-designed control systems include four key steps: establish standards, measure performance, compare performance to standards, and make corrections as necessary.

- A **balanced scorecard** is a comprehensive management control system that balances traditional financial measures with measures of customer service, internal business processes, and the organization's capacity for learning and growth.

15-3 The Changing Philosophy of Control

Managers' approach to control is changing in many of today's organizations. In connection with the shift to employee participation and empowerment, many companies are adopting a *decentralized* rather than a *hierarchical* control process. Hierarchical control and decentralized control represent different philosophies of corporate culture, which was discussed in Chapter 2. Most organizations display some aspects of both hierarchical and decentralized control, but managers generally emphasize one or the other, depending on the organizational culture and their own beliefs about control.

Will you take a hierarchical or a decentralized approach to control as a new manager? Visit MindTap for "Self Assessment: Do You Prefer Organizational Regulation and Control?" to understand your attitude toward organizational control.

15-3a Hierarchical versus Decentralized Approaches

Hierarchical control involves monitoring and influencing employee behavior through extensive use of rules, policies, hierarchy of authority, written documentation, reward systems, and other formal mechanisms.[21] In contrast, **decentralized control** relies on cultural values, traditions, shared beliefs, and trust to foster compliance with organizational goals. Managers operate on the assumption that employees are trustworthy and willing to perform effectively without extensive rules and close supervision.

Exhibit 15.3 contrasts the use of hierarchical and decentralized methods of control. Hierarchical methods define explicit rules, policies, and procedures for employee behavior. Control relies on centralized authority, the formal hierarchy, and close personal supervision.

Pharrell Williams has learned it's better to run his business with decentralization, as described in the "Sunny Side Up" box.

Responsibility for quality control rests with quality control inspectors and supervisors rather than with employees. Job descriptions generally are specific and task related, and managers define minimal standards for acceptable employee performance. In exchange for meeting the standards, individual employees are given extrinsic rewards such as wages, benefits, and possibly promotions up the hierarchy. Employees rarely participate in the control process; any participation is formalized through mechanisms such as grievance procedures. With hierarchical control, the organizational culture is somewhat rigid, and managers do not consider culture a useful means of controlling employees and the organization. Technology often is used to control the flow and pace of work or to monitor employees, such as by measuring the number of minutes that employees spend on phone calls or how many keystrokes they make on the computer during a specific amount of time.

The hierarchical approach to control is strongly evident in many Japanese companies. Japanese culture reflects an obsession with rules and a penchant for bureaucracy that can excel at turning chaos into order. For example, after a devastating earthquake and tsunami struck Japan in 2011, the Japanese efficiently organized evacuation centers for families who lost homes during the disaster. Self-governing committees managed these temporary shelters and laid out, in painstaking detail, the daily responsibilities of the residents. People were assigned specific tasks, including sorting the garbage, washing the bathrooms, and cleaning freshwater tanks. "The Japanese people are the type to feel more reassured the more rules are in place," said Shintara Goto, a tsunami survivor. This hierarchical method of managing the temporary evacuation centers helped survivors find routine and responsibility, which could play a big role in reducing the long-term psychological and physical toll of this natural disaster.[22]

Exhibit 15.3 Hierarchical and Decentralized Methods of Control

	Hierarchical Control	**Decentralized Control**
Basic assumptions	• People are incapable of self-discipline and cannot be trusted. They need to be monitored and controlled closely.	• People work best when they are fully committed to the organization.
Actions	• Uses detailed rules and procedures, formal control systems. • Uses top-down authority, formal hierarchy, position power, quality control inspectors. • Relies on task-related job descriptions. • Emphasizes extrinsic rewards (pay, benefits, status). • Features rigid organizational culture, distrust of cultural norms as means of control.	• Features limited use of rules; relies on values, group and self-control, selection, and socialization. • Relies on flexible authority, flat structure, expert power; everyone monitors quality. • Relies on results-based job descriptions; emphasizes goals to be achieved. • Emphasizes extrinsic and intrinsic rewards (meaningful work, opportunities for growth). • Features adaptive culture; culture recognized as means for uniting individual, team, and organizational goals for overall control.
Consequences	• Employees follow instructions and do *just* what they are told. • Employees feel a sense of indifference toward work. • Employee absenteeism and turnover is high.	• Employees take initiative and seek responsibility. • Employees are actively engaged and committed to their work. • Employee turnover is low.

SOURCES: Based on Naresh Khatri et al., "Medical Errors and Quality of Care: From Control to Commitment," *California Management Review* 48, no. 3 (Spring 2006): 115–141; Richard E. Walton, "From Control to Commitment in the Workplace," *Harvard Business Review* (March–April 1985): 76–84; and Don Hellriegel, Susan E. Jackson, and John W. Slocum, Jr., *Management*, 8th ed. (Cincinnati, OH: South-Western, 1999), p. 663.

Sunny Side Up

Pharrell Williams, Inc.

You might have seen Pharrell Williams winning awards at the Grammys or listened to one of his many hit songs, but maybe you didn't know what an astute businessman he is. The 44-year-old musician with the hat has a number 1 album, 17 top-10 hits, 3 Grammy Awards, and has written songs for movies *Despicable Me* and *Monster Family*, as well as the song "Happy." Williams began to write and produce early in his career and recently produced for Jay-Z and Miley Cyrus. He's also doing fashion labels, a cloud-based musical platform (UJAM), a YouTube channel (iOTHER), and a nonprofit for empowering kids in low-income schools. He also sent letters protesting the lack of diversity on the Recording Academy Board.

How does Williams get more done in a week than most people do in a year? He surrounds himself with smart people. Currently, he has 10 employees, 8 of whom are female. "I would go crazy with an office full of dudes," he says. "What am I going to talk about? Football? I don't know anything about sports."

What Williams does know is how to collaborate, which includes being humble, in order to be productive. Other people have noted how he constantly gives credit to his staff. And because he doesn't get stressed out, he can be more productive, too. Williams likes to do what he calls "Tapping In," which means being open to peripheral ideas that can lead to innovation, and he does the opposite of multi-tasking, preferring something more like fixation.

In decision making, Williams uses his mind and his emotions. He notes that successful apparel companies put taste first, which is his goal as well, to have the aesthetic match the business acumen. His company Bionic Yarn, which is about sustainability and profitability, follows that principle and is now profitable, after only three years in operation. He originally started the company because Rush Limbaugh shamed him and his desire to save the earth. But Williams is unashamedly happy to be called "involved."

Does Williams believe in luck? Not anymore since he's seen what hard work it takes to be productive—and successful. But anyone can figure out how to solve problems. "That's always an option," he says.

SOURCE: Culture Lane, *The Pioneer* (New Delhi, India), February 15, 2018, https://search-proquest-com.proxy.library.vanderbilt.edu/central/docview/2002096757/94E8FB10B83A4542PQ/7?accountid=14816; and Mary Kaye Schilling, "Get Busy: Pharrell's Productivity Secrets," *Fast Company* (December 2013–January 2014), 96–100, 104, 158.

Decentralized control is based on values and assumptions that are almost opposite to those of hierarchical control. Rules and procedures are used only when necessary. Managers rely instead on shared goals and values to control employee behavior. The organization places great emphasis on the selection and socialization of employees to ensure that workers have the appropriate values needed to influence behavior toward meeting company goals. No organization can control employees 100 percent of the time, and self-discipline and self-control are what keep workers performing their jobs up to standard. Empowerment of employees, effective socialization, and training can contribute to internal standards that provide self-control. Nick Sarillo, who owns two Nick's Pizza & Pub shops in Illinois, says his management style is "trust and track," which means giving people the tools and information they need, telling them the result they need to achieve, and then letting them get there in their own way. At the same time, Sarillo keeps track of results so that the company stays on solid ground. He uses open-book management, which will be described in the next section, so that everyone in the company has information about how the company is doing.[23]

With decentralized control, power is more dispersed and is based on knowledge and experience as much as position. The organizational structure is flat and horizontal, as discussed in Chapter 7 with flexible authority and teams of workers solving problems and making improvements. Everyone is involved in quality control on an ongoing basis. Job descriptions generally are results based, with an emphasis more on the outcomes to be achieved than on the specific tasks to be performed. Managers use not only extrinsic rewards such as pay but also the intrinsic rewards of meaningful work and the opportunity to learn and grow. Technology is used to empower employees by giving them the information they need to make effective decisions, work together, and solve problems. People are rewarded for team and organizational success as well as their individual performance, and the emphasis is on equity among employees. Employees participate in a wide range of areas, including setting goals, determining standards of performance, governing quality, and designing control systems.

Recipe for Success } **Campbell Soup Company**

Campbell Soup Company, which controls 60 percent of the U.S. soup market, is piling up profits by implementing cost-saving ideas suggested by its employees. At the plant in Maxton, North Carolina, factory workers huddle every morning with managers to find ways to save the company money. These employees are part of a decentralized culture in which both managers and workers share the company's goals and collaborate on ways to improve efficiency. The daily worker-manager huddles are about "getting everybody involved," says "Big John" Filmore, a longtime plant veteran. "Instead of being told what to do, we get to tell people about our problems," he said.

When challenged to find efficiency in the new Swanson broth line, which processes 260 million pounds of raw ingredients per year, operators and mechanics devised a numbering system for each gasket to speed repairs of the processing equipment. They cut windows into the metal covers over conveyor belts so they could identify signs of wear. They color-coded valve handles to avoid confusion in the settings. With employee-driven changes like these, Campbell says that operating efficiency at the Maxton plant has climbed to 85 percent of what its managers say is the maximum possible, up from 75 percent three years ago. That pays off, as a 1 percent gain in plant efficiency adds $3 million to operating profits.[24]

With decentralized control, the culture is adaptive, and managers recognize the importance of organizational culture for uniting individual, team, and organizational goals for greater overall control. Ideally, with decentralized control, employees will pool their areas of expertise to arrive at procedures that are better than managers could come up with working alone. As described in the "Recipe for Success" box, Campbell Soup is using decentralized control by enlisting its workers to help squeeze efficiency out of its plants.

15-3b Open-Book Management

One important aspect of decentralized control in many organizations is open-book management. An organization that promotes information sharing and teamwork admits employees throughout the organization into the loop of financial control and responsibility to encourage active participation and commitment to goals. **Open-book management** allows employees to see for themselves—through charts, computer printouts, meetings, and so forth—the financial condition of the company. Second, open-book management shows the individual employee how his or her job fits into the big picture and affects the financial future of the organization. Finally, open-book management ties employee rewards to the company's overall success. With training in interpreting the financial data, employees can see the interdependence and importance of each function. If they are rewarded according to performance, they become motivated to take responsibility for their entire team or function, rather than merely their individual jobs.[25]

The goal of open-book management is to get every employee thinking and acting like a business owner. To get employees to think like owners, management provides workers the same information owners have: what money is coming in and where it is going out. Open-book management helps employees appreciate why efficiency is important to the organization's success as well as their own. Laura Ortmann, who owns Ginger Bay Salon and Spa in St. Louis, Missouri, with her husband, discovered that her hairstylists and massage therapists became more motivated to reach their own performance goals once she trained them to understand the company's financial goals. Individual and company goals were recorded prominently on a scoreboard in the break room and listed each employee's daily sales results and whether goals were met. "Behavior changed overnight," said Ortmann. "No one wants their name next to a low number." By helping her employees see how their efforts affected the financial success of the company, Ortmann increased their motivation. "I love the numbers, and I love knowing how I'm doing," says nail technician Terri Kavanaugh.[26]

Remember This

- The philosophy of control has shifted to reflect changes in leadership methods.
- **Hierarchical control** involves monitoring and influencing employee behavior through extensive use of rules, policies, hierarchy of authority, written documentation, reward systems, and other formal mechanisms.
- With **decentralized control**, the organization fosters compliance with organizational goals through the use of organizational culture, group norms, and a focus on goals rather than rules and procedures.
- Campbell Soup uses decentralized control at its plant in Maxton, North Carolina, to encourage employees to cut costs and increase efficiency.
- **Open-book management** allows employees to see for themselves the financial condition of the organization and encourages them to think and act like business owners.

15-4 Total Quality Management

Another popular approach based on a decentralized control philosophy is **total quality management (TQM)**, an organization-wide effort to infuse quality into every activity in a company through continuous improvement. Managing quality is a concern for every organization. In early 2016, the giant food company Nestlé recalled three million boxes of DiGiorno pizza and Lean Cuisine and Stouffer's frozen dinners in the United States because of a suspicion that the spinach in them might contain bits of glass. Around the same time, Perdue Foods recalled around 5,000 pounds of Applegate Farms chicken nuggets because of possible contamination with plastic. Recalls related to foreign materials are less common than those related to food-borne illnesses, but they can sometimes be even more challenging for managers who have to determine what went wrong and how much product was affected. Companies such as Nestlé and Perdue err on the side of caution, pulling a wide range of food off shelves rather than risk missing something.[27] Food safety is of growing concern for consumers, so managers in food companies and restaurants are paying even greater attention to quality.

TQM became attractive to U.S. managers in the 1980s because it had been implemented successfully by Japanese companies, such as Toyota, Canon, and Honda, which were gaining market share and an international reputation for high quality. The Japanese system was based on the work of such U.S. researchers and consultants as W. Edwards Deming, Joseph Juran, and Armand Feigenbaum, whose ideas attracted U.S. executives after the methods were tested overseas.[28] The TQM philosophy focuses on teamwork, increasing customer satisfaction, and lowering costs. Organizations implement TQM by encouraging managers and employees to collaborate across functions and departments as well as with customers and suppliers to identify areas for improvement, no matter how small. Each quality improvement is a step toward perfection and meeting a goal of zero defects. Quality control becomes part of the day-to-day business of every employee rather than being assigned to specialized departments.

15-4a TQM Techniques

The implementation of TQM involves the use of many techniques, including quality circles, benchmarking, Six Sigma principles, quality partnering, and continuous improvement.

Quality Circles   A **quality circle** is a group of 6 to 12 volunteer employees who meet regularly to discuss and solve problems that affect the quality of their work.[29] At a set time during the workweek, the members of the quality circle meet, identify problems, and try to find solutions. Circle members are free to collect data and take surveys. Many companies train people in team building, problem solving, and statistical quality control. The reason for using quality circles is to push decision making to an organization level at which recommendations can be made by the people who do the job and know it better than anyone else. At Carrier Collierville, a manufacturer of residential air conditioners and heat pumps, a quality circle attacked a leak issue at braze joints on a heat pump component. Changes made to the work area resulted in a 50 percent reduction in leaks and associated repair costs.[30]

Benchmarking   Introduced by Xerox in 1979, benchmarking is now a major TQM component. **Benchmarking** is defined as "the continuous process of measuring products, services, and practices against the toughest competitors or those companies recognized as industry leaders to identify areas for improvement."[31] For example, in the original Xerox study, managers compared Xerox to Japanese competitors and found that "it took twice as long as the Japanese competitors to bring a product to market, five times the number of engineers, four times the number of design changes, and three times the design costs." This enabled Xerox managers to identify and allocate resources to specific areas to increase productivity and remain competitive.[32] Organizations may also use benchmarking for generating new business ideas, assessing market demand, or identifying best practices within an industry. A five-step benchmarking process is shown in Exhibit 15.4.[33]

The first step involves planning the benchmarking study, which includes identifying the objectives of the study and the characteristics of a product or service that significantly influence customer satisfaction. The second step involves identifying the source of the information to be collected. For example, the sources of data for a Sherwin-Williams benchmarking study might include national independent lab studies or studies published in *Consumer Reports* magazine. Once the source of information is identified, data are then collected. Xerox collected information on the order fulfillment techniques of L. L. Bean, the Freeport, Maine, mail-order firm, and learned ways to reduce warehouse costs by 10 percent. The fourth step includes analyzing the benchmarking data that has been collected and recommending areas of improvement. The fifth step includes implementing recommendations and then monitoring them through continuous benchmarking.

Six Sigma   Six Sigma quality principles were first introduced by Motorola in the 1980s and were later popularized by General Electric (GE), where former CEO Jack Welch praised Six Sigma for quality and efficiency gains that saved the company billions of dollars. Based on the Greek letter *sigma*, which statisticians use to measure how far something deviates from perfection, **Six Sigma**

Exhibit 15.4 A Five-Step Benchmarking Process

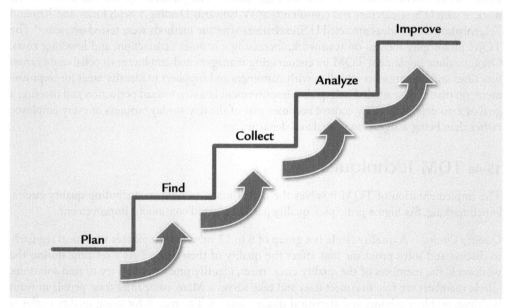

SOURCE: Based on Deven Shah and Brian H. Kleiner, "Benchmarking for Quality," *Industrial Management* (March–April 2011): 22–25.

is a highly ambitious quality standard that specifies a goal of no more than 3.4 defects per million parts. That essentially means being defect-free 99.9997 percent of the time.[34] However, Six Sigma has deviated from its precise definition to become a generic term for a quality control approach that takes nothing for granted and emphasizes a disciplined and relentless pursuit of high quality and low costs. Like other aspects of TQM, Six Sigma is not just for manufacturing organizations. Service firms have reaped significant benefits from Six Sigma and other TQM techniques. Cardinal Health, a distributor of health care products, is a critical link in the health care supply chain and handles one-fourth of all medications prescribed every day. Cardinal embarked on a Lean Six Sigma initiative that has led to a 30 percent drop in the order error rate over a three-year period. Cardinal has now extended the scope of its Six Sigma efforts to its supply chain partners with a goal of achieving zero errors, zero waste, and zero lost revenue.[35]

Six Sigma is based on a five-step methodology referred to as *DMAIC*, pronounced "deMay-ick" (standing for define, measure, analyze, improve, and control), which provides a structured way for organizations to approach and solve problems.[36] Effectively implementing Six Sigma requires a major commitment from top management because Six Sigma involves widespread change throughout the organization. At Honeywell, for example, all employees are expected to understand Six Sigma fundamentals. Six Sigma provides a common language among employees, complements efforts to cut unnecessary costs from the organization, and supports efforts to "get it right the first time." Honeywell explains its dedication to Six Sigma and what it means to reach this high level of performance with these examples:

- If your water heater operated at Four Sigma (not Six), you would be without hot water for more than 54 hours each year. At Six Sigma, you would be without hot water for less than two minutes a year.
- If your smartphone operated at Four Sigma, you would be without service for more than four hours a month. At Six Sigma, it would be about nine seconds a month.
- A Four Sigma process will typically result in one defective package of products for every three truckloads shipped. A Six Sigma process means one defective package for every 5,350 truckloads.[37]

Quality Partnering   One of the drawbacks of a traditional quality control program is that people from the quality control department are often seen as "outsiders" to the business groups they serve. Because they don't always have a strong knowledge of the processes that they are studying, their work may be viewed with suspicion or as an interruption to the normal work routine. The risk here is that quality control is seen as separate from everyday work. Another drawback of the traditional model is that quality control is usually conducted after a product is completed or a service delivered—the time when it's most expensive to make corrections.

As a new manager, will you support TQM by taking personal responsibility for improving the tasks and activities that you work on? Visit MindTap for "Self Assessment: What Is Your Attitude Toward Improvement?" to get some feedback on your attitude toward continuous improvement.

Green Power

The Honeybee Style The honeybee is known for its hard work and wise use of natural resources, as well as for living in a cooperative, interconnected community. Likewise, Munich-based BMW recognizes that true sustainability involves the protection and wise use of not only the environment but also of every resource used to provide quality vehicles for consumers. Dating back to the 1970s, BMW's approach to sustainable growth can be seen throughout its well-controlled production process. Self-managed teams oversee rigorous quality control measurement of sustainability, building for BMW an A+ international sustainability rating. A total of 23 interconnected "honeybee" practices address everything from ethical behavior and social responsibility to quality and innovation. The results include the recycling of production waste and the reuse of scrap from BMW's new carbon-fiber car bodies.

SOURCE: Gayle C. Avery and Harald Bergsteiner, "How BMW Successfully Practices Sustainable Leadership Principles," *Strategy & Leadership* 39, no. 6 (2011): 11–18.

Sunny Side Up } La-Z-Boy

"If we were doing business the same way we did in 2005," said La-Z-Boy manager David Robinson, "somebody else would be here because we would already be closed."

The U.S. furniture industry has been decimated by foreign competition, but a dedication to cost efficiency and continuous improvement has enabled La-Z-Boy to flourish. Robinson, La-Z-Boy's continuous improvement and quality director at the company's Dayton, Tennessee, facility, points out that 23 of the facility's managers and engineers have been trained in Six Sigma, and cross-functional teams have completed 24 *kaizen* events focused on safety, quality, and productivity. A significant process improvement at the Dayton facility is the Flawless Launch Program, which assigns a production engineer to make sure quality and manufacturability is designed into all new products. "Before the product ever makes it to manufacturing, she has been on the front end of the design," Robinson says of the current production engineer. That way, the company knows the tooling and equipment that will be needed to produce the product repeatedly, at low cost, and relatively error free. As an example, he points to the plant's first attempt to manufacture an electric lift chair. It had about a 40 percent failure rate in the field. After reintroducing it using the flawless launch process, Robinson reports, "We now have a fraction of 1 percent failure in the field."[38]

A new approach called **quality partnering** involves assigning dedicated personnel within a particular functional area of the business. In this approach, the quality control personnel work alongside others within a functional area to identify opportunities for quality improvements throughout the work process. This integrated partnering approach to quality makes it possible to detect and address defects early in the product life cycle when they can be corrected most easily. Another advantage of this approach is that quality partners are viewed as "insiders" and peers who are readily accepted into the work group.[39]

Continuous Improvement   In North America, crash programs and designs traditionally have been the preferred method of innovation. Managers measure the expected benefits of a change and favor the ideas with the biggest payoffs. In contrast, Japanese companies have realized extraordinary success from making a series of mostly small improvements. This approach, called *continuous improvement*, or *kaizen*, is the implementation of a large number of small, incremental improvements in all areas of the organization on an ongoing basis. In a successful TQM program, all employees learn that they are expected to contribute by initiating changes in their own job activities. The basic philosophy is that improving things a little bit at a time, all the time, has the highest probability of success. Innovations can start simple, and employees can build on their success in this unending process. A commitment to continuous improvement has enabled furniture manufacturer La-Z-Boy to thrive, as illustrated by the following "Sunny Side Up" example from the company's flagship operation in Dayton, Tennessee.

Thanks to La-Z-Boy's dedication to continuous improvement, operating expenses have been reduced by about $50 million a year. Over a recent three-year period, productivity improved by 42 percent and scrap was reduced by 71 percent. Increases in productivity and decreases in cost mean that consumers can purchase a basic La-Z-Boy recliner for about the same price they might have paid when the Dayton facility first went into operation in the early 1970s.[40]

15-4b TQM Success Factors

Despite its promise, TQM doesn't always work. A few firms have had disappointing results. In particular, Six Sigma principles might not be appropriate for all organizational problems, and some companies have expended tremendous energy and resources for little payoff.[41] Many contingency factors (listed in Exhibit 15.5) can influence the success of a TQM program. For example, quality circles are most beneficial when employees have challenging jobs; participation in a quality circle can contribute to productivity because it enables employees to pool their knowledge and solve interesting problems. TQM also tends to be most successful when it enriches jobs and

Exhibit 15.5 Quality Program Success Factors

Positive Factors	Negative Factors
• Tasks make great skill demands on employees.	• Management expectations are unrealistically high.
• TQM serves to enrich jobs and motivate employees.	• Middle managers are dissatisfied about loss of authority.
• Problem-solving skills are improved for all employees.	• Workers are dissatisfied with other aspects of organizational life.
• Participation and teamwork are used to tackle significant problems.	• Union leaders are left out of quality control discussions.
• Continuous improvement is a way of life.	• Managers wait for big, dramatic innovations.

improves employee motivation. In addition, when participating in the TQM program improves workers' problem-solving skills, productivity is likely to increase. Finally, a TQM program has the greatest chance of success in a corporate culture that values quality and stresses continuous improvement.

Remember This

- **Total quality management (TQM)** is an organization-wide effort to infuse quality into every activity in a company through continuous improvement.
- The TQM philosophy focuses on teamwork, increasing customer satisfaction, and lowering costs.
- **Quality circles** offer one technique for implementing TQM and include groups of 6 to 12 volunteer employees who meet regularly to discuss and solve problems affecting the quality of their work.
- Another option for tracking quality is **benchmarking**, the continuous process of measuring products, services,

and practices against major competitors or industry leaders.
- **Six Sigma** is a quality control approach that emphasizes a relentless pursuit of high quality and low costs.
- **Quality partnering** involves assigning dedicated personnel within a particular functional area of the business to identify opportunities for improvement throughout the work process.
- *Continuous improvement*, or *kaizen*, is the implementation of a large number of small, incremental improvements in all areas of the organization on an ongoing basis.

15-5 Budgetary Control

Debbie Dusenberry was following her dream as a successful entrepreneur. She had opened a beautifully designed store called Curious Sofa and filled its expansive showroom with antiques, offbeat furniture, accessories, and gifts. She had a dedicated staff and sales reaching $800,000 per year. She had borrowed a lot of money and was planning to expand her inventory. Business was growing fast. But Dusenberry was typical of many small business owners who are long on drive and passion but short on financial experience. Caught up in the excitement of growing sales, she was unaware that excessive costs in staffing, inventory, and freight were hurting her profitability. She was operating without a budget and not keeping track of all her expenses. When sales dropped during the economic recession, the glaring weaknesses in her financial system were exposed. Scared and exasperated, Dusenberry began thinking about how she could save her business and realized she needed a new system that would help her monitor and manage her costs. Her first step was to create a budget.[42]

Budgetary control, one of the most commonly used methods of managerial control, is the process of setting targets for an organization's expenditures, monitoring results and comparing them to the budget, and making changes as needed. As a control device, budgets are reports that list planned and actual expenditures for cash, assets, raw materials, salaries, and other resources. In addition, budget reports usually list the variance between the budgeted and actual amounts for each item.

A budget is created for every division or department within an organization, no matter how small, as long as it performs a distinct project, program, or function. The fundamental unit of analysis for a budget control system is called a *responsibility center*. A **responsibility center** is defined as any organizational department or unit under the supervision of a single person who is responsible for its activity.[43] A three-person appliance sales office in Watertown, New York, is a responsibility center, as is a quality control department, a marketing department, and an entire refrigerator manufacturing plant. The manager of each unit has budget responsibility. Top managers use budgets for the company as a whole, and middle managers traditionally focus on the budget performance of their department or division. Budgets that managers typically use include expense budgets, revenue budgets, cash budgets, and capital budgets.

15-5a Expense Budget

An **expense budget** includes anticipated and actual expenses for each responsibility center and for the total organization. An expense budget may show all types of expenses, or it may focus on a particular category, such as materials or research and development expenses. When actual expenses exceed budgeted amounts, the difference signals the need for managers to identify possible problems and take corrective action if needed. The difference may arise from inefficiency, or expenses may be higher because the organization's sales are growing faster than anticipated. Conversely, expenses below budget may signal exceptional efficiency or possibly the failure to meet some other standards, such as a desired level of sales or quality of service. Either way, expense budgets help identify the need for further investigation but do not substitute for it.

15-5b Revenue Budget

A **revenue budget** lists forecasted and actual revenues of the organization. In general, revenues below the budgeted amount signal a need to investigate the problem to see whether the organization can improve revenues. In contrast, revenues above budget would require determining whether the organization can obtain the necessary resources to meet the higher-than-expected demand for its products or services. Managers then formulate action plans to correct the budget variance.

15-5c Cash Budget

The **cash budget** estimates receipts and expenditures of money on a daily or weekly basis to ensure that an organization has sufficient cash to meet its obligations. The cash budget shows the level of funds flowing through the organization and the nature of cash disbursements. If the cash budget shows that the firm has more cash than necessary to meet short-term needs, the company can arrange to invest the excess to earn interest income. In contrast, if the cash budget shows a payroll expenditure of $40,000 coming at the end of the week but only $30,000 in the bank, the organization must borrow cash to meet the payroll.

15-5d Capital Budget

The **capital budget** lists planned investments in major assets such as buildings, heavy machinery, or complex information technology systems, often involving expenditures that occur over more than a year. Capital expenditures not only have a large impact on future expenses but also are investments designed to enhance profits. Therefore, a capital budget is necessary to plan the impact of these expenditures on cash flow and profitability. Controlling involves not only monitoring the amount of capital expenditures but also evaluating whether the assumptions made about the return on the investments are holding true. Managers can evaluate whether continuing investment in particular projects is advisable as well as whether their procedures for making capital expenditure decisions are adequate. Some companies, including Boeing, Merck, Shell, United Technologies, and Whirlpool, evaluate capital projects at several stages to determine whether they are still in line with the company's strategy.[44]

15-5e Zero-Based Budget

Zero-based budgeting is an approach to planning and decision making that requires a complete justification for every line item in a budget instead of carrying forward a prior budget and applying a percentage change. A zero-based budget begins with a starting point of $0, and every dollar added to the budget is reflected by an actual, documented need.[45] 3G Capital Partners LP, a Brazilian private-equity firm that has bought numerous companies in the food industry, including Burger King Worldwide, Tim Horton's Inc., and H. J. Heinz Company, is a big believer in using zero-based budgeting to get and keep companies on track financially.

Many other companies, including Anheuser-Busch and oil and gas giant Shell, have implemented zero-based budgeting to drive significant financial performance improvements. "There's sometimes extravagance that exists at some of these firms, and then there's just bureaucratic waste," said former Anheuser-Busch president Dave Peacock. By forcing managers to evaluate and justify the costs and benefits of each dollar, zero-based budgeting can help companies shave excessive and unnecessary costs from their yearly expenditures.[46]

Budgeting is an important part of organizational planning and control. Many traditional companies use **top-down budgeting**, which means that the budgeted amounts for the coming year are literally imposed on middle- and lower-level managers.[47] These managers set departmental budget targets in accordance with overall company revenues and expenditures specified by top executives. Although the top-down process provides some advantages, the movement toward employee empowerment, participation, and learning means that many organizations are adopting **bottom-up budgeting**, a process in which lower-level managers anticipate their departments' resource needs and pass them up to top management for approval.[48] Companies of all kinds are increasingly involving line managers in the budgeting process. At the San Diego Zoo, scientists, animal keepers, and other line managers use software and templates to plan their department's budget needs because, as CFO Paula Brock says, "Nobody knows that side of the business better than they do."[49] Each of the 145 zoo departments also does a monthly budget close and reforecast so that resources can be redirected as needed to achieve goals within budget constraints. Thanks to the bottom-up process, for example, the zoo was able to redirect resources quickly to protect its valuable exotic bird collection from an outbreak of a highly infectious bird disease without significantly damaging the rest of the organization's budget.[50]

Recipe for Success   3G Capital Partners, H. J. Heinz Company, Kraft Food Group

3G Capital Partners is the major investor and owner of the H. J. Heinz Company and the Kraft Foods Group. Both companies have struggled financially in recent years as consumer tastes rapidly shift away from processed foods, so 3G Capital managers saw that operating costs must be reduced. To lower costs and increase operational efficiency at Heinz and Kraft, 3G Capital implemented zero-based budgeting, requiring managers to justify every dollar they spend from scratch each year. At Heinz, zero-based budgeting led to significant cost cuts from ditching corporate jets and slashing headquarters staff to requiring employees to get permission to make color photocopies. Other companies have also taken the plunge into zero-based budgeting to reduce costs and enforce budget discipline. Coca-Cola and Campbell Soup both plan major cost reductions using this budgeting technique.[51]

- Budgetary control, one of the most commonly used forms of managerial control, is the process of setting targets for an organization's expenditures, monitoring results and comparing them to the budget, and making changes as needed.

- A **responsibility center** is any organizational department or unit under the supervision of a single person who is responsible for its activity.

- An **expense budget** outlines the anticipated and actual expenses for a responsibility center.

- A **revenue budget** lists forecasted and actual revenues of the organization.

- The **cash budget** estimates receipts and expenditures of money on a daily or weekly basis to ensure that an organization has sufficient cash to meet its obligations.

- A budget that plans and reports investments in major assets to be depreciated over several years is called a **capital budget.**

- **Zero-based budgeting** is an approach to planning and decision making that starts at zero and requires a complete justification for every line item in a budget instead of carrying forward a prior budget and applying a percentage change.

- Many companies use **top-down budgeting**, which means that the budgeted amounts for the coming year are literally imposed on middle- and lower-level managers.

- On the other hand, **bottom-up budgeting** involves lower-level managers anticipating their department's budget needs and passing them up to top management for approval.

15-6 Financial Control

"Numbers run companies," claims Norm Brodsky, a veteran entrepreneur and writer for *Inc.* magazine.[52] In every organization, managers need to watch how well the organization is performing financially by watching the numbers. Not only do the numbers tell whether the organization is on sound financial footing, but also they can be useful indicators of other kinds of performance problems. For example, a sales decline may signal problems with products, customer service, or sales force effectiveness.

15-6a Financial Statements

Financial statements provide the basic information used for financial control of an organization. Two major financial statements—the balance sheet and the income statement—are the starting points for financial control.

Think of the balance sheet as a thermometer that provides a reading on the health of the business at the moment you take its temperature.[53] The **balance sheet** shows the firm's financial position with respect to assets and liabilities at a specific point in time. An example of a balance sheet is presented in Exhibit 15.6. The balance sheet provides three types of information: assets, liabilities, and owners' equity. *Assets* are what the company owns, and they include *current assets* (those that can be converted into cash in a short time period) and *fixed assets* (such as buildings and equipment that are long term in nature). *Liabilities* are the firm's debts, including both *current debt* (obligations that will be paid by the company in the near future) and *long-term debt* (obligations payable over a long period of time). *Owners' equity* is the difference between assets and liabilities and is the company's net worth in stock and retained earnings.

The **income statement**, sometimes called a *profit-and-loss statement* or *P&L* for short, summarizes the firm's financial performance for a given time interval, usually one year. A sample income statement is shown in Exhibit 15.7. Some organizations calculate the income statement at three-month intervals during the year to see whether they are on target for sales and profits. The income statement shows revenues coming into the organization from all sources and subtracts all expenses, including cost of goods sold, interest, taxes, and depreciation. The *bottom line* indicates the net income—profit or loss—for the given time period.

Exhibit 15.6 Balance Sheet

New Creations Landscaping Consolidated Balance Sheet, December 31, 2016					
Assets			**Liabilities and Owners' Equity**		
Current assets			Current liabilities		
Cash	$ 25,000		Accounts payable	$200,000	
Accounts receivable	75,000		Accrued expenses	20,000	
Inventory	500,000		Income taxes payable	30,000	
Total current assets		$ 600,000	Total current liabilities		$ 250,000
Fixed assets			Long-term liabilities		
Land	250,000		Mortgages payable	350,000	
Buildings and fixtures	1,000,000		Bonds outstanding	250,000	
			Total long-term liabilities		$ 600,000
Less depreciation	200,000		Owners' equity:		
Total fixed assets		$1,050,000	Common stock	540,000	
			Retained earnings	260,000	
			Total owners' equity		$ 800,000
Total assets		$1,650,000	Total liabilities and net worth		$1,650,000

During the recent economic recession, companies cut discretionary spending, such as travel expenses, to improve the bottom line, and managers are pushing to keep those expenses from creeping back up. If managers keep costs low where they can, they can spend scarce dollars on higher-priority areas, such as salary increases for staff or research and development. To avoid a cost creep in travel expenses, Deloitte reminds employees of company travel policies when managers see costs rising. Employees are discouraged from traveling to meetings that are expected to last less than eight hours and to use video and Web conferencing whenever possible as an alternative to travel.[54]

Exhibit 15.7 Income Statement

New Creations Landscaping Income Statement for the Year Ended December 31, 2016		
Gross sales	$3,100,000	
Less sales returns	200,000	
Net sales		$2,900,000
Less expenses and cost of goods sold:		
Cost of goods sold	2,110,000	
Depreciation	60,000	
Sales expenses	200,000	
Administrative expenses	90,000	2,460,000
Operating profit		$ 440,000
Other income		20,000
Gross income		460,000
Less interest expense	80,000	
Income before taxes		380,000
Less taxes	165,000	
Net income		$ 215,000

Recipe for Success } 7-Eleven

Norman Jemal, an enthusiastic and gregarious 7-Eleven franchise owner in Manhattan, loves crunching the numbers with field consultant Kunta Natapraya. Together, they study the sales data and profit margins for the thousands of snack foods that Jemal sells in his three profitable stores. Some claim that Jemal's success is because his stores are located on busy Manhattan streets. High vehicle and pedestrian traffic produce lots of potential customers. But Jemal's success also comes from his knack for analyzing financial data to spot the most profitable products in his inventory and maximizing profits through efficient ordering.

When faced with reordering decisions, Jemal uses 7-Eleven's proprietary Retail Information System (RIS), which helps him analyze sales and profitability data for each product in his inventory. For example, when corporate 7-Eleven announced it was

rolling out a sugar-free Slurpee Lite and an empanada, Jemal needed to make room for both by eliminating an existing product. Using RIS, he studied the profitability of each snack product and discovered that the spicy beef patty was lagging in sales and profitability, so he removed it from the stores' inventory to make room for the new products.

7-Eleven focuses on its core competence of figuring out what to sell to rushed customers and how to sell it to them. "Other franchises pitch their name," Jemal says. "7-Eleven, which I think has a great name, pitched their [RIS] system." That system is part of a carefully designed financial control model that also includes regular audits. A good audit performance will go a long way toward determining whether 7-Eleven allows Jemal to open more stores. He says he'd like to open 20 more.[55]

The "Recipe for Success" box describes how one successful franchise owner uses a financial control system to manage one of the most profitable 7-Eleven stores in Manhattan.

15-6b Financial Analysis: Interpreting the Numbers

A manager needs to be able to evaluate financial reports that compare the organization's performance with earlier data or industry norms. These comparisons enable the manager to see whether the organization is improving and whether it is competitive with others in the industry. The most common financial analysis focuses on ratios, statistics that express the relationships between performance indicators such as profits and assets, sales, and inventory. Ratios are stated as a fraction or proportion; Exhibit 15.8 summarizes some financial ratios, which are measures of an organization's liquidity, activity, profitability, and leverage. These ratios are among the most common, but many measures are used. Managers decide which ratios reveal the most important relationships for their business.

Exhibit 15.8 Common Financial Ratios

Liquidity Ratios	
Current ratio	Current assets/Current liabilities
Quick ratio	Cash + Accounts receivable/Current liabilities
Activity Ratios	
Inventory turnover	Total sales/Average inventory
Conversion ratio	Purchase orders/Customer inquiries
Profitability Ratios	
Profit margin on sales	Net income/Sales
Gross margin	Gross income/Sales
Return on assets (ROA)	Net income/Total assets
Leverage Ratios	
Debt ratio	Total debt/Total assets

Liquidity Ratios   The **liquidity ratio** indicates an organization's ability to meet its current debt obligations. For example, the *current ratio* (current assets divided by current liabilities) tells whether the company has sufficient assets to convert into cash to pay off its debts, if needed. If a hypothetical company, Oceanographics, Inc., has current assets of $600,000 and current liabilities of $250,000, the current ratio is 2.4, meaning it has sufficient funds to pay off immediate debts 2.4 times. This level for the current ratio is normally considered a satisfactory margin of safety. Another liquidity ratio is the *quick ratio*, which is typically expressed as cash plus accounts receivable divided by current liabilities. The quick ratio is a popular metric to pair with the current ratio to gauge liquidity. "If a business does not have decent liquidity, then one unexpected expense could severely hurt it," said Brad Schaefer, an analyst with Sageworks Inc., a financial information company.[56]

Activity Ratios   The **activity ratio** measures internal performance with respect to key activities defined by management. For example, *inventory turnover* is calculated by dividing total sales by average inventory. This ratio tells how many times the inventory is used up to meet the total sales figure. If inventory sits too long, money is wasted. Dell Inc. achieved a strategic advantage by minimizing its inventory costs. Dividing Dell's annual sales by its small inventory generates an inventory turnover rate of 35.7.[57]

Another type of activity ratio, the *conversion ratio*, is purchase orders divided by customer inquiries. This ratio is an indicator of a company's effectiveness in converting inquiries into sales. For example, if Cisco Systems moves from a 26.5 to a 28.2 conversion ratio, more of its inquiries are turned into sales, indicating improved sales activity.

Profitability Ratios   Managers analyze a company's profits by studying **profitability ratios**, which state profits relative to a source of profits, such as sales or assets. When Alan Mulally became CEO of Ford Motor Company in 2008, he emphatically stressed the importance of profitability. At that time, Ford was a sick company, losing $83 million a day, and the stock price had plummeted to $1.01 per share. Mulally initiated Ford's remarkable turnaround by fostering a new culture of accountability that emphasized the use of consistent metrics to gauge performance. Mulally expected each department head to know and report on how his or her department was performing. His emphasis on data-driven management permanently changed the culture at Ford. In 2010, Ford posted a profit of $6.6 billion, the most money that the company had made in more than a decade.[58]

One important profitability ratio is the *profit margin on sales*, which is calculated as net income divided by sales income. Similarly, *gross margin* is the gross (before-tax) profit divided by total sales. Another profitability measure is *return on assets (ROA)*, which is a percentage representing what a company earned from its assets, computed as net income divided by total assets. ROA is a valuable yardstick for comparing a company's ability to generate earnings with other investment opportunities. In basic terms, the company should be able to earn more by using its assets to operate the business than it could by putting the same investment in the bank.

Leverage Ratios   *Leverage* refers to funding activities with borrowed money. A company can use leverage to make its assets produce more than they could on their own. However, too much borrowing can put the organization at risk for being unable to keep up with repayment of its debt. Managers therefore track their *debt ratio*, or total debt divided by total assets, to make sure it does not exceed a level that they consider acceptable. Lenders may consider a company with a debt ratio above 1.0 to be a poor credit risk.

iStock.com/Agnieszka Gaul

Concept Connection

Research and development of drugs and treatments is a huge expense for pharmaceutical companies, so many managers have implemented **zero-based budgeting** in their research and development (R&D) to improve financial performance. "It really forces you to ask yourself, do you need to spend this," says former Valeant Pharmaceuticals CFO Howard Schiller. "When people have to explain it, and justify it, you often get to a different answer."

- Financial statements provide the basic information used for financial control of an organization.
- The **balance sheet** shows the firm's financial position with respect to assets and liabilities at a specific point in time.
- The **income statement** summarizes the firm's financial performance for a given time interval.
- The most common financial analysis focuses on the use of ratios—statistics that express the
- relationships between performance indicators such as profits and assets, sales, and inventory.
- The **liquidity ratio** indicates the organization's ability to meet its current debt obligations.
- The **activity ratio** measures the organization's internal performance with respect to key activities defined by management.
- The **profitability ratio** describes the firm's profits relative to a source of profits, such as sales or assets.

15-7 Trends in Quality and Financial Control

Many companies are responding to changing economic realities and global competition by reassessing organizational management and processes—including control mechanisms. Two major trends are international quality standards and the use of electronic monitoring.

15-7a International Quality Standards

One impetus for TQM in the United States is the increasing significance of the global economy. Many countries have adopted a universal benchmark for quality management practices, **ISO 9000 standards,** which represent an international consensus of what constitutes effective quality management as outlined by the International Organization for Standardization (ISO) in Geneva, Switzerland.[59] Hundreds of thousands of organizations in 157 countries, including the United States, have been certified against ISO 9000 standards to demonstrate their commitment to quality. Europe continues to lead in the total number of certifications, but the most new certifications in recent years has been in the United States. One of the more interesting organizations to become ISO certified was the Phoenix, Arizona, police department's Records and Information Bureau. In today's environment, where the credibility of law enforcement agencies has been called into question, the bureau wanted to make a clear statement about its commitment to the high quality and accuracy of information provided to law enforcement personnel and the public.[60] ISO certification has become the recognized standard for evaluating and comparing companies on a global basis, and more U.S. companies are feeling the pressure to participate to remain competitive in international markets. In addition, many countries and companies require ISO certification before they will do business with an organization.

Concept Connection

In order to become **ISO 9000–certified**, companies have to work with an independent registrar that will audit the company's practices and procedures according to the certification guidelines. For example, Cleveland HeartLab Inc., which makes medical information management systems for testing and storing data about heart patients, worked with the ISO to earn its certification.

15-7b Electronic Monitoring

Many organizations have moved toward increased hierarchical control with the use of electronic monitoring.[61] A survey from the American Management Association found that 66 percent of employers monitor the Internet use of their employees, 45 percent track employee keystrokes, and 43 percent monitor employee e-mail. Supermarkets can measure how long it takes a cashier to scan items, how many times he or she has to rescan, and how long it takes for him or her to initiate the next sale. Retail workers may have to clock in with a thumb scan, which prevents an employee from clocking in for a colleague who hasn't yet arrived. With today's technology, managers can keep tabs on what employees are doing practically all the time.

Telematics is a term that describes technologies that wirelessly transmit data from remote sensors and GPS devices to computers for analysis. Telematics is projected to be a $30 billion industry by 2018. With the use of telematics that includes handheld delivery-information acquisition devices (DIADs) and more than 200 sensors on each delivery truck, managers at UPS can monitor a driver's speed, seat belt use, stop times, and more. UPS says telematics not only benefits the company but helps the environment as well. In one recent year, the company says telematics saved 1.7 million driving miles, 15 million minutes of idling time, and 103,000 gallons of gas.[62]

Electronic monitoring can have both positive and negative effects. By using an electronic system that assigns and monitors tasks for its warehouse workers, United Grocers, a large wholesaler, says the firm was able to cut payroll expenses by 25 percent while increasing sales by 36 percent. A study of five chain restaurants found that electronic monitoring decreased employee theft and increased hourly sales. However, too much emphasis on close monitoring can damage employee trust, create unhealthy levels of stress for employees, and hurt performance. Employee reactions to electronic monitoring are often negative, so managers should use care when implementing these systems. One UPS driver told of colleagues who found ways to get around the system, such as the driver who buckled his seat belt behind him to save time and help him meet delivery goals. "People get intimidated and they work faster," he said. "It's like when they whip animals. But this is a mental whip."[63]

Remember This

- As global business expands, many companies have adopted a universal benchmark for quality management practices, including **ISO 9000 standards**, which represent an international consensus of what constitutes effective quality management as outlined by the International Organization for Standardization (ISO).
- Many organizations are moving toward increased control from the top with electronic monitoring.

- One survey found that 66 percent of employers monitor the Internet use of their employees, 45 percent track employee keystrokes, and 43 percent monitor employee e-mail.

- **Telematics** refers to technologies that wirelessly transmit data from remote sensors and GPS devices to computers for analysis.

DISCUSSION QUESTIONS

1. You have been hired to manage a 20-person staff for Nightlight Travels, a travel agency in Las Vegas. For five years, sales have been hammered by the global recession, and staff morale has plummeted as star employees have left for positions in more secure industries. Key customer relationships have been damaged by the sloppy and unprofessional work habits of the remaining staff members. Your first responsibility as new manager is to create next year's budget for all planned expenditures. But first you must decide whether you will adopt a hierarchical approach or a decentralized approach to control. Which one would you choose, and why?

2. You're a manager who employs a participative control approach. You've concluded that corrective action is necessary to improve customer satisfaction, but first

you need to convince your employees that the problem exists. What kind of evidence do you think employees will find more compelling: quantitative measurements or anecdotes from your interactions with customers? Explain your answer.

3. Describe the advantages of using a balanced scorecard to measure and control organizational performance. Suppose that you created a balanced scorecard for Walmart. What specific customer service measures would you include?

4. In zero-based budgeting, every account starts at $0, and every dollar added to the budget is reflected by an actual, documented need. Identify the possible advantages of zero-based budgeting.

5. Most companies have policies that regulate employees' personal use of work computers during work hours. Some even monitor employee e-mails and track the Web sites that have been visited. Do you consider this type of surveillance an invasion of privacy? What are the advantages of restricting employee use of the Internet and e-mail at work?

6. Think of a class that you've taken in the past. What standards of performance did your instructor establish? How was your actual performance measured? How was your performance compared to the standards? Do you think the standards and methods of measurement were fair? Were they appropriate to your assigned work? Why or why not?

7. Some critics argue that Six Sigma is a collection of superficial changes that often results in doing a superb job of building the wrong product or offering the wrong service. Do you agree or disagree? Explain.

8. What types of analyses can managers perform to help them diagnose a company's financial condition? How might a review of financial statements help managers diagnose other kinds of performance problems as well?

9. Why is benchmarking an important component of TQM programs? Do you believe a company could have a successful TQM program without using benchmarking?

10. What is ISO certification? Why would a global company like GE want ISO certification?

APPLY YOUR SKILLS: SELF-LEARNING

Is Your Budget in Control?

By the time you are in college, you are in charge of at least some of your own finances. How well you manage your personal budget may indicate how well you will manage your company's budget on the job. Respond to the following statements to evaluate your own budgeting habits. If the statement doesn't apply directly to you, respond the way you think that you would behave in a similar situation.

	Yes	No
1. I spend all my money as soon as I get it.	____	____
2. At the beginning of each week (or month, or term), I list all my fixed expenses.	____	____
3. I never seem to have any money left over at the end of the week (or month).	____	____
4. I pay all my expenses, but I never seem to have any money left over for fun.	____	____
5. I'm not putting any money away in savings right now; I'll wait until after I graduate from college.	____	____
6. I can't pay all my bills.	____	____
7. I have a credit card, but I pay the balance in full each month.	____	____
8. I take cash advances on my credit card.	____	____
9. I know how much I can spend on eating out, movies, and other entertainment each week.	____	____
10. I pay cash for everything.	____	____
11. When I buy something, I look for value and determine the best buy.	____	____
12. I lend money to friends whenever they ask, even if it leaves me short of cash.	____	____
13. I never borrow money from friends.	____	____
14. I'm putting aside money each month to save for something that I really need.	____	____

Scoring and Interpretation *Yes* responses to statements 2, 9, 10, 13, and 14 point to the most disciplined budgeting habits; *Yes* responses to 4, 5, 7, and 11 reveal adequate budgeting habits; *Yes* responses to 1, 3, 6, 8, and 12 indicate the poorest budgeting habits. If you have answered honestly, chances are you'll have a combination of all three. Look to see where you can improve your budgeting behaviors.

APPLY YOUR SKILLS: GROUP LEARNING

Create a Group Control System

Step 1. Form into groups of three to five students. Each group will assume that another student group has been given the assignment of writing a major paper that will involve research by individual group members that will be integrated into the final paper. Each group member has to do his or her part.

Step 2. Your assignment is to develop a list of rules and identify some statistics by which to control the behavior of members in that group. Brainstorm and discuss potential rules to govern member behavior and consequences for breaking those rules.

Step 3. First, select the five rules that you think are most important for governing group member behavior. Consider the following situations that rules might cover: arriving late for a meeting; missing a meeting; failing to complete a work assignment; disagreements about desired quality of work; resolving conflicts about paper content; having differences in participation, such as one person doing all the talking and someone else talking hardly at all; handling meetings that start late; using an agenda and handling deviations from it; and any other situation that your group thinks a rule should cover.

Rules you determine are important	List statistics that could be developed to measure the behavior and group outcomes	How will you know if the group is following the rule and performing as expected?
1.		
2.		
3.		
4.		
5.		

Step 4. Now consider what statistics could be developed to measure the behavior and outcome of the group pertaining to those five rules. What kinds of things could be counted to understand how the group is performing and whether members are following the rules?

Step 5. Discuss the following questions: Why are rules important as a means of control? What

are the advantages and disadvantages of having many rules (hierarchical control) versus few rules (decentralized control) for a student group? How can statistics help a group ensure appropriate behavior and a high-quality product?

Step 6. Be prepared to present your conclusions to the class.

APPLY YOUR SKILLS: ACTION LEARNING

Schoolwork Standards

1. Interview four students not taking this course right now. Make sure two of them are top grade-earners and two are about average. Tell the students you will keep their information confidential, that you will only be reporting results in a paper you will write, that you will not divulge any names. And then stick to that promise.

2. Ask the students questions about how they study, how much they read, how they manage to work on and finish a project or paper, how they feel about grades, and so on.

3. Determine whether any of the students use any of the control mechanisms described in this chapter. See Exhibit 15.1 for the mechanisms.

4. Have the students developed standards for their work? Do they compare the actual performance to the standard? What happens when the performance is less than expected, for example, they don't get as high a grade as they wanted?

5. Write a report for your instructor comparing the top students to the others. Make sure you don't mention the students' names in your report but keep them anonymous.

6. Your instructor may lead a class discussion on the findings. Again, do not mention anyone's names. If you want to talk about your own experiences as a student, that would be fine.

APPLY YOUR SKILLS: ETHICAL DILEMMA

The Wages of Sin?[64]

Chris Dykstra, responsible for loss prevention at Westwind Electronics, took a deep breath before he launched into making his case for the changes that he was proposing to the company's shoplifting policy. He knew that convincing Ross Chenoweth was going to be a hard sell. Ross, the president and CEO, was the son of the founder of the local, still family-owned consumer electronics chain based in Phoenix, Arizona. He'd inherited not only the company but also his father's strict moral code.

"I think it's time to follow the lead of other stores," Chris began. He pointed out that most other retailers didn't bother calling the police and pressing charges unless the thief had shoplifted merchandise worth more than $50 to $100. In contrast, Westwind currently had a zero-tolerance policy toward theft that Ross's father had put in place when he started the business. Chris wanted to replace that policy with one that prosecuted only individuals between 18 and 65 who had stolen more than $20 worth of goods and who had a previous history of theft at Westwind. In the case of first-time culprits under 18 or over 65, he argued for letting them off with a strict warning regardless of the value of their ill-gotten goods. Repeat offenders would be arrested.

"Frankly, the local police are getting pretty tired of having to come to our stores every time a teenager sticks a CD in his jacket pocket," Chris pointed out. "And besides, we just can't afford the costs associated with prosecuting everyone." Every time he pressed charges against a shoplifter who'd made off with a $10 item, Westwind lost money. The company had to engage a lawyer and pay employees overtime for their court appearances. In addition, Chris was looking at hiring more security guards to keep up with the workload. Westwind was already in a losing battle at the moment with mass retailers who were competing all too successfully on price, so passing on the costs of its zero-tolerance policy to customers wasn't really an option. "Let's concentrate on catching dishonest employees and those organized-theft rings. They're the ones who are really hurting us," Chris concluded.

There was a long pause after Chris finished his carefully prepared speech. Ross thought about his recently deceased father, both an astute businessman and a person for whom honesty was a key guiding principle. If he were sitting here today, he'd no doubt say that theft was theft—that setting a minimum was tantamount to saying that stealing was acceptable, just as long as you don't steal too much. He looked at Chris. "You know, we've both got teenagers. Is this really a message you want to send out, especially to kids? You know as well as I do that there's nothing they like better than testing limits. It's almost an invitation to see if you can beat the system." But then Ross faltered as he found himself glancing at the latest financial figures on his desk—another in a string of quarterly losses. If Westwind went under, a lot of employees would be looking for another way to make a living. In his heart, he believed in his father's high moral standards, but he had to ask himself: Just how moral could Westwind afford to be?

What Would You Do?

1. Continue Westwind's zero-tolerance policy toward shoplifting. It's the right thing to do—and it will pay off in the end in higher profitability because the chain's reputation for being tough on crime will reduce overall losses from theft.

2. Adopt Chris Dykstra's proposed changes and show more leniency to first-time offenders. It is a more cost-effective approach to the problem than the current policy, and it stays close to your father's original intent.

3. Adopt Chris Dykstra's proposed changes, but with a higher limit than the proposed $20 amount (say, $50 or $100), but which is still less than the cost of prosecution. In addition, make sure that the policy isn't publicized. That way, you'll reduce costs even more and still benefit from your reputation for prosecuting all shoplifters.

APPLY YOUR SKILLS: CASE FOR CRITICAL ANALYSIS

Five Stars

Cousins Jeri Lynn DeBose, Tish Hoover, and Josephine (Joey) Parks looked forward to meeting up during the Christmas holidays to compare notes on the results of midyear teacher evaluations.

All were public school teachers in districts scattered over the state. In the pressured search for new levels of teacher accountability demanded by legislators, the state department of education had joined 16 other states in implementing a new teacher evaluation system. The goal is to hold teachers accountable for student learning progress in the classroom. Under the guidance of the National Council for Teacher Quality, criteria vary by state, but in most cases, 40 percent of each teacher's accountability score would be based on the principal's evaluation and ranking based on personal observation, 30 percent would be based on personal observation by a master teacher from outside the district, and the other 30 percent would be based on student test score gains. The state department of education would set a performance goal for each school district, and the principal would set a performance goal for each teacher. In preparation, the state conducted intensive training sessions for principals and designated master teachers who would conduct the evaluations based on four class observations per teacher. Officials used standardized achievement tests to derive value-added scores that measure student learning over the year.

Teacher ratings were 1–5, with 1 being the lowest and 5 representing near perfection. The publication of the first year's evaluations stirred interest and controversy, particularly among teachers who worried about the possible long-term effects on job retention and tenure.

Now, with the first-year evaluations in hand, the three cousins pored over their experiences. The three represented different types of school systems within the state. Jeri Lynn worked for a metropolitan system in the state capital. The system included many low-income students whose first language was not English, and several schools within the system were teetering on the brink of state takeover if improvement in student scores didn't materialize this school year. Tish worked in a county system dominated by upper-income residents, and Joey taught in the rural community in which all three grew up. The rural community had high unemployment, and a low percentage of graduates went on to college. As a result, the cousins came to the table with differing teaching experiences.

"The numbers are all over the place," Jeri Lynn remarked as she studied the pages.

"The whole system is flawed and they need to make changes," Joey said. "It's too subjective. The principal and master teacher observations are subjective because there are personal factors that affect a true outcome."

"Yeah, look at the numbers from your upper-income district," Jeri Lynn said to Tish. "How can 60 percent of the teachers score 5s?"

Tish chuckled. "Yeah, lucky us. Our schools are overflowing with children from wealthy families. These are the kids who will apply to Ivy League schools. I can tell you that the principals are going to avoid confrontation on all fronts. No principal is going to give any indication that her or his students are receiving an education that's less than perfect, and that means cramming the rankings with 5s. The principals claim a higher level of motivation for students, and thus the selection of an elite team of educators. So with those pressures, I don't think we get personal feedback that is accurate."

"At the other end of the spectrum, we have my rural district," Joey said. "The big problem is that the principals know everyone and have long-standing relationships with everyone in the county, so I think scores are based on personal history. We could almost predict who would get high or low scores *before* the observations. For principals, it can go back as far as 'his daddy and my daddy hated each other in high school, and now I get to evaluate his daughter.'"

"I think that in many cases, principals feel pressure to align scores with state expectations. The state *expected* my district to have high scores and *expected* rural schools such as yours to be lower," Tish said.

"But isn't that partially offset by lower goals for the rural school districts?" responded Joey.

"The key to the accountability system is the principal in each school," Jeri Lynn suggested. "With several of the schools in Metro teetering on the edge of state takeover by the end of the year, we had lots of strict principals who wanted to hold our feet to the fire with lower scores."

"I thought the whole idea was to provide the teachers with feedback so that we would know the areas where we need improvement," Tish said.

"The principals were supposed to conduct two observations in the fall and two more in the spring," Jeri Lynn said. "I think that's asking too much of them when they already have so much on their plates. I think a lot of them are skimping on their visits. I know I only had one observation last semester, and I'm sure Mr. Talley just faked the second set of numbers. The master teachers make only two observations a year, which may be more objective but counts for less."

"I'm wondering, too, how a principal measures performance in a course area outside his area of expertise, such as math," Joey said. "If the guy has a phobia about math, anything the teacher says or does is going to look brilliant—thus a 5."

Tish and Jeri Lynn looked at each other and laughed. "Maybe we picked the wrong subjects," Tish said.

"My question is one of perception," Jeri Lynn said. "A large percentage of my students are ELL. That affects their scores. How do you measure a 3 in my situation against a 5 for Tish? At the end of the school year, little Carlos is thrilled that his reading in English has improved, but there's no Big Bang here. It's a slow steady improvement that may not actually show up in big strides for a couple of years."

"So the question is *how do they create a system that is fair?*" Tish asked.

"And accurate," added Jeri Lynn.

Questions

1. What do you see as the major strengths and flaws in the feedback control system used in the schools in this scenario? What changes do you recommend to overcome the flaws?

2.   Is a 1–5 grading system by principals and master teachers a valuable part of a feedback control system for teachers? Why?

3.   How might the state control the accuracy of principals who are conducting teacher evaluations? Explain.

ENDNOTES

1.   Kurt Eichenwald, "Killer Pharmacy: Inside a Medical Mass Murder Case," *Newsweek* (April 16, 2015), http://www.newsweek.com/2015/04/24/inside-one-most-murderous-corporate-crimes-us-history-322665.html (accessed May 20, 2016); Sabrina Tavernise and Andrew Pollack, "F.D.A. Details Contamination at Pharmacy," *The New York Times*, October 26, 2012, http://www.nytimes.com/2012/10/27/health/fda-finds-unsanitary-conditions-at-new-england-compounding-center.html?_r=0 (accessed October 26, 2012); and Timothy W. Martin, Thomas M. Burton, and Jennifer Corbett Dooren, "Outbreak Spurs Calls for New Controls," *The Wall Street Journal*, October 9, 2012, A1.

2.   Willaim K. Rashbau, "Inspector Says He Faked Data in New York Building Tests," *The New York Times*, April 26, 2010, www.nytimes.com/2010/04/27/nyregion/27inspect.html?pagewanted=all&l_r=0 (accessed October 2, 2012).

3.   Douglas S. Sherwin, "The Meaning of Control," *Dunn's Business Review* (January 1956).

4.   Anemona Hartocollis, "New York Ties Doctors' Pay to Care Issues," *The New York Times*, January 12, 2013, A1.

5.   Nicholas Bloom, Raffaella Sadun, and Jon Van Reenen, "Does Management Really Work?" *Harvard Business Review* (November 2012): 76–81.

6.   Eric Wilson, "No. 279 Puts on Its Game Face," *The New York Times*, November 22, 2012, E1.

7.   Richard E. Crandall, "Keys to Better Performance Measurement," *Industrial Management* (January–February 2002): 19–24; and Christopher D. Ittner and David F. Larcker, "Coming Up Short on Nonfinancial Performance Measurement," *Harvard Business Review* (November 2003): 88–95.

8.   Jamie Flinchbaugh, "Don't Waste Your Metrics," *Industry Week* (June 2012): 10.

9.   Janet Adamy, "U.S. Ties Hospital Payments to Making Patients Happy," *The Wall Street Journal*, October 15, 2012, A1.

10.   Jessica Bruder, "Can FreshDirect Survive a Crisis and Reinvent Itself?" *The New York Times*, August 11, 2010, www.nytimes.com/2010/08/12/business/smallbusiness/12sbiz.html?pagewanted=all&_r=0 (accessed September 28, 2012).

11.   This discussion is based on a review of the balanced scorecard in Richard L. Daft, *Organization Theory and Design*, 7th ed. (Cincinnati, OH: South-Western, 2001), pp. 300–301.

12.   Andy Neely and Mohammed Al Najjar, "Management Learning, Not Management Control: The True Role of Performance Measurement," *California Management Review* 48, no. 3 (Spring 2006): 101–114.

13.   Robert Kaplan and David Norton, "The Balanced Scorecard: Measures That Drive Performance," *Harvard Business Review* (January–February 1992): 71–79; Chee W. Chow, Kamal M. Haddad, and James E. Williamson, "Applying the Balanced Scorecard to Small Companies," *Management Accounting* 79, no. 2 (August 1997): 21–27; and Meena Chavan, "The Balanced Scorecard: A New Challenge," *Journal of Management Development* 28, no. 5 (2009): 393–406.

14.   Based on Kaplan and Norton, "The Balanced Scorecard"; Chow, Haddad, and Williamson, "Applying the Balanced Scorecard"; and Cathy Lazere, "All Together Now," *CFO* (February 1998): 28–36.

15.   Karen S. Cravens, Elizabeth Goad Oliver, and Jeanine S. Stewart, "Can a Positive Approach to Performance Evaluation Help Accomplish Your Goals?" *Business Horizons* 53 (2010): 269–279.

16.   Juliet Eilperin and Zachary A. Goldfarb, "IG Report: 'Inappropriate Criteria' Stalled IRS Approvals of Conservative Groups," *Washington Post*, May 14, 2013, http://articles.washingtonpost.com/2013-05-14/politics/39248137_1_watchdog-report-tea-party-conservative-groups (accessed May 15, 2013).

17.   Andy Pasztor, "Decisions by Pilots to Land Criticized," *The Wall Street Journal*, March 28, 2011, http://online.wsj.com/article/SB10001424052748703576204576227111818190174 54.html (accessed October 11, 2012).

18.   Geert J. M. Braam and Edwin J. Nijssen, "Performance Effects of Using the Balanced Scorecard: A Note on the Dutch Experience," *Long Range Planning* 37 (2004): 335–349; Kaplan and Norton, "The Balanced Scorecard"; and Cam Scholey, "Strategy Maps: A Step-by-Step Guide to Measuring, Managing, and Communicating the Plan," *Journal of Business Strategy* 26, no. 3 (2005): 12–15.

19.   Nils-Göran Olve et al., "Twelve Years Later: Understanding and Realizing the Value of Balanced Scorecards," *Ivey Business Journal Online*, May–June 2004, www.iveybusinessjournal.com/article.asp?intArticle_ID=487 (accessed October 4, 2010); Eric M. Olson and Stanley F. Slater, "The Balanced Scorecard, Competitive Strategy, and Performance," *Business Horizons* (May–June 2002): 11–16; Eric Berkman, "How to Use the Balanced Scorecard," *CIO* (May 15, 2002): 93–100; and Brigitte W. Schay et al., "Using Standardized Outcome Measures in the Federal Government," *Human Resource Management* 41, no. 3 (Fall 2002): 355–368.

20.   Braam and Nijssen, "Performance Effects of Using the Balanced Scorecard."

21.   William G. Ouchi, "Markets, Bureaucracies, and Clans," *Administrative Science Quarterly*, 25 (1980): 129–141; and B. R. Baligia and Alfred M. Jaeger, "Multinational Corporations: Control Systems and Delegation Issues," *Journal of International Business Studies* (Fall 1984): 25–40.

22.   Daisuke Wakabayashi and Toko Sekiguchi, "Disaster in Japan: Evacuees Set Rules to Create Sense of Normalcy," *The Wall Street Journal*, March 26, 2011, http://online.wsj.com/article/SB10001424052748703784004576220382991112672.html (accessed October 3, 2012).

23.   Ian Mount, "A Pizzeria Owner Learns the Value of Watching the Books," *The New York Times*, October 25, 2012, B8.

24.   Craig Torres and Anthony Feld, "Campbell's Quest for Productivity," *Bloomberg BusinessWeek* (November 29–December 5, 2010): 15–16.

25.   Perry Pascarella, "Open the Books to Unleash Your People," *Management Review* (May 1998): 58–60.

26.   Leigh Buchanan, "Learning from the Best," *Inc.* (June 2010): 85–86.

27.   Annie Gasparro, "Nestlé USA Recalls Products over Possible Glass Contamination," *The Wall Street Journal*, March 10, 2016, http://www.wsj.com/articles/nestle-usa-recalls-products-over-possible-glass-contamination-1457639434 (accessed May 20, 2016).

28. V. Feigenbaum, *Total Quality Control: Engineering and Management* (New York: McGraw-Hill, 1961); John Lorinc, "Dr. Deming's Traveling Quality Show," *Canadian Business* (September 1990): 38–42; Mary Walton, *The Deming Management Method* (New York: Dodd-Meade & Co, 1986); and J. M. Juran and Frank M. Gryna, eds., *Juran's Quality Control Handbook*, 4th ed. (New York: McGraw-Hill, 1988).

29. Edward E. Lawler III and Susan A. Mohrman, "Quality Circles After the Fad," *Harvard Business Review* (January–February 1985): 65–71; and Philip C. Thompson, *Quality Circles: How to Make Them Work in America* (New York: AMA-COM, 1982).

30. Jill Jusko, "Meeting the Efficiency Challenge," *Industry Week* (January 2012): 28.

31. D. J. Ford, "Benchmarking HRD," *Training & Development* (July 1993): 37–41.

32. Owen Ou and Brian H. Kleiner, "Excellence in Benchmarking," *Industrial Management* (November–December 2015): 20–24.

33. Deven Shah and Brian H. Kleiner, "Benchmarking for Quality," *Industrial Management* (March–April 2011): 22–25.

34. Tracy Mayor, "Six Sigma Comes to IT: Targeting Perfection," *CIO* (December 1, 2003): 62–70; Hal Plotkin, "Six Sigma: What It Is and How to Use It," *Harvard Management Update* (June 1999): 3–4; Tom Rancour and Mike McCracken, "Applying Six Sigma Methods for Breakthrough Safety Performance," *Professional Safety* 45, no. 10 (October 2000): 29–32; G. Hasek, "Merger Marries Quality Efforts," *Industry Week* (August 21, 2000): 89–92; and Lee Clifford, "Why You Can Safely Ignore Six Sigma," *Fortune* (January 22, 2001): 140.

35. Dave Blanchard, "Lean Six Sigma Keeps Cardinal's Supply Chain Healthy," *Industry Week* (October 2012): 54.

36. Dick Smith and Jerry Blakeslee, "The New Strategic Six Sigma," *Training & Development* (September 2002): 45–52; Michael Hammer and Jeff Goding, "Putting Six Sigma in Perspective," *Quality* (October 2001): 58–62; and Mayor, "Six Sigma Comes to IT."

37. Jack Bouck, "Creating a Customer-Focused Culture: The Honeywell Experience," *Industrial Management* (November–December 2007): 11.

38. Steve Minter, "La-Z-Boy Never Rests on Continuous Improvement," *Industry Week* (January 2013): 25; and Austin Weber, "There's No Kicking Back at La-Z-Boy," *Assembly* (July 3, 2015), http://www.assemblymag.com /articles/91342-theres-no-kicking-back-at-la-z-boy (accessed May 22, 2016).

39. This discussion is based on Eileen Newman Rubin, "A Partnered Approach to QA Increases Efficiency Through Early Problem Detection," *Global Business and Organizational Excellence* (May–June 2012): 28–37.

40. Weber, "There's No Kicking Back at La-Z-Boy."

41. Clifford, "Why You Can Safely Ignore Six Sigma"; and Hammer and Goding, "Putting Six Sigma in Perspective."

42. Jay Goltz, "The Dusenberry Diary: When Passion Meets Math," *The New York Times*, June 23, 2009, http://boss.blogs. nytimes.com/2009/06/23/the-dusenberry-diary-when-passion-meets-math/ (accessed October 2, 2012).

43. Sumantra Ghoshal, *Strategic Control* (St. Paul, MN: West, 1986), Chapter 4; and Robert N. Anthony, John Dearden, and Norton M. Bedford, *Management Control Systems*, 5th ed. (Homewood, IL: Irwin, 1984).

44. John A. Boquist, Todd T. Milbourn, and Anjan V. Thakor, "How Do You Win the Capital Allocation Game?" *Sloan Management Review* (Winter 1998): 59–71.

45. Jason Gillikin, "What Is Zero-Based Budgeting and How Is It Used by an Organization?" *Houston Chronicle*, http:// smallbusiness.chron.com/zerobased-budgeting-used-organization-22586.html (accessed October 3, 2012).

46. Ibid.; and Gerard Paulides, "Resetting the Cost Structure at Shell," *Strategy + Business* 65 (Winter 2011): 1–4.

47. Anthony, Dearden, and Bedford, *Management Control Systems*.

48. Participation in budget setting is described in a number of studies, including those by Neil C. Churchill, "Budget Choice: Planning Versus Control," *Harvard Business Review* (July–August 1984): 150–164; Peter Brownell, "Leadership Style, Budgetary Participation, and Managerial Behavior," *Accounting Organizations and Society* 8 (1983): 307–321; and Paul J. Carruth and Thurrell O. McClandon, "How Supervisors React to 'Meeting the Budget' Pressure," *Management Accounting* 66 (November 1984): 50–54.

49. Tim Reason, "Budgeting in the Real World," *CFO* (July 2005): 43–48.

50. Ibid.

51. David Kesmodel and Annie Gasparro, "Kraft-Heinz Deal Shows Brazilian Buyout Firm's Cost-Cutting Recipe," *The Wall Street Journal*, March 25, 2015, http://www.wsj.com/ articles/from-heinz-to-kraft-zero-based-budgeting-sweeps-across-america-1427308494 (accessed May 23, 2016).

52. Norm Brodsky, "Balance-Sheet Blues," *Inc.* (October 2011): 34.

53. This analogy is from Brodsky, "Balance-Sheet Blues."

54. Dana Mattioli, "CEOs Fight to Prevent Discretionary Spending from Creeping Back Up," *The Wall Street Journal*, January 1, 1998, http://online.wsj.com/article/SB1000142 405274870360900457535490154556456.html (accessed December 11, 2012).

55. Willy Staley, "How 7-Eleven Plans to Put the Bodega Out of Business," *New York* (May 14, 2012): 38–41, 87–88.

56. Mary Ellen Biery, "Five Metrics You Should Know," *The Washington Post*, May 25, 2012, www.washingtonpost. com/blogs/on-small-business/post/5-financial-metrics-you-should-know/2012/05/25/gJQAuDSjpU_blog.html (accessed October 9, 2012).

57. Lawrence M. Fisher, "Inside Dell Computer Corporation: Managing Working Capital," *Strategy + Business* 10 (First Quarter 1998): 68–75; and Randy Myers, "Cash Crop: The 2000 Working Capital Survey," *CFO* (August 2000): 59–69.

58. Nancy F. Koehn, "The Driver in Ford's Amazing Race," *The New York Times*, March 31, 2012, www.nytimes. com/2012/04/01/business/american-icon-examines-fords-rebound-review.html?pagewanted=all&_r=0 (accessed September 28, 2012).

59. Syed Hasan Jaffrey, "ISO 9001 Made Easy," *Quality Progress* 37, no. 5 (May 2004): 104; Frank C. Barnes, "ISO 9000 Myth and Reality: A Reasonable Approach to ISO 9000," *SAM Advanced Management Journal* (Spring 1998): 23–30; and Thomas H. Stevenson and Frank C. Barnes, "Fourteen Years of ISO 9000: Impact, Criticisms, Costs, and Benefits," *Business Horizons* (May–June 2001): 45–51.

60. David Amari, Don James, and Cathy Marley, "ISO 9001 Takes On a New Role—Crime Fighter," *Quality Progress* 37, no. 5 (May 2004): 57ff.

61. This section is based largely on Esther Kaplan, "The Spy Who Fired Me," *Harper's Magazine* (March 2015): 31–40.

62. Reported in Kaplan, "The Spy Who Fired Me."

63. Ibid.

64. Based on Michael Barbaro, "Some Leeway for the Small Shoplifter," *The New York Times*, July 13, 2006.

Glossary

5 Whys A question-asking method used to explore the root cause underlying a particular problem. The first "why" generally produces a superficial explanation for the problem, and each subsequent "why" probes deeper into the causes of the problem and potential solutions.

360-degree feedback A recent trend in performance appraisal is called 360-degree feedback, a process that uses multiple raters, including self rating, as a way to increase awareness of strengths and weaknesses and guide employee development.

Accountability Means that people with authority and responsibility are subject to reporting and justifying task outcomes to those above them in the chain of command.

Achievement culture A results-oriented culture that values competitiveness, personal initiative, and achievement.

Acqui-hiring When established companies such as Facebook, Google, Yahoo, LinkedIn, and Salesforce.com buy early-stage start-ups, often shutting them down, simply to acquire their engineering talent.

Activity ratio Measures the organization's internal performance with respect to key activities defined by management.

Adaptability culture Characterized by values that support the company's ability to interpret and translate signals from the environment into new behavior responses.

Adjourning The stage during which members of temporary teams prepare for the team's disbanding.

Administrative model A decision-making model that includes the concepts of *bounded rationality and satisficing* and describes how managers make decisions in situations that are characterized by uncertainty and ambiguity.

Administrative principles approach A subfield of the classical perspective that focuses on the total organization rather than the individual worker and delineates the management functions of planning, organizing, commanding, coordinating, and controlling.

Affirmative action Requires that employers take positive steps to guarantee equal employment opportunities for people within protected groups.

After-action review A disciplined procedure whereby managers review the results of decisions to evaluate what worked, what didn't, and how to do things better.

Alienated follower A person who is an independent, critical thinker but is passive in the organization.

Ambidextrous approach Incorporating structures and processes that are appropriate for both the creative impulse and the systematic implementation of innovations.

Ambiguity A condition in which the goals to be achieved or the problem to be solved is unclear, alternatives are difficult to define, and information about outcomes is unavailable.

Anchoring bias When a manager allows initial impressions, statistics, or estimates to act as anchors to subsequent thoughts and decisions.

Application form A selection device that collects information about the applicant's education, previous work experience, and other background characteristics.

Attribution A judgment about what caused a person's behavior—characteristics of either the person or the situation.

Authentic leadership Leadership by individuals who know and understand themselves, who espouse and act consistent with higher-order ethical values, and who empower and inspire others with their openness and authenticity.

Authoritarianism The belief that power and status differences should exist within an organization.

Authority The formal and legitimate right of a manager to make decisions, issue orders, and allocate resources to achieve outcomes desired by the organization.

Avoidance learning Removing an unpleasant consequence once a behavior is improved. Also called *negative reinforcement.*

Balance sheet Shows the firm's financial position with respect to assets and liabilities at a specific point in time.

Balanced scorecard A comprehensive management control system that balances traditional financial measures with measures of customer service, internal business processes, and the organization's capacity for learning and growth.

BCG matrix A concept developed by the Boston Consulting Group (BCG) that evaluates strategic business units with respect to two dimensions—business growth rate and market share—and classifies them as cash cows, stars, question marks, or dogs.

Behavior modification The set of techniques by which reinforcement theory is used to modify human behavior.

Behavioral sciences approach Draws from psychology, sociology, and other social sciences to develop theories about human behavior and interaction in an organizational setting.

Behaviorally anchored rating scale (BARS) A performance evaluation technique that relates an employee's performance to specific job-related incidents.

Benchmarking The continuous process of measuring products, services, and practices against major competitors or industry leaders.

Benefit corporation A for-profit organization that has a stated purpose of creating a positive impact on society; is required to consider the impact of decisions on all stakeholders; and voluntarily holds itself to high standards of accountability and transparency.

Big data analytics Technologies, skills, and processes for searching and examining massive, complex sets of data that traditional data processing applications cannot handle to uncover hidden patterns and correlations.

Big Five personality factors Dimensions that describe an individual's extroversion, agreeableness, conscientiousness, emotional stability, and openness to experience.

Blind hiring Focuses managers on an applicant's job skills and performance rather than educational credentials, appearance, or prior experience.

Blind spot An attribute about a person that he or she is not aware of or doesn't recognize as a problem; this limits effectiveness and hinders career success.

Bottom of the pyramid (BOP) concept Proposes that corporations can alleviate poverty and other social ills, as well as make significant profits, by selling to the world's poor.

Bottom-up approach Involves encouraging the flow of ideas from lower levels and making sure that they get heard and acted upon by top executives.

Bottom-up budgeting Involves lower-level managers anticipating their department's budget needs and passing them up to top management for approval.

Boundary-spanning Links to and coordinates the organization with key elements in the external environment.

Bounded rationality Means that people have the time and cognitive ability to process only a limited amount of information on which to base decisions.

Brainstorming A technique that uses a face-to-face group to spontaneously suggest a broad range of alternatives for making a decision.

Bureaucratic organizations approach Emphasizes management on an impersonal, rational basis through elements such as clearly defined authority and responsibility, formal recordkeeping, and separation of management and ownership.

Capital budget A budget that plans and reports investments in major assets to be depreciated over several years.

Cash budget A budget that estimates receipts and expenditures of money on a daily or weekly basis to ensure that an organization has sufficient cash to meet its obligations.

Centralization Means that decision authority is located near top organization levels.

Centralized network A structure in which team members must communicate through one individual to solve problems or make decisions.

Ceremony A planned activity at a special event.

Certainty A situation in which all the information the decision maker needs is fully available.

Chain of command An unbroken line of authority that links all individuals in the organization and specifies who reports to whom.

Change agent An organization development (OD) specialist who contracts with an organization to help managers facilitate change.

Changing The "intervention" stage of organization development (OD), when change agents teach people new behaviors and skills and guide them in using them in the workplace.

Channel The medium by which a message is sent, such as a phone call, blog, or text message.

Channel richness The amount of information that can be transmitted during a communication episode.

Charismatic leader A leader who has the ability to inspire and motivate people to transcend their expected performance, even to the point of personal sacrifice.

Chief ethics officer A manager who oversees all aspects of ethics and legal compliance.

Classical model A decision-making model based on the assumption that managers should make logical decisions that are economically sensible and in the organization's best economic interest.

Classical perspective Takes a rational, scientific approach to management and seeks to turn organizations into efficient operating machines.

Coalition An informal alliance among managers who support a specific goal or solution.

Code of ethics A formal statement of the organization's values regarding ethics and social responsibility.

Coercive power Power that stems from the authority to punish or recommend punishment.

Collaboration A joint effort between people from two or more departments to produce outcomes that meet a common goal or shared purpose.

Collectivism A preference for a tightly knit social framework in which individuals look after one another and organizations protect their members' interests.

Communication The process by which information is exchanged and understood by two or more people.

Communication apprehension An individual's level of fear or anxiety associated with either real or anticipated communication.

Compensation All monetary payments and all nonmonetary goods or benefits used to reward employees.

Compensatory justice Argues that individuals should be compensated for the cost of their injuries by the party responsible, and individuals should not be held responsible for matters over which they have no control.

Competitive advantage Refers to what sets the organization apart from others and provides it with a distinctive edge in the marketplace.

Competitors Organizations within the same industry or type of business that vie for the same set of customers.

Conceptual skill The cognitive ability to see the organization as a whole and the relationships among its parts.

Confirmation bias The tendency to put too much value on evidence that is consistent with a favored belief or viewpoint and too little on evidence that contradicts it.

Conflict An antagonistic interaction in which one party attempts to block the intentions or goals of another.

Conformist A follower who participates actively in the organization but does not use critical thinking skills.

Conscious capitalism Following organizational policies and practices that both enhance the success of a company and advance the economic and social conditions of the communities in which the company operates.

Consideration Describes the extent to which a leader is sensitive to subordinates, respects their ideas and feelings, and establishes mutual trust.

Consistency culture Values and rewards a methodical, rational, orderly way of doing things.

Content theories Theories that emphasize the needs that motivate people.

Contingency approach A model of leadership that describes the relationship between leadership styles and specific situations.

Contingency plan Identifies important factors in the environment and defines a range of alternative responses to be taken in the case of emergencies, setbacks, or unexpected conditions.

Contingency view Tells managers that what works in one organizational situation might not work in another.

Continuous process production Involves mechanization of the entire workflow and nonstop production, such as in chemical plants or petroleum refineries.

Controlling Is concerned with monitoring employees' activities, keeping the organization on track toward meeting its goals and making corrections as necessary.

Coordination The managerial task of adjusting and synchronizing the diverse activities among different individuals and departments.

Core competence Something that the organization does particularly well in comparison to others.

Corporate governance Refers to the framework of systems, rules, and practices by which an organization ensures accountability, fairness, and transparency in its relationships with stakeholders.

Corporate social responsibility (CSR) The obligation of organizational managers to make choices and take actions that will enhance the welfare and interests of society as well as the organization.

Corporate university An in-house training and development facility that offers broad-based learning opportunities for employees.

Cost leadership strategy A strategy with which managers aggressively seek efficient facilities, cut costs, and use tight cost controls to be more efficient than others in the industry.

Creativity The generation of novel ideas that may meet perceived needs or respond to opportunities for the organization.

Critical thinking Thinking independently and being mindful of the effect that one's behavior has on achieving goals.

Cross-functional team A group of employees from various functional departments that meet as a team to resolve mutual problems.

Crowdsourcing An approach in which many people (sometimes hundreds of thousands of people) contribute to the innovation process via the Internet.

Cultural intelligence (CQ) The ability to use reasoning and observation skills to interpret unfamiliar gestures and situations and devise appropriate behavioral responses.

Cultural leader Defines and articulates important values that are tied to a clear and compelling mission.

Culture The set of key values, beliefs, understandings, and norms shared by members of an organization.

Culture change A major shift in the norms, values, and mindset of an entire organization.

Customers People and organizations that acquire goods or services from a company.

Decentralization Means that decision authority is pushed down to lower organization levels.

Decentralized control A situation where the organization fosters compliance with organizational goals through the use of organizational culture, group norms, and a focus on goals rather than rules and procedures.

Decentralized network A network in which individuals can communicate freely with other team members.

Decentralized planning An approach where top executives or planning experts work with managers in major divisions or departments to develop their own goals and plans.

Decision A choice made from available alternatives.

Decision making The process of identifying problems and opportunities and then resolving them.

Decision styles Differences among people with respect to how they perceive problems and make choices.

Decode To read symbols to interpret the meaning of a message.

Delegation When managers transfer authority and responsibility to positions below them in the hierarchy.

Departmentalization The basis for grouping individual positions into departments and departments into the total organization.

Descriptive An approach that describes how managers actually make decisions in complex situations rather than dictating how they *should* make decisions according to a theoretical ideal.

Devil's advocate A person who is assigned the role of challenging the assumptions and assertions made by the group to prevent premature consensus.

Diagnosis The step in which managers analyze underlying causal factors associated with the decision situation.

Differentiation strategy A strategy with which managers seek to distinguish the organization's products and services from those of others in the industry.

Discrimination (1) Making hiring and promotion decisions based on criteria that are not job-relevant. (2) When someone acts out their negative attitudes toward people who are the targets of their prejudice.

Disruptive innovation Innovations in products, services, or processes that radically change competition in an industry, such as the advent of streaming video or e-books.

Distributive justice Requires that different treatment of individuals not be based on arbitrary characteristics.

Distributive negotiation A competitive and adversarial approach in which each party strives to get as much as it can, usually at the expense of the other party.

Diversification The strategy of moving into new lines of business.

Diversity All the ways in which employees differ.

Diversity of thought Achieved when a manager creates a heterogeneous team made up of individuals with diverse backgrounds and skill sets to provide a broader and deeper base of ideas, opinions, and experiences for problem solving, creativity, and innovation.

Division of labor The degree to which organizational tasks are subdivided into separate jobs. Also called *work specialization*.

Divisional structure An organizational structure that groups employees and departments based on similar organizational outputs (products or services), such that each division has a mix of functional skills and tasks.

Downward communication Messages sent from top management down to subordinates.

E → P expectancy The assumption that putting effort into a given task will lead to high performance.

Economic dimension Represents the general economic health of the country or region in which the organization operates.

Effective follower A critical, independent thinker who actively participates in the organization.

Effectiveness The degree to which the organization achieves a stated goal.

Efficiency The amount of resources—raw materials, money, and people—used to produce a desired volume of output.

Electronic brainstorming Brainstorming that takes place in an interactive group over a computer network, rather than meeting face to face.

Emotion A mental state that arises spontaneously rather than through conscious effort and is often accompanied by physiological changes.

Emotional contagion The tendency of people to absorb and express the emotions, moods, and attitudes of those around them.

Employee affinity group A group based on social identity, such as gender or race, and organized by employees to focus on concerns of employees from that group.

Employer brand Similar to a product brand, except that rather than promoting a specific product, its aim is to make an organization seem like a highly desirable place to work.

Employment test A test given to employees to evaluate their abilities; can include cognitive ability tests, physical ability tests, personality inventories, and other assessments.

Empowerment The delegation of power and authority to subordinates in an organization.

Encode To select symbols with which to compose a message.

Engagement An emotional and mental state in which employees enjoy their work, contribute enthusiastically to meeting goals, and feel a sense of belonging and commitment to the organization.

Equity When the ratio of one person's outcomes to inputs equals that of another's.

Equity theory A theory that focuses on individuals' perceptions of how fairly they are treated relative to others.

ERG theory A modification of the needs hierarchy that proposes three categories of needs: existence, relatedness, and growth.

Escalating commitment Refers to continuing to invest time and money in a decision despite evidence that it is failing.

Ethical dilemma A situation in which all alternative choices or behaviors have potentially negative consequences.

Ethics The code of moral principles and values that governs the behaviors of a person or group with respect to what is right or wrong.

Ethics committee A group of executives (and sometimes lower-level employees as well) charged with overseeing company ethics by ruling on questionable issues and disciplining violators.

Ethnocentrism The natural tendency among people to regard their own culture as superior to others.

Ethnorelativism The belief that groups and cultures are inherently equal.

Euro A single European currency that has replaced the currencies of 19 member nations of the European Union (EU).

Evidence-based decision making A process founded on a commitment to examining potential biases, seeking and examining evidence with rigor, and making informed and intelligent decisions based on the best available facts and evidence.

Exit interview A discussion conducted with departing employees to determine reasons for their departure and learn about potential problems in the organization.

Expectancy theory Proposes that motivation depends on individuals' assumptions about their ability to perform tasks and receive desired rewards.

Expense budget A budget that outlines the anticipated and actual expenses for a responsibility center.

Expert power Power that results from a leader's special knowledge or skill in the tasks performed by subordinates.

Exporting A market entry strategy in which a company maintains production facilities within its home country and transfers products for sale in foreign countries.

Extinction Withholding positive rewards and essentially ignoring undesirable behavior.

Extrinsic reward A reward given by another person, such as a manager, including pay increases, promotions, and praise.

Feedback Occurs when the receiver responds to the sender's communication with a return message.

Femininity A cultural preference for relationships, cooperation, group decision making, and quality of life.

Flat structure An organizational structure characterized by an overall broad span of management and relatively few hierarchical levels.

Focus strategy A strategy where managers use either a differentiation or a cost leadership approach, but they concentrate on a specific regional market or buyer group.

Force-field analysis A technique for determining which forces drive a proposed change and which forces restrain it.

Formal communication channel A channel that flows within the chain of command or task responsibility defined by the organization.

Forming The stage of team development involving a period of orientation and getting acquainted.

Free rider A person who benefits from team membership but does not make a proportionate contribution to the team's work.

Frustration-regression principle Suggests that failure to meet a high-order need may cause a regression to an already satisfied lower-order need; thus, people may move down as well as up the needs hierarchy.

Functional structure An organizational structure in which activities are grouped together by common function from the bottom to the top of the organization.

Functional team A team composed of a manager and his or her subordinates in the formal chain of command.

Fundamental attribution error A tendency to underestimate the influence of external factors on another person's accomplishments and to overestimate the influence of internal factors.

General environment Indirectly influences all organizations within an industry; includes five dimensions.

General manager A manager responsible for several departments that perform different functions.

Glass ceiling An invisible barrier that separates women and minorities from senior management positions.

Global mindset The ability to appreciate and influence individuals, groups, organizations, and systems that represent different social, cultural, political, institutional, intellectual, and psychological characteristics.

Global outsourcing Engaging in the international division of labor so as to obtain the cheapest sources of labor and supplies, regardless of country. Sometimes called *offshoring*.

Global team A group made up of employees who come from different countries and whose activities span multiple countries.

Globalization The extent to which trade and investments, information, ideas, and political cooperation flow between countries.

Goal A desired future state that the organization wants to realize.

Goal-setting theory A theory that proposes that specific, challenging goals increase motivation and performance when they are accepted by subordinates and these subordinates receive feedback to indicate their progress toward goal achievement.

Grapevine A system that carries workplace gossip, a dominant force in organization communication when formal channels are not functioning effectively.

Greenwashing Efforts to portray a company as being more environmentally minded that it actually is.

Grit Perseverance and passion in pursuit of long-term goals.

Groupthink The tendency of people in groups to suppress contrary opinions in a desire for harmony.

Halo effect Occurs when a manager gives an employee the same rating on all dimensions of the job, even though performance may be good on some dimensions and poor on others.

Hawthorne studies A series of research efforts that was important in shaping ideas concerning how managers should treat workers.

Hero A figure who exemplifies the deeds, character, and attributes of a strong culture.

Hierarchical control Involves monitoring and influencing employee behavior through the use of rules, policies, hierarchy of authority, written documentation, reward systems, and other formal mechanisms.

Hierarchy of needs theory A theory proposed by Abraham Maslow saying that people are motivated by five categories of needs— physiological, safety, belongingness, esteem, and self-actualization—that exist in a hierarchical order.

High-context culture A culture in which people are sensitive to circumstances surrounding social exchanges, derive meaning from context, and use communication to build personal relationships.

High-performance culture Emphasizes both cultural values and business results.

Horizontal communication The lateral or diagonal exchange of messages among peers or coworkers and includes team communication.

Horizontal linkage model Means that several departments, such as marketing, research, and manufacturing, work closely together to develop new products.

Human capital The economic value of the combined knowledge, experience, skills, and capabilities of employees.

Human relations movement Stresses the satisfaction of employees' basic needs as the key to increased productivity.

Human resource management (HRM) The design and application of formal systems to ensure the effective and efficient use of human talent to accomplish organizational goals.

Human resource planning The forecasting of human resource needs and the projected matching of individuals with anticipated job vacancies.

Human resources perspective Suggests that jobs should be designed to meet people's higher-level needs by allowing employees to use their full potential.

Humanistic perspective Emphasizes understanding human behavior, needs, and attitudes in the workplace.

Humility Being unpretentious and modest rather than arrogant and prideful.

Hygiene factors Elements that focus on lower-level needs and consider the presence or absence of job dissatisfiers, including working conditions, pay, and company policies.

Idea champion A person who sees the need for change and is passionately committed to making it happen.

Idea incubator An organizational program that provides a safe harbor where employees can generate and develop ideas without interference from company bureaucracy or politics.

Implementation Involves using managerial, administrative, and persuasive abilities to translate a chosen decision alternative into action.

Implicit communication Sending and receiving unspoken cues such as tone of voice or body language as well as spoken words.

Inclusion The degree to which an employee feels like an esteemed member of a group in which his or her uniqueness is highly appreciated.

Income statement Summarizes a firm's financial performance for a given time interval.

Individualism A preference for a loosely knit social framework in which individuals are expected to take care of themselves.

Individualism approach A decision-making approach suggesting that actions are ethical when they promote the individual's best long-term interests, because with everyone pursuing self-interest, the greater good is ultimately served.

Influence The effect a person's actions have on the attitudes, values, beliefs, or behavior of others.

Information technology (IT) The hardware, software, telecommunications, database management, and other technologies used to store, process, and distribute information.

Initiating structure Describes the extent to which a leader is task oriented and directs subordinates' work activities toward goal accomplishment.

Innovation by acquisition A strategy to obtain innovation by buying other companies, recognizing that the cutting edge of innovation often happens with young, small, entrepreneurial companies rather than inside the walls of established firms.

Integrative negotiation A collaborative approach that is based on a win-win assumption, whereby the parties want to come up with a creative solution that benefits both sides of the conflict.

Interactive leadership A leadership style characterized by values such as inclusion, collaboration, relationship building, and caring.

Internal environment Includes elements within the organization's boundaries, such as employees, management, and corporate culture.

International dimension In the external environment, represents events originating in foreign countries, as well as opportunities for companies in other countries.

International management Managing business operations in more than one country.

Internship An arrangement whereby an intern, usually a high school or college student, exchanges his or her services for the opportunity to gain work experience and see whether a particular career is appealing.

Intrinsic reward The satisfaction that a person receives in the process of performing a particular action.

Intuition An aspect of administrative decision making that refers to a quick comprehension of a decision situation based on past experience but without conscious thought.

Involvement culture A culture that places high value on meeting the needs of employees and values cooperation and equality.

ISO 9000 standards Represent an international consensus of what constitutes effective quality management as outlined by the International Organization for Standardization (ISO).

Job analysis The systematic process of gathering and interpreting information about the essential duties, tasks, and responsibilities of a job.

Job characteristics model A model of job design that considers core job dimensions, individuals' critical psychological states, and employee growth-need strength.

Job description A concise summary of the specific tasks and responsibilities of a position.

Job design Refers to applying motivational theories to the structure of work to improve motivation, productivity, and satisfaction.

Job enrichment Incorporating high-level motivators, such as achievement, recognition, and opportunities for growth, into work.

Job evaluation The process of determining the value of jobs within an organization through an examination of job content.

Job satisfaction A positive attitude toward one's job.

Job specification Outlines the knowledge, skills, education, physical abilities, and other characteristics needed to perform a specific job adequately.

Joint venture A strategic alliance or program by two or more organizations.

Justice approach Says that ethical decisions must be based on standards of equity, fairness, and impartiality.

Key performance indicators (KPIs) Tools used to assess what is important to an organization and how well the organization is progressing toward attaining its strategic goal, so that managers can establish lower-level goals that drive performance toward the overall strategic objective.

Labor market The people available for hire by the organization.

Large-group intervention An organization development (OD) approach that brings together people from different parts of the organization (and often including outside stakeholders) to discuss problems or opportunities and plan for change.

Law of effect Asserts that positively reinforced behavior tends to be repeated, and unreinforced or negatively reinforced behavior tends to be inhibited.

Leadership The ability to influence people toward the attainment of organizational goals.

Leadership Grid® A two-dimensional leadership model that measures the leader's concern for people and concern for production to categorize the leader in one of five different leadership styles.

Leading Using influence to motivate employees to achieve the organization's goals.

Legal-political dimension Includes government regulations at the local, state, and federal levels, as well as political activities designed to influence company behavior.

Legitimate power Power that stems from a manager's formal position in an organization and the authority granted by that position.

Line authority The formal power to direct and control immediate subordinates.

Liquidity ratio Indicates the organization's ability to meet its current debt obligations.

Listening The skill of grasping both facts and feelings to interpret a message's genuine meaning.

Locus of control Defines whether an individual places the primary responsibility for his successes and failures within himself or on outside forces.

Long-term orientation Reflects a greater concern for the future and a high value on thrift and perseverance.

Low-context culture A culture where people use communication primarily to exchange facts and information and derive meaning primarily from words rather than context.

Machiavellianism A tendency to direct one's behavior toward the acquisition of power and the manipulation of other people for personal gain; based on the ideas of Niccolò Machiavelli, a sixteenth-century Italian political philosopher.

Making progress principle The idea that the single most important factor that can boost motivation, positive emotions, and perceptions during a workday is making progress toward meaningful goals.

Management The attainment of organizational goals in an effective and efficient manner through planning, organizing, leading, and controlling organizational resources.

Management by means (MBM) An approach that focuses people on the methods and processes used to attain results, rather than on the results themselves.

Management by objectives (MBO) A method whereby managers and employees define goals for every department, project, and person and use them to monitor subsequent performance.

Management science Uses mathematics, statistical techniques, and computer technology to facilitate management decision making, particularly for complex problems. Also called the *quantitative perspective*.

Managing diversity Creating a climate in which the potential advantages of diversity for organizational performance are maximized while the potential disadvantages are minimized.

Masculinity A cultural preference for achievement, heroism, assertiveness, work centrality, and material success.

Mass production Characterized by long production runs to manufacture a large volume of products with the same specifications.

Matching model A human resources (HR) approach in which the organization and the individual attempt to match each other's needs, interests, and values.

Matrix approach A structural approach that uses both functional and divisional chains of command simultaneously, in the same part of the organization.

Matrix boss A functional or product supervisor responsible for one side of the matrix.

Mentor A higher-ranking senior member of the organization who is committed to providing upward mobility and support to a protégé's professional career.

Merger When two or more organizations combine to become one.

Message The tangible formulation of an idea to be sent to an employee.

Mission An organization's purpose or reason for existence.

Mission statement A broadly stated definition of an organization's basic business scope and operations that distinguishes it from similar types of organizations.

Monoculture A culture that accepts only one way of doing things and one set of values and beliefs.

Moral rights approach Holds that ethical decisions are those that best maintain the fundamental rights of the people affected by them.

Motivation The arousal of enthusiasm and persistence to pursue a certain course of action.

Motivators Factors that influence job satisfaction based on fulfilling higher-level needs such as achievement, recognition, responsibility, and opportunities for personal growth.

Multinational corporation (MNC) An organization that receives more than 25 percent of its total sales revenues from operations outside the parent company's home country and has a number of distinctive managerial characteristics.

Myers-Briggs Type Indicator (MBTI®) An assessment that measures a person's preferences for introversion versus extroversion, sensation versus intuition, thinking versus feeling, and judging versus perceiving.

Natural dimension Includes all elements that occur naturally on Earth, including plants, animals, rocks, and natural resources such as air, water, and climate.

Need for change A disparity between actual and desired performance.

Negotiation A conflict management strategy whereby people engage in give-and-take discussions and consider various alternatives to reach a joint decision that is acceptable to both parties.

Neutralizer A situational variable that counteracts a leadership style and prevents the leader from displaying certain behaviors.

New-venture fund Provides resources from which individuals and groups can draw to develop new ideas, products, or businesses.

New-venture team A unit separate from the mainstream organization that is responsible for initiating and developing innovations.

Nondirective interview A conversation where the interviewer asks broad, open-ended questions and permits the applicant to talk freely with minimal interruption, in an attempt to bring to light information, attitudes, and behavioral characteristics that might be concealed when answering structured questions.

Nonprogrammed decision A choice made in response to a situation that is unique, is poorly defined and largely unstructured, and has important consequences for the organization.

Nonverbal communication Communicating through actions, gestures, facial expressions, and behavior rather than through words.

Normative Means that it defines how a manager should make logical decisions and provides guidelines for reaching an ideal outcome.

Norming The stage of team development in which conflicts are resolved and team harmony and unity emerge.

On-the-job-training (OJT) A process in which an experienced employee is asked to teach a new employee how to perform job duties.

Open communication Sharing all types of information throughout the organization and across functional and hierarchical boundaries.

Open innovation A process where people search for and commercialize innovative ideas beyond the boundaries of the organization.

Open-book management Allows employees to see for themselves the financial condition of an organization and encourages them to think and act like business owners.

Operational goal A specific, measurable result that is expected from departments, work groups, and individuals.

Operational plan Specifies the action steps toward achieving operational goals and supports tactical activities.

Opportunity A situation in which managers see potential organizational accomplishments that exceed current goals.

Organization A social entity that is goal directed and deliberately structured.

Organization chart The characteristics of vertical structure are portrayed in the organization chart, which is the visual representation of an organization's structure.

Organization development (OD) A planned, systematic process of change that uses behavioral science techniques to improve an organization's health and effectiveness through its ability to cope with environmental changes, improve internal relationships, and increase learning and problem-solving capabilities.

Organization structure The framework in which an organization defines how tasks are divided, resources are deployed, and departments are coordinated.

Organizational change The adoption of a new idea or behavior by an organization.

Organizational commitment Loyalty to and engagement with one's work organization.

Organizational control The systematic process through which managers regulate organizational activities to meet planned goals and standards of performance.

Organizational ecosystem Includes organizations in all the sectors of the task and general environments that provide the resource and information transactions, flows, and linkages necessary for an organization to thrive.

Organizational environment Includes all elements existing outside the boundary of an organization that have the potential to affect it.

Organizing The deployment of organizational resources to achieve strategic goals; involves assigning tasks, grouping tasks into departments, and allocating resources.

P → O expectancy The assumption that high performance of a task will lead to the desired outcome.

Panel interview An interview in which the candidate meets with several interviewers who take turns asking questions.

Passive follower A person who exhibits neither critical independent thinking nor active participation.

Pay-for-performance Tying at least a portion of compensation to employee effort and performance. Also called *incentive pay*.

People change A change in the attitudes and behaviors of a few employees.

Perception The cognitive process that people use to make sense out of the environment by selecting, organizing, and interpreting information.

Perceptual distortion An error in perceptual judgment that results from inaccuracies in any part of the perception process.

Performance An organization's ability to attain its goals by using resources in an efficient and effective manner.

Performance appraisal The process of observing and evaluating an employee's performance, recording the assessment, and providing feedback.

Performing The stage of team development in which members focus on problem solving and accomplishing the team's assigned task.

Permanent team A group of employees from all functional areas permanently assigned to focus on a specific task or activity.

Personal communication channels Channels that exist outside formally authorized channels and connect people across boundaries for sharing information and accomplishing tasks.

Personal networking The acquisition and cultivation of personal relationships that cross departmental, hierarchical, and even organizational boundaries.

Personality The set of characteristics that underlie a relatively stable pattern of behavior in response to ideas, objects, or people in the environment.

Plan A blueprint specifying the resource allocations, schedules, and other actions necessary for attaining goals.

Planning The management function concerned with defining goals for future performance and how to attain them.

Pluralism An environment in which the organization accommodates several subcultures, including employees who would otherwise feel isolated and ignored.

Point-counterpoint A technique that breaks a decision-making group into two subgroups and assigns them different, often competing, responsibilities.

Political instability Events such as riots, revolutions, or government upheavals that can affect the operations of an international company.

Political risk A company's risk of loss of assets, earning power, or managerial control due to politically based events or actions by host governments.

Positive reinforcement The administration of a pleasant and rewarding consequence following a desired behavior.

Power The potential ability to influence the behavior of others.

Power distance The degree to which people accept inequality in power among institutions, organizations, and people.

Practical approach A decision-making approach that sidesteps debates about what is right, good, or just, and bases decisions on the prevailing standards of the profession and the larger society.

Pragmatic survivor A follower who has qualities of all four follower styles, depending on which fits the prevalent situation.

Prejudice The tendency to view people who are different as being deficient.

Problem A situation in which organizational accomplishments have failed to meet established goals.

Procedural justice Holds that rules should be clearly stated and consistently and impartially enforced.

Process theories A set of theories, including goal-setting theory, equity theory, and expectancy theory, which explains how people select behaviors with which to meet their needs and determine whether their choices were successful.

Product change A change in an organization's products or services, such as the Nike Flyknit Racer running shoe or Robinhood's app-based stock brokerage.

Profitability ratio Describes the firm's profits relative to a source of profits, such as sales or assets.

Programmed decision A decision made in response to a situation that has occurred often enough to enable managers to develop decision rules that can be applied in the future.

Project manager A manager who is responsible for a specific work project that involves people from various functions and levels of the organization.

Punishment The imposition of an unpleasant outcome following an undesirable behavior.

Quality circle A total quality management (TQM) technique that involves a group of 6–12 volunteer employees who meet regularly to discuss and solve problems affecting the quality of their work.

Quality partnering Involves assigning dedicated personnel within a particular functional area of the business to identify opportunities for quality improvements throughout the work process.

Quantitative techniques The use of mathematics, statistics, and computer technology to facilitate management decision making.

Quants Refers to financial managers and others who make decisions based primarily on complex quantitative analysis.

Quasirationality Combining intuitive and analytical thought.

Realistic job preview (RJP) Gives applicants all pertinent and realistic information, both positive and negative, about a job and the organization.

Recruiting Activities or practices that define the desired characteristics of applicants for specific jobs; sometimes called talent acquisition.

Re-engineering The radical redesign of business processes to achieve dramatic improvements in cost, quality, service, and speed.

Referent power Power that results from characteristics that command subordinates' identification with, respect and admiration for, and desire to emulate the leader.

Refreezing The stage of organization development (OD) where people have incorporated new values, attitudes, and behaviors into their everyday work and the changes become institutionalized in the culture.

Reinforcement Anything that causes a certain behavior to be repeated or inhibited.

Reinforcement theory A theory based on the relationship between a given behavior and its consequences.

Relational coordination Frequent horizontal coordination and communication carried out through ongoing relationships of shared goals, shared knowledge, and mutual respect.

Relationship conflict Conflict that results from interpersonal incompatibility that creates tension and personal animosity among people.

Responsibility The duty to perform the task or activity that one has been assigned.

Responsibility center Any organizational department or unit under the supervision of a single person who is responsible for its activity.

Revenue budget A budget that lists forecasted and actual revenues of the organization.

Reverse innovation Creating innovative, low-cost products for emerging markets and then quickly and inexpensively repackaging them for sale in developed countries.

Reward power Power that results from the authority to bestow rewards.

Risk Means that a decision has clear-cut goals and good information is available, but the future outcomes associated with each alternative are subject to chance.

Risk propensity The willingness to undertake risk with the opportunity of gaining an increased payoff.

Role A set of expectations for one's behavior.

Role ambiguity Uncertainty about what behaviors are expected of a person in a particular role.

Role conflict Incompatible demands of different roles, such as the demands of a manager's superiors conflicting with those of the manager's subordinates.

Satisficing Refers to choosing the first alternative that satisfies minimal decision criteria, regardless of whether better solutions are presumed to exist.

Scenario building An approach where managers look at trends and discontinuities and imagine possible alternative futures to build a framework within which unexpected future events can be managed.

Scientific management A subfield of the classical perspective that emphasizes scientifically determined changes in management practices as the solution to improving labor productivity.

Selection The process of assessing the skills, abilities, and other attributes of applicants in an attempt to determine the fit between the job and each applicant's characteristics.

Self-awareness Being conscious of the internal aspects of one's nature, such as personality traits, beliefs, emotions, attitudes, and perceptions, and appreciating how your patterns affect other people.

Self-confidence General assurance in one's own ideas, judgment, and capabilities.

Self-efficacy An individual's strong belief that he or she can successfully accomplish a specific task or an outcome.

Self-managed team A team that consists of multiskilled employees who rotate jobs to produce an entire product or service, often led by an elected team member.

Self-management The ability to engage in self-regulating thoughts and behavior to accomplish all your tasks and handle difficult or challenging situations.

Self-serving bias The tendency to overestimate the contribution of internal factors to one's successes and the contribution of external factors to one's failures.

Servant leader A leader who serves others by working to fulfill followers' needs and goals, as well as to achieve the organization's larger mission.

Service technology Characterized by intangible outputs and direct contact between employees and customers.

Short-term orientation Reflects a concern with the past and present and a high value on meeting current obligations.

Situational model A leadership model that links the leader's behavioral style with the readiness level of followers.

Six Sigma A quality control approach that emphasizes a relentless pursuit of higher quality and lower costs.

Skunkworks A separate informal, highly autonomous, and often secretive group that focuses on breakthrough ideas.

Slogan A phrase, such as Disney's "The happiest place on earth," that succinctly expresses a key corporate value.

Small-batch production A type of manufacturing technology that involves the production of goods in batches of one or a few products designed to customer specification.

Social business Using social media technologies for interacting with and facilitating communication and collaboration among employees, customers, and other stakeholders.

Social facilitation The tendency for the presence of others to enhance one's performance.

Social learning Using social media tools to network and learn informally.

Social learning theory A theory that proposes that an individual's motivation can result not just from direct experience of rewards and punishments but also from thoughts, beliefs, and observations of other people's behavior.

Social media A group of Internet-based applications that allows the creation and exchange of user-generated content.

Social media programs Include online community pages, social media sites, microblogging platforms, and company online forums that enable managers to interact electronically with employees, customers, partners, and other stakeholders.

Sociocultural dimension Includes demographic characteristics, norms, customs, and values of a population within which the organization operates.

Socioemotional role A team role in which an individual provides support for team members' emotional needs and helps strengthen social unity.

Span of management The number of employees reporting to a supervisor; sometimes called *span of control*.

Special-purpose team A team created outside the formal structure to undertake a project of special importance, such as developing a new product.

Staff authority The right to advise, counsel, and recommend in the manager's area of expertise.

Stakeholder Any group or person within or outside the organization that has some type of investment or interest in the organization's performance.

Stakeholder mapping A systematic way to identify the expectations, needs, importance, and relative power of various stakeholders.

Stereotype A rigid, exaggerated, irrational belief associated with a particular group of people.

Stereotyping A performance evaluation error that occurs when a manager places an employee into a class or a category based on one or a few traits or characteristics.

Storming The stage of team development in which individual personalities emerge and people become more assertive in clarifying their roles and what is expected of them.

Story A narrative based on true events that is repeated frequently and shared among organizational employees.

Strategic conversation Dialogue across boundaries and hierarchical levels about the team or organization's vision, critical strategic themes, and the values that help achieve important goals.

Strategic goal A broad statement of where an organization wants to be in the future; pertains to the organization as a whole rather than to specific divisions or departments.

Strategic issue An event or force that alters an organization's ability to achieve its goals.

Strategic management Refers to the set of decisions and actions used to formulate and implement strategies that will provide a competitively superior fit between an organization and its environment so as to achieve organizational goals.

Strategic plan Action steps by which an organization intends to attain strategic goals.

Strategy A plan of action that describes resource allocation and activities for dealing with the environment, achieving a competitive advantage, and attaining goals.

Strengths Natural talents and abilities that have been supported and reinforced with learned knowledge and skills.

Stress A physiological and emotional response to stimuli that place physical or psychological demands on an individual and create uncertainty and lack of personal control when important outcomes are at stake.

Stretch goal A reasonable yet highly ambitious and compelling goal that energizes people and inspires excellence.

Structured interview An interview that uses a set of standardized questions that are asked of every applicant so comparisons can be made easily.

Substitute for leadership A situational variable that makes a leadership style redundant or unnecessary.

Subsystem Parts of a system that depend on one another for their functioning.

Sunk cost effect The tendency to continue investing in a failing project in the hope of turning it around.

Suppliers Provide the raw materials the organization uses to produce its output.

Supply chain A network of multiple businesses and individuals that are connected through the flow of products or services.

Supply chain management Managing the sequence of suppliers and purchasers, covering all stages of processing from obtaining raw materials to distributing finished goods to consumers.

Survey feedback Where organization development (OD) change agents survey employees to gather their opinions regarding corporate values, leadership, participation, cohesiveness, and other aspects of the organization, then meet with small groups to share the results and brainstorm solutions to problems identified by the results.

Sustainability Economic development that generates wealth without compromising environmental responsibility and social stewardship, thus meeting the current and future needs of stakeholders while preserving society and the environment for the needs of future generations.

SWOT analysis An audit or careful examination of strengths, weaknesses, opportunities, and threats that affect organizational performance.

Symbol An object, act, or event that conveys meaning to others.

Synergy A concept that says that the whole is greater than the sum of its parts.

System A set of interrelated parts that function as a whole to achieve a common purpose.

Systems thinking Looking not just at discrete parts of an organizational situation, but also at the continually changing interactions among the parts.

Tactical goal The outcome that major divisions and departments must achieve for an organization to reach its overall goals.

Tactical plan Designed to help execute major strategic plans and to accomplish a specific part of a company's strategy.

Tall structure An organizational structure characterized by an overall narrow span of management and a relatively large number of hierarchical levels.

Task conflict Conflict that results from disagreements about the goals to be achieved or the content of the tasks to be performed.

Task environment Includes the sectors that conduct day-to-day transactions with the organization and directly influence its basic operations and performance.

Task force A temporary team or committee designed to solve a problem involving several departments.

Task specialist role A team role in which an individual devotes personal time and energy to helping the team accomplish its activities and reach its goal.

Team A unit of two or more people who interact and coordinate their work to accomplish a goal to which they are committed and hold themselves mutually accountable.

Team building An organization development (OD) intervention that enhances cohesiveness by helping groups of people learn to work together as a team.

Team cohesiveness The extent to which team members are attracted to the team and motivated to remain a part of it.

Team norm An informal standard of conduct that is shared by team members and guides their behavior.

Team-based structure A structure in which an entire organization is made up of horizontal teams that coordinate their activities and work directly with customers to accomplish organizational goals.

Technical complexity The degree to which complex machinery is involved in the production process to the exclusion of people.

Technical skill The understanding of and proficiency in the performance of specific tasks.

Technological dimension In the general environment, includes scientific and technological advances in society.

Technology change A change in production processes—how an organization does its work.

Telematics Technologies that wirelessly transmit data from remote sensors and GPS devices to computers for analysis.

Time management Using techniques that enable you to get more done in less time and with better results, be more relaxed, and have more time to enjoy your work and your life.

Top leader In a matrix structure, the person who oversees both the product and the functional chains of command and is responsible for the entire matrix.

Top-down budgeting Means that the budgeted amounts for the coming year are literally imposed on middle- and lower-level managers.

Total quality management (TQM) Focuses on managing the total organization to deliver quality to customers.

Traits Distinguishing personal characteristics, such as intelligence, self-confidence, energy, and independence.

Transactional leader A leader who clarifies subordinates' roles and task requirements, initiates structure, provides rewards, and displays consideration for followers.

Transformational leader A leader distinguished by a special ability

to bring about innovation and change by creating an inspiring vision, shaping values, building relationships, and providing meaning for followers.

Triple bottom line Refers to measuring the organization's financial performance, social performance, and environmental performance.

Two-boss employee In a matrix structure, a person who reports to two supervisors simultaneously.

Type A behavior Actions characterized by extreme competitiveness, impatience, aggressiveness, and devotion to work.

Type B behavior Actions that reflect few of the Type A characteristics and include a more balanced, relaxed approach to life.

Uncertainty Occurs when managers know which goals they want to achieve, but information about alternatives and future events is incomplete.

Uncertainty avoidance Characterized by people's intolerance for uncertainty and ambiguity and resulting support for beliefs that promise certainty and conformity.

Unconscious bias Occurs when a person is not aware of the bias in his or her favorable and unfavorable assessments, actions, and decisions toward members of specific groups.

Uncritical thinking Failing to consider the possibilities beyond what one is told, accepting others' ideas without thinking.

Unfreezing The stage of organization development (OD) in which people are made aware of problems and the need for change.

Upward communication Messages that flow from the lower to the higher levels in the organization's hierarchy.

Utilitarian approach A method of ethical decision making saying that the ethical choice is the one that produces the greatest good for the greatest number.

Valence The value of outcomes (rewards) to the individual.

Vicarious learning Learning that occurs when an individual sees others perform certain behaviors and get rewarded for them.

Virtual network structure An organizational structure in which the organization subcontracts most of its major functions to separate companies and coordinates their

activities from a small headquarters organization.

Virtual team A team made up of members who are geographically or organizationally dispersed, rarely meet face to face, and interact to accomplish their work primarily using advanced information and telecommunications technologies.

Vision An attractive, ideal future that is credible yet not readily attainable.

Wage and salary survey A questionnaire that shows what other organizations pay incumbents in

jobs that match a sample of key jobs selected by the organization.

Whistle-blowing The disclosure by employees of unethical, illegitimate, or illegal practices by an organization.

Work redesign Altering jobs to increase both the quality of employees' work experience and their productivity.

Zero-based budgeting An approach to planning and decision making that requires a complete justification for every line item in a budget, instead of carrying forward a prior budget and applying a percentage change.

Name Index

Subject Index